THE WORLD AT FIRST LIGHT

The World at First Light

A NEW HISTORY OF THE RENAISSANCE

BERND ROECK

TRANSLATED BY
PATRICK BAKER

PRINCETON UNIVERSITY PRESS
PRINCETON & OXFORD

Published by Princeton University Press
41 William Street, Princeton, New Jersey 08540
99 Banbury Road, Oxford OX2 6JX

press.princeton.edu

Library of Congress Cataloging-in-Publication Data

Names: Roeck, Bernd, author. | Baker, Patrick, 1976– translator.
Title: The world at first light : a new history of the Renaissance / by Bernd Roeck ;
    translated by Patrick Baker.
Other titles: Morgen der Welt. English | New history of the Renaissance
Description: English edition. | Princeton : Princeton University Press, [2025] |
    Original title: Der Morgen der Welt: Geschichte Der Renaissance. |
    Includes bibliographical references and index.
Identifiers: LCCN 2024040035 (print) | LCCN 2024040036 (ebook) |
    ISBN 9780691183831 (hardback) | ISBN 9780691272153 (e-book)
Subjects: LCSH: Renaissance. | BISAC: HISTORY / Europe / Renaissance
Classification: LCC CB361 .R63813 2025 (print) | LCC CB361 (ebook) |
    DDC 940.2/1—dc23/eng/20250111
LC record available at https://lccn.loc.gov/2024040035
LC ebook record available at https://lccn.loc.gov/2024040036

British Library Cataloging-in-Publication Data is available

Editorial: Ben Tate, Josh Drake
Production Editorial: Elizabeth Byrd
Production: Danielle Amatucci
Publicity: James Schneider (US), Carmen Jimenez (UK)

Jacket Credit: Albrecht Altdorfer, *History Cycle: Battle of Alexander (Battle of Issus)*, 1529, Bavarian State Painting Collections / Alte Pinakothek Munich

The translation of this work was funded by Geisteswissenschaften International—Translation Funding for Humanities and Social Sciences from Germany, a joint initiative of the Fritz Thyssen Foundation, the German Federal Foreign Office, the collecting society VG WORT and the Börsenverein des Deutschen Buchhandels (German Publishers & Booksellers Association).

This book has been composed in Arno

Printed in the United States of America

10 9 8 7 6 5 4 3 2 1

For Gabi.

—B. R.

For James Hankins, *praeceptori humanissimo.*

—P. B.

CONTENTS

Color plates follow pages 360 and 824

PREFACE TO THE ENGLISH EDITION

DEAR READER, the aim of this book is to elucidate the world-historical importance of the Renaissance, the epochal development that was the *sine qua non* of what has been called the "rise of Europe," the "rise of the West," and even the "European miracle" (see pp. 4, 924f.).[1] The original German edition of this book was received very favorably; a translation into Chinese has even appeared.[2] Yet there has also been criticism. Some negative reviews were very instructive, pointing out errors and omissions that I have thankfully had the opportunity to correct in the present edition. For example, one reviewer highlighted a significant fact missing from my portrayal of the "Gutenberg Revolution," namely that Chinese writing employs logograms and not letters, and therefore that moveable type would have provided no appreciative advantage over woodblock printing.[3] This omission has been corrected here (see p. 890).

Some reviewers took exception to the very notion that the West has been "successful," seeing in it a glorification of Western culture and a denigration of others. Yet the attentive reader will note that the "success" spoken of in this volume is not a normative evaluation but rather refers purely to "economic data, innovative technological power, and scientific progress" (see p. 911). Why was the "West" more successful than the rest of the world in this sense? That is the very question this book seeks to answer. But how is one to discover why something did *not* happen somewhere else? As the American Sinologist Nathan Sivin once quipped, "To explain what did not happen is about as rigorous as fiction."[4] The conclusion he draws from this observation accords with the tack I take in this book. Considering the question why modern science first saw the light of day in Europe and not in China, Sivin replies that, although there may be some good answers to the "why not" question, the main task is to ask what actually did happen. Sivin, therefore, concludes, "What did happen was the emergence of early modern science in Europe. It is Europe that needs to be understood." My sentiment exactly. On the other hand, *The World*

xix

at First Light never makes the claim that any specific development *necessarily* had to occur. Instead, it aims to reconstruct the "realm of possibility" in which the "rise of the West" was able to take shape. How would the history of the Americas and therefore of the world have been different if, for example, Columbus's ship had sunk on his first return voyage to Europe, thus burying knowledge of the lands beyond the Atlantic Ocean at its bottom along with him and his men? No one knows (see p. 478).

My book intones no hymns to Europe and its offspring. How could it, in light of the crimes of colonialism and imperialism, to say nothing of the wounds the Europeans inflicted upon themselves? "ISIS executions today pale by comparison," is how Michael Mann, in his book *On Wars*, characterized early modern methods of execution and the atrocities that attended the wars of religion in the sixteenth and seventeenth centuries.[5]

Some authors have claimed that the West's economic, scientific, and technological success was only possible thanks to the profits gained by exploiting the rest of the world. The lapidary formulation of a rather recent—and otherwise admirable—history of the United States reads as follows:

> Before 1492, Europe suffered from scarcity and famine. After 1492, the vast wealth carried to Europe from the Americas and extracted by the forced labor of Africans granted governments new powers that contributed to the rise of nation-states.[6]

But this was simply not the case. Europe continued to be haunted by famine for centuries after Columbus sailed the ocean blue. During the "long sixteenth century" and then the Thirty Years' War, starvation and epidemics claimed millions of victims. Catastrophic food shortages cropped up between 1770 and 1772 and in the late 1840s.[7] The causes of Europe's success were much more complex than is suggested by a formula like "ascendance by exploitation" (see pp. 4f., 917f.). Finally, the Europeans themselves paid dearly for the success of the West, for example, in the early modern wars of religion, on the battlefields of their struggles for independence, and on the barricades of their revolutions.

Despite its drawbacks, the legacy bequeathed to us from antiquity, the Renaissance, and the Enlightenment also continues to confer benefits upon us today, including ideas of freedom, democracy, and tolerance and the enumeration of human rights. The complicated history of the Renaissance also teaches us that, in the long term, it is liberal democracies and not authoritarian states that promote scientific, technological, and economic success.

Democracies are precarious, always incomplete projects that require a great deal of work. Their rules and institutions are supposed to adapt to social change while at the same time working towards the improvement of society—in the spirit of those "truths" enshrined in their constitutions. Democracies must also take precautions to make sure that the tolerance they practice with respect to divergent ideas does not enable those ideas to destroy them. For these reasons, the willingness to engage in radical self-criticism is indeed an essential virtue of open societies, perhaps even the decisive one for their survival. However, a correction must be made to Göle's notion that the capacity for continual self-correction is a key characteristic of modernity in general, in all its manifestations across the globe.[8] In point of fact, it is only the democratic, largely Western variety of modernity that relentlessly puts itself under the microscope and the knife (see p. 934). For only it guarantees the right to the free expression of opinions, without which all criticism would be impotent.

Will history end in a catastrophe or in a renaissance, as one recent critique of modern culture ponders?[9] This must remain an open question. The history narrated in the following pages would suggest that the prospect of a new renaissance is bleak. In premodern Europe, many preconditions had to be met for the possibility of the Renaissance to become a reality. And a great deal of time went by: two thousand years, starting back in antiquity. In part for this reason, *The World at First Light* turned out to be such a long book.

It did not take quite so long to write it, although it was more than a decade in the making. During that time, my family and our dog Gemma suffered no little neglect. Sometimes I worked on the text from the early morning till late at night. Whole passages were deleted, deleted passages rewritten, only for the rewrites themselves to be cut. I hope the traces of this process are no longer visible. Like every book, *The World at First Light* seeks to transmit knowledge and act as an impetus to further thought. Ideally, it will also be a pleasure to read. For that reason, I have dispensed with as much jargon as possible. To the same end, I have sprinkled the text with anecdotes and encouraged the reader to visualize important scenes from the past.

Since the German version of this book was published, I have written three articles focusing on various aspects of its subject. One is an overview of how the concept and periodization of the Renaissance have been treated in German historical scholarship; it appeared in an edited volume on "renaissances."[10] Another article on the "Renaissance of Conversation" came out in 2022, and a third, published in 2024, deals with the iconic turn in the social and cultural sciences.[11]

The fact that my book is now experiencing a renaissance in English is a great honor for me. The titanic labor of translation was shouldered by Dr. Patrick Baker (Berlin), himself an accomplished Renaissance scholar. His feeling for the German language and his attention to detail are admirable. Working closely with him to produce this volume has been a stimulating and abidingly pleasant experience. He not only corrected many errors in the text and the bibliography, but he also made important suggestions for improving the content. In short, Patrick made this a better book. I owe him a huge debt of gratitude. I would also like to thank Sofia Baker for her help correcting the proofs.

In addition, I would like to thank Wolfgang and Jonathan Beck, Detlef Felken, Stefanie Hölscher, Susanne Simor (all at C. H. Beck), and Ben Tate (at Princeton University Press). I also received a great amount of support and unbureaucratic assistance from the Zentralbibliothek Zürich, the Library of Congress in Washington, DC, and the Lauinger Library of Georgetown University (also in Washington, DC).

Special thanks to Lili and Martin in memory of a wonderful summer and our time together in Washington.

The English version of this book is dedicated to Gabi.

Zürich, October 2023

THE WORLD AT FIRST LIGHT

1

Europe's Grand Dialogue

The Portrait of the World

Venice, the summer of 1630. A long day draws to a close. An evening breeze blows in from the Lagoon over roof tiles still warm from the day's sun, the rush of air fanning the foreheads of three men who have gathered in one of the city's palaces. They have spent the day deep in earnest conversation, discussing the two "chief world systems": the model of Claudius Ptolemy, believed since antiquity, according to which the Earth was at the center of the universe, and the theory, not yet a century old, of the Polish astronomer Nicolaus Copernicus, which had demoted the Earth to a planet orbiting the Sun. Sagredo, the group's host, now brings the day's discussion to a close with a speech extolling the human mind and the arts and sciences of his time. He praises the skill involved in removing the superfluous parts of a block of marble, thus revealing the beautiful figure contained therein. He acclaims the ability to mix colors, to spread them across a canvas, and so to portray all visible things after the manner of a Michelangelo, a Raphael, a Titian. He cannot stop marveling, he says, at the age's musical compositions, poetry, architecture, and its art of navigation. But one invention above all he finds worthy of admiration: printing.

> What sublimity of mind was his who dreamed of finding means to com- municate his deepest thoughts to any other person, though distant by mighty intervals of space and time! Of talking with those who are in India; of speaking to those who are not yet born and who will not be born for a thousand or ten thousand years; and with what facility, by the different arrangement of twenty characters upon a page![1]

Behind this fictional Venetian scene was a great author: Galileo Galilei. The episode is found in his *Dialogue Concerning the Two Chief World Systems*, first published in Florence in 1632. Galileo puts his own views into the mouth of a scholar named Salviati, a proponent of the Copernican worldview. The host, Sagredo, plays the role of moderator. Yet he, like Salviati, is a supporter of Co- pernicus and thus also embodies Galileo somewhat. Advocating the old Ptol- emaic system and Aristotelian science is the pedantic Simplicio, whose name means "simpleton." He is dispatched with great irony. Galileo's treatise bubbles over with wit and oozes with sarcasm. The author's aim is to convince an urbane audience. He therefore leads with rhetoric, not mathematics. The arguments put forth by his spokesperson Salviati are not new, nor do they always hit the mark by any means (for example, he thinks he can cite the tides as evidence that the Earth moves). The elegance of the argument is more important than the facts of the matter.

But that is not what concerns us. Galileo's *Dialogue* epitomizes a style of learned discussion that first arose in European culture and that, for a long time, was only cultivated there. Marked by the virtues of curious questioning and serene doubt, it eschewed conflict but embraced booming polemics. Thanks to the printing press, half a continent could participate in the grand dialogue. Galileo's text embodies this novel art of conversation, unparalleled in world history. Its author had not simply discovered something new; he argued in a new way.[2] Admittedly, his model, the Ciceronian dialogue, had deep historical roots, going all the way back to a discussion practice pioneered by Socrates in the fifth century BC. Over time, that ancient manner of seeking wisdom had become a method for gaining scientific knowledge. Socrates and Cicero were thus invisible guests at the summer evening symposium in Venice staged by Galileo.[3]

Many of the developments he praises can be summed up under the heading *revolution*. The first steps towards mechanization in the thirteenth century amounted to a fundamental overthrow of the world that had existed before. Johannes Gutenberg's invention set a media revolution in motion. It was preceded by what we might call a *discursive revolution*,[4] a broadening—initially gradual but ever swifter—of the topics that could be written and spoken about, focused on the secular world and especially on antiquity. With the Reformation, a religious revolution followed. Finally, Copernicus, Kepler, and Galileo revolutionized cosmology and physics. Taken together, these revolutions changed the world. They created what we call *modernity*, or to be more precise, the Western variety of modernity, which has exerted its influence on the entire world.

Without the dialogue with antiquity that was at the heart of the culture of the Renaissance—the subject of this book—these radical changes would have been unthinkable. Without the possibility of conversing and debating with others, of discussing issues critically, of reasoning publicly, democracy never would have arisen, nor would that abundance of technical innovation and scientific knowledge have been achieved that, for better and for worse, marks our day and age. In the words of the German poet Johann Gottfried Herder (1744–1803), "A breath of our mouth becomes the portrait of the world, the type of our thoughts and feelings in the other's soul. On a bit of moving air depends everything human that men on Earth have ever thought, willed, done, and ever will do."[5] Our book is about this *grand dialogue*, this exchange of knowledge, ideas, and practices that shaped the culture of the Renaissance. It was largely restricted to a predominantly male elite. Yet what those few creative minds conceived and constructed changed the world for everyone. Our aim is now to reconstruct how it was possible for the Renaissance to come about and to ponder the consequences it has had. Without its ideas and inventions, the modern world we know may not have been worse off—but it certainly would have been different.

In order to discover how we came to be and what we are, we must journey far and wide. By drawing comparisons with other regions, we hope to reach an understanding of the causes for why the Latin part of Europe underwent a development that gave its culture a worldwide impact. It is a tiny region, comprising not even two percent of the Earth's surface. On three sides, it is bounded by water. To the east, it borders on Russian and Greek Orthodox cultures, a boundary now marked by the Baltic states, Poland, and Hungary, and further to the south by the Balkans.

History of a Possibility

Cultivating the art of conversation and thereby creating a space for disagreement and controversy are among the most important achievements of the Renaissance. Disagreement reveals the weak points of arguments and the cracks in the foundations of theoretical edifices; critical debates have always attended technological innovation. The art of arguing was driven and accompanied by intellectual revolutions. One such was the methodological paradigm shift that is usually designated as *Scholasticism*. Another, indicating the shift in intellectual style, was the diffusion of the revived art of ancient rhetoric that animates Galileo's treatise. What is the essence of the Renaissance? Mining antiquity for its treasures, refining them, using them to create new things, and ultimately surpassing them. Just about every department of knowledge was revolutionized. The Middle Ages, no doubt, did more than debate the sacred, but the Renaissance promoted the wholesale conquest of secular terrain. Across media of all kinds—from books to images, from preaching to disputation—the grand dialogue seized on every topic imaginable. In the lecture halls of universities, in patrician villas and princely palaces, even in monasteries and the Vatican, the heart of the Roman Catholic Church's power, a dialogue unfolded whose dimensions, in terms of the topics discussed and the number of participants, were unprecedented. It is no wonder that during the Renaissance the art of conversation itself was discovered as a topic of conversation.[6]

The expansion of free spaces for thinking, speaking, and writing took place in a world whose comforts may seem paltry to us—a world where the fight for survival left little time for culture and where religious conflict reliably monopolized all human reasoning. How such an environment could nevertheless produce the "European Miracle" (Eric Jones) and with it the "Great Divergence" (Kenneth Pomeranz) of the "West"—a value-free designation referring above all to parts of Europe and the New World—from the rest of the globe is one of the most hotly disputed questions in the discipline of history.[7] Is Europe's "success" primarily a consequence of capitalism, colonialism, and imperialism, and therefore nothing but the shameful product of exploitation? Was its fuel the blood of oppressed peoples?[8] Have Europeans passively profited from the decline of the Asian economy since the seventeenth century? Is the hegemony they enjoyed two hundred years later thus owed not to themselves but to other factors entirely?[9]

Let it be said at the outset that this book sees these issues very differently. It views the intellectual and technological upheavals of the Late Middle Ages as necessary preconditions for the Industrial Revolution. Recognizing this, however, in no way entails celebrating the course of European history. The progeny of the "Christian West" enslaved foreign peoples, committed genocides, and destroyed cultures around the world. Yet in the nineteenth century—a "European century" like no other—the balance sheet has important items in the asset column, e.g., democracy, banishing starvation, victories over diseases, and useful technology. Much of this was exported, with consequences for other parts of the world that were not purely negative.[10] Whether this was all worth the price that had to be paid for it—including by Europe itself, which remained drowned in blood until the dawning of our own time—is a question that will not be addressed here. We intend not to pass judgment on the past or to colonize it, but rather to give an account of it. Our aim is merely to sketch as detailed a picture of the age as possible.

The question of what constituted the Renaissance is the subject of a boundless academic debate, to which no further contribution will be made here,[11] except this: the core of the concept of the Renaissance, as used in this study, is that the reception and further development of ancient thought that began in the twelfth century continued thereafter uninterrupted and in ever-increasing variety and abundance (pp. 923–927). Other times and cultures also experienced renaissances. None, however, involved anything close to the same number of scholars, scientists, and artists. While other cultures, such as China's, treated the ancient world with awe and tried to emulate it, Europe, above all, learned skepticism and the art of critical thinking from its engagement with the great minds of antiquity. Western scientists and intellectuals overcame ancient paradigms (pp. 757–761). No other renaissance around the globe achieved comparable significance; Europe's Renaissance changed the world. As for periodization, our book draws the conclusion that epochs can never be narrowed down to one essential characteristic, nor can their boundaries be sharply drawn (pp. 927–934).

What role the Renaissance played in the prehistory of an ambiguous modernity is not the only question raised by this book, but it is the most important. To ask the follow-up question, namely why nothing similar happened anywhere else, does not entail claiming that some inevitable Western modernity has blazed a compulsory trail for similar developments in the "rest" of the world.[12] With this caveat, we may ask why the Industrial Revolution did not liberate Africa, New Guinea, or South America, whereas a flourishing economy developed in Australia.[13] Why did necessity—little dry land, much water, and frequent flooding—make the Dutch inventive, but not the indigenous

Amazonians or the farmers settled along the Yangtze?[14] No answers are available if we search only in the events immediately preceding modernity, in the Scientific and Industrial Revolutions that paved the way for it. For they were only possible under conditions that developed over a much longer period—conditions that, as a whole, appear to have been peculiarly European.

The best we can hope for from our investigation is to arrive at probable explanations. What can be described are geographically and chronologically definable *realms of possibility*, i.e., frameworks of circumstances that permitted certain kinds of thinking and scopes of action. A historically discernible event, such as a discovery, a revolution, or a work of art, can be thought of as the realization of an opportunity. In the language of probability theory, an *event* emerges from the sample space of possible outcomes. Historical circumstances and conditions are the unscalable walls that encompass the realm of possibility, circumscribing what can (but need not necessarily) be thought or done. Chance—the upshot of complex, unfathomable chains of causes and effects—is also enclosed by the realm of possibility, as are the adventitious, the unnecessary, and the serendipitous. Only a miracle could breach its walls. What will emerge within them we cannot calculate with certainty. For along with other "streams" that flow in the realm of possibility, the power of contingency—i.e., the fact that things happen one way but could have happened another or not at all—is too strong to account for.

Realms of possibility, understood as structures in continuous flux, result from a combination of streams (that often take centuries to form) and individual actions. Events occur in a chronologically circumscribed "window of opportunity."[15] A creative achievement can consist of the crossing of various streams with one another. What results is something new that expands the realm of possibility up to the point that it bears almost no resemblance to its former state. This process can be equated with the concept of *emergence*. Thanks to the working of an invisible hand, the interaction of various elements within a complex system yields outcomes that can be neither completely explained nor predicted from the system itself, that are greater than the sum of the individual causes.[16]

This book begins by tracing the formation of the realm of possibility that gave rise to the Renaissance and the revolutionary innovations it entailed. We will survey vast cultural, political, social, and economic landscapes that provided space for conflict, struggle, and opportunity. Sometimes these opportunities were seized. Yet there were no necessary outcomes in this scenario, just as there was no monocausality. For example, as important as capitalism was for the genesis of Western modernity,[17] it was only one of many factors that stood in a complex interrelationship with one another. Europe's "rise" can be explained by "killer apps" like competition, the rule of law, science, modern medicine, and freedom.[18] Yet this does not tell us why the bundle of these and other factors only appeared in the "West." What circumstances made them possible? This book will also consistently pay attention to detours, slowdowns, and countercurrents: struggles between dispassionate reason and fiery faith, between freedom and high-handed claims to power. When mention is occasionally made of "backwardness," it will always strictly be with reference to objectively measured economic, technological, or similar conditions. The people outside of Latin Europe were not less intelligent than the Europeans. Some cultures—such as in China and the Islamic world—even experienced promising fits and starts. But these eventually led to stagnation, whereas the Scientific and Industrial Revolutions took place in the "West."

The Deep History of an Epochal Emergence: The Seven Pillars of Modernity

We shall first consider the primordial preconditions for the path taken by Europe: *geography and climate*. They represent the *first*, predetermining foundation for everything else.[19] A *second* necessary precondition for Latin Europe's trajectory was the fact that, by the Middle Ages, it had already become a continent of *multiple states engaged in political and cultural competition*. The Middle Ages were also the setting for three more of the seven pillars upon which the grand dialogue of the Renaissance rested, as will be outlined in the following two paragraphs.

Compared with many states in Asia, medieval Europe's government structures were hopelessly inferior in terms of rational organization, economic strength, technology, and military power. The "northern barbarians," as described by a Muslim scholar in eleventh-century Toledo, "lack[ed] keenness of understanding and clarity of intelligence, and [were] overcome by ignorance and apathy, lack of discernment and stupidity."[20] This was to change as the "saddle" from the medieval valley to the modern peak,[21] which began with a gentle slope, grew ever steeper. Economic and demographic conditions improved. The European city and town took shape, and social relations developed there that were unique around the globe. The *urban middle classes and the influence of horizontal power structures* on a broad spectrum of life became the *third* pillar of the Renaissance. Horizontal power structures can be understood in contrast to the vertical organization of authority. Both are ideal types, rarely met with in their pure form. Even in dictatorships and absolute monarchies, opposition to the power that is concentrated in a single individual can be discerned. Civil societies also evince many vestiges of vertical power structures, resulting, for example, from economic inequality and the natural preponderance of executives. That having been said, horizontal power structures prevailed in the cities and towns, and they arose earlier and much more frequently in European societies than elsewhere.

The fact that townspeople enjoyed greater freedom to write and say what they wanted was in part due to the *fourth* pillar: *the containment of religion*. The title of this book—*The World at First Light*—intentionally has several shades of meaning; it alludes to this weakening of religion vis-à-vis the "worldly," understood both as *earthly* instead of *heavenly* and as *secular* as opposed to *holy*. It was indeed this development that the French Enlightenment considered the essence of the Renaissance.[22] Christianity was not per se opposed to science or progress, and religious institutions were indispensable for the preservation and proliferation of knowledge in the Middle Ages. Yet what nourished the growth of dialogue in Europe was the avoidance of excess and the curtailing of priestly power. *The critical dialogue with ancient and Arabic philosophy and science* then became the *fifth* precondition for the revolutions of budding modernity. Europe alone was able to draw from the wells of two world cultures, Greco-Roman and Arabic, both of which preserved traditions from still other cultural areas: Mesopotamia, Egypt, Persia, India, and even a little bit from China. The very possibility of dialoguing with the clever pagans of antiquity and with Muslims was itself due to the first three pillars of Europe we have described above. Without the "rebirth" of knowledge about the speaking and writing practices of antiquity, a discursive culture like the one that developed in the waning Middle Ages in Latin Europe was inconceivable. Of course, the flow of ancient texts never dried up during the Middle Ages, and thus the grand dialogue with the ancients had not fallen entirely silent. Nevertheless, engagement with ancient texts increased dramatically starting in the twelfth century. If this engagement were to be plotted on a curve, this is where the slope would rise steeply.

The *sixth* pillar of European modernity was the *media revolution* set in motion by Gutenberg. Its success mirrored the radical change in speaking and thinking that took place in the High Middle Ages. This new technology provided Latin Europe with communication possibilities that did not exist (or were not used) in any other culture, and they are what gave the grand dialogue of the Renaissance world-changing significance. The European intellectual community was now by far the largest the world had ever seen.

The *seventh* and final prerequisite for true paradigm shifts was *very long periods of time*. In this sense, this book is a manifesto against what the historian of Africa Richard Reid has decried as *presentism*—the notion that it suffices to study a few decades of the past in order to understand the present and that the deepest structures of history can be forgotten.[23] Our enterprise could therefore be called *archaeology* or *deep history*;[24] indeed, historians have long considered the early morning twilight the best time to hunt. The need for "de-sedimentation" (Jacques Derrida) is obvious, as the Renaissance was a culture whose essence lies in recourse to ancient ideas and forms. The term *archaeology*, incidentally, will be used in this book in a way that is the exact opposite of how it was understood by the cunning wordlord Michel Foucault.[25] We shall set the term back firmly on its feet, treating it as a suitable metaphor for the traditional business of the discipline of history. This archaeology uses ground-penetrating radar to map the subsurface and then digs up one layer at a time. It treats words and artifacts as the dusty remains of what were once ideas, calamities, power, work, and war, i.e., as the vestiges of human life. It seeks after the framework of culture and investigates how something as wonderful as rational free dialogue managed to develop out of the chaos of wars, state formation, and waxing and waning empires.

Our archaeology investigates origins and causes, although it knows that the ultimate beginning is lost in seemingly endless chains of causality, in the golden glow of myth or the mist of metaphysics. Monocausal explanations—such as that Christianity was responsible for the "rise of the West"[26]—do not help us gain insight into the origins of grand historical phenomena. Similarly, the provocatively presented and elegantly argued thesis that the Renaissance began with the discovery of a single text, Lucretius's *De rerum natura*, would never occur to a trained historian.[27] The radical changes that marked the beginning of modernity—such as the revolutions of Gutenberg and Copernicus, the Scientific and Industrial Revolutions—were the culmination of overlapping developments that had very different origins, strands of causes and effects that, in turn, became intertwined and mutually influenced one another.

The modernity whose roots we are digging for is a paradoxical enterprise.[28] It contains within itself the communication society and censorship, state capitalism and pluralism, rationality and secularization, fundamentalism and skepticism. Our narrative attempts to identify some of the circumstances that gave rise to it, to capture the moment when, to borrow an image from

Aby Warburg, the butterfly emerged from its cocoon.[29] The focus, naturally, will be on the history of the grand dialogue with European antiquity and Islamic high cultures that reached its fullest potential in the Renaissance. The course of world history would have been very different if the legacy of antiquity had not found its way into medieval Latin Europe. We shall, therefore, trace the paths it took, giving ample consideration to intellectual cross-pollination and cultural transfer.

We shall begin with a tour of the deep prehistory of the "great Renaissance," paying close attention to the origins of Europe's diversity, its bountiful imagery, its realms of memory and its myths, which sprang from epics out of the primordial mist and found an especially impactful narrative vehicle in the legend of Rome. Our first task will be to examine the geographical framework, the well-nigh immutable foundation of all that was to follow.

PART I

Foundations

FROM THE FIRST BEGINNINGS
TO THE TURN
OF THE MILLENNIUM

2

The Luck of Geography

The Phoenix Takes Flight

Renaissance, literally "rebirth," can signify several things: starting over from scratch, a process of renewal and rejuvenation, a mission to recover the radiant purity of one's origins, maybe even resurrection from death. It evokes the ancient Egyptian myth of the phoenix, which rises from its own ashes and grows young again—an allegory of an age-old yearning and an emblem of renewal since ancient Rome.[1] As Rein Taagepera reminds us, however, the very notion of renaissance is ambiguous. "It is as if the scientific-technological-cultural phoenix flew from the Middle East to Greece, then to Rome, and then died, only to arise from the same Italian ashes a thousand years later." Eric Jones concurs, echoing Taagepera: "In reality, the phoenix had gone back to Byzantium, traveled all over the Arab world, picked up some feathers in India and China, and only then returned to Italy."[2] How true this is. If we want to track the flight of the phoenix, we must travel far back in time and all the way to East Asia, to parts of the world without which there would have been no great European Renaissance.

The first thing that made the Renaissance possible was favorable geography. According to the thesis put forward by evolutionary biologist Jared Diamond, the decisive factor was that the Eurasian landmass offered optimal conditions—better than other continents—for the diffusion of cultural innovations.[3] Diamond emphasizes that Eurasia is marked by an extremely vast east-west expanse, by far the greatest on Earth. No massive desert, no insuperable mountain range hinder the spread of cultural innovations. Even the Pyrenees, the Alps, and the Urals can be crossed by means of mountain passes. Large rivers facilitate exchange. It is possible, for example, to cross Russia from the Baltic to the Caspian Sea almost entirely by water. The Eurasian Steppe, which stretches from Hungary to Mongolia, presents no obstacle other than distance. This is how the agricultural innovations that developed in the Near East were able to migrate across the continent along the same line of latitude, albeit over a period of thousands of years. From north to south or south to north, however, exchange is not so easy. Lemons can be cultivated in Spain, Italy, and India but not in Alaska or the Sahara. Transfer along the same line of latitude benefits from the fact that days are more or less the same length, and temperatures and seasons are similar. If certain plants and animals were domesticated in different places, if new techniques were developed in specific locations and not others, thanks to these favorable conditions they could sooner or later spread to the entire landmass. The domestication of animals seems to have begun around 9500 BC in the core regions of western Eurasia, two thousand years later in eastern Eurasia.

European culture began in the heart of Eurasia, in the "Fertile Crescent." The name refers to a region that stretches from Iran to the Mediterranean, that touches Anatolia in the north and Egypt in the south. Early settlement traces in the area date to around 12,500 BC. The favorable Mediterranean climate— mild winters and hot, dry summers—as well as a variegated topography with a wide range of altitudes, facilitated the development of a unique diversity of flora and made farming and animal husbandry easier. It was probably in this region that today's most important crops and domestic animals were first encountered. Societies gradually took shape here in which manual skills were rewarded with economic success. During the "Neolithic Revolution," between 10,000 and 5000 BC, it became possible to produce surpluses and thus to support specialists who did not toil in the fields but rather made weapons, built boats, and so on.

The flood of innovations from the Fertile Crescent soon reached Egypt, Greece, and Sicily. At the same time, it surged in the opposite direction, towards Asia—all the way to the Indus Valley, where a civilization arose equally early. By the mid-sixth millennium BC, the fruits of the Fertile Crescent had arrived in central Europe. Around 3500 BC, they were in England and the southern tip of the Iberian Peninsula. Around 2500 BC, they reached Scandinavia. Along with plants came the wheel, which was already in use in Mesopotamia in the mid-fourth millennium BC. With cattle, milking know-how came to Europe. Milk was followed by beer and wine. Sheep were being shorn in the Near East by no later than the fourth millennium BC. Did Indo-European languages spread along the same route taken by manual skills, domestic animals, and plants? This we do not know. Indo-European is thought to go back to the fourth millennium BC to a region north of the Caspian Sea, perhaps even to Anatolia nine thousand years ago.[4] If societal differentiation is the prerequisite for linguistic differentiation, the latter hypothesis is more likely.

Better diet, so the argument goes, led to an increase in population. Eurasia developed a demographic surplus that holds to the present day. Europe only makes up a small part of the total area of the landmass, yet a multitude of cultures had already crystallized there in prehistoric times. The first cities on the globe also arose on the edge of the Fertile Crescent. Jericho began as a collection of buildings that provided protection to about eight hundred people between 8000 and 6000 BC. In Çatalhöyük in Anatolia, the population may have reached five thousand people between 7000 and 5500 BC.[5] The breakthrough to urban civilization with city-like patterns of settlement occurred in the fertile Sawad, the "black land" south of modern Bagdad that is supplied with water by the Tigris and Euphrates rivers. This is where Ur and Babylon sprang up. The early cities there were home not only to merchants but also to the gods, as they often accreted around the germ cells of holy sites. Fear of predacious neighbors hungry for booty, water, and canals also led to their formation.[6] Uruk was the location of a cultic center to which more and more people flocked. They soon built walls to protect themselves. In the third millennium BC, up to fifty thousand people were already living there.

Trailblazing innovations—the plow, the potter's wheel, the cartwheel, metal money—apparently resulted only from this kind of population density. With cuneiform, which emerged around 3300 BC, and hieroglyphics, which date to almost the same time, the world's first systems of writing were born. Thousands of years earlier, in Jerf el Ahmar (in what is now Syria), images of snakes, birds, other animals, and abstract symbols were cut into stone; these have been interpreted as a "proto-script."[7] There is further evidence that these cities gave rise to complex societies whose political organization could not have been achieved without written language.

The most important factor for all urban civilization has always been access to water. Like pearls on a string, settlements stretched along the Euphrates and the Tigris, the Yangtze, and the Indus. Ur, for example, had two harbors, and Egyptian civilization was a gift of the Nile, which, thanks to favorable winds, was navigable in both directions. The irrigation of the Nile Valley—the only way to engage in agriculture in a desert region—required the division of labor and, thus, organization. Over time, a centrally governed "state" was formed that around 3100 BC encompassed Upper and Lower Egypt. The period known as the Fourth Dynasty, between 2585 and 2511 BC, witnessed the building of the Pyramids of Giza, already admired as a wonder of the world in antiquity. A little later, two city-like settlements located in a far-eastern region of Eurasia, in the Indus Valley—Mohenjo-Daro and Harappa—established ties as far as Mesopotamia.

In the twenty-fourth century BC, Sargon the Great did something entirely new: he created a large city that was then ruled by one dynasty for generations.[8] The conqueror of Mesopotamia, of parts of Syria, Asia Minor, and Elam, was called the "Ruler of the Four Parts of the World." Foundations were being laid everywhere. In Bronze Age Anatolia, at the beginning of the second millennium BC, the trading center of Kanesh was a thriving metropolis whose economic life adhered to sophisticated rules—documented on more than twenty-three thousand clay tablets covered with cuneiform.[9] In Mesopotamia in the eighteenth century BC, the Babylonian ruler Hammurabi created the world's first-known legal code. The legend of Gilgamesh—the first grand epic of world literature—was also a product of the Fertile Crescent, as were ultimately the *Iliad* and the *Odyssey*, which incorporated motifs from the Babylonian text.

Around 1200 BC, there was a mysterious cultural collapse in Asia Minor and the Eastern Mediterranean. Palaces crumbled; even writing systems were forgotten. Scholars have hypothesized causes as various as volcanic eruptions, plagues, droughts, and invasions of foreign armies known as "Sea Peoples." But the crisis was overcome. New dominions were formed, including the kingdom of David and Solomon around Jerusalem. The Assyrian Empire rose again. Around 700 BC, it was perhaps the mightiest state world history had hitherto known—only to be shattered in the following century. Its place was taken by the much larger Persian Empire of the Achaemenids. At its height, it stretched from what are now parts of Kazakhstan, Afghanistan, and Pakistan all the way to the banks of the Aegean and even included Egypt itself.

Europe Learns to Spell

Theories that reduce the past to biology and geography present us with powerful and deep historical explanations. On the other hand, they only show the necessary—and in no way the sufficient—conditions for Europe's world-changing trajectory. Yet without the biological and natural foundations such theories sketch, Europe would not have developed cities and states, nor would it have produced its traditions of thought and writing, its technological innovations, or its arts and sciences. Of particular importance was the fact that Eurasia truly was, and continued to be, one massive sphere of communication. Without contact with the ancient cultures of North Africa and Asia, Athenian philosophy and Alexandrian science would have been inconceivable. The same goes for the high cultures of Rome and the Arab world, which channeled not only Athens and Alexandria but also Persian and Indian civilization. The Renaissance, in turn, profited from all of them. In contrast, Australia, broad swathes of South Asia and Africa, and the Americas fell behind early.

The law stating that truly important innovations require broad, sustainable communication and communications media already applied at the beginning of human history. No society on its own ever could have developed the enormous and diverse quantity of technology that accumulated in Eurasia. In comparison to other parts of the world, the megacontinent was densely populated. It was covered by an ever more tightly knit network of trade. And cultural exchange across large expanses of territory increased. In this way, the number of "creative centers" grew, and with them knowledge that traveled across space and time. Opportunities piled up for discoveries to be made and disseminated. For example, iron metallurgy, which arose in the Caucasus or in Cilicia, had reached the Hittites by ca. 1250 BC. The Iron Age began in Greece and Crete in the eleventh century BC and in Italy two hundred years later. Iron, now widely available, democratized agriculture and crafts—but also war.[10]

An especially important good that spread with traders and warriors was alphabetic writing systems. Scripts were developed in other cultures as well, such as in Mesoamerica and China. The invention of alphabetic writing, however, was of truly world-historical significance, as would become clear in the age of Gutenberg. It is thought to have developed in the western Semitic region between the Sinai and Syria. Thus it, too, was a product of that engine of innovation, the Fertile Crescent, already the source of syllabic cuneiform and hieroglyphics.[11] Nameless language tinkerers recognized the advantages inherent in being able to form words out of a small set of symbols. In fifteenth-century-BC Ugarit, then a flourishing port, a type of cuneiform with only thirty symbols was in use whose names already foreshadow our own alphabet. Its inventors took the initial sound of a word—in the case of *aleph*, or "ox," the *a*; of *bet*, or "house," the *b*—as a symbol for the corresponding sound and put the letters thus formed into a strict order. Since they signified everyday things, they were easy to memorize.

Ugarit was destroyed by the Sea Peoples, but the idea of the alphabet survived. It was picked up by the Phoenicians and the Arameans. The number of letters was reduced to twenty-two. An indication of how important the Phoenicians, a trading people, were for the history of writing is the fact that the papyrus plant was named after one of their most important sites, Byblos. It was used to make the writing material of the same name, *papyrus*, which preceded paper. The Phoenician city is thus the ultimate root of the Greek word for "book": *biblos*.

The alphabet project was completed four centuries later by the Greeks. For the letters *alpha*, *epsilon*, *eta*, *iota*, and *omicron*, they used Semitic symbols whose original signification was not needed, as Greek did not have the corresponding sounds. Various regional systems developed, but it was the twenty-four-character Ionic alphabet that prevailed. The earliest evidence for its use comes from the last quarter of the eighth century BC; it likely originated in Euboea or in the territory of the Ionians or Aeolians. An Aramaic version of the Semitic alphabet was influential in the Orient, providing a model for the inhabitants of Mongolia and penetrating as far as India. It is an ancestor of both Hebrew and Arabic script. The writing system used in China, however, with its thousands of characters, resisted this influence.

Alphabetic writing was much less complicated than hieroglyphics, than syllabic cuneiform, and certainly than Chinese logograms. Once unleashed on the world, this invention soon conquered the realms of commercial communication and literature and inspired variants, the most important of which was the Latin alphabet. With this second media revolution after the invention of writing, an extremely important stone was laid in the foundation of Europe. It freed reading and writing from the privileged domain of specialists. The alphabet could be learned quickly and easily, thus aiding the development of broad educated classes and facilitating the creation of a public sphere that was first manifested in the marketplaces of the Greek cities. The invention of the alphabet was of immediate importance for Europe's grand dialogue, which was born in Mesopotamia, reached a first, isolated summit in Greek philosophy, and still animates our world today. Whether the highly sophisticated dialogue about God and the universe initiated by the Presocratics could have taken place without this system of signs is anyone's guess—but just try to translate Plato's *Phaedo* or Aristotelian logic into hieroglyphics or cuneiform!

The first inheritors of this invention were already aware of its significance. One of the cultural heroes who personified the origins of technology in Greek thought was a certain Palamedes. He was praised not only as the inventor of astronomy, navigation, and board games but also as the inventor of the alphabet, numbers, and the recording of laws.[12] In addition, the alphabet was the prerequisite for a world in which books played an earlier and much larger role than in other cultures. The Mediterranean even flirted with the principle of printing. The 3,700-year-old Phaistos Disc shows that an inventor on Minoan Crete had the idea of using a stamp to imprint symbols for words or syllables on clay and then firing it. The technique was also known in ancient Mesopotamia.

Over the millennia, the entire Mediterranean world was transformed into one large communication sphere, thanks to trade, coastal navigation, slave hunting, piracy, pilgrimages, and finally to regular travel routes.[13] This region became the setting for an unparalleled achievement of the human mind: Greek philosophy. It reached its height during the long half-century between about 800 and 200 BC that Karl Jaspers called an "Axial Age" of world history.[14] This period witnessed the teaching of the Buddha, the compilation of the Upanishads, and the appearance of the Hebrew prophets. As for the Greeks, they bequeathed more to Europe than just myths, temples, columns, and ideals of human beauty. It was they who inaugurated the tradition of a kind of science that is still our own.[15] They became the most important intellectual founders in world history. And they coined words that we continue to use today, from *democracy* and *atom* to *cosmos* and *library*.

The question about the Renaissance's *deepest* origins—and what is more, about the causes of Europe's technological and scientific success—receives its first answer here, on the banks of the Black, Aegean, and Adriatic seas. Without Greek thought, the Renaissance and European modernity would be unthinkable. For it is, above all, Greek thought that was "reborn" and led to the creation of new things. Writing about the Greeks is thus tantamount to reconstructing the genetics of modernity. The Greek gene played a central role in Europe's development. In the words of Ernst Troeltsch, our world is based "not on the reception of antiquity nor on a detachment from it, but on an utter and conscious entanglement with it."[16] We are the heirs of that age, with all the good and bad it produced.

What is the content of this much-vaunted "ancient" heritage? Under what circumstances was this incredibly rich intellectual capital amassed? Some readers may be familiar with the details that are about to be recapitulated, but we beg their indulgence. If we are to understand the trajectory of the West, it is essential to survey the riches that the Greeks, and the Romans after them, piled up for posterity.[17]

3

Greek Thought

CREATIVITY AND CRITIQUE

In the Beginning Was the Polis

In the second millennium BC, people began migrating from central and eastern Europe to what is now Greece and mixing with the native inhabitants there. They hardly considered themselves "Hellenes." Some of them continued on to the islands and Asia Minor, competed with other peoples like the Phoenicians, and learned from them. They no more comprised ethnic entities than did other peoples of the Mediterranean world. As for the "Mediterranean," which literally means "inland sea" or "sea in the middle of the Earth," it did not earn that name until it appeared on medieval maps of the world. There the *mare mediterraneum* was actually portrayed as the center of everything. At the height of the Roman Empire, from the viewpoint of the seat of power it was simply *mare nostrum,* "our sea"; the Jews called it the "Great Sea," *Yam Gadol.* Goods and ideas flowed there from as far off as East Asia, where trade lines stretched all the way to Java and India in antiquity. They traveled on galleys and river barges and along caravan routes, from the Sahara, and from the passes and roads that crossed the Pyrenees, the Alps, and the Balkans.

The Mediterranean is a picture gallery all to itself.[1] It is where Europa, daughter of the Phoenician king, was kidnapped by Zeus, father of the gods. The crafty old shapeshifter turned himself into a bull and carried her across the Mediterranean to Crete, where her son Minos would go on to found a kingdom. In fact, the island is home to the palaces of the first high culture in Europe, known as Minoan. The Mediterranean's waves peter out placidly on the sands of Ostia and Tunisia. They beat against the cliffs of Sardinia, whipped up by winter storms. They break on the volcanic rock of Santorini and the quays of Barcelona and Piraeus. And they lap at the beaches of Dubrovnik, known as Ragusa in olden times. The scorching sirocco blows from historic African landscapes, singeing the soft hills of Tuscany, glinting off the "gray-leaved" olive trees of Andalusia, and spreading the scent of lavender across Provence. In autumn and winter, heavy leaden clouds hang over the land like in El Greco's *View of Toledo,* showering the earth with the rain it so needs and desires. It can be very cold, even in Italy.

The vegetation of the countryside still tells the story of wide-ranging processes of transfer that lasted millennia. Many plants that now seem typical of the Mediterranean are actually foreign. The first cypresses were introduced from Persia. Arabs brought lemons and oranges, peaches and tangerines. Rice came from China, and eggplants immigrated from India. Agaves and figs are New World plants. Tomatoes originated in Peru. Maize, the stuff of immortal polenta, is from Mexico. And eucalyptus was transplanted to Europe much later from the other side of the world—Australia.[2] Only the trio of grapes, olives, and grain is native to the Mediterranean region.

The islands often served as contested bases for pilgrims and merchants, as well as strongholds against attack by foreign peoples: Crete, with its vestiges of Minoan culture, Cyprus, Rhodes, Corfu, and the swarm of smaller islands swimming in the azure sea, many bearing mythical names like Cythera, Ithaca, and Mykonos. Then, to the west, Malta and mighty Sicily, Sardinia and its silver mines, Corsica, and the Balearic Islands. In the fiery mountains, in Vesuvius, Etna, and Stromboli, clefts to the underworld seemed to open up—or *history*, first appeared as an independent endeavor in the form of Ionian natural philosophy. The Mediterranean's communication-friendly geography and the political and social conditions of Greece were now buttressed by another factor that enhanced the development of the grand dialogue: relations with the East.

Great cultures never have autochthonous or national roots. They arise from exchange and productive conflict. Thus, Greek thought owed more to the East than western historians have tended to realize.[9] Athena may not have been Black, as one book title suggests,[10] but she was anything but the color of white marble. Greek sculpture originated in a process of cultural transfer with Egypt, and the Egyptians probably introduced the Greeks to mathematics. Literature and religion also bear influences from the Nile, as well as from Iran and the Near East. Even poetry and philosophy, long considered the pure invention of the Hellenes, were inspired by Eastern sapiential teachings and myths about the creation of the world. From Near Eastern warlords and kings, the Greeks learned how to rule. The Phoenicians not only taught them the alphabet but also served as an example—along with the Sumerians, who, at least in times of emergency, were familiar with processes akin to democracy[11]—of how to build cities and organize political life.

Over time, various places crystallized as centers of the Greek intellectual cosmos. The first, at the time of the Ionian natural philosophers, were the rich trading cities of Miletus and Elea, located in southern Italy. Then Athens became the "teacher of Greece"—a praise put into Pericles' mouth by Thucydides—and finally Alexandria. The vast majority of what the Presocratics and later philosophers wrote has been lost. Only through accounts in the works of other authors, who often lived several centuries later, have fragments come down to us. What survived changed the world.

Greek thinkers were first animated by a sense of wonder—wonder about nature, about the universe, about human beings. Nothing could produce philosophy but wonder, Plato says.[12] Many of these wondering wanderers were, s Diogenes called himself, cosmopolitans: citizens of the world, subject to no ate. Their curiosity drove them to distant lands to explore the world in the eral sense.[13] Hecataeus of Miletus (ca. 500 BC) is said to have traveled to thern Russia and improved Anaximander's map of the world, considered first in Europe. Pythagoras and Plato explored Egypt, searching for the ancient wisdom. Democritus seems to have reached Babylon. Mega- es and Pyrrho went to India, the latter in tow of Alexander's army. In the d century BC, the art of minting elaborate coins made its way to India

so the ancients believed. In their lava-filled depths, the Cyclopes were said to have forged swords and plowshares out of Vulcan's glowing iron.

The Mediterranean did not divide people; it united them—at least in summer when winter storms did not make venturing out onto Homer's "wine-dark sea" inadvisable. Whereas Chinese high culture, in order to survive, needed the muscle of hundreds of thousands of people to build the Grand Canal and thus to transport the fruits of the Yangtze River Valley northward, passage on the Mediterranean was provided by the wind. This made provisioning Rome and Constantinople with grain from bountiful Egypt much easier. The waves of the Mediterranean carried silk and slaves, marble statues and myths, deities and ideas from coast to coast, from island to island. Without the medium of this inland sea, Europe's trajectory would have been very different.

Evidence of the commercial power that fed Greek culture can be found in its money economy. The earliest documented minting of coins there dates to the period between 600 and 560 BC, in Aegina and Athens. Metal currency combines concrete and abstract value, and its conquest of the economy seems to be an expression of the same rationality that manifested itself in Ionian natural philosophy. Fertile Euboea, rich in natural resources and, as its name suggests, herds of cattle, became a great trading power. Its standards of weight, measure, and coinage were used far and wide. In the *Iliad*, Corinth was already called *aphneios*, "rich." Its vases were sold as far away as the western Mediterranean, in distant Ibiza. Miletus, one of the starting points of the Greek intellectual revolution and soon to be one of the wealthiest emporia in the eastern Mediterranean, was augmented by immigration from the Greek mainland. People needed new land; perhaps they were fleeing conflicts in their home cities. These "proto-Greeks" founded autonomous settlements small and large on the banks of the Aegean, many of which became cities. Commercial interests, population growth, and the leaders' desire for power were likely the main causes for the far-flung colonization movement that took place between the eighth and sixth centuries BC.[3] It expanded to southern Italy and Sicily in the eighth century and later reached the shores of the Sea of Marmara and the Black Sea, the Iberian Peninsula, and the coasts of North Africa. Like frogs around a pond, as Plato mocked, the Greeks squatted along the seas.[4] Large cities scattered seeds that grew into daughter cities; they tended to maintain close ties to their progenitors. Miletus alone spawned about thirty colonies (*apoikia* in Greek) on the Black Sea coast. Many of the cities then founded still retain vestiges of their Greek origins in their names: Marseille from Massalia, Nice from Nikaia, and so on.

Their origins must be imagined as humble. With the collapse of the Bronze Age palace cultures around 1050 BC, the age of the polis began. The term, still lurking in words like "metropolis" and "politics," denoted the group of people who maintained a common cult and had a say in issues affecting the community—thus, not only townspeople but also all the inhabitants of a polis's territory. Urban centers probably grew up around meeting places, temples, and the residences of aristocrats who dispensed justice, exercised military leadership, and presided over the cult. Around them accumulated the dwellings of farmers, craftsmen, and merchants, who would go on to form the civic communities and institutions that took on such importance. They emerged around 600 BC as independent entities. Other typical features of the polis included the town hall, theater, and gymnasium, the last of which began as a site for athletic training but, in Hellenistic times, was also an educational institution.

The Greek colonization of far-off parts of the Mediterranean was a process of greater importance for Western civilization than nearly any other single advance made in antiquity.[5] For one, trade with the distant west reinforced—if not outright laid—the economic foundation of Greece's cultural resurrection after the Late Bronze Age collapse. What is more, the colonies in southern Italy were also the conduit by which the rising power of Rome came into direct contact with Greek thought and technology.

In the late sixth century BC, the world of the polis was threatened by the Great Kings of Persia. Whether the Straits of Salamis, where a Greek fleet defeated Persian forces, really was a "bottleneck" through which world history had to pass (as some historians have claimed) is a moot question.[6] Persian rule was not all that onerous. The inhabitants of subject cities could live happily with their gods and enter into alliances with one another. The Persian commander Mardonius even safeguarded democracy in the cities he conquered on the Ionian coast.

The strongest argument for the "bottleneck" thesis is the strange fact that an enduring line seems to have been drawn through the regions bordering on the eastern Mediterranean, dividing them between East and West down to our own day. Democratically organized states and free and open discussion are found almost exclusively on the western side. During the Roman Empire, however, the line was located further eastward. With the relocation of the Roman capital to Constantinople and then the formation of the great Islamic empires (starting in the seventh century AD), it moved westward again. Nevertheless, speculation is futile. The Greek fleet defeated the Persian forces, and victories on land followed. The Greek dialogue was able to continue. Thankfully for the

Hellenes, the massive Persian Empire with its extensive borders had other problems to solve than challenging the Greek frogs for their pond.

In the "Athenian century"—the fifth century BC—the first theories ever about politics (apart from the somewhat earlier teachings of Confucius, ca. 550–479 BC) were developed against the backdrop of the Persian wars, the conflicts between Sparta and Athens, and internal unrest. What the "state" ought to be and how the ideal polity should look were issues first debated in Athens—and at such a high level that the contributions made by the Greeks are still discussed today. It was probably the colonization efforts to far reaches of the Mediterranean that triggered these theoretical considerations; the political order of the new foundations provided ample food for thought. There is much to recommend the thesis that the practice of decision-making on the basis of discussion and majority rule facilitated the breakthrough to a rational philosophy and the study of nature.[7] That not everyone could participate in Attic democracy is another matter. Slaves and foreigners, women, and usually those without property were excluded. In democratic Athens, the right to participate in decision-making as a citizen usually depended on having an Athenian father and mother. Foreigners from outside the Greek world, th so-called barbaroi, were looked down upon with scorn from the heights of Acropolis. Yet only a few societies down to modern times opened so n paths to participation. Until the days of Macedonian rule, no individu local king, no polis, no foreign conqueror, and no priestly caste man become lord of Greece. Instead, power was divided and contested. Athens' defeat in the Peloponnesian War could dissolve its democr severed, albeit with interruptions, down to the second centur Rome deprived the Greeks of their right to wage war.

The idea of being subject to no one had little in common wit universally valid human rights. What it meant was put into wo the Persian menace and the wars between the Greek city-state Aeschylus, Herodotus, Thucydides, and others.[8] The alluri dom," eleutheria, had begun its long journey through wor

Presocratic Fragments: The Cosmo and Human Beings

Like no other people of antiquity, the Greeks p Knowledge and gave names to things. The ver wisdom," comes from Greek. Questioning

by way of the Bactrian Kingdom, the eastern outpost of Hellenistic culture. Conversely, Indian culture sent its influence west. The *Milinda Panha*, the "Questions of Menander," reports a dialogue between the Bactrian King Menander and the Buddhist sage Nagasena.[14]

The Greeks were the greatest inquirers in world history. They were the first to set off in search of truth for its own sake, relying on their powers of reason.[15] Not all the ideas conceived by the Presocratics were unique—one or the other can be found in other ancient cultures around the world—but the diversity of their inquiries was indeed singular. They investigated the soul and discussed the nature of the gods, the structure of matter, and the ordering principles of the cosmos. They developed a natural philosophy in which the divine infused all matter—but also the materialism of Democritus, for whom even the soul was composed of atoms. Presocratic philosophers produced murmuring mysticism and adamantine dogmatism, as well as an aloof skepticism that regarded nothing as holy. In the figure of the physician Hippocrates of Cos, active ca. 400 BC, they founded a tradition of rational medicine, and they began the study of animals and plants. The law of causality was first committed to writing in Greek, as was the art of forming rational premises and conclusions, *logike techne*.

In Ionian natural philosophy, which originated in seventh-century-BC Miletus, laws of nature were already being cited alongside gods and demons as causes of things. Thales of Miletus is said to have interpreted an earthquake as a result of the movement of the sea and not as an expression of Poseidon's wrath.[16] Anaximander of Miletus (ca. 625–547 BC), maker of the first sundial, no longer told stories, as Hesiod had, of deities who created the world. Instead, he searched for a "first principle" that was the basis for all else. Out of what he called *apeiron*, the "indefinite" or "boundless," everything came into being by the division of the opposites hot and cold, wet and dry. The universe became an enormous organism that lives, passes away, and comes into being again. Humankind supposedly developed from a fish-like being.[17] Anaximander was not only a somewhat exotic precursor to Darwin, he was also the first to imagine the world as eternal and, therefore, as not created. His theory resurfaced in Aristotle and would even provide material for discussions of cosmology in the seventeenth century.

The same goes for the teachings of Pythagoras of Samos (ca. 570–ca. 480 BC) and his students, who began living a communal life of asceticism and discussion with their master in Croton around 530.[18] Pythagoras has come down to us in lore as a charming, even divine wise man, as a healer, a sorcerer, and a prophet of the oldest religious truths. At the center of his teaching were numbers. Numbers and proportions, as manifested in the five Platonic solids or the golden mean, seemed to indicate an ordering principle of the universe. From the observation that musical harmonies display correspondences to geometric relationships and from the regularity of planetary motion, Pythagoras concluded that the world was ordered according to laws of harmony. He also taught that immortal souls migrated from one living being to another. Reminiscent of the Buddha's teaching, which also included the transmigration of souls, he taught that people should shape their lives in harmony with the well-ordered cosmos.

In the middle of the Pythagorean model of the world blazed a massive fire. It was the hearth around which the universe was built, around which the Earth, the Moon, the Sun, and the five planets then known revolved at proportional distances and velocities. Since that only added up to nine celestial bodies (including a sphere of fixed stars), the Pythagoreans postulated the existence of a "counter-Earth." This brought the total to the more perfect number of ten. The movement of the celestial bodies, they believed, produced a supernatural music, or harmony of the spheres. A later philosopher, Aristarchus of Samos (ca. 310–230 BC), even promoted the view that the fixed stars and the Sun were immobile and that Earth revolved around the Sun. This ancestor of Copernicus is supposed to have been accused of impiety.[19] Even the possibility of "many worlds" beyond the universe was considered—two thousand years before Giordano Bruno.[20]

Akin to Pythagorean thought was Empedocles, another man of the glorious fifth century BC and one of the founders of the theory of the four elements: earth, water, fire, and air. Along with Democritus, he was a pioneer of atomism. In his view, all things in the physical world were composed of small particles of one of those four indivisible elements. Even god was transformed from an anthropomorphic being into an abstraction. The "obscure" oracular Heraclitus conceived of god as the sum of all things that, like rationally speaking *logos*, unites opposites.[21]

Parmenides of Elea (ca. 520/515–after 450 BC) seems to have been the first to realize that the Earth is spherical in shape.[22] The distinction he makes between appearance and being marks the beginning of all ontology. Parmenides formulated the provocative thesis that only being—and not becoming (which is not yet being)—can be grasped by thought, which is itself being. This was an intellectual revolution: logic, which bows to the law of noncontradiction, which distinguishes "true" and "false," is opposed to "wild thought" and mythology.[23] The acuity of the Greek mind is also exemplified by Zeno of Elea's discussion of paradoxes. Aristotle called him the inventor of dialectics.[24]

The writings of a few of the Presocratics contain a critique of the gods that would still cause scandal in certain countries today. They considered the gods to be figments of the imagination, instrumentalized by people for practical reasons. More than two thousand years before Ludwig Feuerbach sought to unmask God as a creation of man and not man as a creation of God, Xenophanes mocked Homer's and Hesiod's conception of the divine. In his view, if oxen or horses could draw pictures, their gods would look like oxen or horses.[25] He conceived of the divine as a motionless spirit that infuses all things and that moves the universe through the power of thought alone, "like mortals neither in form nor in thought."[26] This was a rejection of mythical explanations of natural phenomena. Xenophanes denied that human beings could have certain knowledge of things; truth was known to god alone, whereas only its image and appearance were available to human beings. Prodicus of Ceos (470/460–after 399 BC) is said to have conceived of the gods as allegorical figures personifying earthly things such as the elements or bread, and Protagoras (ca. 490–ca. 411 BC) soberly observed that it was impossible to know if they existed.[27] He thus distinguished belief from knowledge. And Euhemerus of Messina believed the gods could ultimately be traced back to famous kings, warriors, and learned men whose deeds had been so great that they were declared gods after their deaths. Of course, myth-debunkers of this caliber remained a very tiny minority down to the eighteenth century. Still, their reflections show how radically the Greeks were willing to think—and this at the same time as Israel was fashioning its strict father-god Jahweh and bringing the figure of the Messiah to the world stage.

In addition to god, the universe, and nature, the Greeks also thought a great deal about human beings. Protagoras considered humans to be the measure of all things: "of the things that are, that they are; of the things that are not, that they are not."[28] This was no slogan of a humanist manifesto, although this author did indeed enjoy renewed honor in the Renaissance.[29] Rather it reflected insight into the subjectivity of all perception and a rejection of the exclusive claim to truth that some natural philosophers upheld. Furthermore, it was a prompt to pay attention to the nature of human beings, their possibilities and limitations, their education and upbringing.

Human struggle and suffering are themes of tragedy, which was born at the same time as philosophy. Its father was a figure of the sixth century BC, Aeschylus of Eleusis, a master of drama focused on guilt and the hopeless entanglement in sorrowful fates ordained by the gods. Sophocles (497–ca. 405 BC) and Euripides (d. 406 BC), both Athenians, complete the triad. If these giants of the theater have found numerous modern interpreters, it is because their plays deal with fundamental questions of human existence—themes that also play a role in Greek philosophy: being and appearance, guilt and fate, desire, passion, and reason.

The greatest tragedy of all and the greatest source of material for the stage was history. Thus, a significant form of historiography also premiered in the fifth century. The tradition was begun by Herodotus of Halicarnassus (ca. 485–425 BC), whom Cicero called the "father of history." Along with Hecataeus of Miletus, he is also considered a founder of ethnology and anthropology.[30] Herodotus intended to preserve the memory of important deeds as a source of teaching, imitation, and pleasure, and he sought to write truthfully and impartially. This has been the ethos of all good history writing ever since.

Thucydides (ca. 455–395 BC) claimed that his *History of the Peloponnesian War* was "not a piece of writing designed to meet the taste of an immediate public but was done to last forever."[31] It is a first-rate work of historiography and a literary masterpiece to boot. Thucydides sifts sources critically, investigates causes, considers the motives behind human actions, and analyzes political configurations. He provides a pathology of human violence that is unmatched by other historians, ancient or otherwise. His *Peloponnesian War* may be the first work of history to dispense with the gods. Like in Machiavelli's writing, the place of heaven is taken by chance and necessity. The famous "Melian Dialogue" is a lesson in the cynicism of naked power.[32] Thucydides portrays the desire for freedom and domination as a given of politics and a constant of human existence. He inaugurated a tradition of historiography that, in Tacitus's (ca. 58–ca. 120 AD) formulation, proceeded *sine ira et studio*, "without anger and partiality." Thucydides, Herodotus, and Xenophon, the eyewitness to the *March of the Ten Thousand*, are, however, only the most important founders of a tradition of writing and thought that remains unbroken to our own day.

Historiography and tragedy mirrored the experience of the cleft between a nature bound by crystalline laws and a chaotic unfurling of events. This experience informed the Greeks' desire to find an ordering principle in human affairs, to study the tense relations between nature and *nomos*: convention, custom, or law.[33] *Nomos* appeared as an unnatural tyrant but also a "king over all people" and thus as protection for the weak.

Dialogue and Critique

The Greek world remained a marketplace of ideas and a testing ground for politics. People engaged in conflict, entered into alliances, and experimented with models of federalism. Wars and domestic crises, such as Athens experienced in rapid succession after the death of Pericles (429 BC), were in no way harmful to cultural life. On the contrary, upheaval and chaos expanded the market for philosophers, as they promised guidance and offered a kind of education that increased the chances of success in a complex society. A studious public was willing to pay for erudition and rhetoric—an important tool in the business of politics. A few sophists, learned rhetoricians for hire between 450 and 380, became very wealthy. The celebrity orator Gorgias of Leontini, one of the inventors of rhetoric, claimed that the power of words was equal to physical force. He is said to have donated a golden statue of himself to the Temple of Apollo at Delphi.[34] The fact that marble busts were made of great philosophers like Socrates, Plato, and Aristotle shows the high social status that could be achieved via philosophy. Countless anecdotes illustrate the popularity enjoyed by thinkers. Some philosophers, such as Pythagoras, Empedocles, and later Plato, were even venerated like gods. The sophists applied the analytical method of the Ionian study of nature to the social world.[35] Nothing escaped their critique—not society with its rules and customs, not religion, not even the certainty of human knowledge. The negative connotation of the term "sophistry," which evokes hairsplitting and quibbling, comes from its occasional abuse of the cardinal philosophical virtue of inquiry and criticism, which could get lost on insignificant byways or simply go on forever.

The principle of critical dialogue had a long prehistory. After all, dialogue is a form of philosophizing known to many cultures.[36] Hinduism has *sastrarthas* (debates), and Chinese philosophers discussed the problem of theodicy and the infinity of the universe just like their European counterparts.[37] Yet the debates of the Hindus followed a precise ritual and remained strictly focused on canonical texts, and they were ultimately decided by divine judgment.[38] And Chinese scholars did not argue on the basis of logical proof but rather relied on the authority of classical texts that were at most subject to mild revision. The Greek approach was different, with its inquiry into and irreverent questioning of all things. Thanks to the Greeks, the art of critique—and thus of gaining distance from one's own patterns of thought—has remained a hallmark of Western intellectual history.[39] The falsification and rejection of everyday experience are the essence of science. Critique—to adapt a saying of Heraclitus, the philosopher of opposites—was henceforth the father of all things.[40]

The tradition of the Greek philosophical dialogue begins with the moral authority of Socrates (469–399 BC). His student Plato (427–347 BC) immortalized the discussions in which he engaged. Thanks to his persistent questioning of his own morals and the way he lived and died, Socrates became the founder of practical philosophy and of a technique of thinking and arguing that can only be described as epoch-making. His followers depicted him as a teacher of wisdom on the level of Christ or Buddha. "Saint Socrates, pray for us," are the words Erasmus of Rotterdam put into the mouth of a character in his colloquy "The Godly Feast."[41] The appearance of Socrates and the thought of the sophists marked a break in the history of philosophy; the attempt was now made to predicate the norms that governed every aspect of life on reason alone.[42]

Plato sees dialectic, the method governing discussion, as a gift of the gods that "some Prometheus" brought to humankind along with fire.[43] The Socratic dialogue is the mightiest weapon of all enlightenment, dedicated to the search for truth and wisdom, edifying but also corrosive. It contains subversive elements, flashes of irony, and doses of sarcasm. Much is left unresolved. Often it is difficult to judge which participant or which position has the support of the author. The revolutionary potential of the dialogue is hinted at by its ironic undertone. In contrast, the late-antique Christian version of the genre, one of whose greatest exponents was Augustine, is existentially profound but dispenses utterly with humor and irony.[44]

The technique employed in Socratic dialogue posed a danger to convention and tradition. Giordano Bruno's *On the Infinite Universe and Worlds* and Galileo's *Dialogue Concerning the Two Chief World Systems* illustrate how it works: speeches for and against a position are aired, arguments are deployed, and the more substantive one wins. Doubt is maintained as long as possible. The standard for judgment is reason. Scientific discourse is still based on these principles today. Relentless questioning can ultimately lead to the insight that there are kinds of ignorance and problems that admit of no solution no matter how hard one tries. That was the justification for the division between philosophy and theology, between religion and science. The dictum put in Socrates' mouth, "I know that I do not know," is a call to critically examine everything one thinks one knows.[45] It is the foundation of a defining characteristic of the "West": its culture of critique.

The rediscovery of the skeptical tradition—the term comes from the verb *skeptesthai*, "to investigate," "to examine"—would later provide an impulse for modern philosophy.[46] Skepticism had its major representative in Pyrrho of Elis (ca. 365–275 BC). He denied that value judgments could be made, as they arise entirely from human convention; he even maintained that the existence of an external world could not be proved. Arcesilaus (ca. 315–240 BC), at least, conceded that human beings could judge whether things were probable or plausible. The ethical standard remained what corresponded to reason. Like Pyrrho, he recommended suspending judgment. Only that way could imperturbability and peace of mind, *ataraxia*, be achieved. Nevertheless, skeptics were never supposed to stop inquiring into what was true.

A tradition of skeptical brow-furrowing was not the only thing the Greeks bequeathed to posterity. They were also the inventors of comedy. They taught irony, ridicule, and humor, and their dark brother, cynicism.[47] The comedies of Aristophanes (450/444–ca. 380 BC), for example, provided respite from the atrocities of war and the agonies of everyday life. Greek literature is bursting with anecdotes that put things in a nutshell, aid the memory, and provide entertainment by relating episodes that are human, all too human. The anecdote may not be a Greek invention. Still, the sheer number of somewhat true, artfully embellished, or entirely false vignettes that we know from Cicero, Diogenes Laertius, and others reflects a bountiful and scintillating world of discourse.

Irony abounded, and so did laughter. Xenophanes even poked irreverent fun at such a profound and esoteric matter as Pythagoras' doctrine of the transmigration of souls, claiming to hear the voice of a friend in the whining of a beaten dog.[48] Even the venerable epics of Homer were parodied. Socrates is the greatest ironist of all. He acts ignorant and pretends to think his interlocutor is wise, thereby inducing the latter to expose his own manifold ignorance. In this case, irony is a philosophical method. Usually, however, it is a rhetorical strategy, as it was later in Galileo's dialogue on the two world systems. Even the noble genre of tragedy could be an object of ridicule. Socrates himself was a victim of irony in Aristophanes' *Clouds*. The philosophers also heaped ridicule on one another. Heraclides Ponticus, i.e., "of Pontus," was dubbed *ho pompikos* on account of his solemn bearing and "pompous" clothing. Epicurus called Democritus "Lerocritus," or "judge of nonsense." It is no wonder that it was a Greek—Aristotle, to be precise—who, in his book on the soul (*Peri Psyches*), formulated the first theory of "humans as beings capable of laughter." And Plato's *Menexenus* mercilessly ridicules patriotic boasting, lampooning the notion that it is "sweet to die for one's country."[49]

Had they lived in the wrong place—such as Baghdad, Geneva, or Rome—at the wrong time, Xenophanes, Carneades, and Lucretius would have been burned at the stake. Even Diogenes of Sinope (d. ca. 324 BC), about whom anecdotes abound, probably would have led a much less comfortable life in the Christian West than the one he freely chose to live in a large barrel. Diogenes is the most popular thinker of the Cynic school of Greek philosophy. His grave in Corinth is said to have been adorned with a marble dog, *kyon*, probably an allusion to the yapping aggressiveness for which he was known.[50] No writings of his are extant. Like Socrates, he provided an example of how philosophy can be *lived*. His followers imitated their master by facetiously questioning social norms, denouncing luxury, and criticizing power. Similar to the (admittedly more sober) mendicants and preachers of the Late Middle Ages, they held up a mirror to their world—in this case, the society of the disintegrating polis—caricaturing people in order to induce them to seek the proper path to happiness.

Sages for the Ages: Plato and Aristotle

Over time, dialogue and critique became ensconced in Athens in schools and intellectual centers that would provide a model for the following millennia. Antisthenes (455–360 BC), the first of the Cynics, started a school at the Cynosarges gymnasium that propagated his teachings. Around 390, Isocrates established a training center for rhetoric; it advertised a kind of education that was aimed primarily at preparing aspiring politicians for public life. And around 387/385, in a grove sacred to the hero Hecademus on the outskirts of Athens, Plato opened a school that would become the mother of all intellectual and educational institutions of the following millennia: the Academy.[51] This is where Plato outlined an ideal state in his *Politeia*, or *Republic*, that, like Thomas More's *Utopia*, was the antithesis of the actual state he lived in. The atmosphere of the Academy must have been cosmopolitan and open-minded. Plato tolerated divergent opinions, such as those of his most famous student, Aristotle. Critical discourse, whether outdoors under the shade of the trees or in a lecture hall surrounded by statues of the nine Muses, was the order of the day.

Following the tradition of the Pythagoreans, the Academy elevated mathematics to the highest discipline. This was the ultimate root of math's rise to dominance in the Renaissance, even though Pythagorean and Platonic mathematics did not seek to understand the laws of nature. The immutable truths of mathematics seemed to grant access to a uniquely ideal world of the human mind. Geometry, according to Plato's *Republic*, is "knowledge of what always is."[52] The things of the material world, in contrast, appear as a dull reflection of the light of gleaming ideas. In Plato's oft-cited allegory, human beings can only perceive reality as shadows on the wall of the cave in which they lie, chained and with their backs to the entrance; and so they believe the flitting shadows they see in the gloom are real.

The dialogue entitled *Timaeus* was the most important source for Plato's thought down to the Renaissance. It supplied Christian philosophy with notions of God, the soul, and the universe. Bishop Otto of Freising (ca. 1112–1158) praised Plato's cosmology as so enlightening and wise that one could think he had been steeped in Christian teachings.[53] The *Timaeus* describes the universe as having been created out of an eternal primordial substance by an eternal divine demiurge. Plato believed that the universe was a living being infused by a self-moved, uncaused, and immortal "World Soul." It was the intermediary between mind and senses, being and becoming, and it drove the perpetual, circular motion of the planets, themselves divine beings.[54] The World Soul shaped the cosmos into a whole that was ordered according to geometric principles—and thus that could be perceived with the aid of geometry. Plato gave it the shape of a twelve-sided polygon, the dodecahedron. This notion, which had previously been discussed by the Presocratics, would provide the impulse for one of Kepler's early writings.

According to Plato, the individual human soul is made of the same substance as the World Soul and, like it, is immortal. It animates the mortal body and forms the essence of each and every individual person, which is composed of intellect, will, and desire.[55] It thus participates in the sensual and the intellectual and has a unique "third" form of existence. From the time it was still one with the World Soul, the individual human soul retains dim knowledge of the ideas of pure truth, perfect goodness, and beauty. It is reborn many times in new bodies, and, once it has done good and cleansed itself in its various lives, it may return to its origin. This was a poetic idea that Plato probably got from Pythagoras. It has long been part of the Buddhist and Hindu traditions. Abelard (1079–1142) thought it corresponded to the Holy Spirit.[56] Still, Plato may have been the first thinker to conceive of an independent character able to control its feelings by means of reason.[57]

His concept of the transmigration of souls was not compatible with Christian teachings. His god, on the other hand, was. It was a supreme idea, an absolute good, in short, a *principle* without a human face. Some authors identified Plato's god, or at least the Holy Spirit, with the World Soul, thus turning him

into a grand builder.[58] Pagan philosophers made their own gods his "minions."[59] In this conception, the great creator was not responsible for the obvious defects of his creations. Plotinus (ca. 205–270 AD), the central figure in
the further development of Platonic thought, sublimated Plato's god into a
formless *One*. It was contested which of the many interpretations of Plato the
"theologian" should prevail. Augustine and some of the most important thinkers of the Middle Ages and the Renaissance opted for Plotinus's version. To
the masses, this God, whom Plotinus simply called *to hen*, "the One," seemed
unqualified for the role. He had nothing in common with the ladies' man Zeus
or his colorful cohort of deities.

Even more influential for Europe's future was the monumental oeuvre of
Plato's student, successor, and adversary Aristotle (384–322 BC), who hailed
from the Thracian city of Stagira.[60] He supposedly developed his ideas while
walking to and fro, *peripatein* in Greek. His followers and successors were
therefore called "Peripatetics." The setting for these philosophical strolls was
a covered walkway in a gymnasium dedicated to Apollo Lyceus, the Lyceum—
the source of words for "school" in French (*lycée*), Italian (*liceo*), and other
languages. Aristotle left an astounding wealth of writings. This corpus was of
great consequence for the history of Latin Christendom, as it provided models
of logical argumentation and methods and contained discussions of worldly
topics as well. Aristotle's teachings were often more down to earth than Plato's,
although there is not as sharp a divide between the two as is sometimes
claimed. The worldviews enshrined in the works of these two most important
representatives of Greek philosophy correspond to elementary modes of
human thinking. They can also be found in Confucianism—in the School of
Mind and the School of Reason—and in Scholasticism.[61] Rigorous attempts
were consistently made in medieval Christian Europe to force Plato's thought
and Aristotelian science into harmony with the Good News of the Gospel.

In Aristotle's view, the transcendental is beyond the realm of proof. *Empei-
ria*, "experience," is a keyword of his method, which is focused on what can be
perceived and observed. He does not conceive of human beings as shut up in
a cave but rather out in the midst of reality. Thus it is possible for them to
recognize the beauty of the universe.[62] There is almost no subject Aristotle did
not write about: logic, ethics, rhetoric and poetics, metaphysics, nature, animals and minerals, the cosmos, the stars, the state, history and human beings,
human physiology, physiognomy and psychology, perception and memory,
even dreams. Unlike Plato, he does not have others speak in his works. He
speaks in his own voice.

The connection between these minds from the misty past and the thinkers at the dawn of the modern world is shown in Raphael's *School of Athens*, painted in 1510 in the Stanza della Segnatura in the Vatican (Fig. 3, p. 21). The fresco takes the protagonists of ancient philosophy and places them in the High Renaissance. Plato, holding the *Timaeus* in his left hand, and Aristotle dominate the middle. The former points to the sky, to the realm of ideas, the latter to the earthly world of human beings, open to perception and empirical observation. Next to them is Socrates, Pythagoras with his followers, and many others. When Raphael painted the illustrious gathering, its spirit was as alive as it had been two thousand years before.

The Garden of Epicurus and the Stoa

Alexander the Great's conquest of the Persian Empire fundamentally changed the Greek world. Yet many cities, as long as they remained loyal, retained forms of autonomous civil administration. This work was done by the *demos*, the portion of the population that enjoyed the rights of citizens.[63] Nevertheless, contemplation about the proper regime for the polis lost importance in the wake of constitutional changes and decreased political significance. Cosmology, geography, medicine, and other scientific disciplines came to the fore, but it was, above all, questions of ethics that were now discussed.[64] New schools of philosophy sprang up. One was the *kepos*, or Garden, where Epicurus developed his thought. In this simple orchard outside the gates of Athens, he met with his community of followers, which included women and even slaves, to engage in discussion both serious and jocular—what they called *symphilosophy*, or "philosophizing together."

Not far from the Athenian Acropolis, there was a portico decorated with frescoes and thus known as the "Painted Porch"—*Stoa Poikile*—that lent its name to another school of philosophy: Stoicism.[65] Its ancient history spans half a millennium, from its founding by Zeno around 300 BC to the days of the Roman emperor Marcus Aurelius (r. 161–180 AD). His *Meditations* are the last great product of pre-Christian Stoicism. The teaching of the Stoics may have contributed to the eventual acceptance of Christianity in the Greco-Roman world. Conversely, Christian theologians found many points of overlap with the philosophy of Stoicism.

Zeno considered the mortal body to be unimportant, whereas the mind resembled eternal fire and thus participated in the divine. This stance could ultimately lead to suicide. The Stoic Antipater, for example, chose it as an escape from a life of suffering. The parallels with Christianity ended at this extreme. Stoicism also taught that the universe was ordered by *pronoia*, divine providence, but—in agreement with Aristotle—that it was uncreated and thus eternal. These differences aside, the Hymn to Zeus by Cleanthes (died ca. 232 BC) sounds like a Psalm if the name of "Zeus" is replaced with "God." It begins like this:

> Most glorious of the immortals, invoked by many names, ever
> all-powerful,
> Zeus, the First Cause of Nature, who rules all things with Law
> Hail! It is right for mortals to call upon you,
> since from you we have our being, we whose lot it is to be God's
> image,
> we alone of all mortal creatures that live and move upon the earth.[66]

Zeus is "universal reason," *logos*, and the "creative fire" from which all things flow and all things will be destroyed. History will end with a purifying conflagration encompassing the entire earth—a Stoic prefiguration of the Last Judgment. But that will not be the end of the world. Rather, history will begin anew—a notion common to other cosmologies, such as that of Daoism.

Life and death, praise, desire and pain, wealth, poverty—all such things are marginal to Stoicism. What matters is understanding, self-control, justice and conscience, submission to cosmic forces, to fate, and to necessity. Suffering is not an evil but rather an opportunity to practice virtue.[67] Similar to the Epicureans, the goal of the Stoic lifestyle is to endure the world, not to order or change it. Doing one's duty in life means being in harmony with oneself. Equanimity and imperturbability are the outstanding qualities of the philosopher and the goal of human life: "to fear nothing, to desire nothing," *nihil timere, nihil cupere*.[68] Marcus Aurelius, the Stoic on Rome's imperial throne, gave voice to an idea that would resound in the Christian context of the seventeenth century: life is nothing but a short dream or a stage on which people must play to the best of their ability the role God has given them.[69] The idea of the equality of all people, propagated by Chrysippus (ca. 270–206 BC), fit perfectly with Christian thought. So did the concept of natural law as an eternal rational order that allows all rational people to recognize what is right and wrong.

According to Stoic thought, the contraries that appear in nature and society—male and female, old and young, weak and strong—tend towards harmony by intermixing. Coming into being balances out passing away; everything is in equilibrium. One of the central concepts of Stoicism is *logos*, which denotes not only speech and reason but also the principle at work in nature and human beings. *Logos* is not merely divine; it is divinity itself. This divine reason is interwoven in nature, *physis*, and orders it into a meaningful whole down to the tiniest detail.[70] Since human beings are capable of understanding their own *ratio*—according to Chrysippus—they can make their lives harmonize with it.

Stoicism's enormous influence throughout the centuries—including on Islamic theology and philosophy—was not only due to the fact that it gave order to the universe and taught how to live a good life. In contrast to the Epicureans, who remained aloof from politics, the Stoics also gave advice relevant to the civic world. According to Stoicism, practicing justice and charity, doing one's duty to one's fellow human beings, was a path to freedom. Its influence thus extended far beyond antiquity, into the late Renaissance, and even down to Frederick the Great and Kant.

Just as natural reason was a guide to life in Stoic ethics, it could also be a basis for law. Roman jurists fleshed out this doctrine, and it would deeply influence modern legal thought. On the other hand, Stoicism's emphasis on equanimity did not find a receptive audience among the fiery Protestant Reformers, as can be seen in Martin Luther's snide reference to the "wooden" or "stubborn saints" (*Stockheiligen*) of Stoicism. God, in his view, did not create human beings to be made of stone or wood.[71]

Alexandria

According to a myth reported by Herodotus, the golden, red-feathered phoenix only appears when its father dies.[72] Now that Athens' political dominance was at an end, the phoenix took flight: first to Alexandria and then to Rome. Thus the grand dialogue continued despite all the upheavals of the following centuries. The most important reason for Greek thought's durability was the vast range of topics it addressed and the compelling power of its methods. It required great intellectual robustness to resist the power of rational Greek philosophy, to say nothing of overcoming it. Islam and Judaism had that strength, as did the Orthodox form of Christianity. Latin Europe, on the other hand, succumbed to Greek thought for a long time to come—with massive consequences for world history.

The phoenix first found a new home in Alexandria, in Egypt. Under Ptolemy I Soter, "the Savior" (r. 305–283/82 BC), one of the successors of Alexander, the city already famous for its lighthouse became the most important center of learning in all antiquity. Its Library, along with the works stored in the Serapeum, is said to have contained over half a million texts. The catalog compiled by Callimachus of Cyrene in the third century BC was supposedly five times longer than the *Iliad*. Not even China could boast of such a large storehouse of wisdom at the time.

Alexandria's "Museum," which Cicero referred to as the "workshop of all the arts" (*officina omnium artium*),[73] was what we would now call an interdisciplinary research center. The Egyptian kings appointed its members, paid them, and gave them special privileges such as tax exemptions. It had living quarters, a dining hall, an observatory, a shrine to the Muses, and maybe even a zoo with exotic animals. The rulers generally gave the scholars there the freedom to investigate and discuss whatever they wanted. Poetry and philology reached great heights. The Greek translation of the Old Testament made by Jewish scholars, known as the Septuagint, was produced in Alexandria. But the city was also a byword for mathematics, mechanics, physics, and geography—at the same time, we might note, as a return was being made to materialist explanations of nature in the Garden of Epicurus and elsewhere. Whereas in Athens, philosophers had speculated about "first principles" and constructed systems that were supported by this or that empirical observation, scholars on the Nile focused on individual phenomena in order to develop mathematical models from them.[74] Correspondence with reality was, however, secondary to a model's internal consistency. Alexandrian science did not seek to explain things but rather to describe and prove them with numbers and geometry.

The Museum was a monarchical alternative to the "democratic" Academy. Its organization reflected the changed political landscape after Alexander the Great's death and the wars between his successors. Their competition encouraged innovation—and recourse to ungenteel methods. One of the Ptolemies, likely the founder of the Museum, supposedly ordered that scrolls arriving in the port of Alexandria—on loan from Athens, for example—should be confiscated. Bearing the annotation "from the ships," they then made their way into the Library.[75] The owners at least received copies of their books back. Ptolemy II is said to have imposed a ban on the export of papyrus to Pergamon in order to prevent its famous library from becoming larger and possibly outshining Alexandria's luster.[76] The name of the Attalid capital lives on in the substitute writing material made there out of animal hides: parchment, which derives from the Latin word *pergamena*.

Alexandria was of fundamental importance for science and literature. The physicians Herophilus of Chalcedon (ca. 330–255 BC) and his younger contemporary Erasistratus, two founders of anatomy, started the medical school in Alexandria. Euclid, who was educated in Athens before moving to Alexandria, was one of the fathers of optics. The geometry he developed dominated the field until about 1830 AD. Archimedes, the legendary mathematician known especially for his work in physics and mechanics, was also active in Alexandria for a time. Other leading lights of Alexandrian culture were Apollonius of Perga, the master of conic sections, and the geographer Eratosthenes of Cyrene. The inventions that came out of Alexandria were stunning. Ctesibius, who lived in the third century BC, developed precision water clocks and pumps. The automata he built seem to approximate quite closely the technology of the steam engine.[77] Three hundred years later, Hero of Alexandria actually used heat as a source of power.

Alexandrian astronomers also subjected the movements of the stars to mathematical analysis. The impulse came from astrology, which originated in the East, in Babylon. It was the first attempt to find causality in a model of the cosmos. According to this theory, the movements of celestial bodies and the relationships between them cause all change; they influence the four elements (earth, water, air, and fire) and, through them, human constitution, animals, and even plants. Hellenistic astrologers developed the very influential teaching that the position of the planets had an impact on the abilities, fate, and personality of every individual human being. Astrological theory stimulated astronomical research all the way down to Copernicus's and Galileo's day and beyond.

Even in decline, Alexandria continued to be connected with great names. The physician Galen (ca. 129–ca. 216 AD) of Pergamon, whose medical texts were published in no fewer than 660 editions between 1490 and 1498,[78] spent time in Alexandria before pursuing his career in Rome. Claudius Ptolemy (ca. 100–ca. 170 AD)—another figure in Raphael's *School of Athens*—wrote the *Tetrabiblos* and the *Almagest*, classic works of astronomy and astrology. His conception of the universe, with Earth fixed at the center, was the dominant one until modern times. His geography, along with Strabo's (ca. 64 BC–23 AD), remained the basis for all knowledge of peoples and countries on Earth until the sixteenth century. The Library of Alexandria vanished, however. Its papyrus collection seems to have decayed over time. Already in the first few centuries AD, the funds for making new copies were clearly lacking. It is not known whether fire or looting finished the job.

The Greeks themselves sought to explain the origins and causes of the cultural flourishing they witnessed. Similar to others, such as the Chinese, who

also enjoyed a long period of flourishing, they attributed the glorious development of their culture to gods and heroes. Technology was said to have come
from Hephaestus and Athena, the horse from Poseidon, astronomy from
Hermes, and grain from Demeter. The Greeks' foremost cultural heroes included the aforementioned Palamedes as well as Daedalus, who was considered the inventor of sculpture, the potter's wheel and other useful devices,
even the art of flying. The greatest of all was Prometheus. But the Greeks also
recognized that progress came from human thought and industry as well. "The
gods have not, of course, revealed all things to mortals from the beginning,"
wrote Xenophanes, "but rather, seeking in the course of time, they discover
what is better."[79]

Prometheus is a necessary fiction. It is not possible to explain a Plato or a
Thucydides. Nevertheless, a few circumstances that facilitated the Greek
miracle can be highlighted. The case of Greece shows—and it is not the only
example in world history—that compartmentalized, politically fragmented
regions and open societies offer favorable conditions for cultural development. Radical thinkers had a good chance of finding refuge somewhere. A
further foundation of Greek high culture was the fact that a politically influential class of craftsmen, merchants, and intellectuals had formed in the cities
of the Greek world—a precursor to what we call the "middle classes," a group
of educated, creative people living in relative economic security. They wrote
poetry, built buildings, reasoned; a speech in favor of of a proposition elicited
a speech in opposition, and more and more people joined the discussion.
From the age of Hellenism, no fewer than 1,100 authors are known to us, at
least by name.[80] The number of Greek writers of tragedy and comedy must
have been in the thousands.

From time immemorial Greek society was *agonal*, characterized, for
whatever reason, by a competitive spirit. Races were run and music composed
for prizes. Orators sought to secure a majority by means of better speeches.
Comedies were written for contests. Even sculptors and surgeons hoped to
win something with their hammering and healing. Time was reckoned according to athletic competitions, the Olympiads. Change and innovation were
recognized as human achievements and viewed positively. Hippodamus of
Miletus wished there was a law awarding prizes for inventions.[81] Thus the idea
of the patent was born.

Celebrating progress is a Greek idea. It does not seem to exist in Buddhist
or other cultures of the Far East.[82] The Romans, on the other hand, adopted
this spirit wholeheartedly. Seneca ventured to make a great prophecy:

The day will yet come when the progress of research through long ages will reveal to sight the mysteries of nature that are now concealed. . . . The day will yet come when posterity will be amazed that we remained ignorant of things that will to them seem so plain.[83]

He even predicted the discovery of new continents beyond the legendary Atlantic island of Thule.

On the other hand, excessive curiosity and ingenuity could be condemned as hubris, as is illustrated by an episode from the *Alexander Romance*.[84] Alexander, so the story goes, had two griffins captured and chained to a wagon so that he could fly to the sky. Fastening a horse liver to sticks and holding them out in front of the monsters' beaks, he induced them to take flight. Up in the air, Alexander encountered a bird with a human face who admonished him, "Alexander, you who do not know earthly things are trying to explore heavenly ones?" This caused the king to return to the ground. The story was given a Christian interpretation in the Middle Ages. Now it was God Himself who reined in Alexander's audacity. Like Daedalus and Prometheus, those who try to storm the heavens don't have it easy. Even in Greece, the path from *mythos* to *logos* was anything but straight. Yet nowhere else was it trodden with so much perseverance.

4

Rome

The Phoenix Flies Westward

The beginning of everything else was Rome. In the empire that originated there, Hellenistic culture spread and ultimately transformed through its interaction with Christianity. After the fall of the Western Roman Empire, Byzantium and then the Islamic empires took up this role. All of these powers participated in passing down to posterity the grand dialogue begun by the Greeks. Thus, the culture of the victors of Salamis remained no regional affair but rather exercised an influence unparalleled by any other civilization down to our own day. The phoenix took flight from Greece and flew westward, following the sun.

Rome's meteoric rise was also facilitated by geography. Would the city on the Tiber have managed to become the ruler of the entire Mediterranean without its location in Italy? The long coastlines of the peninsula are open to the east and the west. Italy is in the middle of the Mediterranean: in summery Rimini, early risers swim toward the silvery morning sun; evening strollers along the Gulf of Naples in Posillipo watch it set in a sea of red-gold and then amethyst, in which the islands of Ischia and Capri crouch like giant Cyclopes. The settlement near a ford on the Tiber, the origin of Rome, was probably founded in the late seventh century BC. Farmers and shepherds lived there. Etruscan nobles, their territory centered in what is now Tuscany, conquered it. It is possible that the oldest name of the city—Ruma, which is first attested ca. 330 BC—refers to an Etruscan family. A thirst for territorial expansion likely motivated the wars of conquest in whose course Rome rose to be a regional power. According to Livy (59 BC–17 AD), Rome felt compelled to battle increasingly dangerous foes, starting with the Samnite Wars in the fourth century BC. With the conquest of Carthage in the late third century BC, the path to empire was taken—although no one knew it at the time. Seen from this point of view, John Robert Seeley's remark about the genesis of the British Empire also applies to the Roman Empire: that it happened "in a fit of absence of mind."[1] In point of fact, the "imperial logic" outlined by Livy did not take shape until later.

Machiavelli, who used antiquity like a storehouse of instructive examples, viewed Rome's politics as a model for how to deal best with conquered foes. As he counsels in the fifth chapter of his *Prince*, one possibility is to crush them so utterly that they can never again pose a danger. The other possibility is to pursue reconciliation through moderation, such that the next generation has more to win from being friends than enemies. Rome adopted both strategies. The slaughter of the citizens of Veii and Fidenae, and the destruction of Carthage, Corinth, and Jerusalem, exemplify the first; the tradition of appeasing the losers by giving them freedoms exemplifies the second. Time and again, the system of integration—as in the wars with the Celts or Carthage—demonstrated its reliability. "What else proved fatal to Lacedaemon and Athens, in spite of their power in arms, but their policy of holding the conquered aloof as alien-born?" Emperor Claudius is supposed to have remarked. "But the sagacity of our own founder Romulus was such that several times he fought and naturalized a people in the course of the same day!"[2] If the history of the Roman Empire holds a lesson, it is that freedom, including religious toleration, can replace swords and tanks.[3] Virgil put the political model in a nutshell, musing that Rome's fate was to rule nations, fight the proud, and spare the vanquished.[4]

There is more than just a kernel of truth in the master narrative, fashioned by poets and statesmen, of Rome the frugal republic. Like in Athens, decisions were reached in republican Rome via dialogue, not dictated by a godlike potentate. Allied and free cities, *civitates foederatae ac liberae*, retained their right to exist even under the emperors. In the second century AD, the widely traveled Aelius Aristides still considered the Empire to be a community of poleis, cities with their own territory that, for the most part, governed themselves.[5] In provinces outside of Italy, they were under the supervision of governors who also exercised military command. Nevertheless, like in the city-states of Greece, there was still a certain degree of freedom.

One blemish on the Republic was that it ultimately proved unable to counterbalance social inequality and prevent the decay into monarchy. Augustus's establishment of the Principate completed the latter process. Under Octavian and his successors, Rome also received its marble overhaul. Resources flowed to Rome from every corner of the Empire so that a royal city in the Hellenistic mold could be built. People from all over gathered in this melting pot of nations and cultures. Rome's population grew to over one million. It was the first city in Europe to reach that size and the only one to do so there for almost two thousand years. The impression made by this magnificent display of imperial sovereignty must have been overpowering. Even today, Rome's ruins attest to its once almighty power, to the semi-cosmic order that held the world together.

Rome's Hellenic Yearning

With the incorporation of the Greek states into the Roman Empire in the second century BC, contact intensified between the Hellenistic East and the area that would end up being Latin Europe. To the Empire's credit, it had always engaged profoundly with the knowledge and religion of subject territories and neighboring cultures. An early example is the Senate's decision to have the twenty-eight books on agriculture by the Carthaginian Mago translated into Latin. Most important for Rome's intellectual life, however, was the connection to Greek culture. "Greece, the captive, took her savage victor captive, and brought the arts into rustic Latium." Thus the poet Horace (65 BC–8 AD) formulated the fascination that Greece had for its conqueror.[6] The Roman elite had been enthusiastic about Greek language, culture, and lifestyle long before the proconsul Titus Quinctius Flamininus declared the Greeks a free people in 196 BC. At times it was considered chic to dress and act Greek, to sprinkle some Greek into one's speech, and to grow a "philosopher's beard." Beginning with Hadrian, even the emperors wore beards. Nero renewed Flamininus's guarantee of freedom. Hadrian and Marcus Aurelius—who wrote his *Meditations* in Greek—promoted Stoicism. Antoninus Pius gave all the philosophers in the Empire a tax exemption.

From early times, contact with the culture of Greece flowed through relations with Magna Graecia, the Greek cities in southern Italy, especially Naples and Taranto. This is probably where the Romans first encountered the miracle drug of money. The Latin word for money, *pecunia*, evokes traditional bartering and the most important good that was traded with it: *pecus*, or cattle. The Greek alphabet probably made its way via the Etruscans to Rome, where it was Latinized. It was the source of the Roman letter *c*, which took the place of the Greek *g*, gamma, which in turn moved to later in the alphabet. The Twelve Tables, a collection of laws dating to the fifth century BC, is an early witness to the use of the alphabet in the West. The story goes that three Roman citizens were sent to Greece before the laws were written down, to study the legislation of Solon and the rights of the Greek cities. A statue of Pythagoras was set up in Rome's Comitium, the place where the people met to ratify laws. And Varro (116–27 BC), a public official, military commander, and literary giant well acquainted with Greek philosophy, was ordered by Caesar to compile a library that would include Greek literature.

The classic case of inventing a tradition is the *Aeneid*, in which Virgil (70 BC–19 AD) created the Roman national epic. Reworking the poetry of his predecessors Naevius—who bore the moniker *graecus* or *semigraecus*—and Ennius, he made the Trojan refugee Aeneas into the founder of Rome. The *Aeneid* cast Rome's recent past in the guise of timeless mythology. On its pages, Rome and its leaders appeared as executors of the *fatum*, or fate, willed by the highest divinity, Jupiter. Around the time of the birth of Christ, the Romans were happy to have the rhetorician and historian Dionysius of Halicarnassus tell them that their city was founded as a Greek polis, and thus that they themselves were actually Greeks. They also loved to claim descent from Greek ancestors. The progenitor of the first Etruscan king of Rome, Tarquinius, was said to be Demaratus of Corinth.[7] He was credited with bringing craftsmen from Greece to Italy, and indeed Greek potters and merchants, sculptors and architects were active in early Rome. On the whole, the shape of the young city seems to have owed more to Greek than to Etruscan influences.[8] Greek gods like Aphrodite, Ares, and Zeus were adopted as early as the third century BC, although they were generally given Latin names: Venus, Mars, and Jupiter. That foreign peoples venerated the same gods, just under different names, was a widespread conviction in Greece and Rome.

Resistance to the dominance of Hellenic culture was futile. For example, Cato the Elder (234–149 BC)—historian, profit-minded slaveholder, and the embodiment of ancient Roman virtue—is an early example of how Roman conservatives sought to check the charm of Hellenism. He counterposed strict morality and sobriety to the colorful glitter of Greek culture and its cosmic flights of thought.[9] Yet such a stance could not stem the tide of cultural exchange. A faithful report must emphasize the influence enjoyed by Greek political theory, mathematics, medicine, natural history, geography, music, astronomy, and cosmology. Mention should be made of Aulus Gellius, the antiquarian and teller of tales whose *Attic Nights* was written on the estate of Herodes Atticus outside Athens. Another indication is the enormous importance Greek tragedy had for Rome, where it found a home as early as 240 BC. Above all, Euripides—but also Sophocles, Aeschylus, and lesser lights— entertained, edified, and stirred the Roman soul. A native tradition, aside from insignificant exceptions, was inspired only in the capital.

The Roman art of mosaic was based on Greek models. Etruscan tomb paintings and the decoration of Attic vases, thousands of which have been found in Italy, can only transmit a faint reflection of the Greek-inspired images that we read of in Pliny or in Philostratus's *Imagines*, which recreates a walk through a painted portico in Naples. The situation is different with the more durable art of sculpture. Roman sculptors mass-produced copies of Greek originals—when, that is, the originals (or what passed for such) were not brought over from Greece to decorate palaces in Rome or luxurious villas in the countryside. Scenes from Greek mythology literally stood before the Romans' eyes in the form of massive marble sculpture groups. Better-known examples include the Polyphemus scene in Emperor Tiberius's grotto in Sperlonga, and the Laocoon Group attributed to sculptors from Rhodes. After the latter was rediscovered on the grounds of Nero's palace in 1506, the sculpture became an inspiration for High Renaissance art and the object of a perennial discussion about beauty (pp. 536f., 746f.).

It was not only the myth of Troy that inspired Roman poets. Virgil never could have written his *Eclogues*, for example, without the pastoral poetry of Theocritus of Syracuse. The work of Horace, who lived in Athens in his youth, grew in part out of his study of the Aeolic poet Sappho, of Anacreon, Pindar, and Callimachus. The latter's *Aitia*, translated into Latin by Catullus, inspired both Propertius and Ovid. The Greeks also taught Rome how to laugh. The genre of *fabula palliata*—comedies inspired by Greek originals, performed in Greek clothing, and set in the Greek milieu of their models—soon ruled the stages of the Roman world. Plautus (250–184 BC) and Terence (ca. 195–159 BC) learned from Menander, the master of Greek New Comedy. And Seneca's *Apocolocyntosis*—or *Pumpkinification*, a satire on the apotheosis of Emperor Claudius—was based on a satire by Menippus. Plautus populated the landscape of his plays with parasites and pimps, braggarts, old men mad with love, cunning slaves, and prostitutes. His *Amphitryon* portrays Jupiter, king of the gods, as an almighty Casanova in Greek garb. To prolong a night of amorous ecstasy, he even stops the motion of the stars. A satirist of Plautus's caliber simply cannot be found in Byzantine or Islamic culture. Just imagine a burlesque with Yahweh, Christ, or Muhammad!

By far the most important promoter of Greek thought was the orator and philosopher Marcus Tullius Cicero (105–43 BC), in both his politics and his ideas a staunch defender of the foundering Republic.[10] In Metapontum, he visited the place where Pythagoras died; in Syracuse, he honored the long-forgotten grave of Archimedes. He brought the genre of the dialogue to new heights. Galileo, as we have seen, adopted his model. The interlocutors in his dialogues have occasion to give full voice to their positions. They do not so much discuss each other's views as give speeches. These conversations are set in beautiful estates like Cicero's own villa outside Tusculum—a place that still radiates the aura of the author of the *Tusculanae disputationes*, or *Tusculan Disputations*. The stone stairs of an ancient theater are now a picnic spot for Sunday sightseers. On clear days, Rome can be seen through the olive trees and holm oaks. The silver stripe of the sea sparkles in the distance.

A spring, a spot of grass for lounging under the shade of a plane tree, now became the indispensable setting for a philosophical dialogue. Cicero crafted ideal portraits of serene humanity that still fascinated the Renaissance. He was a master of casual small talk, of sprinkling anecdotes into his discussions. Readers feel that they are the guests of an elegant gentleman who eagerly takes the opportunity to retire to his library, far from the hustle and bustle of the city and affairs of state, to devote himself to philosophy. Cicero was not only one of the most important orators of antiquity. He was also one of the greatest Latin stylists. The technical side of debating, the *form* of speaking and writing, took on paramount importance in his writings. In the Renaissance, it would be infused into the traditional exercise of learned disputation.

As a young man, Cicero studied in Athens with the Platonist Antiochus of Ascalon. There he became acquainted with the teachings of the Academy. The grove of Hecademus had been devastated by Sulla's soldiers in the conquest of Athens in 86 BC, and ever since then the Academy had been located in a gymnasium near the Acropolis. Cicero relates how, a few years later, he took a walk to the remains of the old school in the grove. The erstwhile abode of great minds was now empty and silent. Cicero and his companion traded stories about the memories that hung in the ruins, about the old days of that hallowed ground. They reminisced about Speusippus and Xenocrates, the first heads of the Academy, and about Plato, who was buried there. Cicero thought he recognized the hall where Carneades of Cyrene (214–129 BC), a leading exponent of skepticism, had taught. As part of a Greek embassy to Rome in 155 BC, Carneades had caused a stir by giving a speech in favor of justice on one day, and another speech against it the next. This embassy was the first time Greek philosophy piqued the interest of broader circles of Roman society.

Cicero felt a kinship for the philosophy of this people that, by his own day, had long been part of the Roman world. Despite his obvious vanity, in his works he demonstrates the restraint of a man who knows that there are often two truths, and even more often no truth at all. Against all the complacent *dogmatikoi*, those philosophers who held to fixed doctrines and left no room for doubt, he countered that dogmatism amounted to arrogance and contempt for the truth of others. In this way, he tried to do justice to the great philosophical currents, extract from them the ideas that seemed reasonable, and develop his own philosophy from them. Along with the Peripatetics, Epicurus, and the Stoics, he received the greatest impulse from Plato. Even an ancient defender of Christianity, Minucius Felix, was influenced by Cicero's serene manner of discussing things and treating his adversaries with respect. Cicero, as the clever man in the middle, understandably elicited admiration through the ages.

Rome's historians also learned much from their colleagues from Hellas. The very first historian on the Tiber, Fabius Pictor, wrote in Greek. Sallust took the measure of his style from Thucydides, and the two of them influenced Tacitus, the most important Roman historian, along with Lucian of Samosata (ca. 120–after 180 AD).[11] The first "renaissance" of European history was the Second Sophistic, which began in Asia Minor and lasted from about 60 to 230 AD. It cultivated rhetoric as a public spectacle. It was as skeptical as the model it imitated, and many of its representatives highlighted the reversibility of audaciously aired opinions. The Second Sophistic was tinged with a romanticism common to movements oriented toward the distant past. But like every renaissance, it looked both backward and forward at the same time.[12] One of its leading representatives was the aforementioned Lucian. The written tradition has been kind to this spirited detractor of religion and empty sophistry. Over eighty of his writings are extant. His perennially influential *Dialogues of the Dead* contains imaginary conversations between gods, philosophers, military commanders, and heroes. Another of his works, *True History* (or *True Story*), describes an imaginary adventure through outer space and even includes interplanetary battles—one part satire on mythical historiography, one part science fiction.

It must be noted that, as with Athens, Rome did not enjoy absolute freedom of thought or expression. Violations of moral standards could meet with severe penalties. During the Civil Wars, for example, writings of Varro were destroyed, and later, probably around 8 BC, those of Titus Labienus were burned.[13] The air got even thinner in imperial Rome. The epigrammatist Martial (ca. 40–103/4 AD) hid the identity of the individuals he attacked behind pseudonyms. When Tacitus praised the time of Trajan as one of the few happy ages in history, "when it is possible to think what one likes and say what one thinks,"[14] he was writing of a past that seemed preferable to his own present.

An Empire without Borders

The incredible thing about the Roman Empire is how long it lasted. After the crisis of the Republic and the Civil Wars, the establishment of the monarchy laid the foundation for several hundred years of further survival. Until the reign of Marcus Aurelius (r. 161–180 AD), the Parthian Empire was Rome's only serious competitor. In this sense, it was a "universal" empire. Puppet rulers and client kings from the Black Sea to North Africa helped to create buffer zones along the borders. The emperors could be monsters like Nero or model rulers like Trajan (r. 98–117 AD), but a relatively smoothly functioning administrative apparatus ensured stability across their reigns. Under Trajan and Antoninus Pius (r. 138–161 AD), Rome ruled from Britain to Africa, from the Iberian Peninsula to the Persian Gulf; its trade relations extended to Southeast Asia.[15] The mighty prophecy that Virgil put into Jupiter's mouth, namely that the Empire would be without end, an *imperium sine fine*, seemed fulfilled. Yet Hadrian—Trajan's successor and the second in what may have been the most brilliant series of rulers in all of world history—already had to give up territory in the East and shift gears from expansion to safeguarding prior gains.

In the last third of the second century, it became an effort for the Empire to provide protection. Foreign peoples, who in Roman sources are often simply referred to as *Germani*, "Germanic tribes," swelled across the Rhine and the Danube. On other borders as well—in the Atlas Mountains, on the Euphrates River, in Syria, and in North Africa—Rome was on the defensive. The opportunity was ripe for military commanders to seize control of the government. Beginning with the rule of Maximinus Thrax (r. 235–238 AD), "soldier emperors," many of them hailing from the rural world of the Balkan provinces, determined the fate of the Empire. The Caesars spent less and less time in Rome. They were constantly on the move, putting down a rebellion here and there, fighting off usurpers, and defending against invaders. The center witnessed unrest and fights for the throne. Scenes like the auction of the imperial title after the murder of Pertinax have been burned into memory, as have caricatures of bloodthirsty monsters on the throne. In reality, even in the chaotic third century, Rome could still be ruled by capable men who steadfastly held off decline. Victories were still won that adorned the emperors with resplendent honorary titles: "greatest victor" over the Germanic tribes, Goths, and Carpi, "restorer" of the "Orient" and even of the entire globe. The triumphs, celebrated according to ancient rites, were then clouded by the smoke that rose from the emperors' funeral pyres, carrying their names to the ranks of the immortal gods. Concern grew for the security of the city of Rome itself, as evidenced by the enormous wall erected around it by Aurelian and Probus. The point had long since been reached where the costs of displaying imperial power outstripped its use to society.[16] Even when the hobbled Roman Hercules managed to lop off one or two heads of the barbarian hydra, new heads sprouted immediately from the bloody stumps.

The Empire might have maintained authority over its many foreign enemies had usurpers—including praetorian prefects and generals on the periphery—not disturbed domestic peace with relentless regularity. In one year, five rivals competed for the power and title of emperor. Roman legions battled each other rather than marching against the Goths, Marcomanni, or Sasanians. The Senate still met in Rome, but imperial administration was centered wherever the emperor happened to reside—be it Serdica (now Sofia), Sirmium, or Nicodemia in Bithynia. Diocletian (r. 284–305 AD), who instituted reforms in an attempt to change the course of events, reorganized the defense of the Empire and its rule by dividing both across the shoulders of four men, called "tetrarchs." The form was retained by his successor Constantine (r. ca. 306–337 AD). That this was the first step on the path to the division of the Empire can only be seen in hindsight.

Another step in that direction was taken when the capital was moved. After defeating his rivals for the throne, Constantine founded a new imperial seat on the site of the Greek town of Byzantium, which he called "Constantinople." The location dominated the entrance to the Black Sea so utterly, Polybius (ca. 200– ca. 120 BC) wrote of Byzantium, that no merchant could enter or exit it without permission.[17] Dedicated in 330 AD, the "New Rome" was intended to be a monument to its founder. In addition, it put Constantine closer to the vulnerable eastern edge of the Empire. He entrusted border security to his sons. To this end he created a mobile field army commanded by *magistri militum*, literally "masters of the soldiers," and border defense actually did improve.

Constantine's policy laid the foundation for the creation and rise of the Byzantine Empire, while, to quote Theodor Mommsen, the old capital lived "in widowhood, sulking, grumbling, and criticizing."[18] Its hope lay in two graves that, according to tradition, contained the remains of the apostles Peter and Paul. The former bequeathed to the pope, the bishop of Rome, the power of the keys to bind and loose on earth as well as in heaven. The latter, as the most important propagator of Christ's message, bestowed upon the pope magisterium, the authority to teach religious doctrine.[19] It is strange indeed that the forgotten city's rise to become the capital of Christianity began with a few bones of uncertain origin! The territory of the Western Empire, which had now entered the slipstream of history, was the terrain on which Europe would follow its momentous trajectory.

In the following centuries, many emperors ruled not on the Tiber but in Trier, Milan, or Arles. In the fifth century, Ravenna grew in importance. The pope was separated from the Eastern emperor by two seas. This distance was a prerequisite for the disentanglement of religion from the secular world, for the separation of church and state that began in Latin Europe—and only there. That is what gave the emperors' relocation to the Bosporus world-historical significance. In the embattled West, the papal church gained the freedom to operate that allowed it to become an institution with a universal claim to authority—a process that elicited strong counter-reactions that, after more than a millennium and a half of fighting, ultimately led to a radical curtailment of its political power.

The Greek Christ

The spread of the Christian Gospel was facilitated by the fact that it quickly resonated with Jews of the Diaspora, who were steeped in Greek culture. It therefore not only found an audience among Jews and those who could speak

Aramaic, the language of Jesus, but it also spread in Greek, thus making the Empire a perfect vehicle of transmission. The opening of the movement to the uncircumcised was tantamount to cutting the cord from its Jewish mother. Christianity became a religion rather than remaining a sect—the "heresy of the Nazarenes," as early enemies of the Christian community disparagingly referred to it.[20] By virtue of taking shape in the Greek cultural environment, the new religion enjoyed easy access to its philosophy's ideas and modes of thought.[21] The Greek inheritance was one of the most important preconditions allowing for the dialogue between medieval Christianity and antiquity to even take place, containing as it did the Greeks' unbridled curiosity and their spirit of critical inquiry and methodical thinking.

When it came to religion, the Roman state was usually tolerant. This hands-off attitude was an ingredient in the cement that held the Empire together. Its subjects were free to entrust their concerns to the deity of their choice. There was a wide range to choose from. The rhetorician Themistius, a non-Christian, still counted about three hundred cults in the mid-fourth century. God wants to be venerated in a variety of ways, as he is said to have dryly commented.[22] Rome also left the followers of Jesus unmolested for a long time. Only in the crisis-ridden third century did the pressure mount. Yet persecution did not mute the message of the Gospel. It produced martyrs and, thus, models that strengthened the solidarity of the growing congregations.

The new religion's success in the marketplace of the gods and mysteries is understandable. The Christian message encountered societies that, for whatever reason—perhaps because the monarchical Empire provided a model?—were receptive to monotheism. Its call to charity gave it universal reach, and it accorded men and women, slaves and masters, publicans and prostitutes all equal dignity as creatures of God. Attractive was the tangible benefit of becoming a member of an empire-wide community that provided emergency assistance through a network of "social workers," the deacons. In the form of the Eucharist, Christianity offered a cultic practice that forged a sense of belonging and, unlike the mystery religions of the East, was not re-served to initiates. That was another reason it became a religion for everyone. Nevertheless, specialists were necessary to perform the sacraments; hence the division between the clergy and the laity. This may have planted the seed for the emergence of a unique institution in world history: the Roman Catholic Church under the control of the pope.[23] Finally, the survival of the new reli-gion was aided by the fact that it provided a replacement for the identity that was lost with the decline of the Empire. In its stead, the Church created a religious empire of universal dimensions and fostered a sense of unity based on cultic practice and theology.[24]

What the new religion offered was seductive. As Adolf von Harnack emphasized, it was in essence syncretistic.[25] Its command to love others amounted to an easily understandable code of ethics and provided a rationale for what meaning life and its sufferings could have. It promised redemption and resurrection, providing believers with rituals that were easy to master and that endowed them with renewed purity. The Christian God did not appear to believers merely as an abstract "One," a rarefied "logos," or an ephemeral "light." He was at once infinitely distant and intimately near. He could be spoken to directly and, like his people, knew doubt, suffering, and death. In the fusion of opposites Christianity effected in its fashioning of Jesus Christ, it provided its followers with a two-fold opportunity for identification: with the god and with the man. The latter was a novel, unprecedented feature. Whether pagan Europe's old motley crew of deities could have resisted Islam, with its almighty Allah, the one God with a thousand names, and its enlightened prophet is more than questionable.

The new religion was flexible. The boundaries between pagan and Christian Europe were accordingly fluid. As Jesus resembled the sun god and the father god Zeus, thus many Christian saints shared attributes with pagan divinities. Their quickly growing cohort made up for the loss of the Olympian pantheon. In addition, many Christian rites adopted old pagan traditions. The puzzling Trinity of God could easily be understood as a concession to polytheism; at the least, it must have reminded contemporaries of the Capitoline triad of Jupiter, Juno, and Minerva.

The things that made the Christian god easier for "pagans" to accept could also become problematic as the identities of the gods blurred together. The defenders of pure Christian doctrine thus saw themselves engaged in a multi-front war: against the old gods, against the "mother religion" of Judaism, against the Manichaeans and their differentiation between a world of light and a world of darkness, and against Gnostic currents, which were also imbued with the teachings of Mani in addition to Jewish, Neoplatonic, and Christian ideas. What the enemies of Gnosticism disparaged as "false, so-called knowledge" were often earnest attempts to rationally sift rich philosophical and theological traditions in order to reach knowledge of God and achieve salvation.

With the exception of their refusal to participate in the imperial cult, the behavior of Christians gave no reason to think they might be plotting against the established order. In his letter to the Romans, in words that have stood the test of time, Paul called for Christians to obey the state: "There is no authority except from God, and those that exist have been instituted by God."[26] Of great consequence was the priesthood's development into an independent estate, set apart by consecration and a life of abstinence; it was a prerequisite for the Western Church's rise to a state within the state. From the very beginning, increasing distance from the common people was ensured by the fact that bishops, deacons, and presbyters—divinely chosen intermediaries between this world and the next—for the most part came from the Roman upper and upper-middle classes.[27]

The new religion's survival depended on its connection to the authority of the state. Without this alliance, every religion is destined to live the modest existence of a sect. This was the downfall of Manichaeism.[28] Christianity, in contrast, was recognized as a *religio licita*, a "permitted religion," by Emperor Galerius in 311 AD. Constantine's victory over his rival Maxentius at the Milvian Bridge outside Rome may have provided the final occasion for making it official. The nearly three-hundred-year-old religion boasted so many followers at that point that integrating them into the state seemed inevitable.

Having only just achieved legal status, the Church, then in the process of formation, was rent by internal discord; it is no accident that this happened in Alexandria, the center of theological erudition. The presbyter Arius declared that Christ must have been fathered or created in some way and, therefore, was not eternal, thus degrading him to a kind of demigod.[29] For peoples, such as many Germanic tribes, who believed human beings could be born of gods or become gods themselves, this theology was very attractive. It is remarkable that this controversy played out on the basis not only of the Bible but also of philosophical positions. For example, Plato was the source of important arguments for countering Arius, to the effect that God was One, indivisible, and perfect.

This affair shows that even theological disputes made recourse to the dialectical toolkit acquired from the Greeks. A council called by Constantine in 325 AD in his palace in Nicaea condemned Arius's views as heresy. The emperor, who was not overly interested in theological details, pressured the bishops to adopt the formula that Christ and God the Father were "consubstantial" or "coessential," *homoousios*. The creed formulated at Nicaea, the first ecumenical council in Church history, provided a foundation for the Christian religion from then on. After his death, Constantine was deified like so many of his pagan predecessors. The Christian god may have seemed to him the embodiment of Apollo or Sol, with whom he sometimes identified himself; he appears to have been baptized an Arian.

Fights for the throne among Constantine's successors and within the later Valentinian dynasty made it easier for Franks, Alemanni, and finally Goths to invade the Empire. The Persians threatened from the east. In the late fourth century, pressure mounted on Rome's borders. Huns migrated west from central Asia; some peoples joined them and fought by their side, while others yielded and sought safety in the teetering Empire. A specter arose that did not begin with the Huns but that now took on an elemental momentum: the threat from the steppe, the eternal shadowland between wilderness and cultivation.[30] Legends were told of the offspring of Gothic witches and evil spirits who stormed into the ordered world, wielding death and destruction.[31] China looked westward just as apprehensively as peoples in the West looked eastward. Central Asia became a sinister, eerie place.[32]

Conquering hordes penetrated the borders of the Empire in ever greater numbers. It was no longer possible to integrate them. Land became scarce. Attempts to shut them out militarily failed, such as a Roman army's devastating loss to Gothic warriors in 378 AD at Adrianople. The invaders were perforce given the status of *foederati*, or allies. This recognition lent their control of a part of the Empire a veneer of statehood and legitimacy. As was now clear and would become clearer in the future, the sign of the cross was no guarantee of victory. The triumph of Christianity, on the other hand, was irreversible. Monotheism and monarchy were a steady alliance. Theodosius I (r. 379–395 AD), the last sole leader of the whole Empire, had a council in Constantinople prepare a document that continues to define Christian orthodoxy to this day. It amended the Nicene Creed by affirming the divinity of the Holy Spirit.

In the late fourth century, a forged letter appeared that was a boon to the bishops of Rome. In the document, Clement, a former head of the Roman See, claimed that Saint Peter had named him his successor. This was welcome written confirmation of Rome's primacy. It took centuries for it to be widely accepted, of course. At the same time, the status of the emperor was transforming. From a godlike Caesar and a god-to-be, he became the subject of the Pantocrator, the "almighty" Christ, whose image peered earnestly and unapproachably over the faithful from the apses of churches.

Nicene Christianity was now a state religion. Performing sacrifices to the old gods was high treason. Paganism found a martyr of its own in the mathematician and philosopher Hypatia (ca. 370–415 AD), the first woman to lecture on Plato in Alexandria. She was dragged by a mob into the "Caesareum"—which had been converted into a cathedral—and beaten to death, probably on the orders of Patriarch Cyril.[33] In Athens, things were still calm. In the fifth century, the Neoplatonist Proclus (ca. 410–485 AD), director of the Academy, was able to write his commentary on the first book of Euclid's *Elements*, a history of Greek geometry, and synopses of the astronomical systems of Hipparchus and Ptolemy.

Pagan renaissances occasionally flared up, all leading to nothing. The pagan Symmachus, urban prefect of Rome and scion of an old senatorial family, addressed moving words to Valentinian II when the cult of the goddess of victory was suppressed:

> We gaze up at the same stars; the sky covers us all; the same universe encompasses us. Does it matter what practical system we adopt in our search for the Truth? The heart of so great a mystery cannot be reached by following one road only.[34]

This passage rings with what would become one of the grand themes of the Renaissance: the conviction that a single, great truth is hidden in the multitude of religions.

Symmachus found an adversary in the bishop of Milan, the Church Father Ambrose, who at the same time was fighting the Arians in defense of orthodox Christian doctrine. Ambrose saw himself as the emperor's conscience. When the situation merited it, such as when Theodosius authorized a massacre of citizens in Thessalonica, Ambrose did not shy away from forcing him to perform public penance. This was to become a dangerous precedent for the status of the worldly ruler.

In less than a century, then, the tables had been turned. "Pagans" were on the defensive. The libraries in Rome were as empty as tombs, as no one came to consult their collections. People were probably scared off by the fact that they were located in pagan temples.[35] Jews were allowed to practice their religion, but they were harassed by their former brethren.[36] They could not hold office, Christians were not allowed to convert to Judaism, and marriage between Christian women and Jewish men was forbidden. Circumcision of non-Jews was punishable with death, as was castration in general. Furthermore, traditional anti-Judaism became an even greater threat, as it was now buttressed by a theological system with a claim to universal validity. The soil in which the hatred of Jews and, ultimately, anti-Semitism grew was already prepared by the early days of Christianity.

New divisions flared up around the thorny problem of the Trinity. For example, Nestorius (ca. 381–ca. 451 AD) taught that Mary had given birth not to a god but to a man and that Christ, therefore, had two natures. He was contradicted by the Monophysites, who believed Christ had only *one* divine nature. In vain, the Council of Chalcedon condemned both teachings in 451, proclaiming instead that Christ was both actually God and actually man. This marked the break between Eastern Orthodoxy and the "Oriental Orthodox" Churches, including Armenian, Coptic, Ethiopian, and Syriac Christianity.

Collapse

While the theologians were working on the conundrum of making three equal to one, the Empire fell apart. The collapse provides endless material for bloody historical dramas. It was a true cultural rupture—no mere transformation.[37] The Empire lost its tax base and therewith its military power. This corresponded to a weakening of the emperor's authority. In the latter half of the fourth century, children like Gratian and Valentinian II had been elevated to the purple—only a few pounds of flesh-and-blood legitimacy, helpless pawns of military leaders. Now this became more common. Bishops filled the political vacuum. Actual power devolved to the praetorian prefects and the generals. In 410, while the imperial court in Ravenna was steeped in intrigue, the Goths sacked Rome. It was the first time in eight hundred years that a foreign conqueror had set foot in the city.

In the first half of the fifth century, parts of Gaul and Britain slipped away from the Empire. The Vandals and the Alans established themselves in North Africa. Many of the new potentates who arose on the corpse of the Empire, decked out with Roman titles, were not bent on destruction. The Gothic leader Alaric, for example, managed to combine the title of general in Gaul with the dignity of a king. But his grand plans were buried with him in his mythical grave under the Busento River. Fate was kinder to the Vandal ruler Gaiseric (r. 428–477 AD). He succeeded in fashioning a powerful kingdom with Carthage at its center. He and his fleet attacked Sicily, Sardinia, and the Balearic Islands.

The provinces cared little for pronouncements from Ravenna or Rome, and nothing at all for commands from Constantinople. Flavius Aetius, a Roman general of Balkan origin and one of the most capable military commanders of the Late Empire, used the fierce Huns to destroy Burgundian rule in the territory of what is now Worms. The veterans of his campaign in 436 settled in an area between Savoy and Lake Constance, founding their own *regnum* there. The vestiges of this drama have been captured in one of the most famous epics of the Middle Ages, the *Nibelungenlied*. In 451, Aetius defeated the selfsame Huns and their allies at the Battle of the Catalaunian Plains. This was no victory of the "West" over "uncivilized Orientals"; indeed, in Aetius's diverse army, "Romans," Burgundians, and Visigoths (or "Western Goths"—a term that denotes not an ethnic group but rather a confederation active in the West) fought side by side against the Huns. The death of their leader Attila two years later marked the end of the Hunnish chapter in European history, but not of the age of invasions.

That Valentinian III eliminated Aetius in 454—by his own hand—was a mistake. He himself, the last descendant of Theodosius, was laid low one year later. And with him, the last shadow of imperial legitimacy vanished. A new regime was quickly installed. But Gaiseric seized the opportunity and moved on Rome, which was sacked once more in 455. The Vandals, who were neither better nor worse than others of their kind, earned for themselves proverbial fame as destroyers. But the borders had long since become porous. The Empire no longer stood strong against "barbarian" invaders. Rather, Goths and Vandals fought on the side of "Roman" factions. One emperor after another was proclaimed; hardly one died in bed. A final chance to save the Western Empire was lost in 468, when a massive naval operation against Gaiseric failed.

The last Western emperor, Romulus Augustulus, was the son—and thus, in two senses, the creation—of a general, the Pannonian Orestes. He fell victim to yet another military revolt, led by the Germanic general Odoacer. Odoacer's seizure of power in 476 ended the rule of the "little Augustus," who then lived out a life of luxury on an estate outside Naples. No successor was named this time. Thus ended the history of the Western Roman Empire, although some set the date four years later with the death of Julius Nepos, lawfully recognized as Western emperor by Constantinople. Contemporaries accepted with equanimity the collapse of the mightiest state the Western Hemisphere had ever seen. "Yet we, in the fear of captivity, continue to frequent the games, and shadowed by death, we laugh," wrote the Christian author Salvian in the early fifth century. "You would think the whole Roman people had been steeped in Sardonic herbs: they are dying, but they laugh."[38]

The Empire ultimately collapsed under its own weight. In the end, it proved to be overstretched.[39] Two numbers tell the tale. For a time, the perimeter of the Empire measured a good sixteen thousand kilometers. And during the reign of Diocletian, an army of perhaps five hundred thousand men stood ready to defend it. That was many more soldiers than any one opponent could put in the field, and it outstripped the resources available even to medieval and early modern emperors many times over. Yet it was still too few to master all of Rome's enemies. The mechanism of collapse functioned with relentless precision: new concessions had to be made continually to a growing number of enemies, and each concession meant the loss of a bit of power that could not be gotten back.

Obviously, Rome had forgotten how to wage war. In the early phase of expansion, its military strength was based on a multitude of urban strongholds, a well-developed infrastructure of military roads, and, above all, a loyal citizen army. This last had long since disappeared. More and more often, the emperors were forced to hire mercenaries or rely on the aid of *foederati*. In the third century, "subsidies" and other payments to keep foreign peoples at bay already equaled the budget of the entire army.[40] The cost of maintaining the army overwhelmed the economy, and taxes weighed heavy on the population. Bureaucratic bloating and corruption could no longer be contained. What is more, the binding force of Roman tradition had been lost in the Christian state. The estrangement between the two parts of the Empire increased.

Maybe the collapse was not inevitable. A lucky succession here or there, or the "timely" death of utterly incapable rulers like Honorius, might have held it off for a while.[41] A contemporary like Ammianus Marcellinus, author of the last great work of history in antiquity, was convinced that *Roma aeterna*, "eternal Rome," had survived Cannae, and thus—he reassured his readers, perhaps thinking of the disaster at Adrianople—it would also survive the catastrophes of his own day.[42] He was wrong.

5

The Roman Legacy

Empire and Republic

Neither contemporaries nor future generations wanted to believe that the "empire without end" would actually perish after Odoacer sent Romulus Augustulus's regalia to Constantinople, along with the message that the West no longer needed an emperor. The myth that grew out of the fertile ashes of the empire of all empires was an inspiration for two millennia. No other narrative would be more important, more historically powerful, for modern Europe. Did Rome not demonstrate that the imperial solution was an actual possibility? The dream of humanity living in peace, of a "universal state," seemed to have come true for a short time. Pliny had called Italy the "mother-country of all nations of the Earth."[1] The name of Rome meant immense size and endless power. When, one thousand years after the fall of the Empire, a Portuguese historian saw the giant temple complex of Angkor Wat in what is now Cambodia, he remarked that such a wonder of the world could only have been built by the Romans or perhaps Alexander the Great.[2]

A world order other than empire was unimaginable to Christian historical theology. Many contemporaries were convinced that the fall of Rome meant the end of the world.[3] The notion that the Earth always had to have an empire at its head also retained its force. This point of view found its firmest support in an oft-quoted passage from the Book of Daniel.[4] The text describes the theory of the four kingdoms, the fourth of which will be crushed at the end of days by a fifth, the kingdom of God. Each age had its own interpretation of which empires were meant. In Christian antiquity and the Middle Ages, many exegetes believed the fourth kingdom was the Roman Empire. The fact that the number of empires could shrink to three lessened the model's persuasiveness not one bit. European rulers always had their eye on the monumental *exemplum* of Rome's greatness. It provided them with an imperial ideology, and it spurred them to win back what had been lost or at least to achieve something similar.[5] Even the fascists in Mussolini's decaying Italy conjured its spirit.

The myth of Rome had a second face. Alongside the imperial phantasm, the story of the Republic lived on. The image later centuries had of republican Rome featured farmers plowing fields (the legendary Cincinnatus was supposedly called from his plow to be dictator), industrious citizens, chaste women, honorable priests, and iron-clad soldiers—virtuous people who respected the *mores maiorum*, the customs of their ancestors. This grand narrative provided examples of morality and love of liberty, of patriotism and willingness to sacrifice. Renaissance art often seized on such scenes, using them to teach lessons. There was Mucius Scaevola, who, when held captive by the Etruscan king Porsenna, put his right hand in the flames of a bonfire to show that he feared neither torture nor death. There was Marcus Curtius, who leaped, horse and all, into a pit that had opened up in the Forum. According to a prophecy, the pit would only close again when Rome sacrificed to the gods the most valuable thing it possessed—and that was the bravery and boldness of its men. The legend goes that the gods accepted the sacrifice.

The development of the Republic provided the historian Polybius, a contemporary of the victory over Carthage, with an explanation for Rome's rise. He conjectured that it was not only due to piety and the whim of Tyche, the goddess of fate. Instead, he emphasized the wisdom of Rome's constitution.[6] The fact that the term *republic*—which simply means "state," "commonwealth," "state assets," or "state interests"—could become a modern byword for "democracy" demonstrates the power of the myth of Rome and the fascination that radiated from its idealized model. Indeed, the constitution of the Roman Republic, with its checks and balances between magistrates, senate, and popular assemblies, did provide future times with a model for an ideal political architecture. Inspiration was also taken from Athenian democracy and from theoretical reflections from antiquity about the best form of government. Polybius's cyclical theory of political evolution was very influential. It stated that monarchy will, of necessity, devolve into tyranny, aristocracy into oligarchy, and democracy into ochlocracy, or mob rule. Polybius considered a mixed constitution like Rome's to be the most resilient.

Thus, antiquity introduced both the theory and the reality of democracy into world history. No power could now eliminate it; it was destined to endure, at least as a possibility. Part and parcel of the prehistory of democracy and civil society, finally, was the rich culture of rhetoric, which developed in Greece and Rome and was given a theoretical foundation very early on. Cicero, the *Rhetoric to Herennius* falsely ascribed to him, and Quintilian were, along with Aristotle, the greatest teachers of ancient eloquence.

Cities, Statues, and Statutes

Rome's material remains were an inexhaustible bounty. Statues and ruins of monumental architecture towered over medieval and early modern Europe. Gods and heroes took a fixed place in hearts and minds and later became common themes of the arts.[7] Rome passed down scripts and ink, masonry and viticulture, household utensils of all kinds, even the use of money. The Gothic word for "doing business," *kaupon* (the source of the German word *kaufen*), reminds us that the "barbarians" probably first came into contact with money in taverns; the root of *kaupon* is the Latin *caupo*, "innkeeper."[8] In German, the basic vocabulary of building has Latin roots, including words like *Zement/caementum* (cement), *Mauer/murus* (wall), *Kalk/calx* (lime), and *Ziegel/tegula* (roof tile). This says a great deal about the role that Roman civil planning and engineering played as a model. Rome even overcame geography—with a state-run postal service and communications system and with straight roads, some of which continued to facilitate travel in the Middle Ages. The names of the months in Romance languages are of Roman origin, as is the order of the days according to the planets. Down to the late sixteenth century, the year was reckoned in Europe according to the calendar introduced by Caesar; the same Julius Caesar is the source of words like *Kaiser* and *tsar*.

If Western Europe boasted an urban concentration in antiquity that was rivaled only by China, this was thanks to the Phoenicians, the Greeks, and, above all, the Romans. There were about two thousand cities within the borders of the Empire. The people who came under its sovereignty had not known the earlier urban achievements of Mesopotamia. Aelius Aristides remarked that cities are what distinguished the Roman from the Persian Empire.[9] Parts of Gaul and the Iberian Peninsula, Britain, and Roman Germany received their cities as imports of Roman legions. Many of them grew out of military camps or settlements of subject peoples who did not learn what "urban culture" meant until they were conquered. The spectrum ranged from settlements of wooden houses and a couple of larger public buildings to metropolises like Rome and Constantinople. The visual arts, natural science and philosophy, comedy, tragedy, and literature flourished in cities. Even some provincial nests had a library. There were lecture halls in luxurious bath complexes where clubs met.[10] Gymnasia, which were also often connected to bath complexes, were settings for education, physical recreation, and conversation. In the East, they were so common that the Emperor Trajan could sneer at how much "our little Greeks" loved them.

As earlier in Greece, the larger cities of the Empire competed with each other to see which had the largest population, the most beautiful buildings, and the mightiest, greatest god. Any city containing a temple for the imperial cult was allowed to be called a *metropolis* or the "greatest" "first" city in an area.[11] The infrastructure of Roman cities and the hygiene standards they achieved thanks to baths, water pipes, and sewers would be a dream for many communities in Asia and Africa today. Europe learned how to express power and faith in stone form. Basilicas and palaces, victory columns and triumphal arches provided political architecture with a vocabulary that was used by just about every age down to the twentieth century. Roman law was an intellectual powerhouse of paramount significance. Rome's language, Latin, was by far the most important legacy of the Empire (see pp. 107–110). Europe's access to the cultural, legal, and institutional heritage of the Greeks, Romans, and Byzantines distinguished its process of state formation most starkly from similar developments in Asia and elsewhere in the world.

No state in antiquity was organized as rationally as the Roman one. For a time, the emperors commanded nearly limitless resources. The Empire possessed the knowledge of Athens and Alexandria, and it was able to mobilize a military apparatus of the utmost efficiency. Its architecture achieved unheard-of advances. It devised underfloor heating and built gigantic aqueducts, sewage systems, and bridges, some of which are still standing today. Its engineers designed sawmills and sailing ships. Its scholars read from the forerunner of the modern book, the codex. Still, no true paradigm shifts occurred. Roman agricultural theory was second to none in antiquity, but the three-field system did not sprout until the Middle Ages. Rome knew Hero's automata and Archimedes' "Greek fire," but it did not realize, for example, that steam power could be used to fire projectiles. It understood the magnifying power of lenses, but it did not build any telescopes. Are empires—for whatever reason—infertile soil for inventions? Was there just not enough time for them to develop? After all, Europe needed almost another fifteen hundred years to make use of steam power. Or is the answer much simpler: was Rome simply not blessed with a second Hero or Archimedes?

Honey and Poison: The Christian Inheritance

One late bequest of the Empire influenced the world more than all the rest: Christianity. In Late Antiquity, while various dogmatic, intractable versions of the religion continued to develop, it won over the Roman East and North Africa, and it even managed to break out of the borders of the Empire through Sasanian Persia—where Christ lost out to Zoroaster—and all the way to central Asia, southern India, and China. To understand the significance of its legacy in Europe, we must first turn to the man who, after Paul, was the most influential interpreter of Christ's message: Augustine. Born in 354 AD, he became bishop of the North African city of Hippo Regius in 395. His thought profoundly shaped medieval Christian and Reformation theology. He was well acquainted with Greek philosophy, which was fundamental to his early career as a rhetorician. The most important pagan thinker for him was Plato. By changing a few words and phrases, Augustine wrote, Platonists could be turned into Christians.[12] The denigration of the body that many of his writings exude—and that is common to most religions—may reflect the Platonic celebration of the soul, although it probably owes more to the Manichaeans' demonization of all things material. As a young man, Augustine had himself been an adherent of Manichaeism, but later in life he opposed it vigorously. The process of his conversion is detailed in his *Confessions*. A confession of both faith and sin, it was the first autobiography in world literature.

His chief work, *The City of God* (*De civitate Dei*), was written in the shadow of Alaric's sack of Rome. In its pages Augustine defended Christians from the accusation that their rejection of the old gods had caused the catastrophe. He countered that the Romans themselves were responsible for their destruction. Their gods, he deduced from a Bible passage,[13] were in reality the fallen angels from the first days of Creation. Having mutated into ethereal, airy beings, they did everything in their power to deceive humans, even tempting them to have sex with them. This crude theory, patched together from the Bible and Platonic teachings, would go on to have a dramatic impact a thousand years later when it provided a foundation for witch hunts (see pp. 490f.). On the other hand, Augustine saved the friendlier deities by integrating them into hierarchies of angels, thus preparing the way for their rebirth in the Renaissance. Last but not least, *The City of God* documents Augustine's process of distancing himself from Mani, the guiding star of his youth who had now grown dim. In Mani's conception of the world, evil, the realm of darkness, is an autonomous power equal to that of its adversary, light. Augustine provides an alternative worldview. His god controls all events and can even intervene in the laws of nature as he wishes. He sees the fate of the city of God, in which the faithful are joined with Christ, as inextricably linked to that of the earthly city, the realm of the devil. Only the Last Judgment will separate them. Even the raging of tyrants like Nero has a place in Augustine's view of history; its purpose will be revealed at the end of time.[14]

Augustine developed his theory of grace to combat the views of Pelagius (ca. 350/60–before 431 AD). A British monk who had fled to Carthage from Rome when it was threatened by the Goths, Pelagius ascribed human beings free will and rejected the idea of original sin. Augustine, in contrast, theorized in his later years that a sovereign, divine will determined whether human beings were born for eternal life or, from the moment of birth on, were damned to hell. No one could attain salvation through their own power. This notion also swept away Manichaeism's autonomous force of evil, replacing it with the gloomy claim that the fate of each individual was predetermined from the outset. The cause of suffering and joy was God's wisdom, not individual mistakes or good deeds. Everything depended on the grace that the Lord would grant to his creatures. It alone could free people from original sin, which was spread from one person to another by the lust of sexual intercourse.[15] The Bishop of Hippo described hell as a prison where eternal torments awaited. In his view, even unbaptized children were doomed to suffer there.

Augustine's anthropology is ambiguous. The trinity of the human intellect— composed of memory, insight, and will—turns the poor puppet of predestination into a likeness of its triune Creator. Life in the temporary world of light and filth is compared to a fleeting pilgrimage, and the political order in which it is carried out has no meaning. Compared to the prospect of the eternal realm of light, even the fall of Rome seemed insignificant. Thoughts of this kind may have occupied the bishop's mind as he neared death on August 28, 430. At that moment, his city of Hippo was being besieged by a Vandal army.

Augustine's theology depicts Christianity as a religion of hope and love but also of fear and hatred. Fear of the wrath of God, of the Last Judgment, of the devil and demons. Hatred of pagans, Jews, heretics, and witches—and of all those who are held responsible for evil in the world because they have supposedly brought divine punishments on the state. This theology effected a profound shift in the ancient notion of progress.[16] In contrast to a *vita activa* of industry and action, Stoic serenity and the contemplative life appeared as ideals. A growing number of monks dedicated themselves to such a life. The idea of honoring cultural heroes or erecting monuments to inventors never occurred to the Christian Middle Ages. Now it was God and heaven—not polis or Empire—that provided the foundation for ethical frames of reference. The "Dream of Scipio" that Cicero inscribed at the end of his *Republic* gained new relevance during the crisis of the Empire. Macrobius, a contemporary of Augustine, wrote a commentary on it. In this work, a kind of "moral cosmology," Scipio is imagined up in the Milky Way, looking out upon the universe. From this vantage point, Earth appears smaller than the stars around it. Even the Roman Empire shrinks to a tiny point. Earth as a speck, a nothing in the universe—this was a simultaneously jarring and comforting thought. If the earthly world is so tiny, then our sufferings in it are even less important.

Finally, the Christian god bridled the goddess of fate, whom antiquity had met with Aristotelian reason or Stoic equanimity. What had once been hatched without rhyme or reason by Ananke, Fatum, Fortuna, Moira, Tyche, Heimarmene—fate had many names—was now justified as the unfathomable will of the almighty Christian god. He forced the fickle deity to turn in a perpetual circle. Medieval painters and sculptors took the cue. They depicted fate as a wheel, showing how Fortuna raised rulers to power and let them triumph only to overthrow them in the end. The goddess of fate would not be freed again until the Renaissance. Balancing on a ball, she was then allowed to teeter in whatever direction she desired.

In the final analysis, the Christian religion, now half a millennium old, was both honey and poison. It destroyed pagan cultures with its art, rites, and myths. Its monotheism spawned universal claims that led to oppression and war. On the other hand, it spread the message of the Gospel to foreign peoples and acted as a vehicle for ancient philosophy and natural science. By adopting ancient Latin, it gave Europe a common language. It had a "civilizing" effect, gave weight to the voice of conscience, encouraged self-control, and thus was a mechanism for regulating behavior.[17] Last but not least, the Christian Gospel introduced big ideas to the world, ideas that remain big even though very few people truly live according to them. It called upon people to love their neighbor, it proclaimed the equality of all human beings, and it provided arguments against slavery and oppression.

6

New Powers, Scribal Monks

The Origins of a Kaleidoscopic Continent

The developments that had led to the fall of the Western Roman Empire and caused problems for Byzantium were given a name by the humanist Wolfgang Lazius in 1557—*migratio gentium*, the "migration of peoples." Today the epoch is commonly referred to as the "Migration Period." Rather than "peoples" in their own right, however, it would be more correct to speak of "ethnogenesis" or the "crystallization of peoples." For the hordes that swept over the borders of the two empires were anything but peoples sharing a common "blood" or ethnicity, but rather "imagined communities" like those that are to be found at the beginning of all state formation around the globe.[1] Their origins are lost in darkness. A couple of sentences about some of them may be found in the ancient historians; others may be mentioned in an inscription celebrating the victory of an emperor. All that remains of most are exotic names like Budini, Ruzzi, Marharii, and Vuislane. The shovels of archaeologists have turned up evidence of grave sites, traces of buildings, a piece of jewelry, and little else. Names of tribes like "Gauls," "Celts," and "Germani" actually denote motley mixtures of peoples that probably also incorporated indigenous Italic tribes. It was thus not ethnic groups that formed the nucleus of what would become the European states but rather associations and networks of warrior groups of various origin.[2] They forged a common identity around gods, saints, and heroes. Legends would later shine light on the gloom of their beginnings. For example, Frankish historians would make their people the descendants of scattered Trojan refugees. It was, therefore, not blood that made peoples into peoples, but rather the ink of chroniclers. Genealogies replaced genes.

While the new peoples of Europe were crystallizing, the locals hid behind the walls, long since too expansive, of their old cities. They stayed close to the graves of martyrs, whose magical auras they hoped would ward off danger better than rotten palisades. Some took refuge at the top of hills, fled to the woods—or to the water, as a somewhat later, well-documented episode of Byzantine history illustrates. The story begins with the invasion of northern Italy by the Lombards, stragglers in the great migration. Even powerful landholders were forced to flee with their families to the safety of swampy, malaria-infested islands in a lagoon in the Adriatic Sea. One of them, called "Rivoalto," or "High Bank," was the core of what became the metropolis of Venice. The people there "had abundance only of fish," reports a letter of Cassiodorus, a Roman aristocrat who served the Ostrogothic court.[3] Their boats were "hitched like animals to the walls" of their houses, which stood "like aquatic birds, now on water, now on land." The first Venetians are praised as capable seamen who industriously engaged in salt production. The wild days after the fall of the Western Roman Empire probably witnessed many such foundations.

As illustrated by Venice, the beginning of just about all state formation—including in this period—lies in common work, in a common struggle against nature and, above all, against competitors for territory and plunder. Indeed, war and the preparation for it led to the creation of *states*, i.e., organizations that subjected all other organizations in a given territory to their power, gained a monopoly on violence, and then developed institutions, legal systems, and social networks.[4] In return for their loyalty, the faithful could expect their chiefs to give them gold, land, and protection. Over the centuries, some of these structures turned into *nations*—through common experiences and prejudices, through fear of actual or imagined enemies. Their names might have come from large families with followers who had been influential in the deep past. One example is the term "Franks," which might have simply meant "greedy, fierce people."[5] Late Roman sources used the name to refer to the Ampsivarii, Bructeri, Salians, and others. In the East it was applied to all Western warriors, merchants, and pilgrims, whatever part of Europe they came from.

The reasons for Europe's mass migration are not known with certainty.[6] Perhaps a chain reaction of events connected the continent's fate to that of the Far East. Climatic changes resulting in a reduction of grassland on the steppe and, as a result, loss of pastureland may have led to power shifts in central Asia. The weak were forced to yield. Thus, the Goths who streamed into the crumbling Empire may have been driven there by the Huns. The Avars were pushed westward by Turkic peoples in the mid-sixth century; they founded their own kingdom north of the Byzantine Empire. These and other groups were looking for rich cities and fertile land. That was easier and more profitable than fighting other "barbarians" for their woods, swamps, and grassy plains.

Arrayed in battle formation was not the only way the foreigners encountered the Empire. Since the heyday of its power, they had also succumbed to the embrace of Roman culture. "The barbarians . . . were becoming different without knowing it," observed Cassius Dio.[7] Agrarian communities that had hitherto only had the bare necessities of life developed into complex societies whose elites used the money they had stolen, earned, or received as tribute to indulge in expensive status symbols: perhaps jewelry in the Roman or Byzantine fashion, and certainly *terra sigillata* earthenware. The Empire became their own. Their warriors became less interested in rebelling against it than in rising through its military or administrative ranks. Rome and later Constantinople taught them what money can do, how to write books, wage war, and govern states. This made them able to become their masters' masters.

While the West was sinking into war and chaos, Theodosius II (r. 402–450 AD) surrounded Constantinople with a turreted wall. From then on, the city on the Bosporus was the mightiest fortress in Europe. The Eastern Empire, whose heart it was, saw itself not as a successor to the Roman Empire but rather as the continuator of an unbroken tradition, as the *basileia ton rhomaion*, the "Empire of the Romans." High tax revenues flowing in from flourishing cities created political opportunities. Some adversaries were kept quiet with tribute payments; others were hired as mercenaries and enticed with the prospect of power and honors. In this way, the land-hungry peoples were channeled westward. Constantinople's strength was therefore one of the causes of Rome's weakness.

While the Byzantine millennium was beginning in the East, new states were springing up in the West. Italy first fell under the rule of the Ostrogoths. Their king Theodoric (r. 497/98–526 AD) had been sent to Italy by the Eastern Emperor Zeno, where he defeated Odoacer's forces and killed the usurper with his own hand. As king of the Goths and of Italy he preserved many ancient Roman customs. His image on coins shows him in imperial dress but with a Germanic hairstyle. He is said to have derisively remarked that rich Goths longed "to play the Roman."[8] His cypress-ringed tomb outside Ravenna displays a curious synthesis of Roman and Germanic elements.

The Franks were the power of the future. They had spread throughout Gaul while—around 500 at the latest—the Visigoths ensconced themselves on the Iberian Peninsula. The standard image of shaggy wild men or brawny warriors emerging from the woods to overrun an exhausted civilization is a cliché. Many Franks had long been farmers who performed Roman military service or had settled on Roman lands under other legal titles. Some of their leaders may have spoken Latin and been in contact with the Gallo-Roman elite. This may have been the case with King Childeric I, the scion of a Merovingian clan.[9] He and his son Clovis (r. 481/2–511 AD) managed to establish authority over almost all of Gaul. The Eastern Empire legitimated the rule of the upstarts. The Visigoths yielded to Frankish power, retreating to Septimania in southern Gaul and to the Iberian Peninsula. They, too, were eager students of the Romans. Their *Lex Romana Visigothorum*, also known as the Breviary of Alaric, was a significant legal code. Based on a fifth-century collection, the Codex Theodosianus,[10] its impact continued to be felt in the High Middle Ages. Culturally, the Frankish realm remained divided: the south was heavily Roman, whereas north of the Loire, where Rome had long since lost influence, Germanic culture predominated.

The further development of the Merovingian kingdom displays patterns of conflict that are typical of large empires. After Clovis's death, his inheritance was divided among his four sons. Once again, the kingdom underwent massive territorial expansion, now incorporating Burgundy and stretching all the way to Pannonia in the East. By the sixth century, its history had developed into a drama of domestic infighting and wars with neighbors. Phases of consolidation remained brief episodes.

The Last Romans

Northern Italy, perhaps Pavia, in the spring of 526. A man is writing his last great work, if we can trust what he says, while in prison awaiting death. The goddess of fate had laid Ancius Manlius Severinus Boethius very low indeed.[11] The noble Roman, hitherto chief minister at Theodoric's court in Ravenna, seems to have gotten into trouble because of conspiratorial contacts with Byzantium. The work he penned in his final hours achieved fame under the title *The Consolation of Philosophy*. Philosophy appears in its pages as an allegorical figure. She takes the shape of a very old woman of dignified appearance, yet she is quick-witted and full of youthful vigor. Sometimes she has human proportions; then she grows so large that the top of her head grazes the sky, towering overhead. She wears an indestructible robe of her own making, woven of the finest cloth. In her right hand she holds books, in her left the scepter of a queen. She speaks to the prisoner, arguing that earthly fate, Fortune's gifts and punishments, fade into nothingness compared to the highest good which is comprehended in almighty God. Behind unforeseen coincidences and the daisy chain of destiny, Boethius argues, the same divine reason that rules the entire universe is actually at work.[12]

In support of his reasoning, Boethius makes use of a well-stocked library of ancient philosophy. Plato and sundry Neoplatonists are represented, as are Aristotle and the Stoics, even Presocratics like Parmenides, who is extensively quoted. Boethius also takes comfort in Scipio's view of the Earth as a speck in the universe. He must have known Macrobius's commentary. It is conspicuous that Boethius, whose early writings show him to be a Christian, makes no reference here to the Gospel. We do not know why. Did he lose his faith in Christ the Savior while in prison? We also know nothing about the details of his execution. Still, the *Consolation* spread its author's fame as a martyr far and wide. Edward Gibbon called Boethius the "last of the Romans whom Cato or Tully [i.e., Cicero] could have acknowledged for their countryman."[13]

A belated attempt to jumpstart the Empire failed, albeit in grand style. The last war in this effort was waged by the Emperor Justinian (r. 527–565 AD). His generals defeated the Vandals in Africa and ended the Ostrogothic regime in Italy. They even tried to subjugate the Visigoths in far-off Spain. The enterprise failed due to a lack of financial and military resources. Justinian was also hampered by a pandemic and a threat from Persia that could only be tamed with tons upon tons of gold. In 554, Justinian issued an edict ending the administration of the Western Empire. Its court and the ancient office of consul were abolished. The *hesperium imperium* was now gone for good.

In the Eastern Empire, Justinian continued the process of Christianization. He believed it his sacred duty to root out heretics. One of his laws stipulated that the decisions of church councils had the same force as the Gospels. Mass baptisms were performed, books were burned, pagan temples destroyed. These were hard times for scholarship. The historian Procopius writes of spies who made the free writing of history impossible; he claims the threat of death hung in the air.[14] In 529, the emperor closed the Platonic Academy in Athens. One of its last directors, Isidore of Miletus, who edited works of Archimedes, was also one of the architects of Hagia Sophia. Numerous men of learning fled to the Sasanian Empire. The spirit lost to Byzantium was a boon to Persia and was later bequeathed to the Arabs.

The history of the Byzantine Empire begins after Justinian.[15] Its survival, despite cabals and fights for the throne, was aided by borders that were easier to defend than those of the Western Empire. Other advantages were the urban elite's loyalty to the regime and what Justinian called the "symphony" of church and state. The *basileus* (Greek for "king," "ruler," or "emperor") was its undisputed conductor. He was accorded reverence like an earthly god. Coins portray him as the vicar of Christ, as the apostle of the true faith. Justinian's most important legacy was in the field of Roman law, unparalleled in its systematization and internal consistency.[16]

The codification undertaken at Justinian's command compiled, ordered, and expounded on Roman law and attempted to make its logic harmonize with the legislation of late antique Byzantium. A recent statute casually confirmed Rome's primacy in the West, while according the Patriarch of Constantinople a rank right underneath the emperor. Justinian's *Body of Civil Law* (*Corpus Juris Civilis*) contained fifty books of *Digests* or *Pandects*—tort and civil law—along with the *Code*, a collection of laws enacted by emperors going back to Hadrian, as well as the newer laws of Justinian, the *Novels*, which were supposed to take precedence over older legislation.[17] The whole was rounded out by a textbook carrying the force of law, the *Institutes*, which also structured the study of jurisprudence. Justinian's collection enjoyed a long second act in the Middle Ages, when manuscript copies and then printed books made it a mainstay in universities and council chambers and captured the fascination of scholars (see pp. 192–197). In the nineteenth century, it was the inspiration for the Napoleonic Code and the codification of German civil law. Since then, the influence of Roman law has been felt around the world, all the way to Thailand, Japan, and China.

Broken Traditions

The transmission of Greco-Roman culture was threatened not only by "barbarians" from the forests and the steppe but also by a fundamental criticism of the cultivation of secular studies. It came from clerical circles. Attacks on philosophers went back all the way to Tertullian. He claimed that the advent of Jesus made intellectual curiosity and wide learning unnecessary, asking, "What indeed has Athens to do with Jerusalem?"[18] Jerome (347–420), who translated the Vulgate, the Latin Bible, firmly condemned all pagan literature, even though every page of his own work bears its influence. Even Gregory I the Great (590–604), a monk and the first pope to call himself "Servant of the Servants of God," recommended turning away from secular philosophy. The *Dialogues* composed in his orbit sketch an ideal portrait of Saint Benedict, who may actually be a completely invented figure.[19] It describes the saint's ascent from the grotto of Subiaco to Montecassino, where he founded his monastery. Along with Basil the Great (whose rule governed Orthodox monasteries) and ahead of John Cassian, Benedict—or his inventor—is considered the most important lawgiver of European monasticism.

Gregory, who was himself deeply learned, was of the opinion that philosophy was only useful to the extent that it served pious purposes. The goal, after all, was to purify the world. Like so many before and after him, he knew the prophecy about the end of days from the Book of Daniel and believed that it was near. The *Dialogues* are a collection of reflections on the soul, death, and the fires of hell. Furthermore, they contain a hodgepodge of miracle tales whose heroes are almost all holy monks and bishops. The only book cited is the Bible. Miracles take the place of all technology and knowledge about the natural world. In one legend, a heavy stone is moved not with Archimedean physics but with prayer; it drives away the devil, who had been sitting on the stone, making it too heavy. If Gregory's views had prevailed, science would have traveled a hard road indeed in Europe.

Many pious men were smitten with remorse when they read pagan literature.[20] The fact that monasteries did not turn their backs entirely on "secular" studies but could even be enthusiastic about them was largely due to the authority of Saint Augustine.[21] His theology did not fundamentally rule out an interest in philosophy. He himself valued Porphyry, the author of a frontal assault on Christianity, praising him as *doctissimus*, "extremely learned."[22] Augustine wanted to restore the ancient system of education, putting it on a firm Christian foundation. Obviously, the Bible was his highest authority.[23] To interpret it, however, he used methods developed by pagan philology, such as those applied in late antique interpretations of Homer and Virgil. He emphatically warned against interpreting the Bible literally, in particular when it came to questions of cosmology. Galileo would cite Augustine in this connection when discussing whether the Copernican system contradicted the Bible.[24] Although Augustine repudiated curiosity—another contradiction—he was no destroyer of transtemporal dialogue. Rather, he was an active and, for the extremely pious, an objectionable participant in it. Unlike zealots of his own religion, of Judaism, and later of Islam, he believed that philosophy, while required to justify itself before the truth of the Scriptures, could also lead to knowledge of God. No other monotheistic religion—in no small part thanks to the Bishop of Hippo—permitted such a close relationship with secular disciplines.

Boethius is another symbol of the alliance between theology and philosophy. In happier days, he had supplemented his theological works with a commentary on Cicero's *Topics*, an oratorical manual that, among other things, taught how to find the best argument in court. He was the source for medieval knowledge of Pythagoras' musical theory and the metaphysical speculation surrounding the arcane relationship between musical and mathematical harmony. In addition, he translated and commented on Aristotle's logical writings, as well as on the introduction to them found in the *Isagogue* of the Neoplatonist Porphyry. Last but not least, Boethius's oeuvre, which was widely read in the Middle Ages, was the conduit by which Aristotle entered the world of Christian thought. He taught Christians how to track down causal relationships, expose contradictions, and draw the proper conclusions. He taught them how to think.

In this case, as in so many others, the writings of the ancients reached the hands of their medieval readers in only fragmentary and mutated form. For about eight hundred years, Plato's *Timaeus* was known to Europe almost exclusively in the Latin translation and commentary by the late antique scholar Calcidius.[25] Macrobius's version of the "Dream of Scipio" and his *Saturnalia* transmitted the Ptolemaic worldview to the Early Middle Ages. Martianus Capella, a North African rhetorician in the first half of the fifth century, passed down to Latin Europe the cosmology of Pythagoras and Aristarchus, the Copernicus of antiquity mentioned above.

An extremely long life was enjoyed by the *Physiologus*, a work from second-century Alexandria that was still being studied eagerly in the Baroque period. This short text was based on Herodotus and Pliny, among others. The Sirens mentioned in one of its chapters were known from the *Odyssey*, and the centaurs that appear in its pages also romped through Ovid's *Metamorphoses*.[26] The reader found useful advice for capturing the unicorn—it must be induced to lay its head in the lap of a virgin—and learned that evil spirits and dragons are best kept at bay by burning the hair and bones of an elephant. Like Herodotus and Pliny, the miscellany filled readers with a desire to travel to foreign lands, to see what it described with their own eyes, to search for gold and jewels.

Yet the grand dialogue about God and the universe, which had begun on the Black Sea and continued in the Academy, the Stoa, and the Museum had, for the time being, fallen almost entirely silent. The most important preconditions for it had disappeared: flourishing cities, institutions, and, above all, patrons. A petty king here or there could not replace the Roman elite, much less the emperors, as rich as Croesus with their treasuries overflowing with sesterces. The phoenix found paltry nesting places in cathedral schools, Roman palaces, and Gallic villas; some of their owners employed slaves to copy ancient texts and read them aloud.[27] It also found refuge in bishops' palaces, even though a guide to episcopal lifestyle dating to around 480 forbade the reading of "pagan books."[28] Finally, the miraculous bird alighted in the centers of Christian piety: the monasteries.

A beginning was made by Cassiodorus (ca. 490–583), Boethius's successor and the author of the letter about life on the Venetian Lagoon quoted above.[29] The Vivarium, a monastery he founded near Squillace in southern Italy, was a Christian Tusculum, a cloister cum Academy. Cassiodorus praised the proximity of the Pellena River (now known as the Alessi), which irrigated gardens, powered mills, and restocked the fishponds, or *vivaria*—hence the monastery's name. Oil lamps provided light for nightly vigils. A sundial showed the time during the day; at night and when it was cloudy, a water clock—known as "Clepsydra," the "water thief"—counted out the hours. In this way, prayer times were never missed.[30] There were bath facilities to care for the frail body, a library to sustain the mind. Cassiodorus encouraged the practice of circulating manuscripts and copying them—work that he praised to the skies. Among the Christian authors, who comprised the bulk of the collection, Augustine had pride of place. Homer and the Greek philosophers, physicists, and cosmologists were represented, as was the physician Galen. Cassiodorus, who himself knew the language of all Roman men of learning, had many of these Greek texts translated. The canon of Latin literature spanned from Ennius, Terence, Pliny, Cicero, Seneca, and Quintilian all the way to Macrobius. Horace and Virgil had a home there, as did Varro, Columella, and Sallust, and even the heretic Lucretius.

Cassiodorus's *Institutiones*, or *Institutions of Divine and Secular Learning*, aided the integration of secular studies into schools and then universities. The curriculum it describes is divided into sacred and secular disciplines. The former also include geography, as it helped students learn the location of places mentioned in Scripture. The latter are divided into the "seven liberal arts," the "trivium" and the "quadrivium." The *trivium*, or "three ways," referred to grammar, rhetoric, and dialectic, whereas the "four ways" of the *quadrivium* were arithmetic, geometry, music, and astronomy. At the time, this canon was known mostly from Martianus Capella's *Marriage of Philosophy and Mercury*, which also passed down the literary technique of allegory to the Middle Ages. For example, Martianus personifies the "arts" as seven bridesmaids.

The Vivarium embodied the "other possibility" of monasticism. It was a community of working, reading, and writing monks, not harsh ascetics or self-engrossed hermits. For the time being, it was an exception. For centuries, theology and religion remained the strict lords of all learning. That was the price to be paid for the fact that its refuge was secured by monastery walls. Interest in ancient historiography receded behind the emphasis on sacred history, which already knew everything about the beginning and the end of time. There was little room for the Greeks' enthusiasm for novelty or their probing desire to investigate. People were looking for miracles, struggling to decipher the hidden meaning of natural phenomena.

On the whole, the circle of those who cultivated the ancient tradition, who copied, translated, and wrote commentaries on ancient texts on the soil of the shattered Western Empire, was small. One of them was Bishop Isidore of Seville (ca. 560–636), whose works were widely read in the Middle Ages. The most important was the *Etymologies*, profound and idiosyncratic explanations of the meanings of words. Isidore's corpus gives us a good idea of the sum of ancient knowledge then available. It touches on more or less everything: medicine, zoology, crafts, heresies, monsters, theater, clothing and minerals, cosmology, the order of Creation, home furnishings and natural law, the reckoning of time, theology, architecture and history, literary history and biblical exegesis.

Writing So That Posterity May Learn

The Christianization of Europe was mostly a "top-down" affair. A chieftain or a prince was baptized, and his people followed suit. For example, three thousand people are said to have followed Clovis when he converted to (Catholic, not Arian) Christianity. The religion was indispensable for the creation of stable social systems, as it formulated patterns of social order and provided justifications for them. Christening sanctified power, cloaking it in legitimacy. Baptized rulers could join themselves and their clans to other families of Christian Europe through marriage and by acting as godparents. Their lands were open to missionaries bearing gifts: salvation and literacy, culture and knowledge of the art of government.

The spread of the Christian faith was accompanied and promoted by a further spread of monasticism. The importance of monasteries for the emergence of the Renaissance can hardly be overstated. Their number increased many times over from the sixth to the fifteenth century, from about one thousand to over twenty thousand.[31] They were agents of cultural transmission. While pestilence crept over the walls of cities and the countryside fell into desolation—many foreign conquerors of Europe knew how to fight and plunder but not to plow or sow—the monks preserved *words*. When not engaged in prayer, monks worked in the scriptorium till their eyes were glazed over, their backs bent, their fingers stiff. An experienced scribe could manage to produce seven pages per day of twenty-five lines each. *Scribite, scriptores, ut discant posteriores*—this inscription in the scriptorium of the monastery of Notre Dame de Lyre is said to have spurred the monks on: "Write, scribes, so that posterity may learn!"[32] And that is exactly what they did. They passed down the intellectual cathedrals built by the Church Fathers, recorded saints' lives, and spun yarns about miracles. They copied chronicles that gave their tiny monastic worlds a place in the grand historical drama between the Fall of Man and the Last Judgment. Scribes were assisted by illuminators, most of whom were also monks. Bookbinders put Bibles, Psalters, and books of hours between covers glittering with gold, jewels, and enameled images. This celestial splendor indicated how precious the contents were. Some illuminators proudly signed the product of their artistry, while others immortalized the ordeal of copying. "This parchment is hairy," moaned one. Another sighed, "Thank God it's almost dark!" And a third, "I've finished copying the whole thing. Give me something to drink, for the love of Christ!"[33] The grind of the scriptorium is also encapsulated in the curse that the illuminator Hildebert—

who drew the scene with his assistant Everwin in the foreground—hurled (along with a sponge) at a mouse nibbling at the bread next to him on the table: "Wicked mouse, too often have you provoked me to anger! May God destroy you!" (Fig. 6, p. 70).[34]

Sometimes the scribes received pagan texts to copy. In this way, they kept the spirit of the ancients alive and created an abode for the family of pagan authors, often without intending to do so or even realizing it. They helped keep the works of compilers, encyclopedists, and translators in circulation, thereby preserving the ideas they contained. When they copied Boethius, they simultaneously kept Plato and Aristotle in the world. When they studied writings by the Venerable Bede, they also read parts of Pliny's *Natural History*. It was above all Italian monastery libraries, stores of knowledge for the schools that sprang up around them, where many ancient texts survived. Beginning in the sixth century, a wave of monastic foundations washed back over the continent from England and Ireland, which had been the focus of early Christianization efforts.

The geographer Strabo had speculated that such areas were inhabited by wild cannibals vegetating in the cold, who ate their own parents and engaged publicly in sexual intercourse with any women they chose, including their own mothers and daughters.[35] It is remarkable that Europe now received a civilizing nudge from its own rough borderlands. This was primarily thanks to a missionary impulse sent out by Pope Gregory, who, concerned about the upcoming Day of Judgment, thought it was high time to save souls. The earliest mission was centered in the county of Kent, with Canterbury as its main town. Its bishop rose to become the head of the English Church. Columbanus (ca. 543–615), a monk from the northern Irish monastery of Bangor, founded Luxeuil Abbey amidst the forests of the Vosges Mountains. He also founded Bobbio Abbey outside Piacenza, with its rich library.[36] The Abbey of Saint Gall, originally a hermitage south of Lake Constance, was founded by one of his companions, Saint Gall (or Gallus). Some missionaries, such as Kilian and Boniface, paid with their lives for their holy zeal—the former in the area of what is now Würzburg, the latter in Frisia. Columban monasteries remained free of the control of local bishops and were instead directly subordinate to the pope. Sharing all things in common and renouncing everything but what was necessary for survival required a rational, methodical lifestyle, and it was this that would ultimately enable monasticism's significant achievements in philosophy, art, and economics.[37]

Some monks emerged as transformers of the ancient tradition that was passed down to them. A highly original mind known as the "Irish Augustinian" tried to explain biblical miracles, such as the transformation of Lot's wife into a pillar of salt, with Aristotelian arguments. As he reasoned, God allowed the salt already available in her body—it could be tasted in her tears—to multiply until it took over the whole. In line with the principle of entelechy, the matter then sought to realize the perfection of its nature in the appropriate form. One small intervention on God's part caused Lot's poor wife to solidify naturally.[38]

Ireland's exceptional role in preserving the ancient heritage (and Celtic epics) was also related to the fact that it was largely spared the massive invasions that haunted the island of Britain from the ninth to the eleventh centuries. Many monks—long-haired figures with painted eyelids—had returned home to the islands from their journeys to Italy with books in their baggage. Benedict Biscop, founder of the double monastery of Monkwearmouth-Jarrow in Northumbria, traveled to Rome no fewer than five times—in part, one presumes, to get books.[39] He or his successor, Ceolfrith, brought a magnificent Bible from Cassiodorus's library to the North. Ceolfrith had three copies of it made in the late seventh century, one of which, the *Codex Amiatinus*, is still extant. Its miniatures reflect late antique taste. Along with the early medieval culture of the region, it has led scholars to speak of a "Northumbrian Renaissance." It combined Roman and Irish cultural elements and is symbolized by the Ruthwell Cross, which contains both Latin letters and runes.

The most important representative of this early medieval renaissance of the ancient mind was the polymath Bede, known as "the Venerable" (672/73–735). His literary horizon stretched from the *Aeneid* and the works of the Church Fathers to Isidore's *Etymologies*, the letters of Pliny the Younger, and the *Natural History* by the latter's uncle, Pliny the Elder. His *On the Reckoning of Time* contains a method for determining the date of Easter, knowledge of which was indispensable for precisely calculating sun positions and the path of the moon through the zodiac. This work, which helped spread the use of the birth of Christ as a benchmark for chronology, was a cornerstone of computus, one of the most important scientific disciplines of the Middle Ages.[40] It was the basis for performing rituals at the correct time and thereby pleasing God. Like magicians, priests must be precise for their enchantment to work.

Antiquity also survived in other English libraries. Aldhelm of Malmesbury (ca. 639–709/10), for example, who studied in Canterbury, knew Horace, Juvenal, Ovid, Lucan and, as always, Virgil. The poet was likewise studied in storm-tossed Iona, where monks also passed the time with the insolent Plautus and the gossipy imperial biographies of Suetonius. Of course, it only took one fire to ruin the work of hundreds of years of transmission. What treasures were destroyed in 477 when the Imperial Library in Constantinople, which supposedly contained 120,000 texts, went up in flames! One was a snakeskin several meters long bearing verses of Homer written in gold.[41] Numerous book collections, including those belonging to Cassiodorus and Monte-cassino, were scattered to the winds over the course of time.

If a monk at the monastery of Hirsau wanted to take out a pagan book, there were two signs he could use (when the rule of silence was in force): he could scratch behind his ear like a dog, the symbol for pagans, or he could stick two fingers in his mouth as if he were gagging.[42] No, antiquity was not in good repute everywhere. Nevertheless, the small band of monastic scribes did manage to preserve and pass on a great deal of ancient literature. Admittedly, their legacy was negligible compared to the enormous amount of knowledge that had been scribbled on papyrus in antiquity between Miletus, Athens, Rome, and Alexandria. Yet this trickle of knowledge—soon to be supplemented by new streams flowing to the West from far-flung Byzantium, Persia, and India, and then from Baghdad and other centers of Arab culture—would suffice to change the world.

The Islamic Empire

Slavic peoples and Avars began plundering Byzantine territory in the mid-sixth century. It was only possible to contain the onslaught for a time. The incursions were abetted by Sasanian offensives that occupied Byzantine troops in the south and east. Syria and Egypt were lost. Even Jerusalem fell into the hands of the Persians. At the point of utmost need, relief was finally provided by a series of campaigns against the Persians begun by Emperor Heraclius in 622. Even a siege of Constantinople four years later (that ended in failure) did not dissuade him from his audacious strategy of attacking the enemy on its own ground. A single lost battle could have decided the fate of Byzantium. Yet by 630, the *basileus* had regained the Empire's lost territory; he styled his war a crusade against pagan Zoroastrians. Modern historians ascribe the success of his gamble entirely to luck,[43] and they believe he profited from having the Turkish Khagan on his flank. Contemporaries, however, saw the hand of God at work. The Byzantine Hercules achieved the height of his fame when he brought the relic of the True Cross, freed from the Persian fire worshippers, in solemn procession back to Jerusalem. The tables were also turned in Byzantium's favor in the depopulated Balkans. While the Avar kingdom disintegrated in internal struggles, Slavic peoples settled there. From plunderers they became farmers, from adversaries allies, from pagans Christians. Byzantium's sovereignty replaced that of the Avars for the time being. But a new enemy was rising. A few years after peace was made with the Persians, Arab soldiers invaded Byzantine territory.

This new power began with the figure of Muhammad, born around 570 in Mecca. Later sources describe him as a merchant from Mecca who emerged as the prophet of the true religion of Abraham, which had been tainted by the Jews and the Christians.[44] The revelations given to him personally, as he claimed, by the Archangel Gabriel—*Jibril*—were compiled in the "Holy Quran." Surah for surah, adherents of Muhammad consider it the word of God, *Allah* in Arabic. This Muslim book of books owes much to Hellenistic and Sasanian Persian traditions, and in particular to the Bible. The Quran refers to Jesus as a wise prophet, although not divine. Now the figure of Jesus loomed large in two religions: one that considered him God, and another that appropriated him.[45]

Islamic chronology begins in 622. That is the year when Muhammad and his followers moved from Mecca to Yathrib, later called Medina (shortened from *Madinat an-Nabi*, "City of the Prophet"). This city, where many Jews lived, was more receptive to monotheistic ideas than Mecca with its *Kaaba*, a temple inhabited by all manner of ancient gods. A series of surahs from the Quran provided a strong impetus for expansion. One verse from the second surah could be interpreted as a call to self-defense: "Fight in the way of Allah against those who fight you . . . And kill them wherever you find them."[46] In contrast, verse five of the ninth surah is clearer and more "political," as by then the Prophet was the head of a defined community: "And when the sacred months have passed, then kill the *mushrikun* [polytheists, idolaters, unbelievers] wherever you find them." The Quran is not only a book of peace.

Enthralled by the word or forced by the sword, more and more clans turned to the teachings of Muhammad. Mecca also fell under his control. To the Prophet's great disappointment, the Jews held to their traditional faith. The warriors who now set about conquering half the world had been merchants, craftsmen, and nomads. Nevertheless, many of them had received military training. The fights between the Byzantines and the Sasanians had provided more than enough opportunities to learn to use a sword. Nomadic military units, which had played a central role in defending the Byzantine Empire in the sixth century, now entered the service of Arab leaders, whose gold glittered no less than that of their former warlords. What the warriors lacked in knowledge of tactics, they made up for in burning faith, fighting spirit, and mobility. Their reward was plunder or, for those who fell in holy war, paradise.

Scholars still debate the ultimate causes for the tremendous dynamism of early Islamic expansion. In addition to the religious impulse, there were also systemic pressures to fight. Only fresh conquests made it possible to pay off warriors with land and thus keep them loyal. This was just as much the case here as it was for the empire of Charlemagne; the same mechanism could explain the raiding culture of the Vikings, the Greek expansion, and the rapid colonization of Pacific islands at the hands of Polynesian chieftains.[47] Within a few decades, the Arabs took Syria, Palestine, and fertile Egypt, the erstwhile breadbasket of the Roman Empire. The proud Sasanian Empire was swept away. In the West, North Africa (including the Maghreb) came under the flag of the Prophet. In the first decades of the eighth century, Arab and Berber troops conquered the Iberian Peninsula. Weakened by internal fights for the throne, the Visigothic Kingdom—which itself had called in the Arabs to ward off a usurper—was overrun. Toledo fell without a struggle. The name "Gibraltar" recalls these events. It comes from *Jabal Tariq*, "Mount of Tariq," referring to the leader of the invading army, Tariq ibn Ziyad. Settlers hungry for land followed in the soldiers' wake. In the East, territory was won all the way to the Indus River, to Bukhara and Samarkand. One monument to the Muslim victories over the Jews and the Christians is the Dome of the Rock in Jerusalem. God was too great to have a son—these fighting words were literally spelled out on its walls in mosaic.

This rapid series of successes was facilitated by the fact that the Byzantine and Persian empires had exhausted each other through decades of fighting. Nor was the expansion as violent as the epic Arab historiography of the Middle Ages suggests.[48] Once again, religion was essential for state formation, as it created common ground between local emirates and imperial authority. A mandatory ethical guide was, and still is, provided by the "five pillars" of Islam: the profession of the one God and recognition of Muhammad as his prophet; the five daily prayers at prescribed times; mercy, which must at least take the form of a tax for support of the poor; fasting during Ramadan; and finally, the pilgrimage to Mecca. Common to all Muslims, although interpreted differently by different schools, is Sharia. It is more than just a legal system. It is a comprehensive system of norms.[49]

One reason for the much-lamented fragmentation of Islam, which endures to this day, was that the Quran provides no indication of how the caliph—the "successor" of Muhammad—is to be chosen.[50] The fights that broke out after his death in 632 ended in open war and schism. Clan alliances and lust for power were stronger than all appeals to the faithful to maintain peace. The legitimacy of caliphs was substantiated by kinship to Muhammad through blood, marriage, or both—or by descent from his clan or his first followers. Other qualifications included efforts to protect and promote the faith.

When Caliph Uthman (r. 644–656)—considered the editor of the text of the Quran—was killed, two rivals vied for the title of caliph: Muawiyah (r. 661–680), governor of Syria and a distant relative of Uthman, and Ali ibn Abi Talib (r. 656–661), a cousin of the Prophet and the husband of his daughter Fatima. When Ali decided to reach a settlement with Muawiyah during the Battle of Siffin on the Euphrates River, some of his followers revolted. Their defection led to the creation of the Kharijite sect (the name means "The Leavers"), which would go on to fight for a puritanical form of Islam and against the Umayyad Caliphate. When Ali was killed by a Kharijite in 661 and his son Husayn died in battle, Muawiyah emerged the victor in the struggle for power. Thus, the Umayyad Dynasty came to power, a clan that had long been counted among opponents of the Prophet. In contrast to Ali's people, Muawiyah's followers considered the first three successors of Muhammad to be "rightly guided," and the Umayyad Caliphate therefore to be legitimate. In support, they cited the *sunnah*, the teachings and practices of the Prophet, which served as a model for Muslims to imitate. On the other hand, Ali's supporters, the *Shiat Ali*, were the origin of Shia Islam. In their view, the only mark of legitimacy is descent from the Prophet. In a society that tolerated polygamy and concubinage, this planted the seed for future disputes. Many civil wars among Muslims appeared rather to be wars between brothers. They continue to flare up even today. In the end, confessional disagreements can always be mobilized. One major difference between modern and earlier struggles is that the efficacy of weapons has increased a thousandfold.

While the Sunnis maintained a unified front as a faith community, the Shias splintered again and again. The cause was always fights over the successor to their imam, the highest temporal and spiritual authority—a holy figure who is supposed to have secret knowledge about the true teachings of the Quran. For Shias, it was clear that a worthy candidate had to be a descendant of the now mythologized shining light Ali. Given his own prolific issue, however, this was not a very high hurdle. In addition, one faction of Shias, the "Twelvers," fostered the notion that the true imam had not died but rather had only been "occulted," i.e., removed from visible existence. According to their belief, the Mahdi or Al-Qa'im—the "rightly guided," "rising one"—will return at the end of days and lead the empire to justice.[51] Ever since the death of the eleventh imam in 874, the "Twelvers," today a majority among Shias, have been waiting for the return of the hidden twelfth successor. Other Shia sects, such as the "Fivers" or Zaidiyyahs, considered the succession to have been consummated in the form of "their" last imam. They regarded those who came later as misguided or as charlatans.

The Sunnis, the various Shia sects, and the equally fragmentary Kharijites are only the main currents of Islam. Mahdis and occulted and hidden leaders are common to all of Islamic history. Their followers developed into large faith communities such as the Qarmatians and the Isma'ilis. Many Muslims belonged to mystical, ascetic sects known as the "Sufi" brotherhoods.[52] The Sufis got their name from their simple, humble clothing; *suf* means "wool." The followers of the Prophet included ascetics, ecstatics, and esoterics, as well as literati and no few heterodox thinkers suspected of heresy. Some were inspired by Plato's philosophy, which promises the union of the soul with God. Yet it is the Quran, whose poetic power seems to prove it was indeed dictated by an angel, that shaped—and continues to shape today—justice and law, literature, science, and education for all Muslims.

A Muslim advance to the north failed. However, the Battle of Tours, fought in 732 (or 733), was only a minor event. It was probably no grand invasion that was warded off by the victor, the Frank Charles Martel—his epithet, meaning "the Hammer," was bestowed upon him in the ninth century—but rather an incursion by Muslim raiding parties. The conquest of barren, comparatively poor Gaul may not have seemed worth the effort to the warriors of the Prophet. Arab chronicles ascribe the battle no importance, whereas a Christian contemporary in Córdoba wrote that the *Europenses* had struck back against the sons of Allah.[53] This may have been the first time that Europeans were ascribed a group identity—tellingly in light of the confrontation with "the other," i.e., non-Christian Muslims.

A little later, after enduring a series of bloody conflicts and weakened by a struggle over succession, the Umayyad Dynasty was toppled. The caliphate fell to the victorious Abbasids in 750. The blood of the Prophet flowed in their veins, thus legitimating their title; the Abbasid clan traced its descent back to Hashim ibn Abd Manaf, a great-grandfather of Muhammad.[54] On the Iberian Peninsula—that is, in the distant west, long cut off from central command—a branch of the Umayyads continued to rule under the supreme but remote authority of the Abbasid Caliphate. For the moment, only "Green Spain"— what would later be the kingdom of Asturias in the northwest—resisted the Prophet's warriors.

The two superpowers of the time were the Chinese Tang Dynasty and the Caliphate. The only confrontation between them occurred in the year after the fall of the Umayyads, at the Battle of Talas in what is now Kyrgyzstan. An Abbasid governor defeated an alliance of central Asian troops led by Chinese units. The victory opened central Asia and the Turkic peoples settling there to Islam. Incidentally, this contact with Chinese high culture provided the

Muslims with knowledge of a medium that would later help spread Greek learning and European science throughout the world. Chinese soldiers captured at Talas are supposed to have revealed the technique of making *paper*. It is likely, however, that Sogdian merchants had already brought knowledge of paper to the West.[55] Paper had probably been in use in China since the Han Dynasty (104 BC–220 AD). It changed the world more than a hundred battles could. Paper was easy to make and inexpensive, especially since a method for making it out of mulberry tree bark had been developed.

The vastness of the Abbasid Caliphate prevented its enduring centralization. The fragmentation within Islam was a result of political conflicts grafted onto religious differences. And it had political consequences, as it weakened the Islamic world as a whole. The early Muslim empires never achieved an internal coherence comparable to that of the Roman or Chinese empires, which they exceeded in size for a time. The Abbasids may have ruled the caliphate for a good five hundred years, but its shadow quickly grew shorter. Their rule tended to be a loose authority held together by arrangements with local potentates and tribal leaders. The power and splendor the caliphs were able to display derived from the estates they accumulated through conquest. Yet these resources did not suffice to guarantee their state a monopoly on violence.

The center of power within the empire had already shifted east before the Battle of Talas. The pull of the Far Eastern trade zone, with its centers in India and China, was strongly felt. The vast majority of state revenues was already coming from what is now southern Iraq by the time of the last Umayyads.[56] In 762, the second Abbasid caliph, Abu Ja'far al-Mansur, relocated his capital from Syria, which had been the center of Umayyad power, to a newly founded city. Now called Baghdad, he named it Madinat al-Salam, "City of Peace."

The name was deceptive. A war for the throne soon broke out among the sons of Harun al-Rashid (r. 786–809), the caliph from *The Thousand and One Nights*. In embattled Baghdad, a contemporary poet wrote the following verses:

Behold Baghdad! There bewildered sparrows
Build no nests in its house.
Behold it surrounded by destruction, encircled
With humiliation, its proud men besieged.[57]

Al-Ma'mun (r. 813–833), the victor in the struggle, only managed to maintain the caliphate with difficulty. His successor, Al-Mu'tasim, decided to move his court to Samarra, a hundred kilometers north of Baghdad. A luxurious palace and an entire city were created out of thin air. The caliphs remained there for fifty years, after which Baghdad was restored to its former status and luster.

In 946, the caliphate came under the power of the Buyids, a warrior dynasty that had conquered a conglomerate of states between the Caspian Sea and the Persian Gulf. Their former rulers were now subject to them, useful only to garb their usurpation in legitimacy. The new potentates reigned over a cultural flourishing that has been called the "Buyid Renaissance."[58] Twice a week, theologians, jurists, and scholars met in palaces and gardens in Baghdad, as they would later in humanist Florence, to discuss philosophy and literature. Courtyards and the market where paper and books were sold were also beloved settings for discussion. Participants included not only Muslims but also Christians—there were eleven monasteries in Baghdad alone—Jews, Zoroastrians, and Sabians, allegedly even atheists. In this way, islands of peaceful debate formed in an often unpeaceful world. A pious Andalusian visiting Baghdad in the tenth century was shocked to find so much rationality.[59]

Meanwhile, local governors, generals, and magnates founded their own dynasties far from the capital. They usually ruled as emirs or imams, sultans or even as messianic Mahdis. Not even the title of caliph was holy. In the East, Persian culture gained strength. It nurtured its pre-Islamic heritage, integrated recent Arab literature, and developed its own architecture for mosques and madrasas. In the West, Sicily fell in the second third of the ninth century to the Aghlabids, who then ruled in the eastern Maghreb and were one of the dynasties that broke away from the Abbasids. At least the renegades called their capital outside Kairouan "al-Abbasiyya." The other powers active in the neighborhood of Latin Europe were the Spanish Umayyads and the Fatimids. The latter took their name from Fatimah, the daughter of the Prophet, from whom they claimed descent. They were Shias who had become Isma'ilis, i.e., people who considered Isma'il, the son of the sixth Imam, to be the true Imam. Their empire stretched from the Maghreb across Egypt to Syria and all the way to Yemen. As their new capital city, they founded Cairo, "the Conqueror," in 969. They took Sicily from the Aghlabids but then lost it when their own emirs from the Kalbid Dynasty declared autonomy. The latter would rule the island almost without interruption until 1053.

Byzantium on the Brink and the Rise of the Franks

The thesis of Belgian historian Henri Pirenne (1862–1935), according to which it was not the Migration Period but rather the era of Arab conquests that marked the break between antiquity and the Middle Ages, is now widely considered to have been disproven.[60] The economic consequences of Islamic expansion were not nearly as dramatic for the Latin West as Pirenne thought.

There is no substantive evidence for the theory that it was the cause of a decline in Mediterranean trade in the seventh century. With his dictum, "Without Mohammed Charlemagne would have been inconceivable,"[61] Pirenne argued that it was the destruction of the economic and cultural unity of the Mediterranean world that caused Europe's political center to move northward. What is true, instead, is that the upstart power further weakened the Byzantine Empire, which was already being torn apart by perennial dynastic disputes and internal power struggles. In any case, Byzantium was in no position to prevent the formation of autonomous states in the West.

Italy had long receded to the margins of Byzantine influence.[62] The Lombards had been in control of the territory between the Po Valley and Benevento since 568. They chose Pavia as their capital; the realms of Benevento and Spoleto were ruled by a duke. Rome, too, felt threatened. Inside the Aurelian Walls, their perimeter now too vast, cattle grazed alongside vineyards and fields of grain. The rich, the educated, and anyone else with the means to do so had absconded to Constantinople or sought a livelihood in the clergy. Learning died out among laypeople. Extraordinary times required extraordinary measures; the difficult situation suggested self-help. Pope Gregory paid the Byzantine troops stationed in Rome from his own episcopal treasury. His successors went further, assembling their own armies. Their commanders had to be paid with land. This led to the formation of a local aristocracy whose members fought amongst themselves and, when a pope died, scrapped over the succession. Some pontiffs resembled the head of a mafia-like clan, pursuing their own petty feuds. The Patrimony of Saint Peter, already massive, provided opportunities to favor supporters. In this way, the seeds of enduring patterns of political behavior were sown; the roots of papal nepotism go very deep indeed. On the other hand, a rational bureaucracy based on ancient foundations grew up around the Lateran, the pope's official seat as bishop of Rome. With Gregory's pontificate, the number of documents preserved for posterity increased. Starting in the sixth century, the entries in the *Liber pontificalis*, which recorded the lives and deeds of the popes, also became more detailed.

As Muslims commemorated their caliphs during the Friday prayer, in Rome it was standard to pray for the *basileus* at every papal mass. Yet even though newly elected popes would still long require the emperor's confirmation, his influence melted away. What remained was the sublime radiance of Byzantine culture. It lived on in various monasteries inhabited by Greek monks. Greek merchants dominated trade, and churches were dedicated to Greek saints. Yet there were signs that the cultural influence of the Eastern

Empire was waning. For example, coinage stopped following Byzantine models in the last third of the sixth century. Ancient Roman titles such as "consul" replaced Byzantine designations. The Lateran Palace was expanded as a magnificent seat of political power. The nearby Lateran Basilica, which could accommodate ten thousand worshippers, became the "mother and head" of all churches in Christendom. Latin prevailed over Greek as the language of the liturgy. At the same time, rites and rituals developed that departed from Byzantine customs.

The growing estrangement between Rome and Constantinople manifested itself in dogmatic conflicts that revolved around the old problem of the nature of Christ and a new, related question: What status should be ascribed to religious images, seeing as how they were contrary to prohibitions found in the Bible? Emperor Leo III seems to have forbidden them in 726. Yet the prohibition could not be enforced in Rome. Pope Gregory had provided arguments in favor of religious images. One was that they were useful, as they helped the illiterate to understand and remember biblical history and the story of Christian salvation.[63] Another was that images encouraged humility before God. These views would ultimately prevail in most of the Christian world. On the Bosporus, the iconoclasm dispute escalated into a power struggle between various social groups; it ended in victory for the iconophile monks and the patriarch. It was one of the few times in Byzantine history that the emperor suffered defeat at the hands of his own clergy. The East remained a land of images.

The papacy achieved greater independence by forging an alliance with Francia, the Kingdom of the Franks.[64] Almost contemporaneously with the rise of the Abbasids, the Carolingians succeeded in extending their rule bit by bit. The basis of their power was the office they held as mayors of the palace. Originally responsible for managing the royal household, the mayors of the palace became influential advisers to the Frankish kings and ultimately vied with them for power. Charles Martel's son Pepin unceremoniously deposed the last Merovingian king. In 751, the papacy gave the new dynasty its blessing. The same year, the Lombards took the Byzantine enclave of Ravenna. Pope Stephen II, who visited Pepin in Francia three years later to seek aid against the invaders, anointed him, thus giving his kingdom a sacral aura. Pepin was responsive to the pope's plea. After a successful campaign in Italy, he gave the pope extensive territory including Ravenna and the Lombard Duchy of Spoleto.

This act of generosity looks like a prelude to the "Donation of Constantine," a document that probably dates to a good century later. According to it, Emperor Constantine granted imperial insignia to Pope Sylvester and his successors in gratitude for being miraculously cured of leprosy. It also claims that the emperor gave the pope the Lateran Palace, the city of Rome, and "all the provinces, places, and cities of Italy or the western territories," i.e., nothing less than control over the Western Empire.[65] Along with authentic legal documents, this brazen forgery, the most famous of the Middle Ages, formed the legal foundation of the Papal States.

Further campaigns, including the conquest of Aquitaine, consolidated the Carolingians' position. After Pepin's war, what remained of Lombard power was obliterated by his son and successor, Charles the Great, better known in English as Charlemagne (r. 768–814). Only Benevento survived. Charlemagne shattered the dominion of the Avars. A Byzantine invading force was wiped out in Calabria. After thirty years of war, the pagan Saxons were also overcome. Their god did not intercede when the Franks began the fighting by felling their Irminsul, a holy, "all-sustaining" wooden pillar (or perhaps a tree trunk). Charlemagne had thousands upon thousands put to death or resettled; his warriors were followed by missionaries. In the west, the Carolingian zone of influence only ended at the Atlantic coast. Charles secured his realm against the emirs of Córdoba by establishing the Spanish March, a series of counties that acted as a buffer zone. Of these, Barcelona and Aragon, then called "Jaca," were to have the brightest future.

Moravia and Bulgaria helped themselves to the ruins of the Avar Kingdom. The Bulgarian khan Krum even tried to conquer the Byzantine Empire. After a successful battle, he drank wine from the skull of the fallen emperor. Krum's death in 814 and a victory won by Emperor Leo V (r. 813–820) saved the Byzantine Empire anew. Yet it still had to contend with the new superpower Bulgaria. In the latter half of the century, the Bulgarian Empire adopted Christianity. Tsar Symeon the Great, a deeply learned "half-Greek" who ruled from 893 to 927, had theological writings translated into Old Church Slavonic.[66] A little bit of Aristotle—observations on the wonders of human anatomy—was also translated.

7

First Rebirths and the Striving for a New Order

The Phoenix in Francia: The Carolingian Renaissance

Rome. December 25, 800. What happened is only fragmentarily described by the sources, and they contradict each other in some important respects. The event took place in Saint Peter's Basilica. Originally built by Emperor Constantine, the building was supported by ancient columns; a transept gave it the shape of a cross. The apse was decorated with mosaics. Before it stood a baldachin sheltering the shrine thought to hold the bones of the Apostle Peter. Pope Leo III was joined for the Christmas mass by many laymen, clergymen, and local magnates. Charlemagne was also present. A large, somewhat stout man with a mustache trimmed in the Frankish manner, he had donned a cloak interwoven with gold for the festive occasion. Humbly he knelt before the apostle's tomb, said a prayer, and rose to his feet. At that moment, the pope placed a crown upon his head of full, gray hair. "And from the entire people of the Romans came the acclamation: 'to Charles, Augustus, crowned by God, great and pacific emperor of the Romans, life and victory!'" Songs of praise resounded through the church. According to a Frankish source, Leo honored the new emperor "in the way emperors of old were," namely by prostrating himself before him.

Charlemagne's imperial power grab was the culmination of his de facto status and a favorable historical moment. Just as his predecessor Pepin had been asked for assistance by the pope, Charlemagne acceded to a request from Leo to help him fight off the Roman nobility.[1] The power relations between the new emperor and the pope he was protecting were clear. Before the coronation, Charlemagne, functioning as a judge in a local Roman dispute, had forced the pope to swear an oath of purgation. The events on that day in Rome near the winter solstice of 800 had momentous consequences. Undercutting the claim to universal authority of the "Emperor of the Romans" residing in Constantinople, a western empire raised its head. Charlemagne took his place in the line of Roman Caesars. He claimed to be the protector of all of Christendom; he felt called to spread the Word of God and to protect God's honor. Much ink has been spilled by scholars over an observation by Charlemagne's biographer Einhard, to the effect that the emperor was displeased by the coronation ceremony. He was probably troubled by the fact that the pope had unexpectedly crowned him while he was kneeling, before he had been acclaimed by the Roman people. With this coup de main, Leo had departed from custom and made himself, not the people, responsible for choosing the emperor. The establishment of a Latin emperor revived an old question: Which rights and how much power belonged to secular versus spiritual authority?[2]

Now, on Christmas Day in the year 800, the prophecy that the Roman Empire had to be the final one seemed fulfilled. Europe had gotten back the order vouchsafed to it by God. In the wake of Muslim offensives and Bulgarian attacks, the Byzantine Empire had been reduced to Asia Minor, a few territories around the capital, and its holdings in southern Italy. It had to give up Rome for good; Sicily fell to the Muslims. On the other hand, Charlemagne's bid to become master of Venice was warded off. Constantinople was forced to recognize his status as emperor, although this did not happen until over a decade later. The title he tended to be known by was "King of the Romans," *rex Romanorum*.

Charlemagne left behind more than the memory of a monarch who was equally powerful and pious, resourceful and ruthless. He was dubbed "the

Great" (*Charlemagne* is French for "Charles the Great"), and contemporaries were already calling him *pater Europae*, "father of Europe," in large part because of his steadfast efforts to educate his people and to promote learning and the arts. He himself could read and speak Latin, but he was not skilled at writing.[3] Still, he strived to be learned. In Italy, where the court of the last Lombard king, Desiderius, was populated by educated clergymen, he must have encountered the rich book culture and art of jurisprudence that flourished there. After Desiderius's fall, some of the intellectuals who had worked for him entered Charlemagne's orbit.[4] He also attracted learned men from other corners of the realm to his court. One was the Anglo-Saxon Alcuin, who had been educated at the cathedral school in York by a student of Bede; he served as Charlemagne's teacher. Others included the Irish monk Dungal, the Visigoth Theodulf of Orléans, and Einhard, a Frank from the Main region. The latter's *Life of Charlemagne* was influenced by Suetonius's imperial biographies.

Naturally, this circle was concerned primarily with God and biblical exegesis, as well as the proper form of the liturgy; the latter's standardization occupied Charlemagne's theologians as much as correcting the text of the Bible. At the same time, they cultivated an interest in the classical tradition that went far beyond the reading of ancient *fabulae* that had been practiced at the Merovingian court.[5] They studied Pliny, read the *Aeneid*, and devoted themselves to Sallust and Caesar's *Gallic Wars* in addition to the problems of computus. From what survives of their work, they seem to have been a jovial group whose intellectual banter was studded with ribald humor. Like the Renaissance humanists, they worshipped the Muses and gave themselves ancient names. For example, Angilbert, a lay abbot, was nicknamed "Homer," and Alcuin styled himself an Anglo-Saxon Horace. He signed his poetry with the great poet's cognomen, "Flaccus" (which literally means "floppy ear").

Of course, the more pious among them warned of the dangers of reading pagan authors. Theodulf of Orléans differentiated between the truths contained in pagan literature and the "false mantle" in which they were clothed. Even Alcuin, usually enthusiastic about antiquity, was outraged to hear that monks were being led in singing pagan songs during meals by a minstrel. He remarked, "What has Ingeld"—probably a Nordalbingian chieftain—"to do with Christ?"

> The house is narrow and has no room for both. The Heavenly King does not wish to have communion with corrupt pagans, kings only in name: for the eternal King reigns in Heaven, while that miserable pagan king wails in Hell.[6]

Alcuin went easier on the great Roman poets, although he did find fault with "Virgil's unbridled loquaciousness." He criticized one student for his love of the Roman bard, and he forced another to perform public penance for having read Virgil in secret.[7] But then he went back to admonishing them not to neglect secular knowledge.

Even complex philosophical problems were discussed, such as nothingness and the nature of time. The ancient system of the seven liberal arts was exalted and, like pagan education in general, integrated into Christian doctrine. Those connected to the court knew of Homer and Cicero, devoted themselves to grammar and rhetoric, and contemplated the laws of the universe. The *Liber glossarum*—a lexicon perhaps commissioned by Charlemagne himself—compiled the knowledge of the day in alphabetical order. Its author relied heavily on Isidore's *Etymologies* and other works. Most importantly, however, the Carolingian age rediscovered Aristotle.[8]

Just about all the ancient Latin literature known to us only survived because the chain of copyists remained unbroken down to Charlemagne's time. It is better to copy books than to cultivate vineyards—thus Alcuin exhorted his brothers at the monastery of Saint Martin in Tours.[9] A new script came into vogue: Carolingian minuscule, which evolved from the "New Roman Cursive" of late antiquity. Some humanists considered it ancient and therefore revered it (see pp. 295, 365). Unfortunately for the countless herds of sheep slaughtered for the purpose, but fortunately for posterity, scribes increasingly used parchment. It was expensive—a single missal could be worth as much as a South Tyrolean vineyard[10]—but it was much more durable than papyrus, which quickly fell apart. The codices now written on parchment would provide a stable foundation for the early modern Renaissance. Because of its value—and this was another advantage for textual transmission—parchment was seldom thrown away once it had been written on. Instead, the custom was to scrape off a text that was no longer wanted and to write on the precious skin anew—three times, four times, even more. Such parchments are called "palimpsests," and it is often possible to make out the letters that have been eliminated. In this way, some ancient texts have avoided oblivion.

The miniatures with which Carolingian illuminators decorated manuscripts preserved ancient styles of painting and iconographic conventions, including landscapes in perspective and figures made to look three-dimensional by shading. Centuries later, they would provide inspiration for Renaissance painters. Ancient pictorial style was also revived in large formats. Theodulf of Orléans, for example, had his villa near Fleury decorated with portrayals of the liberal arts. In addition, some ancient institutions and social forms survived, as did economic practices such as slavery, a system of markets, and certain peculiarities of financial administration. People used Roman units to measure land; they adopted ancient political language to describe bonds of personal obligation and governmental systems.[11] There was even an effort to learn from the Byzantine Empire—especially Greek terminology— although this led to competition. A team of intellectuals probably led by Theodulf of Orléans elaborated a position on the question of iconoclasm that was packed with theological erudition. The *Libri Carolini*, or "Charlemagne's Books," branded the iconophile Byzantines as idolaters. Thankfully for European art, no one took this text too seriously.

Ancient architectural forms that alluded to the Rome of Constantine acted as demonstrations of autonomy. Thus, the Lateran Basilica and Saint Peter's served as models for Frankish churches. The Palatine Chapel in Aachen, in contrast, evoked San Vitale in Ravenna and, in turn, the Byzantine churches the latter was patterned on. Some of the columns supporting its arcades were of purple porphyry, the mark of the Byzantine emperors; these columns may have come from Theodoric's ruined palace in Ravenna. Charlemagne had *spolia* brought all the way from Rome. Like relics of the empire, they decorated his palace and its church in Aachen.[12] The language of stone amidst the seclusion of endless forests conveyed a clear message: Charlemagne was an emperor on the same level as the *basileus* in Constantinople and the Caesars of antiquity.

Can the culture surrounding Charlemagne truly be considered a "renaissance"? Support for this view can be found in certain buildings and documents.[13] Theodulf celebrated Charlemagne's rule as a "new spring," and the poet Moduin (ca. 770–840/43) had a young boy in his *Egloga*, modeled on Virgil's and Calpurnius's *Eclogues*, call out,

> Our times follow ancestral custom again
> Golden Rome is reborn and restored anew to the world!

Alcuin echoed this sentiment, claiming that a new Athens had arisen in Francia that, thanks to Christ, surpassed the wisdom of the Academy.[14] This was all horribly exaggerated, and yet Charlemagne and his scholars did play a major part in the genesis of the Renaissance. Still, they did not approach antiquity with a critical spirit; it was too new, too big for that. The period of collecting, copying, and integrating ancient texts into native culture was to last a very long time. Thanks to Latin, parchment, and monastic zeal, the corpus of ancient literature continued to grow. However, huge swathes of the vast intellectual empire of the Greeks and Romans were still waiting to be conquered: almost all of Aristotle, Plato, the Greek physicists, physicians, and natural philosophers, texts of Cicero, Ovid, and so on. Nevertheless, a start had been made.

The concrete world of the *Europenses* also grew larger. Their horizon reached the Balkans, and they brushed up against the culture of Arabia. No one knew what to do with a gilded water clock given to the Frankish ruler by Harun al-Rashid. Nevertheless, this gift, just like the elephant named Abbas that the caliph donated to Charlemagne's zoo, points to new cultural relations—based, of course, on their common interest in collaborating against the Spanish Umayyads and the Byzantine Empire. The two embassies to remote Aachen were not very important to the Muslims; none of their sources mentions them.

Blueprint for a Europe of States

When Charlemagne died on January 28, 814, his body was laid in a late antique sarcophagus from Italy. The spirit of the ancients in no way receded.[15] Walahfrid Strabo (808/09–849), a monk at the monastery of Reichenau (ensconced on an island in Lake Constance), knew the *Histories* of Orosius, a work that relied on ancient authors including Caesar, Livy, Tacitus, and Suetonius. He wrote poetry with a classical flair on topics like friendship and the beauty of nature. His *Hortulus*, or "Little Garden," was a didactic pastoral poem meant to complement ancient literature with his own experience of gardening. It features Zephyrus, the personification of the west wind, as well as several gods: Priapus, the patron of fertility, Saturn, Apollo, and "soul-soothing" Bacchus.[16] The monastery of Fulda became a vibrant center of learning under the direction of Rabanus Maurus (ca. 780–856), head of the school located there and later its abbot. His library was full of ancient authors; along with other Carolingian monasteries, it would be a fruitful destination for humanist manuscript hunters (see p. 374). Rabanus himself did not rely solely on book learning. He wrote a guide to the observation of the heavens, which has its own small place in the history of science.[17]

The Carolingian Renaissance also paved the way for Scholasticism, an intellectual method that, on the one hand, relied on the grand authorities of the past but, on the other, put ideas to a critical test—e.g., by means of disputation—and passed on what had been learned to others via classroom teaching.[18] One of its forerunners was Johannes Scotus Eriugena, a ninth-century grammarian from Ireland.[19] Eriugena wrote a commentary on Martianus Capella. He also helped the notion of God elaborated by Plato and the Neoplatonists make it to the Renaissance, i.e., an unknowable One who reveals himself in his Creation, at once mobile rest (*status mobilis*) and resting motion (*motus stabilis*). Eriugena separated philosophy from revelation. He extinguished the eternal flames of hell, replacing them with the inner, psychological suffering of the sinner; he ascribed human beings free will and thus dignity. In this point, he contradicted the maverick Gottschalk of Orbais (ca. 803–867/69), who drew scandalous conclusions from Augustine's view that humans are predestined to salvation or damnation. If this was the case, Gottschalk argued, then Christ did not redeem all of humanity.[20] And if every individual's fate was already determined from the moment of birth, what was the point in having a Church? The radical thinker was shut away in a monastery for twenty years on account of his heterodox ideas.

Another luminary of the time was Servatus Lupus, abbot of Ferrières (ca. 805–after 861). He was a manuscript hunter reminiscent of a Renaissance humanist.[21] Perhaps the most important philologist of his century, he sought to complete fragmentary texts and compared textual variants. He asked the abbot of Saint Gall for works of Sallust and Cicero, thanked a scribe for improving a manuscript of Macrobius and a Boethius commentary, and hunted for the text of Suetonius, probing as far off as the cathedral library in York. He once refused to send a codex to Archbishop Hincmar of Reims (ca. 800/10–882), a canon lawyer and historian, because books were too precious. The volume was too big to fit inside a robe or a bag, he argued, and might pique the interest of thieves.

The times were indeed dangerous. Under Charlemagne's son Louis the Pious (r. 813–840), the empire had already lost its luster. Power struggles within the Carolingian dynasty did irreparable harm to Louis's dominion. The fraternal feud in the house of Charlemagne continued after Louis's death. The partition of the empire, according to the Treaty of Verdun in 843, created boundaries that would still be felt centuries later when the states of Europe formed. The Capitulary of Coulaines, promulgated in the same year, established a horizontal power structure. This agreement between the king of West Francia and his nobility and clergy, perhaps the first sovereign contract ever, enshrined the horizontal principle in law by stipulating that the king's *fideles* participate in governing the kingdom.[22] Only once more, and only for a short time, would the luck of succession result in a unified Frankish empire.

Meanwhile, the realm became a mere phantom. Vikings and then Hungarians ventured into the feeble heart of the continent. Furthermore, Italy and southern France suffered at the hands of invading Saracens. Their object was usually plunder and nothing more. But Europe's states stood firm.

The Vikings, also called "Northmen" or "Norsemen," ultimately showed themselves to be capable state builders. On the island of Britain, the "Great Heathen Army" of Danish Vikings was withstood only by the Kingdom of Wessex, where Alfred the Great (r. 871–899) organized the defense. By neutralizing the southern English kingdom's competitors, the Danes had unintentionally laid the foundation for its rise. In the decades after Alfred's death, his successors managed to win back territory occupied by the Northmen. Their rule endured in northern France, where Charles the Simple gave them the territory around Rouen, which came to be named for them: Normandy. In return, the Northmen (on their way to becoming Normans) followed their leader Rollo in adopting Christianity.

Sometimes the invasions favored the rise of new dynasties. It was, after all, magnates in border regions who bore the brunt of defensive fighting, thus enhancing their reputation. In East Francia, the Ottonians, a Saxon dynasty, established themselves. Their most important representative, Otto I the Great (r. 936–973), decisively defeated the Hungarians near Augsburg in 955.[23] When Otto went to Rome in 962 to have himself crowned emperor and anointed with holy oil, the title and insignia of an "Imperator Augustus" were once again combined with true power. Yet, as may be suggested by the reduction in written records during his reign and that of his successors, it seems that the force of orations, holy rites, and mounted warriors had again eclipsed the authority of bureaucracy.

In West Francia, the Robertian dynasty prevailed. The final shadows of Carolingian authority vanished there in 987, when Duke Hugh Capet, a descendant of the Robertians' founder Robert the Strong, was chosen king. In direct or indirect line of descent, his family would go on to rule the kingdom, which would ultimately become France, for nine centuries. The Capetians, Valois, and Bourbons could all claim the brave fighter of Bretons and Normans as the founder of their glory. While East Francia evolved into a mixture of elective and hereditary monarchy, the rulers of West Francia managed over the centuries to expand the royal domains, which formed the basis of their monarchical power. In the sixteenth century, "domaine royale" and "France" were interchangeable terms. The West Frankish kings departed from the tradition of dividing their estates among their children. Latter-born sons were given appanages that reverted to the Crown if the collateral line died out. Initially, however, the influence of counts and dukes limited the monarchy there as severely as it did the Ottonians in East Francia.

It is standard to divide medieval Europe into three distinct cultural zones: Arabic, Byzantine, and Latin. However, this division not only ignores the Jews and the Slavs, but it also obscures how richly permeable the boundaries were—and not only in border zones. In the "Middle Kingdom" ruled by Lothair (r. 840–855), one of the sons and heirs of Louis the Pious, regions of exchange and economic and cultural innovation (and admittedly no small amount of bloody conflict) took shape. These included the Duchy of Burgundy with its vibrant late medieval culture, economic hubs like Bruges, Milan, Genoa, Venice, and Florence, as well as the Swiss Confederation. Trade by sea, across the Alpine passes, and along rivers like the Rhine and Po endowed these regions with prosperity. Thanks to their own strength and the jealousy of powerful neighbors, none of whom would allow the others to plunder them, they achieved a high degree of autonomy.

In Italy, the Carolingian bloodline dried up in 924 with the murder of the impotent emperor Berengar of Friuli. Frankish power also disintegrated in Spain. In the north, the Christian rulers of Asturias embarked on the long road to reconquering the peninsula. They gained rich León, by which name their realm would thenceforth be known. The county of Castile split off from León, grew in size and power, and ultimately became strong enough to subdue its former master. This is the origin of the Kingdom of Castile-León. To the east, a petty noble power around Pamplona, the future Kingdom of Navarre, declared autonomy from the Carolingians and stood up to the Arabs. One of its rulers obtained through marriage the neighboring county of Aragon, originally a Carolingian border province; it also rose to become a kingdom. When it united with Castile five hundred years later, a state was formed that first ruled the Iberian Peninsula and then half the world.

Yearning for Rome: The Renaissance of an Idea

The crumbling Roman Empire of Charlemagne was little more than what is known as a "segmentary state." This concept, developed from the study of East African political entities and the Chola dynasty in India, is well suited to describing the empire that fanned out over central Europe. The centers of such states exercise real power only over the territory in which the ruler resides. On the periphery, it dissipates into a ritual sovereignty over more or less autonomous domains.[24] Neither Charlemagne's empire nor the realms of the successor dynasties ever crossed what political scientist Michael W. Doyle has called the "Augustan threshold," a phase in the history of empires during which they transition from expansion to consolidation and let the periphery share in the gains of the imperial center.[25]

For almost a millennium, the imperial crown remained connected to East Francia, which came to be known as the *Regnum teutonicum*, the "Kingdom of Germany." Regardless of the fact that its monarchs could barely rule their own little patch of Europe, their chroniclers placed them in the glorious genealogy of the ancient emperors and the mighty Charlemagne. Theologians and jurists conquered a metaphysical empire for them. This fantasy provided justification not only for the German kings to yearn for Italy in their hearts but also to invade it with an army in tow. The center of the imperial galaxy was Rome. For some it was still the "capital of the world and master of all cities"—a formulation stemming from Otto III (r. 983–1002), grandson of Otto the Great. This youthful emperor was more devoted to the concept of Rome and its promise of empire than any other medieval ruler, even though, like his predecessors, he also sought to extend the influence of his kingdom northwards and eastwards.

In Rome, gigantic ruins recalled shattered greatness. According to legend, the Colosseum would stand until the end of the world.[26] Otherwise, the erstwhile megacity was not all that impressive. Farmers, clergymen, and a few merchants and craftsmen had settled down between the churches and the crumbling palaces.[27] Only pilgrims brought some vitality and money. The surrounding area was unsafe. It was ruled by malaria and noble families feuding over land and power. Inside the city, old ruins like Castel Sant'Angelo, the ancient tomb of Emperor Hadrian, served as fortresses. No one was able to maintain peace, least of all the popes, themselves usually the heads of rival clans vying for power. Many died violently. One of them, Formosus, was dug up and put on trial as a stinking corpse by his opponents in 897. Sources, admittedly biased, portray the papacy at the nadir of its reputation. John XI seems to have been the bastard son of another pope, Sergius III. John XII (955–963), who was not even eighteen when elected, hastened toward a lovely death, killed while in bed with a married woman.[28]

During his brief reign, Otto III spent more time in rundown Rome than any other medieval emperor. He even had a palace built for himself, presumably on the Palatine Hill.[29] "Ours! The Roman Empire is ours!" exulted his adviser Gerbert of Aurillac (ca. 950–1003).[30] In 999, he was made pope by

Otto. He took the name Sylvester II, after the earlier bishop of Rome who was supposed to have baptized Constantine. This was part of a larger political program. Probably on Gerbert's advice, the emperor had decided to undertake a "renewal of the Roman empire": a purification and reform of the Church and the papacy. It did not get past the planning stages, however. Otto died in 1002, not even twenty-two years old, in a castle north of Rome. He had been forced to leave his city swiftly when it became unsafe. His enthusiasm for *aurea Roma*, "golden Rome," had nothing in common with the humanists' romantic view of antiquity. His models were the Christian empire of Constantine and Charlemagne, not the *imperium* of the Caesars.

The procession of German kings to Rome would continue for half a millennium. Some of these "world rulers" did not even manage to fight their way to Saint Peter's and had to make do with a coronation in the wrong location, such as the Lateran Basilica. Those who criticize the German kings, saying they would have done better to invest their energy in colonizing the east rather than dallying around Italy, overlook the magical power that a ritual such as imperial coronation exercised in the Middle Ages. They overlook the ideological significance of the capital of the all-powerful ancient empire. They also forget that it has always been more attractive to pillage high cultures than to clear forests, educate "barbarians," and build states. After all, Italy was part of the booming Mediterranean economy, which, since the Carolingian period, had been connected to the economy of the Muslim world.[31] Silk, ivory, frankincense, and spices docked in Italian port cities. Cities that were big for the time—even shabby Rome had twenty thousand or so inhabitants—amassed wealth that could be funneled off in the form of tribute. Playing politics in Europe perforce entailed trying to rule Italy—or at least making sure that one's opponents did not. From century to century, however, the Germans failed in the attempt. In general, their armies were too small, while the resources of their opponents and the cities and princes of Italy were too great. Yet without Germany's (ultimately destructive) Italian policy, the great Renaissance would have lacked one of its essential preconditions.

While the Ottonians fought for Rome, the decline of the Abbasids allowed the Byzantine Empire to retake the offensive. Nicephorus II Phocas (r. 963–969) reconquered Crete and occupied Cyprus. The imperial standard was soon flying over Asia Minor and Syria once again. The Bulgarians were defeated in a series of campaigns. When Basil II died in 1025, Byzantine influence stretched from footholds in southern Italy to the Euphrates and Lake Van. Sicily remained in the hands of the Muslims for the time being. The religion and culture of Byzantium grew beyond the borders won for it by its armies, all the way to the cities, plains, and forests of the East.

Christ in the Forests: State Formation and Christianization in the East and the North

The origins of the peoples who spoke Slavic languages are thought to lie in various regions north of the Danube.[32] Bit by bit, embryonic states also developed here and in the distant north along age-old trade routes. "Sapphire" furs from central Sweden had warmed freezing Roman matrons since ancient times. In the Early Middle Ages, Arab silver coins glittered in Slavic towns and even under the midnight sun.[33] The people of the north worshipped many-headed gods who hurled lightning bolts; they feared trolls and vampires. Thousands of forts and castles offered protection. Some of them developed into cities. More and more names flash out of the gloom: a ninth-century document fastidiously lists the fixed locations and territories of peoples along the Danube, from the "Nortabtrezi" on the Danish border to the hundred castles of the Khazars, a kingdom between the Black and Caspian seas ruled by a Jewish elite. The eastern border of the Christian world, between nascent states and steppe, was marked by the settlements of the Volga Bulgars, whose culture was shaped by Islam and the Central Asian religion Tengrism. They survived into the Mongol period, whereas the kingdoms of the Khazars and Moravians did not see the eleventh century.

"Bosom of peoples" is the name a Byzantine historian gave to the north.[34] One of those peoples, the "Varangians," was also met with in the east of Europe. Their Finnish neighbors called them "Rus'," probably from the Norse word *roþsmen*, "people rowing boats."[35] Initially feared as raiders, they were later sought as mercenaries—tall, courageous men who had built for themselves panoplies of warrior and agrarian gods and were devoted to a religion of fighting, constant wandering, and doom. They, too, founded fortified settlements. They traveled to the Byzantine Empire and Baghdad to sell furs, swords, and slaves. Soon enough, the areas where the Rus' hunted, traded, and ruled were named after them. Assimilating with a diverse mix of Slavs, Finno-Ugric peoples, and others, they ultimately became the Russian people. The part they played in founding the "mother of Russian cities," Kyiv, is disputed.[36]

The Kyivan Rus', initially a conglomerate of rival principalities, was formed under the rule of the Rurikids, a dynasty of Scandinavian origin. The origins of state formation can be seen, for example, in the way enforced tribute in the form of pelts, wax, or slaves regularly evolved into taxes. As so often, the Christian faith had a unifying effect. A baptism marked the beginning of the integration of the Rus' into the system of European powers. Along with several thousand Varangian soldiers, who would go on to be the personal bodyguard and elite troops of the Byzantine emperor, this was the dowry stipulated by the *basileus* in exchange for giving his sister in marriage to Prince Vladimir the Great (r. 980–1015). Vladimir's conversion, which was followed by a mass baptism in the Dnieper River, laid the foundation for the "Byzantine Commonwealth."[37]

Yaroslav the Wise (r. 1063–1054) founded a theological school and had East Slavic common law codified in the "Rus' Justice." As usual, contact with a neighboring high culture was useful; certain terms and the structure of the work reveal Byzantine influence.[38] Yaroslav's successors expanded the law code. This later form evinces an increasing degree of centralized authority, as it outlaws the right to vendetta and feuds that was sanctioned in the oldest parts. Rule functioned via fealty, which bound the prince to his people as it bound them to him. The council of boyars, the aristocratic elite, exerted influence only for a time and not in all of the Rus' lands.[39]

The Christianization of eastern Europe brought salvation from illiterate darkness. The Glagolitic script invented by Byzantine missionaries was used above all for liturgical books. Russians and other Slavic peoples eventually adopted the Cyrillic alphabet imported from Bulgaria; starting in the eleventh century, Old Church Slavonic developed primarily into a language of religion and literature. The Rus' remained cut off from the tradition of Greek and Latin letters. In part for this reason, Moscow lay outside the Renaissance's realm of possibility and would thus have no share in its innovative potential. As a side effect of Christianization, the territory in which slaves could be found was reduced. For it was forbidden for Christians to sell other Christians to Muslims. This was a reason why Christian traders and princes who profited from the slave business did not always support the missionary impulse with the utmost zeal.[40] Incidentally, Muslim rulers in Africa held to a similar policy, as Islam also forbade the enslavement of fellow Muslims. It was more important to them to earn money from the slave trade than to spread the Word of the Prophet.

State formation and Christianization also went hand in hand in Bohemia and Bulgaria.[41] The former, ruled by the Přemyslid dynasty, followed first Rome and then Constantinople. The ferocious Hungarians also found their place in the "West." After their bitter defeat at Augsburg and an unsuccessful campaign against the Byzantine Empire, they opted to settle down and adopt a tranquil life as farmers. Their ruler, Geza I of the Árpád dynasty, was baptized. On Christmas Day in the year 1000, Stephen I was crowned with a crown sent by the pope; he was later declared a saint, as was Vladimir of Kyiv.

In Poland, Rome had already won out a few decades earlier. Bolesław the Brave (r. 992–1025) expanded the influence of the Piast dynasty first by allying with the Holy Roman Empire, then by opposing it, and, when it was to his advantage, by banding together with pagan auxiliary troops. For a time, he also ruled over Moravia. Attacks on Bohemia and Kyiv failed. According to legend, the coronation sword of the Polish kings was the one he used to strike the Golden Gate in Kyiv; thence, it is said, came the notches on its blade. Shortly before his death, Bolesław, one of the mightiest rulers of *Polonia*, also received the pope's blessing to be crowned king.

In Norway and even in Denmark, the creation of cities and kingdoms also largely coincided with Christianization between 990 and 1050.[42] Their origins are shrouded in fairy tales, under which the contours of a barely Christianized warrior society shine through. Ancient Norse sagas abound with dismembered, mutilated, tortured bodies; seas of blood are spilled. The fact that one of the rulers of the day, Eric, earned the moniker "Bloodaxe" may tell us something about how political disputes were settled. Honor and bravery were exalted as the highest values. The greatest hope of warriors, if they should fall in battle, was to be led to Valhalla by Valkyries.[43] Harald Bluetooth (d. 987), who unified the Danish lands and ruled over a large part of Norway for a few years, began his days as a Viking leader in Normandy. One of the runestones at his seat in Jelling boasts that he converted the Danes to Christianity.[44] Here, as in other parts of the north, however, conversion required the consent of an assembly of magnates and the "people."

After a series of successful campaigns, Sweyn Forkbeard (r. 986–1014) added the English crown to the Danish. What began as plundering raids—the Northmen had resumed their voyages to England in 980—resulted in conquest. By marrying Bolesław I's sister Świętosława, Sweyn was received among the princely families of Europe. A vast Danish empire was cobbled together by Sweyn's son Canute the Great, including the British Isles, Norway, and parts of Sweden, but it was fleeting. The English crown fell to Edward the Confessor; his father was of the House of Wessex, and his mother was a Norman. Sweden, or more precisely parts of central and southern Sweden cut off by impassable forests—Götaland and Svealand, the realms of the Swedes and the Geats— followed their own path. So did Norway.

On Viking Iceland, the "Althing" began meeting in 930. At this proto-democratic deliberative body, held near the summer solstice in the middle of a large lava field along Thingvallavatn, Iceland's largest lake, free, land-owning farmers assembled to discuss their affairs.[45] It was at such a meeting in the year 1000 that the decision was made to convert to Christianity. It was tantamount to deciding to become literate and thus gain access to the culture of Latin Europe. A first Cato quotation appeared between the mid-twelfth and mid-thirteenth centuries, as did fragments of Dioscorides' *De materia medica* (see pp. 127f.) and parts of the Galenic corpus.[46] Even Greenland had its own bishop. A hoard of walrus and narwhal skulls and gigantic cowsheds testify to its wealth.[47]

An increasingly taut web of alliances, marriages, and related gift exchanges connected Europe's princes and contributed to the formation of an ever-growing sphere of communication. For example, Otto the Great gave his sister Hedwig in marriage to the West Frankish Duke Hugh the Great. Otto himself took the daughter of an English king for his first wife and the widow of an Italian king for his second. For his son, he arranged a marriage to a Byzantine princess. Marriages linked Wessex with Normandy, united the Scandinavian powers for a time, and strengthened their alliances with England. The Swedish King Olof Skötkonung wed his daughter Ingegerd to the grand prince of Kyiv. Now as later, kingdoms were founded through advantageous pairings, only to fall apart again in ruinous wars of succession.

Once baptized and crowned, many rulers wasted no time in establishing ecclesiastical jurisdictions of the highest order possible. Only in this way could ecclesiastical independence be achieved, thereby reinforcing political independence. During a visit to Gniezno, for example, Otto III granted the ruler of Poland the archbishopric he sought. Hungary owed the establishment of the archbishopric of Gran to the emperor. Such measures advanced both state formation and culture. Theological erudition was promoted, and—most importantly for the future of Europe—classical Latin enjoyed a revival.[48]

Resuscitation of a Superlanguage

Classical Latin's joints had grown rigid. It was on the brink of death and oblivion, hanging on for dear life in monastic libraries, dried up as ink on parchment, unspoken except in a bare whisper. Only some rhetoricians and grammar teachers continued to speak it. The people communicated in Vulgar

Latin, which developed into a broad spectrum of varieties over time. These became the buds of the Romance languages, which slowly blossomed into their full glory. Meanwhile, in what would become the *Regnum teutonicum*, Germanic tongues prevailed—languages like Old Saxon, Alemannic, and Bavarian, archaic-sounding precursors to modern German. Traditional Latin was barely understood in most parts of Europe, either on the continent or in England. Alfred the Great noted that knowledge of Latin had become so scarce that hardly anyone could follow the mass or translate letters into English.[49] As a consequence, writing in the vernacular was encouraged. After 1066, however, Latin became the language of the clergy and official documents on the island of Britain as well.

Europe's broad linguistic palette was rounded out by Greeks and Slavs in the east and the Arabs in the south, not to mention the Hebrew of Jewish scribes. It must have been difficult at times for traders between Novgorod, Baghdad, and Constantinople to understand each other. People talked with their hands; sometimes they didn't talk at all. The Uralic people on the Upper Volga traded by simply piling up their wares, going away, and only coming back to collect their payment when buyers had put down something of equivalent value and departed. The African gold trade often worked similarly.[50]

There were several reasons why Latin was dying out and other languages were flourishing. The paths of politics were especially important. Millennia later, Europe's linguistic landscape still bears their traces. Latin had followed in the wake of the Roman legions to become the language of Europe, and it lost its dominion with their retreat. Under Justinian, the last Roman on the Bosporus, it continued to be the language of administration even in the Greek East. But Justinian's legal codes, themselves written in Latin, already had to be commented on in Greek under his successors. For when Byzantium lost the West, it also forgot its language.[51] It was not so much coercion as the gentle force of the stronger and thus more desirable power that compelled people to learn certain languages. Over time, love and friendship, hard-nosed commercial interests, and careerism propelled new major languages to preeminence. The Spanish humanist and grammarian Elio Antonio de Nebrija (1444–1522)—the author of a widely used Latin grammar and a Latin-Castilian dictionary—got to the heart of the relationship between languages and states. Without a doubt, he wrote, the Castilian language had always been the companion of the Castilian kingdom: "Together they were born, together they grew up and flourished."[52] In fact, it was thanks to Castile's rise to power that Castellano, originally a variant of Vulgar Latin, became the global language of

Spanish. Every major, widely spoken language was, at one point in its history, the language of a victorious power. The case was no different for Latin. The fact that it survived Rome's decline and returned in the Middle Ages to become the dominant medium of the learned was one of the necessary preconditions for the Renaissance and the "rise" of Europe.

Charlemagne had already included Latin in his educational program. The fiat of rulers alone, however, would not have sufficed to resuscitate the dying language of the Caesars. The decisive agent in its revival was, in addition to law, religion. The language of the Empire became the language of the Church. It was taught by cathedral schools, monasteries, and schoolmasters. Knowledge of Latin was necessary to access the Word of God, the Bible, and the teachings of the Church Fathers. Without knowledge of Latin, it was impossible to properly apply the complex rules of the liturgy and thus unleash its magical power. Translation was aided by glossaries. The oldest of them dates to 765 AD and is the earliest extant work written in Old High German. Called the *Abrogans*, it was used in part for reading the Bible.[53] Its name comes from its first entry: "Abrogans—dheomodi—humilis," i.e., "humble." It was based on a late antique collection of Latin synonyms that might have been assembled at Cassiodorus's Vivarium monastery. With this work by an anonymous Bavarian monk, Europe began its unique career as a continent of translations. Generations learned Latin using the grammar by Aelius Donatus (ca. 320–ca. 380 AD) and the commentary on it by Pompeius, an African with the telling epithet of *grammaticus*. The art of writing letters in Latin was already revived in the Carolingian period. Attempts were made to translate works by Horace, Virgil, Ovid, and the late antique grammarian Priscian.[54]

Engagement with the classics grew more intense in the tenth century.[55] For example, the rule of the (in reality hapless) Berengar of Friuli was celebrated in a panegyric that exhibits the influence of Virgil, Juvenal, and the Latin *Iliad*.[56] Even philosophical topics were taken up. Things got started with Bovo II, abbot of Corvey from 900 to 916, who knew the works of Boethius and may even have been able to read Greek. Notker the German (ca. 950–1022), a monk in Saint Gall, translated *inter alia* two works of Aristotle into German (via the Latin versions by Boethius). The product of a society of farmers, hunters, and warriors, he struggled to find the right words, to reach the proper level of abstraction, and to communicate the texts' logical argumentation. In a nutshell, he struggled to appropriate—in the true sense of the term, i.e., to genuinely make his own, to adopt for his own organic use—the ancient cultural heritage he was trying to share with the Alemanni studying at his monastery school.

The anonymous author of the *Ruodlieb*, a Latin chivalric epic perhaps written in Bavaria and dating to around the mid-eleventh century, certainly knew Pliny and Virgil. And the Benedictine monk Frutolf of Michelsberg (d. 1103) learned of Socrates, Plato, and Pythagoras from his reading of Augustine.[57]

Linguistic diversity often reflects political fissures. In lavish abundance, a majority of the over seven thousand languages in the world today flourish in the tropical regions around the equator, whereas Europe speaks with fewer than one hundred tongues. The differences can be accounted for in large part by geography.[58] Papua New Guinea is a good example. It has fewer inhabitants than Switzerland, but one thousand languages and dialects are spoken there. One explanation could be that part of the population has always lived in New Guinea, which is traversed by jagged, inaccessible mountains, whereas the other is spread across countless small islands. In this case, as in so many others, geography hampered the easy communication that is a prerequisite for linguistic homogeneity. It stood in the way of the formation of an expansive state that could have cleared up the Babylonian confusion. For scientific and technological progress, the fragmentation of writing and speaking represents a massive obstacle. It makes the sharing and discussing of ideas almost impossible. Areas with great linguistic diversity have hardly ever been hubs of innovation. Creole and pidgin languages are little help in solving the problem, as their limited vocabulary and simplified grammar restrict their ability to express complex ideas.

If Europe exhibits relative linguistic poverty, it is partly due to the creation of powerful kingdoms of the kind Antonio de Nebrija had in mind. The linguistic map of Europe ultimately reflects processes of state formation that were more decisive and successful than those that took place in, say, Southeast Asia, the pre-Columbian Americas, or Africa. The small number of languages in Europe facilitated communication across large spaces; the availability of Latin paved the way for the grand dialogue to cross all borders. Thus, despite the continent's political fragmentation—which actually proved essential for its innovative spirit—a vast space with a common superlanguage was created.

Latin Europe's location gave it another major advantage, although it would only be felt centuries later: its proximity to Muslim high culture, which fostered an incredibly rich intellectual heritage. Most importantly, the Arabs had industriously appropriated the treasures of ancient Greek learning. Moreover, they built bridges to East Asia. In this they were supported by a booming economy several times more powerful than that of Latin Europe.

8

Arab Spring, Byzantine Autumn

The Cities of the Prophet

The Muslim conquests created a massive economic zone unprecedented in world history.[1] The followers of the Prophet were great traders, good farmers, and able engineers. They devised sophisticated irrigation systems, improved methods for cultivating crops, and imported new plants from East Asia.[2] The religious revolution was followed by an agricultural one. Thanks to the Arabs' hydraulic engineering, Andalusia turned green and Sicily became the garden of Italy. With the Muslims came cotton, bitter oranges, and watermelon; if not for medieval Arab traders, the sultry summer nights of southern Europe would lack the sweet scent of lemon blossoms. In addition, the art of making silk, which had been known in China and the Indus Valley since the third century BC, spread more widely. From equally far away came sugar. The word encapsulates its origin: the oldest root—*śarkarā*, meaning "sweet"—is Sanskrit. The

Muslim traders who brought the tasty crystals to the West and who soon cultivated sugar cane themselves called it *sukkar*. In Spanish, the Arabic article "al" stuck with the substantive, producing *azúcar*, whereas the Italians left it at *zucchero*. The word contains within itself an entire epic, an odyssey that began in the premodern tropical island world of the Pacific, traversed India, Persia, and Arab lands, and ended up in the Mediterranean. Trade and new technology—as well as pleasant trifles like chess—followed the same paths. The Arab horizon now stretched very far indeed. In order to explain the trading customs of the Ugrians north of the Volga, an Arab geographer compared them with the practices of spice traders on islands in the Indian Ocean.[3] Trade and conquest gave the Arabs access to the overwhelming storehouse of knowledge, art, and literature that the East had amassed over thousands of years.

In addition to sea routes, the main artery of trade between the remote West and the Far East was the Silk Road. The name, an invention of the nineteenth century, refers to a system of caravan paths 6,500 kilometers in length. Here and there, they split off into two or three separate strands or branched off into byways that reached the seas in the south. Thousands upon thousands of robust steppe horses, mules, and two-humped, Bactrian camels carried the marvels of the East and the goods of the West over stony, dusty paths. The journey skirted the "Heavenly Mountains," the Tian Shan range, crossed passes, and traversed the dreaded Gobi Desert, where so many camels met their demise. The Silk Road ended at the western market of the Chinese city of Chang'an. Another route reached Korea. The Silk Road offers truly impressive examples of "cultural transfer." For example, the tomb of the Chinese general Li Xian (d. 569 AD) in Guyuan contained a silver ewer of Persian design that was decorated with a scene of Greek soldiers—probably preparing to embark for Troy.[4]

In the Muslim world, enchanting cities grew up around shrines, fortresses, and palaces, and almost always on the site of age-old settlements—cities whose names evoke the art of rug making and mosques covered in polychrome enameled tiles. In Bukhara and in Samarkand, with its caravansaries, gardens, and palaces, Persian and Arab literature blossomed until Genghis Khan came and put an end to all poetry. Here and elsewhere, potentates who had arranged themselves under the broad mantle of the Abbasid Caliphate adorned themselves with culture, competing for prestige with neighbors and enemies—two groups that often overlapped. Many of their cities had sewer systems. The principal streets were paved, and lanterns supplemented the light of the honey-colored moon. Fez, flush with the water of numerous canals, developed into one of the most beautiful cities in North Africa. It had paved streets that, every day in summer, were doused with water, cooled, and cleaned. It had twenty baths and three hundred mills.[5] Pilgrimage destinations turned into metropolises, such as Karbala and Qom, which contained the tombs of imams, as well as Najaf, the final resting place of the hero Ali. Chroniclers praised Jedda on the Red Sea for its magnificent palaces, as well as Basra, originally established as a garrison. For a time, Basra's luster was said to have outshone even Baghdad's. Shortly before the year 1000, the *Epistles of the Brethren of Purity* was composed there; organized as a series of letters, it was an encyclopedia of all Arabic philosophy and science.[6]

The paths that led from the Gobi Desert across the oases of central Asia and the Iranian highlands ended in emporia on the Persian Gulf—perfect combinations of seaports and transshipment points for land trade.[7] Large merchant fleets set sail from Siraf and let the wind take them all the way to China. In Aden, heavily fortified und unassailable between sea and mountains, trade flowed in from Hormuz and western India, Mogadishu and Jedda. The well-traveled geographer al-Muqaddasi (d. 990) provides a list of goods that were bought and sold in the cosmopolis: Abyssinian slaves, eunuchs, tiger pelts, leather shields, fine cloth. The coast of eastern Africa boasted the gold markets of Kilwa and Mogadishu. The stars of Mombasa and Zanzibar rose after the year 1000. From there, Asia and Christian Europe received slaves, Ghanaian gold, ivory, and mangrove wood. The Red Sea's significance for trade grew and grew. Egypt was a bazaar between two oceans, an emporium for East and West; Alexandria had a million inhabitants at the turn of the millennium.[8]

Often, the splendor of a city depended on the power and money of a military leader. Kairouan, a center of Islamic jurisprudence, had its heyday under the Fatimids and the Zirids, and Aleppo under Sayf al-Dawla (r. 945–967). The Buyid 'Adud al-Dawla (r. 943–983) built a monumental library in Shiraz that had 360 book-filled rooms cooled by a ventilation system; surrounded by gardens and lakes, it was the Shangri-La of bibliophiles.[9] Ghazni owed its splendor to Sultan Mahmud (r. 997–1030). Born a slave, he and his slave army assembled a kingdom that stretched from the highlands of Iran to northern India.[10] The booty from his campaigns of plunder paid for architecture and golden garments, as well as salaries for poets and scholars like the geographer and astronomer al-Biruni (973–1048); such men endowed Mahmud's rule with the noble sheen of learning. Even the Persian Ferdowsi, author of the grand epic *Book of Kings* and one of the greatest writers in his language, joined Mahmud's court, although he only stayed for a short time. In Kashgar, the metropolis of the Karakhanids, a document reflecting the highest degree of civilization was produced: the didactic poem *Kutadgu Bilig*, whose title means "wisdom which brings happiness." It was, so to speak, a kind of *Book of the Courtier* long before Castiglione.

The greatest city of Islam was Baghdad, although it lost its grip over these areas. In its center, the dome of the palace reflected the sky. The caliphs, on certain occasions dressed in the black cloak of the Prophet, withdrew from the eyes of their subjects. They had historians and poets portray them like Great Kings of Persia or equivalents of Alexander the Great, as world rulers and apocalyptic enforcers of justice. In one week, more works of history might have been written in Baghdad than in the Carolingian Empire in a whole year.[11] The treasures the rulers surrounded themselves with rendered even Byzantine ambassadors speechless, men fully familiar with the gleam of gold. In the city of the caliphs, Abu Nuwas (765–815), a poet of the court and the city, sang the praises of life's pleasures: wine and love, including the latter's homoerotic variety. He even mocked the Quran in his works. Baghdad was also the setting for some episodes of *The Thousand and One Nights*. Perhaps of Indian origin and supplemented by additional stories, the folk tales arrived in Baghdad in Persian and then Arabic translation. The story of Sinbad the Sailor reflects the love of travel and adventure of a society of traders and highlights the importance of the Mesopotamian trade network.[12]

The Abbasids even had direct relations with Tang China. Thanks to caravan routes and the Euphrates and Tigris rivers, the Abbasid Caliphate was equally well connected to the Mediterranean, central Asia, China, and the booming economic zone around the Indian Ocean. As one contemporary wrote, Baghdad was the "port of the world." Even Rus' traders did business there.[13] While looking at the river that flowed around the "City of Peace," al-Mansur is supposed to have said, "This is the Tigris. There is no obstacle between us and China; everything on the sea can come to us on it."[14] In the tenth century, Baghdad is thought to have reached 1.5 million inhabitants. Al-Muqaddasi praised Baghdad as the home of "elegance and courtesy. Its winds are balmy and its science penetrating. In it are to be found the best of everything and all that is beautiful." He closed, "All hearts belong to it, and all wars are against it."[15]

In the House of Wisdom

Harran, ca. 860. Thabit ibn Qurra (ca. 836–901), who worked as a moneychanger in Harran (in what is now southeastern Turkey), was a throwback, one of the last representatives of the old paganism of the Abbasid Empire.[16]

He belonged to the Sabians, a religious community originating in ancient Mesopotamia. Sabians venerated the Sun, Moon, and planets and believed spirits moved the stars, mediating between human beings and the divine. In Harran, the crossroads for important caravan routes to Asia Minor, Syria, and Mesopotamia, knowledge of esoteric wisdom from the ancient Near East had been preserved: magical techniques, the secrets of alchemy, and the science of Alexandria. Thabit loved mathematics, the study of the great scholars of antiquity, and translating. Syriac was his native language, but he also knew Arabic and Greek. In cosmopolitan Harran, eloquence was indispensable to men of his profession, considering they had to haggle volubly for every dirham. Thabit must have felt lucky when Muhammad ibn Musa, a fabulously rich favorite of the caliph, recognized his linguistic talent and brought him to Baghdad.

The religion of his fathers was no obstacle. In his *Book of Confirmation of the Faith of Heathens*, a text he wrote in Syriac, he unhesitatingly declared himself a Sabian with remarkable words that underline a fundamental fact. "We are the heirs and offspring of paganism," he wrote.

> Who has civilized the world and built its cities, but the chieftains and kings of paganism? Who made the ports and dug the canals? The glorious pagans founded all these things. It is they who discovered the art of healing souls, and they too made known their art of curing the body and filled the world with civil institutions and with wisdom which is the greatest of goods. Without them the world would be empty and plunged in poverty.[17]

Thabit was right. Without Aristotle and Plato, without Galen and Ptolemy, the Islamic civilization we know today would not exist, nor would modern Europe. And without masters of many languages like Thabit, a man who appears in almost no history books, the vast majority of the tradition would have been unavailable to the West.

He went to Baghdad, the rich, strife-torn city where secular learning was to find a comfortable home. The Abbasid caliphs saw themselves as successors to the Sasanian "Kings of Kings." They were eager to integrate the newly conquered territories into their empire.[18] One way to do so was to adopt the ideology of the Great Kings of Persia, which was steeped in the teachings of Zoroaster. They considered all of Greek literature to be part of the Zoroastrian canon, to actually belong to Persian cultural heritage. Thus, a project was begun under al-Mansur to translate works of Aristotle and others into Arabic. There was a lot of money to be earned by someone with Thabit's abilities.

When he began with his translations, the texts had already traveled twisted paths. The Muslim conquests had united western and eastern Mesopotamia, territories that had previously belonged to the Byzantine and Persian empires. Still, the whole region had been under Greek influence for a millennium. Christians who did not subscribe to the Chalcedonian Creed, Nestorians and Monophysites, for a time even philosophers from the Academy—all had found asylum in the Sasanian Empire. Besides Harran and Merv, there were monasteries and cities like Mosul and Gondishapur where numerous Nestorians worked as physicians. In Nisibis, they appear to have taught Jewish students.[19] Great King Khosrow I (r. 531–579), himself an author of texts on Aristotelian logic and on astronomy, had even summoned scholars from China and India to his empire. "We have not rejected anyone because they belonged to a different religion or people," he once said.[20] The region had a tradition of translating Greek texts into Syro-Aramaic. Bishop Severus Sebokht (d. 666/67) of Nisibis started another translation initiative at the monastery of Qenneshre in northern Syria. In Damascus the Umayyads had established a bureaucracy on the Byzantine model, and so mastery of several languages was also standard there.

Many people heeded the caliph's call and moved to Baghdad as Thabit did, thus making accessible the boundless mass of knowledge available from Greece and the Near East (including India). This knowledge nourished a grand dialogue that now took place in Baghdad, Samarkand, Damascus, Cairo, and Al-Andalus—a dialogue that would be taken up in medieval Europe. In the process, Arabic gained a function similar to that of Latin further west. While the Byzantines were busy squabbling over images and dogma and suppressing pagan literature, the Abbasids—in contrast to the Umayyads—encouraged the study of writings on secular topics. Under al-Mansur's successor, there was also a desire to make Islam the foundation for a commonwealth of subject peoples. It can be no accident that Aristotle's *Topics*, which was useful in part for formulating theological arguments against Christians and Manicheans, was one of the first texts to be translated. On the other hand, Muslim theologians were quick to attack tenets of Aristotelian cosmology that contradicted the Quran. They received support in this effort from Christian critics of Aristotle like the Platonist John Philoponus of Alexandria.

The *Bayt al-Hikmah*, or "House of Wisdom," erected under the early Abbasids served Baghdad for two centuries as a palace library and an archive of Iranian history.[21] Baghdad became a world capital of knowledge and learning on the level of the Tang metropolis Chang'an. The translation project undertaken there was unparalleled. Its patrons numbered not only caliphs and their families but also courtiers, viziers, secretaries, generals, and scholars. Texts were principally translated from Syro-Aramaic, Greek, and Pahlavi (i.e., Middle Persian) into Arabic. Texts originally written in Sanskrit were translated by way of Persian. Embassies were sent to acquire manuscripts; scholars were recruited. Our Thabit was one of them. Given the same salary as the highest civil servants, he translated what was put into his hands: works on mathematics (including Euclid's *Elements*), Ptolemy's *Almagest*, a commentary on Aristotle's *Physics*, and an introduction to arithmetic. He also improved the *Almagest* translation by the polyglot Nestorian Hunayn ibn Ishaq (808–873), a bon vivant who loved wine and wore perfume every day.[22] The automata-maker Hero of Alexandria, Archimedes, the botanist Dioscorides, and the great physician Galen all found their translators; the latter was also translated by Hunayn.

"Occult" subjects that occupied Baghdad's scholars—such as magic, geomancy, and alchemy—were not in any fundamental way opposed to what the Arabs regarded as open disciplines. For they sought to uncover the inner workings of the world. Modern particle physics does nothing different, although it does use different methods. In addition, the knowledge of magical or necromantic techniques promised bountiful practical uses. As a handmaiden to astrology, which boasted knowledge of the future, astronomy was practiced. Al-Ma'mun had an observatory built near Baghdad. The desire to look into the future and explain the historical necessity of the Abbasid regime—did it not accord with the divinely ordained position of the stars?—offered powerful justification for astronomical research, which would then provide reliable, "scientific" results. A priority was placed on practical application; instruments were designed like the large mural sextant built in Ray (near Tehran) in 994. Ahmad ibn Musa began a collection of "ingenious devices" containing a good hundred mechanical toys and automata. Impulses were provided by Hero of Alexandria, Philo of Byzantium, and tinkerers from all over Asia. Ahmad ibn Musa also had ideas of his own. A high point was reached with the machines designed by al-Jazari, who worked for a ruler in eastern Anatolia. He devised water-powered clocks (Plate 1), musical automata, and pumps, employing conical valves, faucets, and crankshafts. A mechanical age seemed about to dawn, although it is unclear if his ideas were ever put into practice.[23] In the twelfth century, Abd al-Rahman al-Khazni's encyclopedia of mechanical and hydrostatic knowledge would treat technology and theory as a unit.[24] Of practical use was also Ibn Qutaybah's (d. 889) book on administration. Based on

Greek sources, it covered subjects from land surveying to civil engineering, from falconry to animal husbandry.

A rich tradition of historiography helped to increase the fame of the caliphs. Source criticism may have been practiced when it came to collecting and interpreting "hadiths." These reports of Muhammad's sayings and actions provided guidance for lifestyle and jurisprudence.[25] A great deal of literature was also translated, including love poetry and fairy tales. A famous example is *Kalila and Dimna*, a collection of fables intended to teach the prince practical wisdom and ethics, as well as an almost Machiavellian art of politics.[26] Of Indian origin, it came by way of Persia to Syria and Baghdad, where it was translated into Arabic. A Greek version later paved the way for it to reach Italy. In total, 450 more translations of the work were destined to follow.

The Arab thirst for translations was slaked with ever more sophisticated texts. This ultimately included *ulum al-awa'il*, the "sciences of the ancients." They were not simply copied down but rather appropriated creatively and critically.[27] The Platonic dialogues were known by way of synopses. By the tenth century, scholars in the Near East had already digested a large portion of the Aristotelian corpus and elaborated upon it. An example is provided by Costa ben Luca, from Syria. His *On the Difference between the Spirit and the Soul* was intensively studied in the Latin Middle Ages. A prerequisite for this process of appropriation was the same open-mindedness in religious matters that had allowed Thabit ibn Qurra to be summoned to the capital. Melkite Christians like Costa, Nestorians, and Zoroastrians worked side by side with Muslims and Jews. Arabs became acquainted with the Bible via the translation by the rabbi Sa'adiah ben Yosef Gaon. Some works of Ptolemy, the Hippocratic Corpus, and others have survived only thanks to the efforts of Jewish translators.[28]

Students of the World, Teachers of Europe

"The sciences which we possess come for the most part from the Greeks." This was the view of Francis Bacon in the seventeenth century, and he was right— but not when he continued that "what has been added by Roman, Arabic, or later writers is not much nor of much importance."[29] The "Arabs" (to call them after the language in which they wrote[30]) were in no way mere intermediaries of Greek thought.[31] Taking an Aristotelian perspective, they discussed the intellect and the soul, spirit and life, and reflected on God and the universe. They developed their own philosophies in critical dialogue with the Greeks.

Ya'qub al-Kindi (ca. 800–837) tried to create a synthesis of Plato and a Platonic interpretation of Aristotle that was in strict accordance with the teachings of the Quran. The writings of this, the first Muslim philosopher, omitted hardly any subject, treating medicine, mathematics, optics, and even the production of perfume and swords. The interests of Abu Nasr al-Farabi (ca. 870–950), praised as a "Second Teacher" following Aristotle, also went far beyond synthesizing what was already available. His encyclopedic approach was in the spirit of Greek universalism. His theory of the ideal state, inspired by Plato, was the first to confront the question of how revealed religion and religious law affected a polity.[32] The strict definition of science to which he adhered excluded medicine and other disciplines that, in his view, had no demonstrable principles.

Nevertheless, medicine was one of the brightest gems in the crown of Arabic science. One of its most brilliant representatives was Abu Bakr al-Razi (865–925/35). From Ray in Persia, he was long in charge of hospitals there and in Baghdad.[33] His comprehensive *Book of Medicine*, which fills twenty-three volumes in a modern edition, engages with Greek, Syrian, and Indian knowledge and supplies countless observations from medical practice. Al-Razi was the first to distinguish between measles and smallpox. He recognized psychosomatic connections. Moreover, he is considered the discoverer of sulfuric acid and sodium hydroxide. He was the first to describe the distillation of *naft*, or petroleum, which many centuries later would become both a blessing and curse for his homeland. His experience as a doctor urged him to correct the almighty Galen, long before Latin Europeans dared to do so. "Rhazes," as they called him, was also one of the most fascinating philosophers of the entire Middle Ages—and not just of the Arabic Middle Ages. He took the tireless questioner Socrates as his model. A Platonist through and through, he understood Creation as the ordering of eternal atoms by an eternal god, and its endowment with a soul as an act of love and mercy. In his view, reason made human beings capable of participating in the divine, and they were thus free to determine their own fate, to embrace or reject base matter. These ruminations, however, did not lead al-Razi to argue for a monastic asceticism hostile to the body. His Socrates was a "well-rounded" man, devoted to beauty and pleasure—indeed, the tradition portrays Socrates as a hard-drinking reveler—and thus one of the rarest birds in the human zoo of medieval philosophy.

Al-Razi's outrageous position vis-à-vis revealed religion made him a heretic. "How can anyone think philosophically," he is supposed to have said in one of his disputations, "while committed to those old wives' tales, founded on contradictions, obdurate ignorance, and dogmatism?"[34] The following views about the Quran are also attributed to him: it was anything but a miraculous work; there were thousands of writings that expressed themselves more fluently, precisely, eloquently, and in more elegant rhymed prose; and it was full of contradictions, without any value or providing any proof for anything. Did al-Razi actually say all that? We do not know, but it was at this time, and probably in the Muslim context, that the story of the "three imposters" arose, according to which Moses, Jesus, and Muhammad used invented revelations and fake miracles to pose as prophets. This negative version of Lessing's ring parable began circulating in Europe in the thirteenth century, appearing, for example, in Boccaccio's *Decameron*. No one was more critical of religion at the time than the anonymous inventor of the tale.[35]

The Arabs' encounter with the "wonderful wisdom" of the Greeks, as one scholar at the Abbasid court put it,[36] made a deep impression on them—so deep that they adopted the word "philosophy." In Arabic, it became *falsafa*. The word connoted a mixture of Neoplatonic and Aristotelian approaches, although it is not always possible to draw a clear distinction between philosophy and theology. The authority of the classics did not overawe Arab readers. They did not simply take note of Eratosthenes' calculation of the Earth's circumference; they calculated it themselves. They admired Ptolemy's astronomy, but they also checked his math and arrived at more precise results for many items. The *Almagest*'s star catalog was considerably improved by Abd al-Rahman al-Sufi (903–986). Once translated into Latin, it would provide a foundation for Western astronomy for centuries. Arab mathematicians discussed problems that would still occupy minds in early modern Europe, and the optics elaborated by Abu ibn al-Haytham (965–1040) in Cairo was still authoritative in Kepler's day.[37] "Alhazen," as the Latins called him, also stands out for performing practical experiments. One tinkerer, Ibn Khalaf al-Muradi, devised a gear-driven water clock, and al-Biruni worked out tables for it with information on various specific weights. In his correspondence with Ibn Sina, al-Biruni questioned axioms of Aristotelian natural philosophy. For example, he speculated that the orbits of the planets did not have to be circular but rather—as Kepler proved in the seventeenth century—might instead resemble ellipses.

Ibn Sina (ca. 980–1037), born near Bukhara and known in Latin as "Avicenna," was one of the greatest polymaths of the Middle Ages.[38] His canon, a summa of systematic medical knowledge, fills twenty thousand pages in print. It elicited a rich tradition of commentary and served as a textbook at the University of Salamanca until 1680. Other achievements of Arabic medicine were equally impressive. Specialists emerged in the fields of ophthalmology, surgery, and pharmacy. False teeth were made out of cow bones. The disinfectant property of alcohol was understood. The anesthetic effects of opium were known, and it was used in operations. Hospitals, often outfitted with libraries, were not only places of healing but also home to research and teaching.

Ibn Sina pursued a science independent of revealed religion. He drew a clear distinction between astrology, which he saw as a part of natural philosophy, and astronomy, which was based on mathematics. Following al-Farabi, he transformed Allah from an omnipotent man speaking to his creatures into an abstract principle. In his view, God is the One in which essence and concrete existence are the same. God is necessity itself. Chance only exists in the human world.

Differently than in Latin Europe, in the Arab sphere the approaches formulated by Ibn Sina and a few others did not develop into a fully worldly science or a purely secular philosophy—although literature was highly prized and elegance and urbanity were recognized social values.[39] Even Kalam, a speculative theology that sought to elaborate the foundations of the faith via dialectic and to defend them against other doctrines, often met with suspicion or outright rejection. One of its opponents was Ahmad ibn Hanbal (780–855), the founder of a very conservative Sunni school of jurisprudence. There were skeptics who spoke out against the belief in miracles and even against Islam and religion in general, claiming they were human inventions, but such individuals remained marginal figures.[40] On the other hand, a rationalist current of Islamic theology did develop in the ninth century, called "Mu'tazila" by its opponents.[41] Similar to the Christian Scholastics, the Mu'tazilites (meaning "those who separate themselves") emphasized the sovereignty of reason—without, however, questioning the truth of the faith. As their opponents saw it, views that seemed to circumscribe Allah's omnipotence were heretical: for example, that He who was just through and through could not send a just man to hell; or the notion that the Quran had been created by God and was therefore not eternal. Caliph al-Ma'mun and two of his successors tried to enforce the elevation of Mu'tazilite theology as a kind of official state doctrine. A few recalcitrants were executed; Ibn Hanbal was tortured for refusing to renounce the dogma of the Quran's uncreatedness. All in all, the Islamic state at the time of al-Ma'mun appeared to be a true torchbearer of Greek learning. As the caliph's ambit saw it, the Greek tradition had been ruined under the aegis of the Christian Byzantines and their absurd belief in three gods.[42] A mythical ancestor of the Arabs was even invented: Qahtan, who was supposed to be the brother of Yunan, the progenitor of the Ionians. In this way, the Greeks would become Arabs, and their glorious tradition of learning would be of Arabic descent.

The passion for translation on the Tigris began fading around the year 1000. Yet Baghdad remained a city of books. A glimpse into the world of reading there is provided by Ibn Sina's recollection of his first encounter with al-Farabi's *Metaphysics*.[43] One afternoon he was ambling through the booksellers' quarter on the east bank of the Tigris. A hawker announced that the book was a bargain, as the seller was in financial difficulty. He pestered the learned man until he finally bought it. No scene of this kind is reported from any Latin European city of the era. In the Muslim world, every city of middling importance from Andalusia to the heart of central Asia had its own library, and many local dynasties patronized the sciences. One bibliophile is supposed to have declined an offer to be chancellor to a Samanid ruler, protesting that it would take four hundred camels alone to transport his books to Bukhara.[44] The Samanid court was itself a significant source of patronage. The blind poet Rudaki (858/9–940/1) was active there for a while. His own poetry and his translation of *Kalila and Dimna* made him one of the fathers of Modern Persian.

Baghdad's role as a center of science and literature was inherited by Fatimid Cairo. Nowhere in medieval Europe could a society so tolerant in religious affairs be found. This legendary openness ultimately had a clear economic foundation: iron and wood, the indispensable raw materials of all power, could only be procured from Italian merchants and other traders from the north. Between 979 and 991, Fatimid affairs of state were directed by Ya'qub ibn Killis, a Jewish vizier who resembled a Renaissance patron of culture. After converting to Isma'ili Islam, he founded a *madrasah*, or university, in Cairo's al-Azhar Mosque where theology, law, and later medicine were taught. When Cairo's Christians celebrated Epiphany or Easter, the Muslims celebrated with them, enjoying the performances of jugglers and shadow plays. The Fatimid Caliph al-Hakim (r. 996–1021) had a "House of Knowledge" built in his palace, a library similar to Baghdad's "House of Wisdom." Over time it would amass one hundred thousand volumes.[45] A monument to this great patron of learning was erected in the form of the "Great Tables of Caliph al-Hakim," a handbook for ascertaining the positions of the planets.

Yet al-Hakim's rule also put an end to the lightness of Cairo's being. The caliph drowned his people in decrees, forbade alcohol, and condemned culinary treats such as the popular coquina clam. Women's faces had to be hidden behind veils. Ultimately, Christians and Jews were forced to wear stigmatizing symbols (wooden crosses and bells). In 1009 al-Hakim demolished one of the most important shrines of Christendom: the Church of the Holy Sepulcher in Jerusalem. When, one night in 1021, he did not return home—he was probably murdered—Islam gained one more "occulted" figure. Al-Hakim's followers developed into a religious community known as the Druze, which still flourishes today in Lebanon.

First Contacts

Western monastic libraries of the time often contained only a few rotting manuscripts. They were no competition for the book emporia of the Near East, which could boast hundreds of thousands of volumes. Only China's imperial palaces had equally comprehensive stores of knowledge.[46] In ninth-century Baghdad, there were supposedly more than one hundred producers of books. The contemporary Ibn al-A'rabi praised books as teachers and advisers: "Were you to say they were dead, you would not be guilty of lying; were you to say they were living, you would not be proved wrong."[47] In the Abbasid Empire, everything was bigger, more magnificent, more monumental than in Europe; even the ideas were sharper and ranged farther. In dialogue with Greek and Indian sources, Muslim scholars developed a superior mathematics that now, after several centuries, moved beyond the arithmetic arts taught at the school of Alexandria. Of the great mathematicians, the greatest was Muhammad ibn Musa al-Khwarizmi. His name is the root of the term *algorithm*; the word *algebra* is derived from the title of one of his books. His *On Indian Numerals*, from 820, is the oldest text to discuss the Indian numerical system, which by then had been known to the Arabs for a good half-century.[48] Thanks to him, the numbers zero through nine are called "Arabic" numerals. Originally outfitted with only nine numbers, the decimal system goes back to the mists of time. Many cultures—the Chinese, as well as the Egyptians and the Greeks—were familiar with the concept; after all, human beings everywhere have ten fingers to count on. Nevertheless, brilliant transformers were necessary for the system to reach its full potential. In the East this role was played by the Indian astronomer and mathematician Brahmagupta (598–after 665), the inventor of the number zero.[49] What a gigantic intellectual achievement this invention represents: a symbol for nothing that also contains a hint of eternity!

What was the status of antiquity in Latin Europe while Arabic science was reaching its zenith? The stream of textual transmission had thinned to a trickle, but it had never entirely dried up.[50] The classics were used more as textbooks for learning Latin than as stimuli for learned debate. When the canoness Hrotsvitha wrote closet dramas based on the comedies of Terence at her monastery in Gandersheim, she did not do so out of enthusiasm for the literary art of the poet—to whom nothing human was foreign—but rather with pious frustration at the lax morality of his plays. For a rosier picture of ancient culture at the time, we must turn to the poet Victor von Scheffel (1826–1886) and his romance *Ekkehard*. It embellishes a scene from a monastic chronicle, in which a monk from Saint Gall reads Virgil with the beautiful Swabian duchess Hedwig while the sun sets over a misty Hegau and Lake Constance.[51]

An exception appears in the figure of Liutprand of Cremona, who knew Greek and was a connoisseur of the Latin classics. As an ambassador of Otto II (r. 973–983), he spent time in Byzantium. His report from there is only a caricature, however, suggesting an experience of alienation.[52] Nevertheless, relations between Byzantium and Latin Europe remained close. The culture of Constantinople radiated to the edges of the continent for centuries. Purple silk, ivory engravings, manuscript illuminations, rituals and titles, even the architecture of churches attest to it. The papacy was represented on the Bosporus by a permanent ambassador, the *apocrisiarius*.

The little we know about the encounter with antiquity in the Ottonian orbit gives hardly any justification for proclaiming an "Ottonian Renaissance." One bright light was an Italian deacon named Gunzo. He seems to have assembled a whole library of classics and brought them to Otto I's court, with works by Sallust, Virgil, Horace, and Juvenal, as well as Plato's *Timaeus* and Aristotle's *Topics*.[53] Even Ottonian book illumination, illustrious in its own right, was only graced with a veneer of the antique spirit. Reflections of ancient forms are to be found, however, in the north of the Ottonian Empire. Bishop Bernward of Hildesheim (ca. 960–1022), who knew Rome well, commissioned a bronze column that was reminiscent of the triumphal columns of old—but only in its form, not its content. Its sculptures depict scenes from the life of Jesus. Not even Gerbert of Aurillac, whom we have already encountered as Emperor Otto III's teacher and adviser, can make the case for an Ottonian Renaissance. The antiquity he knew was that of the Carolingian court. What he wrote and taught remained in the canon of the seven liberal arts. His real significance is as an agent of knowledge transfer.[54]

The age of the Crusades considered Gerbert a kind of Dr. Faustus, a wizard who had in his possession a metal head that could respond to questions with "yes" and "no." He was also said to have spent time with pagans, to have traveled to Córdoba, Seville, and even Morocco to be initiated into necromancy. He was supposed to have won the Holy See with the help of a female demon or, according to another version of the legend, in a game of dice with the devil. In point of fact he was interested in astrology, as evidenced by his acquisition of a copy of *De astrologia*, an ancient didactic poem ascribed to a certain Marcus Manilius. Rumors about Gerbert's journey to pagan lands stem from the fact that Count Borrell II of Barcelona enabled him to study in Catalonia, which was influenced by Arab and Byzantine culture. This is probably where he became acquainted with the abacus, which had been nearly forgotten in Europe since antiquity. He also mentioned Arabic numerals, albeit only nine. In the cathedral school of Reims, he demonstrated a wooden model of the universe, an armillary sphere constructed on Arab models.[55]

At the time, Andalusia was the cultural heart of Europe, and Andalusia's heart was Córdoba, a city of several hundred thousand inhabitants. Even today it has a Near Eastern appearance. Whitewashed buildings, many of them with shady, geranium-adorned patios, provide protection from the summer heat. Amidst the web of narrow streets, the Mezquita, the Mosque-Cathedral of Córdoba, rises above the Guadalquivir River, surrounded by palm and orange trees. It is the result of over a thousand years of building. Underneath and inside it are remains of a Roman temple and a Visigothic church, relics of the two most important levels of Andalusia's deepest cultural foundation. In Gerbert's time, the complex was nearly complete: a marvel of mosaics, inscriptions and reliefs, playgrounds of light and color. After entering its dim interior, one walks through a forest of columns—supposedly 856 in total—and horseshoe arches until a bright Renaissance church suddenly opens up, a symbol of Castile's eventual victory over the Muslims.

Foreign visitors like Count Borrell's envoys must have been overwhelmed when they visited the palace city of Madinat az-Zahra, "the shining city," outside of Córdoba. Scattered across three terraces were administrative buildings, ponds, baths, and pools filled with quicksilver. The caliph's palace rested on jade columns with gilt capitals; ebony and ivory, noble black and white, adorned the interior. The royal residence was a monument to the power of the Umayyads and a cultural bastion against their Abbasid competitors in far-off Baghdad. Wisdom, learning, and education were preserved in the large library. "In four things Córdoba surpasses the capitals of the world," wrote the historian al-Maqqari. "Among them are the bridge over the river and the mosque.

These are the first two; the third is Madinat az-Zahra; but the greatest of all things is knowledge—and that is the fourth."[56]

Gerbert of Aurillac was the first significant European scholar to be familiar with Arabic science. If he ever did go to Córdoba, if he really did spend time with Arabs, we do not know. It is likely, however, that his knowledge of things that "Westerners" considered works of the devil came from texts of Andalusian provenance. On the other hand, Indian-Arabic numerals had already been mentioned by Isidore of Seville.[57] The "book on astronomy" that, according to one source, Gerbert requested from a certain Lupitus of Barcelona, could be a Latin edition of the Arabic version of the *Almagest* prepared by the mathematician and alchemist Maslama al-Majriti in Córdoba.[58]

By whatever paths Arabic science came to Latin Europe, a few preconditions were necessary in order for this point of cultural contact to decisively shape the continent's future. Unbiased intermediaries of Gerbert's stature had to be available, as did translators. So did patrons, to create libraries and schools. Furthermore, channels of communication had to be open. Gerbert's sponsor, Borrell, came to a political arrangement with his militarily superior Muslim neighbor. The friendly relations that developed in this way facilitated open cultural exchange. Finally, *time* was necessary.[59]

Here again, we see a mighty "pillar" of Europe's development: the long period over which it unfolded. For example, the armillary sphere appeared back in the third century BC in Alexandria. It was thought to have been invented by Eratosthenes of Cyrene, who was also the first to arrive at a rather precise calculation of the Earth's circumference. It was invented at about the same time in China. A description of this model of the heavens was provided four hundred years later in the fifth book of Ptolemy's *Almagest* (which Gerbert seems to have hoped to possess). Another five hundred years later, the instrument made its way to Córdoba by way of the Baghdad translators. From there, it could have gone on to Reims. By the time the armillary sphere came to adorn studies and *Kunstkammern*, several more centuries had passed. Responsible for this latter development was the printing press, which made the idea widely available; all that was then needed was the technical ability to craft the device.

Arabic learning thus advanced slowly to Latin Europe, initially in the form of medical works and astronomy.[60] It could take a long time for a context to take shape that favored its adoption. It was, therefore, decisive for Latin Europe's development that the preconditions for the grand dialogue did not disappear as they did in other cultures. What faded or was forgotten in one moment could find more favorable conditions in another. The decimal system and the abacus did not see widespread use after Gerbert wrote about them. Rather, this only happened in the twelfth century, at a time when trade was booming and the money economy had accordingly grown. Gerbert was no Prometheus; he did not singlehandedly bring the light of mathematics to Europe. Still, his efforts are a sign that a mathematical mentality was developing there, and that was a momentous process.

Knowledge took convoluted paths. A prime example is the transmission of the above-mentioned work of pharmacology by Dioscorides, *Peri hyles iatrikes*, which has come down to us under the name *De materia medica*. Cassiodorus had recommended it, and it was still being used in the nineteenth century.[61] Probably written in the first century AD in Asia Minor, this work contained over a thousand medicinal recipes that could be prepared out of plants, animals, and minerals. One copy, which must have been made from a third- or fourth-century papyrus, dates to early-sixth-century Constantinople (Plate 2). Lavishly illustrated, the manuscript was intended as a gift for a Greek princess. It was owned by monks, a French Crusader, Ottoman sultans, and Jewish physicians before a Habsburg diplomat bought it in 1560 for the court library in Vienna. Now known as the "Vienna Dioscorides," the manuscript is one of the oldest extant books in the world.

Strands of the manuscript tradition of Dioscorides ran through Baghdad and Bukhara. One went to Italy, another to Córdoba, where a botanical garden, the first in Europe, had opened in the eighth century. One manuscript, whose images derive from the illustrations in the Vienna codex, was given to the caliph as a gift by the Byzantine emperor's son Romanus (938–963).[62] Since no one on the Guadalquivir could read Greek, *ighriqi*, a monk sent from the Byzantine court had to help translate it. A whole team took part in the process, including Spanish physicians and an Arab from Sicily who knew Greek. It came in handy that Arabic translations of Dioscorides made in Baghdad were available. In the tenth century, the local physician Ibn Juljul wrote a commentary on the work. Then the Córdoba manuscript sunk into oblivion for centuries. Dioscorides lived on elsewhere, however, in monastic libraries and in Byzantium, and also in Salerno. A hospital there, founded in 1080 by the monastery of Montecassino, drew on Arabic sources available in southern Italy. One and a half centuries later a further step was taken by Ibn al-Baitar, who was born in the province of Malaga, served the caliph of Cairo, and died in

Damascus. This "Arab Dioscorides" expanded *De materia medica*, adding about four hundred recipes.

It is easy to see what dangers threatened the ideas of the ancients as they traversed such tortuous paths, clinging to parchment and paper. In the case of many texts, no amount of copying on the part of Western monks would have helped if they had not been preserved by the Arabs. Their contribution to Europe's "rise" is unfathomable. For centuries, the Muslims were cultural donors, seldom recipients. One shrewd chronicler of the Crusades sized up the shabby culture of the "Franks" and their primitive legal system with scorn and unconcealed outrage.[63] Indeed, an observer of our planet around the year 1000 would have had no doubt that the future belonged not to the Europe of the Frankish knights, but to the Muslim world or East Asia, perhaps China or Japan, maybe even India or the Byzantine Empire.

Macedonian Renaissance?

At the time, nothing in the Latin part of Europe could compare with the metropolis on the Bosporus. The intermediary between the worlds of Asia and Europe was much more prosperous than every city further west, flush with craftsmen and businesses. Holy relics lured pilgrims all the way from Gotland. Muslims were allowed to have mosques. Like in antiquity, there were luxurious bath complexes fed by aqueducts. Zoos featured exotic animals; inviting gardens provided refuge from the summer heat. Justinian's equestrian statue in front of Hagia Sophia recalled imperial greatness.[64] The largest church in Christendom at the time, Hagia Sophia served as a shrine and a hall of the emperors, who were priest-kings and styled themselves rulers of the world. When approaching the *basileus* in his palace, ambassadors had to perform *proskynesis*, prostrating themselves three times before the throne such that their foreheads touched the ground. Meanwhile, the throne, flanked by mechanical bronze lions that occasionally roared, would be raised so that the "thirteenth apostle" hovered in silence over them.[65]

During the rule of the Macedonian dynasty (867–1056), a period of economic prosperity and momentary political dominance, the Byzantine Empire basked in the glow of the arts and the sciences. It began with a renewal of the Roman legal tradition. Emperor Basil I spoke of a "purification of ancient law."[66] In the form of the *Basilika*, a Greek reworking and reordering of Justinian's Corpus, Emperor Leo "the Wise" compiled the most comprehensive law code of medieval Byzantium. Constantine VII Porphyrogenitus (whose byname literally means "born in the purple"—referring to the "Porphyra," a room of the imperial palace covered with purple porphyry), himself the author of works on the Byzantine state, its population, and geography, founded a university in the Magnaura devoted to the liberal arts. Euthymius the Athonite's pious novel *Barlaam and Josaphat*, which tells of the conversion of an Indian prince, united various far-flung cultural currents. It was probably based on an Arabic version of the Buddha legend transmitted via a Georgian text.[67]

The theory that there was a "Macedonian Renaissance" finds support in the engagement of a group of learned individuals with ancient mythology, literature, and history. The *Iliad* and the *Odyssey* were copied, as were works of Archimedes and Euclid and Nicander of Colophon's poem on the wounds of venomous animals. The *Myriobiblon* by Patriarch Photius is a guide to Christian and pagan books; we know of many works thanks only to his collection. Michael Psellus (1017/18–after 1078), a man steeped in the knowledge of antiquity, opposed the mysticism of the patriarch with an appeal to rational experience. His contrariness may have come from Terence: "I am an earthly being, made of flesh and blood, so that my illnesses seem to me to be illnesses, blows blows, joy joy."[68] The influential statesman sought to synthesize Neoplatonism and Christianity, making him the descendant of the ancient Gnostics and a precursor to Ficino. His magnum opus is the *Chronographia*, an imperial history bursting with anecdotes that treats the century from 976 to 1077. It is unusual in that it views history as the work of human beings rather than divine predestination. Psellus's contemporary, the Jew Symeon Seth, engaged in astronomy, astrology, and natural science of the Aristotelian stamp; he described foods as well as drugs like hashish and scents like musk. He also translated a mirror of princes of probable Indian origin from Arabic into Greek.[69] One prominent witness to the interest Byzantium fostered for antiquity at the time is the encyclopedia known as the *Suda*, a true "bulwark," as its name suggests, of ancient knowledge consisting of about 31,000 articles in alphabetical order. Striking, because written by a woman, is the work of history penned by Anna Comnena (1083–ca. 1154), daughter of Emperor Alexius I Comnenus. Composed in the style of classical Greek historiography, it is a favorable account of her father's reign. Equally unique is *Timarion*, an anonymous satire dating to the same period. Based on Lucian, it sends its hero on a journey through Hades. There he meets rulers and philosophers of the recent past, including the "sophist" Psellus.[70]

What was written and fashioned in the Macedonian period and afterward, however, does not have much to do with a "Renaissance."[71] From the very beginning on the Bosporus, "antiquity" meant almost exclusively Greek antiquity. It could not be resuscitated since it had never truly died. Nothing really new was created. A few reminiscences of paganism in manuscript illumination and ivory carving do not a Renaissance make. One example is provided by the Veroli Casket. Probably intended as a wedding gift, it features a revival of classical mythology, depicting Dionysus and Aphrodite, Bellerophon, Nereids, and centaurs.[72] The lid shows scenes with Hercules and the Rape of Europa.

PART II

The Development of Possibilities

1000–1400

TURNING POINTS

9

The Centers of the World

INDIA, JAPAN, CHINA

Asia's Mediterranean and Its Inhabitants

Latin Europe and the Mediterranean were in no way the center of the world at the beginning of the second millennium—not in terms of economic and political significance, and certainly not with regard to culture, technology, and science. In the view of one contemporary, an Arab living in India, the emperor he called the *Rum*, i.e. the *basileus* on the Bosporus, was the only ruler in Europe worthy of being counted among the four lords of the world.[1] The illustrious group was filled out with the caliph, the emperor of China, and the Rashtrakuta king of India. As for Saxons, Franks, and other "Westerners" who declared themselves masters of the universe and may have even thought of themselves in such terms, our Arab source says nothing of them. And for good reason. A comparison with the other powers would not have ended very favorably for Latin Europe. Even the Byzantine Empire under the Macedonian dynasty, however large and shiny it may have seemed from the perspective of Latin Europe, was on the margins. The true center of the world was an economic sphere that encompassed East Africa, the Arabian Peninsula and the Persian Gulf, Japan, central Asia, India, and China.[2]

The rise of Islam and its cities created a demand for luxury goods in the remote West. The wonders of the East included bales of silk, coffers of pearls, jade, and gems of all colors of the rainbow (which were considered magical items fallen from heaven), and organza, that fine, airy silk whose name comes from the Turkmen metropolis of Urgench. There was also soap, sandalwood, and sacks of pepper, as well as fragile, finely painted porcelain and bottles of Persian rose water. Its scent was so intense that it even penetrated the wax stoppers of the phials. From the other direction came gold, frankincense, fine horses, African ivory, textiles, and metal goods. Europe had little to offer at the time that could compare with the choice goods of Asia and Africa. Many peoples made their way to the coasts of the Indian Ocean and the China Seas, traded there, and learned from one another. They included Arabs, who had reached China back in the fourth century and founded settlements on the Spice Islands at the turn of the millennium, as well as Indians, Chinese, and peoples of Indochina and the islands. In addition, there were Persian traders who operated between the east coast of Sumatra and Chinese Canton. In the centuries that followed, a system would take shape in which Europe also participated.[3] The symbol of this exchange was the lateen (i.e., Latin) sail, which the Arabs imported from the Mediterranean. This nautical technology, which had also been known in antiquity, used wind power more efficiently and facilitated maneuvering against the wind.[4]

Commerce, abundant human resources, and power laid the foundation for gigantic sacral buildings. In the eighth and ninth century, fifty-six thousand cubic meters of stone were laid to form the terraces of the pyramid of Borobudur on Java, a monument of Mahayana Buddhism. Not far off rose the Hindu temple complex of Prambanan. These and other cosmic centers dominated the smaller political entities of the area. In Bagan in Burma, thousands of pagodas and temples were built—more shrines than the number of inhabitants of most European cities. Like in Europe, the region's power centers were in the process of developing into states. These were, as the historian Victor Lieberman has characterized them, "charter states": communities clustered around a center with their own identities, cultures, and political and administrative patterns that provided a model, or charter, for subsequent formations.[5]

In the minds of Europeans, India, the "Land of the Rose-Apple Tree," evoked images of gemstones, mythical creatures, and sumptuous palaces. No one knew how to forge better swords than the Indians. Indian poetry and music were exalted in far-off Baghdad. Indian cotton conquered Asia's markets.[6] Ancient India was sure of its place at the center of the cosmos. Even today the religiosity of the "holy country" is inspired by the Vedas, written in Sanskrit, the language of the gods and the Brahmins. From India's point of view, the West was populated entirely by uncultivated savages, the East by "barbarians."[7]

From India, Buddha had gone by way of Sri Lanka to China and Japan and, in the other direction, had conquered a vast swath of central Asia. Beginning in the seventh century, learning and religion were centered at the "monastic university" of Nalanda in Bengal. It received patronage from both Buddhist and Hindu dynasties, and students from all over. In addition to sacred texts, medicine, grammar, and philosophy were taught. In the description of one Chinese pilgrim,

> Round the monasteries there flowed a winding stream of azure water, made more beautiful by blue lotus flowers, with wide-open calyxes; within the temple, beautiful *karnikāra* trees hung down their dazzling golden blossoms, and outside, groves of mango sheltered the dwellings with their thick shade.[8]

The place retained its glory down to the end of the twelfth century, when a Turkic warlord demolished the marvelous structure.

Like bees to blossoms, conquerors were attracted to India's riches and fertile land. Persians, Greeks, and Huns got things started; the British finished the job. When the Gupta Empire, which had controlled the north and parts of central India, declined in the early sixth century, regional powers contended for ascendency. They fought off the Arabs, thus preventing an early Islamization of the subcontinent. Around the year 1000, the Cholas were the dominant power in the south. Rather unusual in the history of India, they looked to the ocean. Their fleets carried out attacks on the mighty thalassocracy of Srivijaya, whose center was on Sumatra. Mahmud of Ghazni's heirs in India were conquered in the eleventh century by the Iranian Ghurid dynasty, who extended their control beyond Delhi as far as Bengal. In the following century, they were themselves overthrown by their own slave soldiers, the Mamluks. This was the origin of the Sultanate of Delhi (see p. 205, 576).

In uncertain times, traders hired mercenaries to protect them on their way. Among them, the "Five Hundred Lords of Ayyavole" stands out, a guild active in long-distance trade with Sri Lanka and Southeast Asia. By maintaining mercenary troops to protect their trade routes, they provided what the state could not. They were "famed throughout the world," according to an inscription on a stele in Sumatra,

> born to be wanderers over many countries . . . the horizon as their light . . . penetrating into the regions of the six continents, with superior elephants, well-bred horses, large sapphires, moonstones, pearls, rubies, diamonds . . . ; white umbrellas as their canopy, the mighty ocean as their moat, . . . the nine planets as a belt, . . . the sun and moon as the backers, the 33 gods as the spectators.[9]

The divide between Indian and Islamic ways of life on the one hand and Chinese on the other was formed by the barrier of volcanic fire, with its bastions of Sumatra and Java, that split the Indian Ocean into eastern and western parts.[10] The monsoon winds seem not only to have mapped out trade routes and foodways—grain in the west and the north, rice in East Asia—but also to have carried the words of the Prophet as far as they would go.[11] Muhammad had found a receptive audience on the coast of India as early as the seventh century; a few centuries later, he reached Borneo and the Philippines. While Buddha's influence faded in his home country in favor of the Hindu pantheon, further east it remained strong, such as in China (where, however, it would soon suffer overwhelming competition from Confucius) and Japan.

The "Land of the Rising Sun" was unknown to Europeans at the turn of the first millennium. Marco Polo, who never set foot on the island he called Cipangu, reported that miraculous things were said about it: gemstones and pearls were available in abundance; gold covered the roof of the royal palace and shone from its floors and walls. The governmental apparatus of this eastern Eldorado, modeled on the Chinese bureaucratic state, was as superior to Latin Europe's as that of China itself—at least if central power, the use of written records, and rational organization are used as metrics.[12] A privy council began meeting to advise the emperor at court in 731. There was an office of religious affairs and a chancellor; both had ministries working for them. The massive bureaucracy at times employed over ten thousand officials in the capital and three thousand in the provinces. The scribes in the service of the Japanese central government are said to have painted 350 million characters per year in the tenth century.[13] Meanwhile, the hands of monks were laboriously filling a few sheaves of parchment at Europe's royal courts. Including extant fragments, no more than five hundred manuscripts have been preserved from the Merovingian kingdom. A good seven thousand were then handed down from the sturdier Carolingian Empire.[14]

Centuries before Europeans had the idea, Japan had invented statistics to keep track of those liable to pay taxes and perform service. The earliest extant plans for checkerboard rice fields date to the eighth century, making them some of the world's oldest maps drawn to scale. Provincial governors kept registers containing information about land ownership and liabilities on individual properties. A well-developed network of roads crisscrossed the island. Small family farms dominated the countryside; large estates never played a significant role.[15] Like Europe, Japan had free farmers and unfree peasants. Property rights tended to be strictly respected, and even the homes of simple farmers were considered inviolable. The system seems to have been highly effective. By the eighteenth century, the amount of arable land nearly doubled. Improved irrigation and other measures also contributed to increasing yields. This made it possible to feed a population that grew from about four million to twenty-five million people.

Like the states of the Korean Peninsula, Japan developed its own identity in constructive dialogue with China's culture and governmental system. In the ninth century, the Japanese syllabic script appeared alongside Chinese logograms. The court of Kyoto, a city of soon to be 175,000 inhabitants,[16] developed into a vibrant, impactful center of Japanese culture. Its most exquisite monument is thought to be *The Tale of Genji*, an early-eleventh-century story about love, liaisons, and human transience, with a prince as its protagonist. One of the first novels of world literature, it is thought to have been authored by two ladies in waiting. In the vast palace of the *tennō*, with its gardens, halls, and courtyards, a highly aesthetic, ceremonially circumscribed court culture developed. Besides the imperial residence in Kyoto, there were also palaces belonging to private individuals built from the profits of their estates. Whereas power was displayed in Europe in the form of stone walls, marble-encrusted towers, and copper-green domes, Japan cultivated a more sublime aesthetic: religion became art, and art became a religion.[17] Fujiwara no Yorimichi, Japan's regent from 1017 to 1074, had his residence designed as an image of the "Pure Land," the paradise ruled by Amitabha, the Buddha of "Infinite Light." At the center of Yorimichi's park, named Uji, is the Phoenix Hall of Byodoin Temple, a human-scale, light wooden structure decorated with landscape paintings and set on an island in the middle of an artificial lake. Inside is a gilded wooden statue of Buddha Amida sitting on a gilded lotus blossom in front of a flaming aureole, a masterpiece by the sculptor Jōchō. The Sublime One is portrayed in a very human and approachable way, poised in deep concentration. Only Western arrogance would consider the Christian faith superior to Buddhist teachings, with their striving for inner purification and peace.

There was nothing in Europe at the turn of the millennium that even approached the monumentality and aesthetic refinement of Hindu, Buddhist, and Islamic shrines in the Far East. Compared to the splendor with which some rulers in Asia surrounded themselves, Europe's kings and emperors, shrouded in their bombastic titles, were poor relations; their realms were border regions on the margin of the steppes and the seas. The center of the world was in Asia around the year 1000. And Asia's center was China.

The Center of the Center: China

Cambridge, England, 1937. Sometimes the love of a woman leads to the love of a country. A meeting, a glance, a touch—suddenly life takes an unexpected turn. Something of the sort may have set in motion one of the biggest shifts in the history of scholarship.[18] Dr. Joseph Needham, then a young biochemist at the University of Cambridge, had fallen in love with a Chinese student, Lu Gwei-djen from Nanjing. He became interested in the young woman's distant homeland and undertook the ordeal of learning China's script and language. He even took a job in Chongqing, at the confluence of the Jialing and Yangtze rivers. Today it is a city of eight million people, where visitors to the thousand-year-old Luohan Temple meditate on the wisdom of Buddha in the shadow of skyscrapers.

The fascination exercised by Chinese culture eclipsed Needham's work on embryos and cells. He was one of the first Europeans to take a different view of the global history of science and scholarship. The traditional perspective was now inverted, and China took center stage. Needham realized that, in antiquity and the Middle Ages, China already possessed technology and scientific insights that the West had not even dreamed of yet. He noticed that a huge gap separated China from medieval Europe, one so big that a question presented itself: How did Europe manage to surpass China after the Renaissance, and why did the Scientific and Industrial Revolutions happen there and not in the Chinese Empire, which had been so far superior for so long?

Needham, whose own experience of China was of a poor, starving country torn between Communists and Chiang Kai-shek's Kuomintang, characterized the break in China's development as "one of the greatest problems in the history of civilization."[19] He devoted the rest of his life to the search for an answer to this question, studying the history of science and technology in ancient China down to its tiniest detail. What he discovered was a high culture that, during the European High Middle Ages, seemed to have long since entered modernity and was much more advanced than all other countries on Earth. Needham died in 1995, the same age as his century. Students and collaborators have continued to work on his monumental project, *Science and Civilization in China*. His big question is more relevant than ever, seeing as how we seem to be on the threshold of an Asian century.

Let us, therefore, turn to China. Like India, China was convinced of its superiority to the "barbarians" of the West and the East. Even more, it was certain of being civilization itself. Between the seventh and the twelfth centuries, it experienced periods of artistic excellence and grand inventions.[20] In addition to Buddha, to whom thousands of monasteries and vast estates were dedicated, Taoist gods and Confucius provided the people with rules for life and the state with an identity. Under the Tang dynasty (618–907 AD), the kingdom had become an empire. Its influence encompassed the Korean Peninsula in the west and parts of what is now Vietnam and even reached the borders of Persia. The art of Tang China, its painting and sculpture, is famous. Its enthusiasm for the prancing of beautiful horses is memorialized by elegant green-and-brown-glazed figurines preserved in museums around the world. Most brilliant of all, however, was the poetry of the time, verse about wine, the Moon, and love. With its sensitivity to nature and despair at the human condition, it seems unusually familiar to us. Li Bai, one of the age's greatest literary figures, wrote:

> The living is a passing traveler;
> The dead, a man come home.
> One brief journey betwixt heaven and earth
>
> . . .
>
> Man dies, his white bones are dumb without a word
> When the green pines feel the coming of the spring.
> Looking back, I sigh; looking before, I sigh again.
> What is there to prize in the life's vaporous glory?[21]

But the Tang Empire did not last either. It was broken by foes from abroad— some of whom had learned from their Chinese master, just as the Germanic tribes had learned from the Romans—and by the zeal for power of ambitious generals at home. The Arab victory at Talas ended Buddha's regime in central

Asia and introduced the rule of Islam. New states rose from the empire's rubble. Especially successful were the Khitan people, who succeeded in subduing Mongolia and northeast China. In 947, they took Kaifeng. In the area of what would later be Beijing, they founded a second capital.[22] For two hundred years, Khitans were emperors, referring to themselves as the "Liao" dynasty. They were the mightiest rulers in the region. Further south, the Song dynasty began consolidating its power in 960. For a long time to come, Song emperors would rule over not only the Chinese but also many other peoples.

An ever-expanding bureaucracy dominated Chinese society for centuries. According to Taoism, even heaven was governed by immortal civil servants. In earthly realms, the bureaucracy swelled to over forty thousand during the Song dynasty.[23] Ministries of all kinds mushroomed, their jurisdictions often overlapping. Special agencies oversaw the army of quill-drivers and struggled in vain against the ineradicable virus of corruption. Attempts to pursue new policies in light of the threat posed to the state by "barbarians" failed, such as the ambitious program promoted by Chancellor Wang Anshi (1021–1086). On the other hand, titles and positions could not be inherited. Merit mattered and enabled those with it to rise to the highest posts; the mandarins, the ruling class of the empire, resembled Late Roman senators.[24] Examinations, however, did not test critical thinking but rather emphasized rote memorization and command of the Confucian classics; administrative know-how was not tested. And that is exactly what Wang wanted to change.

The ideal Chinese bureaucrat was honest and loyal, had mastered the art of calm, possessed self-control, and had a literary education.[25] He was—like scholars, artists, physicians, and generals—a trained Confucian, a cultivated man. In short, he was the Chinese version of the *cortegiano*, albeit without the courtier's nonchalant affectation that Castiglione calls *sprezzatura*. Countless calligraphers, poets, and aesthetes belonged to the Chinese bureaucracy, which also mustered the empire's educational elite. Wherever the emperor's court was located, there and only there were all significant decisions made.

Despite all its defects, China's bureaucracy towered above administration in Europe at the time. While its rulers governed in palace complexes surrounded by parks, Europe's emperors trudged around their territory on worn-out nags, a sluggish retinue in their train, to rule from poorly heated monasteries and castles. Most of them were illiterate, able only to add a mark to the signature prepared on documents for them by scribes. Chinese emperors had long spent their leisure penning poetry or crafting masterpieces of calligraphy.

Meanwhile, drought and floods regularly destroyed the livelihoods of farmers. Starvation and poverty affecting large sections of the population were the steadfast, bleak companions of Chinese history.[26] Reports of cannibalism and of human flesh being salted away indicate that China was suffering severe trauma. Demographic pressure forced people to wring from the land whatever it might yield. In the struggle with pale death, however, China developed into a country that, like India, boasted the most advanced agricultural structures of the age.[27] The work done in Europe by harrows, axes, and harnesses was performed in China's different geography by sluices, dams, bucket wheels, and treadmills—but not by windmills, which did not arrive until the seventeenth century. Still, the Chinese began using iron plows before the Europeans. Horse collars and wheelbarrows made the work easier. Trade, transportation, and the irrigation of rice fields were facilitated by a system of canals, which also improved seeds and fertilization methods. Li Ch'u-ch'üan, a poet of the twelfth century, commented:

> Rich lands have been opened up in the surrounding hills,
> Along ten thousand acres wind rice-sprouts like green clouds—
> Clouds that before your eyes turn from green to gold,
> And fill all stomachs with the year's rich harvest.[28]

All initiatives to improve farming were undertaken by the state, not by private individuals. Between 959 and 1021, arable state-owned land quintupled in acreage. Therein—in monopolies and tax revenues—lay the power of the emperors.[29] Thanks to a well-developed road network and despite rampant tax banditry, the various regional centers developed closer and closer relationships. The Grand Canal, whose 1,800 kilometers were dug by a couple of million forced laborers in the seventh century, connected the Huai River to the Yangtze, the north to the south. The latter waterway reached the sea at Hangzhou. The chief goods transported on it were millet and rice.[30]

People had always sought the south. They fled from bandits, civil wars, and burdensome taxes, from drought and the threat of savage riders from the steppe. The gates to the ocean were wide open. Thanks to the integration of Tang China into the trade currents of the eastern Pacific, Guangzhou on the Pearl River delta and other cities on the sea developed into trading centers whirring with activity. Guangzhou (Canton) and Quanzhou, which the Arabs called "Zaiton," formed two corners of a trade rectangle with Samudera Pasai and, later, Malacca.[31] Books, silk, iron, and porcelain—this last often stowed in the hulls of ships as ballast—were exported, while precious goods were imported: elephant tusks and rhinoceros horns, spices, fine woods, pearls, and frankincense.[32] Maritime trade was sometimes organized on a kind of joint-venture model: the state provided the ships, private merchants took care of the business, and profits were shared according to a fixed formula.[33] Craftsmen became entrepreneurs, and retailers became wholesalers. Profits were reinvested—in tea plantations, for example. The most important, most essential import goods were horses.[34] With the "commercial revolution" that began in the ninth century, the traditionally low status of merchants improved dramatically, allowing them to overcome previous legal and social barriers. Officials of rank five and above, however, were not allowed to mix with the people at the market in Chang'an.

Kaifeng, now the capital, had grown so quickly that stores and stands sprawled into public streets. The state gave up trying to prevent uncontrolled development and instituted a "street encroachment tax."[35] The sources paint pictures of urban life. In the summer heat of the glittering metropolis, which was thirteen times bigger than late medieval Paris, countless eateries, tea houses, and restaurants specializing in fine wines accommodated guests. Carafes of water and dainty cloths were put at their disposal to dab the grime of the day from their faces before dinner. Half a hundred theaters offered entertainment. At markets, illuminated when darkness fell, jewelry, lacquerware, and unusually shaped bamboo sticks could be purchased. Visitors encountered finely ornamented wooden houses with curved roofs covered with glazed tiles, temples of Buddha and the sea goddess Mazu, storytellers and water bearers, elegantly dressed prostitutes and court ladies with flowers in their hair, harbors thick with the masts of Arab dhows and native junks, and camel caravans at the end of a long journey.

New things were being made everywhere.[36] The most spectacular invention was printing with moveable type, which dates to the Tang dynasty. It was probably fueled by the needs of the Buddhist mission, as well as by the pious desire to accumulate good karma by spreading sacred writings.[37] One of the oldest printed texts in the world is an incantation dating to after 757 in Sichuan; somewhat earlier prints of magic formulas found in Korea probably also come from China. Precisely datable to 858 is a copy of the *Diamond Sutra* (Fig. 9, p. 133). It was followed by calendars, geographical writings, almanacs and dictionaries, rhymed prose, and translations from Sanskrit and other Indian languages. Under the patronage of the first Song emperors, all of the canonical texts of Buddhism were set on no fewer than 130,000 printing blocks. Extensive literary anthologies appeared before the year 1000, as did the Confucian classics, which civil service candidates used to prepare for their exams. Needless to say, all of this would not have been possible if the printers had not had paper. Only in combination with this invention, already one thousand years old at that point, could the technology of printing unfurl its true potential. Its reach extended far beyond the upper classes. Poetry, religious images, medical writings, legal texts, and handbooks were printed. Even the bronze printing block for a placard advertising a needle store has come down to us.

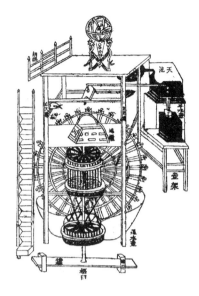

Gunpowder was known from the late ninth century onward. It was initially used to make small bombs and fireworks; cannons and bombards followed soon thereafter. Chinese ships had bulkheads to prevent quick sinking; these would only be introduced in Europe in the eighteenth century. Large stern rudders, known since ancient times in China, held a steady course, and sails set along the line of the keel made it possible to sail hard on the wind.[38] Boats powered by paddle wheels crawled up the Yangtze and Yellow rivers. On the high seas, China's ship captains used a magnetic needle floating in water, "the south-pointing fish," as a compass. It is said to have been invented by Shen Kuo (1031–1095), an inexhaustibly curious man and, like nearly all Chinese scholars, an imperial official. His *Dream Pool Essays* deal with myriad departments of knowledge: the occult, literary and philological questions, mathematics, medicine and biology, astronomy, agriculture, archaeology, and architecture.[39] He described sedimentation and the development of fossils; he was the first to design a purely solar calendar for East Asia. To entertain his genteel readers, he spiced his writing with anecdotes from life at court. He also distinguished himself as a diplomat, military strategist, and hydraulic engineer.

In the imperial palace in Kaifeng, Su Song (1020–1101), another high official, built a water-powered astronomical clock with an escapement and a gear with a chain drive that also powered an armillary sphere and rang a bell (Fig. 10, above).[40] Li Jie, court architect to Emperor Huizong, wrote an encyclopedic work on architecture hundreds of years before the first post-antique work on the subject emerged in Italy. Rudimentary theories of one-point perspective and monetary circulation were even developed.

Much earlier than others, the Chinese used coal as a fuel. They knew how to make steel, and their pig iron production reached dimensions that England would not outstrip until the Industrial Revolution. In porcelain and ceramic production, the manufacturing process was broken up into various steps based on the division of labor. A "large spinning wheel," which could be driven by water, animal power, or the human hand, had thirty-two spindles and could spin a good sixty kilograms of yarn in twenty-four hours. The commercialization of agriculture, by far the true engine of the Chinese economy, made great leaps forward. Paper money, which appeared in Sichuan in 1024—more than six hundred years earlier than in Europe—became a miracle cure for the lack of copper and silver caused by the overheating economy. It soon produced a congenital malady of its own, though: inflation. The iron law of money, formulated in Elizabethan England by Thomas Gresham and named after him, was discovered by the Chinese back in the eleventh century: bad money—in this case, paper money—drives out good money.[41] Meanwhile, China's cultural development reached its zenith. Indeed, in the monumental history of Chinese civilization written by Jacques Gernet, the title given to the section on the Song dynasty is "The Chinese 'Renaissance.'"[42]

Chinese Renaissance

China's ruling classes could afford to live a highly civilized lifestyle. A glimpse into those carefree days of long ago is provided by a scroll painting entitled *Night Revels of Han Xizai*; it was probably based on an original by the painter Gu Hongzhong, finished between 937 and 975 at the court of the Southern Tang. One man beats a drum while others dance. A courtesan plucks the lute, and elegant, lacquered tables are laid out with fine china. A distinguished company listens attentively.[43] Women of the Song dynasty took great pains with makeup and hairstyle. This is how one poet celebrated the artfully staged beauty of a female body:

> In my transparent purple silk nightgown
> my white skin glows
> fragrant and smooth as snow.[44]

They had dry soap, toothpaste, and toothbrushes; young women and men dressed extravagantly. As one eulogist for the past put it, echoing an inveterate lament, "There is no longer the pure simplicity of former times."[45]

THE CENTERS OF THE WORLD   145

The Chinese elite, or *shenshi*, memorialized in Gu Hongzhong's scroll painting was comparable to the English gentry, the upper bourgeoisie, and the lower nobility.[46] It included polymaths, idiosyncratic individuals, bizarre geniuses, artists of all classes, literati, patrons, and, last but not least, lovers of high rank—i.e., brothers of Boccaccio and Leon Battista Alberti, siblings of the Medici, and comrades of François Villon. Su Shi (1036/37–1101), one of the most famous of them, was a calligrapher, painter, essayist, and politician. He wrote poetry about love and wine, about heartache and desire, and extolled skies of jasper and jade. He described ink-colored clouds flying over the hills—elegiac evidence of China's ubiquitous literacy!—and the silent harvest moon pouring its silver out over noisy city life.

China not only sang about the heavens, but it also sought to decipher them. "Although Heaven is high and far away, Heaven inspects the empire daily. Heaven responds to the deeds of the ruler," admonished the Song minister Lü Gongzhu. Conscientious rule guaranteed well-being. If the emperor neglected the gods, if he treated his people poorly, bad luck would follow.[47] When one Chinese scholar speculated that the cosmos might be indifferent to the moral order of human beings, which only a wise man or a "wise ruler" could establish, this was a great exception.[48] The imperial court had an astrology bureau charged with interpreting heavenly signs. Pestilence, starvation and natural disasters, wars and prodigies indicated a disruption in the harmony of the cosmos; they clearly meant that the emperor was not performing his role properly. Religion and politics were thus driving forces for the study of nature in China as well. In passing, so to speak, its astrologers discovered sunspots— long before Western astronomy noticed these flaws in the red giant.[49]

As Zhao Ruyu claimed in 1194, the Song dynasty was an age in which scholars could consider themselves fortunate to have been born.[50] About two hundred academies were founded under the Southern Song, many of them by local officials or the gentry. The first was Hanlin Academy, which opened at the imperial court in 738. It fostered poetry, painting, calligraphy, and Confucian literature.[51] During the Tang dynasty, China had already given birth to a rationalist philosophy that, among other things, disputed heavenly intervention in earthly affairs, demystified solar and lunar eclipses, and showed how the latter could be calculated.[52] As in the European Renaissance, attempts were made to appropriate antiquity meaningfully and to reconcile various religious and philosophical currents. The old writing style—which called for imitating the classical language of the Warring States period, focusing concisely on one theme, and offering a moral lesson—was revived, and along with it the timeless values of the Dao, or "way" of the wise men of the past, figures like Confucius, Mencius, and their predecessors. This was not simply a matter of reconstructing the proper text of ancient classics by means of philological methods. Rather, it was thought that the creative adaptation of a primeval tradition stretching back to Confucius and beyond would lead to a transformation of the self, society, and politics. The old "way" and its values—e.g., goodwill, righteousness, sincerity—were to be accessed in the present day. Polite culture triumphed over the ideals of the declining warrior society.[53] The reformer Wang Anshi was one of those who sought to effect practical change via the return to the ancients.

The engagement with the spirit of the ancients spawned editions of ancient inscriptions and the creation of collections (Plate 3). The official Zhao Mingcheng (1081–1129) collected art, in particular ancient bronzes, whose inscriptions he published and commentated like a humanist.[54] And just as early Italian Renaissance painters used *litterae antiquae* for the texts in their pictures, the painter Li Tang used an archaizing chancery script for his hanging scroll *Wind in the Pines among a Myriad Valleys* (1124). This demonstrated his education and adorned his work with the dignity of tradition.[55] Attempts were also made in the direction of critical historiography. The great historian Sima Guang (1019–1086) rejected the notion that writing about the past should be a mere lesson in morality. Instead, he sought direction in the sources.[56]

Considered as a whole, the skeptical approach to the heavens and tradition, the large spinning wheel, the production of iron, the printed book, and gunpowder all make it seem as if the empire at the center of the world was about to experience major breakthroughs, as if China's modern age had dawned.[57] In the second decade of the twelfth century, the Song also seemed poised to retake the north. A new power had arisen there: the Jurchen people, tribes of hunters and fishermen from eastern Manchuria who set out to conquer the Liao empire. Their mounted warriors forged ahead relentlessly, winning large chunks of Manchuria; their chieftain took "Jin" as the name of his dynasty. At the imperial court in the south, the decision was made to ally with the invaders and to use their help to neutralize the Liao. And indeed, they conquered Beijing together. Their opponents were driven into the steppe, where they carved out a new state for themselves.

Meanwhile, the Song could not control the spirits they had conjured. The Jurchen had acquired a taste for conquest, and they turned on their allies as soon as the Liao were beaten. The Song army could not defend Kaifeng, and it fell in 1127.[58] Emperor Huizong, an aesthete, poet, and calligrapher with no great interest in warfare, was taken prisoner and never freed. One of his sons escaped to Lin'an with 400,000 soldiers. The city that would later be called Hangzhou developed into a splendid capital of the Southern Song. "Up in heaven, there is paradise," the Chinese say. "Down on Earth, there are Suzhou and Hangzhou."[59] Until the Mongol invasions of the thirteenth century, after which nothing in the East would be as it had been before, the Jin remained China's leading power. To keep the border with them quiet, the Song paid tribute: silver and silk by the ton. This practice, while unheroic, accorded with Confucian pacifism.[60] In the long run, the south lost the power struggle. Thanks to its coal and iron deposits, the north had resources that gave it the upper hand for a long time to come. The Neo-Confucian view that only the Chinese emperor had the heavenly mandate to rule over the whole world gave way to a more realistic stance.[61] With the decline of the Song dynasty, China's scientific fire also went out. There were to be no more paradigm shifts in the following centuries, although art and literature continued to enjoy periods of flourishing, and exchange with west Asian cultures was maintained.

At the same time as the Song dynasty experienced the zenith of its "renaissance," wretched Europe began an unprecedented race to catch up. The shift occurred in the late eleventh and the twelfth centuries. But much time would still pass before the German humanist Ulrich von Hutten (1488–1523) could praise his age (see p. 554) in terms similar to those used by Zhao Ruyu.

10

Takeoff under the Sun

Europe Begins to Fly

"At the thousandth year after the birth of Christ," noted one witness to the turn of the millennium, Bishop Thietmar of Merseburg, "a radiant dawn broke over the world."[1] Indeed, the same sunshine illuminated Europe that was gilding China's rice fields at the time. The "Medieval Warm Period," a sustained rise in average temperatures, was a boon to agriculture. In the Alps, the tree line rose to an elevation of two thousand meters. Even in the south of Scotland and Norway, grapevines could be cultivated for wine. As harvests increased, the continent's demographic body also expanded. Europe's population probably doubled between the year 1000 and the mid-fourteenth century to over seventy million.[2] People lived longer, with average life expectancy rising to thirty-five years—a decade longer than in antiquity.

Arable land was needed. Quite a lot of land. White smoke lay over Europe's endless forests; settlements sprang up everywhere. Barren soil was reclaimed, moorland drained. Rye, the grain of the common man, and oats, the fuel of horses, invaded fallow land. White bread was only widespread in the south; along with wine and olive oil, it constituted the glorious trinity of the Mediterranean diet. Fields of grain supplanted pastureland, waving even under the midnight sun around Trondheim. Livestock had to make do with pasturing in marshy areas or on mountain heights.

The Slavic world became more "central European." What has been called the "Europeanization of Europe" forged ahead.[3] German-speaking settlers, Flemings and Dutch, Balts and Slavic peoples, Christians and Jews cleared the East. Princes and manorial lords lured them there with advantageous conditions; old-growth forests and wasteland brought them nothing, whereas farmland bore fruit on which they could impose levies. Along the edges of fields and villages, axes and hoes cut lanes through the undergrowth. People moved into age-old but never populated bishoprics and filled areas over which the German emperors had long claimed an empty sovereignty. From Carinthia to the Baltic, missionaries and warriors converted the Slavs to Christianity, convincing them with the word or forcing them with the sword.

The demographic challenge of feeding more and more mouths required ingenuity. Small, seemingly unimportant technological advances were made. The collar for horses and the head yoke fitted under the horns of oxen increased productivity. The harrow was introduced at the end of the eleventh century. The heavy, wheeled plow replaced the hook plow. This tool, known to ancient Rome, was able to cut much deeper furrows in the earth than its predecessor; it turned the soil and broke it up. It was even effective with loamy and hard soils, loosening them so that plants could breathe and grow better there. Iron became an everyday commodity. Plowshares and horseshoes became weapons against lack, against capricious, resistant nature. So did the shift from the two-field to the three-field system of agriculture, which had first been introduced in Carolingian times. Winter crops were followed by summer crops, after which the field lay fallow so that it could regenerate, be grazed by livestock, and fertilized by their manure. Since now only a third of available farmland was unused at any one time (whereas beforehand it was half), more animals and people could be supported by the same arable acreage.

The close proximity and interplay of agriculture, animal husbandry, and forestry promoted the development of a diversity of trades. The horizontal, treadle-powered loom was used for weaving in town and countryside. It allowed work to be done faster and more efficiently than the vertical warp-weighted loom.[4] This was also the beginning of the millennium of windmills, a technology inherited from antiquity. Precisely 5,624 mills were counted in England in 1086. That amounted to at least one mill operating in each of the more than three thousand villages in the kingdom.

Around the year 1100, one monk raved about how "delightful" it was to "meditate on innovations."[5] Of course, technological progress needed time. Not until the late twelfth century did the horizontal-axis windmill, already known for centuries in Persia, arrive in the North Sea region.[6] More complex versions followed, their inner workings composed of cranks and gears, as did water-driven hammer mills and mills that could be turned into whatever direction the wind was coming from.

Land reclamation and population growth stimulated trade and the money economy. This is attested by a large number of pennies, the capital of the common man. At the same time, a growing number of mints, which made fabulous profits for their owners, reflected the political fragmentation of Europe. Newly discovered silver deposits in Aquitaine, Bohemia, the Harz region, and elsewhere provided the raw material. In addition, trade with Muslims filled Latin Europe's coffers with money. One of the West's most important "export goods" consisted of slaves captured in eastern Europe. Areas previously cut off from long-distance trade, such as southern France, were integrated into the vast networks,[7] whereas England had joined the game early on. More coins are preserved from the tenth century than from all previous centuries combined, including specimens from Afghanistan and Baghdad. Just how extensive trade connections were at the time can be seen in the report of an Arab traveler. In Mainz he saw "dirhams," silver coins from Samarkand, and was amazed that Indian spices were for sale.[8] Thus the "remote West" gained access to the economy of the East. Easily navigable rivers and the long coastline of Europe, the "peninsula of peninsulas," facilitated the transport of raw materials. Barges bore wool from England, grain from Poland and the Baltic, and iron from Sweden to the middle of the continent. A transport network was constructed; what has been called the "road revolution" began.[9] Carts with four wheels appeared, competing with mules. They could carry heavier and bulkier loads than vehicles with two wheels. People looked for things to do with their profits; city-dwellers started investing in property.

In Lombardy, for example, prices for land and houses began rising in the tenth century.[10]

This profound economic transformation provoked a redefinition of the social order. At the beginning of the next century, for the first time in European history, we meet with the notion that society was divided into three orders: those who pray, those who fight, and those who work. This vision entailed a small degree of secularization, as the world was now differentiated into functions and no longer based on a biblical scheme.[11] The daring deed of Eilmer, a monk at the Benedictine abbey of Malmesbury on Avon, was like an exclamation point proclaiming that new things were on the way. In the year 1010, he jumped from the tower of the abbey church with wings strapped to his hands and feet—and managed to fly for a stretch. He said he was inspired by the story of Daedalus and Icarus, and that he designed his wings by watching jackdaws fly.[12] He had been preceded in his pioneering feat by Abbas ibn Firnas, who had attempted to fly two hundred years earlier in Córdoba. Eilmer's undertaking already had all the features that would characterize the triumphal history of European technology: inspiration from the classical tradition, which must have been available to this eleventh-century Leonardo in a well-stocked library, combined with an empirical approach to problem-solving. The first flight of the new millennium is said to have ended with a crash landing, in which Eilmer broke both his legs. But it was a start. Europe had begun to fly.

Deep History: Bridled Passion

Everyday life for the vast majority of people was much more mundane. It took place within a complex framework of economic practices and legal relationships that has been given the name "manorialism": a system of working and living on land that was owned by a territorial lord who exercised wide-ranging rights and privileges. Outside of Latin Europe, this kind of social organization—which may have had late antique or Germanic roots—is rarely found.[13] There is little doubt that the inertia of this system was one of the major hindrances to all attempts at centralization.[14]

In exchange for the use of land, mills, fishponds, and animals, peasants had to pay fees (in coin or in kind) and perform labor. In one very common form of manorialism, peasants and lords each farmed their own land. Vast estates often took shape in which the lord did not oversee the farming himself but rather entrusted its management to a "steward." The manor could survive without a market, but that meant doing without all the comforts that could be bought there. Another peculiarity of the system was that many counts, dukes, and even the king supported churches and monasteries on their land whose affairs they controlled. This is alien to modern ways of thinking, but it is characteristic of how fluid the boundaries were between the Church and the secular world at the time. Priests and even abbots could be appointed by the patrons of these churches and monasteries.

Peasants encountered the "state" above all in the form of their manorial lord or his representative. Be the manorial lord a king or a nobleman, an abbot or a burgher, he was not simply a business partner to his peasants. He punished and protected them, exploited them and helped them when they were sick and in need. The circle of his *familia* encompassed free farmers, who only had to pay fees, and unfree laborers who lived in various degrees of servitude. Some peasants, known as "serfs" or "villeins," were held in bondage—man, woman, and child, all at the utter mercy of their lord. Without permission, they could neither marry nor leave the manor to seek their fortune in a foreign land.

The most drastic change this system underwent between the eleventh and the fourteenth century was that traditional manors were broken up in many regions. The money economy was often the catalyst, as it played an important role in transforming relationships of personal dependence into transactions of farthings and pennies. The odious work in the lord's fields, other labor, and payment in kind were commuted to rent. The dissolution of the old bond also broke the power of the stewards, those agricultural experts who managed operations for the lords. Not a few of these members of the upper class of rural society had succeeded in turning their office into a hereditary possession, making themselves independent of the distant lord. Some had even entered royal service and been knighted. All in all, during the High Middle Ages the economy of the lords and their manors, indeed of all large estates, declined in importance. What they produced could be bought cheaper at the market. In some places, entire manors—including the lord's farm, the "village" of his villeins, and the land farmed by free peasants—disappeared entirely. The estate was divided and carved up into small parcels. The centralization of state power also had an impact, as secular and ecclesiastical rulers gave land to their loyal servants, to their ministers and warriors. Finally, many manorial lords lost their authority to administer justice; this power was gobbled up by the emerging territorial states.

As a consequence of this development, autarchic "households" were replaced by a freer economy characterized by the division of labor and dominated by money. Production benefited. Everyone—peasants and manorial lords—had an interest in garnering the largest possible yield from the soil, no matter whether they grew grain, cultivated vines, or grazed cattle. Surplus ended up at the market, fed the cities, and brought money into the country-side. Peasants became more mobile. Many sought to make their fortune in newly cleared areas or in cities. At the same time, villages consolidated as communities. The three-field system and the practice of animal husbandry necessitated planning, organization, and regulation.[15]

As the historian Michael Mitterauer has argued, this system of agricultural production was ultimately responsible for Europe's unique demographic structure, giving rise to what has been called the "Western European marriage pattern."[16] What does that entail? There is a notional border called the "Hajnal Line," named for its theorizer John Hajnal, which runs roughly from Saint Petersburg to Trieste. In the area to the west of that line, overlapping in part with the territory dominated by manorial agriculture, people got married comparatively late. In addition, the percentage of those who preferred a single life to the pleasures, pains, and responsibilities of marriage appears to have been higher than outside Latin Europe. The age difference between spouses was smaller, and some women were older than their husbands. Periods of marital fertility were therefore comparatively short. As a result, it was not large extended families but nuclear families with few children that dominated.[17] Mitterauer argues that the conditions of manorial agriculture were decisive, or at least very important, for the creation of this marriage pattern. Extended family ties were weakened. When it came to the distribution of land, preference was given not only to sons or brothers but also to the most industrious among them. Very early on, then, labor needs influenced the size and composition of households, which often included farmhands and maids not related to the family running the farm.

The fascinating aspect of Mitterauer's hypotheses is that they seem to lead into the *very deep* past, into the root system of modern Europe. Unfortunately, we do not know how old the pattern identified by Hajnal really is. Precise data before the sixteenth or seventeenth century is lacking for just about all of Europe. It must therefore remain an open question whether the peculiar institution of manorialism—how widespread similar systems may have been in the Early Middle Ages is unknown—really can help explain the "Great Divergence" between the "West" and the "rest" (see Part IV).

There can be little doubt, however, that Roman and canon law bridled human passion. Isidore of Seville and others pronounced a ban on intermarriage within six degrees of consanguinity.[18] Whereas polygamy was widespread in Africa, in Muslim societies, and (at least among the rich upper classes) in China, the Catholic Church insisted on monogamy and tried to bring marriage under its control. In this way, it kept human passion in check and prevented Europe's demographic body from growing unduly.

Urbanization

Nothing changed medieval Europe more profoundly or determined its fate more enduringly than the extension of arable land, which went hand in hand with increased yields, population growth, and the expansion of trade and the money economy. The economic boom laid the foundation for palaces and cathedrals, and it poured coins into the treasuries of kings. It helped their armies grow, such that they felt capable of contending with the warriors of the Prophet. It produced craftsmen and consumers, merchants and taxpayers; it made it possible to open schools, to build castles and churches. In the words of the monk Rodulfus Glaber,

> Just before the third year after the millennium, throughout the whole world, but most especially in Italy and Gaul, men began to reconstruct churches, although for the most part the existing ones were properly built and not in the least unworthy. But it seemed as though each Christian community was aiming to surpass all the others in the splendor of construction. It was as if the whole world were shaking itself free, shrugging off the burden of the past, and cladding itself everywhere in a white mantle of churches.[19]

Indeed, building was going on everywhere. Hence rose Speyer Cathedral, the pantheon of the Salian emperors, San Isidoro in Léon, the cathedral of Pisa and Saint Mark's in Venice. The cathedrals consecrated to Saint Sophia in Kyiv and Novgorod were also constructed in this period, probably under the direction of Byzantine master builders. The novelty of the new cathedrals was that their architects tried their hand at the ancient, nearly forgotten art of vaulting. A very early example is provided by the barrel vaults constructed by Lombard builders in the narthex of the church of Saint Philibert in Tournus. In the twelfth century, the Gothic cathedral was born. It was not easy to find the necessary timber in land that had been cleared of trees, as was the case in the construction of the mother of all cathedrals: the abbey church of Saint-Denis in the Île-de-France.[20] In addition, the art of bronze casting experienced a renewal. Many cathedral churches were outfitted with ornate bronze gates. These portals attest to far-flung commercial contacts. The bronze door in

Mazovian Płock, for example, was cast in Magdeburg. By gift or by grift, it later ended up in Novgorod (Fig. 11, p. 148).

Above all, the newly available farmland nourished new cities and helped old ones to expand. Houses and huts sprung up around royal courts, manorial villas, and monasteries. The skeletons of ancient Roman and Greek cities were once again fleshed out with inhabitants. Like on the Silk Road, pilgrimage sites proved to be seeds of urbanization. Le Puy and Chartres on the way to Santiago de Compostela grew in this way. In dangerous times, the secure castle was the natural center of the city. Habsburg Castle, in the Aargau in Switzerland, even contained the cornerstone of an empire. The nuclei of cities like Ghent and Bruges were formed by the castles from which Flemish counts ruled their land. New foundations were often undertaken on the initiative of princes. Some cities were like giant organisms, spreading seeds over the countryside from which new communities then sprouted. Smiths left villages to shoe the steeds of merchants. Carpenters helped the new townspeople erect cabins. Weavers went to the city to ply their trade. Artisans from the countryside flocked to the great textile centers, supplying the workshops there. Female wool spinners, for example, furnished weavers with thread for their cloth. Towered walls replaced earthen ramparts and wooden palisades, settlements proliferating in their shade. Ibrahim ibn Yaqub, a merchant from Córdoba, reported from tenth-century Prague that the city "of stone and mortar" was visited by Rus' and Slavs from Cracow, as well as by Jews and Turks from the land of the Muslims; they traded slaves, tin, and pelts.[21] It was in Italy, however, that cities grew most dynamically. Otto III's Milan was twenty times bigger than Hugh Capet's Paris.[22]

In the century of cathedrals, the twelfth, the urbanization trend reached its peak. There were about four thousand towns in central Europe alone. They provided work, security, and pleasure—in the form of love for sale, the entertainment of minstrels and jugglers, and sports. In addition to their most important offering, salvation for the soul, churches also provided pleasure for the eye, paintings and sculptures, the smell of incense, and music—something for all the senses. Monasteries offered food for the poor, healing for the sick, and prayers for the dead. Like cathedral schools, they afforded education. Hospitals and charitable foundations supplemented social networks. It could be very tempting to trade an agrarian existence for life in the city.

The economic upturn was also felt outside Christendom. For example, at the end of the eleventh century 8,000 traders from all manner of countries are thought to have crossed the sea routes and caravan paths between Ifriqiya and

Morocco, Andalusia and Sicily.[23] Conversely, European cities gained access to commercial currents in the Orient. Amalfi, which one Arab traveler considered the richest city in southern Italy, was sending traders to Constantinople, Antioch, and Cairo before the year 1000. Even tiny Piacenza was connected with far-off Tabriz.

The money for large-scale commerce grew on farms in the countryside. The inhabitants of the commercial giant Genoa, for example, relied on landowners and tenants on ecclesiastical estates. The peasants who worked their fields generated the capital that, for a time, allowed Genoa's merchants and bankers to compete with Pisa for mastery of the Mediterranean. It was probably first in Venice, and soon thereafter all over the Mediterranean, that trading companies were formed in which various partners contributed capital and then shared the profits proportionally to their investment. The origins of trade fairs, the hubs of wholesale commerce, lay in Flanders and (beginning in the 1170s) in Champagne. They were also the context in which Latin Europe's information society formed, providing as they did the opportunity to exchange new products and share knowledge about the book trade and the money economy.[24]

The first to appear as moneylenders alongside the Jews—who were excluded from the guilds and thus from practicing trades—were ecclesiastical institutions. The first grand fortunes were amassed in the commercial centers of Italy, the spearhead of capitalism, as well as in Flanders and the Baltic region. With and for them, banks appeared. The term comes from the fact that banking transactions were carried out at fairs by specialized traders at a *banca* (Italian), *banque* (French), or *Bank* (German), i.e., a bench or counter. It may have originated in Genoa, the "gates of the world,"[25] where the word *bancherius* first appeared in 1180. Genoa, along with Venice, is also where maritime insurance and bills of exchange were devised. This revolutionary tool—whose principle was known to the Romans and the Chinese, the latter since the tenth century—turned gold into paper and, when needed, paper back into gold. The bill of exchange allowed business to be done on a large scale. It became a silent weapon against the dangers of the road and the sea, against pirates, highwaymen, and marauders. Not without good reason has this financial innovation been compared to the invention of the compass and the discovery of America.[26] The expansion of trade networks is also attested by attempts on the part of confederations to preserve peace and law, at least for specific periods of time. The same goal was pursued by the Peace of God movements, some of which had a millenarian character.[27]

Trade became the driving force behind the legalization of life. For example, a body of international commercial law took shape. One and a half thousand years after its conception, the Rhodian Sea Law was revived, also proving useful for inland navigation. Its imprint can be seen in the town privileges (also called "city law" or "borough rights") of Hamburg and Lübeck.[28] The law codes of some cities acted as models for others, giving birth to "families" of city laws.[29] For example, Magdeburg's laws provided the model for many new settlements in the East, from the Baltic to Poland and all the way to Novgorod and Minsk. Having a written, agreed-upon law code did not just mean ensuring a bit of security for commerce. It also signaled a victory of reason over custom and the circumscription of princely caprice.

Townspeople looked down on country folk with scorn. Renaissance painters would later poke fun at rustic oafs, depicting them in pictures of rural festivals in the act of vomiting or defecating. Still, most medieval towns were just glorified villages, modest settlements in which only a couple hundred people lived. In terms of size, they lagged far behind the grandness of the Oriental metropolises. Only a few European communities, above all big Italian and Flemish cities like Venice, Milan, Naples, and Bruges, exceeded ten thousand inhabitants. Cologne, at four hundred hectares the largest German city, enlarged its walls twice in the twelfth century. In the Late Middle Ages, it still only numbered forty thousand souls.

Compared with today, city life was not comfortable. It was often difficult to keep provisions stocked. Grain, indispensable for the population's daily bread, required a great deal of space to grow even with the three-field system. Cabbage, turnips, and other vegetables competed with grain for land, alongside the large livestock herds pastured outside the town walls. Food became ever more expensive as the population grew, as did the wood and whale oil that provided heating and illumination. In order to save on the latter, people made the most of daylight—although even that was gloomy, since the windows keeping out the wind and cold were made not of glass but of some substitute like oiled parchment. In winter, stifling smoke stung the lungs and eyes. Forgotten was the ancient technology of hypocaust heating, in which hot steam circulating under the floor provided pleasant warmth; the huge bath complexes of the Roman cities crumbled. Life and work took place in the same room, where an open fire smoldered if there was no stove. Depending on the weather, the alleyways were either dusty or full of mud. Systems for waste disposal, a major focus of Renaissance urban planning, developed only gradually. Human waste generally ended up on the streets; dunghills steamed in the morning light. From the butcher's yard and the gibbet, the macabre, sweet smell of death wafted over roofs made of thatch or straw. A history of the human senses could come to the conclusion that our ancestors must have had a very robust sense of smell.

Laws intended to keep cities clean and beautiful first appeared in Italy, at just about the same time as Europe began its chaotic takeoff during the Warm Period. In Siena and then in Florence, building codes unique for the time set the standard for urban beauty. Streets were paved with cobblestones to keep lethal miasmas from seeping out of the ground. Garbage was disposed of, gutters were carved out, canals were dug. Whenever possible, geometric principles were observed in city planning. Straight lines, right angles, and circles were preferred, perhaps with the symbolic value of these elegant shapes in mind. They reflected the order of the universe, just as the plan of cities like Baghdad, Chang'an, and Fatehpur Sikri in India did.

The forms of many cities doubled as stone metaphors of pure, pious communities. The cities depicted themselves as free of evil demons—entirely so, as one fresco in the Upper Church in Assisi portrays Arezzo after Saint Francis exorcized its demons. They also prided themselves on being free of heretics and unwanted foreigners, who threatened to infect the body of the city like dangerous viruses. Purification rituals ensured metaphysical cleanliness as well, stabilizing the community. One example is the *lustratio urbis* in pagan Rome, whose place was taken in the Early Middle Ages by the Feast of the Purification of the Blessed Virgin Mary, also known as Candlemas. Another is the night spell performed in late medieval England to drive evil spirits out of one's home.[30] Some cities modeled themselves on the triumphant Jerusalem of the Apocalypse, the center of the medieval world. Devices on town seals and towered city walls evoked the Holy City. Town gates were reinforced with depictions of Jesus Christ and his saints. Constantinople's Golden Gate alluded to the portal through which Jesus is supposed to have passed to enter Jerusalem. It served as the model for gates of the same name in Kyiv and Vladimir.

The cities sought to be foils to the disordered conditions outside their walls, to the defects and the rot of the wild world. Countless texts paint a bleak picture, including Bernard of Cluny's *De contemptu mundi* (*On Contempt for the World*), a verse satire written around 1140. Everywhere Bernard sees unbelievers and moral decline, sodomy and sexual temptation.[31] With all his heart he yearned for the heavenly Jerusalem, scorned everything female, and prayed for the Last Judgment. Bernard belonged to a spiritual realm that about two hundred years earlier—not coincidentally at the same time as urbanization and the money economy were spreading—had taken up a dramatic struggle against the filth and chaos besmirching the Church and the temporal world.

11

Latin Europe Falls Apart

The Struggle for Purity

The insatiable yearning for purity, the fiercest foe of free thought, has been the obsession of the religious realm at all times and in all cultures—if for no other reason than that religion usually aims for the absolute, the immaterial, and thus also the pure. Christians have the lily as their symbol, Buddhists the lotus blossom.[1] In times of crisis, the desire for purity only intensifies. Medieval Christians began their life with the purification of baptism; they renewed their inner purity through penance. Drawing near to God required purity for the priest as for the layman. At the end of life, the last rites provided a final purification. Even after death, purgatory—that terrifying invention of the Church Fathers—acted as an ultimate stage of cleansing. Only after passing through it could one enter heaven, which is closed to the impure. Living a life relatively free of sin helped to shorten the time spent suffering in purgatory and to prevent one from plunging into the Inferno. Fear of hellfire and the Final Judgment put staves into the hands of pilgrims and swords into the clutches of Crusaders; it caused people to help the poor and the sick, thus fueling not only military enthusiasm but also Christian charity. On the political level, it begot systems of control. The flames of the stake—symbol of the lake of fire and brimstone that awaited sorcerers and idolaters in the Apocalypse[2]—rid the community of heretics, homosexuals, and other "impure" individuals. Europe's Jews also suffered. If they paid heavy taxes, they might be tolerated in light of Augustine's argument that they were witnesses to Christian truth. During the upheavals of the Warm Period, however, they were repeatedly victims of medieval society's ritual atonement.

Purity demands unity. Attempts to compel societies to follow the one pure faith ended, now as later, in war, terror, and division. Most of the dread princes, inquisitors, and rabble-rousing preachers who precipitated what has (with some exaggeration) been called the medieval "persecuting society"[3] were spurred on by their conscience—at least if we take them at their word. In their view, not fighting for the souls of their fellow men was tantamount to sinning before God. Their efforts to cleanse the world were a means of anticipating divine punishment. Had the Lord Himself not purified his Creation by drowning almost all humankind in a mighty flood? In addition, the Old Testament lamented the intermarriage of Israel with sinful pagan peoples,[4] and that could be interpreted as a call to eliminate or destroy everything unorthodox and heretical.

The fight for purity was waged in many arenas. Iconoclastic movements took part, as did reformers who abolished old rituals. Purity was to reign in the city, the home, and the family, above all in holy places. Christ had set the example when he purified Jerusalem's temple. He had come, like Muhammad after him, to renew and purify Judaism, not to found a new religion. The most important setting for the never-ending struggle was the body itself. The Gnostics had already recognized it as the prison of the soul, from which nothing good could come. Interest in the self and its darker recesses took written form, such as the *Book of Temptations* written around 1070 by the Bavarian monk Otloh of Saint Emmeram.[5] Being pure meant improving the self and required, above all, suppressing the desires of the flesh. Monastic rules, the roadmaps to saintliness and the kingdom of heaven, devote great attention to this point. They prescribe practices that seek to dampen an excess of care for the body, including rough clothing, cold baths, fasting, and night prayer. Misogyny of the kind found in Bernard of Cluny's treatise was often lived out in the solitude of the monastic cell. Repressed desires returned to monks in dreams and visions, threatening to turn them away from the path to holiness. Sects, mystics, ascetics, and hermits struggled to reach the unachievable goal of overcoming all earthly things and becoming pure. Only saints could succeed. Some renounced food; all renounced sex. Even in death, so the legend goes, their corpses did not rot but rather emitted ambrosial aromas; lilies sprouted from their graves. Like Indian Brahmins, they already appeared perfectly pure in the muck of the earthly mire.[6]

All religions have their purity fanatics. Starving oneself to death, and thus finally escaping the burdensome body, is the province of both Jain monks and French Cathars.[7] The pioneers of purity seem to be plagued by a kind of religious compulsion to cleanliness that, if given free rein, spares nothing and no one. Mortal bodies and earthly happiness are nothing to them in comparison with otherworldly glory. In this life, however, impurity could only be rendered harmless—if one was not able or willing to blot it out—by means of ritual purification, isolating "filth," or encapsulating it in taboos. Establishing order is always the realistic alternative to the unrealizable ideal of absolute purity. This was the logic behind the creation of Jewish ghettos and the imposition of caste systems, which were meant to keep the pure separate from the impure.[8] It pushed the gallows and the brothel to the margins, such as a corner near the city wall; it dictated that the mad be put into institutions, and that beggars and proscribed groups be stigmatized with special symbols. Coming into contact with such people could sully townspeople, infecting them as if they had touched a leper.

Religions are forced to put up with secularization and the contamination it entails, as they operate in the material world and cannot escape it. That is why even reform movements, which seek to purify and unite, must suffer the inevitable fate of human institutions. They can only survive in the long term as a state—as the Catholic Church succeeded in doing—or in alliance with the state. Both options require making peace with the princes of the world and their evil deeds. When a reform movement succeeds in this way, it usually becomes rich and thus corrupt. It gives birth to institutions that grow, ossify, and deteriorate. Their officials, the descendants of pious ascetics, saintly abbots, or wise teachers, get a taste for the beautiful sides of earthly life. *Doctores* steeped in the art of dialectic inherit the patient word of the founders and appropriate it for themselves. Against every possible criticism they erect rigid orthodoxies, which quickly elicit new opposition. If reforms do not fade silently or end in sectarianism, they generally lead not to purification, renewal, and unity but rather to division. This was the fate of Karaite Judaism's attempt to authorize only the letter of the Bible and not its interpretation by rabbis—a fate shared by attempts at reform undertaken by the Kharijites, Martin Luther, and many others. And in the end, Sisyphus just starts rolling his stone back up the hill again, his zeal increasing when the end of the unclean world seems nigh.[9]

According to Aristotle and a conviction still widely shared in the early modern world, absolute purity only existed beyond the sphere of the Moon, in the light-filled realms above the stars. Medieval theologians agreed with the natural philosophers on this point. Artists essayed to craft at least a reflection of that celestial glory. The most spectacular attempt of the Middle Ages to resolve the contradictions between spirit and matter was the cathedral, that monumental beacon of the rise of the West.[10] It shows the work that was devoted to turning spirit, light, and heaven into an artifact of human construction. The original impetus for the project may have come from Greek antiquity, as can be seen in the notes left by Abbot Suger (1081–1151), the architect of Saint-Denis, which he referred to as an *opus novum*, a "new work." Suger was probably familiar with the writings of a monk from around the year 500 known as "Dionysius the Areopagite." These texts had been translated into Latin in Suger's very own monastery in Carolingian times. They owed their authority to the author's claim that he had been converted to Christianity by none other than the Apostle Paul himself.[11] The metaphysics of light elaborated by this "Dionysius" provided a Neoplatonic framework for the yearning for God. It posited the foundation of being in a "One" that eluded any attempt at precise description and that transcended all multiplicity and all contradiction—a Greek variant of Nirvana. Ascending to this One, reaching enlightenment, and ultimately joining with it, required following the "path of purification," the *via purgativa*, and renouncing all carnality. Thought was supposed to abandon itself. The visible world seemed a mere allegory.

The cathedral in its complete form made the idea of a light-filled heaven a concrete reality. Its windows, glimmering like gems, recall the bejeweled walls of the heavenly Jerusalem. Architectural elements, images, and statues obscure the fact that this compact space is a creation of this world. The walls are both there and not there. The cathedral is an allusion to the great One about whom Pseudo-Dionysius wrote: a metaphysics of glass and stone, a paradox.

Imperfect matter and pure spirit are, of course, just as different as walls and light. Life ultimately takes place in the human body with all its excretions, pains, weaknesses, and desires. Its flesh sets limits to all spiritualization up until the point of death. Even if the purity fanatics achieved all their goals, the body would still remain—and with it, what Christ considered the indelible mark of original sin. All the same, the yearning for purity inspires efforts to reform even reform impulses themselves. In the fifteenth century, it generated the concept of the "blood purity" of true Christians, a prelude to modern racism (see p. 474). The prefix *re-* in the word "reform" means a large step back, a return to the past and thus an erasure of time—the very thing ritual achieves by different means. The idea is to recapture pristine beginnings, such as the time of the first Christians, whose life was piety and whose work was serving God. The ash of history is supposed to be washed away. It is thus not renewal that is usually sought but primitive, apostolic poverty, the pure, clear word near the source and therewith the pure faith of the beginning.

It was not only the approaching close of a century or a millennium, with its signs and prodigies, that fed suspicions that the end times were at hand. Around the year 1000, one scholar wrote that "Satan's millennium" was fulfilled.[12] The Revelation of John is enigmatic, the chronology of the Apocalypse extremely complicated. It was no trouble to locate it in one's own time, whenever that was and whether circumstances were good or bad. Just as premodern Europe abounded in starvation, pestilence, famine, and war, it produced countless saintly heroes who considered themselves the elect rulers of a thousand-year empire preceding the Last Judgment. Thus, not a century went by in which people were not motivated by apocalyptic prophecies. The course of history itself at times seemed to announce the end, whether the Hungarians were invading, tyrants were raging, or heresy was running rampant. By letting all this happen, was God not prompting everyone to prepare for the end, to purify themselves?

Monastic Reform

Before its first half was over, the boisterous eleventh century was already experiencing what has been dubbed the "return to the desert." More and more people were becoming hermits. Retreating to the isolation of the wooded wilderness provided an opportunity to draw nearer to God.[13] Women had themselves walled up in their convent cells, waiting for death and connected to the outside world only by a window. Clerics now called "regular canons" formed communities in order to live like monks. Monasteries performed the work of worship for the state, indeed for all humanity. "The whole world, as far as the eye can see," is how disciples of Saint Francis responded when—in a later allegorical text—they were asked where their monastery was.[14] Like in Buddha's realm, monasteries in Europe were the beneficiaries of generous endowments; many became large landholders. Their power grew, and with it their involvement in the business of the world, such that the cells of renewal constantly saw themselves challenged to return to the purity of their origins. Of the reform movements that struggled for purity in monasteries from Italy to England, the most influential was the one that took its impetus from the Abbey of Cluny, located near the Burgundian town of Mâcon.[15] Cluny stood for a return to the provisions of the Rule of Saint Benedict, apostolic poverty, asceticism and charity, a Christianization of life. And it strove for independence from episcopal authority. In the precarious times after the decline of the Carolingians, Cluny's influence reached all the way to Spain, Italy, and Germany, spawning many new foundations and winning over pre-existing monasteries.

Tens of thousands of paupers and pilgrims stopped in Cluny on their way to Santiago de Compostela, receiving food there (by performing this good work, the monks hoped to shorten their deceased brothers' time in purgatory). The abbey church, finished in 1095 but today largely destroyed, was the largest basilica in Christendom until the construction of new Saint Peter's. It was a fortress against the powers of hell. Cluny sent out a watchword that was soon received far and wide: a call for *libertas ecclesiae*, the freedom of the Church. This meant freedom from the influence of the laity, thus ensuring the purity of spiritual domains unsullied by the filth of worldly power. Indeed, Cluny and other monasteries even received exemption—freedom—from the authority of local bishops. This only strengthened ties between the reform monasteries and Rome, which, for its part, was now also pulled into the orbit of the purification project. The abbots of Cluny had the ear of popes and emperors.

The reform movement was already in full swing by the time of Leo IX (1048–1054). And the fight was not only waged within the Church. Pope Leo attempted to overcome the battle-hardened Normans who had taken over southern Italy. As a reward, he promised his warriors the kingdom of heaven. Nevertheless, the papal force was defeated, and Leo was taken prisoner. Byzantium also refused to submit to Leo, so ties were cut with the "false" faith of the Eastern Church and its "false" rites. Heresy, as one Russian Old Believer warned in the seventeenth century, could "come in by a single letter of the alphabet."[16] The most important theological justification for the schism was a short addendum to the Nicene Creed. It insisted that the Holy Spirit flowed from the Father "*and* the Son"—in Latin, *filioque*. One medieval theologian, Alanus ab Insulis, put the disputed paradox in a nutshell: the daughter conceives the Father and gives birth to him as the Son.[17] Constantinople denied this was the nature of Christ's paternity; Rome accepted it. Excommunications flew from the Tiber over the sea and back from the Bosporus. This was not the first time that the Eastern and Western Churches had parted ways. But this time, in the year 1054, the break turned out to be permanent. The upshot? By throwing off the last vestiges of Byzantine authority, the pope won new power for himself. From now on, whoever dared to question Rome's primacy could be condemned as a heretic and a schismatic.

Reform-minded cardinals like Humbert of Silva Candida, one of the individuals responsible for the break with Byzantium, gained influence, as did monks like Peter Damian; the latter took asceticism to the point of bloody self-flagellation in his monastery. They took aim at simony, a long-bemoaned evil that entailed the selling of church offices and doing business with the instruments of spiritual power—blessings, sacraments, relics, and other magical items. In 1045, one pope, Benedict IX, had sold his office for cash. In 1059 a synod in Rome promulgated numerous reforms. It sought to reduce the circle of the papal electors to the cardinal bishops. It also renewed the fight over the vexatious issue of celibacy. It called on priests to celebrate the mass in chaste purity and not to set bastards into the world who might later claim an inheritance, thus diminishing the property of the Church.

The Empire, now in the hands of the Salian dynasty, had meanwhile reached the height of its power. At the Council of Sutri in 1046, Henry III (r. 1039–1056) presumed to depose three rival popes all at once. In their place, he appointed one of his followers to the Holy See, the reform-minded Bishop Suitger of Bamberg, and had himself immediately crowned emperor by his minion. As Pope Clement II, Suitger retained his own bishopric; the idea was probably that he would be easier to control that way.[18] Sutri, a craggy little town overlooking the Via Cassia north of Rome, became the symbol of a monarchy that claimed power over the Church and the world. Otto the Great had already understood himself to be Christ's vicar on Earth along with the pope, and to have a share in the Holy See.[19] The opposite point of view is symbolized by Canossa.

Earthquake: The Investiture Controversy

In late January of 1077, Canossa, a castle at the foot of the Apennines belonging to Margravine Matilda of Tuscany, was the stage for an outrageous scene. Henry III's son and successor, Henry IV (r. 1056–1106), lay on the cold ground before the pope barefoot and wearing only a hair shirt, begging him for release from excommunication. What had happened in the meantime? The conflict leading up to that day at Canossa began when Henry exercised a right whose legitimacy had long been self-evident: he intervened in the election of Italian bishops, including for the important see of Milan. What ensued was an all-out struggle between emperor and pope which has since been labeled the "Investiture Controversy." Its result—neither desired nor foreseen by its protagonists—was the strengthening of another pillar of the European "miracle": the curbing of religion.

Although it seems exotic to modern eyes, the only thing unusual about the pontifical maneuvering that took place at Sutri was the number of popes deposed. For the emperors had long since been responsible for the Church and the faith. The defense of religion continued to be its most important task into the early modern era. Administering the state had also always entailed administering to the salvation of its inhabitants. Constantine himself, forerunner of the Byzantine *basileus* and the Turkish sultans, considered it his job to set everything in order, including religious affairs. His right to do so ultimately came from his position as head of the Roman college of priests. He convened Church councils, presided over their proceedings as if they were sessions of the Roman Senate, and, although a layman, intervened in the debates of theologians. Ever since Augustus, the office of *pontifex maximus* had been the province of the emperor. Now, on the eve of the great conflict between Empire and papacy (which we are now about to describe), Bishop Atto of Vercelli wrote, "Under the power of Caesar the pope purifies the world!"[20]

What made perfect sense in the late-antique and early-medieval logic of rule became a scandal in the eyes of reformers. The purifiers of Rome viewed the appointment of church offices by laymen as sinful simony. Archdeacon Hildebrand, who ascended the Holy See in 1073 as Gregory VII and who had long been an influential leader of the reform party and, before that, possibly a monk, felt compelled to stand up for these principles.[21] If a document bearing the heading *Dictatus papae* (literally meaning "papal dictation") can be taken as evidence of Gregory's understanding of his office, he did not see himself merely as the liberator of his Church but also as its omnipotent ruler, with primacy over the emperor himself.[22] He menacingly demanded that Henry rescind his episcopal appointments. The latter one-upped him, ordering "Hildebrand, no longer pope but false monk," to abdicate—a demand that met with a papal ban and the excommunication of the king. Unable to mobilize the requisite supporters, Henry's strong words could sire no deeds. Now in a terrible predicament, he put his last hopes in the bitter road to Canossa.

The harshness of the conflict was not only a result of Gregory's pious fervor and Henry's sense of honor. Real power was at stake. Kings and emperors had always diligently supported bishoprics and monasteries, furnishing them with land and rights. In this way, they simultaneously benefited the nobility, from whose ranks the majority of bishops and abbots came. These men of God were supposed to act as counterweights to the great temporal lords of the realm. Incapable of producing legitimate offspring, they could not found dynasties that might undermine royal authority. The emperors received intercession and prayers from their appointees, and they made use of them as scribes, advisers, and ambassadors. Bishops governed cities and commanded their own troops, including in Milan, where the Investiture Controversy began; some even ruled over entire counties. Moreover, bishoprics and imperial monasteries provided substantial contingents of the imperial army, including nearly three-quarters of its mounted troops.[23] Considering the episcopate's manifold functions and economic importance, attacks on the right to "invest" bishops with ring and staff and to place them in office by this "investiture" were a threat to the core of the emperor's power.

In the alliance between crown and crosier, the emperors had long been the senior partners. They made personnel decisions and guaranteed the survival of the Papal States. More than once, Frankish or Saxon swords had been forced to save popes ensnared in local Roman conflicts. Now that Henry lay prostrate before Gregory on the frozen turf, the tables seemed to have been turned. In light of his opponent's ritual submission and penance, the pope felt compelled to lift the excommunication. But the cold peace of Canossa was of short duration. Rival kings were proclaimed; an anti-pope crowned Henry emperor in 1084 once the latter had taken the upper hand militarily. Gregory died a year later, embittered and just as convinced as ever of his righteousness. Only in 1122, after his foe had also finally died, was a compromise reached in the Concordat of Worms. This agreement gave the emperors the right to influence the election of bishops only inside the Holy Roman Empire. The scepter, the symbol of bishops' secular authority, was to be given to candidates before their consecration and investiture with ring and staff. In England and France, where the connection between the episcopate and Rome had been much weaker than that between the emperors and their bishops, solutions were hammered out that gave the kings decisive influence over the filling of bishoprics.

The episode at Canossa provided images that, as if set in stone, animated polemics for centuries to come. Historians diverge in their interpretations.[24] What to some seems the beginning of the end of sacral kingship and the germ of the separation of church and state, appears to others as a diplomatic success for the king. Here Canossa is seen as an expression of the triumph of reform over arrogant secular power, there as the height of clerical hubris. What is certain is that Henry's act of penitence amounted to a profound humiliation of imperial authority. Some historians therefore go so far as to discern in "Canossa" a world-changing shift towards secularization and modernity. Ultimately, the Investiture Controversy can more properly be compared to an earthquake, the release of primordial tectonic tensions from deep under the surface. Was not the crowner of the emperor worthier than the crowned? Were not the emperors Theodosius and Louis the Pious forced to perform penance? The mighty powers that collided were two equally universal claims to authority. And grinding together at the lowest level of the unstable terrain were the contradictions of purity and filth, religion and the secular world, spiritual and political power. They had been buried there ever since Christianity had been recognized as a licit religion in the Roman Empire.

What remained of Gregory's attempts to purify the Church and the world? The war against simony ended in a defeat for moral standards. Nevertheless, criticism of money-grubbing clerics and simoniacs, now increasingly aimed at the papacy itself, never died down. Efforts to restrict priestly sexuality foundered on the rocks of human nature, and the fight against the amassing of benefices was equally unsuccessful. On the other hand, the papacy had gained autonomy and a significance that would soon extend far beyond Rome. The papal court, or *Curia*—called such since the late eleventh century, on the model of the *curia regis*, the "royal court"—became the command center of the Western Church. No amount of purple cloth, once reserved for the *basileus* and the emperor alone, was spared by Rome's tailors on the pope's vestments. The papal monarchy developed into the most modern state of medieval Europe. It was run by hundreds of officials who endeavored to write in elegant, "ancient" Latin. They were soon producing ten times as many official documents as were issued by the imperial chancery.[25]

Rome unwaveringly defended its spiritual monopoly as guardian at the gates to eternity. Outside of the Roman Church, no salvation was to be possible. It alone could determine which rites and formulas were agreeable to God, and which belonged to forbidden black magic or deserved to be condemned as heresy. Those who propagated forms of piety that did not require the intercession of a priest had to reckon with persecution. The ecclesiastical hierarchy doggedly labored to trim back the rank growth of spiritual devotion, to subject religious reform movements to its own rules. The popes even arrogated to themselves the right to name saints—almost like Chinese emperors, who could even create gods.[26]

The import of papal reform and the Investiture Controversy for modern secularization can only be seen from a *long durée* perspective. By not merely remaining a reformer but also challenging the emperor for authority, Gregory VII mired the Church in a political conflict. For the first time, a power raised its head that far in the future would take on awe-inspiring proportions: *the public sphere*. Indeed, the Investiture Controversy initiated the first propaganda war in European history. For example, one supporter of the pope claimed that a ruler as incapable as Henry IV should be chased off like a swineherd who had neglected the animals under his care.[27] In response, those loyal to the king relied on an argument stemming from the late antique ideology of kingship: Henry was the image of Christ, a perfect, anointed "king and priest." New in these exchanges was their sharp tone. If a pope could be denigrated as a "false monk" and a ruler as a "swineherd," what was now taboo? Politico-religious polemics of the kind that raged in the wake of the Investiture Controversy are unknown to other religions. The Investiture Controversy marked an initial high point for a critical discourse about power, religion, and law. The tone of this discourse would remain constant, and then escalate in the Reformation and the Enlightenment.

The perennial conflict between emperors and papacy that began with the Investiture Controversy was so explosive precisely because the popes commanded a large-scale organization that made them immensely powerful secular figures. The price they paid for it was contamination. Religion was diminished in moral authority, the imperial crown in luster. In this battle of heavyweights, it was the lesser powers, the princes and the cities, who were the true victors. The character of the Holy Roman Empire as an elective monarchy—a handicap from the point of view of raw political power—became entrenched. "Blood" never lost its magical force in the Empire, of course. Yet the German emperors had bad luck with biology, *fortuna*, and their fortunes. Dynasties changed every couple of generations, down to the time of the Habsburgs. In 1138, the Salians were succeeded by the legendary House of Hohenstaufen. Among others, it had to ward off the rival House of Welf (or Guelf), which sought to achieve with weapons what it had failed to gain by election.

Age of Crusades: The Origins of Occidentalism

While the fight for the keys to spiritual power was raging in the Holy Roman Empire and Italy, western Europe witnessed the rise of France and England, which since the invasion of 1066 had been ruled by the Normans. The Northmen had also begun constructing another state, this one in Italy under the leadership of Robert Guiscard, whose sobriquet means "the Cunning"—according to a classically educated contemporary, he earned it by being second to neither Odysseus nor Cicero in shrewdness.[28] Robert's Normans defeated Leo IX, took the Lombard principalities in the south, swept away the remains of Byzantine rule, and wrested Sicily from its Maghrebi lords. The reform papacy had quickly sought an alliance with the victors, thus legitimizing their gains. Sicily and the Norman holdings on the peninsula became a kingdom under papal suzerainty. The conquerors transformed the *Mezzogiorno* into a tightly governed model state, even adding cities in North Africa. According to the chronicler Gerald of Wales, Palermo alone yielded greater revenues than all of England.[29] What paths the new lords of the south had traveled! Having set out from forests, fjords, and fells under the midnight sun, they helped found Kyivan Rus', conquered England and a good portion of Francia, and now they inhabited palaces shaded by palm trees.

Their victories had been enabled in part by power shifts in the Near East. The Byzantine Empire was being harried on the Danube border by nomadic peoples; in the Balkans, the Croats—they appear a century later in the sources than the Serbs, namely in the mid-tenth century—were striving for independence. In 1055 the Seljuks, a powerful clan belonging to the Muslim tribal confederation of the Oghuz, conquered Baghdad and imprisoned the Buyid emir. In 1071, their sultan defeated a large Byzantine army near Manzikert in what is now eastern Turkey. In the following decades, the victors occupied Armenia and a large section of the Anatolic Theme, a Byzantine military province that corresponds to modern Anatolia. The Seljuk Empire now stretched from the Mediterranean to Iran. Yet it would soon splinter into many smaller dominions.

Meanwhile, Christians and Muslims also crossed swords on the Iberian Peninsula. The Reconquista, or reconquest of lost Christian territory, mutated into a Holy War. The troubadour Marcabru called Spain a *lavador*, a "wash room" where knights could cleanse their souls.[30] What made the first Christian successes possible were the same conditions that enabled the Normans to conquer their kingdom in southern Italy: discord among their Muslim opponents. After a period of bloody turmoil, the Caliphate of Córdoba fell in 1031, and with it the rule of the Umayyads. They were succeeded by the "petty kings," who ruled for five decades over a good forty different *reyes de taifas*, or independent Muslim principalities.

Alfonso VI of Castile and Léon conquered Toledo in 1085, causing the *taifa* princes to request help from the Almoravids, a militant Islamic Berber dynasty

centered in West Africa. Their warriors succeeded in halting the Christian offensive. At the same time, they disposed of most of the petty kings, who, albeit
Muslims like them, were not as strict in their beliefs. Andalusia became the
possession of an extensive dominion that, with Marrakesh as its center,
stretched from the western Maghreb to Senegal. The Almoravids persecuted
Christians and Jews as well as fellow Muslims whom they suspected of being
too secular. The equally reform-spirited Almohads put an end to Almoravid
rule in al-Andalus. They could not stop the advance of the Christian warriors,
though. In 1212, with their defeat in the Battle of Las Navas de Tolosa at the
hands of allied Christian armies, their fate was sealed. A new phase of the
Reconquista began. It became the heroic age of Spain, with legendary figures
like Rodrigo Díaz de Vivar, known as El Cid, the brave and gruesome warrior
who had made himself lord of Valencia. Even as a corpse strapped atop his
white stallion—so the legend goes—he was the terror of the Berbers.

The Crusades to the Holy Land began in 1095. Pope Urban II called upon
Christendom to rush to the aid of embattled Constantinople and wage war on
the "wicked race" occupying the Christian holy sites. The same spirit that
animated papal reform and the fighting in Italy and Spain also produced the
Crusades.[31] They aimed to purify the entire world of pagans, at a time when
Judgment Day seemed to many to be close at hand. The demographic upswing
produced warriors; freedom and adventure beckoned. Europe's nobility found
an opportunity to win fame and salvation, as well as new land and slaves—
whether the fight was against the Moors or against heretics or idolaters in the
north and the east. "These pagans are most wicked, but their land is the best,
rich in meat, honey, corn, and birds; and if it were well cultivated none could
be compared to it for the wealth of its produce." Thus one text composed at
the time of the Investiture Controversy summarized the earthly and heavenly
enticements with disarming clarity. "This is an occasion for you to save your
souls and, if you wish it, acquire the best land in which to live."[32] Those who
heard the call began the work of purification while still in Christian Europe,
massacring Jews in the Rhineland and elsewhere. Theologians like Petrus Al-
fonsi stoked the fire of anti-Judaism, keeping the flames of the pogroms burning bright.[33]

The warriors of the faith achieved lasting victories only in Europe. For example, Crusaders took Lisbon and other Iberian cities in passing, as it were,
on their way to Palestine. Jerusalem, though conquered in 1099, was lost again
less than a century later. Constantinople, whose plight had been the original
impulse to the Crusades in the Near East, fell prey to its Christian brothers

from the West in 1204. When the knights of the Fourth Crusade found they could not afford the passage to Egypt, they compensated Venice for their transport by winning for it the city of Zara and other sites on the Dalmatian coast from the Byzantines. A very strange fruit indeed of the Crusades and the Reconquista were the orders of knights they spawned, amalgamations of monastic and military communities. Their members saw themselves both as archangels of the pope and as Good Samaritans whose duty it was to take care of sick people and pilgrims. They, too, were ultimately corrupted, grew rich, and built their own states: the Knights Hospitaller on Rhodes, and the Teutonic Order, originally a foundation of northern German merchants, on the Baltic Sea. The emperor and the pope furnished them with privileges and gave them rights to conquered pagan territory. And they actually succeeded in converting pagan peoples to Christianity. The Templars, the "Poor Fellow-Soldiers of Christ," amassed property all over Europe, thus becoming an important financial power active in the money-lending business.

Strategically, the Crusaders failed in the war against the Muslims because it proved impossible to neutralize wealthy Egypt. Attempts to take Cairo were unsuccessful. Egypt and Syria were now ruled by the Mamluks, erstwhile slave-soldiers of the Ayyubid dynasty who had gained freedom and replaced their former masters. When a Mamluk army stormed Acre, the economic hub of the Levant, in 1291, Latin Europe's adventures in the Near East came to an end. Seven times or more, depending on how one counts, the Westerners had invaded the Holy Land. The greatest profit from the Crusading "business" was garnered by the Italian maritime cities, especially Genoa and Venice, whose fleets were indispensable for troop and supply transports. They secured trading bases and gained better access to the flourishing Asian economy.[34] Just how useful the Crusades were for the long-term development of trade is disputed, however. In the more distant future, the experience was a lesson in how to finance and organize colonial enterprises. At any rate, trade with the Muslims was not dampened by the Crusades. Exchange was and remained so lively that the Italians adopted the Arabic term for their branches in the Orient, *funduq*, for related institutions in their own cities. For example, this is how the center for German merchants in Venice, the Fondaco dei Tedeschi, got its name.

It may well be that, while war raged in the palaces, peace reigned in the huts.[35] In some cities a sort of multicultural society seems to have taken shape in which, according to Fulcher of Chartres, who participated in the First Crusade as chaplain to Baldwin of Boulogne, "Occidentals" became "Orientals." In general, however, the Crusades in the Near East sowed the seeds not of symbiosis but of estrangement. For the first time, the Muslim world was confronted with a violent, intolerant, and culturally backward "West." Arab chronicles speak with scorn of the Franks' primitive legal system and its trials by ordeal, of their benighted medicine, of their rude customs. The invaders, albeit regarded as bold fighters, laid the solid foundation for Occidentalism, providing the raw material for enduring prejudices and caricatures of the "West" as an imperialist, money-grubbing, narrow-minded, and otherwise soulless cultural void. Not even the Muslims of Andalusia knew much about the Christian religion and the everyday life of the "infidels."[36]

From the Arab point of view, the Crusades—which in the "West" were the stuff of epics, chansons, and later national sentiment—were almost without significance, hardly worthy of mention by historians. For their part, the Crusaders in the East learned only little about the grand culture of the Muslims. A translation of the Quran and other Arabic texts prepared for Peter the Venerable, abbot of Cluny (1092/94–1156), was meant to serve as a spiritual blueprint for the struggle against Muhammad, that "principal precursor to the Antichrist and student of Satan."[37] The knowledge transfer that was so important to Latin Europe's future took place in the contact zones of Andalusia and southern Italy. The Crusades were less an impetus to Europe's intellectual development than an especially ugly variant of the manifold reactions to the upheavals of the Warm Period. On the other hand, the reality of defeat taught that God apparently did not desire the violent conversion of the world, at least not just yet. Criticism of the Crusades often led to criticism of the papacy, causing the latter to lose even more credibility.[38] It may, therefore, be the case that the Crusades, against every intention of their propagators, were responsible for another step in the direction of secularization. The age of purists like Saint Bernard, one of the most avid proponents of Crusade, was coming to an end.[39]

Fledgling Europe

In the Latin world, the steep slopes of development gradually leveled off. Tacitus's "barbarian Europe" contained almost no more barbarians.[40] The foreign peoples from the north and east had created new political entities, had been integrated into pre-existing ones, or had been wiped out. The "West" was not destroyed by the invasions. On the contrary, it took shape thanks to them, gaining new ideas and powerful arms. The borders of crop-cultivating, field-plowing, and livestock-raising Europe extended ever further into the wilderness of forest and steppe. The continent developed the common language of

Latin and ordered its thoughts according to the Phoenician alphabet. With help from the Arabs, it made progress in the art of mathematics, in medicine, agriculture, and astronomy. It had long since learned to transact business with the magical charm known as "money."

The Christian God gave "fledgling Europe," to use the term pioneered by Jerzy Kłoczowski, an ideological foundation and an embryonic sense of community.[41] Cathedrals, churches, and convents formed a metaphysical map. Pilgrim paths crisscrossed the land like lines of force. The Way of Saint James, or Camino de Santiago, developed into one of the central arteries of Christian Spain.[42] Wayside crosses, shrines, and chapels marked places with a higher concentration of sacredness, where one could feel relatively safe from the influence of the devil and his demons. These were imaginary high-security zones, flickering with magical energy. Mighty saints, some of them deceased kings, protected the countries of Europe, interceding for their peoples in heaven and guarding their borders on Earth. "Territories of grace" sprung up around their relics.[43] These remains called the powers of the saints to life and warded off evil. An army of skeleton *santi* still sleeps in the earth of Italy. The body of Saint James the Moor-slayer stood watch in the remote west. In the north, in Trondheim's Nidaros Cathedral, it was the remains of Saint Olaf. The east was protected by the skull of Saint Adalbert; it was preserved first in Gniezno and then in Prague. The saints created a sense of identity in the long process of nation-formation: Saint Stephen for the Hungarians, Saint Patrick (author of a fascinating confessional work) for the Irish, Saint Wenceslas for the Bohemians, and Saint Stanislaus for the Poles. Europe's eastern border was the end of the Christian world. The other side was inhabited by "pagans" like the Cheremis and the Mordvins, who settled on the Middle Volga, or, north of the Black Sea, the Muslim Kipchaks or Cumans, a Turkic people whose territory extended to central Asia.

A glance at Europe's borders reveals religious hybrids. In 944, Constantinople and Kyiv still solidified a trade agreement with oaths to both the Christian God and the pagan deity Perun, master of thunder and lightning. Europe's prehistory endured in the northern sagas, in songs, and in epic poems like the Old English *Beowulf*, a mix of Christian and Scandinavian traditions that revolves around loyalty, courage, royal hospitality, and gift exchange. In Hungarian territory, it lived on in the stories of the magic stag and the Turul, of Lehel's horn and Botond's battle-axe.[44] Pagan gods survived longest in the northeastern corner of Europe, between Prussia and the forests of Finland—among Old Prussians, Lithuanians, and the eastern Finnic Votes, who were still considered "obdurate pagans" in the sixteenth century.[45] Shamans, sorcerers, and wise-women were available to mediate between this world and the next. Talismans like painted eggs from Kyiv, forerunners of the Easter egg, promised fertility or protection from evil demons. These methods for dealing with the trials of human existence abided into the modern age.

What the "common man" and "common woman" otherwise did and thought is almost totally unknown. By far the vast majority of people inhabited the illiterate countryside. How Christian their faith really was, even if they had been baptized with holy water—this we simply do not know. Which gods, which demons haunted their heads? Considering that their everyday lives were ruled by the seasons, did they foster a cyclical view of history in which the same things happened over and over again? What had they heard about Charlemagne or the pope, much less of the world far beyond the woods they cleared and the fields they sowed and harvested? All civilization depended on their work. They paid the taxes; they provided the food that made it possible for others to write, to pray, and to build, to equip fleets and knights in armor. Without them, state formation would have been impossible.

Territory was ruled above all via personal relationships, by the granting or revoking of favor and estates. The principle of "agnatic seniority" followed in Kyivan Rus' led to the fragmentation of the state during the twelfth century. For a ruler's sons, compensated with minor principalities, gave little thought to the allegiance they owed their eldest brother, who inherited the title of prince of Kyiv—a title, however, that meant only honor, not power. Polotsk, Smolensk (now an episcopal see), and other principalities gained independence, although their status remained contested. *The Tale of Igor's Campaign*, written around 1185 about a prince of Novgorod's raid against the Cumans, bemoans the discord among his people:

> Hard as it is for the head
> to be without shoulders
> bad it is for the body
> to be without head.[46]

At that point, Kyiv's leading role in the Rus' was already history. In 1169 the city was conquered by Andrey Bogolyubsky, prince of Vladimir-Suzdal. The victor took the title of grand prince back to his palace in Vladimir, which was transformed into a capital city on the model of Kyiv.

While Hungary was spared fragmentation thanks to the system of counties instituted by Stephen I and the wealth of the royal domain, Poland under the heirs of Bolesław the Brave was little more than a protectorate of the Holy Roman Empire for decades. Moravia fell to the Bohemian crown. Power struggles also troubled the Piast Dynasty, reaching levels of archaic brutality that included even blinding and castration. The nobility gained power and developed into an estate in its own right. Nearly two hundred years would flow down the Warta and the Vistula before "Polonia" was united under one crown again.

At the same time, the political map of western Europe also changed dramatically. England, hitherto a part of the Scandinavian North Sea Empire, developed in the wake of the Norman Conquest into a state that was deeply entangled in central European affairs. Thanks to marriages and inheritances, a realm had taken shape that stretched from the Pyrenees to England and Ireland; even Scotland fell under the feudal sovereignty of the House of Anjou. The dynasty was also known by the nickname Plantagenet, after one of its ancestors who decorated his helmet with a common broom plant—*genista* in Latin, hence the nickname *Plant Genest*. France's Capetian kings, with their bit of land around Paris and Orléans, saw themselves confronted with a superior vassal. Conflict was unavoidable.

Henry II (r. 1154–1189), the first Plantagenet on England's throne, was an energetic nation-builder. He standardized the common law and endeavored to have the jurisdiction of royal courts recognized. When he also tried to subject the clergy entirely to secular justice, he was opposed by Thomas Becket, archbishop of Canterbury. The latter was murdered in his cathedral in 1170—probably not on Henry's orders, but not to his dismay either. Whereas Becket was canonized only three years after his death, Henry had to make a public apology. The clergy retained the right to appeal to the Curia in Rome.

On the Continent, this conflict had parallels in the disputes between Frederick I Barbarossa (r. 1152–1190) and Pope Alexander III, which sprang from Barbarossa's desire to create a powerful, universal, and above all Hohenstaufen empire based on Roman law.[47] He therefore devoted a great deal of energy to rich Italy, the inveterate object of imperial fantasy. Six times he ventured south. Yet he was always defeated by papal resistance and an alliance of Lombard cities. Alexander survived no fewer than four anti-popes. A peace treaty reached in Venice in 1177 gave the *mundi dominus* ("master of the world"),[48] a pompous title Barbarossa borrowed from antiquity, supremacy in name only. Having learned from the experience of schism, the Third Lateran Council, which Alexander called two years after the peace treaty, formulated the rule of papal election that still stands today: only a candidate with a two-thirds majority of the votes of the College of Cardinals could become pope. In the north, Barbarossa managed to defeat his most dangerous opponent, Henry the Lion. The latter's duchies were broken up. Frederick cut Saxony into smaller pieces; Bavaria fell to the House of Wittelsbach, which continued to rule the white-and-blue principality until 1918. Therewith also appeared the outlines of the later political borders of southern Germany. At the same time, a new group of princes came on the scene who were directly enfeoffed by the king. The age of the "stem duchies" was over. Nevertheless, the House of Welf, which was allied with England thanks to Henry the Lion's marriage to Henry II's daughter, remained the mortal enemy of the Hohenstaufen.

In 1190, while participating in the Third Crusade, Barbarossa drowned in the Saleph (now Göksu) River, which runs through western Cilicia in Asia Minor. His son, Henry VI (r. 1190–1197), ruled over rich Sicily by virtue of his marriage to Constance of Hauteville. In addition, as chance would have it, the new English King Richard the Lionheart fell into his hands while returning from the Crusades. The latter's ransom, tons upon tons of silver, helped Henry to secure his Sicilian inheritance. It was the first time that cold hard cash won a kingdom—evidence for the triumph of the money economy. Leopold of Babenberg, the man who had kidnapped Richard the Lionheart (supposedly in retaliation for his having insulted him at Acre), used his share of the ransom to build a wall around Vienna.

Nevertheless, Henry's attempt to unite the German and Sicilian crowns as a Hohenstaufen patrimony was foiled by his early death. Some historians have seen this as a turning point in European history.[49] Had Henry lived longer, Germany may indeed have embarked upon a path toward supremacy over all of western Europe. As it turned out, the only hope for Hohenstaufen power was the emperor's barely three-year-old son, Frederick Roger. Generals, courtiers, and papal legates, the latter representing the supreme pontiff as Sicily's feudal lord and the legal guardian of the "son of Apulia," now schemed and skirmished over his inheritance.

Magna Carta

The strengthening of states and cities was the most important upshot of the chaos created by the struggles between Europe's leading powers. Their conflicts put organization at a premium. Wars may not have been the father of all things, but they certainly sired very many. They contributed to the consolidation of the state, spawning bureaucracies which, in turn, were capable of taming the wild rule of a warrior class.[50] Power—not the fiercely won and quickly lost variety snatched by the sword, but rather the lasting and undisputed kind—is ultimately the stuff of parchment and signet rings. As far back as ancient China, it was known that an empire can be "conquered on horseback, but it cannot be governed on horseback."[51]

Realms "without a state" gradually vanished. Institutions and legal systems grew, exploded, and entailed greater costs, but they provided a degree of security without which science, technology, and the arts could not flourish. Last but not least, war required money to be raised from the nobility, townspeople, and the clergy, so it became necessary to create public assemblies and parliaments. Ultimately, conflicts were decided by whoever's bureaucracy was better at sustaining the flow of money, grain, and weapons. Most wars were now won or lost in offices, treasure vaults, and assemblies, not on battlefields.

One exception to this rule was the Battle of Bouvines. On July 27, 1214, a Sunday, the army of Otto IV, an ally of the English King John, met the forces of Philip Augustus of France (r. 1198–1223) on the field in what was then the county of Flanders. The buildup to the battle stretched back to the time after Henry VI's death. In 1198, two different men were elected king of Germany. Against Duke Philip of Swabia, who came from the House of Hohenstaufen, the Welf party set up a son of Henry the Lion, the above-mentioned Otto. When Philip was assassinated in 1208, the dispute seemed to have been decided in favor of the Welf Otto, who had himself crowned emperor in Rome by Innocent III (1198–1216). To the dismay of the pope, Otto then invaded Sicily. Yet he failed to conquer it. In the process he made an enemy of Innocent, who dreaded being surrounded by the Welfs as much as by the Hohenstaufen. The emperor then turned his eye on France. Thus was born the conflict that unfurled on the field at Bouvines. Otto had always been an ally of the Plantagenets. In exile, as the protégé of Richard the Lionheart, he had risen to become Count of Poitou and Duke of Aquitaine.

After Richard the Lionheart's death in 1199, the balance of power in western Europe shifted. The new English king, John "Lackland," had to deal with the headstrong barons. In addition, he had gotten entangled in a dispute with the pope over the appointment of the archbishop of Canterbury, who played a key role in English politics. In France, in contrast, the monarchy was gaining strength. Philip Augustus had succeeded in neutralizing the unruly counts and increasing the royal domain. That is why he was able to go on the offensive and seek a resolution in battle. It may actually have been a tiny coincidence that decided the outcome at Bouvines: an arrow struck Otto's war horse in the eye.

After quickly getting a new mount, he was forced to flee. Philip's victory was absolute. The emperor's golden eagle is said to have been placed before him with broken wings. As the story goes, Philip had the imperial standards mended and sent to the young Frederick of Sicily. In this way, the latter gained the Holy Roman Empire without even lifting a sword.[52]

In the country of the loser, however, the nobility rebelled. In 1215, King John was forced to strengthen the rights of the barons in the famous *Magna Carta Libertatum* ("Great Charter of Liberties").[53] New and without parallel was the fact that the charter, which was actually a peace treaty between the king and the barons, did not grant privileges to circumscribed groups like the nobility but rather was addressed to "all the Freemen of our Realm." It required the king to include the barons in governing. It stipulated that taxes could no longer be levied without the consent of the entire kingdom. It was the seed from which Parliament grew. Very forward-looking was the clause that no free man could be imprisoned, banished, or deprived of his property without legal cause. Law reined in arbitrary rule. The cities, chief among them cosmopolitan London, were guaranteed their traditional liberties, as was the English Church. Magna Carta promoted Cicero's notion that the highest law was the good of the people—whereas imperial jurisprudence regarded as law whatever pleased the prince. The influence of the piece of parchment sealed at Runnymede on June 15, 1215 extended to the modern world. The American revolutionaries invoked it in their cry, "No taxation without representation." Three clauses of Magna Carta are still statutes in England today.

King John's attempts to regard Magna Carta as nonexistent misfired in the "First Barons' War." He also failed to regain lost territory on the continent. In the end, all that remained to him was Gascony, as a fief of the French crown. Philip won his sobriquet "Augustus" thanks to the Battle of Bouvines, which also doubled the royal domain. The stabilization of the French monarchy was further favored by biology. Dynasties did not change in the swift tempo that weakened other states. After a long struggle, the perennial resistance of the nobility was finally broken. Saint-Denis, where Philip Augustus's remains are buried, became the pantheon of the French kings, the protectors of the *réligion royale*.

While Otto and Philip were contending for the German throne, the papacy was brought to the height of its power by Innocent III, a trained jurist, shrewd political operator, and author of a work on the sinfulness of human nature entitled *On Contempt for the World, or the Misery of the Human Condition*. He succeeded in vastly increasing the possessions and revenues of the Roman

Church, known as the "Patrimony of Saint Peter." Thinking far ahead of the times, the Curia formulated the notion that the pope, as the inheritor of this legacy, did not merely possess an array of rights and property but rather ruled a concrete territory.[54] His state extended like a bolt across the middle of Italy, stretching from coast to coast.

The Fourth Lateran Council, called in 1215 and attended by European kings, princes, and cities, was a magnificent pageant of the high clergy. The participants negotiated the fate of heretics, called for a new Crusade, and also promulgated reforms. The council required the faithful to perform weekly confession and attend mass, forbade the clergy to engage in untoward worldly behavior— drunkenness and falcon hunts are explicitly mentioned—and declared only marriages conducted by a priest to be legitimate. Marriages within four degrees of consanguinity were prohibited, although dispensations were possible under certain conditions. Those who fought against heretics were granted the same benefits as Crusaders, including plenary indulgence. From that point forward, Jews and Muslims had to differentiate themselves from Christians by wearing special clothing.

The war for purity and order was brought to its culmination by Louis IX, who became king of France in 1234 and was later declared a saint.[55] He was also a ferocious persecutor of heretics and Jews. Their filth, as he said about the latter, was a stain on his realm. He had the Talmud publicly burned and property owned by Jews confiscated. While on Crusade in the Holy Land, he ordered all Jews to be expelled from France. The decree appears not to have been carried out, however. Following in the footsteps of Charlemagne, he continued his predecessors' efforts to consolidate the state. He set about standardizing coinage, created a tax authority and, in the form of the *Parlement*, a supreme court. His attempts to do away with trial by ordeal amounted to a small move in the direction of secularization. The rationality of Roman law gained ground; by means of royal decrees, his famous *ordonnances*, Louis strengthened the power of the crown. In addition, he succeeded in gaining the region of Provence. Even for the pious Middle Ages, he was considered extraordinarily devout. He paid extravagant sums for relics. For the most powerful of them, venerated as Jesus's crown of thorns—it came from Constantinople and reached Venice in 1204—he had a truly royal shrine erected: the Sainte-Chapelle on the Île de la Cité in the River Seine. In no other Gothic cathedral did rose and tracery windows dissolve the walls so perfectly into ruby red, emerald, and sapphire light as in its upper chapel. There, under star-studded vaults, the king talked privately with his God. In 1270, while on his second Crusade, he died in Carthage, himself now ripe for veneration.

The rays of light we have shone on the thirteenth century remind us that the fate of Latin Europe's horizontal power structures hinged on special circumstances and even "accidents." The arrow shot into the eye of Emperor Otto's horse at the Battle of Bouvines is one of them. Would Magna Carta and, later, strong parliaments have come into existence if King John "Lackland" had won that victory? The expansion of horizontal power structures in England and other states on the Continent was in no way a necessary development. Contemporaries thought alternatives were possible. So much is clear from the imperial policy pursued by Hohenstaufen rulers from Barbarossa to Frederick II. If we search for the main reasons why the power of sovereigns remained so fragile, one of the most important is certainly feudalism. Nevertheless, political fragmentation had long been predetermined, ever since states had taken shape on the remains of the Western Roman Empire in the wake of the great migration of peoples.

12

Vertical Power, Horizontal Power

Feudalism

Was there still a chance for empire in Europe? How likely was it that the continent would be ruled by a single monarch? The question is almost laughable.[1] Henry VI did not come close; even Charlemagne only ruled over a small portion of the continent, and that only for a short time. The armies put in the field by the mightiest early modern rulers—perhaps numbering a few thousand cavalry—were ridiculously small when compared to the resources of certain Eastern potentates. Mercenaries, on which Barbarossa and others had to rely, were expensive. In general, the display of power was circumscribed by very tight economic boundaries.

The attainment of imperial dreams was not only thwarted by a lack of people and money. Rulers were caught in a tangled web of rights, duties, and allegiances that has come to be called "feudalism."[2] For a long time, this system of power relations was expressed solely in the form of speeches, gestures, and rituals; only in the late twelfth century would its practices take written form and thus become more concretely comprehensible. In its manifold manifestations, feudalism mirrored agrarian social relations at a higher level. The vassal pledged himself to a lord in a commendation ceremony, paying homage and taking an oath of fealty by folding his hands as if in prayer and putting them in those of his lord, or else by swearing upon holy relics. He was bound to provide counsel and aid and to perform service, above all in war but also, for example, at court. In exchange he received the gift or use of a fief, including land, special rights, and income. The most important difference with respect to the general situation between landholders and peasants was that feudal relationships between freemen were possible and increasingly became the norm. Even nobles of equal rank received fiefs from one another.

The practice of trading land for loyalty was only of benefit to royal power for a certain period of time—namely, while conquests were enlarging the pie that could be dished out. In such a system, during phases of rapid expansion those who distribute the plunder firmly hold the reins. If military vigor slackens, internal crises can quickly arise, especially when bad harvests lead to economic problems and social imbalances. Every evil is then ascribed to the current ruler, and usurpers find fast support. This mechanism destroyed several states in turn: the late Roman Empire, the Carolingian Empire, and later the Ottoman Empire.

Fiefs were increasingly given to relatives or friends of the lord. These vassals then enfeoffed vassals of their own, and those petty vassals imitated their lords in turn, creating their own clientage networks. In this way, vassals acquired their own dependents and negotiated the terms of their relationship with them autonomously, while the remote king, albeit the formal lord of all, was no longer consulted. Some vassals entered the service of many lords, taking manors and rights in fee from several patrons at once. Fiefs, once granted, could become heritable. As early as 1037, an edict of Emperor Conrad II assumes as much, guaranteeing the inheritance of *beneficia* in the male line. The commendation ceremony in which fealty and homage were pledged in return for a fief, originally performed with strict religious observance, became an empty formality. The transmittal of a charter took the place of a personal act. Powerful vassals gained a high degree of independence. The conglomeration of fiefs they accrued could, over time, develop into territorial states. The feudal system did not prevent their creation. On the contrary, it contributed to the fragmentation of power relations, as fiefs were a very secure form of property. Revoking them required engaging in a laborious process.

As time went on, feudal relationships seeped deeper and deeper into society. Farmers, including women, could receive fiefs. Even townspeople became vassals to the crown. In addition, money entered the economy of feudalism. For example, vassals could be paid for their service, such as at the lord's castle, with regular income from rents or with a sizeable sack of silver coins. Conversely, money could take the place of tedious service. The upshot of these developments was that power relations and social life became juridically defined and thus reduced to a state of tranquility—one could even simply say, reduced to statehood. What mattered was who managed to control the distribution of lands and offices. When such goods, once bestowed, became independent of central authority, the latter's power declined. Feudalism did not have to stand in the way of the creation of strong monarchies, as can be seen in the case of France and other nations. Nevertheless, the system turned out to be one of the most important causes for the fragmentation of Latin Europe. For example, viewing an office as a fief protected against arbitrary rule and thus curbed the power of monarchs. The situation was not the same everywhere, however. The same Norman kings who ruled Sicily with the iron fist of a Byzantine emperor governed southern Italy as feudal lords.

European feudalism had almost no parallels anywhere in the world. Most similar to it was the state of affairs in Japan,[3] where the power of the provinces and a clan-based warrior nobility had been growing since the tenth century. By the end of the following century, certain landholders—members of the imperial family, court nobles, religious and state institutions—essentially removed some of their lands, even fishing villages and bays, from the influence of provincial authorities and ruled them as their own.[4] A century later, certain clans were able to stitch together these *shōen* lands and provincial holdings into expansive political entities in a manner similar to European princes. Relationships akin to those that existed between lords and vassals began developing on this foundation in the twelfth century. A landed court nobility, which had originally been involved in military affairs for the government, settled down in the provinces, distributed lands, offices, and rights, and bound the warrior class of *bushi* (later samurai) to themselves. These followers strengthened the nobility's place at court; influence begot greater influence. Local territorial lords gave their land to prominent leaders, receiving it back like a fief. Just as the last Roman emperors were neutralized by Germanic generals, the Merovingian kings by the mayors of the palace, and the Abbasids by the Buyid emirs, the *tennō* lost his authority. It fell into the hands of clan leaders who, in the wake of bloody struggles with competing groups, took control of the state. Following another common pattern, they used the emperor solely as a ceremonial leader and wellspring of legitimacy; they themselves took the humbler title of *shogun*, or "general." Alongside Heian-kyō (modern Kyoto), which remained the official imperial capital, they set up their *bakufu*, or "tent government," in the village of Kamakura (near modern Tokyo). Their rule was also destined to end like that of their counterparts in Europe. The burgeoning money economy weakened the personal ties on which their power depended. As no plunder was won through conquest, the resources for paying off their followers dwindled. Attempts to resuscitate the old imperial system failed.

Guilds, Communes, Confederations

The seals of many European cities and towns prominently feature the city walls; some show only them. Indeed, the walls made the city. Along with the marketplace and the courthouse, they were its essential characteristic. Unwalled villages also existed, but they were rare. Neither the *poleis* of classical Greece nor the cities of Asia had the same strict separation between town and countryside; in the Islamic world, tax structures usually stood as the only line of demarcation.[5] The clearest difference was encapsulated in the pithy phrase, *Stadtluft macht frei* ("city air makes you free"). Despite coming from a later time, the phrase is nonetheless apt, although various forms of obligation did also exist in towns—to monasteries, for example, to which payments had to be made. Indeed, ties to a territorial lord could be cut if one managed to reside inside a town's walls for "a year and a day" without any objection being made.[6] Disputes between towns and territorial lords over runaway bondservants were to form part of the history of urban societies for a long time to come. For example, in 1232, Emperor Frederick II felt compelled to confirm for the German princes a privilege that forbade cities to take in unfree people. Towns were not allowed to have citizens outside their walls, and their jurisdiction remained limited to their immediate territory.[7]

The very name of Freiburg (literally "free town"), founded in Baden in 1120—its foundation is especially well documented in the sources—recalls the fact that it was precisely freedom that made it an attractive place. Those who moved there did have to pay an annual tax on their property to the counts of Zähringen, but they retained their personal freedom. As with Freiburg in particular, the origins of urban liberty in general may be traceable to the fact that the Medieval Warm Period increased the need for workers and settlers. New-comers were able to obtain certain perquisites and gain legal security. Urban freedom meant that city councils, craft guilds, merchant guilds, and confrater-nities could be formed. Corporate entities of this kind offered protection, help, and salvation. Whether they had roots in the Roman Colleges or sprung up spontaneously to meet the needs of the day is unclear. Their appearance, which grew dramatically in the Late Middle Ages—there were 150 in Milan alone—was a silent revolution.[8] They created safe spaces for discussion and brought people from different backgrounds together, closed themselves off to the outer world, promulgated rules for themselves, and often gained political power. Their members worked and caroused in common, prayed together, and buried one another. Town rights in the Baltic Sea area provided for the protection of foreign merchants referred to as "guests" (*gosti*); they were allowed to settle in colonies. In this way, communities with their own law developed beyond the fortress towns. As John of Viterbo summed up the situation around 1250, "a city means the freedom of the citizens, the immunity of the residents."[9]

Urban *communia*, or "communes," which may have been modeled on rural communal structures, sprang up first in turbulent but rich northern and central Italy and somewhat later in southern France.[10] Over time, a civic oath took shape. Regularly sworn by the community of citizens, it enumerated their duties and articulated their commitment to safeguarding peace and law. Communes built city halls and used their own seals. Council meetings could muster several hundred or, as in the case of Bologna, up to four thousand members.[11] Committees and offices were established, and mayors were named to manage all the affairs of civic life from taxation to sanitation. The purpose of the commune was to forge a sense of unity, to create a bulwark against the arrogance of nobles and the power of bishops, and to ensure a peaceful order that protected as many social classes as possible.

It is no accident that the communes had their heyday between the twelfth and the fourteenth centuries, when the early modern state was still in its infancy. In places where rulers waged war with popes or rival kings, a standard game was played: both sides tried to win cities as allies, offering in return privileges and gifts. Once bestowed, such benefits remained with the recipients. The communes were able to boost profits from trade, crafts, and money-lending, whereas the income their noble or ecclesiastical lords drew from their estates could not easily be increased. In times of overproduction, revenues even decreased. Landowners were also weakened by the emigration of farmers who wished to breathe the free air of the cities. In this way, the balance shifted from the countryside to the cities. In the latter, money flowed from many sources including staple rights, customs duties, ground rent, and poll and excise taxes. Some communes grew rich enough to be able to buy up the rights, and thus the power, of their lords, whose influence was generally rooted in property ownership and thus declined with sinking revenues. A few lords even felt compelled to sell off the very city walls. They therewith dispensed with the need to man them, but they also lost an important symbol and a rock-hard instrument of power. Moreover, in competition with the landed nobility and each other, many cities built up their own territories and ruled over them like feudal lords.

Medieval townspeople had little in common with their modern counterparts. They certainly had no constitutional rights to protect them, although for a time the Italian communes did enjoy a degree of "democratic" participation otherwise unknown until the French Revolution.[12] Alongside the bigwigs, family bosses, bankers, merchants, and wealthy craftsmen, there were many who had no voice: newcomers without full citizenship, Jews, beggars, itinerants. The general populace and women did not have much say. The burden of taxes and other obligations left them little room to breathe; in a recurring cycle, lack of resources led to extreme poverty.

In general, only the "best and wisest," those eligible to be councilmen, were considered citizens. To sit on a city council, one had to be wealthy. Ultimately, participation required free time. Those who had to weave or forge had no time for the town hall. Thus the rich and the newly rich crowded into the assemblies. In many cities, power was taken by merchants, craft guilds, or both. Sometimes, old families who had made their name in royal service ruled the field. As symbols of family power, towers rose from the ground that, in part, served a military purpose. They dominated the medieval cityscape. Bologna, for example, had a good 180 towers, making it a kind of medieval New York City. A sense of what the dense forest of urban towers was like can still be gotten in San Gimignano, in Tuscany. In Florence, magnate families were referred to as "those with towers" (*delle torri*). When the *primo popolo*, the "first popular government," came to power there in 1251, one of the first things the new regime did was to cut the towers of the elite families down to size.[13] They were allowed to be no higher than fifty *braccia*, about twenty-nine meters; none could rise above what was then the highest communal tower, that of the Bargello. In other cities as well, when old families fell, their towers fell with them.

Ambition and jealousy, on the other hand, were not so easily kept in check. Laws were as impotent in this regard as the procedure, followed in the Italian

cities, of trying to keep the peace by installing a foreign jurist or nobleman as
podestà, a temporary supreme magistrate. Often enough, the landed elite prosecuted its feuds—a kind of vigilante justice considered legitimate among free
people—within the city walls. The leaders of powerful families took matters
into their own hands, using hired militias or subtler methods like conspiracies,
daggers, and poison. Poverty and starvation, the unavoidable drawback of a
growing population, migration, and economic flux, ensured that the magnates
could always count on having a reservoir of people willing to fight for or
against anything in return for money. The free commune was a fragile project,
under constant threat.

Alliances between cities such as the Lombard League, which had stood up
to Barbarossa, took shape in Spain and northern Europe as well. In 1127, for
example, citizens in Flemish cities formed an alliance to decide the succession
of the murdered Count Charles I of Flanders. In the following year, Ghent
attempted to demote the new count to a kind of constitutional monarch.[14] As
here and in the neighboring Duchy of Brabant, dynastic crises were to the
advantage of horizontal power structures. In the Holy Roman Empire, where
the emperors were often not able to keep the peace and protect trade, townspeople took the initiative. Between Brandenburg and Lake Lucerne, Alsace
and Lusatia, powerful confederations began taking shape in the twelfth
century. Some of them were composed of thirty, forty, or more communes.
They successfully defied the regional nobility, although they also entered into
peace agreements with them if necessary. Accords between merchants ultimately developed into an alliance that, at the height of its power, included
about two hundred cities: the Hanseatic League.[15]

In the Holy Roman Empire, about one hundred communes managed to
attain the status of "free imperial cities" by the end of the thirteenth century.
These were tiny republics subject only to the emperor and the Empire. The
number of these queens among the German cities declined in the following
centuries, however. Similar to the Italian communes, some of them, like Bern,
Nuremberg, and Metz, managed to build up territories of their own. Others,
such as Cologne and Augsburg, controlled little surrounding territory but
were financial centers with massive concentrations of capital, similar to Singa-
pore and Hong Kong today.[16] Writing about the Italian communes, Bartolus
of Sassoferrato, the most famous jurist of the Middle Ages, commented that
their peoples were free and the cities themselves princes (*civitas sibi princeps*).[17]
This characterization also fit many German free cities.

In eastern central Europe, numerous cities also gained rights and, for a while, a bit of independence. This was not the case in the Principality of Moscow, however. "Posad people"—the entire free population settled around the ruler's fortified capital—were jointly responsible for paying their taxes. Yet they did not form a commune, and craft and merchant guilds were unknown.[18] Chronicles of western Russian cities mention "veches," assemblies that were sometimes convoked from above but that also met spontaneously, often during urban uprisings.[19] The most striking alternative to Moscow's vertical hierarchy was found in Novgorod. Like an Italian city-republic, it controlled a territory; during the Late Middle Ages, it stretched from the Arctic Ocean to the Urals. Its free inhabitants swore an oath to one another, and there were merchant guilds. Its veche, called to meeting by a bell, made decisions and passed laws without paying much heed to the words of the prince. Sometimes it was even involved in electing a bishop or choosing a *posadnik*, a kind of mayor. Its sessions were often chaotic, though. It was not the majority but rather the loudest voice that ruled, and blows were often exchanged instead of arguments. Nevertheless, Novgorod added a horizontal timbre to what was otherwise a strictly vertical concert of princes in the Rus'. It was also a byword for the use of written records. Hundreds of charters written on birch bark are extant, not a few of them in Latin.

Political Representation

Democracy is an archetype of political life. The Homeric epics already show that warrior societies highly valued communal assembly and discussion in addition to physical strength. War was thus one of the fathers of Greek democracy and its sophisticated institutions. For it strengthened the influence of those who bore its brunt: the heavily armed foot soldiers. What happened in Athens may have been similar to developments in fifth-century BC Rome, where the infantry stood up alongside the aristocratic cavalry and confidently demanded a say in affairs of state.[20] New in the case of Athenian democracy was that the principle of majority rule triumphed for the first time in a larger society based on the division of labor and written documents. The Greeks were also the first to give serious thought to democracy, until today the best of all political models. Yet their considerations, long the most profound on the topic, were forgotten. The democratic model survived in the countryside and in monasteries of all kinds. There the majority ruled as in other "stateless societies."[21] Democratic forms were also observed in public assemblies of free men in the successor states of the Western Roman Empire.[22]

In the Middle Ages, the idea of freedom was justified on the basis of natural right and the Bible. Eike of Repgow, author of the *Sachsenspiegel*, a legal code compiled between 1220 and 1235, takes from the Gospels the notion that all human beings were originally free. He thence concludes that serfdom and bondage can only result from unlawful violence.[23] Not long afterward, Bologna's popular government used a similar justification to buy the freedom of nearly six thousand serfs, both to undercut the power of their owners, the magnates, and to gain a new tax base for the city.[24]

Early forms of political representation, "one of the major contributions of the western Middle Ages to world history,"[25] are found in Spain. In 1188, probably in Léon, the newly crowned Alfonso IX called an assembly at which emissaries of the cities participated alongside the aristocracy and the high clergy. It is noteworthy that the urban delegates were "the elected citizens of each city," i.e., representatives of the communes.[26] This *Cortes*, an early form of parliament—the term could also denote a general meeting of the citizens of a town—passed resolutions guaranteeing civil liberties. In the sixteenth century, so the legend goes, its oath to the ruler is said to have gone as follows: "We who are as good as you swear to you who are no better than we, to accept you as our king and sovereign lord, provided you observe all our liberties and laws; and if not, not."[27]

Apparently, the king was seeking above all to pacify conquered Muslim cities. In addition, he needed consent for new taxes. Here we already see the three most important causes for the development of the parliamentary embryo: a new ruler seeks to consolidate his power, to quell possible rebellion, and to integrate the people of his cities into his kingdom. Here and in the future, the need for money was another main reason to call an assembly. The tentacles of the young state's bureaucratic octopus were not usually long enough to wring the resources necessary for armies, fleets, and buildings from all the cities, towns, and villages of the land. Only the magnates, clerics, and citizens invited by the king ultimately had direct access to the purses of provincial areas. In exchange for pulling their strings, they could lodge complaints with the king, demand the redress of grievances, and request freedoms and privileges. It was above all property rights with which rulers, who often wanted to wage war but were perpetually short of funds, requited what was granted them, and these rights were very important for the economic development of many cities. Indeed, the private initiative they encouraged had a positive effect on growth.[28]

The first general assemblies of the estates of the realm may have grown out of the duty of vassals to provide counsel. The participation of representatives from the cities at what had been exclusive meetings of the high nobility and high clergy altered their nature profoundly. The path was now taken to understanding such assemblies as proxies for the whole country. The ancestors of modern parliaments have appeared under various designations since their initial appearance in Spain, and thereafter in Portugal, Sicily, then in France and Scandinavia.[29] The first *parlement*, convened by Saint Louis in Paris in 1238, had nothing in common with what is denoted by the modern term, however. It was a court of law and served purely to create a legal basis for the power of the kingship. However, France's "Estates General," its *États-Généraux*, which began meeting with increasing frequency in the fourteenth century, brought together the clergy, the nobility, and the "Third Estate." This body was convened above all when the country was beset by war and the royal treasury was empty. Chaos and misery were good for general assemblies, as the power of princes tended to be weaker in such times.

In the Holy Roman Empire, the principle of horizontal power, first enshrined in writing in the Treaty of Coulaines (see p. 99), initially appeared in practice in the form of *Hoftage*. These "court assemblies," to which the ruler invited the leading princes of the realm, developed into imperial assemblies at which, over time, cities were also given a voice. Some of these meetings featured magnificent displays of the imperial aristocracy, whose support in the form of soldiers and money the emperor hoped to secure. In addition, all manner of issues were discussed, such as rights of succession, the awarding of privileges, and the settlement of disputes. But developments did not go in only one direction. Ties of personal obligation, family relationships, and clan loyalties tended to hold the fledgling states together. The right of primogeniture helped to prevent political division and struggles for succession.[30] Blood thus remained a powerful agent in politics. At the same time, some general assemblies and urban communes emerged that could exercise influence on the level of states. To historians fascinated by modernization processes, especially those in the tradition of Hegel and Ranke, the residues of horizontal power must seem like recalcitrant obstructions to state formation, with its hierarchical structure, bureaucracies, and crowned potentates. Yet they were often both: traditional practices had a unifying effect, and at the same time they provided early, albeit imperfect, patterns for what would much later become the most successful way to structure a regime—and the only way to legitimize one. Citizens won great power in general assemblies of the estates and in the English Parliament. A whole range of opportunities for decision-making was opened up to individuals.[31] Besides, representative bodies and monarchy were in no way antagonistic principles from the get-go. Often enough, they presupposed and needed one another.

In addition to its horizontal power structures, which were actually rather strong from a comparative perspective, thirteenth-century Europe was distinguished from the rest of the world by another institution of phenomenal importance: the university.[32] The disciplines of law, theology, and philosophy gave rise to this *unicum* in the history of human culture. The university was one of the ways European societies responded to the upheavals of the Medieval Warm Period, to urbanization, to the expansion of trade and the money economy, and to general insecurity. For the Church, the universities created a sophisticated theology, one that also made it easier to deal with the general distress of the age.

Universities and the Law of Rome

What it was like to live through this period of change was vibrantly recorded in literature. The ancient theme of the "world turned upside down" was often taken up by the poets of the twelfth century, and it perfectly reflected a society in which nothing remained as it was and little was as it should be. For example, the *Mirror for Fools*, written before 1180 by the Englishman Nigel de Longchamps (ca. 1130–ca. 1200), claimed that the present day turned all history on its head. Chrétien de Troyes (before 1150–1190) portrayed rabbits chasing dogs and lambs hunting wolves.[33] Many evils were pinned on the revolutionary force of money. This view had also been popular in antiquity, as seen in the *Satires* of Juvenal and Persius and some derisive remarks in the works of Horace and Seneca.[34] In the west, Marbod of Rennes wrote that money "is the whole world's master," while in the east Cosmas of Prague called it "queen of evil, friend of deceit, enemy and foe of faithfulness."[35] A dire need for order was felt. And one had to wonder what God's plan for his people was, seeing that He had plunged them into such chaos.

Down to the twelfth century, which turns out to have also been a watershed for the history of learning, education in the liberal arts and theology was firmly anchored in religious institutions. Monastic schools served above all to train novices, the children destined to enter the order; in addition, they were open to secular clergy, the offspring of the nobility, and students from the city (including paupers). Over time, the educational offerings of monasteries lost out to cathedral schools, which were not involved in training monks. Itinerant men of learning also peddled knowledge, and some teachers made contracts with students to coach them in specific aspects of law or theology.

The origin of universities is to be found around 1200 in Bologna and Paris, the latter of which was vaunted as the "city of wisdom"[36] and soon towered above all other centers of learning in France (and, for a time, all of Europe). Universities overshadowed the religious schools but did not sweep them away. At times, a previously existing school for law or theology may have provided an impetus. The University of Bologna, for example, grew out of a local school for jurists. Its rise may have been aided by advantages of location—such as its position on an important road that crossed an Apennine pass—and accidents like the presence of gifted individuals. Decisive was the general environment of the times. One necessary component was a legal system capable of mastering increasingly complex business transactions involving goods, bills of exchange, land, and buildings. The midwives of the new institution were therefore jurists, and it is no accident that it entered the world in the hot economic climate of Italy. Here, in the atmosphere of the communes, of trade, of division of labor and an expanding money economy, the Warm Period had long nourished a growing number of private training centers to cover the need for writing skills and legal knowledge, which could not be met by monastic and cathedral schools. The triumph of jurisprudence was manifested in the increasing importance of notaries. Originally simple stenographers at the court of the Roman emperors, they first appeared in the Early Middle Ages as writers of public and private documents.[37] Their number began to grow rapidly in the eleventh century. They were needed to record and certify wills and business transactions of all kinds. There is much to recommend the thesis that jurisprudence's growing significance in the Italian cities was facilitated by the same factors as the creation of the communes—in a nutshell, the weakness of the Empire.

That Bologna became the fountainhead of modern jurisprudence and thus the birthplace of the very first university was also related to the fact that the conditions were favorable for a true resurgence of Roman law. In all likelihood, Roman law's meteoric rise in Bologna was connected to the discovery of a copy of Justinian's *Digest*, a codex called *Littera Florentina* (after Florence, the place it was later preserved). Probably copied during the emperor's lifetime, perhaps in Italy's "Greek" south, the codex ultimately made its way to Pisa and then to Bologna. At any rate, the city developed into a stronghold of Roman law. The *ius Romanum* had never been completely forgotten here or elsewhere. Now, however, it encountered an environment that needed it and scholars who recognized the intellectual potential of the ancient system.

The reception of Roman law in Italy and then in France, where Saint Louis emerged as its advocate, was the most important renaissance before the Renaissance. Its principles corresponded to "pure reason." The classical jurists had invented technical terms that facilitated the formulation of procedural rules and a language for describing matters of dispute. At the same time as the *Florentina* was inspiring scholars to study the *Corpus Iuris Civilis*, Bologna not coincidentally also became the locus for the systematization of canon law—a body of jurisprudence including papal decrees, rules promulgated by Church councils, and guidelines of the Church Fathers. Around 1140, a trailblazing codification of uncertain authorship appeared: the *Decretum Gratiani*. Its actual title, the *Concordance of Discordant Canons*, reflects that its contents are discussed and arranged in the early Scholastic manner of *sic et non* disputation, i.e., arguments for and against certain positions followed by a conclusion. It was also the vehicle by which natural law entered into ecclesiastical legal thought, namely in the notion that all peoples had equally valid legal norms.[38]

Working with the ancient, new law required technical skills, specialized knowledge, and a critical temper. Logic was helpful, with Aristotle as the most important author. Next in line were dialectic and rhetoric, or at least the *ars dictaminis*, the art of correctly drafting letters and official documents. It goes without saying that a mastery of Latin was a prerequisite. This meant that law could no longer be practiced by amateurs. It was now an occupation, with learned jurists becoming a new fixture at courts and in highly developed urban societies. Their training required an increasing number of specialized teachers, who joined together with their students to form larger communities. Such *universitates*, literally "societies" or "corporations," of masters and students provided the new institutions with their name.

They gradually acquired a legal foundation. A charter of Emperor Frederick Barbarossa, clearly referring to the situation in Bologna, promised protection to students and teachers and provided them with their own law court before their "lord and master" or the local bishop. Once incorporated into the body of imperial law, the document reinforced academic freedom.[39] The imperial or papal privilege that was generally required for the foundation of a new institution mirrored the universal character of university learning, guaranteed the widespread recognition of academic degrees, and secured the right to "teach everywhere" (*licentia ubique docendi*) for those having passed a licentiate examination. Thus was born the intellectual, a figure unique in world history, a person who lives and is paid for one thing and one thing alone: the search for knowledge.[40]

Thanks to a brilliant string of professors, Bologna became the Mecca of jurists. One of the most famous was Azzo (fl. 1190–1220), the author of extensive commentaries on the *Institutes* and Justinian's *Code*. If one did not know one's Azzo, so a proverb warned, it was better not to appear in court: *chi non ha Azzo non vada al palazzo*.[41] The sheer volume of work produced by the Bolognese jurists in only a few decades is attested by the oeuvre of Accursius (1181/85–1260), which collected and critically appraised all of the comments then available on Justinian's *Corpus*; in total it contained nearly one hundred thousand entries![42] This number demonstrates better than anything else what the process of "juridification" entailed.

The first universities organized themselves. Their members developed an esprit de corps, had their own special dress, rituals, and seals, and operated according to their own statutes. Their special corporate status made universities alien elements in the cities, their students mistrusted and suspected of every vice in the world. For the most part, the universities enjoyed immunity from local authorities. After a tavern brawl in Paris during which several students were slain by citizens of the city, Philipp Augustus issued a privilege to the *universitas* of Parisian masters and students similar to the one Barbarossa issued for Bologna.[43] Their status as corporations also clearly differentiated universities from the *Studia* of the monastic orders, Muslim madrasahs, and institutions of higher learning in the Byzantine Empire, India, and China. So did the wide range of subjects they offered, which also included secular science and philosophy of Greek origin.

What Bologna was for the jurists, the University of Paris was for theology and philosophy: an oracle, the highest authority in learning, and home to some of the greatest minds of the Middle Ages. After the founder of one of its colleges, it was later called the "Sorbonne." Its faculty came from the many schools in the city, the most important of which was the cathedral school of Notre Dame, one of the birthplaces of the scientific method. An *universitas* of students and teachers succeeded in liberating itself from the oversight of the chancellor of Notre Dame. The pope and king gave them statutes and privileges that accorded them a status equivalent to clergymen. After 1250, a dispute erupted over the question of whether mendicants could also teach there; the friars prevailed and, from then on, held chairs in Paris, too.

The newly founded university soon became a popular destination. Students came all the way from Uppsala.[44] The University of Paris was divided into four "nations." In Bologna, students were separated into *universitates* from "this side" or "beyond" the Alps. Their numbers continually growing, they organized themselves into seventeen *nationes*: three Italian and fourteen for students from "beyond the mountains." In this way, certain universities acquired the cosmopolitan character that still marks the more important ones today. Speaking Latin was required. A special operative, the *lupus*, or "wolf," was appointed to make sure this rule was followed in student residences and colleges.[45]

With the establishment of theology, jurisprudence, and medicine as academic disciplines, the arts faculty lost status, becoming a kind of preparatory school for the higher subjects. That is where the seven liberal arts were taught, as passed down from Martianus Capella and the classical tradition. In Paris and elsewhere, colleges were established that were often richly endowed and provided students from all the estates with advantageous conditions. Wandering students and masters spread the university model across the continent. Further universities were founded in quick succession: in Vicenza and Padua— alongside Montpellier and Salamanca soon to be an important center for medicine, which had now risen from a lowly mechanical art to become a university discipline—in Oxford and Cambridge, in Valladolid and Lisbon. By the end of the Middle Ages, the West had about eighty universities, thus giving it an infrastructure for learning and scholarship unparalleled around the world. Between the time of the plague and the end of the Middle Ages, an estimated three-quarters of a million *scholares* were educated. For a long time, however, universities had no value as an export good. Only in 1755, with the founding of Imperial Moscow University, did one first appear outside of Latin Europe.

Universities provided cities and states with expert personnel, produced knowledge that was useful for government and administration, and forged weapons for the Church to fight heresy. In all this, they made themselves indispensable. If a dispute with authorities could not be resolved, teachers and students went on strike or left the city for another location. This is how the University of Cambridge began, as an offshoot of the University of Oxford. The University of Leipzig recruited its faculty from the professoriate in Prague. The period of "unplanned" foundations, i.e., those resulting from the spontaneous generation of academic communities, was already over by 1230, however. The papal Curia, bishops, and states then took the lead. The degree of corporate autonomy enjoyed by universities should therefore not be over-estimated. This applied in the long run to all universities, but especially to those of the kind founded by Frederick II in Naples in 1224. Due to tensions with the papacy, the Church had no say in its affairs. The document in which the emperor explained his reasons for founding the university explicitly says it was supposed to be useful to the state.[46]

Universities even provided excellent opportunities to the poor for advancement and upward mobility.[47] In the fifteenth century, ten percent of the students at the University of Cracow came from farms.[48] But the true significance universities had for Europe's future was that they facilitated the growth of an ever-denser network of learned individuals. The result was what Ludwik Fleck called a *Denkkollektiv* ("thought collective"), whose members spoke a common language and shared a common manner of thinking, at least in theory.[49] In the form of public disputations, they practiced giving speeches for and against specific propositions—principles that laid the foundation of all future academic work, even if such argument and discord could be mocked by a poet:

> someone's vanquished, someone's victor
> all's refuted by the teacher.[50]

The "old" was opposed by the "new." The defenders of tradition crossed swords with the *moderni*, pitting realists against nominalists. Even within the various groups, opinions could differ widely. The Middle Ages bubbled over with intellectual vitality, and the university began its rise to becoming a world power.

Triumph of the Ink State

While Europe's jurists were building their legal cathedrals, its states were solidifying under the gauze of the feudal order. Admittedly, antiquity was no stranger to the idea that the state transcended any one individual or ruler: it was the *res publica*, the "common thing" of the people. Nevertheless, medieval Europe had to develop this concept anew. Around the year 1000, Wipo of Burgundy, court chaplain to two emperors, formulated the maxim that the state lived on even when the king died.[51] In this way, the king received two bodies: a frail, mortal one, and an eternal one that embodied the realm from ruler to ruler.

In the thirteenth century, an attempt was made to provide a theoretical basis for the new state. In the wake of the rediscovery and translation of

Aristotle's *Politics* and *Nicomachean Ethics*, and buttressed by a series of commentaries on these works, an increasingly sophisticated theory was developed that put the state not on a biblical or ecclesiastical foundation but rather on a sociological one. Echoing Aristotle, Thomas Aquinas (1225–1274) wrote that human beings are by nature political, sociable animals that form communities with their peers for rational reasons: in order to find protection and compensate for their inadequacies.[52] The sovereign, therefore, rules with a view to the common good. His duty is to ensure that society reaches perfection and that his people live a virtuous and vigorous life. The intensified development of states—along with the increase of economic interdependence and written culture—may actually have contributed to reducing "savage" violence like feuds, civil war, murder, and manslaughter, at least for a time.[53] Thomas argued that the right to wage war could only be derived from the "authority of the prince."[54]

In his history of the English kings, composed in 1136, Geoffrey of Monmouth conceived of their *patria* as "the monarchy of the whole island."[55] This was a forerunner to much later concepts of the state, according to which it has a territory circumscribed by clear borders. Britain, of course, with its entire perimeter delineated by seacoast, was an exception.[56] It was not yet standard to conceive of space as a topographical arrangement. Rather, it was experienced as a sequence of the days it took to travel from one place to another, or as a series of points marked, for example, by cities or castles. Accordingly, rulers were thought of as exercising authority over such points, over people, but not over territory.[57] Philip Augustus was the first to reign as "King *of France*" and no longer as ruler "of the Franks," and Henry Plantagenet styled himself the first "King of England." Still, a "national" desire to expand to "natural borders" was not felt by medieval political entities. Rule manifested itself above all in rights and jurisdictions: in the right to make laws and hold court, in rights to forests, mills, castles, and cities, as well as to payments, taxes, tolls, and customs duties. Every medieval ruler carried around a sack bulging with real and forged documents. Philip Augustus of France led the way. The number of documents issued by his chancery each year rose from an average of thirty at the beginning of his reign to nearly 110.[58]

For advisers, rulers could usually count on a few nobles and clerics, often relatives by blood or marriage. They dictated privileges, undertook diplomatic missions, and hatched schemes. As confessors, they had the ear of power, and some of them rose to be lords of their lords. The *Hofkapelle* (royal chapel), the bureaucratic engine of the emperors, employed hardly more than thirty people in the Salian period. A small group of scribes, most of them clergymen, drew up documents and stacked them in the fireproof vault. Compared to the bureaucratic behemoths of the Chinese emperors, this was nothing. Yet in Latin Europe, different from almost everywhere outside its borders, a trend toward the professionalization of administration took root in the eleventh century. For example, *ministeriales*, originally bondsmen, entered the orbit of kings and emperors and served them as administrators, advisers, and warriors. Their careers advanced not because the right blood flowed in their veins, but because they had amassed expert knowledge about military matters and administrative affairs. Many of them reached the ranks of the nobility. Some of them received fiefs, even achieving a position of independence.[59] More importantly, more and more rulers employed jurists trained in Roman law as well as experts in finance and other sectors. This increased the authority of the sovereign, but also the security of the individual servants and their property. In short, a tedious, indomitable monster named bureaucracy reared its head all over Europe. It created the ink state.

It was in no way the tough opponent of feudalism that previous generations of historians imagined. On the contrary, it made use of feudalism and worked in tandem with it. The upshot of this equally fruitful and conflict-laden cooperation was the territorial state, and with it what has been called the "early modern state." Its post-classical origins can be traced, for example, to documents like the *Capitulaire de villis*, an act of 792/93 by which Charlemagne regulated the administration of the royal estates. The guidelines it contains represent a triumph of written culture. The most advanced administration was practiced by the Roman Curia and the Norman state in England.[60] Another document of early bureaucratic rationalism, similar to Charlemagne's inventories, is William the Conqueror's *Domesday Book*. It recorded which manors the king had distributed and what services he could expect in return for them. What is more, it contains the first statistics gathered in Europe: a registry of populations, manors, plow teams, mills, forests, and other resources. In France and Sicily—where the Byzantine system could be built upon—the Normans also laid the foundations for central authority with strong fiscal administration. Their institutions worked continually, even when the ruler was outside the country—either of his own will or, as with Richard the Lionheart during his imprisonment, against it. In his *Dialogue of the Exchequer*, the Englishman Richard FitzNeal provided a guide to fiscal administration by describing the practices of the treasury set up by the predecessor of his own king, Henry II.

Institutions—that dry term, which we have already encountered in the discussion of universities and in other contexts, denotes something very big and important.[61] Institutions are what first allow the state to become perpetual; without them, it dies. If advisers appear as the mind and memory of the body politic, and the military as its muscles, it is law and institutions that provide a skeleton for the state. They alone are capable of establishing justice over the long term. Only they can set limits to power and arbitrary will. They preserve knowledge of how to achieve success, as well as reminders of mistakes to be avoided in the future. No one knew this better than Cicero, who emphasized the Roman Republic's special ability to gather experience and make decisions based on it.[62] Before the advent of modernity, no section of the globe created institutions as robust and effective as those that developed in medieval Latin Europe. Moreover, these institutions were highly "inclusive." They guaranteed protection under the law and the right to private property, provided education, and were relatively pluralistic (i.e., horizontally structured).[63]

Indeed, Rome owed its success to its institutions. They then provided the states consolidating during the Middle Ages with models of compelling rationality. Ancient Roman names were given to new institutions and officeholders. Senates and *curiae*, consuls (as heads of communes) and quaestors appear in droves in the sources beginning in the late eleventh century. One of the most famous is the royal court in Norman Palermo, known as the *magna curia* ("great court"). Under Barbarossa, the imperial chancery took up the ancient formula "city of god" and equated it with the Empire, calling it "holy," *sacrum*.[64] This description remained with the "Holy Roman Empire" until its demise, when, to quote Voltaire, it had long since been neither holy nor Roman nor an empire.[65]

The work of jurists in Italy and France gradually began to bear fruit. After their initial victory there, Justinian's legions of parchment conquered the southern German trade centers, the southwest of the Empire, and the Rhineland. England's "common law" took its own path. Similarly, northern France, Scandinavia, and other countries were barely influenced by Roman law. Even in areas where it did penetrate, it could take centuries before it prevailed. Local and regional laws and customs retained their force alongside it, often taking precedence.

The creation and development of institutions strengthened the ink state.[66] Beginning in the twelfth century, documents increasingly appear that record which vassals were given which fiefs. Three hundred years later, registers were systematically kept, some decorated with colorful miniatures, that proclaimed the wealth and power of feudal lords well beyond any legal purpose. Since law articulated relationships within the state and provided security for trade and transformation, rulers also felt called upon to observe it. England's Magna Carta was nothing other than an attempt to draw this very conclusion from the "legal revolution" that the realm had experienced under Henry II.[67]

13

Origins of the "Great Divergence"

Mongol Invasions

At the same time as islands of horizontal power were taking shape, and as the conflict-laden fragmentation of the continent progressed apace, portents of the "great Renaissance" began appearing in the twelfth century. The phoenix took flight toward Latin Europe, following the routes of the trade galleys to Italy and France. Meanwhile, things were getting chaotic in the East. Muslim peoples and the Chinese were haunted by invaders. They rocked half the world and upset the balance of power in Asia.

The Mongols came from a territory between the Onon and Kherlen rivers north of what is now Ulaanbaatar.[1] This is where, originally allied with the Khitans, they grazed their livestock, fished, and hunted; they did not practice agriculture. Their herds provided them with meat and milk, bones and skins. Some of them knew tanning and carpentry. The greatest esteem was enjoyed by smiths; iron and other metals had to be traded for, of course. What households lacked could be supplied by raiding. The Mongols lived, so to speak, on the backs of their small, stout horses. It is said that on long rides through barren terrain, the warriors would open a vein in the neck of their mount and drink dark blood from it so as to avoid losing time by stopping to eat. They were phenomenal riders, able to shoot arrows over their shoulders at full gallop. Each mounted warrior kept up to five horses in reserve for battle. Their attacks could develop dreadful dynamics.

The Mongols honed their military capabilities in tribal feuds over pasturelands, not to mention in the fight for survival in a hostile environment. In the description of one Indian chronicler, they had bodies of steel, bald heads covered with felt caps, and faces like fire; their eyes were so sharp they could bore a hole in a metal container, and their stink was more terrifying than their color. European historians moaned that they ate aborted fetuses, afterbirths, and other "impure" meat.[2] The English chronicler Matthew Paris considered them descendants of the ten tribes of Israel and warned that they would collude with their fellow Jews in Europe. In this way, he fortified the already hardy, harmful myth of a global Jewish conspiracy.

The Mongols were initially a confederation of family networks and clans. One of their leaders, named Temüjin (born ca. 1162), used ferocity and tactical genius to force the nomadic peoples of the steppe into the form of a state. He achieved fame under his honorific title Genghis Khan, which means "universal" or "oceanic ruler." As champion of the celestial god Tengri, he felt called upon to create a realm of peace on Earth. This precipitated doom and death, the usual side effects of noble undertakings of this kind. Genghis Khan's hordes—the term comes from *ordu*, "military camp"—first attacked neighboring Turkic peoples and Jin China.[3] Dadu, which later grew into Beijing, was conquered. For one month, so the story goes, the flames of the burning metropolis stained the sky of northern China red. Mongol armies battered the states of central Asia and destroyed cities along the Silk Road. In 1221, this Alexander of the steppe reached the Indus River. Meanwhile, in the west, his warriors crossed the Caucasus. A Russian army that tried to stop them suffered a devastating loss. When Temüjin died in 1227, Mongol power extended from the borders of Europe all the way to Goryeo on the Korean Peninsula, which had become a tributary.

The death of the conqueror did nothing to quench the Mongols' furor. The kingdom of Bulgaria, only recently revivified, was overrun. Moscow, Rostov, and Vladimir fell, as did Kyiv after a brave defense. Divided into three armies, the Mongols attacked Bohemia, Hungary, and Poland, taking Cracow and Wrocław. On April 9, 1241, a reconnaissance force under Batu, a grandson of Genghis Khan, beat a contingent of Silesian and Polish knights at Legnica. Two days later, a Hungarian army was wiped out. The path to Europe's interior was wide open. Once again, it seemed the apocalypse was at hand. Instead, divine grace followed upon punishment. The "Tatars," as the Mongols were called—the reason is unclear—withdrew, and the center of Latin Europe was spared. The Mongols left scorched earth behind them. A million people are thought to have perished, with hundreds of thousands then falling victim to starvation in the wake of the devastation. Craftsmen were kidnapped and taken back to Mongolia; trade died out. French, Walloon, and German settlers filled the empty countryside.

Batu's decision to secure the territory he had conquered rather than continuing westward was due to strategic considerations. To press on into densely populated central Europe, with its castles and walled cities, would have been risky. Furthermore, the death of Temüjin's successor, Ögedei, made Batu's presence in the capital of Karakorum necessary. This highlighted a structural problem of all steppe empires: quarrels over succession eroded cohesion time and time again. The Mongol Empire was first divided among the four sons of the conqueror. This mighty inheritance was carved up into separate khanates, each of imperial dimension and with its own dynasty. By the second half of the thirteenth century, the process of fragmentation had begun. It started with wars between the Kipchak Khanate and the Ilkhanate over supremacy in the Caucasus. The Byzantine Empire engaged in skillful diplomacy to maintain neutrality.

The Ilkhanate fell after 1335, but the central Asian Chagatai Khanate survived into the sixteenth century. The Kipchak Khanate, better known as the Golden Horde, ruled the Rus' princes for two centuries; for a time, it extended as far as Silesia and Moravia. The khans demanded tribute, but they left the Church and religion in peace. They failed to conquer the northwest of what would later be Russia—the "lands of the Rus'"—including the rising power of Novgorod, whose trade relations now reached all the way to the Netherlands. In the shadow of the Mongol threat, its prince, Alexander (r. 1252–1263) of the Rurik dynasty, even managed to defeat a Swedish army on the Neva River and, shortly thereafter, a force of Teutonic Knights on the frozen Lake Peipus. His exploits on the Neva earned for him the honorific title of *Nevsky* (which means "of the Neva"). Alexander Nevsky cut a deal with the Mongols: he acted as their faithful governor, and they repaid his loyalty with the title of grand prince. In the view of Russian Orthodox believers, joining forces with the Tatars, who sought taxes but not souls, was a lesser evil than an alliance with states to the west would have been. The cultural gulf between Latin Europe and the Rus' had grown wide.

The Mongol Invasions also cut deep rifts in Asian history. In the south, Hulagu, a brother of the Great Khan Möngke and the first of the Ilkhans, overthrew the Rum Seljuk Sultanate, the Anatolian branch of the dynasty. In Persia, he did away with the dreaded Assassins—a fundamentalist Shiite sect that rose to prominence by assassinating rulers of every stripe. "Like a darkness chased by a cloud,"[4] the Mongols stormed into the Muslim world. Baghdad fell in 1258. The assault on Egypt was broken by the resistance of the Mamluks. India was only spared thanks to the military might of the Delhi Sultanate and a line of fortresses.

The most spectacular successes were achieved in the East. Kublai (r. 1259–1294), Khagan of the Mongol Empire, now also overthrew the realm of the Southern Song. After Chinese custom, he took the name of Emperor Shizu. He called his dynasty "Da Yuan," meaning "the great primal beginning"; it would rule until 1368. Dadu became the new capital. In addition, Goryeo was added to the empire. After four hundred years of division, China was reunited, albeit in the unaccustomed role as part of a larger whole. An initial Mongol attempt to take Japan was broken off for unknown reasons. A second was thwarted by *kamikaze*, the "divine wind"—a typhoon destroyed two Mongol fleets. Assaults on Dai Viet and Java, where the thalassocracy of Majapahit began its rise, also failed.

Meanwhile, Christian rulers sought to win the Mongols as allies. Saint Louis hoped to conquer the Muslims with their help. Initially, their empire was based solely on the energy of their rulers, clan ties, and the fury of their cavalry. Horses and arrows (and later bombards as well) were now augmented by a much more important instrument of power: a highly efficient communications system with closely staggered postal stations.[5] The Mongols learned from their subject peoples, trading with them and with European merchants. Whereas military opponents normally had to choose between submission or being butchered, the common people were spared. After all, the new rulers needed experts of all kinds. The Confucian art of administration helped them to rule; Chinese, Persian, and Arabic culture taught them how to enjoy and portray their power. Here again we see that when expanding societies outgrow their natural environment and culture and end up in totally new milieus, they are necessarily more open to innovation than others.[6] Typical of the way the Mongols adapted to what they found was how Kublai Khan, a studious Asian Peter the Great, adopted a Chinese lifestyle while at the same time decorating rooms of his palace in Dadu with furs.[7]

The Mongols did not create powerful institutions. They copied or overtook what they found. They themselves did not learn new skills but rather hired specialists for sophisticated procedures and complicated crafts. They did, however, codify their law, and in their *Secret History* they gave themselves an origin story. According to this legend, they descended from a certain Batachikan, the offspring of a blue-gray wolf and a doe. The *Compendium of Chronicles* by the Persian Rashid al-Din, vizier of the Ilkhan, began as an account of the Mongols but was then expanded into a universal history.[8] Its description of Chinese printing was long the most detailed available.

Most of the new rulers were initially adherents of Tengrism, a shamanic faith focused on the celestial god Tengri. Many of them adopted the religions of their subject peoples, but they also retained their own spirituality. The Ilkhan Öljaitü was a religious chameleon. Born a Tengrist, he first had himself baptized a Nestorian Christian, then became a Buddhist, then a Sunni, and seems to have died a Shiite. Herbert Franke, one of the greatest experts on the subject, has speculated that if the warriors of the steppe had stayed in Hungary in 1241, they probably would have become good Christians.[9] But most khanates converted to Islam. For religious minorities which had theretofore been tolerated, the climate became less hospitable. China stayed true to Buddha, although it venerated him in his Tibetan "Lamaist" garb. Alongside him, Confucius, surrounded by incense and gifts, retained his now two-thousand-year-old authority.

China: Walled-In Freedom

Under Mongol rule, the trend toward authoritarianism in China intensified. Corporately organized and militarily equipped elites of the kind found in Europe, capable of circumscribing centralized power, did not exist.[10] The households of the empire were divided into classes according to the productive functions they fulfilled. Mongol and western Asians families were at the top, followed by northern Chinese.[11] Social advancement was nearly impossible. At particular disadvantage were the southern Chinese, who had just been conquered and had to bear an excessive portion of the growing tax burden. The class system was intended to provide the state with skilled craftsmen, teachers, and warriors. The status it enshrined was, therefore, hereditary. That meant once a potter, always a potter; once a soldier, always a soldier. Neither inclination nor ability decided one's occupation.

Like the classes that the conquerors established for Buddhist, Taoist, Nestorian, and Muslim religious scholars, they also provided for "Confucian households"—a good 100,000 in the south and four thousand in the north. They were supposed to act as a reservoir for mid-level administration, which needed people skilled in reading, writing, and arithmetic. Such households enjoyed privileges such as exemption from certain taxes, and they were largely shielded from enslavement and caprice at the hands of military officers. Nevertheless, they could not escape their low status. In this way, two aristocracies developed: one intellectual, and the other political. The old Confucian educated elite, proud of the culture and learning it had inherited over generations, retained influence at the local level. It survived the Mongol period, as did the large landholders with whom the Yuan regime was forced to collaborate; there was no other way to govern the gigantic empire. The Chinese elite faced off with their new Mongol and west Asian leaders. The latter had the advantage of power, but they were also hampered by lack of education and ignorance of bureaucratic procedures. The result of their policies was an unprecedented annihilation of creativity. In the form of the "Confucian households," at least, an intellectual reserve army survived that could contribute to growth and change. Neither, however, would come about until the rule of the Ming emperors.

The attitude of the Chinese elite in the Yuan Empire oscillated between obstruction, cooperation, and apathy. Wealthier elements escaped into sweet idleness and the arts or devoted themselves to pleasure, whereas the less well-off earned their livelihood as teachers, scribes, physicians, and fortune tellers, or they entered monasteries. Thanks to this leisured class, the Yuan dynasty had its share of calligraphy and painting of the highest quality, but the production of printed texts declined drastically.[12] Some artists tried to regain their lost identity through a "restoration of antiquity."[13] Drama and poetry found patronage and a public, and the sciences did not entirely wither and die. Alongside the Chinese astronomical office, a Muslim one was created. In addition, medicine,[14] mathematics, hydraulics, and other disciplines were enriched with "western" knowledge—i.e., Arabic knowledge, transmitted via Persian. Yet the spirit of renewal was slack.[15]

Among the scholars who were permitted to teach and do research under Mongol rule, the most significant was the Persian mathematician and astronomer Nasir al-Din al-Tusi (1201–1274). Hulagu had an observatory built for him in Maragheh (near Tabriz); it became a focal point for numerous scholars and instrument makers, some of them Syrian and Chinese. This gave the East a new scientific center, one whose knowledge radiated all the way to the court of Alfonso the Wise.[16] But nothing is more indicative of the state of learning than the fact that Confucian scholars were placed in the second-to-last of the ten categories into which a contemporary source divided Chinese society—after the common people and before beggars.[17] The civil service examination, initially abolished, was reinstated in 1315, but only few people actually attained office. All ambition was inhibited by the fact that the highest positions—they were now hereditary and endowed with privileges—were largely closed to native Chinese. The Yuan preferred to trust their own Mongols and other "foreigners." Although cultural exchange and the attendant production of knowledge were standard in the Mongolian Empire, Chinese scholars were hardly involved. For example, Muslim astronomy remained almost unknown to them.[18]

The late Yuan dynasty was a dark period marked by an apocalyptic mood, plagued by starvation, chaos, and civil war—a situation not conducive to quiet scholarship. Wild inflation, caused by a flood of paper money, eroded savings. The gap between poor and rich grew wider.[19] The thesis that the Mongol invasions were an important cause of the end of Chinese dominance in science and technology, therefore, has several good arguments in its favor. Opportunities for talent decreased, and with them the chances for innovation.

A Muslim in the Vatican

While Baghdad entered its autumn with the end of the translation boom, followed by a long winter in the wake of Mongol devastation, Muslim philosophy, science, and literature found asylum in cities in Asia, North Africa, and Spain. So did Hebrew mysticism and varieties of Jewish piety.[20] Cairo under the early Ayyubids, for example, accommodated the Jewish physician Maimonides (1135/38–1204), who acted as an intermediary between his religion and Arabic culture. Spain remained the most important gateway to Latin Europe for the latter—and with it the classical tradition it preserved. Moorish architecture reached its zenith in Spain and in the Maghreb; it was later exported to South America, and in the nineteenth century it was the inspiration for a new hybrid style. Echoes of the Arabic history of the Iberian Peninsula can still be heard today in Spanish flamenco and in the melancholic fado of Portugal.

In Andalusia, the *taifa* kings surrounded themselves with courtly splendor. Elegies and pastoral poetry have been passed down, as have works of philosophy and history, astronomy and medicine, agriculture and botany. Long before Latin Europe planted botanical gardens outside monastery walls, they were flourishing in Córdoba and Seville. Abu al-Qasim (ca. 936–1013), the founder of a rational approach to surgery, taught and experimented there. Called "Albucasis" by the Latins, he detailed the tools and methods of the art in his *Kitab al-Tasrif*. Ibn Hazm (994–1064), also known for historical works on Islamic law schools, sects, and the three monotheistic religions, wrote *The Ring of the Dove*, a masterpiece of world literature that ponders the theme of love with sensitivity and realism.

In Toledo, the capital city of a *taifa* dynasty, astronomical tables were worked out and used to calculate calendars and solar and lunar eclipses. The Aristotelian philosopher and poet Ibn Bajja (Latinized as Avempace) of Saragossa, was a long-serving vizier in Granada; he died in Fez in 1139. Ibn Tufail (1105–1185), a physician born in Guadix, also moved to Africa, where he likewise served as vizier, in Marrakesh. His coming-of-age novel, *Hayy ibn Yaqdhan* (literally *Alive, Son of Awake*), was widely read in Enlightenment Europe. It celebrates the power of reason but also enthuses about mystical union with God, thereby defending the path of the Sufis.[21]

Nevertheless, when the twelfth century passed, so did the great age of Arabic science and philosophy (apart from later creative spurts in central Asia and North Africa). An astute and influential attack on the philosophical approach to God had been raised early on by the Persian Abu Hamid al-Ghazali (1058–1111).[22] A Sunni, he achieved brilliant success teaching law in Baghdad. But then he abandoned his worldly career and traveled the land as a Sufi. In his view, inner experience and godliness—in this respect, he was a bit of a Muslim Luther—would lead to a religious renaissance, *nahda*.[23] Al-Ghazali's critique of philosophy was steeped deeply in "Socratic" skepticism about the possibility of *knowing*. He saw no way to bridge the gap between reason and the experience of faith. Thus he also denied natural causality. Instead, he argued, everything that happened—even the burning of a tuft of cotton—was the result of God's will. Al-Ghazali condemned al-Farabi and Ibn Sina as infidels and heretics alongside Plato and Aristotle. His opposition to philosophy culminated in the stance that it would be best if the writings of the "misguided" were not read at all by the people at large. Like al-Kindi before him and Christian theology afterward, he condemned Aristotle's teaching that the world is eternal. The position that it must have been created, on the other hand, necessitated the existence of a creator. Over time, it took on the quality of a proof for the existence of God. Even mathematics was suspect to al-Ghazali, as it tempted people to concede that everything could be proven by philosophy. On the other hand, he exempted moral and political philosophy from his critique, as well as logic, which he considered an aid to theology. For this stance he could cite Abu al-Hasan al-Ash'ari (ca. 873–935), who had recommended an intermediate position between tradition and reason.[24]

Al-Ghazali's Asharite position ultimately prevailed. In contrast, Mu'tazila (see p. 121) died out after renaissances in Buyid Persia, in central Asia, and among the Karaite Jews. It would not be rediscovered until the modern age. Did an early flourishing of reason wither along with it—to the detriment of the Muslim world—in the frozen wind of orthodoxy?[25] Admittedly, the only thing Mu'tazila has in common with the European Enlightenment is its "Greek" dialectical method. It was a thoroughly theological school of thought, and opposition to it was based on the (not necessarily false) view that knowledge of the absolute cannot be gained through syllogisms.

The final bookend to the great age of Arabic philosophy was marked by the work of the unconventional thinker Ibn Rushd (1126–1198), known to the Latin world as "Averroes." He was no less important as a physician and author of a comprehensive medical textbook than he was as a philosopher.[26] Like other Andalusian scholars, he urged the return to a "pure" Aristotle. Furthermore, he maintained that reason should be the judge over controversial interpretations of the Quran. Indeed, as he argued in his imaginary dialogue with al-Ghazali, it must lead to the same conclusions as faith—considering that the world and its first principle, God, are utterly rational. Not acknowledging causality meant rejecting reason. Ibn Rushd argued against "tyrannical" clerical authority and rejected theology's claim to be the master discipline. He viewed it as a mere tool of religion, useful for maintaining social order; a similar justification for theology was given later by "enlightened" thinkers like Machiavelli.[27] Utterly heretical appeared Ibn Rushd's idea that the soul was only immortal as part of the world soul, whereas its material half died with the body. Ideas of its fate in the afterlife, he maintained, were just stories useful to popular religion. In agreement with Aristotle (whom he called "the perfect man") and against Plato and Ibn Sina, he defended human thought's ability to know reality and not only its shadow. In doing so, he provided philosophical arguments in favor of empirical science.

Whereas Muslim culture combatted Ibn Rushd, insofar as it did not simply forget him,[28] he remained a source of inspiration and irritation in the Latin world for centuries to come. A student of the world, he too became one of Europe's teachers. Soon enough, he was known only by the name Dante gave him, *il commentator*, i.e., *the* commentator of Aristotle. Raphael put him in his *School of Athens*, which covered a wall in the Vatican Palace. In this way, the great Muslim thinker received a place of honor in the center of Christianity (Fig. 3, p. 21).

The Byzantine Empire: Learning in the Haze of Incense

In contrast to the East Asian world, four great cultures had the opportunity to learn from the Greeks and Romans: Arabic, Latin European, Byzantine, and Jewish. They made very different use of the ancient legacy, however. Similar to the retarding role played by Jewish orthodoxy, religion hindered a resurgence of the Greek spirit in, of all places, the Byzantine Empire, its motherland. Whereas Muslims worked feverishly alongside Jews, Christians, and even star-worshipping Sabians from Harran to translate and write commentaries on ancient works, and whereas western Europe embarked upon the path to modernity, the Byzantine millennium passed without any truly significant discoveries or intellectual breakthroughs taking place in the former home of innovation between Alexandria and Athens. The case of Byzantium acts as a reminder that, regardless of how brilliant and stimulating an intellectual tradition may be, it still needs the proper environment in order to have an effect. A broad middle class, a communal identity strengthened by membership in corporate structures, to say nothing of autonomy of the kind achieved by the European states—none of this developed in the Eastern Roman Empire. It was ruled, to the detriment of all intellectual freedom, by an adamantine alliance between throne and altar. The dominant role was usually played by the "apostle-like" *basileus*. No one could be made patriarch against his will. Unlike in the West, clerics were not allowed to hold secular office, the basis of political power. No head of the Byzantine Church ever toppled an emperor. One who did try—Michael Cerularius (ca. 1000–1058)—died on his way into exile. Only in the late Byzantine period, when the territory and the power of the emperor melted like snow under the rising Ottoman sun, did the influence of the patriarchs increase. The imperial coronation was as significant an act as in Latin Europe. While the emperor swore to protect the faith before receiving the diadem, in return the high priest of orthodoxy said a loyalty oath to him. The notion that the emperor was simply an administrator and not the master of the state, a mere *despotes*, was a fiction of imperial ideology that bore no relation to reality.[29] The emperor's prerogatives were never fundamentally disputed. The Orthodox Church produced important theologians, but it did not possess a closed theological system. Thus, laymen participated unselfconsciously in the interpretation of Holy Writ. If the *basileus* took a position on questions of faith, it was not considered a problem. "I am emperor and priest"—this statement is attributed to Leo III. And Alexius I, like Constantine in his day, was considered by contemporaries to be a thirteenth apostle.[30]

The short Macedonian autumn had passed without giving rise to a "great Renaissance."[31] In the meanwhile, the Empire had been reduced to little more than a regional power. Some peoples, such as the Pechenegs, it managed to put down; they exited the stage of history. Others were absorbed into the states then developing in the region. Ultimately, constant defensive fighting on several fronts exhausted Byzantium's power. Capable rulers like John II Comnenus (r. 1118–1143) succeeded in staving off decline. Bulgarians and Serbs broke off from the Empire in the final decades of the twelfth century, and Hungary expanded its influence over the Balkans. Byzantine power was circumscribed in the south by the Seljuks, in the east by the steppe empire of the Kipchak Mongols. At least the Greek emperor, his residence then in Nicaea, managed in 1261 to win back the capital in a surprise attack and put an end to the Latin Empire of Constantinople. It was a final triumph before a long period of agony.

Scholarship and science never have it easy in an age of iron. Under the Palaeologus dynasty, which presided over the Byzantine Empire's final act, writers cultivated the classical style, often oriented toward the Second Sophistic. Some scholars like the monk Maximus Planudes (1255–1305) set about translating Latin texts into Greek, such as Ovid's *Metamorphoses* and Boethius's *Consolation of Philosophy*. Planudes' work, however, would have its greatest influence in the West, where his writings, including a book of grammar, were used to learn the language of the Hellenes. He is also thought to have had maps copied from an edition of Ptolemy.[32]

Few people thought of learning from the Latins.[33] Byzantine philosophy—if there was such a thing is disputed—remained firmly in the spell of theological questions, the problem of the Trinity preeminent among them. Works like the *Suda* and the *Bibliotheca* were secular islands in a sea of theological literature. Psellus's history, praised above, was known in only one single manuscript. Even Plato, whose philosophy had found a home in the writings of the Greek Fathers a thousand years earlier, had to step aside for Aristotle. Platonic teachings were now opposed by Palamism, a sublime theology that rose to dominance in the second half of the fourteenth century. A student of Psellus, John Italus, was put on trial for heresy for applying philosophical methods to theological questions.[34] Byzantium's theologians remained exegetes, while the Scholastics in the West subjected sacred texts to logical analysis and critique.

Of high art and architecture, little survives. The imperial palace was left a miserable ruin. Only in the late Byzantine period did architecture open up to international trends. The iridescent mosaics and radiant frescoes decorating the interior of the Chora Church, completed between 1315 and 1321, provide a glimpse of the final flourishing of the art of the dying Byzantine Empire. They depict Christ and the saints with supple bodies, suggesting three-dimensionality. As such, they stand as witnesses to a Renaissance of Byzantine art in the age of Giotto (Plate 4).

The decline of the Empire was contrasted in its late phase by a rich tradition of historiography. At the same time, colorful vernacular literature appeared, including epic songs exalting the fight against the Arabs and the Franks, amusing tales, love stories, and satires. Further development in this direction was hindered by an all-powerful tradition.

Byzantium is a prime example of the dangers that threaten learning, intellectual progress, and discussion when religion's influence is too great. At any rate, the mighty Greek inheritance, rich in scholarship, science, technology, and philosophy, was poorly managed on the Bosporus.[35] In the haze of incense that hung over the "Second Rome," free thought and ingenuity suffocated. Burlesque adventure stories had to hide in the garb of hagiographical legends, such as that of Heliodorus. Religious hierarchy hemmed in all higher learning. The argument went that it would only fill people's heads with pagan ideas.[36] The spirit of Byzantium was meaningless for the intellectual, scientific, and technological breakthroughs of the Renaissance. In the end it played a very limited role, viz., as an archivist of the Greek tradition and an inspiration for (outstanding) art.

The Greek gene inhabiting Christianity, which nourished curiosity and drove the investigative spirit, only manifested itself fully in the Latin world. Soon enough, Latin Europe was thinking Greeker than the Greeks. As intermediaries of Greek literature and a stimulus to original thought, the translators and commentators of the nearby Muslim world gained greater and greater importance. In the West of the Medieval Warm Period, their works now found an audience in a dynamic society searching for direction.

14

First "Renaissances"

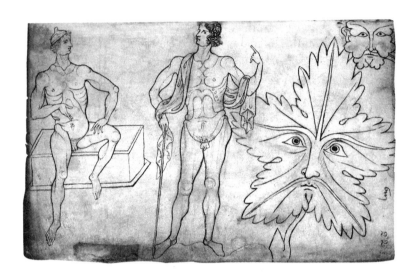

A Revolution of Speaking, Reading, and Writing

Latin Europe's true rise began, as has been noted, in the burgeoning cities and their soon-to-be-much-lamented money economy, with an expanding literary culture, and with war, a commercial revolution, and the ink state. As in every new beginning, chaos reigned. Nothing was certain. "If I had been consulted at the Creation, there are some improvements which I could have suggested to God," was the sentiment expressed by the learned King Alfonso X of Castile (r. 1252–1284).[1] The travelers had not yet found their seats; they had to settle in. The unknown beckoned, and dangers threatened. The devil's star rose. From now on, he climbed more and more often out of the pits of hell, assumed various forms to walk among the people and meddle in human affairs. He was a master of shapeshifting like the old Zeus. As the monk Caesarius of Heisterbach wrote, he is now a giant or a black man, now a big dog or a black cat, now a bear, now a toad or a dragon, now a gentleman or a beautiful, enticing young woman.[2]

The religious and economic fever of the age was mirrored in an intellectual activity that encompassed every field. It can be seen in the development of Scholasticism, in an educational movement that began in the cities of France and Italy, and in the discovery of the science of law. One might also place the rise of polyphonic music in this context of change. Everywhere, from Cracow to Burgos, from Bologna to Paris and Oxford, new thinking, new songs, and new forms of literature were coming to the fore. The discursive revolution that had been initiated exclusively by clerics was now also driven by laymen, many of whom even tried their hand at philosophy. The arts of writing and reading spread ever wider afield. Admittedly, it could take until the mid-thirteenth century for a city council in northern Germany to establish a school. Still, new grammar books were produced. People wrote, sometimes in splendid Latin akin to classical style, about the magical powers of gemstones, discussed rhetorical forms, and rhymed about love. Works on education and tracts about moral conduct and upright behavior were composed. More and more secular themes were taken up.[3] Marie de France, the master of the lay, turned her hand to "Britannic" history when she realized that so much had already been translated from Latin into French by others.[4]

These signs of a new enthusiasm for classical culture were accompanied by a flourishing of vernacular literature. Centers of patronage sprang up at courts, those centers of effervescent lifestyle which were also the germs of state development.[5] The age of "courtly culture" began. Entertainment was welcome, no less so the prestige that patronage bestowed. The splendor of court life sparkled brightest in France. Chrétien de Troyes even sent our phoenix to his homeland. He knew the origins of his cultural tradition lay in Greece, whose importance was clear to him. "Then came chivalry to Rome, and the heyday of learning, which now is come into France."[6] One reason for Francia's pioneering role was its integration in the burgeoning trade and cultural currents of central Europe. In addition, the Investiture Controversy and all the religious commotion it caused had not tainted the air there as it had in Germany and Italy. In both of those countries, the period after the scandal was marked by an aversion to secular concerns that dampened intellectual activity.[7]

Beginning in the twelfth century, more and more *chansons de geste* appeared. These were songs about war and heroes that could, for example, revolve around a romanticized portrait of Charlemagne or be set in the Holy Land of the Crusades. Droves of minstrels and *joglars*, troubadours and *trouvères*, as they were called in northern France, trailed behind the wandering tent cities of kings from castle to castle and from town to town. We know at least the names of four hundred of them.[8] The mere thought of them evokes images of singing contests and grand tournaments where jongleurs, bear trainers, and troubadours performed, of knights with blond curls in shining silvery armor and the noble ladies they hopelessly pined for, of banquets in candlelit halls, of hunting parties and intimate hours in the boudoir. All of that indeed happened. But such festivities were rare in the reality of the court or the everyday life of a singer; rather, the mainstays were *lack* and *want*. Many minstrels whose names have been forgotten had to eagerly perform for a few pennies, for bread and a bed for the night. Hope for reward and fiefs is the theme of more than one of their songs; nor was it always in vain. Moreover, the ranks of the singers included noblemen, princes, even a king (Henry IV) and noblewomen. However, literacy was in no way commonplace, not even in knightly circles. Still, it was new that more and more laymen were able to read.

> A knight there was—so learned he,
> That he could read quite easily
> In manuscripts and books.

Thus Hartmann von Aue described himself.[9] Considering the cost of parchment and scribes, only the wealthy could afford to have manuscript books made. Simply procuring an original to copy must have been a veritable adventure when it came to certain works.

The chansons, epics, and romances of the French enjoyed broad influence. They made their way to Spain, then to northern Italy and Sicily. The English court of the Plantagenets was known as the Athens of the troubadours, and rich Flanders soon took its place in the front ranks of culture. The Britannic cycle of legends surrounding King Arthur, which was taken to the continent by the Normans, found in Francia a new language and, with Chrétien de Troyes, a great poet; the episode with the Holy Grail may be of Byzantine origin.[10] German minstrels also took most of their stories from France. A poet from the vicinity of Maastricht, Heinrich von Veldeke, attempted a Middle High German version of the *Roman d'Éneas*. Contemporaries already recognized him as the founder of German-language literature:

> They award him the distinction
> of having planted the first sprout
> in the Teutonic language,
> from which wide branches sprang.[11]

Chrétien's Arthurian romances *Yvain* and *Erec* inspired Hartmann von Aue, and his *Perceval* moved Wolfram von Eschenbach to compose his *Parzival*, a work that is part translation, part original. The *Mädchenlieder* (literally "Girls' Songs") by Walther von der Vogelweide (ca. 1170–1230) still stir the soul today. Walther sings of love under linden trees, the flowers bent by the lovers' embrace. New is the informal *Du*, which he uses to address a *herzliebes Fräulein* ("sweetheart") instead of the formal *Ihr*.

The heroic tales were the expression of cultures somewhat further along in the process of state formation. They harked back to glory days like the age of Charlemagne, or to a distant, savage past enshrined in legends and stories. More recent events were rarely the subject, but they could be taken up. For example, Walther wrote about the imbroglios of the German throne dispute, and the *Cantar de mio Cid* glorified the story of the warlord Rodrigo Díaz de Vivar. The *Nibelungenlied*, in contrast, was rooted in what one of its manuscripts calls "ancient myths" (*alte Mären*). Like many heroic songs, it is a reflection of the period of ethnogenesis, of stateless societies, of invasions. Now, in the somewhat more refined circumstances around 1200, the legend became a breathless epic of loyalty and betrayal, revenge and love populated by complex characters like Hagen von Tronje and his nemesis Kriemhild. Blood thickened into memory. The struggles and sufferings of yore, of the legendary age of *grôzer manheit* (great courage) when the Huns were fought and the Burgundian kingdom fell apart, crystallized into a beautiful form. A similar instance of aestheticization is the tournament, which now became a glamorous show. Such performances hint at how bloody battle was sublimated as entertaining play. The tournament also doubled as training for the real thing.[12]

States and cities used epics and songs to immortalize their origins. Hunger for the past also animated the great many works of history then being written. Chroniclers flashed back to the prehistoric mist, to the Tower of Babel and even to Noah, or at least to the days of Charlemagne.[13] Their works evince the same murky germs of patriotism that can be detected in the *chansons de geste*— as when the *Song of Roland* speaks of *France dulce*, "sweet France." Singers found ancestors who turned peoples into families, from the Polish Piast to the Welf Eticho to Humble, Dan, and Angul, the progenitors of the Danes. According to Saxo Grammaticus (ca. 1150–after 1216), Angul was also an ancestor of the English. Saxo's *History of the Danes*, written in polished "silver Latin," preserves an oral tradition and ancient songs. It is one of the main sources for the sagas of early medieval Scandinavia, for the worlds of Odin, Thor, and Siegfried's Nordic twin Sigurd, the dragon slayer.[14]

The German empire was given a place in the history of salvation by Otto of Freising, an uncle of Barbarossa.[15] Otto portrays history as a moral event and views political development and decline as an analogy to human life. The title of one of his works—*Chronicle or History of the Two Cities*—consciously alludes to Augustine's masterpiece, *The City of God*. For Otto of Freising, the Holy Roman Empire is the final kingdom, with a line of rulers stretching back to the Roman Caesars; many people continued to hold this view after the Middle Ages had ended. A wide range of historical works was devoted to the fates of German and Italian dynasties. France's kings had their biographers, as did the crowned heads and bishops of England and the rulers of Poland. In this way, the countries of Europe found authors who, in the face of foreign threats and internal discord, helped to create an identity for their peoples—peoples who would ultimately grow into nations.[16] What might be called "pre-nationalist" tones were struck by Cosmas of Prague and others. Further to the east, the *Chronicle of Nestor*, whose first version was written in the isolation of an underground cell at the Monastery of the Caves in Kyiv, laid the foundation for all future historiography about the Rus'. According to its author, the *Tale of Bygone Years* (as it is called, after its incipit) aims to tell "the origin of the land of Rus', the first princes of Kyiv, and from what source the land of Rus' had its beginning."[17]

In the west, too, massive mountains of history piled up. The preferred language was still Latin, with Sallust, Livy, and Caesar as models. Events were often described as the result of miracles. Works written in the vernacular only appeared in large numbers in the Late Middle Ages; the fact that the *Chronicle of Nestor* was composed in Old East Slavic reminds us of the distance separating the "land of Rus'" from Rome and Latin culture. The oldest work of history of the northern periphery, Norway's *Heimskringla* (ca. 1230), was also written in the vernacular. The genre of urban historiography took its first ginger steps in a Genoese chronicle, whose narrative begins in 1099.

As the twelfth century came to a close, the cities also became the setting for theatrical performances. Even jousting tournaments were held in their marketplaces and thus in front of a middle-class audience. However, active participation was restricted to noblemen, who staunchly defended this right as one of the most important privileges of their rank. With the rise of new audiences, who were increasingly critical of chivalry and its fossilized ideals, the courtly love tradition of *Minnesang* faded in the thirteenth century.

Many of the chansons, romances, and poems of the French troubadours, whose words otherwise would have been blown away forever over the blue fields of Provence, were sung on by Italian bards and preserved in the libraries of the peninsula. They inspired literature and art for a long time to come.[18] They embodied the ethics and culture of a noble elite and provided a magical escape from real life. Both of these attributes made them attractive to urban readers in particular.

Meanwhile, traditional religious drama had emerged from the liturgy of the mass as a distinct phenomenon in its own right. It became more entertaining and sought to satisfy curiosity. A cultic service with God as the central spectator transformed into didactic theater for human beings, performed on stages erected outside churches. For example, the New Testament briefly mentions that women purchased spices in order to anoint the body of Jesus—scenes like this could be embellished into full plays. And when the peddler hawked his wares on stage, a familiar experience from everyday life came alive, making it easier for viewers to understand sacred events and feel compassion.[19] Similar strategies were soon used in meditation manuals, as well as by painters, like when they portrayed the passion of Christ with a modern city in the background.

The fact that biblical drama was now performed more often in the vernacular and contained scenes reflecting everyday life was an indication that it increasingly sought a middle-class audience. *Courtois d'Arras*, written in the first quarter of the thirteenth century, is only superficially about the Prodigal Son. Its comic hero is a rustic oaf whose ironic name, *Courtois*, means "Mr. Courtly." The play lampoons his easy life and, in one scene, portrays him being robbed by two prostitutes. Such an episode has nothing to do with the Bible; rather, it is cut right from life in the northern French trade and textile metropolis of Arras. In 1201, Arras also produced the first identifiable author of a religious play in the French language: Jean Bodel.

The literary landscape became more colorful and diverse. Secular dramas and comedies entertained the people and the court; coarse humor, drinking songs, and ballads of love and desire conquered marketplaces and taverns. Singers performed in contests and banded together in associations similar to guilds. Predecessors of Boccaccio and Villon hung around the taverns of Arras and the royal capital of Paris. One of the first was Hugh Primas of Orléans, a sarcastic slanderer and a brilliant poet born at the end of the eleventh century.[20] He still wrote in Latin, interspersed with fragments of Old French. He knew Homer, Ovid, and Sallust, was familiar with Plato and Socrates, and versified about wine, women, and academic wisdom. As the cities swelled, so did the cohort of his peers. Their names alone—one is called *Rutebeuf*, "uncouth ox," another *le Bossu*, "the Hunchback"—evoke a world of taverns choking on smoke and swimming in schnapps where a group of intellectual bohemians sought to earn a living. They sang about brothel-keepers, cuckolded husbands, and swindled swindlers; they poured derision on mendicants who preached against drinking, playing dice, and the poets' own fraternity of gamblers. In *Meier Helmbrecht*, a verse novel written in the second half of the thirteenth century, villages and farmers became subjects of poetry for the first time. The sly fox Reynard, hero of fables that have been passed down in countless versions, became so popular that he supplanted the French word for fox, *goupil*, and bequeathed the name *Reinhard* in German; he even appears in Chaucer's *Canterbury Tales*.[21]

The most popular secular work in the Romanic world was Guillaume de Lorris and Jean de Meung's monumental *Roman de la Rose* (*Romance of the Rose*).[22] It brought classical antiquity a bit into popular vogue. The authors knew Chrétien's lost Ovid translation and Prudentius's fourth-century *Psychomachia*, a spiritual battle between personifications of virtues and vices. The *Romance of the Rose* plays with similar coded messaging. Allegories are ingeniously employed to discuss the art of love, from approaching a love interest to making a conquest to, in barely veiled form, the consummation of desire. The *Renner* (*Runner*), by the Bamberg school rector Hugo von Trimberg (ca. 1230–after 1313), also uses allegory, for example the image of a pear tree "on the edge of a green field . . . full of bright blossoms." Those who think the experience of beautiful nature was not enjoyed until the Renaissance should read the idylls composed by this poet.[23]

Not only cities but also courts, monasteries, and cathedrals remained abodes of culture into the early modern period. This can be seen in one of the most famous sculptures of the Middle Ages, the Bamberg Horseman. Nonchalantly holding his cloak by his finger, he presents himself as the ideal knight of the Hohenstaufen period: a master of the world, set up in a cathedral. He is a king and a saint, if indeed the man portrayed is, as thought, Stephen I of Hungary. The age was not simply marked by secularization, however. Religious literature still ruled the field and would do so for long to come, the most popular work of all being Jacopo da Voragine's *Golden Legend*, written at the same time as the *Romance of the Rose*. The transformation occurred slowly, often barely noticeable, as when Christian heroes, Crusaders, and just rulers displaced heroic saints in French songs.[24]

A perfect example of how secular and religious themes, Latin and German vernacular could stand side by side and even intermingle is provided by the *Carmina Burana*, a collection of sarcastic poems, songs about drinking, love, and the Crusades, pastourelles, didactic verse, and more. Meditations on the transience of all earthly things are interspersed with sex and religious dramas. The triumphant money economy continues to provide occasion for complaint—"Greed reigns supreme and the greedy are in power"[25]—as does the rapacious clergy, rife with the sin of simony. Neither the Gospels nor the sacrament of confession is holy for the authors. One song depicts a life of luxury in a fictional order of layabouts, thus caricaturing the actual lifestyle of monks. The members of the order must sleep late, as morning prayer is forbidden. They must drink wine, eat roast chicken, and waste their time playing dice, an activity condemned by all moralists of the age. For those in search of a burlesque Middle Ages, it is to be found here as much as in the taverns and the marketplaces of Paris.

The *Carmina Burana* also marks the first appearance of the remote land of Cucania, or Cockaigne.[26] A more detailed description would be found in a French comedic story, the *Fabliau de Coquaigne*, and soon in other sources as well. While Europe's cathedrals were rising, providing images of the light-filled, heavenly Jerusalem, the poets created this earthly paradise in which not the soul found happiness but the body. Cockaigne knows neither violence nor starvation. Nature provides all in abundance, the inhabitants celebrate festivals, and work is forbidden.[27] Other countries soon heard of this wonderland. The Italians called it "Cuccagna," the English "Cokaygne," the Flemish "Kokanje." In German, it became known as *Schlaraffenland*, or "Lazy Land." It embodied an inveterate human dream, one that had previously taken shape in the country of the Phaeacians and in the myth of the Golden Age. A predecessor to Thomas More's Utopia, Cockaigne was a mirage that reflected the opposite of a reality in which want and violence were the norm. As one of the authors of the *Carmina Burana* reports, all desire was fleeting there.

> Since the stuff I am made of is a light element
> I am like a leaf that the wind plays with.[28]

Li Bai found a Western brother in this poet.

The Secular World in Ancient Dress: The Renaissance of the Twelfth Century

A gradual uncoupling of the religious and secular spheres began in the most disparate, far-flung settings. For example, canon law gradually broke off from theology. The Church prohibited clerics from participating in dramatic performances and, at the Fourth Lateran Council, in trials by ordeal, which were also unknown to Roman law.[29] Forerunners in this respect were Flemish and French merchants, whose rational economic activity paired poorly with practices like duels and trials by fire or water.

On the one hand, the separation of the clergy from all worldly joys, *werlt-freude*,[30] created a space for them where they could experience a new type of purified spirituality. On the other hand, once drawn, this strict boundary gave the secular world greater leeway to act as it wished on the other side. The literature of classical antiquity had a large share in this process of secularization. The epics and songs of the troubadours were pervaded by the spirit of the Romans and the Greeks. In the poems of the *Carmina Burana*, saints appear side by side with ancient gods, poets, and philosophers, even the scandalous Epicurus.[31] Sometimes the very meter shows that the authors knew not only goliardic poetry but also Ovid and Horace. Even certain passages of the translation of the Quran requested by Peter of Cluny ring with Ciceronian Latin.[32] As early as the eleventh century, the great Roman statesman and philosopher followed Macrobius all the way to the remote monastery in Llanbadarn Fawr on the Atlantic coast of Wales.[33]

In the person of Hildebert of Lavardin (ca. 1056–1133), archbishop of Tours, we encounter someone who could almost be called a humanist. An energetic political operative who never shirked a secular battle, he possessed sophistication and a refined sense of humor. He was closely connected to the highly cultured court of the Plantagenets. He was a virtuoso of Latin style. Open to the thinking of the ancients, it is a sign of his character that, alongside Cicero, he prized the Stoic Seneca in particular, and that he enjoyed camaraderie punctured with witty banter. His great appreciation for stylistic beauty, that is, for the form of language independent of its content, constitutes his closest affinity with the humanism of the Renaissance—his distance from it is encapsulated in his vituperation of curiosity and its temptations.[34] Gazing out from the chaos of his times, he looked with yearning and amazement upon the ruins of the Eternal City and the beauty of marble statues. "In ruins all, yet still beyond compare," thus begins his poem entitled "Par tibi Roma nihil" ("Nothing equals you, Rome"). His Rome is no longer a place that simply promises salvation of the soul. It appears as a symbol of political prudence and law, of military prowess, world peace, and education. New with Hildebert is that, in view of the massive ruins, he sees human beings as shapers of history:

> Man's toil could make of Rome a city higher
> Than toiling gods could wholly overthrow.

A statement of this kind, which gives voice to the proud self-assurance of human potential, supports the view that the twelfth century experienced a true renaissance.[35] People collected ancient remains. Bishop Henry of Blois bought ancient statues in Rome and had them shipped to Winchester. A certain Master Gregorius, an Englishman like Henry, occupied himself with measuring ancient *spolia*. The allure of a statue of Venus fascinated him so much that he repeatedly visited it even though it was two stades from his quarter. Attempts were even made to preserve ancient landmarks, such as when, in 1162, the Roman senate made it illegal to damage or destroy the Column of Trajan.[36]

Another man fascinated by ancient culture was Hugh (ca. 1097–1141), head of the school of Saint Victor outside Paris. In his view, philosophy was the "art of arts" and should comprehend all fields of knowledge. It was a discipline that doggedly explored the foundation of all human and divine things.[37] Hugh did not ask his students to read this or that oration of Cicero, this or that passage of Virgil's poetry, as an exercise in Latin grammar. Instead, he expected them to read ancient works in their entirety, to learn to understand them as literature, and to take pleasure in them. Some authors, usually clerics with knowledge of Latin, took inspiration from classics like Plutarch's (45–after 120 AD) comparative biographies of Greeks and Romans. Vernacular romances took up themes from ancient mythology. One author, Baldric of Dol, imitated Helen's letter to Paris from Ovid's *Heroides* in his rhymed correspondence with a nun.[38] Around 1170, Aesop's *Fables*, which had long been a standard text for teaching Latin in monastic schools, entered French literature. The protagonist of Nigel de Longchamps's *Mirror for Fools* is a donkey seeking to lengthen its tail—a captivating satire on the contemporary academic world; the model was Apuleius's *Golden Ass*.[39] Attempts were made to refine the knowledge necessary to copy Latin texts. In 1199, Alexander of Villedieu compiled a popular grammar book based on Priscian and Donatus. Around 1210, Geoffrey of Vinsauf added a manual of rhetoric, his *Poetria nova*.

Scandinavia also drew closer to central Europe and its ancient legacy. One sign of this is that the *Chanson d'Aspremont*, written around 1190 and set in the Aspromonte Mountains in Calabria, has been passed down in an Old Norse version.[40] Merchants and clerics brought with them knight's tales in Old French and Old English, knowledge of Latin, and works like the *Alexander Romance* and the supposed eyewitness account of the Trojan War attributed to Dares Phrygius, which became the *Trójumanna saga*. Still, some people, such as Anders Sunesen (ca. 1167–1228), archbishop of Lund, warned that classical poetry poisoned the soul.[41] This was just one of the border skirmishes between the earthly city and the city of God that would be fought on many fronts both now and later.

The number of manuscripts containing texts by ancient authors grew dramatically in Europe. A total of 210 manuscripts with works by Cicero are extant from the entire previous millennium; at least 377 were added in the twelfth century. Seneca manuscripts jumped from 68 to 172.[42] The poet of the century was Ovid; hence the epithet *aetas ovidiana*. Chrétien de Troyes is even said to have translated his *Ars amatoria*, or *Art of Love*, an utterly obscene work that was therefore abhorrent to the pious. Many songs and epics focused on stories from the ancient world, revolving around Thebes, Troy, or Rome's founder, Aeneas. Scenes from the *Iliad* were woven into tapestries.[43] The *Alexander Romance* was widely read. It was diffused in many different versions, from Spain to Ireland and Russia. Even Muslim rulers in southeast Asia were in the habit of tracing their genealogies back to the Macedonian king whom they called "Iskandar Zul-karnain."[44] Philosophy, whose most important masters taught in France, also drew on the ancient tradition. In this way, the inventory of ideas that Latin Europe compiled, commented on, and refined grew ever richer. As Bernard of Chartres (d. after 1124) put it,

> With humble spirit, eager learning, and peaceful life; in silence and poverty, to explore the most distant lands; many now endeavor to unlock through study what has long been unknown.[45]

Reason, Faith, and Novelty

The twelfth century was characterized by a manner of thinking that, as the British historian Richard W. Southern has argued, was convinced that Creation could be fully understood by rational investigation.[46] The divine gift of reason made it possible to grasp truths about God and the universe and thus to overcome original sin's darkening of such knowledge. The search was undertaken under the direction of the ancients, above all Aristotle and Plato, the latter of whom was often known via Boethius.[47] Yet the tree of knowledge whose fruit was picked was a pagan plant. The love of ancient literature was, therefore, anything but uncontroversial.

Berengar of Tours, who was active in Chartres in the eleventh century, and Anselm of Canterbury (ca. 1033–1109), often called the "Father of Scholasticism," defended reason and dialectic as paths to the truths of faith. The idea was to discover contradiction and try to deal with it using Aristotelian logic rather than denying it or glossing over it as earlier theologians had. Berengar dismembered the traditional teaching that bread and wine transformed into the Body of Christ during the Eucharist, thereby unleashing a fierce debate. His intellectual kinsman Anselm used ontological arguments to prove the existence of God. He was the first since antiquity to seek God in thought itself and no longer, like Aristotle, in the logic of causality, according to which a first cause had to be at the beginning of every causal chain.[48] In his view, faith and reason could not be in con-

flict but rather had to lead to the same truth. "I do not seek to understand that I may believe, but I believe in order to understand"[49]—this was his shorthand for how the new critical thinking worked. Nevertheless, all knowledge was for him ultimately knowledge of God.

Such thinkers focused their efforts on the text of the Bible, to which they ascribed symbolic meanings. They wrote glosses, commentaries, and commentaries on the commentaries. The notion that knowledge ultimately came directly from divine inspiration gave way to the view that it was necessary to reason for oneself and that the whole truth may well be unreachable.[50] Logic and dialectic, whose use was pioneered by the jurists, now took command in biblical interpretation, for instance in debates over the intractable question of the Trinity. The problem of theodicy—how can a good, almighty God have created a world full of imperfections and evil?—was approached with a Platonic toolkit.[51] The *Heptateuchon* by Thierry of Chartres (ca. 1085–ca. 1155) was a treatise on the seven liberal arts. Based in part on Aristotelian logic, it used Plato's *Timaeus* as a key to discussing the seven days of Creation. It is no coincidence that personifications of the arts were placed at one entrance to Chartres Cathedral, near Mary, the Queen of Heaven. Pythagoras was also depicted there (Fig. 16, above). What a contrast to the view of secular learning that ultimately prevailed in the Islamic world!

Geometry, another inheritance of Platonism, provided a concept of the infinite divine that would still be influential in the Renaissance. God was like a sphere whose center was everywhere and whose circumference was nowhere—this description comes from the *Book of the Twenty-Four Philosophers*, which probably dates to the second half of the twelfth century.[52] Alongside Scholasticism and the pagan classics that informed it, thinkers continued to rely on meditative practices and to search for God from the confines of monastic cells. In addition, somewhat bizarre forms of learning sometimes emerged. People used the Bible to study the geography of heaven and paradise and to discover what it was like in hell, long before Dante gave form to the Inferno with his mesmerizing images.

Peter Abelard (1079–1142)—combative, controversial, and persecuted as a heretic, a representative of the schools and their intellectual activity, and the tragic hero of the most famous love story of the Middle Ages to boot—embodied an early triumph of Scholasticism.[53] He turned it into a critical method that used logical conclusions and discussion to reach new insights. His chief work, *Sic et Non* (literally "Yes and No"), demonstrated this method by comparing contradictory statements made by great authorities. Abelard no longer viewed wisdom as a treasury of truths to be guarded by priests. His method recommended textual criticism and interpretation. He took up the old debate, begun by Boethius, over the reality of general concepts, the famous "problem of universals." The question was whether general concepts preceded the existence of things and possessed a superior reality, as the realists claimed, or whether—the nominalist position—they, like the Aristotelian forms, were inseparable from actual individual things. Abelard, a nominalist, believed that the universality of concepts was merely a sign produced by people via abstraction, and he investigated according to what rules meaning was generated.

This founder of modern semantics was one of the most important of the great medieval theologians who taught Europe to *think*. In a dialogue he wrote between a philosopher, a Jew, and a Christian, he began a conversation about truth and tolerance that is still relevant today. It culminated in a defense of rational discourse as a theological and philosophical method. His thought, however, elicited fierce reactions in his own time. "Peter Abelard teaches new things, writes new things." Thus wrote William of Saint-Thierry in a letter to Saint Bernard. "His books cross the seas, surmount the Alps, and his new statements on faith and new teachings are brought through provinces and kingdoms."[54] "New"—that was dangerous and bad for Abelard's purist opponents. To quote William again, "I am unsettled by the unusual novelties of words about the faith and new inventions of unheard-of meanings." Blazing trails toward a different culture of knowledge was controversial, even among the learned. But new paths were taken nonetheless, and censure—not unimportant, but not all-powerful either—did not prevent it.[55]

For the time being, only a few individuals ventured out into the intellectual unknown. The critical, curious spirit that emerged from the realm of theology conquered ever more disciplines, then nature itself, then the cosmos. In 1128, John of Worcester observed sunspots—the first European to do so—and he included a sketch of them in his chronicle. His compatriot Adelard of Bath traveled to Salerno, visiting the university there, then continued on to Sicily and thence to Asia Minor.[56] He studied Arabic sources, translated mathematical and astronomical texts, and wrote a dialogue about scientific questions ranging from botany to meteorology. Only in exceptional cases did Adelard see God as a cause. He searched for causes in nature and relied on observation. Others did the same. They studied Plato's *Timaeus* and read Boethius, Macrobius, and Martianus Capella. They asked how the world came into being, what the soul was, and how the senses worked. Stoic ethics, which they learned of from the works of Seneca and Cicero, joined Christian moral teachings as a means to cope with the chaos of life. Stoic physics took a place next to Christian physics. Plato's concept of God, which was incomparably more sublime than the notion of a "God the Father" or a supreme feudal overlord in heaven, gained more and more Christian adherents.

On the other hand, Ibn Hanbal and al-Ghazali also found intellectual counterparts among the Christians. "The monk's job is to lament, not to be a learned man," warned Bernard of Clairvaux (1090–1153).[57] "What did the apostles teach? . . . [It was] not to read Plato and obvert Aristotle's sophisms." He attacked the rule of reason over faith and the whole search for innovation (*novitas*), condemning it as "mother of indiscretion" (*mater temeritatis*), "sister of superstition" (*soror superstitionis*), and "daughter of recklessness" (*filia levitatis*). "God's watchdog," as he was known, was especially enraged by Abelard's trust in the power of his own mind. In addition, he admonished the theologian Gilbert of Poitiers for being one of those who, as his contemporary Otto of Freising put it, "adhered too greatly to human reason."[58] Bernard's friend William of Saint-Thierry and others attacked the natural philosopher William of Conches (ca. 1080–after 1154), teacher at the cathedral school of Chartres and author of an encyclopedic overview of the universal knowledge of his time. William was accused of daring to philosophize about God in his scientific study of nature. His response almost reads like an Enlightenment manifesto. He accuses his critics of being ignorant and of wanting everyone else to remain ignorant and, like rustics, ingenuously not seek after causes. "But we say that the reason behind everything should be sought out."[59] It was not only fledgling rationalism but also the reading of the pagan classics that bred suspicion. What use are "Hector's combats, Plato's arguments, Virgil's poems, and Ovid's elegies" for spiritual salvation, the Benedictine monk Honorius of Autun (ca. 1080–ca. 1137) sarcastically mused, considering that those "seduced" by them "now gnash their teeth in the prison-house of infernal Babylon under Pluto's cruel tyranny!"[60] Earlier, Otloh of Saint Emmeram felt like he was being tortured by a monster after reading Lucan.[61] From then on, he abstained from Ovid and Virgil.

Thus, Christian thought evinced the same tensions as Islamic thought. Nevertheless, the power of the purists was not strong enough to control the complex of conversations, thoughts, and ideas—in short, the discourse—taking shape in cities, schools, and universities, at courts, and even in monasteries and cathedrals. The vast majority of intellectuals—ultimately countless numbers of them—disregarded all the dangers and indulged in the literature passed down from antiquity. All over Europe, schools were established, often in cathedrals. Peter of Blois recommended reading the works of the ancients over and over again with increasing devotion, this being the only way to achieve the light of knowledge: "However the dogs may bark, and pigs grunt, I shall always imitate the writings of the ancients; these shall be my study, nor, while my strength lasts, shall the sun find me idle."[62] Women also joined the grand dialogue. Hildegard of Bingen (1099–1179) was the author of a visionary history of salvation as well as scientific and medical texts. Her younger contemporary, Herrad of Landsberg, abbess of Hohenburg Abbey, wrote about the seven liberal arts and the cardinal virtues in a work called *The Garden of Delights*. In the process, she also discussed the great ancient thinkers believed to have initiated the tradition: Pythagoras, Aristotle, and Socrates.[63]

Just as jurisprudence sought orientation in Roman rationalism, philosophy also looked for assistance from antiquity to gain independence from theology. Gradually, the conversation opened up. The price of a diversity of views was the confusion criticized by Stephen of Tournai, abbot of the monastery of Sainte-Geneviève in Paris. "Contrary to the sacred canons there is public disputation as to the incomprehensible deity," he complained, thus shining a spotlight on the discursive revolution in one of its focal points: the city of Paris in the time around 1200. "There are as many errors as doctors, as many scandals as classrooms, as many blasphemies as squares."[64] A little later, Pope Gregory IX (1227–1241) worried that teachers in Paris were turning queen theology into the handmaiden of philosophy.

The lines between religion on the one hand and philosophy and science on the other remained blurred. Throughout the Middle Ages and beyond, monks, cardinals, and even popes were significantly involved in the cultivation of secular, pagan learning. Efforts were made to organize theological knowledge just like Gratian, Azzo, and others had done with the legal tradition, producing *summae* of available knowledge. Authoritative statements on specific topics were drawn from the works of the Church Fathers and organized in collections of *sententiae*, literally "sentences." The most widely diffused of such work was the *Sentences* compiled by Peter Lombard (1095/1100–1160). Largely uninfected by philosophy, it was long a cornerstone of theological education and was still exam material for the young Giordano Bruno.

Gradually, the Athenian gene manifested its entire world-changing potential. No other monotheistic religion turned out to be as open to philosophy as Christianity, thanks to Saints Paul and Augustine. It was not the Crusades that had led to a profound exchange with the Arabs and, through them, the Greeks. Rather it was travelers like Gerbert of Aurillac, Adelard of Bath, and Constantine the African. Hermann of Reichenau (1013–1054), also known as "the lame" because of a medical condition that left him confined to a chair and barely able to speak, was one of the first to measure the universe with the help of Arabic texts. He is believed to have diffused knowledge of the quadrant and to have written a manual for constructing astrolabes.[65]

Hesitant beginnings gave way to dramatic leaps and bounds. The setting was usually the large spheres of contact that had developed over long periods of more-or-less peaceful coexistence between Christians and Muslims: Spain and southern Italy, as well as Pisa, which had excellent trade relations with the Byzantine Empire, then a rich source of inspiration for everything from manuscript illumination to jurisprudence. Alongside James of Venice, the first translator of Aristotle's *Physics*, one of the leading cultural intermediaries was Burgundio of Pisa.[66] A diplomat in Constantinople in 1136, he translated works of Galen, Aristotle, and others, as well as the *Ekdosis*, a synthesis of Catholic teachings by the Church Father John of Damascus.

In Andalusia, Christian Spain captured not only the walls of the Muslim cities but also the knowledge of its new subjects. Toledo, a city of half a million inhabitants, three hundred baths, mosques, and well-stocked libraries, became a kind of Western House of Wisdom; it was one of the most important relay stations for cultural exchange of the entire second millennium.[67] Here, too, patronage played an important role, this time provided by the city's first archbishop, Raymond. He gave benefices to linguists so they could think and write undisturbed by the needs of their bellies. They often collaborated with Jews who had fled the intolerant Almohad regime, as well as with Mozarabs— Christians who had lived under Muslim rule. Amongst one another, they communicated in the vernacular. One translated from Arabic into Castilian, another from Castilian into Latin. A few of them stand out, such as Domingo Gundisalvi and Gerard of Cremona (1114–1187), who is thought to have translated over seventy works from Arabic into Latin. Classical authors appeared in new Latin versions, including Galen, Ptolemy, and, above all, Aristotle. Herman of Carinthia translated the Quran as well as Abu Ma'shar's *Introduction*, a synthesis of Indian, Persian, Hellenistic, and Byzantine astrology that soon found its way to Italy. Outlandish texts were also translated, such as guides to prophesying with the shoulder blades of slaughtered livestock. Another was the *Secreta secretorum*, a tenth-century work from Syria claiming to contain secret revelations written by Aristotle for Alexander the Great. It transmitted magical and alchemical practices, knowledge of physiognomy, and rules for a healthy diet.[68]

The passion for translation was not confined to Toledo. Córdoba continued to host pools of translators even after the city was captured by Castilian troops in 1236. Carriers of Greek, Persian, and Arabic knowledge arrived in Barcelona, where the very productive Plato of Tivoli worked, as well as in Segovia and later in Seville and southern France.

A Millefleur Tapestry of Piety

In many cities of Latin Europe, cathedrals were now reaching completion. In the view of art historian Erwin Panofsky, their rigorously logical architecture expressed the same character as Scholastic philosophy.[69] As stimulating as it is to think that we might be able to discern a kind of overarching cultural superego, the age's broad diversity of discourses ultimately cannot be reduced to a common "Gothic" denominator. The times were characterized not only by sublime intellectual activity and rational thought but also by various forms of piety, mysticism, and Marian devotion (the mother of God was believed to intercede for the faithful in heaven), by pilgrimages and the veneration of relics. Yet Europe's religious history was also ultimately always a history of reform. Attempts at purification often turned violent and bloody, with books and people consigned to the flames. Old monastic orders took up the Sisyphean task of renewal, and new ones were founded in an attempt to oppose decline and secularization.

The Cistercians sought to find the way back to the pristine Benedictine Rule amidst the "horror" and the "deserted isolation" of the woods outside Dijon.[70] A good five hundred Cistercian abbeys between the Ebro and the Elbe, southern England and northern Italy participated in the cultivation of Europe. The monks prayed and worked, as stipulated by their Rule. They played a large part in the clearing of forests during the Warm Period. The plain forms of Cistercian Gothic architecture, which went hand in hand with a frugal liturgy, were another form of opposition—to Cluny, which in the meantime had become too wealthy and powerful to retain its innocence. Yet the Cistercian Order also enjoyed fabulous economic success, and so its ideals paled over time in the shade of mushrooming market production. Saint Bernard was barely in the grave when his brethren started being criticized for being overly materialistic.

Other new orders shot up in the rising sun of the Warm Period, including the Premonstratensians, noted for their extreme discipline. Heresies of all kinds also grew like weeds. Some of the devout renounced the world literally. Monks left the protective walls and full storerooms of their monasteries to live as hermits in a silent fight with the devil and their own flesh. Sometimes communities of hermits formed, and a few of these took on an enduring form. The most famous example is the Order of Carthusians. It began in a mountain valley near Grenoble, where today the Grande Chartreuse cuts into the woods like a holy fortress.[71] Its founder, Bruno, was an adherent of the reform program associated with Gregory VII, who in the years after Canossa was deposed as pope.

A religious yearning was in the air, one that sought fulfillment in a wide variety of forms, often beyond the reach of Rome's authority. This was the same period in which Latin Europe's intellectual revolution began, both in theology and in philosophy; this is when European thought started on its course for "world domination." The love of antiquity that animated the renaissance of the twelfth century gave a strong foretaste of what was to come a few centuries later. Yet all this was only one answer to the upheavals of the epoch. The sources also preserve traces of tortuous spiritual paths. They tell of heretics and of swelling bands of itinerant preachers roving the countryside, including strange saints like Robert of Arbrissel (ca. 1045–1116), the founder of Fontevrault Abbey. In his tattered cowl, with his naked legs and long beard, he must have seemed like a reincarnation of John the Baptist.[72]

Fully outside the realm of the Church were the Bogomils, the most significant heretical movement in the Byzantine sphere of influence.[73] They opposed all formalism, images, the veneration of the saints and belief in miracles, the

Eucharist and baptism, and they gave God two sons: the good Jesus and the evil Lucifer. An abomination to the Orthodox, they considered the entire temporal world to be the work of the devil.[74] From its origin in tenth-century Bulgaria, Bogomilism spread to western Europe, where a similarly dualist yet independent movement grew out of it: the Cathars. The name comes from the Greek *katharoi* and means "the pure." Catharism took the purity project very seriously, even constructing its own ecclesiastical organization. It became the epitome of heresy. The German word for heretic, *Ketzer*, can probably be traced to the Italian word for Cathars, *gazzari*. Innocent III proclaimed a Crusade against them. For the French Crown, the bloody "Albigensian" Crusade, as it was called—named for Albi, a stronghold of the movement—had the advantage of crippling the Provençal nobility connected with the Cathar church. The last traces of "the pure" disappeared in the Late Middle Ages.

In the second half of the twelfth century, people dressed in coarse clothing called *Humiliati* (the "humble") appeared in cities in Lombardy. They formed a religious community and preached although many of them lived at home with their families. Some preferred a monastic existence, and over time an order of priests formed.[75] Rome made sure that their pious zeal was channeled into a monastic life governed by a rule. The *Humiliati* were kin to the Beghards and Beguines of the thirteenth century, pious lay men and women who lived lives of poverty, chastity, and humility like monks and nuns—but without shutting themselves off from the world behind the walls of a monastery. Mistrusted, then esteemed, then banned, and then tolerated again, they were found above all in the cities of the Netherlands and along the Rhine. They came from all social classes but lived together, in their own houses or in enclaves that could be closed off to the hustle and bustle of the city. There, they worked for their living, for example as spinners or weavers, and cared for the sick and the poor. Their frugality held up a mirror to the wealthy Church. The same quality also made the Waldensians a nuisance. Their founder was supposedly a merchant from Lyon who, in the late twelfth century, renounced worldly riches and dedicated himself to a life of preaching. The Waldensians are the only heretical movement from the Middle Ages to have survived until today.

Heresy blossomed everywhere, especially in the big cities. According to the itinerant preacher Jacques de Vitry, Milan was a "hotbed of heretics" (*fovea hereticorum*).[76] Gregory IX went so far as to forbid laymen to own Bibles, especially versions in vernacular translation, prescribing harsh penalties for disobedience. He feared the ignorant might draw the wrong conclusions from scripture. Gregory created a special office to fight heresy, the Holy Inquisition, thenceforth the guardian of the purity of the faith. The mendicant orders worked in its service. The most successful were the Franciscans and the Dominicans, or Order of Preachers, founded by the Castilian nobleman Dominic de Guzmán.[77] In their simple white habits under black cloaks, the Dominicans demonstrated that a life of beatitude could also be led under the umbrella of the Church. They viewed preaching, pastoral care, and battling heresy as their chief duties. "Live like heretics but teach like the Church," was their motto.[78] In the history of the Inquisition and witch-hunting, the Dominicans were dreaded and praised as *domini canes*, "Hounds of the Lord." Their *Constitutiones*, on the other hand, are some of the most impressive products of medieval legal thought. Unlike a monastic rule—the Dominicans followed the Rule of Saint Augustine—these regulations were open to modification and could thus be adapted to the needs of the times. They gave simple friars great influence over the direction of the order and limited local institutional power through a clever system of inspection.[79]

The first Franciscans would have preferred to dispense altogether with a rule or hierarchy and certainly with learning. The story of their founder, Francesco Bernardone, who was born in the Umbrian hill town of Assisi around 1182, is emblematic of life in the Warm Period. It takes place in a world of great wealth and great poverty that has grown large and complicated, against whose temptations the hero rebels. Francesco began as the scion of a prominent family. He learned some Latin, a bit of French too—useful for the career of an international trader, to which his father had destined him. According to tradition, the voice of God called the young man to change course. He retreated to the solitude of a grotto near his native city to repent and pray, ultimately pursuing a life of extreme poverty devoted to caring for others. As he himself wrote, God revealed to him that he should live the form of life described by the Gospels. He found like-minded followers. They gathered around a half-ruined chapel in the middle of a holm oak forest, called Portiuncula (a gigantic Baroque basilica was later built around it). Initially tolerated rather than promoted by the Catholic Church, the order expanded massively within a few short years. Soon it included thousands of members. Women, led by the noble lady Chiara Offreduccio, followed the Franciscan model as well. Their community grew into the Order of Saint Clare, also known as the Poor Clares, which soon also had hundreds of convents.

Following in the wake of the Fifth Crusade, Francis himself took his message all the way to Egypt. His attempt to convert the Ayyubid sultan al-Kamil failed, of course. By the end of the thirteenth century, his order numbered a good 1,600 monasteries. They preached the Gospel as far afield as Beijing. The "Minorites," as the Franciscans were also called, soon entered into competition with the Dominicans.[80] Both of them sought education, indispensable for preaching and engaging with the discourse of heresy. They founded educational institutions (*studia*) and studied and taught at universities. Among the inhabitants of the growing cities, with their bulging underclasses and their intellectually lively middle classes, the sermons of the friars found a keen audience. They were so successful because they offered paths to salvation that met the needs of the overheated market for piety. Even today, the roofs of their mighty churches, under whose vaults their thundering warnings and comforting words of consolation once resonated, rise from the labyrinths of medieval European city centers.

According to legend, Pope Innocent III once dreamed that Saint Francis propped up the crumbling Lateran Basilica on his shoulder.[81] The message for the pope was clear: the works of the humble man from Assisi would keep the Church from collapsing. The story was incorporated into the *Golden Legend*, although now Dominic was the hero. Each version encapsulated a higher truth. Although both orders originated in frustration with the Church's pomp and worldly filth, they nevertheless remained within the hierarchy as servants of papal power. Many of their members lived out the ideals of their founders: poverty, simplicity, humility. In this way they buttressed the credibility of the institution to which they belonged, an institution then suffering attack on many sides.

Ultimately, the Franciscans, too, were overtaken by the fate of all reform orders. Simplicity? The Minorites produced some of the cleverest minds in Europe. Around the year 1500, they operated about one hundred schools across the continent.[82] And poverty? Endowments made the order rich. The legal fiction according to which its property actually belonged to the Roman Catholic Church served only a formalist function. The towering basilicas in Assisi dedicated to *il poverello*, as Saint Francis was known, give clear expression to the chronic failure of all striving for purity. They can be seen from miles away as one approaches the magical town from Perugia. Francis, who wanted to be the poorest of the poor, was indeed laid in a pauper's grave when he died, lying on the cold ground, in 1226. Yet with tremendous effort and at enormous expense, foundations were then laid so that a church could be erected directly over his secluded grave. Francis's radical imperative of poverty was immediately softened by the Church hierarchy, resplendent in its tiara, out of concern for its own well-being and in the realistic awareness that monks, too, are human. The fight over poverty continued. One century later, a pope condemned the claim that Jesus had no possessions, even dubbing it heresy (pp. 281f.). How else could the wealth of Christ's vicars on Earth be justified? Those who took a different view risked being burned at the stake. In the end, the Franciscans split over renewed attempts at regaining the purity exemplified by their founder. Some pious Christians lived out the Franciscan or Dominican ideal without entering an order, essentially realizing the purity project on their own. A few of these members of a so-called "Third Order" achieved sainthood, among them Elizabeth, the wife of Landgrave Louis IV of Thuringia.

Francis ultimately became one of the great saints of Italy and the world and is still venerated today, a perennial source of inspiration and reproach. Some people consider him a founding figure of the Renaissance, in the sense of a movement promoting humaneness and subjectivity.[83] His *Canticle of the Sun*, written in early Italian vernacular, reveals him as a master of a religion of sentiment. It is a movingly simple hymn about the Creation and about life. Francis thanks his *altissimu, onnipotente, bon Signore* for Brother Sun, Sister Moon and Stars, for Brother Wind, Sister Water, Brother Fire, and for

> our sister Mother Earth,
> who sustains and governs us,
> and who produces various fruit with colored flowers and herbs.

Indeed, it is not difficult to draw lines from here to the art of the Renaissance, delighting in the joys of this world but still mindful of its God. Nevertheless, Francis appeared to meet the novelty then erupting over the world with an old yet convincing answer.

The Franciscan ideal of seeking apostolic purity through the renunciation of worldly property never captured the papacy. Detachment from the world was first seen as a remedy for the Church, then failing in its striving for secularization, by a pope of the twenty-first century: Benedict XVI.[84] An exception—and here the dreaded year 1300 was already looming—was the pontificate of Celestine V, a farmer's son and holy hermit whom many identified as the angel pope of the last age of the world. The intermezzo ended after only a few months, however, with the abdication of the overwhelmed pontiff. Unlike Celestine, many popes of the time were utterly worldly men. They snubbed their heavenly bride in favor of earthly beauties, and they sired with their harlots and courtesans numerous children who then had to be supported with benefices. The Curia was highly imaginative in devising new sources of income. In the second half of the thirteenth century, it began cooperating with merchants and bankers who helped it collect taxes from half of Europe. The moneymen stuck to the body of the papal court like leeches, sucking the gold out of its veins. What was left over for the Curia—and that was still quite a lot—was more often put in the service of earthly well-being than heavenly beatitude. A powerful cardinal could draw on up to a hundred benefices to finance his life of luxury.[85] More costly than the patronage of art and the support of scholars were the papal troops. The successor of Peter used his "soldiers of the keys" to wage small wars against noble Roman families and big ones against the emperor. One pope, Boniface VIII (1294–1303), even proclaimed a Crusade against two of his own cardinals (they belonged to the hostile Colonna clan). Dante was not the only one to shake his head at the behavior of this "Highest Priest," as he called him.[86]

That the pope's authority was vested in words alone was already recognized by a contemporary, the Dominican friar John of Paris.[87] By violating this maxim, the papacy lost prestige. The Church, a worldly world power, lost more and more of the quality for which one of its most powerful popes, Innocent III, named himself. The gap between the pristine reputation claimed by the Church and the reality of its nature grew increasingly wide. The struggle between the Empire and the papacy entered a new phase in the second third of the thirteenth century, swelling to a battle of apocalyptic proportions. This time the richest kingdom in Europe was at stake: Sicily.

Sicily's Renaissance

The island's erstwhile, long-lost prosperity is still attested by the golden mosaics created by Byzantine artists in the cupolas of Cefalù and Monreale, as well as in the Palatine Chapel in Palermo. Just how European the deep south of Europe had by then become can be seen in the fact that King Arthur and Saint Thomas Becket found their way into the images decorating its Norman churches.[88] Sicily's kings learned the art of administration from their Byzantine and Arabic predecessors, adding their own accents to the ancient system. Palermo, which had already been one of the great capitals of the Mediterranean world under the Kalbid emirs, remained a cosmopolitan center. King Roger II, a Hauteville by birth and a Sicilian *basileus* and Christian caliph in one, resided there with his harem and his eunuchs. Also significant as a lawgiver, he employed scholars at his court and patronized the medical faculty in Salerno. Constantine the African (1017–1087) was active there (as well as in Montecassino). A scholar from Tunisia who converted to Christianity, he translated works by Arab physicians, writings of Galen, and the Hippocratic Corpus into Latin.[89] It was to him, the "Master of East and West"—he had acquired his knowledge in Kairouan—that Salerno owed its reputation as the *alma mater* of physicians.

Greek antiquity, which was still present in Sicily in the form of the temple ruins in Agrigento and Segesta, was resurrected in Roger's time.[90] Henricus Aristippus, archdeacon of Catania and probably of Greek origin, translated Plato's *Phaedo* into Latin there (albeit rather inaccurately). In 1160, he returned from a diplomatic mission to Constantinople with a manuscript of the *Almagest*. It was translated along with Euclid's *Optics*, Proclus's *On Motion*, and Hero of Alexandria's *Pneumatics*. We see flashes of "modern" curiosity, such as when Henricus Aristippus climbed up to the crater rim of Mount Etna during an eruption, disregarding the danger. Another agent of ancient knowledge at the court of Palermo was al-Idrisi (ca. 1100–1166), an Arab educated in Córdoba. For Roger, he engraved a map of the world on a silver panel, the companion to a work of geography which he entitled "Book of Peregrination of He Who Longs to Penetrate New Horizons." It was based on Ptolemy's geography as well as on knowledge gained from the experience of Muslim boat captains.[91]

With the advent of Frederick II of the House of Hohenstaufen, the beneficiary of the Battle of Bouvines, southern Italy became the most important emporium of the ancient spirit next to Andalusia. The king placed himself in the tradition of the Caesars through works of art, his "augustales" (gold coins minted after the manner of the ancient emperors), and manifestos. On the gate of a bridge near Capua, he had himself portrayed like Augustus, as the "living law" and lord of right.[92] His Constitutions of Melfi are a summa of Roman, Norman, Byzantine, and Lombard jurisprudence. The legal code was meant to help place royal law above oral tradition, as well as to ensure revenues to the fisc. It strengthened the nobility (as long as royal privileges remained intact) and defended the state's monopoly on violence by condemning feuds. It made the king's court the highest authority in the land. The Constitutions of Melfi were the first comprehensive codification of law since Justinian's *Code,* thus earning the man who commissioned them a place among the greatest lawgivers in history.

Although largely ignored by the Muslims, who were quite familiar with learned rulers of his caliber in their own ambit, the Sicilian did not go unnoticed by his European contemporaries.[93] Depending on where one stood, Frederick was either admired as the *stupor mundi,* the "wonder of the world," or demonized as an apocalyptic monster. He was a great patron of the arts and learning, a daunting ruler, and the builder of a bureaucratic state all in one. The same man who employed Jewish scholars, steeped himself in Arabic and Greek learning, and sponsored the creation of emotional love songs, the first products of the *dolce stil nuovo* ("sweet new style"), had his own son locked away in a dungeon. Vilified as a heretic by his enemies, he was himself a merciless persecutor of heretics. The Constitutions of Melfi contain harsh penalties for them.

Frederick found the ideal broker of Greek and Arabic science and philosophy in Michael Scot (ca. 1175–before 1236). From Ireland or Scotland—hence his name—he learned Arabic in Toledo, then spent time in Bologna and perhaps in Rome before settling down at the court of the emperor.[94] Michael's *Liber introductorius* ("Introductory Book") dealt with all manner of questions, treating medicine, astrology, meteorology, and computus. The universal treatise made its author famous, but it also earned him an unpleasant place among the sorcerers in the Eighth Circle of Dante's Hell. Some of the translations of Ibn Rushd's commentaries on Aristotle were probably undertaken by Scot in Sicily. His Latin version of Ibn Sina's edition of Aristotle's *History of Animals* helped Frederick write his famous book on falconry, *The Art of Hunting with Birds*. The treatise, which also offered a totally new study of birds in general, made use of Arabic sources as well. The emperor's most important resource while writing, however, was his own experience as a falconer, which he even credited above the claims of Aristotle, the "Prince of Philosophers."[95] Such critical treatment of authoritative sources was truly exceptional in the world of Latin Europe at the time.

With severity, soldiers, and ships, Frederick II molded his Italian homeland into a mighty state. With genius and taste, he made his court a home of learning. North of the Alps, he sought to forge consensus with the imperial princes. He endowed the Teutonic Order with privileges like no other, thus helping to forge it into a powerful weapon for the fight against the "pagans." He successfully prosecuted a Crusade to the Holy Land—although not, to the disappointment of the pope, with weapons, but rather with words. After negotiating with envoys of the sultan, the emperor entered Jerusalem. It may have been the high point of his life when, wearing the imperial crown, he stood before the grave of the Redeemer on March 18, 1229. He was under papal excommunication at the time, yet he still managed to capture the Holy City without raising his sword.

The conflict with Rome was insoluble as long as Frederick wore the crowns of both the Empire and Sicily, and as long as each side claimed to be the highest power on Earth. Nevertheless, like his grandfather Barbarossa, Frederick failed to conquer the cities of Lombardy. The victory he won at Cortenuova in 1237 meant little; a decade later, troops from Parma captured his fortified storehouse. They butchered the imperial soldiers and won rich booty, including the emperor's seal, crown, treasury, and—perhaps worst of all for the bookworm Frederick—his precious library.

In his final years, Frederick II led campaigns not only against the papacy but also against the clergy as a whole, against its pretensions and its corruption. His manifesto *Illos felices* evoked a pure, primitive church whose priests, imitating Christ, lived poor and humbly like the apostles. The last decade of his life was attended by a no-holds-barred propaganda war on both sides. News of the Mongol invasion nourished apocalyptic fantasies. Frederick no longer sought to free himself from excommunication. Deposed by Innocent IV (1243–1254) in 1245, he died in 1250 neither victorious nor vanquished. Sicily's crown was won by his son Manfred.

The Power of Philosophy and Divine Omnipotence

Alfonso X of Castile, founder of the University of Salamanca, also gained fame as a lawgiver. His *Siete Partidas*, or "Seven-Part Code," contained 550 laws, making it the most comprehensive effort at legal codification in Europe since the age of Justinian. Guided by the basic principle that "all laws of the world have always favored liberty," the code even formulated laws regulating slavery.[96] The court of Alfonso the Wise, as the king was called, was a breeding ground for fledgling Castilian national literature. Alfonso was himself a capable poet, and he commissioned many works, including a history of Spain. The *Alfonsine Tables* computed under his aegis improved upon the *Tables of Toledo*, the work of a Muslim astronomer. They were still being reprinted in the 1540s as an aid to calculating the positions of the planets. Arabic texts were also translated at Alfonso's court, such as the *Lapidario* and *Picatrix*, works containing magical and astrological knowledge.

By around 1240, Aristotle's entire corpus was available in Latin translation.[97] To praise him now seemed superfluous; in the words of one writer of the day, it would be like "helping the sun with torches."[98] A traveler related that an altar had been built over his grave in Stagira and that people venerated him there like a saint.[99] Despite many attempts to repress the teachings of the pagan philosopher, he, his Arabic commentators, and other ancient authors—especially Ptolemy and Galen—enthralled Europe's scholars. When they studied ancient manuscripts, they discovered a methodologically rigorous natural science; they found ethics that did not demand monastic asceticism but rather encouraged balance and moderation. They also became acquainted with a coherent medical science and a cosmology based on observation and calculation. The first to gaze upon the riches glittering in Arabic sources were struck by how impoverished their own culture of knowledge and learning was. From his post in Toledo, Daniel of Morley (ca. 1140–ca. 1210) ridiculed the Parisian *doctores* as "brutes" hunched over their massive folio volumes, their speech sounding childish whenever they tried to appear learned.[100] In the view of Plato of Tivoli, the Europeans had no authors at all in astronomy, and their books were all follies, dreams, and old wives' tales. "That is the reason," he continued, "that has moved me, Plato of Tivoli, to enrich our tongue with that which it lacked the most, by drawing upon the treasures of an unknown language."[101] Latin Europe was being invited to sit at the foot of the masters of Greek, Roman, and Arabic learning. By heeding the call, it increasingly diversified its landscape of learning. Robert Grosseteste (ca. 1168–1253), for example, authored numerous theological works, penned a commentary on Aristotle's treatise on scientific method, the *Posterior Analytics*, and wrote treatments of astronomy and optics. For his work on optics, he relied on Euclid and al-Kindi. In his view, the proper path to knowledge led through the experience of the senses as well as—a novelty—experiments and mathematics.[102]

The age desired summas; it wanted to have the full wealth of available knowledge prepared for it in clear form. Attempts were made to compile overviews of encyclopedic scale. The Dominican friar Vincent of Beauvais (ca. 1190–ca. 1264) compiled his three-thousand-page *Speculum Maius*, or *Great Mirror*, on the basis of Pliny and Isidore, Aristotle, Arabic authors, and recent travel accounts. It was a universal compendium, touching on everything from stones and herbs to demons and mathematics, anatomy, astrology, public administration, and world history. The book reveals a need for a basic ordering of knowledge, as does the similarly encyclopedic *On the Properties of Things* by Bartholomaeus Anglicus (ca. 1200–1272), which is extant in about two hundred copies.[103] The work drew on medieval bestiaries and lapidaries and their knowledge of the hidden properties of animals and stones. Bartholomew the Englishman taught in Paris for a few years and thus had access to the greatest body of knowledge of his day. He, too, deployed an impressive phalanx of ancient and medieval authors. His chief sources were Averroes and Aristotle, as well as scholars who sailed in their wake, such as Michael Scot, whom we have just encountered in Palermo.

Two Dominican friars emerged as the most significant intellectual heirs of Aristotle: Albert the Great (ca. 1200–1280), a forerunner of the Averroists, and his student Thomas Aquinas. Both had a profound impact on society. Albert was born in a small town in Swabia and studied in Padua. As the organizer of the Dominican *Studium* in Cologne, he laid the cornerstone for what would soon become the most important German university. He also served as bishop of Regensburg for a couple of years and taught at the Sorbonne. Albert and Thomas intensely studied Aristotle and his Muslim commentators and also added commentaries of their own.

For Albert, faith and knowledge were two different things. Regarding the Aristotelian doctrine that the world was eternal and thus not, as claimed in the Book of Genesis, created—a position attacked ever since late antiquity by Christian and Muslim scholars alike—he argued that the question ultimately could not be decided.[104] It was not his way to take a literal interpretation of scripture as a substitute for science. But he did believe that the study of nature and theology should equally be able to lead to *one and the same* truth. Still, Albert had to defend his occupation with secular science, even to the members of his own order. "Like unreasoning animals they blaspheme what they do not understand," he once jeered.[105] He earned the honorary title *doctor universalis* both as a theologian and for his study of nature. In the latter capacity his interest ranged from stones to the stars, and he would deeply influence the following centuries.

Thomas Aquinas was likewise a devotee of philosophy, but he was far less interested in the natural sciences.[106] His massive oeuvre had a powerful effect on readers, as he was more resolute than Albert in his attempt to effect a synthesis between theology and philosophy, reason and faith. In Thomas's view, however, revelation retained absolute validity. The mere attempt to drag scripture into the laboratory of reason held substantial explosive power. Philosophy helped to prove the existence of God or the immortality of the soul. Thomas's *Summa contra Gentiles* was aimed not only at Muslims but also at the Averroists active in Paris, as well as at Jews, who still held to the Old Testament. Although an Aristotelian, Thomas in no way subscribed to all the positions that Ibn Rushd had elaborated on the basis of Peripatetic doctrines. Like Muslim theologians, who considered nothing worse than apostasy from Allah, he prescribed the death penalty for Christians who abandoned their faith. Time and again, he involved himself in academic disputes. His unfinished *Summa theologiae* defended the legitimacy of a holy science based on revelation and reason, clearly demarcated from the speculations of laymen and popular piety.

Thomas made theology the queen of all disciplines. His *Summa* recapitulated what medieval theology had to say about God, Creation, and man. In the process, he drew almost inexhaustibly on ancient philosophy, Christian doctrine, and religious experience. In addition to his summas, he wrote commentaries, *quaestiones* (collections of debated questions), and other works on truth, the soul, love, and angels. His theology retained overwhelming significance down to the twentieth century. He also left an unholy legacy, however, in the form of his demonology.[107] Along with Augustine, his most important source, Thomas was chief among the authorities relied on by the *Malleus Maleficarum* (*Hammer of Witches*) and other early modern treatises on witchcraft. Around 1340, probably to commemorate Thomas's canonization, a Sienese master painted an altarpiece for Saint Catherine in Pisa. It depicts Thomas, holding his *Summa contra Gentiles* in his right hand, as the all-powerful doctor in triumph over the pagan Averroes.

As opposed to Muslim cultures, where religion maintained its power and learning independent of the Quran remained unthinkable, the state of affairs was less clear in Latin Europe. The ancient pagan world even made its way into the narratives of simple German city chronicles. For example, the author of an account of a war between his native Strasbourg and its bishop referred to Sallust's *Conspiracy of Catiline*, citing from it a passionate appeal to fight for freedom.[108] The spirit of antiquity roamed free in Bologna and in the medical faculties. In contrast, the theological stronghold of Paris, where the arts faculty added Aristotle's writings to its curriculum in 1255, became the stage for vehement controversies. Monks were admonished to strive for purity and asceticism, not engage in scholarship or teach at universities. Conflict between religious mindsets and philosophical, scientific views of the world erupted everywhere. Arguments were made against excessive reliance on logic and learning, with insistence on greater faith urged instead. Fervid disciples of Aristotle contended with equally determined opponents.

In the person of Roger Bacon (1214/20–ca. 1292), a brilliant outsider appeared on the scene. A Franciscan active in Paris and Oxford, he militated against authority and tradition. In their place, he advocated for methodical investigation based on observation, mathematics, and experiment and directed toward useful ends. Philosophy, however, was still to be the "handmaiden" of theology and the Church in the sense recommended by Gregory IX.[109] Bacon also recommended learning languages. How was one supposed to understand Aristotle without Greek and the Arabs without Arabic, or the Bible without Hebrew? He therefore wrote grammars for these languages, among the first in Europe. They placed efforts to establish the authentic text of the Bible and Jewish exegesis on a firmer foundation.

In Bacon's view, causality occurred in nature undisturbed by spirits. Yet God could intervene in causality whenever He wanted. Bacon occupied himself with semiotics, dreamed of flying machines and submarines, and was a pioneer of alchemy. He considered astrology to be a key discipline, its usefulness demonstrated by how it had helped the Mongols win their victories.[110] He investigated the power of magnets and wrote about the correct mixture of ingredients for gunpowder. He also provided instructions for creating a philosopher's stone (p. 652) and preparing remedies for aging (the recipe contained a strange component, though: flesh of winged dragons from Ethiopia). The optics of Alhazen were as well known to him as Grosseteste's work in the field; he is considered one of the founders of European optics. He seems to have conducted experiments with lenses, burning glasses, and a kind of pinhole camera. Bacon may not have been a medieval Doctor Faustus, and he was certainly a believing Christian, not immune to apocalyptic sentiment. Nevertheless, many of the tones he struck were new. And he paid a price for his boldness: he was locked away in a monastery for more than ten years.

The Church appeared determined to enforce its teachings against all deviation. In 1277, Étienne Tempier, bishop of Paris, condemned 219 "manifest and detestable errors" that he had heard were being professed at the university; the investigation may have been prompted by Pope John XXI.[111] Tempier accused certain scholars—it was probably adherents of Averroism as well as Thomas Aquinas who were meant—of having claimed that theological discussions were based merely on fables, that they added nothing to knowledge, and of asserting that only philosophers possessed worldly wisdom. Tempier's chief target, however, were Aristotelian physics and certain positions of Ptolemy, such as the thesis that all the heavenly bodies returned to the same spot every 36,000 years. They would then have the identical astrological effect, and if that were true, then history would necessarily start over again repeatedly; there would be no Doomsday, no Last Judgment.

In essence, Tempier was concerned to defend divine omnipotence, which was not allowed to be limited by anything, not even laws of nature. For example, he attacked the thesis (number thirty-four on his list) that God could not create several worlds, or (number forty-nine) that he was unable to make the heavens move in a straight line (as it would contradict Aristotle's law that everything in heaven had to move in a circle).[112] If the latter possibility were conceded, a vacuum would necessarily result, as empty space would be left behind whenever the Lord pushed the world a tiny bit ahead. Naturally, the hypothesis that the world was eternal was also rejected. One of the theologians Tempier probably had in mind, Siger of Brabant, had argued that it could not be proven when the world began, as it was a matter of God's free will.

Philosophy emerged victorious from the fight among the university faculties. It survived, as did ancient physics along with it. By questioning the supremacy of theology, it had attacked the clergy's monopoly on explaining the world. Paradoxically, however, the conservative opposition to philosophy expressed in Tempier's suppression also spelled the beginning of the end for the dominance of ancient scientific paradigms. The claim that God had unlimited *potentia* opened the way for alternatives to Aristotelian physics to be discussed. And such discussions indeed took place in the following centuries. Thinkers speculated about the possibility of empty spaces between multiple worlds. They imagined what the consequences of such a vacuum might be, and they conducted yet further thought experiments. Quite unintentionally, then, by forbidding certain ideas, the bishop of Paris had issued a license to think.[113]

Discussions about the universe and nothingness survived because, despite being threatened (as in 1277 in Paris), they always found safe havens. Roger Bacon's changing fortunes furnish a prime example. He was harassed, forbidden to write, and ultimately, as noted above, confined to a monastery. For a moment, brilliant opportunities seemed opened to him when his patron, Cardinal Guy le Gros de Foulque, ascended to the Holy See as Clement IV in 1265. The pope gave him every freedom his work required. Clement died after only three years, however, and so Bacon's freedom was soon curtailed. Still, the episode reminds us that unexpected opportunities for unfettered thought did arise in fragmented Europe. The election of a pope friendly to science and philosophy, or the succession of a ruler of the likes of Alfonso of Castile, sufficed to provide refuge.

A troublesome voice like that of Peter John Olivi (1247/48–1296), therefore, was not in any way silenced.[114] A critic of Aristotle, Olivi argued that certainty could only be achieved through inner experience of God. He was a staunch defender of the Franciscan ideal of poverty—that was suspicious enough—and believed the apocalyptic fight against the Antichrist was approaching. After initially being condemned by the leaders of his order, he was later rehabilitated by them. Pope Nicholas III supported him; Martin IV allowed him to be put on trial. Ultimately, Olivi was permitted to express his views publicly—not in Paris, perhaps, but in Florence and Montpellier. A cult of saintly veneration grew up around his tomb in Narbonne. Two decades after his death, however, his writings were consigned to the flames.

The same fate awaited the books of another free-thinker, Ramon Llull (1232/35–1316). Born in the Kingdom of Majorca, he was the most important lay philosopher of the Middle Ages.[115] Ramon *lo foll* ("the fool"), as he called himself, produced a prodigious oeuvre of over 250 works. Initially a wealthy, married man of the world and a troubadour lyric poet, his life's journey brought him to Paris and Montpellier, Jerusalem and Tunis. Llull wrote in Arabic, Catalan, and Latin, penned highly original works of theology, treated logic, astrology, and medicine, and waged a campaign against Averroes and his adherents. He believed the existence of God could be proven. He hoped to convert Jews and Muslims through rational argument and had two language schools established for this purpose, one for Hebrew and one for Arabic. His *Ars magna et ultima* ("Great and Ultimate Art") was intended as a kind of mathematically based universal science, an unparalleled attempt to arrive at judgments and find truth based on a mechanical combination of basic concepts and attributes. He also constructed an apparatus, a kind of logical computer, to aid in using his system. The concepts were replaced by letters of the alphabet and arranged on concentric discs that could be rotated. By moving the discs, new results emerged.

This overview shows that Europe around 1300 was anything but the abode of dull obscurantists debating theological minutiae with Scholastic sophistry. Its intellectual landscape was arrestingly diverse. Big questions were intensely debated, and both theological and philosophical arguments were exchanged—about what philosophy is able to contribute, and about what only theology is capable of grasping. One problem that occupied the age was whether the biblical God and the god of Plato were the same. In the end, it makes a big difference whether human beings are faced with a deity that resembles them, rewards them, and punishes them or a mysterious principle that it is difficult to pray to or consult. Dissatisfaction first set in when easy explanations were offered for the inexplicable, with everything simply attributed to God's omnipotence.

The prehistory of the division between religion and the secular world has taken us deep into the medieval past. The power struggles between pope and emperor ended with the universalist Holy Roman Empire and the universalist Holy Roman Church as losers. The Crusades initiated by Rome had ended in disaster. Bloody campaigns against heretics had not solved the world's problems either. The only explanation for why God let all this happen was often simply that people were experiencing the final convulsions of the Apocalypse. Over the centuries, however, this argument had lost much of its force. For the world teetered, but it did not fall. It seemed advisable to find a new way of looking at things. Some people found a promise of security in reason and experience. Others put stock in further reform of the traditional Church. Others still sought new forms of piety.

15

New Horizons, New Things

Individuality and Freedom

In the Middle Ages both sides of human consciousness—that which was turned within as that which was turned without—lay dreaming or half-awake beneath a common veil. The veil was woven of faith, illusion, and childish prepossession, through which the world and history were seen clad in strange hues. Man was conscious of himself only as a member of a race, people, party, family, or corporation—only through some general category. In Italy this veil first melted into air; an *objective* treatment and consideration of the State and of all the things of this world became possible. The *subjective* side at the same time asserted itself with corresponding emphasis; man became a spiritual *individual*.[1]

In this oft-quoted passage from Jacob Burckhardt's *Civilization of the Renaissance in Italy*, the age appears as a kind of proto-Enlightenment. And indeed, these sentences smack of Kant and his famous definition of that later movement as "man's emergence from his self-imposed immaturity."

Scholars today are still grappling with the powerful thesis that the Renaissance witnessed the birth of the individual. What is clear is that the "development of the individual" began intensifying in the twelfth century—much earlier than Burckhardt believed. And not only because retreating inside oneself gained greater credence as a pathway to God; that is an option in all times. Much more important was that a reflection of the individual, his feelings, and also his failings emerged in secular literature, too.[2] Walther von der Vogelweide speaks to us at times in the first person, as do the authors of the *Romance of the Rose*. Antiquity supplied the inspiration, and Latin provided the language for expressing it. The learned abbot Wibald (1098–1158) had the words "Know thyself" inscribed in Greek letters above the portal of his monastery in Corvey, knowing full well it was a pagan phrase from the temple of Apollo.[3] Abelard wrote a treatise entitled *Know Thyself*. His *History of My Calamities*, at once a tale of woe and his own life story, is one of the first autobiographies of the Middle Ages. Heloise's letters, with their indulgent reminiscence of lovemaking in the arms of the master thinker, are also indicative of a very personal experience.

Freedom of the will, which Augustine considered impossible in the shadow of an omnipotent, omniscient God, found its defenders. Thomas Aquinas was one of them, as was Albert the Great. The latter even said that human beings, with their individual intellect and capacity for knowledge, were capable of becoming divine.[4] Roger Bacon, one of the combatants in the dispute about universals, emphasized the dignity of the particular or individual, the *dignitas individui*. In his view, the particular surpassed all the universals in the world. In daily life, as he argued, when securing sustenance, clothing, and other necessities, we ultimately seek individual things; universals will not help us. What is more, God created the world for individual human beings, not for humankind. The individual, therefore, and not the species as a whole deserved preeminence.[5]

As a consequence of this view, greater value was ascribed to earthly existence, to life in this world. The Franciscan friar Duns Scotus (ca. 1266–1304) invented a new term: *haecceitas,* or "haecceity," meaning "thisness."[6] He thereby provided his order's mission in the world with a theological foundation. His somewhat older contemporary Dietrich of Freiberg (ca. 1240/50–ca. 1320), a Dominican, literally recognized the Creator of the world in man. In his view, it was the human intellect that ultimately substantiated reality. The intellect *made* reality by rendering it comprehensible in its rationality, by reducing it to concepts in accordance with Aristotle's categories.[7]

A further consequence of the ennoblement of the individual and the new significance ascribed to earthly existence was that more and more freedoms and rights in the state were accorded to individuals vis-à-vis the power of rulers. Cues were taken from the Roman Republic. In his *Policraticus,* for example, a theory of government inspired by Cicero, the theologian John of Salisbury (ca. 1115–1180) contended that it was a personal decision whether to be an active member of a polity. If a ruler undermined law and fairness, the fundamental order of a commonwealth, it was permissible to kill the tyrant. The freedom to question and doubt "as a result of the collision of doctrines," and to make judgments on the basis of rational consideration were human rights for John. Rulers were well advised to let others speak their mind and to guarantee liberty. "And so practice of liberty is excellent, and it displeases only those who live in the manner of slaves."[8]

In no other work of the twelfth century does that magical word appear more frequently than in *Policraticus.* It is a prelude to William of Ockham's (ca. 1288–1347) *Dialogus,* a work that has been described as animated by "the pathos of freedom." "It would lessen the dignity of the human race if all were slaves of the emperor," it argued.[9] Accordingly, Ockham denied the Church coercive power. In his view, God was the God of both laymen and clergy. The truth of faith could be found in every individual. Thus, Ockham also ascribed to human beings absolute freedom of the will—even those who rejected God.

Augustine had taken the negative but realistic position that political domination was a result of human sinfulness. Now, as noted above, Thomas Aquinas promoted the positive Aristotelian doctrine that the state was based on man's natural desire to live in society. Initially established in order to ensure survival, the state served the end of fulfilling and perfecting human nature. According to this view, God's eternal law commanded people to strive for happiness and the common good. Whatever social or political orders human beings created were not permitted to contradict this *lex naturalis.* It was supreme over all earthly power, which was required in particular to respect private property. A 1302 writing by John of Paris entitled *On Royal and Papal Power* emphasized this very point; it has been seen as the beginning of a tradition of thought that centuries later would culminate in the liberal ideas of John Locke.[10]

Individuality was on the rise everywhere. It became increasingly common for people to give themselves surnames, thus enhancing their subjective identity.[11] Artists portrayed themselves in their works and signed them. "Shout out, oh my letter, who I am!" wrote Eadwine, a monk in Canterbury, in a manuscript around 1250 next to a portrait of himself at work.[12] In the second half of the twelfth century, the first two names of composers of polyphonic music are recorded: Léonin and Pérotin. Sculptors created realistic portraits of identifiable individuals, such as that of King John "Lackland" atop his tomb in Worcester Cathedral, or the austere seated figure in the Capitoline Museums in Rome, which portrays Charles of Anjou, brother of Saint Louis, in the toga of a Roman senator.

Italy after the Demise of the Hohenstaufen

The hard marble of that statue corroborates the description of Charles found in written sources: a cold political operator. He was the victor over the last, vain hopes of the Hohenstaufen contenders Manfred and Conradin. The former lost the battle and his life at Benevento in 1266; the latter was defeated two years later in the Battle of Tagliacozzo and beheaded in the market square of Naples. Supported by Urban IV, Charles took possession of the southern Italian kingdom. A popular uprising against his regime, known later as the "Sicilian Vespers," brought the Spanish Aragonese to power on the island in 1282; Charles was forced to retreat to the mainland. Thus, epic plans for a vast Mediterranean empire encompassing even Byzantium, with Sicily at the center—a dream resurrected from Hannibal—came crashing down. The Byzantines had a hand in it, as they supported Charles's enemies in the rebellion. The acquisition of Sicily gave the port cities of Catalonia an advantage over their competitors in Provence. For a short time, Palermo and Corleone, where the rebellion had begun, won the same freedom still enjoyed by the communes in central and northern Italy. Nothing reflects the difference between the "free" cities of the north and the "subject" cities of the south more clearly than the fact that the Mezzogiorno produced no urban chronicles of the kind that flourished in the Italian communes.

The "Vespers" marked the beginning of the long history of the "Two Sicilies." From then on, the Straits of Messina divided two poor kingdoms with the same name. Only Naples, with its royal court, participated in the cultural development that Italy experienced. The rest of the territory, including Puglia, the power base and treasury of the Hohenstaufen, fell into the clutches of the barons. The Anjou did manage to maintain influence in Italy, and some of them won foreign crowns. But the Mezzogiorno, the south of Italy, lost its history. It will now exit our narrative almost entirely. It decayed into a Spanish province from which grain and wood could be exported, taxes extorted, and soldiers recruited. Its cities now had to defer to Anjou and Aragon, just as they had previously cowered under Norman and Hohenstaufen rulers. Trade was dominated by foreigners.[13]

In the mother country, Spain, the Reconquista had progressed apace. Portugal now reached the Algarve coast. Under the "Farmer King" Denis (r. 1279–1325), famous for his promotion of agriculture, Portugal experienced a period of flourishing in which the University of Coimbra was founded, the royal palace in Sintra was begun, and, most importantly, a fleet was built.[14] In 1336, Portuguese ships reached the Canary Islands. Castile had been in possession of Gibraltar, the southernmost point on the continent, since 1309. Alfonso the Wise ventured to send a fleet to North Africa. Of the former Moorish territories, only the Nasrid Emirate of Granada managed to survive, as a vassal of the Castilian crown. In the western Mediterranean region, Aragon began its conquest of Sardinia, then ruled by Pisa. Genoa, on the other hand, claimed Corsica. The maritime republic was sailing to the height of its power, whereas all that remained to Pisa were memories of imperial times—that and the gleaming white marble buildings of the Piazza dei Miracoli, clustered around the cathedral in which trade revenues had been invested since the days of the Crusades. In the meantime, the Genoese had set up bases all over the Mediterranean, in Constantinople, and on the Crimean Peninsula. They exploited alum deposits on the Anatolian coast and traded in slaves that they acquired from the Mongols.[15] Their ships set course for Southampton and Bruges. In the Adriatic and the Aegean, of course, Venice was a mighty rival. Maneuvering between the Byzantine Empire, the Holy Roman Empire, the Normans, and the pope, the Republic of Venice had achieved independence and resolutely pursued the development of its trade empire.

The city was nestled in its lagoon, unassailable, invincible, protected by walls of water and its patron saint, Mark the Evangelist. In wondrous fashion, so the legend goes, his remains came to the city from Muslim Alexandria. The miracle was proof of Venice's divine destiny to be the seat of a patriarch, and it was a promise of the prodigious deeds the republic would perform in the future. In the form of Saint Mark's Cathedral, a monument to cultural exchange with Byzantium, the saint's bones received the most magnificent reliquary imaginable. For the faithful, the most precious item in the cathedral was the Madonna Nicopeia, an icon said to have been painted by Saint Luke himself. It was supposedly captured in 1203 along with a Byzantine general's carriage, although it actually came to Venice decades later. Like Kyiv's "Virgin of Vladimir," it was one of those magical images that helped in any emergency and that endowed the cities and states that possessed them with part of their identity.

Divine assistance against the Genoese was helpful at first. There were alternating phases of open hostility, petty privateering, and truces. The Venetians had long been in the habit of undertaking their trade voyages with escorts, called *mude*, twice a year to provide protection from the Genoese and pirates. Pilgrims took passage alongside the traders and warriors. The engine of Venice's naval power was the Arsenal. In his *Divine Comedy*, Dante recalled the bustling activity of the *arzanà de' Viniziani*, the largest industrial operation of the Middle Ages, when depicting the throng of poor sinners in the blazing Inferno.[16] On the mainland, the *terra ferma*, Venice ruled with a gentle hand—via diplomacy and the contracts that secured its trade interests. Grudgingly, many communes were forced to bend to the economic power of the Serenissima and to accept its dictates; in exchange, they kept their independence. Only Ferrara, strategically located at the mouth of the Po River, was subjected to direct Venetian control, after being conquered in 1240 while Frederick II and the pope happened to be distracted by a quarrel. A quarter-century later, the ancient House of Este took possession of the city.

Italian chronicles of the time ooze with blood. They tell of wars between cities and of struggles between hostile noble families who viewed the communes like apples ripe for the picking. Communal offices, such as the position of *podestà* in Ferrara, often acted as a lever for setting up an authoritarian regime. Frequently it was the populace itself that helped place a strongman in power. Most communes proved incapable of constructing an efficient government, much less of securing law and peace as compensation for the burdens they imposed on their people. The response to chaos was signory, the government of a single ruler—*signore* in Italian—a model that became increasingly widespread beginning in the late thirteenth century. It first gained ground in territories where old noble families wielded power, such as Savoy and Montferrat. Here and there, feudal lords crept out of their castles and forced their way into the city. The Polenta took the late antique Ostrogothic metropolis of Ravenna, the Manfredi Faenza, known for its maiolica. Ezzelino da Romano, a son-in-law of Frederick II—*magister scelerum*, "master of crimes," one chronicle calls him[17]—brought Padua, Vicenza, Verona, and other cities under one regime of terror, whereas Guglielmo Boccanegra subdued Genoa. Some of the dynasties that would go on to play a main role on the grand stage of the Renaissance began their ascent: the Este in Ferrara, the Montefeltro in Urbino, and the Visconti in Milan. Lombardy, once the "stronghold of liberty," was now a "stinking pit" of tyranny.[18]

As the days of the Hohenstaufen grew short, sources began referring to the feuding parties as "Guelphs" and "Ghibellines."[19] The former may have gotten their name from the Welfs, the dynasty allied with the pope, whereas the latter can likely be traced back to the Hohenstaufen town of Waiblingen, then called Wiblingen. The terms first appear in Florence in connection with a conflict between two family networks that had nothing to do with loyalty to the Welfs or the Hohenstaufen. For whatever reason, from then on rival parties were distinguished by these names. Over time, it sufficed for one city or clan to adopt one of these labels for its opponent to take the banner of the other.

An epic struggle between "Guelph" Florence and "Ghibelline" Siena culminated in the 1260 Battle of Montaperti. Siena's victory brought Florence to the brink of destruction. The Ghibellines, who had only recently been sent into exile by their opponents and who now stood on the side of victory, planned to raze Florence to the ground. But their leader, Farinata degli Uberti, successfully pleaded the case of mercy. Yes, he was a Ghibelline, he said, but he was first and foremost a Florentine. The story—perhaps untrue but still a good one—indicates that a seed of patriotism was sprouting in the Italian cities despite all their internecine conflict. This sense of civic pride led residents to beautify their cities; later it would inspire the art of the Renaissance.

After the Battle of Benevento, in which exiled Florentine Guelphs had fought on the side of Charles of Anjou, their party took power in Florence under the aegis of Angevin steel. Yet the city remained restless. A guild regime was unable to keep the peace for long. Nor could the "Ordinances of Justice," the *Ordinamenti di giustizia*. These measures were pushed through in 1293 by Giano della Bella, a noble spokesman for the upper and middle classes, and excluded magnates from government. Membership in a guild became the prerequisite for holding public office. The "great" did not lose all power, as they were tightly interconnected with one another and their military experience made them indispensable. Giano ended up in exile. The factions were reshuffled. The Guelphs, who had long since fallen out with one another, split into "Black" and "White" parties. These were clustered around two families—the

Blacks (who would themselves soon splinter) around the parvenu Cerchi, the Whites around the Donati, representing the old nobility. The Blacks, having long profited from financial dealings with the Holy See, backed close relations with the papacy, whereas the more traditional Whites favored the greatest possible degree of independence. There was no end to fighting and constitutional experiments. Chroniclers lamented them ceaselessly. Taking up an oft-cited simile from Cicero, Dante compared his city to a "sick woman who finds no rest upon her feather-bed, but, turning, tossing, tries to ease her pain."[20]

The German kings seemed to have forgotten the land they once yearned for. In the Holy Roman Empire, the death of Frederick II initiated a twenty-five-year interregnum. The year 1257 witnessed yet another contested election. Richard of Cornwall, a son of King John "Lackland," stood against Alfonso X of Castile. Neither managed to prevail over the other.

The Holy Roman Empire and Its Neighbors

In Bohemia, the rule of the Přemyslids remained largely unopposed. Barbarossa had given the princes of the land a royal crown, and Frederick II confirmed the heredity of the kingship. From then on, the Přemyslids were among the noblest prince-electors of the Holy Roman Empire and the top contenders for the imperial title. Their state reached its greatest expanse under Ottokar II (r. 1253–1278). When the Babenberg dynasty died out, he was able to integrate Austria into his domains, and then, after a war with Hungary, he added Styria, Carinthia, and Carniola. Having become too powerful, he was passed over for election as king of Germany after the death of Richard of Cornwall. War with the successful candidate, Rudolph of Habsburg (r. 1273–1291), a count with massive landholdings in the south of the Empire, was unavoidable.[21] The Battle on the Marchfeld at Dürnkrut, fought in 1278, had consequences as momentous as those of the Battle of Bouvines. Ottokar died, and all of his territory except Bohemia fell to the Habsburg Rudolph and his sons. Ottokar II's demise was the Habsburgs' grand opportunity. Their dynasty took off under Rudolph's rule, eventually becoming a world power thanks to marriage alliances, inheritances, persistence, and a bit of luck on the battlefield.

Yet the Habsburgs failed to keep the imperial crown, despite earnest efforts to do so. It fell yet again to a mere count, Adolf of Nassau. He was deposed, however, his political ambitions having earned him too many enemies. In a first, it was not a pope that removed him from the throne but the same Electoral College that had put him there in the first place. This event underscored the dramatic demystification that had by now befallen the kingship. Adolf died in 1298 fighting for his crown. The victor in the struggle, Duke Albert of Austria, was another Habsburg, but he was assassinated after ten years in office. He was succeeded by Henry VII (r. 1308–1313) of the House of Luxembourg.

Inherited, purchased, or conquered "allodium" was now the actual power base for German rulers. What emperors were able to do depended on what lands, rights, mines, tolls, and wealthy cities they possessed. Jewish communities, whose protection and exploitation had been the province of the emperor since the twelfth century, were another source of revenue. The Empire itself had no tax administration, no legal system with stages of appeal, no army, and no center. Some cities and towns took advantage of the weakness of the monarchy to further loosen the ties that bound them to their ecclesiastical or royal lords, or to cast them off altogether. Sometimes, as in Strasbourg or Cologne, the result was war. The Habsburgs and even the urban nobility offered the townspeople support.[22] It took a long time for such conflicts to be resolved, and the outcome was not always in favor of civic freedom. In Trier, for example, or in Würzburg (in Franconia), where the nobility sided with the bishop, episcopal authority triumphed. Thus, the Holy Roman Empire remained a place of constant negotiation and conflict. The Empire was present where the emperor or the king of the Germans resided, where imperial assemblies or coronations were held. It only took concrete form in its insignia, in rites, processions, and customs, as well as in claims on parchment, most of which never became a reality.

This does not mean, however, that the Holy Roman Empire was one gigantic corpse. In the following centuries, it would spawn institutions, including the Imperial Diet and two supreme courts. A thick web of rights and laws made it a state. The silent behemoth, too weak to conquer anything, was at times invaded and plundered by neighbors. Still, for five hundred years it remained strong enough to survive. At least a stable procedure was developed for electing the monarch. From the great men of the realm, seven "prince-electors" emerged with the right to choose the king (who then had to be crowned by the pope in order to obtain the title of emperor). This Electoral College consisted of three ecclesiastical and four secular lords: the archbishops of Mainz, Trier, and Cologne, the king of Bohemia, the Count Palatine of the Rhine, the duke of Saxony, and the margrave of Brandenburg. The interregnum after the demise of the Hohenstaufen had strengthened their power considerably.

In Bohemia, after a decade of unpopular regency, the estates of the realm took affairs in hand and placed Ottokar II's son, Wenceslaus II, on the throne;

he would go on to win the crown of Poland as well. For a few years, it seemed he would revive the fortunes of the Přemyslid dynasty, especially since he obtained the Hungarian crown for his son after the Árpáds died out, and with it the crown of Croatia, which had been subject to Hungary since the early twelfth century. But Wenceslaus II died in 1305, and his son Wenceslaus III was murdered in 1306. That was the end of the family line, whose power had once reached from Prague to Pordenone. In Hungary, Charles Robert of Anjou ascended to the throne. Under his dynasty, which ruled for eighty years, Hungary drew closer to the cultural spheres of the west and the south. As for the Piasts in Poland, they enjoyed a phase of consolidation but were ultimately diminished by the Teutonic Knights.

The Teutonic Order had created a state under papal suzerainty on territory inhabited by the Old Prussians and other pagan peoples. With Marienburg Castle as the residence of its grand master, it stretched from Danzig (now Gdańsk) to Reval (now Tallinn). In 1237, it absorbed the Brothers of the Sword, who had theretofore ruled Livonia.[23] German settlers and Old Prussians who converted to Christianity in time (i.e., before being forced to do so) comprised an upper class in the State of the Teutonic Knights. This was the root of the later Prussian nobility. Trade and banking were concentrated in cities that possessed their own administration and often their own courts and mints as well.

The great power of the day, however, was Capetian France. Philip IV the Fair (r. 1285–1314) had to mount a new defense against the English vassals. He strengthened his state with the help of a group of advisors chosen on the basis of ability, not birth. It even included jurists of townsfolk stock.[24] He vastly expanded the royal domain. He married Joan I of Navarre, countess of economically prosperous Champaign, thus acquiring her inheritance. And he strove for legal titles of the Holy Roman Empire. To obtain the Kingdom of Burgundy, which had belonged to the Empire since 1033, he became the latter's vassal. The forces of Flanders, however, composed mostly of craftsmen and farmers, managed to defy him. In 1302 at the "Battle of the Golden Spurs" near Kortrijk, they destroyed an army of French knights in shining armor. Although Philip soon took his revenge, the Flemish cities preserved their broad independence. To raise money for his wars, the king taxed the clergy and stole from the Jews, banishing them or seizing their property. Additional gains came from confiscating the property of the Knights Templar. The pope ultimately supported the dissolution of the order, which had become a law unto itself in France. The grand master and many other Templars were condemned as heretics or demon worshippers and burned at the stake.

In England, a group of barons formed that was charged with ensuring that the provisions of Magna Carta were respected—a kind of forerunner to Parliament. Although it was initially hard to distinguish from a royal council, it developed into an independent body. The costs of the fights for Wales and the rest of England's continental possessions forced the king to seek a settlement with the aristocracy. In 1258, at a meeting in Oxford called without the king's consent, the barons sought to institutionalize *parlemenz*, in the sense of "discussions"; it might have been the first time the word was used in this way.[25] The "Provisions of Oxford" called for such assemblies to take place three times a year. The king managed to triumph over the champions of horizontal power in the "Second Barons' War," but he was prudent enough to confirm Magna Carta and to recognize the main features of the new constitutional reality. The assemblies also included knights, often mere "freemen," as representatives of the counties, as well as "burgesses," i.e., free townspeople, and they defended their interests. In this way, a principle of Roman law occasionally cited in connection with tax demands now took force: "What touches all, should be approved by all."[26] They not only talked about money but also censured abuses in local administration and discussed questions of foreign policy. Yet the king's need for funds—occasioned, for example, by wars against the intractable Scots and the Welsh—remained the greatest lever of horizontal power. Assembling in this manner became an established practice. In this way, *parlemenz* gradually evolved into Parliament. In the following century, it even had the power to depose a king: Edward II. Nevertheless, as remarked by one keen observer, the French diplomat Philippe de Commynes (ca. 1447–1511), by levying taxes for the English kings, Parliament increased the power of those very kings.[27]

Kings under the Midnight Sun and a Prince on the Moskva

State formation also occurred in Scandinavia amidst severe convulsions.[28] For example, when the Norwegian King Magnus IV (r. 1130–1135) was captured by his opponents, he was castrated and blinded. They also chopped off one of his feet. The Northmen only obtained a sacral sheen for their kingship late in the day. The first royal coronation in the north took place in 1163 or 1164 in Bergen in Norway, when the archbishop of Nidaros crowned and anointed Magnus V. A coronation took place in Denmark a few years later, in Sweden in 1210. Denmark's kings were a thorn in the side not only of foreign enemies but also of stubborn nobles and even their own brothers. Under Christopher I (r. 1252–1259), Denmark experienced its own version of the Investiture Controversy.

Archbishop Jakob Erlandsen claimed to be the highest power in the realm, with the right even to name the heir to the throne. In the end, ecclesiastical power succumbed. The crown remained weak, however, giving the nobility the freedom it desired and leading the state into anarchy. Only in the middle of the following century did Denmark enjoy a period of calm.

In Norway—a thinly populated, agrarian country with few cities and perhaps 400,000 souls—the Church also got heavily involved in conflicts over succession. After a series of civil wars fought on sea and land, King Haakon IV Haakonsson (r. 1217–1263) obtained recognition for his rule from Rome. In the end, he succeeded in transforming his kingship into a hereditary monarchy based on primogeniture. Iceland and Greenland came under the sovereignty of the crown. The disputed Hebrides, however, were lost to Scotland under his successor. Magnus VI (r. 1263–1280), known as the "Law-mender," created a legal code for the whole country—it is still partially valid in Iceland—that guaranteed protections to foreign traders and abolished serfdom. Magnus also gained fame as a military reformer and founder of a diplomatic network whose web extended all the way to North Africa. The elective monarchy of neighboring Sweden, which long resembled a patchwork of independent territories, was consolidated under Birger Jarl (reigned ca. 1248–1266). He subdued the nobility and undertook a Crusade to win control of Finland's forests, seas, and pagan population. The attempt to expand Swedish influence all the way to the lands of the Rus' was halted outside Novgorod, as noted above. A synod in Skänninge effected the division of ecclesiastical and secular law and—through the introduction of clerical celibacy—of the clergy and the laity.[29] In the sequel, the Church gained exemption from taxation and the right to appoint bishops without consultation with the crown. Thanks to the establishment of the archbishoprics of Lund, Trondheim, and Uppsala, the states developing in Scandinavia managed to escape the gravity of Hamburg and Bremen by the twelfth century. As opposed to most of the countries in east-central Europe, here the principle of individual succession was followed, with the oldest son inheriting the entire kingdom. With the outcome clear, there was no longer any reason for siblings to butcher each other after the death of a king. The immortality of the state was guaranteed by general assemblies of the realm. Administrative organs were developed, their authority slowly extending even to the hinterland, and laws were compiled.

Further east, Lithuania withstood the Teutonic Knights as Novgorod had before. Around 1290, after decades of inner turmoil following the death of its first Christian ruler, King Mindaugas (r. 1238–1263), the last reserve of European paganism began its rise as a major power.

In Russian lands, territorial princes fell to fighting one another after Alexander Nevsky's death in 1263. These rifts provided the Mongol khans with the opportunity to get involved and strengthen their dominion. Yet a power was growing that would not only stop the Lithuanians but also the Tatars: Moscow. The small city, located along the trade route between the Upper Volga and the Dnieper, had been founded during the Warm Period. Its first kremlin, built of wood, dated to the second half of the twelfth century. Under the rule of a branch of the Rurikids that ran through Alexander Nevsky, Moscow's influence now reached the borders of Lithuania, which had absorbed territories once belonging to Kyivan Rus'.

Population growth and Mongol invasions pushed new settlers in Moscow's direction. The city's potentates ate into the surrounding territory in a leisurely fashion, taking a town here, a fortress there. Their princely authority still depended utterly on the Khan of the Golden Horde, though. If they were given an audience in Sarai—a city then animated by Italian merchants but since disappeared, near modern Astrakhan—they had to grovel in the dust to perform the kowtow.[30] Not everyone survived such a visit. The Mongols knew how to rule with ferocity. But they also imported technological expertise from the Arabs, including the science of building dams. For their part, the Rus' learned from the Tatars how to administer a state, collect poll taxes, and run a courier system.

In summary, between the Atlantic Ocean and the Moskva River, the outlines of the modern system of states were gradually emerging. The continuing efforts of the Teutonic Order and the Scandinavian kings to Christianize pagan lands on the Baltic Sea enlarged the realm of possibilities for Latin Europe. In Warmia (also known as Ermland), one of the region's four bishoprics established by Innocent IV, Copernicus would one day earn his living—as Immanuel Kant would later in Königsberg (now Kaliningrad). If Copernicus had been born in Smolensk or Constantinople, Earth would have maintained its place in the middle of the universe for much longer. And one can imagine Kant in Prague, Berlin, or eighteenth-century Paris, but not in Vladimir or Kyiv.

Several European rulers of the age earned considerable, undisputed fame as lawgivers, institutionalizing customs as statutes and compiling law codes. They include Frederick II and his Constitutions of Melfi, Alfonso of Castile as the patron of the *Siete Partidas*, Magnus VI of Norway, Saint Louis with his *ordonnances*, and the English King Edward I. The latter's statutes regulated coinage and the sale of property and set limits to ecclesiastical jurisdiction. All these measures were reactions to the expanding importance of trade and the money economy, and they fostered legal certainty.

Furthermore, the larger cities on the periphery of Latin Europe had long participated in the culture of the center and the south. Nidaros Cathedral in Trondheim, for example, reveals the influence of the cathedrals of Lincoln and Canterbury. Prague, which grew in no small part thanks to the influx of German merchants and colonists, was in the process of becoming a Gothic city. Its castle, whose upper story contained a grand hall, was home to an illustrious court. It is where Ulrich von dem Türlin worked on his revision and expansion of Wolfram von Eschenbach's chivalric epic *Willehalm*. The vain Heinrich von Meißen, nicknamed "Frauenlob" (literally "praise of women"), also found patronage there.

The identity of the states was provided with a firm foundation. Historical, "real" origins emerged from the mists of myth. Individuals whose existence is attested in the sources appeared on the stage: warriors took their place next to saints and prehistoric heroes, and events that actually happened were memorialized in the calendars. Alexander Nevsky, declared a saint at the end of his century, became Russia's national hero. The Cid cemented his place in Spain's national memory. Flanders still celebrates the victory at Kortrijk as a holiday today, and the Germans spirited away the Sicilian Frederick II to the Kyffhäuser, a summit in the Harz Mountains. There it was said he (although legend transformed him into his grandfather Barbarossa) would sleep until his empire was united, at which point he would return.

The World Gets Bigger: Off to Asia!

Genoa, ca. 1298. We do not know how Messer Marco Polo, a merchant from Venice, ended up in a Genoese prison after a long, adventurous voyage. At any rate, he found a good way to pass the time in his disagreeable situation: he dictated his memoirs to a fellow prisoner, a Pisan named Rustichello.

> Emperors and kings, dukes and marquises, counts, knights, and townsfolk, and all people who wish to know the various races of men and the peculiarities of the various regions of the world, take this book and have it read to you.

Thus, Rustichello entices the reader in the prologue.

> Here you will find all the great wonders and curiosities of Greater Armenia and Persia, of the Tatars and of India, and of many other territories. Our book will relate them to you plainly in due order, as they were related by

Messer Marco Polo, a wise and noble citizen of Venice, who has seen them with his own eyes. There is also much here that he has not seen but has heard from men of credit and veracity. We will set down things seen as seen, tidings heard as heard, so that our book may be an accurate record, free from any sort of fabrication. And all who read the book or hear it may do so with full confidence, because it contains nothing but the truth. For I would have you know that from the time when our Lord God formed Adam our first parent with His hands down to this day there has been no man, Christian or Pagan, Tatar or Indian, or of any race whatsoever, who has known or explored so many of the various parts of the world and of its great wonders as this same Messer Marco Polo.[31]

The ghostwriter had earned his literary spurs as an editor of courtly romances, and he knew how to give Marco's account an elegant form. He wrote in French, still *the* language of vernacular literature at the time. Under his pen, the work's great hero Kublai Khan, who outshines all other rulers of the globe in power and glory, speaks like King Arthur conversing with Tristan, and a cavalry battle of Mongol horseman turns into a knightly contest. Nevertheless, this book about the "various regions of the world," later usually known as *Il Milione*, probably recounts actual experiences. It provided Europeans with a glimpse of unheard-of marvels: immeasurable wealth and gigantic cities, foreign customs, and fabulous creatures like the Roc, an enormous legendary bird capable of carrying an elephant through the air. Whether Marco Polo looked upon the wonders of Asia more with the eyes of a merchant, a courtier, or a tax collector—an office he says he held for the Great Khan—we do not know. What is clear is that the man given a voice by a Tuscan troubadour knew how to be astonished. His curiosity appears to know no bounds. In Rustichello's description,

> Messer Marco observed more of the peculiarities of this part of the world than any other man, because he traveled more widely in these outlandish regions than any man who was ever born, and also because he gave his mind more intently to observing them.[32]

After one and a half thousand years, Europe had another Herodotus. It was fascinated by his report, copied it again and again, translated it, and later had it printed. But what about journeys in the other direction?

The medieval Near and Far East also had its share of travelers and writers of travelogues.[33] There was Abraham ben Jacob and al-Biruni, mentioned above, as well as Ibn Fadlan, who visited the Volga Bulgars in the tenth century as part of an embassy from the caliph. Ibn Jubayr (1145–1217) traveled across the Muslim world from Ceuta to Mosul; he spent the turn of the year 1184/85 in Norman Palermo.[34] The itinerary of the most famous traveler of all, the Maghrebi Ibn Battuta (1304–1368/69), took him to Byzantium, India, and China. A fascinating account was written by Zhao Rukuo of China, a trade supervisor from Hangzhou, between 1204 and 1224. His *History of the Various Foreign Countries* describes India, the Pacific islands, and Japan in addition to Baghdad, Mecca, and Alexandria, and even devotes a few lines to the southern coast of Spain.[35] The best informed about Europe was the Nestorian monk Rabban Bar Sauma, a native of Beijing who went to Genoa and southern France on a Mongol diplomatic mission.

Nevertheless, Europe largely remained a blank space on Eastern maps. This had nothing to do with a failure of intellectual flexibility or lack of curiosity. The texts describe trade zones, the worlds of merchants. Ibn Fadlan and Ben Jacob wrote about territories where their compatriots obtained slaves and pelts (four sable furs and one ermine could fetch the value of eighty-six oxen around the year 1200![36]). Much more important than Europe for them was the gigantic Pacific trade zone, including Africa, whose east coast was the western travel horizon for Chinese junks. European travelers to Asia, in contrast, were unwitting scouts of European expansion and, thus, of a first phase of globalization.[37] It began, one could say, with the annotations Columbus scribbled in the margins of his copy of Marco Polo's account. Yet the exploration of the Eastern Hemisphere and its integration into Europe's conception of the world has a much deeper history than that. What is clear is that Europeans in the thirteenth century knew much more about Asia than Asians did about Latin Europe.

Off to Asia! This cry would eventually drive the Portuguese south, the Spanish west. The object was to make a profit, at times also to spread the word of God. By the early fourteenth century, Rome had already managed to establish bishoprics in the Ilkhanate and in southern India. What the first travelers to Asia experienced flew in the face of everything that had been heard and seen before; it could hardly be fit into the scheme outlined by the ancient geographers. The first eyewitness account of the Mongols was provided in 1247 by Giovanni da Pian del Carpine, a disciple of Saint Francis. When the Flemish monk Willem van Ruysbroeck traveled to Karakorum six years later on behalf of Saint Louis, he felt like he had entered "another world," *aliud seculum*.[38] He would have had to be a painter, he mused, to properly portray everything he encountered: the felt yurts of the Mongols decorated with pictures, their dances and songs, their clothing, the court of the Great Khan, their practice of polygamy, not to mention the customs of the Nestorian Christians he met in the land of the Uyghurs. He meticulously described how the Mongols brewed their favorite drink, "cosmos," a fermented beverage made of horse milk. Willem van Ruysbroeck's ethnography was a vast improvement compared to stories and maps, such as the Ebstorf Map (ca. 1300), that featured miraculous creatures and biblical references.[39] The latter reflected not practical experience but rather familiarity with ancient sources and medieval texts like Isidore's *Etymologies*. They transmitted theological rather than geographical knowledge.

Most people still reckoned space in terms of human body parts—such as hands or feet—or experiences such as a "day's journey." Nevertheless, the growing number of travel accounts indicates that maps were finding their way into people's heads. In Prague, the Franciscan friar Giovanni de' Marignolli told Emperor Charles IV about the furthest reaches of the world—about the places where pepper literally grows, i.e., China and India. He believed he had reached the Gates of Eden.[40] In his telling, people there considered carbuncles and sapphires to be frozen tears of the first human beings, shed when they were expelled from Paradise. The Bible and Saint Augustine provided him with categories and names to describe these foreign domains: the rivers of Paradise, the realm of the Queen of Sheba, the grave of the Apostle Thomas. Earth was not a sphere but rather a mass of land, divided into four continents, resting in a vast ocean. Its southern half seemed unreachable to Giovanni. But he still knew that, in the south, the sun was in the north and that the North Star could not be seen.

Diagrams and numbers were now added to the images to describe geographical dimensions. Alongside world maps, another aid to travel appeared, increasingly precise and based on real data: portolan charts. The compass had been known since the late twelfth century.[41] Cogs and large galleys were able to sail in winter, thus driving what Frederic C. Lane has called the "nautical revolution."[42] At the same time, the old myths lived on. Prester John, who first appeared in sources in the time of Barbarossa, inhabited an imaginary realm initially thought to be beyond India, near Paradise.[43] He was reputed to have an army of a million soldiers, ready to cut through the Gordian knot of Europe's chaos and reestablish peace and law. Throughout the Middle Ages and beyond, popes and Christian princes sought to win the phantom as an ally. As Europe's missionaries, warriors, and merchants pushed further afield and the blank spaces on the world map were filled in, the mythical king vanished further east and then finally south. In the end he was imagined to be in

Ethiopia. As one humanist would put it, "We have learned that the miraculous always slips beyond our grasp."[44]

Paper, Eyeglasses, and Earthly Existence: Taking Stock

Rome. February 22, 1300. From the loggia of the Lateran Palace, Pope Boniface VIII announces that all those who come to Rome "in this current year of 1300 and every subsequent hundred years" and who visit the basilicas of Saint Peter and Saint Paul for at least fifteen days will receive indulgence for their sins.[45] Thus was convoked the first jubilee in Christendom. Pilgrims streamed into Rome from all over Europe. They sought redemption, and they were frightened. Was the end of times near, now at the turn of another whole century after the birth of the Redeemer? To purify oneself utterly at the grave of the Prince of the Apostles on the first day of the new (and perhaps last) century was a chance the pilgrims did not want to miss. Along with the rivers of the faithful, gold aplenty flowed into Rome. In the Basilica of Saint Paul Outside the Walls, one pilgrim watched as two monks gathered up the coins day and night that had been thrown onto the apostle's grave.[46] These good works of precious metal were offered to shorten the punishments of purgatory.

The mass pilgrimages to the apostles' graves and the relics of Rome were journeys of salvation in hard times. It seems that it was not the year 1000 that marked a dreaded turning point for people, but rather the advent of the fourteenth century. Their fear was born of the overwhelming changes we have described: Crusades, wars, heresy; population explosion, new states, the large, bewildering cities; money and usury; armies of Muslims and Mongols at the gates of the West. It is no coincidence that more people than ever now lent credence to the prophecies of the Calabrian abbot Joachim of Fiore (ca. 1130/35–1202); Dante put him in Paradise in his *Divine Comedy*.[47] Joachim predicted that the Kingdom of the Father and the Son would be followed, after the apocalyptic struggles foretold in the Bible, by a third "Kingdom of the Holy Spirit." Hopes for this kind of blessed age of love, peace, and ultimate revelation sprouted precisely in periods of upheaval, which were easily viewed as manifestations of the prophesied interim age of chaos. Fear of the Last Judgment did not disappear after 1300. It was the mystical turning of the centuries in particular—the years 1400, 1500, 1600—that caused it to rise again and again.

Despite its confusion, Latin Europe also had several advantages over the rest of the world in the jubilee year of 1300. Its population had increased, a basic precondition for its meteoric rise. At the time, there were perhaps sixty or seventy big cities with more than ten thousand inhabitants. But Europe's demographic body was not bloated, thanks to the fettering of Eros on this side of the Hajnal Line. The agricultural system, and perhaps the limited yields of the grain economy, might have played a part. The political entities resulting from the Migration Period had developed into numerous more-or-less independent states with institutions and multilayered legal systems. Urban middle classes formed. Here and there, horizontal power structures like the general assemblies and the English Parliament gained mass. Private property, trade, and profit even received recognition within canon law. The commercial revolution ennobled trade.[48] Monkish ethics had long since lost their relevance in the dynamic urban societies of the Late Middle Ages. As Albertano of Brescia (ca. 1195–1253) commented, "Thus among men there are distinct duties. For one thing is said to clerics, and another to those remaining in the world."[49] The realities of urban life found another defender in Peter John Olivi. He condemned usury but still allowed moneylenders to be repaid more than the principal on high-risk loans.[50] This cast doubt on the prohibition of interest in canon law. Not that it mattered, as various workarounds were available. For example, a creditor could receive a yearly rent related to a piece of property or a building that, in sum, exceeded the total of the loan.

Philosophy's right to exist was uncontested. Less so was the degree of freedom one had to engage in it, as the 1277 condemnation of Aristotle's "detestable errors" shows (pp. 243f.). Nevertheless, its scope, in the sense outlined by Hugh of Saint Victor, would develop in the following centuries. Once the Arabic summas of philosophy, astronomy, and medicine were available, the translation movement from Arabic into Latin came to an end.[51] Starting in the mid-thirteenth century, translation directly from Greek became increasingly common.

In addition to its sanctuaries of worldliness, Latin Europe also possessed means of communication that, over the long term, would have a revolutionary effect. It had the universal language of Latin, which was now systematized in a growing number of grammars and lexicons. It was also becoming expert in rhetoric, the indispensable tool of lawyers, diplomats, and preachers. And it now had paper.

Those thin, delicate leaves changed the world. Paper carried knowledge and new technologies across time and space, touching off reform movements. An agent of critique and discourse, it showed itself to be a democratic substance. The maturing state devoured it by the ton. Indeed, without paper, the state

would be as unthinkable as modernity itself. Just about everything depended on a few plant fibers and the idea of pressing them into a robust writing material. As we recall, the prehistory of the paper revolution goes back to ancient China, to Samarkand, and then to Baghdad, Damascus, and Cairo. From North Africa, the technology hopped over to Sicily and the Iberian Peninsula.[52] The invention needed almost one and a half millennia to reach Europe. The earliest documents written on paper in the West date to the first half of the twelfth century. From then on, it spread apace, abetted by communication channels long used by merchants. The first paper mills were set up on the Iberian Peninsula and on the Balearic Islands; in 1282, there was one in Xàtiva, a re-Christianized town near Valencia that had been a center of paper production since Muslim times. The mills helped to make paper a mass product. They appeared in France in 1338, in Germany in 1390, and in England a century later. Scandinavia and Russia began producing paper in the second half of the sixteenth century.

Paper was followed by eyeglasses, a tool that allowed older people, and thus more people, to read and do arithmetic. Perhaps the earliest depiction of a man reading with the aid of eyeglasses was painted by Tommaso da Modena in 1352 in the chapter house of a monastery in Treviso, close to the "glass center" of Venice (Fig. 18, above).

Eyeglasses made two major contributions to the world of work: they more than doubled the number of years certain occupations could be pursued, and—as an important precondition for the production of precision instruments—they made it possible to work more accurately.[53] This useful device was probably first produced around 1300 in Tuscany or in northern Italy. The theoretical groundwork had been laid by Roger Bacon, among others. But, as always when it comes to technical innovation, more was required: high-quality craftsmanship. Antiquity had known magnifying glasses made of rock crystal. The Middle Ages gazed at relics through polished panels of quartz that were plano-convex, thus magnifying what was behind them. The same panels were used as *lapides ad legendum*, or "reading stones." In Venice, a venerable center of glass production, a new type of glass was produced for the first time around 1260: *cristallo*. Its basic ingredient was no longer the traditional potash but rather sodium bicarbonate, obtained from Egypt and Syria. Cristallo was much purer than traditional glass, and it was easier to work than hard quartz. Another important innovation was the idea of blowing glass balls and sawing them in half. This process resulted in two nearly identical lenses that only had to be fixed together in a frame. But before eyeglasses could be used to improve sight, a change in medical and physiological perspective was required. Until then, the dominant view was that poor eyesight was a malady that could only be remedied by tinctures.[54] The availability of paper and mass-produced eyeglasses now fired the passion for reading and vice versa, a development driven by writers, learning, and the commercial spirit. It would be a key element in the Gutenberg Revolution's world-shattering impact.

A turning point had been reached in the *history of science*. An excellent illustration is provided by Dietrich of Freiberg's work on the physics of rainbows. He investigated the laws governing the reflection and refraction of light in the individual drops of water that make up a rainbow by studying how light rays pass through a glass ball. His conclusions, which were essentially sound, show that Latin Europe was also catching up in the natural sciences. Dietrich's text treats optics and nothing but optics; it contains no moral or theological interpretations, such as that rainbows symbolize man's covenant with God.[55] It was written independently of an investigation undertaken around the same time by the Persian Kamal al-Din al-Farisi, which reached similar conclusions. If we were to plot the rise of European learning and the decline of Arabic science on a graph, this is where the two lines would intersect.

Many people from an increasingly broad swathe of society participated in the grand dialogue, which often flared up into critical debates. The older view according to which the Renaissance should be seen as a reaction to an ossified Scholasticism belongs on the garbage heap of intellectual history. So does the opinion that it first began, after a prelude in the fourteenth century, in the Italian Quattrocento that followed. Long before that, Paris and Oxford, Padua and Florence were intellectual hothouses for literature, philosophy, and theology. The exchange of ideas in the Mediterranean world was more intense than ever before. Classical antiquity and Arabic literature conquered the libraries of England, North Africa, and Flanders.[56] A simple chronicler like the Franciscan friar Salimbene of Parma (1221–after 1287) could quote Juvenal and Horace at will.

There was no decisive break between the renaissance of the twelfth century and the "great Renaissance" that followed. The paths that would later lead to the four world-changing revolutions of the modern age—the media, scientific, industrial, and political revolutions—had already been embarked upon. An inquisitive spirit had materialized. Trailblazing innovations had arrived on the scene. In addition to paper and eyeglasses, they included Arabic numerals and banking, gunpowder, universities, and Roman law. The compass provided orientation at sea. The Italians credit Amalfi with the invention, others the Frenchman Pierre de Maricourt. In 1269, he was the first to write about the two poles of the magnet, and he attempted to keep a clock in perpetual motion using magnetism.[57]

The realm of possibility for the "great Renaissance" was now wide open. Its origins lay in Italy, which after the fall of the Hohenstaufen had descended yet again into war and partisan conflict, the price of communal liberty and political autonomy. Fermenting in this chaos, it developed into the most intellectually vibrant and artistically creative country in the world. "Not all the arts have been found," commented the Dominican friar Giordano da Pisa. "Indeed, new ones are being found all the time."[58] Giovanni Villani, who joined the pilgrimage to Rome in 1300, sensed where this trend was due to continue: whereas Rome was declining, Florence, its "daughter and creation, was on the rise and would pursue great things."[59] He was right.

16

Italian Overture

Rise of the Notaries

The Renaissance was not all purple and gold, contrary to the starry-eyed "Renaissancist" view of the period from around 1900.[1] Beyond the grand works of art, the material remains of the Renaissance are paper, ink, and printed words.

For its reality, in part splendid, in part dreadful, has long since dried on the pages of books. It is found in the poems of the early humanists of Padua and in the chronicles of the Florentines. It lives in the account books of the Genoese and the balance sheets of Augsburg, in magnificent manuscripts, poisonous pamphlets, and heavy, brown leather-bound volumes with gilt lettering. But this silent parliament of objects does not speak on its own; it must be made to talk. Historians must do the work of necromancers. Their words resurrect the remains of long-deceased individuals, whose last gasp of life and spirit has transmigrated into text. This same, somewhat extravagant metaphor was used by Benvenuto Campesani (ca. 1250–1323) of Vicenza to describe his rediscovery of a manuscript containing poems by Catullus. "Verses on the Resurrection of the Veronese Poet Catullus" (*Versus . . . de resurectione Catulli poete Veronensis*) is what he called the poem he composed to commemorate the occasion.[2]

In the fourteenth century, the dialogue with the ancients intensified. Classical antiquity exercised greater influence on the arts, leaving its first traces in architecture. These were signs of the emergence of the classicizing habitus that would characterize the culture of the following centuries. One development of the utmost significance, found first in Italy, was that a class of laymen formed who, over time, would become decisive agents of Renaissance culture. Until then, the central participants in philosophical and scientific discourse were almost exclusively churchmen. Most of the people joining the conversation now came from the middle classes of the cities. In the beginning, most were jurists. Campesani, whom we just met in Vicenza, is a perfect example. The son of a notary, he practiced the same profession.

It is no coincidence that this development was rooted in the economically prosperous north of Italy during the commercial revolution, when the need for jurists could not possibly be met any longer by clerics alone.[3] Just how quickly the Italians hastened toward the rule of law can be illustrated with a few statistics. In the twelfth century, there were 160 notaries in Bologna. This number was already high compared to conditions outside Italy—evidence of a head start toward modernity. Between 1219 and 1240, no fewer than 1,171 new *notarii* received their license. A few decades later, they had become the decisive power in the "republic of notaries." Thus, the new lay culture of northern Italy took shape as a side effect of economic expansion and its need for legal expertise. Unlike in Francia, in Italy the realm of jurisprudence had always withstood clericalization, remaining an island of worldliness. In northern Europe, the very terms for chancery officials and notaries indicated that clergy dominated the stage. For example, in northern Germany, they were called *clerici civitatis*, literally "town clerks" or "town priests."[4] The etymological path from "cleric" to "clerk" is obvious. Yet here, too, laymen gradually entered the ranks of public administrators, albeit later. In Hamburg, for example, the first notary who was not a priest was recorded in 1236. In the following century, there were jurist poets such as Johannes von Tepl (also known as Johannes von Saaz), author of *Der Ackermann aus Böhmen* ("The Bohemian Plowman"), and Eustache Deschamps (ca. 1345–1404), who wrote over 1,500 poems and produced the first work on poetics in French. Jurisprudence could be linked with other learned interests outside Europe as well. Ibn Sina, for example, participated in legal disputations at the tender age of sixteen.[5]

The arts of reading and writing spread along with the expansion of trade and the money economy. "Legible handwriting in good ink!" Those, in the words of the Florentine merchant Giovanni Rucellai, were the chief aids to his profession.[6] The fact that lay jurisprudence first appeared only in northern Italy was not rooted merely in the needs created by the economic boom; those existed elsewhere as well. There were two other factors: the prospering communes, and the availability of Roman law. As we have seen, this is where Roman law was first revived—a context in which people also used abacuses (with the aid of eyeglasses if necessary) and did their calculations with the creative powerhouse of nothingness, the number zero. Schools in which laymen taught other laymen the tools for careers in the service of the communes enjoyed ebullient support.

The commercialization of education also entailed a certain degree of democratization. Latin and the basic ability to deal with written texts broke through the walls of monasteries and churches. With their training in rhetoric, logic, and Latin, jurists were exquisitely prepared not only to recover Roman law but also to explore other fields of the lost culture of the ancients, even if just as a pastime. As schoolboys, they honed their skills by reading Aesop's fables, the Latin *Iliad*, and the *Distichs of Cato*, a collection of moral teachings by an unknown late antique author.[7] What else might have been written by the people capable of producing something as awe-inspiring as Justinian's *Corpus*? Curiosity of this kind percolates from the dedication which Burgundio of Pisa, also a jurist, prefaced to one of his translations. The books of the Greeks, he says, contained knowledge about the nature of the heavens and everything underneath, about comets, thunder, and lightning. They explained why the sea is salty, and many more things too. At the turn of the fourteenth century in Florence, notaries were translating both French poetry and the classics into Tuscan, including works of Ovid, Seneca, and Virgil.[8]

Very many humanists were trained as jurists. From afar, they resemble the civil servants of Song China, that highly educated administrative elite to whom the Middle Kingdom owed a good portion of its cultural flourishing. The Italians also often had enough spare time to engage in scholarship and the arts. Diplomats and civil servants wrote chronicles and poetry in which they imitated the form and themes of ancient works. They acquired the tools to do so during their education, which also included the study of grammar and rhetoric. Some of them composed learned treatises on the notarial art; others attempted translations from Greek and even from Arabic. They wrote not only for princely patrons but also for a civic elite to whose circle they themselves belonged.

The foundation had been laid by the literature imported from France, most of which arrived by way of Venice (thanks to its extensive trade network). But the chivalric ideals of the troubadours lost relevance in a world of merchant citizens who dealt in bills of exchange and suffered dearly from noble feuds, vendettas, and partisan conflict.[9] The latter discovered the moral philosophy of Cicero and found models in Seneca's serene humanity, which offered advice for dealing with Fortuna's caprice. Albertano of Brescia was one of the first to get things started. His works, which argue for peace, justice, and civic concord based on Christian charity, exude the same spirit that in the following century would animate the most famous painted depiction of the political values of the medieval communes: Ambrogio Lorenzetti's fresco in Siena's Palazzo Pubblico celebrating "good government" (see pp. 291f.).

The First Humanists

Albertano's political versifying was continued by the Florentine Brunetto Latini (1220/30–1294). Chancellor of a divided Florence during the regime of the *primo popolo*, Latini was continually caught up in political disputes and spent time as an exile in France. He translated works of Cicero into the vernacular, thus aiding their diffusion. His Cicero was less a philosopher than a statesman and a defender of republican liberty, which Latini passionately advocated as well.[10] To drink as much as possible from the well of Roman antiquity, to take inspiration from *Italy's own* past—that was Latini's response to the tradition of troubadour lyric and romances, to chivalric stories and heroic epics. Civic pride focused literally on the bell tower of one's local church—a pride nourished by opposition to the ideal of chivalry and the suicidal partisan conflict it inspired in Italy's urban societies—was a cornerstone of early humanism. One of its first exponents was Lovato de' Lovati (1240–1309), a notary and judge in Padua. Unlike Latini, he followed "in the footsteps of the ancient poets," writing primarily in Latin.[11] He endowed the city of his birth with the dignity of an ancient origin. When a skeleton was found during excavations for the building of a foundling hospital, he identified it as the remains of the Trojan prince Antenor, whom Livy, a native of Padua, claimed had founded the city. A sarcophagus for the mythical hero was placed on the spot, sheltered ever since by a stone baldachin.

From time immemorial, the *Iliad* and the *Odyssey* had provided Europe's peoples with explanations of their origins.[12] After all, the inhabitants of unhappy Troy must have ended up somewhere after fleeing to the four winds. Coherent chains of events were reconstructed that stretched from the founding of the city all the way back to the beginnings of time. The humanists zealously forged ahead with this model, giving countless peoples and cities an ancient origin. Antenor, for example, was even integrated into the genealogy of the Poles by one of their historians in the late sixteenth century.[13] The Homeric epics were not available to the High Middle Ages in the original Greek, though, but rather were known primarily via two late antique Latin texts that purported to be eyewitness accounts of the war of all wars: Dictys's *Diary of the Trojan War*, and the *Account of the Fall of Troy* by an author named "Dares."[14] In these versions, however, Padua's Antenor played an inglorious role. Desirous of peace, he is supposed to have opened the gates to the besiegers. In exchange, the conquerors spared his house, marking it with the skin of a panther.

Lovato was one of the best Latinists since antiquity (although he seems to have overlooked this passage from the Latin *Iliad*, with its blot on his hero's reputation). In the opinion of Petrarca,

> Lovato would in recent times have been the prince of all the poets whom our age or that of our fathers knew, if he had not, in embracing the studies of the civil law, mixed the Twelve Tables with the nine muses and turned his attention from heavenly concerns to the noise of the courtroom.[15]

Lovato's poetry betrays French influences as well. Yet he was capable of composing works that breathe the spirit of the great poets of antiquity, including nearly forgotten authors like Tibullus and Propertius. Many of the letters he wrote in classicizing Latin reflect personal thoughts and feelings. One poem, focusing on an illness he had contracted, is a hymn to impermanence and rebirth. It ends not with religious consolation but with earthly happiness.

> Look at the earth flowering with so many thousands of young men: after a short time, the black day may overwhelm them. Nature overturns her own

work and, restless, always fashions matter in new forms. We are mocked by the gods, creations of their hands, and we are not today what we were yesterday. So I want nothing except to enjoy happy times, and when sweet things are lacking, to die sweetly.

Albertino Mussato (1261–1329), another Paduan, continued on the trail blazed by Lovato. Of humble origins and probably of illegitimate birth, he rose to become a notary and a member of Padua's city council.[16] An eloquent defender of communal liberty, he was constantly getting into trouble. Consolation was offered to him by Seneca, who was also a model for his chief work, the *Ecerinis*, which deals with the rise and fall of the Veronese tyrant Ezzelino da Romano and his clan. The *Ecerinis* was the first secular tragedy written since antiquity. What is more, citizens were given a role on stage. They made up the chorus, thus inviting the civic audience to identify with the drama, such as when they praised the restoration of peace. For the premiere, every store in Padua closed. In 1315, Mussato became the first poet since antiquity to be crowned with laurel in a public ceremony. This high point of his career was followed a decade later by a low fall. The Carrara, who took control of Padua shortly thereafter, forced him into exile. In his later years, he seems to have been deeply troubled by the tension he felt between the literary cult of the muses, pagan learning, and Christian faith. He vehemently maintained that his heart belonged to God. He died in exile in the Venetian town of Chioggia.

Lovato de' Lovati and Mussato were two of the founders of humanism, one of the most significant intellectual movements of the early modern world. The term "humanist" may be a product of the nineteenth century, but the Renaissance was certainly familiar with the individuals it denotes. The contemporary term, *umanista*, was translated into German in the eighteenth century as "someone devoted to *schöne Wissenschaften*," literally "the beautiful sciences."[17] The combination of beauty and knowledge connoted by *schöne Wissenschaften* is also encapsulated in the term used for humanism by the Florentine chancellor Lino Coluccio Salutati (1331–1406): *studia humanitatis*. It referred to intellectual pursuits encompassing four liberal arts, namely grammar, rhetoric, poetry, and moral philosophy, plus history. These "humane sciences" or "humanities" taught how to speak eloquently, compose poetry, and act honorably. The canon was not sharply cut off from logic, mathematics, medicine, jurisprudence, or theology. Nor did the humanists comprise a cohesive group, although many of them wrote letters to one another or formed local sodalities. The first may have taken shape in the bars of Padua; Mussato talks about it.[18] These were signs that learned discourse was gradually emancipating itself from monasteries and universities. That Padua, of all places, emerged as a foundational center of humanism might be related to the fact that the city barely attracted any foreign scholars while it was ruled by tyrants like Ezzelino. Notarial services and education thus remained in the hands of locals, most of whom worked for the commune. In this way, knowledge of the classical tradition and local patriotism conjoined, finding models for public life and political stability in the ancient sources. Courses on classical literature seem to have been offered in Padua as early as 1250.

In addition to the new element of town and city residents, the ranks of the early humanists also included monks and high clergy. Some, like Innocent VII, Nicholas V, and Pius II, even ascended to the Holy See. Nevertheless, the relationship between the Christian religion and humanism, with its enthusiasm for pagan antiquity, was never entirely free of tension. The Dominican provincial Giovanni Dominici (ca. 1356–1419) revived a centuries-old debate when he attacked humanism in his *Lucula noctis*.[19] In his opinion, only those strong of faith should be allowed to engage with the writings of the ancients. This view took aim at the introduction of pagan literature as reading material in Florentine grammar schools. At the same time, Dominici's contemporary Cino Rinuccini ridiculed a humanist avant-garde that disdained the "Three Crowns of Florence"—Dante, Petrarca, and Boccaccio—as inferior to the ancients, sympathized with pagan religion, and even shirked their civic duties in favor of easy living. For most people, however, there was no contradiction in pursuing both theological and humanistic studies. For example, Salutati tried to show that the cyclical view of history found in Virgil—the return of a Golden Age mentioned in the fourth *Eclogue*—was consistent with the Bible, and the important Venetian humanist Ermolao Barbaro (1453/54–1494) devoted himself to Christianizing Aristotelian philosophy.[20] He knew two lords, he once wrote: Jesus Christ and learned studies.

Humanism elaborated secular analogs to the perennial hopes of the pious for the purification of the world. Its goal was culture and education in the broadest sense, focusing on good taste, manners, religious and political values, and the acquisition of proper Latin (later Greek and Hebrew as well). As Paul Joachimsen put it, humanism was concerned with "forming and norming" (*Formung und Normierung*), i.e., educating the young and inculcating social norms. For the first time in Europe's post-classical history, eloquence, beautiful language, was cultivated for its own sake. Many humanists shared the conviction that the spirit of the divine emanated from the works of the ancient poets and civilized their readers.[21] Linguistic virtuosos and patriots like Latini, Lovato, and Mussato founded the movement of humanism, which flourished until the dawning of our own age. There is no question that it owed much to the dialogue with Islamic culture, if for no other reason than that it benefited from the tradition enshrined in Arabic texts.[22]

The classics were the standard of elegance in speaking and writing. But the humanists did not stop at the reconstruction of original texts with the aid of critical philology, nor did they indulge in mere interpretation. They also created their own rituals—Mussato's poetic crowning is an example—and hunted down manuscripts containing ancient works. Their searches were not limited to the archives and libraries of Italian cities and monasteries. Rather, they pushed on to the Near East, even to Denmark and Norway.[23] They polished their style, wrote sonnets, plays, and works of history. Their approach to the legacy of classical antiquity was, in a word, creative.

As mentioned, very few *umanisti* thought that what they said or wrote was in acute disagreement with theology.[24] Yet what ultimately made humanism into a revolutionary movement was its engagement with the critical philosophy of the Greeks. Humanism elaborated a civic ethics, reflected on the practice of politics, provided paths to a more pleasant existence, and, with its wondering, inquisitive, and investigative posture, decisively turned toward the world. Knowledge became explainable and communicable. The curiosity of the classically minded humanists is the foundation of modern, secular science. Artists influenced by humanism looked to nature and human imagination for artistic criteria. They elaborated an aesthetics that did justice to Scotus's "thisness." And indeed, greater attention was paid to life here on Earth. The individual looked into the mirror and thought about his or her own self. Perhaps it is no coincidence that the founding figure of Mussato was one of the first medieval men of comparatively low rank who, in the description of a contemporary, appears to us as a flesh-and-blood human being, as a short, healthy, and lively man with a congenial personality. He is also the first person since antiquity who is known to have been in the habit of celebrating his birthday.[25] One's own lifetime was now taken more seriously, at least by the elites.

Campesani's "resurrection" of Catullus, with which this chapter began, is the epitome of humanism. Something long since dead comes back and also provides an impulse for the creation of new things. That is the essence of "renaissance," of "rebirth." People recognized a break between their own time and antiquity, a break filled with what we call the "Middle Ages." The feeling that a new great age of culture had dawned is expressed in a poem that Pace of

Ferrara, a member of Lovato's circle, dedicated to the bishop of Padua: "O Calliope . . . hide yourself no longer," he calls to the Muse of epic poetry. "Take up the pick of the sweet-sounding harp and deign to bind the hair of a new poet with the living leaf."[26]

Epochal Interlude: The *Divine Comedy*

A contemporary of Campesani, Dante Alighieri (ca. 1265–1321), literally brought antiquity to life in his *Comedy* (it would be given its canonical attribute later by Boccaccio, who described it as "divine").[27] As guide and protector on his journey through Hell and Purgatory, Dante chose the universally venerated figure of Virgil; in his native city of Mantua, statues had already been dedicated to the arch-poet of antiquity back in the early thirteenth century (Fig. 20, p. 278). Many well-known individuals appear in the *Commedia*. The scholars, poets, and heroes of the ancient world are granted asylum by Dante in Limbo, a pre-Hell that resembles a paradise garden. Even Muslims—Saladin, Avicenna, and Averroes "of the great Commentary"[28]—are allowed to dwell there. Dante finds himself in a noble castle, in the illustrious company of Homer, Horace, Ovid, and Lucan. On verdant fields, he meets the most highly esteemed men and women of the classical past, including Caesar, Penthesilea, and Lucretia, Socrates and Plato, Democritus and Heraclitus, Cicero, Galen, Euclid, and Ptolemy. In this way, the poet resolves the conflict with which he and other pious Christians grappled, namely that the great masters they venerated were pagans.

The phantasmagoria that Dante evokes in his *Divine Comedy* is burned into the memory of those who have read it. Who could forget Farinata degli Uberti, rising from one of the flaming sarcophaguses reserved for heretics in order to learn the fate of his sons from Dante? Or the story of Ugolini della Gherardesca, who must gnaw the flesh from the skull of his mortal enemy, Archbishop Ruggieri of Pisa, for all eternity—the fitting punishment for a man who, walled into a tower by Ruggieri and raving with hunger, ate the corpses of his fellow prisoners: his own children.[29] All the senses are engaged. We smell stinking excrement, hear the screams and laments of the damned coming from the funnel-shaped pit of Hell, and see black hurricanes and grafters boiling in pitch. A band of bizarre monsters of ancient origin keeps the damned in check. The bulging-bellied Cerberus barks from his three throats. Fearsome Geryon, with the head of a human, paws of a lion, wings of a dragon, and body of a serpent, lurks on the edge of the sea of sand and then

gives the hardy travelers a ride on his back. Centaurs shoot their arrows at murderers and robbers being boiled in a river of bubbling blood. And harpies feed on a forest made of the souls of suicides. Only one medieval pope, the pious Gregory the Great, is given a place in Paradise by Dante. Most of his colleagues roast in Hell. Muhammad, who appears as a religious splitter, is portrayed as savagely beaten, his gut sliced open, bowels dangling between his legs. The last circle of Hell contains traitors, frozen up to their heads in sempiternal ice. Padua's Antenor is also imprisoned there—Dante knew his *Iliad* better than Lovato. At the very bottom, Lucifer grinds up the arch-traitors Brutus, Cassius, and Judas, each in one of his three mouths.

Then the path leads Dante back into the open, under a sky "the gentle hue of sapphire"—to the Mountain of Purgatory and then upwards to Paradise. Once again, the master dramaturge stages unforgettable scenes. He is as expert at depicting the sunrise, the morning light, and a frost-covered landscape as he was at imagining the horrors of Hell. On the seven terraces of Purgatory, the proud carry heavy stones on their backs that force their gaze to the ground. The envious must wander blindly, their eyes sewn shut. The shadowy bodies of the lustful are purified in the fire of a flaming wall. In the end, the poet reaches the Spheres of Heaven. There he receives assistance from Beatrice, the woman he revered, who had died a premature death. Now an allegory for theology or religion, she acts as his guide. For Virgil, unbaptized and thus eternally banned from Paradise, has left Dante. In the Sphere of Mars, the Florentine meets his ancestor Cacciaguida among blessed warriors of the faith, and then several great religious figures from the recent and more remote past: Thomas Aquinas, Siger of Brabant and Bonaventure, Isidore of Seville, Peter Lombard and Saint Bernard, as well as Peter Damian, resplendent in flame. Dante's desire is moved by Plato's *eros*, "the Love that moves the sun and the other stars."[30] Finally, God's Empyrean is reached, where "what I could see was greater than speech can show."

Dante's own contemporaries considered him a "reviver" of the dead art of poetry. According to Guido da Pisa, he "called the ancient poets back into our memory."[31] The *Comedy* shines a light on the factors that gave rise to Europe's superabundant intellectual life. The first classic of world literature created on the continent since antiquity, it must be understood as the product of the lay culture of the cities. Composed in Italian, that is where it found its audience. Commentaries on it were written in Bologna. In Florence, Boccaccio initiated the tradition of public lectures at which the work was read and expounded upon. Without the schools of the city on the Arno, where free thinkers like Olivi taught and Brunetto Latini was Dante's master,[32] the poet never could have acquired the knowledge and the artistic skills necessary for completing his monumental work. He probably also studied at a university. His peregrinations and forced wanderings, which, as he once remarked, led him through the country as a foreigner, almost a beggar,[33] added another element: they gave him the opportunity to study manuscripts and converse with scholars, resulting in the intimate acquaintance with ancient mythology and philosophy that informs the hundred cantos of the *Comedy*.[34] The poem also contains traces of the art of French *chansons* and romances, which must have been in vogue in Florence at the time. The decision to write this epoch-making work in the vernacular was a decisive factor in Tuscan's emergence as the standard language of Italy.

What makes the *Comedy* seem so new is the ease and determination with which Dante introduces himself into the plot. He is not only a first-person narrator but a recognizable individual with fears, joys, and unquenchable curiosity. He speaks to us directly; the reader, *il lettor*, is constantly addressed as if present—just as, a hundred years later, linear perspective would invite viewers inside paintings. The *Comedy*, a drama about all things human and divine, was the culmination of the renaissance that began in the twelfth century. No other verse of the age used such powerful language to create images, both somber and sublime, of what people believed they knew about the cosmos. How different are the worlds of the *Codex Manesse*, a sumptuously illustrated manuscript from Zurich dating to the same period, which contains a collection of high medieval lyric from the north and west of Europe!

No matter how hard one searches, Dante's tomb cannot be found in Florence. Forced into exile as a White Guelph, the poet died in Ravenna. And that is where his remains still lie, all except for a pouch of bone dust possessed by the National Library of Florence. Yet the city of his birth never stopped being a place of yearning for him. It is where he got the language in which the *Comedy* is enshrined, the vernacular "in which even women talk to each other."[35] The *Comedy* was written as an antidote to homesickness and an objection to the injustice Dante felt his exile to be. Contemporary history was woven into all its parts; not a few of its characters have achieved immortality only because Dante placed them in his *Inferno. Italia bella,* "lovely Italy," of whose "green meadows," rivers, and cities he sang, often provides the backdrop. Then he turns again to deploring his homeland's fate: to have been made a slave, an abode of anguish and a bordello, a "ship without a helmsman in harsh seas."[36]

Dante's Emperor, Popes in Avignon, and an Exile in Munich

For a time, the poor poet placed all his hopes in Henry VII (r. 1308–1313), whom he calls "noble Henry," *l'alto Arrigo.* In the *Paradiso,* Dante sees a throne set up for him on the yellow Rose of the Blessed. As Beatrice explains, this throne has been prepared for the one who has come to "show Italy the righteous way."[37] Two years after his coronation as king of the Germans, Henry of Luxembourg descended into Italy to assert imperial rights, to gain the imperial crown, and, like his predecessors, to help himself to the treasuries of the rich Italian cities. Few rulers received as much sympathy from Italy's literary jurists as Henry. Mussato, for example, devoted a work of classicizing history to Henry's three-year sojourn in Italy, inspired by authors like Livy, Sallust, and Suetonius.[38] Henry was the first German king in fifty years to cross the Alps, and he would be the last one for a long time to appear there as a defender of the idea of universal empire. Dante laid a theoretical foundation for this position in his *De monarchia,* written around 1320.[39]

Only a short time before that, in 1302, the papacy had reaffirmed the opposing point of view. During his fight with Philip the Fair over the taxation of the French clergy, Pope Boniface VIII issued the bull *Unam sanctam* against his adversary.[40] "We therefore declare, say, and affirm"—thus its final sentence— "that submission on the part of every man to the bishop of Rome is altogether necessary for his salvation." These were hollow words, although later, in 1516, they did become a general doctrine of the Catholic Church. Only barely escaping capture by French troops, their author died in 1303, a failure. Dante prepared a place for him and his successor, Clement V, in the eighth circle of Hell among the simoniacs, in a special fiery ditch just for popes.[41] In the exhilaration of victory, Philip the Fair boasted he was now king and pope and emperor.[42] He circulated a letter in which he addressed Boniface as "your fatuous majesty." "You should know," he wrote, "that we are subject to no one in earthly affairs. . . . Anyone who disagrees we consider to be foolish and insane."

France continued its successful involvement in Italian politics after Philip's death. Henry VII, on the other hand, although a clever, decisive ruler, could not fulfill Dante's expectations. He failed in his plans to establish an Empire above the parties and, like his predecessor Otto III, make it once again worthy of the ancient name of Rome. He ended up deeply involved in Italian cabals and faced numerous opponents, including mighty Florence. He gained another enemy by attempting, in league with Sicily, to revive imperial suzerainty over Angevin Naples. Only with great effort did Henry succeed in being crowned Holy Roman Emperor. His early death in 1313, in a town south of Siena, spared him further disappointment.

Meanwhile, Italy had lost the papacy. Clement V, formerly archbishop of Bordeaux, was from Gascony and owed his election after a nearly year-long conclave to the French party in the College of Cardinals. He spent the years of his pontificate in southern France. In 1316, his successor John XXII, another Frenchman, took up residence in Avignon where he had long served as bishop. Like his predecessor and his successors, he saw to it that his countrymen, including his own nephews, received cardinal's hats. In this way, a French majority in the College was assured. For more than half a century, the papacy was now located in a fortress-like palace overlooking the Rhone. At least that kept it out of the reach of the tentacles of the Roman nobility. On the other hand, the French crown exercised overwhelming influence. Initially a town of six thousand souls, in the span of seventy-five years Avignon grew to be as large as Rome; its population quintupled.[43] The papal court attracted merchants, intellectuals, and artists. Musicians came from the north, bringing the new polyphonic style of the *ars nova* with them. Once, in 1338, an embassy of Chinese Christians even made its way to the Rhone. Over time, the papal palace accumulated what may have been the largest library of the Latin Middle Ages, with about two thousand volumes.[44]

The still widely practiced abuse of selling benefices shows that Dante had good reason to roast the simoniacs in Hell. The money, which the Holy See displayed exuberant imagination in procuring, helped not only to pay scribes and mercenaries and to feed paupers but also to supply the needs of a sumptuous court. In order to finance their court and wars, however, the popes also needed to take out loans. Franciscan critics of papal pomp appealed to Christ's poverty; Avignon immediately prohibited the view that Christ was poor, dubbing it heretical.[45] Opposition to papal concupiscence arose in England as well, where meetings of Parliament refused to supply the funds demanded by Avignon.

In the Holy Roman Empire, Henry VII's death was followed by yet another contested election. Louis IV (r. 1314–1347) of the House of Wittelsbach was opposed by his cousin, Frederick the Fair of the House of Habsburg. Neither one was recognized by John XXII. Louis's victory at Mühldorf am Inn in 1322 did nothing to change that. When Louis began getting involved in Italian affairs despite the lack of papal recognition, John excommunicated "the Bavarian," as he contemptuously referred to him, and put all the cities and lands that stood by him under interdict. His successors did the same. If we keep in mind the horrors that haunted Dante's *Inferno*, we can begin to imagine what interdiction must have meant for contemporaries: the gates to Hell stood wide open for all who lived in this punishment's shadow. Nowhere could mass be said, children baptized, couples married, or the dead buried. The church bells fell silent. Louis the Bavarian never managed to have his excommunication lifted. Still, the inflation of excommunication decrees, which the popes now handed down for even the most insignificant transgressions, reduced the volume of their terrifying thunderclap to a bothersome background noise. For his part, Louis remained undeterred. He followed the call of the Visconti in Milan and other cities friendly to the Empire and moved to Italy. People there hoped for Louis's support against the pope and his ally, King Robert of Naples (r. 1309–1343) of the House of Anjou. In 1328, Louis had himself crowned emperor in Saint Peter's by excommunicated bishops and representatives of the people of Rome. The episode was unparalleled.

Arguments against papal involvement in secular affairs had been provided a few years earlier by a physician from Padua, Marsilio de' Mainardini (ca. 1290?–1342/43). His Aristotelian-influenced treatise *Defender of the Peace* is a polemic against the papacy. At the same time, Marsilio—or Marsilius of Padua, as he is usually known in English—provided the foundation for a theory of democracy.[46] In his view, the main causes of disharmony and strife were the Church's lust for power and immoderate desire for worldly property. The very status Boniface VIII had claimed for the papacy a quarter-century earlier he accorded to the people, which he dubbed the highest authority and the source of law. Analogously, he declared church councils and not the pope to be the supreme power within the ecclesiastical hierarchy. Secular and spiritual authority were to be kept strictly separate. Marsilius did not, however, see the people as a community of equals. Rather, he described it as the "totality of the citizens" (*universitas civium*) or else their "more powerful part" (*valentior pars*). As for the purpose of the *civitas*, the state, he agreed with Aristotle that it was the "good life." The clergy must have been horror-stricken by the claim that it should receive what it needed for daily existence and nothing more. No wonder Marsilius had to flee Paris when it became known that he was the book's author. He found asylum at the court in Munich, as did other opponents of the pope. The most famous of the group was William of Ockham, who had taken a position diametrically opposed to the papacy in the dispute over the poverty of Christ and its consequences for the property held by the Franciscan Order.

Within the Empire, Louis the Bavarian's policy was to work together with the prince-electors. They agreed with him that the papacy should be excluded from imperial coronation in the future. At the time, a Wittelsbach state seemed on the point of consolidation. Louis increased his allodium, acquired Brandenburg, and, thanks to marriage alliances, strengthened the ties of his family and the Empire, which extended all the way to Denmark and Holland. The rising power of Poland was also incorporated into the Wittelsbachs' marriage strategy. Alliances first with Edward III of England (r. 1327–1377) and then with France were intended to increase revenues in the west. Yet Louis's visionary policy alienated the prince-electors. The golden bulls with which he sealed his documents, suggestive of ancient imperial glory, were meant to obscure the fact that he was merely a prince among princes and anything but a Caesar. In 1346, his opponents named Charles of Luxembourg, son and successor of King John of Bohemia, as anti-king. War was prevented, however, when Louis died of a stroke while hunting the next year. Charles was quickly recognized as the true king, and the conglomerate of lands accumulated by Louis was broken up in the following decades. The Habsburgs won Tyrol, whereas Brandenburg fell to the House of Luxembourg. Charles, who now possessed an extensive allodium, founded what has been called a "hegemonic kingdom."[47]

Italy, Dante's "ship without a helmsman in harsh seas," was farther from unification than ever.[48] In the northern half, the interests of Milan, Venice, Florence, and the Papal States clashed. Survival was only possible by means of clever diplomacy, money, poison, and violence, regardless of whether they were fighting each other or factions at home. Many signories consolidated their position, some with the support of the people, some without it. The office of *capitano del popolo*, literally "captain of the people," was used by some of its holders to become autocrats. The equestrian statue of Verona's supreme tyrant Cangrande della Scala, who was Dante's host and the dedicatee of the first cantos of the *Paradiso*, is a political manifesto. The stone hero and scion of the Scaliger family smiles confidently at passers-by; the eagle hangs resplendent at his side, the symbol of his status as imperial vicar and lord over Vicenza, Brescia, Parma, and other territories. The Gonzaga family, originally from the minor gentry, became lords of Mantua in 1328; they would control the city surrounded by swamps and the Mincio River for three hundred years.

Venice, however, was not willing to sit by and watch as power was consolidated in its backyard. When Cangrande acquired additional cities and set himself up in a castle near the mouth of the Po, a red line had been crossed. Venetian diplomacy assembled a powerful coalition and sounded the drums of war, reducing the Scaliger regime to the mere possession of Verona and Vicenza. Florence extended its influence to the gates of Lucca. Venice kept Treviso, thereby breaking the ground for a mainland state. In addition, the Serenissima set about expanding the Arsenal, quadrupling its size. Nothing more clearly reflects Venice's rise to a Mediterranean superpower. Its ships crossed the Black Sea, anchored off the coasts of Cyprus, Lebanon, and North Africa, and sailed all the way to Lisbon, London, and Antwerp. In 1340, work was begun on the Doge's Palace. No marble was spared in its completion.

The other new ruling families of northern Italy obtained legal title through imperial or papal offices, thereby supplying themselves with the necessary cement for building a state. The Este could now call themselves vicars of the pope, whereas the Gonzaga, despite their Guelph leanings, bore the same title by the grace of the emperor. Other families as well—petty clans like the Pio in Carpi and the Ordelaffi in Forlì, as well as more important ones like the Montefeltro in Urbino—dug deep in their treasuries in order to gild their power with the luster of law. The same was done by the Visconti, who, after a long struggle, had prevailed in Milan thanks to the support of Henry VII; from then on, they could also call themselves imperial vicars. Numerous northern Italian cities contracted with them—first temporarily, then often permanently—to have them as lords and guarantors of peace and order.

The Most Modern City in the World

While the family with the serpent on its coat of arms was constructing its state in Milan, on the other side of the Apennines the *signore* of Lucca, Castruccio Castracani (1281–1328), flamed out after a meteoric rise to power.[49] Allied with Henry VII and then Louis the Bavarian, and like the latter ultimately excommunicated, the mercenary captain had made himself lord of half of Tuscany. He even destroyed a Florentine army. Like an ancient *imperator*, he paraded through his native city of Lucca in triumph. The son of a merchant, he was the first condottiere to attain the title of duke; that is how Louis repaid him for the use of his sword. But he did not have long to enjoy it. Racked with fever, he died of an illness at the age of forty-eight. Guelph Florence exhaled. Castracani's career appears like the herald of a new age, one that would be extremely friendly to vertical power.

Florence's wars in Tuscany were, like Venice's campaigns, motivated not by glory or a desire for sheer power but rather by economic interests. The goal was to neutralize competitors, secure markets, and add subject cities and territories to the tax base. In 1341, Lucca, famed for its silk production, seemed worth starting a new war for. In the opinion of Machiavelli, Florence lost money and gained only ignominy in the process.[50] For its part, Lucca achieved the feat of regaining its status as an independent commune after a turbulent period under various lords.

The international agent of the Florentine economy was the *fiorino d'oro*, or gold florin.[51] First introduced in 1252 and weighing 3.5 grams, it joined the silver lira as a universally recognized measure of value; in the east, Venetian ducats were the standard. The coin with the lily on one side and the city's patron saint, John the Baptist, on the other became the dollar of the Middle Ages, a medium of exchange whose value remained stable for centuries. The precious metal used to mint it often traveled from afar. It was brought via camel caravan from Ghana to North Africa and then shipped to Italy. Florins could be used to pay for grain, which came above all from Sicily, or for luxury goods such as oriental silk. The Florentines ultimately shifted to breeding silkworms to produce the raw material themselves, proof of their entrepreneurial spirit. The most important import good, however, was wool. It was obtained all the way from North Africa and the Iberian Peninsula, and starting in the late thirteenth century from England, whose weather-hardened sheep produced especially high-quality fleeces.

Textile production was by far the largest sector of the Florentine economy. It fed about a third of the ninety thousand people who lived within the city walls, and it provided work to an army of spinners and fullers in the countryside.[52] Florence became one of the leading economic centers of medieval Europe thanks to wool. One could say that the Florentine Renaissance was woven out of it. Around 1338, seventy thousand to eighty thousand cloths left Florence's two hundred textile workshops a year. Weaving, a cottage industry that contained various steps from washing to combing to dying, set mighty streams of capital in motion. Florentine cloth found buyers from Syria to

Seville. Wool dealers tended to provide not only the raw materials but also looms, which they rented out in exchange for money or work in kind. The weavers' guild, the "Arte della Lana," and the cloth merchants' guild, the "Arte di Calimala," were the most powerful in the city. The latter demonstrated its grandeur by commissioning the mosaic that still adorns the massive dome of the Baptistery of Saint John.

Most weavers lived in humble if not downright miserable conditions, and their craft was prone to crisis. However, trade in wool and cloth provided opportunities for upward mobility to those with a little capital, both in Florence and anywhere else the industry was present. The most spectacular example of a career woven out of wool was the takeoff of the Fugger family in late-fourteenth-century Augsburg. It is no coincidence that textile cities and wool regions like Flanders and England were already producing relatively open societies in the Middle Ages. Nevertheless, the gap between rich and poor was extreme. The richest one percent of Florentines possessed more than one-quarter of the city's wealth; the situation was similar elsewhere, such as in Basel.[53]

To contemporaries, it seemed as if Florence, Burckhardt's "Italy of Italy," was everywhere. "You Florentines are the fifth element," Pope Boniface VIII called to a delegation from the Arno during the jubilee year of 1300.[54] Charles of Anjou had waged his war for Naples with Florentine money. Florentine funds were available to the French when they went to war with the English, and to the English when they went to war with France. Florentines regularly visited the trade fairs in Champagne and had offices all over Europe. How far their horizon stretched is documented in a book known as the *Pratica della mercatura*, "The Practice of Commerce" (also called the *Merchant's Handbook*). Its author was Francesco Balducci Pegolotti, manager of the London branch of the Bardi Company. He describes routes from Azov to Beijing and from the Cilician coast to Tabriz, gives practical advice—to grow a beard in Muslim territories, for example—and notes units of weight and measure, prices, products for sale, and much more.[55]

The company Pegolotti worked for was at the forefront of Florentine high finance in the first half of the fourteenth century, along with the consortium headed by the Peruzzi family. The Bardi and Peruzzi had earned their money through trade and moneylending. Profits were invested in buildings and land—and in salvation. No less than Giotto and his workshop were commissioned by the Peruzzi to paint the family chapel in Santa Croce. In 1308, their working capital was nearly 150,000 lire *a fiorino*. A bit later, the Bardi were valued at 1,266,756 lire.[56] It was a tremendous figure, more than all the money ever earned by the other Florentine bankers (including the Medici) combined—four times Florence's annual public revenue.

The Bardi and Peruzzi were not the only ones with chests of gold in their vaults, however. Florentine citizens possessed the greatest amount of private wealth in the world at the time. They invested their money in property outside the city walls. The communal government, in contrast, bought the freedom of bondsmen so as to open up reservoirs of labor to the city.[57] Money multiplied out in the countryside as if it grew on trees. In addition to the cultivation of grain, it enabled the planting of vines and olive trees—investments that needed decades to bear fruit. The city shaped the countryside. The incomparable Tuscan landscape with its scattered farmsteads, its *case sparse*, is a masterwork of capitalism.

The commune's tax revenues—the lion's share coming from customs duties—amounted to 306,500 florins in 1338. It was enough to maintain the city walls, pave streets, and pay officials from the *podestà* to the bell ringer and trumpeter, but it was too little to wage wars. For the campaign against Castracani, Florence had borrowed 800,000 florins. The disastrous war with Lucca upended the city's finances. In 1342, the magnates then at the head of the government hatched the plan of getting a strongman to set things right. The choice fell to Walter of Brienne (ca. 1304–1356), scion of a family of Crusaders and bearer of the title Duke of Athens. It was a hollow honor, as the dukedom, a remnant of the Latin Empire, had long since been snatched away from him and fallen into the hands of the Aragonese crown. This mercenary captain also happened to be related by marriage to King Robert of Naples. Apparently, the idea behind naming him "protector" of Florence was to prevent Neapolitan funds from being withdrawn and to get the Anjou on Florence's side. Good relations with Robert were crucial to the Florentine bankers, whose own fortunes were tied to his finances and who dominated the grain trade in his realm. But when Walter attempted to set himself up as a permanent *signore*, the same clique that had installed him made sure that he disappeared. The alleys rang with calls of "Death to the Duke and his supporters! Long live the people and the commune of Florence and freedom!" The duke's men were butchered, and Walter himself fled after not even a year in power.[58] Nevertheless, the magnates were finished. A last-minute attempt to maintain their position via a coup failed. A revolt led by the guilds—once again, Fiorenza turned over in her sickbed—swept them away, and they were kept out of the new government. A complicated election system was installed with the intention of making future manipulation impossible. Yet it could not hinder the old, antagonistic factions from reorganizing and using patronage to win the allegiance of parts of the *popolo*.

Walter had been the candidate of the Bardi and the Peruzzi, and his failed putsch meant their economic ruin. In October of 1343, the Peruzzi Company declared bankruptcy; its failure dragged a series of other firms down with it.[59] Decline had already set in a decade earlier. The burdens of the Lucca disaster were exacerbated by the Curia's decision to shift its financial business away from Florence's banks. Florentine trade was not disrupted by this crisis, though. New, smaller firms took the place of the bankrupt behemoths, and the Florentine lily continued to circulate in the markets of half the world. The agile Francesco Datini (ca. 1335–1410), for example, cast his nets from Avignon, where he based himself in 1350, and then from Prato and Florence over southern France, northern Spain, and Italy. He traded in all manner of goods, including weapons and wool, ostrich feathers from North Africa, and leather falcon hoods from Paris. Salutati drank wine he supplied.[60] At the end of the century, the merchant and chronicler Goro Dati described the Florentines as having spread their wings over the Earth, with access to novelties and news from every corner.[61] Dati was one of the countless chroniclers that Florence produced at the time. Perhaps no other city in the world had such a rich tradition of *ricordanze* (memoirs) and diaries, which were often continued over generations. Many grew out of account books. They noted grain prices, genealogies, important family developments, business concerns, local events, and words of wisdom from the authors for the benefit of their descendants. *Zibaldone*, or "Hodgepodge," is what Giovanni Rucellai (1403–1483) called his own diary of this kind.

In the offices of Florence and Italy, calculations were now being done with the abacus and Indian numerals, including the mighty zero. Al-Khwarizmi's work had found translators.[62] Books of arithmetic went a long way to securing the victory of the decimal system. The most famous was Leonardo Fibonacci's (1170–1240) *Liber abaci*. It begins with a chapter on the "nine numerals of the Indians." The introduction to its first chapter promises that "with these nine figures, and with the symbol 0 which the Arabs call zephir, any number whatsoever is written, as is demonstrated below."[63] Leonardo probably became acquainted with Arabic mathematics in Béjaïa in North Africa, where his father worked as a notary for Pisan merchants. Italian townspeople practiced thinking in terms of currencies, weights, and measures, regardless of whether it was with Roman or Indian-Arabic numerals. Giovanni Villani (ca. 1280–1348) provides us with a vivid example. A partner in the Buonaccorsi Company, he was a numbers man and a founder of Florence's reputation as the home of modern statistics. Thanks to him, we know that his fellow citizens consumed 140 *moggia* of grain each day—corresponding to a volume of nearly 82,000 liters—butchered 4,000 cows and calves a year, as well as 30,000 pigs and 60,000 wethers and sheep, not to mention the thousands upon thousands of melons that were carted into the city through the Porta San Frediano each July.[64]

The abacus, currency conversion, money, and business dealings— momentous side effects of the economic expansion that banking also had a part in generating—planted what has been called an "arithmetic mentality" in people's heads. This familiarity with numbers was a precondition for the development of the higher mathematics of the Renaissance.[65] Merchants and bankers, therefore, joined jurists in laying the foundations for the Scientific Revolution of the early modern age. Arithmetic thinking may also have influenced the arts in Florence and other incubators of capitalism, as can be seen in the sophisticated proportions that govern certain pictures and buildings, and later in linear perspective.[66] At any rate, the money earned from commerce and crafts was now used to construct monumental buildings. The Dominican church of Santa Maria Novella began rising on the western edge of Florence in the mid-twelfth century. Before the turn of the thirteenth, the cornerstone was also laid for Santa Croce, the Franciscan house of God which would soon become one of the most important religious sites in Italy. The walls of these churches provided free space for frescoes, and the portals and facades required sculptural ornamentation. Also before 1300, Arnolfo di Cambio, son of a provincial notary, began building the city hall that would later be called the Palazzo Vecchio, a fortified monument of guild power and a manifesto of communal liberty. He also initiated the rebuilding of the cathedral, which, as the city council ordered, was to be constructed "for the dignity and honor of omnipotent God, His mother the Blessed Virgin Mary, and Saint Reparata, and for the honor and adornment of the city of Florence."[67] The undertaking was, in part, a response to the megalomaniac cathedral project of Florence's rival, Siena. Between 1330 and 1336, the goldsmith and sculptor Andrea Pisano created bronze reliefs for the south doors of the Florentine baptistery, featuring scenes from the life of the city's patron saint, John the Baptist. The clothing of the figures has an ancient feel to it. A new Athens was in formation.

Europe Enters the Age of Art

Giotto (1266–1337) was the first postclassical artist to be so famous that anecdotes about him circulated.[68] Boccaccio made this man, "who may justly be considered one of the shining glories of Florence," the hero of a story in his *Decameron*. When Dante was writing the *Comedy*, the fame of Giotto, then still alive, was already eclipsing that of Cimabue, another pioneer of the new style of painting:

> In painting Cimabue thought he held
> the field, and now it's Giotto they acclaim—
> the former only keeps a shadowed fame.[69]

Giotto's career took him through the patronage landscape of Italy. The majority of his time was spent in Florence, where he was entrusted with overseeing the cathedral project in his final years. The freestanding Campanile was begun according to a design by him and Arnolfo di Cambio.

At more or less the same time as Florence, Siena entered a new artistic epoch of its own. In Duccio di Buoninsegna (ca. 1255–1318) and his student Simone Martini (ca. 1284–1344), the commune found two masters who likewise broke with the *maniera greca*, the "Greek" or "Byzantine style" that dominated Europe from Cefalù to Canterbury. What they produced for their contemporaries on walls and wood panels must have had a simply sensational effect. People were accustomed to icons or frescoes that had been darkened by the smoke of oil lamps and that had the aspect of large, at times clumsy sketches. The new art embedded scenes in plausibly constructed landscapes, outside cities and buildings, and no longer represented the sky as golden but rather blue and bustling with clouds. Figures were given three-dimensional bodies by means of shading; their faces were endowed with individuality, and they showed emotions. The new direction originated in the cities and courts of Italy. In Assisi, an équipe of painters began adorning San Francesco with frescoes in this entirely new, realistic style in the late thirteenth century. It was hardly a coincidence that Tuscany and Umbria were joined at the forefront of the trend by Padua, the first capital of early humanism. Giotto created a masterpiece for the moneylender Enrico degli Scrovegni (Plate 5) there. Besides ducats, Padua had an open-minded lay public, one that desired images that could not only be prayed to but also admired as "beautiful" and that enhanced the prestige of one's family and the fame of the city.

Byzantine painters had never attempted the kind of naturalism that the artists of Italy were now practicing. They seldom treated secular themes, and they just as seldom made use of lifelike forms from pagan antiquity. In their conception of how images worked, the depiction had a close spiritual relationship with the thing being depicted. It was a prototype of the image, its idea in the Platonic sense. Seen this way, a Marian icon was itself a relic of the Mother of God: a holy object in whose creation God himself participated.[70] In consequence, painters sought to stay as close as possible to the archetype. Innovation, *kainotomia*, was condemned as heretical.[71] In the west as well, icons imported from Byzantium were venerated as primeval charms. Some, like Venice's *Nicopeia*, were considered works of Saint Luke, the first portraitist of the Madonna. Yet in Latin Europe—in stark contrast to the Byzantine tradition—deviation from what had come before, that is the originality of a work, became the criterion of its quality. The complex societies of the fourteenth century embraced the view expounded by Gregory the Great, namely that images were useful for educating the illiterate in the truths of the faith.[72]

Roger Bacon had laid a theoretical foundation for this notion. In his *Opus maius*, completed in 1267, he called for expositions on the Bible to visually portray the things and places mentioned in scripture with the help of geometry, depicting them three-dimensionally.[73] In this way, it would be possible "with one's eyes" to enter the heavenly Jerusalem that only hovered before the prophets as a vision, and thus to grasp the deeper meaning of Holy Writ in a way perceivable by the senses. Although intended as an aid to biblical exegesis and preaching, it reads like a manual for contemporary painters. Their pictures were painted orations for the same audience that listened to the vivid sermons of the Franciscans. Next to the old, magical icons, next to speaking, bleeding, or weeping images, *works of art* appeared.[74] Sometimes, like in Siena in 1311, they even displaced icons. A simple but miraculous image of Mary in the city's cathedral—the Sienese believed its magic had assured the victory at Montaperti—was replaced by Duccio's *Maestà*. Like some of the figures arranged around her, the Madonna looks out at the faithful. Her pose recalls the Madonnas of the Byzantine icons. But Duccio depicts her Cosmati throne in perspective, and she herself, the angels, and the saints are draped in realistic clothing. The traditional gold heightening of the folds is largely abandoned. When the monumental work was completed, citizens and clergy accompanied the image of their queen in triumph into the cathedral. Stores and workshops were closed, and the bells were rung. Whereas beforehand people had paid respect to an ancient, magical cultic icon, now they admired a piece of craftsmanship of the utmost refinement. Later, some painters used tricks—such as painting cracks or holes on the parchment of an illuminated manuscript—to demonstrate that they had created an illusion, literally an *artificial* work.[75]

Latin Europe's painters honed skills that let them portray nature with increasing precision. From there, it was only a small step to developing new genres of painting that occupied secular terrain. One of the first to strike out on this path was Ambrogio Lorenzetti. Between 1337 and 1340, he decorated facing walls of Siena's Palazzo Pubblico with the above-mentioned allegory of communal government, his *Buon' Governo*, and its counterpart *Cattivo Governo*, or *Bad Government*. The frescos attempt to portray Siena and its countryside as they actually were. Never before had secular themes been given a place of such prominence.[76]

Now and for a long time to come, Europe's buildings featured pointed arches and wimpergs. Nevertheless, following in the wake of the literary renaissance of the twelfth century, ancient models began to be imitated in sculpture and architecture as well. In 1210, a portico resembling a triumphal arch was affixed to the cathedral of Città Castellana, a hamlet north of Rome. Famous examples of "proto-Renaissance" architecture in Tuscany include Florence's Baptistery and San Miniato al Monte. But we must look beyond Italy as well. The "sketchbook" of Villard de Honnecourt (ca. 1230) contains drawings of ancient statues (Fig. 15, p. 214). The author was probably also familiar with the geometry of Roman architecture.[77]

More and more often, sculpture portrayed individual human features (although the models were anonymous). All this dovetails with the traces of a new subjectivity and enthusiasm for antiquity that we have noted in philosophy, poetry, and song. However, many themes and beings of ancient origin, such as monsters like sirens and sphinxes, were familiar throughout the entire Middle Ages. They are remnants from antiquity, not evidence of a renaissance.[78] Sirens, maybe even the god of light Mithras, mingle unabashedly with Christian motifs on the capitals of the cloister in Monreale. When the masters of the twelfth century worked with texts rather than stone, they often relied on familiar patterns and structures. Thus, in one commentary on Martianus Capella's *Marriage of Philology and Mercury*, Mars appears as a knight, whereas the divine ruler Jupiter is portrayed as a medieval king. Further evidence of a "renaissance before the Renaissance" is provided by the work of goldsmiths—from Liège and Cologne, for example—as well as by figures adorning Reims Cathedral, where medieval sculpture and antiquity meet for the first time as equals.[79] In Italy, relief sculpture on pulpits in Siena and Pisa by Nicola Pisano (1210/20–1278/87) gives a foretaste of the new style. Nicola may have grown up in Apulia and been trained in the classicizing atmosphere of Frederick II's court.[80] The most famous piece of architecture in Frederick's empire is the marble octagon of Castel del Monte. Blazing white under the blue of the southern sky, it appears to be conceived in the geometric spirit of the Renaissance. Whether it was a hunting lodge, a fortress, or a refuge is still a mystery.

Intellectual Ascent: Petrarca

Malaucène, southern France. April 26, 1336. What an adventure! Mont Ventoux stands mightily before the eyes of Francesco Petrarca (1304–1374).[81] The Italian native has taken up lodging in this small town in Provence and sets out from there to climb the mountain. He was inspired to do so by a passage in Livy's *History of Rome* that records a similar deed, King Philip V of Macedon's ascent of Mount Haemus in Thessaly. Mild spring weather eases the difficulty of the climb, on which Petrarca is accompanied by his brother and two servants. The summit provides a view of the snow-covered Alps, beyond the Rhone to the sea. Yearning with an "incalculable passion" to see his homeland, the traveler casts his gaze in the direction of Italy.

As chance would have it, Petrarca has Augustine's *Confessions* with him. He opens the book and happens upon a passage perfectly suited to deflating joy of an all too earthly nature:

> And men go forth to marvel at the heights of mountains and the vast waves of the sea and the broad flow of rivers and the compass of the ocean and the cycles of the stars, and they leave themselves behind.

Petrarca realizes that only one's own soul is worthy of wonder. Thus, he turns his gaze inward upon himself and climbs back down to the valley with his companions in silence. The moon lights the way.

We do not know if the most famous mountain trek in literary history actually happened as Petrarca described it to a friend. A hike of that kind, for the mere sake of seeing the view from the top, had reportedly not been attempted by anyone for a long time. The landscape was generally arduous, overgrown, and wild. Yet admiration for the beauty of nature was not entirely foreign to the Middle Ages. The mythical Celtic warrior and poet Fionn Mac Cumhaill takes us on a ramble through a "delightful" May morning, accompanied by the nightingale's song and the call of the cuckoo, the "summer-lover." And the troubadour Bernard of Ventadour, for his own joy and that of his love, sings of the green grass and the blossoming trees and flowers.[82] The "modern" aspect of Petrarca's text is its subjectivity, the reflection about his own mental state that he engages in when confronted with the vast panorama. He compares his ascent with the strenuous pilgrimage to salvation, muses about the swift transformation of mores, and ends with the wish that his unsteady thoughts might finally turn to the one, the good, the true, the eternal. The ascent is an allegory for the life of a man who wanders without ever arriving at a destination.

Who was this Francesco Petrarca, traditionally known to the English-speaking world as Francis Petrarch? Born the son of a notary named Petracco in Arezzo in Tuscany—and thus another product of the biotope of the new lay culture—he was originally destined for the dry-as-dust career of a lawyer. But he chose instead to enter the service of the Curia in Avignon and take minor orders. This made it possible for him to accrue the benefices that secured his livelihood. Petrarca lived a life on the move. We find him in Italian cities, in France, Flanders, and Brabant, sometimes on diplomatic missions. In a monastery in Liège, he found a lost text of Cicero, the oration *Pro Archia*—a praise of literary education that must have warmed his heart.

> These studies are the food of youth, the delight of old age; the ornament of prosperity, the refuge and comfort of adversity; a delight at home, and no hindrance abroad; they are companions by night, and in travel, and in the country.[83]

Petrarca praised the life of solitude as the best kind in his *De vita solitaria*, and he regularly retreated to it. One refuge was Vaucluse, near Avignon, where he owned a simple house. The village is famous for its spring, known as "the Sorgue." Petrarca rhapsodized about its "clear, sweet fresh water" in his poetry.[84] The sonnet form, whose origins lay in Frederick II's Sicily, was taken to new heights by Petrarca. His *Canzoniere* would go on to inspire imitation at the hands of some of the most sublime poets for centuries, including Shakespeare, Milton, and Rilke. Never before had Europe produced an author who dealt with the themes of love, death, nature, and solitude as eloquently as Petrarca. His focus was consistently on the tormented self. To find a forerunner, we must go back to Catullus. "I hate and love," we read in his famous poem 85.

> I hate and love—wherefore I cannot tell,
> But by my tortures know the fact too well.[85]

Petrarca most likely encountered the opposite of sweet sorrow in Naples, where he found a patron in Robert of Anjou,

> The good Sicilian king who gazed on high
> And saw far and wide.[86]

The court of the highly educated ruler was a magnet for talent. Robert had already attracted Giotto and the sculptor Tino da Camaino; later on, Boccaccio, whose father was an agent for the Bardi in Naples, would arrive in the city at the foot of Vesuvius. Petrarca's praises did not go unsung in the Castel

Nuovo. On Easter Sunday in the year 1341, his king crowned him poet laureate on the Roman Capitol. The oration Petrarca held on this occasion reveals how he saw himself: as a poet and a scholar determined to revive ancient traditions.[87] He had no interest in hairsplitting theology, and he indulged in invectives against the philosophy of his time. Instead, he sought to produce political poetry modeled on the works of Virgil and Cicero. Impious he was not; he placed his laurel crown on the altar of Saint Peter. As he saw it, he was working in the service of Italy's cultural renewal. He sought Rome's fame and, ultimately, also his own. He exhorted the Romans to finally fight for their freedom.[88] The ruins of imperial grandeur held him in their thrall just like they had Hildebert of Lavardin. He collected ancient coins and hunted successfully for manuscripts. He condemned "Gothic" script as hard to read, indeed disparaging it as "invented for something other than reading."[89] Instead, he used a handwriting based on Carolingian minuscule. It seemed to him to be more practical and more beautiful; whether he also valued it because he thought it was ancient, we do not know, but it is not unlikely.

Like Dante before him and Machiavelli afterward, he railed in vain against Italy's internal strife. More than any of his contemporaries, Petrarca exemplifies how the study of antiquity could be animated by a sense of patriotism and disgust with the sad political reality of the day. In his mind, Italy's grand history demonstrated what it could achieve and how its future should look. "Hail to thee, land most holy, of God beloved. . . . Hail, O beautiful mother, creation's glory," Petrarca addressed his *Italia*.[90]

In Florence, he met Boccaccio; the two men started up a correspondence. During a long stay in Milan, where the Visconti, now the most powerful family in northern Italy, were his patrons, he wrote two of his chief works: the *Trionfi*, or *Triumphs*—once again, love, death, immortality, and glory were the themes— and *Remedies for Fortune Fair and Foul*, a moral-philosophical investigation of the ups and downs of life. Much of what he wrote remained unfinished, such as a collection of biographies of great Romans and biblical heroes, as well as the hero Hercules. His letters, often rhetorical showpieces, were written not only to contemporaries but also to great figures from antiquity like Cicero, Horace, and Homer. In this way, he became a pioneer of the letter as a literary genre. His work spread quickly. By the late sixteenth century, his influence reached as far as Mexico, where the priest Tomás de Plaza decorated the reception hall of his house with frescoes depicting scenes from the *Trionfi* (Fig. 21, p. 296).[91]

The question of whether Petrarca was the first modern poet, with Dante as the last medieval poet, admits of no clear answer. Both were protagonists

in the discursive revolution, and both of their oeuvres are hallmarks of an explosion of creativity sparked by ancient models (although this is less the case with Dante). Petrarca calls Plato the prince of philosophers, placing him above Aristotle.[92] His view of women is different from that of the *Commedia*'s author. In Dante's cantos, Beatrice vanishes into pure theology, whereas Petrarca's Laura—a beautiful woman he claims to have met at church in 1327— has bright eyes, and the wind plays with her blond hair.[93] This Laura, the unfulfilled love of his life and muse of his poetry, might be a fiction, an attractive literary figure like Catullus's Lesbia, and yet she is more real than the ethereal Beatrice. Beatitude was the ultimate desire of both Petrarca and Dante. Yet the latter achieved it as a poetic vision of unprecedented force, whereas the former found it in the solitude of books, in remote villages, and atop a regal mountain, Mount Ventoux.

If we take the differences between the two great poets as our guide, the line between the Middle Ages and the Renaissance seems razor thin.[94] Petrarca distinguishes himself most clearly from his older compatriot in his introspection, which would have parallels in the portraiture of the early Renaissance. He was a bit more oriented toward the earthly world than Dante; he wandered through France and Europe in the hope of seeing things. His antiquarian interests were much more pronounced, leading him to discover Cicero's letters to Atticus in Verona. How close Dante felt to antiquity must remain an open question. In his *Comedy*, heroes and villains from every century exist side by side; the hereafter knows no time and no past, only present. In contrast, Petrarca had a very well-developed historical sense. He viewed his own time as an age of darkness, of *tenebrae*, cut off from the radiant days of ancient Rome, which was the measure of all history. In a letter written to his patron and friend, Cardinal Giovanni Colonna, at the time of his poetic crowning, Petrarca discoursed on the archaeology of downfallen greatness.

> As we walked over the walls of the shattered city or sat there, the fragments of the ruins were under our very eyes. Our conversation often turned on history, which we appeared to have divided up between us in such a fashion that in modern history you, in ancient history I, seemed to be more expert; and ancient were called those events which took place before the name of Christ was celebrated in Rome and adored by the Roman emperors, modern, however, the events from that time to the present.[95]

But Petrarca hoped for a resurrection. His unfinished *Africa*, an epic about the Second Punic War, ends with the vision of a better future:

> My fate is to live amid varied and confusing storms. But for you perhaps, if as I hope and wish you will live long after me, there will follow a better age. This sleep of forgetfulness will not last for ever. When the darkness has been dispersed, our descendants can come again in the former pure radiance.[96]

This passage presages the later division of history into three basic periods: antiquity, a *medium tempus*, or Middle Age, that has far too long been unjustly considered "dark," and modernity, in which the century following Petrarca would locate itself. Petrarca, however, set his hopes on a distant future; the present was a time of melancholy.

> Life flies, and never stays an hour,
> and death comes on behind with its dark day,
> and present things and past things
> embattle me, and future things as well.[97]

17

A World(view) Falls Apart

The Triumph of Death

Dark Ages? Petrarca's estimation of his times was based on real circumstances, circumstances that elsewhere—as in France—also made melancholy and *taedium vitae* major themes of literature.[1] Indeed, the sunny days of the Warm Period were long gone.[2] Temperatures sank, perhaps due to dust hurled into the atmosphere by a volcanic eruption near the equator that darkened the sun. Glaciers advanced on the valleys. Farms were being given up in Sweden and Norway as early as the thirteenth century; the fires used to clear forests died down, the drive to settle new areas slackened. An expedition from Norway and Sweden to Greenland found the villages there abandoned. Food became increasingly scarce and expensive. Famines struck between 1315 and 1317 and on a recurring basis thereafter. Europe's demographic bodies wasted away.

A mechanism inexorably took hold that has tormented many societies, not only those of pre-industrial Europe. The population had expanded faster than could be supported by farm yields. Scarcity and death were the result, when wars and epidemics did not violently establish a new equilibrium. Emigration, the clearing of new land, and technical innovations like the wheeled plow could postpone the disaster, but they could not prevent it. For a while life would get better, until a critical mass was reached and people began dying off again. The "Malthusian trap" was known long before the man for whom the law is named, economist Thomas Malthus (1766–1834), first described it. The oldest Akkadian epic, the *Atra-Hasis*, describes how population expands, making the land "bellow like a wild animal" and disturbing the tranquility of the gods. The solution is birth control and murderous methods: pestilence, drought, and flood inflicted upon the people by the god Enlil.[3]

The first of Enlil's three killers returned to Europe in the 1340s. The plague, or Black Death, perhaps a viral hemorrhagic disease similar to Ebola, crept westward from Asia. In the words of Emmanuel Le Roy Ladurie, microbes united the world.[4] In 1346, the plague arrived at the Genoese colony of Caffa on the Crimean Peninsula. The city had just been besieged by Mongols. The conquerors engaged in biological warfare, catapulting stinking, plague-infested corpses into the city. The pestilence then traveled as an invisible passenger aboard trade ships and war galleys to Italy. It hit Messina in 1347, then Pisa and Genoa. At the same time, Europe was struck by one of its periodic bouts of extreme famine. The starving were easy victims, but the plague soon ceased distinguishing between weak and strong and attacked everything it could. It pushed on to England and sneaked into Scandinavia. The army of corpses it created soon numbered in the millions. Petrarca, whose Laura succumbed to it in 1348, paints a bleak picture in his *Triumph of Death*.

> She scarce had spoke, when o'er the shaded plain,
> Approached, in mournful march, a countless train;
> Beyond the power of prose or poets lay
> To number, or to name. From rich Cathay,
> From India, Spain, and Mauritania's coast,
> Like meeting floods, appear'd the mighty host;
> The sons of every clime and every age,
> And covering far the mighty mundane stage.
> Then Fortune's minions in the press appear'd,
> Pontiffs, and kings, and potentates rever'd;

But now naked, disconsolate, and bare,
They look a ghastly squadron of despair.[5]

Petrarca ascribed these events to an unprecedented conjunction of the planets; they seemed to him to indicate that the end of the world was nigh.

The Black Death was a nameless terror.[6] Symptoms began with a swelling of the lymph nodes. Rashes followed, along with dizziness, chills, and severe pain; some people spit blood. Death set in once the lungs were reached, usually on the same day, sometimes after three days. One chronicler living in Orvieto remarked tersely, "People were healthy one morning, dead the next."[7] And another observed, "Wives fled the embrace of their beloved husbands, fathers avoided sons, brothers eschewed brothers."[8] Some were left to die alone, without the sacraments; no doctor or priest dared to get close. The desperate cries of the sick echoed eerily from the abandoned buildings. In great haste, often unaccompanied by the wailing of women, the tolling of bells, or a funeral mass, the dead were piled up and dumped in multi-leveled mass graves. A little dirt was sprinkled over the top, then another layer of bodies was thrown in, and then another layer of dirt—"like making lasagna," one sarcastic Florentine chronicler observed.[9] People fled to the countryside. In Venice, so many people died that the Great Council could not reach a quorum.

The plague was considered divine punishment for a world turned upside down. Was the Lord punishing his people like he had in biblical prehistory with the Great Flood? The jurist Gabriele de Mussis reported that in China, "where the world begins," masses of hideous snakes and toads had presaged the disaster; in India and in Europe, its arrival had been preceded by earthquakes.[10] Processions and the magical power of relics, penance, and prayer had no effect. Hygienic measures were inadequate, the medical art artless. Bleak columns of pious men whipping themselves bloody were a staple of the Late Middle Ages. So were Jewish pogroms. Scapegoats were found, like at the time the Crusades were launched; it was also an excuse for debtors to shirk their loans. The physician Guy de Chauliac, author of the most famous medieval handbook of surgery, observed that Jews were not the only ones branded "poisoners," blamed for the mass death, and killed. The disabled and, in some places, even the nobility were banished.[11] In the Holy Roman Empire, in France, and in Spain—though curiously not in Italy—Jews were murdered, their property seized and distributed. This sinister zeal had a history; the foundation had long since been laid for the hatred of the Jews. Persecution had

picked up in the second half of the thirteenth century. The victims were accused of ritual infanticide or desecrating the host.

Religious exercises were a way of making God merciful, pogroms of anticipating His purification of the world. Chroniclers also report very different
reactions. The terror of death inspired zest for life. Matteo Villani, Giovanni's
brother, tells us that survivors, who had now inherited a great deal of property, lost all their inhibitions and unrestrainedly indulged in food and drink.
"They loved feasts and taverns, treasured pleasant things, delicacies, and
games."[12] One-third of Europe's population, perhaps even one-half, died of
the plague. For some unknown reason, the majority of the victims were
people in middle age.

The consequences were profound. The money of the dead went to the survivors—a very different case than after a war, which tended to destroy both
people and their property.[13] Interest rates sank, and, since fewer people had to
be fed than before, so did food prices, thus leaving more money available for
luxury goods. Villages were abandoned; occasionally the remains of walls
amidst a secluded wood still stand as a reminder. The land lay fallow. Workers
were nearly impossible to find, especially since the mid-century pandemic was
followed by resurgences of the plague. Laws aimed at keeping wages low had
little effect.[14] The demographic collapse drove the collapse of large estates.[15]
Peasants were often able to secure more favorable conditions and have their
payments reduced. On this account, and because of falling prices for agricultural products, the revenues of the manorial lords decreased. To mitigate their
financial difficulties, the landed nobility had to take out loans and mortgage
their estates. Some lost them altogether. Not a few lords descended to the ranks
of the townspeople or the peasantry. Some resorted to violence to secure new
sources of income, staging raids from their castles and preying on traveling
merchants. Many became leaders of mercenary bands, initiating the great age
of *condottieri*. Others sought employment as civil servants or diplomats.

The money left behind by plague victims was drawn inside city walls by
commerce and crafts. There, despite political upheavals, it funded another
round of lavish building. Town halls and churches were erected. People seem
to have reacted to this period of ubiquitous death, which remained deeply
seated in collective memory, in much the same way as they did when the
plague first hit. Some sought to reduce their time in purgatory and purchase
salvation by doing good works. Others focused on the here and now, seized
the day, and treated fleeting life as a party. All these strategies were good for
the arts, no matter whether a chapel was frescoed, an altarpiece commissioned,

or a sumptuous palace built. The energy now being invested in art was ultimately set free by the accumulation of capital caused by mass mortality. For example, the Florentine confraternity of Orsanmichele inherited 350,000 gold florins from its deceased members; it put 86,000 of them into the tabernacle of its church, Orcagna's marvel of marble, lapis lazuli, glass, and gold (finished in 1359).[16] Some ambitious communal projects came to a standstill, however, as there were no longer enough taxpayers to fund them. The most spectacular example is provided by the incomplete cathedral in Siena. The widely admired church is only the nave of a much larger structure that was never built.

The art inside churches had become conspicuously gloomy, even if the terrible harvest of death from 1347 to 1350 found no painters to immortalize it.[17] The only traces of its memory were left in chronicles and manuscript illuminations. The fresco cycle in the Camposanto in Pisa, which features the same "triumph of death" that Petrarca conjured in apocalyptic word pictures, was completed before the plague hit. It thus perfectly documents the new mentality that climatic change, agrarian crisis, and overpopulation had already brought about in the first half of the fourteenth century. At the end of that period, Johannes von Tepl has his "Plowman" call out, "Grim Destroyer of mankind, vengeful Persecutor of the whole world, frightful Murderer of all men, Thou, Death, be cursed!"[18]

Division Everywhere

The Grim Reaper inexorably drove pestilence and starvation across Europe. Of profound consequence was also a series of wars between the Plantagenets and the Valois, a cadet line of the Capetians that had ruled France since 1328. Although punctuated by periods of peace, the conflicts stretching from 1337 to 1453 became collectively known as the Hundred Years' War.[19] Its deep roots were buried in the strange relationship, mentioned above, that both united and divided the kings of England and France: the rulers of the island of Britain were vassals of the French in Aquitaine, which is what remained of the Angevin kingdom. Then, when his French relative Charles IV died without a male heir, Edward III asserted a claim to the empty throne. This constellation of conflicts resulted in the first pan-European war, its theaters also including Scotland, Flanders, and Castile.[20] In the end, England had been largely driven back to its island, whereas France's borders came somewhat closer to their modern outline.

The great war was a cruel companion of the age. It was waged at tremendous cost, thus increasing the tax burden. The mercenaries it left unoccupied in times of peace brought misery to the people and provoked rebellions. The most dangerous for traditional elites was called the "Jacquerie"—after "Jacques Bonhomme," i.e., "Jack Goodfellow," the derisive name given to peasants by the nobility. The revolt engulfed Paris, the north of the Île-de-France, Picardy, and Champagne. Even townspeople and a few royal officials participated. Out of the twilight of the written record, the merchant Étienne Marcel appears as one of the leaders. He sought to use the dynamic of the rebellion to strengthen the crown against the nobility, and at the same time to subject it to the oversight of the Estates. Petrarca, an eyewitness to events in the French capital, lamented, "One no longer hears the shouts of disputants but of warriors; weapons are piled up, not books; and the walls reverberate not with syllogisms and orations but with vigils and the battering of the ram."[21] Castles in the countryside went up in flames. Aristocrats were killed, their wives raped. According to the chronicler Jean Froissart, one knight was burned by his peasants on a bonfire in front of his family.[22] Only with difficulty did the king prevail. Marcel paid with his life.

Everywhere, things were in motion. The annals record the rise and quick fall of charismatic leaders. One was Cola di Rienzo, who the Roman populace had named "tribune of the people" in 1347.[23] His program—to liberate first Rome and then all of Italy—echoed longstanding yearnings. Petrarca himself offered to sing the praises of the new Rome, to be its new Livy. Dressed in an ancient Roman toga, his hero, the son of an innkeeper and a laundress, paraded around in triumph, dubbing himself "the warrior of the Holy Spirit, exigent and mild, liberator of the city, Italian patriot, friend of the globe, and noble tribune."[24] Cola embodied a bizarre combination of the Renaissance and the apocalyptic beliefs of Joachim of Fiore. Taking on the people and the nobility of Rome, the pope, and the emperor all at once would have been too much for anyone. In 1354, Cola was killed by a craftsman. Thanks to the eloquence of an anonymous author, a Giotto of the word, we have an image of him like no one else of his century: his head bobbing back and forth, the tips of his toes twitching.

France remained restless. Revolts broke out periodically, in Germany as well. To the Sienese chronicler Donato di Neri, it seemed like division was everywhere.[25] There had been power struggles in the burgeoning cities of the Warm Period, but the tension had a different quality now. The people, Jack Goodfellow, had greater power than before. The "people," however, included more than just les misérables, the abject and poorest element of society. An upper middle class of merchants, knights, and dignitaries weary of the battles of Roman noble families had propelled Cola di Rienzo to power.[26] Wealthy farmers and urban craftsmen, even royal officials, supported the Jacquerie. It is not only "bad times" that drive people to the barricades—otherwise half the world would still be in revolt today. More is required, such as the conviction that one is suffering injustice, or the fear of losing everything, and on the other side the prospect of advancement and power, paired with weakness and loss of control on the part of rulers.

When there was no fighting to do, unemployed mercenary bands, called *routiers*, roamed the countryside and tormented the people. The Black Death exacerbated the tension in various ways. Not only did it eviscerate moral standards; it also restructured society to an extent Europe had not experienced since antiquity. The half-empty cities were more attractive than ever to immigrants. Florence's population, for example, which had shrunk to about thirty thousand souls around 1350, numbered seventy thousand again by the end of the century. Whereas the business capital and estates of plague victims accumulated at the upper end of the social stratum, immigration caused the underclasses of the cities to explode. Textile workers did not profit from prosperity, as the death of so many people at once destroyed their market. After all, the dead only need one shirt for all eternity. Poor weavers had no rights and no political voice, and for them immigration meant competition for work and wages. Change of any kind could only be an improvement. Of course, they never sought to utterly overturn the social order. The term "guild revolution" (*Zunftrevolution*), coined to describe the power struggles between craftsmen and patricians in the cities north of the Alps, disguises the fact that it was usually only a few seats on the city council that were at stake, and that at first it was about recognition for the rights and honor of labor.[27] Another deep cause of unrest was the state's insatiable hunger for money. Most funds went not to palaces or feasts, although they were a particularly glaring grievance, but rather down the bottomless gullet of war.[28] Around 1390, a mercenary captain earned 140 times as much as a laborer at a building site.[29]

The Peasants' Revolt in England was fallout not only of the plague but also of the heavy weight of taxes, and the burdens of the Hundred Years' War only exacerbated things.[30] In a short span of time, the English Parliament had approved two new poll taxes. A third caused things to spill over. June of 1381 witnessed an uprising of ten thousand peasants, petty craftsmen, poor workers and other people, some of them rather wealthy. It started in Kent and Essex and then spread to London. The protest widened, demanding fundamental rights: individual freedom and equality. The English may have been inspired by events in Flanders, as the citizens of Ghent had just rebelled against their count.

For the first time, religion also put wood on the fire. John Ball, a follower of the reform-minded Oxford theologian John Wyclif (1330–1384), is credited with an explosive phrase: "When Adam delved and Eve span, who was then the gentleman?"[31] In London, the revolutionaries laid waste to the palace of John of Gaunt (1340–1399), as despised as he was rich and powerful. They precipitated massacres on Flemish merchants, destroyed documents, beheaded judicial officials and even law students. The attacks were aimed at the ostentatious property of elites and irksome competition from the Continent, and at the ink state with its bottomless gluttony for money and its written, incomprehensible law. The rebels wanted justice, not venal attorneys: "The first thing we do, let's kill all the lawyers!" a revolutionary calls in one of Shakespeare's history plays.[32]

The young King Richard II (r. 1377–1399) gave way in the face of the fury. In charters stamped with the Great Seal of England, he proclaimed all subjects of the realm free "by our special grace," declared all forced labor obligations fulfilled, and called an amnesty. On June 15, 1381, one of the most famous scenes in English history took place. Wat Tyler, one of the leaders of the revolt, met with Richard at Smithfield, then outside the city walls but now a district of London. Tyler barely bent his knee, as one chronicler indignantly observed. He gave the anointed sovereign a hearty handshake and called him his "brother." In addition to the abolition of serfdom, he demanded something Wyclif also desired: the confiscation of the wealth held by the great abbeys.[33] The interview ended dramatically. Tyler was struck down by Richard's men and taken to the place of execution, where his head was cut off. In the following weeks, the king quickly managed to quell the rebellion. To a delegation that dared to demand he make good on his promises, he is supposed to have responded, "Rustics you were and rustics you are still. You will remain in bondage, not as before, but incomparably harsher."[34] The executioners were kept busy. The crown punished John Ball with an orgy of ghastly gore: he was hanged, drawn, and quartered. The state was coming into its own, and it would not be trifled with when it came to the foundations of its authority. An important reason the English rebellion and others failed was that cracks formed in the movements as soon as the initial fire burned out, and no "Third Estate" took shape. In contrast, vertical power always reacted quickly and harshly.

The war between vertical and horizontal power was far from over when Ball's dismembered corpse was left to rot in Coventry. The call for "freedom" became a slogan. "The appetite for liberty was burning," complained a monk of Saint-Denis, referring to Paris, "the lust for new things incessant."[35] In modern times, the dead, tortured, exiled losers were resurrected and celebrated as heroes of national mythologies. Cola di Rienzo moved Lord Byron to proclaim, "Rienzi! last of Romans!"[36] and Richard Wagner wrote an opera about him. Étienne Marcel was depicted as the precursor of 1789 and had a Paris Metro station named after him. For the time being, however, fear of Jack Goodfellow and his brothers lodged in the bones of the powerful. Princes and urban tyrants surrounded themselves with walled forts.

Vertical power emerged from the revolts stronger than ever, but cities still enjoyed power here and there. In Spain, rulers' need for funds increased the influence of the Cortes, the descendants of the first representative body called by Alfonso IX. Once again, money-gobbling war was one of the fathers of their freedoms. Castile fought against Portugal and Aragon, which also had to pay for its Italian adventure; here, too, the Cortes had to help raise money. Only in the following century did their power wane. In Brabant in 1356, when the power of the count was weakened by a succession dispute, the Estates succeeded in winning civil liberties and a say in questions of war and peace.

In a few cities of the Holy Roman Empire, guilds took the helm, often for longer periods of time. With more economic weight to throw around, they demanded and won political influence. Meanwhile, the Hanseatic League had become the predominant power on the Baltic, even overcoming the king of Denmark. It traded with Flanders, England, and Portugal. Glory, honor, and greatness for their own sake meant little to merchants. Their aim was to acquire privileges and secure their markets. A peace treaty with Denmark granted them free trade on the Baltic. Further showdowns between townspeople and princes were witnessed in the south and east of Germany. Nearly all of them ended in defeat for the cities. It is hard to say how real the chances were for erecting stable horizontal power structures in the Empire, even at a distance of half a millennium. However, one of the leagues of cities did persevere. It comprised the core of what would later be the Swiss Confederacy. The decisive factor was that the Swiss alliance, as opposed to the Swabian and Rhenish leagues, won its wars against the princes: first against the Habsburgs and later against Charles the Bold. In contrast, leagues of Spanish cities achieved almost no political significance.[37]

In the long run, neither alliances nor economic power were able to help most communes maintain their independence. Ghent, Ypres, and Bruges, which largely ignored the counts of Flanders in the Late Middle Ages and had held over four thousand joint assemblies by the sixteenth century, ultimately ended up as wards of the Habsburgs. Nevertheless, military defeats did not undermine the economic importance of the German cities or the power of their leading merchants. Frankfurt became a center of trade fairs and finance. The Ravensburg Company, founded in the late fourteenth century, had subsidiaries in Italy, in Barcelona and Saragossa, in Avignon, Bruges, Vienna, and elsewhere. Nuremberg's trade relations reached from the mineral deposits of the Carpathian Mountains to Liège and Lombardy. Thanks to its favorable location on a transport route between the Empire and eastern Europe, Nuremberg was one of the most important commercial hubs in Europe.

In Prague, too, craftsmen and merchants gained influence on the city council. They backed the indebted King John of Bohemia (r. 1311–1346), who in exchange for coin provided them with privileges, including the right to collect customs duties and administer justice (*Hochgerichtsbarkeit*). In 1338, the citizens began building a town hall with royal permission. Its tower, seventy meters high, became a symbol of their increased autonomy.

An Emperor in Prague

King John of Bohemia, the heir of Henry VII, was a legend. Although blind, he fought and died at Crécy in 1346, one of the largest battles of the Hundred Years' War. In his own country, however, he remained a foreigner. His son and successor, Charles IV (r. 1346–1378), made Prague a "dear little mother with sharp claws," as Kafka put it;[38] no one who has ever gazed from the Petřin Gardens over the rooftops of Prague, shining silver in the evening sun, can escape the city's grasp. Charles managed to make his city an archiepiscopal see. The center was marked by Saint Vitus Cathedral, begun by a French master builder and continued by a Swabian, Peter Parler. It sat enthroned over the city, the twin of Hradcany Castle, symbol of worldly glory. Prague was to become a large city. Anyone who settled inside the new walls, which enclosed a space three times the size of the old town, could count on favorable conditions. The original core of the city was connected with Malá Strana, the "little side of the river," by a new stone bridge half a kilometer long. In 1348—the city was spared the plague—the first university in the Holy Roman Empire was founded there. It attracted thousands of students. More universities sprang up in German-speaking lands: in Vienna, directly inspired by the model of Prague, then in Heidelberg, capital of the Palatinate, and in 1388 in the commercial center of Cologne. Funded by the city council, the University of Cologne was the first to have both a theological and a law faculty.

With forty thousand inhabitants, Prague was one of the largest cities in Europe and a melting pot of peoples. An important Jewish community grew up around the Old New Synagogue in the Josefov quarter. German merchants constituted a privileged upper class. However, cosmopolitan peace did not reign on the Vltava River. At the end of the century, tensions between Germans and Bohemians mounted. Signs of proto-nationalism emerged. Then as later, national sentiment grew out of opposition to the "other." Charles himself had grown up in France and called himself a successor of Charlemagne; born Wenceslaus, he had taken the name Charles at his confirmation. He could speak Italian, German, and Latin, not to mention his mother tongue Czech. Italy, incidentally, only interested him insofar as its rich cities put gold florins in his coffers.

That he possessed love for learning, *amor studii*, Charles himself once proclaimed.[39] He would have been pleased to ornament his court with Petrarca, who briefly resided in Prague as an ambassador for Milan. Bohemian humanism crystallized around Charles's chancellor John of Neumarkt (ca. 1310–1380), a bishop of middle-class origin who had studied in the south.[40] Classicizing Latin glittered on imperial charters. Charles was the first ruler of the Latin Middle Ages to write an autobiography. More a confession of faith than an account of his life, however, it barely gives a sense of his personality. In contrast, "modern" subjectivity can be found in the work of Peter Parler. His busts of the emperor may depict him as he actually looked. Parler's own bust in Saint Vitus Cathedral is considered the first sculptural self-portrait in post-classical Europe.

Surrounded by jurists, physicians, astrologers, and clerics, most of them of middle-class origin, Charles IV pursued a policy of harmony with the papacy and avoided costly wars. He even sought an arrangement with the Valois. Charles was the classic example of an emperor who exercised power through extensive allodial holdings. He sought to enrich himself in the Empire and in the east, in addition to augmenting his Luxembourg inheritance. He was a pious man, an eager collector of relics and author of a legend about Wenceslaus, patron saint of Bohemia. Heretics, in his view, should be burned at the stake. This group now included Beguines and Beghards. He attempted to restore the sacral aura of his office, for example by establishing a cult of the Imperial Regalia (the Imperial Crown and the Holy Lance) that granted indulgence to initiates. In 1355, during a short stay in Rome, he was crowned emperor by a cardinal standing in for the pope.

Charles's name is associated with the decree that eliminated the pope's right of approbation in imperial elections. The "Golden Bull" issued in 1356 makes no mention of the practice. From then on, a majority of prince-electors and the coronation would suffice to make the emperor.[41] The Bull's prologue emphasizes the intention of establishing unity among the electors and—unusual for an imperial decree—gives classical examples of the dangers of discord: the Trojan War and the Roman civil wars. These passages reveal the guiding hand of a humanist, perhaps John of Neumarkt. The document granted the prince-electors numerous privileges. It guaranteed them the indivisibility of their lands, succession according to primogeniture, the right of coinage, and judicial autonomy. One provision, which, however, never became a reality, called for yearly assemblies of the prince-electors, thus giving the College a say in imperial affairs. One provision *against* horizontal power is headed "On Conspiracies." It prohibited leagues of cities, as they made life difficult for knights, princes, and even emperors. Indeed, it outlawed associations of all kinds unless they promoted the preservation of peace in the realm.

Meanwhile, it looked as if the popes might move back to Rome. From a perch in Venice, Petrarca had criticized the pope for sleeping under a gilt coffered ceiling while the roofless Lateran, the Mother of All Churches, was open to the wind and rain.[42] Nothing under the stars, he admonished, was the equal of Italy. Even its wines were on par with French Burgundy. And indeed, Urban V moved to Italy in 1367—not for the golden Frascati, of course, but rather to escape the ever-tightening embrace of the French kings, who had already seized the Dauphiné. Return seemed possible because a battle-hardened veteran of the fight against the Moors, the Castilian Cardinal Gil Albornoz, had succeeded in stabilizing the Papal States.[43] The laws he issued were so well crafted that some of them remained valid down to the nineteenth century. He died shortly after Urban's acclaimed arrival, however. Charles IV, who was again in Italy—but this time with an army behind him—could offer no protection. As a result, the pope decided to retreat to his fortress overlooking the Rhone. The prudent Albornoz had less-than-prudent successors. Rule via diplomacy, ink, and laws gave way to suppression, blood, and violence.

Petrarca saw all his hopes dashed. He died in 1374, in the peace of old age in the northern Italian town of Arquà at the foot of the Euganean Hills. In accordance with his final wishes, his "cold bones" were entombed outside the parish church of Santa Maria in a classicizing sarcophagus made of red Verona marble. The inscription reads, "May his soul, weary of the world, rest in peace in Heaven's vault."[44] Charles IV followed him to the grave four years later. Thousands of people processed with his body into St. Vitus Cathedral, where it still reposes today. Charles was the first of three emperors to be buried there. His son Wenceslaus, elected king during his lifetime, was an irascible, lazy alcoholic without any political acumen; he quickly lost everything his father had won. He did, however, manage to deprive the cities of their most potent weapon: the ability to enter into alliances. This led to the general peace agreement reached at Eger in 1389. Otherwise, Wenceslaus did not concern himself with the Empire. As one chronicler from Cologne put it, he was content to wallow in Bohemia "like a pig in his sty."[45] He gave no thought to intervening in Italian affairs, much less to acquiring the imperial crown. In 1400, he was deposed as king of Germany by the prince-electors and replaced by an impotent lord, Rupert of the Palatinate (r. 1400–1410). The first flourishing of "golden Prague" had been cut short two decades earlier, by a bout of the plague.

The English Serpent, Feverish Florence, and a Two-Headed Papacy

Anarchy reigned in Italy. Of the mercenaries who roamed the countryside in search of booty, the Englishman John Hawkwood, dubbed the "English serpent," was the most successful.[46] He was immortalized in a fresco by Paolo Uccello on the north wall of the Duomo in Florence. From a modern point of view, the captain does not seem entirely deserving of this tremendous honor. Nevertheless, it shows what extraordinary careers were possible in the chaos of fourteenth-century Italy. Hawkwood was born in the town of Sible Hedingham in Essex in 1320 or 1323. Perhaps a tailor by trade, he learned soldiering as an archer in the English army. Left unemployed after a peace treaty, he and his "White Company" first went to Avignon and then to Italy. In 1363, he became its captain. Like most men in his profession, Sir John—how he attained his knighthood, if he ever actually did, is unclear—served whoever paid him well. The only loyalty he never crossed was to England's crown. He fought now for Milan, now for the pope, often on his own account and always for his own purse. Over time, he became a large landholder and also won the hand of a bastard daughter of Bernabò Visconti, lord of Milan. In the employ of the papacy, he served under Cardinal Legate Robert of Geneva in the reconquest of the Papal States initiated by Albornoz. Florence stood in opposition.[47] Allied with Ghibelline Milan, it went to war in 1375. Using the battle cry of "Liberty!" and appealing to examples of ancient Roman resistance to monarchical tyranny, it tried to incite rebellion in cities in the Papal States. "Remember, dearest brothers, that you are Italians whose right it is to command and not to serve!"[48] The papal troops kept the upper hand, although Florence did manage to buy off Hawkwood. He spared his precious soldiers and fought no battles, but he did help to negotiate a peace treaty. He freed Florence from papal interdict, a menace to salvation and especially to trade. The pope lifted the ban in exchange for 250,000 florins, the going rate for a countship.

Right after the frustrating conclusion to the "War of the Eight Saints"— called thus for the eight magistrates responsible for military affairs in Florence—the Ciompi Revolt erupted in the city on the Arno. The Ciompi, or wool workers, demanded the right to organize in order to agitate more effectively for higher wages. Their opponents were this time the established guilds, not the magnates as in earlier uprisings. For a few months, the Ciompi ruled the city under their leader Michele di Lando, supported by enemies of the mighty Guelph families. But by the end of August 1378, the major guilds succeeded in putting down the rebellion. According to Florentine tradition, its leaders were sent into exile. The regime of the victors included minor craftsmen, but not the Ciompi. It lasted for four years. In 1382, the magnates established a regime that left some influence to the "minor guilds." Real power, however, lay with the major guilds and the Guelph magnates.

Meanwhile, during the War of the Eight Saints, a small miracle occurred. Pope Gregory XI returned to Rome in 1377. The admonitions of the mystic Catherine of Siena (1347–1380) might have had something to do with his decision. She had implored Gregory—"my *babbo* ("dear father"), she addresses him—to reclaim his place on the Tiber.[49] The pope died in 1378, however. The year marked a break in the history of Italy and Europe. Under pressure from a crowd outside Saint Peter's, the cardinals first chose a Roman as successor, but then they elected the archbishop of Bari, Bartolomeo Prignano. Urban VI (1378–1389), as he called himself, seems to have been somewhat muddleheaded. He thought he been chosen by the Holy Spirit, and he noted that the portraits of the apostles in the Lateran Palace, initially somber, had brightened on account of his election. More alarming for his adversaries, he immediately named a large group of Italians as cardinals, thus breaking the French grip over the College. Those who felt crossed deposed Urban as "incompetent" and elected as anti-pope Robert of Geneva. Now notorious as the "Butcher of Cesena" thanks to his involvement in the battles in the Papal States, he called himself Clement, "the mild," and took up residence in Avignon. His Roman opponent held the fort on the Tiber. He took part in the struggles for the Neapolitan throne, employing the services of John Hawkwood as *capitano*. The Angevin prince Charles of Durazzo seized the crown by having his sister-in-law, Queen Joanna, strangled. Urban was yet another monster worthy of his cruel age. Six cardinals were tortured and executed at the command of the paranoid pope because he suspected them of plotting against him.[50]

The Church would remain divided for more than thirty years. One of its popes resided in Rome, a second on the Rhone, and in the end there was a third as well. The legal situation was unclear. One half of Europe—the majority of Italy and Germany, the north, the east, England, and Portugal—stuck with Rome, whereas the west including Castile took the side of Avignon. They were joined by the Scots, who could not support any pope recognized by their archrival England. Fractures soon also appeared in religious orders, cathedral chapters, and monasteries. The Papal States collapsed into chaos, and war raged in many other regions of Italy as well. There was plenty of work for mercenary companies. Changing circumstances and the prospect of profit repeatedly induced our Hawkwood to seek new employers. In his final campaigns and diplomatic missions, he worked once again for the Florentines, this time against Milan. This earned him citizenship and fame via Uccello's fresco. When in 1394 he died in his sleep—a rarity in these times—Florence honored its general with a state funeral. He was a prime example of the *condottieri* upon whom Machiavelli would heap so much scorn.

Italy at the time of the Schism appears a bestiary of human monsters. This was probably not a novelty. Rather, the big cities finally had enough chroniclers who left accounts of such rulers in their works. Their descriptions could be as lifelike as the portraits now being done by painters and sculptors in Prague, Paris, and Naples—at the same time as Chinese artists, incidentally.[51] Hawkwood's father-in-law Bernabò Visconti, heir to the eastern half of Milan, was the classic example of the "tyraunts of Lumbardye" mentioned by Chaucer.[52] His equestrian statue in the Castello Sforzesco in Milan seems to confirm what written sources say about him. Wearing a close-fitting chainmail shirt and a suit of armor, with his hair tied back tightly with a band and a two-pronged black beard, he resembles an Assyrian despot (Fig. 23, p. 313). Burckhardt compared him to the "worst of the Roman emperors."

> The most important public object was the prince's boar-hunting; whoever interfered with it was put to death with torture, the terrified people were forced to maintain 5,000 boar-hounds, with strict responsibility for their health and safety.[53]

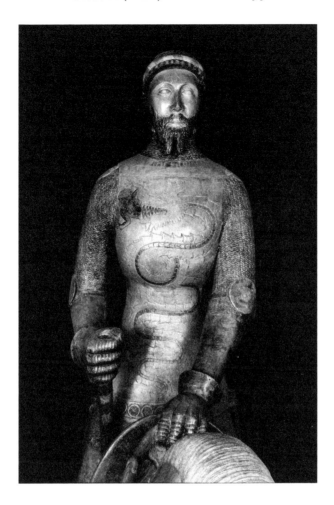

At war with half of Italy and excommunicated several times, he laid the foundation for his family's rule in Lombardy and beyond. His own nephew, Gian
Galeazzo, overthrew him in 1385. Bernabò died a tyrant's death in prison, probably poisoned.

If there was one prince before the nineteenth century with a real chance of
uniting at least the northern half of Italy under one scepter, it was Gian Galeazzo Visconti (r. 1385–1402).[54] He astutely extended Milan's sphere of influence in the east to Belluno, in the south to Pisa and Perugia. He entered into
an alliance with Siena. At the age of eight, he was married to Isabella of Valois.
The amount of money paid for this prestigious union was prodigious, prompting Matteo Villani to remark contemptuously that the king of France had sold

his own flesh and blood. For 100,000 florins, Gian Galeazzo received the title of duke from the languid Wenceslaus. Compared with the stupendous revenues from his lands, this sum did not amount to much. Serious money went into his most ambitious project, the Certosa di Pavia. His ecclesiastical policy amounted to siding with neither Rome nor Avignon, but rather letting them court him. Obviously, a man of his stature was too great a match for the puny German King Rupert. The latter was beaten at Brescia in April of 1402. Thus ended his march to Rome, only barely begun. Visconti, on the other hand, did head south. His object was Florence (p. 367).

The political map of Italy was up for grabs. Milan's ascent was obvious, whereas it must have been unclear whether the Republic of Florence would retain its autonomy. The future of the Church, weakened by the Schism, was anyone's guess. The Anjou, divided by the succession issue, held onto Naples with difficulty. Their attempts to win back Sicily were thwarted by resistance from the locals, who preferred Spanish oppression to French. For its part, Sicily was bleeding out due to constant warfare. Here, too, the Black Death only made things worse. The power of the nobility, with its expansive estates and rights of jurisdiction, prevented reform and modernization. Gibbets erected outside villages reminded the people that local lords had power over life and death. The advent of a learned, cultured king like Martin I the Humane, who took harp lessons and surrounded himself with scholars and poets, did nothing to change the big picture.

Venice had long been gazing beyond the distant horizon of the Adriatic. Its regime remained intact despite grave trials. Two coup attempts by ambitious doges were frustrated by the oligarchy; the conspirators were hanged or beheaded. But there were external difficulties as well. With the Treaty of Zara in 1358, the cities in Dalmatia were lost to Louis I of Hungary. On Crete, a colonial rebellion had to be put down.[55] It had broad support, among both Greeks and Latins; its leaders were noble Venetians. They met with the executioner's sword. In a final, bitter showdown with Genoa, the War of Chioggia, Venice was victorious thanks to the loyalty of its citizens, including even the common people. When peace was made in 1381, Genoa was finished in the Adriatic forever. The crisis became an occasion to admit thirty distinguished *popolani* families to Venice's Great Council, in exchange for having provided financial assistance to the war effort. It was one last tiny victory for horizontal power. The broad masses of citizens remained excluded, however, and Venetian society calcified. In 1297, the noble caste of the lagoon city had already set itself apart by substantially barring new families from entering the Great Council, which had the right to elect the doge. The popular assembly was now on its last legs. In 1426, it was abolished, and not even the word *comune* remained. It was replaced by talk of *signoria* or *dominium*, "dominion."

West, East, and North in the Late Fourteenth Century

Images have a way of lying to us in the most pleasant way. At first sight, the Wilton Diptych, a small, portable altar painted around 1395 by an unknown artist (perhaps French), simply looks beautiful (Plate 6). On a golden background, it portrays Richard II of England. The king, whom we last saw in difficult circumstances at Smithfield, is kneeling in prayer to Mary, the protector of his realm, and baby Jesus. The altar was once in his possession and may have been used for private prayer. The painter was a master at portraying bodies, using foreshortening, and playing with light and shadow. The realistic art of the Renaissance is in the offing. Richard seems tender, almost feminine. The faces of several angels reveal a trace of merriment.

One can hardly believe the historical reality hiding behind this diptych. Richard II, son of the Black Prince, Edward of Woodstock—a hero of the Hundred Years' War—and husband of Anne of Bohemia, was one of the unluckiest rulers in England's history. Not even his claim to the throne was uncontested. The uncertainties surrounding his succession were the root of the War of the Roses in the following century.[56] In 1396, after the death of his Bohemian wife, the time seemed ripe to smother the smoldering war with France. Richard married Isabella of Valois, the seven-year-old daughter of Charles VI. This left him free, he believed, to settle accounts with an unruly Parliament. In his final years, the humble supplicant of the Wilton Diptych had his opponents beheaded and exiled, thus earning for himself the title of tyrant. But his reign of terror did not last long. The year 1399 turned out to be unfortunate for the king. John of Gaunt died, the man who had actually ruled England during Richard's minority. This seemed to Richard an opportunity to avail himself of Gaunt's massive inheritance. He was in desperate need of money; his court alone was one thousand people strong.[57] But Richard had made too many enemies. While he was waging war in Ireland, Gaunt's son Henry Bolingbroke won dissatisfied barons to his cause, as well as the archbishop of Canterbury, whom Richard had deposed and driven into exile. As always in such cases, it was the army that decided the outcome. It abandoned Richard. He was held prisoner in a fortress in Yorkshire, where, probably for simplicity's sake, he was left to starve to death. The successful rebel, although not first in the line of succession, acceded to the throne. With Bolingbroke as King Henry IV (r. 1319–1413), the House of Lancaster came to power.

Meanwhile, the Hundred Years' War had developed a second theater on the Iberian Peninsula. Struggles for the throne in Castile and its conflict with Aragon gave the English and the French an opportunity to supply their mercenaries with meaningful employment. French weapons thus helped Henry of Trastámara (r. 1369–1379) to the Castilian crown. With his own hand, the victor had killed his half-brother Peter the Cruel, who incidentally achieved the rare feat of having three wives at once—archaic lore in the heart of Christian Europe. After the dissolution of the Spanish House of Burgundy, Portugal retained its autonomy under the Aviz dynasty. The first Aviz king, John I, was married to Philippa of Lancaster, a daughter of John of Gaunt. Under his rule, Portugal began its expansion beyond Europe's borders. It was driven by John's fourth son, Henry the Navigator (1394–1460). The prophecy uttered by the chronicler Fernão Lopes would prove correct: a new world and a new race of men would arise.[58]

The House of Anjou was rent by monstrous internal discord. Louis the Great of Hungary (r. 1342–1382) sent an army against Charles of Durazzo. Yet it could not prevent the murderer of Joanna of Anjou from ascending the throne of Naples. In the east, Louis strengthened Hungary's position as a major power, at the expense of Venice and others. He took advantage of the weakness of the Serbian Kingdom, which, after the death of Stefan Uroš IV Dušan the Mighty (r. 1346–1355), had fragmented into a collection of feuding principalities.

In Poland, Kasimir (r. 1333–1370) of the Piast dynasty became king and found a country in "great chaos, full of errors and intrigues."[59] He made an arrangement with the Teutonic Knights, who undertook a new campaign against Lithuania, and also with his Bohemian neighbor. He succeeded in further diminishing the power of the nobility. He was thus free to expand eastward. He acquired Volhynia, Galicia, and the Masovian duchies, nearly doubling the size of his realm. Poland had been depopulated by the Black Death. Now German, Armenian, and Italian settlers immigrated, making the mixture of peoples even more colorful than it was before. Eastward expansion added new subjects of Orthodox faith. The culture and economic activities of the Jews remained significant. Many had fled the pogroms in the west and found a new home in Poland, usually under better conditions than in the old.[60]

The codification of laws and administrative reforms prepared the way for Poland to become a territorial state. The trend was reinforced by a prohibition on appealing to the court of Magdeburg, as it was a foreign city, even though the towns of Lesser Poland followed German law. The notion was even discussed of establishing the principle of "one prince, one law, one coinage" for the whole kingdom.[61] This proto-nationalist conception of the state was promoted by the nobles, who joined together into "confederations" to achieve their goals. The first of these associations was formed in 1353. This was a step in the direction of an aristocratic republic, for which Poland would one day become both famous and infamous.

Cracow emerged as the capital and site of royal coronations. Its Cloth Hall, whose Gothic predecessor was built during Kasimir's reign, still recalls the city's rich trade in English and Flemish textiles. The newly built Wawel Cathedral and Wawel Castle were signs of economic prosperity and royal luster. Outside the walls, Kasimir established a settlement for Jewish immigrants that still bears his name: Kazimierz. He also founded Cracow's university.

The main line of the Piast dynasty died with Kasimir the Great. Poland fell to the Angevin king of Hungary, Louis I, also called "the Great." But for him, it was little more than a tumultuous preoccupation. He wed his daughter Mary to a son of Charles IV, Sigismund, prince-elector of Brandenburg and later German king and Holy Roman Emperor (r. 1411–1437). To secure the succession of his daughter Hedwig (1384–1399), he granted tax reductions, a greater say in government, and other concessions to the nobility, which had been entrusted by his predecessor with the right to choose the king. When the eleven-year-old Hedwig became the wife of Grand Duke Jagiello of Lithuania, the yield from the nuptial contract was tremendous: the baptism of the groom and, thus, the conversion of his people. Europe's last pagans, followers of the thunder god Perkūnas, gradually became Christians. The Polish-Lithuanian union resulted in a large state between the Baltic and the Black Sea, the likes of which the region had never seen before.

A marriage also produced a new kingdom in Scandinavia. It was the work of Margaret (1353–1412), daughter of the Danish King Waldemar IV Atterdag[62] and wife of the Norwegian King Haakon VI Magnusson. After the death of her father and husband, her son Olaf united the two crowns. When the young king himself died in 1387, Margaret was chosen by assemblies of each country to be "Sovereign Lady and Consort and Ruler of the Whole Kingdom" (*fuldmægtig frue og husbonde og hele rigets formynder*). Margaret added a third crown, the Swedish, two years later. In 1397, at the royal palace in Kalmar, she engineered the unification of the realms under the midnight sun. The new entity was a counterweight to the mighty Hanseatic League. From then on, Danish and

German kings determined the policy of the Kalmar Union from the capital in Copenhagen. Norway, for example, had to stand by and watch as one of its foreign rulers hocked the Orkneys and Shetland in order to pay a dowry. In Sweden, portions of the nobility, townspeople, mountain folk, and hut dwellers were against the Union. The country managed to break away during the Reformation. However, the forced marriage between Denmark and Norway would endure until 1814.

Moscow, Mongols, Ottomans

Beginning in the first third of the fourteenth century, Moscow developed into the center of gravity of Rus' lands, the seat of the grand prince and the metropolitan.[63] Its continued rise was aided by the fight against the Mongols. The grand princes, who had to collect tribute for the khans, had secretly set aside a portion of the money and used it to improve their position. Even the plague helped to consolidate Moscow's power, ridding one of its rulers, Ivan II, of potential rivals. Grand Prince Dmitry Donskoy (r. 1359–1389) overcame the last serious challenger to his dominion, the prince of Tver. The time seemed ripe to finally stand up to the Mongols, as they were weakened by bloody rivalries. When Dmitry refused to pay tribute and followed his own mind politically, Khan Mamai launched a punitive expedition. In response, Dmitry forged a broad coalition of Russian princes and—if we can believe his chronicler—a nation.

> Their glory is being sung all over the Russian land: in Moscow, horses are neighing, horns are blaring in Kolomna, drums are thundering in Serpukhov, and Russian banners are lining the shore of the mighty river Don.[64]

In September of 1380, the Russian army did indeed prevail at the Kulikovo Field near the Don, just before the Mongols' Lithuanian allies arrived on the scene. Mamai fled. After losing another battle to his rival Tokhtamysh, he was assassinated by the Genoese on the Crimean Peninsula. Russian sources resound with this first significant victory over the Tatars, who had now completely converted to Islam. The northeastern principalities stood united. "Brothers, boyars, princes, and sons of boyars!" one author has the grand prince call out. "You have given your lives for the sacred churches, for the Russian land, and for the Christian faith."[65] Legends were woven out of words like these, legends that gave the Third Rome its sense of destiny.

The victory may have solidified Russian identity, but it was not decisive. Only a few years later, the Tatars once again attacked Moscow, this time led by Tokhtamysh. They killed, burned, and plundered. Dmitry Donskoy had to eat humble pie and collect massive tribute for the khan. With the advent of a new universal Mongol conqueror, Timur the Lame, historically known as Tamerlane, Moscow again found itself in mortal danger. Its struggle with the steppe now entered its most crucial phase. In addition, new attacks from competitors inside Russia had to be met—Tver rose again as well—before Moscow's leadership position became unshakable.

While the lords of Moscow were forcing Russia together, in the southeast a new Islamic power was forming. In contrast to the Mongolian steppe warriors, it built an enduring state and grew into an empire. Between the shrunken Byzantine Empire and the Ilkhanate, Turkoman peoples driven out by the Mongols had settled and built up small dominions. The most successful of these was the principality of a tribal leader named Osman (1281/88–1324/26) located in northwestern Anatolia.[66] According to legend, a dervish prophesied that he was destined to become a warrior and a future ruler of the world. At any rate, he succeeded in extending his sphere of influence. As usual, the booty was distributed among warriors, relatives, and followers. Osman's son Orhan issued his own coins and was the first of the dynasty to hold the title of sultan. Marriage to a daughter of the Byzantine emperor—princesses on the Bosporus had gotten cheap—gave him legitimacy and Byzantium an ally in its multiple wars. Power was more important than religion for the Ottomans. Without hesitation, alliances were made and wars fought with Christians and Muslims alike. In the mid-fourteenth century, Turkish troops advanced on Gallipoli and Thessalonica as allies of the *basileus*, to support Byzantium against a Serbian attack. But these friends soon turned into deadly foes.

Like all empires in the making, the new kingdom was doomed to expansion. Followers had to be rewarded with booty, and new ones recruited with it. The early Ottoman state has been called a "plundering confederacy" that expanded like a gigantic amoeba, absorbing everything that might be useful to it.[67] Ottoman armies conquered large swathes of the Byzantine sphere of influence. Adrianople, later known as Edirne, became the capital under Sultan Murad (r. 1362–1389). Captured cities were placed under military commanders; this mixture of civil and military administration remained typical of the Ottoman state in general. The Ottomans made Byzantium a tributary and wrested Sofia from the Bulgarians in 1386. Asia Minor also became largely

Ottoman, thanks to money and the marriage of Murad's son Bayezid to an Anatolian princess. At the same time, the sultan's troops invaded the Balkans. A coalition of Slavic peoples, assembled by the lord of central Serbia, Lazar, could not hold them back either. Its army was defeated in 1389 on the Kosovo field near Pristina. Lazar was killed. As a martyr, he immediately attained sainthood and endowed Serbia with a myth that endures to this day.[68] His son Stefan (r. 1389–1427) was demoted to the status of an Ottoman vassal, as was the Duke of Athens, the Florentine Neri Acciaiuoli. In the meantime, Turkish troops subdued Anatolian emirates and got ready to move on Byzantium.

Latin Europe gradually awoke to the threat, but Hungary was in immediate danger. Backed by both the Roman pope and his counterpart in Avignon, King Sigismund assembled a Crusader army. In late September 1396, it was defeated by an Ottoman force at Nicopolis. Thousands were killed or captured. Sigismund only barely escaped the debacle. Nevertheless, further Turkish advance was prevented by far-off events. For in central Asia, Timur the Lame (r. 1370–1405), leader of a federation of Turko-Mongolian tribes based in Samarkand, had set about vanquishing the world—"scourging kingdoms with his conquering sword," in the words of Christopher Marlowe.

Timur the Lame—the name Timur means "iron," and he limped due to a deformity or wound in his right leg—was one of the great monsters of world history. When it came to cruelty, he was in no way inferior to his model Genghis Khan. His warriors were in the habit of piling up the heads of the defeated into pyramids; 28 such structures with 1,500 heads each were counted outside the walls of conquered Isfahan alone.[69] Timur had driven his riders through central Asia at top speed and toppled the forces of the Golden Horde. He had advanced on Moscow, had taken Delhi, destroyed Baghdad, and attacked Aleppo and Damascus. In 1402, he overwhelmed an Ottoman army at Ankara. The sultan died in captivity. Timur used state-of-the-art military technology: flamethrowers, rockets, and siege engines. Christian princes relished the Turkish defeats and rushed to establish relations with Timur. However, he died during a campaign against China in 1405. His dominion disintegrated as quickly as it had been pieced together (pp. 339f.). The Ottomans set about reconquering what they had lost, while Moscow had to defend itself from raids by the Golden Horde and the claims of Lithuania. Latin Europe had been given a reprieve. It did not last long, however, and Byzantium's death was near.

18

Before the Great Renaissance

Decameron, Canterbury Tales

Meanwhile, the late fourteenth century was pondering its reflection in the mirror and thought it saw a new age dawning. What Petrarca hoped for seemed to Giovanni Boccaccio (1313–1375) to already be a reality. Like Virgil, he saw a golden age, a *Saturnia regia*, returning in his own day. Besides Petrarca and Dante, he counted Giotto among the great renewers of culture. In his view,

Giotto brought painting back to the light after it "had been buried for many centuries beneath the errors of those who painted more to delight the eyes of the ignorant than to please the understanding of the wise."[1] These lines by Boccaccio evince for the first time something like the self-awareness of a renaissance that is not confined to literature but also embraces art.

The masses of religious writings were joined by literature that slaked secular curiosity. The *Dittamondo* by Fazio degli Uberti, a restless wanderer through his time, is an account of a world tour from Italy to Greece and Africa. Formally, it is an imitation of the *Divine Comedy*. Virgil's role is overtaken by Solinus, an ancient polyhistor. Ptolemy relates his life story and explains the Earth's geography, while the missionary Fra Riccoldo da Monte Croce (he, too, an actual historical figure) reports on the East. Readers hear about magical gems, monkeys and camels, wander through European cities, see a whole parade of magical Oriental animals like dragons, serpents, and basilisks, and watch the drama of world history unfold from Creation on. Another reporter of this kind was the Bavarian nobleman Johannes Schiltberger, who was held captive by the Ottomans after the disaster at Nicopolis. In a widely circulated work, he describes the princes, lands, and peoples of the East. A main role is played by the cruel "Tamerlan," Timur the Lame, and for the first time mention is made of the land of "Ibissibur," Siberia. Schiltberger tells of sled dogs there "as big as donkeys," and he has heard that the region's inhabitants eat dogs.[2] The account freely mixes true things—the Red Sea "is called red but is not red"—and wondrous details, a reflection of Mandeville's tales. The same goes for the account of a Spanish ambassador in Samarkand. He had heard, he tells us, that an eleven days' journey in the direction of China would bring a traveler to the land of the Amazons, whose ancestors had once lived in Troy.[3]

An urban audience hungry for sensational details and edification devoured novellas set in cities, taverns, and the bedroom. Minstrels inspired by French models sang of distant, exotic lands, of love, struggle, and adventure. Their *cantari* often incorporated ancient elements, such as from Ovid's *Metamorphoses*. Poet-craftsmen emerge from the darkness of the written record. Antonio Pucci (ca. 1310–1388) was a bell founder by trade and a town crier. His poem about Florence's old marketplace is a hymn to the city's ample appetite. He also adapted material from antiquity such as the story of Apollonius of Tyre, of which medieval versions abounded. More and more ancient authors were made available to the people via translations. Boccaccio put Livy and Valerius Maximus into the *volgare*, and he saw to it that the *Iliad* and the *Odyssey* were translated from the Greek original into Latin.

With Boccaccio, a self-described citizen of "the noble city of Florence, the most beautiful of any in Italy,"[4] the literature of the Trecento, the fourteenth century, reached another high point. In the Naples of Robert of Anjou, Boccaccio had gained familiarity with the most important literary currents of his time, with the love poetry of the south and the epics and *chansons* of the French. While residing there, he will have also seen Giotto's paintings and read Petrarca's poetry. Later, we find him at the courts of the lords of Ravenna and Forlì, and finally in his house in Certaldo above the Val d'Elsa. He was also frequently in Florence, whose government entrusted him with diplomatic missions. In the crumbling, overgrown library of the monastery of Montecassino, he hunted for manuscripts. Digging under the thick layer of dust coating the codices, his most valuable find was a fragment of Tacitus's *Germania*.[5] In his works he analyzed love in all its varieties. He wrote lyric poetry, epic poetry, and romances, versified about pastoral idylls and frolicking nymphs. His *Fiametta* is further evidence for Burckhardt's thesis that the Italian Renaissance discovered the individual. Had anyone before Boccaccio offered such a nuanced, introspective portrait of a married, middle-class woman consumed by burning passion for another man? In addition, Boccaccio penned accounts of the fates of famous men from Adam to his own time. He also wrote a comprehensive, fifteen-book treatise on the pagan gods that relates who they are, explains how they relate to one another, and endeavors to interpret the myths about them. His biography of Dante proves that the *Sommo Poeta*, the "supreme poet," was already venerated in the Trecento, and it demonstrates the emergence of a new historical sense.

Boccaccio was famous in his day above all for these works. Today he is known as one of the greatest storytellers to ever pick up a pen, as the author of the *Decameron*.[6] The Black Death provides the frame. A group of high-born Florentine youths gathers in the paradisiacal ambience of a country villa far from the plague-infested city. Respectability and good manners are the order of the day, while, close by, society with all its rules and customs is falling apart. The ten young people pass the time dancing, playing, and enjoying meals accompanied by music and the singing of cicadas. But above all they tell each other stories, ten each day. In the end there are exactly one hundred, the same number as cantos in Dante's *Commedia*. Boccaccio employs a matchless diversity of narrative techniques within his tightly constructed composition. Many of the individual stories are drawn from the *facetiae* tradition, from Arabian tales, troubadour poetry, ancient mythology, and chronicles, but as a whole the *Decameron* is unprecedented. Love and death, money, twists of fate, and

Church corruption are its major themes. The diverse, competitive society of late medieval Italy is depicted vibrantly, now in loud colors, now in nuanced shading. With irony and subtle humor, Boccaccio assembles a panoply of horny churchmen, greedy merchants, ugly aristocrats, betrayed amours, and passionate lovers. We meet with lowborn characters who embarrass great ones with their generosity and cunning, and with great ones who reveal themselves to be stingy and petty.

There is the corrupt notary, a murderer and a blasphemer who indulges in all the desires of the flesh. But since he claims to have lived a chaste and virtuous life at his final confession, he is widely venerated as a saint. There is the horse trader Andreuccio, who is robbed in Naples, ends up naked in the sewer, and, even worse, gets closed inside the coffin of the recently deceased archbishop while trying to steal his ruby ring. We laugh at the clever monastery gardener Masetto, who pretends to be a deaf-mute and sleeps with ten wanton nuns and their abbess. We laugh again at the farmer who is drugged and, upon awaking, believes he has landed in purgatory. We shiver while reading about the girl who hides the head of her murdered lover in a flowerpot and then grows basil in it. Finally, as if Boccaccio had just arrived in his own *Paradiso*, we meet the humble Griselda. But nowhere do we hear the cawing of an anemic moralizer. Rather, this is the work of a consummate writer who knows that people are human, wine tastes good, and sex is fun. Above all, Boccaccio is a master of the art of making people laugh. Modern readers catch a glimpse of an intellectual elite for whom a waggish expression and a witty retort meant more than a requiem. Boccaccio's writing exercised broad influence. In Florence, one of its first admirers was the merchant Franco Sacchetti, whose novellas are very much in the great master's style. In one story, the painter Giotto is asked why Saint Joseph looks so sad in a certain fresco. He answers that Joseph had every right to be sad, seeing that his wife was pregnant and he didn't know who the father was.[7] Sacchetti had as little respect for the holy as his model.

The most important among the European *boccacceschi* was Geoffrey Chaucer (ca. 1340/45–1400), a middle-class Englishman.[8] The son of a wine merchant and a favorite of John of Gaunt, he was a man of many colors: soldier and prisoner of war, justice of the peace, customs comptroller, diplomat, member of parliament, and the owner of a library with sixty volumes. His literary production made him the "father of English poetry." He was the first Englishman to put the notion of "renaissance" in a nutshell: "newe science" from "olde bokes."[9] He translated the *Romance of the Rose* into Middle English, as well as Boethius's *Consolation of Philosophy*. Several political missions took him to Italy. He may have been a guest at the magnificent wedding in 1367 in Milan between a Visconti daughter and a son of Edward III of England; Froissart and Petrarca were also there.[10] He knew Dante as the "wise poete of Florence." The *Dream of Scipio* inspired his *Parliament of Fowls*. His *Troilus and Criseyde*, a long poem about the paradoxes and ambiguities of love, was inspired by Boccaccio's *Filostrato*.

The setting of his *Canterbury Tales*, left unfinished at his death, is different from that of the *Decameron*. Whereas the latter takes place at an estate in the southern countryside, here the background is a tavern, the Tabard Inn, on the other side of London Bridge in a neighborhood of ill repute. No civilized society of modest youths has gathered here, but rather a troupe of thirty pilgrims of all stations. They drink beer, not wine. The innkeeper encourages the group to pass the time on the way to Becket's grave in Canterbury by telling stories. This gives Chaucer the opportunity to portray the society of his time in lovingly detailed portraits, consistently outlining ideals and then challenging them. The poet plays with all manner of narrative forms, including romance, *facetiae*, and fables. He lectures, ridicules, and caricatures, preaches and parodies, is light and earnest—and, despite all the classical learning sprinkled throughout his stories, is endlessly entertaining. Boccaccio's *Teseida* and Boethius's philosophy are the basis for the Knight's Tale. Only superficially about love and honor, what it really does is raise big questions: What is the world? How much freedom do humans have, and how much of life is determined by God, Fortuna, and the stars? We are led back down to Earth—to a small English town—by the burly Miller's Tale, in which bare buttocks and all manner of obscenities bring a rowdy Middle Ages to life. Just like us, contemporary readers of the *Tales* were amused by the chivalrous rooster Chauntecleer, who uses courtly manners with his favorite hen Pertelote, calling her "Madame!" They laughed at a tricky, dishonest indulgence peddler. Incidentally, one need only read Chaucer and Boccaccio to encounter the kind of monks whose behavior would spark the Reformation. The moral of some of the stories is that it's not always easy to find a moral. Chaucer's ethical openness seems incredibly modern. But then the poet of fantasy goes back to describing fairies dancing across fields.

On the Eve of the New Science

The confusion of philosophies and piety movements that reigned in the fourteenth century, the intellectual battles of the learned and the mercurial inventions of the literati, seem to reflect the chaos of politics and war in the world outside. To what extent one influenced the other, how much everyday life moved, disturbed, or animated the spheres of the mind, must remain an open question. Like the arts, philosophy and science have their own laws. They are molded not only by life itself. More often, as in Chaucer's case, it is the works of earlier artists, the intellectual edifices of other thinkers that provide their fuel. Profound piety and lust for life were equally present, then and later. In addition, movements seeking purity took on a new urgency; they would culminate in Luther's Reformation. For rulers, this was manifestly suspect. Charles IV, for one, issued an edict requiring religious books in the vernacular to be scrutinized and approved.[11]

Confraternities that prescribed prayer and penance to their members were founded everywhere. A rich Sienese merchant, Giovanni Colombini (1304–1367), followed Saint Francis's example. He spontaneously gave away his fortune, from then on preaching against wealth and devoting himself to a life of self-denial, chastity, and charity. His followers developed into the Order of Gesuati, or Jesuates—so called because its members constantly called out the name of Jesus. In the mid-fourteenth century, the French Franciscan Johannes de Rupescissa made enemies in the Church by espousing absolute poverty for the clergy. He rebuked his Dominican rivals as "heretical followers of Mammon."[12] His writings joined eschatological prophecies with alchemical revelations intended to offer comfort for the imminent apocalyptic plagues he imagined. In addition, he was the first person to try to put alchemy in the service of medicine.

Around 1355, the young Salutati had an epiphany of a very different sort. From one moment to the next, while reading Ovid's *Metamorphoses*, he was seized "as if by divine gift" by the love of literature.[13] Like him, more and more of his contemporaries took to consoling themselves about the vicissitudes of the day by reading classical texts in their *studioli* (studies), an early refuge of private life. They commissioned works of art, collected antiquities, and searched for manuscripts. The one option in no way excluded the other, just as joie de vivre could coexist perfectly well with piety, rational philosophy with mysticism. For Meister Eckhart (ca. 1260–1328), who was influenced *inter alia* by Neoplatonism and the ideas of Dietrich of Freiberg, God had become the "One": being itself and thus the intellect, the basis of all being. In Eckhart's view, created being was thoroughly infused with God, perceptible as a *scintilla animae*, an "inner spark."[14] In earthly existence, it was possible to attain serenity and perfect, indeed divine, freedom by purifying oneself utterly of the non-divine. In this way, the shrewd logician pointed in a mystical direction. The first to follow his lead was his student Johannes Tauler (ca. 1300–1361), a preacher from Strasbourg who recommended imagining oneself in that enticing, glittering "nothingness," immersing oneself in the depths of the soul.[15] The godlike, creative individual that would be conceived by the Renaissance is also a product of the world where Meister Eckhart advised obliterating the self, or where a Henry Suso (ca. 1295–1366), another Dominican friar, took the path of a latter-day Buddha. Beginning with especially bloody self-mortification, Suso arrived at a serene acceptance of unavoidable suffering.

Intellectual horizons continued to expand. Duns Scotus, the man of *haecceitas*, "thisness," had already plumbed the depths of the knowable, thereby preparing the division of theology and philosophy. Thus, neither the Little Ice Age nor the Black Death is necessary to explain the emergence of critical method. In Scotus's hands, theology had become a positive science that was confined to interpreting Holy Scripture and providing guidelines for human life. Its aura as a participant in God's eternal wisdom was gone. Mind and memory needed no divine illumination to arrive at knowledge. Metaphysics, as Avicenna argued, was about investigating the nature of being and not, as Averroes said, the nature of God.

Scotus's theory of knowledge, steeped in subtle linguistic analysis, is the beginning of a tradition of increasingly radical epistemological critique. Questions like what knowledge is and what we are able to know came to the forefront of a discussion that would culminate in the critical philosophy of Kant.[16] William of Ockham, whom we last met at the court of Louis the Bavarian, agreed with Scotus that causes cannot be indubitably inferred from effects. In general, natural processes followed laws of necessity. Yet to ban divine intervention—i.e., miracles—from nature would be tantamount to denying divine omnipotence. One could never be certain whether what one perceived was real or a deception. In this way, Ockham advanced the "disenchantment of the world" (to use Max Weber's phrase) yet another pace. He also held the view that reason and experience could not lead to knowledge of God. One could believe in the immortality of the soul, but he did not think it was provable. Science based on faith was not science, however: "It is childish to say that I know theological conclusions because God knows the principles that I believe on the basis of God having revealed them to me."[17] Ockham maintained, as Bacon had before him, that universals were not real and that metaphysics was closed to rational comprehension.

In his view, universals were only real as names—hence the term "nominalism" for his philosophy. They are symbols or signs created by human understanding; they are conventions, not the earthly incarnation of eternal ideas. All that is real is the individual thing: random, contingent, and accessible by experience. For Ockham, science deals with logical relationships between concepts and propositions and no longer, as Duns Scotus thought, with being itself. In his view, the simpler explanation was better, and the superfluous must be trimmed away. This has come to be known as Ockham's Razor, whose classic formulation dates to the seventeenth century: "Entities are not to be multiplied without necessity."[18] In light of the insecure foundation of knowledge, some thinkers sought certainty where it seemed most easily obtainable: in the fields of logic, mathematics, and experimentation. This path was taken by a group of theologians who taught at Merton College, Oxford, fittingly known as the *calculatores*. The most famous among them was Thomas Bradwardine (ca. 1290–1349), who sought to describe the way bodies move—the relationship between force and resistance—mathematically. These "calculators," with their counting, measuring, and weighing, stood for an approach to nature that would belong to the distant future.[19]

Conflict with the Church was unavoidable. Some of the most interesting thinkers of the age—Marsilius of Padua and Ockham, for example—were persecuted or, like Meister Eckhart, involved in unpleasant trials. In Paris, Nicholas of Autrecourt, who had questioned doctrines of Scholastic metaphysics and epistemology, was forced to burn his writings publicly. He also lost his teaching position.[20] Many people, however, did not need external pressure to avoid the new paths then being taken. In his invective *On His Own Ignorance and That of Many Others*, Petrarca, the pioneer of classical studies, placed self-knowledge and the will to do good above any rational search for truth. In his view, the highest philosophy was to know God, not the gods.[21]

The sciences were able to escape the stench of heresy by circumventing the citadels of theology and avoiding any ideas that might undermine God's omnipotence. The common phrase that a thesis was being proposed solely *secundum imaginationem*, "as a thought experiment,"[22] granted license to then engage in free intellectual discussion. The French philosopher John Buridan (ca. 1295–ca. 1358) suggested acting as if God had simply withdrawn from the world and left nature to follow its own rules.[23] On that basis, he constructed his natural philosophy, which was heavily influenced by Aristotle and thus by pagan doctrines. For example, he maintained that a vacuum could not exist. Aristotle, not knowing about gravity, had claimed that a body fell faster the thinner the matter was through which it moved. The necessary conclusion would be that an infinitely high speed would be reached in a perfect vacuum—

an impossibility, since then the object would have to be in two places at once. The problem was that logic of this kind restricted divine omnipotence. Was the will of God not subject to the law of noncontradiction? As Kant put it, "A is not non-A." Something cannot simultaneously be what it is not. If this was valid, then not even the lord of the universe could create a vacuum. Buridan, only a member of the secular clergy and never part of a theological faculty, said that God could indeed do it, only he did not want to. His religious scruples thus resolved, Buridan then went on to demonstrate in great detail the impossibility of a perfect vacuum. He asked and asked and asked: "Whether the sky [or heaven] has matter." "Whether it is possible that there are several worlds." "Whether the whole Earth is movable."[24]

Buridan's theory of motion departed from that of his great father Aristotle.[25] The problem, already discussed by late antique and Arabic scholars, was: why does an object that is thrown or launched move after it leaves the hand or the device that has propelled it? Whereas Aristotle defended the position that vortices or vibrations in the surrounding air moved the object, Buridan favored the theory proposed by Philoponus and Ibn Sina, namely that the impetus "imprinted" energy in the object. If that were the case, then the act of a titanic "first mover"—another figure from Aristotelian metaphysics—would suffice to put the spheres into perpetual circular motion. Compared to traditional views, such as that angels moved the spheres (p. 638), this was a very clever idea.[26] Buridan's speculations were forgotten, but not their originator. He must have been a colorful character. Anecdotes about him circulated in Paris, as did highly imaginative tales of scandal—a rare honor for a scientist. He was even said to have been the lover of two queens. According to François Villon's *Ballad of the Ladies of Yore*, one of them ordered him to be thrown into the Seine in a sack (a punishment from which the real Buridan was spared).

The increasingly mechanized view of the world was furthered by Buridan's student, Nicole Oresme (ca. 1320–1382). Like his teacher, Oresme entertained the possibility that Earth rotated on its axis every day along with all its inhabitants, great and small. However, he considered this hypothesis as unprovable as its opposite. He ultimately decided to leave Earth immobile, as tradition had.[27] For his patron, the highly educated Charles V of France, he translated Aristotle's *Politics*, thus making available guidelines for *bonne policie,* a rationally ordered state.[28] In addition, he was the first European to write a theoretical work about money, the *Tractatus de moneta*. He ended his days as bishop of Lisieux.

The work of Buridan, Oresme, and others—including an anonymous professor who thought it more rational to have the Earth revolve around the Sun than to park it in the middle—seems to have inaugurated a shift in the history of science.[29] The study of nature and mathematics developed, haltingly, in the same realm of possibility that increasingly permitted realistic portraits, auto-biographies, and first-person literary personalities, theoretical treatments of the state and classical studies. Still, the number of people debating traditional teachings about nature was small at first, and the diffusion of their works limited. The approach of the "Oxford calculators" to quantities like magnitude and speed was confined to a mental game; it was not a revolution. Science still meant subjecting the statements of ancient authorities to strict logical exami-nation. Experiments were seldom performed. What did point the way to the future were the questions being asked and the doubts being entertained. Étienne Gilson argued that "skepticism" broke out like a "new intellectual dis-ease" in the fourteenth century, thus moving the age closer to modernity.[30] He may have been right, but this skepticism was no disease but rather a symptom of intellectual energy. Ultimately, the history of European modernity is also a history of the triumph of skepticism.

Gunpowder and Capital

The bible of skepticism, a writing by Sextus Empiricus passed down in the philosophy of Pyrrho of Elis, had been available in Latin translation since the thirteenth century. Yet it was ignored. At first, methodological doubt was nourished by the works of Cicero and Augustine.[31] Most philosophers and theologians continued slaving away at the Aristotelian corpus and the com-mentaries written on it, at most adding one or two tweaks of their own. The theoretical edifice of ancient natural science was still entirely stable. For this to change, it would be necessary for the group of participants in the debate to expand, for instance by means of the printing press. It would also take very clever thinkers who dared to challenge tradition and authority—and such people are not born every day. Realms of possibility alone do not suffice for new things to arise.

Nevertheless, the fourteenth century was not content with mere theory. Everywhere, signs multiplied that Europe was becoming receptive to innova-tions of all kinds. It was inconspicuous things and techniques, often barely registered by contemporaries, that signaled that Europe was continuing to close the technological gap with the East. For example, paper had now made its way to England. In 1390, the first paper mill opened in Germany, established by the commercial giant Ulman Stromer—more than half a millennium after paper production began in Samarkand.[32]

Gradually, from all different parts of the world, various essential elements came together without which Gutenberg's great invention, printing with moveable type, would not have been possible (see ch. 24). The most important seems to be that a *market* for books began to take shape. The copying and selling of manuscripts had developed into a commercial endeavor. It had long since ceased to be a preoccupation of monastic scriptoria. With student enrollment rising at universities, textbooks were dismembered and the gatherings given to various copyists so that whole works could be copied more quickly.[33] Paper makers and parchment preparers, illuminators, bookbinders, rubricators, and soon woodcutters, too, worked alongside scribes and authors. A snapshot of the book world of the fourteenth century is provided by Richard de Bury, bishop of Durham and lord chancellor to King Edward III of England. His *Philobiblon*, finished in 1345, is a passionate declaration of love for books, a handbook for how to use them, and a witness to the emergence of a market for all things readable. The well-traveled author recalls a visit to "Paris, the paradise of the world," and the joy he felt walking and looking around.

> There are delightful libraries in cells redolent of aromatics; there flourishing greenhouses of all sorts of volumes; there academic meads trembling with the earthquake of Athenian Peripatetics pacing up and down; there the promontories of Parnassus, and the porticos of the Stoics.[34]

Poets like Boccaccio and Sacchetti wrote for a broad audience. The success of *The Canterbury Tales* is indicated by the number of extant manuscripts: over eighty. As for the *Decameron*, a good sixty manuscripts have survived.[35] The other countries of Europe, however, could not boast writers of the stature of Chaucer and the Italian poets. Bohemia, at least, produced a masterpiece of classicizing rhetoric in Johannes von Tepl's *Ackermann*, that bitter dialogue between Death and a man who has just lost his wife. The tastes of an ever-expanding lay public are reflected in religious writings, saints' lives, and collections of legends in the vernacular.[36] The most successful of the latter, the *Legenda aurea*, was translated into Italian around 1350. Its homespun stories of saints and miracles made it the most widely read religious book of the era in Europe—including the Bible!

There were also other innovations. Hundreds of years after there is evidence for gunpowder in China—again, the time lag—the sound of guns could be heard on the battlefields of Europe. Instructions for mixing the deadly agent of modern power were provided even before Bacon by the *Book of Fire*, written in the first quarter of the fourteenth century. A collection of Arab recipes perhaps assembled in Spain, it taught how to make flammable substances of all kinds, from the legendary "Greek fire" with which Byzantine warriors burned Arab ships back in the seventh century all the way to black powder.[37] The earliest depiction of a firearm, an iron cannon that shot arrows, dates to the year 1326. It was a crucial step toward a kind of warfare that was decided not by muscle and skill but rather by technology and money.

The massive Florentine bankruptcies mentioned above recall the importance that capital now had for the state. Hefty sums were necessary for war, the court, festivals, administrators, artists, and literati. Conversely, state finance required the development of a banking and credit system. The specter of property confiscation always loomed. This danger, however, was not present in the most advanced economy of the time, Italy, as the financial elite was closely connected to political power. Bankers and merchants held key positions in city governments; lender and debtor were often one and the same person. Genoa's regime was so interwoven with the Banco di San Giorgio that it was ultimately the bank that ruled the city and determined its politics.[38]

Dawn of the Mechanical Age

During the boom that began with the Warm Period, Europe learned that time is money. And thus time, too, was tamed. More artfully than ever, it was divided into hours and minutes. Till then, it had flowed sweetly and softly, its passing measured by the position of the sun, drops of water, the burning of candles, or, beginning in the first half of the fourteenth century, by quietly trickling sand. Increasingly, it was now being beaten out by the ticking of clocks; water clocks had fallen out of use in the second half of the thirteenth century. The invention of the mechanical clock was of unparalleled consequence—less because it corresponded to mercantile rationality than because it spread a revolutionary principle: mechanics and machine work.

The Greeks, the Chinese—above we noted the work of the clockmaker Su Song (p. 143)—and the Arabs had already discovered the principle of escapement, necessary for the precise measurement of time. The *Book of Knowledge about Astronomy*, compiled at the court of Alfonso X of Castile, depicts a clock that drove escapement with quicksilver, a more viscous fluid than water. Ibn Khalaf al-Muradi's *Book of Secrets*, which contains a description of a clockwork, made its way to Florence from the same court.[39] The verge escapement, however, which would remain in use even after major innovations were made in the seventeenth century, was probably invented by a western European.[40] This anonymous genius effected a quantum leap in the development of technology.

Its originality alone makes his deed comparable to the invention of the steam engine.[41] How did it work? In order to make the clock tick regularly, the interplay of large and small wheels set a crown wheel with sawtooth-shaped teeth in motion. The teeth gently hit against two tin plates (called pallets) attached to a rod, or verge, causing it to tirelessly oscillate back and forth. How much technological know-how, how much craftsmanship, how much patience were necessary to create a mechanism of this kind! The two metal pallets had to be set against one another at a 90-degree angle, the number of teeth on the crown wheel had to be odd, and a space in the wheel had to be cut exactly opposite each tooth to make sure the verge oscillated regularly. Once the principle was discovered, it wandered throughout Europe—on what paths, one wonders?— and revolutionized time. In addition, it made it possible to build more and more complex apparatuses, especially astronomical clocks, which put the time of the city in a cosmic context.

In Europe, early traces of mechanical clocks can be found in monasteries, where they called the brothers to prayer. Around 1325, the monk Peter Lightfoot installed an astronomical clock in Wells Cathedral. A decade later, Azzo Visconti, lord of Milan, had a mechanical clock placed on the octagonal tower of San Gottardo that rang every hour. The people were so impressed that they called the quarter over whose roofs the bell resounded the "Contrada delle Ore" (literally the "Hours Quarter").[42] The clock became a symbol of power: an instrument that showed the time to the lords of the city in their role as lawgivers. And Europe, the continent of clashing ideas, of books and mills, became a country of clocks from now on and forever more. How strange that the earthly world was becoming mechanized—in Lucca, the mechanical clock appeared at the same time as sophisticated water-driven silk mills—just as philosophy was in the process of exposing the here and now as a realm of godless chaos.

Meanwhile, the prestigious device became the object of theological discussion. Richard of Wallingford (1292?–1336), abbot of Saint Albans (Plate 7) in southern England, wrote a *Tractatus horologii astronomici*, or *Treatise on the Astronomical Clock*. He claims a mechanical clock with a chiming mechanism was built at St. Albans.[43] Richard, who also invented the "Albion," a device for doing astronomical calculations, was consummately prepared for his work. The son of a smith, he was familiar with the art of shaping iron into workpieces. He added theory to practice. Studies at Oxford, then the citadel of mathematics, gave Richard the theoretical knowledge necessary for building his *horologium*. A generation later, the physician Giovanni Dondi dall'Orologio (ca. 1330–1380) of Padua spent sixteen years constructing his astrarium, an astronomical clock of the utmost refinement.[44] He wrote a treatise about his wondrous machine that contains the earliest known depiction of an escapement. Its sources included a writing by Campano da Novara, who was familiar with Arabic texts. Dondi, a friend of Petrarca, was also enthusiastic about ancient monuments. He not only wrote poems about them, he also measured them.

Thanks to engineers of his ability, mechanical time gradually replaced the old method of dividing the workday by the canonical hours. Secularization transformed people's sense of time. The ticking of the clock became the lord of life and death, measuring more precisely than ever the precious minutes of craftsmen. Dante had already cast his gaze back to a quieter age, when his "Florence, within her ancient ring of walls . . . sober and chaste, lived in tranquility," measuring the day by tierce and nones rather than following the dictates of clocks.[45] Somewhat later, the new time made it all the way to Scandinavia. And that region, too, adapted. Of course, clocks were still imprecise enough that, if we can believe Chaucer, the rooster Chauntecleer crowed the time more reliably than it was shown on the monastery clock.

The mechanical clock, whose mysterious existence outlasted that of all previous time-telling devices thanks to its hidden weights, wheels, and escapement, fascinated people for centuries. It served as a metaphor for man, the state, the cosmos. The first to make the comparison was Oresme in Paris—where, by order of Charles V, clocks had to be set by the one on the royal palace on the Île de la Cité.[46] But Oresme's God is not the watchmaker who leaves his finished handiwork and the people he has called into existence to their own devices. Rather he is omnipresent, sustaining and moving his creation. In a bold act of speculation, Oresme identifies God with the infinite space that must surround the outermost sphere. In this way, the path seems to have been taken to a physics where the same rules apply in the heavens as in the terrestrial, "sublunar" sphere. The phoenix had now arrived in Europe, finding nests in Paris and Oxford, in Avignon and Florence.

In the Millennium of Odysseus

Meanwhile, a venerable figure had returned to Europe's literary stage: "wily" Odysseus set sail again. In Canto 26 of the *Inferno*, Dante has him confess,

> Neither my fondness for my son nor pity
> for my old father nor the love I owed
> Penelope, which would have gladdened her,

was able to defeat in me the longing
I had to gain experience of the world
and of the vices and the worth of men.

Neither yearning for his wife nor filial or paternal piety holds him back. He ventures into the unknown, onto the open sea. This passage can be read as an archetypal description of any latter-day Odysseus, an individual who has followed his own spirit and left countless borders in his wake. Here, on this point, Dante is very modern.[47] Petrarca adopted this ideal of boundlessness, aspiring to a life of intellectual freedom. In an enigmatic sonnet, he dons the mask of Odysseus:

My ship, full of oblivion, sails
on a bitter sea, at winter's midnight,
between Scylla and Charybdis: at the helm
sits that Lord, or rather my enemy.

He writes of a "rain of tears," of a "mist of disdain."

Reason and art so drowned by the waves,
that I begin to despair of finding harbor.

But his wanderings in the late medieval mists of time mean at once discovery and experience. They entail love of the old and yearning for the new. They embody that "arduous virtue"[48] that urged him to study ancient monuments and classical texts, that pushed Marco Polo to the edge of the world and caused Fra Riccoldo to look for Paradise.

The crafty traveler had never been totally forgotten. But now the voices invoking him multiply, as does the number of those who compare themselves to him.[49] Baldassare Castiglione would describe him as a man who suffered and endured, a survivor who learned from his own adventures. Lodovico Dolce praised him for virtuously opposing the fickle goddess of fate. Amerigo Vespucci, who gave his name to a continent, liked to think of himself as the Odysseus of his day.[50] The great collector and naturalist Ulisse Aldrovandi (1522–1605) must have understood his first name as a sign (Ulisse, of course, deriving from the Latin variant of Odysseus). Invoking Virgil, he wondered what kind of man he had been named after. "Who was Ulysses?" And he answered immediately: "A man of wide-ranging spirit who wandered . . . long and far."[51] He modeled his life on that of the ancient hero, placing his own journeys across Italy, France, and Spain in the context of that odyssey of all odysseys. Around 1580, he had scenes from the ancient epic painted on the walls of his villa in Sant'Antonio di Savena (near Bologna). Like the Homeric hero, this Renaissance Ulysses placed himself in the protection of Athena, the goddess of wisdom and patron saint of the sciences. Yet he had no illusions. He knew that human effort would always be in vain and that Ithaca, the island of longing for all ancient and modern travelers, is only reached when death comes.

In the fourteenth century, everything else was uncertain—in a word, an odyssey. People did not yet gaze with proud self-assurance beyond the Pillars of Hercules into a new world, as Francis Bacon, the intellectual (but not biological) kinsman of Roger Bacon, one day would. For the time being, the bold innovators and restless thinkers were a tiny group, and their intellectual world—as Petrarca well knew—was threatened on all sides. As at the turn of the previous century, people looked anxiously at the sky. Religious disquiet was everywhere, and the cry for purity reached a crescendo. In the summer of 1399, the "Bianchi," a devotional sect dressed in white, wandered between the Alps and Latium. They anticipated that the following year, 1400, would bring with it an age of peace and piety.[52] In England, Wyclif's teachings were propagated by the "Lollards," a name originally meaning simply "dissenters" of all kinds. They rejected formal aspects of religion like rites, pilgrimages, and the traditional doctrine of transubstantiation, pursuing instead a life of apostolic poverty. The state persecuted and suppressed them. They had no significance for the prehistory of the "great Reformation."[53] In the Netherlands, Geert Groote (ca. 1340–1384) founded the *devotio moderna*, the "modern devotion," another lay piety movement. It spread south as far as Basel and Interlaken. Its religiosity was expressed in one of the most widely read books of the age, the *Imitation of Christ*, which recommended adopting the lifestyle of the Redeemer and reading the Bible devoutly. The search for God could also result in conversion to Islam—as in the case of the Catalan Franciscan Anselm Turmeda (1355–1423), who lived and died in Tunis—but this was quite a rarity.

In France, what Saint Louis had once ordered finally started being put into practice in 1394: the expulsion of the Jews. Many of the survivors opted for baptism. Cities from Strasbourg to Prague and Speyer followed suit. From now on, Jews tended to live in the countryside, as many of those banished from the cities were forced to make a fresh start outside the walls. England's Jews had already been driven out a century earlier. Conflict requires contact, and thus modern anti-Semitism lacked the fertile soil it needed to grow on the island.[54] In Spain, persecution and slaughter began in the last decade of fourteenth century; the epicenter was Seville. Tens of thousands converted.[55]

The universities, now in the firm grip of state and church, lost their significance for a while as centers of intellectual renewal. Outside the lecture halls,
however, at courts and in cities, humanistic studies boomed. Far from the
debates about universals, the tiny insights of the logicians, and the discussions
about subtle points of theology, the humanists approached truth by telling
stories and explaining where things came from. They sought relevance for everyday life in texts, strived for eloquence, and continued to uncover the classical legacy. Standards changed. Domenico Bandini (1335–1418) of Arezzo,
who at the end of his life taught rhetoric and grammar at the University of
Bologna, compiled an encyclopedia that only at first glance resembles a medieval compendium. Bandini's primary focus was on human beings. His book
contains over four thousand biographies of famous men and women—all informed by source criticism. His approach thus reveals humanist tendencies in
the most basic sense of the word.[56]

Unusual, indeed unheard-of positions were taken by the mathematician
and philosopher Blasius of Parma (ca. 1347–1416). A follower of Ockham, he
was the West's al-Razi. He held unconventional views on every topic, earning
for himself the sobriquet *doctor diabolicus*, or "diabolical doctor."[57] Of all the
means of acquiring knowledge, Blasius gave pride of place to mathematics.
Like Descartes much later, he believed there was one certainty that not even
God could subvert: that he himself existed. He taught monstrosities such as
that the soul was probably made of matter, was attached to the body, and was
therefore mortal. Another was that the differences between religions resulted
from differences in climate and the constellations of the planets. God was consigned to the role of an engineer who left the world he created to tick on its
own like a wound-up clockwork. Blasius's thought points the way ahead to
intellectual paths that would only truly widen in the seventeenth century.

The tensions of life that Johan Huizinga described in his *Autumn of the
Middle Ages* also manifested itself in the arts. The "beautiful Madonnas"
(*schöne Madonnen*) found in central and eastern Europe were typical of the
"soft style" (*weicher Stil*) of the age. With their slightly curved posture, their
seamlessly draped robes of many folds, and their sweet physiognomies, they
are courtly ladies of heaven. They seem to have been less an invitation to self-
identification than ideal figures of perfect beauty, similar to the angels on the
Wilton Diptych discussed above. The other side of the epoch and of life can
be seen in the pietàs that began appearing in Germany, particularly in the
fourteenth century. They portray Mary crying, holding the lifeless body of her
son on her lap. Like the *Imitation of Christ*, they were intended to invite the

viewer to feel pity. They thus stood in the service of a devotional technique also practiced by the *devotio moderna*.

Cadaver monuments called *transi* depicted the departed as deceased, dead bodies or skeletons with empty eye sockets, sometimes with maggots, snakes, and toads creeping through them. This horrific art acted as a reminder that life is fleeting, that the most beautiful body is nothing more than future food for worms. The experience of the age of plague is also reflected in the *Danse Macabre*, or Dance of Death, an increasingly common motif. Death is depicted as the great leveler, as a grinning skeleton leading pope and emperor, old hags and beautiful girls, scholars and nuns in a round dance. Gruesome images of this kind started being called "macabre" after the poet Jean le Fèvre wrote about the "dance of *Macabré*" in his *Respit de la Mort* in 1376.[58]

Under the spell of Giotto and in dialogue with the north, the Italians continued their conquest of reality. An entirely new artistic world emerged around 1400, first in the books of hours of the north. These reflections of private devotion must have been produced in the thousands. Some of the miniaturists were masters of an unprecedentedly realistic view of landscapes; they played with light, blurred objects in the hazy distance, and portrayed people in a lifelike manner. Two of the greatest were the Limburg brothers, who produced an incomparably fine book of hours for John, Duke of Berry. Thus, a new view of the world took hold.

Considered as a historical source, the art of the era indicates a massive intensification of cultural exchange.[59] The notion of an "international Gothic" style has been put forward. Numerous *schöne Madonnen* are so similar that an attempt was made to attribute them all to one master. The emergence of common styles resulted from communication. Exchange was facilitated by religious orders and the Curia, by courts and cities with their trade networks, and by universities. The media of exchange included drawings, letters, books, and the eyes of painters. New systems of long-distance communication effectively made Europe a smaller place. Around 1380, a "renaissance of couriers (*staffette*)" began, apparently first in Milan.[60] A postal service developed that did not rely on individual messengers but rather on regular travel along a series of fixed stages. France followed suit, as did the Holy Roman Empire in the final decades of the fifteenth century.

Patriotism, the friendlier predecessor to nationalism, sprouted from more than just opposition to Rome. The *Grandes chroniques de France* narrated the history of the realm for a courtly audience. Its richly illustrated volumes are based on older chronicles, biographies of kings, and other documents.[61] The work was produced in the Royal Abbey of Saint-Denis. A few steps away from the scriptoria lay the kings and queens whose deeds were now being immortalized in ink. It was also the resting place of a valiant commander in the Hundred Years' War, Bertrand du Guesclin. Royal mausoleums were a source of national identity elsewhere as well: Roskilde Cathedral for the Danes, the Jerónimos Monastery in Lisbon for the Portuguese, Westminster Abbey, where Chaucer was also interred, for the English. In the city-republics of Italy, the saints also had to share their houses with a growing number of profane demigods. Santa Croce developed into the pantheon of Florence. Venice buried its doges and maritime heroes in the Dominican church of San Zanipolo and the Frari of the Franciscans.

Europe's Diversity and the Boundaries of Belief

By now, there was also a famous grave in the Far East, in Samarkand. Covered in blue ceramic tiles, the cupola of a mausoleum covers the final resting place of Timur the Lame and his successors. An inscription around the magnificently decorated interior records the ancestry and deeds of the conqueror. He became a legend, his short-lived kingdom the promise of an imperial possibility. In the view of the historian John Darwin, Timur's death marked a turning point in world history.[62] He represented the last (failed) attempt to prevent the division of Eurasia into three parts: the states of the West, Islamic central Eurasia, and the Far East. From now on, the balance of power would be tilted to the Far East and the far West. This was the upshot of Timur's lightning assault on Central Eurasia, as well as of the enduring tribal conditions of the region.[63]

In point of fact, Timur's imperial dream never had a chance of becoming a reality. To be sure, the conqueror's army was no longer composed of wild riders with bows and arrows. He had brought war elephants from India. He possessed infantry, heavy cavalry, and cannons, the most modern weapons then available. He, too, knew that knowledge is power, as his famous exchange with the scholar Ibn Khaldun (1332–1406) in Damascus shows. Timur was obsessed with talking about what is knowable and what is not. But he neither codified laws nor built an administration that could transmit his will to the furthest corners of the realm. His tireless conquering and killing stood in opposition to a time when the future had long since entrenched itself behind the fortresses and walls of ink states. Timur sought legitimacy in Allah. Styling himself Allah's representative on Earth, he claimed all power and authority for himself.[64] Incidentally, his interview with Ibn Khaldun did not stop him from plundering Damascus.

Back in the West, Europe had long since stopped feeling like it was the subject of the Holy Roman Emperor. In the words of the jurist Baldus de Ubaldis (1327–1400), the king is emperor in his own realm: *Rex in regno suo est imperator regni sui.*[65] Admittedly, the *Imperator Romanorum* was still the lord of the last world empire before the apocalypse and the supreme ruler on Earth—at least in the pages of treatises written by authors close to him. And his ambassadors continued to insist on precedence in the diplomatic arena down into the modern era. But none of this corresponded with reality. While the fledgling nations of Europe were creating their places of memory, the line of great monarchs in the Imperial Cathedral of Speyer ended with the Habsburg Albert, murdered in 1308. The universal empire had faded into a fiction. There would never be a German national basilica.

Europe's states—this is the essential point—were not able to enjoy a leisurely existence under the leaden roof of an empire. The continent remained an arena of savage competition, where the weapons were not only swords and cannons but also pens, pictures, and palaces. Ambition and piety fertilized a patronage landscape in which thousands upon thousands of writers, artists, inventors, and scholars found sustenance.[66] The Schism was useful to education and the sciences. For example, popes and antipopes outbid each other in granting privileges to new universities in order to gain their support.

Beyond the religious struggle, a new type of scientist developed who replaced the cleric as the classic natural philosopher of the Middle Ages. His work focused not on dogma, morality and ethics, or the investigation of hidden mysteries, but rather on open discussion of what is "true" and "false."[67] In this way, the practical utility of learning became much more pronounced. Scholars no longer felt beholden to the ideal of forsaking an active life "in the world." The double-headed Church did what it could to prune back uncontrolled growth; it held trials, condemned heretics, burned books and sometimes people, too. Nevertheless, priestly power ran up against limits in fragmented Europe. Rome's monopoly on salvation seemed more threatened than ever around 1400, and social unrest even found theological cover at times. Meister Eckhart had said that it was not ancestry or property that made a nobleman, but rather that it was up to each person to act nobly. If, as he taught—in German, no less—that man had been born of God, his Father, "in the highest part of the soul,"[68] what value could outward honors have? In the fourth book of his

Convivio, Dante also developed a concept of true nobility based on virtue; in comparison, he argued, traditional nobility of birth was worthless.[69]

No doubt, real historical circumstances contributed to the abundance of innovations in the intellectual realm. Starvation and the Black Death, the Church's exile in Avignon and the Schism, wars and uprisings all demanded explanation or at least commentary and judgment. That the birth—or better, the manifestation—of subjectivity in texts and images is related to this seems obvious, even without clear evidence being available. But it did not cause the intellectuals to lose faith in God. On the other hand, some people did consider God to be dead and forgot about the impending Last Judgment—at least such is the charge leveled in a late-fourteenth-century novella by an anonymous author.[70] How widespread such thoughts were, we do not know.

Strong Women

Europe's women had to obey their husbands and seldom had access to higher education. Nevertheless, they enjoyed a few more freedoms than their fellow women outside Latin Europe in the Late Middle Ages. The unenviable position young girls and women still have in many countries of the modern Islamic world has deep historical roots. China also oppressed its female population down to modern times.[71]

We could take Chaucer's Wife of Bath as emblematic of the rising fortunes of European women. She had been married five times, and her tale is a diatribe on the miseries of marriage and the misogyny of monks. It is also a caricature of courtly romances. The long prologue provides the first portrait of an assertive middle-class woman known to literary history. She is a Mother Courage in hard times, eager to live out her God-given sexuality and use it to dominate her husbands (preferably wealthy older men). It would be difficult to find her analog in the literature produced by other cultures, except perhaps for Scheherazade.

There were a few truly free, powerful women in the European Middle Ages. Not only nuns and saints but also rulers like Eleanor of Aquitaine, known as the "Queen of the Troubadours," Margaret of Denmark, Joanna of Naples, and Hedwig of Poland. France's Salic Law, however, excluded women from royal succession. An Elizabeth I would have been unthinkable on the Throne of Lilies. In the urban context, women's right to enter into contracts was usually restricted. Occasionally, we find female merchants who did business freely on their own account.[72] Cologne, Zurich, and Paris had female guilds, including one for silk weavers.

One unlikely advocate of women's freedom was Bernardino of Siena (1380–1444). Although a strict conservative in general, he defended the equality of men and women in one of his sermons: "God did not make a woman out of a bone of Adam's foot, so that he should tread her underground."[73] He must have forgotten the teaching of Thomas Aquinas, who, based on abstruse medical speculations, described woman as a "failed man."

Christine de Pizan (1365–ca. 1430), an Italian who made her way to Paris, has been called the "patron saint" of feminism.[74] She was the first laywoman who, thanks to aristocratic benefactors, managed to live by the power of her pen. Her *Book of the City of Ladies* emphasized that God, in his wisdom, could not have made woman as imperfect and vile as claimed in some passages of the *Romance of the Rose*. In the early fifteenth century, this critique unleashed Europe's first great literary debate. Lined up against Christine were some of the early French humanists, including the most important among them, Jean de Montreuil (1354–1418). Supporters of the popular romance defended it with polemics and wit. Christine defiantly disagreed. She criticized the obvious allusions to male genitalia, the glorification of liberal sexual mores, and the work's theory of love, steeped as it was in Ovidian salaciousness. In her view, literature should observe moral boundaries, including (and especially) female dignity. Her ideal woman was anything but a champion of emancipation. Instead, she was a sensible courtly lady who, when necessary, took offense at the crass comments of men. Or perhaps she was rather the industrious, savvy woman who endured adversity with strength and serenity, a figure we meet in her *Book of the Three Virtues*. It may even be a self-portrait of the author.

Should we not also mention Margherita Attendolo, ancestor of the heroine Caterina Sforza (1463–1509), the ruler of Forlì and Imola who defied Cesare Borgia? With the help of a band of mercenaries, Margherita kidnapped four Neapolitan noblemen and ransomed them for the release of her brother Muzio. Another powerful woman was Eleanor of Arborea (ca. 1347–1404), the energetic ruler and lawgiver of a Sardinian Judicate. She was also a lover of falcons and passed a law protecting them. Writing about the lives of women in medieval Europe also requires focusing in particular on the wives of craftsmen and farmers without much freedom, poor servant girls and prostitutes, midwives, slaves, and daughters forced into nunneries. Female authors like Christine de Pizan, Hildegard of Bingen, and Hrotsvitha of Gandersheim were rare. A bit more common in the Late Middle Ages were female rulers who collected art and patronized learning, as well as wives of rich merchants who prudently ruled the house while their husbands were away on business. Margherita Datini personally cared for the illegitimate children of her husband Francesco.

On the other hand, we could naturally also talk about the love that men felt for their wives or lovers one thousand years ago, just like today. After all, not all men were slavedrivers, oppressors, or bluebeards. To get a sense of the feelings men could have, let us listen to the words of the Icelandic skald Snorri Sturluson (1179–1241), who loved beautiful Gudrun Hreinsdottir. "I came inside, where the woman, the most sublime of all women, sat in the house," he recalls. "This woman was combing her hair."[75]

19

The Sun Sets in the East

The Birth of Ming China

Crisis descended upon other parts of the world in the fourteenth century as well. Japan erupted in civil war in the 1330s. Gangs of bandits roamed the land. Chroniclers recorded nighttime attacks, raids, panic, death, and "parvenus who are turning the world upside down." In the opinion of the chroniclers, it was the lower classes' desire to rule the rulers that was behind the unrest convulsing the whole kingdom.[1] The Kamakura shogunate fell. Power was taken by the Ashikaga, warlords based in the Muromachi district of Kyoto. The period of their rule, 1338–1573, is known either as the Ashikaga shogunate, after the name of the clan, or the Muromachi shogunate, after their residence.

China was haunted by extremely cold years, typhoons, hail showers, and floods. Dragons in the sky portended evil; grasshoppers ate the rice fields bare.[2] In 1344, the Black Death began its devastation there before moving on to the West. The population shrank from one hundred million to sixty million.

High taxes disproportionately levied on the south increased tensions. Reactions were similar to those in Europe: to many people, it seemed that the end of an era was approaching. While Christians in the West awaited the second coming of the Messiah in these times of hardship, China anticipated the return of the bodhisattva Maitreya, who, as a future Buddha, would bring illumination and peace. His analogs in other cultures included occulted imams, Mahdis, and even Emperor Frederick asleep under the Kyffhäuser Mountains. The "Pure Land" dreamed of by the oppressed resembled a Golden Age paradise. This Fata Morgana strengthened opposition to the Yuan. Sects heralding this utopia—including the "Red Turbans"—gained hundreds of thousands of adherents. Their leaders carved out their own domains and gave names to the dynasties they aimed to found—names that resounded with the magic of a better past, like Han and Song. The Mongol overlords lost control. The savior who ultimately emerged from the chaos was no wise god but rather a brutal, pockmarked farmer's son: Zhu Yuanzhang (r. 1368–1398). His military ability had propelled him through the ranks of the Red Turbans. His soldiers eliminated rival warlords and took city upon city. In 1368, he was the master of southern China; the Mongol emperor fled. Yuanzhang declared himself ruler. He named his dynasty "Ming," meaning "bright." Nanjing, a city of one million inhabitants in the deep south, became the capital.

Hongwu, the name he gave himself as emperor, means "great military power." It also described his philosophy of rule. He used his momentum. China became Chinese again. He cleansed the ruling classes and the civil service. He removed the chancellor and abolished the office—a fateful error that would weaken the emperors' position in the long run. One hundred thousand people fell victim to his purges. Foreigners and Buddhists were marginalized; the influence of the Confucian elite was squashed. A system based on suspicion and draconian measures provided for peace. The regime's henchmen beat, tortured, and flayed undesirables, hanging up their stuffed skins as a symbol of terror for all eyes to see. Yet not even this despot could succeed in permanently disempowering the civil service. There was too much work to be done, and the bureaucratic Hercules that managed it was too strong. Supervising Secretary Zhang Wenfu reported that in a span of only eight days the kingdom's offices dealt with no fewer than 3,391 separate matters.[3]

Words engraved on iron tablets proclaimed Hongwu's laws throughout the land. Everywhere—it sounds like sinister irony—concord was to reign. No one was allowed to leave his home village without approval. The Yuan prohibition on changing professions remained strictly enforced. Equally fatal for both the economy and intellectual life was the crackdown on foreign trade. Even within China, the flow of goods was restricted. Agriculture was the only sector that received energetic support. The goal was to make the kingdom self-sufficient. Hongwu committed his successors to a defensive foreign policy. For intellectual sustenance and exam material for aspiring civil servants, all that remained was a handful of Confucian writings. Any statements from Mengzi's commentaries on them that might undermine peace and order were removed by censors. On the other hand, the first Ming emperor undertook massive reforesting efforts throughout China and improved irrigation.

How much power lay hidden in the fettered giant was revealed under the Yongle Emperor (r. 1402–1424), who emerged victorious from the struggle for succession after Hongwu's death.[4] Once again, thousands of heads rolled. Beijing, located on the edge of the dusty North China Plain, was made the capital, its expansion entailing astronomical costs. A canal was dug to facilitate the provisioning of the north, supplying food to the metropolis of 700,000 inhabitants. Walls galore—palace walls, walls around city districts and courtyards—held all freedom prisoner. Three hundred thousand soldiers stood ready to respond to the least twitch of unrest. A dense web of informal controls guaranteed tranquility under Yongle as well.[5] Here in Beijing was the center of the universe. At least, that's how China saw it. In the purple "Forbidden City," which was then closed to the common people, there were over two thousand temples for the heavenly gods and countless shiny golden palaces for the lords of the Earth. In no time, between 1406 and 1420, an army of forced laborers and craftsmen built the largest palace complex in the world. This is where the emperors now lived, surrounded by eunuchs, ministers, soldiers, and beautiful women. The "Hall of Supreme Harmony," where they held court seated upon the Dragon Throne, was surrounded by gardens and small ponds in whose surface pavilions were reflected. Bronze lions still keep watch there as they did six hundred years ago, when the roofs of the palace city were painted imperial yellow.

Even before the first stone of the Forbidden City was laid, Yongle had done a radical volte-face, opting to pursue a dynamic foreign policy. Dai Viet came under Ming sovereignty for two decades. Several campaigns against the Mongols were led personally by the emperor. Gigantic expeditionary fleets dwarfed everything else, seeming to inaugurate an age of expansion into blue horizons (pp. 466–468). But the costly strategy of forward defense was ultimately in vain, and the great periods of learning and technological innovation experienced no renaissance. No mechanical clock kept time for the "Sons of Heaven."

Instead, drums and bells on the north gate tower sounded the hours in the traditional manner. On the other hand, Yongle had a staff of translators and commissioned over two thousand scholars to compile an encyclopedia. Almost twenty-three thousand volumes were produced, filled with knowledge about every subject, with classical texts, and with historical, literary, and philosophical discussions. But the work did not circulate broadly, and outside the court it seems that little of substance was written. The Ming state evolved into a power-hungry leviathan that inhibited all private initiative.[6] The swallows of Maragheh did not make a summer. The economy may have flourished, but no technological breakthroughs were made. Nearly all great ideas continued to be thought elsewhere.

The Decline of Arabic Science

By now, the heyday of Arabic science and technology was also history. Ibn al-Salah, a thirteenth-century master of jurisprudence, literally considered philosophy to be diabolical: whoever studied or taught it would lose God's favor and be overcome by Satan.[7] His stance and that of his kindred spirit Ibn Taimiyyah (1263–1328) were no anomaly of Islamic intellectual history. Christianity also knows such positions. Yet it seems that the words of those opposed to the *falsafa* in Islamic societies held greater weight than in the West. What alienated them was the "unholiness" of the central texts of Greek culture.[8] Beyond dispute is that Arabic philosophy now almost stopped expanding its radius. As far as we can tell from the sources known to us, the focus was on maintaining the tradition, on the exegesis of the classics, and on the writing of textbooks.[9] Even the metaphysics of one of the most important Muslim philosophers of a later time, the Persian Mulla Sadra (1572–1641), merely offers a synthesis of Neoplatonic, mystical, Gnostic, and other teachings. Occasionally, his thought approximates that of Cusanus (pp. 402–406).[10]

   When the decline began is just as contentious a question as what occasioned it.[11] In the view of the Moroccan philosopher Mohammed Abed al-Jabri (1936–2010), one decisive cause was the fact that Muslims did not follow Averroes. In his *Critique of Arab Reason*, al-Jabri called for a critical approach to tradition, for a reading of sacred texts that was exploratory and reflective and not merely commemorative (as was customary). But why, we must ask, did Ibn Rushd lose out in the Islamic world, whereas he spurred the West on to critical thought and rational inquiry? The walling off of the Greek legacy doubtless played a role in philosophy's decline in Islamic societies as well as in the stagnation of science and technology. Yet that does not tell us why this development came about. Admittedly, the search for causes is hampered by many difficulties. Rich source material still lies unread in archives. In addition, the term "Islamic world" comprehends enormous, politically fragmented regions, stateless nomad territory, highly civilized urban areas, rationally organized states, and crude despotisms. As in the case of China, any attempt to identify possible causes for the "great divergence" between Europe and the Islamic world will admit of complex, multilayered answers (see Part IV).

One external cause was the Mongols. They had depopulated cities, ravaged the countryside, and destroyed irrigation systems. In many regions, nomadic existence displaced a life of settled agriculture. It is possible that the invasions of the Mongols and others also brought the "Arab agricultural revolution" to a standstill.[12] When Baghdad was conquered, its thirty-six libraries went up in flames. Decades earlier, the geographer Ibn Jubayr had already described the city as a ruin, as a mere "statue of a ghost."[13] Areas of vibrant intellectual life had been amputated. Muslim southern Italy had fallen to the Normans, and the Reconquista took the intellectual crown jewels of Andalusian Islam. In the first half of the thirteenth century, Córdoba and Seville, old capitals of Arabic culture, were lost to Castile. In addition, wars against Christian armies spurred radicalization. It was religious zealots who then drove Ibn Rushd and others to the Maghreb. Andalusia's relations with the East were broken off. Philosophy then took an esoteric and mystical turn there, losing contact with reality.

Consequently, the topics it dealt with and the boldness of its perspectives remained limited. Only in the sixteenth century—thus argued Hossein Ziai (1944–2011), a scholar of Islamic philosophy—did the reconciliation between religion and classical Arabic philosophy begin.[14] After the Middle Ages, the Islamic world did not produce a Descartes or a Spinoza, a Feuerbach, or even a Schopenhauer. Western thought was given as little attention as sensitive areas of the Latin and Greek tradition (pp. 854–858). Ultimately, people knew they possessed the "right" religion and, in the Koran, the perfect and final book of God. The Koran calls God's messenger Muhammad *Khatam an-Nabiyyin*, "seal of the prophets": the definitive, final prophet until the end of time.[15] From that perspective, what could one learn from cultures which knew nothing of that absolute truth? The first European philosopher that Islam heard of was Descartes. His *Discourse on Method* was translated into Persian at the suggestion of the French consul in 1862.[16] The Islamic world did not learn about Kant and other Western philosophers until Mohammad Ali Foroughi's (1877–1942) *History of Philosophy in Europe*, whose three volumes were published between

1930 and 1940. The contrast with the classical period of Arabic science is stark. For example, there are 237 extant manuscripts in Europe of the Latin translation of the Neoplatonic *Book of Causes*, the *Liber de causis*. Only three copies in Arabic are known.

Another indication of religion's commanding importance is that the vast majority of scientific advances after the thirteenth century came in areas that served religious purposes: astronomy—which adopted a bit of Western knowledge earlier than other sciences via translations—and, closely connected with it, mathematics.[17] The study of the movements of heavenly bodies helped to determine the times of prayer and the dates of Ramadan. Thus, Nasir al-Din al-Tusi was not only an important mathematician but also a theologian. The astronomer Ibn ash-Shatir (ca. 1305–1375) earned his daily bread as a *muwaqqit*, a timekeeper, at the Umayyad mosque in Damascus.[18] Religion also provided the impetus for Muslim scholars to investigate spherical trigonometry, as this knowledge made it possible to determine the direction of Mecca.[19] Only long-familiar astronomical instruments were improved in that late period. The fact that corrections were made to traditional knowledge here and there does little to improve the big picture. Qutb al-Din al-Shirazi (1236–1311), an Iranian physician and Sufi, studied astronomy under al-Tusi in Maragheh. Among other things, he attempted to elaborate a classification system for the sciences after the manner of al-Farabi. He also discovered how rainbows work; his student al-Farisi continued his research in this area.[20] Another late great of Arabic science was Ali Qushji (1403–1474), active in Samarkand and then in Istanbul. Independently of Oresme, he speculated that the Earth rotated on its axis. He sought to eliminate the epicycles by putting the planets in eccentric orbits. He justified his models with empirical observations, not only mathematics. His work could have laid the foundation for a non-Aristotelian physics.[21] Yet the astronomy of Qushji did not initiate a paradigm shift, nor did the ideas of one of his intellectual descendants, the Persian Shams al-Din al-Kahfri (d. after 1525).[22] Medicine also remained largely where it had been in the High Middle Ages.

As always, courts, mosques, and hospitals remained places of learning. Madrasas—schools that could range in size from one teacher to massive institutions—were usually guardians of tradition, not laboratories of innovation.[23] Their function was to transmit religious and practical knowledge, especially Islamic law. Apart from logic, Greek philosophy played no major role in the classroom. Attention might also be paid to grammar and history. And at the madrasa in Shiraz, the subjects included not only philosophy and astrology but also physics, chemistry, and mathematics.[24] In terms of breadth, however, no comparison can be made between the Western *studia humanitatis* and what has misleadingly been called "Islamic humanism," *studia abadiya*.[25] For the most part, it was practically oriented studies that dominated: astronomy, mathematics, and, above all, medicine. This is also the picture we get from what we know about libraries in Muslim India.[26]

What could be thought and studied depended on the whims and preferences of each individual ruler. If a sensitive patron was followed by an uneducated dolt whose only joy was the lion hunt, then it was all over for science and scholarship in his orbit. The situation of many scholars had always been precarious. They had to wander from court to court to find a patron—and sometimes to save their skins.[27] Some of the greatest experienced breaks in their careers because of their views or even because they were involved in cabals at court. Al-Kindi was whipped; Ibn Sina was forced to live a life of restless wandering. Al-Haytham pretended to be insane in order to avoid being stalked by the bizarre Fatimid al-Hakim. Maimonides, as a Jew, was already an outlier; after being chased out of Almohad Córdoba, he had to tramp halfway across the world, first to Fez and then to Jerusalem and Alexandria, until he finally found a livelihood in Fustat. Whether Mulla Sadra also knew the bitterness of exile for a time is unclear.[28]

Similar fates can naturally be found in great number in Latin Europe as well. But there were also more alternatives: more courts located more closely together, rich monasteries and free cities, academies, soon humanist circles as well, printing houses, and public and private grammar schools; and finally, there was the singular institution of the university. It was such places that endowed the Latin European dialogue with permanence—an essential precondition for all significant innovations. It is precisely this that discourse in Islamic culture usually lacked. Arabic astronomers demonstrated errors in Ptolemy and corrected Aristotle, but it would be up to Europeans to remove Earth from the middle of the universe. Ibn al-Nafis (1210/13–1288) may have discovered pulmonary circulation, and one or the other Muslim anatomist may still have cited him in the nineteenth century,[29] but no further insights were made on the basis of his work in the Islamic world. Cairo and Fustat, the gathering places for intellectuals who had fled Andalusia, replaced maltreated Baghdad. And a few great minds did appear here and there between Istanbul and Isfahan. Yet higher-order technological innovations were no longer achieved, nor were major discoveries made. While the Europeans were pursuing unknown lands, Arabic geography barely proceeded beyond al-Idrisi's map until the sixteenth century.[30] One groundbreaking invention, the mounting screw—it was known to the Arabs back in the ninth century[31]—even seems to have been forgotten again (pp. 836f.). Thus, giants like al-Razi, Abu al-Qasim, Ibn Sina, and Ibn al-Nafis were left without dwarves who could climb onto their shoulders. Altogether, the few significant scholars and scientists of the Maragheh period and the following centuries seem like a raggedy band when compared to the quickly growing army of Latin European intellectuals and engineers who were constantly thinking up new ideas and inventing new devices.

At the turn of the fifteenth century, the realm of possibility for the great European Renaissance stood wide open. By now, it reached from Sweden to Poland and the gates of Moscow, from Hungary to Spain, France, and England. Its center was Italy. Niccolò Machiavelli would praise it as a country born to bring dead things back to life, *per risuscitare le cose morte*.[32] This is the role his homeland was destined to play in world history.

PART III

The Realization of Possibilities

1400–1600

20

Florence at First Light

Origins of the Monumental Renaissance

Historians have long been infatuated with painting, sculpture, and architecture. The new classicism of the fifteenth century literally jumps out at them, encouraging them to follow Burckhardt's lead and locate the division between the Middle Ages and modernity in this period. The sight overwhelms the senses, overshadowing the fact that the Renaissance on parchment and paper that we have just sketched long preceded its development in the arts. In the fifteenth century, the visual arts caught up to the intellectual shift, but significantly later and certainly not everywhere. That Florence was the birthplace of the artistic renaissance comes as no surprise. A perfect foundation had been laid for it: a lively humanist scene, rich patrons, connections to other artistic centers in Europe, and mathematical mentalities. The city on the Arno was also in the avant-garde of technology. Florence produced an especially distinctive trademark of the striving for novelty: the patent. One of the first to obtain a patent may have been the architect Filippo Brunelleschi, who received protection from the city council in 1421 for his invention of a cost-saving barge. Venice followed suit in 1474.[1] Another important factor for the classicizing renewal of art was the proximity to Rome's ruins and statues, which provided models for the new style.

The new trend was widespread and would end up conquering the entire continent in the following centuries. Of course, there had been countless responses to the Black Death. Fearing for his soul, one rich merchant paid for the decoration of the chapter house at the Dominican church of Santa Maria Novella.[2] The massive fresco there is like a sermon in answer to the chaos of the times. The pope sits on a throne in front of a domed basilica—a symbol of the universal Church, obviously alluding to the Duomo, or cathedral, then being built in Florence. To the left of the pope is Emperor Charles IV and, on the same level, a Dominican cardinal. In the middle, Saint Thomas points the way to heaven for a motley group of people of all classes lost in celebrating the joys of the world with music and dancing. In the bottom register, a whole pack of dogs with black-and-white spots, the *domini canes*, safeguards orthodoxy. These "Dominicans" watch over a flock of pious sheep, driving off and mauling wolves, symbols of heresy, that are creeping up on the herd. The message is clear: salvation is only possible with the pope, the highest power on Earth, within the Church and the theology of Saint Thomas.

But at the same time as this pious fresco was being painted, something exciting and new was happening in the secular architecture of Florence. Begun in 1374, the Loggia diagonally across from the Palazzo Vecchio outshone all previous structures of its kind in size and elegance. Its function was to provide a worthy frame for public ceremonies and to protect them from the elements. Swiss mercenaries known as *Landsknechte* were later billeted under it, on account of which it came to be called the Loggia "dei Lanzi." Located near the center of power, it was Florence's public space par excellence. This is where the *res publica* did its business for all to see. A little bit later, haltingly at first but then in spectacular fashion, classical antiquity began to appear in sculpture and painting. A start was made—we are now in the last decade of the fourteenth century—when an unknown sculptor placed nudes of Apollo, Hercules, and another figure with his back turned among acanthus leaves on the frame of the Porta della Mandorla on the north side of the Duomo. Classicism, which had never entirely disappeared in sculpture, soon exploded on all fronts.

Classical antiquity apparently provided a cultural code that gave expression to both the republican spirit and the imperial aplomb of the elites. For this to happen, many "streams" had to flow together in the now wide-open realm of possibilities. As always, concrete agents of change were necessary: skillful, educated painters, sculptors, and architects. One of them was Lorenzo Ghiberti (ca. 1378–1455), a young goldsmith who had fled the plague and the threat of Gian Galeazzo Visconti and was now working for the lord of Pesaro, Malatesta di Pandolfo.[3] Friends in Florence wrote him that learned masters from all over Italy were being sought to participate in a "trial and competition." A sculptor was needed to decorate the north doors of the Baptistery of San Giovanni with bronze reliefs.

Next to the Duomo, the Baptistery was the most important holy site in the city. The Florentines liked to believe Giovanni Villani's claim that it was an ancient structure, a temple of Mars.[4] The selection process decided upon by the guild responsible for the building, the Arte della Calimala (the cloth merchants), was accordingly laborious. As far as we know, this was the first such competition in the history of art. It evinces further necessary conditions for the emergence of something new. The contest was not only about ability. Rather, it involved competition, criticism, and thus publicity. In addition, patrons were required who were open to change and who, above all, were willing to pay for the new art. The project also had a religious motive. From the theological perspective, it was a "good work" through which one could hope to garner God's protection from the Visconti and the pestilential angels of the Black Death.

Each participant had to submit a relief sculpture on a predetermined topic: Abraham's sacrifice of Isaac. Ghiberti emerged victorious against stiff competition, including Brunelleschi and Jacopo della Quercia of Siena. In his *Commentaries*, a mix of autobiography, art history, and art theory, he would never tire of celebrating the jury's unanimous verdict. A comparison with Brunelleschi's entry, which has been preserved, shows why Ghiberti won. The latter's composition has a more unitary, organic conception. The naked body of the offering, Isaac, who is saved at the last moment by a heavenly angel, resembles that of an ancient god. From that moment forward, Ghiberti was swamped with commissions. He provided statues for Or San Michele, designed tombs, and developed designs for the glass windows of the Duomo. For the Baptistery, he created the gilt reliefs of the "Gates of Paradise," as Michelangelo called Ghiberti's chief work. He also collaborated with Brunelleschi on the construction of his dome.

Filippo Brunelleschi (1377–1446) was the most important architect of the early Florentine Renaissance. His ancestry will sound familiar, a reminder of the birth of late medieval lay culture from the spirit of the law. He was the son of a notary, who provided him with a solid education and training as a goldsmith.

He won fame primarily as the architect of the dome of Florence's cathedral, which, to borrow oft-quoted words of Leon Battista Albert, still throws its shadow over the peoples of Tuscany. Although without experience as a master builder, his designs won because he invoked ancient models and claimed to have closely studied them in Rome. Theory and practice formed a fruitful union.[5]

The bold innovator was named master builder of the Duomo in 1418, and he seems to have possessed diplomatic abilities that helped him to create classicizing things whenever the chance arose.[6] Many windows of opportunity opened. The silk weavers' guild commissioned Brunelleschi to build a foundling hospital. For the Medici he constructed the Basilica of San Lorenzo, for the Pazzi a funerary chapel. Finally, for the commune he designed the Basilica of Santo Spirito on the other side of the Arno. His younger contemporary Antonio Manetti devoted a *Vita* to him, the first artist biography in Europe.

Brunelleschi's architecture was fascinating for its clarity and geometry in gray and white. His art is familiar to us, not because it is "modern" but because modern art continually borrowed and innovated upon its forms, most recently in the Renaissance Revival style of the nineteenth century. In their own day, Brunelleschi's churches resonated utterly with a spirituality in search of purity and lucidity. They are closer to the piety movements of the Late Middle Ages than they are expressions of modern rationality. It seems that a Platonic aesthetic was taking shape in which light and mathematical relationships played a central role.[7] In the harmonies of the motet that Pope Eugene IV commissioned from Guillaume Dufay for the consecration of the Duomo in 1436, some have heard an echo of the cathedral's proportions—the golden ratio put to music.[8]

A creation of the industrious Brunelleschi, who never commented on questions of theory, stood at the dawn of a new age of painting. What is more, it opened up a view of the world that we, inundated as we are by photographs and films, take for granted.[9] Sometime in the first decade of the fifteenth century, Brunelleschi painted an extremely precise, mirror image picture of the Baptistery executed on the basis of mathematical calculations. In the middle of the thirty-by-thirty-centimeter wood panel, he bored a funnel-shaped hole from the back. Looking through the hole at a mirror mounted in front of the painting, a viewer could see the Baptistery—now no longer reversed—as it really looked. Reality and illusion were interchangeable. It made no difference if one looked at the actual Baptistery through the hole or at the reflection of the painting in the mirror. The experiment was based on the idea, then common, that objects emitted pyramid-shaped bundles of "optic rays" whose points penetrated the eye and created the image. Some people, however, thought the opposite happened, namely that the eye emitted rays that then literally captured images. Perhaps Brunelleschi wanted to check whether reality really was mirrored on the retina like a geometric construction, a cross-section of the optic rays. The experiment demonstrated powerfully that mathematics made it possible to produce perfect illusions of space.

The procedure was first put to practical use by the young Tommaso di Ser Cassai (1401–1428), who, due to his carelessness, was nicknamed "Masaccio," meaning something like "clumsy Tommy."[10] His fresco depicting the Holy Trinity in Santa Maria Novella, only a few minutes' walk from the place where Brunelleschi performed his ingenious experiment, is perhaps the first painting in the world constructed entirely in linear perspective. It probably dates to between 1425 and 1427. At about the same time, Tommaso was commissioned along with an older painter, Masolino, by the merchant Felice Brancacci to fresco a chapel in Santa Maria del Carmine. The subject was scenes from the life of Saint Peter and the expulsion from Paradise after the fall of man. The new perspectival technique opened up spaces and made seemingly solid surfaces of paint, wood, or canvas transparent. They are like thin membranes behind which logically constructed worlds appear. The mountain landscapes seem as realistic as the clouds in the sky and the waves on the Sea of Galilee. Many figures display clear emotions like dread, wrath, and grief. Body movements can be perceived underneath baggy clothing, and shadows are cast—a bit of realism that had still been missing from Giotto's pictures. Masaccio and Masolino continued in paint what Petrarca had begun in his written descriptions of landscapes.

Painting "mathematically" became the passion and obsession of the Quattrocento. "Oh, what a sweet thing this perspective is!"—that is what Paolo Uccello (1397–1475), who employed the technique like almost no other in his day, is supposed to have shouted when his wife called him to bed one night while he was trying to solve geometric puzzles.[11] In sculpture, Ghiberti used linear perspective in his reliefs on the Gates of Paradise. Begun at the same time as the frescoes in the Carmine, they embody Renaissance art in its classic form for the first time. Liberated from the constraints of the Gothic quatrefoil that still bordered the reliefs of the north doors, they relate a pious theme, the story of Joseph, in astounding technical perfection.

Linear perspective was a technique that grew out of the trend toward realism initiated by Giotto and Duccio. The procedure was an expression of the zeitgeist insofar as it came from a world of calculating merchants. Linear perspective put the picture into a subjective relationship with the viewer, as it was calculated to work from just one point of view—his own. It is remarkable that, only a bit later, philosophers reflected upon the perspectival nature of all human knowledge (pp. 404f.). The invention of linear perspective seems to have been an Italian project through and through.[12] Nevertheless, in the following centuries it spread across Europe. Of course, the aesthetic need that linear perspective helped to meet, viz., imitating nature in free composition, was of ancient origin. An echo of this principle can already be heard in Cennino Cennini's *Libro dell'Arte* (ca. 1400), where we read: "Mind you, the most perfect steersman that you can have, and the best helm, lie in the triumphal gateway of copying from nature."[13] The imperative of imitating nature would remain the measure of art for a long time to come. The odd boxlike buildings whose front walls painters had ripped away to provide a view of the inside vanished from fresco cycles. They were replaced by uniform spaces organized according to linear perspective. The custom of painting people large or small depending on their importance also disappeared almost entirely. Artists and humanists rambled through Italy's classical ruins, bringing back to Florence knowledge of how the ancients built. People deduced how ancient buildings looked from written sources, above all Vitruvius's work on architecture, and attempted to reconstruct the theaters of antiquity.[14]

Starting in the 1420s, elements of classical ornamentation were increasingly found in painting. Soon they entwined and framed sculptures and found their way onto buildings. The Renaissance of the page became a Renaissance of paint and marble. Sculpture was brought to its highest heights by Donatello (ca. 1386–1466), a student of Ghiberti who also did a great deal of work in other cities. His reliefs, which likewise masterfully employ linear perspective, are equal to those of his teacher. And he is credited with innovations of his own. His bronze *David* (ca. 1445) was the first free-standing nude figure meant to be viewed from all sides since antiquity. Another first, this time in bronze casting, was his equestrian statue of the mercenary captain Erasmo da Narni, who had conquered Brescia for Venice. Dominating the piazza in front of Padua's basilica, it portrays the so-called *Gattamelata*, "Honeycat," as a mixture of Quattrocento *capitano* and ancient Caesar. Since the days of the Roman Empire, no sculptor had taken on the challenge of casting a bronze figure of this size.

Another novelty, finally, was that all these inventions were attended by an increasingly active theoretical discussion. Until the sixteenth century, it took

PLATE 1. Farrukh ibn ʿAbd al-Latif, "The Elephant Clock." In al-Jazari, *Book of the Knowledge of Ingenious Mechanical Devices* (1315). Ink, gouache, and gold on paper, 30 × 19.7 cm. New York, Metropolitan Museum of Art, accession number 57.51.23.

PLATE 2. Heuresis, the personification of discovery, presenting Dioscorides with a mandrake root. In the "Vienna Dioscorides" (early 6th century). Ink and paint on parchment. Vienna, Nationalbibliothek, Codex medicus graecus 1, fol. 4v.

PLATE 3. Qiu Ying (1494-1552), "Appreciating Antiquities in the Bamboo Garden." Ink, India ink, and paint on silk, 33.8 × 41.4 cm. Beijing, Palace Museum.

PLATE 4. Resurrection of Christ (ca. 1320). Fresco. Istanbul, Chora Church, parecclesion, apse.

PLATE 5. Giotto, Enrico Scrovegni presents the chapel commissioned by him to the Virgin Mary. Detail of a fresco (ca. 1305). Padua, Arena Chapel.

PLATE 6. English or French painter (?), Wilton Dyptich (ca. 1395-1399). Richard II presented to the Virgin Mary by St. John the Baptist, St. Edward, and St. Edmund. Tempera on oak wood, 53 × 37 cm. London, National Gallery, inv. no. NG 4451.

PLATE 7. Richard of Wallingford. Miniature in Thomas of Walsingham, *Gesta abbatum monasterii Sancti Albani* (1390-1394). Ink, paint, and gold on parchment. London, British Library, Cotton Claudius E. IV, fol. 201.

PLATE 8. Hans Memling, portraits of Tommaso di Folco Portinari and his wife Maria Maddalena (ca. 1470). Oil on wood, both 44 × 34 cm. New York, Metropolitan Museum of Art, 14.40.626-627.

PLATE 9. Gentile
Bellini, portrait of
Mehmed II "the
Conqueror" (1480).
Oil on canvas,
69.9 × 52.1 cm. London,
National Gallery, NG
3099.

PLATE 10. Francesco
del Cossa, *Allegory of
March* (ca. 1469/70),
detail of a fresco
showing the first
decan. Ferrara,
Palazzo Schifanoia.

PLATE 11. Antonio del Pollaiuolo, *Hercules and the Hydra* (ca. 1471/75). Tempera and oil on wood, 17.5 × 12 cm. Florence, Gallerie degli Uffizi.

PLATE 12. Guglielmo Giraldi, frontispiece to the *Purgatorio* in a manuscript copy of Dante's *Divine Comedy* (ca. 1474/82) originally in Federico da Montefeltro's library. Ink, paint, and gold on parchment, 49 × 24 cm. Vatican City, Biblioteca Apostolica Vaticana, Urb. Lat. 365, fol. 97r.

PLATE 13. Piero della Francesca, portrait of Federico da Montefeltro (ca. 1472). Varnish and oil on wood, 47 × 33 cm. Florence, Gallerie degli Uffizi.

PLATE 14. Egerton Master and workshop, miniature depicting a blemmya, a monopod, and a cyclops. In Marco Polo, *Le Livre des merveilles* (1410/12). Ink, paint, and gold on parchment, 17 × 16 cm. Paris, Bibliothèque nationale de France, Francais 2810.

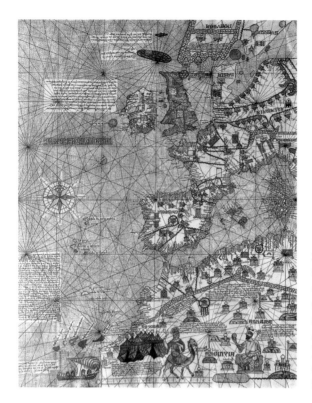

PLATE 15. Abraham Cresque or workshop, *Catalan Atlas* (ca. 1375), detail. Ink, paint, silver, and gold on parchment, 64 × 50 cm. Paris, Bibliothèque nationale de France, Espagno 30, fol 5v.

PLATE 16. Hieronymus Bosch, *The Garden of Earthly Delights* (ca. 1500), central panel. Oil on oak wood, 220 × 193 cm. Madrid, Prado Museum, inv. no. P02823.

place exclusively in humanist Italy. Theory already had a place in the writing of Ghiberti. His treatise on how human vision works, by far the longest section of his *Commentaries*, draws on medieval treatments of optics, including those by al-Haytham, whom he calls "Al-fantem," John Peckham, and Vitello. Ghiberti read al-Haytham in the Italian translation of a (flawed) Latin version.

If it is ever justified to speak of the dawning of a new age of art, then it would be in the first decades of the fourteenth century in Florence. Looking back on that time from much later, Giorgio Vasari (1511–1574) wrote that Cimabue was born by the will of God to give art its "first lights," *i primi lumi*.[15] It is the custom of nature, he reasoned further, when it has brought forth someone excellent in a certain field, to create another person as their competitor so that the two of them can engage in fruitful competition. Later generations would also be animated to strive tirelessly for the same glory as their predecessors achieved, a fame that was on the lips of all. Thus, Florence produced Brunelleschi, Donatello, Ghiberti, Uccello, and Masaccio in the same period, each one a master in his own métier. Vasari writes that Masaccio swept away the crude style that had theretofore been popular, referring to painting influenced by Byzantine art. In addition, the beautiful works of those men spurred later artists to improve further, ultimately achieving that excellence and perfection that one sees "in our day." Vasari's words give a sense of the spirit of competition that must have dominated Florence's cultural climate.

Republican Values, Romantic Classicism

A dense symbiosis of craftsmanship, art, and the sciences developed during the Renaissance. It can be seen in various overlaps between the circles of craftsmen-artists and scholars; Ghiberti and Alberti wore both hats at once. Further evidence is provided by the fact that Paolo dal Pozzo Toscanelli, who taught Brunelleschi geometry and was a friend of Alberti and Cusanus, participated in the theoretical development of linear perspective. Toscanelli (1397–1482) was a leading figure in the intellectual scene that cultivated an atmosphere open to everything ancient, including pagan philosophy. Without it, classicizing aesthetics never could have taken shape, nor could ancient forms and ancient pictorial themes have been developed. A key figure in making Florence the capital of humanism was the notary Salutati.[16] He claims to have taken his path "as a greenhorn," without any teachers and practically without any foundation. For the proud sum of four florins, he bought Priscian's grammar. This was soon followed by Virgil, Lucan, and Horace. With that, he had the beginnings of a library. How many books had been lost, Salutati lamented, in the past six hundred years! So he set about collecting. He provided Boccaccio with a manuscript of Claudian, expecting Macrobius's *Saturnalia* in return. Poggio Bracciolini (1380–1459), for whom he was a father figure, sent him copies of ancient Latin inscriptions from Rome. Salutati sought to reconstruct correct texts and talked about this endeavor with his philologically minded fellows. He was aware from the very beginning of standing at the edge of a gigantic ancient continent: "We create nothing new. We are like tailors who sew together the remnants of ancient garments, presenting them as new."[17] Numerous manuscripts ferreted out by him, including Catullus's poems, Cato's work on agriculture, and a copy of Cicero's familiar letters discovered by Petrarca, still form the basis of modern editions.

Salutati was chancellor of the Republic of Florence, an office that required stylistic, indeed literary abilities. For it was his job to write and polish official documents. During the War of the Eight Saints, he authored rhetorically brilliant pieces of propaganda. They marshaled arguments and examples from Roman history to urge resistance to the pope, painting dark pictures of servitude and telling sweet tales of liberty.[18] The public letters he wrote at the time make Salutati, who personally supported moderate monarchy, look like the prophet of a lay republic. Yet they do not reflect his private views but rather those of the Signoria, the government of Florence, which in the war with Milan styled itself the champion of republican liberty against Visconti tyranny. His literary production was animated by patriotism, his style by the conviction that the classics—Cicero above all—were the best. When it came to history, he emphasized its practical utility: it admonished princes and taught peoples and individuals how to act. Although not a detractor of the religious orders, Salutati prized the active life. He fathered about eleven children and loved good wine. There is even a story of him versifying while enjoying a steam at a Florentine bath complex.[19]

His magnum opus, *De laboribus Herculis* (*The Labors of Hercules*), six hundred pages in a later printed edition and still only a fragment, was similar to Boccaccio's *Genealogy of the Pagan Gods* and developed a theory of poetry based on Aristotle. The author believed that ancient poetry contained profound, encoded truths that accorded with his Christian worldview. Like Dante, Petrarca, and Boccaccio before him, he considered such works to be divinely inspired.[20] Thus the study of ancient myths could reveal ultimate verities. For example, Salutati sees Alcmene, Hercules' mother, as a symbol of the human form and the demigod himself as a symbol of the soul that was conjoined with it. The search for a *prisca theologia,* or primeval theology, hidden in classical texts would remain an obsession of the Renaissance.

Florence's chief bureaucrat possessed little power, but he did have enough influence to promote young humanists like Leonardo Bruni. He had barely been appointed chancellor when he saw to it that the city's *Studium generale,* the predecessor to the university, establish a chair of ancient Greek and fill it in 1397 with the Byzantine diplomat Manuel Chrysoloras (ca. 1350–1415). The intellectuals were ecstatic when "Hemanuel," the one sent by God, arrived on the Arno with his books. Soon they would be able to read Homer, Plato, and Demosthenes in the original! Chrysoloras, who wrote the first introductory Greek grammar and in 1402 produced a translation of Plato's *Republic,* had brought important manuscripts with him, including Dioscorides' *De materia medica.* He only stayed for three years, but his presence contributed to the sustained expansion of Greek learning. Plato, whose God seemed so close to the Christian one, experienced a first revival.

In his later years, Salutati appears to have had doubts about whether he had devoted his life's work to the right cause. In a later writing, *De fato et fortuna,* he used the example of Brutus's tyrannicide to explore the tension between providence, free will, and fate. His last letter defends the introduction of pagan texts as reading material in grammar schools. His arguments were aimed against the fear, enunciated by the Dominican friar and future cardinal Giovanni Dominici, that they would corrupt the young.

Despite such prophecies of doom, it was common around the turn of the century for the sons of leading Florentine families to be educated in ancient literature and history.[21] In this way, the humanist educational movement won hearts and minds among the ruling elite, the wealthy, the top men in the state. Florence's highest educational institution was the *Studium.* In 1414, it was reorganized from the ground up.[22] The commune named influential, financially powerful citizens to the committee responsible for it. In addition, the appointment of locals as masters and professors was forbidden in order to keep the path clear for famous scholars. A classical education, which increasingly included knowledge of Greek, became a status symbol. More and more, writing and the book trade were dominated by laymen and integrated into the guild system. This trend took hold not only in Florence but also, for example, in Bruges and other Flemish cities.

The ideal ruler was now more learned than pious. Ancient history was considered a gold mine of experience, a treasure trove of examples from which maxims for action could be deduced. Yet there was more going on than just reading, writing, and discussion. As the literary tradition was investigated more profoundly and the knowledge and marvels it contained were treated with increasing awe, classical antiquity came to exercise greater influence on the lifestyle of the Florentine elite, giving shape to a cultural habitus. People integrated classical culture into their lives in whatever way possible, including the acquisition of material remains. Poggio Bracciolini collected ancient sculpture and adorned the grounds of his country estate in the Arno Valley with it, including busts of Athena, Hera, and Dionysus that he considered Greek originals.[23] Donatello admired them appreciatively. The "spring" of Renaissance art, of which Donatello's sculptural work is a symbol, was made possible in part by this classically crazed milieu.

One colorful character who embodied the new lifestyle was Niccolò Niccoli (ca. 1364–1437), a rich Florentine bibliophile. He was a friend and patron of numerous artists and humanists: famous men like Brunelleschi, Bruni, Donatello, and Ghiberti, as well as more obscure figures like the book collector Antonio Corbinelli. Niccoli "kept countless medals of bronze, silver, and gold in his house," relates the Florentine bookseller Vespasiano da Bisticci (ca. 1421–1498), author of a series of biographies of his famous contemporaries.[24] "Those who wanted to do him a kindness sent him marble statues or vases made by the ancients, or paintings or marble sculptures, marble epitaphs, paintings by exceptional masters, and mosaics of all kinds." Niccoli is described as a Florentine of the utmost refinement: always dressed in red robes that touched the floor, dining at a table set with a white tablecloth and valuable, antique dishes, and drinking from crystal glasses. The showpiece of his collection was a much-admired gem engraved with a depiction of Diomedes stealing the Palladium. It was later owned by Lorenzo the Magnificent.

His enthusiasm for antiquity caused Niccoli to despise the vernacular. He even presumed to disparage Dante as a poet for "cobblers and bakers."[25] Whether one should write in the vernacular or Latin remained a bone of contention for centuries. The *questione della lingua* required that a decision be made between an idiom connected with one's *patria*—one's native city, then one's nation—and the language of venerable antiquity, whose authoritativeness was approaching its full glory. Both paths were taken in the following centuries. The upshot was that Latin remained not only the language of science and scholarship but also a language of literature.

Niccoli's fervor for everything Greek—he seems to have spent a great deal of money on tutoring and the acquisition of codices—also exposed him to

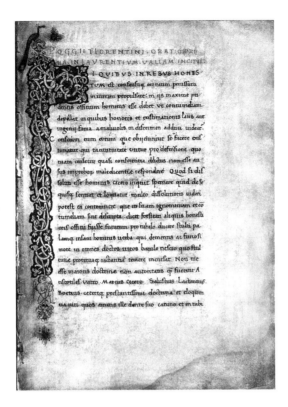

criticism, however. Alberti caricatured him as a cynic who adorned himself with unread books.[26] His personality had a powerful effect on people, and it earned him roles as an interlocutor in numerous humanist dialogues. He bequeathed his books for "the use of all" to the monastery of San Marco, the core of the first public library in Italy.[27] He himself wrote only a few learned works. Yet he still left his mark: as the likely inventor of humanist cursive, the mother of all cursive scripts, which allowed faster writing than Carolingian minuscule. The latter had inspired Salutati to develop his own *antiqua* script; it was characterized by round arcs like those found in ancient monumental inscriptions. The new handwriting was perfected by Bracciolini, the seasoned connoisseur of ancient archaeology. The clear *litterae antiquae* (Fig. 27, above) would serve as the basis for the printed typefaces of the following centuries. Even the font used in the very book you are now reading derives from models developed in Florence around the year 1400.[28]

All'antica was now à la mode. If we believe the poet Franco Sacchetti, even simple Florentines were reading their Livy.[29] That this development entailed a certain amount of tension can be seen in a story reported by Ghiberti.[30] A statue was found in Siena that had been made by the great Lysippus. Painters, sculptors, and everyone who appreciated art flocked to admire the work, probably a statue of Venus. With great pageantry, the statue was ultimately set up in a prominent place, on the fountain in Siena's Piazza del Campo. But the artwork was only able to enjoy its privileged position for a brief time. Reversals in the war with Florence were blamed on the excessive adoration the figure received. "Idolatry is forbidden by our faith," was the admonition in Siena's city council. Military defeats were interpreted as divine punishment for idol worship. As a result, the hazardous object was "executed" and "buried" in the territory of the enemy, Florence. The story reveals a society that could not always distinguish between images and the things they depicted. It treated the statue like an evil demon that was doing harm to the city. The devout city councilors in Siena could not imagine that a statue of pagan origin was only being venerated because it was beautiful. Yet there were clearly others who were fascinated by the artwork as just that, a work of art, and who thus placed it mentally in a religious-free space. About a century after Siena's Venus affair, the man who recorded this story, Ghiberti, achieved a small victory over faith with his Gates of Paradise. Scenes from the life of Christ, which theretofore had adorned the north doors of the Baptistery, were supposed to be given the most distinguished place, the east entrance. But Ghiberti's masterpiece was accorded this honor instead "on account of its beauty."[31] This may be the earliest documented instance of aesthetics trumping theology. Belatedly with respect to philosophy, art was now also demonstrating that realms for free expression and action were beginning to expand, even in the magical circle of the saints. Beauty gained a justification all its own—even if it was of pagan origin, like another statue of Venus seen in a private home in Florence by an envoy of Cardinal Albornoz. He remarked that it was "beautiful."[32] Italy embarked upon the long path to the secularization of art earlier than Europe beyond the Alps. This is well illustrated by the strange story of the Venus of Trier. Displayed at the abbey church of St. Matthias, for centuries the "idol" was ritually chained up and stoned by pious pilgrims.[33]

While the Renaissance was unfurling in Florence, elsewhere the Gothic style was still in its prime. In 1368, the cathedral in Milan, a memorial to Gian Galeazzo Visconti, began rising into the Lombard sky. San Petronio in Bologna was one of the largest Gothic churches in the world. All over Europe, grand hall churches were built—monuments of economic vigor and communal power, an expression of the yearning for salvation and the word of God. The cathedrals rose higher and higher. By 1439, the north tower of Strasbourg Cathedral had reached a height of 142 meters, thus displacing the tower of Saint Stephen's Cathedral in Vienna, completed only two years earlier, as the tallest building in Europe. English and French stonemasons created "Flamboyant" (*flamboyante*) tracery that sprouted into opulent splendor. This style exhausted the possibilities of the Gothic, developing them to their utmost; it was driven by a desire to create something, if not totally new, then at least different.[34] The parallels to the ever more intricate and subtle debates of late Scholastic philosophy, or to the accumulation of corrections to the Ptolemaic world system, are less a reflection of the zeitgeist than of the laws of human creativity. At first, creativity tends to stay within the framework of existing paradigms, until everything has been said. Then, if something new happens to emerge, a revolution is unavoidable. In general, Gothic and Renaissance styles enjoyed a peaceful coexistence—sometimes in the same building. The architect active in Milan known as Filarete, whose given name was Antonio Averlino (ca. 1400–after 1465), praised the Gothic church for exalting the human soul with its soaring form.[35] On the other hand, he vilified pointed arches as the expression of a "barbaric modern style." He stands astride the great divide between two epochs of art history.

The Rotten Republic

On June 26, 1402, Gian Galeazzo Visconti and his allies defeated a force of Bolognese and Florentine troops at the Battle of Casalecchio. Bologna was his. The pass over the Apennines to Florence, now encircled by Visconti mercenaries, stood open. Fear spread along the Arno. Two months later, however, the conqueror whom Bruni called a deceitful monster was carried off by malaria to his castle in Melegnano. A comet had appeared in the night sky, portending the event. In the opinion of some art historians, it was Florence's liberation from fatal danger that suggested the theme for the Baptistery competition—God's last-minute rescue of Isaac. Some have even identified that shocking event as the initial spark for the art of the early Renaissance, seeing its birth in Ghiberti's relief sculptures.[36]

Salutati's protégé and successor as chancellor, Leonardo Bruni (ca. 1370–1444), held up a golden mirror to his city—even before the building boom that would shape the Renaissance metropolis now admired throughout the world.[37] There is no finer city on Earth, he wrote in his *Laudatio Florentinae urbis* (*Praise of the City of Florence*), modeled on the ancient panegyric of Athens by Aelius Aristides. The *Laudatio* put the struggle with Milan in a broader context. Founded by free citizens of the Roman Republic, Bruni claims, Florence had always been the most determined enemy of all tyranny. He extols the city's wise foreign policy and its laws, before which all are equal. He praises its power and its wise, moderate constitution, which allows everyone to participate in public life. And indeed, Bruni's own career and those of many other humanists are evidence of the permeability of Florentine society.[38] Born the son of a grain merchant in Arezzo, Bruni rose to the position of chancellor and held many other important offices.

He had no intention of questioning the regime of the "best and richest" citizens, which he analyzed in a separate treatise. Freedom *from* something, namely foreign domination, was much more central to his concept of liberty than the freedom *to do* something, such as have a say in political affairs. Yet the republican Roman political order propagated by Bruni, Salutati, and Matteo Palmieri had little in common with the values of an aristocratic society.[39] Palmieri (1406–1475) invoked a Roman legal principle when he insisted that civic officeholders must "represent the juridical person of the whole city."[40] This was all more than a vague theory. The system exalted by the Florentine humanists certainly guaranteed more freedoms than the political systems of many European and non-European states. For example, laws had to pass the popular assembly and the Signoria in order to go into force. The highest office, the Standard-bearer of Justice, the *Gonfaloniere di Giustizia*, was only appointed for a period of two months. Power, however, had become focused in tiny circles during the war with Milan. As always, vertical power structures were strengthened by external threats. Whoever wished to prevail in the city's politics had to be a master of rhetoric and possess the resources to create clientage networks.

Bruni's duties left him sufficient time to pursue his literary projects. In addition to his panegyric of Florence, he produced biographies of Aristotle, Cicero, Dante, and Petrarca, as well as translations of Greek classics. He also helped revive the Ciceronian dialogue, that sublime tool of critical reasoning. More decisively than his predecessors, he favored the active life of the citizen over the contemplative life of the monastery. His *Funeral Oration for Nanni Strozzi*, modeled on Pericles' famous eulogy for the Athenian war dead, is a speech in praise of the Republic, the equality of citizens before the law, and liberty.[41]

Bruni's magnum opus, his *History of the Florentine People*, is based on an impressive collection of primary sources. While it justifies the ruling oligarchy, it does not hide its author's sympathy for the middle class. Thus, Giano della Bella, the author of the *Ordinances of Justice* (p. 253), is singled out for special praise.

Bruni's historical writing, whose lodestars were Thucydides, Livy, Sallust, Polybius, and Tacitus, was radically innovative.[42] It is light-years beyond the annalistic style of Villani. Never satisfied with a mere recounting of events, Bruni attempts to identify causes and communicate political experience. He makes sparing reference to the will of God. He staunchly defends Florence's policy of foreign expansion, and he praises the sovereign republic's freedom from the Holy Roman Empire.

After Visconti's death, Florence was able to expand its territory considerably. It took Pisa, once the master of half the Tyrrhenian Sea, Cortona, and, in 1420, Livorno and its excellent harbor. Lucca again resisted, defended by Milanese mercenaries. The failure of this extremely costly undertaking was blamed on the faction led by Rinaldo degli Albizzi. He was the scion of a patrician family that had wielded great influence for decades; his father Maso (1343–1417) had risen to become the most powerful man in the republic. The blame was unjust, considering that the Albizzi family's most dangerous adversary, the banker Cosimo de' Medici (1389–1464), had been involved in important decisions. An attempt to neutralize Cosimo through exile seemed at first to succeed. In 1433, he was forced to flee to Venice. But the next year, a faction friendly to the Medici came to power and recalled Cosimo. Now it was Rinaldo and his allies' turn to taste the bitterness of exile. Among their number was the richest Florentine at the time, Palla Strozzi. Exiled to Padua, where he died in 1462 at nearly ninety years of age, Palla never saw Florence again.

The man now welcomed back to the city on the Arno belonged to a family whose power was based on the "people" and the middle classes and who, moreover, had no especially glorious past to boast of.[43] The golden foundation for its rise had been laid by Cosimo's father, Giovanni di Bicci, and his business dealings with the Curia. Giovanni started out as a petty moneylender, but by 1393 he was able to buy the Roman branch of his uncle's firm. It was a decisive step. Without the assistance of bankers, the Curia had no way to collect the taxes, offerings, and other payments that flowed in from as far away as Iceland and Greenland. A sizeable portion of the money that entered Giovanni's hands never left them. He was able to open his own bank in Florence, which expanded quickly. He had established business connections with the city's old high-finance elite, and he had arranged for his son Cosimo to marry a daughter of the Bardi. When he handed over the reins of his bank to his son in 1420, he was the second-richest man in Florence.

The fact that Cosimo's Venetian vacation did not last even twelve months indicates the robustness of the power framework that the Medici family had slowly built. Cosimo had managed to safeguard his assets before being exiled. After his return, he was the most influential man in Florence—but not its absolute ruler. The complex constitution, and with it the city's tenacious horizontal power structures, forestalled naked tyranny. The material of Cosimo's power was woven from the fine threads of his web of clients. It required a delicate touch to interlink them and pull on them correctly. The most important thing was to get control over the appointment of civic offices. Like in Venice, they were distributed through a mixture of election and allotment. Only those whose names were in the leather pouches from which the officeholders would be drawn were eligible. Thus, the *accopiatori*, literally the "couplers" or "assemblers" responsible for filling the pouches, were of decisive importance. And it was this group of people that Cosimo brought under his control. Money was always useful for this purpose. "He was more cultured than merchants usually are." Thus his contemporary Pope Pius II described him. "Nothing happened in Italy without his knowledge; indeed it was his advice that guided the policy of many cities and princes."[44] Cosimo's cloaked regime lasted about thirty years, a period blessed by fortune. Victory at the Battle of Anghiari on June 29, 1440 secured Florence's rule of Tuscany and Cosimo's stability in Florence. An aura of authority accrued around the old puppet master. After his death, Florence honored its godfather with the ancient Roman title *pater patriae*, "father of his country."

Bruni died in 1444. The new lords of the city had left the lauder of the republic in office—which speaks to either Bruni's flexibility or the Medici's chutzpah or both. Florence honored its chancellor with a public funeral in Santa Croce held "according to the classical tradition, *all'antica*." The eulogy was given by the humanist Giannozzo Manetti (1396–1459); he placed the poet's wreath of laurel on Bruni's head.[45] Bruni's tomb, crowned with the lion emblem of the Guelph Party, was a groundbreaking work of early Renaissance art. Leon Battista Alberti may have been involved in its design. The monument is, so to speak, humanism made marble. The laureate Bruni lies on a bier borne by two eagles, his *History of the Florentine People* in his hands. The epitaph, written in classical letters, was composed by the new chancellor Carlo Marsuppini. It reads:

> Since Leonard departed this life,
> History is mourning, Eloquence is mute,
> and it is said that the Muses, both Greek
> and Latin, could not restrain their tears.

The republicanism defended by Bruni throughout his life had rotted behind the brilliant facade the Medici used to disguise their rule. On the other hand, Florence had become a great Italian power.

21

From Constance
to Constantinople

Constance

In Rome, Boniface IX of the Neapolitan Tomacelli family began ruling in
1389.[1] The abominable Urban had left him surrounded by rubble. Large portions of the Papal States obeyed Avignon and were in the hands of barons or
Bretons, mercenaries in the service of the Avignonese Pope Clement VII. In
the capital, Boniface was confronted by an unruly citizenry. For a moment,
the idea was even entertained of secularizing the Papal States and founding a
"Kingdom of Adria" ruled by a brother of Charles VI of France—that would
have been the price for Clement's return with the aid of French lances. Boniface succeeded in regaining parts of the Papal States. His victory over the
Commune of Rome was definitive. The citizens of the city would have no

power until modern times. Boniface's activist, martial policy was expensive, however. It was financed by fees, taxes and payments of all kinds, and the sale of indulgences. For the first time, we encounter the office of *depositarius*, a banker who took care of collecting these moneys and, in return, lent the estimated sum to the Apostolic Camera, or papal treasury. In other words, the Camera received a permanent loan. It is obvious who profited most from this deal. To be concrete, it was primarily bankers from Lucca and Florence—our new acquaintance Giovanni di Bicci, for example—who held this most lucrative office in the West.

In the jubilee year of 1400, it was not even necessary to make the pilgrimage to Rome to get an indulgence. Coin sufficed. The practice had been pioneered by Clement VI. In 1350, he sold protection from the punishments of purgatory to the residents of an entire island, Mallorca, for thirty thousand guilders.[2] The new holy year still brought pilgrims from all over Europe to the Tiber, and this in turn brought major prestige to the Roman pontiff. Salvation was still sought more in Rome than on the Rhone. Yet Boniface, a master politician, was less a religious leader than a supporter of his family's and his nephews' interests. About fifty members of the Tomacelli clan then residing in Rome are known by name, to say nothing of the networks that sprouted from all manner of marriage alliances with other families. Uncle Boniface showered countless benefices on his relatives, even those of very tender years, and tried to set up Tomacelli signories. As Poggio Bracciolini joked—playing on the word *tomacella*, a name for pork liverwurst—it must have been a very big liver to have produced so many *tomacelli*.[3]

Even in this, the steepest hierarchy in Europe, relief could be found by activating horizontal power. That meant calling a Church council. One by no means disinterested champion of this perennially discussed idea was Cardinal Baldassare Cossa, a Neapolitan "liverwurst" of Boniface IX. Passed over in two conclaves, he saw his chance in an ecclesiastical assembly.[4] The fact that one was called to meet in Pisa in 1409 was very much his doing. The synod was attended by twenty-four cardinals and eighty bishops. It deposed both the Roman and Avignonese popes and replaced them with the archbishop of Milan, who took the name Alexander V. When he died less than a year later, Cossa finally got what he wanted. He was elected pope and took the name John XXIII. To this day, however, he is still considered a mere antipope in Rome, and so there is another John XXIII on the papal rolls but no John XXIV. Of course, neither of the two popes deposed in Pisa thought of submitting to the synod's decree, and both sought support from secular princes. The upshot was that the pious West was now led by an unholy trinity. The Church started resembling the splintered world of Islam.

The turning point came when the Holy Roman Empire got involved in the person of Sigismund of Hungary: one of the losers at Nicopolis, King of the Romans since 1411, and emperor designate.[5] He had defended Hungary against the claims of the Anjou and acquired dominion over Bosnia. In Bohemia, he ruled jointly with his brother Wenceslaus. Sigismund was a spendthrift and a hearty gambler, but also highly educated and a master diplomat. He turned out to be the right man to solve the complex problem of the papal schism. He had good reason to do so: the Church needed to clean house in order for a Crusade to be called against the Ottomans, who represented a constant threat to Hungary. Exerting mild pressure, he got John XXIII to fulfill the terms of an agreement made at Pisa and call a new council. The southern German imperial city of Constance provided a suitable location. The council opened on November 5, 1414.

A decisive element in its success was that Sigismund had managed to get most leading European rulers to cooperate. Even the feuding rulers of France, England, and Burgundy sent envoys. As a result, a veritable parade of Christian Europe was on view in Constance. Participants came from the Scandinavian kingdoms, from Lithuania, from the once wild, unruly Walachia, from Russian lands and Constantinople, even from the Ottoman Empire. Tens of thousands of people crammed into the tiny city. Innkeepers, butchers, and bakers made a fortune. So did prostitutes, who are reported to have numbered at least 1,400. Lobbyists and humanists came, the latter taking the opportunity to search for old manuscripts in the surrounding monasteries. Cardinal Guillaume Fillastre (1348–1428) had copies made of the *Cosmography* of Pomponius Mela, a first-century geographer, and of Ptolemy's description of the Earth.[6] He sent both works to the chapter library in Reims, where they lay, chained to the thirteenth lectern on the left-hand side, to be consulted by readers. Reims also received from him a world map painted on a large walrus skin. The most successful of the manuscript hunters by far was Poggio Bracciolini, who attended the Council as John XXIII's secretary. Somehow, he got the money to travel around the wild countryside of Germany. At the monastery of Saint Gall, located close to Constance, he discovered an early copy of Vitruvius's work on architecture. He found orations of Cicero and Quintilian's treatise on rhetoric. Probably at the monastery of Fulda, the intellectual hub of the Carolingian period, he dug out Marcus Manilius's work on astrology and Silius Italicus's *Punica*, an epic poem about the Second Punic War. His most significant find was Lucretius's *De rerum natura*, henceforth the main source for Epicurean thought (pp. 406–411).[7]

For as long as the Council sat, Constance was Europe's political center. What a reversal of fortune Cossa suffered! Like at the time of Constantine the Great, secular power took matters into its own hands. It demanded unity and reform and, finally, the purging of Christendom of all heresy. Votes were taken not by head but by nation, and the College of Cardinals voted as a block. This checked the influence of the Italian clergy and accorded with the actual political importance of the secular realms.

John XXIII had traveled to Constance in the hope of being confirmed the sole leader of the universal Church. In the end—it was now the spring of 1415—he realized that his pontificate stood in the way of unity. His own cardinals distanced themselves from him. Thus, he took advantage of the hustle and bustle of a tournament to steal away, disguised as a groom. The Habsburg Duke Frederick IV of Tyrol, a sworn enemy of Sigismund, promised him protection. But both men had miscalculated. The Council declared itself the highest authority in the Church, placing itself above the pope. Frederick of Tyrol found himself under imperial ban and was forced to give up his ward. His enemies in Swabia and Alsace seized the opportunity and invaded his estates under title of imperial war. The biggest winner was the Swiss Confederacy; Bern acquired a large territory, the western Aargau.

Sigismund was the absolute master of the Council.[8] John was deposed, and the Roman pope, Gregory XII, was forced to abdicate. His adversary in Avignon, Benedict XIII, the Spaniard Pedro de Luna, would not submit. The Spanish contingent, led by the charismatic preacher Vincenz Ferrer, renounced its allegiance to him. He went to his death, which he met in 1423 in exile in Aragon, insisting that he was the rightful pope. John was imprisoned in Heidelberg, ransomed by the Medici, and recompensed with a cardinal's hat. He died in Florence in 1419. His tomb, by Donatello, was erected in the Baptistery. Again, the bill was paid by Cosimo de' Medici. As the successor to the three popes and now the single head of the Church, the Council elected Oddo Colonna, a member of one of the most powerful families in Rome.[9] He took the name Martin V (1417–1431). After the conclusion of the Council, he first took up residence in the Florentine monastery of Santa Maria Novella. *Papa Martino non vale un lupino*, children on the street called after him: "Pope Martin ain't worth a farthin.'"[10] But the rhyme was wrong. The Colonna pope, secure in his backing by the Medici bank and his own extensive network, went on to restore the Papal States. Gradually, artists like Gentile da Fabriano and Masaccio arrived on the Tiber.

The reestablishment of Church unity was the most important achievement of the Council of Constance. Church reform, on the other hand, was not its priority. It was agreed that the issue would be dealt with at future councils to be called on a regular basis. On the other hand, the fight against heresy was taken very seriously. Wyclif could no longer be called before it. The Council ordered his mortal remains to be unearthed and burnt. But his follower Jan Hus (ca. 1370–1415), a theologian from Prague, was invited with a promise of safe conduct in 1414. His teachings partially anticipated the Reformation. He agreed with Wyclif that the word of the Bible had supreme authority. His zeal for purity was radical. He opposed the veneration of the saints, the display of images, the cult of relics, simony, and the sale of indulgences.[11] He disputed the automatic effectiveness of the sacraments, instead making their power conditional upon the pure lifestyle of those who performed and received them. He rejected the papacy—where was it mentioned in the Bible?—and the ecclesiastical hierarchy. In his view, the Church should be a simple brotherhood of man. Furthermore, laymen should be allowed to read the Bible and preach publicly as long as they were devout and pure. One chronicler reports that Hus's followers had barked "like dogs" against the entire clergy.[12] Hus himself refused to recant any of his beliefs before the Council. On July 6, 1415, it broke its own promise of safe conduct and had the "prince of heretics" burned, his ashes scattered on the Rhine. The next year one of Hus's followers, Jerome of Prague, had to mount the stake. We do not know if King Sigismund was involved in the decision.

The flames from which Hus emitted his final scream ignited a violent counter-reaction of unprecedented proportions. People clamored for the Church to be stripped of all power and property. There ought to be no more pope, it was proclaimed, and only poor priests whose sole job should be to proclaim the word of God. The unifying demand and symbol of the movement was the chalice (*calix* in Latin) of Calixtinism, also called Utraquism, which demanded "communion under both kinds." This practice, according to which the laity receives "both" (*utraque* in Latin) bread and wine during the Eucharist, was first explicitly banned by the Council of Constance. Another complaint was that the king and the magistrates had not pursued the "common good."[13]

The Hussite Revolution began in the summer of 1419 in Prague. The atmosphere was tense after several churches were taken away from the Hussites. Stirred up by a radical preacher, a mob marched on New Town Hall to demand the release of imprisoned members of their movement. Ultimately, some of them stormed the building and threw the burgomaster, several town councilors, and a city functionary out the window. Those who survived the fall were killed by the mob. This ritual act incited an uprising that grew into a mass movement. Criticism of the Church was connected to political interests and the inveterate conflicts between Bohemians and Germans. There was a parallel to the Ciompi Revolt of a half-century earlier, namely that in Prague, too, the revolution fermented among the masses of the people who were excluded from the guilds. In Florence, of course, religion played no role. In Prague, it made the conflict much more brutal.

King Wenceslaus IV died in 1419, leaving a power vacuum. Hussites gained the upper hand in a third of the royal cities. A group of "elect" radicals thought the end of days was at hand. On a mountain in southern Bohemia which they named "Tabor" after the site of the transfiguration of Jesus, they founded a city, lived there in apostolic purity, and prepared for holy war as the spearhead of the Hussite movement. The common enemy drove moderate Utraquists into their ranks: aristocrats and urban middle classes who likewise desired to receive both the host and the chalice at the Eucharist. Thanks to their use of novel military technology—temporary fortifications made of circled wagons called "wagon forts" (*Wagenburgen*) and mobile field artillery, deployed here for the first time ever—the Hussite armies piled up victory upon victory. They advanced to Westphalia, to the Baltic Sea, and deep into southern Germany. Those who resisted their passion for purity were butchered.

Postponed Reforms

Meanwhile, everything built by Boniface IX in the Papal States had now crumbled. The south and Rome were ruled by Muzio Attendolo, a condottiere in the service of the Anjou of Naples. He was known by his military nickname, "Sforza," meaning something like "forcer." The north was in the hands of his rival Braccio da Montone, another mercenary captain and lord of Perugia, Assisi, and other cities.[14] Pope Martin had to come to an arrangement. First, he treated with Queen Joanna II of Naples, who got Attendolo to leave Rome and let the pope enter his own city. Then he dealt with Braccio, who could not be overcome militarily. Martin—gritting his teeth, one imagines—made him a papal vicar, thus legitimizing the power Braccio had amassed for himself. Braccio showed his gratitude by putting down a revolt in Bologna in 1420, thus retaining the city for the Papal States. Martin entered Rome the same year.

But the condottiere's ambition was not yet sated. He turned south, took castles in Abruzzo, and captured Capua and Foggia. Finally, he besieged L'Aquila, the gateway to the Kingdom of Naples. People in Rome and Naples must have held their breath when Attendolo marched out with a large army to relieve the city. But the anticipated duel did not take place. Sforza drowned while trying to cross a river with his army. His illegitimate son Francesco took command. On June 2, 1424, he obliterated the *Bracceschi* under the walls of L'Aquila. Braccio himself was wounded and died a few days later. In Naples, ruled by Joanna II of the house of Anjou-Durazzo (or rather by her lovers), her relative Louis III successfully staked his claim. The childless queen adopted him. He now seemed to have the best prospects for the Neapolitan inheritance.

For Pope Martin, the death of his domineering condottiere was a stroke of good fortune. He made L'Aquila a diocese, came to terms with the commune of orphaned Perugia, established a well-ordered administration of his territory, and set about regaining what he had lost. His choice of cardinals turned out to be quite felicitous at times. They included Niccolò Albergati, who served the Colonna pope and his successors as a capable diplomat, the humanist Domenico Capranica, and Giuliano Cesarini, a jurist who had traveled far and wide in the service of the Church. As agreed in Constance, the pope called a council in Pavia, yet it was meaningless. When it was moved to Siena to avoid the plague, he decided to stay in Rome. "Council" was a dirty word for him and his successors. It meant horizontal power rather than monarchy. It threatened the benefice business and nepotism. In a word, it shook the old pillars of papal power. Shortly before his death, Martin agreed to make another attempt to fulfill the commitment made at Constance. This time the council was set to be held in Basel. It was to be overseen by Cesarini, whom Martin gave the authority to quickly dissolve the pesky congress.

Meanwhile, a reform effort was budding within the Church in the form of the Observantist movement.[15] As its name suggests, it sought a return to the strict observance of monastic rules. Its cause was taken up by the Council of Constance and then by secular rulers. Across Italy and soon north of the Alps as well, apostolic visitors fanned out to exhort monks and nuns to poverty, chastity, and prayer. Reform monasteries provided a model for others. Friars like Bernardino degli Albizzeschi of Siena (1380–1444), a founding father of the Observant Franciscans, introduced reform ideas to the cities. Bernardino captivated the masses, drawing crowds of thousands to public squares. His sermons, emitted from a toothless mouth, could last for four hours. The preacher's trademark was a monogram of Christ set on a sunburst, "YHS": *Jesus hominum salvator*, "Jesus, savior of man." At the conclusion of his sermons, he would call on the people to venerate it. Bernardino owed his success in part to his ability as an entertainer. Cut from the same Tuscan cloth as Boccaccio and Sacchetti, he responded to calls from the audience and salted his frugal moral soup with all kinds of humor. On the other hand, like other preachers he also relied on unfounded prejudices and incited his listeners against Jews, witches, and homosexuals.[16] Accused of heresy for a time, he was ultimately embraced by the Church and declared a saint in the jubilee year of 1450.

Gabriele Condulmer, who succeeded Martin as Pope Eugene IV (1431–1447), granted the Observant Franciscans independence from the rest of the order, the "Conventuals," who for their part were then shielded from excessive reform zeal.[17] Eugene, a Venetian, had the Council of Basel opened according to plan in late July 1431, only to close it, again according to plan, in November. Yet something unexpected happened. Conciliarists, i.e., proponents of the supremacy of ecumenical councils over the power of the pope, refused to comply with the papal bull. The struggle between horizontal and vertical power reached a new climax. A further by-product of the Council was an increased sense of national identity, thanks in part to competition between the Germans and the French.[18]

Sigismund was not idle. Despite the turmoil in Bohemia, he traveled to Italy to save the Council. He promoted peace among the northern Italian powers and interceded personally with the pope. On Pentecost in 1433, he received the imperial crown from Eugene's hands. Skepticism—and some panegyrics—attended his Italian journey, as they had that of Henry VII so long before. Works of art survive as souvenirs. Pisanello painted a portrait of the emperor in Ferrara or Mantua (Fig. 28, p. 372), and Piero della Francesca painted a fresco of Saint Sigismund in the guise of his imperial namesake. Eugene IV backed down and rescinded his bull dissolving the Council. This had less to do with Sigismund's diplomacy, however—the emperor soon felt like a "fifth wheel" and hurried back to Basel[19]—than with events in Rome. At his election, the pope had been enjoined to wrest back some of the spoils his predecessor had showered on the Colonna clan with his benefactions. This led to a final war for Rome and its territory that put Eugene in dire straits. Dressed as a monk and hidden under a sack of tarragon, he had to flee on a galley. He found refuge in Florence, the city of his bankers. He stayed away from Rome for nearly a decade.

In the Papal States, Cardinal Legate Giovanni Vitelleschi—a warrior like Albornoz, only more brutal and a fool when it came to politics—went to work smoking out nests of Colonna support in the Alban Hills. Meanwhile, a chance arose for the pope to regain his position of supremacy. The Ottomans had renewed their offensive in the East. The Venetian outpost of Thessalonica fell in 1430. Growing increasingly desperate, the *basileus*, now little more than a mayor of Byzantium and a vassal of the sultan, looked for help. He was even willing to pay the ultimate price for it, namely unification with the Latin Church. Eugene used the Byzantines' predicament to kill two birds with one stone: to weaken the Council of Basel and to go down in history as the unifier of the Eastern and Western churches. The decisive gambit was to move the Council to Italian soil in accordance with the wishes of Byzantium. In September of 1437, sessions began meeting in Ferrara, and then, when an epidemic broke out on the Po, they moved to Florence, where the Medici bank supplied easy credit to cover the costs.

The Byzantines sent an exalted delegation, including Emperor John VIII, Metropolitan Isidore of Kyiv, and Basilios Bessarion (1403–1472), patriarch of Constantinople. A key role was played by Cardinal Cesarini, who, sensing which way the wind was blowing, decided for Eugene and Ferrara and thus against Basel. The Byzantines agreed to recognize Rome's dogmas. Thus, Christ was accorded paternity of the Holy Spirit. The pope's supremacy was formalized, albeit in obscure terms. The Florentines watched in astonishment on July 6, 1439 as the union was proclaimed beneath the dome Brunelleschi had just finished. For the Orthodox Church, its terms were nothing but a debacle. They were accepted by neither the clergy nor the people, and the Latins never considered paying the price they had agreed to in exchange for Byzantine submission, namely, sending military aid against the Ottomans. Bessarion became a cardinal of the Roman Church. Humanistic Greek studies were nourished by the nearly one thousand manuscripts he had brought with him from Constantinople and later donated to the library of Saint Mark's Basilica in Venice.[20]

But Basel remained recalcitrant. The majority of the conciliarists stayed on the Rhine even though their cause was lost. Yet one positive result was achieved: on the margins of the proceedings, terms for defusing the Hussite conflict were hammered out. The defeat of a Crusader army at the Battle of Taus in August 1431 increased the appetite for compromise. Three years later, an official agreement was signed in Prague. The Utraquists' demand for full lay participation in the Eucharist was met; the right of laymen to preach, however, was not recognized. A hard core of radicals rejected the compromise and fought on, but they were defeated.

Thus ended the bloody "Hussite Wars." The estates of the Bohemian realm emerged from the conflict strengthened. The high nobility was the real beneficiary of the upheavals, winning for itself a significant voice, including in the election of the king. Catholic clergy was not admitted to national assemblies. The new system remained in place until the seventeenth century. A second defenestration of Prague—revolutionaries imitated the Hussite model in 1618—would unleash the catastrophe of the Thirty Years' War. For the moment, however, pious zeal was dampened by insight into what happens when order breaks down and religious fanatics come to power. The Taborite legacy was carried forward by the "Unity of Brethren." At times tolerated and then persecuted in turn, it left a heavy mark on the diverse religious landscape of east central Europe. The task of Church reform remained undone. Many believed it could not be put off for long.

The Hundred Years' War: Reversals and Resolution

In England, horizontal power flexed its muscles when the House of Lancaster displaced the Plantagenets in 1399. Henry IV was king by the grace of Parliament. Only its decree made the removal of Richard II possible and legitimized his successor, in whose veins blue blood flowed a bit too thinly. Notwithstanding, the first two Lancaster kings turned out to be able political operators. Henry IV, an educated, eloquent booklover who kept company with Chaucer and Christine de Pizan, put the royal finances in order. With the help of his son, he quelled revolts and stifled the Lollard movement before it could develop political momentum like the Hussites had on the Continent.

For the time being, nothing was to be feared from his rivals across the Channel. The French King Charles VI (r. 1380–1422) was mentally ill, sinking ever deeper into madness. Regents vied for power: on one side, the king's brother Duke Louis I of Orléans; on the other, Philip the Bold of Burgundy and then, after his death, his son and heir John the Fearless (r. 1404–1419). Then as later, Paris was worth plotting, murdering, and waging war for. In her *Book of the Body Politic*, Christine de Pizan advocated a strong hereditary monarchy based on divine right. But that solution still lay far in the future. The poet Eustache Deschamps lamented his time as an *aage en tristour*, a sad, decadent epoch.[21] His patron, Louis of Orléans, was stabbed to death on the streets of Paris in 1407. The man behind the attack was Duke John of Burgundy. The bloody deed, justified as an act of tyrannicide in a famous tract by the Paris jurist Jean Petit, unleashed a civil war that became intertwined with strands of the Hundred Years' War. The Burgundians, who now controlled Paris, were opposed by an aristocratic coalition around Charles of Orléans (1394–1465), the fourteen-year-old son of the murder victim. Military command was assumed by Count Bernard VII of Armagnac. The Armagnac faction, named after him, succeeded in expelling the Burgundians from Paris. Driven back to his power base of Flanders, Duke John now sought an alliance with Henry V of England (r. 1413–1422), the second Lancastrian king.

No stranger to war—as an adolescent, he had nearly been killed by an arrow in battle—Henry pursued a policy of accommodation at home. As a sign of reconciliation, he had the body of Richard II transferred to Westminster Abbey. He was the first king of Britain to use English as the language of his official correspondence.[22] The object of his ambition was not to construct a nation but rather, in the spirit of his predecessors, to reconquer England's continental domains. John the Fearless did not lift a finger when Henry landed near Harfleur in Normandy. On October 25, 1415, Henry's bowmen annihilated a French army of superior numbers at Agincourt. Normandy was his. The young Charles of Orléans was taken prisoner; he would not be set free for another twenty-five years. In that time, he matured into one of France's great lyric poets.

A unique glimpse at those dark days can be found in a diary that has come down to us under the title *A Parisian Journal*. It provides a worm's-eye view of the Hundred Years' War. "Soldiers appeared without any clear reason," the author writes.[23] He tells of mercenaries who lived "like Saracens," of executions, plagues, and exorbitant prices, but also of miraculous events that proved a higher power had its hand in the chaos. A remarkable contrast to all the horror reported by the anonymous diarist is provided by the *Cour amoureuse* presided over by Isabeau of Bavaria (ca. 1370–1435), wife of Charles VI. Poetic competitions were held, judged by ladies and *damoiselles*. The poetic court, to which non-noble citizens were also granted access, may have been organized with the intention of pacifying a violence-prone elite, with Isabeau playing the role of political mediator.[24]

In late May of 1418, the Burgundians retook Paris. Bernard of Armagnac was killed. The Dauphin managed to escape and held court in Bourges and Poitiers, whereas his Bavarian mother, who sided with the hostile Burgundians, lurked in Troyes. During the course of a meeting between John the Fearless and the Dauphin outside Paris in 1419, the former was killed, probably at the behest of the latter. It was revenge for the murder of 1407. The assassination strengthened the alliance between Burgundy and England that was so dangerous to France.

A response to the confusion was provided by Jean de Terrevermeille (ca. 1370–1430), an expert in Roman law from southern France who served the Dauphin. His *Tractatus*, a series of three essays, developed a precise rule for royal succession that gave the Dauphin rights as a co-ruler. Tattered France was recast as an immortal, "mystical body."[25] Its eternal, immutable fundamental laws bound even the king. He was heir to the realm not on the basis of private law but rather because of his lineage. He was the custodian, not the owner or beneficiary, of the crown. Like so many theories that envision a powerful state or at least conceive of an invulnerable abstraction, Terrevermeille's concept was the product of exceptional circumstances.

It was not possible to resolve the war through diplomacy. Far-reaching agreements that could have led to an Anglo-French dual monarchy under the Lancasters were scrapped when Henry V and Charles VI both died in 1422. France's new king, Charles VII (r. 1422–1461), entrenched himself in the heart of the country, in Bourges. The north of the country was divided among the English and the Burgundians. John of Lancaster, Duke of Bedford and brother of the dead English king, prosecuted the conquest of France all the way to the Loire. In 1428, he laid siege to Orléans. The city was about to fall when salvation literally came out of nowhere, in the form of a farm girl from the town of Domrémy in Lorraine: Joan, the famous Maid of Orléans, a sister of El Cid and Alexander Nevsky, steeped in a piety typical of the century of Catherine of Siena. She claimed to have had visions and heard voices—voices of Saint Catherine of Alexandria, wearing a crown and surrounded by light, and also of the warlike archangel Michael. They had enjoined her to liberate the country from the English and to help the king to his coronation. Orléans witnessed the incredible scene of a young girl in shining armor riding out ahead of a band of iron-eaters. Although she was wounded, Joan led the men to storm the bastions of the besiegers.

After the liberation of Orléans, the French army and *La Pucelle* went on to rack up victory upon victory, clearing the way for Charles to be crowned and anointed in Reims Cathedral. Joan's myth culminated in the tragic end to her story, told countless times. Wounded during the siege of Compiègne in early 1431, she fell into the hands of the Burgundians, who sold her for a hefty sum to the Duke of Bedford. An Inquisitorial court condemned the "scourge of England" to death for heresy and witchcraft. She was burned at the stake on the market square of Rouen, her ashes cast to the winds like those of Hus and other heretics. In those days, the powerful feared few things more than holy women or men who, even in death, could transform religious fervor into military verve. The recapture of Orléans and Charles's coronation represented the turning point in the great war. Decisively, the 1435 Peace of Arras broke the alliance between Burgundy and England. Step by step, the English were driven back, first out of the Île-de-France and Paris, then out of Normandy. Their last offensive failed in 1453. Calais was the only place on the Continent that remained to them. France took on outlines as a territorial state, its power extending beyond the boundaries of the royal domain, its unity embodied in the king. Yet it would be almost two hundred years before a French statesman, Cardinal Richelieu, crossed out the words *Sa Majesté*, "His Majesty," on a diplomatic communiqué and replaced them with *La France*.[26]

Charles VII the Victorious had begun taking steps to buttress royal authority even during the Hundred Years' War.[27] Surrounded by an efficient bureaucracy, he raised money by getting the estates of the realm to approve a tax on all goods and not only on royal domains. His treasurer, Jacques Cœur, got rich in the process. Charles also reconfigured his relationship with the Church. On the eve of the Council of Florence, the beleaguered Pope Eugene was surprised by a declaration, the "Pragmatic Sanction of Bourges," which laid the foundation for the Gallican Church and, thus, for France as a secular state. The king used the discord between the Council of Basel and the pope to gain power over the election of bishops and abbots. The flow of payments to Rome was stopped, and bulls and other papal announcements could no longer be published without the approval of the king—a practice already long in force in England.

In France, willingness increased to accept the crown's monopoly on violence, the essence of the modern state. The mercenaries still roaming the countryside after the civil war was ended by the Treaty of Arras were integrated into a standing army. The rest were driven out of the realm with its help. Neighboring countries got a taste of the dregs. For example, an Armagnac band led by the Dauphin Louis marauded around Basel during a war between Zurich and the other cantons of the Swiss Confederacy. A group of about 1,500 Swiss opposed them at the Birs, a small river. Fighting heroically, they were ultimately surrounded in the garden of a hospital and killed to almost the last man by the overwhelming French force of about thirty thousand troops. Louis decided that such hardy opponents were not worth sacrificing his precious mercenaries for, and he broke off the advance. Saint Jakob an der Birs became for the Swiss what Thermopylae had been for the Greeks, and what the Alamo still is for some Americans. That venerable sacrifice continued to be a source of courage during Switzerland's "spiritual national defense" against Nazi Germany.

The greatest profit from the Hundred Years' War went to Philip the Good (r. 1419–1467), the son of John the Fearless. The old Middle Kingdom of Lothair seemed to be rising again.[28] The territory of Burgundy had been built through inheritance, marriage, and purchase. By the time of Philip's death in 1467, it spanned from Holland to Picardy in the north, encompassing Limburg, Luxembourg, Brabant, and Flanders. It also included the traditional Burgundian lands between the Loire and Lake Geneva. Arras freed Burgundy from vassalage to the French king, making Philip a ruler by his own and God's grace. All that was missing was a royal crown and a way to connect the northern and southern territories.

Midsummer in Burgundy: The Play of Realism

Philip's Burgundy was a young superpower in search of forms of expression and a fitting outward appearance. It shirked no fortune or fuss to portray itself in the greatest possible glory. David Aubert, a calligrapher and miniaturist who served as Philip's librarian, believed his master's book collection, full of classical authors, to be the finest in the world.[29] The colorful culture of Burgundy was set in the same epoch in which Burckhardt had seen the dawn of modernity. Yet to Johan Huizinga, it seemed instead to be the autumn of an age that had achieved full ripeness and that was decaying in overly lush splendor. In point of fact, it was the confluence of old and new, of influences from all over Europe. Situated at the intersection of Europe's most important routes of commerce and communication, Burgundy was, as Gaston Roupnel observed, a generous giver and receiver of cultural goods.[30] The means were provided by a vigorous economy. In the mid-fifteenth century, the dukes of Burgundy ruled over some of the richest cities in Europe, including Ghent and Antwerp, the latter of which was in the process of surpassing Bruges.

What Roupnel meant can be illustrated by the example of the composer Guillaume Dufay (ca. 1400–1474), who in old age served as a canon of Cambrai Cathedral. He spent his life at courts and cultural flash points where, as a famous master of polyphonic music, he built up relationships, obtained commissions, earned a great deal of money, and, above all, taught and learned from others. We find him at the court of the Malatesta, the Este, the Savoy, in Bologna and Rome, and at the councils of Constance, Florence, and Basel. This made his music European, combining Flemish, Italian, French, and English influences; it became a model for later composers. Along with Gilles Binchois, he was a member of Philip the Good's court chapel. He and John Dunstable of England were the leading composers of the Franco-Flemish music that provided the soundtrack for the Renaissance. Piero de' Medici called him "the greatest ornament of our age."[31]

The ceremonial with which the dukes staged their coronations and entrances, banquets and festivals, marriages and funerals made the Burgundian state and its political order visible, portraying it as a "political body."[32] Ceremonial separated the sumptuously black-clad rulers and their courtiers from normal mortals, demonstrating their rank and hierarchy to the public. A wondrous sacral aura was conjured by words, symbols, and music to remind people that sovereignty and the state had an otherworldly foundation. Soon, half the courts of Europe were imitating Burgundy's ceremonial, which for its part reflected French and Spanish customs. At the deepest layer of the ceremonial principle glittered a trace of divinity, preserved in the person of the prince. To disrespect it could mean losing the sovereign's grace—although not one's life, as was the fate of those, for example, who dared to look at the ruler of the Ayutthaya Kingdom in Southeast Asia.[33]

Entertainment was provided by tournaments, celebrated in exotic splendor and fought for the pledge and favor of a fair lady in the stands. Here, traditional knightly combat lived on in the form of festively staged sport. The wars of the age showed that chivalry was a relic. The future belonged to crossbows, harquebuses, artillery, and mercenaries. Traditional courtly culture also endured in chivalric orders like the Order of the Golden Fleece. It was founded by Philip the Good "not for amusement, nor for recreation" but rather to give praise to God and "glory and high fame to the good."[34] The ribbon of the order became Europe's highest distinction. The emblem of the fleece—it may have alluded to the golden fleece of Jason or, more likely, to the fleece of the biblical Gideon—became an attribute of the high nobility. Initially, the dukes of Burgundy were the masters of the order; later on, it was emperors and kings.

The Burgundian dynasty and its noble tradition were immortalized in rich works of history and the funerary monument of the dukes. For the latter, Philip the Bold (r. 1363–1404) had a Carthusian monastery, the Chartreuse de Champmol, built outside Dijon. The order was known for extremely strict discipline. Its monks guaranteed that prayers would dutifully be said for the salvation of their benefactor's soul. As sculptor, Philip chose Claus Sluter, whose work was characterized by monumentality and realism. Sluter created a mystery play out of stone for the Carthusians.[35] Its protagonists, figures of prophets on Mount Calvary, are men of this world who look upon it austerely with deeply lined faces or with serene skepticism. The expressive power of the *pleurants*—"crying," mourning monks—that Sluter and other masters created for the tombs of Philip the Bold and John the Fearless, burst the bonds of convention. Never before had feelings been hewn so realistically into stone. Many of the figures do not reveal the nature of their suffering; instead, they hide their faces.

A similar realism appeared in painting in the last third of the fifteenth century. The new style was pioneered in book illumination. In a parallel development—this time, the cultural current flowed from south to north—the art of the Sienese provided inspiration. Avignon, where Simone Martini was one of the most important artists, served as an intermediary of exchange. The result was spectacular, a revolution that approached the coup effected by Sluter in sculpture. The golden background that tended to dominate sacred scenes disappeared. It was replaced by views of real landscapes, of mountains and broad plains crossed by meandering roads, with hills, castles, and the sea in the distance. Robert Campin (ca. 1375–1444), for example, takes us through the streets of medieval towns, inviting us into the living rooms and workshops of an urban setting. Among the earliest stand-alone portraits of modern art history are two nearly identical depictions by Campin of a portly, noble gentleman (now located in Berlin's Gemäldegalerie and the Thyssen-Bornemisza Museum in Madrid). These works have no sacred context; they show the stout man and nothing more. Jan van Eyck (ca. 1390–1441), like Sluter, was one of those who helped the discursive revolution establish itself in the world of the arts. The man from Maaseik (near Maastricht) was perfectly equipped for the task of painting "according to nature." The magic he performed on wood panels drove from the field all that came before. One thinks of his Ghent Altarpiece, with its large-scale nudes of Adam and Eve, angels in gold brocade playing music, saints, God the Father, and pastoral vistas. The engagement portrait of the merchant Giovanni Arnolfini of Lucca provides a glimpse inside a fifteenth-century home. A bit of graffiti on the back wall doubles as an artist's signature and a statement that the painter himself witnessed the scene: *Johannes de eyck fuit hic 1434.* "Jan van Eyck was here." Objects are depicted as they actually are; even what is not real seems to be so. Like Campin's portrait, this famous picture, one of the first panel paintings with a purely secular theme, is also a kind of worldly conquest. Painting captured reality like Boccaccio's and Chaucer's poetry had in the previous century, and as Machiavelli's political theory would in the next.

Van Eyck's works already fascinated his contemporaries. When the wings of the Ghent Altarpiece were opened on holidays, from dawn to dusk curious people pressed into the chapel that held the marvel. Emperors, kings, and fellow artists like Albrecht Dürer (1471–1528) stood before it in awe.[36] Part of the effect came from the fact that van Eyck did not use traditional tempera as a binder for his paints but rather oil. This medium gave the artist more time to work and resulted in brighter colors. It also allowed for more delicate transitions and for highlights to be added with a fine brush. Van Eyck was a master of the technique. Yet he did not invent it, as patriotic art historians maintain he did. It had been known for a long time.[37]

In the view of his day, Jan van Eyck was not an "artist" in the modern sense of the term but rather a craftsman who, as he himself writes on one of his pictures, worked *als ich can*, to the best of his ability. In contrast to musicians like Dufay, painters were not considered masters of one of the liberal arts. Rather they were practitioners of an *ars mechanica*, a "mechanical craft," and accordingly were paid less than composers. Nevertheless, an exceptional talent like van Eyck, *excellent en son art et science*, as Philip the Good described him, managed to escape the manifold obligations that the guild system imposed on its members.[38] He served his lord as a diplomat. The duke stood as godfather to one of Jan's children, and he seems not to have considered it beneath his dignity to visit the master in his workshop. It was such courts to which painters, sculptors, and architects primarily owed their rise to freedom. Then as later, patronage was the key to the production of significant art as well as serious science and scholarship.

Of the artistic benefactors of northern Europe, one of the most important was Nicolas Rolin (1376–1462), who became Philip the Good's chancellor in 1422.[39] He came from the provincial Burgundian town of Autun and had first worked as a lawyer in Paris and Dijon. Astute marriage alliances had made him as rich as Croesus; his service at court earned him a knighthood. He was the classic example of the social climber: ambitious, greedy, and a committed reformer to boot. He stood by, cold as ice, as Joan of Arc was judicially murdered. Only in his final years did his influence wane. He had every reason to seek to settle his account with his God, and it cost him a princely sum. He had a hospital, the Hôtel de Dieu, constructed in Beaune; Roger van der Weyden (1399/1400–1464) painted a large-format *Last Judgment* for its ward. Earlier, Rolin had commissioned Jan van Eyck to paint a Madonna for a church in Autun that he patronized. There is little doubt that Rolin sought to increase his prestige by engaging van Eyck, the greatest master of his age. Yet one must not overlook the fact that the most beautiful works of art at that time—and the *Madonna of Chancellor Rolin*, with its microscopic attention to detail, was one of them—were first and foremost votive offerings, i.e., good works. As the ever-industrious Rolin wrote in the hospital's foundation deed, the building was donated in the interest of his salvation, in the desire to make a profitable deal: to trade earthly for heavenly goods.[40]

The products of Flanders were highly valued in Europe, both panel paintings and tapestries, for which masters of the highest caliber often provided designs. Their pictures were prized as status symbols and were remunerated accordingly. Thus, Flemish painters followed the musicians south, where patronage was to be had. One of the first whose sojourn in Italy is documented is Rogier van der Weyden.[41] For the holy year of 1450, he traveled to Rome. He was honored by humanists and given a well-paid commission in Ferrara by Marquis Leonello d'Este. One of his contemporaries, Bartolomeo Facio, considered him worthy of a short biography.[42] The Italians were deeply impressed by the perfection of Flemish art, and they apprenticed themselves to it. They learned how to paint microscopically precise portraits and depict gold brocade—so realistically that it seemed to rustle. They added pastel tones to landscapes, discovering the blue haze of the distance and thus aerial perspective. For his *Adoration of the Shepherds*, an altarpiece for the funerary chapel of the Medici general manager Francesco Sassetti, Domenico Ghirlandaio was inspired by a panel painted for one of Sassetti's colleagues, Tommaso Portinari, a representative of the Medici bank in Bruges. Italy's contribution to Ghirlandaio's picture consists of ancient elements such as a triumphal arch in the background and a marble sarcophagus serving as a manger for an ox and a donkey. The same Portinari commissioned portraits of himself and his wife Maria Baroncelli from Hans Memling—a master in Bruges who could paint almost photo-realistically—probably as parts of a triptych (Plate 8).

In this way, the Renaissance art of Italy took shape through a process of cultural exchange and the aid of a massive troop of patrons.[43] The paths of artists followed those of merchants, some of whom, like the aforementioned Arnolfini and Portinari, commissioned work from them. Incidentally, these paintings already reveal a patronage landscape similar to the one in which science and technology would later achieve their breakthrough.

Resetting the Italian Chessboard

A first true synthesis of the various artistic currents was achieved by a painter who gazes out at us earnestly from a self-portrait dating to around 1455: Jean Fouquet, the detail-obsessed illustrator of the *Grandes chroniques de France*.

An altarpiece he painted for Étienne Chevalier, Charles VII's treasurer, depicts the patron with the kind of realism that could only be learned in the north—but in front of an Italian architectural background executed in linear perspective. Indeed, Fouquet spent several years in Italy. In Rome, he painted a lifelike portrait of Eugene IV for the church of Santa Maria sopra Minerva (which has unfortunately not survived).

The pope had returned to his city in 1443. Cardinal Vitelleschi had prepared the way with blood. The capital of the Western Church was not especially impressive. There were fields and hills planted with vines inside the city's far too expansive walls. Perhaps thirty thousand people lived in what had once been a metropolis of one million inhabitants. As one chronicler noted, the pope's absence had made Rome a place for cowherds: "Sheep and cows pastured where today the benches of merchants stand."[44] Eugene took up residence in the Vatican Palace, in the part of the city controlled by the friendly Orsini clan. In case of trouble, a covered passageway, the *passetto di borgo*, provided a means of reaching Castel Sant'Angelo, which was now outfitted with artillery. From now on, the Vatican would be the residence of the successors of Peter, near the grave that contained the foundation of their authority. The myth of the city and its relics had preserved its magical aura. There was no longer any question that Rome was the legitimate abode of the papacy. Amadeus VIII of Savoy, set up as antipope with the name Felix V by the conciliarist opposition in Basel, won few adherents. He resigned in 1449.

The council continued to meet for a bit in Basel and then in Lausanne. Yet the ecclesiastical assembly disintegrated as the dioceses and benefices of those who persevered went to seed. Nevertheless, the council did manage to lay an important foundation for Basel's future as a capital of humanism. To meet the bureaucratic needs of the assembly, a clever entrepreneur had set up a paper mill.[45] It proved to be the basis for Basel's rise as one of Europe's printing hubs. However, the movement for horizontal power within the Roman Church was stopped in its tracks. It was now decided that reform could not be successfully instituted from the top down. More than the renewal of the Church, the papacy was focused on Italian politics. It could not stem Aragon's ambitions in the south. The victor in the eventful war of succession with the Anjou—Queen Joanna departed this life in 1435, Louis III the year before—was Alfonso the Magnanimous of Aragon (r. 1416–1458). Eugene IV had no choice but to accept the facts and grant him investiture. With this crown, Alfonso now unified the Kingdom of the "Two Sicilies." In addition, he ruled Mallorca, Sardinia, and a large part of Corsica, and he attempted to establish a foothold in the Balkans as well.[46] To commemorate his solemn entrance into Naples in 1433, Alfonso added a two-story triumphal arch out of marble to the city's Castel Nuovo.[47] Hordes of artists and humanists traveled to the court of the bibliophile and lover of antiquity, who showered twenty thousand ducats a year on them. Alfonso did not break the power of the barons.

In the north, Venice, Florence, and Milan rebalanced the scale of power. Venice was now pursuing a new policy of establishing a mainland empire. The War of Chioggia had shown how dangerous it was when a powerful rival like Genoa allied with local lords in the Serenissima's hinterland. Venice also sought to prevent Milan from reestablishing its dominance. The opportunity to win territory on the mainland presented itself after Gian Galeazzo Visconti died; his state sank into internal discord and was practically paralyzed for a decade. The Serenissima seized power in cities like Vicenza and Verona; the Carrara in Padua were wiped out. "Dead men wage no wars," the Venetians dryly commented when the clan's leaders were executed.[48] Around 1430, Venice's territory reached Rovereto and Bergamo. In addition, Friuli (including the Patriarchate of Grado) and the Dalmatian cities previously lost to Hungary came under the Banner of Saint Mark. Only the city-republic of Dubrovnik was able, thanks to some diplomatic dexterity, to retain a bit of autonomy— from both Venice and the sultan.[49]

Visconti rule, once brilliant, came to an end in Milan at mid-century. Let us take a closer look at how this happened. Gian Galeazzo's son Filippo Maria Visconti (1392–1447) married Beatrice di Tenda, the widow of his deceased condottiere Facino Cane, thus accruing for himself Cane's orphaned mercenary company and a dowry worth 400,000 ducats.[50] On the same day as the wedding, Filippo's older brother and rival was killed by an assassin—a lucky coincidence. Beatrice enjoyed her marriage only briefly. In 1418, a supposed act of infidelity provided Filippo with an excuse to dispose of his wife, more than twenty years his senior, by beheading. He kept the dowry. The portly, violent, and neurotic Filippo then married a daughter of Amadeus VIII of Savoy, who would later be named Antipope Felix. This political union produced no children, just like the liaison with Cane's widow. For sex and perhaps love as well, Duke Filippo had a mistress who provided him, the last scion of the main line of his family, with a daughter and heir, Bianca Maria.

To lead his army, Visconti first employed Francesco Bussone da Carmagnola. The latter defeated Genoa and even the battle-hardened Swiss, thus retaking Bellinzona for his master. However, fearful of Filippo's distrust and lured by good money, he changed sides and entered the service of Venice. This provided

Francesco Sforza, the victor of Aquila, with his big chance.[51] He had retired from the struggle for Naples in 1425. Now he negotiated a *condotta*, or contract, with Visconti, according to which he was paid to raise a mercenary army. He used it to wage war with Venice. Francesco was a man with political acumen and nerves of steel. Despite setbacks and the opposition of ubiquitous schemers, he earned Filippo's trust. The latter ultimately gave him the hand of his illegitimate daughter Bianca Maria. Carmagnola was less lucky. He suffered a defeat and prosecuted the war hesitantly, causing Venice to suspect him of treachery—whether correctly or not, we do not know. He was beheaded in 1432 between the pillars of the Piazzetta, the traditional spot for executions. Sforza, in contrast, who was now serving the pope and the Florentines, took command of Milan's army upon the death of his father-in-law in 1447. As the general of the "Ambrosian Republic," which sought to reinstitute communal liberty, he continued the war against Venice and advanced his own career. He benefited from the fact that the old fox Cosimo de' Medici bet on him. Florentine money paved his way to power. By now, Venetian expansion seemed more dangerous to the Florentines than the threat of Milan. This led to an inversion of alliances, and it turned out that Florence had backed the winner. Sforza conquered the Venetians and then immediately sent his troops against his own employer. In 1450, he entered Milan as its new lord. Thus Sforza, the illegitimate son of a soldier of peasant birth, won the throne of one of the mightiest states of Italy. It was a storybook rise to power that amazed even his contemporaries.

The history of the genesis of the early modern state normally calls to mind dry topics like Roman law and bureaucracy. Yet, as readers will note, it could from time to time develop into a drama fit for the stage. The fate of the unlucky Beatrice, Filippo Maria Visconti's wife, inspired Vincenzo Bellini to write an opera. And the no less unlucky Carmagnola became the hero of a tragedy by Alessandro Manzoni (1785–1873). Depicting the internecine wars of the Renaissance, it educated Italians of the Risorgimento about the deep historical roots of the peninsula's foreign domination. Indeed, condottieri like Carmagnola were architects of the early modern state. They facilitated the acquisition of power, the drawing of borders, and the clarification of political uncertainty. Many of them dreamt of states of their own, of creating counties or dukedoms, and perhaps even of claiming a royal crown. The few successful ones— Hawkwood and Sforza, later Federico da Montefeltro (1422–1482)—stood out against an army of losers. Fortebraccio was one of the most famous of them. Many others are known by little more than name. A few lived picaresque lives, like Castracani or the swashbuckler Enguerrand VII de Coucy, who fought on three continents and died in knightly captivity in Bursa, in Anatolia.

Those who did manage to fight their way to the top still needed one more thing above all else: legitimacy. A word from the Holy Roman Emperor or the pope sufficed to protect one's gains and pass them on to one's progeny. Accordingly, such a word was recompensed handsomely in gold. Gian Galeazzo Visconti paid the equivalent value of a city for his ducal title. No less painfully did parvenus feel their lack of venerable traditions. Contemporary poets and historians thus elevated them to ancient heights, in line with the style of the age. An especially strange example is provided by Giannantonio de' Pandoni, called Porcellio. He portrayed Francesco Sforza as Hannibal and his opponent, the condottiere Niccolò Piccinino, as Hannibal's vanquisher Scipio.[52]

With enough vigor, the future can be molded. But the past is lost to even the most industrious unless a historian is paid to change it. Even Francesco Sforza's coat of arms was a brazen lie. It features the imperial eagle and the viper of the Visconti, to whom he and his family were not related by blood. Francesco also used the arts and learning to make posterity forget the treachery to which he owed his position. The Visconti library in Pavia, one of the most significant collections in Italy, also received patronage from him. He continued the construction of Milan's cathedral and the Certosa di Pavia and crowned his good works in a manner similar to Chancellor Rolin in Burgundy, commissioning his court architect Filarete to build a hospital. The Milanese soon named the monumental building simply *Ca' granda*, "the big house." Even today, the grim Sforza Castle in the center of the city commemorates the self-made duke. The diamond-shaped studs on the walls facing the city, the massive round towers, and the *Torre del Filarete* convey pure power. Above all, the structure was meant to teach the citizens of Milan to forget their republican sympathies and obey.

22

Children of the Discursive Revolution

Humanist Education, the Rhetorical Revolution, and Textual Criticism

The educational reform begun in the twelfth century was carefully advanced in the schools of the Quattrocento. The ancient classics took the place in the curriculum theretofore held by the *auctores minores*, pagan and Christian authors of late antiquity and the Middle Ages.[1] At the same time, humanism's educational project was systematized. With his *Character and Studies Befitting a Freeborn Youth*, Pier Paolo Vergerio (1370–1444) of Capodistria (now Koper,

Slovenia), a trained jurist, provided an eloquent foundational work of humanist pedagogy that also reads like the manifesto of a new field of learning.[2] It sought to train the proverbial healthy mind in a healthy body, exercised in gymnastics, hunting, and fishing, and refined rationally through learning. It aimed to produce people made free by philosophy and the "liberal arts." That is precisely why they are called "liberal," maintains Vergerio—because they are suited to free people. From the vast number of potential subjects, individuals should focus on those that correspond to their own particular gifts. Singing a new tune, Vergerio praises poetry and music in particular as sources of joy. Astronomy "calls us away from the shadows and murkiness down here and leads the eyes and the mind to that shining home above, adorned with so many lights." Indeed, Vergerio stresses the paramount importance of "knowledge about nature"—at a time when other educational theorists were not even thinking about it. As he explains,

> Through this knowledge we understand the principles and processes of natural things, both animate and inanimate, as well as the causes and effects of the motions and transformations of those things which are contained in heaven and on Earth, and we are able to explain many things that generally seem miraculous to the vulgar.

The civic virtue of ambition and the aristocratic virtue of the desire for glory received justification as drivers of the active life.[3]

Gasparino Barzizza (ca. 1360–ca. 1431), a singular expert on the writings of Cicero, was the author of works that provided instruction in how to write letters. He taught grammar and rhetoric in Pavia, Padua, Ferrara, and Milan. One of his students was Vittorino di Ser Bruto de' Rambaldoni (1378–1446), born in Feltre and thus known as Vittorino da Feltre. He opened his *Casa giocosa*, "House of Joy," on the banks of the Mincio River in Mantua with the support of the local marquis. It was the first boarding school in educational history.[4] There he educated future princes, cardinals, and scholars. He lived with his students in a monastic-style community. He trained them in the liberal arts, took excursions with them, and encouraged them to go riding and play all kinds of games. Vittorino did not write an educational treatise; he made his mark through his personality. His pupil Federico da Montefeltro included Vittorino's likeness among the portraits of great philosophers and poets that lined the walls of his *studiolo*. Andrea Mantegna (1431–1506) shows the pedagogue among the Gonzaga courtiers in his fresco in the Camera degli Sposi of the palace in Mantua. There is no more impressive indication of the value humanist education had now attained. In the form of new grammars and lexicons, including those by the great teacher Guarino of Verona (1374–1460) and Niccolò Perotti, tools were provided for perfecting an elegant style. Giovanni Tortelli's *De orthographia* taught how to correctly spell 3,440 Greek terms and also provided information about philosophers and their schools.[5]

Closely connected to the new direction being taken in education was what has been called a "rhetorical revolution."[6] It had been prepared by medieval books of grammar and rhetoric and the success of the *ars dictaminis* in the studies of the Bolognese jurists, as well as by manuals that taught how to engage in politics. Its most important pioneer had been Petrarca.[7] Ever greater attention was paid to the technique of argumentation, *in utramque partem disputare*— arguing both sides of a question—a fact that clearly reflects the growing significance of public discourse in the states and cities, first in Italy and later all over Europe. It was yet another sign of life for horizontal power. Rhetorical bombards attended wars and competitions to see who had the more beautiful churches and palaces. Ambassadors are often referred to in the sources as *oratores*, as "orators." In this way, rhetoric became a foundational branch of learning.[8] It provided art theory with standards and terms, was useful to jurists and historians, and even made its way into scientific texts—the passage from Galileo's dialogue quoted at the beginning of this book provides an impressive example.[9] As Bruni has Salutati say in his *Dialogues to Pier Paolo Vergerio,*

> By the immortal gods, what is there more valuable than disputation in helping us to grasp and examine difficult ideas? It is as if an object were placed center stage and observed by many eyes, so that no aspect of it can escape them, or hide from them, or deceive the gaze of all.[10]

The shining rhetorical model, achieved by the best of those who imitated it, was the style of Cicero. The orator of all orators was present as an invisible but in no way silent advocate in town councils and courtrooms. He even made his way to Lund in Sweden.[11] Although Cicero was a staunch republican, the political messages contained in his letters and orations did not keep his rhetoric from finding a home at princely courts as well.

A new foundation for rhetoric was laid by Lorenzo Valla (1405/07–1457).[12] His father, a lawyer at the papal Curia, may have put him in contact with the Greek scholar Giovanni Aurispa and thus also with the language of Athens. In the Roman circle around Cardinal Giordano Orsini, Valla trafficked with Bruni, Bracciolini, and other humanists. He relates how they would meet dressed in ancient clothing in order to live out the world of classical Rome—a piece of humanist romanticism.[13] His textbook, the *Elegantiae linguae latinae*, was used all over Europe. He considered polished classical Latin to be the only tool capable of depicting reality—which, he agreed with Ockham, only existed in discrete, individual things.[14]

Valla was a brilliant thinker. The tone of his dialogues is easy and flowing, playful, sparkling with eloquence. He was also a master critic. In this respect, he displayed a special talent for making enemies and fomenting scandal. Hauled before the Inquisition in Naples, he could only be saved by the hand of his patron King Alfonso. His critical mind, honed in the rigorous realm of philological studies, was then aimed at all possible subjects: logic, language, ethics, and the practice of law, with its often imprecise understanding of Roman legal terminology. Valla criticized those who hid behind the authority of Aristotle, scoffed at the "utterly ignorant" Avicenna and Averroes, and gave no quarter to either Boethius or Thomas Aquinas. The latter possessed saintly virtues, he admitted, but the knowledge he had to offer was "of trifling consequence." He devoted himself solely "to the petty reasonings of the dialecticians," without, however, realizing that they were rather "obstacles in the way of better kinds of knowledge."[15] Few things met Valla's high standards. He compared Jerome's translation of the New Testament with the Greek original, found errors, and pioneered a philologically rigorous biblical scholarship. He thus became a forerunner of Luther and the biblical exegesis of Erasmus of Rotterdam, who also highly prized the *Elegantiae*. Valla was the first to realize that the venerated "Dionysius the Areopagite" could never have been in the audience when Saint Paul preached.[16] He became famous, for some infamous, by proving that the Donation of Constantine was a forgery—a discovery that led him to fundamentally criticize all secular power of the papacy.[17] It speaks for the Holy See that Valla was employed as an apostolic scribe and secretary at the Curia from 1447 until his death.

He was interested in this world, in life before death. Considering the question of whether free will was compatible with divine omnipotence, he rehearsed the arguments going back to Boethius but ultimately concluded that no rational answer was possible. In his view, it was a question of faith alone. Otherwise, he relied on reason informed by experience. As a historian, he followed the analytical method of Thucydides.[18] By placing rhetoric, "queen of the world," above philosophy, he sought to promote a free, impartial viewpoint. He aimed it as a weapon of truth against the obscure whisperings of anemic philosophy, which, to his mind, was fettered by the dogmatic chains of its students.[19] His critique of the abstractions of some of the Scholastics helped to dismantle hurdles to a kind of learning focused on the acquisition of useful knowledge. In a word, Lorenzo Valla was a forerunner of the Enlightenment.

Greco-Italian Networks

In this age, however, tolerance was still a foreign word. Anything other than a Catholic world seemed unthinkable, and certainly undesirable, to the intellectuals of Latin Europe. Nevertheless, the most disparate religions thrived between Armenia, North Africa, Byzantium, and Rome, all with their own god and their own beliefs. Crusades against infidels and heretics had done nothing to change that. The notion that there was ever a monolithic "Catholic West" is a myth.

Engagement with the classical tradition led to a new way of dealing with diversity. This was especially the case when it came to Plato's concept of the divine. Might not the various religions contain traces of an original revelation that had been given to humankind at the beginning of its history? And hidden behind the "hundred names" of God, might one not find the ineffable *logos*, the unity of the Word? As we have seen, the philosophy of Plato in particular contained elements that appeared compatible with Christian beliefs. The authority of Augustine concurred. Dante quoted from the *Timaeus*.[20] And Petrarca considered Plato's writings a key to revelation. Till now, they were only available in Latin versions that were often based on Arabic texts that, in turn, had been translated from Syriac. To gain access to the purity of the original, it was necessary to learn Greek. That all Latin learning had spouted from Greek fonts was a truism already known to a chaplain of Barbarossa.[21]

As the Roman Empire was once conquered by Greek culture, now Italy succumbed to the spirit of Hellenism. A start was made in the Byzantine south of the peninsula, which had already been a setting for translations from Greek into Latin under the Norman kings. Greek manuscripts were found in many libraries of Europe, but only a few individuals could read the language. One such book in the library of the Duke of Berry bears the resigned note: "It's Greek; no one can read it."[22] Refugees from the crumbling Byzantine Empire spread knowledge of the language of Homer and Plato in Italy. Boccaccio promoted Leonzio Pilato from southern Italy (or Thessalonica), who taught Greek in Florence and translated Homer.[23] Several hundred Greek manuscripts are known to have circulated in Italy.[24] From his exile in Padua—which was close to Venice, the gateway to Byzantium—Palla Strozzi acquired additional codices, including an illustrated copy of Ptolemy's *Cosmography*. Its translation at the hands of Iacopo Angeli da Scarperia marked a milestone in the history of cartography.[25] Another trailblazer of the revival of Greek was the Camaldolese monk Ambrogio Traversari (1386–1439), who focused on translating works by the Church Fathers.[26] He found a patron in Cosimo de' Medici.

A major player in the Greco-Italian network was Francesco Filelfo (1398–1481).[27] He had worked in Constantinople as a secretary to Venice's *bailo*, the representative of its merchants, and then served the Byzantine emperor, all the while acquiring manuscripts. He learned the language of Byzantium from a brother of Chrysoloras and even married his teacher's daughter. After returning to Italy, Filelfo found employment first in Bologna and then in Florence. There he allied himself with the enemies of the Medici and, when the Albizzi coup failed, had to flee to Siena (p. 449). Later he spent time in Milan, Padua, Rome, and other cities. He was a lifelong friend of Theodore Gaza (ca. 1400–ca. 1475), who translated Theophrastus's work on botany and wrote a Greek grammar. He also forged relations with George of Trebizond (1395–1472/84), a thorny personality who was involved in many conflicts and was a sworn enemy of Platonic philosophy. George had learned Latin under Vittorino da Feltre, in return helping him with translations from Greek.[28]

Another important member of the network was the Sicilian Giovanni Aurispa (1376–1459), a colleague of Filelfo who also acted as a mentor to him.[29] Lorenzo Valla owed him his initial knowledge of Greek. On two trips to the East, Aurispa, a passionate manuscript hunter and an enterprising book dealer to boot, amassed an important collection of Greek writings. The export of theological manuscripts met with disapproval from the authorities, however. The emigration of pagan writings, on the other hand, was tolerated.[30] Aurispa possessed works by Plato—all of them, he claimed. He spent a large portion of his life in Ferrara, which, thanks to him, developed into a center of Greek studies. One of his contributions was to bring Theodore Gaza to the city's university. George of Trebizond also found employment there for a few years. It was thus a handful of men with a strong personal relationship with one another that served as the vanguard in paving the way for the intellectual invasion of the Greeks and especially for Platonism. Gaza seems to have been the first one to teach Plato—in Ferrara. With his spirits and demons, his metaphysics of light, and his enigmatic concept of God, Plato offered an alternative to the "Scholastic" Aristotle.

The Council of Ferrara and Florence left a profound and enduring mark. The waning light of Byzantine imperial splendor had set over an awed Italy.

"The Greek emperor sat on a chair draped in silk, across from the chair of the pope," recalled Vespasiano da Bisticci. "He was dressed in the Greek manner, with a robe of damask brocade, and he wore a Greek hat crowned with a beautiful jewel."[31] The humanists were fascinated by the fact that the Byzantines seemed to be survivors of antiquity. For one thousand years or more, so Bisticci thought, they had not changed their style of dress. This made Emperor John VIII an extremely popular subject for artistic depiction. Pisanello cast a medal with his profile, showing him with a beard, long hair, and the Greek *skiadion* hat. Pesellino and Piero della Francesca used his appearance as a model for the portrayal of ancient potentates.

Archaeology of Wisdom

One member of the Greek delegation was Byzantium's leading philosopher, the distinguished Georgius Gemistus Pletho (ca. 1355/60–1452). In an untranslatable play on words, he announced his intention to combine the foundational principles of thought, *logikai archai*, with the study of antiquity in a comprehensive *archaiologia*, or "archaeology."[32] The goal was to reconstruct the most ancient theology based on what God had said at the dawn of mankind, as well as on Zoroaster, in whose revival Pletho assisted.[33] Must the wisest not also be the most ancient? Pletho masterfully satisfied the early humanists' zeal for antiquity and quenched their thirst for sources. Islam and Judaism were not foreign to him. He is thought to have been a student of the Kabbalist Elissaios at the Ottoman court. His opaquely written texts had the appeal of being esoteric and exotic. They thus contributed to the development of an "occult" Renaissance. Nevertheless, they are also part of the prehistory of enlightened tolerance and of modernity in general.

The search for the ultimate foundation of all religions was a reaction against the fragmentation of Christianity. It drove the archaeologists of wisdom to faraway places in the East and mythical twilight worlds. The Egyptian literary tradition and the teachings of Indian Brahmins were studied, as was Orpheus, who was considered the founder of a cult and the poet of enigmatic hymns to gods, the cosmos, and nature. At the center of all these efforts, however, was Plato. For he had something to offer to rationalists and mystics alike.[34] His universe was ruled by strict geometry and inhabited by demons. His concept of God disappointed neither intellectuals nor pious believers. Generations of theologians and philosophers were not able to imagine that teachings of this caliber were the result of mere human speculation. Divine inspiration had to be involved somehow. Yet the master himself—unlike Moses, Paul, and Muhammad—said nothing about receiving heavenly revelations. It was thus necessary to construct fanciful genealogies that relocated the origin of Plato's teachings in a remote past close to the godhead.

Strange attempts were made to combine the human with the metaphysical on the basis of historical speculation. For example, Orpheus was made the teacher of Pythagoras, who in turn passed the revelations he received on to Plato.[35] Platonic philosophy had been rooted in biblical ground since the second century BC. Hellenized Jews made their Moses, the conversation partner of Yahweh, into the teacher of the Greeks and thus of Plato.[36] Eusebius of Caesarea inserted the prophet Jeremiah into the lineage, claiming that Plato had met him in Egypt and heard God's words from him. In this way, Plato became an "Attic Moses."[37] This view of history seemed to reveal a grand divine plan. Was not Orpheus, who had traveled to the underworld and conquered death for a short while, a forerunner of Christ? Even more so did Pythagoras, the Jesus-like guru and miracle healer, seem to presage the Redeemer.

A first determined attempt to put Plato's philosophy, mythology, and Christian doctrine into harmony with one another had been undertaken by Psellus in the eleventh century.[38] He had discovered a curious text: the *Chaldean Oracles*, a work of Middle-Eastern origin that taught astrological and magical practices. Pletho considered these to be revelations of Zoroaster.[39] In his hands, the prophet of the Persian god of light, Ahura Mazda, mutated into a kind of Platonist *avant la lettre*. This pushed the putative genealogy into deep prehistory, as Pletho believed Zoroaster to have lived five thousand years before the Trojan War—the event that at the time marked the beginning of world history for many people.

This broad survey shows that the groundwork had long been laid for the Christianization of Platonic philosophy and its grand revival in the Florence of Lorenzo the Magnificent, which we will return to later. If Plato's god had driven the biblical God from his throne, then the basic theological problem of the Trinity, including debates about the *filioque*, would have become irrelevant. This did not happen, of course, and, down to our own day, the honorable endeavor to find a common, universal truth behind the diversity of religions has been fruitless. The openness and curiosity of the time around 1450 left a double-edged legacy: a jumble of bizarre "secret teachings" found their way into the world of European discourse.[40]

Those who subscribed to such views easily came under suspicion of heresy, as did some zealous Platonists. Psellus met with the same Orthodox criticism

Pletho did 400 years later.[41] The latter, a central figure in the Platonic revival, was not tolerated in Byzantium. He had withdrawn to the idyllic yet remote Mistra. George of Trebizond condemned him as part of a troika of heretics along with Plato and Muhammad. Only with the help of Aristotle, he replied to Pletho, would Christianity succeed in vanquishing Plato, the author of schism and heresy. George overemphasized the differences between the two philosophies in his polemic. This made him one of the originators of the notion that the two great thinkers were intellectual enemies, as well as of the (incorrect) equation of Aristotle with a "retrograde" Middle Ages and Plato with "modern" Renaissance humanism. Countless attempts were made to resolve the actual and supposed differences between the ideas of the Stagirite and those of his teacher.

Plato's thought retained its appeal despite such conflicts. It stood for the renunciation of Scholastic intellectualism, for a logic of emotion, of "intuitive wisdom," and for a playful engagement with analogical thinking. As such, it shared similarities with late medieval mysticism, which offered its own escapes from the dead ends of "learned" theology. One of those determined to defend Plato and Christianize his thought was Bessarion, who had also been a student of Pletho.[42] Pletho, incidentally, received a grave of honor in a niche in the Tempio Malatestiano, the church of the lord of Rimini, Sigismondo Malatesta—a clear symbol that the Platonic revival was set to begin.

Plato's continuing appeal can also be seen in the philosophy of Cardinal Nicholas Krebs, who was called "Cusanus" after his birthplace, a wine town on the Moselle River called Kues ("Cusa" in Latin).[43] He dealt with the same questions that occupied Pletho; the two men met during the time of the Council of Union in Ferrara and Florence. In the inspired teachings of Hermes Trismegistus, Cusanus thought he could descry traces of the "primeval theology" that, in his view, also underlay Islam and Judaism.[44] This "thrice-great" Hermes was likely a cross between the Greek god of the same name and Thot, the Egyptian god of magic and wisdom. The corpus ascribed to this phantom, a conglomerate of Platonic, Neoplatonic, and Judeo-Christian texts, was probably assembled in the second century. Hermes was known to the Arabs and the Latin Middle Ages, and in one tradition he was believed to actually be three different ancient Egyptians of the same name. He was considered the preserver of the most ancient wisdom and an all-powerful magician, theologian, and cultural hero. His survival required that Lactantius place him back in time before Christianity. One text, falsely ascribed to Augustine, even turned him into a pagan defender of the Trinity. Thus, the clear rejection of Hermetism contained in the

City of God, an authentic work of Augustine, did not keep Trismegistus from making his way into the Renaissance. Nicholas Cusanus sublimated his revelations into a grand philosophy.

The Truth Cries Out in the Streets:
Cusanus's Concordances

Cusanus was born in 1401. As a matter of Church policy, he believed that error had to be wiped out with fire and the sword. He savagely attacked the Hussites. He was also a foe of the Jews, more so than was normal for his time. And yet, his view that a grain of truth was to be found in Islam, in Judaism, in Indian religions, and even among the Tatars was a step in the direction of the notion that East and West, North and South all rested equally in the peace of God. Cusanus regarded ancient philosophy with awe. As he once remarked, some of its representatives had approximated the teachings of the Gospels by the power of their minds alone.[45]

Cusanus was raised in Deventer in the spirit of the *devotio moderna*. He then studied canon law in Heidelberg and Padua. He was the most critical interlocutor that medieval theology found in early humanism. His 1433 *Concordantia catholica*, or *Catholic Concordance*, outlines a vision of a universal hierarchy based on the ideas of pseudo-Dionysius.[46] Populated by spirits, bodies, and composite entities made up of both elements, this hierarchy consists of nine levels, a choir of angels, and the heavenly spheres. They are bound to harmony by the infinite king of Heaven, who is above everything and in everything. In the Church—thus Cusanus's pious hope—consensus animated by brotherhood would soften the hierarchical principle. In his opinion, the judgment of an ecumenical council reached by means of free discussion was of divine origin. The unanimity of its decisions guaranteed truth. Only the Church in its entirety was infallible in questions of faith. Philosophical speculation thus became concrete political theory. Cusanus provided historical examples to demonstrate his position that a Church council had supremacy over the pope. He also argued, entirely in the spirit of his conciliar theory, that what ailed the Empire could be healed by an assembly at which the prince-electors, cities, universities, clergy, and nobility all had a say. A consensus would emerge in the end.

In Cusanus's theory, horizontal power springs from natural right. The consensus of bishops authorizes the position of the pope, just as secular power can only be justified by the consensus of citizens. Following Marsilius of

Padua, he also quotes the maxim that what touches all should be approved by all. The same Cusanus who conceived of a universe full of angels and demons, therefore, also belongs in the prehistory of democratic theory. "In the people," he marvels, "all powers, spiritual and temporal, are latent in potency."[47] Over time, this zealous conciliarist—he realized that the Donation of Constantine was a forgery at about the same time as Lorenzo Valla—became a supporter of the pope. The Council of Union, the most concrete step in the direction of harmony that could be conceived at the time, may have caused him to rethink his position. His about-face won him a cardinal's hat in 1448. Before that, he found time to write other monumental works of philosophy. They deal with the limits of human knowledge, the meaning of life and world history, and human nature.

Those looking for Burckhardt's Renaissance individual will find two things of relevance in Cusanus: first, insight into the subjective, necessarily perspectival viewpoint of human beings, and second, the idea that man is a second god who manifests himself in his works.[48] Adam began the practice of giving things names. By doing so, he intellectualized them, creating them a second time. Whereas God created the actual universe, human beings create a universe of concepts that are both symbols of things and their ideas at the same time. Cusanus viewed Christ as the greatest human being and the most perfect incarnation of the human race. The God-man was so linked with the divine in the highest unity that humankind became identical to the godhead. The unity of reality only disappears through the rational faculty, which thanks to its ability to generate concepts inscribes reality into genera and species; reality is destroyed by the piercing acuity of logic, carved up by reason which—although a finite image of the infinite reason of God[49]—cuts up this unity until it is beyond all recognition. Human reason can rise to see the all-embracing, absolute godhead. Yet it is only possible to understand what God is *not*—not what he is. Philosophy is thus merely "devout human conjecture about divine signs." That is the meaning of *docta ignorantia*, "learned ignorance."[50]

Cusanus's God was not simply the god of Plato, but it was not all that different either. Of doubtless Platonic and Pythagorean origin was his conviction that the ideal path to knowledge was mathematics. Thus, he became one of the intellectual pioneers of the scientific revolution. He was in contact with some of its other forerunners, such as Paolo dal Pozzo Toscanelli, a fellow student of his in Padua, and the astronomer Georg von Peuerbach (1423–1461), who taught in Vienna. In the tradition of Ramon Llull, he tried to square the circle and discovered that a circle conceived as infinite is identical to a triangle conceived as infinite. He also proposed thinking of time as a series of present moments, thus bringing together the infinite and the infinitesimally small. These thought experiments illustrate the chief problem that occupied Cusanus his entire life, namely the unification of total opposites that seems impossible to human understanding. The classic challenge for this brand of philosophy was the problem of the Trinity, i.e., the notion that it is three and one at the same time.

Cusanus identifies the desire to know—curiosity—as the God-given impulse of the human mind.[51] As a thinker who occupied himself not only with infinity but also with concrete nature, he favored a return to focusing on individual experience. It alone could provide access to what really existed. In his view, the study of the universe through what was visible to the eye and ascertainable by reason led to the knowledge of God. In all being, the highest divine being was to be found as the primary cause. The truth is not obscure; rather, as Cusanus said at the end of his life, it cries out in the streets.[52] A theological impetus was now given to empirical research with more incisive arguments than ever before. Cusanus formulated what it should look like in his dialogue *On Experiments with Weights*, his manifesto for a new science. He seeks to weigh and measure things, determine fall velocities, and even discover the relationship between a bell's ring tone and its weight. In short, he seeks to know everything that is knowable, *omne scibile*.[53] By measuring his world, man shows that he is himself the measure of all things; and these things can be perceived because a good God unfolds himself in them.[54]

Earth moves—in this case, the eye cannot be trusted.[55] Cusanus was driven to this dramatic thesis by speculation about the concept of infinity, in which alone all opposites are eliminated. Only God can combine both rest and motion. Only God is absolute—not the universe, which is not endless but rather only without boundaries. Thus, it cannot contain anything that is absolutely at rest, neither Earth nor the other heavenly bodies. Cusanus illustrates these spectacular ideas—we are in the age of images—with a painted *icona* of God whose gaze seems to follow viewers wherever they go; only the image itself is at rest. It was not observation and calculation that brought Cusanus to his insight into the relativity of all motion and thus to the claim that Earth is not at rest. It was the product of a concept of God that was more sublime than the notions of all his predecessors, and that was based on astute philosophical argumentation. Cusanus's cosmology was the fruit of theology, not science. This view in no way entailed a devaluation of humankind or of Earth, even though it stripped them of their place in the middle of the universe. For

Cusanus's intellectualized God was everywhere and nowhere, always omnipresent and thus always equally close to man.

Cusanus helped the discursive revolution achieve new breakthroughs.[56] He had cultivated Socratic doubt. When it came to Aristotle, however, he threw down the gauntlet—not merely at his natural philosophy but also at Aristotle the logician, launching a bold attack on the fortress of the "law of non-contradiction." He urged both the drawing and the expansion of boundaries, and he prepared a theological foundation for a new cosmology. He was the first to explode the crystalline spheres of the fixed stars that, according to traditional belief, encompassed the universe. It was crucial that Cusanus—not just anyone, but a cardinal of the Roman Church—expanded the horizon for impartial reasoning and experimentation, and that his thought, which an ungenerous mind might accuse of pantheism,[57] was even *possible*.

Understanding the Causes of Things: The Return of Epicurus

How different, how free and grand is Cusanus's vision of man compared to the one bemoaned by Innocent III: conceived in sin, made of dust and slime, the product of an "unclean seed"![58] Against the pope's devastating view, two humanists of Cusanus's day raised their voices. The first was Bartolomeo Facio, employed at Alfonso's court in Naples. He was followed by Giannozzo Manetti, the brilliant historian and ugly foe of the Jews who delivered the funeral oration at Leonardo Bruni's catafalque. Manetti's *On the Dignity and Excellence of Man* is a response to Facio, who had promoted the contemplative over the active life, and to Innocent III as well. The Florentine humanist considers the body to be anything but potential worm food. Rather it is a splendid artwork of the Creator and the crown of his creation, wisely constructed from the wall-like nose between the eyes to the thumbs on each hand. Manetti views man as created in God's image and likeness, indeed as divine, as a second creator of the world which has been prepared for him as well as of nature and history,[59] as a sculptor, painter, and architect, as a poet, scholar, and wise man—destined to contemplate his God and to gaze up at the stars. Here we see the "Renaissance man," a fictional character largely invented in the nineteenth century, in his full glory. Human beings are destined to live happily in a beautiful world, not condemned to march a dull pilgrimage to death.

Yet such celebrations of humanity do not simply express the prevailing mood of the time. As usual, things are more complicated. The tradition of contempt for the world continued in parallel, unabated. Poggio Bracciolini not only wrote the *Facetiae*, light-hearted and often erotic short stories. He also composed a long dialogue on the suffering of humankind, which he portrayed as subject to the capricious rule of the dark power of fate.[60] The very first artwork in linear perspective, Masaccio's *Trinity* fresco, includes a skeleton with the following *memento mori* caption, "I once was what you are now, and what I am you will one day be." Flashy self-assurance, the desire for glory, intoxication with beauty, and the yearning for knowledge are only one facet of the fifteenth century. The age's essential characteristic, however, was the ever-expanding horizon of the grand dialogue.

At the same time as some people wandered through the gleaming world of the Platonic ideas, others—and this distinguished the culture of Europe from that of other places—discussed a philosophy that embraced a hard materialism. This development was triggered by Poggio's discovery in Fulda of the didactic poem *De rerum natura* (*On the Nature of Things*) by Titus Lucretius Carus (ca. 97–55 BC). A far cry from the Christian disgust for the world on the one hand and the sublime metaphysics of light on the other, it transmitted the first profound knowledge of the teachings of Epicurus. Up to that point, they were only known in the form of scattered quotations found especially in Cicero, Seneca, and the Church Fathers. Now Epicurean thought could be viewed intact, cast in verse. What was this philosophy all about, which sprung from Democritus's teachings about nature and was one of the extreme poles of Greek thought?

Lucretius enshrined the essence of his thought in about 7,400 hexameters of the highest literary quality.[61] One need only read the opening verses, a hymn to the goddess of love that evokes Botticelli's *Birth of Venus* and *Primavera*.

> Life-stirring Venus, Mother of Aeneas and of Rome,
> Pleasure of men and gods, you make all things beneath the dome
> Of sliding constellations teem, you throng the fruited earth
> And the ship-freighted sea—for every species comes to birth
> Conceived through you, and rises forth and gazes on the light.
> The winds flee from you, Goddess, your arrival puts to flight
> The clouds of heaven. For you, the crafty earth contrives sweet flowers,
> For you, oceans laugh, the skies grow peaceful after showers,
> Awash with light.

The poet portrays Epicurus as the conqueror of religion, the abominable tyrant of human life.[62] One can imagine what effect *De rerum natura* had on an age that was accustomed to mocking monks and viewing Rome's popes as deeply flawed individuals—and in which, at the same time, sinful worms trembled fearfully and penitently in the face of death and the Last Judgment. As Epicurus and Lucretius taught, gods did exist. They were immortal and lived in eternal bliss, but they did not interfere in human affairs. To place one's hopes in them was, therefore, as misguided as it was to fear them.[63] Accordingly, Lucretius also derided the terrifying fairy tales of "fortunetellers," i.e., priests, whose horrors religion used to confound life. His aim was "to unknot / The mind from the tight strictures of religion" by studying nature and its character.[64]

And thus, the poem turns to cosmology. Nothing is created from nothing; there is only the void and atoms, which exist below the threshold of human perception. The number of forms they can take is finite, but there is an infinite number of each kind of atom. Their interplay, not determined by any higher power, is the cause for the diversity of natural phenomena. As letters join together according to rules to form words, thus atoms combine according to laws that, in principle, can be grasped by human learning—although Lucretius admits that he does not know them. In his view, the universe is infinite and full of an infinite number of inhabited worlds. Like Cusanus's cosmos, therefore, it has no center. Lucretius considers it obvious that the universe was not created by gods. Why, indeed, would the blessed give up their easy life to create the world? The mere fact that the world is so imperfect, full of suffering, populated by savage animals, and pervaded by plagues negates the notion that it is a work of divine creation. In this world of particles flowing through the void, in which gods play no essential role, human will is free. No providence determines human fate. What we call mind and soul, Lucretius considers integral, physical parts of the body like hands and feet. Thus, the soul is mortal and death meaningless, since thought and sensation die with the body. Above all it is the fear of the terrors of the underworld that Lucretius considers a result of mere fairy tales. There is no life after death for him. This world is what matters. His poem focuses in depth on the senses, especially the pains and pleasures of love.

In the fifth book, Lucretius provides an explanation for how human societies, forms of technology, and cities may have come into being. He dispenses with primeval cultural heroes, as well as with demons and fabulous creatures like chimeras and centaurs. In his view, it was no Prometheus who brought fire to humankind but rather a bolt of lightning. Language developed like words do from a baby's babbling, and all cultural refinement was achieved through writing and experience. The idea of powerful gods only provides causes for catastrophes and helps to explain the laws of nature. In a tour de force of enlightened argumentation, Lucretius demonstrates the absurdity of the belief that Jupiter punishes the unjust with lightning. Why, he asks, does lightning randomly strike barren places, and why are criminals not struck right after committing their crimes?[65]

The notion that Epicurus equated happiness with unrestrained gluttony and carnal desire is nothing but a vile invention of his Christian opponents. As Lucretius writes in a famous passage of his poem:

> Even at the very moment of having, the raging tide
> Of desire tosses lovers this way and that. They can't decide
> What to enjoy first with hand or eye—so closely pressing
> What they long for, that they hurt the flesh by their possessing,
> Often sinking teeth in lips, and crushing as they kiss,
> Since what the lovers feel is not some pure and simple bliss.

In Lucretius's view, desire can never be entirely fulfilled, and thus the sexual act is consummated again and again.[66]

This philosophy knows no absolutes like Plato's ideas. As it teaches, being is *in* things. History, an endless series of growth and decay, has no purpose. The point of all earthly travail is to live a good life. Epicurus called the desirable state of being *ataraxia*, i.e., imperturbability or equanimity. It entails freedom from passions and compulsion, from fear and pain. To achieve this tranquility of soul, he recommended "living unnoticed," i.e., living a private life aloof from politics and its dangers. Lucretius depicts the philosopher as one who observes others in dangerous waters from his own position on dry land—not with *Schadenfreude* but with the happy knowledge that he has maintained a safe distance from the chaos of worldly affairs.

> But there is nothing sweeter than to dwell in towers that rise
> On high, serene and fortified with teachings of the wise.[67]

At this point, Epicurus's thought coincides with that of Stoicism and Christianity. Thus, Lorenzo Valla could attempt to combine his teachings with Christian ethics.[68] In his *On the True and False Good*, a dialogue finished in 1434, *pleasure* goes from being the whore of chaste virtues to their master. Pleasure and not some anemic "virtue" appears as the powerful driver of all striving, whether it aims at mental or physical achievements. In particular, it leads to self-preservation. False purity, chastity, martyrdom, and even suicide in the service of virtue—all this is questionable for Valla. Especially dubious are those who call on others to die for their country. Ultimately, the dead have nothing from their glory; the benefit actually goes to the living, those who send the glorious to their death. Pleasure, i.e., joy in what is delightful, beautiful, and useful, has a place in life, according to Valla. And thus, in agreement with Epicurus, pleasure is to be countenanced in the body as well. But the *true* Good—now the dialogue enters religious territory—will only be achieved in heaven. Good for its own sake does not exist. Only that which leads to the highest beatitude is good. Christian charity, Good, and pleasure, "joyful movement of the mind and sweet contentment of the body,"[69] are one and the same. Not philosophy but rather faith and faith alone is the standard and the goal of all pleasure. Therefore, only a life lived in Christian charity can be happy and thus called "pleasurable."

When Valla wrote his dialogue, the Lucretius manuscript discovered by Poggio was supposedly still lying safely in Niccoli's library. In his later writings, Valla no longer dared to publicly display his interest in Epicurus. It may have been independent of Poggio's find. Clearly, though, the time had come to engage with Epicurus's teachings. Up to that point, the materialist philosopher suspected of atheism had been persona non grata. Dante roasted him in his *Inferno* in one of the flaming sarcophaguses reserved for heretics.[70] Now, however, as the Quattrocento proceeded, Epicurus and his poet Lucretius were discussed—first in the heartland of Christianity, Italy, and then all over Europe.[71] There is no clearer sign of how much freedom had now been carved out for secular thought. Truly astonishing is the fact that *De rerum natura* was never put on the Index of Forbidden Books, a product of the confessional struggles of the sixteenth century.

The first copy was made by Niccolò Niccoli. All in all, over fifty manuscripts are extant. Printed editions soon followed, usually accompanied by due warnings and claims of dissociation in forwards. The most important thing that could be learned from the poem had already been put in a nutshell by Virgil in a famous verse of his Georgics:

> Happy, who had the skill to understand
> Nature's hid causes, and beneath his feet
> All terrors cast, and death's relentless doom,
> And the loud roar of greedy Acheron.[72]

To understand the causes of things, to observe the world as it is without fear of a vengeful God—this mission was bequeathed to modern Europe by Lucretius. Ariosto, Tasso, Montaigne, and Shakespeare were inspired by it. Its influence extended to the philosophy of Nietzsche. Once God and his angels were dispensed with as movers of the universe, as *De rerum natura* urges, the question of causality was raised with renewed urgency. Yet the cosmology and theory of atoms outlined in the epic poem would have to wait until the late sixteenth century to have a broader impact.

Alberti: Window on the World

The names Lucretius and Cusanus represent two contrary intellectual worlds. In the philosophy of the cardinal from Kues (who admired the ancient poet briefly in his youth), human beings are in absolute proximity to God, but in Epicurean thought they are totally irrelevant. Cusanus's philosophy of a universe pacified by concordance is opposed to Epicurus's abysmal ocean of matter, in which everything is in flow and what we call "being" is an accidental interplay of agglomerated atoms. *De rerum natura* did not unleash an earthquake, however. Lucretius could be coped with by treating him as a poet or, as Valla did, incorporating him into a Christian worldview. Traditional theology and Aristotelian philosophy remained unaffected for a while. But for the first time, European thought encompassed the cosmos of modern physics, which ranges from the smallest of all things, the atom, all the way to the stars and beyond. Furthermore, secularism gained more territory. The terrain could be obscene, like in Poggio's *Facetiae*, whose jokes were mostly about sex, lustful monks, cuckolded and impotent husbands, or men with mighty members. Then again, the landscape could be overgrown with thickets like the soil of Rome, where the same Poggio hunted for ancient inscriptions.

The stony remains of antiquity captivated more and more humanists. Poggio, for example, may have encountered the apostolic secretary Biondo Flavio (1392–1463) during his explorations.[73] This was still an age of insatiable collecting—it was not only Rome's palaces that were filled with ancient statues and reliefs, gems and coins—of sketching what one saw and copying what one read. Biondo endeavored to record Rome's ancient ruins and its Christian churches one neighborhood at a time. His *Italia illustrata*, based on authors like Pliny, Strabo, and Ptolemy, expanded the survey to all of Italy; the idea of combining history and geography was new. With his unfinished history of Italy from the fall of the Roman Empire to the year 1441, he achieved posthumous fame as a predecessor of Gibbon, as the preserver of the memory of Roman greatness and standard-bearer of its renaissance. His widely read

Roma triumphans is a cultural history buttressed by countless primary sources and animated by a critical spirit, focusing on administration, military affairs, daily life, and so on. Biondo approached pagan religions with the understanding of the historian, not the zeal of a devout Christian. Furthermore, he can be numbered among the founders of historical linguistics; to explain the birth of the vernacular from Latin, he pointed to the "barbarian" invasions. He also intended to write a history of the Portuguese voyages of discovery in the Atlantic. This plan never came to fruition, but it did open up very new horizons.

At the same time, new vistas also appeared to those who set off in search of antiquity in its country of origin, Greece. One of the first to describe it was the Florentine priest Cristoforo Buondelmonti (1386–ca. 1430). He set down his impressions in his *Liber insularum Archipelagi* (*Book of Islands*) as well as in a letter to Niccolò Niccoli about Crete. There he recounts meeting a Venetian who was in the habit of reading Dante in a garden full of ancient statues. He tells of ruins and statues, to which he ascribes all manner of allegorical meanings. One of the manuscripts he discovered was Horapollo's *Hieroglyphica*, a late antique interpretation of Egyptian hieroglyphics. Once again, the key to primeval mysteries seemed to have been found. The *Hieroglyphica* became one of the most studied texts of the Renaissance.

A critical spirit rose anew. Was a grave on the island of Chios really that of Homer? Buondelmonti declines to decide the issue.[74] The shrine was clearly a popular tourist attraction. One of those who stood reverently before it was the merchant Ciriaco de' Pizzecolli of Ancona (1391–ca. 1455). Like Biondo, he was an archaeologist and a preserver of antiquity. Somewhat clumsily but tirelessly, he sketched and preserved a great many ancient remains that have long since been lost in the original.[75] Often traveling under an imminent Turkish threat, he reached the Aegean islands, Constantinople, and even Damascus and Cairo. All the while, he drew and described the structure of walls, copied inscriptions, sketched statues, and collected gems, statuettes, and coins. He served Pope Eugenius IV as a guide to Roman antiquities. His drawings provided artists with models for original works. He was an enthusiast, tempted by his engagement with antiquity to curious cultural amalgamations. For example, he invoked both God and Mercury as protectors on his travels, and he claimed to hear Muses and Nereids singing at sea. This Odysseus of Ancona was an outstanding representative of the new art of travel, practiced not (or not only) for commercial profit or spiritual salvation. In the sixteenth century, it would spawn its own literary genre, the *ars apodemica*, which provided useful advice for travelers, everything from medical tips to systematic strategies for getting the most out of sightseeing. Travel became an experience in its own right.[76]

During Ciriaco's lifetime, the humanist project took on new dimensions with regard to intellectual reflection and the systematic exploration of antique remains in the person of one of its principal exponents: Leon Battista Alberti (1404–1472). "I so praise his genius that I would compare no one with him," his fellow humanist Lapo da Castiglionchio said of him. "His genius is of this sort: to whichever area of study he puts his mind, he easily and quickly excels the others."[77] This assessment was not without basis. If anyone ever somewhat resembled Nietzsche's imagined universal human being, it was Leon Battista. Born the illegitimate son of a Florentine exile in Genoa, he studied law but earned his living with a benefice and a post among the apostolic abbreviators, civil servants who prepared bulls, briefs, and other written material for the Curia. In a biographical portrait of him that he himself probably authored, he is described as excelling in everything.[78] Endowed with an iron will, he is at once a scholar, painter, sculptor, javelin hurler, musician, and an accomplished mountain climber to boot. As a rider, the most spirited horses tremble beneath him. He even claims for himself the ability to tell the future. At the tender age of twenty, when his study of law had literally made him sick, he recovered by writing a drama and throwing himself into scientific and mathematical studies. A master of the art of the bon mot, he fit in well in his adopted home of Tuscany. The biography contains pages of witty sayings after the manner of Sachetti and Poggio.

Alberti's physiognomy is known from a medal that he himself probably cast, a profile image based on portraits of ancient rulers. It features his emblem, a disembodied, winged eye floating in the air. It is the eye of the "assiduous inquirer" into everything that pertains to the mind, manual crafts, and the arts. As Alberti writes in the Vita, it takes extraordinary pleasure in observing things.[79] His enigmatic motto, Quid tum—"What now?"—may be a firm prompt to himself to always keep thinking. And that is what Leon Battista Alberti did, from one book to the next. He cannot be tidily summed up as the author of a clear system of thought. Rather, he appears to us, as the humanist Cristoforo Landino (1426–1499) wittily characterized him, as a "chame-leon."[80] His oeuvre, which treats a vast array of topics, cannot be reduced to a pithy description. It shines in all the colors of the rainbow. Alberti was a gossip, a satirist, a serene advisor, then a deep-digging archaeologist, a sedulous collector, a meticulous orderer. He wrote elegies, eclogues, canzoni, love poetry, and a praise of the fly inspired by Lucian, De musca. At the behest of Cardinal

Prospero Colonna, he attempted to raise two ancient boats from the bottom of Lake Nemi south of Rome. He failed in the difficult undertaking, but it did spur him to write a work on Roman shipbuilding, the *Navis*. His satire *Canis*, a praise of his recently deceased dog, is modeled on ancient panegyrics. The dog is a veritable marvel: of the noblest lineage, clever, conscientious, and humble, but also highly educated and eloquent. After doing his duty each day, he sings to the moon at night. Like a saintly monk, he is free of the vice of gambling, never drinks wine, runs without shoes in summer and snow, and is always dressed the same.[81]

His book *Della famiglia* (*On the Family*) heralds similar virtues. It mirrors the perspective of the Florentine middle classes, the intellectual reservoir of Renaissance culture, discussing everyday life, marriage, friendship, and household management. The focus on modest urban existence then gives way to a countryside villa, where peace of mind dwells amidst greenery, flowers, sweet smells, and the singing of birds. The serene location is the inveterate object of yearning for the nervous intellectual, who feels torn between his civic duty to lead an active life and the monastic ideal of contemplation. This was a popular topic. In Landino's *Camaldolese Disputations*, Leon Battista takes the part of defending philosophical reflection and, thus, the contemplative life.

Most of his writings reveal a humanist who marvels at worldly things in order to then investigate and measure them. Even before Biondo, he wrote a precise description of ancient Rome. His treatise *De componendis cyfris* is an introduction to encrypting texts. His *Mathematical Games* may have entertained Mantua's courtly society.[82] Like Cusanus, he tried his hand at squaring the circle. He held forth about raising horses and agriculture and, defender of the *volgare* as he was, wrote a Tuscan grammar. The pleasure he takes in novelty and speculating about paths to equanimity is counterbalanced by insecurity and doubt, a deep pessimism, and caustic sarcasm. His novel *Momus* has a shady hero: the god of slander, the quibbler of all quibblers who instigates atheism and other mischief amongst earthly beings.[83] It is a cynical burlesque of the posturing of vain philosophers. It shines the light on risible deities and masked human wickedness. In the end, the heavenly gods flee a world that has lost its moral compass and its ideals.

Alberti's *Intercoenales*, or *Dinner Pieces*, written about the same time as *Della famiglia*, is another imitation of Lucian. It reveals a different author than the vain, self-confident writer of the *Vita*. In one episode, the shade of the recently deceased Neophronus, whose name means "newly wise," meets that of his "wily" old friend Polytropus, who asks how humanity is getting along up there.[84] They're all "mad," is the answer. Neophronus has a bitter experience when his soul, only just released from his body, undertakes one last flight to his family. Instead of mourning, they are happy that he is dead, and his wife is already lying in bed with the estate manager. Hypocrisy, greed, and treachery are everywhere. Doubts about human nature and the frail mind's capacity to withstand fortune set the tone of the ironic, often bitter *Incercoenales*, whereas *Della famiglia* had a different ring to it (there, hardy virtue was still a match for fate). As Eugenio Garin pointed out, this pessimistic motif remained characteristic of the epoch.[85]

More than any of his great predecessors, Alberti appears to us a secular thinker. The biographical self-portrait never once mentions God. That would have been unthinkable before. The works to which Leon Battista owes his greatest fame deal with thoroughly secular topics: art theory, with a focus on sculpture, painting, and architecture. His discussion of sculpture—*De statua*—is utterly without precedent, and his *On Painting* is also the very first systematic treatment of its subject. *On the Art of Building* has but a single forerunner: Vitruvius. It is one of the most important treatises on architecture ever written.

The treatise on painting offers the first-ever theory of linear perspective. Using the theory of pyramid-shaped visual rays, Alberti developed a new definition of the picture: he defined its surface as the cross-section of the visual pyramid. It is like "an open window through which the subject to be painted is seen."[86] Alberti wanted to portray an objective world. He was an Aristotelian through and through; he put stock in experience rather than dreaming of ideas. In contrast to Cennini, who began his treatise with an invocation to God, the Virgin, and all the saints, Alberti opened his work with an homage to mathematicians and a demand for the autonomy of the painter's point of view.[87]

Furthermore, Alberti was a classicist, a man of the middle and of moderation. Diversity and variety should rule, he argued, but not excessively; no more than nine or ten people should crowd into a picture.[88] Millefleur tapestries and overripe splendor were the opposite of this ideal, which took the rules of rhetoric and applied them to art. The painter should not chatter, as it were, but rather speak in a measured tone. Rhetorical principles were also behind the suggestion to avoid hard transitions, as well as the call to observe *decorum*—decency, propriety—and provide variety, *varietas*. With Alberti, what we call "Renaissance aesthetics" begins to take shape.

In addition to rhetoric, Euclid's geometry and Fibonacci's arithmetic helped create beautiful proportions. By mobilizing the liberal arts in this way for his art theory, Alberti elevated the work of the painter and the sculptor to a higher plane: he turned what they did into a science. He also brought imagination into play. The highest law was to imitate nature, of course. But it was still necessary to arrange what one found, to choose the best from what nature provided, and to combine everything into a harmonious whole. Thus, the painter becomes more than just an "ape of nature." The same Alberti who despairs about human potential in the *Dinner Pieces* asserts that the artist can be considered a "second god," *un altro iddio*, since he is able to make something never seen before, to create whole new worlds.[89]

The virtues of *On the Art of Building* stem in part from the fact that its author himself worked as an architect and an architectural consultant. He gave Matteo de' Pasti advice for the design of the facade of the Tempio Malatestiano in Rimini, and in Florence he designed the facades of the Palazzo Rucellai and the Basilica of Santa Maria Novella (Fig. 30, p. 417). In Mantua he was involved in the construction of Sant'Andrea and San Sebastiano, and he may have had a hand in the ducal palace in Urbino. Although more familiar with ancient architecture than anyone else in his day, he was never content to simply reconstruct buildings of the past. He constantly used the inspiration he drew from ancient ruins to create new things. Other Renaissance architects did the same. No one built exact replicas of ancient structures.

Alberti's treatise on architecture contains a great deal of practical information about building, including the first precise description of the ancient orders. At its core is a theory of the beautiful. Of paramount importance was that a building's parts have symmetry. They should be in the proper proportion to one another and to the whole. "Beauty"—for Alberti, that meant the harmony of all component parts "according to a definite number, outline, and position."[90] The metaphor of harmony is justified, as Alberti indeed has music in mind here. As Pythagoras knew, its harmonies, such as the octave and the third, can be expressed in lengths of string and, thus, in numbers. Pythagorean thought provided Alberti's architectural aesthetics—and thus that of other architects from Francesco di Giorgio to Palladio—with a metaphysical foundation. Euphonious musical proportions and their architectural equivalents ultimately reflected the proportions of the harmoniously composed Ptolemaic universe. Their beauty, therefore, alluded to the eternal, literally "heavenly" beautiful music of the celestial spheres and thus to the art of God.

Beauty was economical in Alberti's view. He accorded with Vitruvius in defining it as regular proportionality, as a "reasoned harmony of the individual parts," as *concinnitas*. A building must be constructed—the definition from

Aristotle's *Nicomachean Ethics* can be applied to other arts as well—such that "nothing may be added, taken away, or altered, but for the worse."[91] What is meant by *varietas*, "variety," is explained by Alberti using the example of the architectural orders. They correspond to the variety found in nature, next to geometry the second authority of his aesthetics. All ornament merely complements the crystalline beauty of a structure with "auxiliary light." Alberti's buildings and paintings are in no way oriented towards their function alone. On the other hand, he argued, if they were not designed to be practical and useful, they could not be elegant. Beauty created in this way would unleash in the viewer feelings that were very much of this world: inner excitement and the very pleasure that Lorenzo Valla had just loosed from its Epicurean foundation.

At the very end of the fifteenth century, Alberti's geometric aesthetics were expanded upon by the Franciscan friar Luca Pacioli (ca. 1445–1514/17).[92] His treatise *Divina proportione* included a discussion of the golden ratio, which had first been derived by Euclid. The fact that Pacioli, in his 1494 *Summa* of mathematics, provided the first description of double-entry bookkeeping reminds us of the liaison between merchant rationality and Renaissance aesthetics. This accounting practice was probably invented in Genoa around 1340, but it did not become standard in northern Europe until the seventeenth century.[93]

A Knight Tilting at Modernity

Somewhere in northern Italy, ca. 1432. The painter engaged by Oswald von Wolkenstein may have learned his craft from Antonio di Pucci, called Pisanello. At any rate, he understood his art and knew how to paint "according to nature." Accordingly, he concealed nothing in his painting: not the fat double chin and certainly not the closed right eyelid, whose weakness was due to a congenital disease (Fig. 31, p. 419). Wolkenstein had his portraitist clearly portray the badges of honor that marked the culmination of an eventful life: the Order of the Jar and the Griffin, a dignity received from Eleanor of Aragon, and the exclusive Hungarian Order of the Dragon, which Emperor Sigismund awarded him at the Diet of Nuremberg. The full, carefully crimped hair of the hale gentleman in his mid-fifties is covered by an exquisite, fur-lined cap. The gold brocade robe also has fur trim. Oswald von Wolkenstein had money, and he clearly thought a great deal of himself. His likeness is the first portrait of a German-language poet ever painted.[94]

The man who seems to be winking at us from half a millennium away was a witness to the epoch we are now traversing. He was born around 1376 at Schöneck Castle in the Puster Valley in South Tyrol, in the heavily wooded alpine region around the pass between north and south. As the second-born son, he had to seek his fortune abroad. The battlefields of Europe were his school. He set off at the age of ten as the squire of a mounted soldier and later continued his travels as a merchant. It became his dream to follow in the footsteps of the poets and singers he met on his journeys from castle to castle and city to city. Oswald must have been a delightful guest, as he was very entertaining. He could "play the fiddle, bang the drum, and blow the pipes,"[95] knew a lot about drinking—"Mr. Innkeeper, we're thirsty. Bring wine! Bring wine! Bring wine!"[96]—and even more about the young women whose "white," "dainty hands" fascinated him.[97] During one sleepless night, he was consumed with yearning for the body of his wife, the beautiful Gret:

> Her mouth keeps me up at all hours
> with a sensuous lament.

Thus, he hopes that she'll soon do everything she can "to make the bed frame creak."[98] What desire!

> Mouth kisses mouth,
> Tongue on tongue, breast on breast . . . [99]

Even if we strip away the poetic license and the tall tales, these verses still provide us with as vivid a portrait of Oswald as the picture of him that graces the frontispiece of Liederhandschrift B, a manuscript in the University Library in Innsbruck. The codex contains songs about heaven and hell, the transience of all earthly things, and the morning that all too quickly ends a night spent in female companionship. We find verses about the burdens of marriage, lovesickness and desire, songs about war and, time and again, of gay days in May. Above all, the knightly poet writes about his journeys in all the cardinal directions, about all the places he claims, in many languages and with great eloquence, to have "gone adventuring" (*geabenteuert*).[100]

If we can believe his songs, he made it all the way to England, Scotland, and Sweden, and even reached Jerusalem. He participated in King Rupert's campaign against the Visconti. He also seems to have been among Henry the Navigator's soldiers when he captured the North African stronghold of Ceuta (pp. 467f.). Wolkenstein entered the service of King Sigismund quite early, visiting Portugal, Spain, and France as his diplomat. He also accompanied him to the Council of Constance. Praise of the city's beautiful women and laments about its expense pervade one of his poems:

> Just thinking of Constance on the lake
> makes my poor wallet ache.[101]

He fought against the Hussites, maybe against Venice as well. In 1432, we find him in Lombardy, where his portrait was probably painted. We meet him at the Council of Basel as a royal adviser.

The other half of this breathless life was spent in his homeland of Tyrol. There he had countless business dealings to attend to and feuds to contend with. For a time, he served the bishop of Brixen, where he owned a house. In 1417, he married a woman from a family highly placed in imperial politics, thus raising his rank. He joined the *Elefantenbund*, an alliance of noblemen against his own territorial lord, the Habsburg Duke Frederick IV of Austria. The duke was the embodiment of the fledgling monarchical state. He was a born enemy of the all-too-free-spirited nobility, which enjoyed the privileges of rule from castles and towers plastered to craggy cliffs. This old elite found itself in the vise grip of history. Mercenary armies scattered their feudal levies. The number of their children increased from one generation to the next, but their territory did not. It had to be divided again and again. Ever-smaller fields and forests had to finance tournaments and hunts, minstrels and mistresses.

Some townspeople had long possessed more ducats than the proud knight in his drafty castle. In one of Wolkenstein's songs, a burgher explains the situation to his counterpart, the courtier:

> About tournaments and fencing
> I never knew a damn.
> My moneybags are full.

Inside I place my hand
and pull out gold, silver, and gems,
as much as I demand.[102]

Indeed, the ability to participate in tournaments was now the last reserve of noble privilege. To distinguish themselves from the rich townspeople, many nobles had to go deep into debt. Thus, Oswald also bans usurers to the sixth chamber of Hell, where they are afflicted by snakes and worms.[103] One alternative was to try one's luck in war or princely service as Wolkenstein did. Another was to make ends meet by banditry.

Violence was often not the last but the first remedy of politics. Sometimes it hid behind the right of waging feuds. Only in the sixteenth century did the state have the strength to abolish this practice. By increasing legal certainty, by suppressing feuds and Vehmic courts, Frederick IV also limited the nobility's freedom a bit. The state, which by now had grown into a juggernaut with its soldiers and bureaucrats, demanded to be fed. It insisted on more and more taxes and payments. The noble lords of shrinking territories sought to pass on the burden in turn, extorting every last penny from their peasants. We had occasion to observe this mechanism as a cause of the revolts of the previous century. Its fatal consequences would long be felt. This interplay of forces, hidden from contemporaries, was what harried Wolkenstein and landed him in bitter disputes over inheritance, land, and money. Once he stole ducats and jewelry from his older brother and almost died in a fight over the plunder. Although he only inherited a third of the castle left by his father, Burg Hauenstein, he hogged all its revenues. Again, it came to a quarrel. His enemies took him prisoner, tortured him, and ultimately handed him over to the duke. In the end, he had to submit to his lord. "I have lived forty less two years long," he dryly observed, "with my raving and rampaging, poetry and song."[104]

Like others, Oswald hoped for assistance from the king and his prince's other competitors. But their arm was not long enough to spare him all his hardship. As a *Freischöffe*, or "free judge," i.e., as a member of a Vehmic court, he tried to go his own way legally.[105] He gives a face to the epoch's bitter struggle over what form the state should take: would it be a strong monarchy or represent the interests of the estates? This conflict was behind the Hussite Wars as well as the formation of noble alliances in France and leagues of cities in the Empire.

The dauntless Wolkenstein faced the challenges of the day as best he could. Yet there was less and less space for men like him in the age—in his view a "sick age" (*kranke Zeit*)[106]—of the consolidating state. We shall now let him rest in peace in his grave in Neustift Monastery near Brixen, where he was buried in 1445. As a poet, he was an exceptional figure, but he was very much a man of his time in his other guise: as one of the last knights who rode out in the twilight of medieval government to wage hopeless war on the colossus of the early modern state.

Beyond Italy: The Origins of European Humanism

Oswald von Wolkenstein's world seems untouched by antiquity and the Renaissance, even though he traveled far and wide and one of the languages he claimed to speak was Latin. Only slowly did the *studia humanitatis* spread across Italy's borders. The first traces of its arrival can be found in Avignon and in Paris, the bastion of theology.[107] A pioneering center was the College of Navarre in Paris's Latin Quarter, founded by Joan I of Navarre (1273–1305), the wife of Philip the Fair.[108] Illustrious names indicate the intellectual depth of the college, which by the end of the century had become the most important in the University of Paris. For a time, its rector was Nicole Oresme, whom we already encountered as one of the most original thinkers of the fourteenth century. One of his successors was Pierre d'Ailly (1350–1420/21), another powerful mind. The son of a wealthy butcher, he became chancellor of the university and ultimately a cardinal.[109] Along with his student and successor as chancellor, Jean Gerson (1363–1429), he was one of the political architects who helped to end the Papal Schism in Constance. His theological writings attempted to resolve the tensions between reason and faith, between the power of the stars—whose influence he saw in all earthly existence—and free will. One must not imagine d'Ailly as being all too secular. In his later years, plagued by apocalyptic moods, he wrote mystical and ascetic works.[110] His *Imago mundi* (1410) compared the shape of the Earth to an apple. He arrived at this view thanks to his study of ancient and medieval sources. A printed edition of this book would end up in Columbus's hands, where it would feature in a chapter of world history (p. 477).

Neither d'Ailly nor Gerson was a product of the *studia humanitatis*, but both were open to the new ideas coming out of their Romance neighbor Italy. Gerson, who in his youth wrote Petrarchan poetry, once intimated that the time was past when France lacked great historians and lagged behind Italy.[111] In the dispute over *The Romance of the Rose*, he took the side of his "intellectual friend" Christine de Pizan.[112] His ambitions as an educator seem somewhat humanistic. His five hundred writings include numerous theological treatises and guides to moral behavior; they were widely read.[113]

Most French humanists were in the service of the crown and the high aristocracy, as well as bishops and the papal curia in Avignon. They apprenticed themselves to Ciceronian Latin and sprinkled a few Greek words in their texts. They studied in Italy or under Italians who—like Ambrogio dei Migli of Milan, a retainer of Duke Louis of Orléans—had come to the country in search of sinecures. Jean Muret, secretary to a cardinal in Avignon, composed his *De contemptu mortis* around 1388. It was one of the first humanistic texts written outside Italy.[114] Boccaccio and above all Petrarca prompted French authors to imitate them and soon—accompanied by patriotic undertones—to gainsay them. Classical authors like Cicero, Plutarch, Valerius Maximus, and Seneca were quickly translated into French. A book-loving jurist at the court of Charles VI, Jean Lebègue (1368–1457), translated Sallust's *Conspiracy of Catiline* and provided miniaturists with a precise description of how the scenes should be painted.[115]

French humanism took on clearer outlines with Jean de Montreuil, educated at the College of Navarre. He was a supporter of *The Romance of the Rose* and thus an adversary of Gerson in the dispute with Christine de Pizan.[116] During a military campaign in Italy—it was related to Louis of Anjou's claim to the Neapolitan throne—Jean became acquainted with Salutati in Florence; later, he met Leonardo Bruni. A small circle of intellectuals gathered around him in the last decade of the fourteenth century. They discussed Cicero, Virgil, and Ovid and argued about things such as Ambrogio dei Migli's supposed Epicureanism.[117] Like many of his companions, Jean expressed love for his homeland France. He praised his countrymen's courage and fomented hatred against the English. Anticipating Machiavelli, he saw history as ruled by fickle fortune. He fell victim to it in the end, one of the many killed during the Burgundians' sack of Paris in late May of 1418.

Times were hard. One wonders how Paris's literati found the peace and quiet to polish their translations, dialogues, and poems while the city was being ripped apart by Bourguignons and Armagnacs. The confusion of war is reflected repeatedly in the work of the most important poet of the time, Alain Chartier (1385–after 1430). He appears as a pessimistic patriot longing for peace.[118] Literary history knows him as the creator of *La Belle Dame sans Mercy*, whose protagonist would be a literary topos from then on: the heartless beauty who remains cool in the face of all courting. The melancholic Chartier was not a humanist in the literal sense of the term, but his poetry was deeply influenced by classical literature. Later generations viewed him as their master in the art of rhetoric and as a new Seneca.

Another master of rhetoric—Cicero's rhetoric—was the first Spanish humanist, the high aristocrat Enrique de Villena (ca. 1384–1434). He was the first to translate the *Divine Comedy* and the *Aeneid* into Castilian and Catalan. He authored a work on poetics as well as theological and medical writings, in addition to giving his views on the dangerous "evil eye" and, curiously, on the art of carving meat. In 1417, independently of Salutati's unfinished work of a decade earlier, he completed a treatise on the twelve labors of Hercules. In line with the art of biblical exegesis, he interpreted them allegorically, making the deeds of the "wise" demigod moral examples for people of all ranks. His interest in astrology and magic ultimately earned him a reputation as a kind of Spanish Dr. Faustus, devoted to the dark arts.[119] After his death, John II of Castile had a Dominican friar purge Enrique's library of all heretical and magical material.

The opposite approach to learning was taken by John's cousin, King Alfonso of Naples.[120] Around the same time, he issued a decree making it illegal to export books without approval. As he explained, they transmit the wisdom and knowledge of the ancients and "make them seem alive to us." Books are a treasury of the arts and sciences. They offer direction in everything related to human existence. Vibrant discussions of Virgil enlivened by refreshments took place at Alfonso's courts in Messina and Naples. The king was in the habit of refilling the reader's glass himself. Even on military campaigns, books were part of his retinue.

Meanwhile, the southern breeze blew north to England. Poggio Bracciolini had been a harbinger of humanist culture there. From 1418 to 1423, he was in the service of Henry Beaufort, bishop of Winchester. His sojourn did not make a deep impression on him, but it was useful to his career in the Curia.[121] Humanist ideas circulated in Normandy thanks to Cardinal Branda Castiglione (ca. 1360–1443) and other members of his family, who maintained relations with Italian humanists.[122] At the behest of Duke Humphrey of Gloucester (1390–1447), Branda's nephew Zanone searched for books by ancient authors while he was in Basel for the council. He also put his patron in touch with Italian humanists who helped to stock his library.

Gloucester, a son of Henry IV, brother of Henry V, and uncle of Henry VI, as well as a minor character in three of Shakespeare's history plays, was one of the founding figures of English humanism.[123] He surrounded himself with Italian secretaries, "agents" of humanism on English soil, and commissioned translations of Boccaccio's *On the Fates of Illustrious Men*, Plato's *Republic*, and Aristotle's *Politics*. In addition, he patronized the composition of a history of the Roman civil war, a biography of his regal brother, and a panegyric of his own military exploits. The point was to provide useful examples: history was to be a teacher to the heir to the throne.

A generation later, another manic collector of classical literature appeared: Sir John Tiptoft, Earl of Worcester (1427–1470]). A participant in the War of the Roses, he was one of the darkest figures of that gloomy time, a man of insatiable bloodlust. In the service of Edward IV, the first king of the House of York—a cadet line of the Plantagenets—he diminished the Lancastrian ranks, having his opponents impaled, quartered, and beheaded. In younger years the "Butcher of England" had studied in Italy, seeing there how beautiful illuminated manuscripts could be. His finely chiseled Latin orations impressed even the humanist Pope Pius II. Back on the island, he translated works by Caesar and Cicero into English. During a short Lancastrian restoration, the brutal bibliophile himself landed on the executioner's block.

In Germany, he had a more peace-loving predecessor in the physician, theologian, and priest Amplonius Rating (ca. 1365–1435), who assembled a library of about 4,500 works. Its catalog bears witness to a lively interest in the ancient and Arabic classics. In addition to Avicenna's *Canon*, Amplonius also possessed Ibn al-Haytham's discussion of optics.[124] One of the first agents of humanist learning in Germany was Peter Luder (ca. 1415–1472).[125] After studying in Heidelberg, this scholar of humble origins traveled through Italy. He stayed with Guarino in Ferrara and studied medicine in Padua. He found a patron in Venice's Doge Francesco Foscari and even won for himself a title of nobility. He claims to have sailed to Greece on a Venetian galley. Finally, he became a professor at his alma mater in Heidelberg. His inaugural lecture on July 15, 1456 sketches a humanist curriculum with a focus on rhetoric, poetry, and historiography. Guarino had provided him with his main themes. Luder claimed for himself the designation of being the first to carry the Muses to his homeland from their Italian heights.[126] In point of fact, he was preceded in that honor by Aeneas Sylvius Piccolomini (1405–1464), later Pope Pius II. Piccolomini's sojourn in Germany, and in particular his abundant correspondence with Germans, was of incomparable importance for the development of humanist culture in the "land of barbarians." He even provided tips on style to a clumsy Latinist, and thankfully his advice was taken.

Luder was so fascinated by antiquity that he named his son Virgilius. That the time was not yet ripe for a man like him, however, may be reflected in his life of wandering—from Heidelberg, he went to Erfurt and then to Leipzig, Basel, and Vienna. On the other hand, he always managed to find jobs and patrons. He had no lack of students and colleagues who shared his zeal for the "modern" Italian approach to learning, nor did he lack opponents. He regarded religion nonchalantly. When a theologian upbraided him about a joke he had made about the Trinity, he replied that he would readily accept a "quadrinity" if it kept him from being burned as a heretic.[127] During a second stay in Padua, he attained a doctorate in medicine, apparently as a way to earn his daily bread. His final days found him at the court of Duke Sigmund of Tyrol. A bundle of his poems, letters, orations, and histories has survived.

The First Academies, Poets in the Cities

Humanists gradually formed learned sodalities, such as the Accademia Romana of the archaeologist and philologist Giulio Pomponio Leto (1428–1498). Its more-or-less regular meetings can be imagined like the gatherings around Cardinal Orsini and Lorenzo Valla, with productions of ancient comedies and discussions about archaeological finds. Similarly informal were the origins of the Accademia Pontaniana in Naples. A circle of public officials, nobles, and clergy met regularly to engage in discussions about language and literature that tended to be characterized more by wit than learning. They often convened in public places, such as under the arcades of Philip of Anjou's palace.[128] Its *spiritus rector* was Antonio Beccadelli (1394–1471), a trained jurist known as *il Panormita*, i.e., "Antonio of Palermo." An earlier attempt to win Cosimo de' Medici's patronage failed miserably. The work he dedicated in 1425 to the Florentine banker, the *Hermaphroditus*, caused a scandal.[129] It is a work of pure pornography. Gigantic, erect phalluses, firm buttocks, and feces play a major role, and everyone sleeps with everyone. Cosimo burned the copy sent to him, and Eugene IV threatened readers of the text with excommunication. King Alfonso, however, was not deterred in supporting the Sicilian humanist, indeed in making him the architect of his foreign policy. After Panormita's death, his protégé Giovanni Pontano (1429–1503) took over the leadership of the sodality, which was then named the "Accademia Pontaniana" in his honor.[130] A native of Umbria, he was as influential at court as his predecessor, served as a diplomat, and wrote works of history, philosophy, astrology, and poetry. As a poet, he found wonderful words to describe the sorrows of a suffering lover, comparing them with the happy fate of the cicada:

The cicada spends his days
Among the leaves . . .
O happy in your birth,
In death still happier.[131]

Humanist sodalities also formed in German cities. The first gathered in Augsburg around the wealthy merchant and councilman Sigmund Gossembrot (1417–1493), who, like Luder, got acquainted with the intellectual world of Italy through travel. Nuremberg followed suit soon thereafter. It was no accident that imperial cities in southern Germany were the first to open up to Italian poetry and the study of antiquity pioneered on the peninsula. For their merchants had maintained close commercial relations with the south since the High Middle Ages. Many had traveled there to study. One of them, Heinrich Steinhöwel (1412–1482/83), a doctor in Esslingen and Ulm and then personal physician to Count Eberhard of Württemberg, attended the University of Padua. He translated works of Boccaccio and Aesop's fables, to which he appended a few of Poggio's erotic stories; it was a roaring success.[132] More chaste was the *Speculum vitae humanae* (*Mirror of Human Life*) by the Spanish theologian Rodrigo Sánchez de Arévalo, which Steinhöwel also translated into German.

In Esslingen, he found a kindred spirit in the Swiss Niklas von Wyle (ca. 1415–1479), who earned his living in the local chancery.[133] Niklas also worked as a painter. A portrait he doodled on a document now preserved in the Esslingen archives may be of himself. He gave Aeneas Sylvius Piccolomini two panel paintings and corresponded with him. He considered the future pope's style, steeped in ancient rhetoric, to be worthy of imitation. Therefore, he took pains to make it available to his fellows, printing Piccolomini's letters as models of the most elegant Latin. Niklas's *Translatzion oder Tütschungen* (*Translation, or Germanizations*) was meant as entertainment but was also supposed to convey the aura of the Latin original. It contained texts by Boccaccio and Petrarca, Piccolomini's *Tale of Two Lovers*, and Lucian's *Ass* (from Poggio's Latin version). Niklas decided to spare his German readers the sex scene contained in the latter work, in which a lustful woman consummates her desire with the four-legged creature.

His contemporary Albrecht von Eyb (1420–1475), a cathedral canon and jurist who lived in episcopal cities in Franconia, also focused on humor. He translated novellas by Boccaccio and comedies by Plautus. Eyb had studied in Italy like Steinhöwel and had risen to the rank of chamberlain under Pius II.

His praise of Bamberg initiated a German genre of civic panegyric. He landed a bestseller with his *Margarita poetica* (*Poetic Pearl*), a collection of ancient, humanistic, and patristic texts for household use. His *Ehebüchlein* (*Little Book on Marriage*), published in 1472, also found a wide readership. Sprinkled with quotations from ancient authors, it discusses infidelity and chastity, dowries, weddings, and parenting, ultimately praising the institution of marriage and women.

Luder and Gossembrot, Steinhöwel, Wyle, and Eyb were pioneers of classical and Italian culture. We should not forget, however, that at the same time a rich culture was also flourishing in German cities that, like Oswald von Wolkenstein's poetry, remained untouched by the classical spirit and *italianità*. Jakob Püterich von Reichertshausen (ca. 1400–1469), adviser to the Duke of Bavaria and a zealous collector of chivalric epics, announced defiantly that he loved the "*old* books." As for "the new ones"—and by that, he meant everything Italian, classical, humanistic—"I don't give them the time of day."[134] Many people besides Püterich read heroic stories, loved religious drama, and laughed at droll tales. One poet who wrote for the urban middle classes was the brass caster Hans Rosenplüt (ca. 1400–1460) of Nuremberg.[135] He inaugurated the poetic tradition of the city that would later be the hub of the northern Renaissance. Rosenplüt penned erotic obscenities, told tales of dirty tricks, wrote toasts, poetic maxims, and a *Faßnachtsspiel*. One of his poems praises his native city. Another uses arguments taken from the Bible to elevate what Rosenplüt and his fellows did to earn a living: hard manual labor. At the same time, Italy's humanists—Poggio, Pontano, Lorenzo Bonincontri—were endowing work with dignity and exalting a nobility of virtue and achievement over the nobility of blood.[136]

One of the most famous heroes of the discursive revolution, the big-city poet François Villon, knew a great deal about ancient literature despite his reputation as a figure of the criminal underworld. His specialty was Neoplatonic love poetry. His works are populated by Averroes and Aristotle, as well as Paris, Helen, and Thaïs.[137] It may be that an otherwise unknown Parisian jurist of the mid-fifteenth century used Villon's name so as to publish his social critique and ribaldries with impunity. The author of the two *Testaments*, the *Grand* and the *Petit* (the *Petit Testament* is also known as *The Legacy*), claims to have come from humble origins but to have studied at a university. A "François Villon" was indeed connected with the Paris underworld and the Coquillards, a band of beggars and thieves that formed during the Hundred Years' War. Involved in a stabbing and an accomplice to a burglary at the College of

Navarre, Villon was banished from Paris. In Blois, he was thrown into prison for unknown reasons. The author claims to have been saved from the gallows by the melancholic Duke Charles of Orléans, the prisoner of Agincourt. In his *Testaments*, he pours biting sarcasm over contemporaries and institutions of all kinds. The "real" Villon, whether he should be identified with the poet or not, landed in prison in Paris in late 1462, was tortured and sentenced to hang. He commented on his prospects in a famous quatrain:

> And from a six-foot rope it's here
> My neck shall learn the weight of my rear.

In the end, Villon's sentence was commuted to banishment. The fate of our sad hero, an outlaw pursued by death, is unknown.

The author's legacy—poetry often reedited and supplemented even in the twentieth century—sings of crime and the sordid love of whores, of poverty, old age, and the fragility of all earthly things. "One pleasure for a thousand pains," the poet complains. All life, all beauty quickly fades: "But where are the snows that fell last year?"[138] Often composed in the gutter talk of scoundrels, his songs are full of obscene allusions and powerful images. Yet they are often tamed by poetic forms, such as the rondeau or the ballad. They shed light on another side of the Renaissance: emaciated hags, the corpses of hanged men blowing in the breeze, their eye sockets being pecked at by magpies and ravens, and—this seems a bit more buoyant—the eloquence of Parisian women. Villon seems modern to us. Not because we feel a kinship with him—we do not know him, and we tend to be neither stabbers nor burglars—but rather because he sings unabashedly and powerfully about many topics that are still meaningful to us, and because he puts the minor moments of everyday life into words. Neither an utter fool nor a wise man, he was the Bellmann, the Belli, the Brecht of his age.

COMPETITION AND CREATIVITY: 1450–1500

23

Le tens revient

Constantinople's Last Stand

When Sigismund, the last emperor of the Luxembourg dynasty, died in 1437, his Bohemian house was anything but in order. The sonless ruler was supposed to be succeeded by Duke Albert V of Austria, the husband of his daughter Elizabeth and a loyal ally in the Hussite Wars. The Habsburg ruler was initially accepted in Hungary, and the prince-electors chose him as King of Germany. The Bohemian nobility rebelled, however, since Albert had been a sworn enemy of the Hussites. He managed to prevail, but in 1439 he succumbed to an illness during a campaign against the Ottomans. To succeed him, the prince-electors chose Duke Frederick, his closest relative. Heir to the thrones of Hungary, Croatia, Bohemia, and the Duchy of Austria was Albert's son Ladislaus, not yet born at the time of his father's death and thus called "the Posthumous." Yet this was not an age of child princes. Ladislaus was merely a pawn conferring legitimacy on those who controlled him. Meanwhile, the Hungarian crown was seized by Władysław III of Poland of the Jagiellon dynasty. Another, albeit fleeting, political factor in the region was Gjergj Kastrioti (1405–1468). Originally in the service of the sultan, he managed to wrest Albania from Ottoman control for nearly two decades as a condottiere for Venice and Naples. His nickname "Skanderbeg" evoked the memory of the gargantuan figure of the great Macedonian king: it derived from *Iskender Bey*, "Lord Alexander."[1]

The Ottoman threat necessitated unity. Cardinal Cesarini assembled a coalition. It seemed useful that Skanderbeg was leading a rebellion against the Ottomans in Albania. Yet the Crusader army suffered a devastating defeat at Varna on the Black Sea. Władysław and Cesarini were killed. Further Turkish successes opened the way to Constantinople.[2] The Ottomans erected an elaborate siege supported by large-caliber artillery. A Christian bronze-caster who flits through the sources but about whom nothing more is known than his name, Urban, helped in its creation and was handsomely rewarded for his efforts. The gravity of the situation emerged in late 1452, when a galley was sunk by Turkish cannons as it tried to cross the Bosporus. Demands for capitulation faded away.

Only a small part of Europe took part in the last battle for Constantinople. A couple thousand Venetians, Genoese, and Catalans had persevered at the side of the Byzantines while an awesome Ottoman army of ultimately eighty thousand men took up positions. In the first days of spring in the year 1453, the siege ring was complete, and the walls of the city came under constant bombardment. A first assault was beaten back. A final bud of hope blossomed when the Christian fleet in the Golden Horn outmatched the Ottoman navy. By the end of April, however, this triumph, too, was rendered moot. Ottoman pioneers managed to pull ships along greased beams over the land route into the Golden Horn, which the defenders had cut off from the open sea with chains. Another assault failed, but supplies and courage were starting to run out. The end came in the early morning hours of May 29. Wave upon wave of Ottoman assaults hit Theodosius's ancient walls. Finally, an elite force managed to break through one of the gates. When the May sun rose over the Golden Horn, Constantinople was in Turkish hands. All those who were able saved themselves aboard galleys of the Christian fleet, which now hastened westward.

The victors won a mighty treasure. Emperor Constantine XI had departed this life; whether he fell in battle or killed himself is uncertain. The prophecy that Byzantium's last emperor would have the same name as its first was fulfilled. The Byzantines had executed hundreds of prisoners and so could not hope for mercy. Countless numbers of them were butchered or carried off into slavery. Blood rushed through the streets of the city like water after a storm, and corpses floated on the sea like melons, one colorful eyewitness reported. "What a city we have given over to plunder and destruction!" Sultan Mehmed II is supposed to have remarked as he rode through his new possession on a white horse.[3]

Istanbul or "Islambul," "full of Islam," was the new name given to Byzantium. The name may also have come from the expression, *Eis ten polin!*—"To the city!" Its new lords attempted, often by force, to get their people to take up residence in the desolate walls. Christians were permitted to keep practicing their religion, although bells could not be rung. Jews were allowed to build synagogues. Venice's merchants had their privileges confirmed, and a strong Florentine colony was established in Galata. Trade with Flanders and the commercial centers of the Mediterranean soon flourished again.[4] Mehmed had his portrait painted by the Venetian Gentile Bellini (Plate 9). The Florentine Francisco Berlinghieri dedicated his geography book, based on Ptolemy, to Mehmed. High above the Bosporus grew a massive palace complex, later called the Topkapı Seraglio. Some of its parts—the central gate and the loggia—betray Renaissance influence. Ancient columns integrated into the building alluded to the conqueror's claim to universal authority.[5] Hagia Sophia was transformed into a mosque. Not far away, the Grand Bazaar sprang up, the heart and belly of the metropolis. Daily life gradually returned to the "city of the world's desire."[6] It was now the center of a quickly expanding Ottoman superpower that threatened East and West.

Athens, meanwhile under Catalan rule, fell a few years after Constantinople. The Parthenon, now a church consecrated to the Virgin Mary and theretofore the crown of a birthplace of European culture, became a mosque. In 1461, when Trebizond was incorporated into the Ottoman Empire, the Byzantine millennium was history. The double-headed imperial eagle found refuge on the coat of arms of Grand Prince Ivan of Moscow, who married the niece of the deceased John VIII. Ivan converted to Orthodox Christianity, and Moscow, the "Third Rome," became its last bastion. The city stood defiantly in the face of a hostile world—and of modernity.

After 1453

Lille, Hôtel de la Salle. February 17, 1454. Europe had not witnessed a feast like the one hosted by the Duke of Burgundy at his palace since the days of ancient Roman decadence.[7] The walls were covered with tapestries that recounted the life of Hercules, a sign that antiquity had long since penetrated the north. A naked statue with long hair may have portrayed Venus; it dispensed to the guests unlimited amounts of the outrageously expensive spiced wine hypocras, the drink of kings. A live lion guarded the lovely statue. On its cage was written, "Don't touch my lady!" There were forty-eight dishes to choose from. Deep red Burgundy—the host, Philip the Good, once called himself the "lord of the finest wines in Christendom"—glowed from gold-rimmed crystal glasses.[8] In moments such as these, Burgundy seems to embody what Clifford Geertz called a "theater state": power served pomp, not the other way around.[9]

The court poet Olivier de la Marche (1426?–1502) tells us a great deal about the feast, his writing as obsessed with details as a painting by van Eyck. He leaves nothing out: horses with blankets of white damask with gold fringe, golden and crimson saddlecloths, dark burgundy silk robes gleaming with gold jewelry and diamonds. Court ladies process through the room, and men in purple robes lined with marten fur appear. The high nobility preens itself with crest-covered coats, gold brocade, blue and gray. A beautiful blond woman floats through the crowd in a violet, gold-trimmed silk dress. Precious colors and exquisite materials are used to upstage competitors for social prestige and emphasize superiority over "lowly" burghers. The table decoration alone, with which Duke Philip portrayed his magnificence for all eyes to see, must have cost as much as a mercenary company. In Olivier's report, we hear silver bells ringing on the harnesses of horses. Chansons and motets reach our ears from half a millennium away. Musicians hidden in a humongous pastry resound with an organ and a choir. Finally, we see living images. One depicts Jason's quest for the Golden Fleece. Another shows the holy Church enthroned in a tower strapped to the back of an elephant. A giant dressed as a Saracen leads the animal by the bridle. Here contemporary history comes into play: Mother Church laments her state and appeals to knights for aid. Knights of the Golden Fleece enter along with a pheasant covered in gold chains. They take the Crusader's Oath to God, the Virgin, and, for some reason, the pheasant as well, which plays an obscure role in the confused legend of Jason.[10] Tambourines, lutes, and harps sound, wine and gingerbread are served. As Duke Philip confided to Olivier, he went to all the trouble of the pheasant feast simply to serve God.

The pious vows were not followed by deeds, and at other courts as well, the news form the Bosporus may have elicited dismay but resulted in no more than lip service. Amidst diplomatic missions and conflicts in his bishopric of Brixen, Cusanus took the time to indulge in a thought experiment. Angels lead the wisest religions of all before divine *logos*, which reveals to them the religion common to all people—the same religion Cusanus had contemplated twenty-five years earlier. The various religions are only separated from one another by ritual differences that arose over time. The result of a return to the one wisdom, a religion that can be grasped rationally—the Christian religion, of course—would be "eternal peace."[11] These were empty hopes. Cusanus died in 1464. His remains lie under a marble slab in the church of San Pietro in Vincoli in Rome. At his request, his heart was interred in the church of St. Nicholas Hospital, which he founded in Kues—a reminder that he, a singular mind of his time, was a man of two worlds: that of the culture of the Scholastic north, and that of the philosophy of Plato, flourishing under the southern sun.

As a "second destruction of Plato," indeed as a "second death of Homer"—that is how Aeneas Sylvius Piccolomini lamented the Fall of Constantinople.[12] Yet it was not so, for the European West and especially Italy reaped intellectual benefits from the epochal event. Many Greek scholars sought refuge in Italy, bringing their language and their knowledge with them. For example, John Argyropoulos, a participant at the Council of Florence and a protégé of Acciaiuoli, became a professor in the city on the Arno. His lectures on Aristotle won him students from the leading families, including Lorenzo the Magnificent.

The Ottoman threat fed the notion that Christian Europe was something "different" from the Muslim world. Thus, a concept of Europe formed that was imbued with fear and animated by the spirit of the Crusades. "Our forefathers often experienced setbacks in Asia and Africa, that is in other regions," Aeneas Sylvius Piccolomini proclaimed at the Diet of Frankfurt in the year Constantinople fell, "but we, today, have been beaten and struck in Europe itself, in our fatherland, in our own home and seat."[13] Europe as a common home—that is what he wanted to beat into the heads of those assembled in Frankfurt. But not even the shock at the fall of the "bulwark of Christianity" could move them to concerted action, to say nothing of building a European army as Piccolomini suggested. The fates of their own small and larger states were a more immediate concern than the distant ideal of a "Christian West." For a long time to come, their own regional entanglements would be more important to the Europeans than the grand cause, no matter how much the popes exhorted and admonished them. Anyway, the patriarch of Constantinople claimed that the Greeks preferred "the turban of the Turk" to "the tiara of the Pope."[14] On the Italian peninsula, at least, the Fall of Constantinople moved the leading powers to come to a fragile arrangement. Venice ended its war with Milan in a peace agreement, hammered out in April 1454 in the Lombard city of Lodi. Soon the pope and King Alfonso joined the treaty. Their alliance, the "Italian League," was the fruit of fear: of each other, of foreign powers—namely France—and of the Ottomans.

In any case, the conquest of the imperial city did little to change the political landscape.[15] Its fall was simply the last nail in the coffin of the body of a long-since-deceased empire. More serious was the economic fallout. The most important emporium for trade with East Asia was no longer in Christian hands, and there was not much sympathy for free trade at the sultan's court. Initially, it seemed it might be possible to evade this difficulty by passing through Mamluk Egypt. But then Egypt was also incorporated into the Ottoman Empire, and this way, too, was closed.

In the long term, the Turkish barrier encouraged Europe to search for new routes to the Far East. Genoa lost its bases on the Black Sea and gradually retreated forever from the eastern Mediterranean world. Only on the island of Chios did a joint stock company belonging to the Giustiniani family persevere. The *maona*, a consortium of investors subject to the Genoese state, and a structure typical of Genoese colonization, combined the economic exploitation of the island with political rule, although it had to pay tribute to the sultan.[16] On the mainland, large portions of Bosnia and Albania fell to the Ottomans. In the East, the sultan succeeded in subjecting the Crimean Khanate, the descendant of the defunct Golden Horde, to Ottoman dependence.

The Italian Mobile

The Peace of Lodi allowed Venice to concentrate on defensive wars against the Ottoman Empire in the Aegean and the Adriatic that broke out in 1463 and nullified its trading privileges. Yet it ultimately fought in vain to stem the decline of its maritime empire. Even on the mainland, Venice was threatened. From the Campanile of Saint Mark's, the Venetians could see columns of smoke rising from villages burning in Friuli—a sign that the Ottoman enemy was nearby. They purchased a humiliating peace that confirmed the 1470 loss of Negroponte (modern Euboea). All that remained, beyond a few bases on the Dalmatian coast, was the island of Corfu. Around 1500, the thalassocracy ceased being profitable. The costs of its maintenance exceeded all profits gained from it. Territory on the mainland, on the other hand, brought in more than 200,000 ducats a year.[17]

On the Italian peninsula, Lodi guaranteed an equilibrium for four decades among the five great powers: Milan, Venice, Florence, Rome, and Naples. Yet it was a cold peace, not a balance eager to maintain itself. The *Italia bilanciata* described by Machiavelli in *The Prince* (ch. 20) had to be continually recalibrated with the help of diplomacy and small wars. Dynasties like the Montefeltro and Malatesta enmeshed themselves in destructive struggles under the umbrella of Lodi in the hope of enlarging their own states. In Rome, humanism ascended to the Holy See after the death of Eugene IV. Tommaso Parentucelli, a trained theologian who took the name Nicholas V (1447–1455), marks the beginning of the Roman Renaissance. Nicholas breathed new life into the Vatican Library. He had thousands of books copied and translated, including classical texts from Homer to Thucydides to Theophrastus. He also initiated an expansion of the Vatican Palace.

The pope's position was now relatively uncontested. A conspiracy led by Stefano Porcari—a Roman from an old family intoxicated by Cicero's ideal vision of the republic—was discovered in January 1453 before it could be set in motion.[18] Frederick III had been crowned Holy Roman Emperor the previous year. It was the last ceremony of the kind Rome would witness, the end of a tradition that went back to Christmas Day in the year 800.

In 1458, Aeneas Sylvius Piccolomini became the second humanist to be elected pope, taking the name Pius II.[19] He wrote geographical and historical works, stylistically elegant letters, and *Commentarii*. The latter reports events and experiences during his pontificate and also contains a good amount of self-reflection. As his first name suggests, Aeneas Sylvius seems to have imbibed classical education like mother's milk. The papal name that he chose, "Pius," emphasizes his connection to Virgil. *Sum pius Aeneas*—"I am pious Aeneas"—is how the hero of Virgil's epic once responds to the question of who he is.[20]

Piccolomini is the unique case of a pope who was not only crowned with the tiara but who had also already been decorated poet laureate. His *Tale of Two Lovers*, told in epistolary form—we recently met its "Germanizer" Niklas von Wyle—combines ideas from Boccaccio with Ovid's love poetry. To the likely surprise of its readers, it justified love as a natural law, indeed as a power of fate—a departure from chaste courtly love and the monastic fear of the body. It did not exactly recommend its author for the Holy See. "Reject Aeneas, accept Pius," he thus said, somewhat contritely, when elected pope.[21] As if he were a Roman emperor, he set up a singular monument to himself: he had the town of his birth—Corsignano, south of Siena—rebuilt as a small ideal city. He named it after himself: Pienza. For the first time, humanist thought formulated an urbanistic program.[22] The idea behind the project probably came from Leon Battista Alberti.

Pius's successor Paul II (1464–1471) earned himself a reputation as an enemy of humanism, although, as a cardinal, he had assembled one of the first great collections of antiquities in Italy.[23] He forbade the teaching of pagan poetry in schools and slashed the number of papal officials, thus robbing learned men and *literati* of sinecures. Poggio Bracciolini had once mocked the papal chancery for being so big that it could defend itself against the Turks without assistance.[24] On the other hand, a monumental Renaissance began taking shape during Paul's pontificate, including buildings like Palazzo Venezia and the Hospital of the Holy Spirit. Sixtus IV (1471–1484) of the della Rovere family continued this building policy, renovating churches and laying out streets. While Roman money was financing the Florentine Renaissance, Florentine artists were fashioning Rome's Renaissance. The walls of the Sistine Chapel, commissioned by Sixtus, were covered in frescoes by great masters from Tuscany and Umbria, including Perugino, Ghirlandaio, and Botticelli.

Otherwise, nothing new happened under the Roman sun. Like always, simony and nepotism thrived, and Sixtus was one of the most successful in these realms. No fewer than six of the thirty-four cardinals he created during his pontificate had the oak tree of the della Rovere on their crest. He incessantly endeavored to supply his nephews with benefices, even states. This led to conflicts with Milan and its ally Florence. This alliance was profitable for both sides. When Cosimo de' Medici's rule began to waver in 1458 due to an economic crisis (whose dimensions are debated), a Sforza army stood at the ready. The same was the case eight years later, in 1466, when a circle around the financial magnate Luca Pitti, originally a faithful partisan of the Medici, led a putsch against Cosimo's son Piero the Gouty. *Il Gottoso* succeeded in outmaneuvering his opponents and securing the succession for his son Lorenzo (1449–1492).

Under Lorenzo the Magnificent, humanist Florence reached its zenith.[25] At the same time, the authoritarian character of the Medici regime grew stronger. It became increasingly clear that the family had designs beyond Florence's

walls and intended to marry into the feudal nobility. For Lorenzo, a marriage
was arranged with Clarice Orsini, daughter of a family with estates around
Bracciano north of Rome. Ducats wed tradition. What raised eyebrows among
Florentines and nobles alike ultimately became the rule with the succeeding
generations of Medici. The way toward a dukedom emerged, and magnificence
helped to pave it.

Feasts that converted civic moneys into chivalric splendor were only slightly
less extravagant than Philip the Good's pheasant banquet. They made it possible for the Medici to escape the grayness of their middle-class origin. Burgundy
provided the model. At a tournament held and fittingly won by the recently
wed Lorenzo in front of Santa Croce in 1469, the House of Medici presented
itself in all its glory, on the same level as the nobility. Lorenzo's robes, adorned
with pearls, bore an image of a sun and a rainbow and the motto *Le tens revient*,
"The age returns." The fact that the motto was in French reminds us that all
chivalric pageantry derived from the world of chansons and romances. Luigi
Pulci, the court poet of the Medici, connected the motto with the idea that the
world was being renewed, that a Golden Age was returning.[26]

What was new was Lorenzo's foreign policy. In the name of the republic, he
had a hired band of mercenaries led by Count Federico da Montefeltro crush
recalcitrant Volterra. The reason for the 1472 military action was primarily the
desire to maintain the Medici monopoly on alum, which seemed threatened
by the discovery of a new deposit in the town's territory. Things got out of hand
after Volterra was stormed. The soldiers turned to murder and plunder, thus
tarnishing Lorenzo's reputation. In addition, his bank encountered difficulties.
It had given excessively lavish loans to kings and princes who now were not
making their payments. The Medici manager in Bruges, Tommaso Portinari,
whom we have already met as a patron of Memling and van der Goes, fell into
disrepute. He was responsible for the bank's overly cozy relationship with
Charles the Bold, one of the great political busts of the century (pp. 441f.),
even serving him as a diplomat.

The moment to settle accounts with the Medici seemed to have arrived. But
in 1478, the conspiracy led by Jacopo de' Pazzi and Francesco Salviati failed.
They played the main role, while Sixtus IV pulled strings behind the curtains.
Lorenzo de' Medici dealt ruthlessly with his enemies. He had clearly taken to
heart the saying attributed to his grandfather Cosimo, namely that "states were
not held with paternosters in hand."[27] A few constitutional modifications ensured the family's power. It did not matter that the bank was in the red; if
necessary, the city's treasury was available.[28]

Lorenzo's excessive vengeance precipitated a war that pitted Naples and the papacy against Florence. When the situation became critical, Lorenzo dared to enter the lion's den. He visited his enemy in Naples—alone. King Ferrante, one of Jacob Burckhardt's exemplary monsters, was on the throne then. He is supposed to have indulged a macabre passion, keeping his enemies near him—either alive in a dungeon or dead, embalmed and clothed.[29] Somehow, Lorenzo managed to convince the brute to leave the anti-Florentine alliance. He returned to the Arno from the diplomatic mission of the century crowned with the glory of a halo. Historians portrayed him as the guarantor of equilibrium in Italy. In 1481, Florence stood at the side of its former enemies Rome and Naples when Venice tried to take Ferrara. The trio managed to block the Serenissima. The Italian mobile had begun to wobble a little; now, it was brought back into balance. Sixtus IV died the same year the War of Ferrara ended. In Rome, an anonymous poet wrote:

> Though no power with wild Sixtus could vie
> At the mere word "peace" he did die.[30]

Alliances were realigned. Lorenzo the Magnificent wed one of his daughters to an illegitimate son of Sixtus's successor, Innocent VIII (1484–1492). In return, his own son Giovanni, then only thirteen, was named a cardinal. This exchange of gifts bound Florence to Rome. The Sforza maintained power in Milan, although there was no shortage of machinations and murder in the city of Saint Ambrose. Francesco Sforza's son Galeazzo Maria, a notorious spendthrift and tyrant, was assassinated. His heir Gian Galeazzo, still a minor, was placed under the strict guardianship of the regent, his uncle Lodovico. Known as *il Moro*, "the Moor," on account of his dark skin, he sought an alliance with Ferrante of Naples by marrying his ward to a niece of the Aragonese king. The artistic director of the wedding feast, another excessively sumptuous affair, was Leonardo da Vinci. Gian Galeazzo Sforza died in 1494 after only recently reaching the age of majority, thus ending the marriage and the alliance. Il Moro, immediately and probably not wrongly suspected of having murdered him, was now able to enjoy full power in Milan. King Ferrante died in the same year of 1494.

Most of the small wars that up till then had been waged to maintain—or upset—Italy's equilibrium had had the dimensions of gigantic tournaments. The Battle of La Molinella on July 23, 1467, one of the bloodiest engagements of the century due to the massive use of artillery, was broken off at sundown per the agreement of the opposing generals Bartolomeo Colleoni and Federico da Montefeltro. They sealed the stalemate with a handshake as if they had just concluded a sporting event. Mercenary soldiers were capital, after all. They were needed alive. Economic considerations set narrow boundaries for all fighting; wars were limited affairs. On the other hand, hopes for unity under a single Italian scepter proved illusory. No Italian state could have come close to mobilizing the means necessary to assemble the massive army the task called for. To do so would have required the resources of vast royal domains or conquered territory.

In 1461, the king of Bohemia, George of Poděbrady (r. 1458–1471), asked Antoine Marini, a merchant, inventor, and diplomat from Grenoble, to think of peaceful ways to unify Europe.[31] Like in earlier designs of this kind, the first thing he urged was to build a united front against the Ottomans. Marini promoted a Europe of independent states controlled by neither the emperor nor the pope. The plan seems visionary and belongs to the prehistory of a "Europe of Fatherlands," although participation on the part of the horizontal power of citizens was probably not foreseen. Marini envisioned a kind of organization of states with its own bureaucracy. The assembly of the states, a permanent body meeting at rotating locations, would be given the highest, albeit voluntary, jurisdiction. According to this plan, the rulers of France, Germany, Spain, and Italy—here, Marini names Venice and the cities—would each have one vote. Decisions should be made by the majority. As events shaped up, such ideas did not have the slightest chance of being put into practice.

The European Framework

Italy was able to enjoy four decades of little significant violence thanks to the international political situation. Frederick III (r. 1440–1493) of the House of Habsburg, the longest-reigning Holy Roman Emperor ever, barely got involved in entanglements on the peninsula. His name is connected with neither glorious victories nor clever diplomatic maneuvers.[32] He depended on the legitimacy of his crown and, thus, the secure possession of titles and honors. Despite being reduced to his patrimonial lands in Inner Austria and often being in a seemingly hopeless position, he held with incredible tenacity to his claims, such as his claim to the Hungarian crown. His chancery virtually flooded the Empire with parchment and paper; between thirty thousand and fifty thousand documents are extant. Frederick's administration of about five hundred bureaucrats increasingly relied on jurists. Astrologers also weighed in on decisions.[33] Frederick inscribed himself more enduringly into the imperial constitution than any other emperor.

When the young Ladislaus the Posthumous, holder of two crowns and the Duchy of Austria, died in 1457, the political deck was reshuffled in the turbulent game of states around Frederick III's core territory. In Bohemia, George of Poděbrady became king despite initially being installed there by Frederick as an administrator. An adherent of the moderate wing of the Hussites, the Calixtines—literally "Chalicers," named after their desire for laymen to receive the chalice (Latin *calix*) of wine at the Eucharist—he was the first non-Catholic ruler in Europe and was therefore opposed by Rome. All that remained to Frederick was a claim to the succession. In 1462, he was besieged in his palace in Vienna by rebellious citizens and his own brother, Archduke Albert the Prodigal of Austria. While the bombards thundered against the walls, the Holy Roman Emperor and his family had to survive on dogs, cats, and birds, so the chronicles tell.[34] But Albert died in 1463. His demise came in the nick of time, giving Frederick his inheritance. However, he still lacked silver-rich Tyrol and the territories in Sundgau and Vorarlberg. They were still ruled by his cousin Sigmund.

The emperor achieved his greatest coup in the west, where developments in Burgundy provided him with a once-in-a-lifetime opportunity. The duchy was now ruled by Charles (r. 1465–1477), the son of the feast-giver Philip. The young prince, soon to be known as "the Bold," invested his money not in pastry and capons but in powder and cannons. He was driven by two major goals. First, he sought to unite the northern and southern parts of his state by conquering a bridge between them. Second, he strived for a royal crown and, if possible, election as emperor. Frederick was able to field an army of imperial troops to defend Neuß, a city on the Lower Rhine that had been besieged by Charles since 1474. He forced the Duke of Burgundy to break off the campaign. Charles worked out a peace agreement with Frederick, promising his daughter Maria in marriage to the latter's son Maximilian, who would himself later become emperor. Imperious, daring, and indeed characterized by extraordinary courage, Charles the Bold now went far beyond what seemed possible, conquering Alsace and attacking Lorraine. His successes and ruthless subjugation of the vanquished provoked opposition. Ultimately, defeats at the hands of the Swiss and deft diplomacy by Louis XI of France reversed Charles the Bold's fortunes. At the Battle of Nancy in January 1477, Swiss mercenaries cut his army to pieces. The body of the man so heavily in debt to Lorenzo the Magnificent[35] was found, its head split open, frozen in the ice of a pond. Swiss liberty was once again saved. In the same year, Habsburg and Burgundy wed in Ghent. As time would tell, Frederick had assured the dazzling rise of his dynasty.

Part of the Burgundian lands and other territories fell to the French monarchy, which continued to consolidate under Louis XI (r. 1461–1483)—a devious political player whose well-deserved nicknames were "the Cunning" and "the Spider." He also added Provence to the royal domain, which gradually transformed from the private estate of the king to the property of the state. Naples, too, which had once belonged to the Anjou, piqued his greed. But the French aristocracy was not yet tamed, and England was lurking in Calais.

After the Hundred Years' War, the English kingdom had descended into the chaos of the War of the Roses between the houses of York and Lancaster. Defeat at the hands of France had fed dissatisfaction and rebellion; with the war's end, a battle-hardened warrior class lost the objects of its ambition. The fury with which the English nobles went at each other's throats seems archaic, even self-destructive. When the dust settled, the grim figure of Richard III (r. 1483–1485) of the House of York emerged—in Shakespeare's famous description, "deformed, unfinish'd, sent before my time into this breathing world."[36] Fighting valiantly, the historical Richard died in 1485 at the Battle of Bosworth Field. With him, the last Plantagenet, the sun of York set forever. The victor, Henry Tudor (r. 1485–1509), Earl of Richmond and heir of the Lancastrians, founded a new dynasty. He was the last English king to win his crown with the sword. His marriage to Elizabeth of York, a daughter of Edward IV, was intended to reconcile the White Rose of York with the Red Rose of Lancaster. Parliament confirmed their issue's right to succession. The island kingdom gradually regained stability.

In the West, the trend was toward the consolidation of states and the enlargement of realms—not only in France and England but also on the Iberian Peninsula, where the Reconquista was nearing completion. This opened the Renaissance's realm of possibility even wider.[37] In northeastern Europe, Poland-Lithuania had obliterated the army of the Teutonic Knights at Tannenberg in 1410, thus initiating the process by which the latter ceased to be a great power. The Crusader state had become a retirement community for second sons of the nobility. Since Lithuania had been missionized by its own princes, the Crusaders lost their function and their legitimacy. Their campaigns were now of the standard variety, waged against Christian competitors: the Poles, the Lithuanians, and the Danes as well. The nobles and burghers who settled in the State of the Teutonic Order, however, were all too happy to dispense with its parasitic rule. They thus became natural allies of the Polish crown. Thirteen years of protracted war ended in 1466 with the Second Peace of Thorn, according to which the western half of the Teutonic state became a possession of the Polish crown, as did the bishopric of Ermland (also called Warmia). The eastern part remained in the hands of the grand master as "Ducal Prussia," but it was now under Polish suzerainty. During the Reformation, the area would be converted into a secularized Protestant duchy directly enfeoffed by the Polish crown.

The Polish kingdom developed into a limited monarchy in which the nobility enjoyed extensive freedoms. One of the nobility's peculiar features was its numerical strength. It represented about 8 percent of the total population, whereas in France it was only 0.3 percent. As mentioned above, it possessed the right to select the king. No one of noble birth could be imprisoned without legal cause. This right was enshrined in the Polish Magna Carta, the Privilege of Jedlno, negotiated in 1430. The senate, originally an advisory council to the king, became an institution in its own right that set limits to royal power. This representative body also included Catholic bishops, castellans, and voivodes, governors of administrative provinces. Of the cities, only Danzig (Gdansk), Elbing (Elbląg), and Thorn (Torún) could send representatives. The parliament, called the Sejm, brought together the senate, the nobility, and the king.

The union of Poland and Lithuania continued under Casimir IV (r. 1445–1492), the brother and successor of Władysław III, who had fallen at Varna. Lithuania's aristocracy managed to achieve substantial equality with the Polish nobility under the Jagiellon monarch. Casimir's marriage to a Habsburg princess gave him prospects for the thrones of Bohemia and Hungary, and his son actually became king of Bohemia as Vladislaus II (r. 1471–1516). The Hungarian crown fell to King Matthias (r. 1458–1490), son of the regent John Hunyadi, the most powerful aristocrat of the kingdom and famous for saving Belgrade from the Ottomans. Like his father before him, Matthias "Corvinus"—the name came from the raven (Latin *corvus*) on the family crest—won renown from victories over the Turks. He succeeded in adding Moravia, Silesia, and Lusatia to his state, which, as he himself said, he ruled with an iron fist.[38] After a long conflict, he and Vladislaus II agreed to the Peace of Olomouc in 1479, according to which they shared the kingship of Bohemia. A few years later, Matthias even took Vienna. What the Raven King lacked was a legitimate heir. Neither his first marriage nor his second, to Beatrice of Aragon, the daughter of King Ferrante of Naples, produced the desired offspring. All Hunyadi glory died with Matthias and his notorious "Black Army" of mercenaries.

Italy, Land of Patronage

The arts and sciences did not perish in the war-torn fifteenth century. On the contrary, the political relations and social dynamics in and between the cities and states of Europe promoted all-around competition, the mighty driver of cultural flourishing. It emerged throughout the continent, but nowhere more than in rich Italy. The condottieri wars had a significant effect on the creation and development of Renaissance culture: they set enormous streams of money in motion, flowing from the centers of power into the treasuries of the *capitani*, who then invested in culture. One of them, Federico da Montefeltro, is depicted on a marble relief along with his brother Ottaviano. They stare at each other as equals. Ottaviano has books and a laurel branch as attributes, Federico a helmet. The reconciliation of art and war, of *ars* and Mars, that was a side effect of Italy's petty wars is symbolically portrayed here—just like in a painting by Pedro Berruguete showing the condottiere with his young son Guidobaldo. Federico, wearing shining armor and a sword under an ermine-lined robe, is engrossed in reading a book.

Only a handful of specialist scholars would still know about once famous mercenary captains like him or his rival Colleoni had they not dispensed lavish patronage, the classic social strategy of "big-men."[39] Colleoni had a monumental mausoleum built for himself in the heart of Bergamo. More than anything else, he is commemorated by Verrocchio's equestrian statue of him in Venice. The determined man of bronze sits firmly in the saddle upon his striding horse. With a grim look, his elbow thrust out defiantly at fate, he seems to be gazing out upon a new world. The palaces of the smaller Italian rulers, more-or-less free satellites of the major five powers, were intellectual and artistic universes of their own. In Mantua, Alberti built, and Pisanello and Mantegna painted. In Cesena, a branch of the Malatesta collected a library of exquisite books. Ferrara's university had a European format, and its court was among the most radiant in Italy. Duke Borso d'Este was in the habit of wearing clothing interwoven with gold even while hunting.[40] A sign of the interest in ideas from far-flung places and times, and also a reminder of the intellectual resources of the Este court, is the Hall of the Months painted around 1470 in Ferrara's Palazzo Schifanoia (Plate 10).[41] The portrayal of the "decans of the planets"—rulers of ten-day periods within each month that derive from Indian or Babylonian astrology—is based on the *Great Introduction* by the Persian astronomer Abu Ma'shar (787–886), which came to Ferrara by way of the translation by Pietro d'Abano (1250/1257–1316).

Antiquity was now increasingly enshrined in painting. Long before their like was actually constructed, the imagination of painters created buildings in linear perspective with classical decor. The master of this art was Piero della Francesca (1411/13–1492), who built imaginary spaces designed with mathematical precision into works like his *Flagellation of Christ* and a votive image for Federico da Montefeltro. A budding sense of the historical distance of antiquity is evinced in the ruins that Andrea Mantegna, a Gonzaga courtier, placed in frescos and panel paintings. Piero di Cosimo attended to mythological themes. Antonio del Pollaiuolo specialized in naked heroic bodies. One of his paintings depicts a sinewy Hercules fighting the Hydra (Plate 11). The most enduring fame of all was won by Sandro Botticelli (1445–1510), whose enigmatic *Spring* and *Birth of Venus* have found a place in the timeless museum of world art.

To understand the psychology of patronage, we must not ignore the simple view of it taken by the Florentine merchant Giovanni Rucellai (1403–1481), according to whom it is sweeter to spend money than to make it. Rucellai was thinking above all of the art he commissioned, of the Palazzo Rucellai, the facade of Santa Maria Novella, and the Chapel of the Holy Sepulcher in San Pancrazio.[42] Art is enjoyable; contemplating it passes the time. But it can also be a devotional act. Cosimo de' Medici was once described as a contrite sinner conscious of having earned money with dubious business dealings. In addition, he had to reckon with the envy and ambition of his competitors in Florence, and he could not simply give orders as he would have liked.[43] As a patron, however, he was utterly free to demonstrate his social and political standing by means of "conspicuous consumption," even though formal honors were out of reach.

The capitalist spirit always had to pay its dues to Christian ethics. Fear of the afterlife could be attenuated by doing good works—and Cosimo's construction of a monastic library was certainly a good work. Piety and pride moved him to build monasteries and a whole church, his family palace in Florence on what is now Via Cavour, country villas, and much more. His favorite artists included Fra Angelico and Donatello, his "personal sculptor." Wherever Medici money was converted into marble and paint, the family's symbol, six balls, was to be seen. Other patrons did the same, guilds and tycoons alike. The wool weavers had their lamb, the Strozzi their half-moons, and the Tornabuoni their lion.

Cosimo exhibited a princely habitus. Along with generosity, beneficence, and hospitality, demonstrating *magnificenza* was one of the key virtues of the high aristocracy. Education was also necessary. This could be evidenced best by the books one owned. Vespasiano da Bisticci, known as the "prince" of Florentine booksellers, helped the Medici to assemble the works that comprised the core of the library housed at the monastery of San Marco. "I immediately set 45 copyists to work," he recalls about the early days of the undertaking, "and in 22 months I had produced 220 volumes."[44] By the end of the century, the Medici library numbered a good thousand.

Extravagant patronage helped parvenus and usurpers to veil the often-dark details of their rise to power behind a beautiful veneer. Those who could pay for whole churches and huge palaces demonstrated that God's grace sanctioned their success. Physical structures in mortar and stone seemed divinely ordained, their existence justified. Large buildings, monuments for eternity that were raised, so to speak, by God himself, demanded and reinforced the respect of the people—Giannozzo Manetti put these very words into the mouth of the pope in his *Life of Nicholas V*.[45]

What triumph or failure in the constellation of states in the Italian mobile meant can be seen with a journey into the rugged Montefeltro territory in the Apennines. Its lord, Federico da Montefeltro, was of illegitimate birth and only came to power when his half-brother Oddantonio was assassinated.[46] In 1465, he conclusively defeated his archenemy Sigismondo Malatesta. Now, in his last remaining fifteen years, he showed what it meant to be a winner. In that short span of time, his humongous palace rose above Urbino. The triumphal arch on the southwest façade, set between two slim towers, faced in the direction of Rome, to which Federico owed *condotte* and his office as apostolic vicar. The building itself was without parallel in Italy. The classically proportioned cloister with its elegant Corinthian columns is one of the most beautiful architectural structures of all time. Majestically wide steps lead to the upper story. The pride of the prince, his greatness communicated by marble, gold, and richly inlaid doors and wall paneling, is everywhere announced by his monogram: "FE DUX" (standing for *Federicus dux*, or "Duke Federico"). All this communicates more or less the same thing that Timur the Lame had written on his palace of Ak Serai one hundred years before: "If you have doubts about our grandeur, look at our edifice."[47]

In contrast, the gloomy *castello* of the defeated Malatesta, who in his final days was merely lord of Rimini, is a memorial to decline and fall. Less than two decades earlier, Sigismondo had been one of Italy's most sought-after condottieri and had engaged some of Italy's foremost artists. Federico da Montefeltro perfected his victory on the battlefield by commissioning works from the very same artists, including Piero della Francesca and Leon Battista Alberti. Sigismondo, once celebrated as *magnifico*, was thus roundly beaten in the tournament of art patronage.

In Urbino, a humanist court in its purest form took shape. Five hundred *bocche*, or "mouths," made up Federico da Montefeltro's "family," from the stable master to the barber and physician, from court musicians to astrologers. A comprehensive manual detailed their duties and described the ceremonies that were to be performed on any number of occasions, such as when the duke dined before the eyes of the people. During Lent, sacred works were read aloud during meals; otherwise, it was Livy's *History of Rome*. When the day's work was done, Federico listened to lectures on the main works of Aristotle, theology, the natural sciences, and other subjects. His library included over nine hundred volumes, making it one of the most important collections in Italy, along with those of the Vatican and the Medici.[48] It was open to anyone who could give a good reason for their desire to use a book. A librarian kept a catalog, combatted vermin, and saw to the needs of visitors.

> He is to carefully show the books to individuals of authority and education, point out to them the beauty and nobility of the script and the miniatures, and take care that no page gets bent.

Thus reads the court manual. "If uneducated people show up who only want to see something out of curiosity, if they are not of very high rank a quick glance will suffice."[49] New was that the duke had the books installed in his palace and not in a monastery, as had previously been the rule. In another departure from tradition, the volumes were not chained to individual spots on lecterns but rather could be consulted freely. This made it possible to compare several works with one another—an advantage for philological studies.

Yet the library was not merely a practical institution in the service of learning. "What script! What books! What magnificence!"—thus Vespasiano da Bisticci once enthused.[50] Pages of the finest goatskin parchment were gathered in red bindings studded with silver. The message conveyed by the outlay was clear: the owner is a man who prizes learning above all (Plate 12). This is exactly how the famous portrait by Piero della Francesca depicts him (Plate 13): the eagle-beaked warrior and cunning political operative is crowned with the red beret of a scholar. This accorded fully with the theory of *magnificenza* once formulated by Giovanni Pontano.[51] The patron of the arts and learning is himself portrayed as a man of letters and a connoisseur of the arts.

As in Urbino, it was often one or two decades of patronage dispensed by a single ruler that brought a forlorn nest to life, after which it once again sank back into slumber, where it still remains today. For example, what would Castiglione Olona in Lombardy be without its patron Branda Castiglione, who had a palace built there and a chapel decorated with frescos by Masolino? What would Pienza be without Pius II? Pictures and buildings have endured, but ceremonial entrances, feasts, and opera performances are preserved merely in a few drawings or in fleeting references in chronicles—despite the fact that top-notch artists often painted the scenery, devised the machines, and played master of ceremonies. These must have been spectacles that the eye never forgot.[52]

Like Federico's magical palace in the Apennines, countless Renaissance residences united patronage of the arts and learning under one roof. Both had long become part and parcel of the princely habitus. The great significance of the tight alliances between power, the arts, and learning that existed all over Europe can be illustrated by the history of the Scientific Revolution, in which courts would go on to play a leading role. Natural science and technology in particular became increasingly important in light of the struggles over state formation; rulers did not need Francis Bacon to tell them that knowledge is power. The agents of exchange now included countless book hunters and antiques collectors, artists and intellectuals. There were broad, tight networks of epistolary communication and manuscript lending. The active use of princely libraries—the Medici seem to have been just as liberal in this sense as Federico da Montefeltro[53]—is attested by librarians' notes about their special cross to bear: books lent out for years or never returned at all. Sometimes creative minds lived together, discussing and intriguing, under the roof of a royal residence or patrician palace. Bearing devout dedications and letters of recommendation, they sought to secure a living. The ascension of a new ruler or the death of a pope could ruin the best-laid plans, and the game had to begin anew. Without interruption, men of letters invented stories, composed verse, wrote histories, and cobbled together all manner of learned material to please a magnificence, an excellency, or a holiness.

Let us take as an example the life of a humanist of the second rank, Pier Candido Decembrio (1399–1477) of Pavia.[54] His father Uberto, a humanist and trained jurist in Milanese service, was known for a translation of Plato's *Republic* that he undertook with Chrysoloras. The son inserted himself into the close-knit networks of the new culture. He met Gasparino Barzizza, the teacher of Alberti, Vittorino da Feltre, and Francesco Filelfo. To the doge of

Genoa he dedicated a youthful work, *On the Inventors of the Seven Liberal Arts*. He served Filippo Maria Visconti for three decades, traversing Europe as a diplomat and translating classical texts into the vernacular, including works of Caesar and Curtius Rufus's *History of Alexander the Great*. He corresponded with prominent individuals, including Bruni, Valla, and Humphrey of Glouces-ter, to whom he sent a copy of his own translation of Plato's *Republic*. He once asked the duke for money to buy a villa that had been owned by Petrarca. It seems, however, that he did not receive a penny for his work.

In 1447, Pier Candido made the mistake of entering the service of the short-lived Ambrosian Republic. He did not manage to then win the favor of the new strongman Francesco Sforza. Nicholas V rescued him with a post as apostolic abbreviator. Under Nicholas's stingy successors, though, he had to search for a new source of sustenance. He found it in the Naples of the generous Alfonso and then, during the chaos that followed his death, in Ferrara. As a sign of gratitude, he dedicated a book about the plague to Borso d'Este. From 1467 on, he lived in the humanist enclave on the Po. Efforts to return to Milan only bore fruit in 1477, shortly before Decembrio's death. His life of wandering shows how many opportunities were open to an agile spirit like his in the pa-tronage El Dorado of Italy. According to the inscription on his grave in Sant'Ambrogio, he wrote more than 127 books. The most important of them was a biography of Filippo Maria Visconti.

Service at court could be a proverbial hell on earth, a reality that Pier Can-dido and his fellows had to experience with regularity. One false word, and favor and money were lost. At least humanists seldom had to fear for their lives. One who did was Francesco Filelfo, about whose itinerant life we have already heard. He wrote a scathing satire about the Medici during the brief period when it seemed the putsch organized by Luca degli Albizzi would be successful. In response, Cosimo de' Medici ordered that he be assassinated in 1433.[55] A scar on his face reminded him of the attempt on his life for the rest of his days. A second attempt, after Filelfo had fled to Siena, also failed. Unique in the history of humanism, the scholar now engaged his own hit man to wipe out the assassin along with his employers, including Cosimo de' Medici. But the plan came to light while it was being forged in Siena. The Sienese hacked the hands off the would-be killer, a Greek from Athens. If they had caught Filelfo, they would have cut his tongue out—a terrifying punishment for a professor of eloquence! The land of humanism's birth certainly had a barbaric aspect. The figure of Filelfo—this hotheaded schemer, would-be murderer, satirist, and author of a treatise on moral philosophy—illustrates the two sides of an age in which Jacob Burckhardt thought he could see the origins of his own time.

In Plato's Heaven

"The tone is elegiac, but the subjects of the picture are both savage and sublime." That is how the historian Hayden White characterized Jacob Burckhardt's book on the Renaissance.

> The 'realism' of the subject-matter stems from the refusal to hide anything crude or violent, yet all the while the reader is reminded of the flowers that grew on this compost heap of human imperfection. But the purpose is Ironic. Throughout the work, the unspoken antithesis of this age of achievement and brilliance is the gray world of the historian himself, European society in the second half of the nineteenth century.[56]

This industrialized world was not only gray but also nervous. Burckhardt's master narrative is ultimately an anatomy of this modern unpleasantness. *The Civilization of the Renaissance in Italy* was also a tale of yearning written by a man who sensed he had been abandoned by God.

In addition to art, he focused on the Renaissance's celebration of the philosophy of Plato. Burckhardt gives a privileged place at the end of his book to the revival of Platonism in the Florence of Lorenzo the Magnificent. The final sentences of his magnum opus are written in the muted pathos that is typical of his style:

> Echoes of medieval mysticism here flow into one current with Platonic doctrines and with a characteristically modern spirit. One of the most precious fruits of the knowledge of the world and of man here comes to maturity, on whose account alone the Italian Renaissance must be called the leader of modern ages.[57]

In the second half of the Quattrocento, interest in philosophy does indeed seem to have gotten stronger in Florence. The Plato of past times, the framer of open, critical dialogue and the teacher of rhetoric, gave way to the theologian. The morally dubious parts of the *Republic* were glossed over, for example where Plato recommends that women be held in common.[58] On the other hand, teachings that seemed suitable for uniting faith with wisdom enjoyed a breakthrough. A circle was thus closed that Augustine had begun to sketch.

Emblematic of the renaissance of speculative philosophy is the work of Marsilio Ficino (1433–1499), a frail, somewhat hunchbacked, lisping, and stuttering man from Figline in the Arno Valley.[59] At an estate at Careggi, whose revenues Cosimo de' Medici gave him, he met regularly for discussions with friends, benefactors, and students. This group, referred to as the "Platonic Academy," included Alberti, Lorenzo de' Medici's court poet Angelo Poliziano (1454–1494), Cristoforo Landino, and Luigi Pulci (1432–1484), the author of a parody of chivalric epic called *Morgante*. Ficino venerated the ancients so enthusiastically that he adopted vegetarianism in imitation of Pythagoras. When the morning sun rose over the Tuscan hills, he plucked a lyre. In his view, playing music in harmony with the celestial spheres fostered good health.[60] He devoted his writings equally to the body and the soul, reflecting his double professional identity as a physician and a priest. His *Three Books on Life* contained recipes and advice for living a long and, above all, a good life. Similar to Nicholas Cusanus and Pletho, who he said was "like another Plato,"[61] he sought to reconstruct a primeval theology from the writings of Hermes Trismegistus and thereby to overcome the "Mosaic distinction" between the true faith and false religions.[62] The fact that God, the world-creating *logos* of the Gospel of John, had allowed himself to be worshipped in different times and places by different rites did not seem a defect to Ficino but rather a divinely willed augmentation of the universe's beauty.[63] Such were the teachings Burckhardt revered as the "most precious fruits of knowledge."

Cosimo de' Medici commissioned Ficino to translate into Latin a Hermetic manuscript that surfaced in 1462. The wisdom of Hermes, whom Ficino called "the greatest philosopher, the greatest priest, and the greatest king,"[64] seemed to him the consummation of the longed-for *prisca theologia*. Combining it, Neoplatonism, and Christianity, he tried to construct a single system.[65] His translations of Plato's works remained unsurpassed until the nineteenth century. Ficino also integrated into his system Aristotle's shadow world of the passions and the Stagirite's empirical method.[66] He describes the immortal soul as an intermediary between mind and matter, unity and multiplicity, rest and motion, as the "knot of the world" that binds the cosmos to unity. Since the soul is a mirror of its creator, self-knowledge leads to knowledge of God.

Ficino's universe is the cosmos of Ptolemy and Pseudo-Dionysius the Areopagite: hierarchically structured, guarded by angels, inhabited by demons, and infused by the "One," Plotinus's *to hen*. The light that floods Ficino's cosmos is divine truth and the divine Good, indeed God himself. All the soul's desire is directed towards unification with him.[67] Intellect and will are the "wings" with whose help the soul can return to him, its origin. According to Ficino's 1484 work *De amore*, the universal energy that effects this ascent is *eros*, love. It is the energy that drives human beings to perform glorious deeds, that feeds their yearning for knowledge and even for wealth. It gives form to chaos and manifests itself as a desire for beauty and thus for God, the absolute Good, whose "radiance" or reflection is utter beauty. On Earth, "beauty is, in fact, a certain charm which is found chiefly and predominantly in the harmony of several virtues."[68] It has to do with looking, less so with touching, and least of all with sex. The sixteenth century would develop these teachings in all manner of different directions.

Ficino viewed himself not merely as a philologist or theologian but also as an instrument of providence destined to heal souls and the state. He was, at times, illuminated by visions. He talked with the dead, including the recently deceased Cosimo de' Medici. His work is full of abstruse and obscure statements. For example, he claims it is possible to animate objects such as statues by means of heavenly power.[69] He also elaborated a sophisticated theory of demons. On the other hand, no one before had ever provided as eulogistic an image of love and love-death, of dissolution of the self in the highest power, as this poetic philosopher whose work was now being diffused throughout Europe.

Ficino had a younger intellectual kinsman in Count Giovanni Pico della Mirandola (1463–1494).[70] He also set off in search of what was common to all revealed religions. He endorsed the remarkable view of a Castilian priest according to whom everyone, whether Christian, Jewish, or Muslim, could be saved in their own religion.[71] He was one of the first humanists to acquire knowledge of Hebrew, and he tried to integrate the Jewish tradition into his monumental religious unification project. In no fewer than nine hundred theses, many of which betray the influence of Cusanus, he listed competing views. The list is a *summa* of the philosophical knowledge that had so far been accumulated: doctrines of Scholasticism, the Greeks, Arabic philosophy, the Kabbalists, and Hermetism. Pico presents over half of the conclusions as his "own opinions:"[72] propositions about God and mathematics, the Orphic hymns, the Chaldean Oracles, and magic.

He planned to hold a public disputation of his views in Rome in 1486, but it was blocked by Innocent VIII. Pico was now suspected of heresy and had to flee. He found asylum in Medici territory, in Fiesole near Florence. There he wrote *On Being and the One*, the prelude to an ambitious attempt to finally reconcile the views of Plato and Aristotle. It is a "negative theology" that merely paraphrases God as the "One," the "True," the "Good," and "Being."[73] Dating to the same period is the *Heptaplus*, an esoteric interpretation of Genesis that attempts to decipher hidden meanings in the words, letters, and numbers found in the Scriptures. In this work, Pico also applied Kabbala, the mystical discipline whose origins, according to Jewish tradition, lie in the words God spoke to Moses on Mount Sinai. Pico was the most important founder of its Christian interpretation. In his final years, he was moved to devote himself to a life of contempt for the body and the world by a new actor on the Florentine stage: the prior of the monastery of San Marco, Girolamo Savonarola (1452–1498), who envisioned transforming Florence into a theocracy.

Pico's philosophy fulfilled yearnings for harmony and truth in times that experienced an excess of dialectic, criticism, and religious anxiety.

> Oh God, oh highest good, now how can it be
> that I never succeed though I only look for thee?

Thus wrote Lorenzo the Magnificent in one of his most beautiful sonnets:

> *O Dio, o sommo bene, or come fai*
> *che te sol cerco e non ti truovo mai?*[74]

Ficino, Pico, and Savonarola gave very different answers, as Luther would later, to how this anxiety should be met. In 1520, as the Reformation was already well underway in Germany, Gianfrancesco Pico, the nephew and biographer of Giovanni, would lash out at all pagan philosophy, Plato included, as an unreliable product of the senses and reason.[75] Only Christian doctrine, he argued, led to truth. Thus, this possibility, too, remained open.

The discussions in Careggi may have given expression to an attempt to gain distance from the business and other dealings of the world. While they talked of light and love, enjoying cool drinks on a shady loggia—this is how we might imagine them, at any rate—in nearby Florence, Cosimo de' Medici's puppet show was reaching its finale. The republican facade crumbled under the regime of his grandson Lorenzo; war and vendetta were the words of the day. A remarkable contrast to this savage reality is provided by the verse written by the prince of terror himself, Lorenzo: love lyrics, witty rhymes, religious pieces like the sonnet quoted above, and poetry describing a beautiful natural world inhabited by nymphs, fauns, and shepherds. The most famous trace of this lost time is the refrain of a *canzone* about Bacchus and Ariadne. It betrays an awareness on Lorenzo's part of the fragility of the idylls of which he sang:

> Youth is sweet and well
> But doth speed away!
> Let who will be gay,
> To-morrow, none can tell.[76]

At the Close of Fair Days

Careggi, outside Florence. April 8, 1492. Lorenzo—poet, patron, and murderer—is dying, surrounded by the magnificence of his villa. In the fading light of the late afternoon, ancient vases gleam on the shelf; a tapestry woven with gold decorates the wall. The armchair in which the deathly ill man rests is surrounded by his poets and scholars: the elderly Ficino and Pico della Mirandola, Poliziano and Pulci, and Lorenzo's personal physician, the astrologer Piero Leoni da Spoleto. Lorenzo's mistress, the enchanting Fiore, has made sure that another guest is present in his final hours: Girolamo of Ferrara. Fiore had once been the latter's lover. Abandoned by the beautiful woman, he had taken the cowl in desperation. He is no other than Savonarola. He would soon rule Florence. Lorenzo, already in the grip of fever, suspects the threat that awaits his city. He makes a frenzied appeal, defending humanistic culture and its open-mindedness, speaking up for curiosity and debate, art and spirit, the great wings of life. "I will break them, these great wings," the friar announces. Lorenzo counters, "It is death whom you proclaim as spirit, and all the life of life is art. I will prevent you. I am still master." It is no use. His strength ebbs. Lorenzo dies. And with him goes the Florence of the early Renaissance. In vain, Fiore exhorts Savonarola to eschew power and remain a simple friar. "Then hear this: Descend! The fire you have fanned will consume you, you yourself, to purify you and the world of you."

The scene just described never actually occurred. It comes from Thomas Mann's play *Fiorenza*, written in 1906 but never performed.[77] Fiore, the beautiful mistress, symbolizes Florence, Lorenzo's city, which is now handed over to Savonarola. Lorenzo's son and successor, Piero de' Medici, another character in the drama, actually was as Mann describes him: a political lightweight and an inhuman despot. His brother, Cardinal Giovanni—later Pope Leo X (1513–1521)—was also as described here: a great patron of the arts. Savonarola's presence at Lorenzo's deathbed is attested, too, although he was only there as a confessor in his capacity as prior of the Medici monastery of San Marco.

Thomas Mann had carefully studied his Burckhardt. Interiors like those he described for Lorenzo's villa were familiar to him from his father-in-law Alfred Pringsheim's mansion in Munich, where he spent time while working on the piece. Mann was profound even in his weaker efforts, among which *Fiorenza* certainly figures. The dialogue between Lorenzo and Savonarola highlights tensions that would shape Europe and beyond for centuries to come, and that continue to do so today: the rival claims to power of religion and the secular world, of philosophy and faith, and the antithesis between piety and asceticism on the one hand and uninhibited joy in the pleasures of this world on the other. These conflicts stood out in much starker relief in Renaissance Florence, the capital of the discursive revolution, than elsewhere. Fiorenza was a "city eager to speak," *città di parlare avida*,[78] that loved mockery and scatological language. And yet it also stood silent in prayer before the altars of its saints. It seems rational and esoteric, pious and godless all at once. While Ficino and Pico were flying through the cosmos, Luigi Pulci was denied a Christian burial because he disputed the possibility of miracles and, in Epicurean fashion, called the soul a "pine nut in hot white bread."[79] Finally, the young Machiavelli, a contemporary of the burning, pious absolutist Savonarola, copied Lucretius's didactic poem from the first line to the last. This scribal drudgery was preparation for an ice-cold secular coup.

Lorenzo's Florence was not destined to be known for Epicureanism, murder, and costly petty wars but rather for the myth of a man who became the epitome of the perfect patron. And yet he was not only a brutal powermonger but also physically an exquisitely ugly specimen, with olive skin, a flat nose, and a frog mouth. In a 1479 dialogue on freedom, Alamanno Rinuccini dubbed him a "Florentine Phalaris," after the cruel tyrant of Agrigento. It was above all to Machiavelli that Lorenzo owed his posthumous fame as a patron of the arts and a peacemaker.[80] In the *Florentine Histories*, Lorenzo is described as providing Florence with a perpetual feast, complete with tournaments, triumphs, and theater in the ancient manner. This panegyrical portrayal was self-serving, however, as the work that contained it was commissioned by a nephew of Lorenzo (p. 514).

Things changed for the worse after Lorenzo the Magnificent's death. In 1494, Charles VIII of France (r. 1483–1498) invaded Tuscany with a large army and the support of Lodovico il Moro and the pope.[81] The goal was Naples, where the king intended to support his kinsmen in their fight against Aragon.

Piero de' Medici, who had inherited his father's unscrupulousness but not his political cunning, rightfully earned for himself the sobriquet "the Unfortunate." He opened the gates of the city to the king. It was too much. Piero and a large portion of his family were driven out of the city amid cries of "the people and freedom!" The family bank collapsed. For nearly two decades, the city's fate was then guided by a Great Council of over 1,000 men and a smaller Council of Eighty. However, the new government was not able to prevent the loss of Pisa, which had willingly submitted to the French king. While Charles led his army south, the hour of Savonarola struck on the Arno. Pico della Mirandola did not live to experience the friar's rule. On the same day Florence fell, he died, only thirty-one years old. Beforehand, he had written a polemic against astrology. In his view, such a system was opposed to a conception of humankind that assumed freedom of the will as a precondition for drawing closer to God.[82]

The French invasion put an end to the balance of power in Italy forever. The peninsula became an arena of competition for the great powers of Europe. Its ailing republics and monarchies could no longer oppose them. Charles VIII's army, with its mobile field artillery, its heavy cavalry, and its battle-tested Swiss mercenaries, provided a foretaste of the coming doom. Despite these political convulsions, the arts reached new heights. In Italy's darkest hour to date, what we call the High Renaissance took shape. At the same time, novelty upon novelty broke over the world. The foothills of modernity rose steeply.

24

Media Revolution

IMPRESSIO LIBRORVM.

Potest vt vna vox capi aure plurima: Linunt ita vna scripta mille paginas.

Innovation in Mainz

Italian scholars and artists had given Europe its antiquity back, albeit in the guise of a creative transformation. They had expanded the domains of the secular world and helped a critical, open style of thought take hold. Thanks in part to their activity, the discursive revolution could no longer be reversed. Yet now, the context for world-changing events shifted northward. The first venue was a small German city smack in the middle of the Latin-European realm of possibility: Mainz.

The town, founded in Roman times, numbered no more than seven thousand souls in the mid-fifteenth century.[1] The commune's catastrophic economic situation and resulting quarrels between guilds and dynasties shifted the balance of power in favor of the archbishop, one of the three spiritual prince-electors of the Holy Roman Empire. Now the citizens were losing the rest of their liberty. In 1462, after the "Mainz Diocesan Feud"—a bellicose conflict over the appointment of the archbishop—this liberty was gone for good. That Mainz was a holy city was immediately obvious to any visitor. Prayers ascended to heaven from sixteen monasteries, ten abbeys, the cathedral, and numerous churches and Beguine and Beghard houses. At Altmünster Abbey, pilgrims venerated the sudarium of Christ, the city's most valuable relic. The Rhine and Main rivers provided Mainz with everything a late medieval community needed. The city's best-known export product seems to have been ham, the *jambon de Mayence*, whose mention in Rabelais's *Gargantua and Pantagruel* propelled it to literary fame.

It was thus a somewhat cramped and provincial atmosphere that gave birth to one of the most important inventions in human history: the printing of books with a press and moveable type. Johannes Gutenberg, whose name is attached to the invention, came from the Gensfleisch family, a prosperous patrician clan. He took his last name from the Gutenberg estate, where he was born around 1400.[2] His father may have enabled him to study in Erfurt, which was then part of the Electorate of Mainz. Gutenberg acquired his abilities as a craftsman during an apprenticeship as a goldsmith. He spent the years between 1434 and 1444 in Strasbourg; the reason is unknown. There he organized the production of *Wallfahrtsspiegel*, devotional articles sold everywhere. They contained small mirrors in which devout travelers on the Great Pilgrimage to Aachen hoped to capture the optic rays emitted by Mary's cloak or Christ's swaddling clothes, thus creating what may be termed "optical relics" to take home with them. The method employed to manufacture these *Wallfahrtsspiegel*—they were made of lead and tin—was probably the same one Gutenberg later used to cast his letters. The latter were 83 percent lead and 9 percent tin, the rest being a mixture of antimony, copper, and iron. Once back in Mainz, Gutenberg was experimenting with moveable type. He tested its viability with a work that was sure to sell well: the widely used Latin grammar of Aelius Donatus. Indeed, it seems that up to ten thousand copies were sold. An appeal to undertake a Crusade against the Turks, printed by Gutenberg, can be dated to 1454. A year later, a letter of indulgence was also printed using the new technique.

Only little is known about the beginnings of this media revolution, the third after the invention of writing and the alphabet. Important preconditions for its emergence were access to trade routes and thus the availability of metal, inks, and, above all, the still relatively new material paper. Without the Chinese invention, there would have been no Gutenberg Revolution. A simple calculation makes this clear: if parchment had been used instead of paper for the 27,000 incunables that appeared in the fifteenth century in average print runs of 400, it would have required the hides of over 216 million animals![3] Also necessary were highly skilled craftsmen of various trades who knew how to fabricate instruments and cast metal. All this was found even in tiny Mainz.

The media revolution did not necessarily have to ignite there. Experiments in the art of printing were being carried out in many places in the large European realm of possibilities. The first steps toward the new printing technology had already been taken. Letterpress printing was an ancient technology, as we have already seen with the Phaistos Disk. Woodblock printing had been known in China at least since the ninth century. And block books, in which each page contained images and text printed from a single woodcut, may have been available in Europe. Carving letters inversely in relief on hard wood was a laborious process, of course. A common alternative was to simply leave space between the images and write the words by hand. It is possible that Europeans were inspired by almanacs, calendars, and paper money imported from China.[4] The sources say nothing about this. As one Spaniard reported, people in the Middle Kingdom seem to have thought that "Iuan Cutenbergo" saw books brought by merchants and deduced the art from them. According to this view, he was in no way the inventor of the new technology.[5]

Alongside woodcuts and the printing press, another technology was coming into its own: copper engraving, which had first been invented around 1420.[6] Its origins are obscure but are probably also to be located in Germany. In the second quarter of the fifteenth century, a craftsman likely active in Alsace carved playing cards into metal and created prints of them. A little later, between 1450 and 1467, he was followed by a master known by the initials "E. S." The latter seems to have worked in the Upper Rhine region; a good hundred engravings from his hand are extant. In the western German town of Bochold, Israhel van Meckenem (ca. 1430/40–1503) copied the copper engravings of "E. S." and others. Israhel and his homonymous father—a goldsmith who produced ornamental engravings—were the first copper engravers to make a name for themselves. The work of art now definitively entered the age of mechanical reproduction. What is more, there may have even been direct links between the rise of copper engraving and Gutenberg's invention. At any rate, the playing card master used a pattern book created in Mainz for his work, and it is quite possible that Gutenberg learned from him. Imagine it: a flash of genius that changed the world may have burst forth during a card game! As always with highly complex innovations, Gutenberg's achievement was to bring together a wide variety of technological currents.

It is one thing to undertake a project. It is another to help it reach maturity. For a single individual to take several decisive steps at once is extremely rare. In the case of the printing press, there were three: first, the production of types for each individual letter; second, the use of metal, which allowed many more prints to be created than with wooden letters; and third, the use of a press like the screw press employed by Mainz vintners. The history of this tool goes all the way back to Roman times.

The press made it possible to apply the ink uniformly to a piece of dampened paper. To manufacture the types, a casting device and a matrix had to be developed. The latter was created by hammering a steel rod with a letter inversely carved on its tip onto a copper plate. The letter then appeared on the copper plate facing the right way. Any number of new inverse letters could then be cast in these molds; the majority were cast in lead. In addition, composing sticks, frames, tympans, platens, and other components had to be fashioned. The rest was then less complicated. The letters had to be assembled into text. For ink, Gutenberg used a mixture of soot, varnish, and egg white. He probably got the recipe from a painter in Mainz.

At first, printers tended to put text on only one side of a piece of paper. They soon started using the other side as well. Ultimately, they printed up to sixteen pages on one large sheet that, if arranged properly, could then be folded, cut, and bound into a book. The procedure had been perfected by the time Gutenberg decided to print the Bible, an obvious bestseller. At this point, another element necessary for every great innovation had to be found: capital. For Gutenberg's project was taking on monumental proportions. The printed Vulgate had 1,282 pages of forty-two lines each, requiring the use of about 100,000 types and 108 reams (a unit of five hundred sheets) of paper. During the two and a half years it took to finish the 180 Bibles Gutenberg is thought to have produced, wages had to be paid to twelve or more printers, four to six typesetters, and all manner of journeymen. Just the paper imported from Italy and the vellum on which a portion of the run was to be printed cost over one thousand guilders. In the end, Gutenberg was in debt 2,020 guilders to his main creditor, Johannes Fust, including unpaid interest. He also forfeited all of his equipment and the books he had already produced. It seems to have taken him little time to ward off bankruptcy, though. For in the autumn of 1454, the first copies of his Bible were offered for sale at the Frankfurt Book Fair. We know this thanks to Aeneas Sylvius Piccolomini, who marveled at the "very neat and legible" script, remarking that it could even be read easily without eyeglasses.[7] In addition, he reports that the whole edition was already sold out. The invention seemed so incredible that, when Fust peddled his Bibles in Paris, he was accused of making a pact with the devil. How else but with demonic power could one man produce so many books in such a short time?[8]

Fust continued the undertaking in collaboration with one of Gutenberg's journeymen, Peter Schöffer. In 1457, they produced a complete, color-printed edition of the Psalter. It was followed by texts on canon law and another Bible edition. The master now focused on smaller projects. He eventually gained the favor of Archbishop and Prince-Elector Adolph II of Nassau. Exempted from taxation and corvée and provided with lavish allotments of clothing, grain, and wine, he spent his twilight years in Mainz. He died there in 1468. Neither a portrait nor a gravestone remains of the man who changed the world more than anyone before him—and anyone since.

The Gutenberg Continent

Initially, journeymen trained in Gutenberg's orbit brought the new art to the rest of the world. There were also instances of industrial espionage. Charles VII is supposed to have sent his mint master to Mainz to find out what was going on in Gutenberg's workshop.[9] By about 1460, the invention had spread to Bamberg and Strasbourg. In 1464, it gained a foothold in Cologne, Augsburg, and Nuremberg thanks to a journeyman from the print shop of Fust and Schöffer. It crossed the Alps with two German printers and found a home in the Benedictine monastery of Subiaco. There, for the first time, an *antiqua* typeface based on ancient Roman monumental inscriptions was used. Shortly thereafter, Gutenberg's art made its way to Rome—where it impressed Alberti[10]—and then, in 1469, to Venice. In Paris, the first printing shop was run jointly by the Savoyard Guillaume Fichet, author of a comprehensive manual of rhetoric, and the German theologian Johann Heynlin.[11]

The speed with which the invention from Mainz conquered Europe was breathtaking. Of course, its usefulness and the profit opportunity it promised were obvious.[12] It captured the Sorbonne in the 1470s and advanced to Naples and Messina. Florence and Foligno, Lyon, Albi, and Toulouse followed, as did Buda further eastward. A printing office was operating in Valencia in 1474. In the same year, the first books in English appeared in Bruges, two years before they did in London. The merchant and diplomat William Caxton, who had learned the art of printing in Cologne, served as translator and publisher. For their part, merchants from Cologne invested in Venetian presses. In the city on the Lagoon, the Frenchman Nicolas Jenson (ca. 1420–1480) had developed *antiqua* letters whose elegance surpassed all previous fonts, setting the standard from then on. The press of Aldus Manutius (1449–1515) became the most important in Venice. Its specialty was Greek literature. The foundation for the typography had been laid by two Greek immigrants from Crete.[13] Printers even worked with Cyrillic letters in Venice. On behalf of the lord of Zeta, a priest and monk named Makarije bought a press in Venice, which, starting in 1493, he used to print liturgical works, Psalters, and the Gospels in his homeland of Montenegro.

Over 250 printing offices were operating in Europe around 1500. They changed the media landscape of the continent forever. Until then, in the same time it took Gutenberg's workshop to print 180 Bibles, a single scribe could only make one copy. Thanks to larger print runs, the cost per copy sank, and, thus, so did prices. Around 1470, folio volumes of 250 leaves could cost as much as a small house. The five-volume edition of Aristotle printed by Aldus between 1495 and 1498 only fetched the price of a good saddle horse, fifteen to twenty guilders, or one to two months' wages for a university professor.[14] The number of titles in print increased rapidly. For example, by the time he was fifty, a man born the year Constantinople fell could look back on a period in which more books had been produced than all the scribes in Europe had copied since the founding of the city on the Bosporus.[15] To put it in numbers: in the Early Middle Ages, an estimated twelve thousand manuscripts were created each century; in the fifteenth century, it was five million plus 12.5 million printed books; around 1600, between 150 and 230 million books were in circulation. Bookselling hubs included the trade fairs in Venice, Lyon, Antwerp, and Frankfurt. The humanist Konrad Celtis quipped that there were now so many printed books in Germany that the sacred scriptures could be found in every inn. "Everything finds its way to the printer; there are no secrets anymore, and we know what Jupiter does up in Heaven and Pluto under the Earth."[16] As early as 1474, Venice felt compelled to pass a law granting the printer Johann von Speyer a five-year monopoly on the printing and selling of books. The first printing privilege, an early form of copyright, was granted for twelve years to Marcantonio Sabellico for his history of Venice.[17] Oases of woodblock images soon enlivened the deserts of leaden text.

The decisive reason for the dramatic success enjoyed by Gutenberg's invention was that it met with a receptive market. The discursive revolution had prepared it through the interplay of paper and the money economy—in the bosom of societies that possessed capital and were populated by literate middle classes and the educated laymen they produced. The growing thirst for reading is reflected by the fact that since the fourteenth century it had become common to read silently and thus ever faster.[18] Chaucer's work already portrays a world jammed with readers.[19]

There was plenty to write about in the wake of the radical changes in reading and writing that attended the High Middle Ages. The catalogs of the first printers reflect the broad, diverse spectrum of topics that had developed since the twelfth century. Many printers knew exactly which titles promised to bring a profit. They included religious texts, especially the Bible. Among the books in English published by the savvy businessman Caxton, it is no coincidence that in 1483 a translation of the *Legenda aurea,* the most popular work of the entire Late Middle Ages, already figured alongside the *Canterbury Tales* and a chess manual. His first efforts were a collection of stories from the Trojan War and *Jason,* a chivalric epic written in the orbit of Philip the Good by Raoul Lefèvres. Profit could also be expected from handy calendars and herbals (including Dioscorides[20]), fables and classics. Cicero's *De officiis* was published in Cologne in 1465, his letters a bit later in Rome. Virgil, always a popular author, received his first printed edition in 1469. The *Decameron* and Petrarca's *Canzoniere* were printed in 1470, followed by Dante's *Divine Comedy.* Villon's poetry went to press in 1489, as did less significant yet amusing works like Albrecht von Eyb's *Ehebüchlein.* In Strasbourg, Johannes Mentelin sold works of Virgil and Terence's comedies. Lucian and Lucretius found publishers, as did Plautus and Ovid, including the latter's *Art of Love.* Ptolemy's works also now appeared in print, propelling them to the furthest corners of Europe.

The teeming market was filled with legions of consumers: pious readers who sought devotional literature and bought letters of indulgence, scholars, the educated, and individuals of nearly every rank hungry for education. There were universities with their bands of book-thirsty students, cities with reference libraries in their town halls, and royal bureaucracies that required legal texts and rained printed mandates down on the people in growing numbers. More and more individuals were therefore reaching for books, including a growing number of older readers. As a result, the demand for eyeglasses also swelled. It could no longer be satisfied by Italian spectacle makers. Eyeglass production was soon booming north of the Alps, and with it—an important side effect—more glass of increasingly higher quality was made. The first workshop, that of the *Parillenmacher* ("spectacle maker") Jacob Pfüllmair, is attested in 1478 in Nuremberg, where book printing had already been at home for nearly a decade. There were eleven more masters of the trade by the end of the century. Without the technological know-how accumulated in the spectacle makers' workshops, further inventions, especially precision instruments like the telescope and the microscope, would have been inconceivable (pp. 791–794, 822). This is one of the causal chains that connects the "deep history" of the Scientific Revolution to the discursive revolution of the High Middle Ages and the media revolution of the fifteenth century.

Dams could not break because there were none. Censorship, the unwanted guest at the boisterous, inchoate forum of a new public sphere, had not yet reared its head. The first edict in this direction was issued in 1485 by Berthold von Henneberg, archbishop of Mainz.[21] It called for all books printed in German to be inspected at the Frankfurt Book Fair. The Fifth Lateran Council issued a similar decree. In particular, writings in the vernacular were in the crosshairs. This scrutiny was motivated simultaneously by fear of the masses and by concern for their souls. But there were always places where one could buy what had been forbidden by the priests in Mainz or Rome. The printing shops, teeming with typesetters, correctors, woodcutters, and authors, evolved from workshops into intellectual spaces and venues of learned debate. The most famous examples are Froben's printing shop in Basel and the Aldine press in Venice.

Gutenberg's invention initiated the most radical transformation of the conditions for intellectual life in the history of Western civilization.[22] Without it, the Americas never would have been "discovered" in 1492. Without it, in all likelihood, there would have been no Copernican Revolution—at least not in the sixteenth century—no new physics, no new anatomy, nor would the Industrial Revolution have come as quickly as it did. On the other hand, books were and still are vehicles for both good and evil. One early example of the latter is the *Fortress of Faith* by the Spanish Franciscan Alonso de Espina, which contained a compilation of long-familiar anti-Jewish clichés. This shabby production was also a handbook for fighting Muslims, heretics—including "rationalists" like Aristotle—and dangerous demons. Several editions were published in the fifteenth century alone.

Almost no critical voices were raised against the new technology. Vespasiano da Bisticci condemned printing, remarking that "all the books" in Federico da Montefeltro's library were "of the utmost beauty, all written by hand. None are printed, which would be beneath his dignity." But this is hardly surprising, considering that Vespasiano earned his money with the production of luxury manuscripts.[23] The world of scribes like Diebold Lauber, who added "pretty" (*huebsch*) pictures to his books at Hagenau Castle, passed irretrievably out of existence. Most commentators praised printing as a godsend. Knowledge was not so easily lost as in the manuscript age. The continuation of the dialogue was ensured—Latin Europe developed into a single, gigantic intellectual laboratory. Thanks to Gutenberg's invention, Europe's realm of possibility gained thousands and, ultimately, millions of minds for its grand dialogue.

25

New Worlds

Nanjing, Ceuta: World History Shifts Course

Nanjing. October of 1405. The Armada dispatched by the Yongle Emperor to the West from Nanjing under the command of the "Three Jeweled" eunuch Zheng He was the largest that had crossed the ocean since antiquity.[1] Entire forests had to be chopped down to build it. The tree trunks were floated down the Yangtze River to the sea, where at the Longjiang Shipyard they were fashioned into mighty ribs, fitted with planks, and glued, painted, and caulked. The fleet consisted of 317 ships, including nine-masted monsters eighty-five meters in length, and 28,000 seamen.[2] Thousands of red silk sails billowed against the gray monsoon sky of late autumn. The large treasure ships transported gifts for princes and items to trade: gold, porcelain, and silk. In addition to soldiers and horses, there were also astrologers, physicians, and craftsmen on board.

The armada traveled by way of Java, Sumatra, and Sri Lanka to the southeast coast of India. Another six expeditions followed, reaching Malindi in East Africa, the Maldives, the Red Sea, and the Persian Gulf. A Chinese delegation made it to Mecca, where it marveled at the aroma of rose water that wafted from the Kaaba and at the happy people living according to the laws of their religion. The ships were decorated with imperial dragons. Their names, such as "Pure Harmony" and "Eternal Peace," camouflaged political aims: unpopular potentates were deposed, pirates captured, and tribute demanded. Upon their return, the ships were laden with curiosities, jewels, and exotic animals. A furor was caused by two giraffes from Africa. The admiral inscribed his pride on a memorial tablet:

> We have traversed more than one hundred thousand li of immense water-spaces and have beheld in the ocean huge waves like mountains rising sky high, and we have set eyes on barbarian regions far away hidden in a blue transparency of light vapors, while our sails, loftily unfurled like clouds day and night, continued their course [as rapidly as] a star, traversing those savage waves as if we were treading a public thoroughfare.[3]

The mission of the Ming navy, by far the largest in the world at the time, did not only have supporters at the imperial court. Yongle's short-lived successor Hongxi halted further expeditions, whereas his son, Yongle's favorite grandchild Xuande, followed in his grandfather's footsteps. He sent Zheng He on another distant voyage between 1431 and 1433. It was his seventh and last. After the Xuande Emperor's death, China retreated to the mainland for a long time. The "yellow" bureaucratic China of the interior, focused on farming its rich soil, had the upper hand over the "blue" China of the coasts, with its individualism, its entrepreneurial spirit, and its merchants. The fleet was decommissioned; the emperor even had shipyards destroyed. Dai Viet, Champa, and others took advantage of the situation, exporting their products, including millions of plates and cups, to the rest of Southeast Asia.[4]

Things developed quite differently in Europe. In August of 1415—Zheng He's armada had moored on the coast of East Africa a few months earlier—a Portuguese naval unit dropped anchor at the other end of the continent, near the Berber city of Ceuta. It was a couple of ships under the command of Prince Henry of Avis, son of John of Portugal.[5] There were knights on board, including the young Oswald von Wolkenstein, and mercenaries as well. They mustered under the sign of the cross, preparing as they were to fight Muslims. All of the soldiers had been promised indulgence. They stormed Ceuta on

August 24. According to Christian chronicles, only eight Portuguese fell in the victory, whereas thousands of Muslims were butchered. Supposedly, Ceuta's defenders tried to repulse the Europeans with stones. In addition to salvation and Ghanian gold, the victors won for themselves a base from which further conquests could be organized. While the enterprises of Yongle's dragon fleet, seemingly the beginning of a great undertaking, turned out to be the endgame, the performance on the Straits of Gibraltar was the overture to the establishment of a commercial empire. In 1580, Ceuta became part of Spain; it has remained a piece of Europe in Africa.

As in the age of the Crusades, competition among the European states spilled over the borders of the continent. In the following centuries, it would be taken to the furthest corners of the globe. The world-historical tragedy whose curtain rose with the conquest of Ceuta became increasingly dramatic. Holy wars became intertwined with struggles for secular power. Initially, the Spanish and Portuguese fought against each other. Then others joined the mix, especially the Dutch, the English, and the French. The goal was to gain resources for wars at home or at least to prevent one's rivals from capturing them. It was this concept that was foreign to Chinese strategists. The dragon fleet was not sent out to conquer or to convert. In matters of religion, the Middle Kingdom was wise, not zealous. Zheng He's mission seems intended primarily to show his country's colors. The voyages were displays of imperial power, used by China to demonstrate who was master in East Asia. China's decision to turn its back on the ocean was ultimately due to pride: the notion that it might need anything at all from anywhere else was beneath the empire's dignity.[6] Never again in premodern times would Chinese junks sail beyond the regions reached by Zheng He.

At the time Ceuta fell, the Europeans' conception of the world was also abundantly undefined. They were still ignorant of large portions of Africa, the far north, and the northwest. They knew nothing about the antipodes and their mysterious southern continent.[7] Even Asia remained covered by a mythical mist more than a century after Marco Polo's travels. There was vague knowledge of Buddha. At least the *Legend of Barlaam and Josaphat*, which tells the tale of an Indian prince's conversion to Christianity, was widely diffused among medieval Europeans.[8] Notions of far-off lands were still fed by the writings of ancient geographers, medieval encyclopedias, and works of imaginative fabulists like the author who called himself Sir John Mandeville.[9] For a long time, the yarns spun by the putative English knight from the realm of Prester John were taken at face value—tales of Lotus Eaters, which, as

Homer claimed, subsisted on aromatic flowers, of monopods (one-footed humanoids), of cynocephali (dog-headed humanoids), and of rebirths of the phoenix. Mandeville's fables were extremely entertaining and well suited to inciting the credulous to explore the wide world for its miracles and monsters, or perhaps even the golden hills of Tapobrana, a legendary island mentioned by Megasthenes. Most of this was pure fantasy, perhaps copied from Vincent of Beauvais's *Mirror* or the travelogue of the Franciscan friar Odoric of Pordenone (d. 1331).

In addition to Mandeville's myths, clues about what could be discovered in the West were provided by miraculous stories like *The Voyage of Saint Brendan the Abbot*. The legend, which probably dates to the tenth century, tells of a voyage to the Isle of the Blessed that the saint is supposed to have taken with several monks.[10] After seven years of adventure—once the holy men believe they are on an island, but it is actually the hump of a monster, the gigantic fish Jasconius—they reach their desired goal: an island bereft of human beings and full of aromas. No matter how much of this account followed literary models and how much came from the experience of actual travel, it suggested one thing for certain: there were islands far out in the ocean, places of incredible beauty, that were worth searching for. People may have heard of the Vikings' "Vinland"—Newfoundland or Labrador, i.e., a part of North America—or the island of Thule. The latter, as reported by Pytheas of Massilia in the fourth century BC, was supposed to be located six days' journey north of Britain, on the outermost edge of the world. The imaginary place was still mentioned in the seventeenth century, identified variously with Iceland, the Shetlands, or Telemark in Norway.[11]

Yet the legends were now accompanied by more concrete geographical knowledge.[12] The Catalan Atlas, created in Mallorca in the 1370s, is the first map of the world based in part on Marco Polo's account (Plate 15). It delineates the coastlines of the Mediterranean and the Atlantic and includes the Canary Islands, Madeira, and the Azores. In addition, it depicts phantom places like the island of Antillia, which Columbus hoped to find as a relay point for his westward journey to India.

But let us return to Portugal, where it all began.[13] Prince Henry, the victor of 1415, had earned his spurs and the title of Duke of Viseu in Ceuta. Thereafter, he only seldom set foot on board a ship. Yet he was not undeserving of his title, "the Navigator." For he was the one who laid the cornerstone for Portugal's position as a maritime superpower, albeit without intending to do so. His mind was on Crusading and knightly combat when he put his fleet to sea. First, it reached Madeira, and then a decade later the Azores. Both archipelagos were placed under the prince and the Order of Christ.

The religious motive faded during subsequent Portuguese expansion. Portugal set its sights on Africa: its land, its gold, and its people, who could be turned into slaves and thus also into gold. The humanist Pope Nicholas V blessed the enterprise with a bull.[14] Furthermore, Henry recognized the profit that could be made from sugar production. He can be considered not only the founder of the Portuguese slave trade but also of the Atlantic sugar industry. Only around the end of the fifteenth century did the goal emerge of finding a sea route to India and thus of bypassing the Ottoman Empire, the profit-sucking middleman of the silk and spice trade, and avoiding the dangers of the road. That it was possible to sail around Africa was already evident on the map of the world produced in the mid-fifteenth century by Fra Mauro, a Camaldolese monk in the monastery of San Michele on an island in the Venetian Lagoon.[15] He relied on the reports of "experienced sailors" and "trustworthy men who have seen with their own eyes."[16] Ventures southward had so far failed. Two Genoese galleys that had tried to navigate the dreaded Cape Bojador had foundered.

Those who now sailed into the unknown must have been extraordinarily brave: men like Gil Eanes and João Dias, who overcame this "Cape of No Return"; Lopo Gonçalves and Rui de Sequeira, the first Europeans to cross the equator; and Diogo Cão, who went up the Congo River in the belief that it was finally time to go east and thus in the direction of India. But it was necessary to sail still further south. And so Portuguese captains and their pilots—that is what the seamen were called who bore the actual responsibility for navigating and organizing the voyages—continued down the coast of West Africa. Their fleets left behind outposts, some of which grew into markets for trade with the interior. The Cape Verde Islands were discovered by accident around 1456. A storm had blown the ships their way. The Venetian merchant Alvise Cadamosto (ca. 1432–1483), who was in Prince Henry's service and chronicled the Portuguese expeditions of the time, provides a lively report of the incident. He also describes the land and people of Africa, which he calls "another world."[17]

The number of the enslaved quickly rose into the tens of thousands. On the Cape Verde Islands and Madeira, they were set to work on sugar plantations—the model for the Caribbean—while others were shipped off to Portugal.[18] In 1460, the year of Henry's death, the coast of what is now Sierra Leone had been reached. The pace of exploration briefly slackened when King Alfonso V diverted his resources to North Africa, ordering that Tangier be conquered. But the oceanic project had long since become an institution with its own agencies. In the sixteenth century, they would be merged as the Casa da Índia. Funding for the voyages came from merchants prepared to take risks in exchange for the right to exploit the conquered.

In the early 1470s, the Portuguese took possession of the islands of São Tomé and Príncipe. In 1482 they set up a fort near the gold fields of Ghana, São Jorge de Mina (or Elmina for short), which served as a base for subsequent advances southward. Crosses and stone stele marked areas that were claimed for the crown. Thus began the history of the "Atlantic World," and with it a singular process of creolization. A culture emerged that was not simply the product of governments, capital, merchants, and slave traders but rather was just as much the creation of native Africans and Americans, of black and white women and men of many different cultures.[19]

Birth of a Catholic Empire

The construction of the Portuguese maritime empire was initially undisturbed by the ambitions of Spanish rulers. During the long regency for the infant John II (r. 1406–1454), Castile was weakened by rebellions and struggles for the throne. No thought was given to adventures at sea. Even during John's reign proper, beginning in 1419, the country found no peace. In 1433 and again thirty years later, conspirators even thought there was a realistic possibility of transforming Seville into a city-state on the Italian model. The nobles allied with Aragon also revolted. The Constable of Castile, Álvaro de Luna, a nephew of Antipope Benedict XIII, only barely preserved his king's crown. The noble rebellion led to his downfall in 1453; he was executed by beheading. King John died a year later. His successor, Henry IV (r. 1454–1474), was a weak ruler mistrusted because of his predilection for men. On account of his inability— in whatever sense—he was called *el impotente*, the Impotent. Castile's history at the time has thus been described as "cosmic chaos."[20]

Aragon's affairs were in similar disarray after Martin the Humane died without an heir in 1410, thus putting an end to the House of Barcelona. The Cortes of Aragon, Valencia, and Catalonia had a say in choosing the successor, Ferdinand the Just of the House of Trastámara. He died after only six years on the throne. His heir, Alfonso V, concentrated on expanding Aragon's Mediterranean empire with its center in Naples (pp. 390f.). John II (r. 1458–1479) first had to make good on his claim to Navarre, which had fallen to him by marriage.

From 1462 to 1472, war raged over Catalonia, whose estates wanted to preserve their liberties. Louis XI of France sought to exploit the dissension. In return for supplying the embattled John with funds, he was given possession of Roussillon and Cerdagne for several decades.

In light of the situation, an alliance between the two leading Iberian realms seemed advisable. What started out as cabals and marriage maneuvers ended up making world history.[21] Considering how consequential it was, let us review the details. Henry IV's only issue was his daughter Joanna, whose paternity was not certain. She was derisively called *la Beltraneja*, after her putative sire Beltrán de la Cueva, the lover of her mother Joanna of Portugal. Another candidate for the throne was Isabella, a daughter of John II and Henry's half-sister. The timely death of potential husbands selected by the king saved her from numerous undesired marriages. Having reached the age of majority, she also resisted union with a Valois. The lucky man ended up being her cousin Ferdinand, heir to the throne of Aragon. Lest King Henry try to hinder them, the seventeen-year-old ladies' man—despite his tender age, he had already fathered two illegitimate children—disguised himself as a stable boy, traveled to Valladolid, and wed Isabella there in 1469.

Things came to a head when Henry IV died. Only half of Castile recognized Isabella's claim to the throne. In addition, her rival Joanna was able to count on assistance from Portugal as well as from Louis XI of France. Nevertheless, the forces arrayed by Isabella and Ferdinand prevailed in a war of large armies. The peace agreement reached in 1479 cost Portugal old claims to the Canary Islands but preserved its monopoly on all trade farther south. Isabella remained queen of Castile. John II died in the year of the treaty, making Ferdinand king of Aragon. In this way, a superpower was created that quite soon would overshadow all other European states. On the Iberian Peninsula, only Portugal and Navarre retained their autonomy. The connections between Castile's wool merchants and northern Europe became interwoven with Aragon's commercial relations, which reached all the way to the East. The monarchy consciously promoted the "lower" nonhereditary nobility, the *hidalguía*, in order to keep the old families in check. The cities were dominated by the crown via alliances with local aristocrats. Trained jurists, *letrados*, gained the upper hand over the high nobility in the royal council, the courts, and the bureaucracy. The latter's horrendous pensions were drastically cut, but not so radically that the kingdom would lose their support. The Church was a reliable servant and ally of the monarchy.[22]

Isabella was a politically savvy ruler, both pious and educated. She was as worthy of the title of "Catholic Queen," granted her by the pope, as her husband was of his epithet of *rey católico*. Spain's politics became "catholic" in the other sense as well, i.e., universal in scope. It firmly asserted a religious claim to power and rooted its legitimacy in religion. From the very beginning, the unifying power of faith was used to draw the two kingdoms together, although each continued to "belong" to its own ruler.

In 1478, the Catholic Monarchs received the pope's approval for the creation of an Inquisition tribunal specifically for Castile and Aragon. Whereas the Inquisition was under the control of the Holy See in other states in Europe, the Spanish version developed into an institution directly responsible to the crown. The estates and cities of Aragon resisted its machinations, albeit in vain, as it seemed a tool of Castile. What is more, it was perceived as the spearhead of vertical power, of a monarchical campaign against the estates. The office of the Inquisitor General of Spain was conferred upon Isabella's confessor, the Dominican Tomás de Torquemada (1420–1498).[23] The *Suprema*, the "Supreme Council of the Inquisition," cared for souls—at the cost of bodies if necessary—and endeavored to induce the people to morality and the uneducated to the true faith. With fire and torture, it persecuted everything un-Catholic, irreligious, and superstitious. It burned its victims at the stake or doomed them to a life of torment on the galleys. However, it was never the mighty kraken with inescapable tentacles it was portrayed as. It was too small an institution for that, lacking the necessary funding and personnel, even if the twenty thousand or so *familiares* who served it as spies are counted. That it worked in secrecy, the object of hatred and suspicion, was a conscious strategy, making it seem more powerful than it really was.[24] Most of its functionaries were dull bureaucrats, often high-level civil servants who were trained jurists and theologians. They were a banal evil, not fiery fanatics. Occasionally it produced reasonable men like Don Alonso de Salazar y Frías, who put a stop to the witch trials in Spanish Basque regions because he was convinced of the defendants' innocence.

The Inquisition contributed to the foundation of the nation's sense of itself as the most Catholic of all. Yet even though its bad reputation may have been exaggerated in many respects, it still stood in stark contrast to the Renaissance's eagerness for discussion and open-mindedness. It has left a bleak legacy. The notorious *autos-da-fé* were performances of terror, carnivals of piety held at town squares. Barefoot victims dressed in penitential clothing—*sanbenitos*—were forced along in a sad procession with burning candles and made to publicly confess their sins. While priests offered them the cross as a final comfort, the stakes blazed away. Especially vulnerable were *conversos*, converted Jews, as they were suspected of secretly continuing to adhere to their "diabolical"[25] religion and tempting Christians to convert. The usual accusations also circulated, allegations that Jews had desecrated the host or even crucified a Christian baby.[26]

Early on, Spanish anti-Judaism acquired a characteristic that can be called racist: the concept of "blood purity," *limpieza de sangre*. It disadvantaged Christians whose ancestors included Jews or Muslims and thus all *conversos*. The fact that this devalued the sacrament of baptism did not matter. The rule restricted access to university colleges, cathedral chapters, religious orders, guilds, and city councils, and it made a lengthy Christian lineage a requirement even for midwives in the service of the royal household.[27] The first city to enshrine it in statute law was Toledo in 1449.

The resoluteness with which the Spanish realms were cleansed of everything non-Catholic stemmed from centuries of confrontation with the Muslim "other." It was a response to a challenge from a religious culture that harbored its own strict conceptions of purity.[28] A 1462 notice for Mudéjars—Muslims living under Christian rule—prescribed barbaric punishments for all transgressions against morality: death for infidels living in secret, stoning for blasphemers, rapists, and homosexuals, and whipping for all who drank wine during Ramadan or "fornicated" outside of marriage.

With the exception of pogroms towards the end of the fourteenth century, *conversos* had long lived in pragmatic, peaceful co-existence with Jews, Old Christians, and Muslims.[29] Christian rulers had never disdained entering into alliances with Muslim potentates when it promised to be useful. Christians had ruled over Muslim vassals and Muslims over Christians. Jews were also guaranteed a right to exist. They did not live on terms of equality, but there was peace. Muslim musicians played at Corpus Christi processions in Tarazona in Aragon, and during one famine there were common processions of supplication.[30] There were also converts from Christianity to Islam and tepid Christians who behaved like Muslims. Now, however, this period of *convivencia* came to an end.

Isabella and Ferdinand were determined not only to lead their own realms to orthodoxy but also to make their entire peninsula Christian. They prepared arms against Granada, Allah's last unconquered citadel. With fiery words, Sultan Yusuf III had once exhorted his fellow Muslims to join him "in this victorious city of ours, Granada, over which God watches with his own eyes," and prepare for holy war.[31] So far, altercations had been limited to reciprocal raids in which livestock or harvests were at stake, not existence or annihilation. Ballads turned these forays into the heroic struggles of holy warriors.[32] In the shadow of the Christian threat, the emirate had grown into a modern, court-centered administrative state with an efficient tax system. Its powerful military organization included a budding system of general conscription and barracking, as reflected in writings like Ibn Hudhayl al-Andalusi's *Kitab Hilyat al-fursan wa Shi'-ar al Shuj'an* (*The Finery of the Knights and Emblem of the Brave*) and *Kitab Tuhfat al-anfus wa-shi 'ar sukkan al-Andalus* (*The Prowess of the People of al-Andalus*).[33]

In 1481, the last war of the Reconquista began—waged in the spirit of Crusade, financed by the pope, and lit by the fire of the *autos-da-fé*. Discord among the Muslims aided the Christian troops in their endeavor. One city after another fell. Malaga, the base for reinforcements from North Africa, was taken in 1487. Four years later, the siege of Granada was complete. On January 1, 1492, the Andalusian metropolis surrendered. From then on, the view from the Alhambra, as described by the poet Ibn Zamrak, was a mere memory for Muslims. "Stay awhile here on the terrace of Sabīka [i.e., the Alhambra] and look about you," he wrote.

> This city is a wife, whose husband is the hill:
> Girt she is by water and by flowers,
> Which glisten at her throat,
>
> Ringed with streams; and behold the groves of trees which are the
>   wedding guests,
> Whose thirst is being assuaged by the water-channels.
>
> The Sabīka hill sits like a garland on Granada's brow,
> In which the stars would be entwined,
> And the Alhambra (God preserve it)
> Is the ruby set above that garland.
> Granada is a bride whose headdress is the Sabīka, and whose jewels
>   and adornments are its flowers.[34]

Columbus: Westward to the East

When the lions and castles on the standards of Isabella and Ferdinand were raised above the Alhambra, one of the spectators at the ceremony was a man from Genoa named Cristoforo Colombo. The Spanish called him Cristóbal Colón; we know him as Columbus.[35] The young man was one of many adventurers then seeking to gain the favor of the courts of Europe—with their ability and with their good and, more often, extravagant ideas. Shortly before, he had managed to attain Queen Isabella's support for a fantastical project: to search for a sea route to India, not around Africa like the Portuguese but rather in a westward direction.

Born in 1451, Columbus could be described as a man with oceanic sensibilities—a man who inhaled travelogues, bent over marine charts, and fiddled with nautical instruments. Wherever he was, he gathered knowledge about the rhythms of the sea, studying winds, currents, and the positions of the stars. He gained his first experience of the sea in his youth, on a voyage to the Aegean island of Chios, which then belonged to Genoa. Once, he seems to have found work on a ship that brought him to London and Bristol and ultimately to Iceland, although the journey is not documented. He might have heard the rumor then that still more land was to be found far, far to the west. Later he made it to the sugar island of Madeira. He married a young Portuguese woman from an impoverished noble family and lived for a time on the island of Porto Santo. His wife may have helped him to make useful connections at the court in Lisbon. Columbus rose to become the commander of a fleet, sailing with it to Fort Elmina. There he got a taste for fresh gold. He would never lose his appetite for it. Around that time, he must have come up with the idea that Asia could be reached by crossing the other side of the globe, following the setting sun.

For him to be able to seriously pursue his plan and ultimately discover a continent theretofore unknown to Europeans—although not the route to India—many different "streams" again had to flow together. Indispensable were technological devices like the astrolabe, dry compass, and quadrant. The plummet was useful for navigating shallow coastal waters. The ship's log made it possible to measure the speed of the journey, thereby approximating the distance a ship had traversed. Columbus would record it each day on the voyage westward but always give his crew a lower number. Thus, whenever their spirits sank, he could always tell them they had not yet gone far enough, that it was only a few miles more.

Another decisive factor was the existence of a kind of ship that could cross the Atlantic. Galleys advanced slowly along the coast, even in the rather peaceful Mediterranean, and rarely braved winter storms; they could not navigate the high seas. The caravel could. It was designed on the basis of the experience garnered by Portuguese pilots on their voyages of discovery in the Atlantic. Caravels maneuvered well but still had up to one hundred metric tons of cargo space. Their two or three masts were rigged with triangular lateen sails or, depending on wind conditions, with square sails. The stern rudder the Europeans used to steer their caravels might have been copied from Chinese junks.

Columbus was more than an experienced seaman familiar with various nautical cultures. Thanks to Europe's excellent communication structures, he had had the opportunity to accrue a great deal of book learning as well. For the first time, Gutenberg's invention and the work of the humanists led directly to world-changing events. For example, Columbus owned Pierre d'Ailly's *Imago mundi*, which was first printed in 1480.[36] He studied it assiduously, as can be seen by the notes that fill his copy. He found confirmation there of what Marco Polo had written about the riches of Asia. The book also calculated that the portion of the Earth covered by water was much smaller than that covered by land, thus giving Columbus the courage to seek a waterway to the other side of the "apple," the metaphor d'Ailly used to describe the world.

This was in accordance with what Strabo claimed. His *Geography* was first printed in 1469 in the Latin translation by Guarino Guarini. Even today, we continue to be fascinated by the critical spirit of this work, which compiled all the geographical knowledge available at the time of Christ's birth. Columbus was able to read there that the Earth had a spherical shape.[37] Strabo also concluded that all inhabitable land was an island surrounded by the ocean. Furthermore, the Atlantic was not divided into two different seas by isthmuses but rather was continuously navigable by ships.[38] Above all, Columbus might have been electrified by a comment stemming from Strabo's critical engagement with Eratosthenes: "If the immensity of the Atlantic Sea did not prevent it, we could sail from Iberia to India along one and the same parallel over the remainder of the circle."[39] According to Strabo, the distance was not 200,000 stadia but rather, as Posidonius claimed, only 70,000 stadia, i.e., about 8,000 miles. Therefore, "if you sail from the west in a straight course you will reach India."[40] Seldom did credence in ancient authorities have more momentous consequences.

Other ancient sources and perhaps also Marco Polo's account encouraged Columbus to trust Strabo. He had exchanged letters with Paolo dal Pozzo Toscanelli, probably in an attempt to use the famous Florentine scholar's authority to convince financial backers. Toscanelli affirmed that the voyage to India was possible, calculating that it was only three thousand nautical miles from the Canary Islands to Japan, and from there another two thousand to China (in reality, the distance is over ten thousand). Columbus made the fateful decision not to simply sail in the wake of the sunset but instead to take a southwestern route. It would take him, he thought, to rich lands inhabited by monstrous humanoid creatures. He considered it legitimate to enslave such brutes.[41]

Almost all experts disavowed the project initially. A Portuguese commission to which Columbus proposed it in 1484 considered his grandiose promises unrealistic, as did an expert panel in the service of Isabella of Castile. A second appeal in Lisbon was also unsuccessful. But Columbus was undaunted. He pondered bowing and scraping in England or France. Ultimately, he was received again in Santa Fe, in the headquarters of the army besieging Granada, by Queen Isabella. Now, in the winter of 1491, the omens seemed more propitious. However, when he demanded to be made viceroy of the newly discovered lands and appointed admiral, he was sent packing.

The following scene represents a turning point in world history. We see—a few weeks before the episode described at the beginning of this chapter—a crestfallen Columbus riding to France on the back of a gray mule. In Pinos, a village north of Santa Fe, a messenger reached him with the news that the queen had changed her mind. Columbus's courtly network had come through in the end. And he had found something that would turn out to be decisive for the enduring success of his enterprise: a state, indeed one of the mightiest states in Europe.

Isabella's fateful change of mind seems to have been the work of King Ferdinand's treasurer, Luis de Santángel.[42] Pointing to the successful endeavors of the Portuguese competition, he maintained that Castile could not afford to fall behind. Isabella might also have been convinced by the argument that it was a pious work, now that the heretical Moors were being driven out, to envisage the conversion of the peoples of Asia. The queen endowed Columbus with extraordinary privileges, including the rank of admiral, hereditary noble rank, and the title of viceroy. Furthermore, the crown helped to finance the expedition. Private capital also launched the three ships that now set sail to find the new route to India: two caravels, the *Niña* ("Girl") and the *Pinta* ("Painted Lady"), and the *Santa Maria*, the flagship. Probably a carrack, Columbus referred to her simply as his "*nao*," his ship.

What would have happened if Columbus were subtracted from the equation? For example, he easily could have gone to the bottom of the sea in 1476. The Genoese fleet he had hired onto was attacked off the coast of Lagos by a squadron of Portuguese and French ships. He narrowly escaped to land, clinging to a rudder. Indeed, there was no lack of dangerous situations in Columbus's eventful life. If he had died in any of them, a key figure would have been missing without whom things certainly would have turned out differently. To be sure, the time was ripe. The compass and the caravel were available, and at some point, another Odysseus would have succeeded in finding the continent that lay between Spain and India. Yet if the voyage to the Americas had happened only one or two generations later, the Catholic Monarchs would not have been able to pursue their imperialist designs, retain their Italian possessions, and curb Protestantism. Perhaps people from Brazil to Chile might be speaking English today—and the indigenous peoples would have been spared suffering, exploitation, and repression, at least for a few decades.

This counterfactual thought experiment highlights the element of time. *When* an event happens is not unimportant. It is only through the efforts of individuals that a possibility becomes a reality. What is more, figures like Columbus are few and far between. He was a highly trained seaman and a hard commander. He combined stubbornness, boundless faith in God, and equally boundless optimism with a sense of mission and an eschatological outlook.[43] To this were added a thirst for knowledge, audacity, and faith in ancient authorities. Such qualities were necessary to argue for the westward sea route to the East in the face of nearly all expert opinion. For there was a very real danger of reaching a point of no return—when water and food would run short, thirst and scurvy decimate the crew, and a hurricane bury what was left of the expedition beneath the waves. The knowledge available at the time did not even make it possible to rule out that an abyss opened up at the western edge of the world, a maelstrom that would devour the ships and all hands on deck. Moreover, it was in no way settled that the Earth was spherical. No doubt, d'Ailly's apple model corresponded with the positions taken by ancient and Arabic scholars. It was opposed, however, by the authority of a Church Father, Lactantius. If the Earth were a ball, the saint had pointed out, heaven would be both above and below every point on its surface. As a result, things on the other side of the ball would fall into heaven! And that was impossible.[44] Thus Hartmann Schedel's 1493 *Weltchronik* left it an open question whether the Earth was in the shape of a disk (*gescheybelt*) or a sphere (*kugelt*).[45] At about the same time, the painter Hieronymus Bosch portrayed the Earth as flat as a pancake (Fig. 36, p. 486).

In addition, dangerous creatures might prowl the ocean depths—the monstrous fish mentioned by Brendan, gigantic kraken, and hybrid beings like the echeneis, a fish that, according to Aristotle, had feet. Pliny said that it had magical powers and could even stop ships; it was still feared around 1600.[46] Understandably, Columbus had difficulties recruiting manpower. The crew included representatives of the crown, a notary, physicians, and a *converso* who could speak Arabic as a translator. The group probably had mixed feelings during the final mass said before departure in the church of San Jorge in Palos. Half an hour before dawn on August 2, 1492, the tiny fleet weighed anchor and departed on the greatest sea voyage of all time.

1492

In early October, there was still no land in sight. The critical moment was approaching. Columbus took every bird, every lump of seaweed, as a sign that land was near.[47] Only with difficulty did he keep the crew from mutinying. Deliverance came over two months after the voyage had begun, on October 12, 1492. A cannonball shot from the lead ship, the *Pinta*, shattered the morning calm over the Caribbean. Then came cries of "*Tierra! Tierra!*" The flotilla had reached one of the Bahamian Islands. Columbus named it San Salvador after Christ the Savior, Spain's pilot to his New World. The admiral went on land with the captains and a few others and took possession of the island, erecting banners with the sign of the cross and the initials of the Catholic Monarchs. In his description, the people he met on the island were "naked as when their mothers bore them,"[48] painted in bright colors or gray, and shapely. They were friendly and bestowed parrots, cotton balls, and spears on the foreigners, whom they took for gods. They gladly received cheap bric-a-brac in exchange.

The Spanish continued from island to island, in search of spices, gold, and more gold. First, they discovered only tobacco, mastic, aloe, and cotton, as well as pine trees whose wood could be used to build ships. They saw unknown plants and trees, heard of strange gods and myths, and encountered societies from another time. Columbus writes of elegiac landscapes in his journal; he rhapsodizes about the chirping of birds, enticing aromas, flocks of parrots, and trees green in late autumn "like April in Andalusia."[49] He was the first European to set foot on Cuba, convinced that he had finally found the gold country promised by the ancient geographers, and he ultimately reached Hispaniola. There he lost the *Santa Maria*, which hit a sandbar and sank. His carpenters fashioned a fort from the salvaged planks. He called it "Christmas," *La Navidad*, to commemorate Christmas Day, 1492, which witnessed the foundation of the first European settlement in America since the Vikings. A group of volunteers stayed behind, provisioned with a year's supply of wine and bread as well as seeds for crops.

After a difficult journey, in which a storm nearly consigned the two remaining ships to the deeps and thus the great discovery to oblivion, Palos was

reached on March 15, 1493. The admiral now claimed he had found "the extreme East," *el fin del Oriente*, the location of the "terrestrial paradise."[50] Received by his patrons with the highest honors, he promised them that the lush
country would soon yield a profit.

> And I shall labor to make all these people Christians. They will become so
> readily, because they have no religion nor idolatry, and your Highnesses
> will send orders to build a city and fortress, and to convert the people.[51]

Christendom, but above all Spain, "to whom the whole country should be
subject," would be able to trade with the people there. Columbus's logbook is
rife with contempt for the "Indians," whom he believed to be incapable of
fighting and easy to rule.

Columbus forged grand plans as soon as he returned. He wanted to bring
two thousand settlers to the newly discovered islands, found cities, and search
for gold, while his queen and king hoped new souls could be won for their
Christian empire. An armada of seven ships was assembled and loaded with
breeding animals, seeds, and tools. Horses and soldiers were also taken on
board, as well as five monks. Venetian galleys led the armada out of Cadiz: the
great power of the old Mediterranean saluted the future superpower of the
western ocean. Again, new islands and heavenly country were discovered. On
the other hand, the remains of cannibal feasts reminded the voyagers that the
idyll had its dark side. A harsh surprise was in store for the Spanish when they
visited La Navidad. All they found was charred timber. The colonists had been
slaughtered to the last man by the natives. More and more often now, contact
gave way to conflict, exploration to conquest. No gold was found. The Spanish
rounded up human capital instead. They carried captives off to the slave markets, built forts—including Santo Domingo, which would ultimately grow into
a city of millions—and laid out plantations.

In 1498, Columbus undertook his third voyage. When he landed on the
coast of what is now Venezuela, he set foot for the first time on the mainland
of the American continent. There was unrest among the colonists on Hispaniola, who learned the hard way that even in paradise gold did not grow on trees.
The admiral and his two brothers could not get the rebellion under control
and were ultimately replaced by a governor sent by the crown. In Spain, a
newly created body (later formalized as the Council of the Indies) assumed
responsibility for overseeing administration and justice for the overseas territories.[52] In imitation of the Portuguese model, another agency subordinate
to it, the *Casa de la Contratación* in Seville, oversaw trade and emigration.

Thousands upon thousands of simple lives were now inscribed in its records. The crown wanted the newly discovered land to remain pure. Vagabonds, criminals, and, later, people of "impure" blood were not to find their way there.[53]

In 1503, Columbus succeeded a fourth and final time in getting a small fleet approved. He added Martinique and Jamaica to his list of discoveries and then sailed down the Central American coast to the mouth of the Orinoco River. The next year, he returned home, again without any gold to show for his efforts. He spent his final years, plagued by gout and greed, futilely seeking compensation and the confirmation of his viceroyalty.

He died on May 20, 1506. No representative of the court was present when the man who had opened up a new world to Spain was laid to rest in the crypt of the Franciscan monastery in Valladolid. To the end, he was convinced he had been close to the gates of paradise and thus to China and India. He had constantly sought to understand the foreign by describing it in terms of what he knew, such as Spanish landscapes and Portuguese coastal forms. Pliny's *Natural History* helped to give names to the unknown. So did mythology, like when he thought he had seen three sirens in a bay of Hispaniola—they were probably manatees. Mandeville's wonders of the Orient also crop up in his drawings.[54] From the word that his sources used for man-eaters, *caniba*, he keenly deduced they must be the dog-headed monsters of Asia reported by the ancient geographers and their student Pierre d'Ailly. For *canibal* must have come from the Latin word for "dog," *canis*. Once, when he was stranded in Jamaica but thought he was in Asia, he defiantly declared, "The world is small."[55]

Spain: A Pure Country

For Ferdinand and Isabella, 1492 was a miraculous year whose events seemed to provide confirmation of their mission. They had taken Granada, and lush, fairy-tale islands inhabited by throngs of future Christians had fallen into their laps. The royal couple likely understood their luck as an invitation to continue with their efforts at purification and conversion. These were aimed first at Spain's Jews and *conversos*, and later at Sinti and Roma as well. The pressure had previously come not from the royal court but from the Cortes and city councils. Now that the Emirate of Granada was history, Ferdinand and Isabella adopted that anti-Jewish position as their own.[56] In March of 1492, Torquemada convinced them to issue a decree that gave Jews a choice: be baptized or emigrate. Mass conversions followed. Yet tens of thousands of the ca. eighty thousand Jews then living in Castile and Aragon preferred to leave. Children were ripped from many families and taken to sugarcane plantations off the coast of West Africa, where they were raised as Christians. In 1497, Portugal was obliged to follow Spain's example, forcibly converting Jews and expelling Muslims. The purification of the population was one of the conditions upon which King Manual received the hand of a daughter of the Catholic Monarchs in marriage.

Spanish Jews sought asylum everywhere on the coasts of the Mediterranean in the following decades. They were called "Sephardim," after the Hebrew word for Spain. They brought in tow their faith, an elaborate carpet design from Muslim Andalusia, and their Castilian mother tongue. It could still be heard around 1600 in Thessalonica.[57] The *conversos* who remained in their homeland lived an arduous existence. Suspected of heresy, many of them fell into the hands of the Inquisition. *Conversos* constituted a large portion of the ca. two thousand individuals executed as heretics before 1520.[58] The country's purification of non-Catholic subjects was mirrored by reforms of religious orders and the secular clergy.[59] The crown, whose influence on ecclesiastical affairs was stronger than elsewhere in western Europe, played an active role. Church and kingdom existed in a nearly Byzantine symbiosis, sometimes allied with the pope in far-off Rome, sometimes against him, and always supported by the Inquisition. The Catholic faith shaped the nation, justified its wars, and gave comfort to its people.

A good example of Spain's Catholic fervor is the Janus-like figure of Francisco Jiménez de Cisneros (1436–1517), archbishop of Toledo, Inquisitor General, and ultimately a cardinal. Using the influence he enjoyed as the queen's confessor, he sought to increase the educational level and moral purity of the clergy. He founded schools and expanded the *studium* of Alcalá de Henares— known as the *Complutense* after the Roman name for Alcalá, Complutum—into a full-fledged university. He won posthumous fame as a patron of the polyglot Bible produced there. Cisneros's piety was influenced by mystical and reform ideas. The curriculum of his university, however, remained guided by Thomas Aquinas, Duns Scotus, and Ockhamist nominalism. He read works by Catherine of Siena and Savonarola but also by Erasmus of Rotterdam, whom he even invited to Spain. He assiduously administered the Christian mission to the islands discovered by Columbus. He financed a mercenary company and sailed with it to Africa, where he conquered the city of Oran for the cross.

A rebellion in December 1499 in the Muslim quarter of Granada, precipitated by forced baptisms and followed by revolts in other cities, provided the occasion to employ harsh measures against the Mudéjars as well. Cisneros thought they ought to be baptized and enslaved—then the country would forever be peaceful.[60] Thus the final hours chimed for Muslim Spain not even ten years after the conquest of Granada. Mass baptisms were intended to produce even more new Christian souls. A few Muslims were allowed to emigrate. Mosques were turned into churches; Arabic books were burned. Granada was "purified" in 1501. In subsequent years, purification efforts were extended to all of Castile. Aragon, however, did not yet join in; its nobles and Cortes checked the zeal of piety. After all, the Mudéjars were still needed for cheap agricultural labor.

The conquest of Granada and the discovery of routes to a new world mark turning points in Spanish history. Cardinal Cisneros and his ilk wiped out an exceptional culture and the chance to be a living example of coexistence with the "other," Islam. Granada, on the border between two worlds, had long since established its own iridescent identity. The city had been neither solely Islamic nor exclusively Christian, neither entirely Arab nor totally Spanish. One of the ballads written about it takes the form of a conversation between King John II and Yusuf, a pretender to the throne of the Emirate who ruled Granada in 1432 as a puppet of Castile. Then the city herself speaks, telling John that she does not need his affections:

I am a married woman, King John,
A married woman and no widow,
And the Moor that keeps me
Loves me very dearly.[61]

A sign of what was destroyed is visible right outside Granada's Alhambra. Surrounded by rose gardens with a view of the snow-covered peaks of the Sierra Nevada is the magical Nasrid palace. On the outside, it is unassuming, resembling a fortress. Inside, it is an allegory of the utmost civilization, albeit somewhat decadent. Around the Court of the Myrtles and the Court of the Lions, paved with marble and lined by slender columns, some of the most beautiful rooms in the world are found. The eye is dazzled by sparkling, elaborate ornamentation and Arabic inscriptions that line the ceilings and walls, proclaiming the glory of Allah and his Prophet. A few decades later, Emperor Charles V celebrated his marriage to Isabella of Portugal in the gardens of the Alhambra.

26

Witches, High Finance, and the Authority of the State

Hellfire

In the beginning was the Word. "For he spake, and it was done; he commanded, and it stood fast." This verse from the 33rd Psalm provides the caption for one of the most mysterious pictures in the history of art: Hieronymus Bosch's late-fifteenth-century painting *The Garden of Earthly Delights*.[1] The words appear on the back side of the two exterior panels that, when closed, cover the central image (Fig. 36, p. 486). The universe is depicted in the state it was on the third day of Creation, in white, gray, and black colors. Light and dark, day and night, have already been separated, and the firmament has been erected "in the midst of the waters." The cosmos, in the shape of a glass ball, hovers in the void. The Lord is enthroned high above, wearing a royal cloak and crowned with the tiara like his vicar on Earth. In his left hand, he holds a book that might show a sketch

of the plan of Creation. The Earth below is still uninhabited. But the barren land illuminated by the glow of the world's dawning is sprouting with the first vegetation, as described in Genesis. The next day, God will fix the Sun, Moon, and stars in the sky. For now, it is only the luster emitted by the distant Creator that spreads pale light over the primeval landscape.

The first viewers must have reeled when, as happened on special occasions, the outer panels with their somber grisaille were folded back to reveal the richly colored theater of the world on the inner panel. Bosch continues telling the tale of Creation, from the first human beings down to the brink of his own day. The story of Adam and Eve is populated by exotic creatures like unicorns, three-headed amphibians, armies of mailed piscine people, gigantic flying fish, an elephant, and an eerily gray giraffe. Without precedent, Eden is depicted with springs, mountains, and rivers flowing through rock formations, with bizarre organisms in spectacular colors, pink and blue, seemingly from another world. "And it came to pass," reads the caption of the center panel (Plate 16), again from the Bible,

> when men began to multiply on the face of the Earth, and daughters were born unto them, that the sons of God saw the daughters of men that they were fair; and they took them wives of all which they chose.[2]

Indeed, they enjoy each other's company, naked, in all manner of positions. A Dionysian procession rings a pond in which dark- and light-skinned women bathe. The mortals unabashedly eat luscious fruits, the first of which decided humankind's fate: gaining access to divine wisdom but, in consequence, having to toil and suffer. The unfettered existence of earthly paradise must have an evil end, as Genesis teaches. The right interior panel, a virtuoso night scene again without precedent, depicts demonic armies, blasts of fire, the gate to the flaming underworld, and a frozen lake upon which naked people shiver. All of the senses are offended. Bosch paints infernal music, the stink of a latrine, the torture of human bodies, and various mortal sins, including gamblers and a naked, beautiful woman representing lust; she looks at herself in the mirror, her reflection reddened by the fires of hell. At the bottom right, where the painting's narration reaches its end, a sow dressed in the habit of a Dominican nun is blandishing a naked man. Is she trying to convince him to put her order in his will?

The Garden of Earthly Delights dates to the middle of the period that is the subject of this book. Bosch's captivating, shocking visions come from the same time when Perugino painted his serene Madonnas in distant Italy, while in the circle around Marsilio Ficino the dawn of a "first Enlightenment" appeared to be breaking. All that seems far away from the gloomy worldview communicated by Bosch's art. Commenting on one of Bosch's depictions of hell, the art historian Ernst Gombrich once noted that the artist succeeded in concretely and vividly picturing the monstrosities of a tortured fantasy that terrified the medieval mind.[3] Actually, the Inferno that Bosch conjured on the right panel cannot merely be a reflection of medieval texts like the *Vision of Tundale*, the popular report of a journey to the afterlife printed in 1484. No one is able to create a painting of that kind without having seen flames and destruction with their own eyes. But oppressive phantasmagorias did not only haunt the Middle Ages. The Renaissance was more terrifying than Leonardo's smiling Mona Lisa would lead us to believe.

If people of the time imagined hell as Bosch portrayed it, then their fear for their souls and efforts at salvation make perfect sense. The striving for godly purity even played out in Renaissance Florence. Savonarola tried to establish a theocracy there. Not Luther but the friar from Ferrara was the first to use the printing press for the purpose of religious polemics. He had over a hundred texts in Italian printed.[4] He called for a frugal Christian life of prayer and penance. He wanted to abolish the theater and gambling, the cardinal sins of the age, and do away with feasts. During Carnival in 1496, he sent the children of the city to gather alms rather than parade around in masks. He preached rebellion against humanistic Florence, the city of artists and poets, of homosexuals, of libertinism. Despite being a major killjoy, the hollow-cheeked Savonarola won a following among the people. He acted like a prophet and considered himself a man of the Apocalypse. While Bosch was painting his picture, rumors circulated that the end of time, a "last battle," was nearing—just like at the turn of previous centuries.[5] The whispering seems counter to the rationality infused into time by clocks, into the economy by money and accounting, and into philosophy by thinkers like Machiavelli. Yet the age contained all these multitudes. It knew desperation, enjoyed elegance and beauty, burned heretics and searched for primeval wisdom, glowed with piety and no less with passion for old manuscripts and ancient statues. Thus, Savonarola did not simply embody a triumph of the Middle Ages over the Renaissance. Rather, the preacher was one of those archetypal figures known to all times. He descended from the clan of Bernard of Clairvaux and Bernardino of Siena, Gregory the Great and Gregory VII, and he was an ancestor of the human incinerator Calvin and the frenzied zealots of our own day. His *On the Simplicity of Christian Life* explains what it was all about: "The whole of Christian life tends toward one thing, to be purified of all earthly contamination."[6] In this way, man (as an intellectual and corporeal being) and the world would become the holy temple of God. Savonarola also proclaimed that Florence would rule Italy as God's elect city.

No better world followed, although a plague did. The city was soon riven once again by partisan conflict. And just like Robespierre let heads roll when his Revolution and purification efforts went off the rails three hundred years later, Savonarola resorted to flames to do his work. During Carnival in 1497, a "bonfire of the vanities" was set up on the Piazza della Signoria. Wigs and perfume bottles, makeup and playing cards, sumptuous clothing, ostentatious furniture, harps, busts, and paintings went up in smoke.[7] The old Carnival tradition became a reckoning with all Renaissance secularism. Among the books that fed the flames were literary works, writings by Boccaccio and Petrarca and Pulci's *Morgante*, which contained a sharp polemic against Savonarola or those like him.

But the great fire burnt itself out. Internal tensions were compounded by external pressures. Alexander VI did not want a charismatic prophet at his side, and he was dead set against Florence's alliance with France. He excommunicated Savonarola, who in turn tried to unmask the supreme pontiff as the Antichrist. When the prophet organized another bonfire of worldly vanities in 1498, he met with resistance. Young nobles sought to block the pious happening. Florence gradually grew weary of the preacher. A trial by fire was proposed, but he refused. It was his last chance. On May 23, 1498, he was hanged and his body burned. A plaque set into the Piazza della Signoria marks the spot where the friar who sought to turn Florence into a heavenly Jerusalem went up in smoke. Some people continued to romanticize him, honoring him as a man of the people who opposed the luxurious life of the rich, pagan philosophy, and worldly art.[8]

The times seemed to call for a strong ruler. The Florentines thought they found one in Piero Soderini (1452–1522), who had served the city as ambassador to Charles VIII and as a prior. He was made Gonfaloniere for life. He would remain in power for ten years.

Hammer of Witches

Some Florentines continued to have a penchant for eschatological thinking. This is illustrated by a mysterious painting by Botticelli, the *Mystical Nativity*.[9] It includes a text written in Greek saying that the picture was painted in 1500 "in the troubles of Italy . . . in the second woe of the Apocalypse," i.e., war (Plate 17). It seems that the intellectual world of the hell-painter Bosch and that of Botticelli, the master of Madonnas, the beautiful Venus, and the rose-breathing Chloris, were not as far apart as they may at first seem. A third painting might also have been inspired by the same source as the other two, i.e., the book of Revelation: Luca Signorelli's *Last Judgment*. Painted on the walls of a chapel in the cathedral of Orvieto between 1499 and 1502, it depicts muscular, greenish and grayish devils tormenting the damned.

Indeed, the "evil enemy" seems to have been up to his old tricks again. The Inquisition had lots of work on its hands. In the diocese of Lincoln alone, over three hundred people were accused of heresy after 1500.[10] Augustine, Thomas Aquinas, and Neoplatonist demonology were the chief sources on demons, according to which they had to be whirling about in the billions in all possible guises. The troubles of the world alluded to in Botticelli's painting seemed the best evidence for their existence.

People also thought that countless women and men served Satan as accomplices—as witches. The traditional hatred reserved for heretics was reinforced by dread. In 1486, not long before the ominous year 1500, one of the darkest books ever written appeared: the *Malleus maleficarum*, the *Hammer of Witches*. Yet it did not start the terror that would seize hundreds of thousands of women and men down to the eighteenth century, putting them on trial and perhaps costing sixty thousand of them their lives.[11] Belief in witches existed before, and there were isolated executions. In the early fifteenth century, for example, people in the western Alps believed that a coven of witches was at work. The danger of witches was also a topic of discussion at the Council of Basel.[12] The *Hammer of Witches*, therefore, met with a primed audience. Its significance was that it combined what Augustine, Aquinas, and older theories said about witches with what the late fifteenth century thought it knew about demons and hags. Peter Drach, a printer in Speyer, smelled success when he invested in the thick tome—a modern edition numbers almost seven hundred pages.[13] There were no fewer than thirteen editions by 1523. Explanation was required for the bad weather that damaged harvests (actually caused by climate change), as well as for the fact that eerie pestilences were plaguing the land. The work of witches seemed to provide it.

The *Hammer of Witches* was written by the Dominican friar Heinrich Kramer (ca. 1430–1505), from Sélestat (Schlettstadt) in Alsace. He saw the catastrophes of his time as signs that the end of the world was nigh. He cited the same passage from Revelation to which Botticelli alluded with his ominous inscription.[14] He traced all evil to the misdeeds of the devil, released for one last period of time; Satan was the one responsible for the "heresy" of witchcraft. Kramer's book, jam-packed with evidence, offered advice for coping with the enemy of humankind. Its authority was buttressed by a prefatory bull issued in 1484 at Kramer's request by Pope Innocent VIII, *Summis desiderantes affectibus*. The bull confirmed the mandate the Holy Father had given his witchcraft inquisitor to help him efficiently wage a war of extermination against the powers of darkness.

Kramer's book paints a panorama of terror across hundreds of pages full of panicky fear of the devil, sadism, and obsessive misogyny. Cringing readers are taught about sexual intercourse between people and demons. They learn about spell-casting midwives who destroy fetuses, weather witches who brew up storms and make it hail, and hags who rob men of virility and kill cattle. There are descriptions of night flights of witches on anointed wood and ghastly Sabbaths where dissonant music pounds the ears and the cooked bodies of children are served for dinner. The idea that sexual union with the Prince of Darkness sealed the pact was a standard accusation in countless trials. The *Hammer* provides a detailed description of the formal rules for holding witch trials, a secular analog to the day's heresy trials. Torture played a very important role. It transformed harmless women into super-predators and peaceful men into dangerous sorcerers. Once their joints were dislocated or their thumbs were pressed until blood issued from under their fingernails, people confessed to whatever the judge wanted to hear. Just as heretics and Jews were suspected of forming networks and hatching conspiracies,[15] a gigantic web of witches was feared. It existed only in the minds of the persecutors.

Many of the victims were poor and old. A physical anomaly such as red hair or a hunched back could brand them as outsiders, opening them up to suspicion for causing all kinds of misfortune. There were mass trials that widened to ever greater circles, including children and young women, thanks to the fatal idea that witches met on the Sabbath. To discover who the demonic worshippers at the black mass were, name after name was forced out of the tortured until ten, twenty, and ultimately hundreds had been implicated. Their greatest crime was that they had supposedly renounced God and thus insulted his "honor." Yet the Lord's omnipotence had to be preserved intact, a feat the *Hammer of Witches* achieved by resorting to convoluted theological arguments. It emphasized that the rampaging of witches and the devil all took place with divine approval. It was the means for activating the mechanism of punishment and grace that was necessary for salvation. If the premise is accepted that a physical devil, demons, and witches existed, then the *Hammer of Witches* has a certain internal consistency. It evinces a perverse variant of the same rationality that characterizes Renaissance science.

Kramer actually succeeded in having women burned at the stake—about two hundred of them, as he once boasted. With or without his assistance, witch trials became increasingly common in Italy and southern Germany in his lifetime. The manic witch-hunter may have been a frustrated celibate fighting to maintain his own purity and striving for holiness. Maybe that explains why his book is imbued with hatred for everything female. The mere fleeting thought of womanly temptation may have given him a guilty conscience. Searching for guilt in women and not in one's own lecherousness was a source of relief and exoneration. Kramer seems to have been certain that it was Satan who used women as bait and filled their heads with unchaste thoughts. The strange opinion that women were constantly lusting after men—even old monks like Kramer—was a timeless commonplace.[16]

Not daring to fight the devil and his human agents meant angering the Lord. This was also a source of the ardor with which Kramer and his ilk preached witch-hunting. The same spirit animated the Inquisition's expulsion and extermination of *conversos*, inspired pogroms against Jews and Crusades against Muslims, and drove preachers to the pulpit to condemn all of sinful secular existence, its joy in the small things of life and its desire for beauty.

It is no wonder that Kramer was also an enemy of the Jews. In a ritual murder trial against the Jewish community of Trent, he assisted the prosecution by providing information on similar Jewish "crimes."[17] The Jews had been the classic scapegoats from time immemorial. People accused Jews of anything and everything to absolve themselves of their own responsibility.[18] The fires lit by the Inquisitors and witch-hunters were a form of appeasement, sending sacrificial smoke to heaven to keep God from punishing society for having tolerated his enemies in its midst.

In the decades around the jubilee year of 1500, optimism mounted in tandem with apocalyptic anxiety, contrition with mania for purity.[19] Looking back at those years, the history professor Christoph Cellarius (1638–1707) identified them as the epochal threshold between the medieval and early modern periods. The *Hammer of Witches* soon provided popular preachers with material for their sermons, but it would enjoy its greatest influence in the second half of the sixteenth century (pp. 665–670).

When this book was published, Gutenberg's invention definitively lost its innocence. For the first time, printing became the tool of terror and death.

Turnaround: Population, Economy

Far from the world of the explorers and intellectuals, common men and women performed their daily labor by the millions. When the work was done, they prayed or caroused. At sundown they sank into straw mattresses, while the night outside belonged to the stars, owls, and demons. Little has come down to us about their dreams, hardly anything about their conversations, and nothing about their conceptions of the cosmos and nature, which may have seemed to them to be full of mysteries and interwoven with magic. The peaks of some mountains were believed to be perilous places where witches reveled, the haunts of winged dragons and dangerous demons.[20] Ghosts still lived in the gloom of forests, in treetops, in crevices and springs, as did elves, giants, very real robbers, and hermits seeking the kingdom of heaven. The classic forest outlaw was the Robin Hood sung of in ballads and poems of the fifteenth and sixteenth centuries. This imaginary figure was pious but—or perhaps, therefore—a sworn enemy of avaricious monks. What is more, in the semi-darkness of his wild Sherwood Forest, which could be thought of as an "otherworld,"[21] Robin Hood was a rebel against the late medieval state, which attempted to discipline even the trees with its rules and regulations. He was, thus, literally an outlaw. He only became a "noble bandit" and good Samaritan in the time around 1600.

On the edges of the darkness, charcoal makers did their fiery work, excluded from society as untouchables. The woods meant adventure, danger, deprivation, and isolation. They were considered such a tangle that, when it came time to illustrate a wilderness in Marco Polo's travelogue (Plate 14) or in legends of holy hermits, it sufficed for miniaturists to symbolize it with just a few trees. The woods also had some use to the common man and woman, who gathered brushwood, herbs, mushrooms, and berries there.

The Renaissance was intimately familiar with poverty and misery. Plagues and famine recurred regularly.[22] The Dance of Death remained a major theme of art. Bernd Notke in Lübeck, Hans Holbein in Basel, and many others depicted a grinning grim reaper leading the final round. Far to the west, Jorge Manrique, who would himself soon die in the war for Castile's crown, wrote:

> Our lives are fated as the rivers
> That gather downward to the sea
> We know as death.[23]

Starting around the mid-fifteenth century, however, more people were born than died, despite the unfavorable weather and the bad harvests. In the ruins of once-abandoned villages, new life stirred. Like at the height of the Medieval Warm Period, hard hill country was made arable in certain areas such as Tuscany. If the fertility of the soil permitted, all kinds of plants cropped up next to fields of grain, such as woad and madder, which were used in dying textiles.

The profitable business of raising sheep—expanded in times of low population, which had ruined grain prices—flourished in Spain and especially in England. It was so widespread in the latter country that Thomas More could sarcastically remark that the sheep grazed on people, villages, and cities.[24] He considered it especially problematic that lords put fences around arable land to reserve it for their own herds. This was a reference to the notorious "enclosures," which cut pastureland out of what had once been commons. The conflict over enclosures would soon erupt into revolts. It was the age-old, indeed biblical dispute: between Cain, the forward-looking farmer and ancestor of all agrarian capitalists, and Abel, the shepherd with his land-killing livestock. Massive swathes of territory were eaten up in the Late Middle Ages just by huge oxen trails leading from Scandinavia and the East—from Hungary, Poland, and Ukraine—to the large cities of the south and the west. Those cattle ate grass on land that, therefore, could not be used by farmers to grow grain and turnips, and where otherwise cows, sheep, horses, and smaller livestock would graze.

Farmers tilled the soil under various systems of law and rule.[25] Sharecropping had been widely diffused in Europe since antiquity, and it was common in Asia as well. The lord of the manor provided tools and seeds, the tenant his labor. The yields were then split. Furthermore, in addition to the form of manorialism described above (pp. 152f.), which is known as *Grundherrschaft* and which was more common in the west of Europe, in parts of Germany, England, and the Netherlands, there was another, more centralized form, *Gutsherrschaft*, which was found in the east. There were also many intermediate forms of manorialism.

Gutsherrschaft, a relic of the colonization campaigns of the High Middle Ages, created states within states in the fifteenth century. The Black Death and emigration had benefited the territorial lords. When land became empty, they added it to their own holdings. The *Gutsherr*, or lord of the manor, was a kind of god on Earth to his peasant families: judge, ecclesiastical authority, and employer all in one, although he could also be a helpful paternal figure in times of need. He had absolute control over the economy of his lands. Bands of peasants bound to forced labor, some of them serfs, worked the fields to fill his barns. He sold the fruit of their labor at the market. How much air was left for the peasants to breathe depended greatly on how strong or weak the prince or king was; most of the latter lived far from the fields. They were the only ones who could rein in caprice—if they chose to do so. Power interests made alliances with the magnates natural, usually at the expense of the subservient. The conditions of many peasants who worked under *Gutsherrschaft* became even worse during the following centuries. They were mute and despondent. The land in the east remained almost utterly silent when the great Peasants' War swept over the country (pp. 593–599).

In western and central Europe, there was usually at least a higher class of peasants who lived a better life. In many regions, they were free, thus providing an example to those who were not. The abolition of serfdom was a demand often heard, as in the great English Peasants' Revolt. Free peasants could usually pass their farms down from generation to generation in exchange for a special payment. Money payments replaced personal bondage and forced labor. Everyday life, including conflicts with the manorial lord, was regulated at assemblies of the village community. Peasants and lords intensively farmed their lands, which were tiny clods of earth in comparison to the massive estates of the east. The means of doing so were paid laborers, technical innovations, and enhancing the fertility of the soil as much as possible. All this required a certain amount of ingenuity and capital. Like Asia, however, Europe also had hordes of peasants with little land and bulging lower classes in the cities that were threatened with death in times of famine. Furthermore, a sizeable portion of the yields of large and small farmers alike was eaten up by manorial lords— be they noblemen, clergy, or burghers. To prevent emigration, wage laborers at least had to be paid well.

Labor was initially in short supply, in particular in the towns and cities. They were consistently hit harder by plagues, as the higher population density increased the risk of infection. As one late-fifteenth-century saying had it, two masters chased after one journeyman.[26] Craftsmen received more work, especially from the upper classes, who had grown rich from inheritance and trade—unless a long war had wiped out capital along with people, as in France and England. Wages rose, whereas interest rates fell in societies where capital had been amassed in the wake of the plague. Thus the ostentatious, beautiful culture of the Renaissance was accompanied and driven by a further integration of the market economy.[27] By 1500, however, the gap between wages and prices closed that until then had been such an advantage to craftsmen. It opened again in the sixteenth century, now to their disadvantage.[28] The reasons were population growth and immigration from the countryside to the cities. With the arrival of more and more consumers inside the walls, the prices for grain and other crops rose. The population of Naples, for example, is believed to have quintupled in the first half of the sixteenth century.[29] The masses who came to the city brought their misery with them. The trend was similar in other towns, although booms like that experienced by Naples were the exception.

Although the gap between rich and poor widened, there can be no doubt that more-or-less robust, wealthy middle classes survived all over Europe. It was ultimately their hunger for books that made the printing press such a roaring success. They fulfilled their pious needs with mass stipends and donations to churches, their bodily desires with sumptuous food. The consumption of meat, wine, and fruit reached record highs. Townsfolk wore luxurious clothing in imitation of nobles. A rising tide of authoritarian regulations attempted to limit extravagance in a bid to at least maintain an outward appearance of social order. It was of little use.

Silver, Iron, Paper: The Consolidation of the Ink State

The last few chapters have been devoted to what appear to be wildly disparate aspects of the past: belief in witches, humanist philology, Atlantic expansion, the history of printing, and the rise of sophisticated craftsmanship capable of producing mechanical clocks and eyeglasses. It is impossible to report on all of this without artificially distinguishing these themes from one another. In reality, they were interwoven in highly complex ways, and they also interacted with other powerful trends, the most important being demographic development, the spread of capitalism, and the consolidation of the early modern state. A glance at the mining boom of the fifteenth century shows in stark relief how these and other factors mutually influenced one another.

More people needed more money. Merchants and explorers needed ships and thus money, and ships needed nails and anchors of iron. States needed guns with iron barrels and bronze cannons for their armies—and for all this, again money was needed. So was metal: iron, copper, silver, and gold. Thus, the search for new deposits intensified, starting in 1430 in Tyrol, then in Saxony, Thuringia, and Hungary. The burgeoning mining sector stimulated ingenuity. It also favored production processes that relied on the division of labor and required highly skilled specialists as well as manual laborers. An improved smelting technique called the Seiger process—in which lead was added so that silver could be extracted from ore when heated—facilitated silver production. It has been described as the "most significant and consequential innovation in mining" since the ancient invention of a process for making brass.[30]

Complex technology was required to drain deep mineshafts. Waterpower had been providing assistance since the late thirteenth century. It powered hoists, kept hammers striking in tireless tempo, and breathed air into the bellows of the smelting furnaces. Before a shaft could be sunk into the "dark underworld filled with floating stars"—as Konrad Celtis once described a salt mine[31]—capital had to be secured. Similar to overseas trade, in which shares in ships could be bought, mining was also financed by the sale of shares in shafts.[32] These *Kuxen*, as they were called, were often tiny, thus spreading the risk across many shoulders. The smelting of ore required a high capital investment. As with paper production, Nuremberg was in the vanguard of progress. A silver smelting furnace was built outside the gates to the city in 1419; fifty years later, similar operations began in the Thuringian Forest. The capital was usually supplied by consortiums of patricians or merchants. They purchased the raw material, had it smelted, and sold the resulting metal for an often astronomical profit. Production increased massively in line with market demand. It is estimated that European silver production quintupled between 1450 and 1540, while the annual production of pig iron increased in the second half of the fifteenth century from twenty-five thousand to forty thousand metric tons.[33]

The vigorous development of mining produced a rich theoretical literature that had a reciprocal impact on practice. Albert the Great's work on minerals was followed by handbooks (*Kunstbüchlein*) dealing with technical questions, the digging of shafts, smelting, and the analysis of mineral resources.[34] Highlights of the genre included Georg Agricola's 1530 *De re metallica*, a dialogue in twelve books on mining, and Vannoccio Biringuccio's *De la pirotechnia*, a foundational work on metallurgy published ten years later. Thanks in part to Agricola's book, the piston pump spread from Saxony and Bohemia to all of Europe. Details of the smelting process, however, were kept secret. Innovation thus had to be based on practical experience. A great deal had been accumulated from the attempt to turn base metals into gold via alchemy and the attendant process of assaying (also called "docimasy"). The need for capital, the printing press, technological innovations, alchemy, and mining thus all mutually influenced one another. Another factor was the ongoing process of state formation, for it was the state that had by far the greatest need for metal. Buildings, royal courts, diplomacy, bureaucracy, and, last but not least, war all had to be financed. The mints needed raw materials.

The state's constant need for credit led to an increasing number of alliances with major business enterprises. States paid for loans by giving their creditors control of mines or mining rights for a certain period. Sovereignty over mineral resources was a royal prerogative, a right that originally belonged to the king or emperor. In the Holy Roman Empire, it had devolved to the prince-electors, princes, and other territorial lords—i.e., to wherever states were consolidating. Nowhere outside Europe did a capital market of even remotely comparable size develop. Nowhere did similarly professional bureaucracies grow. With the help of Roman law, which now began to gain a foothold in the north as well, the economy received the support of a framework of norms and standards. Large projects in mining and overseas trade, which required massive loans to be carried out, were thus facilitated and indeed enabled. For only law and bureaucracy could guarantee the security necessary for doing business

smoothly. In unison with the expansion of legal systems came a massive increase in documentation—an indicator of the concentration of state power. This was made possible not only by growing armies of civil servants but also because cheap paper progressively replaced expensive parchment.

The sovereign state was only just now coming into being. The age of itinerant rulers was not yet over. Nor was there yet a framework of permanent embassies, although there was a great deal of diplomacy. It focused on negotiating alliances and peace agreements, as well as on gathering information—spying, one might say. Emperor Maximilian I, for example, spun a broad diplomatic web that extended to England and even the Teutonic Knights and the grand princes of Moscow. He employed a good three hundred ambassadors during his reign. They took on enormous significance in the prehistory of Europe's first world empire.[35]

Father of an Empire: Maximilian I

Maximilian was born on March 22, 1459—under an ominous star, he believed, whose power he hoped to oppose with God's grace.[36] The young Habsburg archduke won his spurs on a glorious August day in 1479 at the Battle of Guinegate. Fighting in the front ranks of his *Landsknechte*, a great share of the victory over a French army was due to him. This success was a major step toward claiming the inheritance of Charles the Bold. Maximilian's young wife Mary, daughter of the Duke of Burgundy, died three years later during a falcon hunt. But she was survived by two children, Philip and Margaret, who were valuable marriage assets and who embodied the legal claim to Burgundy. More wars would have to be fought to assert it. These were decisive years in the history of the Habsburg dynasty. In 1490, Archduke Sigmund of Austria, in debt up to his ears, was forced to cede his dominions—with Tyrol as the crown jewel—to his cousin Maximilian. That same year Matthias Corvinus died in Vienna, the last Hunyadi and a more dangerous enemy to the Habsburg ruler than the sultan himself. In a surprise attack, Maximilian took back his Austrian territories. But he could not conquer Hungary, which supported the Bohemian King Vladislaus II. The attempt to defeat the Jagiellonian ruler militarily failed. After a short war, a peace treaty was signed in Pressburg (now Bratislava) in 1491 that confirmed the co-rulership of Hungary and, should Vladislaus's line die out, a Habsburg succession.

The Peace of Pressburg was one of countless such deals, an uncertain bet on the future. Only in hindsight did it turn out to be an important brick in the wall of the later Austro-Hungarian dual monarchy. For the moment, the arrangement relieved pressure in the east for war in the west, where high taxes had driven townspeople in Flanders to rebel. The revolts were put down but with difficulty. The last city to fall was Ghent. The 1493 Treaty of Senlis confirmed Maximilian's claim to all but the western part of Burgundy, which the French crown was able to retain. The borders of the Holy Roman Empire now ran farther westward than ever before. And with that, a conflict was cemented that would determine events in Europe for long to come: the rivalry between the House of Habsburg and the kings of France, Valois and Bourbons alike. Increasingly the duel was fought out in the arena of Italy, the ancient seat of the Empire.

Maximilian gained the imperial crown in 1493 upon the death of Frederick III. The next year he married again, this time to Bianca Maria Sforza, the niece of Lodovico il Moro of Milan. It was a poor match but one that opened up the prospect of possessing the duchy. For a monstrous dowry, supposedly one million ducats, the "Moor" bought himself more than the honor of being related by marriage to the imperial dynasty: he acquired the title of duke.

Compared to modern times, Maximilian's empire was a thinly populated territory.[37] After the losses of the plague, it may again have numbered ten million souls by the last third of the fifteenth century. The Holy Roman Empire, a curious mixture of monarchy, confederation, and representative state, was increasingly referred to as "German," just as there were French, English, and Spanish kingdoms. It had no capital and no army and was more fragmented than Italy. Nevertheless, taken as a whole, it possessed boundless economic power and an inexhaustible reservoir of brilliant craftsmen, as well as an abundance of courts, cities, and first-rate minds. Just who belonged to this entity was seldom uncontroversial. The hardships of the Hussite Wars had prompted an imperial assembly in Nuremberg in 1422 to compile a register of all the entities liable to taxation: bishoprics, abbeys, principalities, lordships, counties, and cities. Further lists of this kind followed. The imperial constitution, a bundle of laws, treaties, and customs, was constantly in flux. Every Imperial Diet made additions.

This *Sacrum Imperium* took shape not only in the form of mountains upon mountains of paper but also in the colorful processions resplendent with gold that attended coronations and Diets. It was also embodied in a symbol, the double-headed eagle, which could be seen by the thousands on banners and city gates, town hall facades, and stove tiles. Did the two heads refer to kingdom and empire, or did they indicate that the Holy Roman Empire, like the ancient Roman Empire, encompassed both east and west?[38] Imperial privileges were part of the constitution, as was the Golden Bull of 1356, the decree outlining the governing framework of the Empire. So, too, was the concordat that Maximilian's father Frederick had reached with Pope Nicholas V shortly after being elected.[39] It governed relations with the Holy Sea down to the nineteenth century and allowed, among other things, the chapters of metropolitan and cathedral churches to freely elect their archbishops and bishops. The pope retained the right to veto or confirm them and the possibility of filling canonries in metropolitan and collegiate churches that fell vacant in uneven months. Townspeople gained a greater voice in the Empire thanks to the imperial cities. Accountable only to God and the emperor, their envoys were admitted to Imperial Diets starting in the last third of the fifteenth century, where they joined in discussions about taxes and laws.

The Estates demanded reforms at an Imperial Diet in Worms in 1495, although they were not always of one mind. The upshot of months of negotiations was a general peace that was supposed to be "perpetual" but that lasted no longer than its predecessors. More important was the decision to establish a supreme imperial court, the later Imperial Chamber Court (*Reichskammergericht*). Half of the sixteen justices were to be nobles, the other half trained jurists. In this way, the ancient law of Rome penetrated the inner sanctum of imperial jurisdiction. The "legal Renaissance" reached a climax. The Chamber Court developed into a powerful consolidator of the imperial confederation. It opened avenues of legal redress even to humble subjects. To maintain peace and justice, however, the reforms were utterly insufficient.

Austria became a world power not as master of the fragile Empire but rather, once again, through marriage alliances. Two unions were celebrated in 1496 and 1497. A shared opposition to the House of Valois brought Trastámara and Habsburg together. First, Philip the Handsome, Maximilian's son from his marriage to Mary of Burgundy, took the hand of the infanta Joanna. Then Margaret was joined with the heir to the throne, John, who, however, died the same year, still only eleven. Since Ferdinand and Isabella's other children also met premature deaths, the sole heir was Philip and Joanna's son Charles, later Charles V (r. 1519–1558). He was destined to become lord of half the globe. Of course, no one could have known that in 1500. Maximilian undertook campaigns in Italy and attempted to conquer all of Burgundy, but to no avail. He was also unable to achieve anything against the Swiss Confederacy, which had refused to accept the decrees issued at Worms. After a war with the Swabian League—an association of princes, nobles, prelates, and cities—that had grown out of border conflicts in 1499, the Swiss emerged stronger than ever. This loose confederation of urban and rural communes continued to formally be part of the Empire. As a provisioner of mercenaries to the armies of half of Europe, however, it had become a power in its own right.

A Crusade against the Ottomans, who by then had advanced as far as Venetian territory, was beyond Maximilian's reach. But thanks to good fortune in battle and diplomacy he did manage to bridle the Estates, which had utterly neutralized him for a time. He had himself proclaimed Holy Roman Emperor in 1508 in Trent; the pope consented. A war against Venice that he waged with varying allies brought the Serenissima to the brink of destruction. France, Aragon, the emperor and the pope had joined together to fight Venice as the League of Cambrai. After defeating the main Venetian army in 1509 at the Battle of Agnadello near Cremona, their troops were poised on the banks of the Lagoon. But they lacked the fleet required to overcome Venice's wall of water. In addition, the cities of the mainland, which already enjoyed a great deal of autonomy, stayed true to their master.[40] Savvy diplomacy, ceding the Romagna to the Papal States, and surrendering ports in Puglia to Spain took care of the rest. Venice managed to extract its head from the noose. The league of convenience fell apart when the pope pulled out.

Maximilian failed to win the great prize in northern Italy. But he did manage to secure the Spanish succession for his grandson Charles. He kept his eye on Hungary in the east. A Habsburg-Jagiellonian union seemed to be the only means of countering the Ottoman menace. Thus, another double wedding was arranged. A Spanish grandson of Maximilian, Ferdinand, married King Vladislaus's daughter Anna. And Vladislaus's son Louis, King of Hungary and Bohemia, had been chosen before birth to be the husband of Mary of Castile. Louis's death after the Battle of Mohács (p. 563) gave Ferdinand and the House of Habsburg both of the crowns that had belonged to the Jagiellonians.

Maximilian was a man of grand, fantastical plans. Once he even seriously considered having himself elected pope and thus resolving the perennial tension between tiara and imperial crown in the Byzantine manner. The Count of Auersperg, a poet of the *Vormärz* period, called him the "last knight." The emperor himself cultivated this very image in semi-autobiographical works written with the help of members of his court: *Weißkunig* (*The White King*), *Theuerdank*, and *Freydal*. He energetically administered the churches in his territories, although he enriched himself from them whenever he could. The brunt of his imperial policy was borne by his hereditary lands. Their administration, which relied largely on experts from the towns and experience from

Burgundy, never overcame the avalanche of debt. It was incurred from ostentation and art patronage but most of all from war, which Maximilian regarded as the first rather than the last remedy of politics.[41] It was the ruinous cost of war that reined in Maximilian's ambitions. The West could not be conquered with one thousand mercenaries, and the emperor often lacked the money even for that many.

Big Business: The Fugger Family

Maximilian spent more time in Augsburg than any other imperial city. He even bought a house there. The Swabian city had been the point of departure for the emperors of the High Middle Ages when they traveled to Rome to be crowned, and for traders on their way to Venice, the bazaar of the Mediterranean. The merchants and craftsmen of Augsburg had everything an emperor's heart desired: fine work in gold, astronomical devices, art, books, and weapons and armor to outfit warriors, enthusiastic hunters, and knights competing in tournaments. Augsburg—for a man of rank, it meant music and *danse basse* in gentleman's taverns or dance houses, tournaments at the court of the episcopal palace, or crossbow shooting outside the ramparts. And it meant a connection to the wide world. In Augsburg, business was done with Bruges and London, Lisbon and Budapest, and enterprises were hatched whose horizons went beyond the islands discovered by Columbus. As an inscription on the town hall said, it was a *wahrhaft königliche Stadt*, a "truly royal city." One contemporary considered it the richest on Earth.

It was not only pleasure and the business of Imperial Diets that drew Maximilian there. Even more, it was his need for money. In addition to trade and the key industry of weaving, Augsburg owed its wealth to mining and banking. Between 1470 and 1500 alone, revenue from the wealth tax quadrupled. Augsburg's merchants, including the future global company of the Welser family, had quickly invested in the silver and copper mines of Saxony and Tyrol, set up smelting furnaces, and produced brass. They were also quick to feed the state with silver. Georg Gossembrot (ca. 1445–1502) had been Sigmund of Tyrol's financier before serving his successor Maximilian in that capacity. At the turn of the century, he and a consortium of other merchants sought to establish a copper syndicate. One member of that group was a family that had beat out Gossembrot to become the leading banker to the court in Innsbruck: the Fuggers.

They were of humble origin. The founding father was a weaver who had moved to Augsburg in 1367 from a small village to the south and had quickly amassed great wealth in textiles. While one branch of the family went bankrupt and thus lost its honor for a time, the "Fuggers of the Lily" enjoyed a meteoric rise. The mastermind of the business was Jakob Fugger (1459–1525), known as "the Rich." He forged a relationship with Maximilian, borrowed money to buy mining shares in Thuringia, and built smelting furnaces and hammer mills all across the Habsburg sphere of influence between Tyrol and Hungary. The sale of silver was transacted via Venice. The profits were dizzying. In only one silver deal lasting three years, Fugger made almost one million ducats. All the while, he never lost sight of the textile business and trade with Italy. In 1505, the Fugger family invested four thousand ducats in three ships that sailed to southern India along the route that had now been discovered over the Cape of Good Hope (pp. 575f.). The flotilla returned to Lisbon heavily laden with spices, pearls, and cloth. In Rome, the company established a relationship with the papacy, earned profit from the sale of indulgences, and ultimately was able to take over the papal mint. Fugger money paid for both the Swiss Guards and the magnificence of the Habsburg-Jagiellonian wedding feast in Vienna. Branches of the Fugger company could be found in cities all over Europe by the beginning of the sixteenth century.

The family's rise was set against the backdrop of the dramatic expansion of long-distance international trade.[42] Southern German high finance was heavily involved in that development. In Antwerp alone, there were over fifty Swabian companies during Maximilian's reign. The Fugger company was the greatest of them all. Like the Medici, the Fugger family sought to rise socially and ultimately acquired estates and dominions. Jakob the Rich bought himself the title of count, and his successor Anton became an imperial prince. The castles from which forests and fields were administered were status symbols for the new aristocracy. Land did not only confer nobility. It also yielded profits and provided security in times of trouble. What a Fugger did, he did wholeheartedly.[43]

The family had a palace built along Augsburg's wine market. It was the company headquarters, soon a hoard of costly collections, and, when necessary, an imperial lodging. Everything about it said money: the copper roofs, the marble, the lavish pomp of the rooms. In 1516, Jakob the Rich undertook an unparalleled charity project. In a suburb of the city, he had a neighborhood built, the *Fuggerei*. Its fifty-three houses were opened to the "respectable poor." Prayers for the salvation of the benefactor were more important than the rent of one guilder per annum. The great banker used the donation to settle accounts with his God. Albrecht Dürer painted his portrait, an emblem of capitalism. His closely cropped hair is tucked under a Venetian cap interlaced with gold—a reminder of the company's ties to the Rialto, where the tycoon had once done his apprenticeship. Dürer's Fugger is an earnest, shrewd man with sharp features. No one would want him for an enemy.

When the portrait was painted, during the 1518 Diet of Augsburg, Fugger had just achieved his greatest coup. He had amassed the money necessary to help Maximilian's grandson, Charles V of Spain, become Holy Roman Emperor. The amount is fastidiously noted in his account book: 851,918 guilders. Even a highly paid craftsman would have had to work nearly thirty thousand years to earn that much money.[44] The lion's share, more than half a million, came from the Fugger company's own capital. The money helped the prince-electors to vote unanimously. From then on, however, it inextricably bound the company to the fortunes of its all-powerful debtor. Fugger once even coolly reminded the emperor that it was money and not God that had made him: "It is well-known and for all to see that Your Imperial Majesty could not have secured the Roman crown without my assistance."[45] A statement of that kind could have cost the speaker his head in China or Russia.

The Fugger company's support already bore fruit in Jakob's lifetime. With the emperor's help, an antitrust suit against the family and other Augsburg business magnates was quashed at the Imperial Chamber Court. The connection to the Habsburgs and thus to Spain was reinforced under Anton Fugger (1493–1560), Jakob the Rich's successor.[46] Of the twenty-eight million guilders the emperor borrowed during his reign, over one-third came from Augsburg. The loans were risky for the creditors but guaranteed by state revenues of all kinds. The Fuggers were most richly rewarded by their highly profitable lease on the *Maestrazgos*, the estates of three Spanish knightly orders; they had devolved to the Spanish crown in the wake of the Reconquista.[47] The most valuable part was the cinnabar mines of Almadén. They provided quicksilver, which was used to coat mirrors, as an element in the gilding process, and, above all, to amalgamate silver. The Iberian Peninsula became the most important trade arena for the company from Augsburg. From there, the Fuggers shipped Swabian cloth to America, Fugger copper to the New World via Seville, and Fugger brassware to West Africa via Lisbon.

The liaison between capital and state power—the emperor's brother Ferdinand and numerous other princes also oiled their financial machinery with money from Augsburg—was advantageous to both sides, at least in the beginning. It made it possible for metal to be dug out of the ground in previously unheard-of quantities. The craving for money continuously spurred the development of technological improvements, thus increasing mining revenues. In the other direction, large loans helped to develop state structures and wage wars. They endowed Maximilian with an empire. In the long run, however, German high finance's connection to the state attenuated audacity and innovative zeal. The future belonged to more flexible capital and to companies that operated in societies with stronger horizontal power, like the Netherlands and England.[48] Pioneers of market liberalism could already be found in the Catholic milieu of the Fugger age: in its view, the selfishness of individuals seemed the best basis for the common good. And thus, greed gradually lost its place of honor among the mortal sins. Nevertheless, Jakob Fugger the Rich built his social housing project because fear of the afterlife had driven him to do so. This fear could still be assuaged a bit by the magic charm of the old Church: good works.

But let us turn our attention once again back across the Alps—where the Fuggers had made a great deal of money, and where German guilders helped finance cultural goods of global significance.

27

Raison d'État Is Born

The Triumph of Hierarchy: Renaissance Popes

The ascendancy of the papacy, which had bucked the demands of the conciliar movement—and thus missed the chance at reform occasioned by it— continued in the second half of the fifteenth century. An uprising planned in the circle around Pomponio Leto in 1468 was simply a final flare-up of the dying republican ideal. The scheme was betrayed just as Porcari's conspiracy had been. The strengthened monarchy standing on the graves of Peter and Paul gave Rome a new face. Streets cut through the center of the city and provided thoroughfares for the masses of pilgrims who arrived for the holy year. Since Sixtus IV, the whole commune had been ruled by the Apostolic

Camera. The popes had long acted like princes, and their retinues were often stocked with more laymen than clergy. The weddings of their numerous children were celebrated publicly and with pageantry.

The tiara remained the object of hot competition among the Roman nobility. Their property meant access to money, land, and benefices. A cardinal's hat and even prospects for the papacy were the dowry of some marriages in the orbit of the Roman nobility. Cesare Borgia, a son of Alexander VI and the most famous of all papal minions, was showered with benefices by his father. If we can believe the Master of Ceremonies Johann Burchard, the venerable walls of the Vatican Palace witnessed wild excesses. He describes an orgy with fifty courtesans. According to his account, they danced naked for the lecherous pope and then crawled on all fours through Cesare's room, after which the prelates slept with them. Whoever could "do it" most often won the prize.[1]

Beyond the debauchery and the religious worship, political prudence was called for. Charles VIII's invasion of Italy had been a great danger to Alexander's pontificate, as his opponents within Rome—the Orsini, Colonna, and Caetani—had allied with the French king. But the European system reacted. An alliance of Italian states, joined by Emperor Maximilian, opposed Charles. Seeing the league on the march, he sought safety in a hasty retreat. An uncanny enemy had weakened his army: syphilis, which gnawed at the bones of his mercenaries. France's powerful position in Italy crumbled as quickly as it had been built. It could not hold the south, which returned to Spanish hands in 1502.

Barely had the danger evaporated when the pope sought solidarity with France. His partner was Louis XII, who ascended the throne upon Charles's death in 1498. The accord was reached in the style of the times. Cesare Borgia renounced his religious offices and received the hand of a French princess, the Valentinois, and the title of duke; thereafter, the Italians called him "Valentino." Earlier, Alexander had obliged his French partner by annulling his childless marriage. In this way, Louis was able to wed his predecessor's widow, Anne of Bretagne, thus paving the way for the incorporation of her duchy into France. The Roman-French alliance, strengthened by a pact with Venice, also helped him to conquer Milan by 1500. Lodovico il Moro ended his days in a French dungeon.

After the demise of his brother Juan—who had been stabbed to death and dumped in the Tiber—Cesare Borgia became the undisputed protagonist of his father's politics. At the head of the papal troops and a mercenary company supplied by Louis, the duke got to work. His weapons were cunning, murder, war, and favor. He wiped out his Roman opponents, now defenseless without their French protector, and overthrew the signòries of the Romagna. What until then had been proud dominions under loose papal supremacy, citadels of petty power and grand culture, fell like dominos. The victims included Forlì, Pesaro, Rimini, Faenza, and even Urbino. In 1502, Cesare led French troops in a war against Naples and conquered Piombino in Tuscany for himself. He waged his wars in the Romagna under the legal title of a commander of the papal army and as a vassal of the French crown. In reality, he was interested in the same things as his "holy" father: the establishment of a Borgia state.

But when Alexander VI died in 1503, this dream evaporated. The papal throne was ascended by Julius II (1503–1513) of the della Rovere family, mortal enemies of the House of Borgia. It soon became clear that Valentino's power had depended entirely on that of his father and the support of France. He fled Italy and ultimately entered the service of the king of Navarre. He died in 1507, suffering from syphilis and forgotten in Italy, during the siege of a fortress near Pamplona. Posterity has been haunted ever since by the ghost of this monumentally nefarious figure who tried to have his way with Fortuna. Machiavelli stylized the political bankrupt as the ideal prince. Burckhardt painted a portrait of him that was as powerful as it was profoundly mistaken. He and Nietzsche both turned Cesare Borgia into the superman—that absurd antithesis of the pale, utterly mediocre philistine of the *fin de siècle*.

Julius II was able to pick up where Cesare left off. He energetically went about winning back everything Borgia had taken, and he conquered the long-sought prize of Bologna. Milan fell into his grasp; in 1512, he handed it over to Massimiliano Sforza. Genoa shook off French rule. Contemporaries called the pope "the Terrible"—more out of respect than contempt. He paraded high on horseback, decked out in full armor, amidst his troops. Once when Michelangelo was working on a statue of him, Julius is said to have asked to be portrayed with a sword rather than a book in his hand. "I know nothing of learning," he supposedly said.[2] The fact that he tried to restrict the sale of ecclesiastical offices and could occasionally be humble and affable did almost nothing to change Julius's reputation.

He prudently protected himself from the Roman nobility. As a precaution, he removed its men from the palace watch and surrounded himself instead with a cohort of reliable Swiss mercenaries, the above-mentioned Swiss Guard. The League of Cambrai's victory over Venice brought him no profit, however, nor did his allies benefit from it. Opposing French designs in northern Italy seemed more urgent. Politics followed the model of chemical reactions. Without embarrassment, the pope now formed a bond with his most important partners from the League of Cambrai against his erstwhile ally France, creating a new "Holy League." In response, Louis XII tried to have Julius deposed by a council called in Pisa. However, the latter deftly outmaneuvered the schismatics with a well-attended synod of his own, the Fifth Lateran Council of 1512.

Julius's art patronage knew no bounds. He adorned the Belvedere Courtyard with ancient statues, including a figure of Apollo that was found in 1489 and would soon be famous. He laid the foundation stone of New Saint Peter's Basilica with his own hands. Without his commission, Michelangelo would not have painted his frescos on the ceiling of the Sistine Chapel; in that sense, they are, in part, the work of the pope. Julius died shortly after the scaffolding was taken down. For the tomb he also commissioned from Michelangelo, one of the legendary projects of world art, only a few figures were produced: a *Genius of Victory*, unfinished *Slaves*, and the wrathful *Moses* now in the Roman church of San Pietro in Vincoli, a portrait of the fear- and awe-inspiring patron (Fig. 37, p. 506).

Meanwhile, France and Spain's Italian wars continued. In 1515, at the Battle of Marignano, south of Milan, French artillery exploded the myth that Swiss mercenaries were invincible. The new French king Francis I enjoyed possession of Milan for a decade; the rule of the Sforzas was history. Meanwhile in Rome, the Medici Pope Leo X had succeeded Julius II. Appointed an apostolic protonotary at the tender age of seven and named a cardinal six years later, he was the Renaissance pope par excellence. The procession leading to his coronation at the Lateran was lined with statues of Apollo, Bacchus, Mercury, Hercules, and Venus.[3] In 1517, a conspiracy to assassinate Leo failed. The pope immediately enlarged the College of Cardinals to include reliable Medici partisans. Beforehand he had closed the Lateran Council. Reform should have been on the agenda, but the synod had achieved little. Its one significant decree affirmed the immortality of the individual soul. In the last year the council sat, Luther published his Ninety-Five Theses.

When Leo X died in 1521, Germany was in turmoil. Italy was also without peace, its fate now decided in Spanish, Dutch, and French palaces. The south of Italy remained in the hands of the Habsburgs, despite vain attempts by King Louis to add it to his Milanese possessions. Affairs in the north were unsettled. Venice had learned the lesson of Agnadello: the battle remained a traumatic memory that inhibited further adventures. Defying reality, the Serenissima's artists painted a romantic picture of diplomatic success, portraying the doge of the crisis period, Leonardo Loredan, as the arbiter of Europe. With the aid of its boundless riches, Venice decked itself out as a Renaissance metropolis that could vie with Florence itself. In the view of Philippe de Commynes, its painted buildings and marble structures made it "the most triumphant city that I have ever seen." He dubbed the Grand Canal "the fairest and best-built street . . . in the world."[4]

Machiavelli

On the Arno, events unfolded in the Medici's favor. After dangerously waffling back and forth in international politics, at the decisive moment the Soderini republic found itself on the wrong side, that of France. In the late summer of 1512, a Spanish army led by the Neapolitan viceroy invaded Tuscany, captured and plundered Prato, and ultimately entered Florence. Spanish mercenaries opened the city gates to the Medici, and Piero Soderini fled. A conspiracy was uncovered in February 1513. It gave the new regime the opportunity to clean house among its enemies. The only remnant of the republic was the "Hall of the Five Hundred" in the Palazzo Vecchio.

Among those suspected of taking part in the conspiracy was a man who would subsequently achieve worldwide fame: Niccolò Machiavelli. Taken prisoner and tortured, he was lucky not to be executed but rather only banished to Chianti, south of Florence. He was born in 1469, the son of a lawyer. A small library in his father's house provided him with a decent humanist education. Savonarola's ashes had barely blown away when the intelligent young man was named the head of Florence's "second chancery." The office was devoted to the administration of domestic affairs but also required close coordination with the first chancery, which was responsible for foreign affairs. The secretary of the second chancery had hardly any influence. But he did have access to the secrets of politics and the opportunity to study the alchemy of power. He made good use of his time in the chancery. It was a place where information was gathered and a center of lively discussions about Florentine and international politics.[5] "The fifteen years I have been at the study of the art of the state," Machiavelli once wrote in a letter to Francesco Vettori, "I have neither slept through nor played away."[6] Diplomatic missions brought him together with key figures, including Louis XII and Emperor Maximilian. While on a mission to Cesare Borgia, he witnessed a murderous scene at Senigallia. The duke invited four disloyal condottieri to a feast of reconciliation, only to have two of them strangled and the other two imprisoned (and later assassinated).

In exile in Chianti, specifically in Sant'Andrea in Percussina near San Casciano, Machiavelli now had all the time in the world. He wrote comedies and musical compositions and his chief works: *The Florentine Histories, The Discourses on Livy,* and above all *The Prince.* In crystal-clear language, this thin volume transmitted techniques for gaining, maintaining, and expanding power. This "drastic experiment in secularization" had nothing in common with its immediate predecessors, handbooks for morally good, Christian rule known as "mirrors of princes."[7] Where previous thinkers thought they had descried God's "unfathomable will," Machiavelli saw *Fortuna,* fate. In his view, fortune was like a capricious woman who must be coerced, beaten, and knocked to the ground if necessary. To become her master required *virtù.* In Machiavelli's lexicon, this word connotes prudence, courage, strong nerves, and perseverance. Yet in extreme situations, all the virtue in the world cannot break the power of fate.[8] The prince must therefore always consider the circumstances, the possibilities available, and the limits of action. He must recognize necessities and know how to seize opportunities. Until the bitter moment when fate proves itself all-powerful, he can rely only on himself. He must be both fox and lion, cunning and strong. For the lion does not look out for snares, and the fox does not frighten off wolves.[9]

Machiavelli's *Prince* contains dryly delivered principles of the following kind. Rebellious populations must either be showered with benefits or wiped out. It is much safer to be feared than to be loved. Just as medicine only works when it is taken at the right time, evils must be met immediately, and necessary wars must be waged without delay. To become the master of a state, all necessary atrocities must be carried out in one blow. The prince must never take the property of his subjects for himself "because men forget the death of a father more quickly than the loss of a patrimony."[10] Machiavelli was a cool observer of events. The past may be promising or exasperating; either way, for the reader of Lucretius, it is not in the hands of a beneficent father who would straighten everything out in the end. That was the true revolution in Machiavelli's thought: he separated politics from religion, and he removed God from history. Religion appeared only as an instrument of power. Fear of God is useful, as it disciplines the people and helps to maintain the state. It is immaterial, however, whether the ruler himself believes in the deity that is invoked.[11] He does not wield the scepter by the grace of God but by means of prudence, deceit, lies, and murder. History does not progress from bad to good. Rather it repeats itself in an eternal cycle: order gives way to chaos, and chaos gives way to order.

Machiavelli was not blinded by Savonarola's sermons. He saw through the rhetorical strategies of the "new Moses" and ultimately wrote a contemptuous poem about him. For the papacy, he reserved harsh judgment. He viewed it as the wedge keeping his homeland divided. The Church was too weak to subject all of Italy, but it was strong enough to keep others from doing so.[12] Insight into the fragility of institutions would lead the Reformation to conclude that they must be returned to their original purity, while people should have faith and hope for divine grace. In contrast, Machiavelli urged people to rely on their own abilities. Individuals were the one and only creators of their world, although they were also bloodthirsty wolves consumed with ambition. "They are ungrateful, fickle, pretenders and dissemblers, evaders of danger, eager for gain."[13]

Machiavelli's work reflects the experience of the suffering endured by Florence, an enfeebled community that had given up its constant aspiration for expansion and was now locked in a struggle of life and death. It was the Renaissance state that—in the form of the French and Spanish crowns—had grown into the deadly opponent of the medieval republic. The ultimate moral foundation of Machiavelli's political theory is the ethics of emergency. If the state perishes, then all else is lost. Regardless of whether it is a republic or a monarchy, its own preservation must be its highest priority. Machiavelli never said that the ends justify the means. Yet a dangerous argument does pervade his writings: crimes are allowed when they are necessary to avoid worse outcomes. And as another infamous, albeit less famous, political theorist observed, only the sovereign can decide when such a "necessity," and thus a state of emergency, is at hand.[14]

In Machiavelli's view, the only means to preserve the state is a strong army. "Without its own arms no principality is secure; indeed it is wholly obliged to fortune."[15] He filled in the details in the *Discourses* and his dialogue *The Art of War*. Machiavelli relies on empirical evidence—a method handed down from antiquity—and on examples from history, especially ancient history. He seeks to draw conclusions from both. He is convinced that compulsory military service nurtures patriotism and peace, whereas mercenaries were expensive and unreliable—a danger even to the hand that fed them.[16] Along with Sun Tzu's *Art of War*, the most important theoretical treatment of warfare from ancient China, Machiavelli's dialogue is a classic of the genre, on par with the works of Thucydides, Vegetius, and Clausewitz.

In practice, however, his theory was a failure. Convinced that a homeland could find no better defenders than its own citizens, he mustered an army of townspeople and farmers when the Spanish approached in 1512. In the first true test of its mettle against highly trained professional soldiers, it scattered in panic. This was not the only time Machiavelli's analytical skills let him down. He did not recognize the military potency of the rising world power Spain. His boundless enthusiasm for all things ancient blinded him to the importance of artillery and thus to the terrifying trend toward the mechanization of war. Nevertheless, his thought, which insisted on practical effectiveness, shows better than that of any humanist before him how great an impetus to modernization could be won from engagement with ancient literature. The idea that native citizens would be better protectors of their own homes than hired lances had much to recommend it. It provided a foundation for the principle of general conscription.

Machiavelli, antiquarian and reporter all in one, represented a humanism of action. In his view, studying the ancients meant learning about politics and the art of war. Rome taught how to establish empires and subjugate peoples. Machiavelli was a Renaissance man through and through in another sense as well: he advised that decrepit states, especially Italy, could be healed by returning to their origins. His *Prince* ends with a passionate appeal to Italy's "new prince" to free the country from barbarians. The last words quote Petrarca:

> Virtue will take up arms against fury,
> and make the battle short,
> because the ancient valor in Italian hearts
> is not yet dead.[17]

Less well-known is the fact that Machiavelli was also a defender of horizontal power. In his view, a time in which each individual was entitled to have and defend their own opinion was a golden age.[18] In his *Florentine Histories*, he has one of the most "daring" and experienced of the Ciompi voice an opinion that must have sounded outrageous to the ears of aristocratic readers. Taking up an old Florentine discourse, the rebel argues that all those who had achieved great wealth and power did so either by deceit or through violence. To hide the hideousness of their ill-gotten gains, they dressed them up as honorable profits.

> Do not let the antiquity of blood, with which they will reproach us, dismay you; for all men, having had the same beginning, are equally ancient and have been made by nature

—not by God!—

> in one mode. Strip all of us naked, you will see that we are alike; dress us in
> their clothes and them in ours, and without a doubt we shall appear noble
> and they ignoble, for only poverty and riches make us unequal.[19]

Machiavelli's reputation as an engineer of tyranny is therefore undeserved. At
the end of the sixteenth century, the jurist Alberico Gentili lauded him as a
"praiser of democracy."[20] Even a socialist manifesto was able to invoke
Machiavelli.

His political experiences had made him a proponent of republicanism. The
people, which he once characterized as a "brute animal," are accorded a more
positive role in his *Discourses* than the prince or the grandee faction that supports
princely rule.[21] He viewed the Medici as destroyers of Florentine freedom. Yet
he was "Machiavellian" enough to dedicate his *Prince* to the "magnificent" Lorenzo di Piero de' Medici, then the most powerful man in Florence. This gesture,
however, did not even earn the exile permission to return home. Nevertheless,
another Medici, Giulio—later Pope Clement VII—did commission him to
write the city's history.[22]

For a political mind and a Florentine patriot like Machiavelli, exile in contemplative Chianti must have been a kind of hell on Earth. In one of the most
famous letters of the Renaissance—sent to the diplomat and Medici intimate
Francesco Vettori—he describes his daily life there: rising with the dawn,
hunting birds, taking a walk, checking on woodcutters, then some reading—
Dante, Petrarca, Tibullus, or Ovid—and chatting at the *osteria*.[23] After a frugal
midday meal, he goes back to the inn to play boisterous games of *tric trac* or
cricca with a butcher, a miller, and two bakers.

> Thus involved with these vermin I scrape the mold off my brain and satisfy
> the malignity of this fate of mine, as I am content to be trampled on this
> path so as to see if she will be ashamed of it.

But then follows a scene of great significance, and not only for the
Renaissance. It is doubtless a piece of calculated self-fashioning, but it is also
the description of a sensibility that cannot be totally foreign to any literary
man or learned woman, regardless of where and when they live.

> When evening comes, I return to my house and go into my study. At the
> door I take off my clothes of the day, covered with mud and mire, and I put
> on my regal and courtly garments; and decently clothed, I enter the ancient

courts of ancient men, where, received by them lovingly, I feed on the food that alone is mine and that I was born for. There I am not ashamed to speak with them and to ask them the reason for their actions; and they in their humanity reply to me. And for the space of four hours I feel no boredom, I forget every pain, I do not fear poverty, death does not frighten me. I deliver myself entirely to them.

For a moment, Machiavelli takes us into the inner sanctum of the workshop of humanism, which is essentially a dialogue and an aesthetic performance in an ugly world—and at the same time an escape from that world. It had been the same for Petrarca. Whenever he wanted to forget his own time, as he wrote in a fictive letter to Livy, it seemed to him that reading brought him into fellowship with Scipio, Laelius, Fabius Maximus, Brutus, and Decius; in those great names, he sought consolation for his miserable existence in an abysmal age.[24]

The free space in which Machiavelli could think what he wanted had grown small, restricted to a farmstead between Pesa and Greve. Yet the medium provided by Gutenberg would soon give one of the most disputatious and controversial thinkers of modern times a legion of conversation partners. In death, at least, he was permitted to return home to Florence. He was laid to rest in Santa Croce. *Tanto nomini nullum par elogium*: "No praise is equal to such a great name." Only in the eighteenth century did someone dare to inscribe these words into the marble slab that commemorates him.

28

Travels to Utopia, Art Worlds

Beautiful Cities

Sabbioneta. Mid-August. Giorgio de Chirico painted several pictures of cityscapes that do not exist anywhere: endless series of arcades, a round temple ringed with columns before a green-gray horizon, empty squares; monuments, anonymous statues, few people, and then a child determinedly pushing a hoop. The phantasmagoric dreamscapes seem a bit more real if you ever spend a hot Sunday afternoon stranded in Sabbioneta. The air rising from the pavement shimmers in the heat, stifling even in the shade. Churches, palaces, and bars are all dead. The square is utterly peaceful, the shadows thick as lead. Lost is the knowledge that time continues to flow and that there is a loud, busy world beyond the stillness.

The town near Mantua seems like one of de Chirico's metaphysical settings. Not that the layout is boringly uniform. Bastions of seemingly irregular shape encircle a network of orthogonal streets that is interrupted by numerous protrusions.[1] And yet, the visitor is indeed standing in the middle of a work of art. The whole thing is planned down to the last detail—according to ancient Roman proportions, it seems. The bastions are inscribed in a square, and the town's central axis is aligned with the position of the Sun on December 6. That is the birthday of the founder, Duke Vespasiano Gonzaga (1531–1591), who hoped in this way to activate the star's powers for his city. Astrology, alchemy, and antiquity were the guiding lights for the construction of Sabbioneta, which began in 1554. Vespasiano, who had had a significant military career and risen to the post of viceroy of Valencia in the service of Philip II of Spain, styled himself a new Caesar. Allusions to golden Rome are found throughout the city, in the ducal palace, in a long gallery that once held the duke's sculpture collection, and in the form of a theater based on ancient models. An academy was also built. Although Vespasiano did all he could to assure the success of his foundation—he even tried to force some of his subjects to settle in Sabbioneta—the planned city died with him. Too much geometry is never good for real life.

In three curious pictures that were probably painted for Federico da Montefeltro and that now hang in museums in Baltimore, Berlin, and Urbino (Fig. 38, p. 516), people seem largely superfluous. Although the purpose of these works is unclear, they show us how the Renaissance imagined ideal architecture. In strict linear perspective, they depict palaces, round buildings, fountains, a triumphal arch, and high columns capped with statues. It is all pretty to look at, but it does not seem an inviting place to live. It is far, far removed from the urban ideal promoted by Leon Battista Alberti in the previous century. His book on architecture mustered a rhetorical argument against the wasteland of the geometric city: it praised *varietas*, demanding streets slightly curved in soft arcs so that the eye would constantly be provided with new buildings to see—and thus with variety.[2] The idea was realized in Pienza, Pius II's city, where the main thoroughfare is indeed slightly curved. Nevertheless, Alberti's essentially humanistic view—in the sense of taking human beings as its touchstone—remained an exception. The urban planners of the Renaissance tended to desire strict symmetry, using the circle, the octagon, or the rectangle as the basic forms of their designs. In support of this practice, they could cite the authority of Vitruvius, whose ideal city is organized according to the rationality of geometric and astrological principles. Geometric, pure communities like Sabbioneta symbolized political and perhaps even cosmic order. Moreover, they proclaimed the glory of their founders, seeing that the foundation of cities was an undertaking worthy of ancient emperors and one pope. Thus Filarete even named the ideal city he conceived—it was never built but rather remained an architectural fantasy—*Sforzinda*, in honor of his patron Francesco Sforza. The plan is dominated by merciless uniformity. A nod is at least given to human needs in the variety of the buildings, which is meant to reflect the diversity within the individual.[3] Like Sforzinda, most of the urbanistic dreams of the Renaissance remained mere texts and drawings.

A love of geometry and a propensity for symbolism were also nurtured by the city-builders of other cultures. One thinks of the checkerboard layout of Beijing and Cusco or the circular design of Al-Mansur's Baghdad, based on Persian patterns. Its plan was supposed to be an image of the cosmos. In the same vein, the architect and urban planner Francesco di Giorgio named his ideal city a "small world," *piccolo mondo*.[4] When treating architecture in relationship to the human form, his ideas, again based on Vitruvius, reflected the holistic thinking of the age: the notion that the cosmos, man, and even the city existed in an analogous relationship (pp. 649–651).

Renaissance Italy's theoretical engagement with urban planning was entirely new—another aspect of the discursive revolution. It emerged within the same cultural context that had produced sophisticated, in part aesthetically minded building regulations, that had affirmed communal identity with chronicles, and that had celebrated cities in panegyric writings.[5] Europe discovered that cities could be "beautiful" and were therefore worthy of being portrayed.

The cityscape came into its own as an artistic genre in the late fifteenth century. Cities had long since outgrown their traditional portrayal in symbolically abbreviated form. They were now depicted as concrete, individual places with identifiable buildings and hints at their geographical location. Nevertheless, "realistic" cityscapes were always accessories to holy scenes and other historical tableaus. The first cityscape in its own right, the so-called "Chain Map," portrayed illustrious Florence, Dante's "great city" on the "lovely Arno" (Fig. 26, p. 355).[6] The plan might be based on an original from the fifteenth century. In the year 1500, Jacopo de' Barbari's brilliant bird's-eye view of Venice appeared. The number of such cityscapes, often in the form of colored woodcuts and then engravings, would soon explode into the thousands. And *Städtebücher*, books containing views of various cities that represented a laborious undertaking for printers, invited viewers to travel around the world in their imagination.

Ideal cities, urban panegyrics, and cityscapes are largely a peculiarity of Latin Europe. Cities were portrayed artistically in other cultures as well, but in nowhere near the same number as in Europe. Furthermore, non-European artists seldom seem to have been concerned with depicting their cities "realistically." Do these differences reflect the special status of the "Western city"? Many European renderings doubtless evince patriotic pride in their own, often autonomous community. It was not rare for them to be commissioned by municipal authorities. Their producers and consumers often came from the same urban circles that had fought for their independence from bishops and princes—social classes that did not exist elsewhere. Yet there were also many depictions of unfree cities whose purpose was to demonstrate their possession by princes. An important attribute of texts and artworks devoted to cities is that they focus on their mundane, human aspects. They thus represent a kind of demystification of European art, one that would also make itself felt in the emergence of other genres (p. 540).

In addition, the history of cities and buildings now attracted the attention of painters and woodcutters. Emblematic of the fascination with the power of time is the ruin. With all its deficits, it is the opposite of the out-of-time ideal city. Its mysterious underground passageways, its faded feasts, its walls whispering of lost greatness and doom make the ruin both a charming and a sad place. Along with the growing sense of history, it aroused romantic feelings of *eros* and death. An impressive example is provided by one of the most beautiful books ever printed: the *Hypnerotomachia Polifili*, published by Aldus Manutius in Venice in 1499. It is thought to have been written around 1467 in nearby Treviso, perhaps by Francesco Colonna, a Dominican friar from Venice.[7] Like few other works, it reflects the culture of the time, its obsession with antiquity, and its dreams.

Arcadian Dreams

In clear *antiqua* type, the *Hypnerotomachia* tells a love story. Exquisite woodcuts (Fig. 39, p. 520) are sprinkled throughout the text, whose title has been translated as *Poliphilo's Strife of Love in a Dream*. It begins with Poliphilo suffering a sleepless night because his beloved Polia has left him. At dawn, he is overcome by a deep slumber. He awakens in an overgrown forest—one thinks of Dante's *Inferno*—gets lost, and again falls asleep. The story becomes increasingly removed from reality: Poliphilo dreams he is dreaming. Searching for Polia, he wanders through lovely valleys, encounters nymphs, and, in a magnificent palace, meets Queen Eleuterylida, the ruler of the realm of free will. Led by the nymphs, he finally finds his beloved. Their betrothal is celebrated in the temple of Venus. Poliphilo and Polia then wander through a necropolis containing the resting places of unfortunate lovers and ultimately reach a harbor. From there, they take a ship to Cythera, the mythical island of love. Having arrived at their destination, they are permitted to consummate their union at the Fountain of Venus. At the climax, Cupid shoots an arrow through a curtain inscribed with the word *hymen*—the imagery is not very subtle. Venus enters the scene in all her glory. At the grave of Adonis, Poliphilo tries to

embrace Polia, but she disappears in a puff of pink smoke. Poliphilo wakes up and bemoans the brevity of his sleep. This is only an allusion to death, which will overtake the lovers in the end.

At first glance, the *Hypnerotomachia* seems to be a romance indebted to models like the *Romance of the Rose* or Boccaccio's *Amorosa visione*, another allegorizing poem. At the same time, the book is deeply erudite, which does not enhance its readability. Its author had a downright erotic relationship with the architecture of antiquity. There are pages upon pages of descriptions of ancient monuments, palaces, tombs, and ruins, as well as sophisticated machines. The author parades his education for all to see. The vernacular is intermixed with Latin passages and Greek words, Hebrew and Arabic letters, and hieroglyphics. Parts of the story turn out to be a kind of commentary on Vitruvius's architectural theory.[8] At any rate, the author must have known Alberti's *On the Art of Building*. The magnificence of the ancient buildings ultimately leaves the narrator speechless. In the face of the mighty grandeur and beauty of one such structure, he is so overwhelmed that all he can do is cry.

The spectacle made of knowledge, the dexterous, playful engagement with symbols and images, with codes and emblems, with revelations and disguises is just as typical of the intellectual culture of the time around 1500 as the rapturous enthusiasm for all things ancient that the *Hypnerotomachia* exudes. It, too, is utterly open to the things of the world and unabashed in the face of the monstrosities of pagan culture. The narrator evokes a panoply of nymphs, fauns, and gods. Satyrs gambol across fields, and Venus builds her own paradisiacal realm—all in a society imbued with Christian faith. But in the end, it is all just a dream; even more, it is a dream within a dream. The work's refined literary artistry surely helped it gain the approval of censors.

Poliphilo's Strife of Love in a Dream is a key text of the Renaissance. Polia—whose name alludes to an ancient epithet of Athena—is probably a personification of ancient wisdom. Kidnapped from a nunnery, she is carried off by a reborn Minerva to the realm of a sensuous goddess of love.[9] As the second part of the book explains, in "real life," this Polia was a young woman of patrician birth, Lucrezia de Leliis, who had consecrated herself to the cult of Diana during plague times. The pagan goddess is a disguise for the mother of God, however. Lucrezia-Polia does not need to be reborn, as she will live on in Mary. She therefore enters a Marian convent. In fact, in the symbolic language of the Renaissance, the mother of the Redeemer was equated with Athena, a defender of wisdom, as the *virgo sapientiae*. Poliphilo, a true Renaissance man, seeks wisdom with all his will. In the end it disappears in a puff of smoke, i.e., it remains unattainable. In this reading, the *Hypnerotomachia* would be nothing other than a picture of Renaissance culture as it saw itself at its high point.

Before assuming that the age was cheerful and worldly, however, we would be wise to read this exquisite book to the end. It closes with two epitaphs. One reads, "Fortunate Polia, you who live in death." In the second, the deceased girl responds to her lover, who is trying to restore her to life with his tears: "Alas, Poliphilo, give up. A flower this shriveled will never be revived. Farewell."[10] Ambivalence belongs not only to the late Renaissance. Death is present even in Arcadia.

The distant world of dreams remained the most important of the many literary escapes created by the Renaissance. Ovid, Theocritus, Homer, and again and again Virgil provided settings and characters: Pan, nymphs, and satyrs, shepherdesses and shepherds. The most successful work in the genre was not the labyrinthine *Hypnerotomachia* but rather the *Arcadia* of the Neapolitan poet Jacopo Sannazaro (1458–1530), published in its final form in 1504.[11] It tells the story of a young, lovelorn poet—Sannazaro himself—who leaves bustling Naples and retreats to Arcadia to find consolation among the shepherds. The pastoral romance is a celebration of carefree existence in harmony with nature, in which clear springs bubble forth and limpid streams flow. It is a hymn to free, innocent love and merry feasts. The catastrophe in Naples, the invasion of Charles VIII's troops, causes the "pilgrim of love" (*peregrino di amore*) to return to the capital, where he must learn of the death of his beloved. The whole is imbued with the nostalgic reminiscence of a lost Golden Age. "Our muses are perished," complains the epilogue addressed to the poet's panpipes. "Withered are our laurels; ruined is our Parnassus; the woods are all become mute; the valleys and the mountains for sorrow are grown deaf; Nymphs and Satyrs are found no more among the woods; the shepherds have lost their song."[12]

Sannazaro's book inspired poets all over Europe. In the late sixteenth century, it was imitated by Philip Sidney's kindred novel of the same name. And it put paintbrushes in the hands of artists. Giorgione was one. So was Titian, who painted a portrait of Sannazaro. The literary model's enduring success was probably due to the fact that it expressed archetypal desires. It contrasted geometrical cities and the ugliness of politics with nature and the simple life; the intellectualism of academic disputes with innocence and naive joy in the tones of the flute; the burden of history with dreamlike timelessness. Another thing that made Sannazaro famous in his own time, and which indeed even won him a place in Raphael's *Parnassus* (p. 537), was that he interwove pagan and Christian elements. The *Arcadia* is full of allusions to religious values and biblical stories.

Beautiful landscapes and enchanting nature had been an integral part of the Renaissance long before Sannazaro wrote his *Arcadia*. Travelers in search of broad vistas no longer carried Augustine's *Confessions* with them, however. What had changed since Petrarca's famous ascent of Mont Ventoux can be seen in a visit to Pius II's palace in Pienza, which has a grandiose loggia on the piano nobile. The entire architecture of the building is designed to provide a view of the countryside from its vantage point. The vista sweeps over pines, silver olive trees, and vineyards toward the soft triangle of Monte Amiata. Pius loved taking picnics in the countryside and spending time in nature just for the fun of it, with no pious motive.[13] He was able to give expression to his bucolic emotions. He wrote of the yellow broom of the Cimini Hills, the blue flax around Viterbo, and the singing of birds without ever losing sight of ancient ruins and columns. Relaxing, taking a break from everyday life and its business—not only popes could do that in such idyllic places. They made it possible to live the dream of Arcadia, at least for a bit. A rich theoretical literature provided instructions for doing so. Those with the necessary resources built beautiful country villas in imitation of classical models and took refuge

there after the manner described in Cicero's *Tusculan Disputations* and Boccaccio's *Decameron*.

With its officials and its soldiers, the early modern state had made the countryside safe. The buildings used for administration and celebrations increasingly lost their fortress-like character. Cosimo de' Medici's citadel in Careggi
outside Florence is an example of the older variety. In contrast, Lorenzo the
Magnificent's villa in Poggio a Caiano, further up the Arno, is wide open to its
surroundings. On the outskirts of the big cities, the patrician class adorned its
estates with villas and framed them with artfully designed gardens.[14] The vacation landscape of the Venetian mainland state was the most magnificent of
them all. Its dazzle, incidentally, was the flip side to a darkening political horizon. The Turkish advance in the Mediterranean restricted the possibilities for
earning money with trade and made business ventures riskier. The alternative
was to invest in land. And that is what the Venetian elite did, covering it with
villas. The learned discussions and classicizing pageantry that once filled these
monuments to their owners' magnificence have vanished with the memory of
their participants. Yet we can still imagine timeless moments, far removed
from everyday life and close to Arcadia. After all, Arcadia is always located
somewhere else.

Nowhere Lands

Arcadia could be described as an earthly paradise pervaded by the spirit of
antiquity. Its burlesque counterpart was the land of Cockaigne. At the same
time as Sannazaro was polishing his *Arcadia*, the legendary land of milk and
honey was enshrined in literature by the Alsatian writer Sebastian Brant
(1457/58–1521).[15] His *Ship of Fools* depicts "Narragonia," the "fool's paradise,"
the Arcadia of the people. The "other" portrayed by Brant is not a foil for the
life of a humanistic wordsmith or a hypercivilized courtier but rather for a
hard, dreary existence of starvation that was filled with anything but roast
chicken, goose, or pigeon. For some people, the dreams of Cockaigne or Narragonia demanded fulfillment. The rebellions and turmoil of the age are witness to that fact.

One of the most surprising answers to the questions plaguing society was
provided by the Englishman Thomas More (1478–1535). To denote a perfect
place in *this* world and not in the hereafter, he coined the word "utopia." The
son of a London lawyer and himself a trained jurist, he had considered becoming a monk but ultimately opted for a civic career and marriage. When he

published his *Utopia* in 1516, a grand path with a tragic end (p. 608) still lay ahead of him. He wrote his most famous work amid the hard reality of Machiavelli's Europe, with its wars, intrigues, and lies. Before whisking his readers off to the island of earthly beatitude, he used the narrative frame—a dialogue set in Antwerp, where the author had actually lived for a time as an envoy—to sketch the state of his times. It looks gloomy. A growing number of poor, including those crippled by war, is beset by a mix of vulturous nobles, lazy monks, and idlers, as well as by states engaging in costly wars of conquest. More knows that excessive taxation can cause unrest and revolution, and he is also aware of the connection between poverty and criminality.

Everything is better on the island of Utopia. More's narrator is the well-traveled Raphael Hythloday, who claims to have landed there after being blown off course on one of his voyages. There is no private property in Utopia, just like in the ideal state of Plato's *Republic*, the chief model for More's story. The classic argument against such a communist society is also aired, put into the mouth of the first-person narrator: namely that it would dampen acquisitiveness and thus result in general laziness. But in Utopia, the socialist model works. There is a police force that makes sure no one lazes about. Since everyone works, everyone works less. In this way, the means are generated to sustain a mild welfare state. Those who prove capable of higher learning are freed from physical labor in a secret vote of the people. The basis of the Utopian economy is agriculture, which everyone, even craftsmen, must engage in by turns along with their actual profession. The community is organized as a republic headed by a prince. If he develops autocratic tendencies, he can be deposed.

Utopia's cities look like ideal cities. As foils for the chaotic behemoth of London, they are built with perfect regularity. The buildings are robust and fireproof; one is just like another. All Utopians wear the same clothing. Like in Plato's *Republic*, they dine together. They do not have money, and like the noble savages of America they despise gold. In order to discredit it, they use it to make chains for slaves, toys, and chamber pots. Sexual morality is strict. Adultery is punished with slavery, repeat offenses with death. Thus, in contrast to Plato's ideal state, women are not shared in common in Utopia. Permission from the authorities is necessary to travel, and everything everywhere is done in public. What Hythloday reports about Utopian religion sounds more pleasant: whereas elsewhere it is earnest, sad, and severe, Utopians—recalling Lorenzo Valla, whose position More knew—treat faith as a source of pleasure. It provides joy taken in a well-lived life and reward for it in the beyond. The god of Utopia is similar to Plato's. He is an "unknown, eternal, infinite, inexplicable" power that spreads itself over the whole world.[16] The Utopians are tolerant; they abhor religious wars and fanatics. A Christian missionary who had once zealously sought to convert them was sent into exile. One of their oldest legal principles is that no one should suffer disadvantage on account of their religion. Only materialism of the Epicurean variety—the vicious philosopher is not named, however—is forbidden. Otherwise, the cult of the Utopians, which they venerate in expansive temples bereft of divine images, recognizes the possibility that God takes pleasure in the diversity of religions.

Although *Utopia* can occasionally seem like a draft of the *Communist Manifesto*, it is anything but a political pamphlet calling readers to action. Rather, More offers a detached, ethereal essay whose tone is often ironic. His brilliant intellectual experiment is addressed to thinkers who understand nuance and know that desire is not enough to change reality. In the epilogue, the author even distances himself from the views of his narrator Hythloday, although he does not say which ones. Even the name "Hythloday" connotes aloofness. It contains the Greek word *hythlos*, meaning "nonsense" or "empty drivel."

The values that undergird Utopia come from the deep past. The notion that a good state rests on agriculture, military virtue, and simple living could be found in the eulogists of republican Rome, and the community of goods and charity are supposed to have been practiced in the earliest Christian communities. On the other hand, the Utopians are "Renaissance men," exuding curiosity. As soon as Hythloday acquaints them with the printing press and paper, they immediately adopt the inventions.

Nothing like *Utopia* had been written since antiquity. It was an attempt to describe an ideal state *in the real world*, to supply it with an economic foundation that was not utterly fantastical, and to develop a model for society based on it.[17] More's book coined a term and launched a literary genre. The point was to think the unthinkable and to expand realms of possibility beyond the boundaries of the possible. From then on, countless utopias of all kinds held up the mirror to the societies that spawned them. By showing how things ought to be and claiming that they could indeed be that way, they questioned the status quo and called for change. The measures they recommended tended to be quite radical. For that reason alone, the genre could only flourish in states where there was at least a minimum of freedom and where censorship did not stifle everything. Latin Europe, where such freedoms did exist—as did the printing press and a large, educated audience that appreciated this kind of literature—therefore earned a special place in the new literary field. Nowhere else was a similar variety of utopian schemes elaborated. Elsewhere people stuck to pious visions, such as the Shambhala of Tibetan Buddhism and the Pure Land of the Buddha Amitabha, or the paradises and theocracies imagined by Islamic writers.[18]

The curious word "utopia" literally means "nowhere." Accordingly, Europe's utopias were initially located in remote areas, usually on islands. But in the following centuries, as the furthest corners of the globe were explored and the space for imaginary realms diminished, utopias started cropping up in the future. They were outfitted with the most amazing technology and placed on distant planets light-years away. The Arcadian tradition, with its joyous nature and pleasant anarchies, was joined by geometric, strictly organized states on the model of Plato and More. These fantasies were reflected in the ideal cities that were being planned and built at the time.

Lenin once emphatically refused to classify Marx's vision as a utopia. As is well known, he considered it a necessity of natural law that history would produce communist societies.[19] Another difference between More's imaginary island and Lenin's paradise was that Utopia could not survive without a rigid political order, whereas the state was supposed to be superfluous in the mature phase of communism. It is no small irony that in the very place where Utopia became at least a bit of a reality—between Beijing and Moscow—it resembled less the communist model than the vision of the peaceful Christian Thomas More.

The Utopia of Urbino: Castiglione and the Civilizing Process

Urbino, Palazzo ducale. September 25, 1506.

On the slopes of the Apennines, almost in the center of Italy towards the Adriatic, is situated, as everyone knows, the little city of Urbino. Although it is surrounded by hills which are perhaps not as agreeable as those found in many other places, none the less it has been favored by Nature with a very rich and fertile countryside, so that as well as a salubrious atmosphere it enjoys an abundance of all the necessities of life.[20]

Thus the diplomat Baldassare Castiglione (1478–1529) described one of the most significant centers of the Renaissance. He was present when Pope Julius II entered the city after his successful campaigns to consolidate the Papal States. The pope was given the keys to the city, and the gates were ripped down to signify that it now belonged to him.

Julius confirmed Guidobaldo, the only son and heir of the great Federico da Montefeltro, in his role as lord of Urbino. Yet he now entrusted title to the city to his own family, the della Rovere. The childless Guidobaldo was 35 in that year, 1506, but plagued by severe gout. Only two painful years remained to him. The final flourishing of Urbino's courtly culture was therefore overshadowed by gloom. Thoughts turned to the better days under Duke Federico, when the land was securely protected by Francesco di Giorgio's fortresses, and Italy's princes could still hash out their rivalries without foreign interference.

That was the somewhat somber backdrop to another key work of the Renaissance, Baldassare Castiglione's *Cortegiano* (*Book of the Courtier*). It also has utopian features. Its author compares it to efforts to describe the perfect state, the perfect king, and the perfect orator.[21] Castiglione was born in 1478, the same year as Thomas More. When he began writing in 1513, he had accrued nearly a decade of experience as a diplomat in the service of Urbino. He was thus intimately familiar with the setting for his narrative, Duke Federico's palace—he calls it "more like a city than a mere palace."[22] In the book, a circle of court ladies, humanists, and courtiers gathers there for evening conversations. How some of them looked is known from extant portraits, a few of which are attributed to Urbino's native son Raphael. They include pictures of the hostess, Elisabetta Gonzaga, Giuliano de' Medici (a son of Lorenzo the Magnificent), and the humanist Pietro Bembo (1470–1547).

The *Cortegiano* is a game, *un gioco*, with words. It addresses the old question of whether poetry should be written in Latin or Italian, describes the qualities of the ideal prince—the interlocutors conclude that he must provide his subjects with a peaceful, safe existence lived in freedom—and discusses love and women. The atmosphere is jocular and relaxed. Everyone was entitled to speak and make jokes, Castiglione writes, although the greatest freedom was attended by the best behavior. Issues of life and death were not on the agenda. They laughed, but not loudly—that would be uncivilized.[23] They argued, but without zeal. At the close of the conversations, when the sun had set behind the hills around Urbino, they danced.

The dialogic culture of the Renaissance reaches a high point in Castiglione's work. The *Cortegiano* has a lot to say about what proper language is. It addresses not only what can be said but also how it should be said. Castiglione describes the utmost refinement and cultivation, which joins apparent opposites and avoids extremes: earnestness and levity, learning and wit, rules and freedom. The courtier knows how to sing, write poetry, and paint. He can fight and dance. He is an adviser, even a teacher to his prince, whose favor he seeks.

He acts naturally but not coarsely. He is cultivated but without affectation. He is a master of the high art of making his charm seem effortless. He is neither a dandy nor a prude, neither ignorant nor erudite. He lets his spirit shine without showing off. He possesses tact, stoic serenity, and moral rectitude. Yet he is no wet blanket. The key term for what characterizes ideal behavior in Castiglione's view is untranslatable: *sprezzatura*. It is easier to say what it does *not* mean. It is not carelessness or nonchalance or coolness, certainly not contempt—*disprezzo* in Italian—but rather a calm, secure, yet unforced behavior. It contains old chivalric virtues like "moderation," *mâze*, as well as Cicero's *urbanitas*: worldly education, beauty, elegance, and good manners.

If everyone were like that, the world would be in order. Castiglione was forced to experience firsthand that the world was not in order. The *Sacco di Roma*, the sack of Rome by hordes of *Landsknechte* unleashed on the city in the year 1527, was a bacchanal of barbarity (p. 601). Castiglione, who was then serving as papal nuncio to Charles V in Spain, was judged complicit in the disaster, accused of being too close to the emperor and insufficiently informing the pope of his plans. The *Cortegiano* appeared in 1528 from the Aldine Press. The next year its author died. But the book made its way through Europe in a variety of translations. Spin-offs appeared, no longer only providing models for behavior at court but also attempting to transmit guidelines for good behavior in general. Castiglione's spirit left palaces and villas, inspired handbooks on the *Art of Conversation*—thus the title of an especially successful book by Stefano Guazzo, published in 1574[24]—and came to animate bourgeois homes. If they could not be courtly, people now wanted to at least become courteous.

In the German-speaking world, the printing press facilitated the diffusion of books on table manners and general conduct. The century of the *Cortegiano* was also their heyday. The most famous example is the German minister Friedrich Dedekind's *Grobianus*, first published in 1549. The author provides colorful caricatures of filthy behavior and slovenly dressed, uncombed oafs. Page after page is filled with drinking, eating, spitting and vomiting, farting and burping, animated gestures, loud talking, and boisterous laughter. Dedekind describes the antithesis of the courtier—and yet still manages to offer a kind of *Cortegiano* for the people.

> Read this book day and night
> Do not as it says, and you'll do right.

Thus admonishes the title page of the German edition of 1553.[25]

Like Castiglione's work and countless of its offshoots, the *Grobianus* is evidence for what Norbert Elias called the "civilizing process."[26] "Civilization" became a principle. Its job was to give a form to societal coexistence, to make it pleasant, decent, and good.[27] But the development did not follow the pattern traced by Elias, i.e., a straight line from an ostensibly burlesque, shameless Middle Ages to the civilized court society of the Age of Absolutism. An early precursor to the *Cortegiano* is the *Welsh Guest* by Thomasin von Zerklaere (ca. 1186–1238?).[28] Written in Middle High German around 1215, the work is a guide to noble virtues and refined courtly behavior intended for "pious knights, good women, and wise priests."[29] There are many more examples of this kind. One is the *Siete Partidas* written by Alfonso X of Castile in 1265. It exhorts the ruler to maintain self-control, comport himself properly, and not gesticulate. Eating with one's hands was still the standard, but not all the fingers should be used, and they should be washed before and after the meal.[30]

Urbino was an emblem of an advanced phase of state formation and the peace, albeit still precarious, that it preserved. Castiglione's work also signaled worldliness. Religion is utterly on the margins of the courtiers' conversations. One of the interlocutors, Giuliano de' Medici, once mentions almost by way of apology that he prefers not "to confuse divine things with these foolish discussions of ours."[31] The *Cortegiano* also provides the model for enlightened conversation among equals. This is made possible by the narrative device of sending the sickly Duke Guidobaldo to bed, thus permitting the lady of the house, Elisabetta Gonzaga, and her sister-in-law, Emilia Pia, to guide the discussion. Urbino is the perfect opposite of the Burgundian court in Dijon, with its polished ceremonial, to say nothing of Versailles two hundred years later, where everything revolved around the Sun King. Castiglione's utopia depicts the opposite of the strict geometric order desired by More and by many of his successors, as well as by the lackeys of absolutism: builders of ideal cities, strongmen, and pious fanatics.

The Art Market

In her portrait, Elisabetta Gonzaga appears before a lyrical background: the hills around Urbino are illuminated by the fading light of day (Plate 18). Above the duchess's carefully trimmed eyebrows, the artist depicts a headband with a scorpion on it. It could be the Gonzaga impresa, or maybe it was a talisman with which the duchess tried—in vain, as we know—to force the stars to give her the offspring she so desired; according to traditional belief, the constellation Scorpio rules the reproductive organs.[32] The Renaissance loved allusions of this kind, indeed any pictures that invited deciphering and facilitated conversation for the enjoyment of educated patrons and their guests. As one humanist remarked on such discussions about art, "Everyone has a different opinion and nobody agrees with anybody else. This is more delightful than the pictures themselves."[33]

Most of the more significant artworks of the Renaissance were still the products of formal commissions.[34] As with the *Gates of Paradise* for the Baptistery in Florence, competitions were often held. This was the case in 1490 in Milan, for example, when the possibility of adding a dome to the cathedral was considered. Operating between patrons and artists were often dealers, agents, and advisers, each of whom took their cut. It was not rare for patrons to take a hand in the planning process. The resulting artwork was therefore also a product of their mind.

The contracts drawn up for the creation of paintings, for example, often specified minute details, dimensions, and things like delivery dates. Above all, they included precise instructions for the use of costly materials like marble, gold, or ultramarine (which was made from lapis lazuli).[35] It was not unusual for a gilded frame to cost more than the painting it bordered. A figure whose robe was painted a costly color must, for that reason alone, have immediately seemed like an important person and attracted the gaze of contemporaries.

Painters and sculptors were still considered craftsmen and nothing more. They were organized into guilds that, in Italy and elsewhere, oversaw the amount of their wages and the prices of their works. In the case of disputes between artists and patrons, an arbitrator might help resolve things. If a contract stipulated, as sometimes happened, that the master was supposed to carry out the work himself "with his own hand," it was the quality of the execution that mattered and not a big name. Even Dürer, when quarreling over the price of an altar with the Frankfurt merchant Jakob Heller, employed the prosaic argument that the panel included nearly a hundred heads.[36] By doing so, he emphasized the work and time it had taken to paint so many portraits, not the aesthetic qualities of his painting.

"Art markets" for the people, at which hardly anything other than images of saints were sold, had existed since the Late Middle Ages.[37] Merchants dealt in ancient sculpture as well as plaster copies of famous artworks. They also had terracotta Madonnas, manuscripts, mirrors, and devotional images on offer. Around 1480, Neri di Bicci sold small *all'antica* tabernacles for home use containing holy scenes in painted plaster relief. These mass-produced trinkets

made him the richest painter in Florence at the time.[38] Churches and museums all over Italy and around the world contain the white and blue, sometimes
colorfully glazed terracotta reliefs produced by the della Robbia family business, headed by masters Luca and Andrea. Most of it is mass merchandise and
would be called kitsch if it were not a product of the Florentine Renaissance.
Great art often provided models for the makers of majolica plates, stove tiles,
and small bronze figures.[39] This brought the Renaissance into bourgeois living
rooms. The massive mountain of handicrafts of this kind that has come down
to us is only a modest remainder of what was produced.

The chance for social elevation made courts attractive to artist-craftsmen.
Some painters attained titles of nobility and great fortunes or, like van Eyck,
were sent on diplomatic missions. Once the desired sinecure or status as
court painter or court composer had been secured, however, new forms of
dependency appeared. Those who held such posts were generally not allowed
to accept commissions from outside the court, and they often could not travel
without permission. They had to put up with princely moodiness and engage
in boorish work, such as painting theater backdrops or staging feasts. Each
change of ruler could mean the loss of one's job. In this respect, the situation
of Western artists—and scholars—differed from that of many of their
counterparts in Asia. One must also keep in mind that not all courts were
equal. It made a big difference if one found employment with the pope, in
Milan, or in Paris, or if one ended up in Cesena, Forlì, or some minor court
in Germany.

The south was still very different from the north. Dürer famously put it in
a nutshell during his stay in Venice: "How I shall freeze after this sun," he wrote
to a friend in Nuremberg. "Here I am a gentleman, at home only a parasite."[40]
This may have been nothing more than moody exaggeration, but there is no
doubt that what we call "artists" emerged in Italy. That is where the first quirky
individuals appeared who bucked bourgeois conventions, the first extravagant
geniuses who had to be treated with kid gloves if their creativity was to flourish. In the form of the glorious trinity of Leonardo, Raphael, and Michelangelo, their number included three gods of creation made flesh. We must be
careful, though. This exaggerated vision of the superstars of the High
Renaissance is entirely the product of later writing about art and Renaissance
romanticism. Indeed, it is nearly impossible to distinguish the outlines of real,
historical individuals beneath the thick overpainting given them by enthusiastic aesthetes and novelists. By far the most influential constructor of these
and other artist golems was a latter-day member of their own ranks: Vasari.

From anecdotes that were often freely invented and *barzellette*, or jokes, he created a fictional character that soon came to life: the modern artist.

The Ungodly: Leonardo

A work of art that approximates like no other the human ideal expressed in the *Cortegiano* is the *Mona Lisa*, the most famous portrait in the world. The legendary Florentine woman's smile is unique; equally unique is the masterful technique of its painter. To create the illusion of physicality and distance, he applied countless layers of varnish. He worked on outlines like Cusanus had attacked the problem of opposites, erasing the distinction between the not-yet and the no-longer, creating an infinitely delicate border approaching invisibility. Outlines evaporate into indefiniteness.

The painter of the *Mona Lisa*, Leonardo di Piero, was born in 1452 in Vinci (outside Florence). His father was a notary, and his mother was probably a farm girl. He learned his craft in the workshop of the sculptor and painter Andrea del Verrocchio (1435–1488).[41] He quickly made a name for himself, working first in the orbit of the Medici and then, starting in 1482, at the court of the Sforza. When Milan was taken by Louis XII, he had to look around for new patrons. In 1500, he went to Venice, Mantua, and Florence. He spent some time in Cesare Borgia's retinue and ultimately found another post in Milan, which was then in French hands. A sojourn in Rome, where the biggest commissions could be won, remained an *intermezzo*. Leonardo spent his final years in France. Far from home, he died in 1519 at the Clos Lucé chateau near the royal residence of Amboise. Some of his works ended up in the possession of the patron of his later years, Francis I, and thus of France. That is why the *Mona Lisa*, the *Virgin and Child with Saint Anne*, and *John the Baptist*, Leonardo's most perfect meditation on outlines, now hang in the Louvre.

This genius—in his exceptional case, the term might be justified—today symbolizes "Renaissance" more than any other artist or scholar of his time. Leonardo's reputation hardly stems from his mastery as a painter alone but also from his forward-thinking inventions and theoretical investigations. What we do not know about him, or only suspect, has made him even more of a legend than what we do know. His drawings are among the most beautiful in the history of art. A handful of his paintings are extant beyond those already mentioned, including the battered *Last Supper* in the refectory of the monastery of Santa Maria delle Grazie in Milan, an object of admiration and inspiration for generations. Preliminary sketches remain for lost or unfinished projects, such as the equestrian monument for Francesco Sforza or the tomb for the condottiere Gian Giacomo Trivulzio. The Battle of Anghiari (p. 370) provided the subject for a fresco in the "Hall of the Five Hundred" in the Palazzo Vecchio. Commissioned by the Soderini regime in 1504, it was to immortalize a Florentine victory over Milan. Leonardo probably experimented with the ancient method of encaustic, in which wax is used to bind the pigments; the idea was to yield shinier colors. Despite two years of effort, however, he could not master the technique. The paint fell off the wall, and the project ended in disaster. What remained was the myth of a masterpiece.

The painter from Vinci was a strange mix of nervous tinkerer and genius, perfectionist and experimenter. Brilliant ideas gushed out of him. While the solution for one problem had not yet been found and a second had already been attacked, he started working on a third. He also developed mechanical devices. Some of them worked. Once, he built a functioning robot for a Sforza feast.[42] Other projects were never realized, such as plans for a massive encyclopedia, unfinished technical fantasies like flying machines, gigantic catapults, crossbows, a diving suit, and unbuilt churches and fortresses. Leonardo must have been a convincing salesman of quixotic projects. Once, he imagined diverting the Arno by means of a large canal in an attempt to deprive Pisa of its source of water. The only thing left high and dry by the failed endeavor was the Florentine treasury.

Leonardo surpassed all others in combining theoretical reflection with the skill of a craftsman. For example, he conducted experiments on friction, discovering that this troublesome impediment to all mechanical work was not the result of the size of the surfaces rubbing against one another but rather of the pressure applied to them.[43] Leonardo was the most curious man of his century. He studied plants, animals, and geological formations, water currents and whirlpools.[44] His anatomical studies went far beyond the needs of a painting workshop; he skinned corpses, cut them open, and dissected them. The drawings he made of human bodies and their inner organs were far superior to all that had come before in terms of technical quality and precision. He dissected bodies in part as a means of studying human proportions, calculating them as precisely as possible.[45] But he was also interested in the functions of the organs, their shape, and the innermost parts of human beings. References to antiquity do not play any great role in his notes—not because it had lost its significance as the measure of all art, but rather because its authority had meanwhile become self-evident, internalized. Thus, when Leonardo did not make recourse to the measuring of "real" people for his understanding of proportions, he relied on Vitruvius and likely the *Doryphorus* or "Speer-thrower" of Polyclitus, the Renaissance's ideal of proportionality.[46]

As a scientist, Leonardo was more the heir of Gerbert of Aurillac, Roger Bacon, and Eilmer of Malmesbury than a precursor to Galileo. He played no role in the history of the Scientific Revolution, in large part because his research and designs were never published in his lifetime. Not that he slaved away in secret and isolation, eschewing the light of publicity like some sorcerer. Rather, he was probably aware of the inchoate, unfinished nature of his work. Only in a few of his paintings did he achieve a level of perfection that took even his contemporaries' breath away. The jokes and riddles contained in his notes might have been aimed at entertaining a courtly society. This could also be the case for some of his singular caricatures.

Leonardo must have had a winning personality.[47] Those whose portraits he drew were entertained by lute music, and "readers of various and beautiful works"[48] gathered in his studio for delightful conversation, like in Castiglione's Urbino circle. Yet the *sprezzatura* cultivated by Leonardo, perfumed with lavender water, was the veneer of a profound mind. He refused to be dismissed as an unlearned man, a *homo senza lettere*.[49] He knew ancient books of marvels and had heard of Presocratic philosophy. The longest and most polished text of his that has come down to us, a treatise on painting, shows that he had worked through contemporary theories of perspective and writings on optics, including that of al-Haytham.[50] He was an Aristotelian and put stock in experience. The Platonic realm of ideas was foreign to him. It might be symbolized by the allegory of exploring a cave that is found in his notes.[51] He writes of digging ever deeper into the darkness, full of fear but also driven by the expectation of finding something wonderful there. The famous text reads like an inversion of Plato's allegory, which seeks to see what really exists in the glaring light outside the cave. In contrast, Leonardo searches for it deep in the earth, in the form of hard matter accessible to experience. He did not believe in the existence of bodiless spirits either.[52] In his view, the essential characteristic of human beings is the ability to think and work; other than that, they are just producers of excrement, simply a special species of animal.[53] Yet they can achieve divinity through art. The hands of the painter create nature—better and more completely, in Leonardo's view, than poetry or sculpture could. Adapting Dante, he sees the painter as a grandson of God.[54]

It is strange that the creator of some of the most beautiful religious paintings of all time was not a devout Christian. Neither eternal beatitude nor the Last Judgment represented the end of all being for him. Alluding to the Presocratic philosopher Anaxagoras, he remarked, "Everything comes from every-thing, and everything becomes everything, and everything returns to every-thing."[55] His visions of the end of the world are inspired by Ovid, not the Apocalypse of John. Still, he was moved by metaphysical questions. In the affairs of the world, he observed a power that renewed itself and yet sought its own death. Who was its author?

> Look at the light and behold its beauty. Now close your eyes and observe: what you saw is there no longer, and what you will see is not yet there. Who is it who makes it anew when its maker constantly dies?[56]

The Divine: Michelangelo and Raphael

Florence. January 25, 1504. It was perhaps the most illustrious gathering in the history of art.[57] The heads of the "Opera," or governing board, of the cathedral and the wool guild had invited about two dozen artists and craftsmen to assemble, including the painters Cosimo Rosselli, Sandro Botticelli, Filippino Lippi, Lorenzo di Credi, and Pietro Perugino, the architects Giuliano and An-tonio da Sangallo, as well as Andrea della Robbia and Leonardo da Vinci. They were there to discuss the venue for a statue whose sculptor, Michelangelo Buonarroti, then not yet 30 years old, only referred to as *il gigante*, "the giant" (Fig. 40, p. 536). He meant the *David*. Over the space of two and a half years, Michelangelo had chiseled it out of a block of marble over five meters high. Florence was amazed. The victorious youth did not stand triumphantly over the head of Goliath as was customary. Instead, Michelangelo showed the hero in the moment before his decisive shot, as naked as described in the Bible passage. With fierce determination, his gaze seeks the imaginary foe. Attentive observation reveals that the head seems a bit too big. The figure was originally intended to be placed high up on the cathedral and was, therefore, designed to be seen from below. After a long debate, the commission of artists decided to erect it outside the Palazzo della Signoria, the seat of the Soderini govern-ment. The *David* was a political manifesto: it stood watch, on the lookout for enemies of the republic. At the time, that primarily meant the Medici, whose return was expected at any moment.

Michelangelo was born in 1475 in Caprese, near Arezzo. His "giant" made him the foremost sculptor in Florence, indeed in all of Italy. As the protégé of the very same Medici family that his *David* now threatened with a deadly sling-shot, he had received commissions in Florence and had also enjoyed success

in Bologna and Siena. His breakthrough came in Rome just before the turn of the century with his *Pietà*. In Florence, in the large hall of the Palazzo Vecchio near Leonardo's *Battle of Anghiari*, he was supposed to paint a fresco depicting another battle, Florence's victory over Pisa at Cascina in 1364. It was not carried out. Nor were figures of the apostles for the cathedral. Michelangelo preferred to seek commissions from the greatest of all patrons: the pope.

The reigns of Julius II and his successor Leo X were the apogee of art patronage on the Tiber.[58] In addition, in 1506 an ancient sculptural group of exceptional quality was discovered in a Roman vineyard, one that would provide inspiration to generations of sculptors and elicit admiration for centuries to come: the *Laocoon*. "Learned antiquity beheld no nobler work," mused the humanist Jacopo Sadoleto. "Now, freed from the darkness, it again beholds the towering walls of revived Rome."[59] The papal city was then in the process of overtaking Florence as the capital of the Renaissance. Palaces like the Palazzo della Cancelleria—the residence of the powerful Cardinal Camerlengo Raffaele Riario, a great-nephew of Julius II—were just the beginning. Around 1500, Donato Bramante (1444–1514) made his mark. The *Tempietto* he erected in the courtyard of the monastery of San Pietro in Montorio, based on ancient round temples, was financed by the Catholic Monarchs of Spain. A perfectly circular building, it marks the spot where Saint Peter was thought to have been crucified. A few years later, the architect received the most prestigious commission then for the having: the construction of New Saint Peter's Basilica.

In the figure of Raphael, a new generation achieved artistic ascendance in Rome. The son of the painter Giovanni Santi came from talent-rich Urbino, where Bramante—who worked for Federico da Montefeltro's architect Luciano Laurana (ca. 1420–ca. 1479)—also received his training. It was Bramante who then recommended his younger but already distinguished colleague to the pope. In 1509, Raphael began painting the *Stanze*, an apartment in the Vatican Palace; Julius seems to have dictated the pictorial program. The *Stanza della Segnatura* contains Raphael's *School of Athens*, on the opposite wall the *Disputation of the Holy Sacrament*, and next to it the *Parnassus*. In the latter fresco, Apollo is surrounded by the nine Muses and poets of ancient and more recent times, including Homer—whom the painter has made to resemble the *Laocoon*—Virgil, Dante, and Sannazaro. In this way, one and the same room combines pagan science and poetry with the cosmos of the Christian faith, with the Trinity, saints, and theologians.

Bramante, Raphael, and Michelangelo were the constructors of the "High Renaissance" in Rome. The term is not meant to indicate that the summit of beauty and perfection had been reached. Like all names for stylistic or chronological periods, it is a heuristic device. It is most meaningful when used to indicate that an elite group of artists, writers, and scholars now possessed a more-or-less complete mastery of the lexicon, grammar, and knowledge of antiquity. Michelangelo could sculpt like Polyclitus or Lysippus. Bramante's architecture dreaded no comparison with classical buildings. The process of *re*-birth was finished. The object, in the arts as well, was now increasingly to create new things. The market was accordingly very competitive. The prizes were prestige and money. Lots of money. For the tomb he commissioned from Michelangelo, Pope Julius promised to pay over ten thousand ducats. Indeed, Buonarotti is thought to have become the richest artist of his day. He received 3,200 ducats for the ceiling of the Sistine Chapel alone.[60]

Julius, notorious for his irascibility, was now faced with a sensitive, distrustful, and impulsive artist who knew what his ability was worth. Michelangelo once abandoned Rome, upset for one reason or another. He and Julius reconciled in Bologna, where the latter was headquartered during his campaigns in the Romagna. When the pope ordered Michelangelo to postpone his work on the tomb project in order to fresco the ceiling of the Sistine Chapel, the master only complied reluctantly. He had trained as a painter in the workshop of the Florentine Domenico Ghirlandaio, but he drew his pride from being a sculptor and thus the master of an art that, in his eyes, was more important. The commission put him in direct competition with the ambitious Raphael, who was then the most sought-after artist in Rome.

The competition between these two greats is without parallel in the history of art. Over the span of four years, between 1508 and 1512, Michelangelo painted prophets, sibyls, and the story of Genesis in shining colors and complicated perspective on wet plaster. It was his first experience ever with the difficult technique of fresco; what he achieved in such a short time is well-nigh miraculous. Even those who take no pleasure in the complex theological content of the paintings will not be able to deny the incredible creative power that streams out of them. Incidentally, the idea that Michelangelo painted the whole thing without assistants is a legend. Raphael included a portrait of his brilliant rival in his *School of Athens,* in the guise of the brooding Heraclitus resting against a block of marble.

The rivalry ended on Good Friday in the year 1520, the day Raphael died. He, too, had been showered with commissions and, as Bramante's successor, had been named chief architect of Saint Peter's. The banker Agostino Chigi had commissioned him to decorate his palace with frescos and to design his funeral chapel. On the order of Julius II, he painted a high altarpiece for the church of San Sisto in Piacenza: the *Sistine Madonna,* the most famous of his numerous Marian paintings. For Pope Leo X, he continued work on the *Stanze,* now supported by a disciplined team of assistants. In addition, he provided large-format designs for ten tapestries, intended to be hung in the Sistine Chapel, depicting scenes from the lives of the apostles Peter and Paul. Popes, cardinals, and beautiful women had their portraits painted by Raphael. Like other artists, he was a student of antiquity. He personally ordered a translation of Vitruvius's work on architecture into Italian. The fact that the pope named him curator of Rome's ancient monuments is a sign of the growing sensitivity for the significance of the physical remains of the classical legacy—"of this ancient mother of the glory and the greatness of Italy," as Raphael and Castiglione wrote.[61] Without giving it a second thought, the Roman people had long been in the habit of grinding down any marble they found to create new building materials. Meanwhile, what had once been treated as garbage was now handled as collectibles and accessories for the luxury abodes of the Roman aristocracy.[62]

The funeral held for Raphael was extraordinary. His body was laid out in his workshop underneath his final, almost finished painting, the *Transfiguration.* He was laid to rest in the Pantheon, at the foot of a Madonna modeled on an ancient statue of Venus. His epitaph reads (in the masterful translation of Thomas Hardy):

Here's one in whom Nature feared—faint at such vying—
Eclipse while he lived, and decease at his dying.[63]

Thanks to his phenomenal ability, Michelangelo, the survivor of the contest, never lost favor in Florence or the papal court despite all the political changes involving the Medici. For them he sketched designs for the facade of San Lorenzo and the Biblioteca Laurenziana. He spent ten years working on figures for the family mausoleum. The monument was completed during the last Republican interlude in Florence, between 1527 and 1530. From 1534 until his death, Michelangelo was back in Rome, where he was entrusted with redesigning the piazza on the Campidoglio and continuing work on Saint Peter's. Its dome, hovering over the Eternal City, stems from his design.

Michelangelo produced works of equally exceptional quality in sculpture, painting, and architecture. In addition, he was a gifted poet. His sonnets provide insight into an intellectual world imbued with Ficino's philosophy. For him, beauty, inextricable from love, reflected the truth and love of God.

> Love is a conception of beauty
> (that friend of virtue and of graciousness),
> that is imagined or seen within the heart.[64]

The striving for beauty thus approximates the search for God. The great art of the Renaissance is founded upon the same yearning as the period's most important branch of learning. Michelangelo wanted to portray ideas, not just depict nature. That explains his contemptuous remark about Flemish painting, which he said merely tried to deceive "the naked eye."[65] The goal had to remain unreachable. Ideas cannot be carved in stone. The most beautiful work is only their shadow.

Michelangelo's struggle with stone seems to become violent in a few unfinished sculptures: the *Prisoners* (or *Slaves*) and the *Matthew*. Perhaps by seeing their *non finito*, or unfinished state, as a reflection of Rodin's "perfect incompleteness," we overlook the fact that the sculptor simply ran out of time and was overworked. However that may be, they are symbols of colossal ambition. Our imagination is free—again taking a cue from one of Michelangelo's sonnets— to approach the sublime hidden in unformed matter:

> Not even the best of artists has any conception
> that a single marble block does not contain.[66]

Artistic work had now been exalted to metaphysical heights. Ficino saw the soul and the intellect of the artist shining through his work—and God himself reflected in them.[67] His student Cristoforo Landino opened up a new dimension in poetry, elevating it from a mere intellectual and didactic game to the revelator of ultimate truths.[68] The revelation was proclaimed by the poet inspired by Platonic "divine madness." He was followed by the sculptor and the painter, whom Alberti had already said could become "a second God." Deifications now piled up. Dante and Petrarca, even contemporaries like Titian, were declared *divini*. But the most divine of all was Michelangelo. Ludovico Ariosto (1474–1533) called him "Michael, more than mortal, a divine *angelo*"—an angel.[69]

Italy, Capital of Culture

When it came to the arts, literature, the sciences, and even technology like irrigation systems,[70] the sixteenth century belonged to Italy. It did not matter that the peninsula was at the mercy of foreign armies. As with architecture and sculpture, Italy's painting maintained the highest rank. Contemporary critics were already praising the Venetians as masters of coloring (*colorito*), whereas they accorded Tuscany preeminence in the art of *disegno*, or drawing. New genres took shape. Starting in the 1520s, the first autonomous landscapes appeared alongside cityscapes, and genre painting followed soon thereafter. The arts mutually influenced one another. For example, the laws of harmony in music can be detected in architecture and painting.[71]

It was not only the great centers of Rome, Florence, Milan, and Venice that came to the fore, although the creative elite did focus their careers there. The luster of Urbino had not yet faded. Mantua found one of the most inventive architects and painters of the century in Raphael's student Giulio Romano. In nearby Ferrara, the Este court was a magnet for artists and humanists. The cultural sheen of the city, resplendent with its renowned university, had overshadowed its political significance since the Quattrocento. Ferrara's traditional focus on first-rate music—it could boast not only Dufay but also the Dutchman Rudolph Agricola (1443/44–1485), who was furthermore the author of an influential textbook on rhetoric—continued with Josquin des Prez, the most famous composer of his day. He only ended up staying from June 1503 to April 1504, as a pestilence broke out on the Po. Nevertheless, he was paid a princely sum despite being considered a difficult personality and, as one courtier complained, tending to compose when he felt like it and not when he was supposed to.[72] Thus an artistic world of a seemingly modern stamp began to take shape in the field of music.

In the Cinquecento, the sixteenth century, the Este court was one of the great cultural centers of Europe. Isabella d'Este (1474–1539) had the ambition to collect not only clothing, gems, antiquities, and precious vases but also pictures by the great masters in her studio.[73] After extensive haggling, she snagged a painting by Jan van Eyck in Venice. In vain she begged Leonardo to paint her likeness. The best she got was a color drawing; the busy artist finished it in 1499 while stopping over in Mantua on his way from Milan to Venice. Isabella bought a *Cupido* by Michelangelo from Cesare Borgia. As her portraitist, she engaged Titian. She thus experienced the pleasure and pain of collecting in full measure. For her brother Duke Alfonso I, Giovanni Bellini painted *The Feast of the Gods*, which now hangs in Washington, DC. It was an unusual subject for the master of tender Madonnas. The lush forest in the background was added by the young Titian after Bellini's death in 1516.

The court also boasted Ariosto, one of the leading poets of his age. Three different versions of his *Orlando Furioso* were issued between 1505 and 1532. Ariosto dressed up the outdated genre of the chivalric epic in humanist clothing.[74] He juggled with the old forms and added new adornment, allusions to ancient and more recent literature that were appreciated by an educated court audience. The author felt free to play a literary, perhaps even ironic game with the provincial Italian princes' purported descent from Trojan heroes; Italy's petty rulers loved grandeur. *Orlando Furioso* is at times funny, at times a meditation on the relationship between appearance and being, historical truth and fiction. Various plotlines intertwine to tell the story of a war against the Saracens during the reign of Charlemagne. Sorcerers, harpies, winged horses, and other mythical creatures appear amid battles, sieges, and amorous mishaps.

The hero, Orlando, is one of the great mad figures in world literature. When he discovers that the object of his love, the intoxicatingly beautiful princess Angelica—daughter of a Chinese king—has given herself to the simple squire Medoro, he rips his clothes off, falls down weeping, and wallows in grief, hatred, fury, and violence. He is only healed when his reason is restored to him—by the Moon, where everything lost on Earth ends up. He is then able to help the Christians triumph in battle over the Muslims. The whole wild story is told in perfect hendecasyllables and Tuscan Italian. *Orlando Furioso* had a huge impact. Painters like Tiepolo, Boucher, and Delacroix were inspired by it, as were composers—Vivaldi, Handel, and Haydn, for example—and poets from Lope de Vega to Shakespeare.

Ariosto's intention to buttress the vernacular's importance as a language of literature was also a concern of his friend Pietro Bembo, whom we have already met as an interlocutor in the *Cortegiano*. Bembo's best-known work, the dialogue *Gli Asolani*, was also written in Ferrara, between 1497 and 1502. It is set in the garden of a castle in Asolo in northern Italy, hence the title.[75] The lady of the house, the Venetian Caterina Cornaro, assembled a literary court there whose prehistory extends far across the Mediterranean Sea. Before feeding poets and commissioning works from painters on her estate at the foot of the Alps, the hostess had been married to a Lusignan bastard and, as his widow, become queen of Cyprus. Asolo was a gift from Venice, compensation for the fact that Caterina had given Cyprus to the republic in 1489. She had been encouraged to this act of generosity by a Venetian fleet cruising off the coast of her island.

Back to Bembo. His *Asolani* continued the discourse on love that had been taken to its zenith by Ficino. One of the interlocutors bemoans love's sufferings—*amare senza amaro non si può*, "one cannot love without bitterness"—whereas another praises it as the source of all joy. The synthesis is proposed by a third speaker, who contrasts base physical lust to the sublime Platonic theory of love. In this way, a theory of *eros* develops over the course of a seemingly spontaneous dialogue. For his part, the author was able to draw on ample practical experience, which he had gathered in the bed of the young Lucrezia Borgia, among others. The carnal side of *eros* was explored extensively in the *Ragionamenti* of Pietro Aretino (1492–1556), which was published in 1534 and 1536 and was soon banned. This discussion between two whores omits hardly any shameless details. Its classical model was Lucian's *Dialogues of the Courtesans*. Marcantonio Raimondi provided sensual illustrations for Aretino's work.

This overview of Italy's literary production during the first decades of the Cinquecento shows that the perennial theme of love was accompanied by a broad interest in literary style, rhetoric, aesthetics, and, in the wake of the *Cortegiano*, the criteria of civilized comportment. Bembo himself had written his *Prose of the Vernacular Tongue* while in Urbino. It recommended Petrarca as the master of poetry and Boccaccio as the model for prose. First in Florence and Ferrara, Italian conquered the theater in the form of comedies revolving around love, deceit, and money, and of tragedies about power, guilt, and fate. The *Sofonisba* by Giangiorgio Trissino of Vicenza earned its place in literary history as the first tragedy in Italian to be written in line with Aristotle's *Poetics*.

The common man, with his weaknesses and difficulties, seldom appeared on stage. The noble audience preferred pastorals (and thus Arcadias) to the gutter. Exceptions were provided by the Paduan playwright Angelo Beolco (1496/1502–1542), nicknamed "Ruzzante" after one of his rustic characters.[76] He devoted two dialogues to the misery of the life of mercenaries and poor farmers, ancestors of *Lazarillo de Tormes* and *Simplicius Simplicissimus*.

Cultural exchange between Italy and the rest of Europe grew more and more intense.[77] The two trips to Italy taken by Albrecht Dürer of Nuremberg, in 1494 and 1505–1506, are only the best-known in an endless procession of artists that stretched into modern times, including the likes of Goethe, Thomas Mann, Joseph Brodsky, and Cy Twombly. Conversely, more and more Italians went north, drawn by commissions and inspiration. Simply having an Italian name could be reason enough for receiving a post, regardless of how much talent one had.[78]

29

South Wind

THE RENAISSANCE CONQUERS EUROPE

Paths of Art and Ideas: Western Europe, Eastern Europe

One of the southerners who enjoyed success moving north was Francesco Laurana (ca. 1430–1502), a sculptor from Zara in Dalmatia. In southern France, he worked for the erstwhile king of Naples, René; two raised Renaissance tombs reveal his involvement. One, for Charles IV of Anjou, is in the cathedral of Le Mans. The other is found in the crypt of Sainte-Marthe in Tarascon, although the attribution to Laurana is not entirely certain. The man whose bones it holds, Giovanni Cossa, was a senior official in the same Neapolitan court for which Laurana worked. In northern France, the Florentine Renaissance first arrived in the Abbey of Saint Bertin in Saint-Omer. Its abbot, Guillaume Fillastre, the illegitimate son of a cardinal of the same name—who had hunted for manuscripts at Constance—commissioned a polychrome glazed tomb from the della Robbia around 1467.[1] The work, of which only fragments survive, was a monument to a humanist. Aristotle and Euripides, i.e., philosophy and poetry, commemorate the rhetor and writer interred there.

Classical scholarship had survived the Hundred Years' War in the orbit of the dukes of Orléans, Anjou, and Berry. In Paris, Gregorio Tifernate (1414–1464) was the torchbearer of humanism. This friend of Valla, correspondent of Decembrio and protégé of Nicholas V, taught Greek and rhetoric at the Sorbonne. He had learned Greek during a sojourn on the Hellespont.[2] Another agent of cultural exchange between north and south was Cardinal Jean Jouffroy, bishop of Albi (d. 1473).[3] He was a diplomat and courtier in the service of Burgundy, the Roman Curia, and France and was a true man of the Renaissance: a collector of benefices, a drinker of wine, a gourmand, a friend to women, and once even a military commander. He was imperious, irascible or pious (depending on the circumstances), and highly educated. He had studied under Valla. His eloquence impressed even the Italians.

A later generation of humanists was represented by the theologian Jacques Lefèvre d'Étaples (ca. 1460–1536).[4] The bishop of Meaux entrusted him with the mission of reforming his diocese; this did not turn Jacques into a French Luther, though. Indicative of his mildness as a theologian, he edited Ficino's translation of the Hermetic Corpus with its "most ancient wisdom." He was a trailblazer as one of the inventors of the humanist commentary, which replaced the traditional long-winded questions and objections with short explanations sprinkled with classical quotations. Lefèvre's contemporary Guillaume Budé (ca. 1468–1536) was a jurist and perhaps the most significant Greek scholar of his time. He is considered the founder of the *mos gallicus*, a method that dealt critically with Justinian's *Corpus* and tried to understand Roman law in its historical context.[5] This critical, historical approach to the revival of ancient jurisprudence was part of a broader European trend. Alongside Budé and Lorenzo Valla, it was exemplified by Ulrich Zasius (1461–1535) in Germany and Andrea Alciati (1492–1550) in Italy.

In the realm of literature in France, the discursive revolution also continued to unfold in dialogue with Italy. The final decades of the fifteenth century were dominated by a group of poets that the nineteenth century would refer to as *rhétoriqueurs*, or "rhetoricians." One of them was Jean Lemaire de Belges (ca. 1473–after 1515), who gained fame with a retelling of the *Iliad* and his *Épitres de l'amant vert* (*Letters of The Green Lover*).[6] The "green lover" was a parrot, a favorite pet of Margaret of Austria, regent of the Netherlands. To the dismay of its owner, the bird was eaten by a dog. The poet transformed the tragic event into a lament inscribed in two verse letters, a genre that would soon come into fashion. Lemaire has the deceased bird claim it had been so distressed by its lady's absence that it had offered itself to the foxhound as a meal, thus heroically committing suicide. The parrot writes Margaret two letters from the afterlife, declaring its love and confessing to having regarded her beauty covetously while she performed her toilette. In the end, like some feathered Dante, it tells of the horrors and monsters of the underworld and the paradisiacal beauty of the Isle of the Blessed. The new literature of the discursive revolution now contained light humor and literary games with erotic undertones.

Another "journey to the underworld" was put into verse by Clément Marot (1496–1544). Accused of having broken the fasting rules during Lent with a meal of bacon—the Reformation was casting its shadow—he was thrown into a Parisian prison in 1526. His classicizing work *L'Enfer* recounts the experience in satirical form. In his country, Marot was considered a pioneer of *italianità*. He wrote the first French sonnets and helped revive the epigram in its classical form as known from Martial. His elegant, slightly cutting style gave the name to a type of poetry: *style marotique*. Marot was the classic courtier. Long in favor with Francis I, his Protestant leanings consistently got him into trouble. He eventually found protection with the king's sister, Margaret of Navarre (1492–1549), who had assembled poets and scholars at her court in Nérac in southern France.[7] The queen herself was a distinguished author. Her *Mirror of the Sinful Soul* evinces a kinship with Lutheran thought. In addition, she wrote the *Heptameron*, a collection of novellas inspired by Boccaccio that were admittedly more edifying than their model and somewhat verbose.[8] But we have gotten ahead of ourselves.

Burgundy maintained a distance from *italianità* and antiquity.[9] The halls of its palaces were adorned with tapestries portraying ancient myths (Fig. 42, p. 547). They showed gods and heroes in modern clothing, not in ancient garb or totally naked, as was permitted in the south.[10] At least Boccaccio, *messire Jehan Bocace*, found interpreters and translators there. Chroniclers imitated Livy's style, and the Portuguese scholar Vasco da Lucena translated Curtius Rufus's *History of Alexander the Great* into French for Charles the Bold. The architecture of the southern Netherlands did not receive the adornment of *antics wercken*, ancient style, until the 1530s.[11]

As in Burgundy, humanism remained a marginal phenomenon in Spain.[12] The field of literature was dominated by chivalric romances. Joanot Martorell's *Tirant lo Blanc*, printed in Valencia in 1490, was praised by Cervantes as the

"best book in the world"—because its *caballeros* were real people and not dolls. Like the poetry of the country, the work bears no trace of the humanist spirit.[13] In contrast to Italy, the study of the classics remained the preserve of a noble elite. Plato and Florentine Platonism, however, managed to find their way into libraries. Yet, like everything pagan, they were soon suspect in the eyes of religious authorities. Once the shockwaves of the Reformation were felt in Iberia, their time was up. A few significant humanists did emerge on the Iberian Peninsula. Alongside Antonio de Nebrija there was Alfonso de Cartagena (1384–1456), a native of Burgos and translator of Seneca. Another was Alfonso de Palencia (1424–1492) of Castile, who wrote a history of Spain and compiled a Latin-Castilian dictionary.[14] Drawing on a wide variety of ancient sources, it explains *inter alia* the geographic designations for pre-Islamic Spain. Finally, Pietro Martire d'Anghiera (1457–1526), a cleric active in Granada, can also be considered a representative of Spanish humanism. His eight *New World Decades* are among the foundational documents of modern anthropology. For example, he takes a strikingly relativist approach to the various assessments of skin color, regarding them as a question of taste that, according to the arbitrariness of fashion, prefers "the bearded man" here but "the beardless" there. As he writes, "The Ethiopian considers that black is a more beautiful color than white, while the white man thinks otherwise."[15]

Renaissance architecture and sculpture had a much greater impact on the land of the Catholic Monarchs, making their mark as early as 1480.[16] One of the first figures to pave the way in this regard was Pedro Gonzáles de Mendoza (1428–1495), the "Great Cardinal of Spain." His name and that of the Italian-trained architect Lorenzo Vázquez are connected with Renaissance buildings in his home province of Guadalajara, in Valladolid, and in Toledo. Mendoza's tomb in Toledo Cathedral is probably the work of the Tuscan Andrea Sansovino, who worked in nearby Portugal from 1492 to1501. Otherwise, the reigns of Isabella and Ferdinand were adorned with the flowery Plateresque style—an elaborate variety of Gothic literally designed "in the manner of a silversmith" (*platero*)—which competed with the ornate Mudéjar style. Only in death was the royal couple associated with Renaissance art. Their raised tombs in the Capilla Real of Granada Cathedral were completed in 1517 by Domenico Fancelli (1469–1519) of Settignano. In 1527, Charles V then had construction begun on a palace inspired by Roman models near the Alhambra.[17] Compared to the ornate Muslim architecture of the Nasrid palace, the monument to imperial might seems downright clunky. Interestingly, the Christian conquerors refrained from entirely demolishing the Alhambra, the stone souvenir of Muslim culture.

On the eastern end of Latin Europe, in Hungary, an early foundation had been laid for humanism and the new art by Emperor Sigismund. He had employed Vergerio as secretary and the Florentine Filippo Scolari, nicknamed Pippo Spano, as a military commander. The Renaissance was ultimately ushered in under Corvinus and his wife, Beatrice of Aragon. In Buda, the king assembled his library of two thousand manuscripts, the famous Biblioteca Corviniana.[18] Many of its sumptuous codices had been made in Italy. Plato arrived in the country with Francesco Bandini, a student of Ficino. A few unconventional thinkers arrived as well, such as Galeotto Marzio, a reputed Epicurean who held the scandalous opinion that Turks and Jews, heretics and pagans could be blessed without baptism.[19] An équipe of Tuscan masters decked out Corvinus's palace and his summer residence in Visegrád as Renaissance enclaves. As one contemporary wrote, they turned Hungary into a second Italy.[20] There was still much to do, of course. Hungary's leading humanist, Janus Pannonius, who had studied with Guarino and became bishop of Pécs, sneered that the Latin spoken in Hungary would leave Virgil or Cicero speechless.[21]

Corvinus's cultural politics followed the standard strategy of dignifying power with a veneer of education and learning. Further playing the role of the ambitious climber, he had obliging historians ennoble the Hunyadi family tree. His court historian Antonio Bonfini traced the Corvinus family back to the ancient Roman clan of the Corvini, thus giving the ruler a glorious genealogy.[22] How useful could such historical tinkering be when it came to polishing the gloomy glimmer of power? So useful that even the Russian tsars adopted the procedure. Generally not infected with the humanist bug, they had family trees constructed around 1555 in the *Gosudarev Rodoslovets*, literally "The Sovereign's Pedigree Book," that traced their own genealogies and those of the leading noble houses back to ancient Roman imperial greatness.[23]

Little has remained of Hungary's Renaissance. Corvinus's library was scattered to the four winds, and much was destroyed by the Turkish wars. Still extant is the funerary chapel that Archbishop Tamás Bakócz added to Esztergom Cathedral in 1506. It brought the Florentine Renaissance to the Danube. How curious that death markers introduced the "style of rebirth" to the architecture of many regions! This was the case in Germany as well. The first Renaissance structure erected there is thought to be the Fugger Chapel in Saint Anne's Church in Augsburg, finished in 1512.

The Renaissance in art also made its way to Poland in the early sixteenth century, beginning with the frame that Francesco Fiorentino carved for John I's raised tomb in Wawel Cathedral. Its distant ancestor was Bruni's tomb in Florence. Shortly before this, the German sculptor Veit Stoß (ca. 1450–1533) had brought late Gothic sculpture to its acme with the high altar he created for Saint Mary's Church in Cracow. This spectacular work recommended him for commissions in Nuremberg, the city he later chose to call home.

At first, the Renaissance import on the Vistula was a preoccupation of the crown and the bishop.[24] The founding figure of Polish humanism, Gregory of Sanok (1403–1477), later bishop of Lemberg, had spent two years in Italy and collected a significant library. Other intermediaries of Italian culture included

Lorenz Rabe, "Laurentius Corvinus"—who has garnered interest among scholars due to his connection to the young Copernicus—and Sanok's protégé Filippo Buonaccorsi (1437–1496), known as Callimachus. Stocked with men like these, the University of Cracow was reformed in the spirit of humanism. It and the academy founded in Poznań in 1559 developed into citadels of the *studia humanitatis*. Piotr Tomicki (1464–1535), archbishop of Cracow, was a passionate collector of painting and sculpture—a rarity outside Italy and beyond the orbit of royal courts. The Cistercian monk Stanisław Samostrzelnik, Poland's first Renaissance painter, did his portrait (Plate 19). The Italian style then reached grandiose dimensions: in the tiered arcades of the courtyard in Wawel Castle (Fig. 43, above) and in Sigismund's Chapel in Wawel Cathedral. Both were the work of teams of local and Italian artists.

Bona Sforza (1494–1557), the wife of King Sigismund I, imported Italian court culture (including refined cuisine) to Poland-Lithuania. Comedies of Terence and others were performed at her court.[25] Whereas the Renaissance came to Cracow from Rome and Tuscany, it was architects from northern Italy and southern Switzerland that brought it to Silesia and then further to Mecklenburg and Sweden. A wine merchant in Lviv (in Ukraine) had a family chapel designed by a German architect who was likewise active in Silesia. Finished in 1615, it is a prime example of a "hybrid Renaissance"—a phenomenon that would also be found in South America and northern Germany.[26]

In general, the Renaissance in stone had a harder time spreading across Latin Europe than the humanist spirit did. In the early sixteenth century, idiosyncratic variations of it popped up in France, first on the Loire. In 1536, construction began on the Duke of Bavaria's residence in Landshut, the first Renaissance palace in Germany. In England, Italian influence emerged more clearly towards the end of the century, apart from accessories like the terracotta medallions with portraits of Roman emperors that Giovanni da Maiano provided for Cardinal Wolsey's Hampton Court Palace in 1520. In many cases, it was social climbers like the cardinal who used the avant-garde style as a symbol of their success—men who had grown rich and powerful like Matthias Corvinus, Cardinal Mendoza, or the Fuggers. The style lent them an air of venerability and imperial luster. It was a sign of education and familiarity with modern fashions. In order to adorn oneself "classically," it was necessary to break free of the Gothic tradition and to be receptive to the humanist spirit. The new and the old style were often close neighbors, as in Cracow. Another example is the monastery of Brou in Bourg-en-Bresse, where Margaret of Austria commissioned the German sculptor Conrad Meit to make a lavish tomb for her deceased husband in 1526. Putti frolic and realistic faces engage the viewer amid late Gothic beauty. The recumbent, nearly naked figure of the late Duke Philibert, sculpted in Carrara marble, could commemorate an ancient hero.

Bohemian architecture's long rejection of humanism and Renaissance style could have to do with the absence there of the preconditions we have outlined. On the Vltava, Utraquism and patriotism worked together to hinder the open-minded study of antiquity. Apart from initial flirtations during Charles IV's reign, contact with Italian culture remained ephemeral. The Hussite-minded University of Prague eschewed it.[27] In contrast to neighboring Poland, not even plays inspired by classical drama were performed. The humanism of the statesman Bohuslav Lobkovic of Hasištejn (1462–1510) was limited by his strict Catholic piety, the style of his poetry marred by an imperfect mastery of classical Latin.[28] Yet he knew Italy from his studies in Bologna and Ferrara. His inherited wealth allowed him to build a library and embark on a five-year journey that brought him all the way to Tunis.

In contrast to the Neo-Latin of the "Bohemian Odysseus" Lobkovic, the Utraquist Viktorin Kornel (ca. 1460–1520) pursued humanistic studies in Czech. He translated works of classical literature and was an enthusiast for republican ideals, which for him primarily meant freedom of religion.[29] Recourse was seldom made to the original texts in Bohemia. The pagan spirit raised suspicions. Only Plato's *Republic*—in Ficino's translation—and Seneca's Stoic philosophy enjoyed popularity, no doubt thanks to their kinship with Christian thought. The most impressive work of history about Bohemia was not the writing of a native son but rather Aeneas Sylvius Piccolomini's *Historia Bohemica*. A selection of stories from Boccaccio's *Decameron* was translated into Czech, probably by a son of George of Poděbrady, Henry the Younger (1452–1492). The translation was based on a German version and, betraying the spirit of its model, extolled traditional chivalric ideals. Even learned treatises of the time continued to cite medieval natural philosophers and not the ancient *auctoritates*. Only 8 percent of the texts printed in Bohemia between 1480 and 1526 were secular in nature.[30] Bohemian intellectuals never developed the freedom and insolence that was able to lift the spirits of even the melancholic German humanists.

In contrast to Bohemia, humanistic studies in Germany penetrated ever deeper into university life, although they did meet manifold resistance. Italy remained the cultural exemplar. People imitated Petrarca's *canzoni* and sonnets, read Boccaccio, and studied Ficino. Personal connections furthered cultural exchange. The southern German humanist Johannes Reuchlin and Lefèvre d'Étaples met Ficino and Pico on journeys to Italy. The encounters left a deep mark on their writings. English intellectuals such as John Colet and William Grocyn also learned Greek in Italy and brought that knowledge back with them to their island.[31] The physician Thomas Linacre (ca. 1460–1524) studied under Poliziano, one of the founders of critical philology; one of his fellow students in Florence was Giovanni de' Medici. Linacre translated texts by Galen and *On the Sphere*, a work attributed to Proclus, into Latin.

Physicians knowledgeable in ancient medicine like Linacre and jurists who could find their way through the labyrinth of Justinian's *Corpus* had good prospects for finding posts at court. They served as educators, advisers, and diplomats, cared for the mortal body of princes and secured the immortal body of the state with the armor of Roman law. And they wrote its history, thus giving it an identity. Mariano Siculo did so for the kingdom of Aragon, Polydore Vergil of Urbino for England. Jan Długosz's *Annales seu cronicae incliti regni Poloniae* told the history of the "illustrious kingdom of Poland" in the style of Livy, and Paolo Emilio and Robert Gaguin chronicled France's past. Claude de Seyssel (ca. 1450–1520), who at the highpoint of his career was chancellor to Louis XII, wrote the *Grande Monarchie de France* (*Grand Monarchy of France*), a mixture of administrative handbook, political theory, and mirror of princes.[32] The glorious past of the modern nation took its place alongside the master narrative of the ancient empire, whose legacy was shared in by all Europeans.

O tempora, o mores! Humanism in the Holy Roman Empire

This same idea fueled Konrad Celtis's unfinished project to provide a description of Germany, the *Germania illustrata*. The author hoped to renew his homeland with the spirit of antiquity. In his most famous ode, he calls on Apollo to abandon Italy, just as he had once moved there from Greece, and to take his lyre to the Germans. In this way, their raw speech and everything dark would disappear.[33] Born the son of a vintner in Franconia in 1459, Celtis's life was literally an educational odyssey. He studied in Cologne and Heidelberg and taught at numerous universities, traveled through Italy from Padua to Rome, and visited Cracow and Buda. He encountered several important and indeed singular figures of his time, met Ficino and Pomponio Leto, visited Manutius in Venice, and won the favor of two Holy Roman Emperors. Frederick III crowned Celtis poet laureate at Nuremberg Castle. Maximilian appointed him professor in Vienna. Upon his death in 1508, a gravestone with his epitaph was set in Saint Stephen's Cathedral in Vienna. This shows just how important a humanistically educated scholar could now become in the north.

Celtis was the most important intermediary of ancient thought and poetry for the Germany of his day. He edited tragedies by Seneca, Tacitus's *Germania*, and Apuleius's *On the Universe*. In addition, he produced a Greek grammar. His odes, elegies, and epigrams reveal an intimate knowledge of Plato and other classical authors. Furthermore, he attempted to revive ancient music and theater. For Dürer and other artists, he developed iconographic programs. Celtis was also a tireless networker, and he established several "sodalities"— loosely organized clubs—in Heidelberg, Vienna, and Cracow. His editions of works by Hrotsvitha of Gandersheim and a description of Nuremberg testify to the patriotic sentiment that was now also growing in Germany. His *Carmen seculare*, chock full of numerology and astrological references, was inspired by Horace's ode of the same name. A response to the apocalyptic mood of the pious, it celebrated the holy year 1500, praising deities and individuals of merit and culminating in the invocation of an incomprehensible God.[34] It lauds Emperor Maximilian, the poet's patron, as the ruler of a Golden Age.

Meanwhile, Celtis's countrymen had discovered the wonders of archaeology. The soil of Germania on the Roman side of the *limes* contained copious remains from the empire, and Germany was seen within that tradition. One of the first to praise the science of the shovel was Dr. Conrad Peutinger (1465–1547), a *Stadtschreiber*, or town clerk, in Augsburg. He had studied law in Bologna and Padua and was an adviser to Emperor Maximilian. He collected antiquities and copied and published inscriptions.[35] His name is connected with the medieval copy of a late Roman road map, which Celtis found in a monastic library and gave to his friend in Augsburg. Hence the name of the document, which measures over six meters in length: *Tabula Peutingeriana*, i.e., "The Peutinger Map."

In Nuremberg, the humanist and physician Hartmann Schedel (1440–1514) published a large collection of inscriptions.[36] His city was now one of the hubs of the northern Renaissance. The artistic style of its most famous citizen, Albrecht Dürer, was influenced by the thought of Alberti and Ficino.[37] Dürer's painting was decisively shaped by his acquaintance with the art of the south. The tomb of Saint Sebaldus in the church named for him in Nuremberg, sculpted by Peter Vischer and his son between 1506 and 1519, puts an idiosyncratic northern version of the Renaissance on display. At the same time, late Gothic sculpture also reached singular heights: in Nuremberg with Veit Stoß and in the nearby Mainfranken region with Tilman Riemenschneider.[38]

The age also seemed propitious for learning. "What times! What erudition! It is a joy to be alive!" wrote the humanist Ulrich von Hutten in 1518 to the Nuremberg patrician and humanist Willibald Pirckheimer.[39] The declaration certainly does not reflect Hutten's personal wellbeing, as he was poor and plagued by syphilis. Rather, it evokes the fact that humanism had now grown into a broad movement in Germany as well. It was at home at courts, in cities, and at universities; Heidelberg, Vienna, and Erfurt were the leaders. Rudolph Agricola's 1484 treatise *De formando studio* outlined the first systematic education program for the north. Many more writings on the subject were to follow. Agricola had emphasized instruction in moral philosophy, theology, and rhetoric. The study of nature, in contrast, was assigned only marginal importance. Its pursuit seemed to him, a pious follower of the *devotio moderna*, of limited use.[40] Celtis saw things differently. In 1501, he succeeded in founding an independent *collegium* in Vienna for poetry, rhetoric, and mathematical and scientific subjects: geometry, architecture, and astronomy. Its graduates were to be crowned poets laureate.

The sodalities were like "humanist assemblies," representing the movement and its interests into the Reformation period.[41] Like-minded groups
formed around pivotal figures like Peutinger in Augsburg, Celtis and Pirckheimer in Nuremberg. They met to engage in discussion, ate in common, and
performed plays. From one town to the next, they wrote each other polished
letters. They also saw to the publishing of learned treatises and literary texts.
Just like the Italians, the Germans played at being ancients. They dressed up
their coarse names with Latin monikers: a man named "Hundt" ("dog," in
Latin *canis*) became "Canisius"; a "Krachenberger" called himself "Gracchus
Pierius." Celtis's real name was "Bickel."[42] The patriotic historiography pioneered by Celtis was also engaged in by two outstanding humanists from
Alsace, Jakob Wimpfeling and Beatus Rhenanus, panegyrists of the freedom
and military ability of their ancestors.[43]

The classics found their German audience. Two thousand years of European
culture were summarized by the frontispiece to a 1536 translation of the *Odyssey* (Fig. 44, above). It shows Homer, the "father of all poets," breathing his
inspiration into the triad of the great Roman bards Virgil—the Westphalian
painter Ludger tom Ring portrayed him as a scholar with eyeglasses (Fig. 41,
p. 544)—Ovid, and Horace. The message communicated by the picture is
clear: the Greeks had bequeathed their concept of literature to Europe, then
the Romans had cultivated it, and now it had arrived in the North.[44] Even the

world of craftsmen was affected by the ancient spirit. Wimpfeling's compatriot Jörg Wickram wrote numerous dramas and farces, and he published an edition of Ovid—he himself was ignorant of Latin—based on a translation from around 1200. Hans Sachs (1494–1576), the most famous of the *Meistersinger,* incorporated humanistic models and ancient material into his work. Countless allusions can be found in the more than six thousand poems, plays, and *Fastnachtsspiele* that the shoemaker from Nuremberg found the time to write. He borrowed from Aristophanes, Plautus, and Terence, and knew Apuleius, Plutarch, and Pliny. He did think it necessary, however, to explain to his Nuremberg audience what satyrs were.[45]

The Apogee of Humanism: Erasmus of Rotterdam

Hans Holbein the Younger (1497/98–1543) provides us with a portrait gallery of the great men of his time. Active in the humanist hub of Basel and then in London, he immortalized mind, money, and might in art, painting pictures of merchants and patricians, diplomats and courtiers. In 1523, he produced a profile likeness of Erasmus of Rotterdam. The painting, probably intended for his friend Bonifacius Amerbach of Basel, is an emblem of intellectual concentration. It shows the scholar entirely focused on his writing, dressed in gray and black, his left hand decorated with costly rings. When Holbein painted the portrait, his subject was an intellectual authority. Courts and universities from England to Spain had sought to ornament themselves with his presence. He wrote letters in the thousands, including to popes, kings, and the Holy Roman Emperor. He had them printed, thus enhancing his charisma.[46] Erasmus was for scholars what Michelangelo was in the art world: a star. A note from his hand warmed the heart; a fleeting encounter remained a memorable occurrence.

He was not to the manor born. He came into the world in 1466 or 1469 near Rotterdam or in Gouda, the bastard son of a cleric. After being educated in a grammar school run by the Brothers of the Common Life, he was put in a monastery and then consecrated as a priest in 1492. Only at the height of his fame did he manage to get a papal dispensation from his vows. The religious world of his youth was informed by the mild piety of the *devotio moderna.* It harbored almost no opposition to the study of antiquity. In Deventer, a center of the *devotio moderna* movement, entire libraries of pagan literature were printed, including even works of the frivolous Plautus.[47]

Erasmus gave himself the humanist epithet Desiderius. Like most of his fellows, his life was an odyssey. He was always writing in search of patronage and was the recipient of many invitations himself. While studying in Paris, he learned about—and learned to hate—Scholastic philosophy. If all the works of Duns Scotus and others like him perished, he once wrote, it would be easier for him to bear than the loss of the writings of Cicero and Plutarch.[48] Through hard work, he became the best Latinist of his day and one of the most significant Greek scholars. Paris and England—where he became friends with Thomas More and John Colet—were the first stations on his life's journey; he would return there often. Erasmus spent three years in Italy. In Venice, he collaborated with Aldus Manutius. It was the beginning of his European career, for his books were now being diffused throughout the continent by one of the most respected publishers. He extended the scope of his activity to his Dutch homeland and finally to Basel, where he lived with short interruptions from 1514 until his death in 1536. He rejected the cardinal's hat offered to him by Paul III, just as he rejected Luther's cause.

Erasmus was deeply influenced by Latin culture, as can be seen in his *Adagia*, a collection of ancient proverbs and idioms. It was a huge commercial success, especially as it provided preachers, diplomats, and writers with a useful arsenal of quotations. There were over four thousand in the third edition of 1533, all of them explained and outfitted with references.[49] Many entered common parlance, e.g., "to pour oil on the fire" (from Horace), "sending owls to Athens" (Cicero), "shoemaker, not beyond the shoe" (Pliny), and "make an elephant out of a mosquito" (from Lucian, one of Erasmus's favorite authors).

Erasmus was a caustic critic of monks and the papacy. This made him a saboteur of the bastions of the old Church, although such was not his intention. He wrote a satire of the warlord Julius II in which the pope dies but is not let into Heaven; the pearly gates remain closed to the vicar of Christ. The famous *Praise of Folly* contains a pungent caricature of a monastic sermon.[50] Even the *Enchiridion*, the "Handbook of the Christian Soldier," belongs in this context. It teaches how to live a godly life and exhorts the reader to fight against corruption—in the world and in one's own self. Erasmus also produced an edition of the New Testament, based on Valla's earlier work. With a critical edition of the Greek text, a Latin translation, and a commentary, it was the cornerstone of a project of theological renewal.

Erasmus promoted a moderate, respectable religiosity, one that contemned the flesh but did not require asceticism, and that preferred heartfelt belief to empty rituals and relics but was not overly zealous. His Christianity does not bicker over doctrines of the Trinity; instead, it promotes peace. Erasmus is never on fire. His *Enchiridion* recommended itself more as a model of Latin style than as a passionate call to piety.[51] Incidentally, the Renaissance would have been much poorer as a period in art if people like Erasmus had been in control of the building and decoration of churches. A wonder of the world like the Certosa of Pavia appears in one of his *Colloquies* as a mere symbol of *ambitio*, "vanity." As his literary alter ego snidely remarks, the money spent on it should have been given to the poor instead.[52]

He countered aristocratic arrogance with "Democritic laughter." The highest nobility, he argued, is to be reborn in Christ, and true nobility means having contempt for empty nobility.[53] Yet this did not lead Erasmus to then urge rebellion against aristocrats, but rather to emphasize the ennobling power of education.[54] He was convinced that people can be improved by learning. Valla had written that better Latinists were better people—a bold hope that only a dyed-in-the-wool philologist could harbor.[55] Erasmus's *Education of a Christian Prince* was the antithesis of Machiavelli's *Principe*.[56] The two authors drew diametrically opposed conclusions from their lived experience of just about the same era. Machiavelli taught cool *raison d'état*, whereas Erasmus promoted the politics of peace, charity, justice, and morality.

Erasmus's most famous work is the above-mentioned *Praise of Folly*. It was written during a stay at Thomas More's house in London in 1509. Inscribed in a literary tradition stretching back to Lucian, the work is an ironic panegyric of self-deception, self-love, and error. Folly, daughter of wealth and the queen of kings, proclaims a praise of herself. The love of glory, itself a form of folly, nevertheless appears as a powerful driver of all culture, as a precondition for the creation of states and empires. War, the summit of all folly, makes heroism possible. And self-love, the sister of folly, produces music and poetry.[57] Human life and coexistence and civilization are simply inconceivable without a variety of emotions, irrationalities, and thus follies great and small—and all this happens to the delight of the gods. Is not the beginning of all life marked by the folly of love and marriage, including the boundlessly foolish act of procreation?[58] Folly reaches its summit in the ecstasy of lovers and in pious rapture. Seen this way, supreme happiness is nothing but the uttermost folly.[59]

Erasmus observes his world from on high. He sees the sufferings of human life from the pangs of birth to the pain of death. He sees poverty, torture, and deceit. In short, he sees disaster upon disaster, like grains of sand by the sea. Only folly could allow people to delude themselves about the nature of things, could offer hope and oblivion. Fools are happier than wise men. What is more, the *Praise of Folly* is a hymn to doubt and a praise of knowledge about ignorance. What absolute claims are made by foolish theologians about the cosmos and Jesus's nature as the son of God, about transubstantiation, divine omnipotence, *quiddities*, and *haecceities*! The apostles themselves would have understood none of it.[60] Along with other writings by Erasmus, the *Praise of Folly* ultimately landed on the Index of Forbidden Books. In religiously impassioned Bohemia, it was quickly given the honor of translation.

In matters of faith, Erasmus was a devotee of the Sermon on the Mount. His works contain numerous appeals to tolerance and balance. He even viewed the Turks with unusual sophistication. They, too, he argued, were ultimately human beings and half-Christian to boot.[61] A shadow falls on only one aspect of Erasmus's thought: his denunciations of what he called the "criminal" (*sceleratissima*) Jewish people.[62] The *Complaint of Peace*, in contrast, a timeless document of pacifism, is one of the great works of European intellectual history. It portrays war as an aberration contrary to the commandments of Christ and the laws of the cosmos.[63] Vipers do not bite vipers, nor do lynxes tear at other lynxes. Even evil spirits—the enlightened Erasmus was well acquainted with the demonologies of his time—made common cause to establish their tyranny. Christians, however, attack each other with "weapons invented in hell."[64] The *Complaint of Peace* reserves special contempt—Valla had taken a similar stance—for those who preached peace but propagated war: the pope and the cowl-wearing warmongers in the pulpits. The summit of absurdity, in the author's view, was that Christians waged war on Christians, even marching into battle under the sign of peace, the cross.[65] War gave rise to more war, and vengeance only bred vengeance.[66] Now, however, good should multiply good, and grace beget grace. People should see "that this world, the whole of the planet called Earth, is the common country of all who live and breathe upon it."[67]

Erasmus developed this moving work for a congress planned for early 1517 in Cambrai, at which some hoped a general peace would be declared, thus creating the conditions for a Crusade against the Ottomans. The pope was already issuing belligerent bulls. But the meeting never took place. Hopes for peace were dashed by political interests, by the old antagonisms between the Holy Roman Emperor and France and their allies. The same year the peace process failed, 1517, events in Germany took a dramatic turn, one that deferred the dream of peace in the Christian world further into the future than ever before.

NEW EMPIRES, NEW KNOWLEDGE, RELIGIOUS SCHISM

30

Empires and Emperors

The Ottoman Empire at Its Zenith

It seems that societies cannot survive without a clear idea of who or what their enemies are. The evil that they paint in vibrant colors is an "other," a contrast that lets them see themselves as good or better.[1] Enemies reinforce the identity of the community. They legitimize the establishment of systems of control, the maintenance of armies, and sometimes persecution, torture, and murder. The supposedly evil "others" that people in the sixteenth century believed they saw infecting the community—witches, Jews, and heretics—were now joined by the Ottoman enemy. Since the fall of Constantinople, it had drawn dangerously near. It became an object on which to project fears and prejudices. The victories of the Turks were hard to fit into a Christian worldview. While God's empire was winning souls in western Europe and across the ocean, it was losing them in the East. The Turkish war seemed to be more than mere divine punishment. Many thought it was Armageddon, the final battle before the impending Last Judgment. Behind the papacy's numerous attempts to bring about peace and organize Crusades was the notion that Christendom must unite in the shadow of the Apocalypse, so to speak, in order to resist the invasion of the infidels.

Latin Europe faced a powerful opponent. Since the overthrow of the Crimean Khanate during the reign of Mehmed the Conqueror, the entire coast of the Black Sea had been in Turkish hands. In addition, Albania was conquered— Skanderbeg had died in 1468—as was eastern Anatolia. The Ottoman Empire now extended to the Euphrates River. The tribal union known as the "White Sheep," which dominated the region between Syria and the Caspian Sea, had initially managed to resist the Ottoman assault. But it had fallen in the wake of a heavy defeat at the hands of Mehmed and after the death of its leader Uzun Hasan (r. 1453–1478). Venice's alliance with the enemy of its enemy was now over.[2] The Ottoman advance seemed unstoppable. When Otranto in Puglia was conquered in 1480, even the road to Rome, and thus to one of the "Golden Apples" desired by the sultans, seemed open. But the outpost could not be held. Mehmed's son and successor, Bayezid II (r. 1481–1512), conquered the two Moldavian port cities of Kilia and Akkerman. His army checked Polish ambitions in the region.

In 1499, the Ottoman fleet defeated Venice at the Battle of Zonchio in the Ionian Sea. In the following years, the Serenissima lost most of its Greek possessions, including Coron and Modon. Till then, the "eyes of the Republic" had stood watch over both the Adriatic and the Aegean. Actually a peace-loving, melancholic man,[3] Bayezid otherwise pursued a foreign policy of restraint. He equipped the army with firearms, which benefited his successors, and increased the bullion content of the coinage, which profited the economy. He also patronized the arts, building a magnificent mosque in Istanbul as befitted a sultan. However, none of this saved him from a swift, likely violent death after he abdicated in favor of his son Selim.

A new opponent rose to challenge the Ottomans as the Safavid dynasty grew stronger under Shah Ismail (1487–1524), a grandson of Uzun Hasan. The charismatic leader of a Sufi movement known as the Kizilbash (literally "red heads") took what was left of the "White Sheep" and created a large state with its center in Iran. The new kingdom was enmeshed in wars with the Uzbeks, a central Asian people, and in conflict with Mughal rulers. On all fronts, political differences were exacerbated by religious ones: the Safavids were Shias, whereas the Mughals of India and the Ottoman sultans were Sunnis. For the European opponents of Istanbul, flare-ups with the Safavids were convenient, as the Sublime Porte sought to avoid fighting wars on multiple fronts. In 1560, one imperial diplomat concluded that only the Persian threat saved Europe from conquest.[4]

In the second decade of the new century, Selim I the Grim (r. 1512–1520) returned to the policy of Ottoman expansion. After a fierce campaign, the Mamluk Sultanate was defeated. Syria, Palestine, and parts of the Arabian Peninsula—including the holy cities of Mecca and Medina—had to recognize the sovereignty of the Ottoman sultan, as did other princes of the region. The most significant gain was rich Egypt, among whose spoils was a moral victory: the title of caliph. The last Abbasid, who was now residing in Cairo, supposedly officially transferred the empty title to Selim. The Ottoman Empire assumed the role of intermediary between the Mediterranean world and the Indian Ocean. It experienced its own age of exploration. Ali Akbar's 1516 *Khatay-nameh* (*The Book of China*) provided the most precise description of Ming China then available. The next year, Admiral Piri Reis presented the sultan with a world map that not only looked east but also revealed knowledge of the discoveries made by Columbus—Piri Reis calls him "Qulünbü"—showing the coasts of South and Central America (Plate 20).[5]

Suleiman I the Lawgiver (r. 1520–1566), one of the most important rulers of the Ottoman dynasty, ascended the throne as the sole surviving son of Selim I.[6] In his day, it was customary in the House of Osman—in line with a directive of Mehmed the Conqueror—for the question of succession to be resolved in a brutal manner: the newly installed sultan had his brothers and all their sons killed. This normally happened quietly, by means of strangulation or a silk garrote. The procedure was meant to prevent civil wars and divisions of the realm. In the mid-seventeenth century, it was replaced by the principle of agnatic seniority. From then on, the successor was the oldest offspring of the dynasty.

Once in the saddle, the sultans ruled with nearly absolute power. The core of their army, then the biggest in Europe, was composed of battle-tested cavalry and, starting under Murad I, Janissaries. The Janissaries (*yeñiçeri*), or "new soldiers," were an elite corps recruited from young Christian captives and sons of Christian farmers in Anatolia and the Balkan Peninsula. The latter were taken from their families by force as tribute, although they did not necessarily have to break off all contact with them. The victims of this notorious practice, called *devshirme*, were distributed among Muslim farmers, learned their language, and grew up in the Muslim faith. The cohort, which was placed under the Sufi Bektashi Order, was a sworn brotherhood. Janissaries were also used in state administration and at court. As slaves of the sultan with no loyalty to any family, they were a reliable buttress of his power.

The Ottoman Empire was an ink state. It had a sophisticated bureaucracy that piled up mountains of documentation. Its treasury was fed by a share of the spoils of war: one-fifth of all goods taken, including the value of captured slaves. The land was largely the property of the sultan; it could be parceled out as a reward or taken away as punishment. The management of estates was entrusted to officials, military leaders—usually cavalry officers, who had to finance their equipment in this way—and sometimes also religious scholars and jurists. Upon the death of their holders, these "timars" returned to the state, where they could be handed out again as rewards to faithful servants.

One Habsburg envoy reported that the sultan himself distributed offices and posts. Clearly accustomed to a different system at home, he added,

> And in doing so [he] pays no attention to wealth or the empty claims of rank, and takes no account of any influence or popularity which a candidate may possess; he only scrutinizes the character, natural ability, and disposition of each.[7]

Assuming this observation was not entirely false, it helps us to understand the Ottoman Empire's extraordinary political success. In subject territories, rule functioned as it did in other empires: through arrangements with local leaders.[8]

Like his predecessors, Suleiman was a great conqueror. His armies captured Belgrade, which had previously withstood an Ottoman siege, and defeated a Hungarian force in 1526 at Mohács. The fact that the young King Louis II drowned while fleeing the debacle was a bit of a silver lining for the Habsburgs, as Louis's death placed the kingdoms of Hungary and Bohemia in the hands of his sister Anna's husband, Ferdinand. It was an early harvest of the double marriage celebrated ten years before (p. 501). The new possessions were under extreme threat, however. Suleiman's army made inroads as far as Vienna but could not take the strongly fortified city. Ferdinand was only able to lay claim to the west of Hungary. Loans from the Fuggers helped him to pay for the necessary army. Relief came inadvertently from the Uzbeks and the Safavids, who resisted the Ottoman advance against them and thus drew troops away from the western front. The Safavid Empire, long a trading partner of Latin

Europe, remained an important player in Middle Eastern politics. On the other hand, even the Habsburgs' Christian enemies, France in particular, went to grovel in the Topkapı Palace.

In the Mediterranean, Ottoman forces took Rhodes from the Hospitallers. The order retreated to Malta. In 1538, Istanbul's mastery of the sea was secured at Preveza by its victory over the combined fleet of a "Holy League." The ships, mostly provided by Venice, Spain, and the pope, were under the command of the emperor's admiral, Andrea Doria. Venice's last bases in the Aegean, on the Peloponnese, and in Dalmatia fell. Banners bearing the lion of Saint Mark now only flew over Crete and Cyprus. In addition, Suleiman managed to wrest from the Safavids their territories east of the Euphrates, including Baghdad. By the end of his long reign, the Ottoman Empire contained about twenty million subjects and stretched from the Caspian Sea to the Carpathian Basin, from Yemen to the coast of North Africa. Vassal kings paid tribute. Their number included the khan of the Crimean Tatars and the Christian rulers of Transylvania, Walachia, and, as of 1538, Moldavia.

Only after the conquests in the East did the Ottoman Empire become a state with a predominantly Muslim population. Muslims remained a minority in the Balkans. The Christians who did not convert were accorded a large degree of religious freedom—a policy guided by *raison d'état*. They still had to pay the customary special tax, however, and they suffered a few legal disadvantages. Other religious minorities also enjoyed a high degree of autonomy. Diversity thus remained a mark of the empire. Those who converted to Islam could rise in the administration or the army without restriction. Not a few of the previously Christian aristocrats of the Balkan region and former Byzantine territories became grand viziers after professing themselves followers of the Prophet.[9] Any religious dissent combined with political goals, however, was dealt with harshly by the authorities. Islam remained the cornerstone of the state. Religious scholars controlled higher education and the legal system. Just as the subjects of the Holy Roman Emperor could appeal to the Imperial Chamber Court, so too was a legal path to the Imperial Divan open to simple farmers in the Ottoman Empire. This supreme civil court also functioned as an advisory council to the sultan.

Suleiman, who loved intimidating envoys from foreign courts with excessive pomp, was called "the Magnificent" by the Latins. Pursuing the standard strategy of dynasties on the rise, the House of Osman surrounded itself with art and learning. It had itself glorified in all the languages of its empire. Sinan (ca. 1490–1588), who entered the court by way of the *devshirme*, served the

Ottomans as an extraordinarily capable architect. He built monasteries and palaces, mausoleums and mosques, as well as infrastructure like aqueducts, schools, and hospitals. Without Sinan's buildings, Istanbul would be a different city—and a much less beautiful one. The architect himself praised the Süleymaniye Mosque as

> a meeting place of the lovers of purity,
> a joy-giving abode like paradise.[10]

Suleiman's countrymen honored him with the epithet *Kanuni*, "the Lawgiver." Indeed, he continued with the legal codification begun by Mehmed the Conqueror. He had laws drawn up that regulated taxes and finances as well as property rights. For the first time, sultanic law, or *kanun*, attained primacy over Sharia. Not without reason, the sultans saw themselves as successors of the Roman emperors, as *Kayser-i Rum*. They drew prestige from their position as "servants of the two shrines," Mecca and Medina, and as champions in the war against the infidels. Inscriptions celebrate them as defenders of Sunni Islam and conquerors of the Shias.[11]

With a population of about 600,000, Istanbul had grown into the largest city by far in the entire Mediterranean world, a center of politics, economics, and culture. Bibliophilic rulers had treasure troves of books sent to the Bosporus from conquered lands. Artists, scholars, and craftsmen were urged or forced to settle in the capital.[12] The spice trade, which followed routes from Southeast Asia via Egypt to Venice and was controlled by the Ottomans, reached its maximum volume in the second half of the century.

Moscow: On the Path to Empire

At the same time, the Principality of Moscow was transforming from an emporium into a continental agrarian state, where wealth was created by land ownership and not trade and tribute.[13] The grand princes of Moscow commanded thinly populated territory. Protected by no natural boundaries, it was bordered by the endless world of the steppe nomads. This forced them to accumulate resources and to build up a strong military—at first to hold off invaders and later to engage in expansion.

Wars and power struggles with rivals dominated the politics of Russian rulers in the Late Middle Ages more than anything else. A flexible policy toward Lithuania, which included war as an option if necessary, allowed the great power to be held at a distance. Its decline began in the late fifteenth century.[14] Whenever possible, Moscow's princes sought to take advantage of disunity among the Tatars. In this way, they gave themselves greater room to maneuver, whereas the Golden Horde fragmented into rival khanates (p. 204). Nevertheless, a Tatar army defeated Grand Prince Vasily II (r. 1425–1462), who lacked sufficient support from his Russian neighbors. Despite being blinded in both eyes during fights with his brothers, he managed to overcome his opponents. Supported by the Church and the boyars, Vasily the Blind mercilessly defended Moscow's leadership and the principle of primogeniture, a prerequisite for the principality's consolidation and rise as a state. Opponents had their arms, legs, or heads chopped off. Vasily's son Ivan III (r. 1462–1505) succeeded to the throne without any opposition. Times were hard. The situation resembled Italy in the previous centuries.

In the past, Dmitry Donskoy had regarded the state and the title of grand prince as his own personal property, as a "patrimony." Ivan did the same. Over time, Moscow's rulers succeeded in tying all property ownership to royal service. The boundaries between private property and state land blurred. The weakening Golden Horde could no longer check the rise of its erstwhile vassals. In 1480, its forces surrendered to a Russian army without a fight after weeks of eyeing each other on the Ugra River. The Tatars did not try to subdue Moscow again. A disastrous defeat at the hands of Poland-Lithuania wiped the once terrifying power off the stage of world history. From then on, the "liberation from the Tatar yoke" was an important chapter in the story of Russian identity.

The Muscovites had long since ascribed a vital portion of their success to the "Virgin of Vladimir," yet another Byzantine icon believed to have been painted by Saint Luke himself. It had miraculously gone to Vladimir from Kyiv and then, in 1395, was taken to Moscow by the metropolitan. It immediately proved its magical power, as Timur the Lame spared the city. The icon's 500-year journey through time reflects the path of the Rus'. Once it arrived on the Moskva River, the image symbolized the unity of the state.

Ivan earned the epithet "the Great" not only as the victor over the Mongols but even more so as a conqueror of territories and a collector of cities. Lithuania lost a majority of its East Slavic principalities. The greatest prize was Novgorod, where a Muscovite army easily prevailed. The slight liberties of the city-state were now history. Ivan had the church bell that had summoned the veche, both a tool of communication and a symbol of power, taken to Moscow, where it continued to peal.[15] The Hanseatic kontor in Novgorod was closed in order to free Russian trade from competition. Tver, long a rival of equal standing, surrendered in 1485. The military campaigns were funded by a tax on ecclesiastical property.

Around the turn of the century, an apocalyptic mentality developed in Moscow similar to the one in Latin Europe. Indeed, the Orthodox considered the year 1492 to mark the seventh millennium since Creation and thus to forebode disaster.[16] When, to great surprise, life went on anyway, a new eon seemed at least to have dawned. Ivan III was portrayed as its Constantine. The title of *tsar*—derived from *caesar* and *Kaiser*—had already been used by Vasily II. Along with the newly introduced symbol of the double-headed eagle, it now placed Moscow, like Istanbul, in the tradition of Rome and Constantinople. The decline of Byzantine Christianity was also interpreted as an order from God to now preserve and spread the true faith. The grand princes saw themselves as secular defenders of the Orthodox Church. In Poland-Lithuania, an independent church with its own hierarchy developed.

Heresy was suppressed. After a bit of a delay, Ivan acquiesced to the wishes of his archbishop to follow the pious example of the Catholic kings and persecute "heretics" who were supposedly flirting with Judaism.[17] The first Rome fell because of its heresies, the second, Byzantium, because it entered into a union with the first, wrote Filofei, a monk in Pskov.[18] The third Rome, Moscow, would live forever, and there would be no fourth. That is how Filofei expressed the historic mission his tsar felt called to fulfill.

Ivan's son Vasily III (r. 1505–1533) brought the "gathering of the Rus' lands," as Moscow's expansion was euphemistically and cynically described, to a provisional close. In 1510, Pskov lost its *veche* bell and received a governor from Moscow in its place. The entire ruling class, 300 families, was deported and replaced with officials from Novgorod. Smolensk was taken from Lithuania, and then the Principality of Ryazan was conquered. These foreign-policy successes solidified Moscow's power. One helpful strategy for taming the elite was to turn the princely court into a social and cultural magnet. An elaborate system of ranks and titles, whose allocation lay in the hand of the tsar, bound courtiers closer to their ruler or created distance from him. It encouraged people to fight for distinction—a trend useful to the monarchy.[19] If a nobleman became too powerful, he ended his days on the executioner's block or in a monastery. The tsars had copied aspects of financial administration, the courier system, ceremonial, and military strategy from the rulers of the steppe. Otherwise, their autocracy developed according to its own laws. It was no mere child of "Oriental despotism."[20]

From the very beginning, the Muscovite state contained only a few big cities and none that could compete with the splendor of western metropolises. The share of Russia's population that lived in cities has been estimated at only four to seven percent. For the state was not based on an ancient, advanced civilization like the one that had created Rome.[21] Rather, it had grown up amidst forests, swamps, and steppe. Only Moscow, Novgorod, and a few other cities reached the size of, say, early modern Cologne. Moscow was protected by no walls. Like all Russian towns, it was made almost entirely out of wood—fuel for large fires that could be sparked by lightning, carelessness, or the conniving of Tatar plunderers. Few stone buildings, mostly churches, rose above the gray thicket of homesteads, cabins, storehouses, and sheds. The borders of the city were distended by numerous spacious gardens and squares, such that from a distance it seemed bigger than it really was.[22] The roads were not paved, and there was no running water. Wooden planks, which the Russians referred to as "bridges," offered protection from mud but also helped to spread fires. Russian travelers were accordingly amazed when they saw cobblestones in Western cities.

Opposition from townspeople was not a concern of the lords of the capital. Civic autonomy was not desired, and there were no communes. The Russian cities had burdens to bear, not privileges to collect. Lay Orthodox confraternities were the sole semblance of horizontal power. Only in cities west of the Dnieper did an ambition for autonomy raise its head for a while.[23] On the other hand, the tsar increasingly called on leading merchants as advisers, especially in economic affairs, starting in the second half of the sixteenth century. He conferred administrative posts on them, sent them on diplomatic missions, and granted them economic concessions—only to then squeeze the *gosti* dry.[24]

Despite the efforts of important rulers like Peter the Great, Russia would never succeed in catching up with Latin Europe in terms of rational administration, technology, and learning. Art, knowledge, and weapons were mostly imported from Latin Europe. For example, the notes of the Habsburg diplomat Sigmund von Herberstein (1486–1566) make mention of a gunsmith named Niklas, a German version of the bronze caster Urban who had helped the Ottomans in their conquests.[25] Indeed, the walls of Smolensk supposedly crumbled under the blast of 140 cannons. Germans were also imported to practice the art of healing as physicians and apothecaries, whereas Italians arrived as architects in 1462. Aristotele Fioravanti, an engineer and architect from Bologna who also knew how to cast cannons and mint coins, rebuilt the Dormition Cathedral in Moscow's Kremlin.[26] He did not employ a Renaissance aesthetic, though, but rather adhered to the model in Vladimir. For the "Virgin of Vladimir," the beneficent icon displayed in Fioravanti's church, had to feel at home there. Nevertheless, the Renaissance debuted rather early in Moscow: in the Palace of the Facets (Fig. 46, p. 569) and the Cathedral of the Archangel Michael—both of them the work of Italian im-

migrants. The red, towered walls of the Kremlin were designed by Milanese architects. They even recall the fortifications of the Castello Sforzesco. Moscow was now an outpost of the new style in the East.

Conquistadors

At around the same time as the Spanish Inquisition was burning heretics and Spanish ships reached the Caribbean, an attempt was made in the southern German city of Nuremberg to summarize the geographical knowledge of the day. It was the final snapshot of an already outdated view of the Earth. In collaboration with the major printer Anton Koberger and the merchant Sebald Schreyer, Hartmann Schedel produced his *Weltchronik*, or *Nuremberg Chronicle* as it is known in English, a universal history that promised to capture the whole world in one lavish folio volume. Contemporaneously, and also in Nuremberg, a team of craftsmen under the direction of Martin Behaim—the son of a merchant who had emigrated to Lisbon—built a globe, finished in 1494 (Fig. 45, p. 560).[27] The geographical knowledge it encapsulated was based largely on Strabo, Pliny, and Ptolemy's *Geography*, which had been available since the early fifteenth century. It shows Saint Brendan's Island in the extreme west, along with Antilia and other nonexistent places, although it also includes the Cape Verde Islands and outlines the West African coast south to Cabo Ledo in modern Angola. There, the continent ends. Mandeville's gold paradise of Taprobane is sketched as an oversized island off the coast of India. In the Far East, Japan is included under the name given to it by Marco Polo: "Cipangu." According to the caption, gold and spices were to be found there. The interior of Asia is also drawn in line with Marco Polo's account. North and South America are missing.

A new geography developed in the wake of Columbus's explorations and the voyages of the Portuguese, a sense of which is provided by a 1502 map brought back from Portugal to Italy by Alberto Cantino, a Ferrarese diplomat. It provides a rather accurate picture of Africa, and it also shows Hispaniola, Cuba (which it calls "Isabela"), and parts of the coasts of Florida and Brazil.[28] Independently, the southern German Carthusian monk Gregor Reisch (ca. 1470–1525) created a world map that is found in his 1503 *Margarita philosophica* (*Philosophical Pearl*). A caption on the lower margin, south of the depiction of the Indian Ocean, reveals that he recognized the rift that had opened up in the traditional conception of the world: "There is no land here but rather sea, in which there are islands of remarkable size that were unknown to Ptolemy."[29]

The year Columbus died, two German cartographers, Matthias Ringmann and Martin Waldseemüller, produced their famous map of the world. They had gotten hold of travel accounts by the Florentine navigator Amerigo Vespucci (1451/54–1512), written in epistolary form, including a letter to Lorenzo di Pierfrancesco de' Medici entitled *Mundus novus*, or *New World*. Vespucci took the position that it was not islands that had been discovered in the West but rather a continent containing more people and animals than Europe, Asia, or Africa.[30] On the far left-hand side of their 1507 world map, which otherwise followed Ptolemy, the cartographers accordingly drew a thin strip of land longer than Africa and Europe combined. Only the east coast has a definite outline. Beyond that, as a caption indicates, was *terra incognita*, "unknown land." In honor of Vespucci, they named the continent "America." That is how the "New World" got its name.

Amerigo Vespucci had worked in Cadiz and Seville as an agent of the Medici, where he gained knowledge of Spain's oceanic discoveries. It is unclear which of the voyages he described were actually undertaken by him. His talent for showmanship took Amerigo far. He even went down in world literature as a character in the narrative frame of More's *Utopia*. His letters, which circulated in print, fascinated readers with descriptions of the land and peoples of South America. Vespucci writes of nude savages who disdained money and trade.[31] Satisfied with what nature provided, wealth meant nothing to them. In matters of religion, he considered them worse than pagans, a godless folk equivalent to Epicureans. Worse still, they practiced the custom of eating their enemies. Thus, Vespucci's letters provided material not only for white lies about the Americas but also for dark legends. Although their author was certainly not the brilliant navigator he boasted of being, the king of Castile named him *piloto mayor*, a kind of chief bookkeeper for discoveries. The idea was to gather new knowledge and create maps of newly discovered lands. Amerigo's letters, along with more and more accounts of the New World, turned the Americas into a place on Europe's mental map. Perhaps as early as 1504 and certainly by 1510, it was found on globes, which now also increasingly provided orientation about the Earth's surface.

In 1494, two years after Columbus's first voyage, the superpowers Spain and Portugal set about dividing up the world between them. The Treaty of Tordesillas between John II of Portugal and the Catholic Monarchs of Spain drew a line from pole to pole. The Portuguese succeeded in pushing the line so far west that part of South America belonged to their half. Discoveries west of the line were to be the property of Spain. The deal was brokered by Alexander VI, who, as the successor of Saint Peter, considered himself the proprietor of the whole globe. The pope's claim to ownership also formed the basis of the so-called *requerimiento*. The "Requirement" of 1513, a text edited by Spain's royal jurist Palacios Rubios, announced Rome's claim to sovereignty over all people in the world. A text to this effect was customarily read to the peoples of "discovered" territories, explaining that Saint Peter had given the islands of the ocean as well as the mainland to the Catholic Monarchs as a gift. The appropriate thing for them to do now was submit to Spanish authority; otherwise, war and slavery could be expected.[32] The indigenous auditors could not have understood a word of it. Even contemporaries considered the procedure a farce.

The fate of the affected populations hardly worried the Europeans. Their concern was for gold, spices, and God—in that order. The Spanish rooted for gold like starving pigs, as one Aztec contemptuously observed.[33] In addition, they searched for drugs and medicinal plants.[34] Incidentally, the reason that spices were unimaginably precious and that they had always been more important for trade than most other goods was not simply because they tasted good.[35] Contemporaries believed that they carried the scent of paradise, in whose vicinity they were thought to grow. Consuming them enhanced one's prestige. It proved that one belonged to the nobility or to the upper classes of the towns and cities.

In Tordesillas, the treaty was drawn up in the absence of the other major players—England, France, and the Netherlands. They did not recognize the agreement. The British were the first to set sail. Equipped with a letter of safe conduct from Henry VII and funded by other Italians living in London, Giovanni Caboto of Venice undertook three voyages westward from Bristol between 1496 and 1500.[36] The last one might have brought him not only to Greenland and Newfoundland but also, sailing down the North American coastline, to Venezuela. He died shortly after his return. His expeditions were not followed up. Neither were Portuguese voyages that may have reached Newfoundland.

The colonization of the Americas began as a mixture of state-sponsored wars of conquest and private enterprise. Daring and, above all, wealthy individuals received licenses from the Casa de la Contratación entitling them to subjugate specific territories. One-fifth of the profit was to be paid to the crown. The contracts usually gave the crown a mechanism for dispossessing the conquerors of their spoils in the end.[37] The economy of the Spanish colonies was regulated by the *encomienda* system, which resembled Ottoman military feudalism. Royal officials distributed land and indigenous people to colonists as payment for their services. The latter were supposed to be free and receive fair payment for the work they performed on plantations and fields, in mines and pearl beds—and be converted to Christianity as well. In reality, the *encomenderos* treated them like slaves; conditions were the same in Portuguese colonies. Likewise ignored in practice was the rule that the natives were only to be used for a certain amount of time.

Businessmen and soldiers of fortune followed the explorers. Trading capital saw profit opportunities on the other side of the ocean. And bankrupts and swindlers were lured by the chance to escape predicaments at home. The other types of wayfarers to the New World were thus joined by the *pícaro*. This shrewd, devious, small man who cheated his way through the jungle of the cities now became a literary character with the rise of the *novela picaresca*. Hundreds of thousands of such people would immigrate to the New World during the sixteenth century.

Thanks to their Caribbean beachheads, the Spanish could explore the mainland step by step. In 1509, they landed on the north coast of Colombia. Their gaze soon extended over the Pacific. The first to see the legendary "South Sea" was Vasco Nuñéz de Balboa, a petty noble from Galicia. In search of precious metals—stories were told of entire rivers of gold—he had crossed the Isthmus of Panama with a small detachment of soldiers. It must have been an incomparable moment when the coast was reached in September of 1513 after a strenuous march through jungle and swamps. From a mountainside, the Spaniards saw the panorama of a blue bay in the Gulf of Panama, which they called "San Miguel." Balboa claimed the "South Sea," along with all the coasts and lands that bordered it, for the crown of Castile in the name of God.[38] After that, the explorer's fate was infelicitous. Pedro Arias de Ávila, his father-in-law and successor as governor of the area around Darién, had him executed in 1519 (the year Panama City was founded), thus putting an end to a long-smoldering power struggle.

Two years later, Juan Ponce de León set sail from Puerto Rico to Florida, driven by the hope of finding the legendary Fountain of Youth.[39] Yet he was struck by an arrow in a battle with the indigenous population, putting a sudden end to his dreams. The exploration of the Gulf of Mexico was continued by his compatriots, whereas the French followed the English example and headed for North America—initially in the hope of reaching Asia. Sailing for the French crown, the Tuscan navigator Giovanni da Verrazzano explored the east coast of North America. He was the first to describe the mouth of the Hudson River, where New York City would later grow up. The real prize beckoned further south, however.

Between 1519 and 1522, Hernán Cortés (1485–1547), a petty noble from Medellín, overthrew the Aztec Empire. He had amassed considerable wealth in Hispaniola and Cuba, which allowed him to finance a profitable *conquista* on the mainland. Cortés was a man of many qualities, at once an evangelist and a butcher. Ambitious and courageous, a diplomat with a winning personality, and a crafty businessman as well, he showed himself to be a monster in critical situations. He was a gambler through and through—one of the most successful ever, if the effort he invested is compared to the outcome. He quarreled with his superior, Diego Velázquez, the governor of Cuba. In 1519, he founded the settlement of Veracruz, which would become Mexico's chief Atlantic port. It served as the base for his march into the interior of the country. He put all his eggs in one basket: either he would win an empire, or he would lose his head.

An insane desire for gold was at the root of one of the most bizarre episodes in world history. It pushed Cortés into an endeavor whose chances of success must have seemed extremely thin by any rational reckoning. A handful of foreign mercenaries attacked an empire of several million people that possessed cities, sophisticated systems of administration, and a road network. But Cortés saw that there were cracks in this grand edifice. In reality, the Aztec Empire was a federation of three city-states. Tenochtitlán was the leader. Tributary peoples were all too ready to throw off its oppressive yoke. Furthermore, a struggle for the throne had weakened the power of its ruler, Moctezuma. This gave the Spaniards an opportunity to gain allies among his opponents. It was a situation that would often repeat itself: the invaders faced numerically far superior opponents who were, however, disunited and let themselves be played off against one another. Many of them contributed to their own downfall by lining up with Cortés's army.

In the first clashes with the "*indios*," the element of surprise was with the Spanish. It was the Renaissance against the Bronze Age. The European warriors, clad in armor and accompanied by bloodhounds, rode their horses—an animal as yet unknown in the Americas—into the interior and found reinforcements among the locals. A dramatic skirmish took place in Cholula, a large city at the foot of Popocatépetl. Probably afraid of being attacked, Cortés's soldiers killed thousands, including the highest-ranking individuals. Nothing in their experience could help the Aztecs understand what was happening. Moctezuma hoped for divine aid, then gave in to resignation. He could not act, not even when the news of the massacre in Cholula reached Tenochtitlán.[40]

Perhaps the Aztec king identified the foreigners as Quetzalcoatl and his retinue. The stars had foretold the return of the feathered serpent god for the very year the Spanish came. The course of events seemed predestined. How could one oppose the universe? Was it, then, unswerving faith in the language of signs that caused the *indígenas* to accept their destruction? Or did they invent the story that Cortés had exploited the myth in order to make their defeat explicable?[41] However that may be, Tenochtitlán belonged to the conquerors. An eyewitness was reminded of the magical stories of *Amadís de Gaula*, a popular chivalric romance of the time, when he first saw the city in the middle of the since-vanished Lake Texcoco.[42] With its temples, palaces, and gardens, it seemed like a dream. On the other hand, it was infused with the stink of corpses from the sacrificial altars where priests offered thousands of young men to the gods each year.

Moctezuma received Cortés and his people with great honor. The conquerors ruthlessly took him captive, destroyed temples, toppled idols, and killed several hundred Aztecs. Cortés was not in the city when this happened. He had had the chutzpah to hurry to Veracruz and defeat a force sent by Velázquez to make the bold conquistador see reason. Those who survived the battle joined Cortés.

When he returned to Tenochtitlán in June 1520, the city was in turmoil. After heavy fighting in which Moctezuma was killed and the Spanish suffered great losses—the slaughter went down in history as the *Noche Triste*, or "sad night"—the invaders were forced to retreat. But Cortés entered into new alliances and recruited reinforcements. His army cut a bloody path through the land. Tenochtitlán was starved out, then conquered and destroyed. The victory was owed in part to an epidemic of smallpox, a disease introduced by the foreigners. People died in the tens of thousands. The Spanish compared their victory to the conquest of Jerusalem by the Romans, thus styling themselves the successors of ancient glory. Cortés appeared as both a new Alexander and a new Caesar.[43] He had also opened the way to the Christianization of Central America. In 1523, a dozen Franciscans began their pious missionary work. They were called the "Twelve Apostles of Mexico."

Beyond the Cape of Good Hope

On the other side of the world, the Portuguese had now broken through to India. In 1488, Bartolomeu Dias was the first to round the cliff-lined, storm-tossed Cape of Good Hope. Yet it was not he, the conqueror of the Cape, but rather Vasco da Gama (1469–1524) who, in 1498, was tasked by King Manuel I with finishing the grand project. On the final leg of the voyage, his ships were guided by an Arab pilot. In May of 1498, they moored in Calicut on the Malabar Coast, modern Kozhikode. Two ships returned to Lisbon the following year, laden with pepper and cinnamon—two others had not survived the voyage. Of the 180 men who are thought to have set sail for India, one-third of them never saw home again. Manuel now styled himself—perhaps outlining a program for future aspirations—"By the Grace of God, King of Portugal and the Algarves on this side of the seas and beyond them in Africa, Lord of Guinea and of Conquest, Navigation, and Commerce of Ethiopia, Arabia, Persia, and India."[44]

Immediately, another fleet was sent under the command of Pedro Álvarez Cabral, consisting of 13 ships and over 1,200 crewmen. After Easter of 1500, it landed in Brazil, whose coast had once been sailed by Vicente Yáñez Pinzón, the commander of Columbus's *Niña*. In line with the Treaty of Tordesillas, the land was claimed for the crown of Portugal. This "discovery" of Brazil was the result of an accident. Cabral was actually on his way to the south of Africa, but he had guided his fleet far to the west in order to avoid the doldrums that often quieted the Gulf of Guinea. Continuing on, four ships were then lost in heavy storms south of the Cape of Good Hope. A fifth was also damaged but reached Mauritius and La Réunion. For the first time, Europeans caught sight of Madagascar. By September, Cabral was in India.

From the very beginning, the Portuguese voyages to India were of a differ-ent character than Columbus's expeditions. The captains were not sailing into uncertainty. In the Indian Ocean, they could follow much-traveled routes. They were familiar with their destination and knew what was to be had there. "Roses are sold everywhere," a Persian diplomat reported from Vijayanagara in the fifteenth century. "These people could not live without roses, and they look upon them as quite as necessary as food. . . . The jewelers sell publicly in the bazaars pearls, rubies, emeralds, and diamonds."[45] In growing numbers, European traders and missionaries reported on the local customs, goods, and gods, as well as on the widespread practice of burning widows, *sati*, which forced women to follow their husbands beyond the pale of death.[46] Just how close India had now become to Europe is indicated by the observation of the widely traveled Niccolò de' Conti (ca. 1395–1469), to the effect that Venetian ducats were in abundant circulation there.[47]

Like Cabral's fleet, the ships on which Vasco da Gama set sail on his second expedition to India were loaded with weapons. An attack by Indian and Arab ships off the coast of Calicut was repelled by its cannons. Portuguese coloniza-tion, driven by desires for profit and a Crusading spirit, now developed an enormous energy. Even before Cabral arrived back in Lisbon with the rest of his fleet, further expeditions had already set sail, financed in part by merchants from Augsburg and Florence. After Hormuz was taken in 1507, it was possible to control trade across the Persian Gulf.

India's political fragmentation made it easy for Europeans to gain a foothold on the coast. In the north of the subcontinent, the Muslim Delhi Sultanate was only a shadow of its former self. Timur's campaign of conquest in 1398 had hastened its decline, a process long since begun by the rise of Ma'bar, Bengal, and Bahmani as independent entities. Bahmani, in turn, split into five sultan-ates after fierce fighting in the late fifteenth century; they shared the Deccan Plateau. Further south, the Hindu Vijayanagara Empire dominated down to the second half of the sixteenth century. The coastal areas, where pepper plants grew and ginger blossomed, were shared by numerous petty kingdoms.

No great power stopped the Portuguese from setting up forts here and on Sri Lanka. From a base on the island of Diu off the west coast of India, they defeated a Mamluk fleet in 1509. It happened to be carrying financial aid from Christian Venice, who hoped to neutralize competition from Portugal. The victory opened the Indian Ocean to the Portuguese. From Bijapur, one of the central Indian sultanates that had bucked the sovereignty of Bahmani, they wrested the territory around Goa. The city became the administrative center for a string of bases that now went by the name of the State of India, *Estado da Índia*. In 1511, its governor Alfonso de Albuquerque took Malacca, the relay point for trade at the intersection of routes between the Spice Islands, China, and India. In the view of Tomé Pires, an apothecary who wrote the first description of the region from a European perspective, whoever controlled Malacca had their fingers around the neck of Venice.[48] The Portuguese also took Pasai, but they were driven out a few years later. Asia's traders had no intention of bowing to the new regime, so they headed for the north of Sumatra. Aceh, ruled by sultans—both male and female—and soon to be allied with the Ottomans, assumed Malacca's role and remained an adversary of the Europeans. China did not lift a finger.

Portugal was now enmeshed in far-flung economic relationships that stretched to Cairo and Venice in the West, and to China and Japan in the East. Cambay, the commercial center of Gujarat, had two arms, as Pires wrote. One stretched out toward Aden, the other toward Malacca. Merchants from Cairo supplied goods from Venice, whereas opium, rose water, pearls, and more came from Mecca and Aden.[49] In 1517, Portugal sent a diplomatic mission headed by Pires to make contact with the Chinese court and pave the way for economic relations. After a few years, however, the attempt failed dramatically when Europeans violated holy Chinese ceremonial, thus making themselves unacceptable partners. There were military clashes in the Pearl River Delta. In addition, the conquest of Malacca had displeased the Chinese. Rumors also circulated that children kidnapped by a Portuguese pirate had been eaten by Christians. Several members of the embassy were tortured or executed. Some of them died in prison. Pires was likely one of the victims. Only after the middle of the sixteenth century were the Portuguese permitted to set up a trading post in Macao (p. 727).

At sea, only the Ottoman Empire could have checked them. Despite warning voices, however, the Sublime Porte decided not to build a Pacific fleet, probably for economic reasons.[50] It was content to defend its bastions in the Persian Gulf and its control of the Red Sea along with Jeddah, the gateway to Mecca and Medina. Portuguese influence in the Pacific should not be overestimated, though. Muslim merchants ruled trade around the Indian Ocean, and Muslim rulers protected it.[51] They and the Chinese continued to play a more important role than the Europeans.

Portugal's activity in Asia did not cause it to lose sight of Brazil. Three ships under the command of Gonçalo Coelho sailed into a bay on January 1, 1502. It was mistaken for the mouth of a river and thus called Rio de Janeiro, "January

River." In subsequent decades, bases and missionary posts would be established there and on other sections of the coast that eventually developed into cities. In addition to Rio, these included Recife, Salvador, and Sao Paolo. The most important industries were trade with wood used for dyes and, later, sugar production.

If any proof was still necessary that the Earth was shaped like a ball, the last shreds of doubt were now swept away. The discoverer of the passage from the Atlantic to the Pacific, which ever since has born his name, was a battle-tested captain who had spent time in India: Fernão de Magalhães (1480–1521) or, as he is known in English, Ferdinand Magellan. Magellan's goal was the spice fields of the Moluccas, which he thought must be easier to reach from the east than from the west. This belief may have been reinforced by a map made by Martin Behaim that showed a southwest passage.[52] Magellan was not able to convince Manuel of Portugal about the project, and the king brusquely rejected him. But the Spanish competition jumped at the idea. In September of 1509, Magellan set sail with a fleet of five ships. Always mindful to avoid contact with Portuguese ships, it carefully made its way down the east coast of South America. Every river mouth and every bay was explored to see if it led to a passage. Strange animals were sighted: seals, penguins, flying fish. And, as the Venetian crewman Antonio Pigafetta reports, they encountered huge men, mysterious natives. Pigafetta believed they worshipped demonic hordes whose leader they called "Setebos."[53]

The story of the first circumnavigation of the globe reads like an adventure novel.[54] The longer the search went on, and the less food was available, the more restless the crews became. A mutiny was ruthlessly put down by Magellan. Two captains were executed. The royal inspector and the ship's chaplain were abandoned in the wasteland of the Patagonian wilderness, doomed to a slower death. Over one year after departing Spain, they finally found the passage they were seeking. We might imagine the caravels' voyage to the end of the world as it was described by the poet Stefan Zweig, who wrote a romantic biography of Magellan: along barren shores, windswept tundra, and dark mountains, under the alien firmament of the deep Southern Hemisphere.[55] On beaches across from the mainland, the mariners saw flickering points of light, distant fires around which unknown people huddled. It was the furthest outpost of humanity. The island was called *Tierra del Fuego*, "Land of Fire."

One month later, the sailors were once again on the open sea. Pigafetta describes a hellish three-month voyage across the murderous Pacific Ocean, entailing starvation, scurvy, and death. The crew chewed on hardtack full of maggots and soaked in rat urine, survived on ox hides, and drank putrid water.[56] When the ships landed on one of the Philippine islands, only one hundred of the original 270 men were still alive. Magellan himself was fatally wounded during a clash with the natives. The voyage continued to Borneo and then to Tidore, one of the Moluccan Islands, thus reaching the intended destination. From there, they sailed around the Cape of Good Hope and back to Spain. On September 6, 1522, the *Victoria* arrived in Sanlúcar, Spain with a crew of eighteen and fully loaded with spices; it was the only ship to survive the entire voyage. The process that we call "globalization" was now underway, driven inexorably and mercilessly forward by European rovers for whom— differently from others—their world was not enough.

The Habsburg World Empire

The empires whose creation or rise was witnessed in the early modern period were special cases of a general process of state consolidation via bureaucracies and armies that elsewhere progressed on a smaller scale. The logic of power demanded expansion, pushing states when possible, as in some phases of the Ottoman Empire, toward universal rule and the construction of corresponding ideologies. In Europe, the era of leagues of cities and city republics was coming to an end. Galaxies of power were forming whose gravity sucked in the smaller stars. When imperial spheres of influence overlapped, the result was turbulence. Russia and the Ottoman Empire, which had expanded to the mouth of the Dniester on the Black Sea, entered into direct confrontation in the last third of the seventeenth century. Meanwhile, to the west, an opponent of the Ottomans was on the rise that would ultimately vanquish it after several centuries of struggle: the Habsburg Empire.

As mentioned above, the Habsburgs' ascent was prepared by marriage alliances. The most consequential was the union between Philip the Handsome, the son of Maximilian and Mary of Burgundy, and Joanna, the heiress of Castile. Their first-born son, Charles of Burgundy, was heir to the greatest fortune of all time. From his parents and his grandparents, Ferdinand of Aragon and Isabella of Castile, he inherited the Spanish crowns. When Emperor Maximilian closed his eyes forever in January of 1519, after a lifetime of high-flown plans, bitter disappointments, and grand successes, his patrimony also fell to Charles: Austria, Burgundy, and more still. There were great expectations for the pale, wooden Habsburg with the oversized chin that a beard and the art of painting did their best to hide.

The man crowned on October 23, 1520 in a solemn ceremony in Charlemagne's cathedral in Aachen first saw the light of day in Ghent in 1500.[57] His
native language was French. Over time, he learned Spanish, later a little German and Italian. He went through adolescence without a father and far from
his mother, as Joanna was overwhelmed by mental illness after the death of
Philip the Handsome. Called "la Loca," "the Mad," she continued to deteriorate in her widow's residence in Tordesillas until her death in 1555. Nevertheless, decrees from the Castilian crown were still issued in her name.

The future Holy Roman Emperor was entrusted to the care of his aunt Arch-
duchess Margaret, later regent of the Netherlands, and educated in the ways of
chivalry. He may have acquired his piety during his youthful years in Mechelen,
where the *devotio moderna* had many adherents. His firm faith was to have far-
reaching consequences. When he had reached the age of maturity and assumed
the government of his Burgundian lands, a court humanist invented a motto
for him that would become famous: *plus oultre*, in Latin *plus ultra*. This "ever
further" or "ever onwards" was meant as a response to the *non plus ultra*, "no
further," that, according to myth, Hercules had inscribed on the pillars at the
end of the world.[58] The future proved Charles's motto right. Beyond the Pillars
of Hercules, beyond the Strait of Gibraltar, he acquired one land after another
during his reign. Cortés's conquests—Charles quickly blessed the conquistador's actions—and the subjection of Central America were only the beginning.
Indeed, the emperor would endeavor far beyond the limits of the possible—and
not to the benefit of his realms. The desire for glory and honor was a powerful
driver of his policies. At times, it followed the laws of the tournament. Charles
once even challenged his opponent Francis I to a duel, just like Ariosto's *furioso*
Orlando challenged the Saracen king Agramante. Charles observed that it was
not seemly for a prince to think of money when engaged in heroic action, and
that one's own safety and wealth should be put on the line in matters of honor.[59]
This ethos continued to animate his successors. In the following centuries it
drove Spain's armies to a couple of victories and defeats, the state into bankruptcy, and the empire into decline.

Charles was now the fifth of his name to be "Emperor of the Romans, forever August." He bore the empty title of a king of Jerusalem, but also the by-
no-means empty title of King of Spain, the Two Sicilies, the Balearic Islands,
the Canary Islands, and the "Mainland of the Ocean Sea." In addition, he was
Archduke of Austria, Duke of Burgundy and Brabant, Count of Flanders,
Tyrol, and more. He also styled himself somewhat nebulously as "Lord in Asia
and Africa." He had his Austrian lands governed by his brother Ferdinand, the

future master of Hungary and Bohemia. Charles was the first Holy Roman Emperor to have to sign a "capitulation," an agreement with the prince-electors that put limits on his sovereignty, bound him to the laws and customs of the Empire, and, above all, prohibited its transformation into a hereditary kingdom.[60] It also declared that decisions of war and peace should not be made without a vote of the Imperial Estates or at least of the prince-electors. According to the capitulation, the emperor was not even allowed to enter into alliances without the assent of the prince-electors. Charles did not honor these agreements.

Despite all efforts to keep the imperial double-eagle from flying too high, the coronation ceremony celebrated the office and person of the Holy Roman Emperor with traditional pomp.[61] It inaugurated the rule of a man who made one final, earnest attempt to create a universal Catholic monarchy. He was inspired to this dream of world rule by his "grand chancellor" Mercurino Gattinara. The jurist from Piedmont certainly did not have autocracy on the Russian or Ottoman model in mind. In his conception of empire, the point was not to become an actual sovereign here or there, but rather to be venerated by the rulers of the world.[62] The massive space far to the west that Spain's mercenaries were subjugating at the time of the coronation in Aachen was still at the edge of Gattinara's mental map. In Mexico, Charles might seem to be a savior called to heal the New World, the *mundo nuevo*. But that did not make him emperor of the Aztecs.[63] Nevertheless, the conquistadors' grand narratives incorporated models from classical antiquity. The conquerors gazed into the ancient mirror and saw themselves reflected there as greater than even the titanic Romans had been. The Americas, incorporated into the realm of Castile as a conquered territory, were to become the province of a reborn Roman Empire.[64] Gattinara's sense of world order recalls Dante's *Monarchia* and its ideal of an Augustan emperor of peace. As the defender of the faith, Charles acquiesced to coronation decorations that depicted him as subordinate to the Church.[65] Yet the debate over primacy between him and the pope had long since been decided in the Europe of nation states. The lord of a world empire had nothing to fear from such symbolism. Gattinara saw the key to success in his homeland of Italy. He wanted Charles to exercise loose dominion there.

Peace within Charles's realms was quite fragile, as was revealed after he set out for Germany for his coronation.[66] *Germanías* (literally "Brotherhoods") in Valencia and Mallorca, guild militias that had actually been formed to fight pirates, rose up against the nobility and the Muslim minority. At the same time, the Revolt of the Comuneros broke out in Castile, involving nobles and townspeople alike. Charles had broken agreements made before his departure with the Cortes of Castile and Aragon, according to which locals would not be passed over when important offices were filled. Furthermore, the burdensome taxation entailed by imperial aspirations nourished unrest. Initial military successes added dangerous fuel to the movement; even peasants joined it. The rebellion was quelled by 1522, but only with difficulty. The following year, the last stirrings of the *germanías* in Mallorca were stifled. The failed uprising strengthened the monarchy. Spain's future belonged to it, not to the horizontal power of representative government.

The groundwork for Gattinara's project was not as stable as the two pillars on the imperial emblem. Nowhere did Charles V rule like a tsar—not in Spain or Italy, not in his hereditary lands in the east, and certainly not in the Holy Roman Empire. He had not conquered one square meter of his own lands by himself. Everywhere the imperial will was thwarted by thickets of customs, privileges, and exemptions, fenced in by the silent power of financiers, the less silent power of princes, the Estates, and the Church, and even by the stubbornness of Spanish sheep farmers, who had organized as the "Honorable Council of the *Mesta*." It was impossible to create a uniform administration for this diverse political conglomerate. Nevertheless, fanciful ideas were connected with Charles. Hernán Cortés thought he could even conquer China for him, thus making Charles master of a world empire, a *monarchia universalis*.[67]

He was not as remote from his subjects as a sultan or a Chinese Son of Heaven. Yet he was still surrounded by an intricate ceremonial, its shimmering aura creating a distance between him and everyone else. The people watched in awe as the emperor, silently and without paying any attention to his audience, dined on pâté, calf's head, or suckling pig, beckoning to his servants with quick waves of the hand. The jokes of the court jesters were able to tease a slight smile from him at times.[68] The art created in his orbit extolled him as an ancient *imperator*. The Habsburg Caesar, in this sense a true Renaissance prince, was at the same time Dante's last emperor. Some people hoped the election of the mighty new ruler would signal the beginning of long-awaited Church reform. A few months before the coronation in Aachen, one of them wrote, "God has given us a young man of noble birth as head of state, and in him has awakened great hopes of good in many hearts."[69] The man, named Martin Luther, would turn out to be mightily disappointed.

31

Religious Revolution

Luther

Wittenberg. October 31, 1517. No, Professor Luder probably did not go in person to the north door of All Saints' Church armed with hammer and nail to post a broadsheet announcing the ninety-five theses he proposed to argue in an academic disputation. That was customarily the task of the caretaker.[1] The scene so often depicted in painting and film is, therefore, only a legend, that of a monk with a hammer whose blows echo far beyond the sleepy town of Wittenberg—a place Luther described as "on the edge of civilization"[2]—beyond Saxony, even beyond Europe. Such portrayals show the writer of theological works endeavoring to shatter the thousand-year-old edifice of the Roman Catholic Church, the man of the Enlightenment beginning the task of driving the Middle Ages out of his religion. In reality, things were more complicated.

Luder was born in Eisleben in 1483 and grew up in a middle-class home. His mother belonged to a reputable burgher family. His father Hans was the son of free farmers. When not working in the fields, he was involved in the booming copper mining business. He rose to become a town councilman in the city of Mansfeld, and he was able to send his son to a university to study law. But Martin entered Saint Augustine's Monastery in Erfurt in 1505 and studied theology. He quickly won the trust of his superiors. In the service of the order, he traveled to Rome for a few months. The culture of the High Renaissance had no effect on him. After returning, he rose to the post of provincial vicar. In 1512, he was awarded a doctorate by the University of Wittenberg, founded only ten years earlier, and made professor of biblical exegesis there.

Let us now review the prosaic reality behind the publication of his *Ninety-Five Theses*. Dr. "Luther," as he now called himself—after *eleutherios*, "the free man"—sought to elicit interest in his disputation not from the people at large but from a small circle of colleagues. The theses he proposed to discuss, which were written in Latin and actually posted on the doors of several churches in Wittenberg, dealt with indulgence and grace. The debate was, therefore, to focus not only on theology but on a venerable, flourishing business practice. By purchasing an indulgence, one could buy one's way out of purgatory or shorten the time one had to suffer there. Money seemed to make actual penance and contrition superfluous, at least in the eyes of the more simple-minded, especially since Pope Sixtus IV had sanctioned the practice of issuing indulgences for those who had already died. Considered soberly, the sale of indulgences generated considerable profit all around. The purchasers acquired, in the words of Thomas Kaufmann, a "universal insurance policy for the living and the dead," a kind of passport to heaven[3]—and thus a little peace of mind. And the Holy See obtained means to fund beautiful art. Saint Peter's, for example, was built largely on indulgences.

It is strange that this monumental building, the symbol of the Church's claim to universal authority, was also the cause of its deepest crisis. The cathedral in Rome recalls an especially egregious business deal built on the fear of hellfire. Albert of Brandenburg (1490–1545), only recently selected as archbishop of Mainz, was in need of money. In order to retain the other bishoprics he already possessed, which was against canon law, he had to pay high fees to the Holy See; money made many forbidden things possible. Pope Leo X helped get the project funded by supplying indulgences for Albert's bishoprics. The interim financing was provided by the Fuggers. Half of the revenues went to service the debts

Albert incurred in order to pay off Rome. The other half went into the walls of Saint Peter's. Preachers, accompanied by Fugger agents, fanned out to try to convince people to buy indulgences. It was this commercialization of the relationship between individuals and God that caused Luther to raise his voice. He had long regarded the sale of salvation with a critical eye. What finally drove him to pick up his pen was the indulgence business that sanctioned Albert to be the bishop of several sees at once.

After much inner struggle, Luther had developed convictions steeped in mystical piety and the bleak thought of Augustine. Ockham was also one of the inspirations for his theology, as was the fear of sudden death.[4] When Christ said, "Repent!"—thus the first thesis states—he meant that all of life should be repentance. Luther thus pointed another way to salvation, an alternative to the mechanical recitation of a few Our Fathers or the purchase of a piece of paper. The idea was to look inside oneself and feel contrition, i.e., to do mental, emotional, and spiritual work. Holy Writ alone, *sola scriptura*, sufficed to arrive at faith. And faith alone, *sola fides*—and therefore not reasoning about, say, Aristotle's *Ethics*—was the root of all good. Alone through God's grace, *sola gratia*, finally, could one become free of sin. Faith in grace abided in a depraved, chaotic world. This left no room for good works and certainly none for indulgences. The disputation Luther had announced was never held, for reasons unknown. But his theses spread far and wide. Soon printed, reprinted, and reprinted again, they found a passionate audience.

Rome was less enthusiastic. A trial for heresy was initiated—by Dominicans who hoped thereby to damage their Augustinian competitors. At stake was essentially the scope of the pope's authority. His jurisdiction extended all the way to purgatory itself, one of the theologians entrusted with reviewing Luther's theses boldly claimed.[5] Nothing came of the trial, however, thanks to Luther's territorial prince Frederick III the Wise (r. 1486–1525). He was the lord of the Electorate of Saxony, which after the hereditary division of Saxony was ruled by the "Ernestine" line of his house. The Duchy of Saxony, with its capital in Dresden, was ruled by the "Albertines."

Elector Frederick was a very pious man. He possessed an exquisite collection of relics.[6] Among its highlights were pieces of the tablecloth used at the Last Supper, including leftover breadcrumbs. He saved himself over 100,000 years in purgatory with this holy treasury. It may have been this deep religiosity, which exceeded the already high standards of the time, that caused Frederick to take the reservations of his young theology professor seriously. After all, the questions at stake affected his own salvation.

Another factor aided the survival of the reform discourse: the impending election of a new Holy Roman Emperor. The elector of Saxony's vote was being courted. Neither Leo X, who favored the French king, nor Charles of Habsburg wanted to alienate Frederick. Thus, Luther was permitted to continue publishing his ideas. In disputations and other writings, the theology behind his criticism of indulgences gained clearer and clearer outlines. Luther had to explain himself to a papal legate on the margins of an Imperial Diet at Augsburg; the latter could not bring him to recant. A disputation at the University of Heidelberg won him many adherents among the masters and students of the arts faculty. A few of them appeared later as Reformers of imperial cities in southern Germany.

Between late June and mid-July of 1519, Luther and the Roman Catholic Church exchanged blows at Pleissenburg Castle in Leipzig. The Church was represented by Dr. Johannes Eck, professor of theology at the University of Ingolstadt and an intellectual—and physical—heavyweight. His booming voice reinforced the thrust of his arguments. Not unknown as an opponent of the Church's prohibition on usury, he attained fame as one of the most astute German theologians. Finally, he became notorious as an agitator against the Jews and one of the initiators of the fateful legend of a worldwide Jewish conspiracy.[7] Eck proved himself a match for the young Luther. He succeeded in eliciting dangerous statements from him, such as the assertion that scripture offered no proof of purgatory's existence or that the pope's authority rested solely on the consent of the faithful and did not flow from divine right. Eck ultimately got his adversary to assert that even ecumenical councils could err. As an example, Luther cited the Council of Constance and its condemnation of some of Huss's beliefs, which, he claimed, were perfectly in line with the Gospels. And with that, Eck had his opponent cornered, affiliated with a heretic. From then on, Luther could not shake the stink of heresy. The Albertine Duke George was present for the debate. As a result, he became a determined foe of the Wittenberg faction, even though he was actually a proponent of Church reform.

The outcome of the debate in Leipzig marked a further step in the direction of Luther's break with the Roman Catholic Church. The universities of Leuven and Cologne condemned his opinions. From Liège to Mainz, his writings were burned. The conflict escalated. Driven and elated by the impact of his words, Luther wrote treatise upon treatise, most of them in German and thus for the common people. Like the Hussites, he demanded that the laity receive bread and wine at Communion. In three texts, all dating to 1520, he waged a frontal assault on the old Church: *An Address to the Christian Nobility of the German Nation, On the Babylonian Captivity of the Church*, and *On the Freedom of a Christian*. They outlined a program for the reformation of religious life and the reorganization of state and society. The treatises could not be printed fast enough. A readership formed that went far beyond intellectual circles.

If the goal of the theses of 1517 was to renew and thereby to save the Church, the *Address to the Christian Nobility* burned all bridges with it. Luther dealt harshly with the "Roman See of avarice and robbery," denouncing the massive sums of money Rome sucked out of German lands.[8] He sought to reduce the pope to a mere theologian and break his monopoly on the interpretation of Holy Writ. Two further walls had to fall: the pope's right to call ecumenical councils and, first and foremost, the supremacy of spiritual over secular power. Luther wanted Rome to lose all of its influence over worldly things. He branded acts of deference like kissing the pope's feet as signs of "devilish pride." He attacked pilgrimages and the cult of the saints—"I would rather the dear saints were left in peace"—criticized the excess of mendicant churches, and demanded the abolition of excommunication and indeed of all canon law. On the ruins of the ecclesiastical hierarchy, he wanted to build a common priest-hood. He claimed that all the baptized were priests. As a result, there was no longer any need for the clergy; the community of the faithful would replace the institution of the Church. Luther had heaps of suggestions for reforming education and ethically overhauling society. He argued against usury, prostitu-tion, and even holidays, which, in his view, only invited people to engage in all manner of sin. Furthermore, he demanded the abolition of clerical celibacy. He himself got married soon thereafter to Katharina von Bora, a nun who had escaped from her Cistercian convent.

On the Babylonian Captivity of the Church views matrimony not as a sacra-ment but rather as a mere secular institution.[9] The tract only recognizes the sacramental character of baptism, the Eucharist, and penance. As Luther ar-gues, they are the only "sacramental signs" (*signa sacramentalia*) that have a basis in the text of the New Testament, and faith alone turns the bread and wine into the body and blood of Christ. This view robbed priests of their shamanic status and magical power. What is more, Luther dubbed Holy Orders, confir-mation, and extreme unction as deceptions of Rome, required to lend credibil-ity to the fable that the clergy was necessary for salvation.[10] Finally, he claimed that denying the blood of Christ to the laity was godless and tyrannical.

The third treatise, *On the Freedom of a Christian*, is addressed directly to Leo X. Despite his previous attacks, Luther still calls him "most blessed father."

For his part, the pope had taken Eck's advice and issued a bull threatening Luther with excommunication should he fail to recant his heretical teachings within sixty days. It was, of course, illusory—or a mere rhetorical ploy—to try to convince the pope, whom Luther called "a lamb in the midst of wolves," to undertake fundamental Church reform, much less to abolish the Curia. Christians were free in their hearts through their faith, Luther admonished him. Only on the outside are people bound to their fellows out of Christian charity. In this way, individuals can act like Christ towards others even if, in the order of things, they are servants and subject to his authority.[11]

The stormy year of 1520 came to its furious end with an unforgettable performance put on by Luther outside Wittenberg's Elster Gate at the town's *Schindanger*, the place where animal cadavers were disposed of to maintain purity inside the city walls. His colleague and comrade-in-arms, the Greek scholar Philipp Melanchthon (1497–1560), had publicly announced that the ceremony would take place on December 10. Students and some professors were therefore witnesses to what took place: a book burning. The texts consumed by the flames included the corpus of canon law, writings by Eck, and the *Summa* of the Franciscan theologian Angelo Carletti, a guide to ethics and theology containing 659 articles. Luther would have liked to add works by Thomas Aquinas and Duns Scotus. Yet the librarian, who felt sorry for the precious folios, refused to produce them. As the fire climbed higher, Luther threw the papal bull on it.

Not even one month after this spectacular event, Pope Leo excommunicated "Martinus" along with his followers and protectors. It was no longer possible to simply burn the quarrelsome monk now that his orations and writings had found such a broad audience. Plus, he was still being protected by the elector of Saxony. Luther was thus invited to an Imperial Diet in Worms. Only thanks to extraordinary courage, faith in God, and the absolute certainty of his righteousness did he heed the call.

On April 18, 1521, Luther stood before the Holy Roman Emperor and the Estates, a mere monk and professor from the provinces. He explained that he would not recant unless forced to do so by Holy Writ. The scene has left a deep imprint on Germany's national consciousness. His famous final words were supposedly, "Here I stand, I can do no other. God help me. Amen." They are not authentic, but they are in line with the short speech that Luther made to the assembly.[12] No less famous is the answer given by Charles V the following day, a statement written in his own hand that was read out to the Imperial Diet. A single monk, it said, opposed to the entirety of more than one thousand years of Christianity had to be in error. He, Charles, would pledge his realms, friends, body and blood, life and soul to defend the Christian faith.

No other reaction could have been expected from a ruler infused with the culture of Reconquista Spain. A few weeks later, he issued the Edict of Worms, making Luther an outlaw. In response, Elector Frederick staged an abduction of Luther and had him taken for safekeeping to Wartburg Castle outside Eisenach. There he found the time to begin his translation of the Bible, based on the Vulgate. In 1534 it appeared in its entirety in print. A work of powerful verbal imagination, from then on it was a handbook for Protestants and much more successful than previous versions. God's word was to be made available to everyone. "I was born for my Germans," Luther once wrote, "and I serve them."[13] Meanwhile, a storm was breaking beyond the walls of the castle in Thuringia. "All of Germany is in an uproar," a papal nuncio wrote to Rome.[14] The people had a new saint. Various engravings depict him surrounded by an aura, with the dove of the Holy Spirit over his head (Fig. 47, p. 583).

A German Realm of Possibility

Luther's speeches and writings met with a society that had come unhinged.[15] Chronicles recorded a rapid increase in peasant revolts and urban unrest. Their spokesmen opposed burdensome taxation and demanded the redress of economic grievances. Considering the incredible importance religion had in German society, it is no surprise that the Church was attacked. Yet people wanted only purification, not revolution. Most critics of religious affairs were also the fieriest supporters of a lost apostolic Church.[16]

An anonymous writer at the time of the Council of Basel had even proclaimed the restoration of the apostolic Church. To give his arguments greater force, he claimed for them the imprimatur of Emperor Sigismund.[17] His tract, the so-called *Reformatio Sigismundi*, puts social and ecclesiastical abuses in the context of economic hardship—conditions that would facilitate the Reformation's success. The author bemoans violations of the law and seeks especially to put a stop to rampant vigilante justice. Noting that Christ ultimately died for everyone, he anticipates social reforms like the abolition of serfdom. He demands protection for the common man from the excesses of the money economy, from monopolies, middlemen, customs duties, and usury. The tone is gruff. "Religious law is sick; the Empire and every part of it is in the wrong. Its power can only be broken by force, and it must be broken. When the great sleep, the small must wake." The "small" are the "holy" imperial cities, not the people in general. The main problem is the clergy, its power, and its property. "The priesthood is responsible for the damage." The author thus calls for the separation of church and state. "Spiritual and temporal life must everywhere be divorced from one another, as clearly as they were in the beginning and as was demanded by our ancestors and as today's law prescribes."[18] No fewer than seventeen manuscripts and eight printed editions of this work are extant—a sign that the views it promoted resonated profoundly with readers.

The society that brought forth the Reformation asked questions and harbored doubts. One Holy Roman Emperor, Maximilian I, could serve as a prime example of this attitude. He had several common-sense questions about religion, and he turned for answers not to a theologian but rather to Johannes Trithemius (1462–1516), abbot of Sponheim and an expert in magic. Why did God want to be believed in by people and not recognized by the angels? Why did Holy Writ speak in riddles? Did God see to human needs, and was he omniscient?[19] An excellent source of certainty was available in the realism of the new art. One example is Matthias Grünewald's 1515 *Isenheim Altarpiece* in Colmar. The brutalized, crucified figure is obviously dead, just as the radiant risen Christ unquestionably transcends all earthly mortality.

We have already seen just how deep the yearning for salvation was in pre-Reformation Europe, in our exploration of the millefleur tapestry of piety—that alien yet fascinating world of pilgrimages, sermons, belief in miracles, mysticism, and the cult of relics that the sources reveal to us. Information about how to lead the "right" kind of life could be found in writings like *The Imitation of Christ* or in the preaching of charismatic individuals like Saint Bernardino. From Rome, at least, no answers could be expected. That was where popes celebrated the wild weddings of their bastards, and cardinals constructed palaces. It was the home of all that had little to do with Christ-like existence or apostolic poverty. Many monasteries administered by lay trustees were under the control of noblemen who had themselves tonsured not out of piety but in order to enjoy a carefree life. Some monks were forced into a monastery as children. It was not rare for parish priests to be more expert in the anatomy of their concubines than in the reading of the Bible, considering that they knew no Latin.

The sources might be exaggerating. Everyday life is less often recorded in them than scandal. Nevertheless, there can be no doubt that rampant anticlericalism was one of the sparks that lit the Reformation. Diatribes against lusty monks and stinking cowls,[20] criticism of the avaricious Church and simoniac popes had been known for centuries. The ridicule of monks resounded from

Dante's Florence to Chaucer's London.[21] For example, one of the early humanists in Paris, Nicholas de Clémanges, wrote a work denouncing the Curia's craving for worldly things.[22] At the top of the Church hierarchy, Cardinal Nicholas Cusanus remarked to Pius II,

> If you can bear to hear the truth, I like nothing which goes on in this Curia. Everything is corrupt. No one does his duty. Neither you nor the cardinals have any care for the Church. . . . All are bent on ambition and avarice. If I ever speak in a consistory about reform, I am laughed at.[23]

Perhaps Rome underestimated the "Luther problem" precisely because it had been accustomed to similar attacks for centuries. Yet it should have taken notice. Denunciations flowed from more than the pens of poets. Calls for reform of the "head and limbs" of the Church were to be heard at the Council of Vienne in 1311.[24] A little later, Ockham had chastised John XXII as a heretical pope. Wyclif, finally, held positions that made him look like a Lutheran *avant la lettre*. He argued that Christ himself, and not the pope, was the rock on which the Church was built, that human fate was subject to predestination, that scripture was the highest authority, and that nearly everything depended on God's grace. On the other hand—and this is a major difference—he did admit the efficacy of good works.[25]

When attempts to renew the Church from the top down failed, the river of *gravamina nationis germanicae*, the complaints of the German nation, began to swell. They found a forum at ecclesiastical synods, meetings of the Estates, and Imperial Diets. The attacks focused on the accumulation of benefices, the selling of indulgences, and the money drain they entailed. By rejecting money-grubbing Rome, Germany discovered part of its identity. *Viva libertas!* With these words Ulrich von Hutten began a letter to Luther; the "freedom" he referred to was freedom from Rome.[26] The Reformer's brilliantly formulated attacks expressed what many people already thought. His teachings fell on extremely fertile ground. The Empire had been the main stage for the Investiture Controversy; that is where townspeople and princes fought with their bishops for power. Nowhere else was the clergy as deeply entrenched in secular politics—and accordingly as in conflict with it—as in Germany. Some bishops and even abbots, most of whom came from powerful noble families, ruled small states; the long prehistory of this oddity has already been traced (pp. 165f.). In some areas, the Church owned more than half the land. In cities, too, clashes between burghers and clergy were common. They fought over taxation, the appointment of preachers, and whether town councils could set up schools. Against this background, anticlericalism became almost axiomatic. Other countries also had to give the clergy its due, and yet the stormy atmosphere that darkened Germany was absent there. In Spain, where the Church had been reformed from the "top down," a man like Luther would have had no chance. In the Revolt of the Comuneros, for example, criticism of the Church played no role. Only the abolition of the Inquisition was sporadically called for.[27]

Just how explosive the mood was in the pre-Reformation Empire can be illustrated by a spectacular conflict that came to a head in 1511.[28] Johannes Pfefferkorn, a baptized Jew who was now a full-blooded Christian and Dominican friar, advocated the burning of Jewish books. He was opposed by Johannes Reuchlin (1455–1522), a jurist and humanist who had written a Hebrew grammar. How could one engage in Christian theology, he asked, without knowing the language of the Old Testament? Like Salutati and others before him, he was convinced that primeval wisdom lay hidden in the Talmud and Kabbalah. He saw Hebrew texts as witnesses to the one God venerated by Christians and Jews alike. Like Pico, he believed no realm of knowledge vouched for the divinity of Christ more than magic and Kabbalah.[29] The affair became dangerous when the Cologne Inquisition initiated heresy proceedings against Reuchlin. His cause, however, found the support of a German humanist elite. They chose the keenest weapon available for battling fanaticism: humor. In 1515, they published fictional letters written in barbaric Latin and purporting to be written by Pfefferkorn, the inquisitor, and various professors in Cologne.[30] These "obscure men" (viri obscuri) were caricatured as lazy, boastful, and lustful, as gluttons and boozers who got bogged down in absurd theological debates. The controversy ultimately got lost in the din of the Reformation. Yet it had shown how quickly an intellectual public could be mobilized against monks, university theology, and "Rome."

Decisive for Luther's success was the availability of the printing press, which could transform an intellectual debate into a popular movement. The number of pamphlets published between 1520 and 1526 rose into the millions.[31] Thus Luther's message found its first audience in the turbulent world of German towns and cities, with their literate middle classes and humanist scholars skilled in critical debate. From the very beginning, supporters and opponents of the Reformation fought with gloves off. For example, an anonymous "Karsthans"—the pen name means something like "rube" or "country bumpkin"—cast a simple peasant as a clever, Bible-savvy disputant against Thomas Murner (1475–1537), a Franciscan friar and an enemy of the Reformation. The latter, a humanist by training and a gifted polemicist, countered in 1522 with his satire *On the Great Lutheran Fool* (*Von dem großen lutherischen Narren*). It betrays an awareness of the social forces that had unleashed Luther's rebellion. The Lutherans flouted all human laws and conventions, Murner wrote under the heading "Banner of Freedom" (*Banner der Freiheit*). They recognized no master but God and hoped the Lord would permit them to do whatever they wanted.

> If the ox threw off his yoke
> And the horse his collar broke
> And the yeoman left his plow
> Who would the land be farmed by now?[32]

Shadows of the Apocalypse: Peasant Revolution

Luther had supporters in the cities as well as in noble circles, especially among the imperial knights—a class that felt like it was being crushed between the economically prosperous burghers and the territorial princes, who no longer based their power on knights but on mercenaries, artillery, and jurists. Most knights adjusted to the times. Only their tournaments retained the splendor of an earlier era. One of those who bucked the trend was Franz von Sickingen (1481–1523), a knight with lands in the Middle Rhine region who was a successful mercenary captain for various lords. His fellow knight Ulrich von Hutten, an early supporter of Luther and a poet and polemicist, had converted him to the new doctrine. Sickingen provided asylum to persecuted Reformers. In one of his castles, he had sermons given in German and wine served to the laity at the Eucharist. A joy in feuding, desire for booty, and the project of conquering his own principality were infused with the nobler goal of liberating the "fatherland" from Rome's tyranny. He overestimated his strength, however, when he attacked the Electorate of Trier. An army of allied princes defeated the knights and breached the walls of Sickingen's refugee castle. Sickingen lost his life in the effort, and the Reformation lost any chance of infiltrating Trier. Another battle was won for the early modern state.

This episode shows that the explosive nature of Luther's teachings was a danger to more than just the pope and his priests. Another example is provided by the hotspot of Wittenberg. During Luther's absence, supporters of a more thorough purification of Church and society had gotten the upper hand. The dean of the theological faculty, Andreas Bodenstein von Karlstadt (1486–1541), a friend of Luther, had taken the side of the radicals. He spoke out against clerical celibacy and followed his words with action, getting married himself. Priests were exposed to attack. Monks left their monasteries. Pictures and statues were piled up and burned. After all, a revolution is only completely successful when it triumphs over old rites and fetishes.[33] By purifying the churches in this way, Karlstadt and his ilk were ultimately concerned with salvation. In their view, the Lord wanted to be venerated in the "right" way. Praying to pictures and statues was nothing but idolatry, the devil's pleasure. Furthermore, they argued, art was a hindrance to pious contemplation.

Meanwhile, at the Wartburg, Luther observed with growing consternation the havoc being wrought by the spirits he had unleashed. He immediately grasped that his project would be threatened if it were co-opted by radicals. First, he published a treatise warning against rioting and insurrection; in the spring of 1522, he then returned to Wittenberg. He managed to pacify the situation. Now as later, he insisted on caution and on consideration for the weak, not on force. The word of God would suffice to win the day—of that, he was certain. Again and again, he emphasized that obedience was owed to temporal authorities. Karlstadt, now excommunicated like Luther, fled Wittenberg and then Saxony. He had a hard life of wandering ahead of him, although in his later years he did enjoy a quiet professorial existence in Basel. He was not a "leftist."[34] Nor were the "Zwickau Prophets," three lay preachers who had been driven out of their home city and sought refuge in Wittenberg. Under the influence of the preacher and theologian Thomas Müntzer (ca. 1490–1525), they had developed a mystical religiosity that dispensed with priests and scriptural exegetes. They also rejected child baptism.[35] Luther viewed them as the spawn of the devil, who was using them to destroy the incipient work of the Reformation. With corresponding decisiveness, he rejected the teachings of the "false brothers" and saw to it that they were expelled from his city.

Another variant of the Reformation took shape at the same time in Zurich. The city's *Leutpriester* (literally "people's priest") Ulrich Zwingli (1484–1531), a man steeped in humanism and Scotist Scholasticism, praised Luther as a "second Elijah."[36] The break with Roman tradition came in 1522 at the beginning of Lent, when Zwingli attended a sausage dinner, thus giving it his approval and condoning the eating of meat during the traditional period of fasting. This act was meant as a symbol of Christian freedom.[37] In two disputations, Zwingli convinced the Zurich town council to adopt his project: church reform, the confiscation of ecclesiastical property, and the abolition of the Eucharist, sacred images, and clerical celibacy. Councilmen and parish priests sat as judges on a marriage court, whose bailiwick soon expanded to include monitoring the manners and morals of all. A rising tide of edicts was issued against fornication, excessive gambling, games of chance, dancing, and other offenses. Similar trends soon tormented the citizens of many cities that took up Luther's cause. The Reformation provided means for making the holy community of burghers[38] even holier, and thus for securing God's blessing and avoiding punishments like plagues and starvation.

The primacy of the text of the Bible championed by Zwingli and Luther in no way led to a new certainty in matters of faith. It removed the words from their ties to tradition, the decisions of ecumenical councils, and papal decrees. Nevertheless, as Luther concluded from the thirteenth chapter of Paul's letter to the Romans, secular authorities had to be obeyed.[39] Their kingdom and the kingdom of God were separate entities, as Augustine had argued. Luther only permitted resistance to secular government within narrow bounds. Yet the leeway that the Reformer allowed to conscience demands closer scrutiny. How can his position be reconciled with the fact that he defied the emperor, the Empire, and the pope? The answer is that Luther believed the Last Judgment to be at hand.[40] In his *Address to the Christian Nobility of the German Nation*, he had unmasked the pope as an apocalyptic Antichrist—a view that was soon spread far and wide by Protestant polemics. The "common enemy and destroyer of Christendom" acted as if he were the successor of the apostles. Sadly, "the rule of the apostles and of the pope have as much in common as Christ has with Lucifer, heaven with hell."[41] If the Roman high priest had indeed been unmasked as the final nemesis of Christ, then the gates to eternity would have to be wide open. Then one could fight without fear of death. As for whether war against the Antichrist was permitted even though all secular authority deserved obedience—no justification was necessary for that.

Luther was not the only one who thought the world was coming to an end. The apocalypse was also proclaimed by Thomas Müntzer, who had been disgraced by the "Zwickau Prophets" affair and consigned to a life of wandering that took him all the way to Prague. He ultimately seemed to find a quiet existence in the small Thuringian town of Allstedt. Originally an adherent of Luther, he applied the Reformed spirit to the mass. He introduced German into the liturgy and had the congregation sing German hymns he himself had written.[42] His piety was deeply rooted in the same mystical thought he had infused into the "Zwickau Prophets." Like Luther, he hoped to recruit political authorities for his purification project; meanwhile, Luther agitated furiously against the apostate. One of Müntzer's sermons, preached before Duke John of Saxony and his son on July 13, 1524 at Allstedt Castle, revolved around an interpretation of the Book of Daniel. Like Joachim of Fiore before him, Müntzer believed the last of the world empires prophesied by Daniel was embodied by the crumbling Holy Roman Empire of his own day. He called on the princes to protect the persecuted elect, to destroy the godless—they had no right to live!—and to return the Church to its origins.[43] If they did not act, he warned, the sword would be taken from them.

That was a very thinly veiled threat indeed. When Müntzer united with a band of like-minded fanatics intent on inaugurating God's kingdom on Earth, the authorities intervened. Once again, he was forced to flee. In pamphlets, he badmouthed Luther as "Dr. Liar," "living high on the hog in Wittenberg." He publicly attacked the princes, the "seedbed of usury, robbery, and thievery" who wanted everything for themselves: "the fish in the water, the birds in the sky, the produce of the earth."[44] This clearly went beyond a reform of religious affairs. As Thomas Murner had predicted, the fundamental order of society was being challenged.

The German "Peasants' War" marked the high tide of revolutions that had been sweeping the region between southern Germany and Hungary.[45] The "structural" causes of this, the most significant assertion of horizontal power in European history, were mounting tax burdens and everyday suffering that worsened as the screws of the Malthusian crisis tightened. Resistance was also spawned by a growing preponderance of written laws that were incomprehensible to the unlettered. The Reformation added another, novel element: by emphasizing the message of freedom contained in the Gospels, it nourished the notion of a divine right that superseded all human law and tradition. An ominous alignment of the stars foreboded terrible events for the year 1524, a "great flood" of anger, calamity, and bloodshed—all thanks to *luterey* ("Lutherism"), as the abbess of one Nuremberg convent wrote.[46]

It was clear from the very beginning that the Reformation was adding fuel to the fire. Right when the first unrest broke out, in 1523 and 1524, loud calls were heard for the unadulterated word of God to be preached. In January 1525, isolated uprisings in southwestern Germany coalesced into a broad movement that ultimately involved thousands upon thousands of people. The "Twelve Articles" formulated in March in the imperial city of Memmingen summarized its demands.[47] At the top of the list were the free election of preachers by the entire congregation, the preaching of the pure Gospel "without human additions," and the abolition of serfdom—after all, Jesus Christ had redeemed everyone, great and small. Yet the Articles in no way called for a total reordering of society. "Not that we want to be entirely free, with no authorities over us," their authors emphasized, as if seeking to counter Murner's admonition. Rather, they continued, they were concerned only with justice and fairness, with the redress of grievances. They desired the abolition of illegally instituted taxes and forced labor, as well as the right to once again use forests and commons that had been usurped by lords against ancient custom. They also demanded the right to hunt and fish freely, as well as legal proceedings that were not decided by favor or caprice. The justness of their demands was to be decided—and now we hear the echo of Luther—by the text of Holy Writ alone.

From then on, the Twelve Articles pointed the way for the rebellion. At stake were the honor of God, the right of God, and the Word of God. These were the slogans that provided revolt with legitimacy. People no longer opposed individual territorial lords. Entire towns and regions rose up. In no time at all, the revolution seized an area stretching from Upper Swabia and Alsace to Tyrol and Salzburg. It enveloped Franconia and the Palatinate, penetrating thence into central Germany, Luther's domain. In April 1525, Thuringia was in turmoil. Müntzer, who had taken refuge in the south of the Empire, hurried back to his homeland and preached war: "Strike, strike while the iron is hot. . . . Strike, strike while the light lasts! God is leading you. Follow him! Follow him!"[48] Monasteries were stormed, fortresses breached. Some regions, however, such as Bavaria, northern Germany, and almost the entire east, remained peaceful.

The revolts were prosecuted not only by peasants and miners but also by some preachers like Müntzer. Cities followed their banners only when pressured by irrepressible waves of peasants. One imperial prince, Ulrich of Württemberg, made common cause with the peasants, but he had his own special reason for doing so. After attempting to take the imperial city of Reutlingen by force, he had been expelled from his duchy in 1519 by an army of the Swabian League. The peasants seemed to him useful reinforcements for the Swiss mercenaries he had employed to win back Württemberg, now in Habsburg hands.

In most regions, the revolution only lasted a few months. Although strong in number, the peasant armies were tactically inexperienced and poorly armed. Furthermore, they were often internally divided. By late summer, the troops of the Swabian League and the princes had stamped out most of the flashpoints and butchered the rebels. Ulrich of Württemberg's adventure had failed quickly in March. The Peasants' War in central Germany ended on May 15, 1525 at the Battle of Frankenhausen. The threat of the masses had united the pro-Lutheran Philip of Hesse and the anti-Lutheran George of Saxony. Their army made short work of the peasant forces. Müntzer was captured, brutally tortured, and beheaded. Did he really harbor the Communistic, apostolic Christian sentiment that "all things should be held in common," or were these words forced from his mouth by torture? We do not know.[49] What is certain is that he was known to be someone who "stood with the common man and not with the great lords." His thought does not belong to the prehistory of Communism but rather was derived from mysticism and millenarianism.[50]

Initially, Luther urged both sides to peace. When Thuringia erupted in rebellion, however, he distanced himself from Müntzer, calling him a "lying devil" and a "devourer of the world." Now he wrote against the "predacious and murderous mob of peasants," calling for the rebels to be stabbed, beaten, and strangled to death.[51] He knew that his Reformation could only survive in concord with the world and with Saxon support. Müntzer's teachings lived on in secret, above all in Anabaptist circles. After the prelude in Zwickau, the movement began in earnest in 1524 in Zwingli's Zurich. Citing the authority of scripture, the "Anabaptists"—as they were called by their enemies—rejected child baptism. In their view, the profession of faith in Christ should be a free and conscious choice. They were soon connected with Karlstadt, who had already opposed baptizing infants in Wittenberg. Despite being peaceful, the Anabaptists were mercilessly persecuted. The first executions took place.

The Peasants' War remains the souvenir of a slim possibility of how German history could have gone. For a brief moment, incredible prospects had opened up. When the revolution was just about finished militarily, a peasant parliament met in Heilbronn to draft a new imperial constitution. The main points were supplied by Wendel Hipler, who had gained political experience as chancellor to a south German count, and Friedrich Weygandt, a public official in Mainz. In the view of these two men, not only scholars and burghers but also peasants, along with the emperor, the imperial princes, and the nobility, should be involved in reorganizing the Empire. These plans remained a pie in the sky. So did those of the Tyrolean peasant leader Michael Gaismair. The new world order he envisioned included equality before the law and the abolition of the Church's secular power. Gaismair's hope of founding a republic of peasants and miners was forward-looking indeed.[52] In 1526, the Swabian League put an end to his democratic reveries. Pursued for many years by bounty hunters eager to win the price on his head, Gaismair was ultimately stabbed to death in Padua.

The Peasants' War is thought to have resulted in about seventy thousand casualties. The victors imposed fines on rebellious villages and had ringleaders mutilated or blinded.[53] Yet the peasants did not shed their blood entirely in vain. In some places, unjust taxes were repealed and serfdom abolished. A few peasant federations were recognized as legitimate political entities. Meanwhile, the experience of the war remained engraved deeply in the collective consciousness. At times, it was only the prospect of another uprising of the common man that kept the state and territorial lords in check. In fact, the series of uprisings did not end in the following centuries, either in Germany or elsewhere in Europe. And Luther's Reformation took root far and wide without opposition. This was in part due to international political developments. Charles V's wars, victories, and defeats had repercussions for the struggles for purity and reform in Germany.

Roman Graffiti and the Nightingale's Song

Near Calais, at the Field of the Cloth of Gold, June 1520. At about the same time as Luther was correcting the page proofs for his sermon on "Good Works" in Wittenberg, and as the bull of excommunication against him was being issued on the other side of the Alps, a glittering display was put on between Ardres and Guines near the port of Calais. An outdoor meeting was held between the young kings of France and England, Francis I (r. 1515–1547) and Henry VIII (r. 1509–1547). A Renaissance palace constructed of timbers and painted canvas provided the stage; out front, wine flowed from ornamental fountains. A whole city of tents—those belonging to nobles were made of silk—accommodated 10,000 guests. Meetings between the monarchs took place from June 7 to 24, all choreographed down to the last detail and ornamented by a program of tournaments, banquets, masked balls, and masses.

Those days in June showcased the level of refined civility the old warrior states of Europe were now capable of. It would have taken nothing at all for the cavalry on hand—one chronicler counted over three thousand horses on the English side alone—to wipe out a few peasant armies. But war remained at the level of play, in the form of tournaments. Unobserved, ignoring ceremonial, Francis stole into the bed chamber of his English counterpart. Yet he did not kill him. It was a demonstration of power, of clemency, of noblesse. We are in the age of the *Cortegiano*—not in Moscow or Sarai, and certainly a far cry from the huts of chieftains in "the state of nature" who were wont to assassinate each other by their own hand. Perhaps people were momentarily entranced by the illusion that an Anglo-French alliance could lead to universal peace.[54] At the same time, the pageant witnessed a subtle showdown fought with the weapons of beauty. The participants competed for prestige, the most important resource of kings at all times and in all places. Those present did not simply see two handsome young rulers but rather the glory of their crowns, which symbolized immortal states: that of the Tudor monarchy, which had risen from the ashes of the War of the Roses; and Valois France, which seemed to be resting safe and sound on its crown lands.

In the following decades, and thus also during the Reformation, both men played leading roles alongside the Holy Roman Emperor. Henry and Francis were both what Renaissance princes are popularly imagined to be: Machiavellian power brokers, patrons of the arts, and lovers of all things female. Their portraitists depicted them accordingly. Hans Holbein painted Henry with his legs apart and elbows defiant (Plate 21). Jean and François Clouet showed Francis in three-quarter profile, cloaked in shimmering silk and with a coy smile. The agreement reached by the two rulers was ultimately as ephemeral as the Potemkin palace on the Field of the Cloth of Gold. Why did the festivities not mark the beginning of a beautiful friendship? The reasons lay in the logic of power. On his own island, Henry had to watch out for the Scots. Traditional enemies of the English crown, they were also the traditional allies of the French. In addition, Britain's rulers still bore the title of the King of France, a reminder of a not-so-far-off past and a constant provocation. Initially, Henry took the side of the emperor. This made sense in light of their common commercial interests, as the cloth industry of the Habsburg Netherlands was one of the largest importers of English wool. Nevertheless, the grand plans forged by the two rulers did not result in any significant military collaboration.

The differences between Charles V and Francis I were deep and longstanding.[55] Gattinara claimed various imperial titles—for the Spanish crown, for the Empire, for the Habsburg family—including half of southern France, Burgundy, Milan, Genoa, and Asti. After eventful encounters, in 1525 Charles's army succeeded in conquering French forces at the Battle of Pavia and taking King Francis prisoner. The latter placed the interests of the state above his chivalric honor, breaking his word not to take up the struggle again after his release. Along with the Medici pope Clement VII, the Duke of Milan, Venice, and Florence, he formed the League of Cognac, which Henry VIII also now joined. Once again, international politics followed the usual laws: too much power on one side, in this case the Habsburgs, led to the formation of a counterweight. What had been gained by the victory at Pavia was lost. On the other hand, in 1526 the emperor married the Portuguese princess Isabella. One year later, the couple had a son: Philip, the future king of Spain and the heir to Portugal.[56]

In Italy, the war between the imperial forces and the League of Cognac remained a stalemate. The *Landsknechte* won a hollow victory, but they were not paid. Leaderless, in the spring of 1527 they marched on Rome, where rich spoils waited to be won. In early May, twenty thousand or more of them stormed through the Aurelian Wall. The Swiss Guard covered the pope's escape to Castel Sant'Angelo, fighting to the last man. The foreign mercenaries took what they found, raped women, and demanded ransoms. Like wolves, they also tore each other apart over the booty. Some of them clamored for Luther to be named pope, and someone scratched the Reformer's name into a fresco in Raphael's *Stanze*. Rome was sunk in chaos for nine months. Bodies rotted in the streets, and an epidemic abetted the soldiers in their killing. Clement escaped to Orvieto, where Signorelli's fresco depicted the end of the world. In nearby Florence, the Medici regime, now bereft of its papal protector, fell apart. Once again, the republic was given a chance.

Some saw the Sack of Rome as an apocalyptic judgment upon the capital of the Renaissance, the Babel of courtesans, sumptuous feasts, and humanistic debates devoid of all theology. One eyewitness dubbed the events a "Lutheran storm."[57] Was the end now truly at hand, as many people wondered? The Ottomans threatened from the east. The Renaissance culture that had once flourished in Hungary under Matthias Corvinus was literally crushed.

In Germany, the Habsburgs, busy waging war against the Turks and in northern Italy, were unable to stop the further advance of the Reformation. To be sure, a host of enemies quickly rose up against Luther and his cause. Yet the Reformation also won several mighty fortresses, Wittenberg and the Electorate of Saxony most important among them. At times, a popular revolt led to the decisive steps being taken; at others, the Imperial Estates seized the initiative. The attitude of monasteries was important; decisive were the decisions of rulers and the stance taken by civic communities. In general, town councils followed rather than determined the will of citizens.[58] Although the Reformation did not penetrate certain areas—such as Bavaria, Habsburg lands, and the ecclesiastical states—it won out not only in Saxony, Hesse, and other principalities but also in nearly two-thirds of the imperial cities.[59] Outside of Germany as well, it tended to triumph first among the inhabitants of towns and cities. In Poland, it conquered cities with large German populations. In Norway, a country that still had no universities or printing presses, it gained a foothold in the trading center of Bergen. Here, too, it was supported by the powerful community of German merchants.[60]

The sentiments of craftsmen in Nuremberg, which had decided early on in Luther's favor, were captured by Hans Sachs in a long poem. In it his "Wittenberg Nightingale," namely Luther, sings about the dawn of a sunny day and then heaps withering scorn on the clergy.[61] Catholic minorities survived in some places. One was Augsburg, where the Fuggers, financial backers of the anti-Reformation Habsburgs, defended the old faith along with the health of their account books. When the Prussian territory of the Teutonic Knights became a hereditary dukedom in 1525, it was the first state outside the imperial realm—its duke was a vassal of the crown of Poland (see pp. 442f.)—to pledge fealty to the Reformation.

On the opposing side, those loyal to Rome closed ranks. In 1529, an Imperial Diet in Speyer approved measures intended to check the Reformation's advance. The Lutheran princes lodged a formal protest, thus earning for themselves the name "Protestants." The Holy Roman Emperor was still a force to be reckoned with, despite his preoccupation with the Ottomans. Clement VII had made peace with him again in June 1529. Shortly thereafter, France joined them. Francis I's mother, Louise of Savoy, and Charles's aunt, Margaret of Austria, negotiated the Treaty of Cambrai, which cemented Habsburg supremacy in Italy. On February 24, 1530, the pope crowned Charles emperor in Bologna. It was the last ceremony of its kind in European history.

One of the things Clement got in return was support in the reconquest of Florence for his family. Once again, Spanish mercenaries marched into Tuscany.[62] Michelangelo was named head of the city's defenses, but it was no use. On August 12, 1530, Florence fell. Its new lord, Alessandro de' Medici, was named duke by the Medici pope—the first of the family to receive the honor. Seven years later, he was murdered; the assassin was a family member who styled himself a defender of republican freedom. Yet there was no alternative to the clan with the balls on its coat of arms. The new lord was the politically astute and militarily gifted Cosimo de' Medici (1537–1574), the scion of a cadet branch of the family. Both pope and emperor confirmed his title as duke. Feverish Florence had decided once and for all to take the medicine of vertical power. In foreign affairs, the pope won room to maneuver by promising his niece Catherine in marriage to Francis I's son, the future King Henry II. Originally a banking family, the Medici had long been accepted into the European high nobility.

Splintering of the Splinters: Wittenberg, Zurich, Münster

The siege of Florence was still underway when Emperor Charles V entered Augsburg in mid-June 1530. An Imperial Diet was announced. In addition to war with the Turks, religion once again dominated the agenda. The Protestant estates submitted a statement of their beliefs to the emperor. The so-called Augsburg Confession began by emphasizing the many commonalities between their views and Catholic dogma. The differences were described in the second part of the document. It is rather doubtful, however, that there was any real hope of accommodation. The economic and political gains to be made by a zealous Reformation program—or, on the other side, by alliance with the emperor, who perforce had to show his gratitude—were too significant.

The prospect of reconciliation was also frustrated by the fact that Luther's movement was fraying at the edges. Irreconcilable doctrinal differences had arisen between Wittenberg and Zurich. The disagreement was rooted in conflicting interpretations of the Eucharist. Lutherans believed that the bread and the wine really were, as Christ had said, his body and blood. Zwingli, on the other hand, who, as a connoisseur of Plato's philosophy, was indifferent to the material aspect, understood Communion as a merely symbolic expression of faith.[63] The two groups were only united in their rejection of the Catholic notion that the host transformed magically, so to speak, into a different substance. A religious colloquy in Marburg, which Luther and Zwingli both attended, was inconclusive. As a result, the Diet of Augsburg was presented not only with the "Confession" of the Lutherans but also a personal confession from Zwingli as well as confessions of faith from the imperial cities of Lindau, Constance, Memmingen, and Strasburg. The emperor and the majority of the Diet reaffirmed the hard line of the Edict of Worms, rejecting the confessions as heretical. Now, the Protestants were under threat of imperial ban. There was vague hope, including on the part of the emperor, that a church council might reestablish concord. Yet now as later, it was obvious that religions were too concerned with the absolute and the eternal to master the art of compromise in questions of dogma. Indeed, the controversy over the Eucharist was wrapped up in a problem that stretched back more than a thousand years: the question of the nature of God.[64] To preserve what they considered to be true, the theologians even sacrificed the unity of the Reformation movement.

In Bavaria, around Salzburg, and in the Netherlands, the Reformation had by now found its first martyrs. The first religious war took place in the Swiss

Confederacy.[65] It pitted Zwingli's Zurich against central Switzerland, which remained loyal to Rome. An initial armed engagement in 1529 barely managed to be defused before hostilities began. A second ended in a defeat for Zurich. Zwingli was among the dead. The peace agreement reached in 1531 could have served as a model for the rest of Europe: each locale in Switzerland was allowed to choose its own confession. As contemporaries probably realized, a continuation of the war might have drawn powerful neighbors into the conflict, thus spelling the end of Swiss independence. It was not tolerance but insight into political necessities and dangers that recommended such a settlement.

In Germany, the time was not yet ripe for the Swiss path. A first step toward war was taken when the Protestant princes and cities formed the Schmalkaldic League.[66] Its political purpose was to oppose Habsburg hegemony, its religious aim to defend the reforms achieved so far. Since the emperor needed the help of the Empire against the Ottomans and wanted his brother Ferdinand to be elected as his successor, war with the Lutherans was still inconceivable. Nevertheless, one thing was clear: power politics and questions of faith were intertwining so tightly that they could not easily be unraveled.

For the concrete arrangement of religious affairs, many places followed the lead of Luther's Wittenberg. In Protestant territories, the old mass with the magic of the Eucharist, with incense, Latin formulas, and recitations, gave way to a form of Communion that continued to include prayers and hymns but that now revolved around a sermon delivered in German. In contrast to Luther's original intention, the decisive role in all religious affairs, especially in the appointment of preachers, fell to the state or to city authorities and not to the congregation. Prelates withdrew from representative assemblies. The newly established *gemeine Kästen*, iron-bound "community chests," filled up with revenues from confiscated ecclesiastical property. The money was supposed to pay the salaries of preachers, fund the activities of the congregation, and also support the poor—at least in theory. Often it ended up padding the finances of the authorities.

The Reformation infiltrated schools and universities. It influenced family and married life. It produced cultural milieus, giving rise to Protestant iconography, hymns, and sacred architecture that corresponded with the new liturgy and the significance of the sermon. The premium placed on the written word, embodied in the German Bible and the two catechisms Luther had compiled even before the Diet of Augsburg, was a call to reading and thus a spur to the acquisition of literacy. The Reformation now joined the mutually reinforcing interplay of paper, eyeglasses, and the printing press. Literacy increased dramatically, especially in Protestant lands.

Better education for an ever-increasing number of people was yet another component of Europe's modernization, as was the religious pluralism that the Reformation spawned (to the horror of its initiator Luther). Itinerant preachers traversed Germany and Europe, spreading the ideas of the Reformation far and wide. Some, like Luther himself,[67] murmured about the end of the world and admonished repentance. Prophets appeared and proclaimed their visions. They desired an even more thorough purification than the one achieved by the alliance of states and followers of Luther or Zwingli. One especially eloquent "dreamer of the absolute"[68] was Melchior Hoffmann, a furrier from Swabia who was active in the Baltic region, in Sweden, northern Germany, and the Netherlands. Originally an adherent of Luther, he developed into a radical Anabaptist. He spoke of the coming of the kingdom of God, which, in line with the Apocalypse of John, would precede the Last Judgment. And like Müntzer, he preached a final struggle against the godless. The Lutheran town council of Strasburg had him imprisoned. Nevertheless, his ideas found numerous supporters.

They had a powerful impact on the city of Münster in western Germany.[69] In 1534, a militant group of Anabaptists managed to take control of the government there. They chose a learned tailor named Jan van Leiden as their king, who went about constructing an Old Testament utopia. He instituted the community of goods and polygamy, the idea being to increase his new Jerusalem's population, making it capable of renewing the entire world. The Anabaptist king surrounded himself with a grand retinue and exotic ceremonial. Of his sixteen wives, he is supposed to have beheaded two with his own hand for insubordination. While an army belonging to the bishop of Münster set up a siege around the city, the rule of the pious fundamentalists turned into a reign of terror. There was a moral code based on the Ten Commandments, and Jan van Leiden had violations punished with death. Churches were purged of their paintings; statues had their faces hacked off (Fig. 48, p. 606). The Anabaptist king sent out missionaries to convert the world. The journeys of almost all of them ended on the executioner's block.

In Münster, this piece of bizarre theater lasted little more than a year. In June 1535, the city was betrayed. The people shuddered to see the bodies of the rebels after they had been interrogated and tortured, put in iron cages, and left to rot. Even today, the cages remain hung high on a church tower, a reminder of the potential consequences of the alliance between the desire for power and

religious delusion. Anabaptism lived on as an underground movement, utterly discredited and condemned by papists and Lutherans alike. Meanwhile, Melchior Hoffmann starved in his Strasburg prison until his death in 1543.

The troops that put an end to the nightmare in Münster included contingents under Catholic and Lutheran command. Just like during the Peasants' War, religious differences receded into the background when it came to defending the social order. Under the walls of Münster, yet another victory was won for the early modern princely state. In a similar development, Ulrich of Württemberg had managed to win back his dukedom the year before, thanks to help from Philip of Hesse and mercenaries from the Schmalkaldic League. The turning point was a victory over the occupying force of the Habsburg governor. Württemberg developed into a fortress of Lutheranism.

As in the battles of the Peasants' War a decade before, neither the emperor nor the Empire played a role in the struggle for Münster. The victor in the conflicts between faith and power was the territorial principality, which, whether it stood with Luther or against him, expanded its influence over religious affairs. While Philip's cavalry overran Württemberg and the Anabaptist Zion in Münster fell, Charles V was in distant North Africa, far from all European developments. He was with a powerful army outside Tunis, the target of Spanish ambitions since the time of Ferdinand of Aragon. In July 1535, the imperial forces breached the city walls. The victory was immortalized in bombastic propaganda: triumphal processions, pamphlets, and a costly series of tapestries by Jan Vermeyen that can still be admired in Madrid and Vienna. The Ottoman ruler of Tunis, grand admiral and former corsair Hayreddin Barbarossa, a clever strategist and soon again to be the scourge of the Christian coastal cities of the western Mediterranean, had absconded in time. An imperial assault on Algiers, Hayreddin's power base, failed miserably a few years later. Like the imperial coronation in Bologna, the campaigns in North Africa seem like the final scenes in the history of the medieval Empire. For the very last time, a Roman emperor personally led his army into battle against the "infidels."[70]

Divorce English Style: Henry VIII's Reformation

Events in Münster were less important for the history of the Reformation than developments on the edges of Christian Europe. Sweden found itself on the path toward Lutheranism ever since a diet at Västerås Castle in 1527. Denmark, where Luther's friend Johannes Bugenhagen was an apostle of the Reformation, followed suit, as did Norway along with it. As of 1537, the "supreme pontiff" of the two countries was the Danish king, who used confiscated ecclesiastical property to cement his power. The parts of Hungary that had not become Ottoman also aligned with Wittenberg.

In England, the Reformation was triggered by Henry VIII's desire to divorce his wife.[71] On the one hand, she had produced no male heir; of the children born to Henry's wife Catherine of Aragon, only the future Queen Mary survived. On the other hand, the king was infatuated with one of Catherine's court ladies, Anne Boleyn; the price she named for sex was marriage. Only the pope could dissolve the existing union. Yet negotiations went nowhere. The first victim of the affair was the once all-powerful lord chancellor, Cardinal Wolsey, whom the king blamed for the failed talks. Only a timely natural death saved him from the scaffold. On the advice of Thomas Cromwell (ca. 1485–1540), who now became his most powerful minister, Henry tried to put pressure on the pope. The risk of a break with Rome was known and acceptable to him. In 1532, the clergy was forced to sign a document stipulating that Church edicts required the king's approval to be enacted. Moreover, the House of Commons drafted a law depriving the pope of his most important source of income in England: "annates," i.e., the revenue from a benefice in the year it was awarded. The king threatened to enact the law if Rome did not give in. But Clement VII stood firm. It cost his church a kingdom. For in 1533, Henry went ahead and married Anne Boleyn anyway, who—if her growing belly was any indication— had meanwhile acceded to the king's desires.

The king's next steps were well planned. To obviate any and all objections, Cromwell formulated and Parliament passed the Act of Appeals. Following a timeless tradition of insulating English jurisprudence from foreign authorities, this law practically forbade legal appeals to the Curia. An ecclesiastical court presided over by the newly minted archbishop of Canterbury, Thomas Cranmer (1489–1556), nullified Henry's marriage to Catherine of Aragon and certified his union with Anne Boleyn. This ensured that their daughter Elizabeth, who entered the world on September 7, 1533, was born legitimate. She would eventually wear the English crown. Her ascension to the throne—ahead of her older half-sister Mary—was stipulated by the Act of Succession. This law was ultimately void, as new women and new children by them entered Henry's life, but its central tenet remained valid: namely, that involvement by the "bishop of Rome and the Holy See" was absolutely impermissible in questions of succession.

In 1534, the series of anti-Roman laws was crowned by the Act of Supremacy. Its short text made the king the head of the Church of England and accorded him the authority to decide what constituted proper doctrine. This made Henry what the Habsburg emperor Maximilian gladly would have been: pope and king in one. A subsequent law made opposition to the new measures high treason. It was his refusal to take an oath to the Act of Supremacy that led Thomas More, once lord chancellor and author of *Utopia*, to the scaffold. He was a victim of the same inexorable *raison d'état* that he himself had championed against heretics. Six of them had been burned with his sanction.

Meanwhile, Chief Minister Cromwell pressed ahead with separation from Rome. The Church's special legal status and the clergy's privileges vanished, as did pilgrimages and the veneration of relics. The overgrowth of late medieval holidays was trimmed back. Ecclesiastical taxes no longer flowed to Rome but rather to the royal treasury. A pro-Catholic revolt broke out in northern England in October 1536, aimed also at restraining the crown's growing power. Henry managed to defuse it with skillful diplomacy. As soon as the rebel army was disbanded, he had its leaders massacred. The "Pilgrimage of Grace," being largely financed by abbots, provided the occasion for continuing the dissolution of monasteries on a grand scale. Monastic life in England was soon defunct. Statues were smashed, paintings destroyed, and abbeys used as stone quarries.

Cromwell is generally considered the architect of the English Reformation. Some even see this son of a craftsman from Putney as one of the creators of the English nation, whose sovereignty was now embodied by the "king in

Parliament."[72] Trained as a jurist, Cromwell rose to fame as an administrative reformer. The inner circle of royal advisors, the Privy Council formed by his predecessor, now also contained men of middling station. The nobility retained its significance above all in the army. By elevating countless individuals to the peerage, Henry created counterweights to the old aristocracy.

The English Reformation was a revolution from above. It conquered with statutes, with the weapons of law. Never before had horizontal power played such an important historical role in Britain as it did between 1529 and 1536, when the king and Parliament worked together to fundamentally transform the state. Religious reforms proceeded relatively smoothly, as the expulsion of the papacy was welcomed by the majority in Parliament. The English Reformation never developed into a popular movement as it had in Germany, although unrest stemming from friction between townspeople and clergy seemed to erupt in English towns more often than elsewhere.[73] Factions such as Anabaptists and Lollards played no role during the English Reformation.[74] Nor did the realm simply become Lutheran. Henry remained conservative with regard to dogma and doctrine. He persecuted Lutherans and papists alike. For example, he ordered William Tyndale, who had finished his English translation of the Bible in Wittenberg, to be seized in exile, imprisoned in a castle in Brussels, and executed. Cromwell was the head of the Reformation party at court, and after his fall papal theology regained ground for a time. In 1543, the common people were even forbidden from reading the Bible.[75] The king knew how malleable Holy Writ was and how explosive the mixture of social protest and religious conviction could be. The English Peasants' Revolt had taught this lesson just as forcefully as the German Peasants' War.

Henry was educated in theology and a patron of humanists, historians, and playwrights. He also composed music. His song "Pastime with Good Company" was all the rage in London taverns in the Age of Elizabeth, and it is still known today. He won grim fame as a judicial murderer by God's grace and as a sex maniac. When Anne Boleyn in turn failed to produce the desired male offspring, he sent her to the scaffold as well. The same fate was suffered by his later love Catherine Howard. After supposedly having an affair, she had a rendezvous with the executioner. Henry divorced the German Anne of Cleves because she was too ugly for him. Apparently, upon signing the marriage contract, he had only seen a flattering portrait of her by his court painter Holbein. Cromwell, who had arranged the marriage in order to forge an alliance with Anne's powerful family on the Lower Rhine, lost his office and his head over the debacle in 1540. Before that, Henry's third wife, Jane Seymour, had borne him an heir, Edward. She died not by the blade but in childbirth. Catherine Parr, Henry's sixth and final wife, had the good fortune to outlive him; he died in 1547. This Bluebeard had tried with all his might to provide his realm with an ordered succession. The memory of the War of the Roses was still fresh. For that reason alone, a shred of rationality hangs over his behavior.

The English Reformation completed a process set in motion by strong kings in the fourteenth century: the subordination of the Church to the crown. With a determination unparalleled by other rulers of his time, Henry forged the sovereignty of his nation into an iron throne. The preamble to yet another law forbidding appeals to Rome, formulated by Cromwell, was a milestone along this path.

> Where by divers sundry old authentic histories and chronicles it is mani-festly declared and expressed that this realm of England is an empire, and so hath been accepted in the world, governed by one supreme head and king ... with plenary, whole and entire power.[76]

The destruction of Thomas Becket's shrine in Canterbury in 1538 symbolized the upheaval in the relationship between church and state. Not even the heavenly aura of a saint could restrain the national crown from dispossessing the arrogant Rome of Gregory VII and Boniface VIII, or prevent it from scuttling papal pretensions to worldly power.

In foreign policy, the antagonism between the Habsburgs and the French gave the Tudor king a choice between glorious isolation on his island and profitable partisanship abroad. When the two powers went to war again in 1542, Henry once more took the side of the Holy Roman Emperor, thus gaining himself recognition from the latter as head of the Church of England. Otherwise, an analysis of his reign remains ambiguous. The Scots were beaten at Solway Moss, but they were not utterly defeated. Wales was further integrated into the kingdom. A mixture of brutality and beneficence brought Ireland somewhat to heel. Henry now styled himself "king" of Ireland, not just its "lord." The campaign in northern France only brought him the brief possession of Boulogne, despite a massive deployment of troops and astronomical expenditures. Along with another war with Scotland, it cost over two million pounds, about ten times the yearly revenues of the crown.[77] The "Great Enterprise" of which Henry once dreamt—splitting up France and sharing it with the Holy Roman Emperor—now lay beyond the realm of possibility.

The balance of power between the crown and Parliament was far from certain at the time of Henry's death. The confessional question also seemed open. Henry's successor Edward VI (1547–1553) was a nine-year-old boy with a strict Protestant upbringing. For a few important years, the Reformers around Archbishop Cranmer now gained a free hand. Rebellions against the new order stood no chance. In the person of Mary Tudor (1553–1558), however, Rome's papists had a future Catholic queen, and Spain seemed all too ready to undertake a Crusade against the island's heretics. Peace with France was declared in 1550. Boulogne was returned to the Valois in exchange for reparations, thus also opening the way to settling affairs with the Scots.

Stunted Reformations

The arenas where struggles over dogma and Church reform played out were distantly removed from the worlds of the High and late Renaissance, which were now coming into their greatest glory. In the year Luther issued his Ninety-five Theses, Mario Equicola, a courtier of the Gonzaga, published a praise of women. In Mantua, Giulio Romano's Palazzo Te was being built, and in Rome Giuliano da Sangallo's Vatican Palace was taking shape. Titian's star was rising in Venice. In 1517, he painted his *Assumption of the Virgin*, the *Assunta*, for the high altar of the Frari. The same year, Raphael completed work on the *Stanze*, and in Florence Andrea del Sarto (1486–1530) put the finishing touches on his *Madonna of the Harpies*. The year 1521 witnessed the publication of the Milanese architect Cesare Cesariano's elaborately illustrated edition of Vitruvius. And in 1525—as peasants were being butchered in Germany— Equicola's *Book on the Nature of Love* appeared in Venice. It was not only infused with knowledge of classical authors, but it also harked back to the tender love poetry of the troubadours.

There is no doubt that secular themes became more popular in the art and literature of Italy. Yet that should not blind us to the fact, copiously documented by the number of titles alone, that religious writing dominated the market. The same was the case for art. As the analysis of one inventory of dated paintings informs us, the proportion of "secular pictures" increased from 5 to 22 percent from 1480 to 1539.[78] That means, however, that nearly 80 percent still revolved around sacred themes, albeit more beautifully, more technically adept, and more imaginatively than ever before. In Parma and its environs, Correggio (1489–1534) painted his holy scenes, airy pictures that played with light and color, along with mythologies and frescoes shining with bold fore-shortenings. In Florence, the brilliant Pontormo (1494–1557) embarked on his career. His *Deposition from the Cross* is one of the greatest paintings of the century.

Italy was, therefore, neither a pagan nor a holy land. Even Aretino, then the brightest star in Italy's literary firmament and a savvy commercial author, not only described pleasurable sexual positions but also wrote biographies of the Virgin Mary and Saint Catherine. Still, the religious renaissance engendered by the Reformation and the Catholic response to it does seem to have caused some poets to have undergone a change of heart. Ariosto, for example, added five pious cantos to the last version of his *Orlando Furioso*, which otherwise offered entertainment not intended for moral edification.

Italy's aristocracy, intellectuals, and artists were intimately linked to the Curia—by ties of marriage, benefices, or the money paid out to them by the chamberlain. They had not the least intention of turning the papal court into a pious, ascetic monastic community. Adrian VI (1522–1523), a Dutchman steeped in the *devotio moderna*, tried to suppress simony and nepotism and even issued a confession of guilt for the papacy's transgressions. He met with little applause.[79] At the Pasquino—an ancient torso set up in the center of Rome, to which people attached pieces of paper containing often caustic commentary about political developments—Romans aired their frustration with the grump from the north. Italy exhaled noticeably when God called Adrian to him after a pontificate of only one year. From then on, the reform spirit lived on in provincial synods and in the monastic orders, including a newly formed society of regular clergy, the Theatines.[80]

The heartfelt alliance between the Curia and culture can be illustrated by an example that reached almost monstrous proportions: the career of Pietro Bembo. After his years in Ferrara and Urbino, we find him in the service of the Curia and as the possessor of numerous benefices. In order to retain them under the pious Adrian, he quickly took monastic vows. Nevertheless, he maintained his relationship with a woman who, although married to another man, bore him three children. He was fertile as an author as well, producing sonnets, elegant letters, and a history of Venice that traced events from 1487 to 1513. He unabashedly mixed the pagan with the sacred, such as when he compared the Virgin Mary to a "radiant nymph."[81] Despite his not-very-holy lifestyle, he was named a cardinal in 1539. It is no surprise that an ecclesiastical prince of his stamp harbored little interest in theology and none at all for a man like Luther.

The nexus between elites and the papal court, along with the former's satura-tion with humanist ideals, were among the most important reasons that Lu-ther's ideas had such difficulty penetrating Italy. One Italian traveling through pre-Reformation Germany noticed how much attention the locals paid to the mass and the construction of churches. In contrast, he was saddened by the "scant religiosity" of his countrymen.[82] Another reason the Reformation gained no foothold in Italy was the weakness of the communes. They lacked the very power that was essential to the development and survival of Germany's Refor-mation: a public sphere driven by the urban middle classes, tolerated by local authorities, and motivated by a yearning for salvation. No Pasquino could re-place it. Italy also had its share of pamphlets, but the number of titles and copies printed was nothing compared to the German market.[83]

Repression was also a factor. As a result, many people hid their religious leanings, earning for themselves the reproachful epithet "Nicodemites." Some felt forced to flee. Pietro Bizzarri, born in Umbria in 1525, tried to make ends meet as a historian and served the English crown as a spy.[84] We find him in Genoa, at the court of Saxony, in Augsburg, Antwerp, and The Hague. All trace of him disappears after 1586. Some individuals had to pay for their "heretical" views with their lives. One such was the apostolic protonotary Piero Carnesec-chi. When he climbed the scaffold in Rome in 1567, he is said to have worn a bright white shirt and white gloves.[85] It was as if rabid religious zeal were put-ting humanist civility to death.

Carnesecchi belonged to a circle of idiosyncratic thinkers that flocked to Juan de Valdés (ca. 1490–1541) in Naples. The Castilian was the intellectual product of a movement whose members were known in his native Spain as *alumbrados*, "the Illuminated."[86] We encountered similar piety movements in the Late Middle Ages. Their ideal was a life of humility, love, and reading scrip-ture. Like Johannes Tauler, they sought God within themselves. There were affinities with the thought of Erasmus and Luther's theology, as well as with Platonic philosophy. When the Spanish Inquisition took a harsher stance toward the advancing Reformation—about 130 *alumbrados* were executed—Valdés fled to the quiet viceroyalty of Naples. While he himself was shielded from consequences by the position of his twin brother Alfonso, an intimate of Charles V, other members of the circle were, like Bizzarri, forced to flee to the four corners of Europe. They included the quondam vicar general of the Ca-puchin Order, Bernardino Ochino (1487–1564), and the Augustinian canon Pietro Martire Vermigli (1499–1562), he, too, a high official of his order. Both later joined the Reformation. Vermigli found a home in Zurich, whereas

Ochino had problems there as well and had to move on to Austerlitz, in Moravia, where he died of plague. Also influenced by the spirituality of the Valdés circle was one of the most famous—and according to Paolo Giovio's description (see p. 734), one of the most beautiful—women of the century: Vittoria Colonna (1492–1547). Her Platonic poetry was already fêted by contemporaries.[87] It may have been under her influence that some of Michelangelo's sonnets took on their pious, contrite tone.

The states of Europe that remained in the old faith essentially had two options for responding to the challenges of the Reformation. On the one hand, they could resort to violence, expulsion, and perhaps even execution of Lutheran heretics. On the other hand, they could undercut the movement with their own reform efforts. Bavaria, which had been united under primogeniture since the War of the Succession of Landshut, opted very early on for both routes at once. A decree was issued against the new doctrine in March 1522, threatening its partisans with expulsion from the realm. Five years later, a Lutheran theologian was burned as a heretic. At the same time, the dukes had met with their bishops to see about curtailing ecclesiastical abuses. As for the Protestants, the most important tool at their disposal was church visitation. Since the clergy itself lacked the necessary will, the state took over this role.

Spain went its own way, as noted. It became perilous to read Erasmus, even Plato, Ficino, or Pico.[88] Spain's rock-hard Catholicity was the result of the Reconquista, early reform—Cisneros was its symbol—and a deep piety steeped in mystical experience and the love of Jesus. One example is provided by Teresa of Ávila (1515–1582), whose devotion could apparently rise to the level of a sexual encounter.[89]

A towering representative of Spanish Catholicism emerged in Ignatius of Loyola (1491–1556), the product of a Basque noble family. He was severely wounded in 1521 at the Battle of Pamplona—part of the Spanish conquest of Iberian Navarre—and experienced an existential crisis during his long period of convalescence. Ignatius the soldier traded his courtly romances for writings like the *Golden Legend* and Cisneros's *Ejercitatorio*. Epiphanies moved him once and for all to a pious conversion. He took a pilgrimage to Jerusalem and eventually studied theology. Ignatius developed into a Catholic brother of Luther. His piety was likely based on spiritual foundations similar to those of his countryman Valdés. For a while, at any rate, he was suspected of being an *alumbrado* and perhaps even a disciple of Luther.[90]

Like the Reformers, Ignatius yearned for purity. He agonized over his sins and searched for a gracious God. As with Luther, piety was not a posture for him but a project that required constant confrontation with his own self. His *Spiritual Exercises* recall late medieval picture cycles. They helped viewers to visualize suggestive scenes from the life of Jesus and thus to imitate it with humility and love. Their goal was to help people renounce their own interests and dedicate themselves to God's will.[91] In contrast to Luther, Ignatius was initially satisfied by his turn inward. It did not lead him to criticize the "Jesus of the page" of the theologians or the weaknesses of ecclesiastical institutions. On the contrary, the order founded by the short saint with the lifelong limp developed into the most powerful force to come to the aid of the beleaguered Church.

France also remained Catholic. The Sorbonne had condemned Luther's teachings from the very beginning. One adherent of the Reformer was even burned. But initially the royal court let things take their course. Across the land, Reformation-minded circles were allowed to form. A harder line was taken in the wake of a scandal known as the "Affair of the Placards." On the morning of October 18, 1534, surprised residents of Paris and a few other cities awoke to find manifestos complaining of the "horrific" abuses of the papal mass.[92] It was an unprecedented conquest of the public sphere that Francis I interpreted as a frontal assault on the crown. Twenty-five suspects were executed. A series of royal edicts endeavored to prevent further Protestant activities. Religious affiliation became a question of life and death. A special court for trying heretics—it was gruesomely referred to as the *chambre ardente*, "burning chamber"—had plenty of work. Protestants left the country in growing numbers. For example, not even Margaret of Navarre could afford adequate protection for Clément Marot. He was forced to flee, seeking refuge in Ferrara (where he met Rabelais), Venice, and Geneva. He died in 1544, the most important French poet of his generation, in Turin in Savoy.

God's Sheepdog: Calvin

Similar escapes—to Margaret's court, to Ferrara—also marked John Calvin's (1509–1564) biography.[93] His father, a high official of the bishop and cathedral chapter of Noyon in Picardy, had provided him with thorough legal training and a humanistic education. Calvin was fascinated by Reform ideas early on, so much so that he was threatened with arrest for heresy. In late 1533, he made a narrow escape from Paris, lowered from the window of his accommodations while bailiffs pounded at the door. He gave up the benefices in Noyon that had theretofore nourished him, and after the Affair of the Placards he left France for good. In 1535, we find him in Basel, where his *Institutio Christianae religionis* (*Institutes of the Christian Religion*), appeared a year later. The book made an overnight celebrity of its author. He revised it continually until his life's end, expanding it to monumental proportions. Initially containing six chapters, it ultimately had no fewer than eighty. His theology was inspired by Augustine, Duns Scotus, and others, but above all by the "preeminent apostles of Christ" Luther and Martin Bucer (1491–1551), the Reformer of Strasbourg. Calvin's scorn for theological hairsplitting has a humanistic flavor. His thought revolves around the tension between the God-man Christ, who confers grace and comfort, and the conception of a God that transcends all human comprehension. Calvin was a popular preacher, thanks to his short, clear sentences and penchant for everyday subject matter.

His theology focused firmly on the question of predestination. He was utterly convinced that all of human life is foreordained from the moment of birth.[94] The reasons that condemned one person to hell and lifted another to heaven were, in his view, inscrutable. He did not even think it permissible to investigate them. Like Luther, he believed people must rely on faith alone. In contrast to some of his supporters, Calvin did not take the position that success or failure in life provided insight into God's judgment.[95] Human beings may have been debased worms subject to the will of the Lord, but Calvin did not, therefore, consent to their leading a passive existence. Rather, he called for a relentless struggle against sin and pleaded for Christian charity, fraternity, and a zealous exaltation of the Lord, which everything in life, including food and drink, should serve. As for the practice of lending money at interest, he agreed with Luther that the Ciceronian principle of equity pertained. Of the sacraments, only baptism and the Eucharist met with his sanction.

The place where Calvin's work developed world-historical importance was Geneva, a commercial center that had adopted the Reformation in 1536. He settled there in 1541. A kind of Protestant Savonarola, his charisma as a preacher made him the dominant figure in the city. Yet he created no Byzantine theocracy on Lac Léman, but rather a republic that sought to be pious and pure. The city government's job was to serve the Church, thereby fulfilling its divine duty. Furthermore, it was to safeguard the moral lifestyle of the congregation entrusted to it. The highest authority in ecclesiastical affairs was the Consistory. Initially, it was composed of the pastors of the city and twelve laymen, known as "elders," chosen by the city council.[96] In Calvin's view, secular power had no business interfering in church affairs. He considered it a Christian right to resist a government that flouted God's law.[97] This was not a call to revolution. Rather, resistance was the job of elected popular representatives, "lesser authorities." This doctrine provided theological support to future popular movements against monarchical hybris. As such, it gave rise to a historical curiosity: the thought of a religious zealot and constructor of a moral state would go on to play a significant role in the prehistory of democratic thought—and concretely in the ideology of American democracy. Calvin thought the ideal regime should contain a mixture of aristocratic and democratic elements; Geneva's constitution provided the model. Theologically, Calvin's emphasis on horizontal power manifested itself in the priesthood of all believers.

Calvin thought of himself as a "sheepdog of God."[98] The academy he founded in Geneva soon attracted theologians from all over Europe. Sermons were delivered daily in three churches. Communion, however—the bread and the wine—was only given four times a year, as the city council directed. In light of Geneva's tension with foreign neighbors and the darkening of the European horizon, including the conflict between England and France, the Schmalkaldic War, and the Ottoman wars, Calvin's moral politics hardened. Homosexuals were sent to the scaffold. Adulterers were subjected to public humiliation. So were people who had merely indulged in a bit of harmless dancing. Preachers and elders visited townspeople in their homes to check on their lifestyles. Not even baptismal names could be freely chosen now, but rather were assigned according to a list. For example, one priest angered a couple by naming their child "Abraham" instead of their preference, "Claude."[99] For a few weeks, the council even closed down the city's taverns. "Abbeys" were opened in their stead, with special rules such as that grace had to be said properly. That was one reform too many. Established Genevans clamored against Calvin and the streams of French exiles settling in the city so loudly that the Reformer risked suffering the same fate as Savonarola. Yet he persevered. For despite his moral severity, he was not stubbornly doctrinaire, as can be seen in the compromise he reached with the natives of Zurich over the question of the Eucharist.

His thought harnessed the cold reason of a jurist to the ideal of purity. Like Luther, Calvin glorified vocation and work. Just like everything else in life, they were a form of service to God. Not even music—an art that he happened to appreciate deeply—was allowed to be cultivated for sheer pleasure. Churches had to be austere, stripped bare of all worldly glitter. When it came to reshaping the world according to the text of the Bible, Calvin was even stricter than Luther.

In an enormously influential study, Max Weber sought to demonstrate that Calvinism's call for "inner asceticism" generated a specifically capitalist work ethic.[100] He argued that there was an affinity between Calvinist positions and the capitalist mentality. There may be a kernel of truth to this thesis: by engaging in competition with one another, all the variants of the Reformation and the Catholic countermovements to it fostered a disciplining of European society. Along these lines, it was not Calvinism per se but rather a constantly reforming Christianity that facilitated the creation of Latin Europe's "spirit of capitalism."

Rather powerful forces were at work in the structure of Europe's relatively open, competitive societies, as well as in the spaces for free thought that opened up within them—in part in reaction to the upsurge of the religious sphere driven by the Reformation. Calvinism owed its global success to the fact that its doctrines sought to mobilize an omnipotent God against the uncertainties and threats inherent in the coming of modernity. Calvin's God was greater than even Plato's abstract divinity, and yet he still kept watch over the fates of individual human beings. This very ambivalence is one of the factors that made Calvinism a distinctly modern religion. What personal experiences and wounds were responsible for the dynamics of Calvin's theological turn? Was it the early death of his mother? The fact that his father was denied a Christian burial because of a small dispute with the cathedral chapter of Noyon? We will never know. One thing is certain: Calvin was an exile his whole life, and that must have been the source of at least some of his theology's asperity. It was a response to the life he lived—like all religions.

War and Council

Calvin had tried in vain to win Francis I to his side and turn him into a Frederick the Wise of his Reformation. The *Institutio* is dedicated to the king. But France remained Catholic. Its ruler achieved fame not with war but rather with the arts and sciences: as the patron of Leonardo; as the builder of Chambord and the Palace of Fontainebleau, which was decorated by a brilliant équipe of Florentine artists; and as the founder of a library and the patron of the "College of the Three Languages," namely Greek, Latin, and Hebrew. The latter institution developed into the Collège de France. Its famous students included not only Rabelais and Ignatius of Loyola but also Calvin. The sheen of art and learning, the triumphal entries and parties at the "perfect palace" of Fontainebleau[101] communicated the crown's claim to absolute power. One contemporary already recognized that such scenes were nothing but drugs to keep the people compliant.[102]

Four wars on land and in the Mediterranean against the Holy Roman Emperor did little to change the political map. In the course of these conflicts, Francis, who (like his predecessors since the twelfth century) styled himself "Most Christian King," did not shy away from making deals with the Turks. As part of the Treaty of Crépy, which marked the end of the duel between the two powers—as we saw, Henry VIII had allied with the Habsburgs—Francis substantially gave up his Italian ambitions. In exchange, the emperor renounced his claim to the western part of Burgundy. After the treaty was signed, the Dauphin let it be known that he had no intention of respecting the losses it formalized once he became king.

Charles V was not satisfied to play the role of moderator among the various parties in the Empire. What was the point of being emperor if one could not protect the true religion? The idea of keeping politics separate from faith was utterly foreign to his sense of right and wrong. Such had indeed been the suggestion of an Urban Diet held in 1524. It assured the emperor of its obedience in secular affairs, but not when the Word of God, human salvation, and thus issues of religious conscience were at stake.[103] Lutherans saw Charles as an enemy not only of religion but also of the state.[104] He was, no doubt, utterly certain of acting in his God's interest by planning a war against the Protestants. His goal was to force the heretics to attend a Church council that would then press ahead with ecclesiastical reform and reestablish religious unity. In a secret accord appended to the Treaty of Crépy, Francis I was required to support this course of action.

Alessandro Farnese, who then occupied the Holy See as Paul III (1534–1549), seemed as little predestined as most of his predecessors to cleanse the Church of worldly filth and offer the Protestants an olive branch.[105] He owed his rise in the Roman hierarchy to the fact that his sister Giulia, known as *la bella*, had once charmed Cardinal Rodrigo Borgia, later Pope Alexander VI. The liaison turned out to be extremely helpful for his own career. The pope made his beauty's brother a cardinal. Alessandro then snatched up as many benefices as he could, crowning his efforts with the bishopric of Parma. Notes attached to the Pasquino mocked him as *Cardinal Gonnella* ("Cardinal Petticoat") and *Cardinale fregnese*, an epithet better left untranslated. The power of his loins was attested by several children. Having become pope himself, he bestowed favor upon his own children and grandchildren to a degree that dwarfed even the scandalous practices of his predecessors. Titian depicted

Paul in a painting, now in Naples, that has become a portrait of nepotism. The frail old pope is hunched in the middle, looking up somewhat suspiciously at his elegantly clothed grandson Ottavio (1524–1586), Duke of Parma, who approaches him obsequiously. To Paul's right stands Ottavio's older brother Alessandro (1520–1589), the *gran cardinale* ("grand cardinal"). At the tender age of fourteen, he was raised to the purple by his grandfather and given the bishoprics of Avignon and Monreale. He would go on to become one of the leading art patrons in late Renaissance Rome.

Paul was fully aware that the Church needed reform. As usual, purification efforts began in the monasteries. The pope also appointed to the cardinalate men who were considered open to reform. A commission, headed by the diplomatically skilled Venetian Gasparo Contarini (1483–1542), was formed to generate suggestions for "improving the Church." Yet all it produced was a document of twelve small pages. Nothing more happened. Rome's strategy was now aimed in a different direction: reinforcing Catholic dogma and wiping out heretics. A little bit should change so that everything could stay the same. The way the wind was blowing was signaled by the creation of the Holy Office under the auspices of the Neapolitan Cardinal Giampietro Carafa, later Pope Paul IV. It was set up in 1542 as the supreme organ of the Inquisition, with a remit extending to the entire world "on both sides of the Alps," thus including Germany. The change of mood toward a more austere religiosity was marked by a first-rate work of art: Michelangelo's newly finished *Last Judgment* in the Sistine Chapel. This universal drama, originally commissioned by Clement VII, pope during the Sack of Rome, is a reminder that all earthly action and inaction would ultimately be subject to God's tribunal.

In foreign affairs, Paul in no way pursued closer ties to the Holy Roman Emperor and thus to the Catholic superpower of Spain, although such would have been in the spirit of his religious politics. He sought instead to gain from the conflict between Charles V and Francis I. "The whole world knows that the pope is the sole cause of all your past and present woes," Charles's ambassador in Venice judged. "What other prince has done you greater harm? Blind men can see that he is responsible for everything the French king has done to you."[106] Charles tried to create a bond with the pope by aiding his familial aspirations. An opportunity arose when Paul, of his own accord, enfeoffed his son Pier Luigi Farnese with the duchies of Parma and Piacenza. The emperor legitimated the act. In return, Paul III agreed to call a Church council. And it was indeed inaugurated in December 1545 in Trent—a city within the boundaries of the Empire but close to Italy and part of the patriarchate of Aquileia. Luther died not two months later. He was given a princely burial.

Meanwhile, dark clouds were gathering over Wittenberg. Charles V had neutralized Francis I and gotten the pope to call a council. That was a lot, but still too little. For the Protestant princes had no intention of sending their theologians to Trent. The emperor's envoy, the layman Francisco de Toledo, was so influential at the council that its detractors called it the "Council of Toledo."[107] The Lutherans had nothing to expect from a meeting of this kind except the rejection of everything they had been fighting for since 1517.

The emperor decided to take up arms. Within the limits set for him by economics, tradition, and current circumstances, Charles prepared for battle with remarkable strategic savvy. The resulting Schmalkaldic War was a diplomatic success for him before the first cannon was fired. In effect, the conflict was already over by the end of April 1547, when the Schmalkaldic army was defeated by imperial forces at the Battle of Mühlberg on the Elbe River. The Elector of Saxony, John Frederick I, was imprisoned. Maurice, lord of Albertine Saxony, had allied with Charles. As a reward he received the title of Elector previously held by his defeated cousin. A diet in Augsburg, convened in September of the same year, cemented the victory in law. For eight months, the Swabian city became the center of events. Even Titian traveled there from Venice. He painted a portrait of Charles as a defender of Christianity, sitting astride a horse and holding the Holy Lance in his right hand. No Holy Roman Emperor since the High Middle Ages had achieved so much power within his own realm. A Spanish chronicler compared his lord with Caesar, having him say, "This is the Elbe—so often spoken of by the Romans, and so seldom seen!"[108] The morning before the battle, the fog had risen and given a view of the opponents encamped across the river.

At the Imperial Diet, Charles was domineering and arrogant. Representatives from the imperial city of Ulm, from the very beginning a champion of religious freedom, had to remain in the presence of the silent *imperator* for a half hour with their eyes fixed on the floor.[109] He was contriving nothing short of a conservative revolution. His plan was to reorganize the Empire as a federation, bringing it more in line with a true monarchy, to have the council make the Protestants see reason, and in the process to renew the Church.

Even before the victory at Mühlberg, however, this plan had little chance of success. The council was anything but universal, rather like a rump parliament loyal to Rome. Immediately it began to build dogmatic walls. Creating even more hindrances to consensus, Pope Paul moved the assembly in

March 1547 to Bologna, a place under his direct authority, under the pretext of avoiding an epidemic. It is highly unlikely, however, that this maneuver destroyed the one final chance for reconciliation with the Protestants, as was argued by Hubert Jedin, a historian of the council.[110] Indeed, politics and theology had long been inextricably interwoven. German princes of all confessions gained from Rome's weakened authority, as well as from the equally significant blow dealt to the emperor's power by religious strife. The final break between pope and emperor came when Paul's bastard son, Duke Pier Luigi, was murdered in September 1547—not at Charles's behest, but certainly not without his knowledge. Nothing substantial was achieved in Bologna.

Meanwhile, at the Diet of Augsburg it became clear that Charles was a master of spinning diplomatic webs and winning battles, but that he did not know how to press his advantage sensibly. The new imperial federation, intended also to include territories in Austria, the Netherlands, and Italy, would have meant re-Catholicization, in addition to new taxes for its members and the loss of all political independence. Spaniards as lords of Germany? Even for allies of the emperor, it was a nightmarish prospect. Charles's plans met with widespread rejection. Little of the federation project saw the light of day. Furthermore, the Protestants were dissatisfied with the concessions that had been made to them. As a temporary solution until the council could work things out, the Diet permitted clerical marriage and allowed the bread and the wine to be served at Communion. But it also decreed the reinstitution of Rome's "ancient ceremonies" and reinforced papal and episcopal powers.[111]

Charles's first concrete actions spelled nothing good. Nearly thirty renegade imperial cities were forced to accept fundamental changes to their constitutions. Guild regimes—the emperor spoke disparagingly of *Ochsen und Pöbel*, "the beastly rabble"—were replaced by aristocratic governments.[112] In many places, churches and monasteries had to be returned to their old owners. Not only Protestants trembled, however, when at another Imperial Diet in Augsburg in 1550 the emperor set to work engineering his son Philip's succession to his office and estates. The latter was a Spaniard through and through and even more pious than his father. The princes complained that Charles intended to abolish the principle of free election and transform the Empire into a hereditary monarchy, placing his son, a foreigner, on the throne.[113] Charles's brother Ferdinand remained loyal, although he hoped to have his own son Maximilian become the next emperor. Yet things took a turn for the worse for the Habsburgs. Despite the truce, the corsairs renewed hostilities in the Mediterranean. In Hungary, Temesvár fell to the Ottomans.

At this moment, the newly minted Elector of Saxony, Maurice, took advantage of the Imperial Estates' discontent. In league with various Protestant potentates and France's new king, Henry II (1547–1559)—as mentioned above, Francis I had died in 1547—he led a rebellion against the emperor in 1552. The fact that Henry II was feeding Protestants to the flames in his own country was no matter. As the secret treaty of Chambord declared, at stake was the ancient freedom of the "beloved fatherland of the German nation," which had to be saved from "brutish" slavery to Spain.[114] Clearly flabbergasted, Charles had to flee the city of Innsbruck, where he had made a stop. Now the gouty ruler of two worlds had himself carried to Carinthia on a litter. The leaders of the Schmalkaldic League, held prisoner as hostages, were released. Without consulting the emperor, the rebels met with Ferdinand in Passau in 1552, and it was agreed that both confessions would tolerate each other until a final arrangement—thus the pious hope—could be reached at an Imperial Diet. Yet Charles did not simply accept defeat. Once again, he mobilized the resources at his disposal and marched against France. This time he did not even manage to retake Metz, an imperial city that had been given to King Henry in the Treaty of Chambord against imperial law.

With this war going on in the background, the council, which had returned to Trent in 1551 after the intermezzo in Bologna, broke up. Under the heel of the pope, no agreement could be reached, to say nothing of Church reform. Paul's successor, Julius III (1550–1555), was an enemy of all things Protestant and incidentally also of the Jews, saving his love for the arts, hunting, good food, and young men. Maurice of Saxony saw a political future at the side of Charles's brother Ferdinand, who represented a "German" alternative to Spanish servitude. Yet the Elector died, only thirty-two years old, in a battle against the outlawed Margrave Albrecht Alcibiades of Brandenburg-Kulmbach. Allied at times with his Protestant fellows, at times with the emperor, and always a threat to the public peace, this ill-fated gambler tried to patch together a Franconian principality via plunder. The political order of Europe still seemed open to the formation of new states. In reality, as Albrecht's example shows, this was less and less the case.

At the height of his power, Charles's armies had fought in various theaters at a total strength of 150,000 troops. This number marks by far the most significant mobilization of military power west of the Ottoman Empire. Yet it was in no way up to the task of waging war with the Turks, the French, and the Protestants all at once. The emperor's struggle for unity and purity was no match for the realities of the day. At the 1555 Diet of Augsburg, whose place and date had been set at the meeting in Passau, Charles no longer participated. He was succeeded in the Holy Roman Empire by Ferdinand of Austria (1556–1564), in the west by Philip of Spain. The division of the House of Habsburg into an Austrian and a Spanish line became a reality in spite of all earlier planning.

Luther's Legacy, Humanism, and Renaissance

In mid-May 1548—Spain's illustrious infantry had just taken Wittenberg—Charles V stood at Luther's grave in the city's castle church.[115] For whatever reason, he resisted the demands of a few zealots to at least dig up the heretic and have him burned now that it was no longer possible to do it while he was alive (the Fifth Lateran Council demanded this archaic post-mortem punishment). Was it a sign of respect for the greatness of the adversary fate had dealt him? At any rate, the Protestants were able to keep their shrine.

In later years, the daring monk of old fossilized into a monument to himself. It is easy to admire the young Luther—easier than the older Luther, who agitated against the peasants and wrote cringeworthy tracts against the Jews.[116] In his 1543 pamphlet *On the Jews and Their Lies*, Luther argued they should be treated with Augustinian "harsh mercy." It is a testament to disappointment. In an early writing, he had expressed the hope that the Jews could finally be converted by rational arguments after having been alienated and defamed for so long by the depraved papacy. Now he demanded that the Jews' homes be destroyed, their synagogues burned, their books confiscated, and their rabbis forbidden to preach upon pain of death.[117] His call for the Jews to be driven out of the country was widely heeded, causing them great suffering. Like Eck before him, Luther believed the Jews were involved in a grand conspiracy, prepared to harm Christians and murder their princes. Thanks to his authority, this kind of blustering was much more effective than that of other enemies of the Jews. That is why Luther plays a special, fateful role in the prehistory of anti-Semitism. Those who attempt to exonerate him by pointing out that his anti-Judaism was in line with the standards of the time should not overlook the fact that the Renaissance also produced a Pico and a Reuchlin. That having been said, few others could have uttered the latter's great words, "The Jew belongs to our lord God as much as I do."[118]

Luther was another of the countless missionaries of purity constantly produced by Christianity and other religions, a brother of the Cluniacs and Gregory VII, Saint Bernard and Saint Francis. He wanted to cleanse the world of superfluous words, false rituals, and futile works. He wanted pure faith and trust in God's grace. But he understood—and this distinguished him from other apostles of purity—that human beings are imperfect creatures, not made for the absolute, and that it is not good to deprive them of too much of what they are used to. Like the successful religious founder Buddha—who is said to have tested himself with harsh asceticism but later to have avoided extremes[119]— Luther desired improvement, but he was not a purity fanatic. He liked eating and drinking, and he did a lot of both. He had a sense of humor that could be crude at times. And he fathered six children with his wife Katharina. He preached in his professorial gown, which thus became the model for the vestments worn by Protestant pastors. When celebrating the Eucharist, he even put on a chasuble. He considered images to be inconsequential. He did not demand their destruction and even condoned their use in teaching and as a memory aid to divine history. Admittedly, he made penance a focus of Christian life. Yet he did justice to the secular world, what he called the *Scheißhaus*, the "outhouse," of earthly existence.[120] The "evangelical parsonage" that he lived out with his family developed into a legendary cultural biotope. His social views did not champion monkish ideals but rather prized vocation in a very general sense: all people should do their work as well as possible, wherever God placed them. This was not so much a celebration of industry as a call to humility and respect for the order of society. One key reason that Luther's Reformation survived, therefore, was that it preserved a human countenance.

It was the sufferings of Sisyphus that turned the young Martinus into the Protestant pope Dr. Luther. He saw that his once lively Reformation was spiraling into murder and war, into factions and factions of factions. He sensed Satan's machinations everywhere, and he ultimately believed himself to be wrestling directly with the devil. The world had not gotten significantly better since his reform movement had begun, and the word, of whose overwhelming power Luther was so convinced, seemed to have no power at all—not with the Jews and certainly not with the pope or the emperor. Violence was thus necessary; the final battle had to be fought.

The outlines of the ambivalent figure that Luther became had been visible as far back as the Peasants' War. In his appeal *To the Christian Nobility of the German Nation*, he had still argued that heretics should be convinced with writings, not overcome by fire. Now he made no objection when a 1529 Imperial Diet in Speyer established the legal basis for executing Anabaptists.[121] The Augsburg Confession had then condemned the Anabaptists in its ominous sixteenth article, which is often printed in redacted form in modern editions.

Himself considered a heretic in half of Christendom, Luther now stood with the persecutors. All things radical or uncontrollable threatened his alliance with the state.

To monitor orthodoxy and morality, Protestant towns and states used the same tool, albeit more enthusiastically, as was customary during the Middle Ages: visitation. Commissions of theologians and public officials visited congregations to check on conditions there. They tested the preachers' knowledge, examined financial records, judged the steadfastness of the people's faith, and sniffed for heresy, witchcraft, and magic. Despite the initial idea that all believers in Christ were priests, Lutherans also formed rigid hierarchies. Theologians dissected the Bible as they always had, and as always they bent its words, now using the tools of humanist philology, to mean all manner of things. The new Reformed currents, the most important of which was Calvinism, maintained their own interpretations. They were countered by a Lutheran orthodoxy that saw itself as the Praetorian Guard of proper belief: "We are not in Plato's Academy but in a church of God!"[122] Censorship was in no way a peculiarity of Catholicism. Even in tolerant Basel, the body of the Anabaptist David Joris was exhumed in 1559 and burned along with his books.

As usual in difficult times, people sought their own paths to God outside the narrow bounds of the major religions. These paths were also taken by mystics in the European Middle Ages and by Greek and Russian hesychasts (who practiced a kind of mystical pietism), by Sufis and by the Hindu Bhakti movement of South Asia.[123] The latter opposed the Brahmins just like the European Reformers rose against the priests of Rome and the Anabaptists against the Reformers. All of them yearned to be close to God or simply for some ineffable transcendence of the world.

Christian mystics searched for the divine spark in the soul, and for the serenity that was described by both Tauler and Müntzer. Their heirs include the Spiritualists of the sixteenth century. One of the most important of them, Sebastian Franck (1499–1542/43), fostered an utterly nondogmatic religiosity that sought inside the self for the light emanating from the Holy Spirit. Confessional bickering and squabbling over heresy were just *Taubendreck*, "pigeon droppings."[124] In his view, heresy was nothing but deviation from what was sanctified by the majority. Anyone who sought God uprightly and did not claim to be "master of his head"—whether papist, Lutheran, Anabaptist, Turk, or Jew—was his *lieber Bruder*, his "dear brother." Furthermore, pagan and Jewish wise men like Hermes, Moses, and Plato had all spoken about one and the same divinity. Similar things were to be heard on the Catholic side, too. Agostino Steuco (1496/97–1548), bishop of Kissamos (on Crete) and later a participant at the Council of Trent, published his *De perenni philosophia* (*Perennial Philosophy*) in 1540. It also made the old argument that all the forms of wisdom to be found in oracles, revealed writings, and philosophical works were simply variations on the one Christian truth.[125]

In the thought of Sebastian Franck, humanistic individualism wholly embraced religion but also disentangled itself from the latter's power. "I am just a man among men,"[126] Franck once said; he sought to live by his conscience. Like him, the Silesian nobleman Caspar von Schwenckfeld (1489/90–1561) and his disciples also focused on personal experience of God, not the "Jesus of the page" of the theologians. For Schwenckfeld and Johannes Arndt, who belonged to the next generation, the goal was not primarily to purify the state and society but rather to achieve an inner, personal purification, to imitate Christ. It is no surprise that religion's official functionaries were loath to share their monopoly on salvation. Like Spain's *alumbrados*, the Schwenckfeld circle was persecuted and embattled, as were other dissenters like the polymath Guillaume Postel (1510–1581) and the shoemaker Jakob Böhme (1575–1624), one of Germany's most original mystical thinkers.

One idiosyncratic response to the state of the times was provided by the *Cymbalum mundi*, or *Timpani of the World*, probably written by Bonaventure des Périers. Its tone was inspired by Lucian. The author, a protégé of Margaret of Navarre, heaped scorn on the bickering of theologians of all stripes. In one chapter, Luther and Bucer, transparently disguised by the anagrams "Rhutelus" and "Cubercus," claim they know how to find pieces of the philosopher's stone. The work closes with a dialogue between two dogs, clearly wiser than their owners, who discuss the gullibility of human beings.[127]

The historical Luther bequeathed a theology somewhere between formalistic Catholicism and the heartfelt piety of the mystics. Those who followed him were directed to heed the Bible and sermons. His disciples had a more direct relationship with their God than orthodox Catholics did. No saints interceded, good works had no effect, and not even prayers were effective. If a storm approached, processions did not help, nor did the blessing of Saint Vitus, the emergency responder responsible for helping Catholics faced with bad weather. One could not even be certain of God's grace. All that remained, as Muslims would say, was to engage in constant jihad—a term that also denotes the inner striving for the good and true faith.[128] Freedom of the will was sacrificed on the altar of terrifying necessity, divine omnipotence, and omniscience.

Luther's conception of man was diametrically opposed to that of most humanists. This was the issue at stake in a hefty dispute he had with Erasmus. In 1524, smack in the critical years of the Reformation, the Dutch humanist published his *On Free Will*, or more precisely, on the free "choice" between two different options. It was a duel between two worldviews. A peace-loving interpreter of events entered into a debate with a rumbling prophet who saw himself as God's instrument in an apocalyptic struggle. This war, in which life and death really were at stake, required *Landsknechte*, not literati. Erasmus met the gruff certitude with which Luther presented his interpretation of various Bible passages with a Socratic skepticism that was keenly aware of the limits of exegesis.[129] He pleaded for tolerance, considering that the alternative, as he perspicaciously realized, was unrest and war. To strip human beings of free will was to make them nothing more than a piece of clay in the hand of a potter god.[130] As he argued, it was *more likely*—nothing more!—that human beings were capable of anything with God's grace. And thus, all their works could be good.[131] A deity that shellacked his own creatures with arbitrary punishments from the very beginning would be a gruesome tyrant. All on account of original sin, which Luther magnified to the extreme, he would rage against all of humanity. What sense would the Last Judgment have, Erasmus asked, if there was no merit to reward or fault to punish?[132] Furthermore, if God alone was the source of all good, would he not also have to be the cause of all evil?[133] And if that were the case, where was human fault to be found?

Luther responded with his *On the Bondage of the Will*. He compared Erasmus's rhetorically ornate argumentation to "refuse or ordure being carried in gold and silver vases." His escape from the labyrinth of the problem of theodicy was to reject reason, "the devil's whore"—at least when it went too far.[134] For the resolution of all contradictions, Luther waited for the glorious light at the end of days.[135] Like so many who sought to unveil the mystery of "God," Luther used reason to engage in the astute textual exegesis that formed the foundation of his theology. Yet once it ceased to be useful in resolving contradictions, it became a whore of Satan. Erasmus was not fooled. He saw that the integrity of Luther's grand paradox relied on many ancillary ones.[136] The Dutch humanist agreed with Lorenzo Valla that the creature had no business judging the will of the Creator. He thus appealed to faith at a much earlier point in his argumentation than Luther did.

Luther's stance toward free will and scholarship does not belong to the Middle Ages, as that period was much more open to a variety of points of view. Nor does Luther's work mark the beginning of something new. Instead, he was one of the countless warriors in the battle between religion and the secular world, faith and reason, that belonged to no one particular time but rather had endured for over a millennium and still endures today.

The tense relationship between Erasmus and Luther might suggest that irreconcilable differences separated the Renaissance and humanism from the Reformation. Yet such was not the case. Both currents sought answers to the same theological challenges.[137] One might also wonder if Luther's project could have been successful had the trail not been blazed for him by humanists who had fought against authority of all kinds. Many Reformers had been given a humanistic education. More importantly, they shared the humanists' philological interests. *Ad fontes*—"back to the original sources!"—was the battle cry inscribed on both their banners.[138] Those who wanted to found their theology on God's word ultimately had to know what the Lord had actually said. For example, Lorenzo Valla's textual criticism provided an indispensable tool for the Reformers' philological work, and Luther used Erasmus's New Testament when translating the Bible.

The education reform initiated by Melanchthon aimed at unifying humanist pedagogy and teaching with the principles of the Reformation. The foundation of *Gymnasien*—in 1526 under Melanchthon's direct involvement in Nuremberg, in 1531 in Augsburg, and in 1538 in Strasbourg—was an important step in this direction. The curriculum included subjects from mathematics to Latin and Greek, rhetoric, dialectic, and ancient Roman literature. In this way, the rich tradition of pagan antiquity was integrated into the Christian worldview. Ancient texts sometimes underwent marvelous transformations. Plato was made a crypto-Christian, Virgil a Catholic.[139] The poetry of Ovid, certainly no Puritan, had long been given a Christian interpretation. For the view of humanistically educated artists, we can turn to Dürer. "Art is great, grave, and good, and we use it with great reverence to praise God," he wrote.[140] In his view, attributes ascribed to Apollo in antiquity could be applied equally well to Christ, as he was the "most beautiful man in the whole world."[141] Furthermore, he argued that Venus was an appropriate model for the Virgin Mary, just as Hercules was for Samson. In a self-portrait dating to 1500, Dürer painted himself in a presumptuous frontal view as a Christ-like creator.[142] Not even three decades later, the wind had shifted. Erasmus, whom no one would have accused of zealotry, attacked Rome's casual approach to pagan antiquity in his *Ciceronianus*.[143] He viewed it as a secularization of faith, and he derided the humanists for trying to imitate the style of their hero, "Saint Cicero." In this way, Erasmus lent support for individuality in the field of literature. The point of writing, he argued, was not to imitate antiquity but rather to create something of one's own.

Luther's approach to scholarship and the arts was that of the pious man who cared about his relationship with God and otherwise for not much else. It never would have occurred to him to admire paintings simply for their beauty. He prized music as one of God's greatest gifts because the devil hated it deeply and because it could chase away many of the greatest temptations.[144] Holy Writ, he believed, nullified all knowledge. This view made him a fellow of Bonaventure and al-Ghazali. He studiously kept his distance from Greek philosophy. Only Plato occasionally received his approval. He condemned Aristotle as a "blind pagan master" whom God had put on Earth to punish humankind for its sins.[145] He thus also rejected Thomas Aquinas's teachings about Holy Communion. For the latter had used the distinction between the substance of a thing and its changing, "coincidental" qualities, the "accidents," to explain the miracle of the Eucharist.[146]

One of the harshest accusations Luther could hurl at anyone was to call them an "Epicurean." This epithet was used for Erasmus and the pope, Turks, Italian cardinals, and indeed all Italians.[147] It is unlikely that Luther knew very much about Epicurus's philosophy, though. He did support educating the young. And art and learning had their justification, but only when they—like music—provided protection from evil, helped to spread God's word, or were useful for ruling. Luther's approach to natural science was circumscribed entirely by the text of the Bible. In his view, too much curiosity and intellectual freedom led people away from what mattered most.

And Erasmus? He remained forever a son of the Catholic Church. The fact that he was buried in 1536 in the Protestant Basel Minster symbolizes his position between the fronts. The catastrophic development taken by subsequent events proved the skeptical humanist right more than the Reformer, who was so convinced of himself and his cause. Yet even Luther's voice mellowed in the end. "Do not seek to explore this divine *Aeneid*, but rather bow down and worship its traces," he wrote in notes for a sermon. It is the last thing known to have come from his hand.[148]

32

Revolution of the Heavenly Spheres

Prometheus

For a long time, the most influential interpretation of the Reformation was provided by the German philosopher Georg Wilhelm Friedrich Hegel (1770–1831). In his *Lectures on the Philosophy of History*, he celebrated the Reformation as "the all-enlightening Sun, following on that blush of dawn"—the Renaissance—"which we observed at the termination of the medieval period."[1] Actually, the Reformation represented a break in the history of the humanist project. In many countries of Europe, the free space carved out for worldliness was restricted again for over a century. Questions of faith and theological controversy took center stage in the grand dialogue; at times, war and persecution of the "other" shut it down almost completely. By contradicting the universalist claims of both the pope and the emperor, the Reformation became a contributing force to the formation of national consciousness. On the other hand, its call to read the Bible in the vernacular streamlined with a trend already underway in Catholic Europe. In both Italy and France, literary debates obsessed over whether classical Latin or native languages should have precedence. One might also recall that, by decree of Francis I, French replaced Latin as the language of law in 1539.[2]

The Reformation did not create "modern man." Only with regard to Christ did it open space for subjectivity. It freed individuals to choose their faith, but in doing so it made them prisoners of the word of God.[3] It did not unloose the chains that bound them to the transcendent—on the contrary. Taking the individual as the index of modernity, one could say that Catholic tradition and even the Council of Trent were more "modern" than Luther. For unlike the Reformer, they left some room for free will.[4] Luther's notion of the human condition is a world away from the bold constructions developed by Nicholas of Cusa and Rudolph Agricola, who made man a creative demiurge of things and concepts. Very different from Luther were also Petrarca, Manetti, and Leon Battista Alberti, who spoke of man as a "second god." Leonardo, who was as exceptional in his anthropology as in so much else, replaced God with the creative force of Nature, maker of the soul and the body, and with the "wonderful necessity" (*mirabile necessità*) of the law of causality.[5] As for who enacted that law, he left it an open question.

Nevertheless, the anthropology of the Renaissance was never merely a proud celebration of the *uomo universale*—the universal man—that fictional character created by the cult of the Renaissance, who desires to know all and whose ability knows almost no limits. At first glance, this statement seems to be contradicted by Pico della Mirandola. "We have given you, Adam, no fixed seat or form of your own," he has God say to the first human being,

> no talent peculiar to you alone. This we have done so that whatever seat, whatever form, whatever talent you may judge desirable, these same may you have and possess according to your desire and judgement. Once defined, the nature of all other beings is constrained within the laws We have prescribed for them. But you, constrained by no limits, may determine your nature for yourself, according to your free will, in whose hands We have placed you. We have set you at the center of the world so that from there you may more easily gaze upon whatever it contains. We have made you neither of heaven nor of earth, neither mortal nor immortal, so that you may, as the free and extraordinary shaper of yourself, fashion yourself in whatever form you prefer. It will be in your power to degenerate into the lower forms of life, which are brutish. Alternatively, you shall have the power, in accordance with the judgment of your soul, to be reborn into the higher orders, those that are divine.[6]

That indeed sounds like an anthem of modern subjectivity. Yet if we continue reading, we find that the highest goal of divinely created human beings is not mastery over the world but rather the soul's union with God.

So too, emulating the cherubic life on earth, curbing the drive of the emotions through moral science, by dispersing the darkness of reason through dialectics (as if washing away the squalor of ignorance and vice) may we purge our souls.[7]

Ultimately, "we shall no longer be ourselves, but He Himself Who made us."[8] With the kiss of death, the *binsica*, and the demise of the body, the individual will die a second death and dissolve in the beauty of God.[9] None of this is very earthly or worldly. Pico's oration is, therefore, only superficially a humanistic manifesto, despite abounding with Greek quotations and deploying a host of gods and learned authorities.

While Luther was starting his revolution, Pietro Pomponazzi (1462–1525) was also thinking about the limits of human desire and knowledge.[10] In a writing dating to 1516, he defended the thesis—against the view propounded a year earlier at the Fifth Lateran Council—that the immortality of the soul could not be proven rationally. That doctrine, he concluded, was an invention intended to make people good and submissive and thus to preserve the social order.[11] Furthermore, God could not act upon nature directly; he needed the planets as an intermediary. Moreover, apparent miracles could be explained by natural causes. At one point, Pomponazzi compares the philosopher with the archetype of modern man, Prometheus, and channels himself through the latter. "These are the things which disturb me, anguish me, make me sleepless. This is the true interpretation of the fable of Prometheus, whom, when he wished secretly to steal the fire of Jove, Jupiter sent to the Scythian rock."[12] Pomponazzi turns Prometheus into the image of the philosopher because he, too, wants to steal the secrets of the gods and therefore is plagued by concern and misgivings. The philosopher, he writes,

> does not drink, desire food, sleep, eliminate. He is mocked by all and even considered stupid and sacrilegious; he is pursued by the inquisitors and made a spectacle for the common people. These are the payments of the philosopher and these are his rewards.[13]

Here and in other late works, Pomponazzi depicts himself as a Socratic skeptic, a philosopher who knows that his science allows no more than conjecture. "In philosophy, you must be a heretic if you want to discover the truth," he once said.[14] On his deathbed, he supposedly evinced Stoic equanimity, not Christian certitude. "I leave happily," he comforted those gathered around him, as one source reports. "Where are you going, master?" one of them asked. "And where do all mortals go?" The master responded, "Where I am going and all the others have gone." To one last attempt to learn more, he answered with his final words, "Let me be, I wish to go."[15] Pomponazzi's thought, which met with great hostility during his lifetime, drew boundaries between philosophical and theological truth. It influenced dissenters and freethinkers of all stripes. Bembo once had to defend him before the Inquisition. All the while, "Peretto"—"little Peter," as the diminutive Pomponazzi was nicknamed—routinely emphasized that human knowledge was limited, and thus that one had to adhere to the rules of the Church, guided as it was by the Holy Spirit.

We have now entered the age of Dr. Faustus. The "amazing necromancer" (*wunderbarlicher Nigromanta*) was first mentioned in 1507 in a letter of Johannes Trithemius, who notes that there was a Master Georg Sabellicus in Gelnhausen who called himself "Faust the Younger."[16] This Faust seems to have embodied a very different kind of Renaissance. He was a master of magic, astrology, and alchemy and a practitioner of black magic. According to Trithemius's report, he posed as the most learned man of all time. He claimed to have memorized all the works of Plato and Aristotle and to be the consummate alchemist. He could even outdo the miracles performed by Jesus. In contrast to this boasting, the scattered sources sketch a miserable existence. Faust was expelled from a city here, paid a few guilders for a horoscope there. For gullible monks, he exorcised a ghost and drove it out of their monastery. He probably died in an explosion while performing alchemical experiments. All the same, it made sense to suspect that Satan was personally involved in the death of his servant. Faust was no archetype of German identity, a man who sold his soul to the devil for knowledge. He was a charlatan who hustled people just to get by. He was lucky during his lifetime merely to have been mistrusted as a fraud and not persecuted as a sorcerer.

Thinkers like Pomponazzi, Pico, and Reuchlin walked a thin line, as did shady figures like Faust. Just how thin is illustrated by an episode from the life of the energetic reform abbot Trithemius, our principal witness for the historical Faust. His passion for stenography and secret code—Trithemius is thought to have discovered a manuscript with Tironian notes, an ancient form of shorthand—almost earned the abbot an accusation of witchcraft; the abbreviations were considered symbols of black magic. His *Steganographia*, which contained descriptions of the all-powerful spirits of the planets, landed on the Index. And yet Trithemius also gained prominence as the author of a book against the "bog of witches," the *Antipalus maleficiorum*. It fell to his student Agrippa von Nettesheim (1486–1535) to feed a ravenous market with his *Three Books on Occult Philosophy*, a standard work on white magic.[17] It took pains to distance itself from witchcraft of any kind. The master of white magic seemed to have limitless powers. Agrippa's universe was, like Ficino's, full of angels and demons, and he knew recipes of Arabic and Jewish origin. He also knew how a mandrake could be used to create an artificial human known as a homunculus, a cousin of the golem.[18] The idea made an impression on Goethe, as did the black dog Agrippa owned. It was the inspiration for the poodle that follows Faust and Wagner on their Easter walk. And Agrippa himself was the true inspiration for Goethe's Faust. Yet, in a later work, the historical Agrippa acknowledged the uncertainty of all knowledge. In his view, only the study of the Bible and faith in Christ would lead to truth.

It was hardly a coincidence that Prometheus now became the subject of two panels (Fig. 49, p. 631) painted by Piero di Cosimo (ca. 1462–ca. 1521) of Florence, or that Pomponazzi made him the image of the inquisitive philosopher.[19] Pomponazzi had Boccaccio's interpretation in mind, which imparts to Prometheus a double identity. On the one hand, he symbolizes nature and the divine creator. On the other, he is a learned man who brings the fire of the mind to humankind. Boccaccio invented a story according to which Prometheus was not chained to a mountainside but rather had wandered through the Caucasus to steal the secrets of nature. As for the eagle that in the original myth gnaws at the liver of the bound Prometheus, it was merely an allegory for the lofty thoughts that haunt the wise man.

Like Odysseus, Prometheus is both a classic hero of the Renaissance and an ambivalent figure. He educates people. He sheds light on reality. At the same time, he is a Lucifer, a rebel against God. The fire he brings provides warmth and light, but it also destroys, and knowledge can be dangerous. Lorenzo the Magnificent once complained that Prometheus's curiosity had robbed the world of its happy Golden Age. As a virtuoso of power, he recognized that "too much knowledge leads to unrest."[20] A few decades later, one of the great innovators of medicine, Paracelsus, replied, "Rest is better than unrest, but unrest is more useful than rest."[21]

Paradigm Shift

Scientific activity, doing research, discovering new things—this work is often just a long, hard slog. Isolated slivers of knowledge are gathered up, and various problems are worked out. The basic assumptions, methods, and approaches to problem-solving accepted by the community of experts—what, in a heavily debate book, the historian and philosopher Thomas S. Kuhn (1922–1996) called a "paradigm"—do not change in the process.[22] Yet sometimes facts are discovered that defy classification. Normally, attempts are then undertaken to make the anomalies compatible with the old system in some way and thus "to save the phenomenon."[23] Over time, however, contradictions pile up. The bridges connecting the two intellectual edifices crumble, resulting in incommensurability. In the face of so many contradictions, only violence is ultimately effective. The hour of the destroyers strikes. The old paradigm becomes irredeemable; something entirely new is required. The defenders of the old are forced to the margins, although this process can take a long time and be accompanied by fierce resistance. In the end, the "paradigm shift" is complete. What for a millennium seemed as strong as steel collapses in a heap. The facts are fit into the new pattern, which explains what they mean in its own way.

Columbus's stubborn attachment to his initial hypothesis, namely that he had reached Asia, provides an example of the dilemma of incommensurability. Despite the truly revolutionary insights that his expeditions had made available to him, the Genoese sailor held fast to his old worldview. If what the ancients had passed down about the expanse of the ocean was accurate, then he *had* to have reached India. Vespucci, in contrast, understood the import of his decision to call the "islands" in the west a new continent. In his own words, "We discovered much continental land and islands without number, and a great share of them inhabited, of which no mention is made by the ancient writers; because they had no knowledge [of them,] I believe."[24]

The most famous "paradigm shift" of the early modern period was the "Copernican Revolution," which will be traced in the following pages. What scientific and sociological conditions gave rise to the heliocentric model? This question has parallels in the investigation into the emergence of the new art of the Renaissance and the rise of new ideas in philosophy and technological innovations like Gutenberg's; it regards the riddle of human creativity itself. The central question is how new things come about.[25]

Science proceeds at a glacial pace. For example, Gregor Reisch had also observed that there were lands unknown to Ptolemy, but he did not conclude anything from it. The worldview of the *Philosophical Pearl* continued to be informed by ancient and medieval authorities, both Arabic and European, even in its second edition in 1583.[26] Citing the "divine Augustine," Reisch disputed the existence of the antipodes. Based on Herodotus and others, he believed in exotic African populations: headless beings with their faces on their chests (Plate 14), and snake-eating "troglodytes" who more hissed than spoke. Naturally, Reisch thought the Earth was at the center of the universe, with hell blazing in its chasms and the heavenly spheres arched overhead. An army of authorities stood opposed to anyone who questioned the traditions propagated by such works.

And that is exactly what, a few years after the dutiful Reisch and Vespucci had undermined the Ptolemaic worldview, was done by an even greater mind on the eastern edge of Latin Europe's realm of possibility: Nicolaus Copernicus (1473–1543). Between 1509 and 1514, he wrote a *Commentariolus*, a short commentary on astrological questions.[27] It laid out the following arguments: all planetary motion occurs around the Sun; it and not the Earth is the center of this motion; the apparent motion of the stars and the Sun results from the Earth's motion; the Earth rotates each day on its own unchanging axis, along with the water flowing over its surface and the air surrounding it; the sphere of the fixed stars and the outermost heavenly sphere are stationary. These were claims that seemed to contradict all experience. The Earth upon which people stood firmly with their own two feet was actually a wandering star engaged in two different kinds of rapid motion at once? The Sun, whose daily path from east to west could be observed every single day, was actually the fixed center around which everything revolved?

The Music of the Spheres: The Premodern Sky

The ideas about the structure of the universe held by Gregor Reisch and just about all other learned men of his day were derived from a Greek thinker we have often had occasion to mention: Claudius Ptolemy. His cosmology was one of the most successful scientific paradigms of all time. His *Almagest* provides a mathematically precise description of the—apparent—orbits of the Sun, Moon, and planets around the Earth. The name of the work is indicative of the circuitous route by which it arrived in medieval Europe. The Greek words *mathematike syntaxis* or perhaps *megiste syntaxis*—i.e., "mathematical" or "greatest collection"—became *al-megiste* in the hands of Arabic scholars, which the Latins then appropriated as *Almagestum*.[28] Gerard of Cremona translated it into Latin in the twelfth century, after which information about its contents could also be gleaned from various excerpts and commentaries. The most important source, however, was John of Holywood's *Sphaera*, written in 1230 in Paris.[29]

Just like Macrobius and Boethius, the Middle Ages and the Renaissance saw the Earth as a small point at the center of the heavenly spheres, upon which the Sun, Moon, and planets were supposedly fixed. These heavenly bodies abidingly followed their circular paths under the sphere of the fixed stars, in this way, according to Pythagoras's teaching, creating the eternal music of the spheres.[30] Like their ancient intellectual ancestors, Renaissance cosmologists were convinced the universe had to be the work of a perfect creator, furnished with ideal proportions. The imperative that the human world be at the center followed from the Aristotelian principle of entelechy: all matter contains its own end within itself. The energy of each kind of thing insists on manifesting in a specific form.[31] This is what makes the tree grow, the limb fall, and everything strive for its natural place. Therefore, the heavy Earth "wants" to be down in the center, whereas light things—air and fire—strive upwards.[32] Above the sphere of the Moon, different natural laws were thought to pertain than underneath it. According to the ancient physicists, heavenly things, including the stars and the planets, were made of a fifth element, the mysterious *quinta essentia*. Neither heavy nor light, neither dense nor rare, the quintessence defied description. Still, people were convinced that everything in the heavenly spheres was perfectly pure and immortal. Chaos and change, transience and death, the occasionally joyful but more often depressing confusion of earthly existence—this was all only part of the sublunar world. One important law for the history of the astronomical revolution stated that all motion on Earth occurred in a straight line towards the center; in the heavens, in contrast, the natural philosophers believed circular motion reigned—in accordance with the perfection of the spherical form of the heavenly bodies and the substance they were believed to be made of.

One heavily debated question was what force moved the spheres and thus the Sun, Moon, and planets. Slight demystification ensued with the waning of the strange notion, found in Plato's *Timaeus* and other writings, that the heavenly bodies possessed souls and intelligence that let them find their way through the universe.[33] As in Buridan's work, it was replaced by Aristotle's "prime mover" (pp. 328f.). Human thought always searches for a beginning. The Chinese found it in Tai chi (the "greatest ultimate"),[34] modern cosmology in the "Big Bang." According to some, the continuous motion of the heavens was the work of angels. Since the winged creatures consisted almost entirely of air, they performed this labor through the power of their will alone. As late as the seventeenth century, people discussed whether the angels got tired and whether energy was even necessary to keep the celestial dance in motion. Around 1650, one Jesuit theologian calculated the number of angels required for the task at over one thousand.

Above the planets, the astronomers placed the sphere of the fixed stars. Some put an additional sphere of water above that. Although not compatible with Aristotelian physics, its existence was inferred from a passage in Genesis.[35] Beyond the *primum mobile*, the "prime mover," was the abode of God and his court, the "Empyrean" or "fiery heaven," an immeasurably vast region of pure light.[36] According to the mystic Heinrich Seuse, that is where the soul would shed all temporal elements and unite with the Trinity. Before this orgiastic moment was consummated, even as sober a spirit as Calvin hoped there would be time for a calm discussion with Luther and a party with Melanchthon.[37] As for Luther, he and some Catholic scholars doubted whether God's heaven even had a fixed orb.

The eight or nine spheres that surrounded the Earth in the Ptolemaic model were not the end of the matter, however. There was a problem: as clear and beautiful as the system appeared, it did not accord with what could actually be seen in the sky. If the Sun revolved around the Earth in a circle at a constant rate, why were the days of unequal length? Why did the brightness of the planets change? And how to explain, again assuming circular orbits, that the planets of the "upper" spheres, those further away from Earth—i.e., Saturn, Jupiter, and Mars—seemed to stop and even go backward before they continued their forward progress? We know that this odd behavior results from the fact that Earth actually passes those outer planets along its tighter orbit around the Sun, whereas Venus and Mercury pass it in the same way. Yet this was beyond all comprehension at the time, as was the tilt of Earth's axis with respect to the ecliptic, which causes the change of seasons.

In order to maintain the dogmas of circular orbit and harmonious proportion in the face of observational data, numerous auxiliary hypotheses were required.[38] Only thus was it possible to "save the phenomena." Apollonius of Perga, Hipparchus, and then Ptolemy had explained the variation in the length of the day by placing the Earth slightly off the center of the Sun's orbit. That contradicted the Aristotelian concept of perfectly concentric spheres, but it allowed the Sun to keep its circular orbit. In addition, the existence of "epicycles" was hypothesized. According to this theory, the planets revolved not only around the Earth but also around the path of their own orbit, called the "deferent." Thanks to such hypotheses, apparent retrograde motion and loops in the planetary orbits observable in the night sky could be described as overlapping circular motions. The traditional law was saved. To explain the apparent change in speed at which the planets traveled, Ptolemy had introduced the concept of the "equant," a mathematically derived point from whose perspective the speed of the epicycle center's orbit was entirely constant.

None of this was very elegant. However, the survival of this Gothic construction did have an advantage: when checked against observational data and refined in light of it, it enabled planetary motion to be very accurately predicted. On the other hand, differences between the calendar year and the solar year had grown more pronounced since antiquity. It was necessary to bring them into alignment again, at the very least so that holy feasts and commemorations of the saints could be celebrated on the right day. Astrologers, too, needed the most precise dates possible. Indeed, it may have been tiny imprecisions as well as the hypercomplexity of the Ptolemaic system that nourished the first doubts as to its validity. How could the work of an omnipotent artificer contain discrepancies? Why had he been so uneconomical, indeed so inelegant, in his creation? One possible conclusion was that either Aristotle or Ptolemy (with the eccentric location he gave Earth) had to be wrong. The possibility that *both* might be wrong did not occur to anyone for a very long time.

One of the first to entertain doubts that the mathematically constructed cosmos had anything to do with physical reality was Averroes. "Present-day astronomy does not deal with realities, and is suitable merely for computing unrealities," he wrote.[39] Indeed, it was difficult to imagine how mathematically calculated models were supposed to function in nature—if one assumed the existence of fixed crystalline spheres. Fifty or more were necessary to account for all the orbits and orbits of orbits. The attempt of the physician Girolamo Fracastoro (1476/78–1553) to avoid the system's inelegant eccentricities resulted in a confusion of no less than seventy-seven spheres.[40] Yet exercising Averroes's nuclear option—i.e., doing away with the epicycles and deferents and returning to Aristotle's perfect concentric spheres arranged around the Earth—did not do the trick, as that system no longer agreed at all with observations.

In the Arab world, astronomers had been criticizing Ptolemy and trying to reconcile mathematical astronomy with natural philosophy for centuries.[41] In Andalusia, Nur ad-Din al-Bitruji made the outermost sphere the motor of all other celestial motion, thus already thinking in a mechanical direction. However, his attempt to master the epicycles by hypothesizing spiral orbits for the Sun and planets required complicated auxiliary constructions of its own.[42] Using an ingenious geometric technique, Nasir al-Din al-Tusi showed that two circular motions, one inscribed inside the other, could produce oscillating motion in a straight line.[43] The "Tusi couple" made it possible to dispense with all the linear motion in the Ptolemaic model. It seemed the key to a "grand unifying theory" of the two major systems. Ibn al-Shatir thanked Allah for the insights that enabled him to abolish the bothersome equants by adding an extra epicycle.[44] His model of the orbits of the Moon and planets resembled the one proposed by Copernicus—except that it left Earth in the middle.

Only in the second half of the fifteenth century did Latin Europe's astronomers reach the level of the Muslim masters. Now, however, they possessed more precise Latin translations of the original Greek texts. For example, Cardinal Bessarion patronized the improvement of a defective translation of the *Almagest* that George of Trebizond had completed for Nicholas V. To aid in this project, Bessarion called on the Viennese professor of astronomy Georg Peuerbach and his student Johannes Müller (1436–1476). Müller, who called himself Regiomontanus (derived from the Latin name of his birthplace, Königsberg, literally "royal mountain," in Franconia), was the most significant mathematician of his time. As a member of Bessarion's entourage, he became acquainted with Italy and several humanists, including Toscanelli and Alberti.[45] For a few years he was employed at Corvinus's court in Buda. In Nuremberg, he set up a print shop with the help of Bernhard Walther, a merchant and himself an accomplished astronomer.[46]

Patronage and communication created the realm of possibility for the revolution in European astronomy that took place in the following centuries. Regiomontanus's print shop published Manilius's *De astrologia* and Peuerbach's *New Theories of the Planets*, which detailed the current state of astronomical knowledge. By the mid-sixteenth century, the latter would be reprinted more than fifty times. No less successful was the *Epitome* of the *Almagest* that Regiomontanus prepared with his teacher. His *Ephemerides*, which predicted the position of the planets from 1475 to 1506, found its way not only into Copernicus's library but also into Columbus's. Marginal notations in the admiral's copy attest to his intense engagement with the text.

The printing press enabled cultural transfer of epic proportions. For example, Peuerbach's *New Theories of the Planets* transmitted the teachings of Muslim astronomers, including al-Battani, who in turn relied on knowledge from India. By way of Nuremberg and other cities, advances in science made their way all over Europe, indeed all the way to remote Prussia, from southeast Asia, Harran, Baghdad, and Vienna. Without the work done by Eastern astronomers, Copernicus's astronomical revolution would have been unthinkable. Exactly what the Polish scientist borrowed from their writings is debated; the fact that he knew some of those writings is not.[47]

Copernicus

Copernicus's *Commentariolus* was not printed in his lifetime. However, one of his students, Joachim Rheticus, published a report about it.[48] For decades, Copernicus had sought evidence for the heliocentric theory, recording observations and making calculations. The result ultimately appeared in 1543, in the form of a book that would literally change the world: *On the Revolutions of the Heavenly Spheres*. Who was the man who had taken on the "Herculean task"— thus it was described by one of his critics, Petrus Ramus—of dragging the Earth out the middle of the universe?[49]

Nicolaus Copernicus (Niklas Koppernigk) was born in 1473 in the Hanseatic city of Thorn, then subject to the Polish crown. His father was a wealthy merchant. Nicolaus's aide-memoire on coinage, which anticipated certain elements of Gresham's theory of monetary value (p. 667), reflects this milieu. During his studies at the University of Cracow, he became acquainted with the works of Peuerbach and Regiomontanus and thus with the latest advances in astronomy.[50] In the autumn of 1496, he went to Italy, where he probably stayed off and on until 1503. In Bologna he studied canon and civil law, in Padua medicine. He studied mathematics under Domenico Maria de' Novara, a pupil of Regiomontanus from Ferrara. The University of Ferrara awarded Copernicus a doctorate in canon law. Thereafter, he spent most of the rest of his life in Frombork (Frauenburg) in Poland, the center of the small bishopric of Warmia. He earned his living as a cathedral canon, a position secured for him by his uncle. The duties that fell to the holder of this benefice seem to have been modest. In his residence, a tower in Frombork Castle, he found the conditions necessary for any scientific career: money for his daily bread, freedom, peace and quiet, and time.[51] In addition, he was embedded in communication networks. Without access to the library at the University of Cracow, he would not have been able to pursue astronomy.

In the preface to his magnum opus, he gave eloquent voice to the confusion he found at the beginning of his undertaking.[52] He realized, he wrote, that the astronomers did not agree with one other. Furthermore, they were unable "to establish anything certain" from their observations that "would without doubt correspond with the phenomena." And they had failed to discover the "chief thing, that is the form of the universe, and the clear symmetry of its parts."

> They are just like someone including in a picture of hands, feet, head, and other limbs from different places, well painted indeed, but not modeled

from the same body, and not in the least matching each other, so that a monster would be produced from them rather than a man.

He therefore read the writings of all the learned men he could find in order to arrive at a different, better explanation than those provided by the theoretical mathematicians.

With Copernicus's "preface" to Pope Paul III and the debates that surrounded his work, rhetoric entered into the style of discussion.[53] The writings of the great astronomers and mathematicians of the age—we got a taste of Galileo's rhetoric at the beginning of this book—shine with ornate quotations and images from mythology and the great literature of antiquity. What we call "Renaissance" also flashes forth from every page of Copernicus's preface. When grappling with Ptolemy, Copernicus first calls upon Cicero, who reports Hicetas of Syracuse's hypothesis that the Earth rotates around its own axis. Another ancient author he relies on is Martianus Capella, a native of a Roman province in Africa, according to whom Mercury and Venus—although not Earth or the other planets—orbit the Sun.[54] The weightiest authority Copernicus cites is the Pythagorean Philolaus, who believed that the Earth, Sun, and Moon revolved around a "Central Fire."[55] Finally, he reports that Heraclides of Pontus and the Pythagorean Ecphantus claimed the Earth spun like a wheel around its own center, from west to east. "I therefore took this opportunity and also began to consider the possibility that the Earth moved."

Not satisfied with hypotheses, Copernicus attempted to calculate the consequences of the Earth's double motion, namely around its own axis and around the Sun. In so doing, he created a model of the universe that contradicted Ptolemaic astronomy and Aristotelian physics in essential aspects. Nevertheless, the paradigm shift remained incomplete. For Copernicus did not intend to overthrow the old systems completely. Rather, he tried to "save" them by means of (very significant) corrections. He obstinately worked on the construction of an elegant "world machine." In his view, the apparent retrograde motion of the planets could be explained more easily by assuming the Earth moved. In addition, this trick made it possible to dispense with the equants.[56] And was it not simpler to make the tiny Earth move than to put the Sun and the whole, massive sphere of the fixed stars in motion?

By the time *De revolutionibus orbium coelestium* was finally in print, the theory had again lost a good deal of its elegance. The circular orbits of the planets were "saved"; not until Kepler would it be proven that they actually correspond to elliptical conic sections (pp. 787f.). Yet the center of the orbits calculated by Copernicus in no way coincided with the location of the Sun. Rather, the heavenly bodies revolved around the center of the Earth's orbit. That once again put the center of the universe a bit off-center. Copernicus was thus himself forced to entwine epicycle upon epicycle—at least there were now five fewer than in the old cosmos[57]—and to have the Earth's axis spin conically in order to make his system accord with observational data. Nevertheless, he trumpeted the most important result of his deliberations.

> In the middle of all is the seat of the Sun. For who in this most beautiful of temples would put this lamp in any other or better place than the one from which it can illuminate everything at the same time? Aptly indeed is he named by some the lantern of the universe, by others the mind, by others the ruler. Trismegistus called him the visible God, Sophocles's Electra, the watcher over all things. Thus indeed the Sun as if seated on a royal throne governs his household of Stars as they circle around him.[58]

In the new system, the Earth's distance from the Sun was used to determine the space between all the other planets. Mercury was placed closest to the central star, while Saturn followed the furthest orbit.

> We find, then, in this arrangement the marvelous symmetry of the universe, and a sure linking together in harmony of the motion and size of the spheres, such as could be perceived in no other way.

In the eyes of many contemporaries, Copernicus's book did no more than propose a rather unlikely alternative to the Ptolemaic system. Objections galore could be made. For example, it could be noted that according to the prevailing Aristotelian teaching, all heavy elements tended downward—exactly where the Earth had resided till then. How could the Sun, the natural abode of the lighter element of fire, suddenly be the home of all that was heavy? This view even found support in the theology of Thomas Aquinas. His universe combined a physical hierarchy with a moral one, beginning with the heavy and evil and culminating in the spiritual and most perfect and thus in God.[59] How, then, could hell hover *above* the Sun, which seemed to shine forth in immaculate purity? Another problem was the observation that the fixed stars twinkled away in stoic serenity. If the Earth revolved around the Sun, thus moving closer to and further away from them, should they not at times appear larger and brighter, at times smaller and darker, which they manifestly did not?

Another strong argument had been proposed back in antiquity by Ptolemy himself, in opposition to Aristarchus's heliocentric thought experiment: if the

Earth moved at high speed, must not everything that was not nailed down fly westward?[60] Copernicus countered that clouds, birds, human beings, and all other physical things belonged to the Earth and therefore shared in its natural motion. As for the objection that the fixed stars lacked parallax—evidence to the contrary was not provided until 1838—Copernicus sought to undermine it with a clever argument: the Earth's distance to the fixed stars was too great for changes in the latter's size to be perceptible; from the stars' point of view, the Earth's entire orbit would itself look like a mere dot.

Indeed, Copernicus's calculations massively increased the size of the universe circumscribed by the sphere of the fixed stars: from Ptolemy's 20,000 Earth radii to 1.2 million, or, converted to modern measurements, from 90 million kilometers to 7.4 billion kilometers.[61] The unsettling upshot was that a gargantuan empty space now opened up between Saturn, the outermost of the planets then known, and the edge of the universe.[62] The apparent sense-lessness of such a design again contradicted the conviction that God created nothing without reason.[63] It was still utterly unclear how the "moresca" of the heavenly bodies—the metaphor is from Celtis[64]—worked in practice if one assumed the existence of transparent and yet somehow solid spheres. Copernicus could provide no evidence for his model. Instead, he offered his rhetoric, which focused on "simplicity," "harmony," and economy as design principles of the universe. The Polish astronomer agreed with Aristotle that "God and nature do nothing in vain."[65]

Copernicus expected to be attacked by the Church. "There may be triflers," he wrote in the preface to his book, "who . . . because of some passage of Scripture wrongly twisted to their purpose . . . will dare criticize and censure this undertaking of mine." Even Lactantius, "a distinguished writer in other ways but no mathematician, speaks very childishly about the shape of the Earth when he makes fun of those who reported that it has the shape of a globe."[66] Probably to defend Copernicus, the Nuremberg theologian Andreas Osiander added another preface to the book in which he downplayed the new model of the universe as a mere hypothesis. In so doing, he toed the line that had been prudent for dealing with dangerous ideas since the Paris verdict of 1277: to discuss scientific propositions that did not harmonize with the faith as thought experiments. Indeed, while Osiander was writing his preface, out in the Holy Roman Empire the Schmalkaldic War was brewing. Caution was therefore advisable.

Copernicus died on May 24, 1543. We do not know if he ever held the printed copy of his *Revolutions* in his hands, and thus it is unclear if he approved of the preface added by Osiander. The vast majority of scholars preferred to remain on the firm foundation of Ptolemaic Earth. The two editions of *De revolutionibus orbium coelestium* that appeared before 1600—all in all, one thousand copies may have been printed—were overshadowed by the one hundred or more editions of books with a Ptolemaic worldview.[67] The Oxford professor of mathematics Sir Henry Savile (1549–1622) once said that the Earth is moved in a circle, but such a remark was a great exception. So was the globe labeled "mobilis" that was shown during the newly elected Holy Roman Emperor Rudolph II's entrance into Vienna in 1577.[68]

The Books of God

Acceptance of the heliocentric theory was hindered in Protestant circles by the fact that Luther personally rejected it. He compared what he called *astronomia confusa* ("confused astronomy") with a person riding on a ship or wagon who thinks he is standing still while the land and trees move. "I believe the Scriptures," he wrote. "For Joshua commanded the Sun to stand still and not the Earth."[69] This biblical allusion was often cited in opposition to Copernicus. According to the story, God made the Sun stand still for the Israelite general Joshua, thus enabling a complete victory over the Amorites.[70] Luther's friend Melanchthon added that wise rulers should tame mischievous minds like the "Sarmatian stargazer," who moved the Earth and bound the Sun. Other Reformers, including Calvin, also rejected the new model of the universe.[71]

Copernicus's provocation prompted others to compare the old cosmology and Aristotelian physics with another book whose author was no less than the Creator himself: the book of nature. Alan of Lille (ca. 1128–1202) reduced the metaphor to a formula:

> Every creature is for us
> Of the world an image and a book
> And a mirror in which to look.[72]

According to Nicholas of Cusa, the Lord wrote this book "with his own finger."[73] To read it meant to draw closer to his revelations. That is why Saint Augustine approved the study of nature.

Much intellectual energy was devoted to creating a concordance between the two books, the Bible and the book of nature. The foundation for deciphering the hidden messages of Holy Writ was provided by the late antique teaching of the "three senses of scripture." The same principle was used to interpret the works of Virgil and Homer. Origen had taken the first steps in this direction in the third century when he distinguished between a "somatic" (i.e., bodily or literal) sense for simple readers, a "psychic" (i.e., soulful or moral) sense for advanced readers, and a "pneumatic" (i.e., spiritual or divine) sense for perfect readers. This approach to reading the Bible opened up a broader scope for interpretation. Those expert in applying it, such as Calvin, transformed the ominous sphere of water above the ninth sphere into simple clouds.[74] In his view, this accorded with common sense.

What happened in God's second book, nature, was also open to interpretation. God was the master of living creatures, of plants, stones, and planets. He made the rules and also determined the exceptions. He could stop the Sun, perform miracles, create monsters, and admonish or threaten by means of dramatic heavenly signs. Just like Allah and the gods of China—the weather continued to comment on the work of provincial authorities there down to the eighteenth century[75]—the Christian God was disinclined to silently stand by and observe what his creatures did or failed to do. In principle, all things and all events were suspected of not simply existing in themselves but also of being signs of something else. Nothing in nature, the work of a perfect, almighty Creator, could be without meaning. This extended even to the lines on one's face, which were the subject of their own science, "metoposcopy." The art combined physiognomy with astrology.[76] Practitioners divided the forehead into regions, each of which was supposedly governed by a planet, and then attempted to predict one's character and future fate from the furrows. Even warts and birthmarks could say something about those who had them. A step toward secularization was taken in the sixteenth century when scholars began to distinguish between signs that came directly from God, supernatural signs, and others that had natural causes.[77]

History could also be interpreted in this manner, considering that it, like everything else, was the work of God. It was seen as the great author's third book. This view was common to both "Western" historians and non-European chroniclers.[78] For Christians, the beginning of history and its end were certain. It all started with the fall of man, and it would end with the Last Judgment. What happened in between could be assigned meaning with the aid of Holy Writ and the study of nature. In this way, the three books commented on each other. An earthquake heralded "earthshattering" events or helped their significance to be understood. Flooding was a symbol of the Great Flood and thus an admonition from God in the face of moral decline or heresy. A comet was a warning sign that presaged war and rebellion. And the meaning of the greatest historical event, the death of Christ, had been indicated by a solar eclipse.

Hermeneutics often proceeded on the basis of analogies to everyday life. For example, the tail of a comet was interpreted as the image of a rod and thus as a threat of divine castigation. And considering that the celestial rovers seemed to follow no fixed orbit, it made sense to see them as heralds of chaos and calamity. As we read in Shakespeare's *Troilus and Cressida*,

> but when the planets
> In evil mixture to disorder wander,
> What plagues and what portents! what mutiny!
> What raging of the sea! shaking of earth!
> Commotion in the winds![79]

Less remarkable things than comets also elicited interpretation. When a rainbow appeared above the battle lines at Frankenhausen on May 15, 1525, Müntzer is said to have interpreted it as a sign that God was with the peasants. In the book of Genesis, did God not use a rainbow to promise a covenant with Noah after the Great Flood?[80] Monstrous births and "sulfur rain"—probably clouds of pollen wafting over the land in May—even blood-red sunsets and strange cloud formations were subject to interpretation. "Books of wonders," which appeared in increasing numbers and enjoyed brisk sales, helped to make sense of such phenomena.[81] Yet the grand meaning of everything would only be revealed in the final act of the universal drama with which God concluded his greatest book: the heavens. This was the perspective within which "the sense of an ending," as described by Frank Kermode, became a fundamental constant of Western thought.[82]

33

The Great Chain of Being

Renaissance Magic: The Power of Words and Things

Magic is a universal human practice. In all ages and in all cultures, it has been considered a way to ward off pain and danger or to gain an advantage. Shamans, Buddhist monks, and Taoist priests counted as magicians, just like Jewish wonder workers and the healers, treasure hunters, and "wise women" of Europe did.[1] Thinking in analogies, adjacencies, kinships, and affinities was a method for bringing order to the physiognomy of the inchoate early modern world and discovering the meaning of things. Human beings saw themselves as a microcosm of the larger universe—in Latin Europe as in China or India.[2] As Foucault put it, "The universe was folded in upon itself: the Earth echoing the sky, faces seeing themselves reflected in the stars, and plants holding within their stems the secrets that were of use to man."[3] The search for similarities, Ficino's "congruences," became the focus of the episteme.[4]

The external was considered a sign of the internal; a thing's appearance was thought to correspond with its qualities and powers. Symbol and symbolized were not two separate things. Rather, they were believed to be connected to one another by spiritual forces. Thus by pricking a fetish, one simultaneously pricked the thing of which it was an image. It was an imperative of Renaissance learning to analyze similarities, explore hidden properties, and put them to use. As Ficino taught, magic was the art of combining "vapors, numbers, figures, qualities"—nothing other than a technology based on the knowledge of nature and geometry.[5]

The power of the words used by magicians and priests was also based on this special brand of logic. Words seemed to be an inseparable part of what they denoted. Only in modern times would this symbiosis break down.[6] The potential of mere words seemed massive, indeed infinite. So much could be seen in the book of Genesis, where God created the universe using *logos* alone—a highly complex term generally translated simply as "word." Pico della Mirandola was convinced that human beings could attain the creative power of God by deciphering the meaning of numbers and words in the Bible or Kabbala and thus unveiling God's mystery. Words, symbols, and rituals could make one the master of the universe as long as one knew how to handle the powers of nature. One would become, in Pico's view, the "lord and master" of nature.[7] The only limits to this power were set by God's omnipotence.

Reverence for the almighty word was also a motive for Johannes Reuchlin's defense of Jewish books. His writings *On the Art of Kabbala* and *The Wonder-Working Word* were meant to provide knowledge of it to Christian humanists.[8] For the practice of magic, words were of paramount importance even in the form of Christian prayers, which along with obscure formulas were part of occult rituals. Rare and difficult-to-find or disgusting things—body parts of executed people, for example, or snakes or bats—were often necessary as well.

Just as the holy could be helpful or dangerous and thus commanded reverence, magic rituals required the utmost precision. That was the only way to keep the forces it unleashed from turning destructive. The slightest deviation could render the ritual ineffective, just like a mistake in a "normal" prayer that offended the divinity. If one wrong word slipped out, the demon might enter the protective chalk circle and wring the conjuror's neck.[9] A mistake made the inviolable area permeable. When practiced regularly, occult rituals *compelled* demons to do one's bidding, whereas prayer could merely make requests of God. As hard as magicians tried to affirm that they only used natural powers and therefore were no different from physicians, they were quick to be accused of making a pact with the devil. The Church certainly viewed their activity with suspicion. After all, Catholic priests themselves disposed of magical charms of tremendous power, such as the host, relics, and rites. In the sixteenth century, they kept an increasingly jealous watch over magicians, male and female alike, to make sure they did not become competitors.

The Power of Stones and Stars: Alchemists and Astrologers

In the Renaissance, the word "occult" did not denote anything supernatural or demonic. Rather, in line with the meaning of the Latin term *occultus*, it referred to powers that were "hidden" in things, powers that could be activated by virtue of the model of analogy and, according to Ficino,[10] with the life-giving principle of love. The host of the Eucharist unleashed these forces just like a magnet, a plant, or a gem. For example, carnelian, itself red, was thought to affect the humor of blood and thus soothe a violent temper or help with nosebleeds or menstrual pains.[11] Works like Albertus Magnus's *Secreta* had compiled knowledge of such powers. The material came not only from medieval sources but also from the ancient and Arabic traditions.[12] Printers with a good catalog of *secreta* literature stood to earn high profits. One of the most successful works of this kind was the *Secreti*, published in 1555 under the pseudonym Alessio Piemontese. The book contained recipes for all kinds of remedies, soaps, and even paints and jams. It was translated into many languages and appeared in more than one hundred editions before 1700.

Renaissance alchemy oscillated between hocus pocus, experiment, and empiricism. The founding document of the field was the *Emerald Tablet*, or *Tabula Smaragdina*. Its myth reached Europe from Arabic sources. According to one variant of the legend, it was found in the grave of Hermes Trismegistus, which was believed to be in the Pyramid of Cheops. The text on the tablet supposedly contained all the knowledge of the primeval sage.[13] "Miracles are worked by One, just as the things of that substance are created from one single process," we read in a Spanish translation of the twelfth century. "Take the earth away from the fire, and it will shine for you!"[14] Numerous commentaries interpreted these words. The techniques of alchemy—pulverizing, distilling, melting—had the aim of refining raw materials to obtain an absolutely pure substance called *prima materia*, and then using it to act on the hidden processes of nature.[15]

Whereas the *Corpus Hermeticum* had been in circulation since the fifteenth century in the translation by Marsilio Ficino, the Greek tradition of alchemy was not available until much later, with the publication of Domenico Pizzimenti's *Ars magna* in 1573.[16] The appearance of this and many other texts inaugurated an age of alchemy that would culminate in the following century. The practical goal of alchemical experimentation was to attain all manner of remedies, gold, and, ideally, the "philosopher's stone."[17] More properly the "stone of the philosophers," it was supposedly a complete microcosm that contained the properties of all the elements. Whatever came into contact with the stone would, following the law of entelechy, be infused with the need to reach perfection. Silver would turn to gold, and the sick would become healthy. Roger Bacon said animal blood was the chief component of the stone, whereas the Arab Jabir ibn Hayyan, a man of the eighth century and the author of a widely diffused book of alchemy, favored quicksilver.

From the perspective of magic and alchemy, nothing in the universe stood alone. Everything was directly or indirectly connected to everything else. "What is above comes from below, and what is below comes from above," murmured the *Emerald Tablet*. According to another of its rumblings, "The fine is nobler than the rough—cautious and wise. It rises from the Earth to Heaven and seizes the lights from above; it descends back down to Earth in possession of the power of above and below."[18] The great chain of being ranged from dirt, clay, and human beings to angels and God. It was the model and justification for social hierarchies.[19] Angels and demons—rational, immortal beings capable of suffering—supposedly acted as intermediaries.[20] Since the order of the universe prescribed that the mightier and the higher should have power over the weaker and the lower—thus wrote Bonaventure (1221–1274)— the stars had power over the elements and the bodies composed of them.[21] In the Renaissance, people were still also generally convinced that it must be possible to harness energies from the upper spheres down on Earth.[22] To do so, it was necessary to access the hidden powers of the elementary world with the aid of medicine and philosophy, those of the spiritual world with the rites of religion, and those of the heavens using mathematics and astrology. Alchemy was close kin to this last discipline. One scholar called it "terrestrial astronomy."[23] As for the celestial variety, its significance was not affected by Copernicus's attacks on the Ptolemaic model of the universe. It is even possible that the Polish astronomer began his studies with the intention of repudiating Pico della Mirandola's criticism of astrology, with which he may have become acquainted in Bologna.[24]

For astrologers, human beings were the point of reference for all that happened in the heavens.[25] The movements of the planets took place as a moral theater for human eyes alone. Heavenly bodies admonished, threatened, and made promises, but they also caused things to happen. Heralding and influencing human fate was the purpose of their dance. Affecting life under the moon was supposedly the aim of the powers emitted by the stars. Their influence was thought to have a profound impact on nature and, thus, also on the human body. Ptolemy had already expressed the opinion that the diverse physical attributes of individuals are related to the positions of the planets at their birth.[26] To quote Hans Sachs, the *astronomus* knew

If the harvest would be good next year
Or prices would rise and war draw near
And various diseases set in.

Like magic, "astral rays" worked according to the rules of analogy and sympathy. For example, if a magical amulet bore the symbol of the sun, its power would be activated when it was ritually placed in the sun's "energy field."[27] An essential aspect was the position of the wandering planets in the sky with respect to the signs of the zodiac. The symbols formed in this way were assigned binding power. The character traits of the populaces of entire cities were derived from the powers of the planetary constellation under which those communities had initially been founded. Some thinkers even believed the course of history to be generally subject to the stars. For example, Pietro d'Abano connected upturns in world history with harmonious conditions in the heavenly spheres. Accordingly, decline was supposedly related to the precession of the equinoxes, which since antiquity had been observed as a disturbance in celestial order.[28] The notary Cecco d'Ascoli (1257–1327), a contemporary of Pietro d'Abano, was doomed when an Inquisitor deemed that he thought "everything" was subject to the power of the stars. He even believed that the planets determined the life of Christ, whose horoscope he had cast.[29] Cecco was burned at the stake as a heretic.

The astrologers' intellectual model had always been controversial.[30] In Chaucer's view, their art was worthless.[31] Theological misgivings stemmed from concerns that belief in the power of the stars called God's omnipotence into doubt. Supporters of the astrological path to knowledge countered that the stars indeed ruled human beings, but that it was God who guided the stars. They had an effect on people, but they could not compel them. Pomponazzi had argued in like manner, and Kepler agreed as well.[32] Accordingly, astrological speculation had to ultimately lead to knowledge of divine will, just as the observation of planetary motion did.[33] Thus, religious conviction provided a deeper motive for relentless questioning—even on the part of some of the heroes of the Scientific Revolution.

Scholars, Charlatans, Science

Since astrology promised manifold uses and even mastery over the future, it was underwritten by rulers in all times and many cultures. In Latin Europe, astrology or astronomy—the terms were interchangeable in contemporary usage—had been established in universities since the Late Middle Ages.[34] For example, the holder of the professorship established in Cracow in 1459 had to cast one horoscope every year. He also lectured on Abu Ma'shar's *Great Introduction to Astronomy*.[35] In the early sixteenth century, the astrological system was expanded further on the basis of more precise translations of Ptolemy's writings.[36] Even military commanders were advised to learn astrology, as it could help them assess the strengths and weaknesses of their enemies and determine the proper time to wage war.[37]

From the very beginning, Copernicus's search for a coherent model of the universe was primarily intended to create a new foundation for prognostication and calendrical calculation. Even critics of his main thesis valued his book because it did, in fact, provide more precise data than other writings. Belief in the auguries and power of the stars was in no way weakened when forecasts turned out to be wrong. In any case, the complicated system of astrology was clear only to experts. And if a prediction proved false, then it was assumed the data underlying it had simply been too imprecise. Thus, when a foretold event did not occur, Regiomontanus did not argue against astrological thinking itself but rather urged the improvement of observational methods.[38] Astronomical data initially recorded for astrological purposes was also used to create calendars and to aid ocean voyages. Unintentionally and adventitiously, "serious" knowledge was thus amassed that helped to demolish a millennial worldview.

The same factors that helped astrology endure also buttressed the survival of magic. Its procedures were also highly complex. One wrong word at the wrong time, one missing substance—if necessary, even the intercession of God—could explain any failure. Moreover, no one knew the ultimate source of a given problem or to what extent human intervention could help. Nor could it ever be excluded that an illness had moral causes and was, accordingly, divine punishment. It therefore made sense to seek errors not in the system itself but in individual concrete applications and the empirical foundation for using them.

Alchemy, the sister of astrology and magic, had been forbidden by the Church in the fourteenth century—in vain, of course, as it promised as tremendous results as magic: wealth, health, and youth, perhaps immortality if the alchemical masterstroke of finding the philosopher's stone was achieved. In addition, alchemy forged bonds with Christian mysticism, as can be seen in the *Buch der heiligen Dreifaltigkeit* (*Book of the Holy Trinity*), written at the time of the Council of Constance. Governments and even highly rational businessmen like the Fuggers invested "venture capital" in alchemical experiments. It seldom paid off. Masters of the occult like Dr. Faust did not know how to make gold but rather only how to draw it from their patrons' coffers. If they were not careful, they might end up reaping their final reward under the gallows.[39] Vannoccio Biringuccio, a trailblazer of metallurgy, said in his *Pirotechnia* that he did not understand how anyone could believe what the alchemists' promised.[40]

Nevertheless, alchemy also had a legitimate place in the prehistory of the Scientific Revolution.[41] Its distilling and sampling produced actual knowledge just as astrology did, since the search for the philosopher's stone and the occult properties of things motivated experimentation. In this way, the alchemical laboratory contributed to the development of the research laboratory. Accordingly, John Dee (1527–1608)—astrologer to Elizabeth I, mathematician and geographer, magician, conversation partner to angels, eclectic Aristotelian and Platonic mystic all in one—saw magic as an experimental science and not as an "art" or a diabolical practice.[42] In fact, valuable things were discovered. Experimenting with quicksilver brought to light its propensity to combine with other metals, an important insight for the amalgamation of silver and gold. The most famous example of a discovery made accidentally via alchemical experiments is the early-eighteenth-century reinvention of porcelain by the Saxonian "gold-maker" Johann Friedrich Böttger. Of course, the number of false paths the alchemists went down was legion.

The forward-looking aspect of alchemical practice was its method of achieving progress by means of experimentation and making mistakes. Learning by trial and error is still a foundational principle of scientific activity today. Yet modern science and especially medicine were only able to develop because angels and demons, thinking in analogies, and belief in God's miracles were ultimately banned from scientific discourse. But that lay far in the future.

34

The Dissection of Man

The Rise of the *Medicus*

Printing increasingly turned medical knowledge into common knowledge. To take one example, let us turn again to Dioscorides' classic herbal. By now, it had been roused from its 700-year hibernation in a library in Córdoba by the humanist Juan Páez de Castro (ca. 1510–1570). The hunter for lost literary treasures made the *antiquissimo codice Griego*, the "ancient Greek manuscript," available to the Converso physician Andres de Laguna (1499–1559).[1] The latter was the right reader for the manuscript. For Laguna was not only a botanist and apothecary but also a philologist. He translated the text into the Castilian vernacular, supplementing it with information about newly discovered plants from Asia and the Americas. The work was printed in 1570, allowing Dioscorides to finally leave his Latin ivory tower in Spain and make his way to physicians who only understood *vulgar castellan*. At the same time, Dioscorides' tortuous history of transmission provides an example of how humanist elite culture could become useful to broader swathes of society—and how the new medium of print stole the secrets of popular medicine. The work and methods of its practitioners—female herbalists, "wise women," barbers, surgeons, and midwives—may have been of more practical use to people than academic medicine, which, however, was expert at appropriating "folk" knowledge.[2]

The art of medicine was still founded on principles from antiquity and Arabic culture. Yet the Renaissance put an immortal Platonic soul into the mortal Aristotelian body, like a pearl into an oyster.[3] The most important authority by far continued to be Galen. His "humoral pathology," whose deepest roots may have been in Indian Ayurveda (p. 865), was the basis for a kind of psychological materialism. It was premised on the belief that the human body, like all substances of the sublunar world, was composed of the four elements of air, fire, earth, and water. Inside the body, four humors (i.e., fluids) corresponded to these elements: blood to air, yellow bile to fire, black bile to earth, and phlegm to water. These humors had specific qualities, namely cold, hot, dry, and moist. They intermingled in all manner of ways, thus producing the various temperaments. When we say today that a cheerful person is "sanguine," that is a relic of humoral pathology. The term denotes a surplus of life-giving, stimulating blood.

According to Galenic teaching, health meant the harmony of humoral fluids, whereas illness indicated an imbalance. All of a physician's efforts were aimed at restoring this balance, for instance by bloodletting, the weapon of choice in the therapeutic arsenal. If an unsound body was excreting fluids such as blood, pus, sweat, or vomit, it was an indication that nature was trying to heal itself. The doctor came to its aid. Bodily excretions, especially urine, were to be examined carefully. "Uroscopy" was such a common medical procedure that artists, when portraying physicians, tended to show them holding a glass of urine as a symbol of their trade.

In the view of Renaissance doctors, the composition of the humors was influenced by many factors. Even witnessing a disturbing scene could provoke an imbalance and result, for example, in the birth of an ugly child.[4] Experts were convinced that climate, diet, and even the power of the stars could upset humoral composition, thereby injuring one's state of health. For doctors, therefore, astrological knowledge was not only useful but also necessary. When syphilis started spreading, the calamity was ascribed to a planetary conjunction. The evil planets Mars and Saturn—so the theory went—had converged in the sign of Scorpio, the ruler of the genitals, and overcome benevolent Jupiter. A remedy was thought to be available in the quicksilver of Mercury, which suppressed a few symptoms (but tended to do more harm than good).

In accordance with the relationship between the microcosm of the body and the macrocosm of the universe, the body's organs and their products were all thought to be under the influence of their own specific celestial counterparts. For example, the blood produced in the liver was believed to belong to air and to the signs of Libra, Aquarius, and Gemini. Also related to this humor was the planet Jupiter, the partner of tin. The star of geniuses and melancholiacs, artists and inventors, was thought to be sullen Saturn, whose God, according to myth, had eaten his own children.[5] Saturn was the father of depression and creativity. It caused melancholy by thinning out and concentrating the humors from the height of its sphere and by making the spleen boil over with black bile. It was aided in this malignant business by Earth, by its metal, lead, and by its preferred season, gloomy autumn. Magicians and physicians had to take all these factors into account.

To restore health, they could try to intervene in the "great chain of being" on all manner of levels. The treatment had to take place at the right time. Planetary power and the hidden forces of things could be mobilized to activate the potential of herbs, gems, metals, and amulets. There was no agreement as to what helped best. In addition, Galen had given the sound advice that prevention was better than healing. He recommended moderation, taking baths and exercising, listening to music, or observing pleasing colors. Alberti believed he had once been cured of a fever in this way.[6]

Galen's suggestions, the theory of the temperaments, and finally the authors' own experience informed a rich body of advice literature. These "health manuals" helped people to heal the body, just as the *ars moriendi*, instructions in the "art of dying," helped to care for the soul.[7] Translations into the vernacular made this knowledge available to an ever-larger audience. The genre began in Italy with the *Libellus de conservatione sanitatis* (*Brief Treatise on Preserving Health*) by Benedetto Reguardati (ca. 1398–1469), Sforza's personal physician.[8] An example from England was Thomas Elyot's (1490–1546) *Castell of Helth*, full of macrobiotic tips. German contributions included the richly illustrated herbals produced by the physician and botanist Leonhart Fuchs (1501–1566; Plate 22).

Medical knowledge and teaching were now no longer the province of hospitals and their libraries but rather could be found at universities. "Modern"—

i.e., learned—medicine had begun its career. Class consciousness and the desire to communicate with colleagues caused academically trained doctors to form guild-like associations. In 1518, the Royal College of Physicians was founded in London at the suggestion of the physician and humanist Thomas Linacre. A clear line separated the new *medicus* from the surgeons and barbers, who worked with blood, festering flesh, and phlegm. The *medicus* gingerly held the urine sample, drawing conclusions from its color and consistency, wearing a knowledgeable expression and probably speaking in Latin. During dissections, he stood genteelly to the side while journeymen did the dirty work. That meant that he possessed a great deal of book learning but had barely any practical experience with patients.

Vital Spirits, Holistic Medicine: Fernel, Paracelsus

In the sixteenth century, the professional field of the physicians also split off from that of the theoretically minded natural philosophers.[9] Yet there were some who rounded out their practical work by exploring the underlying conditions that determined health and sickness. These studies delved deep into dim areas of knowledge, as can be seen in the writings of Jean François Fernel (ca. 1497–1558), the personal physician of King Henry II of France and his wife Catherine de' Medici.[10] Fernel's search for "hidden causes" of illnesses led him to tackle big questions. A "fiery substance" like the mind needed sustenance. Where did it come from? The soul and the body had to be connected somehow. But by what? How did life come about? And how much power did magic have?

Fernel was a capable anatomist, as well as an avid mathematician. In 1542, he broke new ground with the publication of his *Physiology*—a term he is thought to have coined. He was the first to describe the spinal canal, the heart's pumping mechanism, and the symptoms of endocarditis. In addition, he speculated that *spiritus*, literally "spirit," was at work in the body. According to Aristotle, this very fine substance was where heat resided and was the generator of all life; it also participated in the divine.[11] Fernel believed that "natural spirit" ran through the veins from the liver, whereas "vital spirit" was sent out through the arteries from the heart. Spirit responsible for perception and motion floated through the nerve fibers from the brain and the spinal cord. As the binding agent between body and soul, Fernel hypothesized an oily "essential humor" (*humor nativus et primigenius*) that was both fatty and airy and supposedly invisible. Death resulted from its depletion.

Fernel's ideas influenced physicians down to the seventeenth century. The basic outlines of the physiology he sketched came from Plato, Aristotle, and Galen. To explain the mystery of life, the latter's medicine called upon not only *spiritus* but also the *pneuma* of the Stoics, a fine, animating breath. On the other hand, Galen had also developed rational models to explain disease. In contrast to contemporary healers of the East, he did not make recourse to theological explanations but rather sought natural causes.[12] That was another thing Galen taught questioners like Fernel. Groping and fumbling their way forward, they sought "natural" explanations for bodily functions and life. By positing sublime substances (such as *spiritus* or *pneuma*) in direct communication with the divinity, they believed they had found mediums that transformed spirit into motion and channeled the power of the distant heavenly spheres into human bodies.

The first physician to decisively break with ancient medicine was a veritable hothead: Theophrastus Bombastus, the fabled Paracelsus (1493/94–1541).[13] He had studied, so he claimed, in Italy, perhaps in Ferrara. By nature a traveler, and not always a welcome one, he did not stay anywhere for long. In 1527, he threw Avicenna's *Canon of Medicine* and Galen's corpus into the Saint John's Fire outside the University of Basel. In response, his opponents then burned his books.[14] Yet Paracelsus, a scion of a noble Swabian family, was no rationalist. His medicine is thoroughly imbued with the holistic thinking of the era, with Platonic and Gnostic thought. He expressed his ideas in forceful German, not Latin. For in his opinion, it was God's will that nothing remain unknown to us "students of the stars,"[15] as all things had been created for our sake. Paracelsus viewed Creation as a massive alchemical undertaking.[16] He believed the material world to be mere slag left over from the heavenly one, made from the clear waters of the upper sphere. His goal was to explore nature, to read it like a book.[17] He, too, saw man as a microcosm, possessing a fleshly body and an astral one, the intermediary to the soul. Human individuality, growth, and sex were determined by *archeus*, a vital spirit that inhabited everything before it entered the world. In addition, its power caused illness, which thus no longer appeared as a disruption of Galenic humoral composition.[18] Sickness could be the result of poisons, the stars, or an unhealthy environment. It could also have moral causes, i.e., it could be a punishment from God—a notion, as we have seen, that reflected widespread beliefs. In Paracelsus's view, sinful thoughts transformed into a volatile substance that rose to the corresponding planet: envy to Saturn, for example, or deceptiveness to Mars. There it activated the seed of illness with which the star infected the air and could even bring about an epidemic.[19]

In the first half of the sixteenth century, only Luther wrote more than Paracelsus. Fortunately for the latter author, much remained unpublished. Although some of his positions were close to the Reformer's, his religious thought was generally unorthodox. He scornfully claimed that Zwingli, the pope, and the Anabaptists were all "cut from the same cloth."[20] He entertained the notion that God had created a female form of himself in order to create the second person of the Trinity—a view that could have sent him to the stake. In later years, he advocated a peaceful Christian life, wrote against war and the death penalty, and pleaded for a just allocation of the fruits of labor. Equally modern to our ears sounds his claim, found time and again in his labyrinthine oeuvre, that he relied on experience and experiment. He was the first to describe occupational diseases, as well as illnesses that resulted from *tartarus*, a deposit in the blood vessels and the organs named after the tartar found in wine casks. He called for the antiseptic treatment of wounds, conceived remedies, herbal therapies, and spa treatments, and developed surgical practices. On the other hand, he presumed to give the recipe for making an artificial man, a homunculus, which in turn could supposedly create fierce people like giants and pygmies.[21] Rather than the four elements of Greek natural philosophy, the world seemed to him to be composed of three other substances, all of which were related to constellations: fatty, combustible sulfur; smoky, volatile quicksilver; and finally crystalline salt. To deal with them, Paracelsus believed alchemical medicines were necessary, which he tried to obtain through a process of separation. He is rightfully considered the founder of iatrochemistry, or "chemical medicine," and thus of modern pharmacy.

Just how ambivalent this highly vaunted and highly controversial man was—his compatriot Thomas Erastus called him a beast, a grunting pig[22]— can be seen in his approach to madness. He believed it was not the work of Satan but rather had natural causes. Encouragement, fasting, and bed rest were sure to help. That sounds reasonable, but not his suggestion for what to do with the mentally ill should treatment fail: burn them so that the devil had no chance to take their souls.[23] Analogies that doubled as signs—heart-shaped things healed diseases of the heart, prickly thistles helped against stinging pain in the chest—replaced causality in Paracelsus's thought. His worldview was compatible with esoteric speculation, but it also prepared the way for a rational science that sought to harness the power of an autonomous nature.[24] As Galileo would soon do in physics, Paracelsus completed the turn in medicine toward systematic experimentation. While he was touting his at times opaque, at times illuminating cosmological medicine, the hour of the specialists struck.

Anatomical Revolution: Vesalius

The most important of the specialists was Andreas Vesalius (1514–1564) of Flanders, Fernel's premier student.[25] Right in the title-page engraving of his folio volume *On the Fabric of the Human Body*, he portrayed himself as an alternative to the book-learning of the Galenists (Fig. 51, p. 656). Surrounded by a dense crowd of spectators, he presents the uterus of a dead woman. And he does it himself, thereby styling himself an empiricist who, although a doctor of medicine and professor at the University of Padua, dissects bodies with his own hands instead of having it done for him. The study of the macrocosm was thus now accompanied by a fascination with the inner workings of the microcosm, the human body. The microscope had not yet been invented. Vesalius, therefore, sensibly agreed with Berengario da Carpi (ca. 1470–1530), one of his most important predecessors: what could not be seen—things that were too small—he refused to consider as objects of speculation.[26] His book symbolizes the gradual departure from holistic medicine à la Paracelsus. It provides a factual description of the body and the functions of the organs. Its more than seven hundred folio pages reflect the experience of a highly professional expert, one who describes and measures and no longer searches for spirits and the soul—at least not primarily. *On the Fabric of the Human Body* features clear typography and masterful graphic technique. It earned its author a post as personal physician to Holy Roman Emperor Charles V. Thanks to an abridged version, the *Epitome*, it enjoyed long-standing influence on medical practice. It served as a manual for teaching and surgery. *On the Fabric of the Human Body* marks a break in the history of anatomy, splitting it into ages before and after Vesalius.

Contrary to popular belief, the late medieval Church did not strictly forbid the dissection of human bodies.[27] At first, in Salerno, only pigs were dissected. But soon enough, Mondino de' Luzzi (1275–1326), author of the most important book of anatomy before Vesalius and an expert in Arabic medicine, dissected human bodies in Bologna without opposition. Just as astronomers hoped to decipher the words of God in the night sky, many anatomists believed human dissection was tantamount to seeking God and his miracles.[28]

The amazing fact is that the "spiritual" conception of the body did not keep Europe's doctors from cutting—as opposed to Ayurveda doctors in India, for example.[29]

Evidence of human dissection increases in the fifteenth century. By its end, Padua, the citadel of medicine, had an "anatomical theater." Built like an amphitheater, the room centered on a raised table where a corpse lay. Dissection also became the province of artists, especially sculptors. Leonardo was driven by scientific curiosity, whereas Michelangelo was more interested in its advantages for sculpting and painting the human form. It was not easy to procure a corpse (ideally fresh). Vesalius took the bodies of those who had been executed or committed suicide and who were therefore not allowed a proper burial. In Padua, his students stole the body of a monk's mistress from the cemetery, removing the skin from the head to keep her lover from identifying her should the robbery be discovered.[30]

As Columbus had explored the world and Copernicus had moved the Earth, Vesalius now investigated the almost wholly undiscovered country of the human body. He wanted to do the investigating himself, not simply believe what his predecessors told him. In the preface to his great work, dedicated to Charles V, he criticized earlier authors' slavish dependence on Galen. The latter, he remarked, often contradicted himself, and his knowledge came from the dissection not of human beings but of apes.[31] Yet Vesalius did not intend to uproot the entire system that had been passed down to him. He ferried the anatomical *practice* of the ancients into the Renaissance, justifying its fundamental significance for teaching and research.

Vesalius's anatomy book was published in 1543, the same year as Copernicus's *Revolutions*. It provides the most spectacular evidence of how important the technical advances of Renaissance painting could be for medical progress. Never before—except for Leonardo's as yet unpublished drawings—had art so precisely captured a subject of science. About two hundred woodcuts, probably produced by Jan van Calcar, a student of Titian, augmented the *Fabric*'s comprehensive text. They show what the knife had laid bare: bones, muscles, blood vessels, and organs. Some pages depict skeletons in the typical pose of the melancholiac, propped up on their elbows. Others feature skinned musclemen in exalted stances. At times it seems like surrealist art.

Despite Vesalius's trailblazing efforts, the path toward a new medicine was still long. His contemporary Fracastoro also remained in the Galenic paradigm. What is forward-looking in his work, as in Fernel's, can only be found in the details. Against the ancient view that effluvia rising from the earth were responsible for the outbreak of diseases, Fracastoro formulated his clever theory of infection via tiny particles, which he called *seminaria,* or "germs." On the whole, however, his work continues to consign human beings to a cosmos ruled by the stars and animated by an all-pervasive world soul. In his didactic poem about syphilis—it accomplishes the feat of describing a gruesome disease and all its symptoms in perfect poetry—the germ theory of infection shares space with astrological speculation. According to the latter, the plague of 1348 was related to fiery Mars and somber Saturn.[32]

Attempts to "save the phenomena" were also undertaken in the field of Galenic medicine. One example is the fate of the *rete mirabile.*[33] Galen had discovered this "miraculous web," or dense complex of arteries and veins, in his dissection of animals. He believed it supplied the brain with vital pneuma. Vesalius was not the first to note that this feature is absent in human beings. It was one of the two hundred errors he pointed out in Galen's oeuvre. The ancient authority was then defended by Jacques Dubois (1478–1555).[34] The Parisian was too good an anatomist not to agree that Vesalius's observation was correct. His way out was to assume a kind of degeneration of the human race. In antiquity, he argued, human beings must have been more perfect and therefore still had a *rete mirabile.* Dubois may have been thinking of the ideal bodies chiseled out of marble by ancient sculptors. He was not alone in ascribing perfection to antiquity, as is indicated by a strange episode reported from the year 1485.[35] It revolves around the discovery of the body of a Roman woman from the time of Augustus on the Via Appia outside Rome. Thanks to a coating in an antiseptic essence, it had been preserved perfectly. It was brought to the Capitol, where people came in droves and were amazed: finally, they had seen a person from antiquity in the flesh! The dead woman was "more beautiful," in one chronicler's estimation, "than could be said or written." Apparently, some Renaissance contemporaries could not imagine the people of the venerated Golden Age as anything other than marvelous.

ICY TIMES

35

European Tableau I

WESTERN EUROPE—CONFESSIONS, WARS, COUNTRIES OF THE FUTURE

Climate Change, Starvation, Witchcraft Craze

As the sixteenth century progressed, Europe and the rest of the world got colder. Average temperatures began to decline gradually around 1540 and then more dramatically after about 1560.[1] Large bodies of water like the Thames and Lake Constance froze over. The year 1573 witnessed the iciest winter of the century and the coldest in half a millennium; 1587 went down in the chronicles as a summerless year. Glaciers crept down into the valleys. Grain rotted in the rain; hail stormed down from yellow clouds. Floods became more common, and wolves wandered through frozen towns and villages. A memento of the temperature plunge is provided by the first large-format winter paintings in the history of European art, one of which is Pieter Bruegel's *Hunters in the Snow*, painted in 1565 (Fig. 52, p. 665). At the same time, the number of astrological writings jumped. People feared for the future and wanted to know what to expect.[2] The physician Michel de Nostredame (1503–1566), the famed "Nostradamus," found a wide audience with his cryptic prophecies.

The disastrous weather was the low point in a long-term cooling of the Earth's climate known as the "Little Ice Age." It began around 1300 and lasted until 1850. Only during the eighteenth century did the sky brighten for a while. In all likelihood, the great freeze was global. It is now thought to have been caused by a decrease in solar activity, as well as by a burst of massive volcanic eruptions. There were also warm days and beautiful summers; problems arose when there were two or three bad years, and thus bad harvests, in a row. Town granaries tended to hold enough stores for the population to survive for nine months. If the shortage continued, bread was baked in smaller loaves—and sold for the same price. Grain imports from the Baltic region, where a repressive manorial economy enabled higher yields,[3] did not suffice to close the supply gap. Firewood also grew scarce.

The ice age had especially dramatic consequences because Europe's population had grown, having pretty much reached the limits of the possible. Now the Malthusian mechanism set in. Starvation returned, more intense and more dire than ever before. It made lifespan even shorter than it already was due to epidemics and wars. Some people wasted away till they looked like walking skeletons. As one contemporary reported, privation turned the skin ashen, sometimes almost black; it induced hallucinations; greedy death lay in wait.[4] The killing was abetted by inflation, which was spurred on by the influx of precious metal from the Americas and even more by population growth. Real wages stagnated while prices rose.[5] When the demographic curve dipped again in the final third of the century, craftsmen were not able to react immediately to sinking demand. Especially in the notoriously volatile textile sector, production outpaced the needs of consumers. As a result, large numbers of weavers and other craftsmen involved in the making of cloth and clothing sank into poverty.[6]

Social tensions were increased by the state's hunger for money. It levied taxes, chiefly on those who barely had anything to eat anyway and who watched as inflation chipped away at what they had saved for even rainier days. In this way, state expansion, war, and climate entered into an unholy alliance.

Starting in the second half of the sixteenth century, this troika caused an increasing number of states to collapse, fomenting revolutions and revolts all over Europe and around the globe: from Mexico to Japan, from the Philippines and India to Brazil.[7] Most of these did not aim at fundamental change in the system but merely at combatting starvation and want, and perhaps at restoring prior, better conditions.

People at the time did not understand the complex mechanisms behind their misery. At least the French jurist Jean Bodin (1529/30–1596) recognized that the silver streaming out of the New World was involved in the mysterious phenomenon of currency depreciation. His contemporary, the financier Sir Thomas Gresham (1519–1579), advisor to Queen Elizabeth I of England and founder of the Royal Exchange, formulated the law that would later be named for him: bad money drives out good, i.e., coins whose face value exceeds their precious metal content drive good coins from the market. They are spirited out of the country or are socked away. But rational explanations of this kind were an exception. Instead, most people ultimately saw the punitive hand of God behind the climate crisis and its dreadful consequences.

When searching for an immediate cause of poverty, contemporaries unfailingly blamed it on the poor themselves. Their supposed laziness, the sin of sloth, was thought to have called forth the wrath of God. If the Lord, as one German preacher at the turn of the seventeenth century taught, was a member of the *Arbeiterzunft*, or "workers' guild," then Satan represented the league of loafers, who were assisted by their own special demon, the *Faulteufel* (literally "lazy devil").[8] The fight against laziness was also prosecuted by a plethora of treatises. Work, which had long been seen merely as the irksome upshot of original sin, now became a civic virtue. Amidst the crisis provoked by climate change, a veritable "industriousness campaign" unfolded that would remain a constant of the bourgeois society then in formation.[9]

Responses to the Little Ice Age ranged from the rational to the mad. Starting in the second half of the sixteenth century, people systematically recorded climatic observations with great frequency and sought to make meteorological forecasts.[10] It was widely supposed that destructive weather conditions were the work of witches. As temperatures sank, belief in their black magic reached the heights of hysteria.[11] Conjuring up devastating hail had long been one of the ills ascribed to witches. The *Hammer of Witches*, reprinted many times in this period, also lists it. In addition, people still tried to blame all sorts of evils on the enchantments of malicious women and dangerous magicians, including epidemics, the sudden death of animals and children, and impotence. There had been waves of persecution before. But now major panics broke out, more or less contemporaneously with the nadir of the Little Ice Age. The worst period was between 1560 and 1630.

The demons that Latin Europe created with the help of its theologians, jurists, and torturers absolved society of guilt. Like the Jews, these supercriminals—mostly female but also male—were scapegoats. They thus served essential functions in the emotional economy of those who persecuted and killed them. They helped to explain adversity, and they afforded a steady opportunity to act even when there was nothing much to be done—be it against cold or flooding, sickness or death. The belief that the heavens had awful punishments in store deterred neither Christendom nor the followers of other religions with similar systems of punishments and rewards.[12] Indeed, witches and warlocks, ghosts from the depths of the human psyche, appear in all corners of the world and at all times. We find them among the Navaho in America and the Chewa in East Africa, among the Aboriginal Australians, the Aztecs, and the "Argonauts of the western Pacific," the Trobriand people.[13] What distinguished the witch hunts of Latin Europe from pogroms elsewhere was that they were carried out by states in possession of relatively sophisticated legal systems, "expert literature" like the *Hammer of Witches*, and police forces.

Denunciations, which often led to trials with ultimately hundreds of victims, usually came from the accused's immediate social setting. The persecutory fervor was especially intense in petty lordships with a weakly developed state apparatus and in villages that had wide-ranging jurisdictions. Formal rules of procedure were often flaunted; these were little more than show trials.[14] On the other hand, some governments used witch trials to demonstrate their efficiency as a sovereign power.

Nowhere did pogroms against witches have as many victims as in Europe. According to conservative estimates, between fifty thousand and sixty thousand people were executed. There were also a few critical voices that decried belief in witches as an empty delusion and even questioned the existence of demons, such as Johann Weyer's *De praestigiis daemonum* (*On the Illusions of the Demons*, 1564), Thomas Nashe's *The Terrors of the Night* (1594), and Benedict Pereira's *Adversus fallaces et superstitiosas artes* (*Against the False and Superstitious Arts*).[15] But they were exceptions, as was the Jesuit father Friedrich Spee's famous *Cautio criminalis*, or *Precautions for Prosecutors*, printed in 1631. Just about everyone was convinced of the power of magic, both beneficial and harmful, from intellectuals like Ficino and Bodin to the country herbalist who charmed away a gouty man's pain with her mumbled incantation.

In contrast to actually existing minorities like Jews, witches could be produced in any number. Indeed, to account for the abundance of disasters that arose in the late sixteenth century, it was necessary to conjure hosts of evil that outmatched Asian armies. In 1589, one chronicler from Augsburg calculated the number of participants at a witch's sabbath to be 29,400. At the same time, one work of theology put a precise number on the total of all existing demons: 2,665,866,746,664.[16] In addition, people of the time imagined that werewolves roamed the land, along with vampires—in regions bordering the Ottoman Empire—who sucked blood and honey and devoured grain. All of them were blamed for privation and misery. God, the great educator, allowed them to rampage as a punishment and a warning.

The authorities felt obliged to purge state and society of all verminous witches and demonic filth. The religious commotion of the post-Reformation age enhanced moralizing zeal. People closed whorehouses, thundered against fornication, games, and gambling, and even fought against the devil himself, his minions, and his accomplices. Once again, wood was piled up for the stake. Purification had to be thorough. Witches and warlocks were burned like heretics, as if they were cancers on the sacred body of city, state, and Church (Fig. 35, p. 485). At least some executioners shortened the suffering of the condemned, strangling them before the flames climbed high or tying a small bag of gunpowder around their neck to hasten their end. The witch burnings may have ultimately been sparked by an archaic idea: a vengeful god must be propitiated with sacrifices. In this way, life was destroyed to bring forth life, and order was restored to the universe.[17]

The Church defended its monopoly on magic so decisively during the Little Ice Age in part because the mere toleration of heresy and witchcraft was an affront to God's honor. God wanted to be venerated "properly." Tolerance for those who broke the rules could incite the divine wrath that brought cold, starvation, and pestilence to the land. What was abided in less precarious times—for example, white magic—increasingly fell into the persecutors' field of vision. Salvation was always at stake. Holy warriors, visitators, Inquisitors, and even simple pastors worked to make the world clean and pleasing in the sight of God.

From Augsburg to Trent

No one in the Renaissance could count on reaching a peaceful old age. Death threatened every age group, even in normal times. A small infection was all it took. Taking into account infant mortality, life expectancy averaged between eighteen and twenty-one years.[18] No matter what one did, therefore, the after-life had to be kept in mind. After all, eternity awaited; in comparison, one thousand years on Earth were nothing but a passing breeze. From this perspective, the fight against witches and heretics made as much sense as the resolute defense of "pure teachings." The confessions consolidated, and the prospect of a settlement faded. The pace quickened.

The sting was felt by the Spanish physician Miguel Servet, more widely known as Michael Servetus, whose idiosyncratic views on the Trinity placed him in theological no-man's-land. Citing scriptural and Arabic sources, he proclaimed that the historical Jesus was a mere man and no God. Persecuted by Lutherans and Catholics alike, he was recognized during a stay in Geneva and seized. Calvin saw to it that he was executed outside the city gates on October 27, 1557. Servetus was burned alive. God's honor was restored. Even Melanchthon, usually so peaceable, applauded the act. Sebastian Castellio, a former student of Calvin and now his opponent, found fitting words: "To kill a man is not to protect a doctrine, but it is to kill a man."[19] In a much darker time, 1936, the writer Stefan Zweig would celebrate Servetus as a defender of conscience in the face of violence. Meanwhile, Calvin continued preaching his fiery sermons: against all aberration, against anti-Trinitarians, Anabaptists, spiritualists, Jews, the indifferent, and humanists who indulged in the joys of this life. After his death in 1564, he was succeeded by Théodore de Bèze (1519–1605), a theologian and an excellent Greek scholar from Burgundy.

Calvinism turned out to be the hardiest child of the Reformation. Its teachings spread much more dynamically than Luther's did.[20] They conquered a few German states and penetrated the Netherlands, Scotland, and England, in each of which independent churches formed. France's persecuted Protestants took refuge behind the *Confessio Gallicana*, or Gallic Confession of Faith, formulated by Calvin. Waldensian congregations also followed Geneva. Spain, in contrast, remained immune. Only two translations of Calvin's works appeared there, as opposed to more than two hundred in France.[21] Despite occasional overtures, Calvinists and Lutherans remained almost as hostile to each other as to the papists. Their dispute continued to be fed by divergent opinions about the nature of the Eucharist.

The quarreling Germans negotiated a religious peace at the Diet of Augsburg in 1555. It guaranteed to Lutherans recognition under imperial law, although it excluded other confessions—a seed of later conflicts. It was the prerogative of each prince to decide the faith of his own territory. The Latin formulation adopted somewhat later was *cuius regio, eius religio*, literally "whose region, his religion." Subjects whose conscience drove them to reject the "state confession" enjoyed the small human right of emigrating. For a string of imperial cities, the Peace opened the way for the coexistence of Catholics and Lutherans.[22] Cause for continuing conflict was provided by the "Ecclesiastical Reservation," a unilateral declaration of King Ferdinand. It required an ecclesiastical prince to renounce his secular authority and forfeit all his revenues from church property if he adopted a new confession. A Catholic was to be chosen in his stead. In return, another declaration of the king, the *Declaratio Ferdinandea*, protected the Protestant faith for knights and some cities in ecclesiastical territories where it had long been practiced. As for who controlled what lands, the status quo in the year of the Peace of Passau, 1552, was to be the norm.

Pope Paul IV (1555–1559), a zealot with psychopathic tendencies, refused to recognize the peace agreement.[23] He threatened the Holy Roman Emperor with excommunication and even dared to join forces with Henry II of France in a war with Spain. It was not a good idea. Troops commanded by the Duke of Alba occupied the Papal States, and Paul had to eat humble pie. In the Holy Roman Empire, in contrast, more pacific conditions returned. The fragile peace of 1555 would last until 1618. Its trailblazing significance consisted of prioritizing political considerations over religious scruples. Both sides agonized over it. King Ferdinand once moaned that he had no less of a Christian conscience or sense of honor than the Protestants, and that he was just as loath to compromise against his as they were against theirs.[24] Nevertheless, he signed the document. Charles V, however, did not. Directly after the Peace of Augsburg was agreed upon, he abdicated. He transferred the lands and crowns of Spain to his son Philip. In the empire, Ferdinand was to succeed him.

The retired ruler spent the three years that remained to him in the Hieronymite monastery of San Jerónimo de Yuste in Spain's barren southwest. He did not live in a cell there but rather in a fancy Renaissance villa built just for him, surrounded by a six-person court and provided with choice foods. In his final days, he contemplated Titian's *Gloria*, which portrays him in the white robe of a penitent, perhaps already the habit of the Blessed, surrounded by his family and the choir of angels (Plate 23). The powerful, powerless man raises his hands to the Trinity in a pleading gesture. He has laid his crown down next to him. Hardly any other work of art plumbs the depths of an individual of the sixteenth century quite as profoundly as this picture. Charles had the best painter of his day portray the vision of his afterlife for him. When the hour of his death came on September 23, 1558, he was fully conscious of having achieved a place close to God.

The early reign of Charles's successor as king of Spain, Philip II (r. 1556–1598), seemed blessed by fortune. Twin victories over the French—in 1557 at Saint-Quentin in northern France and in 1558 at Gravelines—induced the archrival to seek peace. In addition, it looked like England could be brought into Spain's imperial system. In 1554, Philip had married Mary Tudor, daughter of Henry VIII and Catherine of Aragon; she was eleven years his senior. The future queen's education at the hands of Erasmus had not kept her from becoming a militant Catholic in the Age of the Reformation. In 1553, after the death of her half-brother Edward, she triumphed in the struggle for succession and promptly departed from the Protestant-friendly politics of previous years. She wanted England to be Catholic again, with the pope as the head of its church. Medieval heresy laws were passed. Nearly three hundred Protestants ended up on the executioner's block. Among them was Thomas Cranmer, who had performed the divorce of Mary's parents, thus reducing their daughter to the status of a bastard. Philip's marriage to "Bloody Mary" could now have made him the heir to England's crown as well, but the queen remained childless. She died the same year as Charles V. Mary's successor and half-sister Elizabeth, daughter of Henry VIII and Anne Boleyn, rebuffed Philip's courtship. She let it be known that she already had a husband to whom she was lawfully wed: England. Her Protestant subjects awoke from their nightmare. Meanwhile, in Seville, half a hundred Lutherans were delivered to the flames.

Mary was barely in her grave in Westminster when Philip sought accommodation with Henry II, whose coffers were as empty as his own. The Peace of Cateau-Cambrésis, which was directly followed by the bankruptcy of the French state, ended the weary war in Italy and northeastern France.[25] In addition, it marked England's renunciation of Calais, the last remaining bit of the Angevin Empire on the Continent. Thus ended a bloody chapter in English history whose centerpiece was the Hundred Years' War. England gained valuable decades to expand its fleet and establish new trade routes and markets. One indirect consequence of the peace was that England ended its alliance with Spain, which had been entirely pragmatic, born of their common opposition to France.

Meanwhile, power struggles became intertwined with confessional strife in France as well. After Henry II's death—he succumbed in 1559 to wounds received during the tournament celebrating the Peace of Cateau-Cambrésis—the monarchy staggered into a phase of instability. Henry's son Francis II, already king of Scotland thanks to his marriage to Mary Stuart, died in 1560. He had not even reached the age of seventeen. His successor was Charles IX, a ten-year-old child. The regent was Catherine de' Medici (1519–1589), Henry's widow. She had to manage conflicting parties: on the one hand, a polypoid family network around the brothers François and Charles of Guise—the former a duke, the latter Cardinal of Lorraine[26]—and on the other hand, the Protestant high aristocracy consisting of the houses of Bourbon, Condé, and Châtillon. For all the pious convictions she may have harbored, ultimately the crown of France was at stake. Approaching calamity soon cast its shadow. In early 1560, a conspiracy of Protestant aristocrats was put down, the so-called "Tumult of Amboise." Over one thousand people were hanged for their involvement.

For the moment, the regent sought accommodation. The same year, she saw to it that the jurist and Erasmian humanist Michel de L'Hôpital (1503–1573) was named chancellor. He and others who preached toleration were suspected by hardliners of Machiavellian machinations. They were called *politiques*, i.e., "politicians"—it was not a compliment. Nevertheless, the Huguenots were led by a spokesman who was also willing to compromise, Admiral Gaspard de Coligny (1519–1572). The big showdown was postponed.

Developments in the land of the "Most Christian Kings" induced Europe's Catholics to close ranks. After difficult negotiations, the great powers put aside their political differences to revive the suspended Church council. Its third and final term opened in January 1562, once again in Trent. No Protestants attended. More than two hundred cardinals, bishops, generals of monastic orders, and abbots did. Italians made up the overwhelming majority. The participants had no intention of building bridges with the Protestants. Rather, Rome sought a clear line of demarcation, a consolidation of its own doctrine, and, at long last, reform as well. When the closing *Te Deum* rang out in Trent Cathedral on December 4, 1563, the council fathers could look back on eighteen years of work.

The Catholic Church had rediscovered its identity. It was put into concise form in the Tridentine Creed and the Roman Catechism, which was an exact response to Luther's catechism. The seven sacraments were maintained, and Christ's actual presence in the host was asserted. The validity of the Church Fathers' teachings and older Church council decrees was reaffirmed; this contradicted Luther's principle of *sola scriptura*. Opposing his doctrine of *sola gratia* was the famous Decree of Justification. It recognized that the faithful indeed needed God's grace. Yet, in contrast to Luther's teaching, it also maintained that they could increase grace through actions of their own—which were guided by free will and accompanied by grace—or diminish it through sin. The Decree was a theological masterpiece. Yet it did not end debates on how much God's omnipotence, divine grace, and human will each figured into the calculus of salvation.

The council also reaffirmed the existence of purgatory and original sin, as well as the doctrine of Mary's "immaculate" conception. One of the abuses it tried to suppress was the selling of indulgences. It required bishops to reside in their diocese, to preach sermons, and to carry out visitations. In addition, it provided for the establishment of seminaries for priests. The spirit of humanist education was at work here. Secret weddings were prohibited. From now on, marriages could only be performed after a pastor had announced them publicly three times.[27] Concubinage remained strictly forbidden. Numerous decrees dealt with reforms of the Church's inner workings, including the choice of abbots and bishops and conditions in monasteries. The traditional liturgy was to remain in force, with Latin as the language of the mass and the Vulgate as the standard version of the Bible. Further decrees permitted the cult of the saints and the veneration of images.

Not all of these reforms enjoyed success. Prelates continued to stockpile benefices, and some of them continued to hold court like secular princes. Children of priests and concubines remained a thorn in the side of the more prudish. On the other hand, selling indulgences could be punished with excommunication from now on. Priests received better training. The Roman liturgy and Catholic doctrine took on clearer outlines. The Index of Prohibited Books, introduced by Paul IV, was revised by the council and published anew in 1564. A new congregation was created specifically to monitor all reading material. Additional blacklists followed, as did manifestos against humanism, heresy, humor, and tolerance.

The provisions adopted by the Council of Trent for the construction and decoration of churches were not very concrete. Their general tenor was to foresee stricter regulation. Provincial synods formulated precise rules. A Catholic theory of art developed around the topic, advocating renunciation of the superfluous and the frivolous and—taking a page out of Luther's book—guidance from the scriptures.[28] One of the first post-Tridentine sanctions had repercussions for the nudes in Michelangelo's *Last Judgment*. Daniele da Volterra was tasked with chiseling away the offending genitalia and painting billowing robes in their place. In 1573, the painter Paolo Veronese (1528–1588) had to answer to Church authorities for including dogs, a parrot, and a dwarf in a *Last Supper* destined for a Venetian monastery, as these characters were not mentioned in the Bible.[29] "We painters take the same liberties as poets and madmen," he defiantly remarked.[30] Rather than change the painting, he simply changed its name to *The Feast in the House of Levi.*

Trent was not only a source of austere reforms. It was also an inspiration to create a new architectural style out of the spirit of the Catholic Renaissance. The Church of the Gesù in Rome, begun in 1568, served as a very influential prototype. Commissioned by Cardinal Alessandro Farnese, it was like the Council of Trent in stone form. Entering the Gesù today, one gets an impression of where Catholicism was heading then. The wide-open space, abounding with gold, marble, and lapis lazuli, overwhelms the senses. The cupola is transformed by a fresco of Giambattista Gaulli into a heaven populated by saints and angels. In this building, the Catholic offensive manifested itself as a celebration of God in the form of a lavish, extravagant good work. The faithful had no need to imagine transcendence there. The Empyrean was visible, just as God seemed to be present in the flesh during the Eucharist. In line with Tridentine thought, the tabernacle, the abode of God, was the focus of the church's interior.

Catholic Renaissance

The Gesù enjoys special status in the history of the Catholic Renaissance, as it is the mother church of the Jesuit Order.[31] One of its altars is said to contain the bones of the founder, Ignatius of Loyola. The community that grew up around him was recognized as a religious order in 1540 by Paul III. By the end of the century, the Society of Jesus had grown to 8,500 strong. Like the Theatines, its members did not follow the standard monastic life of seclusion and the liturgy of the hours. In addition to the standard vows, the elite of the order pledged special obedience to the pope. The *patres* lived among the people, traveled to Asia and America, and set up missions. Not a few Jesuits found the ear of the powerful as confessors. The movement, which grew out of the yearning for the beatific vision and the desire to imitate Christ, became the epitome of religious rationality and militant reaction to the Protestant challenge. A sign of what was to come can already be seen in Ignatius's *Spiritual Exercises.* There the former soldier compares Christ with a military commander who gathers apostles around himself in order to take the field against Satan's forces.[32] A correspondingly harsh military tone developed. In 1554, Ignatius wrote an incendiary letter about the "poison" of the Reformers' "evil teaching" to Peter de Hondt (also known by the nobler moniker "Canisius"), a professor of theology in Ingolstadt and the future Jesuit provincial for Germany.[33] In his view, it was necessary to preserve what was healthy and heal what was sick. Ignatius considered schools and concise treatises that spread the true faith among the people to be the best means of keeping the Protestant "cancer" from spreading.

Catholic education, "learned piety," seemed the ideal remedy for the temptation presented by the Reformation and heresy.[34] Thus the Jesuits founded colleges, first in Padua in 1542 and Messina in 1548, and then all over Europe. Initially intended for training novices in the order, they soon attracted students from further reaches of society. They became successful competitors to the Protestant *Gymnasium*. Some took on the character of universities. The curriculum focused primarily on ethical education, with philosophy, mathematics, and natural science rounding out the program. Among the texts used to practice Latin and rhetoric, Cicero's writings stood out. Not even during the height of the confessional struggle did the classical spirit recede. The *Ratio studiorum*, a guideline for the organization of "studies," provided a structure for the Jesuit schools erected around the globe. Their fight for souls extended to many arenas and media. They put holy dramas on the stage, preached, and erected lavishly decorated buildings. One of the composers who worked for them was the great Giovanni Pierluigi da Palestrina. Even the peoples of the overseas missions were to be converted to the cross by means of music.[35]

Competition was good for the young generation of all confessions, encouraging them to aim high. More and more saints and would-be saints populated the world of Rome. Carlo Borromeo (1538–1584), appointed a cardinal by his uncle Pius IV, endeavored with all his might to make his archbishopric of Milan a model diocese of Tridentine reform. Filippo Neri (1515–1595), known by contemporaries as "good Pippo," took pity on the poor, the sick, and pilgrims stranded in Rome. Once, while praying in a Roman catacomb, his heart filled with divine love, supposedly swelling so much that his rib cage could no longer contain it. He was also known to levitate.[36]

Rome felt compelled to do something about the excess of saintliness. In 1588, an agency was founded specifically for this purpose, the Sacred Congregation of Rites. It now decided who would be given a halo and who not. "Pippo" received one in 1622, along with Ignatius of Loyola, the missionary to the Far East Francis Xavier, and Teresa of Ávila. Filippo Neri went down in the history of the Church as the founder of the Congregation of the Oratory. In the next generation, Francis de Sales, himself the founder of an order, was a living example of Tridentine reform as the spiritual leader of the Diocese of Geneva. New pious communities like the Salesians, along with exemplary individuals who embodied asceticism and charity, became the vanguard of a militant church. Divine science also went on the offensive. The University of Bologna, the old stronghold of civil law, had only one professor of theology in 1550; a century later, there were nine.[37]

Late medieval culture seemed to experience a revival in Catholic countries. As always, conviviality and salvation were pursued in religious confraternities. Miracles became more frequent. Pilgrimages and processions spread God's grace across the land. Relics emitted their magical power, and foreheads were moistened with holy water. Churches filled up with paintings that were larger and more colorful than ever. A new age of art began: the Baroque period. It manifested itself differently in different religious contexts, leading to the formation of different confessional cultures in Europe. Churches from the Gesù to palatial monasteries in southern Germany were the antithesis of the Calvinist chapel. Paradigmatic of the Lutheran Renaissance is the decoration of the chapel in Neuburg Castle, the palace of a Protestant princeling. The ceiling and walls are painted with Bible stories. The central fresco depicts Christ ascending to heaven in a bold *sotto in su*, a foreshortening technique that means "as seen from below." Without knowledge of Italian models, this artwork would not have been possible.

Over time, confessional divergence seeped into everyday life, influencing the choice of given names, reading material, and sexual behavior.[38] Europe's diversity became even richer than before. What is now commonly called "confessionalization" was not only imposed from above by churches and civic authorities; it was also imbued in people by multigenerational processes of learning, internalization, and exclusion. In this way, the various confessions took on separate identities. They were tempered in the fire of controversial sermons, the stake, and, above all, the religious wars that would now engulf Europe for a century.

Darkness Descends: The French Wars of Religion

Les Baux. April 8, 1633.[39] In the previous year, the small town located on a steep spur of the Alpilles had withstood a siege by troops of Louis XIII (r. 1610–1643). Now the citizens opened their gates to the soldiers in the hope of receiving mercy. But Cardinal Richelieu, the king's chief minister, would not countenance this thorn in the south of his realm. The fortress and its bastions were to be razed. The final charges were detonated on April 8. With the white smoke of the explosion, the power of Les Baux wafted away forever. In the High Middle Ages, it had been the home of a prosperous noble house, its court famous for its troubadours. Now it fell to the crown. Later on, Louis XIII gave Les Baux to the Grimaldis, the princes of Monaco. It returned to France during the Revolution, but it was ultimately left to ruin, a ghost town belonging to the mistral, the Provençal sun, and Romantic poets.

Its drab ruins recall the victory of the monarchic state, which five years earlier had captured La Rochelle, the principal stronghold of the so-called "Huguenots." The name, which first appeared in 1560, means "sworn brotherhood" and may be a corruption of the German word *Eidgenossen*, or "confederates." Now the war against them entered its final phase. The hope of the persecuted, namely that light would follow upon darkness—*post tenebras lux*—was in vain. This phrase was inscribed on a ruin in Les Baux, next to the year "1571" above a stone Renaissance window frame. A biblical quotation, it was originally stamped on Genevan coins when the city was on the point of throwing off its episcopal lord. Now it became the motto of the persecuted and repressed Protestants of France. Les Baux is thus one of the last *lieux de mémoire*, or "sites of memory," of the French Wars of Religion. These wars were fought to settle two things: the faith of the country and a power struggle among the great noble houses. The constitution of France was at stake.

In 1562, Catherine de' Medici issued an edict of toleration in St. Germain-en-Laye that had been formulated by L'Hôpital. In March, however, it was rendered moot when soldiers of the Duke of Guise butchered more than sixty worshippers at a Reformed church service. Violence begot violence: Guise was murdered the following year. The road to civil war was open. Calvin had warned about this possibility from the beginning. He recommended passive resistance and, if necessary, martyrdom. Otherwise, as he predicted in a letter to Coligny, a stream of blood could flow that would drown all of Europe.[40] This prudent warning was not heeded. Hardliners prevailed at court, and L'Hôpital fell. He withdrew to Belesbat, his chateau south of Paris, where he lived the life of a scholar. A quotation of Horace on his portrait, painted by Giovanni Battista Moroni, suggests that he was aware of living in a world overshadowed by misfortune (Plate 24):

> If the heavens fractured in their fall,
> still their ruin would strike him, unafraid.[41]

Indeed, the conflagration had by now spread beyond the realm of the Valois. Next door, in the Netherlands, another war had broken out.[42] Causes included the Spanish ruler's meddling in traditional privileges, increased taxation to support distant wars, and religious repression. Iconoclastic riots broke out in Flanders in 1566, signaling a dramatic renunciation of the old Church. Philip II sent the Duke of Alba, Fernando Álvarez de Toledo (1507–1582), to the rebellious province to restore order. The brutal and arrogant soldier made short work of things. After staging show trials, he sent thousands to the scaffolds. He went too far, however, when he had the counts of Egmont and Hoorn executed on the market square in Brussels. These two men of great service to the Spanish crown were beheaded for the lone crime of being open to compromise. The war unleashed by these judicial murders would last for eighty years. Various conflicts became intertwined—after all, the Netherlands were of enormous strategic importance. Whoever controlled them, wrote the humanist Benito Arias Montano to his sovereign, Philip II, could hold Germany in check, conquer France, and contain England.[43]

The year 1571, chiseled into the window frame in Les Baux, marked a high point in the display of Spain's power. At Lepanto in the Gulf of Patras, an armada of Catholic forces commanded by Don Juan de Austria (1547–1578), a bastard of Charles V, defeated the Ottoman fleet. Catholic Europe celebrated the victory in poetry and painting as the triumph of the militant Church. No one doubted that it was owed to the Virgin Mary. Paolo Veronese's depiction shows the Virgin Mary amidst a gathering of saints above the clouds, with rays of fire shooting down upon the Turkish ships (Plate 25).

In France, too, Catholics took the offensive. The year after Lepanto, the Huguenots suffered their darkest hour. In the circle around the regent, plans were hatched to behead the Reformed opposition.[44] The occasion was provided by the wedding of Catherine's daughter to Henry of Navarre (1553–1610), which had brought many Protestant grandees to Paris. Before first light on August 24, St. Bartholomew's Day, Coligny and other Protestant leaders were killed. The liquidation of the Huguenot elite was just the beginning of a wave of violence. Things spun out of control. Long pent-up tensions between Paris's majority Catholic population and the Reformed minority boiled over. Terror ruled the city for three days. There and in the countryside, thousands fell victim to the unfettered mob. Even respectable citizens forgot all civility, joining in the slaughter. Philip II was pleased. The pope ordered thanksgiving services to be held, and he had the events immortalized in a fresco cycle in the Royal Hall of the Vatican.

In the aftermath of the Parisian nightmare, Protestants were embittered but not broken. The war flared up again. Periods of peace imposed by lack of funds, not by better judgment, punctuated the fighting. Foreign powers got involved: Spain on the Catholic side, and German princes, England, and the

Netherlands on that of the Huguenots. Only in the last decade of the sixteenth century did L'Hôpital's political descendants prevail. They realized that religion must have its own space outside of politics. This was a new idea, one that long remained strange in Europe as well. Another novelty was the claim—put forward in an anonymous pamphlet in 1579—that freedom of conscience was an inalienable, fundamental right of the individual.[45]

The eighth and final war of religion in France, which began in 1585, was long and bloody. In the view of the philosopher Montaigne, it "[ate] and destroy[ed] itself with its own venom."[46] The crisis was overcome by Henry of Navarre, the groom in the bloody wedding. He secured the support of the *politiques*. He managed to win more and more soldiers to his cause and drove out the Spanish in hard-fought battles. The decisive step came in 1593 when he, theretofore the head of the Huguenots, converted to Catholicism. It was the sixth conversion for the confessional chameleon. The first was forced upon him by the Saint Bartholomew's Day massacre, but now Henry was moved by reason of state. His flexibility in the question of religion signaled a move toward the secularization of the political arena. It also bid adieu to the notion that power without power over the faith was no power at all, and that a ruler stood as guarantor to his subjects' salvation before God. Clement VIII quickly gave the convert absolution and recognized the kingship of the first Bourbon monarch of France. In 1598, the pope negotiated the Treaty of Vervins. Philip, deathly ill at the time, had to accept that France would essentially maintain the status quo that had been established at Cateau-Cambrésis.

The same year, the promise inscribed in stone at Les Baux before France descended into its long, dark night finally seemed fulfilled. Henry IV issued his famous edict of toleration in Nantes, which guaranteed legal equality to Protestants and the freedom to worship publicly, albeit with limitations.[47] In addition, the Parlement set up an ecumenical commission responsible for adjudicating potential disputes over the interpretation of the edict. To ensure that toleration was more than just a mere word, the Huguenots were given control of over one hundred military strongholds.

His land in shambles, "Good King Henry" was determined to rebuild. He was adept at expanding the crown's power, and he enlarged the bureaucracy. In so doing, he paved the way for absolutism but also increased venality. Like elsewhere, commoners entered state administration. Many of them bought titles of nobility. This *noblesse de robe* ("nobility of the robe"), an aristocracy based on high office holding rather than blood, developed into the state's most important bulwark. Henry was also a builder in a very literal sense, ordering the construction of the Place Dauphine and the perfectly square Place des Vosges—then called Place Royale, or "Royal Square." The Grande Galerie, which runs along the Seine and connects the Louvre with the Tuileries Palace, is also his monument. In the years remaining to him, he set the course for an active foreign policy that, in the face of all confessional solidarity, returned to hostility with Spain. First, Henry amputated parts of strategically important Savoy. He would have gotten heavily involved in the War of the Jülich Succession in neighboring Germany, but he was stabbed by a fanatic Catholic on May 14, 1610. Two weeks later, the regicide was drawn and quartered at the Place de Grève, the usual place for such gruesome spectacles. The big war with Germany, which the conflicts on the Lower Rhine easily could have ignited, was postponed for eight short years.

Nantes, therefore, marked anything but the happy ending to the story of a good king. The path to absolutist France led through Cardinal Richelieu's defeat and disarming of the Huguenots—through La Rochelle, the symbolic Protestant refuge, and even through tiny nests of resistance like Les Baux. France's Protestants had a hard future ahead of them. Once again, the old oppressive dream of purity was pursued. By now, Spain was a mere shadow of its former greatness. The baton had been passed to France.

Night Falls on Spain

Madrid. April 23, 1616. Convent of the Discalced Trinitarians. After a life of adventure and misery, he now finally found peace. The man buried, doubtless without pomp, somewhere in the church of the pious nuns had been one of Europe's greatest poets: Miguel de Cervantes Saavedra. Four centuries later, a search for his mortal remains turned up nothing. No portrait shows his visage for certain. Like his contemporary Shakespeare, he speaks to us almost solely through his writing.

Cervantes was born in 1547 in Alcalá de Henares.[48] His father, a surgeon from an impoverished noble family, provided him with an education tinged with humanism. At the age of twenty-two, Miguel went to Rome, perhaps because he had wounded an opponent in a duel. In 1571, he had a date with history, serving as a soldier on a man-of-war in the Battle of Lepanto. He seems to have fought courageously. One shot hit him in the chest, and another shattered his left hand. With coy pride, he henceforth called himself *el manco de Lepanto*, "the one-armed man of Lepanto." On the voyage home four years later, his ship was captured off Spain's coast by Algerian corsairs. Cervantes was taken hostage. He made four unsuccessful escape attempts from his prison, the *bagno* in Algiers. Only five years later was the ransom paid to buy his freedom. He made his living as a tax collector, tried his hand at all sorts of business, and landed in jail several times. The prison in Seville is where he claims to have begun the book that would make him immortal: *The Ingenious Gentleman Don Quixote of La Mancha.* The mortal Cervantes profited little from it. The end of his life found him sick and almost broke.

The first part of *Don Quixote* appeared in 1605, the second in 1615. The novel can be read as a historical source. For it tells us much about the conditions of the period its author lived though, generally considered the Golden Age of Spain. It shows the dark side, the world of the streets, of peasants, whores, officials, and barkeeps. Dulcinea, whose beauty the merchants in the book *must* believe in, although they have never seen the dumpy peasant woman, is a Spanish sister of Dante's Beatrice. She is an allegory of religion—a religion in which one had to believe on pain of death.[49] The main character of the novel is a *hidalgo,* a member of the "working class" of the nobility. This type of Spaniard had fought for his country for centuries. Yet in a time of increasingly rationalized state power, there was no longer any place for him. Barely able to get by, he now had to sell his services, for instance as a *conquistador.* Don Quixote is an urbane relative of Wolkenstein, Sickingen, and Hutten: a somber man of chivalry in unchivalrous times. His story is a parody of the still popular romance genre, filled with warriors, courtly love, magic, and heroic fighting. But that is not what makes the work a jewel of world literature. Nor is the fact that it is constructed with incredible artistry.[50] Rather, it continues to fascinate us because it can be read as an allegory of human life. The foolish, daydreaming don and his sober squire Sancho Panza fight a fight that is universal, one that belongs just as much to little men with their wish for a tiny slice of happiness as to big, blood-stained battlers like Spain's rulers.

Only in hindsight do Charles V's and Philip II's attempts to purify and order the world appear quixotic. They may have prevailed at Tunis and Mühlberg, at Saint-Quentin and Lepanto, but in the end it was all for nothing. Their multifront wars were like battling sheep and tilting at windmills. In their view, Spain had to stay Catholic, and Europe had to become so. Thus, time and again, *Kaiser* and king involved their lands in wars for orthodoxy and power, only to fail time and again. Yet their defeats, as the historian James Tracy has argued, were more useful to Europe's future development than a victory would have been. For the continent remained politically diverse.[51] A Spanish Europe—even contemporaries considered that prospect a nightmare.

A policy of mass forced baptism had supposedly made King Philip's lands free of Muslims. But that was only the official interpretation. Moriscos, in some parts of Andalusia comprising the vast majority of the population, continued to practice their faith and preserve their traditions. Many developed a kind of syncretism, practicing both Christianity and Islam.[52] Pleas for tolerance received no hearing. One rebellion that broke out in Granada in 1568 was put down by Juan de Austria after two years of fighting. Thousands were sold into slavery. An end was put to the precarious coexistence of those who remained in Christian Spain in 1609 when Philip III (r. 1598–1621) decreed their expulsion. Around 300,000 people were impacted. They found a new home in northern Africa.

The process of Catholic consolidation was inextricable from the continued construction of the Spanish state. The clearest expression of the latter lay in the fact that the royal court had been fixed in Madrid since 1561. Like the medieval Holy Roman Emperors, Charles V still exercised power by traveling with an itinerant court. Reflecting on his reign at the time of his abdication in Brussels, he summarized,

> In the course of my expeditions, sometimes to make war, sometimes to make peace, I have traveled nine times to Germany, six times to Spain, seven times to Italy, four times to France, twice into England, and twice into Africa. . . . I crossed the Mediterranean eight times, the Spanish sea twice.[53]

Solo Madrid es Corte—"only Madrid is the court"—now became a common saying.

The actual symbol of Philip II's government, however, was El Escorial, located in the Sierra de Guadarrama northwest of the capital. Finished in 1584, it was a palace and monastery all in one. The floor plan, designed according to a precise geometrical scheme, resembles a gridiron in honor of Saint Lawrence, on whose feast day Philip's army had prevailed at Saint-Quentin.[54] The sober structure seems to have been built more for prayer and work than for ostentatious representation. Nevertheless, diplomats and petitioners must have held their breath as they approached the monument in the heart of the universal empire. When not traveling, the king worked here surrounded by a large bureaucracy, dictating documents, tirelessly reading and writing, in old age with spectacles perched on his nose. The *rey prudente*, or "clever king"— thus he was called in a massive overestimation of his disastrous policies—was also a *rey papelero*, a "paper king" who micromanaged his realm and had comprehensive statistics gathered about its cities, towns, and villages.[55] His library in the Escorial, numbering fourteen thousand volumes, was one of the most significant collections of the century.

In his day, Philip II was the most powerful man in Europe. Yet the orders issued by his pen had only a very delayed impact. The speed at which news traveled was limited by the power of horses. A message from Madrid needed between twenty-two and eighty-five days to reach Venice. In addition, its path over land and sea was very costly. As Fernand Braudel has noted, news was a luxury good. But the mightiest windmill at which Philip and other European rulers tilted was the economy. Bastions built according to ballistic calculations made sieges increasingly drawn-out, expensive affairs. Guns and artillery gobbled up ungodly amounts of bronze. Iron, gunpowder, and lead were equally expensive.[56] It was expensive to maintain the most important type of weapon: the infantry provided by mercenaries. Even more expensive was cavalry. And the most expensive of all was the fleet. Even so, the armies that Philip fielded at the height of his power were never comparable to those of Song, Ming, or Ottoman rulers. War finance was aggravated by a factor that affected not only Spain's economy: inflation. Henry VIII of England felt its sting acutely, as his second invasion of France cost perhaps ten times as much as the first.[57]

Like the Later Roman Empire, the Habsburg conglomerate crumbled due to "strategic overstretch."[58] Philip waged perpetual war: against the Ottomans in the eastern Mediterranean, against privateers and Elizabeth I's navy in the Atlantic, in Flanders against the renegade Dutch, in Paris against France's king, and at home against rebellious Moriscos. It was a vicious cycle. Multifront war increased taxes, which in turn, along with religious suppression, was the main cause of revolts. Putting them down required more and more money. Four times during Philip's reign—in 1557, 1560, 1575, and 1596—the crown was unable to pay its debts. Of course, the competition, France in particular, was beset by equally grievous problems.[59]

Spain's wars put it into financial straits from which it could not escape. It was a hand-to-mouth existence. Money from Genoa or Augsburg might help to send a couple of thousand soldiers here or there. Battles might be won or lost. But no matter what, the mountain of debt grew a little higher. Nevertheless, the great war for the countries of Europe and the souls of its people continued decade upon decade, with the scarcest of resources. The Army of Flanders, which grew to the monstrous size of 67,000 men, devoured one-quarter of the Spanish Empire's revenues.[60] Lack of funds was therefore the greatest ally of peace, which from time to time the king was forced to accept.

More than any political maneuvering, it was the economy that guaranteed the survival of a Europe of competing powers.

The primary cause of Spain's decline lay in the ideologically rigid hegemonic politics of Charles V and his son. The military drained the local economy of capital. What silver remained was only rarely put into investments. Instead, it tended to be shipped by the ton via the Philippines to eastern Asia (pp. 718, 728f.). Furthermore, the country lacked an international banking system, dynamic merchants, and entrepreneurs. For such entities to form, a certain amount of political freedom and upward social mobility would have been necessary. Both were available in the "republican" environment of southern Germany, northern Italy, Flanders, and England—but not in Spain. In the eyes of the Dominican friar Diego Durán (ca. 1537–1588), a chronicler of the conquest of the Americas, even Spain's truly rigid social structure seemed to be falling apart. As he wrote, one could no longer tell who was a knight and who a muleteer. In contrast, he preferred the iron value placed on social hierarchy by Aztec civilization.[61]

Madrid failed to develop an economic policy that integrated the various parts of its empire. Internal customs duties hindered trade, and there was no common currency. The government gave little thought to agriculture. Some regions were dependent on grain imports and thus had to bear the weight of rising prices. Production of goods declined. The expulsion of Jews, Conversos, and Moriscos was not only inhumane; it was also stupid. For with each emigrant, the already thinly populated country lost more minds, money, and industry. Foreign creditors charged a high price for the risk they took. The Fuggers got shamelessly rich. Profits per hundredweight of Peruvian and Mexican silver, for which they received prospecting rights as security, could reach 100 percent.[62] One enduringly fatal consequence of the policies pursued by the crowned Quixotes Charles and Philip was the isolation of their empire from the rest of Europe. Philip's agents kidnapped exiles who converted to Protestantism, even abroad.[63] Foreign scholars and craftsmen were invited to work in Spain, but they and the arts they practiced had to be Catholic. Spain's universities responded to the skepticism embodied in Cervantes's work and many other literary products of the *Siglo de oro* with a renewed Aristotelian Scholasticism. In the confused context of religious division, it sought certainty in ancient authorities and the Sacred Scriptures. Spanish Scholasticism spread far and wide, even influencing seventeenth-century German academic philosophy. Its most significant exponents included the Dominican friar Francisco de Vitoria (ca. 1483–1546) and the Jesuit Francisco Suárez (1548–1617).

The two men also brought glory to the "School of Salamanca," a *spiritus rector* of modern international law. For the multifaceted Juan Luis Vives (1492–1540), known in part as the author of pedagogical writings—including a treatise on the education of girls—there was no place in Spain. For he came from a family of Conversos. His father had been burned alive. "Our country is a land of pride and envy," a compatriot wrote to Vives when yet another humanist was imprisoned. "One cannot possess any culture without being suspected of heresy, delusion, and Judaism. Thus silence has been imposed upon the learned."[64]

God's Iberian country had to be protected from books that could endanger salvation. Yet the Inquisition did not manage to completely dry up the stream of suspect writing; in practice, censorship was often lax. Nevertheless, foreign-language literature remained largely unknown. Before the depressing period during and after the Reformation, no duties had been placed on printed matter.[65] Now, however, the works of Erasmus, once so popular, were suppressed along with everything that smacked of Lutheranism. Even Spanish authors had difficulty finding a press. An average of three print shops operated in a sixteenth-century Spanish city, as compared to two hundred in Venice alone. Even paper had to be imported for a while[66]—in the country that had boasted the first paper mills in Europe. Conversely, almost no Spanish literature made it to the Frankfurt Fair.[67]

The theater, which would reach a high point in Lope de Vega's plays, was neither critical nor edifying. Rather, it acted as an apology for the status quo.[68] The sciences stagnated for the most part, except for descriptions of animals and plants discovered in the Americas and works about navigation and shipbuilding.[69] Universities functioned primarily as training grounds for the bureaucracy. The important humanist Sebastian Fox-Morcillo (1526/28–1560)—one of those scholars who sought to unite Platonic and Aristotelian philosophy—was chosen by Philip II as a tutor for his hapless son Don Carlos, but he died in a shipwreck on his way to assume the post.

Philip himself was highly educated, an art connoisseur, and a collector of paintings by Titian and Hieronymus Bosch. He spent his final years, plagued by gout, fevers, and colic, in a cleverly constructed wheelchair (Fig. 53, p. 687).[70] The master of the universe was now a bald little man with a white beard, no more than a pitiable invalid. Gout had frozen his joints; he could no longer even sign his name. The imperious *Yo el Rey*, "I, the King," that had long marked his documents gave way in September 1596 to authentication by a secretary. Two years later, as Cervantes was polishing his masterpiece in Seville, Philip was brought to the Escorial, where his father lay and where a fantastic

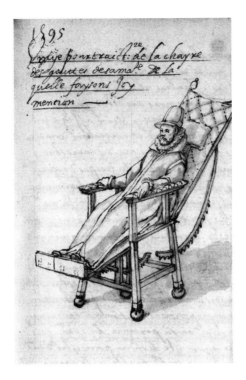

treasure of holy relics could offer salvation for his soul—but not for his body.
Witnesses described his final days as an ordeal. He suffered from abscesses all
over, unbearable pain at the slightest touch, paralysis, diarrhea, ichor, and the
rough butchery of the doctors, who bled him and cut open his festering sores
while monks gathered around to chant prayers. In the end, it was feared the
patient might regurgitate the host he requested each day. Thus, the mightiest
man in Europe wasted away in one of the thousand rooms of his palace on a
feculent, lice-infested bed amidst agony and malodor. In the early morning of
September 13, 1598, a Sunday, his suffering ended.

Philip's legacy was a despoiled, albeit purely Catholic, country in which the
clergy had preserved its privileges uncontested (and bore more than a third of
Castile's tax burden[71]). The Dutch provinces were in revolt. There was even
unrest at home. The victory at Lepanto had not managed to smash Turkish
hegemony in the Mediterranean. Cervantes's captivity in Algiers reminds us
that the proud Spanish fleet could not even guarantee safety off its own coast.
On the other hand, when the House of Aviz died out in 1580, Portugal and its
entire sea empire had fallen to Philip. Nevertheless, the attempt to conquer

England with a massive armada failed (pp. 694–696). The Treaty of Vervins with France concluded during the king's final months was tantamount to a capitulation. Pomponne de Bellièvre, later Henry IV's chancellor, called it the most advantageous peace France had negotiated in five hundred years.[72] Without Spain's involvement in multifront wars, France's consolidation would have been inconceivable.

Dutch Daybreak

These wars also favored the movement for Dutch independence; indeed, they facilitated its success.[73] The yearning for freedom had roots that went much further back than the days when Hoorn and Egmont were beheaded. The Duke of Alba sought to conquer a country whose rich, large cities had already stood up to the dukes of Burgundy. There was a tradition of rebellion and, accordingly, of horizontal power.[74] The leader of the resistance was now William of Orange (1533–1584), descended from the German House of Nassau-Dillenburg, who had managed to escape the court in Brussels and find safety in exile. Initially a favorite of Charles V, then stadtholder for Philip II in three provinces, he ultimately took on the role of *pater patriae*. Like Henry IV, he was a man who sought accommodation. Raised a Lutheran, given a Catholic education, and ultimately married (for the fourth time) to a daughter of the Huguenot leader Coligny, he ultimately opted dispassionately for Calvinism. His dynasty continues to represent the Netherlands today.

The Spanish army could not be beaten in open battle. The only option was a "small," asymmetric war, the classic tactic of the weak against an overwhelming enemy. It was fought on the sea by privateers called *watergeuzen*. William had given them letters of marque. The term, which contains the French word *gueux*, or "beggars," was an ironic name the freedom fighters gave themselves. Aristocrats and merchants also helped to finance the revolution. A major moral victory was won in April 1572 when the first city, Den Briel, was captured from the Spanish. Zeeland and Holland fell, and, finally, Leiden. William of Orange founded a university there that would become the leading such Protestant institution. The brutal Duke of Alba was recalled. Yet neither his successors nor the rebels were able to achieve a conclusive military victory.

The Catholic provinces of Wallonia and Flanders favored a settlement with Spain. In Arras in 1579, they banded together to form an alliance. In response, the Protestant provinces of the north created the "Union of Utrecht." In 1581, they took the daring step of deposing Philip II as their sovereign. His image disappeared from coins and seals. One of the writings cited in justification of the break was the *Defense of Liberty against Tyrants*, an anonymous Huguenot publication.[75] It advocated resistance against a ruler who broke divine and human law and destroyed the state. In its pages, the true king appeared as a servant of the people, which, as a body, is sovereign over the man it has entrusted with rule.

The divide between north and south turned out to be irreversible. An armistice agreed with the Ottomans in 1580 gave Spain new room to move politically. Alessandro Farnese, the son of Margaret of Parma—an illegitimate daughter of Charles V—was now in command of the army. He advanced on Flanders and Brabant, capturing city after city. Some were taken by siege. Others freely capitulated. Others still were betrayed. In July 1584, William of Orange was assassinated. The next year, Farnese took Antwerp. The rebels' cause seemed lost, especially since Farnese proceeded more prudently than Alba. For example, he allowed Calvinists in Antwerp to emigrate if they were not willing to convert. Yet he could not win back the north. The "great bog of Europe,"[76] marshland interspersed with lakes, waterways, and canals, helped to hold off the mightiest army in Europe at the time. Maurice of Orange (1567–1625), the decisive figure in the northern provinces after his father's death, would ultimately succeed in driving the Spanish out.

Besides geography, a reform of military training and strategy also contributed to victory.[77] Regular drilling, increased use of firearms, and other principles caught on all over Europe. With Maurice's reorganization of the Dutch States Army, military affairs also experienced a "renaissance." Indeed, some of the changes—like splitting armies into smaller, more agile units—were copied from the Romans. In addition, the rebels had strengthened their forces. The army numbered over fifty thousand men in 1600. A belt of fortified cities with strong garrisons protected the new state created by the seven allied northern provinces. The border between the free Netherlands and the southern provinces—which remained Spanish and thus Catholic, and which correspond more or less to modern Belgium—remained contested until the final recognition of the former's sovereignty in 1648. Neither side was able to force substantial changes.

In the north, the search for a crowned monarch that might have provided legitimacy was unsuccessful. In consequence, a decentralized republic emerged. While the individual provinces saw to their own internal affairs, decisions about war and peace were made by the assembly of their representatives, the "States General," which remained continuously in session from 1593.

The "general stadtholder," the national counterpart to the stadtholders of the provinces, commanded the army and the fleet. Especially in times of war, he possessed extraordinary power. The office was not hereditary, but it almost always fell to a member of the House of Orange. The office of the "land's advocate" of Holland, the most important province, evolved into the position of the "great pensionary," who, as president and chancellor of the States General, could have enormous political influence. But the greatest power lay with the cities and their wealthy merchants. They dominated the provincial assemblies and, through them, the States General in The Hague. From their number also came the ca. two thousand *regenten*, a political elite that held state and city offices. More a union of the estates and cities than a federal state, the Dutch Republic joined the Swiss Confederacy as one of the first examples in world history of a polity in which citizens (and in some provinces, even farmers) exercised political power. Its institutions were much more firmly joined than the loose network of Swiss cities, whose only common organ was the *Tagsatzung*, or Federal Diet. Offices comparable to the general stadtholder or the great pensionary were unknown to the Swiss.

The "United Netherlands" was officially a Calvinist republic. Yet its Church was not the official state church but rather the church officially sanctioned by the state.[78] Followers of other faiths were allowed to practice their religion, although not publicly at first. Jews who had immigrated from Portugal were allowed to build a synagogue in the middle of Amsterdam. As the printer Christophe Plantin noted in 1585, Catholic students at the University of Leiden were not exposed to coercion.[79] A debate over the doctrine of predestination— the "Remonstrants" around the Leiden theologian Jacobus Arminius opposed the hard Calvinist version—remained an isolated episode. Admittedly, many Arminians were forced into exile. Yet the execution in 1619 of their leader, Land Advocate Johann Oldenbarnevelt, had less to do with his religious convictions than with the fact that the theological dispute had developed into a power struggle with the Calvinist stadtholder Maurice of Orange. The latter's victory contemporaneously marked the shift to a military offensive overseas.

Commerce never indulged in religious fanaticism, however. Tolerance, albeit within strict limits, became a competitive advantage. The T of tolerance was joined by two more: talent and technology. These "three T's" were the Netherlands' primary contribution to enlarging Europe's realm of possibility. Many books that could barely be published in Italy and definitely not in Spain would be printed there, including Galileo's *Discourses* and Descartes's *Discourse on Method*. The Spanish provinces, in contrast, suffered terribly at the loss of the "three T's." Antwerp ceded its role as a commercial center. Christophe Plantin's print shop did good business, however. At times sixteen presses pounded away, worked by eighty printers. Thanks to his "labor and constancy"—*labore et constantia* was his house's motto—Plantin could afford a mansion in town with an ornamental garden.

Down to the nineteenth century, Holland blocked the mouth of the Scheldt River, thus cutting Antwerp off from the open sea. Refugees from territories reconquered by Farnese streamed into the northern provinces. The cities there grew dramatically. For example, Amsterdam went from thirty thousand inhabitants in 1570 to 140,000 by the mid-seventeenth century.[80] The urbanization trend in the north was exceptional. About half of all people lived in cities. The economy grew by leaps and bounds.[81] Holland's cloth weavers kept pace with competition from India. Blue-white Delftware elevated Europe's table manners, and all over Europe tobacco smoke was puffed through clay pipes fired in Gouda. Mass-produced ships called "fluyts" transported cargo at unbeatable prices. They required only ten deckhands to operate—in part because pulleys were used to raise their sails—while others needed three times that number.[82] The Hanseatic League lost its western trade as a result. Despite the wars at home, Dutch ships sailed to Africa, competing there with the Portuguese. They cruised the Mediterranean and reached Narva in the Baltic and Spitsbergen in the north.

Life was hard for the common man, although wages were higher on average in the Netherlands than in the rest of Europe. Those left behind by the boom were supported by the soup kitchens, orphanages, and hospitals of the Protestant ethic. The workhouse established in Amsterdam in 1595 subjected its residents to strict discipline. There was unrest caused by high taxes and rising prices, but it was rare and resulted in only a few deaths.

Regenten, shipowners, and merchants stood at the apex of society. The aristocracy was much less significant than in neighboring countries, the *burgerij*—the middle classes—much more so. The social universe was divided into groups like shooting clubs and guilds. In literary societies called *rederijkerskamer*, or "chambers of rhetoric," poets of all stripes met. Education was provided by newly founded universities: in Franeker, Groningen, Utrecht, and Harderwijk. The University of Leiden was home to the botanist Carolus Clusius (1526–1609) and the mathematician Rudolph Snellius (1546–1613), among others. In the person of Justus Lipsius (1547–1606), Leiden could boast of a first-rate philologist, philosopher, and political theorist. His successor Joseph Justus Scaliger (1540–1609) was no less important as an editor of classical texts and was an expert in Oriental languages to boot. He was paid the king's ransom of 1,200 guilders per annum, an expression of the high esteem for humanist learning.[83]

Many farmers, most of whom were free and owned their own fields and pastures, had a share in the prosperity that flowed from the seas. Grain was largely imported from the Baltic region, leaving muscle power and capital free for livestock raising, dairy farming, and cheese production. Purpurin and flax, raw materials of the textile industry, were also cultivated. Often in the form of investments by townspeople, capitalism conquered the flat land, helping to improve farming techniques, build dikes, and ameliorate the soil. The new nation was so economically sound that the state was able to bear the high cost of the war of independence against Spain without ever going bankrupt.

A Woman on the Throne: Elizabeth I

On the other side of the Channel, it became clear that Spain's hopes had been in vain. Queen Elizabeth was not going to find the true faith and return to the policies of the Catholic Mary. Advised by the jurist William Cecil, Lord Burghley (1521–1598), a clever pragmatist, the queen set to work rebuilding the Church of England. The clergy had to take an oath to her as "the only supreme governor of this realm . . . as well as in all spiritual or ecclesiastical things or causes, as temporal."[84] The *Book of Common Prayer* compiled by Cranmer, which delineated the liturgy, was reinstituted with slight alteration. However, Elizabeth balked at all the radical demands made by purity fanatics, this time in the form of the Puritan movement—with its joyless morality, endless sermons, and dreams of returning to apostolic Christianity. The Puritan cause had been wholly discredited by the Scottish Reformer John Knox (1514–1572). In 1558, he published a pamphlet that not only raged against Catholic queens but also unleashed a "blast of the trumpet against the unnatural rule of women" in general.

Elizabeth's Church retained a Catholic sheen. At any rate, the queen never lost sleep over questions of dogma. She was perfectly pious, but her main concern was for the authority of the crown. Major decisions were made in the Privy Council, which met regularly and to which a bureaucratic apparatus had now accreted. Numerous courts provided the state with a framework of rational jurisprudence. The close working relationship between the government and the judiciary can be seen in the Star Chamber—named after the ceiling decoration of its meeting room in the Royal Palace of Westminster—whose membership was largely identical to that of the Privy Council. Printed matter was subject to (rather unsystematic) censorship, less for religious than for political concerns.[85] After Elizabeth was excommunicated by Pius V (1566–1572), things got more serious. Even popular Robin Hood dramas were banned, as the cheerful Friar Tuck embodied a bygone, folksy monasticism that could inspire unwanted nostalgia.[86]

During Elizabeth's reign, Parliament retained the status it had acquired under her predecessors, its members keeping the "free voice" they considered their most precious good.[87] The House of Commons even once dared to make its approval of financial support dependent on an issue of succession: it wanted the "Virgin Queen" to marry. That was clearly a bridge too far. Elizabeth snapped back with words that would go down in history:

> Though I be a woman, yet I have as good a courage, answerable to my place, as ever my father had. I am your anointed Queen. I will never be by violence constrained to do anything. I thank God I am indeed endued with such qualities that if I were turned out of the realm in my petticoat, I were able to live in any place of Christendom.[88]

She was an intelligent ruler, at times vindictive and quick-tempered, but always focused on the possible. Her deft maneuvering and foreign threats made sure that the constitutional problem did not become a crisis. The situation was complex. France was sinking into its civil wars, and Alba had been let off his chain in the Netherlands. To make matters worse, there was a Catholic rival in Mary Stuart (1542–1587); Francis II's young widow had become ruler of Scotland in 1561. Her reign was ended in 1567 by an aristocratic conspiracy, and her one-year-old son James inherited the Scottish throne. The toppled queen had to seek asylum in England. She was held under arrest for nineteen years in castles in the interior of England, embodying hopes of a Catholic restoration. At first, only skittishness about the magic of legitimacy could have kept Elizabeth from eliminating Mary. A 1569 aristocratic plot to bring the so-called Queen of Scots to power shows just how dangerous she was. Elizabeth's mercenaries quashed the rebellion.

Realistically assessing the resources of her country, the queen did not dare to openly challenge the supremacy of Spain. At first, she stuck to a limited cold war, providing aid to Philip's enemies and promoting piracy with letters of marque. In response, Madrid imposed economic sanctions. The decisive battle for England, the true faith, and the question of who would rule the seas was only postponed because the Spanish Gulliver was tied down in its wars on the

Continent. In 1585, however, plans were hatched at the Escorial to finally put an end to English heresy and the plague of piracy. An armada, the likes of which Europe had never seen, was to invade the island and enable the reinstatement of Mary, Queen of Scots. Elizabeth's effective spy network—organized by the jurist Sir Francis Walsingham—had ears in Madrid and all over Europe; it sent alarming reports.

The duel now entered its decisive phase. Elizabeth pursued a policy that would later become doctrine: to maintain division on the Continent with diplomacy and, if necessary, with war in order to win the seas. Troops were sent to the Netherlands and France. They achieved little in either place. The greatest expense was occasioned by campaigns in restive Ireland, which was tearing itself apart in fighting between local clans. This was unavoidable, as the Emerald Isle could otherwise be used as the base for a Catholic invasion. It had already been necessary to thwart attempts by Spanish and papal mercenaries to establish bridgeheads in concert with rebels.

Fears of a fifth column at home prompted the crown to take harsher measures against Catholic missionaries who had infiltrated the country, as well as against those who gave them shelter. Several hundred paid for their religious zeal with exile, prison, or death. Mary Stuart also met her destiny now. Conspiracies against Elizabeth involving Mary were uncovered by Walsingham's agents at the last moment; in 1587, she was beheaded. At least the Scottish front remained quiet when the great war with Spain broke out. Mary's son James was already eyeing England's crown, which would fall to him if Elizabeth died without issue. Meanwhile, Philip focused all his resources on the invasion project. If successful, it would mean the restoration of Catholicism on the island, as well as the safeguarding of Atlantic sea routes and probably a final victory in the Netherlands as well.

The balance of power was unequal. England's land army, a ragtag band of recruits from the shires, was of questionable military value. It would not have been much of a match for an invading Spanish force. The fleet, on the other hand, had been assiduously expanded under the direction of the erstwhile pirate John Hawkins (1532–1595).[89] The job of his lean, well-equipped navy was to preemptively attack Spanish treasure fleets in the Caribbean and the Azores, thus depriving Philip's empire of silver. Such privateering voyages, with or without royal license, were not normally undertaken with the national interest at heart. Rather, they were motivated by profit. For example, Hawkins, financed in part by Elizabeth's privy purse, had cut into the Portuguese slave trade and bargained for captured human beings in western Africa. He took his victims to Haiti, where he sold them to Spanish buyers.

His cousin Francis Drake (ca. 1540–1596) achieved hero status. His fame reached all the way to southern Germany.[90] The farmer's son from Devonshire had risen through the ranks to become an accomplished sailor and pirate, first in the English Channel and then as Hawkins's accomplice in the Caribbean. Drake became a legend thanks to his circumnavigation of the globe between 1577 and 1580, the first such voyage survived by a single captain from beginning to end. Off the coast of Ecuador, the English captured a Spanish galleon despite its daunting nickname—*Cacafuego*, i.e., *Spitfire* or, more literally, *Fireshitter*— and stole its load of silver. In the end, the voyage netted 150,000 pounds; Drake was made a knight.[91] Showered with ducats and jewels by the upstart, the queen even agreed to a banquet on his ship.[92] A contemporary portrait shows the newly minted "sir" as a ruddy fellow with a weather-beaten face. His right hand imperiously grasps a globe, as if the world were his to rule.

The privateering stridently pursued in the leadup to the decisive battle cost the already depleted Real Hacienda, the royal treasury, a great deal of money. Drake pursued an aggressive strategy. He razed Spanish bases in the Caribbean to the ground. In 1587, he pulled off an especially daring escapade, entering the port of Cadiz with a strong fleet and destroying thirty Spanish ships. On the way home, he had the chutzpah to take a detour to the Azores and capture a Portuguese carrack laden with treasures from Africa. The booty was lavish and brought the underwriters of the campaign a good profit. In this way, war was financed by war.

Much was at stake for Spain and everything for England. The fleet was the island's only defense. The ideological dimension of the battle was reflected in the names of the ships. The English side featured *Bull*, *Tiger*, *Revenge*, *Golden Lion*, and *Dreadnought*. The Spanish fought with *Santa María de la Rosa* (*Saint Mary of the Rose*), *San Juan* (*Saint John*), *San Pedro* (*Saint Peter*), and *Nuestra Señora del Rosario* (*Our Lady of the Rosary*). Elizabeth entrusted command to experienced captains. Serving under Lord High Admiral Charles Howard of Effingham (1536–1624) were Drake and Hawkins, among other seasoned fighters. In command of the Armada was Alonso Pérez de Guzmán (1550–1615), Duke of Medina Sidonia. Inexperienced at sea, he had accepted the post against his will. Nevertheless, he was surrounded by capable officers. The upcoming battle was like a duel between parvenus and the old high nobility. The aristocrats on board the Spanish ships were dressed in sumptuous, colorful clothing as if they were going to a ball and not a dance with death.[93]

The Armada that sailed north from Lisbon in late May 1588 and reached England in July arrayed itself in a half-moon formation, the ships close together to protect themselves from broadsides. It advanced through the English

Channel like a floating fortress, surrounded by nimble English galleons that peppered it with artillery fire. The beginning of the end came the night of August 8, off Calais. The Spanish had failed to find secure harbors in time, and so they had to anchor in a vulnerable position off the coast. The Armada was now near the Spanish Army of Flanders, which it was supposed to ferry to the island. England's fate hung by a thread. But Admiral Howard seized the moment, sending fireships into the slumbering colossus. Confusion spread, and anchor lines were cut in panic; the protective formation disintegrated. The main battle broke out the next day near Gravelines, in which Howard's galleons, the enemy seeing only scattered ships, enjoyed all the advantages. Four of Spain's ships were sunk, and most of the rest were too damaged to continue fighting. The weather took care of the rest. Storms drove what remained of the "invincible Armada" past England and Scotland, out into the Atlantic, and then toward the cliffs on the west coast of Ireland. Only a few ships made it back to La Coruña. A portrait of Queen Elizabeth, wearing a dress covered in pearls and jewels, shows the final scenes of the battle in the background (Plate 26). The monarch's hand rests on a globe, right atop the Americas, the target of British expansion.

The victory of 1588 in no way put an end to the war. A massive English counterattack one year later was thwarted off the coast of Lisbon. Two more Spanish fleets were dispatched northward, but they were stopped by storms shortly after setting sail. Privateering could not win the war. Many English buccaneers found the gallows instead of gold. Drake died of an infection on board his ship in 1596 during a stalled campaign against Panama.

Compared to the tons of precious metal that reached the Spanish motherland, the losses inflicted on the Catholic empire by piracy were insignificant. Nevertheless, the economic consequences of the war were grave. Spain's trading houses suffered losses. This meant lower tax revenues and thus less money in the royal budget. Ten million ducats went to the bottom of the Atlantic with the Armada. All this contributed to the financial collapse mentioned above. Philip's successors continued his quixotic policies. Their armies' victories here and there only veiled the fact that the economic foundation of a once awe-inspiring superpower had now crumbled.

England was also embroiled in costly wars in support of Henry IV and the Netherlands. The Irish conflict was smoldering as well. Most of Elizabeth's subjects now practiced a moderate Protestantism that differed from the Continental variety in its ceremonious liturgy, which harmonized with the majesty of Britain's cathedrals. Richard Hooker's *Of the Laws of Ecclesiastical Polity*

(1585) provided the inchoate Anglican Church with its theology. Philip II had succeeded in utterly discrediting all things Catholic on the island. The war with Spain had also strengthened Parliament, since Elizabeth was constantly forced to request that new taxes be levied.

Debates in Saint Stephen's Chapel in Westminster, the chamber of the House of Commons, were contentious and often tumultuous. The world had not experienced such training for democracy since the best days of the Roman Republic. In the shadow of the Spanish threat, Parliament generally cooperated loyally with the crown. Contemporaries considered it England's "most high and absolute power of the realm." Parliament had claimed to work for the good of the *entire* realm since the thirteenth century.[94] The queen treated the Commons with reverence in her famous Golden Speech, delivered to a delegation from that body on November 30, 1601. "There is no jewel, be it of never so rich a price, which I prefer before this jewel—I mean your loves. . . . And though God hath raised me high, yet this I count the glory of my crown: that I have reigned with your loves."[95] In return, she assured the gentleman of her deep devotion to them, and she bid all the members kiss her hand. It was to be her last Parliament.

The Elizabethan world still lives on in the arts: in John Dowland's melancholic songs and William Byrd's church music, in Nicholas Hilliard's miniatures of pale, yearning lovers, in Edmund Spenser's *The Faerie Queen*, which immortalized Elizabeth's glory, and above all in Shakespeare's plays. Half-timber buildings and the manor houses of the landed gentry and the ministers, whose steep late Gothic architecture here and there betrays the timid beginnings of Italian Renaissance influence, reflect the economic prosperity of an age that was glorified by those that followed.

36

European Tableau II

THE NORTH, THE EAST, THE CENTER, AND ITALY

Patriots

When Elizabeth I died in March 1603 at the age of 70, she bequeathed to her successor, James of Scotland, a stable state. Its elite may have already thought of themselves as part of a nation. The successful war with Spain had provided an opportunity to celebrate battles and newfound prosperity in the certainty that God's grace lay upon all, that one belonged to a chosen people.[1] This is an utterly absurd and dangerous notion, one still harbored by some religions and states today, nourished by military victories, imperial dominance, and even by repression (which can be interpreted as a "test" from God). It has been argued that England's budding national sentiment was the "spirit" behind the growth of the English economy. Yet this is as dubious as the thesis that an English identity had existed since before the early medieval invasions.[2]

In England as in France, wars over religion, freedom, and the throne created communities of experience. Before there was a word for it, they fed what we would now call "patriotism." The good of the fatherland, the *patria*—one's city, the place one came from, and ultimately an entire country or empire—gained greater significance as a political and moral value.[3] The speech Henry IV delivered to the Parlement to justify his toleration policy pointed far into the future. In his own party, he said, he had met men who sought war out of ambition or because it was in the interest of Spain and others who saw only an opportunity for theft—none of these especially honorable motives. "We should no longer distinguish between Catholics and Huguenots," he concluded. "We should all be good Frenchmen."[4] Henry's words show that the Europe of dynasties and patriots, of Catholics and Protestants, was slowly beginning to transform into a Europe of nations.

The peoples of the continent recognized each other's peculiar characteristics. Gradually, national stereotypes emerged: proud Spaniards, deceitful Italians, sullen, boozing Russians, German pigs.[5] Writers attempted to create literature in their native languages to rival the hegemonic Latin of the classics and the dazzling poetry of Petrarca and other Italians. Thomas Elyot (1490–1546) translated ancient authors and texts by Pico della Mirandola into English. He wanted to write for his own country, he claimed, and thus did so in his mother tongue.[6] The magnificent 1532 edition of works by John Gower and Chaucer may reflect the printer's calculation of what would sell, but it also shows that people were beginning to think in terms of a homegrown literary tradition. After midcentury, English translations of Virgil's *Aeneid*, Ovid's *Metamorphoses*, and Seneca's tragedies appeared. In France, Clément Marot published a modernized version of the *Romance of the Rose* and produced a new edition of François Villon's poetry. In addition, the *Pléiade*, a group of poets around Michel de Ronsard (1524–1585), an admirer of Marot's poetry, sought to equal the greatness of classical and Italian literature in French. During the civil wars, the construction of a cultural nation—on which the French had only begun to work—countered the fragmentation of the homeland.

Similar endeavors were undertaken elsewhere. The Dominican friar André de Resende (ca. 1500–1573), Portugal's first archaeologist, brought his home country's deep past to light and therewith the identity of some of its ruins.

Luis de Camões's (1524?–1580) *Lusíadas* became the national epic. A kind of Portuguese *Aeneid*, it sings of the discoveries of Vasco de Gama and other great captains. The "Polish Horace" Jan Kochanowski, a correspondent of Ronsard and an expert on Italy, wrote poems and histories in the style of Boccaccio—but in Polish. His Dutch counterpart was Hendrik Spiegel (1549–1612), who considered himself a defender of his *moedertaal*, or mother tongue. In the Holy Roman Empire, learned societies devoted to fostering the German language were not founded until the seventeenth century. They, too, stood opposed to the fragmentation and devastation of the fatherland wrought by the Thirty Years' War.

In Italy, patriotic sentiment developed in earnest. Giorgio Vasari's *Lives of the Most Excellent Painters, Sculptors, and Architects*, whose first edition appeared in 1550 in Florence, is not only a monument to the dawn of art history. Every line of the *Vite* gives voice to the awareness of Italian, and more specifically Tuscan, greatness. The author is proud to belong to a people that is gifted with dazzling imagination and boundless creativity, and that has brought forth an artistic epoch without compare. The Flemish painter Karel van Mander (1548–1606) was no less proud of the glorious line of Dutch masters. Starting with biographies of the van Eyck brothers, he tells their life stories in his 1604 *Schilder-Boek* (*Book of Painting*). Many of his compatriots decorated their sitting rooms with maps of their fledgling, hard-won state. These, too, it has been argued, emanated patriotism.[7]

In the sixteenth century, nations gradually completed the process—very familiar to us—of delineating themselves literally, of drawing fine lines on maps, thereby giving themselves a precise territory and thus a clear shape. What had once been a jumble of rights and privileges became a territory. The old genealogies of the homeland's saviors and heroes were updated, now including the new heroes produced by fights for throne, faith, and freedom: Henry IV in France, Drake in England, and in Venice Marcantonio Bragadin, who defended Cyprus and was flayed alive by the Turks. These men were honored in the customary fashion, given graves or monuments in prominent churches. For example, the Dutch buried William of Orange in Delft's New Church. The *Wilhelmus*, which would become the country's national anthem, praises him for dedicating "undying faith to this land of mine." Bragadin lies in Venice's San Zanipolo and Henry in Saint-Denis. Not all the mortal remains of the celebrated great men made it home. Drake was buried at sea somewhere off the coast of Panama, and the bones of Luis de Camões, who died of plague after a picturesque life, were dumped in a mass grave.

The Baltic Region and Siberia

Sweden's great revolutionary hero was Gustav Vasa (1496–1560). After a short war, he brought an end to the Kalmar Union, thus securing his country's independence from Denmark.[8] Further fighting after Gustav's death could not reverse the situation. The foundation for Sweden's rise as an independent power was laid by iron and copper, wood, pitch, and tar—i.e., the building blocks of sea power. Exports to Holland and England filled the coffers of the new dynasty, and foreign businessmen—Dutch, Germans, Walloons— brought capital and credit to the country.

In domestic affairs, the Vasa rulers cooperated with the clergy, townspeople, and farmers to the detriment of the aristocracy. Social mobility was relatively fluid, and the educational system was well-developed thanks to state initiatives. Sweden thus joined the vanguard of Europe's nations. Like its neighbors, it adorned itself with an ancient identity. What the Trojans, Teutons, or Batavians were for the others, the Goths were for Sweden: erstwhile masters of half of Europe. The Goths had been discovered as ancestors of the Swedes in the mid-fifteenth century. Archaeological interest developed relatively late under the midnight sun. Not until the reign of Gustavus Adolphus, king during the Thirty Years' War, was the magician, mystic, and rune historian Johannes Bureus (1568–1652) made "imperial antiquarian" and thus master of runes and ruins.[9] Bureus was a somewhat esoteric propagandist of Gothicism, which provided an ideological bulwark for Sweden's foreign policy. Its agenda was focused on the fight for predominance in the Baltic region, *dominium maris Baltici*. After the Hanseatic League's power waned, Sweden was challenged by Denmark, Russia, and Poland.

In 1587, Poland's crown was also donned by a Vasa, Sigismund III (r. 1587– 1632).[10] The last Jagiellonian had died in 1572, followed by the one-year reign of Henry of Valois (r. 1573–1574) and then the rule of the Transylvanian Prince Stephan Báthory (r. 1576–1586). Then Sigismund was chosen as king. Dynastic rivalry now intensified the fight for control of the Baltic Sea, as Sigismund and his successors also consistently pressed their claim to Sweden. A confessional element increased the tension even more. Unlike the Swedish Vasa, the Polish line remained loyal to Rome.

Poland-Lithuania was still a great power. In the face of the threat from its Russian neighbor, in the final Jagiellonian years the nobility had decided to turn the personal union into a true commonwealth, unifying the land into a single state. Nevertheless, the sheer size of the realm and a few military successes under Báthory only veiled the internal weakness of the aristocratic republic. The capital was now Warsaw, which had fallen to the crown along with Masovia, the land of the Piasts, when that line died out in 1526.

While the rest of Europe was tormented by religious wars, Poland-Lithuania remained an island of tolerance down to Báthory's reign—a "land without stakes."[11] Roman Catholics lived peacefully alongside Orthodox Christians, Lutherans and Calvinists, Muslim Tatars, Jews, Anabaptists, Bohemian Brethren, Socinians (who rejected the Catholic doctrine of the Trinity), and many more groups. One statute, passed by an aristocratic alliance in anticipation of Henry of Valois's election, drew a lesson from events in France and obligated its signatories to maintain peace in religious affairs. The goal was to preserve the unity of the state.[12] Under the Vasas, however, Catholic supremacy was reestablished; Jesuits preached against the sin of tolerance.[13] The division of the Orthodox caused by the foundation of a unified Catholic-Orthodox church—it followed Slavic rite but accepted the pope as its head—lightened the load for the Roman mission. Poland developed into a Roman Catholic stronghold, surrounded by Protestant Sweden, Orthodox Russia, and the Ottoman Empire. The powerful Polish chancellor Jan Zamoyski (1542–1605) fought in vain to prevent the erosion of tolerance. Formerly rector of the University of Padua, he was one of the patrons of the Polish Renaissance. His monument is Zamość, an ideal city like Sabbioneta planned by an Italian architect.[14]

Another participant in the Baltic power game ruled in Moscow: Ivan IV "the Terrible" (r. 1547–1584). His foreign policy initially cast its eye on the restive Tatar territories to the south and east. He succeeded in conquering the Khanate of Kazan. Other successor states of the Tatar superpower, including even the Khanate of Sibir, preferred to pay tribute rather than bear the risks of war. Astrakhan was annexed in 1556, and the Circassians south of it capitulated a few years later.

The dynamics of this expansion were tremendous. At the beginning of Vasili III's reign in the early sixteenth century, Moscow had ruled over a territory of about 430,000 square kilometers. Now it was 5.4 million, albeit sparsely inhabited. The motives behind this policy were complex. Moscow gained control over massive economic zones, and the Orthodox Church hoped to win more souls for Christ. Encouraged by his initial successes, Ivan now decided to roll the dice of war in the west. The target was Livonia, once the domain of the Teutonic Order. If victorious, he stood to win port cities and thus the opening of a trade route from the Baltic coast to the Caspian Sea.

Poland and the Scandinavian powers opposed the tsar. The campaign quickly got bogged down.

His defeats, not to mention failed harvests and epidemics, could have been seen as admonitions to prayer. But Ivan, sensing treachery everywhere, reacted with terror. Actual and presumed traitors were executed, even from the circles of the high nobility. The tsar declared half of the empire to be his *oprichnina*, an extraterritorial state within Russia's borders over which he had sole personal authority. Boyars with lands there were dispossessed.[15] As a personal bodyguard he engaged 1,500 mounted troops, the *oprichniki*. Dog skulls jangled from the bridles of their horses, and wooden rods entwined their whips like the fasces carried by ancient Roman lictors[16]—a rare glimpse of the Renaissance in Russia. Whole swathes of the *oprichnina* burned or were depopulated by massacres and expulsion. The tsar ultimately ordered Novgorod plundered. To frighten all possible enemies, two thousand people were tortured, impaled, flayed, and quartered. In one of the most bizarre episodes of Russian history, Ivan, like an abbot, gathered his black-robed *oprichniki* for masses lasting hours and even issued monastic rules. Only when Crimean Tatars set fire to Moscow did Ivan change course. Without local support, he believed, the Tatar raid would have been nearly impossible. So he arrested his death squads, now turning the terror on his own terrorists. At the same time, in the summer of 1572, the Russian army defeated the Tatars at Molodi, south of the Oka River. Moscow breathed a sigh of relief. Thanks to the destruction of the old elite, the upshot of the *oprichnina* was to bolster the power of the tsar. Meanwhile, the Livonian War ended in 1583 without anything to show for it. In contrast, spectacular victories were won in Asia. They had been prepared by Timur the Lame's wars of annihilation. Besides Sarai, the chief city of the Golden Horde, he had destroyed important trading centers in central Asia, thus cutting off the Khanate's economic blood supply.

By expanding into the Slavic world and conquering peoples who spoke other languages and worshipped strange gods, the Russian state under the tsar, who claimed for himself overlordship of all Orthodox Christianity, had crossed the threshold into empire. It was an epochal development in the history of Eurasia.[17] Not that it was the product of a grand design—opportunities were seized, and power sought greater power. The tsar became the true heir to the Mongol dynasties. His empire expanded ever further, following the path into the steppe and forests east of the Urals, with their inexhaustible wealth of natural resources and forest fruits. Furs were a coveted good, the true gold of the east.

The spearhead of the conquest of Siberia was the Stroganov family, a merchant clan that had grown rich thanks to a salt monopoly. Ivan IV furnished them with trade privileges. In return, they rented a private army with five hundred Cossacks at its core. In a swift campaign, they overthrew the Siberian Khanate. A counterattack was initially successful and claimed the life of the leader of the mercenary troops, the Cossack ataman Yermak. The Russians had to retreat. But now Moscow took the initiative and sent reinforcements. The key to controlling this vast territory was the building of bases fortified with wooden palisades, which offered protection in times of need. The steppe remained hard-fought. After the conquest of Kazan and Astrakhan, Russian settlers pressed into the area and took the most fertile land for themselves. For the moment, the Crimean Tatars remained unbeaten. Another showdown with their protectors, the Ottomans, did not take place. Both sides wanted to maintain the lucrative trade that flowed through Azov and Caffa.[18]

Ivan's legacy was an impoverished, divided land.[19] Many farmers had emigrated; entire villages lay deserted. The state lacked tax revenues. A brutish remedy was to prohibit peasants from leaving their masters, thus tying people to the land. This was one step closer to serfdom, a condition to which an originally free population of farmers was increasingly reduced.[20] When Ivan died, the succession was unclear. For the irascible tsar had killed his own firstborn son during a fight. This left only his younger son Feodor, who was mentally ill and childless. He died in 1598. The successor to the last of the Rurikids was chosen by the Zemsky Sobor, the parliament of the tsardom, on the recommendation of the Patriarch. The lucky candidate was the provincial nobleman Boris Godunov (r. 1598–1605), who had already served as Feodor's regent.

The new tsar gained more glory from Pushkin's play and Mussorgsky's opera than from his actual deeds. His policies were initially crowned with success, though. He was victorious against a Tatar army and won back territory lost to Sweden. But he was stymied by a familiar, titanic enemy: the Little Ice Age, which had also plagued Ivan IV. It destroyed two harvests in a row, causing the death of thousands. Rebellions resulted, with people fighting for bread and against serfdom. During Godunov's reign, the tsardom slipped into a "Time of Troubles." Pretenders to the throne cropped up, with Sweden and Poland adding to the chaos. In 1610, Polish troops occupied the Kremlin. It was the first time in Russian history that foreign arms pierced the heart of Russian power. Yet the crisis brought together everyone able to hold a weapon. The Church gave its blessing to the fight against foreign domination and Catholicization. Moscow was liberated. Once again, in 1613, the Zemsky Sobor chose a new tsar: Michael I, a descendent of the boyar House of Romanov and the son of a metropolitan imprisoned by the Poles.

In the following century, Russia become the hegemonic power in the Baltic region. Denmark was forced to give up all pretensions, whereas Sweden tried to keep playing its tired role as a major power down to the time of the Great Northern War (1700–1721). Poland was able to celebrate a few final victories, but less because of its own strength than because of Russia's weakness in the Time of Troubles. What had once been one of Europe's mightiest states sank to the status of a protectorate of the tsardom. Warsaw could now place its hopes in only one counterweight: Turkey. When war raged on the Bosporus, peace reigned on the Vistula.

The Holy Roman Empire

The notion that the *Kaiser* of the Holy Roman Empire was the master of the world and sovereign above all princes and kings had long been a mere chimera. It must have seemed exotic in Moscow. In 1488, when Frederick III offered the Grand Prince a royal crown in exchange for his aid against the Ottomans, the latter replied sharply that his ancestors had always been rulers by God's grace and had no need of such a trinket.[21] Closer contact between Vienna and the Russian autocracy did not develop again until the time of Emperor Maximilian II (r. 1564–1576).[22] Ivan IV sent an embassy to the Diet of Regensburg in 1576; it was the first time that Russians appeared before the Holy Roman Emperor and the representatives of his *Reich*. They traveled with a grand retinue, bringing whole "timbers" of sable furs—each containing forty skins—as gifts. A cavalcade of five hundred horses demonstrated that a superpower was paying a visit.

The emperor whom the Russians met in Regensburg was less Catholic than the other Habsburg rulers.[23] There is no doubt that Maximilian II harbored sympathy for Luther's teachings. He disapproved of Queen Elizabeth's excommunication. The Saint Bartholomew's Day massacre appalled him. Yet he married a Spanish princess, a daughter of Charles V, and consented to have his sons grow up in Madrid under Catholic influence. A music lover and book collector, he was interested in science. He seems to have been an amiable companion. A friend of stuffy court ceremonial he was not. He kept his true beliefs to himself his whole life. What is certain, however, is that dynastic—i.e., Catholic—solidarity was more important to him than his private religious sentiments.

With that limitation in mind, Maximilian understood his role to be that of moderator. He was committed to the Peace of Augsburg and respected the checks and balances of the imperial constitution. This was an imperative of *raison d'état*. A rigid religious policy on the Spanish model was not an option in Germany. To wage war and get the money necessary for it, the emperor needed the support of the Diet. The Ottoman threat even drove him to make concessions to the nobility of his own hereditary lands. The 1568 Peace of Adrianople, bought at the price of high tribute payments, took the pressure off the Holy Roman Empire for twenty-five years and gave it the opportunity to improve the line of fortresses that secured the border between the Habsburgs and the Ottoman state. In Germany itself, however, peace was threatened by confessional and political tensions. Under the fragile aegis of the religious peace, Protestantism continued to gain ground, secularizing previously religious territory. Catholic regions like Bavaria purified themselves by expelling dissenters. Within the Reformation movement, Calvinists—who were not included in the Peace of Augsburg and thus enjoyed no legal protection—competed with Lutherans. A danger was presented by the fact that confessional networks extended beyond the borders of the Empire. This made it easy for conflicts to quickly take on international dimensions and draw foreign troops onto imperial soil, as then happened in the Thirty Years' War.

The desire for peace still predominated. Lazarus von Schwendi (1522–1583), a successful general in the Ottoman war, wrote a memorandum encouraging Maximilian to pursue his policy of restraint. It is imbued with a profound understanding of the historical justification for the Reformation. Schwendi, who, like his lord, remained Catholic his whole life, saw its causes in an obstinate papacy incapable of reform. The path of violence was hopeless, as events in France and the Netherlands showed. If the coals were stoked in Germany, foreign nations and the Ottomans would not miss the opportunity. The Empire would fall into their "jaws and hands."[24] Schwendi, therefore, advised maintaining distance from Spain and the papacy, which was always adding fuel to the fire. Unfortunately for the German people, this advice was not heeded.

After Maximilian II's death, tensions rose in Germany as well. When the archbishop-elector of Cologne, Gebhard Truchsess von Waldburg (1547–1601), breached the Peace of Augsburg by converting to Protestantism in 1582 without abdicating his office—so that he could marry a noble canoness—the Catholic party took up arms. Bavarian and Spanish soldiers drove out the lovestruck prelate and set up a Wittelsbach prince in his place as archbishop of Cologne. Only the House of Orange supported Gebhard. With alarming swiftness, the conflict on the Rhine escalated into an auxiliary theater of the Dutch Revolt. It was a warning sign of coming entanglements.

While this trouble was brewing in Cologne, Catholics and Protestants even lost their common sense of time.[25] Supported by a commission of astronomers and mathematicians, Pope Gregory XIII had introduced a new calendar. It was to replace the Julian Calendar worked out in Caesar's time, as the latter diverged too flagrantly from the solar year. Tiny imprecisions had piled up over a millennium and a half. Now, for example, the full moon illuminated the land days before it was calculated to do so. The observational astronomical data currently available made it possible to align the calendar more precisely with reality. The most important of the remedies required was to simply skip ten days. Concretely, this meant that October 4, 1582, was followed directly by October 15. Now spring could once again be ushered in on March 21, and Christmas and Easter could again be celebrated on Christmas and Easter. This course of action was sensible, its motivation purely technical. But it had the disadvantage of being decreed by the pope. Setting the proper time was ultimately the province of a universal authority. In Riga, Augsburg, and other cities, riots broke out when the new calendar was introduced. Protestant lands held fast to the Julian calendar for a long time. For example, England and Scotland adhered to it until the mid-eighteenth century, and some Orthodox churches still do today.

Opinions about Rudolph II (r. 1576–1612), Maximilian II's successor, are as widely divided as those about his father.[26] The new emperor was born under Saturn: melancholic and shy, indeed moody—at times jovial, at times irascible. He was highly intelligent, which is no help for depression. And to his distinct disadvantage as a sovereign, he was anything but a bureaucrat. From 1583 on, he spent his life ruling from the heights of Hradčany Castle in Prague. To the displeasure of the papal nuncio, he did not shy away from friendship with a circle of heretics, including Lutherans, Calvinists, and even a Utraquist and a converted Jew. He also kept Jesuits out of the University of Prague. He took refuge from complicated reality in his cabinet of curiosities, a museum full of precious items, artworks, and rare objects. He was surrounded by hundreds of alchemists, astrologers, and magicians, some of them charlatans, others prominent scholars. Rudolph is said to have had a long discussion with the rabbi Judah Löw, who, according to legend, created the golem, an artificial man.[27]

Rudolph's Prague developed into a center for the sublime, bizarre, virtuoso art of the late Renaissance. The emperor was especially fond of precious clocks, perhaps because their precise mechanisms were the antithesis of the chaos of the world outside. In his hereditary lands, he was careful to enforce his authority against the obstinacy of the estates and, albeit without excessive zeal, to restore the old faith. He had no interest in the intricate affairs of the Holy Roman Empire. The Hungarian nobility's yearning for freedom was aided by the resumption of the Ottoman wars in 1593. This installment was known as the "Long" Turkish War. For thirteen years, castles and cities were taken and lost again. Rudolph celebrated his petty victories to the skies with ostentatious works of art. Under him, Habsburg policy in the east became highly expansionist, casting its eye all the way to Moscow, the potential ally against the Ottomans. Even a Persian embassy paid a visit to Prague.

The expansionism of the Safavids and unrest at home urged the Sublime Porte to seek peace with Rudolph in the early seventeenth century. For his part, the emperor was moved to end the war by his dynasty's notorious lack of funds. Heavy taxation and quartering, the scourge of the age, had put Hungary, Moravia, and Austria in revolt. The rebellious lands, which persevered successfully in their struggle for a degree of autonomy, also pushed for a peace agreement with the Ottomans. The Peace of Zsitvatorok, negotiated in 1606 on an island in the Danube River, would last for seventy-five years. Without peace in the east, Rudolph never would have been able to pursue his agenda in central Europe. The future of Germany's Catholics would have been dark indeed if Isfahan had not indirectly sent them military aid.

The momentous peace negotiated in Zsitvatorok was not owed to the emperor. He was ensconced in the dreamworld of his castle and increasingly seemed to be losing his mind. In secret, he had been deprived of power by his brothers. As there was no legitimate offspring—Rudolph had remained a bachelor—the oldest of the plotters, Matthias (r. 1612–1619), took control. When Rudolph II died in Hradčany Castle in 1612, all that remained to him was an empty title and one of the most beautiful art collections in Europe. The deterioration of imperial authority came to a precarious head: war was brewing in Germany.

Increasingly, proponents of violent confrontation had been setting the tone. Disputes about the interpretation of the Peace of Augsburg and breaches of law led to paralysis in the imperial judicial system. In 1608, an Imperial Diet ended its session without issuing any decrees. There were no longer any discussion forums or authoritative bodies capable of tackling disputes and bringing about peace. As a result, the confessional parties ignored the imperial constitution and organized themselves into competing alliances: the Protestant Union and the Catholic League. Cardinal Klesl, bishop of Vienna and a leading statesman at the imperial court, now once again located in his diocese, tried in vain to de-escalate the situation by political means. The revolt of the Protestant nobility in Bohemia—like in France, the issues were religious self-determination and political privileges—put an end to all peace efforts. The rebellion was quickly quashed; Frederick V, Elector of the Palatinate, wore the kingly crown given him by the Bohemians in 1619 for only one winter. The victors set about the work of decapitation, confiscation, and Catholicization with gusto. Protestant princes and Spain got involved, as did the Habsburgs' opponents throughout Europe, thus dragging Germany into a war that would last for thirty years.

History of a Mythology: Italy

The massive changes to the framework of the world ushered in by Columbus's voyages to America and the discovery of the route around the Cape of Good Hope were first sensed on the Rialto, one of the most important information exchanges in Europe. In August 1499, the patrician Girolamo Priuli noted that Portuguese ships had been sent to find spice islands "whose lord is Columbus," and that they had arrived at "Calicut and Aden in India."[28] In his clear-sighted judgment, "this news and its significance seem gigantic—if it is true." However, pepper prices did not crash until the late sixteenth century. Caravan trade along the Silk Road, which the Portuguese could not control, once again gained greater importance. In their desperation, the Venetians contemplated the fantastic plan of digging a water route between the Mediterranean and the Red Sea, a Suez Canal ahead of its time. The project was never seriously pursued.[29]

In the eastern Mediterranean, the Serenissima was embroiled in defensive battles against the Ottomans. There was also trouble with Uskok pirates, Serbian and Croatian refugees that had settled down between the great powers. The same year Lepanto was won, Cyprus was lost, and in the following century Crete fell as well after a long war. The Dutch and the English cut into the trade with the Ottomans. The Thirty Years' War caused German markets to crash. Venice's status as an international commercial hub was gradually becoming a thing of the past, part of a general trend in which the age of commercial empires based on urban economic power was ending. The decline of the Hanseatic League is just as symptomatic of it as the sharp fall-off in Venice's Levantine trade. The fine but expensive wool clothing sent from the Rialto to the East was driven from the market by cheaper products from the Netherlands and England.[30] Many people preferred to take their money out of high-risk trade and invest it in rural estates instead. Population increase made cereal cultivation lucrative, both in the Veneto and in Lombardy. Hardly any grain now made its way to northern Italy from the Ottoman Empire, which had its own ravenous megacity of Istanbul to feed. The game was now to close supply gaps and make as much money as possible in the process.[31]

Of the five powers that once ruled the peninsula, the republic on the Rialto was the only one that still had a bit of room to maneuver. It successfully defied the papacy. In a dispute with far-reaching consequences, it challenged the Curia's right to exempt clergy from secular jurisdiction and put a stop to the further expansion of ecclesiastical territory. Paul V (1605–1621) excommunicated Venice, putting it under papal interdict. In response, the city punished the publication of papal decrees with death and expelled Jesuits and members of other religious orders. In the end, Rome had to give in. Medieval papal supremacy succumbed to modern state sovereignty. Defiantly, the Bible verse used to justify the pope's absolute status was inscribed in mosaic in the cupola of Saint Peter's, in letters two meters tall: "Thou art Peter"—the Latin word also means "rock"—"and upon this rock I will build my church. . . . And I will give unto thee the keys of the kingdom of Heaven."[32] In a symbolic act, Paul sainted the pope of Canossa, Gregory VII, in the same year of 1606. A little later, Suárez and other Spanish Scholastics confirmed that the pope, and never a council, enjoyed full sovereign power (*plenitudo potestastis*) in the Church.

Rome had grown to more than one hundred thousand souls. The shepherd ruling over them, now surrounded by a bloated bureaucracy, was the pope. His power continued to be circumscribed by the old families, which were buoyed by their privileges, their feudal holdings, and their networks. Trade was of no significance to the capital of the Papal States, and the city had little in the way of industry.[33] As before, Rome lived on rivers of revenue that flowed to the aristocracy from estates in the hinterland, on pennies from pilgrims, office seekers, and tourists—but above all, on ducats that were collected all over Europe and then piled up in the Curia's treasury and the coffers of the cardinals. Trent had addressed some grievances, but the old nepotism was as strong as ever, hardly less present around 1600 than before the council. Still, the days of a Cesare Borgia were history. Not even the mightiest condottiere could now dream of establishing his own state in the peninsula's rigid political scheme. And yet the Papal States did grow somewhat, gaining Ferrara in the late sixteenth century (when the Este lacked a male heir) and Urbino in 1631 (after the della Rovere died out).

Florence persevered. After the nadir marked by Alessandro de' Medici's murder, his clan, now related by marriage to half the noble houses of Europe, climbed to new heights. In the Pitti Palace on the far side of the Arno, now expanded to the imposing size we are familiar with today, Cosimo de' Medici's wife, Eleanor of Toledo, established a magnificent court. Ever since, the old seat of government in the city center has been known as the Palazzo Vecchio, or "Old Palace." Like the Venetians and the Lombards, the Florentines moved to the countryside and lived on the income provided by olive trees, wine, and grain. Technological innovation ground to a halt.[34]

Florence no longer needed to wage major wars. Duke Cosimo fought only one significant battle his whole life, at Marciano in the Val di Chiana on August 2, 1554. Won with Spanish support, the victory over the Sienese and the French opened the way to Siena. After a year-long siege, the old rival fell. And with it went France's most important bastion in Italy. Giorgio Vasari celebrated the event with a monumental fresco in the Sala dei Cinquecento, the pantheon of the Medici and their city. In 1569, Pius V (1566–1572) elevated Cosimo's tiny patch of land to a grand duchy. A few years earlier, Cosimo had purchased the hand of a daughter of Emperor Ferdinand for his son Francesco.

In those days, all of Florence's glory flowed from the grace of its overpowering Spanish ally, in whose wake the Tuscan state continued to navigate under Cosimo I's successor. Philip's power lay heavy over the peninsula. Spain ruled in Milan and Naples, and on Sicily and Sardinia. Fortresses along the Tuscan coast and on Elba, the "State of the Presidi," provided protection from the Ottomans, from pirates, and from the local population. Strategically important Savoy had to obey Madrid, as did Genoa, which had switched to the Spanish side under the leadership of its naval hero Andrea Doria. The Peace of Cateau-Cambrésis had given Corsica to the Ligurian republic; on the other hand, it lost the Aegean colony of Chios to the Ottomans in 1566. Militarily well-equipped Savoy remained a source of unrest under the ambitious Duke Charles Emmanuel I (1562–1630). Yet his policy of shifting allegiance between Spain and France brought no real profit. His attempt to take Geneva in a sneak attack was also unsuccessful. The War of the Mantuan Succession (1628–1631), a secondary arena of the struggle between the Habsburgs and the Bourbons in central Europe, only brought Savoy insignificant gains in Montferrat.

Spain's Italian lands were as bereft of a politically powerful middle class as the motherland, although the economy still hummed along. The Spanish overlord regarded Italy as a money supplier—the chief financial center was Genoa—and a defensive wall. Territories in the south and west protected against the Ottomans and in the north against France. The decline of southern Italy, in the High Middle Ages the richest region in Europe, continued accordingly. To fight Spain's wars in France, Flanders, and the English Channel, ships had to be withdrawn from Sicily and garrisons abandoned. As a result, the shoreline was visited more often by privateers from the Barbary Coast. In the interior, the strong helped themselves. On Sicily and on the mainland, brigands took with violence what a corrupt state had claimed as its right and the barons thought they legitimately possessed. For their part, the barons made use of the brigands from time to time to engage in feuds and intimidate their peasants. The hard-won produce of the countryside permitted a parasitic aristocracy to live a life of luxury in the cities. The urban population grew, in part thanks to immigrants from the area of the Balkans conquered by the Ottomans. Meanwhile, pestilences raged, e.g., in Messina in 1575 and Palermo in 1624, rebalancing the scales between the number of mouths to feed and available resources.

Sicily's parliament was little more than a rubber stamp of the viceroys. Delegates from the cities were selected from on high. They had as little political say as the Church, which was a ward of the crown. The suzerainty of the pope had evaporated in the Two Sicilies. Madrid appointed bishops and controlled the Inquisition. Higher education was available only at Jesuit colleges and the venerable universities in Salerno and Naples. During a revolt in 1547, Viceroy Pedro Álvarez de Toledo (r. 1532–1553) closed the Neapolitan Academy, which he suspected of being a hotbed of revolution. Roads and bridges in the hinterland crumbled; only the capital enjoyed urban renewal.[35] In places where the distant state failed to offer protection, people took refuge in families and clientage networks. Social relations ossified. It was as if time stood still in the south of Italy. Deforestation for masts and planks eroded the terrain, as did the ubiquitous goats that ate the land bare. Rivers changed their course unobstructed, trickling away in the summer and returning to flood the dusty country in the spring. Swampland expanded, spreading malaria along with it.[36] In his novel *Christ Stopped at Eboli*, Carlo Levi, exiled by the Fascists to a village in Basilicata, describes a rural world unchanged for eons: "There should be a history of this Italy, a history outside the framework of time, confining itself to that which is changeless and eternal, in other words, a mythology."[37]

37

Beyond the Pillars of Hercules

The Wrath of God

The displacement of the world's economic axes initiated by Columbus's American adventure marked the beginning of the end of the great age of the Mediterranean. The Atlantic Ocean became Europe's new "middle sea." Carlo Levi's forgotten land was one of the losers in this shift. Already on the edge of the Spanish empire, the advent of the new, multicenter world economy consigned it to the status of a kind of secondary periphery, for the Mediterranean stopped being the center.[1]

By about 1550, Spain's colonial possessions in the Americas had reached the extent they would have down to the nineteenth century. Contact had given way to conquest and domination.² After six thousand years, so it seemed to a courtier of Philip II, world history had been fulfilled. Catholic Christendom and the Spanish universal empire were now one and the same.³ Leading a cohort of barely three hundred men, the conquistador Francisco Pizarro (1476/78–1541) managed to overthrow the Inca Empire and extort tons of gold and silver. Once again, disunity facilitated the Spanish undertaking—a power struggle had broken out among the indigenous people of Peru right before the conquistadors arrived—and once again, Spanish steel dripped with blood. Even the Inca leader, Atahualpa, was killed after being taken hostage. Further north, shock troops had pressed all the way into what is now Texas. The city-states of Yucatan put up fierce resistance. The last one, Chichén Itzá, would not fall until 1697.

In Seville, "the sea that swallows everything and where everything goes to end," adventurers gathered to undertake the journey into the great unknown.⁴ Timeless motivations for migration are mentioned in a 1564 letter written by a tailor from Puebla to his wife back in Spain: "Here we can live according to our pleasure, and you will be very contented, and with you beside me I shall soon be rich."⁵ Many real brothers of "Lazarillo de Tormes"—the poor devil who lived by his wits in the 1552 novella that bore his name—sought their fortune in the New World. The curious hoped to make discoveries, bankers and merchants profit. Fairy-tale careers like that of Cortés and Pizarro beckoned from the far-flung New World. Some of the conquistadors came from the lesser Spanish nobility, which had to find a new role in the changing social environment. After the fall of Granada, the chivalric struggle against the Moors no longer provided a path to honor and riches, *honra y provecho*, on the Iberian Peninsula.⁶ Besides hidalgos, craftsmen, and traders, the main body of the conquerors was made up of sailors, soldiers, and *letrados*—all of them people of urban origin.⁷ By around 1800, eight to nine million people had emigrated overseas.⁸ Their number included few women. They accounted for one-quarter of those who went to Spanish America.

This quickly growing band of soldiers of fortune was engaged in a struggle for survival. Many were lost without a trace in the malaria-infested swampland, in the jungle, somewhere on the seas, or on the icy peaks of the Andes. Countless of them starved, fell victim to poisoned arrows, or were laid low by the musket balls of competitors. One man who left nothing behind but revulsion and a grim myth was Lope de Aguirre (after 1510–1561). Admittedly, the portrayal of him as a power-hungry madman who killed for the sake of killing, who had his captain crowned king of Peru only to then have him murdered, comes from biased sources. Aguirre—"Lope the Wanderer," "rebel until death"—wrote a letter to Philip disavowing him as sovereign. It must be the most outrageous letter a Spanish ruler ever received from a subject. Accompanied by his *"marañones,"* he set up a realm of terror on an island off the coast of Venezuela before ultimately meeting the fate that generally awaited men of his kind: execution, quartering, and defilement of his mortal remains. He is said to have dubbed himself "Wrath of God, Prince of Freedom and the Kingdom of Tierra Firme and the Provinces of Chile."[9]

Easy gold, such as fell to the conquerors of the Inca city of Cusco, remained an empty hope for Aguirre, as for nearly everyone who went to the New World. This was experienced bitterly by Diego de Almagro (1479–1538), a former lieutenant of Cortés and a participant in the Peru campaign. While Pizarro took the titles of governor and captain general and made his brother Hernando lord of Peru, Almagro was left out. To avoid a duel with his partner, he went south with a strong force all the way to Itata. There he was prevented from continuing by warriors of the indigenous Mapuche people. The majority of his troops had not survived the march across the Andes and the bone-dry Atacama Desert. The Spaniards had no idea that they had passed by one of the richest silver deposits in the world, in the territory of Chañarcillo. Weary and with little booty to show for their effort, they returned to Cusco. But they were the first Europeans to see Chile: "the fertile and famed land in Antarctica," as the eyewitness Alonso de Ercilla y Zúñiga described it in his *Araucana*.[10]

In the following decades, Spain secured the territory along the Pacific coast with forts and settlements. The first to be founded was Santiago—named after the patron saint of the Conquista—followed by Concepción and Valdivia. Almagro ultimately did try to seize power from Pizarro and was executed (by hanging and garroting). The result was a war among the conquistadors, pitting Almagro's followers against Pizarro's. Pizarro was killed, and his brother Gonzalo continued the fight. It took until midcentury for Viceroy Pedro de la Gasca to finally succeed in pacifying Peru.

Europeans ventured ever deeper into other regions of South America, following rumors of El Dorado, a king supposedly covered in layers of gold dust.[11] Land in what is now Venezuela, opened up by mercenary troops of the Welser company, was claimed by the Spanish crown. In the 1530s, the Río de la Plata was explored. In 1546, the treasures of Cerro Rico were discovered near Potosí. Along with deposits found in Mexico shortly before that, they unleashed a veritable silver rush. The mining camp developed into a metropolis of over 100,000 inhabitants.[12] Starting out from the Andean Highlands, the Amazon was explored at the same time. The sources tell of phantasmagoric marshes and river journeys through hails of arrows from hostile peoples. But El Dorado remained hidden. Not until the late seventeenth century were gold and diamonds found in Brazil's Minas Gerais. Meanwhile, the Portuguese asserted their authority over the coastal regions of Brazil. They successfully hindered the French project of founding a *France antarctique*. The attempt by Huguenots to settle in Florida was thwarted by Spanish muskets in 1565.[13]

A few conquistadors sought legitimacy for the power they had amassed: a governor's title, a military command, or, as Francisco Pizarro managed, both. Cortés, who broke the mold in this respect as well, won the rank of a *marqués* and the hand of a noblewoman (in his second marriage). Such opportunities faded after the whirlwind years of the Conquista died down. Social relations calcified and approximated existing hierarchies at home. Since the crown could offer little money to pay professional soldiers, the colonists enslaved the natives and enforced tribute. Border wars developed into a lucrative business.[14] The indigenous high aristocracy was for the most part eliminated.

The challenge entailed by subjecting the massive colonial territories to a uniform administration was unique in world history. With remarkable energy, the Spanish crown strove to gather *entera notiçia*, "full knowledge," of what had been conquered.[15] In fast motion, Spanish America underwent a process of state formation that had taken medieval Europe centuries (although the pace was different in different areas). The most important step was to establish a second viceroyalty with its center in Lima, the capital of Peru, founded by Pizarro. It was first given bureaucratic stability under Viceroy Francisco de Toledo (r. 1569–1581). He ruled with a heavy hand. *El Solón Virreinal*, as he was called, laid a legal foundation for Spanish colonial rule. In 1572, he conquered Vilcabamba, to which the Inca people had retreated. He had the young Túpac Amaru executed, thus creating a martyr whose name is still used by modern guerilla groups. The last bastion of the Inca Empire was razed to the ground, left to be reclaimed by the jungle.

With the establishment of further viceroyalties in the eighteenth century—Neugranadas and Río de la Platas, both carved out of Peru—the basic division of continental New Spain was complete. The motherland provided the model for administrative structures. The provincial bureaucracies were overseen by *audiencias*, superior authorities with wide-ranging powers that also acted as appellate courts for the administrative districts subordinate to them. At the local level, a small voice was given to horizontal power. Leadership of town councils, of which only full citizens could be members, was in the hands of royal functionaries.

Spanish colonial identities gradually took shape. So did a class of "mestizos," the children of native women and European men or, much rarer, of native men and European women. These individuals felt accepted by the culture of neither parent. African men and women also produced children with the indigenous population, so-called "zambos," and with Europeans, referred to as "mulattos."[16] A minimum of autonomy was available in "Indian republics" and "pueblos," in which Spaniards and mestizos usually also lived, although the *indios* were required to perform labor for their *encomenderos* on such reservations as well. In general, the indigenous population was exploited both by the Spanish and by their own aristocracy. The least intolerable living conditions were probably found in the thirty "Jesuit reductions" in the territory of what is now Argentina, Brazil, and Paraguay. In these regularly laid-out towns, native people—several thousand in each—lived and worked under the pious and strict, albeit not cruel, regime of the Jesuit fathers. They provided relative safety from slave hunters. Within their boundaries, people who had lived by hunting, fishing, and agriculture, or who had roamed as nomads, were supposed to become Europeans. The heyday of the *reducciones* was the seventeenth century. By the next century, however, the experiment had already failed.

Religious affairs were regulated by Madrid. Spain's king acted like a kind of "vice-pope" for America.[17] He made decisions about the appointment of bishops and had to personally approve the decrees of provincial synods. The Inquisition was headquartered in Lima, in Mexico City—built atop the ruins of Tenochtitlán—and ultimately in Cartagena as well. The victims of its stalking tended to be alleged "Judaizers," Protestants, and native "pagans." Mendicants and later Jesuits wandered about missionizing, and secular clergy streamed into the land. By 1520, it had been divided into thirty-five dioceses. Blessed Mother Mary helped in conversion efforts. She appeared in visions—first in Guadalupe—and, like in Europe, provided a role model and identification figure, particularly for women.

It took a long time to stamp out the old cults. "They believed in God and also followed their old heathen rites and customs," the Dominican friar Diego Durán (ca. 1537–ca. 1588) stated.[18] His book provides information on a literary tradition going back to "Chronicle X," a long-lost work of Aztec history. The historians and painters, he wrote, had inscribed the feats of great men "with fine brushes and vivid colors in their books" so that "their fame would grow and spread like the brightness of the sun throughout all the nations."[19] In Yucatan, however, it seems that human sacrifice was still being practiced in 1560, even in churches.[20] The Franciscan provincial Diego de Landa (1524–1579) claimed to have stopped the killing of a young boy at the last minute. Contrary to all law, he had 4,500 natives tortured in order to uncover circles of secret "idolaters." Of those, 158 did not survive the ordeal; some were so scared they committed suicide before it began. In 1562, Landa staged an auto-da-fé in which thousands of "idols" were thrown into the flames. Yucatan's bishop, Francisco de Toral, had an investigation conducted and concluded that the victims of the spectacle were "very simple, even more obedient, charitable, free of vices." Landa had to answer for his actions in Spain, but he was rehabilitated and became Toral's successor after the latter's death in 1571. In 1585, a Mexican council forbade the *indios* once again from singing "the songs of their ancient histories and false religion."[21]

If the Spanish viewed the catastrophe they brought upon the *indígenas* as divine punishment for "evil and depraved" pagans, it was the product of a European idée fixe. "Who can deny," Gonzalo Fernández de Oviedo (1478–1557) wrote, "that the use of gunpowder against pagans is the burning of incense to Our Lord?"[22] People even wondered if converted *indios* were worthy of receiving the Eucharist. What is certain is that the weight of the Spanish world empire was now pressing down on them, whether they toiled on plantations or at an elevation of four thousand meters on the "Rich Mountain" of Potosí. Silver finally gave the Spanish a commodity that the Asian market craved, especially after China's paper money system went up in the flames of inflation. Silver became the fuel of a nascent worldwide super-economy, powering the imperialism of the Catholic kings.[23]

The Holy Roman Emperor, traveling among his European holdings, and the paper king in the Escorial could hardly keep tabs on what their conquistadors were conquering or whom they were defeating. Religious commandments meant little when the game was exploitation and enslavement, raping and pillaging. Even more dangerous than the Europeans' swords were the viruses and bacteria they brought with them. The indigenous peoples, whose immune systems had no defenses against them, died en masse on both the mainland and the islands. "The wild people," one English captain observed in Florida in 1585, "died verie fast and said amongst themselves, it was the Inglisshe God that made them die so faste."[24] Holes in the labor force were filled with imported Africans. Each year, up to ten thousand slaves were shipped to the New World from São Tomé alone. By the end of the sixteenth century, they may have numbered a quarter million. In the following century, there were nearly five times as many.[25]

A triangle trade was established across the Atlantic. Europe shipped textiles, weapons, tools, and bric-a-brac to Africa. There, they picked up slaves and brought them to the Caribbean and the Latin American mainland.[26] Markets in Europe and later in North America then received the produce of the plantations, including cacao, tobacco (looked down on as "low-class" and diabolical), and, above all, sugar. The latter was soon being consumed by all social classes. One German traveler to England noted that Queen Elizabeth had very black teeth. He dryly remarked that the English ate too much sugar.[27]

Exchange changed both worlds, the Old and the New. The *condition nègre* ("Black condition"), in the words of Achille Mbembe, became transnational.[28] Epidemics spread around the globe. In the early sixteenth century, syphilis was already being transmitted by lovers in libidinous Guangzhou.[29] A century later, the silent murderer named tobacco traveled across the sea on European ships, reaching Japan, Korea, and (by way of Siberia) northern China. Green beans and tomatoes were shipped to Europe from the Andes. A phenomenal plant, the potato, arrived in Japan in 1600; in Europe, it would feed the Industrial Revolution. In return, the old continent supplied wheat and wine, merino sheep, pigs, horses, and cattle.[30] The Mexicans were already praised for their prowess as riders by Don Quixote's Sancha Panza.

Latin American Renaissance, *Tristes Tropiques*

Some Renaissance Europeans, readers of Herodotus and other ancient geographers, observed the New World with an anthropologist's eye.[31] Nevertheless, they were often at a veritable loss for words when it came to describing the new things they experienced. Therefore, they appropriated the unknown with the known—thus llamas became large sheep and Aztec pyramids became mosques—and with familiar stories. Indigenous peoples did the same thing, like when a horse became a "tapir of Castile." Diego Durán traced the native peoples back to a lost tribe of Israel, and he transformed Peru into the golden land of Ophir. The Americas could also become Atlantis, the large island in the ocean mentioned by Plato that was supposedly swallowed by an earthquake.[32] Pliny was helpful for describing nature. The planning of colonial cities followed a checkerboard scheme, as Vitruvius recommended.[33] The layout of the old town of Santo Domingo provides an example. The façade of the cathedral, built between 1521 and 1540, resembles a Roman triumphal arch with Charles V's coat of arms in the middle. The presence of Habsburg rulers was suggested everywhere in Spanish America by portraits, statues, tapestries, and public rituals.[34]

Models for describing the Inca Empire, its cities, its majestic roads, and its history were provided by the Roman Empire. Strange parallels were drawn. The vestibule of a house in Cusco is decorated by a mural, painted in 1600, showing Caesar and Pompey fighting each other on horseback. It is probably an allusion to the Peruvian "civil war" between Pizarro and Almagro (Fig. 56, above).[35] Even the mighty Amazon owes its name to humanist education. A travelogue written in 1542 identifies women who fought the Spanish on the banks of the river as "Amazons." The battle-ready women excited the male imagination time and again: in central Asia, in Africa, and on islands in the Indian Ocean.[36]

Latin America's idiosyncratic Renaissance evinces hybrids of cultures from the pre-Spanish past and the Christian present.[37] Pictures by European painters, such as works by Simon Pereyns (ca. 1530-ca. 1600), a Flemish immigrant to Mexico, visualized Christianity for the native inhabitants. For a memorial service to honor the recently deceased Charles V, a cenotaph was set up in the monastery of San Francisco in Mexico City, decorated with a strange gathering of gods, heroes, and rulers: Jupiter, Apollo, and Huitzilopochtli (who would later morph into the devil "Vitzliputzli"), Caesar and Cortés, Alexander VI, Ferdinand the Catholic, Moctezuma and Atahualpa.[38] An image of Hercules fighting the Hydra symbolized Charles's battle against Lutheran heresy.

An impressive example of a "hybrid Renaissance" is provided by murals painted during the last quarter of the sixteenth century in the Augustinian monastery of Ixmiquilpan on the Silver Road.[39] They were the work of indigenous painters called *tlacuilos*. The term originally referred to pictographs. Their style reveals the influence of the European Renaissance, but without the artists giving up their traditional forms of expression. The subjects were chosen by monks with a classical education. In one, an exotic centaur crops up in a battle scene (Plate 27). The presence of Perseus likely betrays knowledge of Ovid's *Metamorphoses*.

The success story of the great ancient poet's masterpiece now started a new chapter beyond the Atlantic. The first American edition was printed in Mexico City in 1577. The Colegio de Santa Cruz in Tlatelolco, founded by Franciscans in 1536, declined after a short period of flourishing. But it possessed a library stocked with many Latin classics.[40] The University of Mexico City, founded at mid-century, also became a training center for the sons of indigenous aristocrats. Their hunger for learning soon made the Spaniards uneasy. "Reading and writing are as dangerous as the Devil," one of them warned. Day by day, he continued, there were more *indios* who could write Latin as elegantly as Cicero. Aesop's fables were translated into native Nahuatl; the fox became a coyote and the jackdaw a parrot. Virgil made it all the way to the South American end of the world, as the *Aeneid* provided the model for Ercilla y Zúñiga's *Araucana*. The epic stood as a monument to the courage of the Mapuche. It portrays their chief Caupolicán as a mixture of noble savage and saint who, brave to the last, endures martyrdom by impaling. In contrast, Alonso depicts his Spanish compatriots as cruel and brutal.

The Europeans found justification for their crimes in caricatures whose tired ideas were provided by travelogues. For example, Hans Staden (ca. 1525–1576), a German mercenary in the service of Portuguese settlers in Brazil, wrote a "true history" of the "wild, naked, fierce man-eating people."[41] It tells of flying fish and Saint Elmo's fire at sea, of the native inhabitants' headdresses and hammocks, their rituals, food, and dwellings. The climax is a description of the author's imprisonment by the Tupinambá people. It provided readers with a chilling scene of ritual cannibalism (Fig. 55, p. 713).

The most influential constructor of the cliché of uncivilized pagans was the Walloon Theodor de Bry (1528–1598).[42] The title page of a volume of his collection of travelogues—it contains Staden's account—shows a pair of naked natives before an *all'antica* architectural backdrop feasting on a human arm and leg. Above them are men praying to an idol. Was it not a Christian duty to subjugate such savages, who supposedly committed incest with their daughters and even with their mothers,[43] and convert them to the true faith? One of the many people who followed that logic was the Spanish theologian Juan Ginés de Sepúlveda (1490–1573).[44] Relying on the authority of Augustine, Aristotle, and St. Thomas, he gave the "Indians" a place in the "natural order" under the Spanish conquerors, thus legitimizing the invaders' inhuman behavior.

This treatment also came in for no small amount of criticism, however. In 1511, the Dominican friar Antonio de Montesinos dressed down his fellow Spaniards in an Advent sermon. "You have all committed a mortal sin with the cruelty and tyranny you practice against these innocent people," he cried to them. He opposed the forced labor imposed upon the natives without their being given adequate nourishment or medical care when they were sick. "You kill in order to pile up gold each day!"[45] A legal argument was put forth by Francisco de Vitoria. He emphasized the status of "Indians" as subjects of international law. The pope was in no way the sovereign lord of Christians or pagans outside the borders of the Papal States, he reasoned. Therefore, there was no legal justification for waging war on "barbarians" and stealing their property.

Best known are the writings of Vitoria's fellow Dominican Bartolomé de Las Casas (1485–1566). His *Short Account of the Destruction of the Indies* vividly describes the atrocities of the conquerors.[46] The Spanish appear as the true barbarians, foils for the charitable and prudent indigenous rulers whom they murdered and whose societies they destroyed. Las Casas had a large share in getting laws passed in 1542 to protect the *indios*. These *leyes nuevas* prohibited the establishment of new *encomiendas*. Those already in existence were to revert to the state upon the death of their owners. The laws also forbade the conversion of tribute payments to labor requirements, as a means of halting the enslavement of the native population. When plantation owners resisted and even rebelled, however, these provisions were immediately relaxed. Nevertheless, to the end of his life, Las Casas never tired of fighting for human rights. His view of the *indios* as innocent, childish beings was its own form of discrimination, of course. It was also false. The Aztecs had treated the peoples they subjugated hardly better than the Spanish now treated them.

A more nuanced approach to the world of the *indios* can be found in the work of the Franciscan friar Bernardino de Sahagún (1499/1500–1590), who spent a good 60 years in Mexico. He regarded the Aztecs as an ethnologist, without idealizing them.[47] His *General History of the Things of New Spain* paints a picture, in both Nahuatl and Spanish, of a grand culture facing collapse. He took the view that Christianization had done more harm than good to the Aztecs. Once their gods and customs were taken from them, their society's entire ethical framework was uprooted. Sahagún did not share Sepúlveda's opinion that the *indios* were inferior to the Europeans. "It is most certain all these people are our brothers, stemming from the stock of Adam, as do we. They are our neighbors whom we are obliged to love, even as we love ourselves."[48]

Sahagún could not escape his own cultural context. Thus, he compared the Aztec deities to the gods of classical mythology, equating Chicomecoatl with Ceres and Tlazolteotl with Venus. A related approach—similar to how the Muslims bestowed the status of prophet on Jesus—was taken by Toribio de Benavente Motolinía (1482–1568), one of the "Twelve Apostles of Mexico." He turned the serpent god and mythical ruler Quetzalcoatl into a noble ascetic and preacher of natural law—just as others inserted the old deceiver Satan into the pantheon of the indigenous gods.[49] Sahagún even worked out his own justification for human sacrifice: he argued it was a way for the *indios* to give to their deity, whom they thought was real, what it considered most valuable. Stories from the Bible, which were new and incomprehensible to the natives, were appropriated by them in their own way. For example, the lamb of the Last Supper was transformed in eighteenth-century paintings—such as in the Cathedral of Cusco—into a familiar animal: a guinea pig.

The critical self-reflection of Las Casas, Sahagún, and others like them provided welcome ammunition to Spain's enemies. Europe now produced its first interstate anti-imperial ideology: the "Black Legend," the story of a dark Catholic power that burned heretics and exterminated *indios*.[50] At the same time, we can see the roots of a seminal cliché: the "noble savage." What had seemed shameless nudity became innocence, wilderness transformed into paradise, and "barbaric" existence metamorphosed into life in harmony with nature and the universe. The "second discovery of mankind" made by the Europeans—on the Canary Islands, where they encountered the Stone Age in the fourteenth century—was now followed by a third. David Abulafia has equated its significance with the discovery of the individual traced by Burckhardt.[51] Unusual inversions resulted. Besides classical texts, it was the conditions of the aboriginal inhabitants of the Canary Islands that influenced perceptions of the indigenous peoples of the New World. Conversely, their peaceful conversion, seemingly ordained by God and favored by a miracle, provided the foil for the violent Christianization of the Americas.

The *leyenda negra*, the "Black Legend," was anything but an evil fairy tale. The Spanish really did enslave and murder the indigenous peoples, and they obliterated their memory by destroying their places of worship and burning their revered ancient writings.[52] The Book of Chilam Balam, a collection of

Mayan texts written between the sixteenth and the nineteenth century in Yucatan, recalls the break signaled by the arrival of the foreigners. "With the true God, the true Dios, came the beginning of our misery. It was the beginning of tribute, the beginning of church dues, the beginning of strife," it reads. Beforehand, there had been no sickness, no "aching bones" and no high fever, no smallpox, no "burning chest" or headache. It was the "mighty men from the East" who "first brought disease here to our land, the land of us who are Maya."[53] Their own gods, thus the authors of these texts believed, had fallen silent and no longer safeguarded the future. The beautiful "land of the turkey and the deer," as the Maya called Yucatan before the arrival of the Spanish, was gone. The history of the *Tristes Tropiques*, literally "sad tropics," described by Claude Lévi-Strauss had begun the moment Columbus set foot on San Salvador.

Spending one's everyday life in a foreign culture, perhaps for decades, inevitably means being influenced by it. At some point, one begins to *understand* it. Even the iron-hearted Cortés beheld Tenochtitlán with awe, albeit more with the pride of a conqueror than with the melancholy that overwhelmed Petrarca when he viewed Rome's ruins. His companion Bernal Díaz del Castillo thought he had been transported to Hell while viewing the sacred images of the Aztecs. Yet the beauty of some of their painting also reminded him of the art of Berruguete and Michelangelo.[54] Even Durán, who wanted to eradicate all things pagan, was deeply moved by Aztec hymns. "I have wished this my history to preserve the fame and memory of those heroes," he wrote. "Let their memory be a blessing, since such men are the loved ones of humankind and of God, similar to the saints in Paradise. This is the only type of fame that is worth perpetuating."[55] Tenochtitlán's beauty even fascinated Dürer. When designing an ideal city, he was inspired by a woodcut of the Aztec city found in the printed edition of Hernán Cortés's letter to Charles V.

A few indigenous Americans won voices that can still be heard today. Guaman Poma de Ayala, who wrote a chronicle illustrated with nearly four hundred drawings, denounced Spanish brutality. Yet he also attempted to reconcile the Incas' fate with a Christian view of history.[56] He traced the Andean peoples back to Noah. In his scheme, Jesus Christ heralded the dawning of a fifth age of world history—when *Julio Zezar monarca* ruled, *Aristotiles* and *Tulis* (Cicero) philosophized, and the Inca Sinchi Roca reigned in the Andes. In his account, Christ's message reached the Andes by way of the Apostle Bartholomew (others ascribed this deed to the well-traveled Apostle Thomas). The arrival of the Spanish marked the last age for Ayala. One of his drawings

shows the Pillars of Hercules, the same image found on Charles V's blazon, above the mountains of Potosí. They are born aloft by the Inca ruler and the four kings of the *suyu*, the districts of the Inca Empire (Fig. 57, above). Charles appears as their lord whom they support, not as their conqueror.

Similar lines of thought can be found elsewhere, such as in the mestizo Fernando de Alva Ixtlilxóchitl's *History of the Chichimeca Nation*. Garcilaso de la Vega (1539–1616), author of a history of the Incas and the Spanish conquest of Peru, is a representative of an "indigenous Renaissance." In his work, the Inca realm becomes a South American *imperium* with Cusco as its Rome, an *otra Roma*. The ancient parallels suggest that the Inca Empire shares in the function ascribed to Augustus's *Pax Romana*: to have prepared the way for Christ's reign, now in the New World as well. It was a tragedy, in the author's view, that the logic of the history of salvation necessitated the destruction of his culture.[57]

"Inca," as Garcilaso called himself after many name changes, was a man with an iridescent identity.[58] His father was a conquistador and his mother a niece of an Inca ruler in Cusco. When his father died, he used his inheritance to set himself up in Andalusia. His first literary endeavor was a translation of Leone Ebreo's (1460/65–before 1535) *Dialogues of Love*. To put this in perspective: an Ibero-American mestizo Christian translated into Castilian the work of a Platonist Sephardic Jew who had long lived in Naples and Venice. Garcilaso de la Vega was the first true son of nascent globalization.

Spain Grasps for East Asia

Spain's attempt to hold the world in its hands was not limited to Central and South America. Isolated forays northward had already gone to Florida and beyond. One expedition reached the area around El Paso, where a mission would be founded only much later. Hernando de Soto marched with initially well-equipped troops to the area of what is now Memphis, reaching the Mississippi. He went to his grave there in 1542. At the same time, another expedition from the Gulf of California reached Llano Estacado. When neither the Seven Golden Cities of Cibola, rumored to exist by the natives, nor any precious metal was found, exploration lost momentum. Only at the turn of the century were the next campaigns sent into what is now Texas. In 1598, Juan de Oñate, a late and especially execrable exemplar of the conquistador genre, claimed the territory around the Rio Grande for his king. Thanks to the brutal style of warfare favored by Oñate, the name of Spain was anathema among the Pueblo Indians for many years to come. Santa Fe was founded a decade later. Yet "New Mexico" would long remain a contested peripheral province; for a while, it was even given up.

After the disappointment of these initial expeditions, Madrid was not very interested in the Pacific coast of North America. In 1542 and 1543, one detachment pushed all the way north of what is now San Francisco, again in search of Cibola's Cities of Gold as well as a northern passage from the Pacific to the Atlantic, the legendary Strait of Anián. This journey was without consequence for the moment. The chain of bases and missions that would grow into the major cities on California's coast—from San Diego and Los Angeles to San Francisco—only came into being much later. At the same time, Spain was looking not only north but west: out over the Pacific Ocean, which the crown had considered its own ever since it was claimed by Balboa. Cortés had already asked Charles V for permission to organize a voyage from Mexico to the Spice Islands in order to break the Portuguese trade monopoly there. Attempts to turn this idea into a reality failed, entailing high losses. And once the islands were reached, conflict with their Portuguese masters ensued. Charles V ultimately decided to let his competitor have his Moluccas. The 1529 Treaty of Saragossa augmented the Treaty of Tordesillas. The initial boundary line, now shifted a bit westward, was joined by an Asian demarcation. Spain preserved its American claims, with the exception of Brazil. In exchange, Africa and the majority of Asia were recognized as a Portuguese sphere of influence. To seal the deal, John III (r. 1521–1557) gave Charles

350,000 ducats. That was not even half of what the latter had paid for his election as Holy Roman Emperor, and anyway, it only sufficed for a couple of months of war. On the *Kaiser*'s mental map of the world, one Italian fortress probably loomed larger than half of Asia. At any rate, he did not have the men. According to the estimate of one royal official, there were no more than 25,000 Spanish households in the New World.[59]

Nevertheless, more and more expeditions put out to sea.[60] In 1565, a fleet from Mexico made it to the Philippines; the archipelago had already been named for Charles's son, the future king, on an earlier voyage. The Spaniards hopped from island to island, fending off natives and Chinese pirates and establishing bridgeheads. In 1571, they conquered a rich settlement under the control of a sultan, whose aboriginal name they corrupted to "Manila." The city, a transshipment point for goods from China, Siam, states in Malaysia, and Japan, became the center of the new colony. Missionaries managed to convert many native Filipinos to the cross, in large part because the baptized hoped their new brothers in faith would become brothers in arms against local rivals. Still, the process of state formation proceeded much more peacefully than in the Americas.

The Europeans owed their victories not only to their weapons and the disunity of their opponents but also to the fact that there were no solid states arrayed against them. *Barangays*, alliances of up to several hundred families, banded together under the supremacy of a sultan into loose confederations. The sultanates of Mindanao, the Sulu Islands, and Palawan resisted attempts at conquest. Unlike the Portuguese, who simply built fortified bases on the sea, the Spanish constructed a territorial state whose framework grew over time to consist of more than one thousand missionary settlements. Manila became the residence of a governor subordinate to the Viceroyalty of Mexico. In 1579, it became the seat of a bishop. When the Iberian crowns were joined, the city was integrated into the Portuguese trade network, which now extended all the way to Japan.

Nagasaki became the focal point of the so-called *Nanban*, or "southern barbarian," trade. The gate to China was the port of Macao, located on the Pearl River Delta. It was given to the Portuguese in 1557. In this way, the Iberians profited from Beijing's gradual opening after the period of self-sufficient isolation that had followed the Yongle Emperor's display of maritime power. Of course, the interior remained closed to them, and the idea of conquering China was nothing but an absurd fantasy.[61] The Europeans sensed they were dealing with a gigantic empire. "Distant things often sound greater than they really are," wrote the Dominican friar Gaspar da Cruz (ca. 1520–1570), but in this case it was different: "China is much more than it sounds."[62] The report published by the Augustinian Juan González de Mendoza in 1587, soon translated into many languages, depicts a rich, tidy country with bejeweled palaces and massive armies. Mendoza's description of Chinese courtesy and table manners is the epitome of civility. He writes of people eating from painted porcelain with silver and golden chopsticks, music playing in the background.

Missionaries sought to bring the Good News of the Christian Gospel to East Asia. The Jesuit father Francis Xavier (1506–1552), a companion of Ignatius who was later declared a saint, preached in India and Malacca, on the Spice Islands, and in Japan. Yet the efforts of the Portuguese and their wars tended to have the effect of rallying the threatened natives to the banner of the Prophet.[63] The Christian God may have conquered the deities of America, and he also found adherents in Japan, but Allah was a more stalwart opponent.

Since Beijing had prohibited trade with Japan—one reason was the danger presented by Japanese pirates—the Europeans found a lucrative opening. They transported Chinese luxury goods, gold, and other raw materials to Nagasaki, returning with their hulls full of the Japanese silver popular in China and India. Before moving on to Goa, they loaded more Chinese gold on board in Macao. Conversely, Chinese traders and Japanese Christians turned up in Manila. The Philippine metropolis was the first truly global city.

Right after landing in the Philippines in 1565, the commander of the Spanish fleet dispatched his navigator, the Augustinian monk Andrés de Urdaneta, to find a favorable route for the return journey. Urdaneta, a first-rate astronomer and mathematician, used monsoon winds and the Japan Current. After three months, he reached the California coast around where Los Angeles would later be founded, and then sailed on to Acapulco. He had discovered a passage that is still one of the most important sea lanes on the globe today. Regular ship traffic developed between Manila and Mexico. Each year, a galleon—a ship with a cargo capacity of up to one thousand metric tons—made the trip between Spain's new and even newer world. American silver streamed via Manila and Macao into Asia. The Europeans used it to buy silk, porcelain, and tea.[64] By way of Mexico, even European architectural forms made their way to the Philippines.

Initially, the Iberians were left almost entirely unmolested by the other European powers in their Latin American and Pacific holdings. The Dutch were the first to then take the African route to East Asia. The English followed. Up to that point, they had tried to find gold, establish trade relations, and found colonies far afield of the Spanish giant's sphere of influence. They navigated the North American coast, searching for good harbors and alternatives to the Strait of Magellan. England's crown had been less directly invested in such undertakings than Spain's. The share of private capital in their financing was high. The same consortium of London merchants behind the search for a northeast passage contemporaneously underwrote a trading voyage to Guinea.[65] In addition, the Russian Empire was now becoming integrated into global trade relations.

The Magic of the Capes

In the winter of 1553/54, unexpected guests turned up at the court of the Russian tsar: the English captain Richard Chancellor and a few companions.[66] They were received with honor and lavishly entertained. Their ship was the only one of a small fleet to survive the voyage that took them up the Norwegian coast, around North Cape, and down to the White Sea. Without further ado, Chancellor then traveled the one thousand kilometers from there to Moscow. As a direct result of the expedition, the English established a trading company—the Muscovy Company—which would cut right through the Hanseatic and Scandinavian cogs on the Baltic Sea to do business with Russia. Tsar Ivan furnished the merchants from London with privileges, allowing them to displace the Hanseatic traders.

The original purpose of Chancellor's voyage into the cold was to search for the northeast passage, a sea route along the continent's northern coast to the Pacific. Despite considerable efforts, it came to nothing. The city of Archangel at the mouth of the Dwina River, which began crystallizing around a monastery and a fortress in 1584, owed its growth to trade with the English and soon the Dutch too. Furs upon furs, honey, bric-a-brac, potash, and similar wares were shipped to the west. In return, the Russians received weapons, cloth, sugar, and spices.

Despite the slim profits from the Russian venture, England pursued its oceanic passion. The dynamic forces behind its initial forays were the same economic boom that powered Holland's trade and the same spirit of anxious competition and unbridled appetite that drove the Europeans to America. It found expression, for one, in a dramatic increase in cloth production in the countryside, as well as in the expansion of coal mining in Newcastle. Low wages favored the amassing of capital, which in turn sought investment opportunities and found them in overseas projects. However, persistent inflation unsettled the national finances, gnawed away at savings, and led to higher prices for food and rent and, thus, to social imbalances. All these problems were exacerbated by the global climate crisis. They affected more than just England.

Queen Elizabeth no longer paid attention to complaints from Portugal about violating its sphere of influence. The Peace of Cateau-Cambrésis expressly did not extend to territories west of the Canary Islands and south of the Tropic of Cancer. Conflicts there need not have consequences in Europe. It was a license to wage war in the Caribbean and the Pacific. Francis Drake put it in a potent nutshell: "No peace beyond the line."[67] The search for sea passages in the north was motivated not only by the wish to find a shorter route to the Pacific but also by the desire to bypass the Spanish and Portuguese zones of influence. The northeast beckoned first, but now the northwest also lured those in search of a passage.[68] A third possibility was pursued in the deep south. Ptolemy had spun yarns about a "southern continent." On world maps by Ortelius and others, a landmass was placed south of what is now Chile, stretching all the way to beneath Indonesia.[69] Not until James Cook's (1728–1779) voyages of exploration was it shown that the area contained mostly water and a few islands. Australia was also there, of course; its name still recalls the spectral *terra australis*. The coasts of this fifth continent had probably already been sighted by European seafarers in the sixteenth century.

With these voyages to the north, the English continued the work begun by Caboto and the Breton Jacques Cartier (1491–1557), who had explored a good portion of the Saint Lawrence Seaway under the flag of Francis I. Chancellor's voyage to the Arctic Ocean had opened sea lanes to the northeast. From then on, ever-deeper forays were made into the labyrinth of frozen islands in the Polar region. This, if anywhere, is where "Renaissance men" were to be found: famous heroes and failures, soldiers of fortune and pirates, brilliant navigators and foolhardy risk-takers. One was the professional privateer Martin Frobisher. He dropped anchor several times in northeastern Canada between 1576 and 1578, found only fool's gold, took an Inuit family back to England, and later fought against the Spanish Armada. Other pioneers included John Davis, who explored northwestern Greenland, as well as William Barents and Henry Hudson, who sailed in Chancellor's wake and made it all the way to the island of Novaya Semlya. Barents went to his grave there in 1596 after starving through an Arctic winter. Hudson's last known whereabouts were somewhere in the ice of James Bay.

The saga of these searches illustrates the psychology of the restless Europeans, who risked life and limb and would not be stopped by anything or anyone: not by the frost of the endless Polar night, not by starvation, scurvy, polar bears, or seemingly invincible pack ice.[70] One could speak of the magic of the capes, of the excitement felt during the approach to a piece of land jutting out into the sea, where it was still unclear whether the land ended and the longed-for passage to the ocean actually opened up behind it—or if high hopes would be disappointed and nothing more had been reached than a large bay or the mouth of a broad river. Jacques Cartier gave the name "Cap de l'Espérance" to a piece of the northern coast of Miscou Island. The brave Barents dubbed the northern tip of Novaya Semlya "Hoek van Begeerde," "Cape Desire," not knowing that beyond it lay yet another small sea and not the passage to the Far East he had hoped to find.

Many of these seafarers are still memorialized in place names: Barents Sea, Frobisher Bay, Davis Strait, Hudson River, and Baffin Bay. Some wrote down what they had experienced or compiled works of geography that inspired further voyages. Humphrey Gilbert (ca. 1537–1583) published speculations about a "New Passage to Cataia," encouraging Frobisher to set off on his own voyages. Gilbert had been governor of Ireland and earned infamy as a butcher of rebels. In 1583, he reached Newfoundland and claimed it for England's crown. He met his fate on the return journey, off the ship-slaying coast of Sable Island.[71] Buoyed by his firm Calvinist belief in divine predestination, he is supposed to have weathered a violent storm on the quarterdeck of his frigate *Squirrel*, reading a book and repeating the phrase, "We are as near to heaven by sea as by land!" Around midnight, one eyewitness on a nearby galleon reported seeing the lights go out. The poor *Squirrel* was swallowed by the Atlantic, and its owner along with it.

Around 1600, it was not clear that English settlers would one day be masters of nearly all of North America. They encountered no well-organized states there, unlike in the south. A powerful tribal confederation like that of Powhatan, arrayed along the James and York rivers, was an exception. The biggest problems were the intractable land and the lack of settlers. An attempt in 1585 to establish a colony on Roanoke Island off the coast of North Carolina—it was to be called "Virginia" in honor of Queen Elizabeth—initially failed.[72] Four years later, no trace was left of the settlers, who had numbered about one hundred. Their fate was unclear. Jamestown, founded in 1607 and maintained with considerable effort, was the first English colony to survive.

The transoceanic adventure found more and more chroniclers. The most conspicuous French example is Samuel de Champlain (ca. 1570–1635), who took meticulous notes about modern Canada. On one end of the spectrum, there were accounts like Andrés de Urdaneta's description of his voyage through the Strait of Magellan to the Spice Islands. On the other were the long, sober letters in which Captain Arthur Barlow informed his employer, Sir Walter Raleigh (1552/54–1618), the intimate of Elizabeth I, about a first expedition to Roanoke. In 1550, the Venetian Giovanni Battista Ramusio (1485–1557) began publishing his collection of accounts of voyages to Africa and Asia. They inspired Richard Hakluyt (ca. 1552–1616), among others. His twelve-volume compilation of *The Principal Navigations, Voyages, and Discoveries of the English Nation* is an invaluable historical source.

History and Truth

It was not only exotic experiences in far-off lands that set pens moving but also developments at home. The fact that history writing reached remarkably high methodological heights in the late Renaissance was not simply due to the plethora of great events. Events are always happening. Rather, the increased number of texts by countless past authors made available by the printing press had the effect of increasing quality. This trend was also buttressed by competition among the nations and their growing cognizance of their own pasts. Hakluyt, for example, wrote not only for England but also against Spain.[73]

The Elizabethan Age found its Tacitus in the antiquarian William Camden (1551–1623). Lord Burghley commissioned him to write an account of the reigns of the "Virgin Queen" and King James of Scotland. His dry annalistic chronicle sought to defend the queen and king from Catholic attacks. This work was predated by Camden's *Britannia*, dedicated to the same Burghley, which provided England with what Biondo Flavio and others had given Italy: a description of the country that married geography and history.[74]

A historiography that no longer traced the course of divinely ordained events or adduced examples for imitation was still the exception rather than the rule. Catholics and Protestants had their own truths, just like the chroniclers of the Spanish conquests who sought to fit hitherto unknown peoples into the familiar history of Christian salvation. For example, the view was taken that the acquisition of the new continent was God-given compensation for the losses suffered due to Luther.[75] On the other side, the intention of the *Magdeburg Centuries*, initiated by the strident theologian Matthias Flacius Illyricus (1520–1575), was to tell the story of how the Church had fallen away from its pure apostolic beginnings. The *Centuries* only made it to 1298; if it had been completed, Luther was going to be the hero.[76]

Beneath the level of universal history, a pragmatic historiography developed on both the Protestant and the Catholic sides that tried to stick to the sources. Johannes Sleidan's (1506–1556) political history of the Reformation, commissioned by the Schmalkaldic League, would be widely influential.[77] Sleidan had the last of the four world empires culminate with Charles V, and with the perfection of religion brought about by Luther. The fact that the work pleased neither Protestants nor Catholics speaks for the author. Laborious consultation of sources was the basis for the history of the French Wars of Religion written by Jacques-Auguste de Thou (1533–1617), who was close to Henry III and Henry IV. It concluded with a plea for lawfulness, tolerance, and strength in foreign affairs—factors that de Thou saw as mutually dependent. Rome honored the work by adding it to the Index of Prohibited Books. On the Catholic side, Cardinal Cesare Baronio (1538–1607) responded to the *Centuries* with his *Ecclesiastical Annals* (1588), based on a critical survey of a wide variety of sources. Another historian of the first rank was Paolo Sarpi (1552–1623), an ascetic but sublimely educated Servite monk. His account of the Council of Trent turned an assembly of divinely inspired church fathers into a human, all too human diplomatic congress.[78] Only a Venetian like Sarpi, with a congenital distaste for everything Roman, could write a work of this kind.

Florence, the city of the great pioneers Salutati and Bruni, boasted outstanding representatives of secular historiography in Machiavelli and Francesco Guicciardini (1483–1540).[79] The works of both men reflect their experience of the *calamità d'Italia*, a development that seemed to turn the world upside down. For Guicciardini, a Lutheran at heart and a republican, the decline prophesied by Machiavelli was a fait accompli. In his view, a low point was reached with the Sack of Rome, which occurred while he was writing his twenty-volume *History of Italy*. The work focuses on the period from Charles VIII's invasion to 1534. The wrath of God, mentioned briefly on the first page, retained only marginal significance for explaining the woes of Italy. Portents and prodigies meant nothing to Guicciardini. Instead, he soberly described *what happened*. His work was balanced between obvious love for his homeland and acute source criticism, making his *History of Italy* and *History of Florence* milestones in historiography.

One trend toward secularization was the division of time into periods of one hundred years, as practiced in the *Magdeburg Centuries*. It caught on. In 1583, Joseph Justus Scaliger constructed a chronology that was based on a critical analysis of sources and not on a biblical framework.[80] The same Scaliger was one of the destroyers of the historical confabulations of the Dominican friar

Annius of Viterbo. In the late fifteenth century, Annius tried to prove that Italy's culture was the oldest in human history and thus nobler than that of Greece. His flawed evidence was founded on the misidentification of the mythical first king of Italy, Janus, with Noah, the progenitor of humankind.[81]

Putting one's own country or community in the right light was the intention of many authors. For example, Paolo Paruta (1540–1598), an official historian of Venice, portrayed the republic in his *Istoria veneziana* as the counterpart to imperial Rome: an aristocratic commonwealth, balanced at home and peaceful abroad.[82] Origin myths and foundation legends were often treated as the source of a mandate for greatness. The Batavi inspired the Dutch, the "Germani" inspired the Germans, the Sarmatians inspired the Poles, and the Romans inspired everyone.

The purpose of history writing was to provide examples of right behavior, bring the past experience of humankind to light, and herald glorious deeds. Its goal could be to justify actions or ascertain past laws.[83] No historian of the time would have admitted to being a mere entertainer. And yet, as Petrarca and Machiavelli claimed for their own work, history should help the reader forget the misery of the present during happy hours of leisure. One who achieved just that was Paolo Giovio (1483–1553) of Como, a leading Italian historian of his day.[84] His work hazards strong judgments, and it is colorful as can be. It makes brocade shimmer, describes a Venetian wedding, discusses fish sauce in ancient and contemporary Rome, and even devotes attention to Vittoria Colonna's breasts, "whiter than shining silver," "like little turtle-doves sleeping." This latter passage, incidentally, is not the product of its author's having seen, much less touched, his subject—a privilege Giovio concedes only to Colonna's husband. Rather, it belongs to a literary tradition going back to Boccaccio.

Alongside the ancient past, the Middle Ages also increasingly became a subject of historical writing. For example, the genre of universal history from Creation to the present day enjoyed a resurgence. A massive number of new sources, the raw material of all historiography, was made available. One trailblazing accomplishment was Étienne Pasquier's 1560 publication of sources related to French medieval history.[85] A remarkable feeling for medieval history was evident in the painter John White (ca. 1540–1593), one of the settlers at Sir Walter Raleigh's "lost colony." He used his own watercolors of "Indians" to reconstruct what the prehistoric Picts and Britons looked like.[86] His depiction of a member of the Secotan tribe is based on a highly modern Renaissance model, Giambologna's statue of Mercury, cast five years previous (Fig. 58 and 59, p. 735).

Like medicine and mathematics, history writing strove to be seen as scientific. Melanchthon wanted it to be integrated into the university curriculum. For he believed, echoing Cicero, that a man without history would always be a child.[87] Camden managed to have the first chair of history created at Oxford; it still exists. Methodological guidelines were provided by Cicero—history was the witness of the ages, a teacher of life, and the light of truth[88]—as well as by Tacitus and Livy, the latter of whom was especially revered in Catholic circles. The dictum that the historian must not only narrate facts but also that all historiography must evince rhetorical qualities is, more than anything, what distinguished Renaissance historiography from traditional chronicles. Yet it also provided grounds for uncertainty. For if it were true, then no matter how scientific history was, it would remain linked to poetry. It is no secret that this connection, so inspiring but so threatening to objectivity, has often been sought by historians. The humanist Maffeo Vegio, a student of Leonardo Bruni, put the difference in a nutshell. Whereas the poets were inspired by "divine frenzy," historians performed "menial slave labor."[89] Down to today, their job has been the one prescribed to them by the humanist Francesco Robortello in 1548: to tell what happened and how it happened.

The sixteenth century ultimately produced a rich literature on historiographical theory.[90] François Baudouin (1520–1573) recommended that historians employ the method of a jurist—weighing eyewitness testimony, discerning motivations, and investigating the causes and consequences of events. In his *Method for the Easy Comprehension of History* (1566), Jean Bodin distinguished between human history, sacred history, and natural history. In Bodin's view, the ultimate end of historical developments is the creation of political orders that enable a "good life." Their highest form was monarchy, a reflection of divine unity. Bodin also says that human history should be narrated and explained soberly, with distance from the subject and without any rhetorical ornamentation. Like Baudouin, he argues that the impact of geography and climate must be taken into consideration, and also that history should approximate jurisprudence. He knows that the best the historian can achieve is verisimilitude, not truth itself.

The nature of *veritas historica*, historical truth, was investigated by Francesco Patrizi (1529–1597), he, too, like Bodin, an admirer of Tacitus. In his *Ten Dialogues on History* (1560), he defined this truth as the correspondence between subjective understanding and actual events. The historian is an anatomist of what happened; he should not say any more or less than what the matter bears. Patrizi found certainty about what was true in history writing in the conviction that the "book of his soul"—again, that fruitful metaphor!—which could be compared with the external book of history, was written by God himself. What accorded with it was true; what did not was false.[91] Therefore, only the prudence and the conscience of the historian, through which God's voice spoke, could guarantee certainty. What happens in the world outside, however, is left to itself; truth is here itself historical. As such, it is different from the truth of the philosopher or the theologian. "Is history the work of God?" Patrizi asks. "No. Is it the work of nature? Again, no. Is it the work of human beings? Indeed it is."[92] In this sense, history is no longer a divine sign or a collection of *exempla* but rather the realm of human freedom. It is where people, to adapt a quote of Ficino, become creators of themselves, masters of their future—with all the possibilities and imponderables it entails.

38

Autumn of the Renaissance

Gardens of Melancholy

Bomarzo (near Viterbo), 1580. Vicino Orsini's *Sacro Bosco*, or "sacred grove," had just been finished.[1] In the wilderness at the foot of Mount Cimino north of Rome, the lord of Bomarzo had a park full of statues, benches, and buildings laid out. The work of three decades, it included a theater, a grotto of Isis, sphinxes, Psyche, sirens, a giant turtle and other monstrosities, a house that looks like it is about to fall over, and a fountain with a Pegasus taking flight. The gray peperino stone of the once brightly painted sculptures is weathered, overgrown with moss, almost reclaimed by the very nature it sought to reconcile with art. Of the allegory of glory, prancing on the turtle's back, only a torso remains, and Pegasus has lost its wings. Undamaged is a giant *Orlando Furioso* defeating an opponent. Time has erased words from the numerous inscriptions, making them seem like poems by Mallarmé. One seems to say, "And watch closely . . . Who well . . . eyes . . . tower . . . heaven . . . I am . . . order." And another: "The cave, the spring . . . From all dark thoughts." Above a man-sized mouth of hell that threatens to swallow anyone who enters it, sun and rain have nibbled so many letters away from a Dante-esque inscription that all that remains is *Ogni pensiero vola*, "All thoughts fly."[2] Inside there is a stone table that was once used for picnics.

Prince Vicino Orsini (1523–1585), the inventor of all these wonders, had had a less-than-spectacular military career before retiring to Bomarzo. He was among the papal troops that helped Charles V defeat the Schmalkaldic League; then he fought for the French against Charles's son Philip. Taken prisoner after the fall of the French city of Hesdin, he was freed after two years by the Peace of Cateau-Cambrésis. Vicino's decision to turn his back on military service may have been occasioned by a shocking experience. In 1557, while in the service of Paul IV, he witnessed a massacre perpetrated by papal mercenaries against inhabitants of the rebellious nest of Montefortino—an episode from the absurd war that the Carafa pope had provoked with Spain (p. 671). For two decades, Vicino now devoted himself to laying out the garden and building a palace in Bomarzo, an antidote to boredom and the diabolical dangers of melancholy.

Is there a key to interpreting this labyrinth of images and signs? No one knows. The puzzle itself was the point, the solving of learned mysteries a pleasure that the inventor and proud owner of the enchanting garden enjoyed with his friends and guests, so long as the weather of the Little Ice Age did not ruin their plans. On beautiful summer evenings, while the heat of the day slowly dissipated and the August moon of Latium rose, people may have gathered here for soirées: for conversation, delicacies, and erotic play accompanied by the gurgling of the fountains, the music of the cicadas, and the calls of exotic animals. Against the grain of his time, Vicino professed himself an Epicurean. As his letters reveal, sex was as much an obsession of the aging lord of Bomarzo as literature and flushing wine.[3] His installation can also be read as a résumé of the Renaissance. Even in its remote location, it disposed of a mass of ancient and more recent texts that provided the plot for cryptic narratives. And it reflected familiarity with ancient worlds and the inkling of new ones—knowledge that could now be engaged in playfully and without regard for convention. The sculptures of the grove elicited thoughts of Egypt and recalled the Etruscan past of the countryside surrounding Bomarzo. Some of them betray knowledge of the art of India and Latin America. They take their impetus from Virgil, Plutarch, and Apuleius, as well as Sannazaro's *Arcadia*, the *Hypnerotomachia Polifili*, and Ariosto's *Orlando Furioso*. The world of astrology is also present.

We can get an idea of Orsini's spirituality by mentioning his appreciation for Apollonius of Tyana, who was notorious in the Late Renaissance as a magician and charlatan who had made a pact with the devil; some thought he had discovered the Emerald Tablet.[4] The confessional controversies of the age likely left Vicino cold. His grove was a place of refuge from the world, one of many the Renaissance created for itself.[5] The dream park resembles Thélème somewhat, the utopian "anti-monastery" in Rabelais's *Gargantua and Pantagruel*. The abbey, lavishly supplied with everything, is the antithesis of a life of dreary, ascetic seclusion. The only maxim there is to "do what you will"—*Fay ce que vouldras*—to drink, read, play music, and go for a walk: no different from what people did in Orsini's sacred grove, far removed from the quarrels of the world.

While time stood still there for happy hours, out in the rest of Europe its pace quickened. At least, that is how it felt to those who experienced it. Joachim Du Bellay lamented the Eternal City in his sonnets:

Rome, living, was the world's sole ornament,
And dead, is now the world's sole monument.[6]

At the same time (the turn of the century), Calvin's friend Pierre Viret wrote that the world was at an end.

When I look at this world, I see an old, decrepit building whose sand, mortar, and stones, and every day pieces of brick, crumble bit by bit. What else could we expect from such a building than sudden collapse—and at just the moment we least expect it?[7]

Similar tones could be heard from Italy and England.

The pleasant years that seem, so swift that run
The merry days to end, so fast that fleet,
The joyful nights, of which day daweth so soon,
The happy hours, which more do miss than meet,
Do all consume, as snow against the sun,
And death makes end of all that life begun.

These lines are found in *Tottel's Miscellany*, a collection of English poetry published in 1557.[8] Under the gray clouds of the Little Ice Age, melancholy, that "fearefull disposition of the mind," found its analysts.[9] Timothy Bright, a scholar who barely escaped the Saint Bartholomew's Day massacre, investigated its various guises. In 1621, Robert Burton published his exceedingly popular *Anatomy of Melancholy*, a footnote-studded summa of the knowledge amassed about the saturnine sickness since Hippocrates.[10] And Shakespeare put the melancholiac par excellence on the stage in the form of Hamlet.

We have already had occasion to meet several famous melancholiacs, including Petrarca, Henry III of France, and Rudolph II. Another member of the club was Torquato Tasso (1544–1595).[11] Born in Sorrento and for a time a law student, he ultimately pursued the life of a poet, going from court to court and traversing Italy's entire patronage landscape. His epic poem *Rinaldo* gave him an entrée to the Este court in Ferrara. One July day in 1573, his *Aminta*, a pastoral play populated by nymphs and a satyr, premiered on an islet in the Po. It is a tribute to all-conquering love, to the liberties of the long-lost Golden Age when "what was pleasing was allowed."[12] As Sannazaro had once offered his Arcadian idyll as an antidote to overcrowded Naples and Charles VIII's war, Tasso's drama provided a foil for the steely world of states and decadent court life. *Aminta* gainsaid the high civilization of the Renaissance while at the same time being one of its most beautiful literary products. Tasso's masterpiece *Jerusalem Delivered* (1575) struck the nerve of the generation of Lepanto. Set in the time of the First Crusade, it is an epic of love and war, a work of the utmost ambition that stands shoulder to shoulder with the works of Virgil, Homer, and Ariosto.

The author may have been thrown off kilter by overwork and nitpicking at his magnum opus. Tormented by doubts about his own art, he forgot his role as a courtier, grew violent, and ultimately had to flee. His inner demons drove him across the land. He spent seven years locked away in a hospital in Ferrara. After his release, he again roamed around restlessly. In vain, he sought consolation in faith. He died on April 25, 1595 in Rome, the day before Pope Clement was set to honor him with the laurel crown. Near the monastery of Sant'Onofrio, his last refuge, the withered remains of an oak tree can still be seen; there in its shadow, Tasso supposedly meditated on the divine.

The Painting of the Self: Montaigne

Fifteen years earlier, in November 1580, the wretched Tasso met the philosopher Michel de Montaigne (1533–1592) in Ferrara. The Frenchman sought out Tasso in his room at the Hospital of Sant'Anna. The summit between the chief philosopher of the day and one of its greatest poets was a disappointment. Tasso, whom Montaigne valued as "one of the most judicious and ingenious of men, a man more closely molded by the pure poetry of antiquity than any other Italian poet has been for a long time," no longer knew who he was or what he had written.[13] The visitor felt more disgust than pity. His diary—it is the best travel account of the century, full of clever observations about mores and everyday life—does not mention his visit to the invalid. As a memento of Ferrara, he took a rose picked for him from a bush that miraculously bloomed all year long.[14]

Montaigne was the product of nouveau riche nobility. His father was Catholic, whereas his mother seems to have been born into a family of baptized Sephardic Jews. She is said to have been sympathetic to Calvin. The tone at home must not have been very strict, then, when it came to questions of religion. This was one of the factors that made the philosopher, a Catholic his entire life, one of the greatest teachers of tolerance. The tower of the family château in Périgord was for him what the "sacred grove" was for Vicino Orsini, Tusculum for Cicero, and the Vaucluse for Petrarca. Montaigne seldom left its walls. He sold his position in the Bordeaux Parlement in 1570—it was standard practice to treat offices like property—but later assumed the post of mayor of Bordeaux for a few years. He was friends with de Thou and went hunting with Henry IV, details that highlight how disposed he was to peace and tolerance. He was wont to wander around the bookcases in his library, lost in thought, aimlessly reading now in this book, now in that, and then putting his "fancies" down on paper.[15] From day to day, he worked on his *Essays*, a word literally meaning "exercises" or "attempts." Even after the final printed edition during his lifetime appeared in 1588, they remained a work in progress. Consisting of meandering, serenely skeptical reflections, the collection inaugurated a literary genre and won the author fame.[16] It is a kind of associative philosophizing, one that seems postmodern and that was certainly out of step with its own hard age: a not entirely consistent, often ironic conversation between the author and himself and us: "The world is but a perennial movement," Montaigne wrote. "All things in it are in constant motion—the earth, the rocks of the Caucasus, the pyramids of Egypt—both with the common motion and with their own." And like in the Caucasus Mountains—thus his philosophy has been described—the earth shakes a little everywhere.[17]

Of greatest concern to Montaigne, who coquettishly claimed not to be a philosopher,[18] is the investigation of his complex, fractured self. The goal of the undertaking was not religious. It was more than the distance of a thousand years that separated it from Augustine's *Confessions*. The command to "know

thyself," a leitmotif of the Renaissance since the twelfth century, is here taken
to extremes to include a confrontation with one's own psyche, one's body,
one's own sexuality. By dissecting himself to the bone with his words, the essayist studies "the entire form of man's estate," the *condition humaine.*[19] The
result is not a self-assured individualism. Rather, the *Essays* give voice to the
devastating experiences of the time. The texts reflect the insight that the marvel of "Renaissance man," despite all his divine qualities, has achieved little
more than war and religious strife. In Montaigne's eyes, this fictional creature
is merely a shadow whose iridescent self can change its behavior at any moment. "I do not portray being: I portray passing."[20] The only knowledge he
talks about is that of not knowing. Montaigne's motto, *que scay-ie?*, "What do
I know?" leaves the answer open.

In his view, universal history is an account of human mental states. It shows
on a grand scale the fleetingness, mutability, and unpredictability that characterizes even individual fates.[21] He points to the Roman Empire, whose imposing ruins he admired during his visit to the city on the Tiber. He noted the
heavy layers of dirt that had accumulated over the ancient city through the
centuries, even burying entire buildings.[22] The observation illustrates Lucretius's famous words, which Montaigne then also quotes:

> Nothing remains itself, but all things range;
> Nature modifies all and changes all.[23]

Montaigne exhibits only moderate need for the Bible and none for theologians. His philosophy is humanist in the truest sense of the word. Its most
important authorities are philosophers of antiquity, Stoics and Skeptics: Seneca, Plutarch, and the dangerous Lucretius, but above all the prince of the Skeptics, Pyrrho of Elis. In 1562 in Geneva, Henri Estienne had published Sextus
Empiricus's *Hypotyposes*, which transmits Pyrrho's philosophy.[24] Still, these
authorities were not of exaggerated importance for Montaigne. They provide
the mere impetus to seemingly playful flights of fancy. His view of things is clear
and sharp. Amidst the wars of religion, "this notable spectacle of our public
death," the author tries to strike a Stoic pose. The ideal is to "belong to oneself,"
to be steadfast and calm.[25] Since he cannot prevent the decline, he at least wants
to learn from it. To withstand the avalanche of knowledge that overwhelmed
his time and the antagonism between differing positions, he aims his discerning
lens at the limits of all understanding. "You are the investigator without knowledge," he has the god of Delphi address mankind, "the magistrate without jurisdiction, and all in all, the fool of the farce."[26] In this way, he emerges as the

pioneer of a line of thinking that rejected systematization and Scholasticism and that took the self as the yardstick of knowledge.

His "Apology for Raymond Sebond" deals with the Catalan theologian's opinion that God's two books—the Bible and nature—are in harmony with one another. At first glance, the text seems to be a defense of the Thomist doctrine of the unity of faith and knowledge. Subtly, however, it becomes an indictment of all claims to absolute truth. This essay, the longest in the collection, culminates in a plea for toleration. Religious war is portrayed as a scandal. "Nothing is more deceptive in appearance than a depraved religion, in which the will of the gods is offered as a pretext for crimes."[27]

The watchman Montaigne was the most ardent relativist of the dawning modern age. "Savages" are not savage for him, just different. "Barbarism" is merely a byword for what is unusual at home.[28] The "Apology" reviews all possible concepts of God, in which the author recognizes nothing but reflections of the people who devised them. He even attributes his own faith to the Catholic education he received, comparing its adherents to the goose mentioned by the irreverent Xenophanes: it believes it is the center of the universe and proudly thinks the people who feed it are its servants.[29] Montaigne, who was incidentally a Copernican, gave the faith of human "geese," with their equally limited understanding, freedom in its own realm outside that of reason. Echoing Athens in the time of Socrates, the latter's French admirer Montaigne praises open discussion as "the most fruitful and natural exercises of our mind."[30] And he knows that death, although the outer limit of life, is not its end. Rather, the meaning of life— and this was a very unusual view in that time—is found in itself.

Perhaps the best insight into Montaigne's unorthodox thinking can be gleaned by taking a look at the roofbeams of his tower library.[31] The master of the house had maxims and affirmations carved into them in Latin and Greek letters, including quotations from classical authors and the Bible. They make him look like one of us. One phrase—a quote from Terence—reads, "I am a human being and believe nothing human is foreign to me."[32] A walk around reveals the following sentiments: "I determine nothing. I understand nothing. I withhold judgment. I deliberate. I grasp nothing."

Mannerism: The Arts in the World

Montaigne's "painting of the self"[33] is the high point in the long history of subjectivity. It has a counterpart in the introspection of painters that culminated in self-portraits by Titian, Tintoretto, and even Tobias Stimmer (Plate 28).[34]

More and more biographies appeared, soon biographical lexicons and autobiographies too, including that of the Venetian Jew Leon Modena (1571–1648)—a
rare autobiography by a Jew before the eighteenth century. They document
how people, surrounded by a topsy-turvy world about which they knew more
than ever but thought they knew less than ever, took the path into the darkness
of their own psyche. Autobiographical accounts were now written not only by
intellectuals—Montaigne was joined by the polymath Gerolamo Cardano
(1501–1576) of Pavia—but also by craftsmen and artists, such as the Augsburg
painter Jörg Breu and, much more importantly, Benvenuto Cellini (1500–1571),
the greatest of all goldsmiths.[35] In his *Vita*, the hothead Cellini presents himself as a defender of the city during the Sack of Rome, as a thug and thrice a
murderer, but above all as a gifted craftsman and technician. Goethe's very free
translation of his autobiography portrays a self-assured swaggerer. Cellini tells
of imprisonments and escapes, of his work for popes, dukes, and Francis I,
who paid him the consummate compliment of visiting him in his workshop
near the Louvre. The sources tell us that he continued to father children in his
sixties and also had a predilection for his own sex. More than once, his art
alone saved him from the noose.

At times exuberant and at times sensitive, at times bizarre and quirky, often
brilliant and always interesting, the figure of the modern artist took shape—if
not in flesh and blood, then at least on paper and in print. The most important
fashioner of this creature was Giorgio Vasari. His artist biographies contain
countless anecdotes that, if not true, at least make for good stories. He tells of
a magical leather jacket made from the skin of a hanged man by the sculptor
Silvio Cosini—a man both clever and *capriccioso*, "bizarre"[36]—as well as the
painter Sodoma, who, always extravagantly dressed, lived in the company of
badgers, a dwarf donkey, a speaking raven, and other animals. *Mattaccio*, "the
madman," was the name given to him by the monks of San Oliveto. Thanks to
anecdotes of this kind, the figure of the painter or the sculptor, who wanted to
be an artist but was still just a craftsman, took on clearer outlines and sometimes the aura of genius. Eccentricity, the mark of artists down to our day,
came into fashion then.

The best way to escape the straitjacket of the guilds was to attain a position
at court. Another helpful strategy was to insinuate artistic work, which still
belonged to the lowly mechanical arts, into the vicinity of the liberal arts, as
Alberti and others had done. Painters, goldsmiths, and architects were depicted in portraits with a drawing compass as their attribute, thus claiming
expertise in geometry. Not a few distinguished themselves as authors of theo-

retical works. In 1563, Grand Duke Cosimo founded the *Accademia* of drawing at Vasari's urging. Two decades later, the Academy of San Luca was established in Rome. Thus began the age of art academies.[37] Artistic work won recognition as an intellectual activity. Effort was devoted to investigating its wellspring, the mystery of imagination. The new appreciation for imagination, which has parallels in contemporary poetics and the theory of history,[38] can be seen in the improving status of drawing. As the most direct manifestation of inspiration, it went from being a tool used in the workshop to an art form in its own right, hallowed as the relic of its creator. The first "prince" of the Roman Academy of San Luca, the painter Federico Zuccari, devoted a treatise to drawing.[39] He distinguishes external drawing, the material thing on paper, from internal drawing, the *disegno interno*. In line with Platonic thought, he ascribes a divine cause to this "sun of the soul." He places drawing at the beginning not only of all art but of all human activity.

As originality became the chief criterion for judging art, the artist and his work melded into the unity that is familiar from modern usage. Indeed, today it is standard to admire not just a picture but rather, for example, "a Picasso." The art collector Isabella d'Este asked Bellini to paint a "pagan fantasy" for her. All she got was a Birth of Christ—but it was still "a Bellini." Accordingly, the number of signed paintings increased during the sixteenth century, a further indication of the rise of the subjective. The same trend can be seen in the primacy given to the "judgment of the eye"—with its vagueness, its "feeling"—over objective geometry, no matter how much the art of the compass and the set square endowed the aura of learning on the artist-craftsman. Michelangelo, for one, did not appreciate the strict mathematical spirit behind Dürer's theory of proportion.

During Titian's lifetime, we can see the beginning of what could be called "the Renaissance shift" or, to use Hiram Haydn's term, the "counter-Renaissance."[40] Its protagonist was the humanist, cleric, and physician François Rabelais (1494?–1553). His novel *Gargantua and Pantagruel*, published between 1532 and 1552, tells the tall tale of the birth, education, and deeds of two massive giants, a father and his son.[41] The third volume deals extensively with the question of whether one of the novel's shady characters, Panurge, should get married or not. The fourth volume describes a sea voyage to the "Divine Bottle," the oracle that is to decide the matter. The fifth part, in which the *Dive Bouteille* is reached, appeared posthumously in 1564. Only its outline, at most, is based on Rabelais's ideas. At any rate, the plot of the book barely matters; it is merely a stage for lighting the fireworks of the imagination and unbounded creativity.

The wild work is satire, grotesque, utopia, and a parody of romance literature all in one. Incredibly humorous, it offers fun and seriousness, pornography, wisdom, and nonstop nonsense. Rabelais levels attacks against the learned stupidity of the University of Paris, against monks, the papacy, lawyers, and zealots. Nothing human and certainly nothing bodily is foreign to the author. With relish, he describes the voiding of seas of urine, overactive digestion, and defecation. One long chapter is devoted to the fine art of "ass-wiping." Rabelais's stories are an eloquent adieu to order, harmony, and purity—an orgiastic potpourri of the pleasures of the body and a celebration of anarchy. The doors are blown off moderation.[42] Pantagruel's tongue alone is miles long, and entire cities sit in his mouth. He wages war against an army of 42,000 sausages and keeps a black flee as a pet whose care costs over 600,000 guilders. Using deceit, Panurge induces 600,014 dogs in heat to follow a woman who has spurned his advances. At the same time, the novel is as stuffed with humanist learning as its insatiable heroes are with food and drink. The prologue begins with an ironic take on Socrates that is more irreverent than anything dared before. Countless classical quotations, some real and some invented, pervade the text. Antiquity is omnipresent but does not command respect. Alexander appears as a pants-patcher, Xerxes sells mustard, and Cleopatra trades in onions. Mention is once made of Florence, its cathedral, and its palaces. "These old statues are very well put together, I agree," one character says. "But by St. Ferreol of Abbeville . . . the pretty girls back home are a thousand times better-looking."

Emblematic of the shift from the boundless veneration of antiquity to a more distanced approach is a caricature of the Laocoon group, engraved in 1500 and perhaps based on a design by Titian (Fig. 61, p. 747). Instead of the priest and his sons, it shows an ape fighting with the serpent. In a similarly facetious vein, the poet Annibale Caro (1507–1566) caricatured the all too solemn adoration of "gigantic art" à la Michelangelo, celebrating the oversized nose of a friend in a kind of litany.

> It would not be strange . . . if some Apelles painted this nose, some Polycleitus chiseled it, or Michelangelo immortalized it in one way or another. . . . Perfect nose. Princely nose. Divine nose. Nose, be thou blessed among all noses, and blessed be thy mommy who made thee so long, and blessed be all that thou breathe in."[43]

The first to truly embody the new type of artist was indeed Michelangelo. In Vasari's eyes, the arts had reached their zenith in him alone.[44] The pomp with which "the Divine One" was laid to rest in the Florentine church of Santa

Croce in 1564 was beyond compare. When the coffin was opened again, it supposedly emitted a scent that was otherwise known only from saints.

Conditions in the overcrowded art market of the Little Ice Age reflected the competition among poets, scholars, scientists, and inventors. Tintoretto used sophisticated marketing strategies to get major commissions.[45] Specializations became even more specialized. There was no other way to distinguish oneself in a market that required virtuosity and intellect. Some painted only landscapes. Others focused on winter scenes, stormy seas with boats, picture puzzles, or still lifes. Others devoted themselves to scenes of hell after the manner of Hieronymus Bosch. The Milanese painter Giuseppe Arcimboldo (ca. 1526–1593) struck it big with a single, albeit highly original idea: he deftly combined vegetables and fruits, flowers, coral, shells, and other objects into compositions that at a distance coalesced as portraits.

Buyers wanted not only a work of art but also a piece of its creator. For a work to be a product of the master's own mind seemed just as important—indeed more so—than for it to come from his own hand. The parallels to Erasmus's insistence on the stylistic individuality of the poet are obvious. Of course, it was nearly impossible to guard against imitators. Copyright was only in its infancy. A dispute about it had flared up at the beginning of the century in Venice. Marcantonio Raimondi copied Dürer's engravings, even retaining the latter's signature "AD." Dürer complained to the Signoria.[46]

The "manner" of a master became his trademark. Some groomed teams of assistants who could perfectly imitate their style. The most famous example is the Antwerp workshop of Peter Paul Rubens (1577–1640), a painting factory of mass (but high-quality) production. Beyond supplying designs, the great Flemish artist's contribution may have been limited to a single brushstroke. It is usually impossible to distinguish his hand from those of the many assistants in his workshop. Yet it is still immediately clear that it is all "Rubens." Signatures were superfluous.

The sumptuous autumn of the Renaissance was centered in the palaces of Fontainebleau and Prague—where Arcimboldo found his patron—in Munich and Florence, in town halls and patrician *palazzi*, in parks from Bomarzo to Aranjuez. Nature was challenged and pressed into service by unbridled creative passion. Seashells and coral were cemented into Genoese grottos, nautilus shells were set into the masterpieces of goldsmiths, and water was forced to perform tricks at the Villa d'Este in Tivoli or in the garden at the Villa Lante in Bagnaia. In the competition with nature, art emerged the victor. Now it played with the vanquished, creating flaming figures coiled like snakes or looming giants—like the Apennine Colossus in the park of Pratolino—that stood shoulder to shoulder with Pantagruel. Gods hovered over glittering fountains while the scent of hyacinths and daffodils wafted up from the flowerbeds.

The painters answered with bold poses, overlapping figures, and complex foreshortening. They sought out difficulty to show that they were able to overcome it. No nudity—not even obscenity—was taboo. The masters pieced together monsters, played with mirror images, and whispered profound secrets. In Venice, Titian created his stunning late work. Paolo Veronese painted his banquets bursting with color, mythological scenes, and depictions of saints. El Greco (1541–1614), later so revered by the Expressionists, came from Crete. His amazing career spanned the Mediterranean. After apprenticing with Tintoretto in Venice, he moved on to Rome and then Spain.

Venice gradually deteriorated into a museum of itself. The city developed into Europe's pleasure dome. From the days of Claudio Monteverdi onward, it was a center of European opera. On the mainland, its aristocrats populated their estates with villas whose architecture was inspired by classical buildings. The idea was to endow their residents with an "ancient" *je ne sais quoi*. The chief among northern Italy's master architects was the Paduan Andrea Palladio (1508–1580).[47] Many of his buildings were commissioned by humanists, including Giangiorgio Trissino, the above-mentioned author of the *Sofonisba*, and Daniele Barbaro (1513–1570), patriarch of Aquileia. Collaborating with Palladio, who contributed illustrations, Barbaro issued an Italian edition of Vitruvius's architectural theory, which was now applied to actual structures. For him and his brother Marcantonio, Palladio constructed a villa in Maser (north of Venice) with two expansive wings—as usual, on a raised, majestic position that afforded a view of the land surrounding it. The interior was decorated with lavish frescoes painted by Veronese. The building thus united the painting and architecture of two of the greatest masters in art history.

Palladio's *Four Books of Architecture* (1570), a theoretical work supplemented with stupendous woodcuts, spread his art throughout the world. The Palladian style conquered Europe, especially England, and reached the United States and colonial Cuba. Some of what Palladio built was pure aesthetics; the proportions of his buildings were meant to correspond to musical harmonies.[48] His Villa Rotonda outside Vicenza subordinated all practical needs to symmetry and geometry. Il Redentore on Venice's Giudecca, an offering of thanks made to God after an epidemic, is a sophisticated innovation on ancient temple architecture. And the Teatro Olimpico, built between 1580 and 1585, brings to life what an ancient theater was thought to look like.[49] Along with Vincenzo Scamozzi's theater in Sabbioneta, it was one of the first permanent structures for drama in the Renaissance. Up till then, it was customary for provisional stages to be set up in churches, palaces, and town squares. Now, around 1600, architects were tasked with building theaters, abodes for a new public that had a major future ahead of it.

Rome also built villas, fountains, and palaces. The cupola was placed atop Saint Peter's in 1602, and ten years later Carlo Maderno's façade was finished. Caravaggio's (1571–1610) paintings entranced viewers with spectacular chiaroscuro and thinly veiled erotic titillation that exploded all Renaissance conventions. Meanwhile, the popes transformed the shape of the city. Pius IV and Sixtus V (1585–1590)—an energetic man who had risen from humble beginnings—had broad streets laid out that connected the city's main churches for the convenience of pilgrims. Sixtus's legacy still looms large today in the Egyptian obelisks he set up on important squares. They were crowned with crosses; statues of Peter and Paul were placed atop the columns of Trajan and Antoninus Pius. *Roma Christiana* presented itself as the victor over the pagan empire and, thus, in a certain sense, over the Renaissance.

Florence vied with its old rival. Cellini cast his *Perseus*, which was set up under the Loggia dei Lanzi. Vasari set to work building the Uffizi, and Bartolomeo Ammannati (1511–1592) erected the marble mass of his Fountain of

Neptune in sight of Michelangelo's *David*. It alluded to the expansion of Florentine sea power, with its base at Livorno. The water god resembles the Grand Duke. In the Pitti Palace, the first opera in music history whose score has been preserved was staged: Jacopo Peri's (1561–1633) *Daphne*. The genre, which united music, architecture, painting, and poetry, seemed to provide a solution to the problem of reigniting the high emotion that ancient sources enthusiastically ascribed to the theater. The opening scenes of Peri's *Euridice* momentarily spirited the audience away into a different, beautiful world:

Nymphs, whose beautiful golden hair
is loosened by the playful wind
And you, whose great treasure
Is hidden by beautiful burning rubies,
And you, who are more glorious than the dawn,
Come all of you, pastoral lovers;
In this dear countryside, covered with flowers
Happy voices and happy songs resound.
Today to consummate beauty
Blessed Hymenaeus joins consummate valor.
Adventurous Orpheus, Fortunate Euridice,
Heaven joins you together: o happy day!⁵⁰

Despite the country's political malaise, Italy's culture radiated across the continent. Other richly illustrated architectural treatises now joined Palladio's *Four Books of Architecture* in spreading Italian design. Especially successful was the *Seven Books* by Sebastiano Serlio (1475–ca. 1554) of Bologna, of which six appeared during the author's lifetime and one after his death. Outside Italy, new hybrids of Renaissance art continually emerged. Architects and painters like Lancelot Blondel of the Netherlands and Wendel Dietterlin of Germany formed crossbreeds that did not disavow their Gothic paternity. The walls and vaults of castles and town halls were decorated with grotesques, ornaments featuring strange chimeras and vines modeled on decoration found in the ruins of Nero's "Golden House" in Rome in the late fifteenth century. Pious art critics, Catholic and Protestant alike, were horrified by such painterly "dreamworks."⁵¹ Also typical of the art of the age were emblems, combinations of cryptic texts and images, *picturae*, each of which provided a key to unlocking the meaning of the whole. Emblems were conceived in the hundreds, diffused in printed books—one of the countless examples is the jurist Andrea Alciati's *Emblemata* (1531)—and found their way into oil paintings and frescoes.

As the century progressed, these one-of-a-kind, somewhat crazy, somewhat learned but technically brilliant artists operated in a divided art world. In the pre-Reformation age, when paintings were largely uncontroversial, boundaries were not drawn between the spheres of the holy and the profane. The whole world seemed more or less holy, more or less profane. Even in churches, stalls for selling wares were set up, documents were issued, town councils met.[52] Now confessional competition caused people across the spectrum to consider what should be allowed in the most sacred centers and what not. Beyond the protected sphere of the holy, secular spaces opened up.[53]

Yet there were still skirmishes in the border zones between religion and the secular world. The state of affairs is illustrated well by what the Catholic Raffaello Borghini, in his 1584 dialogue on art, has one of his interlocutors say about an indecently "salacious" (*tanto lascivo*) angel (Plate 29) painted by Agnolo Bronzino (1503–1573): it had no place in a church, but he would be happy to keep it at home. He considered this particular messenger of God to be "one of the most agreeable and lovely figures one could lay eyes on."[54] But even art displayed in the private, secular realm could sometimes elicit shock. Thus, Cardinal Otto Truchsess von Waldburg was criticized for having "shameless statues and paintings" in his castle in Dillingen (near Augsburg) that "offended chaste eyes."[55]

The Abundance and Order of Knowledge

The variety of Mannerist art was not simply the product of market conditions, nor were its wild play with anamorphosis (the artful distortion of images according to precise rules of perspective), monsters, and trompe-l'oeil merely the mirror of a labyrinthine age. Its overwhelming abundance, its bizarreness, capriciousness, and elegance are signs of the late period of a style, which is generally followed by a classicizing reaction. The arsenal of forms and concepts available to painters and sculptors had grown to the sky. The same applied to literature. In Rabelais's novel, Gargantua praises the level of education attained in his day, remarking that the world is full of learned people. "Thieves and highwaymen, hangmen and executioners, common foot soldiers, grooms and stableboys, are now more learned than the scholars and preachers of my day."[56]

Indeed, learned men in Europe had grown beyond number. Some might have bequeathed to posterity an idea or two, but most—like the alchemist Alexander Seton, who wandered Europe around 1600—left little more than news of their death. They included oddballs and esoterics like John Dee and Robert

Fludd, as well as loudmouths who passed themselves off as masters of nature. Cardano claimed to have solved 240,000 problems in his lifetime.[57] Minds great and small corresponded feverishly with one another; around 1500, they started feeling like they belonged to a republic of letters, a *respublica literaria*.[58]

Thanks to the printing press, unprecedented heaps of knowledge had piled up. According to one contemporary, there were now so many inventions unknown to the ancients that that it would take more than one book to list them.[59] Books became thicker and began to appear in more and more volumes. At 964 pages, Robert Estienne's *Thesaurus* (1543) anthologized quotations from over 30 ancient authors. In 1572, his son Henri published a four-volume *Treasury of the Greek Language,* and the Zurich physician Conrad Gessner (1516–1565) produced a richly illustrated work of zoology that ran 4,500 pages. The name of the legendarily polyglot king Mithridates was used as the title for a comparative description of about 130 languages, including outlier idioms like Rotwelsch and fictional tongues like the one Thomas More invented for the Utopians.

Gessner and others inaugurated the great age of polyhistors. Gessner distinguished himself as a linguist and the founder of the genre of botanical geography. Cardano produced about two hundred books on medicine, astrology, physics, philosophy, and politics. He wrote about dreams, teeth, lightning, sea monsters, music, and fossils, and he also wrote accounts of the lives and works of great figures of antiquity, from Theophrastus to Cicero. Association with magic and his unorthodox approach to religion brought him problems with the Inquisition in later life. Another polyhistor was Ulisse Aldrovandi (1522–1605). The "Aristotle of Bologna" filled thirteen volumes with natural science.[60] As director of the botanical garden in Padua, he became a distinguished expert on plants. Of the numerous museums in Italy, Aldrovandi's in Bologna was one of the most famous. He supposedly amassed eighteen thousand objects, in addition to an herbarium with seven thousand specimens.

Collections, museums, and cabinets of curiosities—the boundaries were fluid—were now to be found everywhere.[61] Even burghers indulged in the passion for collecting. In Basel, the cabinets of the jurist Basilius Amerbach (1533–1591) and the physician Felix Platter (1536–1614) could be viewed. They were places of curiosity, amazement, and study, containing a rich diversity of monstrosities and medals, real and fake antiquities, mandrakes and astrolabes, machines, ostrich eggs and elephant bones, fossils, gems and artworks, exotic and erotic memorabilia—objects that glowed with a special aura on account of their age, distant origin, rarity, or the fame of the artists who had made

them. Some patrons had the ambition to arrange their museum as a microcosm of the entire universe.

Ancient raw material was supplied by a now vast multitude of antiquaries
and art dealers. They provided paintings and sculptures, rarities and curiosities. One of the leading names, Jacopo Strada (1507–1588) of Mantua, grew
rich off the trade. He could afford to have his portrait painted by Titian (Plate 30).
Antiquities were anything but cheap. In 1588, two medals from the second
century cost seventy-five scudi, about the annual salary of a university teacher.
According to one contemporary, a figure by Apelles was double the price of
one by Raphael.[62]

In princely circles, cabinets of curiosities formed part of ensembles including botanical gardens, fishponds, libraries, workshops, and alchemical laboratories.[63] Their proud owners wanted to show what they were able to afford,
thus demonstrating their superiority to social competitors. The cabinet of
curiosities was a variant of the treasure chamber, a secular counterpart to the
reliquary chapel, and a precursor to the scientific study collection. In the sixteenth century, a system emerged that classified objects into *artificialia, natu-
ralia, exotica,* and *scientifica*: works of art and craftsmanship, wonders of nature,
exotic things from distant lands, and finally clocks, automata, astrolabes, and
the like. Gradually, catalogs were compiled; the very first may have been for
Paolo Giovio's museum in Como.

In the tradition of Alberti and Peutinger, ancient objects, long since discovered as historical sources, found their editors and analysts. In a 1542 publication,
Aldrovandi cataloged the ancient statues to be seen in Roman villas, gardens,
and palaces; it has remained an invaluable source for art history and archaeology
down to our own day. His contemporary Pirro Ligorio (1513/14–1583), a Neapolitan architect and painter, planned a monumental collection of images of
Roman antiquities. Ligorio's interest was aesthetic. In his view, only those with
a profound understanding of the ancient world could create good art.[64] One lone
volume appeared in print in 1553 in Venice. Yet richly illustrated material remained in manuscript form, enough for more than forty volumes.

An urge was felt to order not only things but also knowledge in general. Or,
to borrow an image from Francis Bacon: the blind scavenging of ants had to
give way to the ordering work of bees.[65] The first thing that needed to be done
was to make books more user-friendly. The principle of adding page numbers
became standard in the sixteenth century. Indices also became more common.[66] Bibliographies grew in size and quality. In 1545, Gessner published his
Universal Library, a milestone in the craft of bibliography. His collection

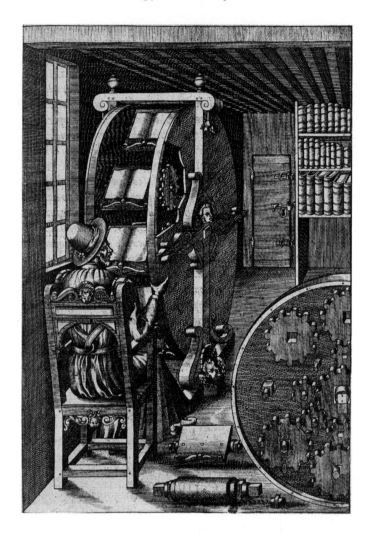

included ten thousand titles of works in Hebrew, Greek, and Latin. It was in demand everywhere and soon appeared in expanded editions.[67]

This flood of knowledge stimulated a Renaissance of the venerable practice of mnemonics, the art of memory.[68] It also prompted a curious invention: the "book wheel," pictured in Agostino Ramelli's book of engineering and machine designs (Fig. 62, above). The device combined ten or twelve movable lecterns that always remained at a constant angle. It allowed the reader to consult the pages of several folio volumes at once. Its complicated gearing was adapted from astronomical clocks.

Last but not least, "creating order" was also the focus of a discussion about method that had been reaching a crescendo since the Late Middle Ages.[69] Now, in the sixteenth century, a host of learned men set about structuring knowledge, elaborating methods for all possible disciplines from botany to mathematics. The success of the philosophy of Petrus Ramus (Pierre de la Ramée, 1515–1572), a victim of the Saint Bartholomew's Day massacre, was in part due to its promise to quench the overwhelming thirst for order and systematization.[70] Ramism was a philosophy oriented toward practical application. Its focus was entirely on this world and thus on consciously perceptible things. The ordering of knowledge that Ramus undertook proceeded from the general to the specific. It took clearly defined general concepts such as "politics" or "music" and subdivided them into narrower and narrower subconcepts. The influence of Ramus's philosophy of education, which dealt with such principles, was massive—less so at the old universities than in grammar schools, but that made its impact even greater.

There was no lack of polemics against the quibbling and quarreling that dominated much university teaching and writing. The Burse in Tübingen, built around 1480 as a student dormitory, even had separate entrances for adherents of the "new way" of the nominalists and the "old way" of the realists; a wall divided the two conflicting realms. This symbol is deceptive, however, as it was often universities that overthrew tradition and offered a stage for the open fighting between competing theories and the struggle for consensus.[71] Nearly all the leaders of the Scientific Revolution completed a university degree or held academic positions.[72] Furthermore, not all universities were the same. Padua, with its cutting-edge medical faculty and international atmosphere, cannot be compared with a small, provincial German university.

In addition, learned discourse found a home in academies.[73] In 1583, the Accademia della Crusca, literally the "Academy of the Bran," was founded in Florence; its mission was to separate the wheat from the chaff of the Tuscan idiom, thus purifying the language. A scientific research institute was then founded in Rome in 1603, the "Academy of the Lynx-Eyed," or *Lincei*. Naturally, not all such institutions of this kind should be imagined as laboratories of knowledge. They provided a refuge from the world, an oasis for artists and intellectuals—romantic settings that recalled the ancient Athenian model. "Science shall sit in a shady courtyard or in the countryside, with a villa surrounded by plane trees . . . to engage in enjoyable learned discussions," mused Cesare Ripa, author of the *Iconologia* (1593), a very popular lexicon of allegorical symbolism.[74]

The Renaissance academies probably had their roots in southern Italy. An "Accademia Segreta" seems to have formed in Naples around 1560, whose goal was to discover the secrets of nature. Its results were to be "publicized" in order "to elicit the noblest rivalry from every true Lord and Prince in his state, and from every beautiful and sublime mind." Thus wrote its alleged founder Girolamo Ruscelli.[75] It is not quite clear whether it really existed. At any rate, Ruscelli provides an ideal plan for a Renaissance academy, saying that the Accademia Segreta maintained a botanical garden, a laboratory, and a team of experts and assistants including goldsmiths, apothecaries, and perfumers. What we know for sure is that an informal circle took shape after mid-century in Naples around Giambattista Della Porta (1535–1615), himself an incredibly productive scientist and dramatist.

Della Porta still belonged to the era of scientists who had to find their bearings in nature as it was described by Aristotle, Plato, and Pliny, the Arab scientists, and the European Middle Ages: a world of sympathies, analogies, divine signs, spirits, and occult powers. According to his *Phytognomica*, a work of botany, the "signatures" or external forms of plants indicated inner qualities and their effects. His (in)famous physiognomy followed the same pattern of thought: people who looked like oxen acted like oxen.[76] In addition, Della Porta practiced voodoo. Its logic follows the same law of relationships and similarities: sticking a needle into a doll supposedly makes the person the doll resembles feel pain in the same spot, even if they are located far away.

What distinguished Della Porta's science from the work of earlier authors was that he sought to bring order to the discourse of magic and used experiments to try to figure out how hidden powers could be harnessed beneficially.[77] His twenty-volume *Natural Magic*, whose second edition appeared in 1589, towered above all its predecessors. Spells, prayers, and rituals had no place there. The power of things may have come from God, but the effects they brought about were no miracles, and the *magus* was anything but a shaman. Rather, he was a humanist, alchemist, astrologer, and mathematician, as well as a craftsman who was handy with a scalpel and a distillation flask. Della Porta practiced a natural science that, while in the process of conquering new frontiers, still felt at home within old ones.

Similar transitions from "untamed" thinking within old paradigms to an ordering and systematizing tendency can be seen in the science of Ulisse Aldrovandi. A prime example is his idiosyncratic natural history of monsters—in the thinking of the time, hybrids of animals and humans whose body parts seemed to come from different species, even including winged dragons, bats, and flying fish. The precursor to Aldrovandi's work was the 1560 *Histoires prodigieuses* of Pierre Boaistuau (ca. 1520–1566). But while the Breton considered monsters to be ominous products of God's wrath,[78] Ulisse approached them with cool rationality. Page after page, he sought to define what monsters actually were, after which he soberly classified and ordered them according to their abnormal body parts, such as having two heads or split tails. Winged creatures he divided by habitat, diet, and beak form. Of course, he made mistakes even with actual animals. While another pioneer of zoology, Oxford professor Edward Wotton (1492–1555), agreed with Aristotle that bats were mammals, Aldrovandi counted them among the birds. Impressive were the illustrations he produced in collaboration with various painters, foremost among them Jacopo Ligozzi of Bologna. Here, brilliant technique—Ligozzi's temperas seem almost photorealistic (Plate 31)—and science merged into one of those characteristic syntheses that would accompany Latin Europe's Scientific Revolution.

At times tentative, at times energetic, and baldly self-promoting, these incursions into the murky realms of the unknown undertaken by Della Porta and his ilk produced not only curiosities but also windows onto the future. Della Porta's *Physiognomy* and posthumous *Metoposcopia* were precursors to psychosomatic psychology, as well as to biological racism and eugenics. Gessner described sphynxes and satyrs, as well as dog-headed and hoofed, forest-dwelling humanoids (Fig. 83, p. 929). Nevertheless, he is justly considered a pioneer of modern zoology.[79] Cardano did not merely consider the mosquito a relative of the elephant on account of its proboscis. He also pioneered probability theory and was one of the first to get a handle on negative numbers, cubic equations, and binomial coefficients. He has gone down in the history of technology as the inventor (or at least the first theorizer) of ingenious devices like the gimbal and the universal joint.[80]

Fall of the Titans

An especially impressive example of how opposite tendencies could coexist in close proximity is provided by Aldrovandi's *Dracologia*, a natural history of dragons. It just so happened that the day Gregory XIII was elected—whose crest featured a two-footed dragon—a monstrous amphibian was found outside Bologna. Aldrovandi dissected it in front of a rapt audience. He carved the miracle up, thus turning a heavenly omen into an object of scientific curiosity.[81] The monster's remains ended up in his cabinet of curiosities (Fig. 63, p. 758). The demystification of the dragon was one of those hairline cracks that had been

appearing between the old and the new, the ancient and the modern. Another example is provided by the process of Filippo Neri's canonization. Anatomists examined his corpse, arriving at the conclusion that its broken ribs and other injuries had unquestionably resulted from supernatural causes.[82] In this way, the new art of anatomy was put in the service of the pious belief in miracles.

The medicine of Paracelsus and Fernel also evinced tradition and innovation side by side. The human body was not simply a machine of bones, flesh, and muscles; rather, it seemed to them and their contemporaries to be connected to the cosmos. Their conjectures about vital spirits in the body were similar to the vitalistic models of learned Chinese physicians, who used acupuncture, acupressure, and moxibustion in an effort to improve the circulation of qi vapors in the body. Like them, most Europeans believed in witchcraft, astrology, and geomancy.[83] Even the idea of achieving immortality on Earth was not foreign to Europe. Differently from the Chinese, however, some leading thinkers in Europe drove a twofold paradigm shift. By adopting Greco-Roman philosophy, they had undermined the religious model; by smashing the ancient systems of knowledge, they blazed the trail for modern science.

The fact that Europe's learned men did not remain in awe of ancient monuments but rather dared to topple them is one of the most astounding aspects of the history of science. Ironically, the technology required for this demolition had been supplied to them by the Greeks, in the form of the Socratic dialogue and Aristotelian logic. One of the founders of modern skepticism, Herbert of Cherbury (1583–1648), would use Aristotelian philosophy to figure out how to achieve cognition of what is true.[84] Had not Aristotle himself eschewed all regard for authorities? "Plato is a friend," goes his oft-quoted comment, "but truth is a greater friend."[85]

The hierarchies of being constructed by the Middle Ages collapsed, and the powers of nature broke free of their metaphysical constraints. One important insight gained ground, namely that truth is not something once possessed by humanity that must be rediscovered, but rather a goal located somewhere in the future that may actually be unattainable.[86] The basic description of things, now undertaken ad nauseam, the dissection of bodies, and the collection of objects gradually robbed them of the aura of the unknown.

Ancient systems were now being attacked on all fronts. In the field of botany, doubts had already arisen in the fifteenth century about whether Pliny had correctly translated the Greek names of plants. In the case of medicinal herbs, this was not merely a philological problem. People set about observing and comparing, based their work on experience and experimentation, and ventured out directly into nature. "Should Pliny, or Theophrastus's translator Gaza, have such authority that we believe them rather than our own eyes?" remarked the physician Niccolò Leoniceno (1428–1524), the leading botanist of his generation.[87] In his view, Avicenna was a gruesome tyrant whose followers trusted their leader implicitly and held doggedly fast to things they had not learned by experience. The anatomist Realdo Colombo (ca. 1516–1559) crisply stated his intention to contradict "the ancients and the moderns alike."[88] Even Aristotle, Europe's great teacher of rationality, came under fire. He was accused of proclaiming uncertain things, expressing himself unclearly, and hiding like an octopus in his own ink.[89] Petrus Ramus went so far as to attack the core of Aristotelian philosophy: logic.

Devastating arguments against the teachings of the titanic ancient authorities were brought back by sailors from their voyages. What they reported further widened the cracks in the traditional understanding of geography that could already be discerned in Gregor Reisch's map. The physician Garcia de Orta, who lived in Goa, wrote in his work on botany that more knowledge could be acquired in one day from a Portuguese sailor than the Romans had stacked up in a century.[90] In fact, sea captains wrought a "revolution of experience."[91] Contrary to ancient teachings about the equator, according to which it was home to murderous heat, the Portuguese crossed it without event. José de Acosta (ca. 1540–1600), who sailed to South America in 1571, reported that it was frightfully cold there.[92] "What could I do," he wrote, but laugh at Aristotle's *Meteorology* and his philosophy? In that place and in that season where, according to his rules, everything ought to be scorched by heat, my companions and I were freezing.

Clearly, he concluded, Ptolemy and others had not known even half the world.

The precious mountain of ancient knowledge and ancient art had been scaled, and from its summit people could see farther. As poetic patriots had rebelled against the dominance of Latin and Italian, political patriots against Spanish imperialism, and religious patriots against the papacy, the gauntlet was now thrown down to ancient thinkers and their medieval successors. What continued to shore up the crumbling Peripatetic empire was its alliance with theology. As a result, new ideas germinated alongside Aristotelianism, not in place of it. In midcentury Venice, Giunta issued an edition of the available writings of Averroes in Latin translation. In 1597, Jean Bodin published his *Theatrum naturae*, a bulwark of ancient philosophy buttressed by the Bible. It took a stand against natural magic and Epicurean atheism, opposed all doubts about the immortality of the soul, and defended the Aristotelian doctrine of the eternity of the universe.[93] Newton would still receive his scientific education from a textbook informed by Peripatetic positions.[94]

In philosophical discourse, the seismograph of the intellectual zeitgeist, Montaigne's doubts sent out tremors. In his 1581 work entitled *That Nothing Is Known*, the physician Francisco Sanches (1550/51–1623) argued that not syllogisms but only precise observations could lead to knowledge—and even then, only for individual questions.[95] Where could certainty be found? In the perception of the senses, Bernardino Telesio (1509–1588) claimed.[96] In his view, this was the only reliable authority. A second royal road to knowledge was thought to lead through mathematics. Of the natural philosophers of the late Renaissance, it was Cardano, that curious mixture of bold thinker, tinkerer, and ingenious mathematician, who put stock in it. He recognized that what can be known is limited. Yet in his view, mathematics allowed the boundaries set by the senses to be expanded and even the infinite to be grasped. Still, Cardano knew that not even the synergy of observation, experimentation, and calculation could lead to absolute knowledge about the nature of the universe. His autobiography reveals him to be a profound pessimist.[97]

Fierce opposition to all things new came from the astronomers. The vast majority of them toiled undaunted—and uninfluenced by Copernicus's arguments—to "save the phenomena." More and more spheres were posited in the cosmos. Their number rose to 12, 14, even 77 or 79.[98] Someone hatched the odd idea that the planets moved—like rabbits in their burrows—through celestial "canals."[99] What existed beyond the Empyrean remained an open question. Infinity? Nothing? But, it was asked, if there was "nothing" beyond the universe, how can this nothing border on "something?" Copernicus had avoided taking a stand on the issue. "Therefore let us leave the question whether the universe is finite or infinite for the natural philosophers to argue."[100] After him, Thomas Digges (1546–1595), a student of the abstruse John Dee, hinted at the possibility that the universe was infinite.[101] Nevertheless, Digges's boundless sphere of the fixed stars, a woodcut of which appeared on the title page of his 1576 treatise on the celestial spheres, is still the old biblical "home of the elect" and the "court of the great god"—just without borders. Around the same time, Francesco Patrizi contradicted Aristotle by formulating the idea of an "absolute space" that *preceded* all being. This construct is as little deducible from what is perceived by the senses as another concept discussed by Patrizi: that of "absolute" time. Both had been theorized earlier by Telesio. Thus, philosophical premises for the model of an infinite cosmos were being formulated—at the same time as cosmology was considering the question of the boundaries of the universe.[102]

Winter Journey to Infinity: Giordano Bruno

Rome. February 16, 1600. The hooded figures appeared at dusk. For the man huddled in a windowless cell in the Tor di Nona, the papal dungeon not far from Castel Sant'Angelo in Rome, their arrival foreboded nothing good.[103] The black-robed individuals were angels of death, there to shepherd the man through the awful moments between life and its harsh, violent end. Members of the Brotherhood of Saint John the Beheaded, they were sworn to provide comfort to those condemned to death. All night long they talked to the prisoner, a short, skinny man with a chestnut-brown beard, grown pale after long incarceration, and tried to sway him from his heretical beliefs. "Yet he persisted to the end in his damnable obstinance," one source reports.[104] All that remained were the usual prayers for those condemned to die. Finally, the man was led out into the early dawn, its rays breaking through the pine trees on the Janiculum Hill to chase the last vestiges of twilight from the cupolas of Rome.

The group made its way to Campo de' Fiori. It is not far from the Tor di Nona, no more than thirty minutes at a leisurely gate. For the doomed man, the march through the narrow city streets must have felt like the Road to Calvary. For he knew exactly what awaited him. In the middle of the square, a stake had been set up surrounded by a pyre—in the very place where a monument now stands to the man who met his fate there. The name of the bronze figure who looks down earnestly from his pedestal upon passersby is famous throughout the world: Giordano Bruno.

Ettore Ferrari's statue is a manifesto against papal Rome, which had just been overcome by the Italian state united during the Risorgimento. In the eyes of the fledgling nation, the bronze Bruno stood as a martyr to the truth, a hero of civil society. That was an exaggeration, of course. Giordano Bruno was certainly no standard-bearer of liberalism. Yet his life embodied a conflict that we have been tracing in this book ever since Canossa. It revolved around the question of who should have more rights and freedom: the Church and its claim to absolute possession of the truth, or the secular world in which science and philosophy had their place and critical discourse had taken hold.

Born the son of a soldier in the Campanian town of Nola in 1548, Bruno joined the Dominican Order and received a thorough humanist education.[105] He was brilliant, a restless spirit, a book-devouring Pantagruel. He soon gained a reputation for heresy. His life's path became a winter journey through the gloomy Europe of the Late Renaissance. He sought and found supporters— including Henry III and Rudolph II—and money. He seldom departed anywhere in peace. "Thus have I come to wander through your cities," he once noted before leaving yet another one, this time Wittenberg in 1588:

> A foreigner, an exile, a renegade, a plaything of fate, slight in stature, a have-not, abandoned by fortune, beset by the hatred of the mob, and therefore despised by dumb and common people.[106]

By then, Bruno had left his monastic order. He published constantly—on the art of memory, cosmology, physics, magic, and geometry. He wrote sonnets, didactic poetry, and a play. Many considered him a heretic, some a magician, a prophet, or a revolutionary. He was excommunicated three times: by Rome, in Calvinist Geneva, and even in Lutheran Helmstedt. He gazed upon both Catholic and Protestant skies through the iron bars of prison windows.

What was the nature of the "thousand errors and vanities" imputed to Bruno?[107] His attacks were leveled initially against Ptolemy and, with foaming virulence, against Aristotle, whom in one of his texts he depicted as a jackass.[108] Bruno saw himself as the perfector of Copernican cosmology and as a Prometheus bringing enlightenment. He rated himself greater than Tiphys, the creator of the Argonauts' ship, greater even than Columbus, for releasing human thought and knowledge from the bonds that held them prisoner. He forced his way into the heavens, crossed the boundaries of the universe, and "dissolved the fictitious walls of the first, eighth, ninth, and tenth spheres, as well as any others that idiotic mathematicians and the blindness of ignorant philosophers felt the need to add."[109] Bruno produced dialogues of singular brilliance, texts full of irony, satire, and sarcasm. He was a master of ancient mythology and the art of deciphering allegories.

His *Ash Wednesday Supper*, published in 1584, is equal parts godlessness and piety, cheer and fury, mastery and puerility, earnestness and folly. It takes place in the house of Sir Fulke Greville, in real life an eminent figure in Elizabethan England, a friend of the poet Philip Sidney and Francis Bacon.[110] In their attempt to get to the supper, the guests wander around London, a metaphor for the confusion found in Scholastic dialectic. They try to take a shortcut, spend a long time on a slow ferry, get stuck in the mud, and lose their way. Bruno comments, "O wily dialectics, O knotty doubts, O testy sophisms, O petty squabbles, O dark riddles, O tortuous labyrinths, O frenzied sphinx—reach a solution, or one will be reached for you!"[111] Ultimately the wanderers turn up at a feast. Fortune comes to the rescue, opening the door of the mind with the aid of reason and ordering free choice to allow the journey to continue. And that is exactly how Bruno saw his own thought: aided by rational resolve and intellectual freedom, it overcame the sophistries of Scholastic philosophy and shed light on what was obscure. In Bruno's view, reason made human beings mature and free—even capable of conceiving of the infinite, which transcends all experience.

The *Ash Wednesday Supper* proclaims all of Bruno's central arguments. The universe is infinite, as is the number of stars and planets it contains. Therefore, it has no center. Some stars that seem to be close together are actually farther from each other than the Sun is from the Earth. It is not fictitious spheres that move but the planets themselves. The latter are not fixed in the heavens, nor is the Earth or the stars. For its part, the Earth rotates from west to east in a period of about twenty-four hours and revolves around the Sun. Bruno enlarged upon these ideas in his treatise *On the Infinite Universe and Worlds*, published in the same year of 1584, and in a few other writings. The steadily twinkling stars beyond Saturn, he once wrote, were actually suns that were orbited by other planets, other "Earths."[112]

The thesis that the universe could include a multitude of inhabited worlds, which has still not been either refuted or substantiated, was postulated back in antiquity. Yet it had never before been formulated so eloquently.[113] Its rationale was provided by a concept of God steeped in Platonic and Hermetic thought. Bruno's God is the paradox of an infinite limit. As such, the universe is an image of God, who at the same time contains it within himself and appears in it like in a mirror in which he is himself omnipresent (and not only as an image).[114] Bruno hypothesized that the far reaches of the universe may contain planets whose inhabitants enjoy a more blissful existence than that of Earth-dwellers. God's sublimity is "glorified not in one, but in countless suns; not in a single earth, a single world, but in a thousand thousand, I say in an infinity of worlds."[115] Beyond the infinite universe, however, there was nothing at all, neither space nor fullness nor emptiness nor time.[116]

Bruno's infinity admits of no center, no hierarchy ascending from the bodily to the spiritual and ultimately to the divine, no order of elements. "Where then is that beautiful order, that lovely scale of nature?" he has Burchio, an interlocutor in his dialogue *On the Infinite Universe and Worlds*, ask. Fracastoro, to whom Bruno erects a true-to-life monument here, responds, "You would like to know where is this order? In the realm of dreams, fantasies, chimeras, delusions."[117] Bruno's cosmology appears as a radical refutation of the universe of the *Divine Comedy*, a contradiction of the cosmos of the theologians with its Empyrean, choirs of angels, and phalanx of the saints. Bruno's God is eternally creating the cosmos;[118] its creation, simultaneously the self-creation of its creator, unfolds in perpetuity. Thus, the universe is simply there, one with the equally infinite principle that works within it down to the tiniest detail. Change and rebirth are experienced only by forms, but their matter is eternal. Therefore, nothing can truly pass away; nothing can truly die.[119] Thoughts of this kind are behind the Bible verse that Bruno inscribed in the album of the University of Wittenberg: "Solomon and Pythagoras. What is that is? The very thing that was. What is that was? The very thing that is. There is nothing new under the Sun."[120]

In contrast to the far-reaching influence he had on philosophy, in the history of modern astronomy, Bruno played no special role. For his ideas were based on neither observations nor calculations. The expansion of the universe he theorized corresponded solely with his concept of a mega-god. Still, it drove home the possible consequences of Copernican cosmology. If the Earth was not the center, then the center of the universe could be anywhere or nowhere.

Clearly, dogma lost all significance in the face of Bruno's abstract, totalizing concept of God. In the *Ash Wednesday Supper*, he dismisses Jews, Christians, and Muslims as "three utterly different, antagonistic sects" that have each split "into countless even more different and even more antagonistic ones."[121] During his trial, he said that Luther, Melanchthon, Calvin, "and other ultramontane heretics" deserve the name not of "theologians" but of "pedants."[122] It was not his far-out cosmology that sent Bruno to the stake but rather his attacks

on religion. His polemic entitled *Expulsion of the Triumphant Beast* was one of
the most outrageous things to be written against Christianity (Bruno once
called it *sant'asinità*, which could be loosely translated as "Christi-ass-ity")
before Nietzsche.[123] Christ appears in the guise of the "Divine and Miraculous
Orion," who "causes the heavens to 'orionate' from fright."[124] Bruno caricatures
him as a presumptuous ape of divine wisdom who performs all sorts of tricks,
sleight of hand, and other good-for-nothing miracles.[125] Bruno's condemnation of pious zealots reflects the conditions of the age. "While they utter greet-
ings of peace, they do . . . carry, wherever they enter, the Knife of Division and
the Fire of Dispersion," he wrote.

> They call themselves ministers of one who resurrects the dead and heals the
> infirm, [but] it is they who, worse than all others whom the earth feeds,
> cripple the healthy and kill the living, not so much with fire and with the
> sword as with their pernicious tongues.[126]

From our perspective today, the life of this philosopher seemed to lead
straight to the stake. Yet that was not the case. He found patrons and money
everywhere. His scandalous treatise was published in London. In the succeeding years, he taught and fought, bowed and scraped in Paris, Marburg, Wittenberg, Prague, and Helmstedt, in the imperial city of Frankfurt, in Zurich,
and in Padua, where he vied for the professorship that Galileo would soon be
given. Disaster only came when he accepted an invitation from the Venetian
patrician Giovanni Mocenigo. They fought about something or other. His host
denounced him to the Inquisition, which, rather unusual in liberal Venice,
extradited him to Rome. That sealed his fate. People built bridges for his escape, even in the final months, but he refused to cross them. Under the eyes
of his torturers, he dared to make outrageous claims, such as that Moses was
a magician who invented the Ten Commandments. The Bible he called a mere
"dream."[127] When his death sentence was announced, according to one source
he simply responded, "Perhaps you proclaim my sentence with greater dread
than I receive it!"[128] Then the final scene was nigh. As the flames rose from the
crackling wood, licking at his body with a foretaste of the agony to come, did
Bruno have the peace of mind to think of his infinite universe in which there
was no death but only transformation and rebirth? With his last words, he
supposedly said that he died a martyr and gladly so, and that his soul would
rise to Paradise with the smoke.[129]

Bruno thought a tradition through to the end that had begun with the
Presocratics. This tradition included Lucretius, for whom nothing existed but

atoms in motion. It included Plato, the creator of the God who permeated Bruno's universe. It included Aristotle—yes, even Aristotle, whom Bruno heaped high with scorn—who taught that the universe was uncreated. Finally, it included Cusanus as well, whose cosmos is boundless, albeit not infinite. In this sense, Bruno was a thinker of the Renaissance. And he even identified himself as such, characterizing his own science as "ancient and obsolete views . . . renewed."

> They are amputated roots which germinate, ancient things which return yet again, occult truths which are discovered; it is a new light which after a long night riseth over the horizon in the hemisphere of our knowledge and little by little approacheth the meridian of our intelligence.[130]

We should not make Bruno more modern than he was. Some have tried to characterize him as a kind of learned Mannerist whose thought, similar to the painters of the late sixteenth century, turned things on their heads. That is a novel view, but it applies to the essence of creative imagination in general more than it captures Bruno's particular way of thinking. He arrived at his insights by means of "medieval"-seeming speculation (indeed, it came from the renaissances of the twelfth and thirteenth centuries). In some of his writings, he appears to be here an eccentric mystic, there an ecstatic Platonist. His concept of the universe is vitalistic and magical.[131] His view of the stars and planets as ensouled beings, a belief that would long remain widespread, simply seems quaint today.[132] On the other hand, he developed the revolutionary idea that all life forms—from oysters to human beings—were alike with regard to their substance.[133] What is traditional about Bruno, and what amounts to the swan song of ancient thought, is that he did not base his work on mathematics and empiricism but rather argued as a philosopher. But in that field, he ran up against the limits of the European realm of possibility. Galileo would also explore those limits, although in a very different way. Only he and the other greats, Kepler and Newton, would heed the call Bruno sounded to himself at the end of his dialogue on infinity.

> Rend in pieces the concave and convex surfaces which would limit and seperate so many elements and heavens. Pour ridicule on deferent orbs and on fixed stars. Break and hurl to earth with the resounding whirlwind of lively reasoning those fantasies of the blind and vulgar herd, the adamantine walls of the primum mobile and the ultimate sphere. Dissolve the notion that our earth is unique and central to the whole."[134]

Winter's Tale: Shakespeare

London. Around 1600. The city, which with perhaps 187,000 souls had grown to be one of the five largest in Europe, was full of potential and growth, a future center of world trade, a global port.[135] A panorama engraved by Claes Visscher in 1616 shows London unfurled along the Thames over a space of two meters. The river is crowded with galleons, barges, boats of all kinds. Veritable forests of masts rise above Saint Katharine Docks. The city behind them is presented as a muddle of gables and steeples, with Saint Paul's standing in high relief. Right in the middle, the widely admired London Bridge can be seen. Like the Rialto Bridge, it was outfitted with buildings where needles and other bric-a-brac were peddled on the ground floor. Travelers from Southwark were greeted by the grimacing heads of the freshly executed—Visscher included this detail as well—who warned those entering the city what was in store for them if they disturbed the peace. Harrow on the Hill, Hackney, and Stepney are still villages on the horizon, as is Hampstead, surrounded by pastures and populated by windmills. Guildhall is captioned in the center. So is the Royal Exchange, which received its noble title from Queen Elizabeth in 1570. Along the waterfront, Visscher depicts a row of aristocratic residences, including Lord Burghley's palace and Somerset House, where the Renaissance had established its first bridgehead in London in the mid-sixteenth century. Closer to the center, the city gets more commercial. On the bank of the Thames is the Steelyard, formerly the base of the mighty Hanseatic League. Not far upriver, the guild house of the fishmongers can be discerned.

We can hear the calls of the captains, the groaning of the cranes, the hammering on the dockyards, and the "Eastward ho!" or "Westward ho!" of the ferrymen. We might imagine yearning glances cast down the Thames, following the galleons as they sailed to far-off lands, or the impatience on the sun- and salt-burned faces of returning sailors, who for months had dreamt of nothing but the city's brothels, taverns, and play dens. Even then, some Puritans considered London a modern Babylon. Humanist scholars, in contrast, still thought of it as a daughter of Troy.

The property of "papist" institutions had been sold off at bargain prices. The garish residence of the archbishop of York, which had previously belonged to the benefice collector Cardinal Wolsey, remained in the possession of the crown. It was renamed "Whitehall" and was now the queen's residence. Goldsmiths, silk dealers, and others who sold luxury goods settled in its vicinity. Other areas were taken over by courtiers and capital. The Savoy, once a hospital for the poor, became a glass factory; glassblowers from Murano worked nearby. Where monks had once prayed and bishops resided, arsenals, sugar mills, tennis courts, and even a bakery specializing in hardtack sprang up. Monastic property was not subject to the city's jurisdiction, making it a particularly attractive investment. John Stow, the chronicler of Elizabethan London, sneered at the palaces of the nouveaux riches. With their little towers and chimneys, he wrote, they resembled Midsummer processions. Pointless, only for show and pleasure, they betrayed the vanity of the human spirit.

Like all beautiful depictions of cityscapes, Visscher's panorama hides what London was like at night, its poverty, its dirty suburban slums, the gray smoke hanging over the roofs that mingled with fog in autumn. Huts cobbled together out of wood, clay, and plaster provided makeshift accommodations for immigrants. No pictures show the narrow alleys impenetrable to sunshine, like tunnels underneath the protruding upper stories of the half-timber buildings. And let us not forget the stink of feces and rotting flesh outside the slaughterhouse of Saint Nicholas within Newgate or along Butcher's Row, home to black rats and thus the plague. The pestilence had broken out again between 1592 and 1593, creeping through the overpopulated city. Yet there was also educated, literate London, the London of schools that taught medicine and mathematics and jurisprudence. A college endowed by Thomas Gresham in 1597 not only taught merchants the law but also gave them a classical education. Booksellers were at the service of all readers. Their main marketplaces were Paternoster Row and Saint Paul's churchyard.[136] On neighboring Fleet Street, later home to London's newspaper industry, printers had had their presses for a century. There were twenty-four in 1585, sixty around 1650.

A certain poet from the provinces probably spent a lot of time there: William Shakespeare (1564–1616) of Stratford-upon-Avon.[137] For a time, he lived very close by, in Cripplegate. In light of the skepticism of scholars, we shall resist the temptation to place him in Italy between 1585 and 1592—a period that has left so few sources for his life that it is known as the "lost years." At any rate, he does not really seem to have been familiar with Italian geography. Yet his verse is inspired by Italian meter, and he knew the literature of the south. For example, the plot of *The Merchant of Venice* was probably taken from a novella by the Trecento poet Giovanni Fiorentino. Shakespeare was extremely well educated for a man of his birth; his father was the son of a farmer, although he had risen to become the mayor of Stratford. Shakespeare's oeuvre draws on Plautus, Ovid, and Plutarch, Boccaccio and Chaucer, as well as all sorts of chroniclers and contemporary poets. In Stratford, he had only attended a grammar school, where he learned a little Latin and even less Greek.[138] Where else could he have gotten everything if not from London's booksellers?

For a man like him, for whom the whole world was a stage, and the stage his whole world, the road to the capital was probably the only one available. Every day, two or three comedies were performed somewhere in the city, as one traveler tells us.[139] Nowhere else provided a better prospect for finding powerful patrons for an acting troupe; nowhere else had more theaters. Two of the most famous appear in the foreground of Visscher's engraving: the Swan, which had space for three thousand spectators, and the Globe, whose mere name proclaims its cosmopolitan aspirations. Nevertheless, we should not think of theaters as especially elite institutions. Shakespeare's art came from the margins, from disreputable entertainment districts where whores sold their bodies, syphilis lurked, and prisons stood ready. The stage had about the same status as the animal baiting that took place in the "Beargarden," located next to the Globe. People smoked during performances, ate fruit, drank beer and wine. The theater directors and their actors—including wild men, poor devils, and a few rogues—fought to survive in a tough market. They were permitted many things, but being boring was not one of them. Scenery was sparse at best; the eye was delighted by costumes and fireworks. On stage, people fought, danced, killed, conjured the devil, and told dirty jokes. As is well known, Shakespeare cast witches, fairies, and demons, and his tragedies are full of characters staggering across the stage; madness was all the rage in the age of melancholy. But what images did the poetic champion's words put in people's heads!

Shakespeare's theater was frequented by London's middle class and in no way only by its most refined stratum. After all, nearly everyone could pay the one-penny entrance fee. To the amazement of foreign guests, women were allowed in, too. In the seventeenth century, wealthier elements already started trying to distinguish themselves from the common people by patronizing private theaters, which charged significantly higher ticket prices.[140] Nevertheless, the Elizabethan theater symbolizes the beginnings of a new public, one that formed in contradistinction to the audience for sermons. It was thus condemned—not only by puritanical clergymen but also by prissy citizens—as a hotbed of immorality and unrest. More than once, politically sensitive passages brought censors onto the scene. In fact, the theater of the time seems to have been the laboratory of a society caught between the early modern and the modern world. Indeed, Shakespeare's plays frequently reflect this ambivalence.[141]

The bard was not received by everyone with open arms. One competitor, John Greene, disparaged him from his deathbed as an "upstart crow."[142] But this seems to have reflected a minority opinion. The newcomer found a patron in the third Earl of Southampton. As was then fashionable, he began writing sonnets. In 1593, his narrative poem *Venus and Adonis* became a bestseller and won him favor at court. The next year we find him among the Lord Chamberlain's Men, an acting company that, after Queen Elizabeth's death, restyled itself under James I as the King's Men. Financial success was secured. Shakespeare could afford the luxury of procuring a coat of arms and buying an imposing estate with orchards and fields in Stratford. He now belonged to the landed gentry.[143] To that, he added part ownership in the Globe and another theater, Blackfriars. Shakespeare spent his later years in Stratford-upon-Avon. He died in 1616, ten days after Cervantes. Ben Jonson honored his friend and rival in a foreword to the first folio edition of his plays with the oft-quoted words: "He was not of an age, but for all time!"

That was both true and untrue. To the displeasure of his Romantic admirers, the few extant historical documents reveal no titan but rather an enterprising businessman. If the portrait bust adorning his funerary monument in Stratford-upon-Avon's Holy Trinity Church can be believed, the author of *Macbeth* and *A Midsummer Night's Dream* was no Romeo but rather a balding distinguished gentleman with a Van Dyke beard and the makings of a double chin. His massive oeuvre flowed less from feverish creative furor than from an impresario's need to constantly produce new material for his sizeable acting troupe. And yet, Shakespeare may have had occasional moments of abandon in which "he would forget himself, putting the real world at a distance, and losing himself in the cold snows of his dream."[144]

Shakespeare is an analyst of power and a keen observer of human life, which he once described as the path from a first to a

> . . . second childishness and mere oblivion,
> Sans teeth, sans eyes, sans taste, sans everything.[145]

He understands a great deal about desire and passion, about eros and its accompanying happiness and despair:

> Before, a joy proposed; behind, a dream.
> All this the world well knows; yet none knows well
> To shun the heaven that leads men to this hell.[146]

He creates highly complex characters—Brutus, Hector, and Hamlet—and strong women like Titania, wrathful ones like Lady Macbeth, and fragile ones like the Danish Queen Gertrude. Some of his characters are still as vivid as they were four hundred years ago, such as Sir Toby Belch and the giant hulk of flesh Falstaff. Shakespeare's comedies still make us laugh; scenes in his tragedies still take our breath away. Machiavelli's unscrupulous prince has several brothers in the Englishman's dramas, foremost among them Edmund, who vies deceitfully and violently for Lear's vacated crown. Here as elsewhere in his history plays, however, Shakespeare is concerned less with what actually happened than with what he can teach us.

Nevertheless, a modern source-critical approach reveals insights into a phase of state formation in which a kingdom could no longer be administered as the sovereign's private property, could no longer be carved up like a wedding cake. The timeliness of this theme can be seen in the fact that James I did indeed regard the crown as his family property. In a speech in 1610, he described Parliament as a kind of advisory body to himself and his vassals. James saw himself as a king by divine right, indeed a godlike lord who should be accountable to no one for his behavior.[147] Decades later, a similar view would cost his son Charles his head.

In his history plays, Shakespeare avoided illustrious (and thus boring) episodes in favor of darker chapters from the medieval past of England and Scotland. The audience could shake off all the murders and atrocities with a cozy shudder. The great wars of the fifteenth century were the stuff of yesteryear. Spain had been conquered, and things were looking up. The inchoate nation— in the words of John of Gaunt, "this dear dear land, dear for her reputation through the world"[148]—seemed poised to conquer new frontiers, serene at home and triumphant on the seas. Nevertheless, once again the vision of history that Shakespeare put on the stage seems close to Machiavelli's. Not God but human beings make history. The director of the drama is blind Fortuna— here a friend, there a foe. Only occasionally do grand themes like guilt and mercy, predestination, necessity, and free will crop up.[149] In the passage of history, human beings—even if the cosmos is reflected in them—are nothing but the "quintessence of dust."[150] "To the gods," as Gloucester says in *King Lear*, we are "as flies to wanton boys. They kill us for their sport."[151] Do such lines reflect the experience of the times, or are they dictated by the plot?

Shakespeare's plays provide evidence for the notion that a firmly established concept of the universe was falling to pieces around 1600. The old concepts of fate, freedom, and providence were losing ground to the idea that everything was determined by the law of nature.[152] In the face of fathomless injustice on Earth, a devastating thought could be uttered: the possibility that there is no God. Let us quote *King Lear* again.

If that the heavens do not their visible spirits
Send quickly down to tame these vile offences,

we hear the Duke of Albany say,

It will come,
Humanity must perforce prey on itself,
Like monsters of the deep.[153]

No *deus ex machina* descends to put things in order. Edmund indeed meets the fate he deserves, but Lear dies of grief, and his realm falls to pieces. The play ends with a funeral march.

Shakespeare asks many questions but provides no simple answers. After hearing Puck's soliloquy at the end of *A Midsummer Night's Dream*, the audience may have felt unsure as to the nature of reality and truth—just like the readers of *Don Quixote*, the visitors to Vicino Orsini's sacred grove, and the viewers of Arcimboldo's illusions. With its nested levels of reality, its play within a play, the structure of *A Midsummer Night's Dream* recalls somewhat the journey Polifilo took a century earlier. But the retreat to a Marian convent—the device used in the *Hypnerotomachia*—no longer brings things to a harmonious conclusion. Nor does death. Everything remains unresolved. If necessary, thus the closing recommendation of the court jester Puck, one must treat it all as a dream.

Like Montaigne, whose essay *Of Cannibals* left its mark on *The Tempest*, Shakespeare may have been a man of deep skepticism. Without a doubt, he was a master of ambiguity, contradiction, and irony. He knew very well where Bohemia was, but he still called it a "desert country near the sea" in *The Winter's Tale*.[154] What did he mean by that? Every age, of course, finds meanings in great poetry that the author himself need not have been aware of. For one possible interpretation, let us close with verses from Ingeborg Bachmann's "Bohemia Lies by the Sea":

And err a hundred times,
as I erred and never withstood the trials,
though I did withstand them time after time.
As Bohemia withstood them and one fine day
was released to the sea and now lies by water.[155]

SCIENTIFIC REVOLUTION

39

Observation, Experimentation, Calculation

1600: In the Shadow of the Volcano

Naples, Castel Nuovo. Spring, 1600. Did the prisoner in the castle on the Gulf of Naples, the Dominican friar Tommaso Campanella, hear of Giordano Bruno's horrible end in nearby Rome? He himself had been imprisoned there a short time before.[1] The same fate threatened him, although for a different reason. He had taken part in a rebellion against the Spanish overlords—not out of cool political calculation, but rather out of a conviction that violent change was on the horizon and that he, Tommaso, had been called upon to be God's prophet.[2] Grandiose plans were attributed to him, including the intention to found a republic and preach a new religion. He is said to have considered himself the Messiah of truth and to have planned to rename the mountain at his birthplace, the Calabrian town of Stilo, as "Fertile Mountain."[3] *Libertà, libertà*—"Freedom, freedom!"—was then to be shouted perpetually from its summit. The Antichrist was to be expected in 1630.[4] As it turned out, the rebellion was quickly put down, and the Apocalypse did not arrive.

The old world remained, and it was not good. While being tortured on the rack, Campanella screamed at his tormentors, implored God and the Blessed Mother, swore by *Santo Diavolo* (the "Holy Devil"), begged, and cried. The transcript of the session lets us listen in for a moment on the awful reality of early modern legal practice: "Oh, I'm dying! Traitors, sons of cuckolds, whores. . . . Let me down and I'll tell you whatever you want. . . . Oh, I'm dying! Oh, my balls! Oh, you've killed me. . . . I'll piss myself, brothers. . . . I'll shit my pants if you don't let me shit. . . . I can't take it anymore!" During the interrogation, he muttered incoherently, started singing, and mumbled, "The pope must come, and if the pope doesn't come to set things right, there'll be hell to pay."[5]

Campanella's years in prison are the stuff of a Kafkaesque novel. On a scrap of paper, he scribbled the following verse:

In this dark tomb I cry out my pain,
Echoing between iron and stone in vain.[6]

We can imagine the scene. Outside the castle: the Gulf of Naples, softly swaying from Posillipo to Vesuvius, the blue sea under the shimmering southern heat, the sails of the ships, the calls of the fishermen, the palms, the loud, colorful life of the big city. Behind walls meters thick: the prisoner, images swimming in his head, full of agonizing thoughts, close to madness or feigning it to cheat the executioner.

Campanella actually did manage to survive. He would spend a quarter-century in Neapolitan strongholds, patrons providing him with writing materials and literature. Despite his insanity, or behind the mask of the madman, he retained a maximum of inner freedom during his confinement in the shadow of the volcano. A prisoner through and through, he thought of himself as entirely free.[7] And he wrote continually: on theology, metaphysics, astrology, and magic, in favor of worldwide Spanish monarchy—a political about-face right after his imprisonment—and against atheism, Aristotle, and Machiavelli. His phantasmagorical utopia, the *Città del sole*—*City of the Sun*—makes the

Copernican system the model for a totalitarian, agrarian, communist state with a command economy.

Campanella was one of the great imprisoned writers of modernity. The wise must save the world whose sins have caused it to go mad—thus urges one of his poems—by speaking, living, and acting like madmen, even if in secret they think differently.[8]

> Accompanied and alone, free and bound,
> Screaming and quiet, the haughty mob I confound.
> To the mortal eye of the lower world deranged,
> To the divine spirit on high a sage.[9]

Things turned out unexpectedly well. In 1626, Campanella was released from prison thanks to the intercession of influential admirers and placed as a ward in a Roman monastery. He escaped renewed persecution by fleeing to France, where he received the protection of the almighty Cardinal Richelieu. In 1639, he died in the care of a Parisian monastery.

Campanella's story, a drama about madness, reality, and science, puts the trends of the late Renaissance into high relief. Everything was in turmoil; things that had long been believed without question were up for grabs. Uncertainty was everywhere. *Mutazione*, "change," is a key concept in Campanella's work, as "mutability" is in Shakespeare's plays. Astronomy, equipped with observational data and mathematics, had sprung the universe from its hinges. Earthquakes, new stars, blood rain, plagues of locusts, and monstrous births forebode nothing good. Against this backdrop, the historical theology of Joachim of Fiore attracted renewed interest. The pope was now joined by the Turk as a candidate for the part of the Antichrist, whose appearance must precede the apocalypse. In 1598, the Jesuits of Coimbra even presented a theory of how the end of the world would have to proceed "technically." God would command the heavenly intelligences to stop moving the spheres. Thus all motion would stop, and time along with it.[10] At any rate, Campanella was in no way alone in his hopes for purification and general reformation, which now, in light of the hastening end of the world, was necessary.[11] The causes of uncertainty were not only related to the confusion produced by confessional conflict. There was also a global crisis: a millenarian mood was on the rise outside the Christian *orbs*, too—in southern and western Asia, North Africa, and elsewhere.[12]

Cause for a more optimistic view was occasioned by the boom in scientific activity. Even the apocalyptic visions that haunted Campanella in his tomblike prison took on a note of desperate hope.[13] He was a student of Telesio, whose works were placed on the Index in 1593. As a natural philosopher, he was an empiricist and a Copernican. Before his imprisonment, he had belonged to Della Porta's circle. The news of new worlds, new stars, new systems, and new nations strengthened his belief that a new age was dawning.

Experimental Science, Systematic Research

The paths of the natural sciences had become similar to Columbus's voyages: thought, too, now crossed all horizons. The journey was not without danger. In the days of Bruno and the great witchcraft panics, the question of what was permitted to science had become much more fraught. In 1580, Jean Bodin had published his *Daemonomania magorum*, one of the century's truly hellish books on witchcraft. In 1588, Dr. Faust celebrated his rebirth.[14] In the *Historia von D. Johann Fausten*, published by Johann Spies and soon translated into English and other languages, he sold his soul to the devil for two dozen years and traveled with him through the celestial spheres. He made the most accurate calendars and prognostications, was the master of nature, and amused himself with different women every day. Yet he met a terrible fate. His journey to hell put an end to a life that had literally taken the German Icarus to the stars.

Ultimately, the fictional character of Faust became emblematic of modernity. The scholar who sacrificed his soul for the sake of trifling magic tricks—thus Christopher Marlowe (1554–1593) portrayed him—was transformed in the following centuries into a man struggling for knowledge and freedom, a transgressor of boundaries who wanted to be like God and was doomed tragically to fail. For authors of the late sixteenth century, however, the moral of the story was simpler: good Christians must be on their guard against the demonic power of magic.

The attempt to unlock the secrets of the imaginary world with learned rationality was not without risk. One of those who dared was Giambattista Della Porta, who studied the effect of witches' flying ointments. He mixed them using bat's blood, the rendered fat of dead children, celery, poplar leaves, and hallucinogenic plants like nightshades and aconite.[15] Yet he did not want to use this horrific blend to perform magic. Rather, he intended to show that the supposed night flights of witches were mere hallucinations induced by natural substances. What could have cost Della Porta his head was the fact that his endeavor questioned a core aspect of established witchcraft theory. Dr. Johann Weyer (ca. 1515–1588), a physician from Brabant, based his 1563 book *On the Tricks of Demons* on Della Porta. He sought to demonstrate that supposed witches were actually melancholiacs, i.e., that they were mentally ill and certainly not candidates for the stake. In this way, he provided potential arguments for denying the existence of the entire world of evil creatures and for calling off the war on Satan. The pious were appalled. What a victory for the devil, whose hellish hosts would then be free to rampage unchecked! Bodin's *Daemonomania* offered a response. Weyer's book landed on the Index. At the end of the century, the Jesuit Martin Anton Delrio (1551–1608) corrected the errors of all the wimps and skeptics like Weyer in a three-volume treatise. His work, praised highly by Protestants as well, even criticized the practice of simply beheading witches and not burning them, calling it too mild.[16] In a subsequent edition of his book on magic, Della Porta considered it prudent to remove the passage about witches' ointments. From then on, the Inquisition kept a close watch on him. He had to submit everything he wrote to its review.

It was thus the "rationalist" Della Porta who was in real danger, not Faustian figures. The latter went on their way uneventfully, for the most part far from the dangerous darkness with which Della Porta flirted. One of his intellectual kinsmen was Jacopo Zabarella (1533–1589) of Padua, another great "orderer" of knowledge. His theory of method, based on Aristotle, developed some of the logical foundations for the science that was now in the process of becoming modern. Zabarella asked in what way new things could be known with certainty. He favored a combination of analytical and synthetic methods, which he called *regressus*: a dynamic process that combined the observation of phenomena, the analysis of their causes, and then the explanation of their effects. Galileo was aware of it.[17] It is unlikely, however, that he required Zabarella's work to develop his physics. The mathematics that would be of decisive significance for Galileo did not interest Zabarella.

The collecting and observing recommended by the latter had long been practiced by natural philosophers. A further step in the direction of the scientific method was taken with systematic experimentation.[18] After uncertain indications in medieval sources, there is increasing evidence in the latter sixteenth century that it was turning into a method. For example, the Flemish mathematician Simon Stevin (1548–1620) discovered through a series of experiments that the downward pressure exerted by a fluid did not depend on the shape of the container but rather solely on the water level. Thus hydrostatics was born.

The first person known to have performed whole series of experiments was William Gilbert (1544–1603), Elizabeth I's personal physician. In his 1600 work *On the Magnet*, he went far beyond the foundation previously laid by Pierre de Maricourt.[19] *On the Magnet* is a milestone in the history of experimental science. Gilbert noted the deviation of the compass needle from the geographic North Pole—this had been attributed since the Middle Ages to the existence of a mysterious magnetic mountain between Asia and the Americas—and observed how the force of a magnet got weaker toward the edge of its "sphere of influence," its *orbis virtutis*. Gilbert, therefore, had a rudimentary understanding of what we would now call a "magnetic field."[20] On the other hand, he still assumed the Earth had a soul and believed "magnetick force" was animate. His most significant discovery was to recognize that magnetism is a distinct force from static electricity, such as is produced by rubbing amber. He also invented an apparatus to measure such static electric effects: the *versorium*, an early form of an electroscope. Gilbert's work opened up an entirely new field of research.

More and more support developed for a type of science that did not deduce conclusions from general theories but rather observed individual cases and designed experiments. It is called "Baconian," after its leading exponent. A nephew of Lord Burghley, a trained jurist, a member of Parliament, and, at the peak of his career, lord chancellor to James I, Francis Bacon (1561–1626) was a pioneer of experimental science. He rejected the criteria of age, authority, and common knowledge, arguing instead that the only way to prove something was to demonstrate how it had been discovered.[21] He had as little regard for contemporary university teaching as he did for the learned writers of antiquity. In his view, their knowledge of the past was based on fables, their acquaintance with geography poor, and their experience with printing, gunpowder, and the compass nil.[22] Nevertheless, Bacon made no blanket condemnation of Aristotle or Plato. Copernicus's model of the universe seemed "an absurdity" to him.[23] The cosmos in which Bacon believed, animated by Platonic spirits, was still that of Ptolemy.

His *Novum Organum*, or *New Organon*—whose subtitle promises "True Directions concerning the Interpretation of Nature" (*Indicia vera de interpretatione naturae*)—called upon the reader to acquire the knowledge that nature itself provided in unadulterated form. He sought to understand nature on its own terms: "Nature is only subdued by submission."[24] The illusions produced by the human mind's dreams and delusions, he continued, had to be dismissed, especially those that arose from imprecise language and faulty reasoning. Bacon compared the old books and dogmas with idols. And those *idola* in the temple of wisdom had confused human understanding. He considered nature to be something objective, something that had to be recognizable and explicable to the human mind. Systematic series of experiments would increase the odds of accidental discoveries, which, in his view, were behind all the great inventions of the Middle Ages. *Experimentum* forced nature to reveal things that were not necessarily obvious to casual observation.

Like Della Porta, Bacon conceived of magic as applied science. His chief objections to it were of an ethical nature, as a reliance on the powers of spirits and the force of fantasy seemed to make work and effort superfluous.[25] Analogical models and Paracelsian "dreams" were not his thing. "Final causes," knowledge of which had been the old natural philosophers' great object of yearning, he calls "barren virgins."[26] In contrast to Bodin, for example, who sought explanations for familiar phenomena, Bacon marched into unknown territory to discover new things.[27] For him, natural science was rooted in reason, highly precise observation, and comparisons that led to the formulation of rules. One single exception sufficed for him to reject the rule. That entailed a radical turn away from superstition. Bacon's publisher and first biographer, William Rawley, put his approach in a nutshell.: "Your Lordship's course is to make Wonders Plaine, and not Plaine things Wonder."[28]

Rawley edited Bacon's incomplete utopian novel *New Atlantis*, which contains the description of a large, state-sponsored research institution that is as impressive as it is frightening. This vision had a precursor in Campanella's *City of the Sun*, which features technical marvels like speedy wind-powered wagons and flying machines. Bacon writes of new, artificially created metals and animal species, human-designed plant mutations, and technologically induced climatic change.[29] At "Salomon's House," located on his fictional island of Bensalem, no fewer than 18 teams were at work in underground caves, mile-high towers, gardens, and buildings, all experimenting, distilling, and tinkering.

Bacon suggested clever experiments. Yet he only performed one himself, and it would have been better if he had not. He attempted to discover if a chicken stuffed with snow decomposed slower than an uncooled animal. The endeavor ended in pneumonia for the investigator. Bacon died as a result, and thus the first theorizer of experimental research also became its first victim. In 1621, political intrigues had toppled him as lord chancellor, but he had been allowed to retain his titles and his property. The ensuing free time was devoted to his scientific writing, including the *Instauratio magna* (*Great Instauration* or *Great Renewal of Learning*). This work was intended to provide nothing short of a system and a theory of method for a new science. Only one section of it, consisting of the *Novum Organum*, was finished. Bacon's tireless pen produced incredibly influential appeals for systematic experimentation and the atheoretical collection of observational data. The imaginary Salomon's House described in the *New Atlantis* appears like a blueprint for the Royal Society, a formal academy founded in 1662 that was devoted entirely to scientific research. Like its Parisian counterpart, founded in 1666, it promoted science as an autonomous activity practiced by expert specialists. Members could experiment and publish more or less independently of ideological constraints. In London and especially Paris, the potential benefits to state and society were in the foreground.

Bacon was a purveyor of the idea that knowledge is power.[30] "It is the glory of God to conceal a thing," he wrote, "but it is the glory of a King, to find a thing out.[31] In his view, the ultimate purpose of all research was to improve human life. Science offered the prospect of overcoming original sin and creating for humankind a new world that was the product of technology and experimental research—an actual paradise on Earth, one whose realization would precede the end of the world. Bacon's methodological revolution has no equal, not even in antiquity. He cut a humongous gash right through the old theories. In practical terms, the most impressive advances in astronomy, physics, and medicine were already made in his day.

Turning against Galen

Insight into the standard medical practice of Bacon's day can be gained by looking at what Lady Grace Mildmay (ca. 1552–1620) preserved in the library and pharmacy of Apethorpe Hall, her estate outside Peterborough. In addition to religious literature and the writings of Avicenna and Giambattista da Monte (and maybe Paracelsus as well), she owned a wide assortment of medicines: twenty-four types of roots, sixty-eight types of herbs, flowers, laxatives, very strong wine and vinegar, almonds and violet syrup, quicksilver for syphilis, and opium for madness. A human skull that had never been buried was also used as a healing aid. The most important remedies, however, were prayers, as Lady Grace considered sin the true cause of illness.[32]

Professional physicians continued to treat patients on the basis of Galen's humoral pathology. Yet an avant-garde was also rearing its head, advancing Vesalius's anatomy and raising more and more doubts about Galen's system. One inconsistency after another caused physicians to pick up a scalpel and see for themselves. An especially egregious discrepancy was revealed by a closer look at the heart. According to Galen, blood was produced in the liver and then flowed via the heart and lungs to the brain. Enriched in this way with vital energy—*pneuma*—it supposedly nourished the body and was ultimately consumed. Fresh supplies of blood, so went the theory, were yet again provided by the tireless liver. Vesalius had already noted that, *pace* Galen, there were no openings between the two chambers of the heart to permit blood to flow from one into the other. How Vesalius and his followers dealt with this problem shows once again, now in the realm of medicine, the fine line between the old and the new science. Vesalius initially attempted to find an explanation for the absence of holes that was commensurate with the ancient teaching. One of the arguments he deployed to "save the phenomenon" was that the senses were not capable of perceiving these pores.[33] The second edition (1555) of his work, however, reveals that Vesalius had come to harbor more serious doubts as to the sufficiency of such exculpatory hypotheses. Realdo Colombo—first his student, then his bitter enemy, and finally his successor—thought in the right direction by relieving the blood of its detour through the lungs. (Incidentally, this conjecture had been made three hundred years earlier by Ibn al-Nafis, whose work was not known to Colombo.) For the time being, however, the problem remained unsolved. New insights in other areas of medicine prompted experimentation.

Colombo was a supporter of vivisection. As test animals he recommended dogs and not pigs, in part due to the latter's "horrible-sounding squealing and their grunting."[34] To find out whether the voice ultimately resided in the heart, as Aristotle claimed, he cut one out of a dog. The poor animal still howled for a few seconds before giving up the ghost. On the question under discussion, Aristotle's view was now as dead as the dog.

Ratio and eccentricity were combined in the work of the Fleming Jan Baptist van Helmont (1580–1644).[35] He was also an anti-Galenist, as well as a nervous, devout man who believed he had been enlightened by visions. To hasten their arrival, he seems to have used psychotropic aconite. The Inquisition regarded him as a heretic, placing him under house arrest on his estate outside Brussels for years. One novel aspect of van Helmont's scientific practice was that he performed experiments to verify the recipes of his guiding light Paracelsus. He grasped the principle of specific weight, was the first to investigate the relationship between acids and bases, and tested the narcotic effect of ester on chickens. He coined the term "gas" for the fumes emitted, for example, from burning charcoal, which he considered a "wild spirit." The rational potential of van Helmont's methods, despite their esoteric character, can be seen in their influence on a later scientific pioneer: Robert Boyle (1627–1691, p. 821) of Ireland.

The decisive breakthrough to a new physiology was achieved by William Harvey (1578–1657), whose career brought him to the courts of the English kings James I and Charles I. By recording weights and other measurements, he discovered that the heart's main task was to contract, not to expand, and that this activity pumped more blood through the vessels in a half-hour than the whole body contained in total. If this amount was not expelled—which it clearly was not—it had to be recirculated somehow. In this way, Harvey arrived at the insight that the blood flowed through the body in a constant circuit from birth to death. He believed he had discovered a universal principle: as the stars preserved the world through their movement, the circulation of blood disseminated life, thus preserving the individual.[36] Yet Harvey's discovery did not downgrade the heart, the "Sun of the Microcosm" called man, to the status of a mere pump.[37] Rather, it remained part of the ensouled cosmos of antiquity, in which all of nature was infused with a universal vitality. Like his teacher Girolamo Fabrizio, who discovered venous valves and founded embryology, Harvey was an undeterred follower of Aristotelian natural philosophy. Nevertheless, his medicine constituted yet another step taken in the direction of secularization. Like Bacon's science, Harvey's anatomy dispensed entirely with metaphysics. He sought no traces of the grand artificer God in the human body. Rather, he simply wanted to know how the heart worked.[38]

The story of the discovery of blood circulation highlights further preconditions for the looming paradigm shift in medicine: time and discourse. The latter thrived in academies and universities. Harvey presented and discussed the results of his series of experiments over the course of two decades in lectures before finally publishing his chief work, *On the Motion of the Heart and Blood in Animals*—just as Copernicus had anticipated his magnum opus with the *Commentariolus*. Thanks to the debate about the hypotheses proposed by the "circulator," as Harvey was derisively known, his arguments became more incisive. Ultimately, the idea of blood circulation was accepted not because it was "true." Rather, it was considered true because it was accepted.[39] One important authority, the anatomist Arcangelo Piccolomini (1525–1586), who worked in Rome, emphatically identified debate as an important requirement for scientific progress. As progressive as Harvey was in his own field of research, however, he, like Bacon, remained skeptical about the Copernican model. He even considered blood circulation to be an analogy for the way Aristotle's heavens revolved around the Earth. Nevertheless, decisive evidence had now been found that the Polish astronomer had been thinking in the right direction.

40

The Sun Rises in the West

Tycho Brahe: The Luck of Patronage

The preface to *De revolutionibus orbium coelestium* provides us with an opportunity to highlight certain preconditions for one of the most significant scientific upheavals in human history. There Copernicus wrote that it was his engagement with ancient astronomy that had inspired his ideas. He read the pure, ancient sources, came to terms with ancient cosmology, and improved upon it. Thus, he preserved the uniformity of the cosmos and the circular orbits of the heavenly bodies.[1] His project could be viewed as an attempt to use Aristotelian physics and Ptolemaic mathematics to save Ptolemy, thereby also saving both of these pillars while preserving ancient cosmology. In that sense, Copernicus would be the epitome of Renaissance astronomy. Yet to portray him as a mere restorer of an outdated theory would not do justice to his intellectual achievement. From the standpoint of mathematics, the premises that he changed may seem nothing more than cheap tricks to "save the phenomena." From the point of view of theology and philosophy, they were not. Rather, they constituted a revolution of dramatic proportions. A devout Christian had to be truly audacious and radical to turn the world upside down in that manner. It is no coincidence that Copernicus had only one precursor, Aristarchus of Samos, but never mentioned him. For according to tradition, the Greek thinker had been accused of atheism in his own day.

Copernicus's theory entailed a monstrous consequence: human beings, the crown jewel of Creation, made in God's image and the object of God's plan, now found themselves in the middle of nowhere between the Sun and Saturn. On this very point—removing Earth from the center of the universe—Copernicus's view differed from that of all his Christian predecessors, from Arabic cosmology, and from all available concepts of the cosmos apart from Aristarchus's. In the Islamic world, Earth retained its privileged place for several more centuries. The great astronomers of the Late Middle Ages had no successors there. As a result, Copernicus's sun rose not in the Muslim East but rather in the Latin West. Yet it was no simple task for Europe to complete the paradigm shift either. Nowhere can the importance of debate for the creation of new things be seen better than in the battles over Copernicus's system. His student Joachim Rheticus compared them to the great war fought between the Greeks and the Trojans over the beautiful Helen. The printing press spread knowledge about the new cosmological theory far and wide, thus also increasing the number of people who could discuss it. The fact that Copernicus's book was banned by the Church in 1616 barely hampered debate about it in Catholic Europe, and in Protestant Europe not at all. In every corner of Latin Europe, people were able to develop and refine its ideas.

The decisive figure in preparing the final breakthrough was the Danish nobleman Tycho Brahe (1546–1601).[2] The most important astronomer of the sixteenth century after Copernicus, he was a man of instruments and regular, laborious observation of the night sky. Brahe studied in Copenhagen and at German universities. He traveled extensively, bought books, and maintained a lively correspondence with scholars that—a first in the history of science—he also published. In Augsburg, he had a copper celestial globe and other equipment fashioned by the clockmaker Christoph Schißler. In Kassel, he received help from the astronomy enthusiast Landgrave William IV of Hesse, who recommended him to King Frederick II of Denmark. The king provided Brahe with lavish support, giving him an island in the Øresund as a fief and funds to build two observatories. In addition, Brahe received income from additional fiefs and a salary as a canon of Roskilde Cathedral. His patron even lent him a ship from the royal fleet. According to the order, it was to be "as good as new, and not too old."[3]

No other astronomer in early modern Europe could mobilize anything close to similar resources for their research. Four years after the foundation stone had been laid (at an astrologically propitious moment), Uraniborg's somewhat bizarre construction was finished. Four years after that, the underground observatory Stjerneborg was built. One of Brahe's first biographers remarked that his entourage was like a prince's, only that he was surrounded not by knights and soldiers but by able mathematicians, observers, and instrument makers; his weapons were not spears and bows but instruments and a printing press. Uraniborg anticipated Bacon's vision of a large-scale research institute. Brahe worked there until 1596. His most important duty was to cast a horoscope for the royal family every year.

The powerful equipment at his disposal was meant to resolve inconsistencies between calculations and what could be seen in the night sky. For example, he had noticed that the conjunction of Jupiter and Saturn took place one month before its expected date. So he set to work revising Copernicus's tables of planetary positions, using instruments he worked intensely to improve. The equatorial armillary sphere pictured in his *Mechanics of Renewed Astronomy* shows Brahe's portrait along with Copernicus's: a statement of his adherence to the new astronomy and evidence of the author's sense of his own importance. Brahe was one of the first to use mechanical clocks to measure time precisely for astronomical observations. In this way, another legacy of Europe's medieval past came to bear in the cosmological paradigm shift.

When a "new star" appeared in the constellation Cassiopeia in 1572—an event that whipped all of Europe and even China (p. 897) into a frenzy—Brahe argued that the star had to be beyond the moon and thus in those regions of the heavens that according to Aristotle must be immutable.[4] Yet another stone fell from the Stagirite's monument. The greatest yield of Brahe's work were star catalogs and models of planetary motion that were more precise than anything astronomers' eyes had yet worked out.[5] The upshot was that Copernicus was to be preferred to Ptolemy in many respects. Yet Brahe believed removing Earth from the center of the universe contradicted the wisdom of the Creator. In addition, he disapproved of the large distance between Saturn and the fixed stars, which in his view contradicted the Creator's sense of economy.[6] He therefore contrived his own model of the universe that left the Earth in the center. The Sun and stars revolved around it, whereas the other planets revolved around the Sun. One concession required by his observational data was that the Sun became the center of the planetary orbits. This made the uneconomical empty space beyond Saturn no longer necessary.[7] On the other hand, the model had the disadvantage that the Sun's orbit had to cross the path of Mars twice, as well as those of Mercury and Venus. This caused Brahe to take a radical step: he did away with the planetary spheres, which made such orbits impossible—after all, opinions differed wildly as to what they were made of and whether celestial matter was similar to earthly— and left the planets floating in the ether.[8] Brahe's compromise cosmology was still highly complex. But it was acceptable to many people because it could be reconciled better with the Bible than Copernicus's model. Furthermore, since it was based on extremely accurate observations, it depicted the movements of the heavens more convincingly than Ptolemy's model.

Brahe was one of the big winners in the European patronage system. When he lost the support of the Danish king in 1596, he found succor at various way stations before ending up at the court of the starry-minded Emperor Rudolph.[9] He set up an observatory in Benátky, near Prague. Yet he did not have much time left. In 1601, he died. Shortly before the end, he is said to have asked his assistant Johannes Kepler to complete his observational work.

Kepler Conquers Mars

Kepler was born in 1571 in Weil der Stadt, a city in Württemberg. In 1600, he arrived in Prague a nearly penniless refugee, where he was taken in by Brahe.[10] Up to that point, he had taught mathematics at a school in Tübingen and then worked as an astrologer and calendar-maker for the region of Styria. Its lord, Archduke Ferdinand of Inner Austria, later Holy Roman Emperor, had recklessly taken up the cause of the Counter-Reformation. For example, Kepler had to pay a penalty when he had his deceased daughter buried by a Protestant churchman in a neighboring town not in the domain of the Habsburg zealot.[11] Emperor Rudolph's court, with its relatively tolerant atmosphere in questions of religion, provided a very different scope of opportunity than the tiny principality ruled by the strict, intellectually limited Catholic Ferdinand.

Kepler brought order to the mess of numbers Brahe had left behind. The "Rudolphine Tables" he produced would be the foundation for calculating the orbits of the planets and the Moon for two centuries to come. The Swabian enhanced them with something they had hitherto lacked: mathematical genius.[12] His mind was only one part of the equation, however. The other was hard work continually subjected to critical self-reflection.

Kepler made seminal contributions not only to astronomy but also to physics. For example, he discovered the basic law of photometry—the measurement of light intensity—and developed a theory of vision that was the first to go far beyond Ibn al-Haytham. One of his insights was to recognize that the eye is like a lens.[13] His greatest coup, however, was to discover the actual, regular paths that the planets' orbits followed around the Sun. He began with the orbit of Mars, whose apparent retrograde motion had stymied astronomers forever. Kepler noted that the positions of the red planet ascertained by Brahe and his team deviated by eight arcminutes—1/2700 of a circle—from those required by his theoretical assumptions. It was a minuscule difference, within the tolerance range accepted by ancient astronomy. But Kepler did not accept it, instead regarding this trifle as a "divine gift."[14] He would later realize that those ominous eight minutes alone had shown the way to the renewal of all astronomy.[15] Trust in the Creator's economy conquered Greek rationalism.[16]

The eureka moment that produced the first mathematically based laws of nature cannot be reconstructed.[17] After what Kepler called "infinitely complicated" calculations that had to be compared again and again with observational data, he first postulated an oval-shaped model before finally arriving at the elliptical shape of Mars's orbit. Unlike Brahe and Copernicus, he assumed that the Earth was also in motion. Only these two assumptions—an elliptical orbit and a moving Earth—could provide an explanation for Mars's apparently serpentine path, which Kepler compared to a Lenten pretzel. Epicycles and other clumsy notions such as "latitudes," supposed lateral movements of the planets, could now be dispensed with. On June 4, 1609, Kepler proudly announced his conquest of Mars to Emperor Rudolph, which simultaneously meant a triumph over Aristotle: "I am now at last exhibiting for the view of the public a most Noble Captive, who has been taken for a long time now through difficult and strenuous war waged by me under the auspices of Your Majesty."[18] It had taken him ten years and seventy attempts to solve an arithmetic problem for which a modern computer would need fractions of a second.[19]

The discovery that Mars and the other planets followed elliptical orbits was the true break with the old astronomy and its dogma that the heavens knew only circular motion. Kepler's work on the orbit of Mars led him to formulate his three laws of planetary motion, the first two of which appeared in his *Astronomia nova* of 1609; the third was first published a decade later in his *Harmony of the World*. The three laws state the following: (1) The planets move in elliptical orbits around the Sun, which is one of their foci. (2) The area created as a line between the Sun and a planet sweeps across the latter's orbit is proportional to the time it takes to move that distance. (3) The squares of two planets' orbital periods are in the same proportion to each other as the cubes of their distance from the Sun.

Kepler was the first to regard the orbits of the planets as a physical problem and to formulate rules governing them.[20] His approach was novel in that he did not merely work out mathematical equations; he also asked whether they accorded with observable reality. Gilbert's book on magnets helped him to see calculable forces at work behind the movements of the heavens. The explanation Kepler gave for their enormous magnitude still followed traditional lines: they came from motive "souls" or intelligences. He also worked with abstract concepts of physics. In his view, the elliptical shape of the orbits was formed by the counteracting forces of attraction and repulsion, as well as by the axial rotation of the Sun and the planets. Planets closer to the central star moved faster, and those farther away moved slower, since, as Gilbert taught, magnetic force decreased with distance. Kepler also hypothesized that the Sun's axial rotation produced a vortex that pulled the planets into its orbit. Here we can discern a rudimentary understanding of the force of gravity.

Kepler's epochal *Harmony of the World* makes for strange reading.[21] Chains of mathematical reasoning stand side by side with hymns to God and the ensouled cosmos. The author tenaciously attempts to save the thesis of a perfectly harmonious arrangement of the heavenly bodies; accordingly, observational data is not always in the foreground. His universe still literally reverberates with the celestial music of the spheres, which human ears cannot hear. Now that the planetary orbits' elliptical shape has been proven, a curious reason is given for relieving the angels of their role as movers of the stars: they surely would have chosen perfectly circular orbits.[22] The planetary intelligences also gradually retreat from the new astronomy.

Like Bacon, Kepler distanced himself from the shadowy mysticism of the Hermetists and Paracelsians. He contrasted their thought with the luminous clarity of mathematics.[23] In the midst of the magical speculation of the Faustian age, he distinguished between thinking in terms of analogies and in terms of causalities, between symbols and the symbolized. "I, too, play with symbols . . . , but I play in such a way that I do not forget that I'm playing. For nothing can be proven by symbols."[24] Now the line was drawn between faith and astrophysics as well. Kepler once wrote that he wanted to show that the machine of the universe was not like a divinely ensouled creature but rather a clock.[25] Furthermore, he was a student of the ancients. The investigation of conic sections undertaken by Apollonius of Perge in the late third century BC provided an indispensable foundation for his calculations of the planets' orbits, and Pappus of Alexandria's mathematical *Collection*, written around 300 BC, helped him elaborate methods that paved the way for infinitesimal calculus.

God as a Mathematician

Mathematics, the key discipline of the Scientific Revolution, had long scraped out a meager existence at universities.[26] It had been mostly a technical aid to music or astronomy, helped painters with perspective, sailors with navigation, traders with currency exchange, and artillerymen with their aim. Only in the second half of the fifteenth century was it elevated to a science. In the following century, the first chairs of mathematics were established. Europe's arithmetic artists now stood eye to eye with their Indian and Arabic masters. The trend began in Protestant Germany. In Catholic Europe, Jesuits played a leading role. Foremost among them was Christoph Clavius (1538–1612), one of the scholars who had prepared Pope Gregory's calendar reform. He helped give mathematics an important place in the curriculum of Rome's Jesuit university, which served as a model for its sister institutions. In a new development, math was now to concern itself with empirical facts. Mathematical proof, as known from Euclidean geometry, joined the Aristotelian syllogism and enjoyed the same level of prestige. Expertise in nature and mathematics now complemented one another.[27]

The boom in mathematical studies had been buoyed by the Platonic renaissance of the latter fifteenth century. The Platonic-Pythagorean tradition assumed that the universe was arranged according to measure and number and that the divinity manifested itself in it, its regularity, and its beauty.[28] God, the architect of the world, mutated into a mathematician. Ultimately, natural science and especially astronomy appeared as a search for the equations according to which the Creator had structured being. The idea inspired the greatest minds of the time. Copernicus graced the title page of his chief work with a variation of the motto that was thought to have been inscribed above the entrance to Plato's Academy: *Medeis ageometretos eisito*—"May no one enter who is ignorant of geometry." Kepler believed he had been possessed by "inspired frenzy"—a kind of divine inspiration described by Plato—when he thought he had grasped the principles underlying the structure of the universe.[29] Indeed, the Book of Wisdom says that God ordered everything according to measure, number, and weight.[30] The most profound motivation behind Kepler's and others' calculation efforts was thus the hope of deciphering the language of the Creator in cosmological phenomena. In Kepler's view, the fact that Ptolemy, a pagan, had been unable to grasp the key to God's massive design was the decisive difference between ancient cosmology and his own.[31]

The yearning to understand God's geometry sometimes set him on strange paths. The fact that five empty spaces gaped between the six planets then known electrified him: were there not the same number of perfect Platonic solids, namely the cube, dodecahedron, tetrahedron, icosahedron, and octahedron? Thus Kepler, then just a twenty-five-year-old novice, sought to prove that the planetary orbits could each be inscribed perfectly in one of these solids, which should also be harmoniously proportional to one another. His *Mysterium cosmographicum* depicts the universe as harmonious, elegant, and therefore beautiful.[32] This astronomical aesthetics corresponded to the same criteria according to which Alberti, in a totally different context, had defined beauty. Just as nothing could be added to or taken away from a beautiful building without making it uglier, the cosmos must also be constructed such that nothing was in it without reason. The economy of the universe's architecture, which clearly resembled a Renaissance building, consequently had an aesthetic basis that, for its part, rested on religious convictions. Nothing in nature should ever be idle or superfluous. Meaning was everywhere; pure reason was ubiquitously at work.[33]

The iron laws of mathematics even set limits to the power of divine creation. The Lord is not the lord of the mathematically impossible. Therefore, the structure of the universe did not seem random to Kepler either. He nearly said that God created what he could and omitted what he could not.[34] This touches upon a fascinating riddle that was then being discussed by Italian humanists and that still occupies cosmology today: how is it possible, insofar as human observation and experimentation can tell, that natural phenomena obey mathematical laws? Is God perhaps not a mathematician, but rather the universe a system of mathematics?[35] Kepler was convinced, as Einstein later would be, that God does not play dice. For the Renaissance, the solution lay in the still intact belief that it was ultimately the Creator who granted the ability to know truth, descry perfection, and thus understand his books, i.e., nature and the Bible.

Kepler's new universe was indeed possessed of classical clarity. Epicycles and deferents had become superfluous, as had the constant speeds and circular paths of planetary motion. On the other hand, his cosmos was two thousand times larger than Ptolemy's. The Copernican universe would have extended more than 247 billion kilometers. Around 1245, Gossuin of Metz thought Adam, the first man, had been capable of reaching the sphere of the fixed stars via daily marches of 25 miles in 713 years, which corresponded to a diameter of only about 6.5 million miles.[36] Galileo calculated the distance between Earth and the sphere of the fixed stars to be 49,832,416 kilometers; Kepler said it was 142,746,428 kilometers. He had to reject Bruno's view that the cosmos was infinite—agreeing with Cusanus, on whose philosophy he steadily drew in his work.[37] The infinite was not only invisible, immeasurable, and thus incapable of proof. More importantly, the notion of a limitless and thus shapeless cosmos contradicted Kepler's aesthetics.

The tone of his *Dream* is playful and cheerful. It is the first-ever work of science fiction and a demonstration of the new world system.[38] It anticipates that noble moment, Christmas 1968, when human beings first saw the Copernican cosmos with their own eyes from a spaceship orbiting the Moon. Kepler conceives of the instant the Earth rises behind the Moon as the most incredible event his fictional astronaut can witness. The home planet appears in shifting shapes, now a crescent, now a sphere—and for the same reason the Moon does to observers on Earth, namely the varying degrees to which it is illuminated by the Sun.[39]

The Invention of the Telescope

One of the first closer looks at the Moon was had on a July night in the year 1609. We are rather well informed about it. Galileo Galilei, then professor of mathematics in Padua, aimed his telescope at Earth's satellite. At about the same time, Thomas Harriot (ca. 1562–1621) of England sketched an astonishingly precise topography of the Moon, he, too, with the aid of the recently invented telescope. Yet he never published this or other discoveries. Galileo was different. "Great indeed are the things which in this brief treatise I propose for observation and consideration by all students of nature." Thus began his *Sidereus nuncius*, or *Starry Messenger*, of 1610.[40]

> I say great, because of the excellence of the subject itself, the entirely unexpected and novel character of these things, and finally because of the instrument by means of which they have been revealed to our senses.

The work is dedicated to Grand Duke Cosimo II de' Medici of Tuscany (1590–1621), who had invited Galileo to his court.

The "great things" Galileo writes about were, first, the discovery of countless fixed stars never seen before, "in numbers ten times exceeding the old and
familiar stars"; second, his view of the "rough and uneven" surface of the
Moon, which looked "just like the Earth's surface, with huge prominences,
deep valleys, and chasms"; and third, new "planets," the moons of Jupiter,
which the author named the "Medicean Stars" in honor of his patron. Further
staggering discoveries followed: the rings of Saturn, which Galileo also
thought were moons at first, and the phases of Venus. With a precision not to
be exceeded for a long time, he calculated Venus's diameter and then that of
Jupiter. The view through his telescope's lens suggested to this first Columbus
of the cosmos that the physics of the heavens was, in contrast to what the ancients held, in no way fundamentally different from that on Earth. Cracks
could be seen on the Moon's surface, as could black spots on the Sun—the
latter was an observation Galileo made at the same time as Harriot and the
Bavarian Jesuit Christoph Scheiner; John of Worcester's observation in 1128
(p. 227) had been forgotten. The moon's imperfections, which could hardly be
overlooked by the naked eye, had been attributed by the Middle Ages to the
satellite's position between the heavenly and the earthly realms. "It shares the
nature of both," Robertus Anglicus explained in the thirteenth century, and
thus both "clearness . . . and darkness appear in it."[41] The undeniable discovery
of spots on the Sun, a body that ought to consist of the purest quintessence,
destroyed yet another axiom of ancient natural philosophy. "You have opened
our eyes and shown us a new Heaven and a new Earth!" Campanella wrote to
Galileo from his Neapolitan dungeon.[42] The instrument that had enabled Galileo's celestial sojourns was described right on the first pages of his *Sidereus
nuncius*.

It is emblematic of a symbiosis without which there would have been no
Scientific Revolution: the collaboration between expert craftsmanship and
book learning.[43] Many "streams" had to flow together for the telescope to be
invented. Its prehistory extends far back and includes the long birth of eyeglasses, as without knowledge of their optical principles the telescope could
not have been constructed. Indeed, it was spectacle-makers who developed
concave and convex lenses and worked to improve the quality of glass. It was
noticed that the proper technical specifications allowed distant objects to be
enlarged. The first to ponder a telescopic system seems to have been Fracastoro. The decisive idea probably came from Hans Lipperhey (ca. 1570–1619),
a spectacle-maker in Middelburg. He realized that an aperture was indispensable for obtaining clearly focused images. Equally important was refractive

power—at least two or three diopters—and the quality of the glass. Experiments have shown that, of the fifty-seven eyeglass lenses still extant from the sixteenth century, only five would have lent themselves to making a telescope. No wonder that it was ultimately a craftsman who made the breakthrough, as he had a full stock of lenses at his disposal in his workshop.[44]

Europe adopted the telescope with the same lightning speed as it had the printing press.[45] Its usefulness—for navigation and war—was too obvious. Galileo himself improved the invention.[46] His version magnified images twenty times, as opposed to the three times magnification of its predecessor. While the Swabian Sisyphus Kepler was knee-deep in calculations, the telescope gave Galileo the "coup de main of intuition."[47]

The *perspicillum* was a revolutionary invention. After millennia, astronomy entered into a new phase of its history, one we still find ourselves in today. For the acceptance of the heliocentric theory, the view through the telescope was decisive. It made visible what had theretofore only been brought to light by numbers. In 1603, Galileo was still giving his astronomy lectures on the basis of Ptolemy. What the telescope, soon in increasingly improved versions, showed to the eye confirmed what Copernicus had observed and calculated.[48] Jupiter and its moons were like a miniature solar system, and the phases of Venus were indicative of the planet's orbit around the Sun. When doubts were raised about what he had seen, Galileo was ready with a response. If the body of the Sun appeared spotty and imperfect, then one had to call it such. The nature of a thing should not be adapted to its name but rather its name to its nature. His discoveries, he proudly wrote—Galileo possessed no shortage of self-confidence—signified nothing less than the burial, indeed the Last Judgement, of Aristotelian "pseudoscience."[49] After gazing through a telescope for the first time, Kepler cheered, "O *perspicillum*, instrument of great knowledge, more valuable than any scepter! Is not he who holds you in his right hand king and master of God's work?"[50]

Despite this new perspective—literally, this new way of seeing things—the Copernican model did not lack opposition. The arch-Aristotelian Cesare Cremonini is said to have refused to even look through the telescope.[51] Clavius said it would be the demise of all natural philosophy if the methods that had led people to believe in epicycles and eccentricities were challenged.[52] He was right about that.

Galileo personally embodied several core aspects of the European Renaissance. First, as we have just heard, he was a powerful force in overcoming the old Aristotelian worldview against the objections of conservative thinkers. Second, as his telescope shows, he combined theoretical knowledge with practical craftsmanship. Finally, when he was offered a position at the Medici court in 1610 and therewith a professorship in Pisa—where he had taught mathematics in his early days—Tuscany, the grand old home of reason and novelty, once again became the stage for world-changing discoveries.

Galileo's New Physics

Galileo was born in Pisa in 1564. He was introduced to the world of science very early on. His father, Vincenzo, a cloth dealer from a family with somewhat noble roots, nurtured musical, scientific, and mathematical interests. The first seeds of the revolution in physics that Galileo started may have been planted by Vincenzo's teacher Gioseffo Zarlino (1517–1590). For he attempted the same thing in his field, music, that Galileo would do in the field of physics: to combine theory and practice and compare each in light of the other.[53] The mathematical beauty of a musical harmony was not enough for Zarlino. He wanted to know if what had been calculated actually did sound good, and that was often not the case. Thus, regardless of its internal consistency, he abandoned the time-honored Pythagorean system and developed an alternative.

In Galileo's case, it was a critical engagement with Alexandrian mathematics that spurred his intellectual development. His teacher during his university studies in Florence, Ostilio Ricci, was himself a student of the great mathematician Niccolò Tartaglia (1499/1500–1557), who had edited the writings of Archimedes. The latter's physics was of central importance for Galileo's work. Archimedes embodied a method: analyzing natural processes and deriving rules from them. Experiments had led him to formulate the principle now named for him, according to which the buoyancy of a body floating in water is equal to the force exerted by the fluid it displaces. Galileo built upon that principle when he dealt with the problem of determining specific weight.

He combined the gifts of a brilliant mathematician and observer with those of a pragmatist. He was always thinking about practical applications. He had compasses of his own design fashioned, of which he sold about one hundred for the price of thirty-five *lire* each.[54] In addition to his telescope, he developed a hydrostatic scale, a thermometer, and a pump. In his later years, he even worked on a design for a pendulum clock. He had laid the foundation for it with experiments conducted on the laws of the pendulum during his early years in Pisa.

His horizon stretched far beyond that of a physicist and inventor. He was interested in poetry, painting, and sculpture. He held a lecture in Florence on the topography of Dante's *Inferno*, which he reconstructed using methods of geometry—an intersection of modern science and medieval cosmology. As a scholar, Galileo was a specialist and, thus, the opposite of a polyhistor. In an attempt to demonstrate his beloved Ariosto's superiority to Torquato Tasso, he used a comparison that sheds light on his self-understanding as a scientist. He caricatured Tasso's poetry as a cabinet of curiosities belonging "to some small, curious man" who collected random objects: a petrified crab, a desiccated chameleon, a fly and spider trapped in amber, Egyptian clay figures, drawings by Baccio Bandinelli and Parmigianino. In contrast, Ariosto's museum was a kingly gallery of ancient statues, paintings, and precious gems.[55] In this sense, Galileo's own brand of rational science corresponded to the classic High Renaissance, devoid of all mysticism and Mannerism.

Galileo's eye-popping achievement, like that of his contemporary Kepler, consisted in exploding the foundation of a two-thousand-year-old paradigm. In contrast to Clavius and his ilk, it was not clear to them *a priori* how the world in which they lived and worked was constructed. That had to be discovered. Like the Presocratics, the Athenians, and the Alexandrians before them, they marched into entirely uncharted territory. The appearance of these two heroes of the Scientific Revolution shows once again that the farthest realm of possibility requires "great individuals" who indeed realize what is possible: radical free thinkers who unite various "streams" and follow them down wherever their united force flows. For centuries, people had speculated about the rules that govern motion. But Galileo was the first to systematically perform experiments for which he created conditions that were as close as possible to an ideal mathematical context. For example, he reduced disruptive influences on a path of motion as much as possible in order to see whether observation accorded with mathematical tenets. He asked what exactly happened when a stone is dropped versus a feather, and why one falls faster than the other. The difference, he realized, was simply aerodynamic drag. In 1971, the astronaut David Scott repeated Galileo's experiment under nearly perfect conditions—on the Moon. He dropped a falcon feather and a hammer. In a vacuum and thus unimpeded, both landed in the gray dust at his feet at the same time. "Mr. Galileo was correct in his findings," Scott reported from outer space. This was also powerful evidence for Galileo's hypothesis that the physics of the heavens obeyed the same laws as the physics of the sublunar world.

Mr. Galileo did not ask *why* objects fall to the ground.[56] What force pulled them down remained an open question. He counted and calculated and repeated his experiments until he achieved a satisfactory result. A manifesto for his new physics appeared in 1623 in the form of a polemic entitled *Il Saggiatore* (*The Assayer*). It dealt with the appearance of a comet five years earlier. In its pages, Galileo attacked the position of various Jesuit astronomers articulated by Orazio Grassi. Grassi's view was actually closer to the truth than Galileo's, who interpreted the comet as a reflection in the vapor of Earth's atmosphere, but that is a mere ironic footnote to a controversy that was a highlight in Europe's grand dialogue.[57] Like Kepler and Copernicus, Galileo believed that the universe was constructed according to mathematical principles. Science, *filosofia*, he wrote, was no work of the human imagination like the *Iliad* or *Orlando Furioso*. To be able to read the book of the universe, one had to learn the language in which it was written.

> It is written in mathematical language, and its letters are triangles, circles, and other geometric shapes. Without these tools, it is impossible for human beings to understand a word. Without them, one must inevitably wander aimlessly through a dark labyrinth.[58]

These sentences recall how Copernicus banned those ignorant of geometry from his astronomy.

Galileo in no way understood mathematical laws as an ideal framework beyond the world experienced by the senses. Rather, in his view they constituted the essence of things. His and Kepler's revolutionary achievement was to establish mathematics in its place at the center of the makeup of the real world.[59] The calculating mind is capable of figuring out what remains hidden from the senses and correcting them when they err. That is why Galileo bowed down before Copernicus. As he put it, "I am infinitely amazed at how the power of reason in Aristarchus and Copernicus was able to bridle the senses so well that it took their place as master of their views."[60] Galileo's cosmos required no more intelligences to animate magnets or heave planets through the night sky.[61] In contrast to Kepler's cosmos, his universe was no longer anthropocentric. Instead, his model was conceived according to mathematical necessities and was therefore equally elegant.

Now that Aristotle was history, the physical laws of the heavens and the sublunar world no longer differed.[62] On this firm foundation, Galileo investigated laws of free fall and motion and, ultimately, a new model of the universe. Hot and cold no longer resided in matter. Like taste, smell, and color, Galileo saw them merely as labels that human beings affixed to things.[63] He banned the sphere of the fixed stars from his cosmos, as it was irreconcilable with observation and calculation.[64] The universe seemed to him unique, true, and real. It could not be other than it was. Was it infinite or not? He, too, considered the question undecidable.

Apprehending reality—for him, that meant asking question after question, raising doubts, discerning probable things, plumbing possibilities.

> When I ask what the substance of clouds may be and am told that it is a moist vapor, I shall wish to know in turn what vapor is. Peradventure I shall be told that it is water, which when attenuated by heat is resolved into vapor. Equally curious about what water is, I shall then seek to find that out.[65]

Through a process of asking questions and observing phenomena, the qualities of far-off bodies like the planets could be perceived, as could those of the tiniest corpuscles, *corpicelli minimi*.[66] The *Saggiatore* based a remarkable hypothesis on the latter: the author was "inclined to believe" that what we feel as "heat" is nothing other than "a multitude of minute [fire] particles having certain shapes and moving with certain velocities."[67] In one of the final chapters of the treatise, he speaks of "truly indivisible *atoms*"[68] as the smallest building blocks of matter. Galileo left it at these speculations. He did not seek to penetrate any closer to the ultimate core of physical phenomena. Nevertheless, he admits that the solution would fascinate him. Modern particle physics is still trying to figure it out.

Galileo's frontal assault on the old physics was anything but harmless. What he wrote about atoms must have reminded contemporaries of the godless Lucretius. The stench of Bruno's stake still hung over Rome's Campo de' Fiori. In 1619, Giulio Cesare Vanini, a follower of Pomponazzi's philosophy, was executed in Toulouse. When his tongue was cut out so that he could never again proclaim heresies, he is said to have bellowed like a bull on the block.[69] The answer that Vanini was accused of giving to the question raised by the existence of misery and unhappiness in the world—"Why do I suffer?"—was supposedly that there may not be a God.

The Trial

The times were such that Galileo easily could have ended up in a dungeon or worse. Yet Rome left him in peace for a long time. He was first put on trial in 1616, relating to his attempt to harmonize biblical interpretation with the knowledge of nature. It seemed to blur the distinction made by Cesare Baronio, according to whom "the Holy Spirit sought to teach how to go to Heaven and not how the heavens go."[70] Galileo's bold concordance had threatened the

Church's monopoly on biblical expertise, which had only recently been bolstered by the Council of Trent. Should mathematicians and astronomers possess the authority to interpret the Bible in light of their discoveries? The trial ended in leniency. Following the line established in 1277, Galileo was permitted to put the Sun in the middle of the universe *hypothetically*. A mathematical model might be acceptable. Treating the thought experiment as physical reality would have been heresy.[71] Largely responsible for the trial's outcome was Cardinal Roberto Bellarmino (1542–1621), famous as a commentator of Thomas Aquinas and as a co-founder of the Jesuit theory of education—in addition to being one of the loudest controversial theologians of his time.[72]

Only in 1632 did the Inquisition get serious. One reason for the Holy See's increased rigidity may have been the escalating war in Germany, which at the time seemed to be turning in the Protestants' favor. Furthermore, the competition between Dominicans and Jesuits was to Galileo's detriment, as neither order was willing to be outdone by the other in terms of religious fervor. The second trial was occasioned by the *Dialogue Concerning the Two Chief World Systems*, perhaps the most significant work of popular science of all times and the text with which our history began. Only a small amount of ill will is necessary to identify the simpleton "Simplicio" as Pope Urban VIII, originally a supporter of Galileo.

Once again, the physicist was opposed by no confederacy of dunces but rather by highly educated individuals. His judges were simply not willing to give up a type of science that was broadly accepted and that also harmonized with accepted religious dogma. For one, Galileo's corpuscular theory of matter shocked readers because it seemed irreconcilable with the Catholic interpretation of the Eucharist.[73] Indeed, if all things were composed of immutable corpuscles, then due to bread corpuscles bread would stay bread, and due to wine corpuscles wine would stay wine. This kind of physics made transubstantiation impossible and, if one did not simply hope for a miracle, played into the hands of the Protestants.

Decisive for the trial's outcome, however, was Galileo's Copernican position. The tribunal suspected him of heresy because he considered true a teaching that, in its eyes, was false and contradicted Holy Writ, namely "that the Sun is the center of the world and does not move from east to west and that the Earth moves and is not the center of the world."[74] The verdict was not meant for Galileo alone. It was a signal sent out against the modern zeitgeist. It was a way to rebuke intellectual circles in Rome in which it had become modish to stand with Copernicus. Even more alarming, an axe was being taken to the

Aristotelian system and thus to the Scholastic philosophy built upon it. Its chief exponent, Thomas Aquinas—Trent rears its defiant head again—had officially been declared a Doctor of the Church in 1567.

Galileo's condemnation in June 1633 took place in the Dominican monastery of Santa Maria sopra Minerva in Rome and thus, so to speak, under the watchful eyes of Thomas himself. In one of the church's side chapels, a fresco cycle by Filippino Lippi celebrates the saint in triumph over the heretics.[75] In his hands he holds his *Summa contra gentiles*, the mightiest weapon forged in the Middle Ages against Jews, Muslims, and other "unbelievers." One of their number, Averroes, would appear barely two decades later in Raphael's *School of Athens*, in which pagans and Christians gather peacefully. At that moment, the balmy breeze of the High Renaissance was blowing, even through the columns of the Vatican. At the time of Galileo's trial, in the cold of the Iron Century, theology once again triumphed over modern science—and not only in Lippi's fresco. Galileo was forced to abjure his "heresies" on his knees, his head bowed, a noose around his neck. After this bleak ceremony, legend has it that the tragic hero of science uttered the words, *Eppur si move*—"And yet it moves."[76] Recorded for certain, however, are proud words he wrote in a copy of his *Dialogue*:

> In the matter of introducing novelties. And who can doubt that it will lead to the worst disorders when minds created free by God are compelled to submit slavishly to an outside will? When we are told to deny our senses and subject them to the whim of others? When people devoid of any competence whatsoever are made judges over experts and are granted authority to treat them as they please?[77]

The act of penance in Santa Maria sopra Minerva signified the fall of a courtier who had risen to become an intellectual star.[78] For Galileo, endowed with winning manners and sparkling wit, had made his career as a *cortegiano*. Now he barely saved his skin. The Holy Office placed him under arrest and enjoined him to engage in neither "public nor secret conversations."[79] He was exiled to an estate in Arcetri, outside Florence. Students surrounded him. Visitors turned up, including Thomas Hobbes and John Milton. His daughter Virginia had found a home in a nearby convent. In the decade that remained to him, he wrote his chief work on physics, the *Discourses and Mathematical Demonstrations Relating to Two New Sciences*.

In 1630, Kepler died during a stay in Regensburg, where he had gone to approach Emperor Ferdinand about back pay. Although Kepler was Galileo's most significant supporter, the latter never did him justice. In his *Dialogue Concerning the Two Chief World Systems*, Galileo defended the (incorrect) thesis that the tides were evidence that the Earth moved, meanwhile ridiculing as "childish" (*fanciullezze*) Kepler's correct hypothesis that they were caused by the Moon's attractive force.[80] Nor did he adopt the elliptical orbits Kepler assigned to the planets, if he even knew about them at all. After Rudolph II's death, Kepler moved to Catholic Linz. In 1626, he found a patron in Emperor Ferdinand's general Albrecht von Wallenstein. The epitaph on his tomb, written by Kepler himself, reads,

> I used to measure the heavens, now I measure the shadows of the Earth. Although my soul was from heaven, the shadow of my body lies here.[81]

Kepler and Galileo drove a development from a world of "approximation" to a "universe of precision."[82] More and more frequently, the metaphor of a clock was used to describe it.[83] Galileo, who had seen farther than any astronomer before, was destined to go blind in his final years. He died on January 9, 1642, still suspected of heresy. The Church forbade any official ceremony honoring him, so his burial in Santa Croce had to take place in silence. He only received a tomb much later. And that is where his mortal remains lie: in the pantheon of the Florentines, also a memorial temple to the Renaissance, the eternal resting spot of several protagonists of our story. Nearby, Leonardo Bruni awaits the Resurrection, while across the way, Machiavelli's bones turn to dust. Michelangelo is buried a few steps further.

The Phoenix in Europe

Kepler and Galileo's true achievement did not consist merely in their idea of correlating mathematics with observable reality. Others before them, including Ptolemy, had attempted the same. The difference was that now, around 1600, *they succeeded*.[84] Even today, modern physics continues to be based on the pillars they erected: empirical knowledge, experimentation, and calculation. The discursive revolution intensified. In the opinion of the Jesuit Paulus Hoffaeus, "It is in the natures of these things and the nature of the best talents that they cannot do otherwise than always to discuss something new."[85] One mind learned from another, and another still from both of them. People wrote letters to each other, and they fought about everything, until the century's end and even in far-off Mexico.[86] That is how ideas in the mind became machines, how presumptions became procedures. Some discoveries were made twice, nearly contemporaneously. For example, we find notes in a diary of Isaac Beeckman, a friend and encourager of Descartes, that indicate he had developed a theory of motion in 1613 that was very similar to Galileo's.[87] The law of refraction, discovered in the tenth century by the Persian scholar Ibn Sahl, was rediscovered three times in short succession: by Descartes, Willebrord Snell, and Thomas Harriot. Conflicts increasingly arose over who deserved credit for inventing something new. For example, Della Porta said he was the first to build a telescope. The same was claimed by Zacharias Janssen of the Netherlands.[88] The notion that there was something like intellectual property was expressed in numerous book privileges. They did not tend to be especially effective, however. Vesalius had already complained that they were not worth the paper they were printed on.[89]

Finally, the star of mathematics rose in response to confessional conflict and philosophical skepticism. Geometry became fashionable, in the form of the crystalline beauty of fortifications, facades, and Baroque parks. Gone were the ambiguities and riddles of Bomarzo, gone its surreal wonderlands, its moss-covered melancholy. Nature was trimmed in circles and straight lines. The spirit of geometry left its mark in the measured steps of dances and in painting. Soon after Caravaggio had played the overture to the High Baroque in Rome, the English architect Inigo Jones (1573–1652) and the French painter Nicolas Poussin (1594–1664) commemorated their classical preferences. Poussin believed that colors could be compared to the emotive expression of musical keys; he was thinking of the theory of harmony elaborated by Vincenzo Galilei's teacher Zarlino. Thus, mathematics found its way into the palette of paintings.[90] Campanella's circular *città del sole* was reflected in the ideal cities of Italy and in Freudenstadt, a square-shaped planned town in Württemberg whose construction began in 1599. "Christianopolis," the ideal state designed by the theologian Johann Valentin Andreae, adopted the latter's form,[91] whereas the geometric philosophy of René Descartes (1596–1650) could be seen in Jones's classicizing architecture, which was also influenced by Palladio's art.

Descartes embodied the *other* possibility of philosophizing, as opposed to a *philosophie de la conscience*, or philosophy of the self—that subjective, experience-based philosophy of the senses[92] whose preeminent forerunner we have already met in Montaigne. Descartes hoped, albeit in vain, that the rationality of his system would put an end to the baleful quarrel between theologians and philosophers.[93] It was intended to be based on clear arguments and certain principles. In his *Discourse on Method*, printed in 1637, he emphasized the certainty that arises from systematic doubt—an insight first attained by the clever Blasius (p. 337): if one *thinks*, one can be sure of existing. Thinking proves being, and being can be experienced as thinking.[94] The Cartesian system distinguishes *res extensa*, matter that requires space, from *res cogitans*, intellectual substance with its thinking and desiring. Any psychic power attributed to things, all animation via spirits or occult energies, is obliterated.[95] Space and matter are the same thing, infinite and infinitely divisible; there is no such thing as a vacuum, i.e., space entirely devoid of matter. Descartes's universe functions like a machine. Even the human body is like a machine. All events are governed by natural laws. The tiniest building blocks of the material world are corpuscles of all different kinds. They are surrounded by spaces filled with the finest matter. Descartes explained the motion of heavenly bodies as a vortex in the "ether" that fills outer space. Motion occurred when corpuscles changed their position and, since there was no empty space in his natural philosophy, displaced others and were replaced in turn.

Descartes's universe was no less a perfectly geometric construction than the cosmos of Kepler and Galileo.[96] For Descartes, the prime mover and lawgiver of nature was its heavenly Creator. He believed he could prove the latter's existence with his method. He took God, certainly no deceiver, as a guarantor for human reason's actual ability to grasp truth. Yet this God was no longer present in his Creation. At most, his angels were at work in his place.[97]

Cartesian physics, with its colliding corpuscles and counteracting vortices, was closer to Epicurean thought than any other scientific model the age had to offer. From there it was only a small step to letting the perfectly constructed clockwork run on its own, and maybe even to questioning the very existence of God. Calvinist and Catholic zealots alike regarded it with mistrust. How things had changed! The same Aristotle whose teachings had been condemned in 1277 was now being protected by the Church against "modern" thinkers like Descartes.[98] The French philosopher had to watch his step. He devoted acrobatic efforts to proving that the magic act of the Eucharist could be reconciled with his physics.[99] His chief works landed on the Index anyway. He abandoned thoughts of publishing a synthesis of his philosophy, *The World*, when he heard the news of Galileo's trial. After fierce controversies with Calvinist authorities in his adopted home of the Netherlands, Descartes preferred to move to Sweden. The next year he departed this life.

41

In the Age of Leviathan

Between Renaissance and Baroque

For the common man and woman, life was not easy in the icy, iron seventeenth century. The number of the poor, the number of those at acute risk of starvation in any period of famine, was extremely high in urban societies. For example, London, the city of Shakespeare, Bacon, and Newton, was, for thousands of immigrants, nothing but an overpopulated, foul-smelling deathtrap. Revolts, unrest, and revolutions become more frequent—not just in Europe but also around the globe. The sturdier among the poor were confined to houses of correction and workhouses. Such institutions were set up in increasing numbers as a means to combat idleness and disorder. A complete picture of the society of the outgoing age would include outsiders: vagrants, the insane, the handicapped, and knackers. A reflection of the glory of high stagecraft was provided to the people by traveling comedians, such as the English acting troupes that could be encountered all over Europe. Besides farces featuring the indispensable clown "Pickelhering," they might also perform scenes from Shakespeare or Marlowe. Mechanical clocks helped to carve time for leisure— free time—out of the workday. Beginning in the seventeenth and eighteenth centuries, the middle classes also participated in "the conquest of the night."[1] Some of their hours were increasingly devoted to reading and amusement, whereas simpler folk would continue for a long time to rise with the sun and rest when it set.

No matter how much the cosmologists demystified the universe, the old notion of the hierarchy of being still held the day against all attempts at emancipation, against pleas for democracy, the abolition of slavery, and civic freedoms. It also provided arguments for the repression of women, portraying them as incomplete versions of men and the latter as the measure of humanity.[2] Reality occasionally overcame such discrimination. In fact, we have already encountered significant stateswomen like Elizabeth I and Catherine de' Medici, as well as patrons of art like Isabella d'Este and Margaret of Navarre, protector of the persecuted. In general, however, women took only little part in shaping Renaissance culture.[3] Universities, academies, and thus scientific discourse were largely closed to them, as was guild membership. Their everyday place was in the home, their usual tools the wooden spoon, broom, and spinning wheel. The history of philosophy proceeded without women, as did the history of architecture and that of the Scientific Revolution. A few female poets are known. In addition to Margaret of Navarre and Vittoria Colonna, we have verse from Olympia Fulvia Morata, Louise Labé, and Isabella Whitney, among others. Nevertheless, in comparison to men their work was marginal and their number few. Of course, this had absolutely nothing to do with a lack of talent and very much to do with social conditions and with role models that, from our viewpoint, seem absurd. The same can be said of female artists, like the sculptor Properzia de' Rossi and the painters Sofonisba Anguissola and Catharina van Hemessen. The most important of them, Artemisia Gentileschi (1593–ca. 1653), belonged to the generation after the conjuror of light, Caravaggio.

The scenery of the new century also continued to include the self-representation of the ascendant Baroque state. Supplied with sovereignty, ink, and armies, it seemed invincible. It portrayed itself with ceremonial entrances, hunts, parades, and parties, with dance, music, plays, banquets, and fireworks. A justification for all this had been found back in the fourteenth century in Aristotle's *Nicomachean Ethics*. As the Dominican friar Roger Dymock wrote in a treatise dedicated to Richard II, lavish displays visually communicated the prince's magnificence to the common people, encouraged respect for him, and intimidated rivals.[4]

The Baroque Age celebrated the ruler's magnificence to excess. The cost exceeded anything seen before. Princely palaces vied with each other in grandeur and splendor, no matter how much strain this luxury spending put on the fisc. It was the decadent climax of a cultural style that had first appeared in the western European Middle Ages and the Italian Renaissance. The Leviathan also continued to demonstrate its power via public executions. They provided spectacle with real blood and death, congealed into a legal act. Pickpockets and bandits were dragged to the scaffold, as were homosexuals, witches, and wizards. Impaling, burning, and quartering remained in the repertoire, even in this enlightened age. Spectators were admonished and entertained. The dead body was an object of fascination—in the grim remains of the executed, the mummified husk of the saint, and the carved-up cadaver in the anatomical theater. The corpse played a leading role in literature and art, which made use of it to recall the impermanence of all earthly things.

Confessional divides put their stamp on Europe's physiognomy. Parsonages, courts, and universities became biotopes of Protestant intellectual culture. In the lands of Luther, Zwingli, and Calvin, the saints had abandoned the heavens, relics had lost their magic, and the throne of the Holy Mother stood vacant.[5] This change was reflected in the arts. Secular themes became more common. They dominated production in Protestant regions, most strikingly in the Netherlands. The number of pictures painted there reached fabulous heights, an estimated two and a half million by around 1650.[6] Artists depicted ribald feasts and wild carousing in every color of the rainbow. They portrayed middle-class tidiness, turning the marble floors of townhouses into mirrors, and captured in oil the sea and the glorious naval battles that took place on it. Dutch windmills—in reality technical, utterly unromantic structures—joined the scenery, symbols of the young nation's pride in its modernity. Above all, however, painters unfurled sweeping landscapes above which white, gray, and rose-colored clouds played their games. A blaze of sun breaking through the murk—as in Jacob van Ruisdael's (1628/29–1682) *Ray of Light*—might mean that God's grace lay upon them. In this way, religion found its way in coded form back into an art that seemed utterly devoted to the beauty of the world. Reminders of the world's transience and vanity were hidden in still lifes and even in depictions of children playing with soap bubbles. Dutch art had long been in intense dialogue with the humanist culture of Italy, which taught it how learned allusions could be put into pictures.

As for spiritual life, the major religions and their organs continued to care for the needs of the masses. Here and there, in the Swiss Confederacy and in various German imperial cities, mixed-confessional societies developed in which strict laws forced citizens to keep the peace. Unlike its Protestant opponents, Catholic Europe built thousands of Baroque churches that, inspired by Trent and often imitating the Gesù in Rome, became stages for *theatrum sacrum*. They were gilded, colorfully painted machinery for creating Catholics or bringing heretics back into the fold of the old faith. Spain, politically exhausted and economically broken, slipped into its long slumber of *decadencia*. Only painting and poetry flourished; after all, it was the century of Velázquez and Calderón.

The Demystification of Politics

Many had grown tired of confessional conflict. As a remedy, political theorists recommended strengthening the state, which seemed the only entity capable of ending the endless fighting. The first to think in this direction was Jean Bodin, in his *Six Books of the Commonwealth* (1579). To counteract the erosion of state authority which he had personally experienced in the wars of religion, he proposed the revolutionary concept of *sovereignty*. This term denoted supreme, indivisible, and temporally unlimited power.[7] In Bodin's view, only the state possesses it. Without it, there is no state. The sovereign, whose authority derives from God's endless authority, decides over war and peace. He has a monopoly on lawgiving but is himself not bound by the laws. He is *legibus solutus*. The Latin formulation, which is contained in the term "absolutism," is in line with the definition of the prince in Roman law. Yet Bodin's sovereign is no despot. He is still subject to natural law, i.e., God's law. He must respect family and property.

The times called for a politics driven not by religious fervor but rather by cool, geometrical thinking. Despite being demonized everywhere and suppressed by censorship, Machiavelli's sober analysis had given rise to a rich tradition of writing. The principles he said should dictate political action were encapsulated by another Italian, Giovanni Botero (1540–1617), in the term *ragione di stato*, "reason of state." It was a theory of how to obtain, retain, and expand power. Like others, Botero masked his disreputable "Machiavellism" by citing not the Florentine but rather Tacitus. The latter's historical works provided lessons about the mechanisms behind the transition from republican freedom to tyranny, or put more positively, from chaos to order.[8]

Steeled with the shimmering sword of sovereignty and endowed with the mind of Machiavelli, the state's task was to quash the chaos of the wars of religion and constitutional struggles. A repressive regime might take hold at home, but anything seemed better than the breakdown of all order. Justus Lipsius, at heart a peaceful Stoic, thus viewed confessional unity as the highest imperative. In his *Six Books on Politics*, he suggested dealing with dissenters who endangered peace by "burning" or "cutting" them out of the commonwealth,[9] whereas his compatriot Hugo Grotius (1583–1645), grand pensionary of Rotterdam, recommended recognizing only one ecumenical religion. Its truly essential tenets, to be guarded by the state, were that there was only one God and that he guided human affairs. Grotius's chief work, *On the Law of War and Peace* (1625), conceived of the state as a system of institutions and powers—no longer as an organism connected to the cosmos.[10] The commandments of natural law, derived from reason and the needs of the community, were adamantine. Not even God could change them. They applied even in the (very hypothetical) case that God did not exist or did not concern himself with human things.[11] Wars could only be waged for defensive purposes, to press legitimate claims, and to punish crimes. As a result, religious grounds no longer sufficed to make war seem just.

Like Bodin and the Dutch thinkers, Thomas Hobbes (1588–1679) also erected a strong state against the war of all against all. His theory of the state was the product of an emergency situation. "My mother dear did bring forth twins at once," he wrote, "both me and fear." This is an allusion to the year of his birth, 1588, when the Armada attacked England.[12] Terror at the approaching Spanish fleet caused his mother to go into premature labor.

Hobbes made use of a geometric method. It subjected human beings, society, and the state to a mathematical regime. In contrast to Bodin, he made a *contract*—i.e., an arrangement with horizontal power—the foundation of all statehood. Individuals, the corpuscles of society, joined together to form a "body politic," transferring their power to one single person or to a representative body. Hobbes's *Leviathan*, published in 1651, does not elaborate a theory of absolutism. Rather, it describes the state as it was actually composed. Hobbes calls it a "mortal god." "No power on Earth is its equal," announces a caption on the title page, a variation of Job 41:33 (Fig. 66, p. 803).[13] The state, not some distant deity, now ensures peace. Its immeasurable power has been given to it so that it can provide its people with security and a pleasant life.[14] In particular, it is to be lord over religion.[15] The citizen owes obedience to the secular sovereign alone. Otherwise, violence and civil war will ensue. For Hobbes, peace is more important than religious truth. The nature of that truth is for the sovereign to decide. And what of freedom?

> There is written on the Turrets of the city of Lucca in great characters at this day, the word LIBERTAS; yet no man can thence inferre, that a particular man has more liberties, or immunitie from the service of the Commonwealth there, than in Constantinople.[16]

The freedom of the individual and the freedom of the state are two separate things. Contrary to what the humanists thought, Hobbes argued that the individual freedom of the citizen did not necessarily have anything to do with active participation in the commonwealth or "virtue." With a scornful tone, Hobbes buried this ideal of Renaissance political theory and, as Quentin Skinner has argued, said goodbye to it forever.

In political reality, the early modern state had continued to expand its apparatus. The number of government departments grew, as did that of legally trained bureaucrats at all levels of power. In France, for example, most Royal Councils under Louis XIV's (1643–1715) reign were composed of nobles "of the robe" (*noblesse de robe*), not of blood.[17] The age of condottieri and mercenary bands hired on demand was over; that of standing armies dawned. One of the causes of this development was the Thirty Years' War (1618–1648), which still counts as the last interstate war in Europe in which religion played a major role (at least in certain phases).

The adieu to religious war was a dramatic process. Conflicts wretched and writhed in terrible death fugues. Ultimately, the Thirty Years' War suffocated itself. It had eaten up the last ducats of the princes, robbed the cities of power, and laid such waste to the land that armies could barely find anything to eat. It caused more casualties on German soil than any war before or since. Once again, proof was offered that the attempt to create heaven on earth led straight to hell.[18] Muskets and cannons, and even more so starvation and pestilence, killed up to a third of the population.[19] The 1648 Peace of Westphalia, a masterpiece of European diplomacy, guaranteed the sovereignty of the Netherlands and the Swiss Confederacy. France and Sweden won territory and reparations, the German territorial princes a high degree of independence. To defuse the confessional bomb, the year 1624 was established as the status quo for territorial possessions, and fair procedures were introduced for resolving religious conflict. Subjects no longer had to adhere to the religious conversions of their lords. Ironically, the only one who refused to sign the treaty was the envoy of Pope Innocent X (1644–1655), whose coat of arms bears a dove of peace.

Spain continued to prosecute its conflict with France for over another decade. Only the 1659 Treaty of the Pyrenees put an end to the grand duel. The proud kingdom had long been considered a declining power. "The monarchy of Spain is a sleeping ogre," one Italian observed even before the Thirty Years' War, "a vast, flabby, vulnerable bulk, a colossus of straw."[20] Portugal had split off in 1640, and rebellions were on the rise in the rest of the country. As the war in Germany was dying down, the Count of Olivares, a minister and a favorite of Philip IV, concluded melancholically, "This is the world, and so it has always been, even though we thought we could perform miracles and turn the world into something it can never be."[21]

Power Play for the World

England sallied forth to fill Spain's role. Elizabeth I had bequeathed the means to rule over the oceans' waves: a fleet fit for the high seas and a "blue water" strategy.[22] The first foundations for colonial expansion and inklings of an imperial ideology had been provided by Hakluyt. His 1584 *Discourse on Western Planting* emphasized the opportunity to spread the true Christian faith, as well as the necessity of halting Spanish power and genocide overseas. High profits could be expected from the exploitation of new territories and the export of domestic goods to them. Jobs would be created, and safety valves to relieve population pressure would be opened.[23] Walter Raleigh warned that if the king of Spain possessed all of America, there would be no way to stop him.

The escapades of Hawkins and Drake had been mere overtures to the global showdown. The old tournaments became world wars. Since there was no understanding of economic growth, the prevailing view was that one could only make gains at the expense of others. The fear was that leaving territory to one's opponent, even just savannas or bays where no gold was to be found, would mean falling behind at home in Europe. Thus, commerce often led to war. "Trade cannot be maintained without war, nor war without trade," as one contemporary put it in a nutshell in 1614.[24] High taxes were the flipside of a policy that saw profits as a function of military might.[25] On the other hand, while military security for colonial enterprises and infrastructure usually had to be provided by states—Portugal's crown went bankrupt for that reason in 1650—profits flowed mostly into private hands.

The dynamics of competition drove the global expansions of European states further and further, igniting a "financial revolution."[26] In addition to the Muscovy Company, similar entities were set up for trade with Spain, Portugal, Scandinavia, and the Levant. The East India Company followed in 1600. The crown gave it privileges that amounted to rights of sovereignty. Holland answered two years later, establishing the United East India Company (*Verenigde Oostindische Compagnie*, or VOC for short) and setting up a commodities exchange.[27] The VOC brought 6.5 million guilders together, ten times what was available to competitors at the time. Its powers made it a state within the state. It, too, was able to wage wars, make treaties with foreign rulers, and erect fortresses. A virile, virtuous cycle was set in motion. Money in search of investment was lent at low interest rates, which supported technical know-how in shipbuilding and entrepreneurship, thus driving new investment. The Bank of Amsterdam, set up in the old town hall, allowed cashless payments in all manner of currencies. The ambition and capital of the Dutch far outsized the minute geography of their state.

By 1596, during the war with Spain, Dutch ships reached fertile Java. The VOC established a network of bases and foreign trading posts that stretched from the Persian Gulf to Japan and included Sumatra and Timor. In 1616, Surat was added, the richest port in the Mughal Empire and perhaps in the world at the time. Jayakarta (today a quarter of Jakarta) was definitively won in 1619 and renamed "Batavia" by its new lords. It became the bulwark of Dutch trading power. The VOC pursued its profit interests with utter ruthlessness. In 1621, Governor-General Jan Pieterszoon Coen (1587–1629) had the entire indigenous elite of the Moluccan island of Banda massacred and the rest of the population enslaved. Two years later, on nearby Amboina, the VOC's governor sent twenty-one men, including ten English merchants, to the scaffold for their supposed involvement in a plot. The VOC's reward was the dominance it desired over the nutmeg trade, but the price it paid was a chronic quarrel with the British.

In the following decades, the VOC continued to expand its area of influence in East Asia, a boundless realm of luxurious flavors and beguiling scents, adding the cinnamon empire of Sri Lanka, the pepper country of Malabar, and the nutmeg and clove domain of Sulawesi, conquered between 1660 and 1669. Having its own spice islands and taking territory on Java only interested the company as a means to establishing monopolies. Ultimately, building states was expensive and troublesome. In general, the Dutch attached themselves to the shoreline like barnacles on a boat, built forts, and established a loose dominion over regional potentates. Often, they simply set up trading posts, first on the sea and then in the interior. They forced the Portuguese to retreat to

Goa, Macao—which managed to repulse a Dutch attack—East Timor, and a few spots on the mainland.

A legal mantle was provided to Dutch mercantile imperialism by Hugo Grotius. His 1609 *Mare liberum*—*The Free Sea*—established a foundation in natural law for unchecked commerce. The aim of the book was to show "shortly and clearly" that it was "lawful for the Hollanders, that is the subjects of the confederate states of the Low Countries, to sail to the Indians as they do and entertain traffic with them."[28] Grotius developed the tenet that the sea was free and could not belong to any kingdom. His book was a frontal assault on the principle of Tordesillas, a rejection of all papal and Spanish universalism. On the other hand, when his countrymen attempted, in contravention of their own ideology, to gain a monopoly on the clove and nutmeg trade, they had to hear the following words from the sultan of Aceh: "God made the land and the sea; the land he divided among men and the sea he gave in common. It has never been heard that anyone should be forbidden to sail the seas."[29]

In 1621, the year of the Banda massacre, the States General founded a "West Indian" counterpart to the VOC that was responsible for Africa and the Americas. Its purpose was to wage war against Spain in the Atlantic and Pacific, as well as to establish trading posts between the coast of West Africa and New Guinea and to conquer land for settlement.[30] In 1652, the Cape Colony was founded, later an important port of call for Dutch voyages to Asia and the germ of the future state of South Africa. Spain retained Cuba and Puerto Rico, while the English established themselves in the Bermudas, Jamaica, and Barbados— then the most important producer of sugar in the world. The Dutch had to make do with territories on the "Wild Coast" between the Amazon and the Orinoco, in what is now Guyana and Surinam. The small nation with its two million inhabitants possessed what was then the greatest merchant marine on the globe, accounting for more than half of all tonnage on the oceans.

Yet England proved a powerful competitor in the war for the world. The East India Company had trading posts in India, in what is now Thailand, and on the islands of Sumatra, Sulawesi, Borneo, and Java. For a decade, between 1613 and 1623, it had a base on the Japanese island of Hirado. Meanwhile, in 1622, the Safavid Shah Abbas I helped a fleet belonging to the company to break Hormuz out of the Portuguese *Estado*. That secured the English position in the nearby port city of Bandar Abbas, a hub between branches of the Silk Road and the Persian Gulf. Fort Saint George, a fortified settlement on the Coromandel Coast, was built in 1641, thus establishing a robust English bridgehead on Indian soil. It grew into the city of Madras, later renamed Chennai. In

1660, English trading companies supported by the crown also began breaking into the gold trade and slave markets of West Africa.

English ambitions were primarily aimed at the Atlantic world.[31] It was in the purview of the Virginia Company and the Somers Island Company, responsible for Bermuda. In 1620, the "Pilgrim fathers," a group of radical Calvinists, had sailed to what is now Massachusetts on a fluyt called the *Mayflower*. Their colony of Plymouth was the first in a series of settlements that would develop into the New England states of America. They were initially separated from Virginia and Saint Mary's, the birthplace of Maryland founded in 1634, by a Dutch territory: New Netherland, with its settlement of New Amsterdam on Manhattan, an island at the mouth of the Hudson River.

When its civil war ended, England was able to address the North American challenge. In 1651, the protectionist Navigation Acts laid the foundation for opposing Dutch dominance; more such laws were to follow. In the first act of an intermittent naval war, the Dutch could not manage to force their English competitors to reconsider their policy. Confessional solidarity no longer meant anything.

In 1655, the Dutch under Governor-General Peter Stuyvesant overpowered a Swedish colony on the Delaware River. A decade later, however, the hunters became the hunted. In the course of renewed hostilities, an English fleet forced them into submission in 1664. New Amsterdam and New Netherland ultimately evolved into the city and state of New York. Shortly before that, the States General had been forced after a long war to give their Brazilian holdings back to Portugal. They also lost Fort Zeelandia in Taiwan to the Chinese warlord and Ming loyalist Zheng Chenggong. From now on, the east coast of what would become the United States was in British hands, from the current state of Maine down to the deep south. A third Anglo-Dutch War, from 1672 to 1677, did nothing to change this situation.

Among British merchants, the view began to take hold that the transaction costs imposed by war were too high. "Our business is trade, not war," the directors of the East India Company maintained.[32] This was not a universal view, however. For example, power struggles within India in subsequent decades affected the English stance. In 1687, Sir Josiah Child, governor of the East India Company, concluded it was necessary to finance a "state" strong enough in civil and military power to ensure English sovereignty in India "for all time to come."[33] It is debated whether this was the first step toward Britain's colonial empire on the subcontinent.

After losing ground during the wars of religion, France also joined in the competition for the globe. Bases in Senegal and the Gulf of Guinea served the slave trade. In addition, various islands in the Caribbean were occupied, including Martinique and Guadeloupe. Réunion in the Indian Ocean and the eastern part of Guyana (with Cayenne) followed shortly thereafter. On the eastern coast of India, a French company modeled on the VOC acquired Pondicherry, the first step in the direction of building a protectorate. This was all small fry, however, compared to the foundation of New France in North America. It built on the pioneering efforts of Jacques Cartier and Samuel de Champlain, the founder of Quebec.[34] Missionaries, traders known as *coureurs de bois* (literally "runners of the woods"), and fur trappers explored the massive territory. Branching out from bases in and on the Saint Lawrence Seaway, they went down the Mississippi River all the way to the Gulf of Mexico. The Sun King claimed it all for himself. Yet there was a lack of settlers. Only a few thousand arrived in the first decades of the colonial foundation; they did not even number 100,000 by 1770. In contrast, England's North American colonies welcomed a steady stream of newcomers, starting with the Pilgrim fathers.[35] The first scouts were already heading west, constantly expanding the borders.

Moscow sought to penetrate the sparsely populated East. The conquest of Siberia was completed by the tsars in the mid-seventeenth century. Farmers, hunters, and traders followed on the heels of soldiers. Christ came as well, clearing a religious wilderness in which strange syntheses of Asian traditions and the written religions of their neighbors flourished. Forts developed into settlements, and settlements into cities. Russia signed the Treaty of Nerchinsk with Qing China in 1689, establishing a clear border between the two states. The language of the official text of the treaty was Latin, thanks to Jesuit translators.[36] By 1700, Russians and other "white" people composed the majority of the Siberian population. Russia was the last significant participant in the competition for global hegemony.

Leviathan's Triumph

Back in Europe, courts and cities remained gravitation centers of politics and culture. The Holy Roman Empire, with its many component parts, emerged from the Thirty Years' War as a lively political union and a vibrant cultural zone. Sweden, along with France a winner in the conflict, established itself for half a century as the major power in the north. Poland's Vasa king renounced his claim to Sweden's crown for good. Prussia, long dependent on its neighbors as the runt of the State of the Teutonic Order, became a sovereign duchy. It was another step toward the status of a kingdom, achieved by the Hohenzollerns in 1701.

Louis XIV harvested and spoiled the fruits of Richelieu's policy. After the Habsburgs had been contained and the nobility subdued, France rose to hegemony for several decades. Yet it never managed even to defeat the Dutch. Within the country's borders, the Huguenots met their final fate. The Edict of Fontainebleau, issued by Louis in 1685, meant the victory of the principle of "One God, one king, one faith, one law"[37] and the definitive demise of Henry IV's policy of toleration. The Sun King's state approached the ideal of a pure, strictly geometrical monarchy in which only the Catholic religion was allowed to exist.

In the east, the Ottomans reached Vienna one last time in 1683. After achieving victory at Kahlenberg Mountain, Austria was able to go on the offensive in the following decades. A war over the succession of the last Spanish Habsburg engulfed central Europe from 1701 to 1714, once again disturbing the rather peaceful conditions that had settled upon northern Italy. England entered the Habsburg alliance, which opposed Louis XIV's expansionist policy. The upshot of the carnage—containment of France and a balance of power on the Continent—corresponded to England's war aims. Its interests were on the seas. London gained a monopoly over the transatlantic slave trade and took Menorca and Gibraltar.

The War of the Spanish Succession did not merely put an end to Louis XIV's ambitions on the Continent. France also lost part of its Canadian territories. France's power was broken in North America once and for all with its defeats in the Seven Years' War (1756–1763). That conflict also put an end to France's Indian ambitions. Victor on three continents was England. The vision of Britannia ruling the seas, Neptune in supplication before her—the image adorned John Selden's 1635 *Mare clausum*, an apology for English thalassocracy (Fig. 67, p. 815)—had gained a foothold in reality.[38]

The Europeans' decisive advantage was that their overseas projects were buttressed by the eternity of bureaucratically organized states. Wherever they encountered technologically inferior societies with weak states, they easily had their way. Yet as we have had occasion to observe, they often conquered not because of their own strength but thanks to divisions among their opponents. The pursuit of private profit and state fiscal policy tended toward the same goal: to make a profit and increase tax sources. Only under these conditions would the money flow in to finance fleets and soldiers. Quickly mobilized capital helped the Dutch to overcome the Portuguese. Superior economic resources contributed to England's ability to defeat the French in India and America and to conquer Bengal.[39]

Paradoxically, the Europeans benefitted from their political fragmentation overseas as well. If a unified European empire had set out to the east or west, every new ruler could have ended the colonial enterprise—as had happened in China after Zheng He's expedition. In Europe, there was no emperor or sultan who could beach his ships with a single word. It made no difference that Brandenburg and Sweden gave up their maritime ventures after timid attempts, and Portugal's exhaustion was immaterial. Others—first the Dutch, then the British—picked up the slack.

The true winner in the wars around the globe was thus the early modern European state. It was hardly a coincidence that Japan, which also possessed a strong state, long held pace with the Europeans in the competition for Asian economic zones.[40] Its ships, whose red seals indicated their state license to trade, traveled the seas and did commerce with Siam and other places. The Japanese maintained a dense network of trading posts in the emporia of southeast Asia and even reached Acapulco, more than sixteen thousand kilometers from Nagasaki. Copper and silver, the latter from the Iwami and Ikuno mines, streamed into China until a surplus caused prices to fall around 1635. While the glut of silver was stimulating Asia's economy, exports slowed inflation back in Europe. Without them, the Habsburgs never could have pursued their imperial policy for so long.[41] Conversely, when demand fell, the fisc was weakened. Thus, Spain lost its part in the Thirty Years' War not only on the battlefield at Rocroi, but also in Macao and Nagasaki.

Yet the Europeans were never masters of the world. Their power in Asia was based essentially on a few ships, on fortresses built on the Italian model, some of which—like in Manila—reached enormous proportions, and on bureaucracy and diplomacy. As a result of this expansion, the rest of the globe became a bit European, for better and for worse. European weapons and strategy, European taste, Europe's ideas, its Christianity, and its capital penetrated every continent. Symbolic of this process is an exotic performance of Hamlet that was staged on board an English ship anchored off the coast of Sierra Leone. Sailors played the parts, while the audience included the rest of the crew and Africans supplied with a translator. It was probably in Temne, their native language, that the latter learned that something was rotten in the state of Denmark.[42]

Of course, Europe exported more than just Shakespeare to the rest of the world. It also spread its racism, its dangerous national dreams, and—more felicitously—its democratic ideals. In the other direction, a deluge of foreign things flowed back to Europe, teaching at least brighter minds that their way of seeing the world was not the only one conceivable.

The Dawn of Civil Society

The immediate prehistory of modern democracy, like the beginnings of the Industrial Revolution, unfolded in the domain of Camden's *Britannia*. This was probably owed in no small part to the island's protected position. Shakespeare's John of Gaunt alludes to it when he praises his country as a "fortress built by Nature for herself" and as a "precious stone set in the silver sea, which serves it in the office of a wall."[43] The nation could retreat into "glorious isolation" and pursue its pragmatic foreign policy. The sense of mission that Hakluyt had sprinkled into his concept of colonial policy did not hurt. Profit as reason of state[44] may not always have been in the interest of the common good. Yet it was ultimately preferable to the wars required by the old value codex of princes. Political bankrupts like Charles V, Philip II, and Louis XIV yearned for honor, glory, and pure religion, but in the end they racked up only death, destruction, and debts.

There is good reason to believe that the differential between the economies and standards of living of North and Latin America is related to their different colonial histories. The Spanish wanted vassals, the British land.[45] The Iberian legacy left a corresponding mark on the south. Indigenous peoples and natural resources were exploited by a European elite on the old model of the *encomienda* system; no rural middle class emerged. A slave economy also developed in the north, of course. Yet many colonists themselves worked, and they created enduring and relatively impartial institutions.[46] The settlers in Jamestown managed to break the absolute power of the governor of the North Virginia Company, a corporation with a royal charter whose purpose was to develop the land in the colony. Virginia's "Great Charter" of 1618 provided for the establishment of two bodies to advise the governor, a Council of State and a General Assembly for affairs of a "very extraordinary and important" nature.[47] The latter was to represent all the settlements in the colony, meet once a year, and make decisions by majority vote. This process, "one of the most momentous steps in the history of North America" (as Wolfgang Reinhard put it), set an early precedent for the democratic constitution of the United States.[48] The settlers in Plymouth followed suit. The Mayflower Compact, penned in 1620 on Cape Cod, based the commonwealth on "just and equal laws" in order to prevent fights among the colonists.[49] In this way, the wolfish wilderness of Hobbes's fictional state of nature was tamed by a bona fide social contract. Horizontal power was further buttressed by distance from the home country, as well as by the weakening of central authority effected by the Civil War and the Interregnum. Most colonies developed a mixed constitution, a triangle formed by a governor, his council, and the assembly, the colonial equivalent of the House of Commons.[50] Power relations took different forms. In Rhode Island and Connecticut, the assembly could elect the governor and his council, whereas the norm elsewhere was for him to be appointed by the crown. In addition, London retained veto power over the legislature and remained the highest authority in legal disputes. As in England, the franchise depended on property. Only landowners could vote.

The path to democratic civil society in North America was still quite long. Most of the indigenous population died of disease or fell in war. Tens of thousands were enslaved. Along with viruses and bacteria, the steady stream of settlers that started in 1620 also carried the familiar European diseases of greed for profit, intolerance, and religious zealotry. Was not this pristine land the right place to finally get serious and establish pure Christian communities, earthly images of the heavenly Jerusalem? The immigrants to America practiced all manner of faiths, some of which—like Anabaptists and Schwenkfelders—were persecuted in Europe. Nevertheless, religious zeal took a deadly toll here as well. In Boston, four Quakers (three male and one female) were hanged between 1659 and 1661. Only the intervention of the crown could stop the pious purge. A mania for purity was also behind the witch trials in 1692 that gripped Salem, a community in Massachusetts. One of the mainsprings of the trials that claimed nineteen victims was the Boston clergyman Cotton Mather (1663–1728), who saw Satan lurking behind secularization and the erosion of Puritan orthodoxy.[51]

An alternative to the heavenly Jerusalem on Earth was provided by the division between religious and civil affairs. It was promoted by Roger Williams (1603–1683), the founder of the Providence colony—the nucleus of Rhode Island.[52] In secular affairs, he believed all religions, including the cults of the Native Americans and even "antichrists," should be unmolested and enjoy liberty of conscience. Williams himself, a wayward Puritan and a father of the American Baptist movement, rejected all institutionalized religion. The principle of the separation of church and state was carved into legal stone in 1791, in the first amendment to the American Constitution. It codifies the prohibition against establishing a state religion and restricting the exercise of religion. Furthermore, it guarantees freedom of speech and of the press as well as the right to peaceful assembly.

Back in England, horizontal power had won the day with the Glorious Revolution. More than anything else, it was the longstanding parliamentary tradition, Magna Carta, and habeas corpus acts that distinguished the country from the rest of Europe—not, as has been claimed,[53] an early development of individualism, social mobility, or market-oriented economic rationality. No king since the Late Middle Ages had managed to rule without the support of Parliament for any great length of time. As early as the fifteenth century, the island's special symbiosis of monarchy and "republic" was praised as the foundation of prosperity at home and displays of power abroad.[54] As we have seen, the need for money, especially in the face of continuous warfare, had time and again forced the crown to come to terms with horizontal power. Furthermore, the common law bridled monarchical authority. Serfdom had ceased to exist around 1600. In the form of the Leveller movement during the English Revolution, a kind of radically democratic party, complete with mass appeal and a propaganda apparatus, appeared for the first time in world history.[55] The "freeborn Englishman," the creation of the Leveller John Lilburne (ca. 1614–1657), took the stage. He was now a *citizen*, not a subject.

The upshot of 1688 was that Parliament would remain the dominant political force. William III of Orange (r. 1689–1702), grandson of the decapitated Charles and son-in-law of the deposed James II, was given the crown but not the authority that had once gone with it. The ascendance of horizontal power was enshrined in the Bill of Rights directly after the victory was won. It expressed the expectation that the new monarch would halt attacks on religion, rights, and liberties. The fact that the only civil freedoms it enumerates are the right to petition and the right to bear arms—only for Protestants, incidentally—can be explained by the historical situation that produced it: opposition to the Stuart monarchy. The spirit of the document lives on today in the Constitution of the United States. The Bill of Rights saw the monarchy as an office entrusted to a ruler's care, not as a self-evident inheritance. A French attempt to reinstall the Stuarts on the throne failed in 1692, at the sea battles of Barfleur and La Hogue.

Of course, tolerance had its limits in England, too. More than one manuscript was left unprinted because the author feared reprisals by guardians of the faith, and witch hunts were inflamed by Puritan zeal as in North America. Yet religious tensions became less important.[56] John Locke (1632–1704), who as a standard-bearer of parliamentary sovereignty had persevered in Dutch exile from 1683 till the Glorious Revolution, embodied the intellectual trends of his country. An empiricist and anti-absolutist political theorist, Locke was accordingly a proponent of tolerance—a view that he expressed in his *De tolerantia* (1689).[57]

What may seem in hindsight like the logical conclusion of a process that had begun with Magna Carta and parliaments was in reality a tortuous path. Women still did not have the right to vote. Furthermore, large cities were vastly underrepresented in the legislature. On the other hand, the House of Commons took a big step in the direction of democracy when it let the Licensing Act lapse, a censorship law introduced at the beginning of the Restoration. Compared with conditions in other countries, it should be said that England was already the closest to approximating an "open society" in the sixteenth century. As Marlowe's *Tamburlaine the Great* taught, a shepherd may rise to the rank of emperor. And according to the diplomat Sir Thomas Smith (1513–1577), gentlemen were "made good cheape in England." For anyone who studied law, attended a university, and could live a life of leisure was considered one.[58] In addition, Smith viewed the erosion of the social pyramid as an advantage to his country—an opinion of no little merit.

The openness of society and the interests of merchant capital favored innovation. Science was now chic for larger swathes of society. Performing experiments became the expression of a new culture[59]; doing research and making discoveries developed into a sport. The Royal Society presented spectacular experiments to high-ranking visitors. After becoming the first woman to see the hallowed halls of Gresham College, Lady Margaret Cavendish, Duchess of Newcastle and herself a littérateur and natural philosopher, is supposed to have cried, "I am full of admiration!"[60] The new empirical science gained preeminent status in Scotland, whose universities soon numbered among the leading thought centers in the world.

As in the Netherlands, in the British Isles—the union of Scotland and England created the kingdom of Great Britain in 1707—public lectures were organized to spread knowledge of mathematics and astronomy among craftsmen, sailors, and soldiers.[61] The eighteenth century witnessed an increase in journals detailing physical phenomena and technological advances. Mechanics even became a subject in schools for girls. Businessmen learned to speak the same language as technicians and engineers, whose social status seems to have been higher on the island than anywhere else. Gradually, the scientific mentality spread on the Continent as well. This appears to have happened first in Protestant societies, thanks to their culture of the word.

The English realm of possibility provided a bundle of favorable conditions for the Scientific Revolution and the Industrial Revolution that flowed from it. In hindsight, it is clear that England was one of the more likely settings for these developments to have unfolded in the early modern period. And yet, none of these factors—parliamentary government, a public sphere, tolerance, mature capitalism, or competition—could have spawned the Industrial Revolution *on its own*. Nor could the profits reaped by colonial expansion, the close relationship between science and commerce, or the economic growth that had clearly taken root long before industrialization set in.[62] Finally, while the *inventions* indispensable to the Industrial Revolution indeed came from England, they could have sprung up elsewhere in Europe.

42

The Mechanical Universe

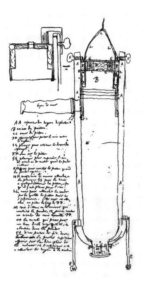

Inventive Passion

In all possible disciplines and in many countries of Europe, new discoveries and inventions were now cropping up. Robert Boyle realized that under certain conditions the pressure of a gas is inversely proportional to its volume (Edme Mariotte of France achieved the same insight shortly thereafter, and the law stating such has been named for both of them). Along with Johan Baptist van Helmont, Boyle laid the foundation for analytical chemistry.

Another pioneer was Christiaan Huygens (1629–1695) of the Netherlands. He was the first to hypothesize the wave character of light. Evidence that the speed of light is finite was sought by his Danish contemporary Ole Rømer. Huygens refined Rømer's methods, arriving at an estimate that was more accurate but still nearly one-third slower than the actual speed of 300,000 kilometers per second. Among other things, Huygens formulated laws of collision and set about combining Descartes's vague notion of floating corpuscles with Galileo's method.[1] He was also a brilliant technician. He drew up a design for a combustion engine (Fig. 68, p. 821) and invented a pendulum clock whose accuracy long remained unsurpassed. Using the law of refraction worked out by Descartes and Willebrord Snell, he improved the telescope. He descried Saturn's moon Titan and the planet's rings, which beforehand had only been visible as blurry bulges. On the eastern edge of the European realm of possibility, Johannes Hevelius (1611–1687), a brewer and mayor of Gdańsk, went about exploring the topography of the Moon using a telescope forty-seven meters in length. His *Selenographia* describes the lunar surface with greater precision than ever achieved before.

As the telescope revealed myriad moons and stars, the microscope, invented in the late sixteenth century—again in the Netherlands—provided insight into tiny worlds of wonder. Pioneers espied protozoa in pond water. They studied fly eyes, bacteria, and the capillary system, whose existence explained how blood flowed from arteries into veins.[2] Robert Hooke (1635–1703) not only discovered something very big, namely the Great Red Spot on Jupiter, but also very small things. He used his microscope to examine the compound eyes of insects and the tiny structures on the point of a needle. His 1665 *Micrographia* included astoundingly precise engravings (Fig. 69, p. 823).[3] Of course, the new device could not show the smallest building blocks of matter, Lucretius's atoms or Galileo's corpuscles. Debates about ancient theories intensified all the more.

Like the Ptolemaic worldview, other ancient axioms also lost authority. Francesco Redi (1626–1697), a physician from Arezzo, disproved the Aristotelian concept of "spontaneous generation," according to which flies, maggots, and leeches developed from decomposing matter thanks to the warming of animating *spiritus*. He noticed that no maggots appeared in rotting meat protected from flies by gauze. Therefore, they must hatch from eggs laid by the insects.[4] What is more, Antonie van Leeuwenhoek (1632–1723) observed human sperm for the first time under the microscope. As he realized, life can only come from life.

In the face of the dramatically swift increase in knowledge, the polymath became an endangered species. One latter-day exemplar—and oddball—was Athanasius Kircher (1602–1680), a lifelong member of the Jesuit College in Rome. Kircher was a tireless experimenter, producer of folio volumes, builder of machines, and decoder of hieroglyphics. He wove magical, religious, and modern experimental approaches together into a bafflingly variegated mé-

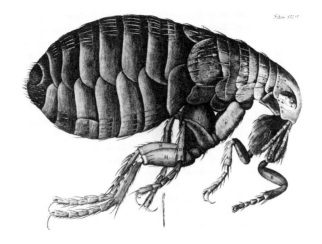

lange.[5] He invented speaking statues and a magic lantern, contrived a universal language, and reconstructed the blueprint of Noah's Ark. He also performed linguistic and geological research, studied magnetism, and devoted a monumental work to describing the interior of the Earth and the demons that supposedly lived there.

Lost Center

The Copernican cosmos destroyed the certainty of being safe in a privileged spot at the center of everything. Kepler already sensed that an infinite universe, whose possibility had become conceivable in his time, changed everything. It held "some kind of secret, hidden horror," he wrote, continuing, "We wander about in this immensity, which has neither boundaries nor center and therefore no secure places."[6] One is tempted to say he felt the icy breeze of European modernity blowing through the new universe he himself had helped to build. He felt alone and abandoned there, like human beings in Patrizi's realm of historical freedom. The interlocking of human and cosmic order seemed to be lost.

> And new Philosophy calls all in doubt,
> the Element of fire is quite put out;
> The Sun is lost, and th'earth,

as his contemporary John Donne (1572–1631) wrote,

> 'Tis all in pieces, all coherence gone.[7]

Skepticism was even budding with regard to science itself, which claimed to know everything. As Shakespeare's Lafeu opines,

> They say miracles are past; and we have our
> philosophical persons, to make modern and familiar,
> things supernatural and causeless. Hence it is that
> we make trifles of terrors, ensconcing ourselves
> into seeming knowledge, when we should submit
> ourselves to an unknown fear.[8]

The power of the stars—at least so much is attested by a scene in *King Lear*—had become more questionable than ever, the words of the book of nature illegible.[9] God seemed strangely distant, and the heavens above Caesar, once a reliable source of guidance, were silent.[10] In his essay on meteorology, "Les Météors," Descartes robbed the clouds of their ancient function as divine signs. A few philosophers even tried to force the devil out of existence. As skepticism and critical thought penetrated courtrooms, advisory councils, and cabinets, the fires for burning witches died down and went out; events in Massachusetts and isolated trials in the eighteenth century were exceptions. Even the Bible was bathed in the acid bath of critical philology.[11] Citing the "ancient philosophers"—Epicurus and Aristotle are meant—an anonymous writer concluded in 1659 that there was no God. The world was eternal, the soul mortal, hell a fairy tale.[12]

Yet the hale old man, as Michelangelo had painted the Creator on the ceiling of the Sistine Chapel, was in no way banished. Without him, as Jacques Monod put it, people would have been left with nothing but a cold universe deaf to their music and indifferent to their hopes, sufferings, and crimes.[13] People feared God, but even more so, they feared a world without him. At the same time, Earth was shrinking. Compared to the cosmos it was just a point, Campanella reported from his dungeon. And yet he insisted defiantly: "*For us* [it] is not a point."[14] Still very much a man of the Renaissance, he continued to see human beings as the measure of all things. Bacon, too, felt compelled to defend an anthropocentric perspective. "If man were taken away from the world, the rest would seem to be all astray, without aim or purpose . . . and leading to nothing."[15]

What if Adam was indeed only an extra in the drama that we call "being?" On his utopian voyage to the Moon and the Sun, Cyrano de Bergerac (1619–1655) deprecates Earthlings' belief that nature was created for them alone. "As if it were likely that the Sun, a vast body four hundred and thirty-four times

PLATE 17. Sandro Botticelli, *Mystical Nativity* (1500). Oil on canvas, 108.6 × 74.9 cm. London, National Gallery, inv. no. NG 1034.

PLATE 18. Raphael (?), portrait of Elisabetta Gonzaga (ca. 1505). Oil on wood, 52.5 × 37.3 cm. Florence, Gallerie degli Uffizi.

PLATE 19. Stanisław Samostrzelnik, portrait of Bishop Piotr Tomicki (ca. 1530). Tempera and gold on wood, 142 × 241 cm. Cracow, Church of St. Francis of Assisi.

PLATE 20. Piri Reis, world map (1513), fragment. Ink and paint on parchment (camel skin), ca. 86 × 62 cm. Istanbul, Topkapı Palace Museum.

PLATE 21. After Hans Holbein the Younger, portrait of Henry VIII of England (1536/37). Oil on wood, 239 × 134.5 cm. Liverpool, Walker Art Gallery, inv. no. 1350.

PLATE 22. The "illustrators of the work" Heinrich Füllmaurer and Albert Meyer, and the "wood engraver" Veit Rudolf Speckle. From Leonhart Fuchs, *De historia stirpium* (Basel, 1542). Woodcuts on paper, 37.9 × 24.4 cm. Ames, Iowa, Iowa State University Library.

PLATE 23. Titian, *La Gloria* (1551-1554). Oil on canvas, 346 × 240 cm. Madrid, Museo Nacional del Prado, P00432.

PLATE 24. Giovanni Battista Moroni, portrait of Michel de L'Hôpital (1554). Oil on canvas, 185 × 115 cm. Milan, Biblioteca Ambrosiana, inv. no. 196 1984 000196.

PLATE 25. Paolo Veronese, *Allegory of the Battle of Lepanto* (ca. 1573). Oil on canvas, 169 × 137 cm. Venice, Galleria dell'Accademia, inv. no. 212.

PLATE 26. Unknown artist (George Gower?). Elizabeth I ("Armada Portrait," ca. 1588). Oil on oak wood, 133 × 105 cm. Woburn, Bedfordshire, Woburn Abbey.

PLATE 27. Fresco with a centaur by an unknown artist (last quarter of the 16th century). Ixmiquilpan, Mexico, San Miguel Arcangel.

PLATE 28. Tobias Stimmer, self-portrait (ca. 1563). Chalk, ink, and watercolor, 19.7 × 15 cm. Schaffhausen, Museum zu Allerheiligen, B 5924.

PLATE 29. Agnolo Bronzino, *Resurrection* (1552). Oil on wood, 445 × 280 cm. Florence, SS. Annunziata.

PLATE 30. Titian, portrait of Jacopo Strada (1567/68). Oil on canvas, 125 × 195 cm. Vienna, Kunsthistorisches Museum, G 81.

PLATE 31. Jacopo Ligozzi,
Psittacus ararauna
(1580–1600). Black chalk
and colored tempera on
paper, 67 × 45.6 cm.
Florence, Gallerie degli
Uffizi, inv. no. 1988 O.

PLATE 32. Keisuke Ito, *Seal and Mermaid*. In *Kinka Jūfu* (*Book of Beasts*)
(ca. 1850). Watercolor drawing on paper. Tokyo, National Diet Library.

bigger than the Earth, had only been kindled to ripen their medlars and plumpen their cabbage."[16] Huygens and Fontenelle—the latter in his *Conversations on the Plurality of Worlds*—followed Bruno in considering the possibility that the fixed stars were nothing but far-distant suns, themselves orbited by planets.[17]

These were still just the thought experiments of a few individuals. They are emblematic of the dialectic of rationalism: the more zealously people heeded Bacon's call to accumulate knowledge, the more uncertain their place in the universe seemed to be. The measuring sticks broke. The view through the telescope and the microscope revealed human beings to be tiny and gigantic at the same time. Blaise Pascal (1632–1662) demonstrated that "empty space" did exist, thus disproving the traditional conviction about nature's *horror vacui*, or abhorrence for "meaningless" nothingness. Unlike Descartes, he drew a very sharp distinction between faith and knowledge, emotion and *ratio*. In his view, reason was necessarily restricted to knowledge of the finite. Neither infinitely large nor infinitely small things could be perceived by it, and therefore nor could final causes. In contrast, the "logic of the heart" ascertained knowledge about things that the *esprit de géométrie* could never grasp. Pascal did not consider the existence of God to be provable. Nevertheless, he recommended believing in God. There was no risk involved in the famous wager he proposed: bet on God's existence, and endless profit may accrue; if he does not exist, you have lost nothing. Those who deny God, however, have nothing to gain in either case.[18] Pascal united in himself both logics, that of emotion and that of reason. As a theologian, he was conservative; as a scientist and technician, he was one of the foremost "moderns" produced by his century. He invented a calculator and designed a simple barometer. He also continued the experiments on air pressure and vacuums that had been begun by Galileo's student Evangelista Torricelli, the inventor of the mercury barometer. Along with Pierre de Fermat, he founded probability theory, an area in which Huygens dabbled as well.

How acceptable the possibility of a universe without a benevolent father had become can be seen in the concept of God elaborated by Baruch Spinoza (1632–1677).[19] For him, God is also nature, none other than the causeless, eternal, and infinite substance of which everything is composed. His God has as little to do with the Christ of revelation as Bruno's. As a result, even the cosmology of his day could live with Spinoza's concept of God. In his own century and beyond, this son of a Portuguese Sephardic Jew was demonized as a pantheist, an atheist—which he certainly was not—and a materialist. He was expelled by the Jewish community in Amsterdam, the city of his birth; his writings were forbidden everywhere but England. A century earlier, he would have been a sure bet for the stake. Only later did Enlightenment thinkers discover him as a founder of modern philosophizing, a champion of freedom— he argued it was the ultimate purpose of the state—and religious tolerance. His thought and that of his followers produced a European movement that disavowed the legitimacy of all monarchy, aristocracy, the subjection of women to men, ecclesiastical authority, and slavery.[20]

There was no shortage of attempts to embed new discoveries in the traditional biblical worldview. Jan Swammerdam's (1637–1680) physicotheology celebrated as proof of God the wonders that the microscope revealed in even the smallest things.[21] In 1726, the Swiss naturalist Johann Jakob Scheuchzer interpreted a petrified salamander as the remains of a sinner who had died in the Great Flood.[22] The new physics was activated to provide a natural explanation for the miracles recounted in the Bible. Thus the theologian and philosopher Pierre Gassendi (1592–1652), incidentally a highly significant proponent of Epicurean atomism, argued that the walls of Jericho had fallen under the impact of vibrations caused by the sounding of trumpets.[23] Bartolomeo Mastri (1602–1673) and Bonaventura Belluti (1599/1600–1676), both Franciscans, still made use of spiritual intelligences to set the planets in spiral motion. In support, they mustered whole armies of Greek, Arabic, and Scholastic authorities, including Michael Scot's translation of al-Bitruji. Along with hordes of kindred spirits, they went down old paths and got lost on intellectual byways. It was people like them whom Galileo ridiculed in his *Dialogue*. He did not aim his scorn at Aristotle, for whom he had great respect, but rather at the herd of learned sheep that bleated after him.

Of a much higher caliber was the model that the German philosopher Gottfried Wilhelm Leibniz (1646–1716) proposed in opposition to Cartesian physics and Spinoza's theology. He sought to put God back into the universe by animating Descartes's dead corpuscles as ensouled "monads." Immortal, without extension or shape, they were capable of perception and desiring changes in their state.[24] God programmed them so that a synchronicity would eternally exist between them and the movements of bodies, like that between two perfectly aligned automata. This was the essence of his famous "pre-established harmony." Of the infinite number of conceivable universes, a good, perfect Creator could only have brought the "best of all possible worlds" into existence. Everything that happened in it must serve a good ultimate purpose—even evil, without which good is inconceivable. Like Descartes, Leibniz trusted in the power of reason. He worked tirelessly for the development of a universal language that would make it possible for people to understand each other across all national boundaries and to seek political and religious peace.[25]

"Reason" became the magic word of the dawning Enlightenment. Another was "critique," the legacy of Pyrrho and Montaigne. Firmly in that tradition stands Leibniz's contemporary and adversary Pierre Bayle (1647–1706).[26] Whereas the one sought to develop a cosmology that seemed compatible with his Christian worldview, the other regarded the concept of "pre-established harmony" with skepticism. His response to the challenge posed by the problem of theodicy was radical and heretical, seemingly akin to Manichean and Cathar thought: evil must be a powerful first principle, just like good.[27] Yet both Bayle and Leibniz saw that reason and ecumenism were the only ways out of the crisis in which fights over the true and pure faith had culminated.

Dispensing with all philosophical contemplation, Isaac Newton (1643–1727) completed the Scientific Revolution.[28] His 1697 *Principia Mathematica* (*Mathematical Principles of Natural Philosophy*), along with the *General Scholium* appended to the second edition, founded the classical physics that was considered universally valid until the theory of relativity and quantum mechanics. Newton also adopted the method of doubting everything not demonstrated by experiment or observation. Unlike Descartes, however, he based his natural science entirely on mathematics. As he conceived of it, space was infinite, just as absolute as time, and empty. The movements of particles and the bodies they composed came from forces whose effect Newton inscribed in simple laws. His universe, like that of Copernicus and Kepler, functioned on principles of economy. God was the God of order, not of confusion, he once wrote.[29] The curtain came down for good on Aristotelian circular motion and Descartes's vortices in the ether, whose dynamics had required the influence of external forces; they were also irreconcilable with Kepler's laws.

In the person of Newton, the Swabian astronomer had found the reader of all readers. The Englishman was the first to recognize the supreme significance of his "conquest of Mars." Thus, what Kepler predicted in his *Harmony of the World* came true:

See, I cast the die, and I write the book. Whether it is to be read by the people of the present or of the future makes no difference: let it await its reader for a hundred years. If God Himself has stood ready for six thousand years for one to study him.[30]

Newton got a grip on celestial mechanics by assuming the existence of a force working at a distance: gravity. He recognized its effect in the relationship between the masses of two objects and the distance between them; a heated conflict developed with Robert Hooke over who achieved this insight first. Newton succeeded in expressing it in a mathematical formula and providing initial confirmation of its existence in the form of observational data. As to what this ominous gravitation was and where it came from, he did not speculate. The Cartesians and Leibniz objected that this was just another occult force and, therefore, simply a return to the Scholastic universe that Descartes had just smashed to bits. Newton replied coolly that he might not know the nature or cause of gravitation, but he was more than capable of calculating the effects of such a force and reducing them to laws.[31]

The universal mechanics Newton proposed could be reduced to a simple formula; it had none of the magic of the old models. Planetary intelligences and angels gave way to centrifugal and gravitational forces. Even comets lost their status as wild desperados and heralds of doom. In two writings about a comet that flickered across the sky in 1680, Bayle had already worked to demystify them. The final proof for the fact that comets followed paths according to Kepler's laws came when one of them appeared in Britain's night sky in 1758, exactly when it had been predicted by a computation of its orbit undertaken in the early eighteenth century. It was named for the man who foretold its return, Edmund Halley (1656–1742). Halley's *Opticks* also completed the process of demystifying rainbows that had been started by Kamal al-Din al-Farisi and Dietrich of Freiberg.[32]

If one hundred years earlier, as the historian of science Richard S. Westfall claims, the focus of Western civilization had been on Christianity, it was now on modern science.[33] Unintentionally, a universe had emerged that functioned like a clock and no longer needed God. Newton himself was far from drawing such radical conclusions. He considered it obvious that "this most beautiful system of the Sun, Planets, and Comets, could only proceed from the counsel and dominion of an intelligent and powerful being."[34] Nevertheless, so he thought, the divine mechanic would occasionally have to correct irregularities and make repairs to keep the cosmological clock working.[35]

Newton seems to have been a neurotic man driven by scientific demons. It is curious that the same thinker who had reduced the mystery play of the heavens to mathematics devoted himself very intensely in secret to alchemy, Hermetism, and the Apocalypse, which he believed was close at hand.[36] He was profoundly convinced that the ancients had known or suspected many things and that his contemporaries needed to rediscover the "primeval wisdom" they had possessed. This was all a legacy of the "other Renaissance." Newton filled thousands of pages with his thoughts on such matters. Yet he published none of it. In the final analysis, he was as much a Prometheus of European modernity as he was the last great magician of the Renaissance.

43

The Archaeology of Modernity

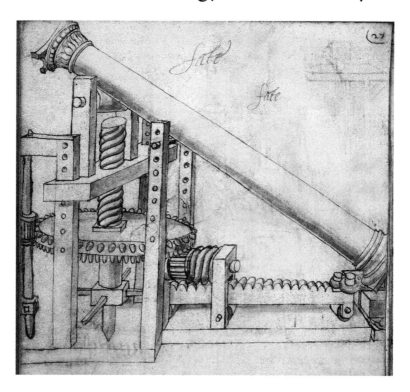

The Great Divergence

Somewhere in the world. Today. You are not freezing while you read these lines. Perhaps you're sitting in a toasty room or a balmy backyard. There is running water and electric light in your home. Mechanical devices like a washing machine and a refrigerator make life easier. Reliable healthcare is available if you get sick; a social safety net is there should you be in need. You have received a decent education. You can write and, of course, you can read. What is more, you can publicly say what you want as long as you don't break any laws. In your world, the media is not censored. Legal avenues exist to settle disputes. You can belong to the religion of your choice, or you can believe in nothing at all. Every couple of years, you vote in an election. Ballots, not bullets, decide who will govern your country and how. If you suffer violence, the perpetrator becomes an enemy of your state, the mighty Leviathan. Human dignity is supposed to be inviolable in your world.

If this is all more or less true for you, then you live in the "West." Your world is anything but perfect, of course. Who could deny it? It, too, knows poverty and injustice. It owes a substantial portion of its prosperity to dirty business with weapons, the exploitation of "others," the destruction of the environment. . . . The list of sins committed by the "West" is long and could be extended ad libitum. Nevertheless, the vast majority of those at home on the islands of democratic civil society live a better life than most people elsewhere. Starvation, poverty, and war drive millions upon millions of refugees from their homes. Religious fanaticism feeds violence as in sixteenth- and seventeenth-century Europe. In many African and Asian countries, kleptocracies and dictators exploit their peoples more efficiently (thanks to sophisticated technology) than the crowned potentates of yesteryear and even monsters like Timur could.

The differences between your world and the "rest" are ultimately the consequence of a process of elemental force: industrialization. By the mid-nineteenth century, the "great divergence" was obvious. Today, the richest economies are many times richer than they were in the pre-industrial age. Other countries have gotten poorer. Whereas industrialization has decreased inequality in general within Western societies, it has clearly increased the gap between industrialized nations and those that did not keep pace.

The classic explanation for the "great divergence" goes as follows: it was Europe's special economic and cultural conditions, its legal systems and its capital, that caused the gulf to widen starting in the seventeenth century. Some historians have disagreed, objecting that economic conditions and standards of living around the world barely differed from one another until around the year 1800.[1] Furthermore, some have claimed to see in Asia as well—i.e., in Japan and China—traces of a phenomenon that in European economic history is referred to as the "Industrious Revolution."[2] According to this view, there was a widespread increase in the amount of work performed without wages keeping pace. The desire for sugar, tobacco, and other luxury goods encouraged people to trade leisure hours for work time. This created new markets for consumer goods, which in turn made their industrial production attractive. Were not

China, Japan, and perhaps other flourishing national economies on the verge of industrialization in the eighteenth century? And was not Western imperialism mainly responsible for smothering Asia's industrial revolution?

There is no shortage of dissent to these arguments. For example, the hypothesis that the "great divergence" first began in the nineteenth century has been challenged.[3] What exactly do we know about living conditions, per capita income, or gross domestic product (GDP) in African, Asian, and even European societies in the medieval and early modern periods? The statistics compiled by the economist Angus Maddison (1926–2010) in an oft-cited publication are not universally accepted.[4] For example, it is unlikely that China enjoyed the same level of prosperity as the most prosperous Latin European societies in the eighteenth century.[5] In any case, a mere glance at growth rates and standards of living cannot explain why the economy of the "West" took off in the nineteenth century.

We cannot sketch here the entire spectrum of conditions that structured the Industrial Revolution's realm of possibility. The key points are well known. First of all, a warming climate after the end of the Little Ice Age favored population growth. Agricultural reforms helped to feed more people. More people needed more to eat, which led to an increase in agricultural production.[6] These people needed shirts, trousers, and skirts, and so more textiles had to be made. Better fed and dressed people could also work more. They would form the army of the industrial workforce. Starting in the Late Middle Ages, developments can be observed that have been grouped under the—much-debated—heading "proto-industrialization."[7] This term refers to the rise of regions with handicraft production in rural areas and not only in urban contexts dominated by guilds. Merchants and businessmen provided capital, machines, and materials, organized the work, and sold the products. Ultimately, the seventeenth century witnessed the appearance of manufactories, small-scale predecessors to mammoth factories. All this, however, would not have sufficed on its own to create what was the essence of the "Industrial Revolution" and, therefore, the factor that ultimately caused the "great divergence": the replacement of muscles by machines powered by steam and fed on fossil fuels. Economic growth became uncoupled from population growth, which had only been able to increase production with the work of more muscles.

Without the use of steam as a power source, there would have been no Industrial Revolution—that is the most likely formula.[8] Steam power was first harnessed for pumps and looms. Once the principle of converting steam to mechanical energy was shown to be practicable, there was no stopping it.

A positive feedback loop emerged in which innovation led to a boom in production, which caused increasingly significant investment to be made, which resulted in yet more innovation.[9] In the end, Europeans were better prepared than all others for the challenges that emerged in the eighteenth century due to population growth. Victory over starvation was achieved in part by agricultural reforms (including the mass planting of potatoes) and in part by railroads. They were faster and cheaper than horses for transporting food from regions with surpluses to those with shortfalls. The last time a mass famine struck Europe was 1846/47, with exceptions in Ireland, Spain, and Finland.

The availability of capital, including profits from colonial enterprises and slavery, was of secondary importance for the *beginning* of the Industrial Revolution.[10] The appearance of the decisive inventions was not owed primarily to money but rather to knowledge and ideas and their communication.[11] Only once steam-powered machines were used on a large scale in transportation and production did capital gain ascendance.

Like the invention of the compass, the cogwheel clock, eyeglasses, the printing press, and the telescope, the birth of the steam engine has a *deep history*. It represented the culmination of a project begun back in Alexandria. "Industrial" modernity—one of the "multiple modernities" as envisioned by the sociologist Shmuel Eisenstadt[12]—had mighty foundations in the epoch traced in this book.

Screws and Inventors: The Completion of an Alexandrian Project

The tinkering of Hero of Alexandria, whose *Pneumatica* and *Automata* were known to the Renaissance and medieval Byzantium (p. 128),[13] had at least shown the power that steam could unleash, thus putting latter-day imitators on a path to the future. Yet only in the fourteenth century, with John Buridan's considerations on the vacuum, did the modern history of the air pump begin. It deserves a place in the prehistory of the steam engine just as much as the Renaissance's *teatri di macchine*.[14]

Experiments performed by Torricelli and Pascal showed that we are surrounded by an "ocean of air."[15] Otto von Guericke (1602–1686), mayor of Magdeburg, used the forces it contained to construct the first piston pumps. The great power of vacuum pressure was demonstrated by a famous experiment that he conducted in 1654. Two teams of eight horses each were unable to separate the two halves of a sphere from which the air had been pumped out and that were thus held together by "nothing." The next step was taken by the landscape architect Salomon de Caus (1576–1626).[16] This heir of Hero was probably the first to construct a steam-powered pump. In 1650, Edward Somerset, Marquis of Worcester, is said to have used the new energy source to spray a water fountain forty feet in the air.[17] Three decades later, the Flemish Jesuit missionary Ferdinand Verbiest appears to have displayed a model of a steam-powered vehicle at the Chinese imperial court.

Meanwhile, Huygens in the Netherlands, who had read about Guericke's experiment, and Boyle in England were investigating the power that could be harnessed from air and vacuums.[18] Boyle and Robert Hooke collaborated to build an air pump; the motor that Huygens sketched in 1673 was supposed to run by means of metal cylinders (Fig. 68, p. 821). The explosion of the gunpowder would push air out of the cylinder through leather valves. The vacuum created in this way would pull the piston down. Denis Papin, a French student of Huygens and an assistant to Hooke and Boyle, embraced the principle. Yet he focused on steam. And indeed, he succeeded in creating a steam pump, thus providing a foundation on which Thomas Savery (ca. 1650–1715) and Thomas Newcomen (1663–1729) could build improved versions. They, in turn, prepared the breakthrough embodied by James Watt's (1736–1819) steam engine.

The engineering competition continued after Watt's patent expired in 1800. From that moment on, developments were continuous and quick. Synergy with the broader industrial takeoff powered the steam engine to greater and greater perfection. It was first put to practical use in mining, where groundwater had to be pumped out of shafts. Savery, therefore, called his (not yet very efficient) product the "Miner's Friend" in an attempt to boost sales.

A new dimension opened up when the "stream"—in the sense used by John W. Kingdon (p. 6)—that had led to the development of the steam-powered pump joined with another one: the mechanization of weaving.[19] For millennia, people had been improving the loom and distaff, those emblems of all culture since time immemorial. The spinning wheel was introduced to Europe in the thirteenth century. Three hundred years later, William Lee invented a stocking frame knitting machine. The process hastened forward in the eighteenth century, too. In 1733, John Kay (b. 1704) invented the flying shuttle, which sped up the process of weaving many times over. Three decades later, James Hargreaves's (1721–1778) spinning jenny revolutionized the spinning of wool. A steady stream of improved machines, initially powered by water, stimulated weaving and inspired thoughts of further innovation. How could the mountain of yarn now available thanks to new production methods be woven immediately into cloth? In 1785, the clergyman Edmond Cartwright (1743–1823) received a patent for a mechanical loom powered first by water, then by steam. It was a union, one could say, that sired industrial modernity.

In the following decades, this innovation edged out handweaving, first gradually and then fiercely. In the early nineteenth century, around 2,400 looms were in operation in England. Thirty years later, it was 100,000.[20] Without letup, further improvements were made—to smelting techniques as well as to the steam engine, which was receiving ever more applications. For example, locomotives and steamships revolutionized transportation and, therewith, space and time. The flood of innovation, however, did not have an immediate effect on economic growth or standards of living. Yet it would eventually change everything. Between 1700 and 1900, English cotton cloth production grew seven hundred times, pig iron production three hundred times.

Steam was nearly the whole game. The acceptance and further development of this key innovation was driven by other factors. Some were specifically European, some specifically British. Like other European countries but unlike most outside Europe,[21] England possessed a sophisticated, legally secure system of credit and firmly entrenched property rights.[22] All this had been useful to colonial enterprises and had consolidated liberties. Now it provided succor to the Industrial Revolution. Patent law protected inventions better than anywhere else—in England, thanks to the 1624 Statute of Monopolies—thereby lessening the risk of investment, albeit also limiting the chances for the invention of superior alternatives for a time.[23] The market conditions that provided a stimulus at the start and helped innovations to achieve a breakthrough were specifically English.

For example, the success of the steam engine also indirectly stimulated the puddling process, which was widely used around 1800. It made it possible to produce high-quality iron suitable for forging, but it required a significant energy expenditure. Wood was expensive and relatively difficult to procure. This situation, in turn, led to the intensification of coal mining. Furthermore, it made the capital expenditure necessary for constructing steam-driven pumps economically viable, even though such was quite high in comparison to building a water wheel.[24] There was yet another, literally down-to-earth factor: England's coal deposits were located deep underground. It was therefore very labor-intensive to keep groundwater from continually seeping into mineshafts. As a result, it made sense to buy even the wimpy "Miner's Friend" or its more potent successors, thus letting them take care of the drudgework.

To explain the absence of an Industrial Revolution in China despite its long history of superiority, some have argued that its "subterranean forests" were located closer to the surface than in England.[25] Consequently, so the thinking goes, the Chinese lacked the challenges whose mastery called for the construction of steam-powered pumps. Yet would it not have made sense here and in India to use steam power in cloth weaving or in rice farming? In China, a water-powered spinning device had been invented back in the Late Middle Ages; India became the world's leading exporter of textiles by the end of the seventeenth century.[26] Still, no one had the idea of using steam to replace the muscle power necessary for weaving. The availability of cheap labor in densely populated regions may have been another impediment to looking for new technologies. But these factors are of secondary importance. Challenges like the coal crisis or competition from Indian textile imports[27] might have hastened developments from time to time, and their absence might have retarded them. Yet to design a device as complicated as a steam engine, mere incentives were not enough by far.

In the realm of possibility that had produced the mechanical loom and the steam engine, the demands of the day flowed together with ancient streams. The revolutionary device was not the result of long-term planning. Nor did Europe's spectacle-makers, busy grinding their lenses, have a telescope in mind before the sixteenth century. The same goes for pioneers like Somerset and de Caus, who were not thinking of English coal mines drowning in groundwater when they devised their machines. Their projects were aimed at powering fountains and technical merriments, and Guericke's experiments were linked to the debate over Aristotle's arguments about the existence of a vacuum. Only later did what he discovered turn out to be useful knowledge.[28] As for whether his experiments were necessary for pumps to be built, or rather if the tinkering of technicians had gained a momentum of its own, that is a separate issue.

It is easy to overlook the fact that the development of certain components necessary for building machines also took a long time. While scholars were making much ado about "nothing," i.e., the vacuum, thereby preparing the way for the invention of the air pump, in a totally independent development the mechanical clock was being invented, thus ushering in Europe's mechanical age. Highly specialized craftsmen hammered and filed away at parts and tools without which the masterpiece theater of the "Industrial Revolution" never could have been staged; in a few larger early modern European cities, there were over fifty shops just devoted to specific metal products. These included cogwheels[29] and universal joints. One especially useful object indispensable to the machine

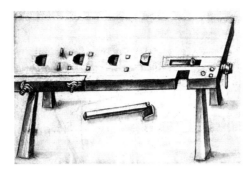

age experienced its European renaissance after a complicated prehistory in the fifteenth century: the *screw* (Fig. 71, above).[30] For a long time, screws had to be cut one by one in a laborious process and were initially a luxury good used in costly jewelry like brooches and bracelets. Starting around 1490, screws increasingly replaced the leather straps and rivets that had traditionally held together suits of armor. The triumph of firearms eventually made armor obsolete, but the tiny fasteners proved to be immortal. They were screwed into medical instruments, telescopes, and microscopes. The German *mechanicus* Jacob Leupold (1674–1727) praised them as "one of the most useful inventions in the world." A new profession emerged: a smith who specialized in making screws. At the end of the eighteenth century, Henry Maudslay (1771–1831) designed a lathe that made it possible to mass-produce precision screws.

Finally, let us not forget that the production of steam engines required resilient materials. Closely corresponding with economic cycles and the needs of craftsmen, smelting and casting techniques had been improved upon during the Renaissance. The art of casting was so advanced in Europe that the Venetians melted down artillery captured from the Ottomans at the Battle of Lepanto because the bronze was "of such poor quality." The metal gained in this way was turned into new cannons that were safer and more effective.[31] Was iron produced anywhere else in the world at even close to the same level of sophistication as in high medieval Italy?

In the "West," therefore, a critical mass of knowledge of all kinds had been accumulated by the eighteenth century.[32] Only its availability enabled the technological breakthroughs that were necessary for the Industrial Revolution. As Karl Marx observed, Latin Europe's old society was long pregnant with a new one.[33] To take just the case of the steam engine, the driver of the Industrial Revolution, the period of pregnancy and infancy lasted more than half a millennium—and that is only if we ignore the ancient prehistory of the invention, which was probably indispensable for its development. This hissing creation did not spring fully formed from the head of James Watt. Rather, it was the fruit of an ancient, pan-European discourse that ultimately reached maturity in the age of print, took shape in all manner of intellectual circles, universities, and academies, and traversed many paths, the majority of which turned out to be dead ends. Most of the institutions of this kind were unknown to other cultures. In Europe they acted as agents of sustainability, contributing to the perseverance of the grand dialogue.

The Butterfly Effect

Various attempts have been made not only to measure and compare the economic data of Europe, China, and other countries over long periods but also to do the same with their cultural achievements and innovative power.[34] Such an undertaking is doubtless problematic for any one individual metric, but not with regard to large trends. All of the truly significant scientific paradigm shifts between the end of the Middle Ages and the nineteenth century took place in a geographical area that extended from Naples and Marseille to Glasgow and Copenhagen, from western France to Silesia. All of the more important inventions came from the same territory. This is where most of the essential components that went into making the steam engine were invented; this is also where the Industrial Revolution started. The fact that it began in England was owed primarily to the fact that "creative streams" were fed by an especially favorable and, at the same time, challenging context, one that included capital, a countryside that produced textiles, and, in the case of the steam engine, deep coal deposits. One could go into greater detail, perhaps citing patent laws or the Calico Acts passed by Parliament. Starting in the first decades of the eighteenth century, the latter banned textile imports, thus fostering the boom in domestic production that was a key sector in the Industrial Revolution.

The preconditions for it were not forged in Great Britain alone, nor was that country the only stage for fateful innovations. At the same time as Englishmen were developing the steam engine, the Swede Carl Linnaeus elaborated his botanical and zoological taxonomies, the Frenchman Buffon wrote his monumental work of zoology and conducted geological research, while Albrecht von Haller founded experimental physiology in Bern. In 1783, the first balloon flights in Lyon and outside Paris ushered in the age of aviation. That same year, again in Paris, Antoine Lavoisier demonstrated that water is not, as had been assumed for two and a half millennia, an element but rather could be divided into hydrogen and oxygen. The list could go on and continue into later times, to the early days of the telephone, the automobile, or bacteriology. All this and much, much more was the legacy of a tiny patch of scientific Europe.

The big question—*why* did the Scientific Revolution and, therefore, the Industrial Revolution start in Latin Europe?—will never be answered with absolute certainty. The methodological problem is that it is impossible to synthetically separate events or actors from the historical process as if they were chemical agents in a laboratory experiment. "What would have happened if . . ." is as impossible to say as *why* something happened, as mysterious as what conditions *exactly* contributed to a specific event. All we know is what actually did happen; we know the here and now. In the words of Schiller, coincidentally uttered in the world-changing year of 1789, just weeks before the outbreak of the French Revolution:

> Even that *we* found ourselves together here at this moment, found ourselves together with this degree of national culture, with this language, these manners, these civil benefits, this degree of freedom of conscience, is the result perhaps of all previous events in the world: The *entirety* of world history, at least, were necessary to explain this single moment.[35]

Not even the beating of a butterfly's wings in Brazil, as chaos theory teaches us, can be seen as unrelated to the prehistory of a tornado in Texas. What good or evil thing has *not* happened thanks to some or other accident of history that no one will ever know about? Decisive situations with enduring consequences are as impossible to eliminate from what happened as seemingly secondary processes that attended the dawning of momentous chains of cause and effect.[36] Would England have become a parliamentary democracy without the fatal arrow shot at Bouvines in 1215? Likewise, heaven only knows whether the island kingdom would have become the first industrial nation in the world without the screw—or without Max Weber's Protestant work ethic, for that matter, although the screw was probably more important. On the other hand, *one* key factor, the lack of raw materials, probably retarded industrialization in the Netherlands until the late nineteenth century. The acquisition or construction of steam-driven pumps offered no immediate prospect of profit there. Obviously, without the initial spark of the steam engine itself, an essential precondition for the further development of its technology was missing.

It may be true that the beating of a butterfly's wings can contribute to the development of a tornado. Nevertheless, it is very unlikely to be the main cause. The upshot for the history of the Scientific and Industrial revolutions is that a series of factors was more important than the butterfly effect. Long paths and periods of time were necessary for them to come together and turn European modernity's realm of possibility into a reality. All the essential inventions were due to the culmination of science, entrepreneurial spirit, and, last but not least, "genius." The prehistory of the steam engine is as unthinkable without screws as it is without the small cluster of inventors who actually brought about the decisive turning points. They contributed hard work, calculations, corrections of partial solutions, observations, and tests. At some point, a moment must have come that we cannot reconstruct: the moment in which thought shifted and something truly new arose—when Gutenberg began playing with letters; when Copernicus stopped the Sun (it must have been around 1514); when Watt invented the ingenious mechanism (in 1784) now named after him. Of course, a role was also played by *serendipity*: a happy coincidence from which further inferences could be drawn.[37] The closer we get to the ideas, however, the more the causes of invention become inaccessible to historians. Artistic and scientific creativity are very closely related in this sense. After the decisive moment, connections become clear, and things appear in a different light. To put it a bit more theoretically: in hindsight, we observe complex, interconnected streams that flow together into realms of possibility and bring about radically new things.

As David Landes has observed, "big processes call for big causes."[38] An economic head start—if indeed it really existed—cannot explain why Lilliputian Latin Europe became the center of unceasing novelty for centuries. No intensity of demand or economic boom could have led to the invention of a steam engine in eighteenth-century China. Such things do not happen overnight. Not even screws were known in the Middle Kingdom until Jesuit missionaries introduced them.[39] The view that China was on the verge of industrialization at the end of the Song Dynasty does not have much going for it. Here and elsewhere outside of Latin Europe, the conditions that existed within the latter's borders were missing—be it this factor or that or all of them together. Comparisons can help to highlight what distinguished this patch of land between the Atlantic Ocean and the Mediterranean Sea from the rest of the world, and what conditions brought about *its* modernity. We have paid special attention to certain forms of state formation. For without a modicum of the order guaranteed by a state, technological progress and science are unimaginable. Regions that knew only weak systems of rule remained lost. On the other hand, a strong state was naturally not sufficient on its own for good science and technological progress to mature. The case of the sluggish giant Russia shows this with all possible clarity.

PART IV

Conclusions

THE "WEST" AND THE REST

44

Vertical Power, Sky High

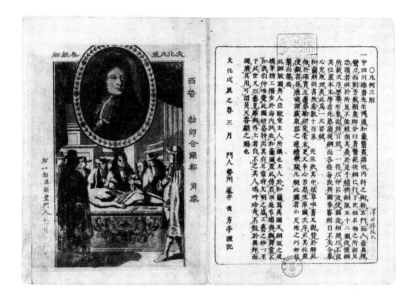

Russia: Tsars and Patriarchs

"We thought that you lord it over your domain, and rule by yourself, and seek honor for yourself and profit for your realm. And it is for these reasons that we wanted to engage in these affairs with you," wrote Tsar Ivan IV to Queen Elizabeth in 1570. Yet he did not seem satisfied that she was a partner on equal footing.

> But now we see that there are men who rule beside you, and not only men but trading boors who concern themselves not with our sovereign safety, and honors and income from our lands, but seek their own merchant profit.[1]

No clearer statement could be made as to how different Russia was from Elizabeth's England. Indeed, horizontal power had a tough going in the state centered in Moscow. It survived somewhat in the form of the Duma, composed of up to two dozen men, most of them boyars. The tsar had to listen to their counsel, but he was not bound by what they said. The high point in the slim history of Russian horizontal power was achieved in the brief period when general assemblies had elected first Boris Godunov and then Michael Romanov as tsars. Townspeople were invited to the first, and even farmers to the second. Yet even here, the nobility and the clergy had the decisive power.[2] Motions toward a little freedom on the village level were halted by the burdens brought by times of war. As Giles Fletcher of England, a man used to very different conditions, observed at the end of the sixteenth century,

> As for Burghers or other to represent the communalitie, they have no place there, the people being of no better account with them than as servants or bond slaves that are to obey, not to make lawes, nor to knowe any thing of publike matters before they are concluded.[3]

The Muscovites had to learn their faith from the stories illustrated by their icons, for both the nobility and the people were largely illiterate. Even some priests could neither read nor write. This was to the tsars' benefit, as it was easy to rule over a pious, uneducated people. About 250 monasteries were founded between the fourteenth and sixteenth centuries alone, indicating that Christianization was forging ahead in the now gargantuan tsardom. Alongside it, as in Latin Europe, all manner of magical practices proliferated, as did superstitious and even demonic customs, as church leaders irately observed. On Saint John's Eve, they claimed, witches and wizards collected deadly grasses and poisonous herbs, and Satan paraded in triumph through the cities and the countryside.[4]

Attempts to introduce the Reformation were fruitless, and even Gutenberg needed more than a century to reach the banks of the Moskva.[5] The first work to be printed there was the *Apostol*, in 1564, containing the Acts of the Apostles and letters from the New Testament (Fig. 73, p. 845). Ivan Fyodorov, the printer of the work and a deacon, initially received support from the tsar but was then driven out, perhaps by monks fearing the threat he posed to their monopoly on copying books. In Ostroh, Ivan printed a Bible in the Cyrillic alphabet. Its importance for Orthodox Christians would soon equal that of Luther's Bible for German Protestants. Meanwhile, the limits of the Gutenberg galaxy's expansion highlighted the hard cultural border between West and East. Poland was on the western side; books were already being printed in

Cracow in the late fifteenth century. Moscow, in contrast, lay deep in the East. Nonetheless, the image of Saint Luke in Fyodorov's *Apostol* is framed by beautiful Renaissance architecture.

The Russian empire was said to be under God's protection. Its rulers would thrive as long as they obeyed his law, gave the metropolitans their ear, and supported the Church.[6] Down to the Revolution, the alliance between church and state was wrought of iron. Of the two powers, the tsars were always in control. Sigmund von Herberstein recorded in amazement that priests were subject to secular jurisdiction.[7] The tsar could depose insubordinate patriarchs without much ado. In 1551, Ivan IV presided over a council like Constantine the Great once had. And he forbade monasteries from accepting bequests, in order to stem the further accumulation of already massive ecclesiastical property.

Ivan's exaggerated autocracy provided his country with a model for future rulers, in addition to leaving it with a heavy burden. Even princes he regarded as mere servants. His successors imitated him in ruling their multiethnic empire as one large estate. They governed through alliances with the aristocracy and against the people, who ultimately came to prefer heavy-handed order and exploitative institutions to the uncertain chaos of freedom. In this way, the Romanovs ruled an empire whose society was without intellectual vigor or notable secular science, to say nothing of the capacity to bring forth technological innovations. Only in the eighteenth century did "modern" intellectual life begin to develop.[8] The quarrel between reason and faith that shook up Latin Europe was not felt in Muscovy. The classical tradition remained almost entirely unknown. A figure like the diplomat Fedor Karpov, who knew Homer, Cicero, Ovid, and Aristotle, was a white raven. Russian literature followed the Byzantine tradition.

Almost exclusively the product of learned monks, it dealt with religious topics and specialized in the rhetorically polished biographies of saints, heroes, and princes. A critical historiography on par with Latin European standards did not exist; Russian chronicles focused on Moscow's rise and the resplendence of the dynasty. One exception to the trend appeared around 1550: a revision of the *Domostroy*, a set of household rules for Christian family life. Painting remained mesmerized by Byzantium. Portraits showing individualized features first appeared in the late seventeenth century. Only slowly was an opening made to the West. Technology and learning were gradually acquired from all over Europe, foreign trade grew, and the population increased. Yet the nature of the economy barely changed. In the Late Middle Ages, furs were still used as currency instead of coins.[9]

The endless horizon encouraged a profligate relationship with the land. Like migratory birds, it was said, farmers roamed from one place to the next, clearing fields by fire and settling, then moving on yet again when the soil was exhausted. According to one historian of Russia, its peasants had a unique talent for "ravaging the land."[10] Only tentatively, centuries later than in central Europe, does the three-field system seem to have been adopted. The lack of lush pastureland, in addition to long winters during which animals had to be fed, limited opportunities for raising livestock. As a result, too little manure was produced. Since there was a lack of big cities and, consequently, there were hardly any townspeople to feed, there were no incentives for market production or for developing new devices or new techniques that might increase yields. Mills, the motors of Latin Europe's economic boom, only began to populate Muscovy in the sixteenth century, i.e., five hundred years later than farther westward. There was a lack of capital and available labor, to say nothing of daring entrepreneurs or an enlightened intelligentsia. Under Peter the Great (1689–1725), the state stepped in. Its needs—i.e., the needs of the fisc— determined the logic of economic policy. The tsardom was poorly prepared to take the path to modernity. The same can be said of the other great power on the edge of Latin Europe: the Ottoman Empire.

The Sick Man on the Bosporus

Like in Muscovy, the opulence of rulers in the Ottoman Empire was paid for by the common people, scorned by elites as *reaya*, i.e., the "herd."[11] The ruling class of *askeri*—officials in state service largely exempt from taxation—was composed mostly of military men, jurists, religious scholars, and high Christian clerics and rabbis. It was not impossible for humbler folk to rise to this status. It was in the power of the sultan to effect an elevation in rank. Before the eighteenth century, however, craftsmen and merchants were hardly ever promoted. An educated, politically influential middle class was unknown even in the capital.

Suleiman's conquests and Sinan's buildings should not blind us to the fact that the empire's foundations began to crack, albeit imperceptibly at first, even during its period of greatest splendor. Its Achilles heel was the economy. Compared to western competition, the empire was underdeveloped economically, an old-fashioned giant. Sparks of a capitalist economy based on trade and industry were smothered by the practice of awarding land to followers in order to bind them to the central authority. Rents were largely paid in kind, in part a result of the price revolution that affected the Ottomans and the Safavid Empire.[12] Hardly anything was left for the market.

The Ottoman Empire's gross domestic product remained constantly low between 1500 and 1800.[13] The importance of the former capital of Bursa as a transshipment point for Persian silk or for trade in spices and, starting in the seventeenth century, coffee, did little to change the big picture.[14] As in other Muslim states, literacy and thus legal certainty had always been much less developed than in the "West." Large fairs and markets of the kind that took place in Latin Europe in Champagne, Frankfurt, and many other places were as unknown to the Ottoman Empire as joint-stock companies, stock exchanges, insurance, and the stout protection provided to private property by sophisticated laws. A stable banking system did not develop until the mid-nineteenth century.

The legal system disadvantaged producers, financiers, and merchants. It neither prized nor protected corporations.[15] Only waqfs—charitable endowments that followed religious aims and financed large projects of all kinds— were of a corporate character. A comparison of Muslim and Genoese trading companies in the High Middle Ages shows that the Italians, buttressed by impersonal institutions and abstract law, developed increasingly complex commercial structures, whereas the Muslims remained within their own ethnic and social networks.[16] Inheritance law, based on the Quran, encouraged the fragmentation of fortunes. Capital could seldom be held together over several generations in the manner achieved by family trusts like the Medici or the Fuggers. Moreover, real estate, one of the most important sources for accumulating grand fortunes in the "West," could not be sold or bought at will; most land was owned by the state anyway. In short, business ventures in the Islamic world were not adapted to meet the challenges of the increasingly complex markets in which traders of all different origins and religions participated.

The state's economic policy remained fiscalist and provisionist. Its priorities, therefore, were to rake in the highest revenues possible and to care for the masses, thus keeping them quiet. This was reflected in widespread practice, although a strictly anti-mercantilist policy was not pursued. Imports were facilitated by low customs duties, and exports were hindered by high ones. Domestically, internal tariffs hampered trade. Long-distance commerce across the Mediterranean was controlled by foreigners. The trade privileges bestowed for political reasons upon foreign merchants—the French in 1536, for example, who were united with the Ottomans against the Habsburgs—led to cheap imports flooding markets to the detriment of local craftsmen. This was one reason for a long-term decline in the diversity of crafts practiced, an important indicator of the division of labor and thus of economic development. Meanwhile, the number of specialists in the state bureaucracy tripled between the Middle Ages and modern times. All in all, Ottoman economic policy remained deaf and blind. No permanent embassies were maintained in any of Latin Europe's large capital cities. This would only change in the eighteenth century.

With the conquest of Muslim territories where Islamic law was strictly applied, the legal system lost flexibility.[17] The situation worsened under the series of weak sultans that ruled after Suleiman's death. The cost of reconstructing the fleet after the loss at Lepanto—no matter how much the grand vizier played it down[18]—emptied the state's coffers, as did expenditures for land wars against the Habsburgs and the Safavids.

The victory the Turkish army won over Habsburg forces at Keresztes in 1596 would be its last in open battle. As a result, there was no more conquered territory to mete out.[19] The timars had to be cut smaller. The lack of land was intensified by the fact that, due to the silver shortage, civil servants and soldiers were no longer paid in cash but rather were rewarded with benefices. To meet the need for money, taxes were increased and the treasury plundered. Yet not even these measures sufficed. By the late sixteenth century, Anatolia was

plagued by marauding mercenary bands; in some territories, the state no longer had the power even to collect taxes.[20] Offices and military commissions
were for sale; one could even buy one's way into the Janissaries. The army lost
men and fighting power. Contrary to tradition and law, the land of refugees or
indebted farmers fell into the hands of benefice holders, tax farmers, moneylenders, and civil servants.

Animal husbandry dominated, to the detriment of the more labor-intensive
cultivation of grain. Sheep, which we have already met as the killers of English
and southern Italian agrarian structures, now ate their share of the Ottoman
future. The usual consequences ensued: migration to cities, brigandage, rebellions, and putsches. The once ultra-loyal Janissary corps became a law unto
itself. Its leader, the Agha, gained decisive power—as long as the harem was
not in control. Capable grand viziers, such as Köprülü Mehmed Pasha and
Köprülü Fazil Ahmed Pasha, a father and son who held office from 1656 to
1678, could not turn things around.

Like others in the Mediterranean world, the Ottomans were confronted by
insoluble problems caused by the shift in global trade to the Atlantic. The Red
Sea and Persian Gulf, the Ottomans' inland waters, lost their importance as
emporia of two global economies. Yet no response was made to the changed
situation. A 1568 plan to dig a canal through the Isthmus of Suez, similar to the
one once contemplated in Venice, was not pursued.

Like all states beholden to bureaucracy and religion, the High Porte only
valued the sciences when they yielded useful results or adorned the court. The
government gave scant attention to promoting innovations and inventions.[21]
Furthermore, there was no hereditary aristocracy to step in and provide patronage. Large estates, elsewhere the nobility's chief source of power, could
not be accumulated, as the timar benefices were only granted in usufruct.[22] In
consequence, scientific funding was almost exclusively to be had from the
sultan and a handful of viziers. Western technology and inventions were
scarcely adopted. Among thousands of estate inventories from the eighteenth
century, only twelve pairs of eyeglasses and five books are listed.[23] Even military technology was bought rather than developed at home. On the other
hand, recognition must be given to the smallpox vaccination campaigns undertaken in Istanbul starting in the final decades of the seventeenth century.
In Latin Europe, inoculation had to overcome manifold resistance before its
effectiveness was widely recognized.[24]

Now and again, religious authorities vetoed what they saw as overly zealous
research efforts. In 1580, for example, the Istanbul observatory, which had only

been built five years earlier, was destroyed due to pressure from religious cir-cles.[25] A quarter-century went by before observations of the night sky were undertaken again. Nevertheless, Muslims made use of the telescope neither on the Bosporus nor anywhere else. Although their astronomy had laid the decisive foundation for the astronomical revolution in Latin Europe, the latter only made its way to them late in the day. In 1732, the diplomat Ibrahim Mute-ferrika (ca. 1674–1745) wrote a treatise on the Copernican system, which he knew about secondhand. In the same breath, however, he declared the helio-centric theory to be wrong and charged Muslim scholars with disproving it.[26] At the same time, a provincial scholar in Anatolia requested a *fatwa*, a legal opinion, as to whether the rising of the Sun in the west, supposedly a sign prophesying the coming of the Last Judgment, was even astronomically pos-sible.[27] His contemporary Newton would have had a clear answer.

A short time before, Muteferrika had set up a printing shop in Istanbul, where previously only Armenians and Jews had operated presses. However, it was not allowed to print religious texts; God's word did not tolerate moveable type. From the very beginning, religious scholars opposed the introduction of the new technology. In 1485, Sultan Bayezid II prohibited printing with Arabic letters on pain of death.[28] The religious proviso was fateful, considering that scriptures and pious tracts had always helped printing to establish itself—in Korea and Japan as in China and Germany.[29] In the lands of the Prophet, the Quran would naturally have been the trailblazing text—and yet, *the* holy book of Islam that was not allowed to be printed.

The ban also had political motives. The state considered the free diffusion of knowledge to be dangerous; only experts were to be allowed to discuss scientific questions.[30] At any rate, there were many fewer potential readers in the Ottoman Empire than in Latin Europe. The sad fate of Muteferrika's print shop, which shuttered its doors after a bit more than a decade, shows that not even cosmopolitan Istanbul had a market for Europe's super-medium. A grand total of seventeen books had been published. Another attempt failed thirty years later, this one by James Mario Matra (1746–1806), secretary of the British embassy.

The Ottoman Empire remained cut off from the great intellectual currents of the West. For example, Machiavelli found a translator in 1825 but not a printer.[31] While Europe was piling up millions upon millions of books, in Muslim cultural space a handful of scholars studied manuscripts just like a thousand years before—to the delight of scribes and miniaturists, who were still able to subsist on their tranquil labor.[32] Yet for science and technology, the long-term consequences were devastating—in Turkey as well as in other states of the Islamic world, which all shied away from the art of printing.

Clever ideas remain mere ideas when they only blossom in the dark. In Latin Europe, Leonardo da Vinci provides us with a case in point. He knew much and invented even more, but he did not print any of it. As a result, his ideas simply faded away. The historiography of an Ibn Khaldun was as unknown in the Muslim world as al-Khwarizmi's revolutionary thesis that the planets followed elliptical orbits. The same goes for the invention of the Istanbul polymath Taqi al-Din, an intellectual descendant of al-Jazari. In 1551, he described a rotating spit powered by steam.[33] Yet his idea remained unpublished. Nobody pursued the project further; no entrepreneur turned up to recognize the potential of the device and invest in its development.

The chance for bold projects to be begun and pursued for decades, indeed centuries, was a thousand times better in Latin Europe (with its sophisticated communications media) than in the Ottoman Empire. There is no doubt that the observation made by the historian of science Edward S. Kennedy holds true: Tycho Brahe could indeed have had a Turkish name.[34] Yet could this Turkish Tycho have found a Turkish Kepler as a reader, and this Turkish Kepler, in turn, a Turkish Newton? In Europe, in contrast, the idea of using steam as an energy source had meanwhile been developed by many individuals over a long period of time. The first viable locomotive gathered speed in Wales in 1804. A few years later, steamboats chugged through a Scottish canal and along the Hudson River between New York City and Albany. And in 1830, England's Royal Navy launched its first steam-powered warship.

45

Pastoral Power

STATE, SOCIETY, RELIGION

Painful Separations, Crippling Connections

The bugbear of confessional antagonism was still accepted as a justification for war down to the latter half of the eighteenth century. Yet colonialism and imperialism had to search for new rationales.[1] More flagrantly than ever, Europe's states waged their wars for power and people, renown and resources. The old utopia of a "pure country" took on nationalist and then racist overtones. It continued to haunt Europe in the twentieth century, through its longest, darkest night.[2] But the taming of religion—*a process that took a millennium*—was one of the most significant preconditions for the two massive upheavals that we are wont to style as revolutions: the Scientific and the Industrial.

The religious wars of the sixteenth and seventeenth centuries—more specifically, those wars whose causes included religious differences—were part of the price that the West had to pay for its modernization. It was a high one. To adapt an infamous phrase of Samuel Huntington: Christianity also had bloody borders, perhaps even bloodier than Islam.[3] This mad, mutual butchery was one of the preconditions for the reinforced political neutralization of religion that now took place in Latin Europe, as well as for the progressive separation between church and state, science and religion. This trend did not mean that religion ceased to be part of life nor that its stewards lost all influence. Nevertheless, "pastoral power"—in a narrower sense than the one in which Foucault used the term[4]—was broken. Whether a book was listed on the Index seemed negligible in the eighteenth century, even in Catholic France. The clergy was reduced to caring for souls. After its first outlines took shape in the Renaissance, "enlightenment"—the project of using reason and discussion to get closer to truth—now received a second chance.

In Orthodox Muscovy, the Ottoman Empire, and other states ruled by Islam, these painful acts of separation did not take place. Likewise, there was no need for it in the realms of Buddha, Shiva, and Confucius (pp. 901–904). The Reformation, an initial trend toward enlightenment (composed of the Renaissance and the long runup to it), and the second, great Enlightenment remained European peculiarities. Nowhere else were philosophical foundations laid for such a break; nowhere else was the division between religion and politics a state-sponsored, legally safeguarded project.

Just how crippling an excess of pastoral power and internalized religious tradition can be for the sciences is demonstrated by the history not only of Byzantium or Spain but also of Judaism. The latter made almost no contribution to the decisive paradigm shifts of the Scientific Revolution, except for the significant role Jewish scholars played as intermediaries in transmitting Arabic and Greek science and philosophy to Christian Europe.[5] Max Weber argued that Judaism was essential for the shift in the West to a rational view of the world, but the only support this thesis finds is in Judaism's involvement in the development of the capitalist economy.[6] One reason for this was the social marginalization that generally excluded Jews from universities, academies, and guilds.[7] Furthermore, rabbinical authorities had the same mistrust of secular philosophy as those of other religions. For example, the Neoplatonist teachings of Solomon ibn Gabirol (1021–1058/1070) survived above all in Christian Europe—and then only because their author's faith was unclear.

The Aristotelian Levi Ben Gershon (1288–1344), a mathematician, theologian, and inventor of the Jacob's staff, reaped the whirlwind from pious Jews for his book *The Wars of the Lord*. They caustically characterized his attempt to reconcile the Talmud with Peripatetic philosophy as a "war *against* the Lord."[8] Rationalistic currents appeared now and then, such as in fourteenth-century Prague and late-sixteenth-century Poland, but they seemed to be inspired from outside, namely through contact with Italian culture.[9] Moses ben Isserles (1525–1572), a rabbi in Cracow and an accomplished astronomer to boot, felt compelled to justify the very fact that he was interested in Greek science.[10] The only work of theoretical astronomy written in Arabic by an Andalusian Jew was Joseph ibn Nahmias's *Light of the World* (ca. 1400).[11] One searches its pages in vain for new ideas.

There were hardly any Copernicans among early modern Jewish astronomers. Their number did not even include David Gans (1541–1613), a Jew in Prague who wrote a systematic astronomical treatise and conversed with Brahe and Kepler.[12] One exception appeared in the next generation: the physician Joseph Delmedigo (1591–1655), who lived on cosmopolitan Crete and had studied in Padua. He was at least willing to treat Bruno's and Galileo's teachings as hypotheses worth considering. Ultimately, however, he believed that absolute truth could only be found in God and divine revelation.[13]

Only with the *Haskalah* (Jewish Enlightenment) and Jewish emancipation in the eighteenth, nineteenth, and twentieth centuries did Jews take part in the grand scientific dialogue. As is known, they made contributions of phenomenal importance.

Words of Wax

The words of scripture are not very helpful when trying to understand the reasons for hostility to science or for openness to learned discourse. The Old and New Testaments and the Quran contain contradictory statements that admit of all manner of interpretations. "What is man, that thou art mindful of him?" rings out one praise of God in the Psalms. "Thou madest him to have dominion over the work of thy hands; thou hast put all things under his feet." In stark contrast stand the fateful consequences suffered by Adam and Eve for eating the fruit of knowledge. As Bonaventure, minister general of the Franciscan Order, wrote in the thirteenth century,

> But if we incline toward knowledge of things through experience, investigating them more than is allowed, we deviate from true contemplation and

taste instead of the forbidden Tree of the Knowledge of Good and Evil as Lucifer did.[14]

The tension highlighted here between religious revelation, the human pursuit of gain, and the thirst for knowledge beyond mystical meditation and faith is born of the conflict between religion, which knows all from the start, and science, which seeks to know what it does not know. Pietro Martire d'Anghiera warned that those who went too far in the search for truth could burn their wings and crash like Icarus.[15] However, where exactly the boundaries of knowledge lie and where that dangerous "more" begins—theology, the Church, the pious, and doubters all gave different answers to that question. And they in no way needed to be hostile to science.

Just as Christian investigators of nature sought divine signs, there is a concept in Islam, *ilm*, that can denote the desire for knowledge and that could be understood as an attempt to read in the book of nature written by Allah.[16] On the other hand, the twenty-seventh Surah emphasizes that Allah alone has knowledge of what is hidden. Such statements also provided ammunition to the opponents of deep-seeking science, to the rejection of Mu'tazila or Averroist positions. As one hadith says, "The truest word is the Book of Allah and the best guidance is the guidance of Muhammad. . . . Every innovation is going astray, and every going astray is in the Fire."[17]

Nevertheless, the view that Islamic doctrines erected insurmountable barriers to all science is not accurate.[18] The Prophet himself is supposed to have encouraged inquiry, calling out to his followers: "Seek knowledge, even if it is in China."[19] And Timur the Lame's grandson Ulugh Beg (1394–1449) had the following words inscribed on the wall of a madras he established in Samarkand: "To strive for knowledge is the duty of every Muslim."[20] Ulugh was himself a distinguished scholar. He had an observatory built in Samarkand, for a time making the city a world center of mathematics and astronomy.[21]

Then as now, we occasionally meet with bizarre attempts to demonstrate the absolute agreement between the Bible or Quran and the insights of modern science.[22] For example, Muslim exegetes could interpret "The Immutable," one of Allah's ninety-nine names, as a paraphrase of natural law. According to this point of view, God creates specific conditions anew in every moment.[23] An object does not burn because it has been ignited by fire but rather, as al-Ghazali taught (p. 209), because Allah continually creates the burning. He causes things, but what looks like causality actually flows from his will. Every single phenomenon, no matter how great or small, is brought to pass by him. Some Christian thinkers believed something similar about their God.[24]

In sum, the words of scripture appear to be made of wax. Giordano Bruno got to the heart of the matter: "Everyone finds in Holy Writ exactly what pleases them and suits them best. And they interpret the same passage not only differently but also utterly discordantly, turning a yes into a no and a no into a yes."[25] Ultimately, what matters is who has the authority to say what holy texts mean and the power to impose that view on others. Dramatic episodes illustrate the boundaries that the guardians of religion drew to contain the will to know, such as the destruction of the observatory in Istanbul and the trials of Bruno and Galileo. Apart from that, how many clever thoughts may have been neutralized by the "silent censorship" whose purpose is to keep the guardians of religion at bay—or by the conviction, internalized over centuries, that knowledge beyond that transmitted by the Bible, Torah, or Quran did not exist?

"Pastoral power"—regardless of whether it is exercised by Catholic Inquisitors, imams, or ultra-orthodox rabbis—also requires specific social and political conditions in order to produce its crippling effects. Neither malleable words nor the religious system alone can explain why the sciences began to stagnate in the lands of the Prophet in the Late Middle Ages and technological breakthroughs ceased. In fact, the influence of religious officials stemmed from the same preconditions that hindered the development of freer thought in general: overwhelming vertical power, and no middle class or "civic" public sphere to rein in the authority of rulers.

Kant Stopped before Bagdad

Admiration for Arabic learning can somewhat obscure what its masters were *not* interested in. For example, the Latin tradition was almost entirely neglected. Exceptions to this rule were found above all in al-Andalus, where Latin texts on agriculture were known, among others. Lucretius and Epicurus were largely unknown, as was the skepticism of Pyrrho.[26] Thucydides and Tacitus were ignored by Muslim historians from the very beginning; so were Cicero's political theory, Seneca's Stoicism, and the poetry of Ovid and Virgil. Not even Aristotle's *Politics* was translated. The tragedies of the ancients remained foreign to the Muslims, their comedies disregarded. Can a writer like Luigi Pulci—one of whose heroes in the *Morgante* utters blasphemies, claiming to believe in butter, beer, cider, and especially wine, which saves everyone who trusts in it—be imagined in Bagdad or Istanbul?[27]

Of course, there was and is no such thing as monolithic Islam. Its diverse variants evince contradiction and coherence.[28] As opposed to Christian

Europe, where dogma, ecclesiastical law, and religious rites were more or less controlled by the pope (until the Reformation and wars of religion changed everything), Islam had no clergy with a high priest. Only Iranian Shia Islam produced a kind of clerical caste in the sixteenth century, as did the Sunni variety in the Ottoman Empire. The teachings of Muhammad were safeguarded by *ulama*—many-headed bands of mostly local religious authorities. Their power was (and is) wide-ranging, its limits unclear. They served sultans and caliphs, issued fatwas, interpreted the Quran and hadiths, and preached morality.

There is no doubt about Islam's ever having been mere religious window dressing. It was and is a *way of life*. In the Middle Ages, all of Islamic society was referred to as a "church," as a community of the faithful protected by the state.[29] That did not preclude accommodations between religion and everyday life. For example, Muslim traders knew as well as their Christian counterparts how to circumvent bans on charging interest.[30] Nevertheless, it was a serious disadvantage that the rules of Islamic law were the product of a distant past and thus had to be adapted creatively to the present.[31]

The influence of religion may have buttressed political stability, but it did not bolster free speech or probing research, since these did not serve religious purposes. Criticizing rulers, or even revealing the mistakes and weaknesses of others in general, would have run counter to deeply rooted social and religious norms. Critique could cost one's head. It was engaged in accordingly seldom.[32]

Insofar as they aimed at purifying the faith, some of the reform attempts experienced by Islam resembled tiny Reformations. Yet as in Christendom, they resulted in division and sectarianism. The lack of a supreme doctrinal authority to determine what counted as orthodoxy and what as heresy encouraged a retreat to tradition.[33] With corresponding zeal, the guardians of religion opposed everything new. Those constantly forced to search for arguments in favor of a pre-established truth are not open to doubt or free discussion. It could be dangerous to use the critical analytical toolbox provided by Greek philosophy since, in combination with the malleability of words, it could be employed to undermine any truth. Logical arguments can be questioned, articles of faith and feelings not. Contempt for the teachings of Averroes, which relied on reason and bowed to no authority, ultimately stemmed from this imponderability.

While the free spaces for secularism and thus also for debates about science and technology expanded in Latin Europe, with the number of those participating in them skyrocketing, the same kind of civil society never seems to have had a chance in the Islamic world. Before the nineteenth century, Arabic did not even have a word for what is denoted by the term "secular" in Western languages.[34] Profound secularization of the kind seen and suffered in Europe would have rocked Muslim societies to the core. Even today, many if not most Muslims reject it. There have been exceptions, such as intellectuals like Mohammed Abed al-Jabri (1935–2010) of Morocco. He opposed the insistence on early medieval exegetical approaches to sacred texts and philosophical traditions, promoting instead a secular understanding of science, independent thinking, the use of reason, and critique.[35] Yet the Arabic world never witnessed the development of a critical public sphere that could have helped an Islamic Enlightenment to survive. Authoritarian systems of rule with little respect for private property hindered the formation of a middle class. Meanwhile, in Latin Europe, it was above all members of this social element that engaged in independent scientific research, defended its right to exist, produced the Reformation and the Enlightenment, and created the public sphere.

According to an estimate by the World Bank, around the turn of the millennium all Arab states combined had fewer exports (not counting petroleum) than Finland.[36] So far, only three individuals from Muslim countries have been awarded a Nobel Prize in a scientific discipline, as opposed to twenty-two recipients from tiny Switzerland and almost three hundred from the United States. In the view of Abdus Salam of Pakistan, one of those three scientists, "There is no question but today, of all civilizations on this planet, science is weakest in the lands of Islam."[37] A United Nations report identified three deficits in the Arab world as of 2002: knowledge acquisition, freedom and good governance, and women's rights.[38] Pretty much the same diagnosis could have been made for the early modern period. Some Muslim intellectuals see a way out of the dead end by returning to a purified, holistic Islam.[39] If that really presents a solution is anyone's guess.

No Middle Class in Sight

Nowhere in the premodern Islamic world were there popular assemblies that could have acted as vehicles for cities to demand a say in government affairs; nowhere were there city republics. The Muslim city did not comprise a "political body" on the European model. At the most, the rich chronicle literature reveals occasional examples of local pride.[40] Almost all of the realms of the caliphs and sultans, from the Delhi Sultanate to the North African dominions threatened by nomadic warriors, resembled military dictatorships.

With their large spaces dedicated to public life, Europe's communes even physically looked like the antitheses of the cities of the Prophet.[41] The classic forum for dialogue—the *Platz*, piazza, or agora—the space that played host to haggling and chatting and also embodied the public sphere itself, was not usually laid out in Muslim communities.[42] Town halls were absent too. The centers of the Muslim city were the bazaar and the mosque. Dead-end streets (which, unlike broad roads, did not count as public), buildings without windows, and courtyards closed to outside eyes ensured privacy. Monumental structures attest not only to architectural genius, economic conditions, and the world of religion but also to brutal regimes that "could squeeze blood out of stones if the stones were numerous enough."[43] Enthralling and threatening at the same time, they were silent sentinels standing watch over the people.

Caliphs and sultans ruled by means of alliances with urban notables that, without exception, came from the commercial elite. Such dignitaries had their roots in local groups, such as schools of jurisprudence, that were not always friendly toward one another, in neighborhoods, and sometimes in tribal associations. In general, they acted as vicars of state power and not as representatives of a community of citizens that, in case of conflict, would defend their independence. They can hardly be compared with the communal governments that mediated between princes and people in European cities.[44] Only during periods of weakened central power and in peripheral zones of the empire did trends toward the development of communal autonomy appear.[45]

Things seem to have started to change in the eighteenth century, however. One example is offered by Ottoman Aleppo, where an urban culture developed that did not have much in common with the traditional values of Islam and, indeed, was often antithetical to them.[46] In Tripoli and other cities, landowners, merchants, and members of respected guilds achieved relative autonomy from central power. The organ of home rule was a council, the *jama'al-bilâd*, which also chose the mayor. Future research is likely to further refine our understanding of the Muslim city.

Finally, reservations about city life were related to the fact that urban activities, the striving for material goods, and the satisfaction of earthly desires departed from the ideal of a blessed life as theorized by Arab philosophers. "Freedom" was not a positive value. In the "collective city," which most closely approximates democracy in al-Farabi's conception, freedom means licentiousness. "The aim of its people is to be free," he writes, "each of them doing what he wishes without restraining his passions in the least."[47] In Averroes's opinion, urban societies lacked a common purpose, viz., the highest good. In his view, every household pursued its own interests, which tended to be of a material nature. A few magnates shared power and profits, whereas the people—in Iran as well as "in many of these cities of ours," as he argued—were exploited.

How different the situation was in some lands of the Prophet is illustrated by Ibn Khaldun's reflections.[48] In his magnum opus, the *Muqaddimah* (literally "Introduction"), he offers an explanation from the Maghreb perspective for the decline of Islamic culture. He argues like a sociologist. He identifies an inflection point in the invasions of the Banu Hilal, a tribal confederation that began attacking cultivated Muslim land in the mid-eleventh century. In Ibn Khaldun's view, the Banu Hilal were made superior by their iron system of values, *asabiyyah*, a blanket term for the fidelity, loyalty to the federation, and resulting sense of honor that were forged by blood and religion. He believed that the Arabs conquered by the Bedouins had lost these very values, thanks to their urban lifestyle, its luxury, and its customs which destroyed all tribal and family ties. Fear of laws and punishments sapped courage and strength. Impoverishment, corruption, and deviation from the true faith were the evil consequences. In contrast, power, military success, and *asabiyyah* were closely connected. He theorized a kind of generational decline: from father to son to grandson to great-grandson, possession of all-powerful *asabiyyah* slipped away bit by bit. That is why it was lost. Rulers rose and fell, rose again and declined once more, all based on the vigor or weakness of *asabiyyah*; this was his version of the Western metaphor of the wheel of fortune.

Ibn Khaldun's animadversions on human civilization portray a chivalrous tribal community as the ideal and modernization as the problem. It seemed inevitable to him that the world of pure beginnings would be eaten away by the cancer of decadence that nestled in the cities. In the civic world of medieval Latin Europe, people were already starting to see things very differently. For example, the Franciscan friar Berthold of Regensburg (1210–1272) celebrated the city as the place where security and conveniences provided citizens with the freedom to serve God joyfully.[49] In addition to Ibn Khaldun's faith in the ethics of the tribal bond, the most important difference between his political theory and that of his younger counterpart by a century, Machiavelli, was the central role he assigned to religion to preserve and expand power. Homage is paid to Allah on every page of the *Muqaddima*. Philosophy, logic, and the study of nature also seemed to Ibn Khaldun to present a danger to faith. Such a line of argumentation had deep roots. Back in the tenth century, a follower of the Umayyads had reproached the detested Abbasids for patronizing Greek learning, blaming this for the decline of Islam.[50] Learned rulers like the Ottoman Sultan Mehmed II, who was receptive to Greek learning, became increasingly rare in the Late Middle Ages.

Was Ibn Khaldun's analysis correct? In his own day, the idea that "decadent" cities were responsible for Arab weakness was already inaccurate, considering that it was inside their walls that the techniques were devised and the weapons forged that alone made it possible to overcome steppe and desert. As a modern observer could now coolly point out to the Tunisian scholar, it was trade and commerce, technology and science—Ibn Khaldun had no problem with the latter, incidentally—that made states powerful, not blood, tribal honor, or modest agriculture. And it was Greek thought that prepared Europe's technological takeoff.

A not insignificant role in the process was also played, finally, by the art of realistically depicting the world, picked up from antiquity and perfected by the Dutch and the Italians. It, too, remained a largely European peculiarity. Allied with printing, it entered into the service of science and technology early on. The contrast with other cultures was spectacular, especially in the field of anatomy. Once again, such differences were often enough dependent on religion.

Apollo Stopped at Gandhara: Religion, Art, Anatomy

One Japanese scholar's eyes nearly popped out of his head in 1771 when he got his hands on a Dutch edition of the anatomical charts originally created by the German physician Johann Adam Kulmus. They were far superior to anything he had ever seen, including works in Chinese. He immediately commissioned a translation.[51] Muslim societies had no anatomical writings of a quality comparable to those of Latin Europe either.[52] One example is provided by the 1390 work of anatomy by the Persian physician Mansur ibn Ilyas (Fig. 75, p. 862), whose images are useless for any practical application. It was still being copied down to the seventeenth century, as clearly nothing better was available. On the other hand, at least one Muslim anatomist, Shams al-Din Itaqi, did copy drawings from Vesalius's work.[53]

Naturalistic art had always been largely a European phenomenon. Masterpieces like Vesalius's Fabric of the Human Body had a long, complex prehistory that stretches back to Greek antiquity and the early centuries of Christianity. The technical ability that made it possible was not developed overnight. The fact that others did not engage in naturalistic art or did so less often was due to divergent aesthetic conceptions and, thus, to different understandings of what purposes images served.

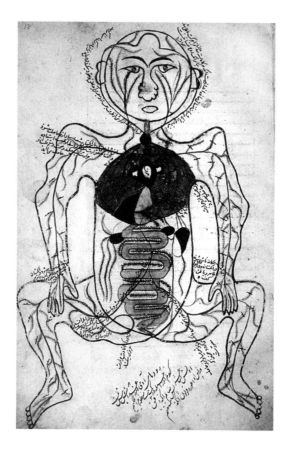

In Islamic societies, as in Judaism, the prohibition on images in the Deca-
logue was a retarding force—although taken literally, the ban applies only to
sculpture.[54] Muslims were not overly enthusiastic about images, although they
did not dispense with them entirely either; sculptures of human beings were
a rarity.[55] The hadiths' unfriendly stance toward images in stone or paint was
probably a relic of the religion's early days when Muslims had to deal with
pagan "idolaters"; the Quran does not say much on the subject. The hadiths
let it be known that images were impure like dogs; they enticed people to worship idols and distracted them from prayer. Painters who dared to depict living
human beings or animals were seen as brazen rivals of the Creator-God and
thus had to fear hellish punishments. Indeed, Islamic art preferred to focus on
presenting the pure word of God. Inscribed into exquisite ornaments, the letters were as beautiful as the content of the Surahs they transmitted. Human
images were rare and almost always reserved for the private sphere.

In contrast, Christendom arrived early on at a much more relaxed relationship with images, especially with those depicting its deity. Portraits of Christ and his mother replaced the usual portraits of the imperial cult back in the fourth century, indicating that it was now their duty to protect the state.[56] Yet people still wondered how something as awesome as a universal creator could be rendered in paint, wood, or stone. Far Eastern religions adopted a concept similar to that of the Byzantines, who imbued their icons with the "idea" of Christ or—as in the case of the Mandylion of Edessa—suggested a heavenly origin for portraits. For example, one Daoist text claims that artists receive lightning visions of formless, colorless gods and saints that they then use to create their images.[57]

At any rate, the biblical prohibition on images could be circumvented by focusing on Christ's *human aspect*. Not the divinity was depicted but the man. Tellingly, the Byzantines, who were amenable to images and versed in theology, only painted the Son of Man, never God the Father. The latter, likewise Christ, would technically have to look like the Son. Admittedly, only a few people consistently implemented such ideas. One was Enguerrand Quarton (ca. 1410–ca. 1466) of France. His *Coronation of the Virgin*, now in Villeneuve-lès-Avignon, was theologically correct in that it depicted God the Father and Christ identically. This was very different from God the Father as painted by Michelangelo, who portrayed him in the traditional manner as a bearded old man in the mask of the prince of the gods, Zeus.[58] Perhaps Christian art was willing to make pictures of its god because the Greeks and Romans had done the same with their gods. In other words, the Christian god reflected the same classical world whose legacy had nourished the painting and sculpture of Christians. In addition, they were guided by words of scripture to the effect that God had created human beings in his image and likeness. Portraying God as a man—thus Dürer argued—required at least making him as beautiful as possible.

In sum, religion in Latin Europe was never fundamentally opposed to depicting real-life human beings in all their corporeality. The "Greek Christ" never vetoed the portrayal of nudity. In spite of objections here and there, physicality and the naked body found their place in the pictorial world of Latin Europe.[59] From time immemorial, it had been the unquestioned standard to show Adam and Eve naked. The tradition of large-format sculpture and painting began with figures of the first humans on Bamberg Cathedral's *Adamspforte* (literally "Adam's Gate"), i.e., before 1237. The Renaissance then rendered thousands of naked bodies in marble and paint. If sculptors and

painters did not themselves study anatomy, they had a large supply of models in ancient statues.

The overwhelming power of Greek sculpture even helped to inspire images of Buddha in the first century. Before that, artists in India had shied away from carving him in wood or stone. The earliest statues of the sage appeared in Gandhara, on the border between Afghanistan and Pakistan, in what had once been a Diadochi kingdom (Fig. 76, above). Indian, Persian, Greek, and Roman influences melded into a fascinating synthesis. Some of the figures could be mistaken for Roman gods, if not for their stylized physiognomy or inapposite accessories like gems on their foreheads.[60]

Apollo stopped at Gandhara. And even there his power diminished with the invasion of the "White Huns" in the fifth century. Naturalistic art experienced a late flourishing in Mughal painting, with high points under Akbar and Jahangir. However, anatomical portrayals are also rare in Indian art. The hundreds of thousands of medical manuscripts written there contain almost no pictures.[61] The colored drawing of an "Ayurveda Man," created around 1700 and now in the possession of a British library, seems to be influenced by Tibetan models. Lhasa is also the likely origin of the exceptional scroll paintings commissioned by Sangye Gyamtso (1653–1705)—the learned *desi*, or regent, of the fifth Dalai Lama. They illustrated his *Blue Beryl*, a compendium of traditional Tibetan medicine.

The refusal of most "others" to engage in what Craig Harbison has called the "play of realism"[62] is irrelevant to an aesthetic judgment of their art—but not to the history of scientific or technical illustration. Ultimately, the invention of highly complex equipment required, as Eugene S. Ferguson has noted, not so much mathematical knowledge but rather the ability to think and communicate in pictures.[63] Just try to describe in words the construction of a water-powered organ of the kind designed by Salomon de Caus!

The reasons that the lands of Muhammad, Buddha, and Shiva largely avoided creating images of anatomical findings are rooted deep in their social orders and spirituality. Let us take Ayurveda as an example.[64] India's multimillennial history of medicine does not treat the body as an isolated unit. Rather, it regards it as being in constant osmosis with its natural and social environment. In a very tiny nutshell, health, according to Ayurvedic teaching, means that the three "doshas" of a given individual—first, water and earth; second, fire; third, air and ether—are in equilibrium with one another and in harmony with the macrocosm. Healers know the location of "marma" points, mysterious energy centers. They know the dangers of injuring them and the positive effects that result when they are touched or massaged. Therefore, Ayurveda is not just medicine but rather, as the Sanskrit term denotes, "knowledge of longevity." It does not merely facilitate survival but rather helps people lead a good life. Thus the concept embraces physical, psychological, and ethical aspects, such as the proper treatment of one's fellow human beings. Anatomical knowledge is utterly superfluous for its practice. Apparently, it was the British colonial regime that first introduced India's doctors to the dissection table. The first autopsy was performed in 1836 in Calcutta. Western medicine took hold not in place of Ayurveda but rather alongside it. Within the Ayurvedic system, India's physicians have always practiced medicine with a rational, scientific spirit. They have relied on observation and experience since time immemorial. Their rationality is *different*, not worse, than that of Europeans.

46

Lost Civilizations, Stubborn States

Beyond the Realm of Leviathan

Montaigne could have written similar sentences.

> So cross each bridge as you come to it; gaze at the moon, the snow, the cherry blossoms, and the bright autumn leaves; recite poems; drink saké, and make merry. Not even poverty will be a bother. Floating with an unsinkable disposition, like a gourd bobbing along with the current—that is what we call the floating world.[1]

This timeless perspective on history comes from the Tokugawa poet Asai Ryōi (ca. 1612–1691). It gives voice to the ancient Buddhist conviction that the world is in a constant state of flux; one must seize the day. This is a good idea in light of the civilizations that have been lost around the world, civilizations of which barely a memory survives: ruins, a few bits of a wall, graves, soil discolorations.

We catch a glimpse of them in sculptures like the enigmatic moai on Easter Island or earthworks like those of the "Mound Builders" of North America. The cities of the Maya, inventors of writing and mathematicians, are marked only by ruins. Almost nothing remains of Tenochtitlán. The Inca left little, but at least we still have Machu Picchu and its sophisticated irrigation system.

Often it was internal conflicts, epidemics, or invasions of foreign conquerors that led to collapse.[2] Climate change, environmental overexploitation, the loss of economic outlets, and the exhaustion of natural resources could result in decline or collapse, as could the lack of institutions. It was usually a combination of several factors. By all means, Maya culture was allotted seven hundred years—but even that was too little, considering, for one, that the key material of paper took much more than one thousand years to go from China to Europe. In contrast to Europeans, the inhabitants of the Americas could not draw on the inventory of ancient cultures, including the legacy of Asia.

Long periods of time and sophisticated state structures are necessary if opportunities are to develop for the sciences and the kind of "Promethean" (to quote the economist Deepak Lal)[3] growth enabled by new technology. These two foundational conditions were missing in many regions of the world.

Let us first look at precolonial Africa, behind the dark curtain of contempt and racism that later centuries drew across the continent.[4] Islam assisted in state formation and the organization of urban life in those territories it conquered. Like Christendom in its domains, it bestowed a certain amount of literacy and scientific education.[5] For example, the gold city of Ghana already had bath complexes and twelve mosques in the eleventh century; it provided a home to scholars and nourished jurists.[6] Islamization often remained superficial, however. In the Hausa Kingdoms, the jihadi Usman dan Fodio (1755–1817) witnessed the worship of trees and rocks, fortune-telling, magic, and the mixing of potions.

Only a few of the political entities that had developed between the Sahara Desert and the Limpopo River after the year 1000 were comparable with the ink states of Europe.[7] One example of the different paths followed by most African states is provided by the savanna Kingdom of Lunda, which emerged in the sixteenth century. Its political system was ingenious. Every ruler, regardless of his origin, assumed the identity of his predecessor and thus the latter's family network, which now became his own. He was able to maintain authority independent of tribal ties.[8]

Firearms endowed some states with power and political heft. Equally helpful was the possession of horses. One Portuguese chronicler reports—a boundless exaggeration, no doubt—that the Kingdom of Wolof raised an army of 100,000 infantry and 10,000 cavalry.[9] The Songhai Empire, which initially rose in pre-Islamic times and was one of the dominant states in Africa in the fifteenth and sixteenth centuries, used cavalry to carve out its enormous territory around the Niger River under Sunni Ali (reigned ca. 1464–1492) and Askia Muhammad I (r. 1493–1528). The might of Oyo, also in the territory of modern Nigeria, was likewise accrued on horseback. Further to the south, the deadly tsetse flies checked the cavalry.

In some kingdoms—their number was estimated at two hundred around 1500 and still a good one hundred around 1850[10]—the rulers barely outshone the ruled. Lively impressions from North Africa are provided by a 1526 travelogue by the Andalusian al-Hasan al-Wazzan (ca. 1494–after 1532), who was baptized a Christian in Rome, adopted by Pope Leo X, and thereafter known as Leo "Africanus"—"the Berber."[11] He claimed that every Italian nobleman had better manners than any ruler in Africa. On the other hand, Ibn Fadlallah al-Umari reports that anyone who did not remove their shoes before entering the chamber of the king of Mali, Mansa Musa, was executed.[12] Anyone beheld by the Songhai ruler had to cover himself with dust. Only his *djina-koï*, a kind of generalissimo, was allowed to perform the act with flour.[13]

Christendom had bastions in Ethiopia and—down to the Late Middle Ages—in Nubia. Missionary successes were limited in the west and the south. The first diocese was established at São Tomé. One of the few Christian enclaves on the mainland was the Kingdom of Kongo in Central Africa; its rulers had converted under the influence of Portuguese missionaries. The Christian god became Nzambi a Mpungo, as the creator of the universe was known there.[14] Alfonso I, who ruled Kongo from 1506 to 1543, corresponded with Lisbon and was recognized as king. He made efforts to attract teachers and craftsmen from Portugal. European fashion became a status symbol of the upper class. The decay of the Kongolese state, which for a time possessed an army outfitted with firearms, was ultimately the work of its Portuguese "friends." The copper deposits in its territory animated the spirit of greed, as did the opportunity to obtain slaves. Around 1530, between four thousand and five thousand slaves a year were "exported." Rivalries in the interior facilitated Kongo's subjugation. When a Kongolese army was defeated by a combined Portuguese and African force in 1665, the three-hundred-year-old kingdom was history. Nevertheless, an "Atlantic creole" culture survived in West Central Africa that produced Africanized forms of Catholicism. It was the source of—Christian!—slaves that were shipped off to Caribbean and

North American colonies, thus forming a founding generation of African Americans.[15]

States in Africa were also familiar with horizontal power, for instance in the form of councils of elders, youth associations, and secret societies. The most important social formation was usually the ancestral group or lineage. It provided succor and protection, made kings or impeded them. Many individual decisions, such as marriage, required their consent. Some African societies allowed for upward social mobility, such as when someone proved their worth as a warrior, hunter, or ritual specialist.[16] In others, however, there was no way out of the caste into which one was born. Money economies hardly existed;[17] banks, currency exchanges, and the like were utterly absent. The economy of Africa never achieved noteworthy increases in productivity without becoming inefficient in the process. Agricultural production was extensive, usually assisted by slaves. The latter were, in addition to gold and salt, Africa's most valuable "commodity."[18] Indigenous elites were among the buyers as well. Ultimately, it was not the possession of material goods on which reputation was based but rather the possession of human beings.[19]

Only a few African languages, such as Swahili, achieved written form before the colonial period. Even in places penetrated by religions of the book, literacy was restricted to a small circle. Only in the nineteenth century did missionary schools provide locals with a little instruction in reading and writing. Some African dignitaries continued to reject such arts even after 1850.[20] Nowhere beyond areas in contact with Islam or Christianity did state administrations based on written records take shape. Leo Africanus took a decidedly Eurocentric view, however, when he wrote that cities were not properly ordered nor courts well organized "in the land of black people."[21]

Africa's economy was conservative, its productivity low. Foreign, more sophisticated technology was seldom imported. The loom and firearms were adopted, but not the wheel. It was therefore impossible to transport goods over long distances at a price that made sense, except for rare raw materials, luxury goods, and slaves.[22] The spinning wheel also went unnoticed. It had enabled Europeans and Indians to increase textile production dramatically. Domestic production in Africa could not displace imports, only supplement them.

On the other hand, many realms of the continent produced outstanding indigenous art and architecture—such as the monolithic rock-hewn churches of Lalibela, the earthen clay buildings of Aït Benhaddou, the massive Bou Inania Madrasa in Fez, and Dogon and Kuba masks. The ban on resemblance that has been ascribed to African art[23] was in no way universal. African sculptors were fully capable of making naturalistic statues when they wanted to, as evidenced by the spectacular bronze heads produced in West African Ife in the fifteenth century (Fig. 77, p. 866). They could have come from the workshop of a Renaissance Florentine sculptor.

Early on, European travelers laid the foundation for enduring clichés.[24] Antonio Malfante of Genoa, who crossed the Sahara in 1444, portrayed Africans as sexually deviant savages who did not shy away from incest; they were great wizards and conjured demonic spirits with incense.[25] Leo Africanus said they lived like animals, without laws or rules.[26] Only in the large cities did they possess a "little more rationality and a hint of humanity." In addition, he said they were always joyful and liked to dance and feast. In his 1602 description of the Gold Coast region, the Dutch merchant Pieter de Marees reported that the inhabitants of West Africa "learn easily" and "understand quickly"—so not everything that Europeans wrote was imbued with racism. However, portraits depicting black Africans in the habitus of Renaissance European lords, endowed with dignity and gravity, were an exception. So was the career of Juan Latino (ca. 1518–ca. 1594), a freed slave who became a Latin professor at the University of Granada.[27]

Around 1600, there were hardly more than thirty cities in all of Africa with a population of twenty thousand. In the following two centuries, the number dwindled even further.[28] All Marees could say about the cities on the Gold Coast is "that they are ugly places and stink like Carcasses because of the rubbish which they throw out on the roads in heaps." If the wind was right, he claimed, the stench could be smelled from miles away.[29] In sub-Saharan Africa, larger settlement conglomerates crystalized thanks to trade and around natural resources, farmland, and pastures. Sometimes the gods helped, as when a cult site attracted people. Among the cities of the south, Great Zimbabwe was one of the most significant of the Middle Ages, with a population of eighteen thousand. Its prosperity derived from neighboring gold mines and exchange with port cities on the Indian Ocean. The elite fed on beef and beer, used Chinese porcelain, and lived in monumental granite buildings. Settlements of the dimension of Great Zimbabwe were found only in a few regions. They included Dia (in what is now Mali) and Timbuktu, a center of Islamic learning, as well as cities on the Indian Ocean like Mombasa. Kilwa boasted "many fair houses of stone and mortar" with ornately carved wooden doors. Here, too, Portuguese intervention put an end to cultural flourishing and urban freedoms.[30] Like other cities on the east coast of Africa, Mombasa and Kilwa fell under the rule of Oman in the seventeenth and eighteenth centuries.

Long periods of time for development were not granted to most African states. Ghana decayed in the thirteenth century; Mali, the gold state's successor as the great power in West Africa, splintered in the late fourteenth century in the wake of dynastic conflicts. The weak Marinid Sultanate, the inheritors of the Almohad Caliphate, also lapsed into infighting in the second half of the thirteenth century. When Sultan Abd al-Haqq II (r. 1421–1465) fell, so did the state. The heyday of Great Zimbabwe ended at the same time. Perhaps its decline was due to overexploitation of the environment, perhaps to shifts in the gold trade.[31] Ife's place had been taken by Benin by the time the first Europeans arrived.[32] Surrounded by mighty ramparts, the city sat enthroned in the middle of a small state whose king possessed a palace and a rudimentary administration. Its significance declined in the seventeenth century. Before that, the Portuguese had conquered Monomotapa, a successor state to Great Zimbabwe. Songhai, weakened by fights for the throne, was powerless to oppose the harquebuses of the sultan of Morocco's army in 1591.

Things were quieter only in regions of the interior, which had been reached by neither Islam nor slave-hunters. A few dynasties in more exposed regions survived for a longer time as well, such as the House of Solomon in Ethiopia, which ruled until 1974, the Hafsids in what is now Tunisia, and the Sayfawa dynasty, which assumed rule in Kanem in the eleventh century and then in Bornu. Ottoman advisors helped the Sayfawa kings to muster a corps of musketeers. Idris Alauma (r. 1564–1596) used this force to secure for his country an important route through the Sahara and to subdue neighboring powers, including a few Kotoko city-states south of Lake Chad.[33] The Sayfawa dynasty endured until 1846.

The different rules by which African societies played provide models for how communities without Western-style states can be organized.[34] In the early modern period, the European presence on the gigantic continent was largely limited to bases on the coasts and, all in all, was not very important. Not until the nineteenth century did Africa get sucked into the vortex of Western modernization. It metamorphosed from a slave supplier to a market for European goods, to a terrain that was exploited by the West and ultimately conquered militarily. Only then did a dramatic population explosion take place—a main cause of the continent's problems today. In the past, the opposite was the case. Around 1750, population density was still between 2.3 and 5.8 people per square kilometer,[35] as opposed to a maximum of 27 in Europe. That was the chief reason for the low level of urbanization in precolonial Africa, with all its consequences: an almost complete lack of educational infrastructure, few repositories of knowledge, little or no literacy in most places, and thus no bureaucracies or sophisticated legal systems.

The early modern European state and its nucleus, the city, are in no way the gold standard of human development. Nevertheless, a look at these non-European societies and civilizations helps us to understand how fundamental strong state structures were for the emergence of "Western" science and technology. Ultimately, they guaranteed a minimum of security—an indispensable parameter for research and discussion. This security was missing in many Asian states as well.

Parallels, Divergences: Central Asia, Southeast Asia

Like Africa, Central Asia and regions of the Middle East played a passive and not an active role in the process of global economic change touched off by the Industrial Revolution.[36] The center of the Eurasian continent had been haunted time and again by invasions and wars. In the process, libraries, archives, and scriptoria went up in flames, and with them knowledge and memory. Al-Biruni called the destruction of the city of Kath at the hands of a regional strongman a "crime against ancient culture."[37] The metropolis of Nishapur, numbering over half a million souls, was, for a time, one of the leading intellectual centers in the world. Toward the end of the rule of the last Seljuk great sultan Sanjar (reigned ca. 1084/86–1157), it was plundered by Turkmen nomads along with Merv and other cities of the crumbling empire. The Mongols and the Black Death finished the job. The notion of a *pax mongolica*, once floated by scholars, has not stood the test of time.[38] Genghis Khan and Timur looked eastward to India and China. The culture of Europe and that of the Muslim West were far from their minds.[39] In the wake of ensuing catastrophic events, intellectual life in many places sunk into rabid Sufism—at the same time as universities were rising in Latin Europe and enclaves for secularism were expanding.

Despite intense conflicts that redounded to the benefit of the Ottomans and the tribal confederation of the "White Sheep" (p. 561), Timur's descendants maintained power in eastern Iran and Transoxania. The Timurid states set up tollgates, using the revenues to fill their empty coffers. They have been called early "Renaissance monarchies," as they possessed secular regimes equipped with administrative know-how, facilitated merit-based social mobility, and established a diplomatic network that spread as far as Egypt and China.[40] The old splendor flashed forth here and there. Astronomy produced powerful minds, although the observatory in Tabriz lay in ruins after the first Mongol invasions. Under Ulugh Beg, the sciences experienced a period of renewed flourishing in Samarkand. And under Husayn Bayqara (r. 1469–1506), who enhanced his prestige with (both Persian and Turkish) literature and the arts, Herat also enjoyed a second heyday. The sultan's death spelled the end of the Timurids, though. One of them, Babur, went to India, where he inaugurated a postscript to the history of the dynasty (pp. 877f.). Otherwise, what remained were nomad federations in the north and the "oasis states" in East and West Turkestan. Some, like the Cossacks living in the border regions of the Russian Empire, opted for the lawless life of the steppe and sought to escape centralized power. The Ukrainian Cossacks managed to maintain their freedom until the reign of Catherine the Great (r. 1762–1796).[41]

That same period witnessed the end of the late flourishing of the once mighty Safavid Empire, of the caravanserais on the trading routes between Turkey and the Indian Ocean.[42] It had regained its former strength under Shah Abbas I "the Great" (r. 1587–1629). While monumental architecture was erected in the capital of Isfahan and illumination, artisanal trades, and literature emanated far and wide, the sciences were regarded with suspicion by the Shia clergy and thus neglected. In 1722, the city of 600,000 residents fell after a long siege to the Ghilzai Afghans. During the reign of Catherine the Great, only about fifty thousand people were left there.

As in Central Asia, the Middle East, and Africa, most political entities in *Southeast Asia* did not endure for a long period of time—i.e., for more than a few centuries.[43] One exception was the mighty Khmer Empire, which ranged from Dai Viet to the Malay Peninsula. It reached its zenith around 1200. A hundred years later, one Chinese envoy was still awed by the pageantry that surrounded the Khmer kings, observing, "The people know what a ruler is."[44] By then, however, the empire's future was already growing bleak. A period of drought seems to have done great damage. The Thai pushed back against its authority. In the fifteenth century, it fell under the rule of the rising Ayutthaya Kingdom. The Khmer retreated to the area around Phnom Penh. Their former power is memorialized by Angkor Wat, once the largest sacral complex in the world; one of its temples was covered in gold. In the same period, many other states enjoyed shorter periods of flourishing, including the Sukhothai Kingdom, Muang Mao, and Ava. The latter took the place of the mighty Pagan Empire, which began to wane in the mid-thirteenth century.

Leviathan's iron grip did not reach into the territories of the "savages" of Southeast Asia, as city dwellers in the region disparaged them. Some lived in

Stone Age conditions. The Portuguese historian João de Barros (ca. 1496–1570) mentions the mysterious "Gueos," a mountain people in northern Siam. He describes them as cannibals, their entire bodies tattooed and branded, who waged mounted war against neighboring peoples.[45] Rice cultivation, rivers, and, above all, proximity to the sea favored the creation of networks of smaller power centers that developed their own identities: "mandala states," systems of concentric circles dominated by a central power.[46] These had to continually negotiate their authority with satellite powers, which, in turn, were often centers of smaller mandalas. Whenever the center showed weakness, the smaller powers sought affiliation elsewhere. As in Europe, marriages helped to cement alliances and unite dominions, while population growth and trade could increase the gravitational pull of the central star. Some of them even evinced the development of "national" identities. After the successful end to a war with Ming China in 1428, whose activist Yongle Emperor had invaded and annexed the country (p. 346), one author wrote, "The soil is again the soil of the Southern kingdom. The people are again the people of the Viet race."[47] The victor Le Loi, founder of a new dynasty, lived on as the hero of his nation. Incidentally, the Vietnamese had already defeated a superpower once, at the end of the thirteenth century: the Mongols. The Yongle Emperor would have done well to take notes.

On the Bay of Bengal, Arakan (Rakhine) rose to power. Centered in Mrauk-U, it gained independence from the Bengal Sultanate in the sixteenth century. Its Buddhist rulers embodied cosmopolitan culture. They had Muslim titles, fostered Persian literature, and had Brahmins officiate at ceremonies.[48] Here as in other areas of Southeast Asia, conditions somewhat recall those of Renaissance Italy. A few dominions located on the coast developed a high degree of independence. Profits from long-distance trade provided the means to expand militarily. Firearms were obtained first from China and the Islamic world. In the sixteenth century, European gunners and mercenaries were called in along with their technologically superior equipment. An Asian Gian Galeazzo Visconti appears in the form of the "Victor of the Ten Directions" (i.e., world ruler) Bayinnaung, a scion of the Burmese Toungoo dynasty.[49] The "Lord of Many White Elephants" used western cannons to assemble a realm that included Pegu, which had been conquered by his predecessor and extended far beyond Burma. Yet the state collapsed soon after his death in 1581.[50] Ayutthaya, briefly conquered by the Toungoo, also threw off their yoke.

The national hero of Siam was Naresuan (r. 1590–1605). The warrior king reconquered Ayutthaya and subdued Cambodia and Chiang Mai, the capital of Lan Na, the "Kingdom of a Million Rice Fields." Cosmopolitan Ayutthaya was a kind of Thai Venice. Located at the confluence of three rivers, criss-crossed by canals, and well supplied by international trade—the Dutch had a trading post there—it boasted three royal palaces and nearly four hundred temples within its walls. Here, too, the sun over Siam was reflected in gold upon gold.[51] Its potentate, to whom all the land belonged, seemed to João de Barros to be the most absolute ruler on Earth.

As in Europe, power sheathed itself in religion, art, and architecture. From Angkor Wat to the "Temple of 90,000 Buddhas" in Mrauk-U, monumental palaces, temples, and mosques communicated the grandeur of rulers, the greatness of gods, and the gains made from international commerce. Europe's saints, relics, and icons had equivalents in Southeast Asian communities in tutelary deities, Buddha's canine tooth, and the divinely worshipped white elephants of Siam, which also served as important symbols of power. Statues worked miracles. One was the Phra Bang, the royal Buddha image of the Lao state of Lan Xang. Another was the "Emerald Buddha," which, after a series of adventures, found a home in Bangkok.

The medieval empires of Srivijaya and Majapahit were distant counterparts to Italy's sea powers. As the doge married the sea by throwing a ring into the Venetian Lagoon, the maharaja of Srivijaya sacrificed a bar of gold to the Musi River, which flowed through his territory. "Look," he called out, pointing to the water, "there lies my wealth!"[52] The Southeast Asian tableau included is-land kingdoms like Gowa-Tallo on Sulawesi, as well as countless tiny domin-ions and small thalassocracies like Ternate and Tidore, each of which ruled over (or at least tried to rule over) a smattering of isles with their own different languages, religions, and cultures. One Chinese observer regarded the indig-enous inhabitants of Timor with contempt. According to his report, they ran around half-naked, a sight nearly too ugly to behold. Here and on other islands that supplied spices and sulfur, limited fresh water and a lack of anchorages for large ships hindered the development of trading centers. There were also well-organized states like the Sultanate of Maguindanao, Sulu, Aceh, and Johor. The Italian traveler Antonio Pigafetta stood in awe before the palace fortress of the Sultan of Brunei. As he fastidiously noted, it was defended by fifty-six bronze cannons and six iron mortars.[53]

In the early seventeenth century, Dai Viet (later Burma and Ayutthaya)—the blueprint for Siam—dominated the mainland. By then, Dai Viet had split into two warring kingdoms under the nominal sovereignty of shadow emperors of the Le dynasty.[54] Until the end of the century, its southern part, Cochinchina (including what was left of Champa), stretched to the Mekong Delta. Cultural identities solidified. Thai, Javanese, and other peoples gradually took on the names we know today.

It is disputed whether the gulf between Southeast Asia and the West already started widening at this point in time—with the Little Ice Age and the global crisis—or not until between 1750 and 1850.[55] However, there is little question that the seventeenth century marked an inflection point in Southeast Asian history. Natural disasters and periods of drought, wars, and rebellions left its systems of rule fragile. In 1645, a massive earthquake ended Manila's heyday. Fifteen years later, Aceh was hit by a devastating tsunami. There was one famine after another. Regions destroyed by nature or war did not recover for a long time. The port cities of the archipelago, weakened by population loss, could not maintain control over the hinterland. Local and regional leaders gained greater power. The Portuguese mercenary captain Filipe de Brito e Nicote (1566–1613) even managed for a few years to revive the old condottiere dream of creating his own state, wresting Syriam from Rakhine and setting himself up as king. Anaukpetlun, one of the heirs of Toungoo rule, put a violent end to the adventure.

Not everything went downhill. The northern and southern parts of Vietnam reached an agreement in the 1670s. Lan Xang enjoyed relative peace and prosperity until the century's end. Ayutthaya also had a phase of stability under the authoritarian rule of King Narai. Aided by the recent presence in the region of the French, it ended when a putsch expelled the unpopular Europeans in the weeks before Narai's death in 1688. The Dutch, who had abandoned Phnom Penh, now energetically penetrated the archipelago. They wrested Malacca from the Portuguese, conquered Makassar between 1660 and 1669, and brought Java and the Java Sea largely under their control. After internal conflicts and a regicide in 1699, Johor's period of greatness was over. Bali remained divided into warring entities, and Ternate became a mere vassal of the VOC. The latter's authority waned as administrative and military costs piled up in the following years, and it was ultimately broken by massive incursions from British competition. Yet the fate of the VOC, once the mightiest trading company on Earth, was not sealed for good until the defeat in the Fourth Anglo-Dutch War (1780–1784).

As the historian Victor Lieberman has noted, some of the types of state formation just mentioned evince "strange parallels" with European developments: the subjection of the smaller at the hands of the larger (the Indians spoke of the "Law of Fish," *Matsya Nyaya*[56]); the centralization of power through murder and violence; the construction of mercenary armies and bureaucracies; and the erection of splendid palaces and the staging of the state with sumptuous ceremonial entries. Sophisticated systems of alliances and counter-alliances seem "European," as does cultural integration effected by religion or history writing. The parallels fade, however, when one considers Europe's university-trained public officials, its representative assemblies and parliaments. None of that existed in Southeast Asia, except perhaps for the *ruma bechara* (literally, "house for speaking") on Sulu, an assembly of local clan chiefs and other influential individuals.[57] It is incredibly difficult to find parallels to Europe's educated middle class and its scholars. The "Renaissance man" Karaeng Pattingalloang, chief minister of the Indonesian Kingdom of Gowa-Tallo, was an exception. He spoke fluent Portuguese, understood at least Spanish and Latin, collected books, and studied European mathematics and astronomy.[58] Nevertheless, telescopes, clocks, and other precision instruments had to be imported.[59] All the high civilizations in Southeast Asia were as far from achieving technological breakthroughs or jumpstarting their own Industrial Revolution as they were from the Moon. Investment in innovation via venture capital was hindered by exorbitant borrowing costs. Interest could be as high as 400 percent per annum, whereas in sixteenth-century Europe it had sunk to between 5 and 6 percent or less.[60] In addition, the money economy developed at vastly different paces in different regions, and capital was not secure. Printing, brought to Dai Viet by missionaries, was not well received. One legacy of the missions is that the Latin alphabet is still used in a few Southeast Asian countries.

Whereas dynasties and constantly growing bureaucracies gave longevity to states in Europe, the states of the Southeast Asian mainland wore each other down in regional wars. For example, Burma and Siam fought for supremacy for two hundred years. A supranational order of states, such as unfolded on a small scale in Renaissance Italy and on a large scale in eighteenth-century Europe, did not develop. None of the more significant dynasties in the region survived. Qing China's far-reaching economic expansion gave Southeast Asia its "Chinese Century" between 1740 and 1840—a sign of the weakness of the region's own states.[61]

India

In the "Land of the Roseapple Tree," a new great power had arisen: the Mughal Empire.[62] The name recalls its Mongolian roots. Its founder was the aforementioned Zahir al-Din Muhammad Babur (b. 1483, Great Mughal 1526–1530), a

Timurid from Transoxania steeped in Persian culture. In the shadow of Safavid expansion and the construction of the Uzbek kingdom under the Shaybanids, he had set his sights on Afghanistan and then, seeking his fortune in northern India, taken rich Delhi and Agra. He secured enduring glory with his autobiography, a first-person narrative notable for self-criticism, self-dramatization, idyllic garden scenes, and landscape descriptions.[63] The most important of Babur's descendants was Akbar (r. 1556–1605). After a brief interregnum under the Afghan Sur dynasty, he is considered the second founder of the Mughal Empire. Upon his death, it stretched from Kabul and Gujarat to Bengal. Akbar ruled with the aid of a military elite, the bureaucracy that buttressed it, and an army of millions. He did not exercise power arbitrarily on the model of the sultans but rather via agreements between governors and local leaders.[64] The empire's capitals, the most beautiful being the wonder of the world Fatehpur Sikri, communicated an image of rule that depicted the state as the expanded household of the emperor, indeed as a microcosm of the universe.[65] The caste system, based on religious values and degrees of ritual purity, was a hindrance to all civic freedom, as was the power exercised by kinship networks. Local city administration only existed in rudimentary form; villages alone enjoyed a degree of autonomy.[66]

India's rulers were generally unconcerned with who engaged in ocean trade as long as customs and taxes filled their treasury. The firm foundation of their power rested on agrarian yields. Down to the colonial period, India remained a center of global trade buoyed by capital inflows yet bled dry by its money-hungry rulers. Indian and Chinese merchants were omnipresent in the coastal cities. Compared with them, the number of Europeans remained infinitesimal. Property rights took root, and the late Mughal Empire showed signs of a budding middle class composed of city dwellers, traders, and a bureaucratic elite.[67] In the commercial hubs along the Coromandel Coast, a kind of merchant capitalism developed that seemed to be paving the way for the transition to industrial production. The necessary capital—in the form of rupees coined in Latin American silver—would have been available. Nevertheless, no part of India showed signs of "Promethean" growth.[68]

The grand tradition of Indian astronomy and mathematics had long since disappeared. The study of nature, being of no benefit to religion, was consigned to craftsmen and thus the lower classes.[69] The *Hortus Malabricus*, a work of botany that appeared between 1678 and 1693, was produced with the aid of local experts by a European—Hendrik van Rheede, the VOC governor of the coastal province of Malabar.[70] The Maharajah of Jaipur, Jai Singh II (r. 1700–1743), had observatories for astronomical study built, but that fact does little to change the overall picture. Isolated heights were also reached during the Mughal period in book illumination and architecture—one need think only of the tomb built for Shah Jahan's wife, the Taj Mahal in Agra.

The quality of artisanal craftsmanship was impressive, such as lacquer work, ceramics, and fine textiles. Yet the trades in India, like everywhere else in the world, did not achieve nearly the same level of diversity and specialization as in the cities of Latin Europe.[71] Ram Singh Malam, who was employed at a western Indian court in the eighteenth century, was one of the few who sought to bring European technology to the country. After being shipwrecked off the east coast of Africa, he ended up in the Netherlands. There he had nearly two decades to learn Western crafts, from glass blowing to the production of clocks and guns.[72] Yet Ram Singh Malam does not seem to have passed on the arts he acquired. More sophisticated equipment—clocks, telescopes, even eyeglasses (p. 898)—continued to be imported to India, as to the rest of Asia, from Europe.[73] And no wonder, as people there did not know how to make glass. A miniature from the time shows the aged Great Mughal Aurangzeb (r. 1658–1707)—the ruler of northern India, part of Afghanistan, and the conqueror of the Deccan Sultanate—reading the Quran. His back bent, he huddles closely over his book (Fig. 78, p. 880). A pair of glasses would have allowed him to assume a more majestic posture.

His realm also lacked the incentives, time, and money to invest in the development of innovations. Merit and economic success only enabled upward social mobility on a small scale. At any rate, higher status could be hoped for in the next reincarnation, and good karma was better amassed by making peace with current conditions than by trying to change them. Not even clever Akbar had recognized the significance of printing when he was shown movable type with Persian letters. India remained in the manuscript age down to the nineteenth century.[74] As a result, an essential precondition for the advancement of useful knowledge was missing.

Other countries in East Asia ignored printing too. In the first half of the sixteenth century, presses had been set up by Jesuits in Goa and Macao and by Dominicans in Manila. However, the number of secular titles they printed was vanishingly small. Three had been published in Goa by 1679.[75] Outside Christian communities, religious reservations seem to have hindered the spread of printing down to the twentieth century. Ultimately, the rejection of

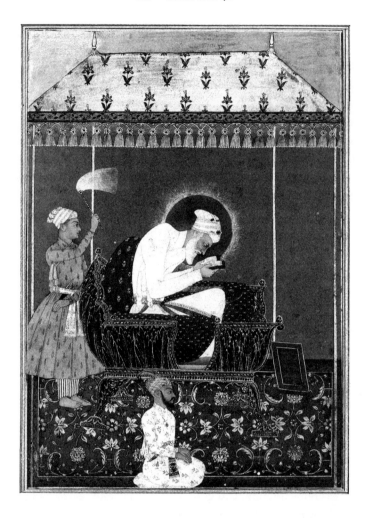

Gutenberg's invention locked India out of the European intellectual legacy, just as it did the Lands below the Winds and the Persians, who conquered Delhi in 1739, thus sealing the fate of the Mughal Empire.

Japan: Tokugawa Renaissance?

The modern history of Japan, Marco Polo's mythical "Cipangu," evinces especially striking parallels to that of Europe. In the fifteenth century, the Ashikaga shogunate steadily declined. In 1467, a feud between powerful vassals plunged the country into over a century of chaos. During the Sengoku, or "Warring States," period, the dominions of provincial warlords achieved a nearly autonomous status similar to that of the states of Italy's "new princes." Rural communities and cities bolstered their right to self-government.[76] They joined together—one thinks of late medieval leagues of cities and confederacies—into alliances covering entire provinces, enacting debt moratoria and lowering taxes.[77] At assemblies, mass discussions (*shūchū dangō*) were able to develop. Majority rule prevailed.

Like in the German Peasants' War, religious motives exacerbated the zeal of those in revolt. An example is provided by the *ikkō ikki*, leagues formed from the Buddhist Hongan-ji school. Their military might continued to grow into the late Muromachi period. Their faith promised those who fell in battle rebirth in the Pure Land, a joyous paradise.[78] Craftsmen, merchants, and local leaders participated in the *ikki*. The word connotes "single-mindedness," "popular contention," and "political protest." In 1485, a union of thirty-six samurai lords from all over Yamashiro Province was created that lasted for several years; one Japanese historian called it a "people's parliament."[79] The assembly, one of many, was the expression of a political culture and the possible beginning of a federative tradition. Examples of the survival of urban freedoms are provided by the fortified city of Kanazawa, ruled by a military commander and merchants, as well as Sakai, whose constitution one Jesuit compared to that of Venice.[80] Japan even had city halls, *kaisho*. Political competition was a spur to patronage. The magical world surrounding Kyoto's Silver Pavilion, poetry and plays, refined tea ceremonies, and ink painting—all this was a product of the wild "Warring States" period.

Firearms had been known since 1543.[81] The famous *Teppoki*, or *Gun Chronicle*, narrates an Asian culture's first encounter with Western weapons. It tells of two Portuguese traders driven off course by a storm to the island of Tanegashima. In their possession was an object made of a "heavy substance," a pipe three *shaku*—about one meter—in length that was closed at one end.

> There was an aperture on its side, through which fire was applied. Its shape could not be compared with anything else. When used, some mysterious (medicine) powder (*myoyaku*) was put into it and a small lead pellet was added.

Its potential for war and hunting was immediately obvious. "One shot from this object can make a mountain of silver crumble and break through a wall of iron." When the master of the island, Lord Tokitaka, asked how it worked, the Portuguese gladly instructed him. When the gun was then fired on a day identified as propitious, "people were at first startled, then they became frightened.

In the end, however, they all said in unison: 'We would like to learn!'" The "wonder of wonders" was copied. In 1558, muskets were first used on the battlefield. It is interesting that the Asian nations that would later become the continent's leaders seem to have been the only ones to produce firearms themselves and not rely on imports.

Nonetheless, technological breakthroughs did not follow. As the missionary Francis Xavier observed in 1552, no one there knew about the shape or the motion of the Earth. At the same time, Luís Fróis noted that all the work performed in Europe by water, windmills, or animals was done in Japan by human beings.[82]

In 1580, the *ikkō ikki* were defeated. The Hongan-ji was monitored carefully. Like in Italy, where the age of communal freedom was followed by an epoch of strong princely rule, the establishment of the Tokugawa shogunate in the early seventeenth century spelled the end of horizontal power. In light of the tensions in the country, those who had converted to Christianity were persecuted as scapegoats. A few missionaries suffered martyrdom. In the 1730s, the *bakufu* went about turning Japan into a closed commercial state—a concept familiar to some European economists.[83] The regime issued a series of laws motivated by both fear and pride. With few exceptions, the Japanese were forbidden from leaving their homeland on pain of death. All foreign relations were now subjected to strict governmental control. Those who had lived abroad for a substantial period were no longer allowed in the country, and trading voyages were limited. The Portuguese, with their Crusader mentality, had to pack their bags in 1639. Their place was filled by Chinese traders; the Dutch were all too happy to jump in as well. Yet they had to do their business on an artificial island off the coast of Nagasaki. The shogunate feared a Spanish attack from Manila. Often enough, missionaries had merely been the vanguard of mercenaries.

Japan sought security in an unstable world by reinforcing ties in East Asia. It successfully pursued the same strategy as other states in the region: strengthening internal cohesion, building traditions, and gaining greater independence from the volatility of international trade.[84] There was an ideological aspect as well. In a challenge to China, Tokugawa Japan maintained the fiction that it was the center of the world.[85] In light of the Manchu takeover, so the argument went, barbarians from the north now ruled in Beijing. Therefore, universal order could no longer be centered there. Should not the lords of a true center, the "land of the gods," have things supplied to them rather than supplying others?

Jesuits shipped a printing press from Macao to Kyushu in 1591. A short time later, printed works and moveable type were brought home as spoils from the invasion of Korea. A Japanese printer set up shop in Kyoto, eventually printing a Japanese version of Aesop's fables. Yet the technology was not widely adopted, perhaps because the first books tended to be Catholic in nature. Japan, then, which had at least as long a tradition of printing as China, remained mired in the laborious media of block printing, handwriting, and drawing.[86] As for works that could have spread "foreign" science and learning, they were marginal to the canon.

The policy of closing the country off to the outside world in no way meant keeping it under lock and key. Rather, it led to a restructuring of relations with Asian neighbors. And it graced Japan with a long period of foreign peace. The shogun, whose capital was now in Edo (modern Tokyo), granted yearly audiences to VOC officials during which he was informed about global political events and scientific developments. Confucian teachings, which became the official ideology of the Tokugawa, contributed to inner tranquility. The social pyramid, with the shogun and the nobility at the peak, was thought, as in medieval Europe, to be rooted in the rational order of the universe. Also similar to Europe, the foundation of a developing market economy was based in part on competition within the system of cities and regional domains ruled by the shogunate and cemented in law.[87]

Japanese society was in turmoil in the eighteenth century.[88] The merchant class, contemptible in the view of Confucianism, developed into the primary creditor of the state. Markets and money grew in importance. While large centers like Edo and Osaka began losing population at mid-century, harbor towns and fortified cities expanded. Japan was the opposite of Africa: one of the most highly urbanized regions on Earth. A good twelve percent of the population lived in cities, including the country's intellectual capital. This was one of the reasons that Japan modernized much more quickly than all other states in Asia in the late nineteenth century.

Like in Shakespeare's London, the theaters were packed—with both men *and* women, rich and poor. Paintings and especially color woodblocks in a native artistic genre called "pictures of the floating world" give us insight into an urban culture, depicting courtesans, sumo wrestlers, and genre scenes: a bourgeois civilization without parallel in Asia. Literacy was probably more widespread than in Europe, as the schools at Buddhist temples were open to boys and girls of all ranks. Yet book production lagged far behind that of Europe. In the Netherlands, 538 books per million inhabitants were printed, and in England it was 198. In Japan, it was a mere seven.[89] On the other hand, the market was flooded with printed pamphlets containing both text and images. They informed readers about important events, wars, and natural disasters. Their main object was to entertain. In addition, there were Buddhist and Confucian texts, books of arithmetic and how-to manuals, plays, comedic material, and classics like the *Tale of Genji*.

Japan had been in dialogue with ancient Chinese culture since time immemorial. Now this process intensified. Private academies and schools educated hundreds of eager students from the entire socioeconomic spectrum.[90] Like the humanists and the Reformers—and similar to developments in neighboring Qing China—the *kogaku* ("ancient learning") movement sought to bypass the Chinese commentaries and go back to the pure texts of the classics. In the seventeenth century, a class of professional scholars with high social standing first appeared. They went about ordering and classifying animals and plants, producing encyclopedias, and demystifying nature. Their work became the object of awed fascination and a prize for collectors.[91] As Aldrovandi had categorized and dissected monsters, the cool light of rational research was now shone on Japan's fantastic beasts, such as mermaids (*ningyo*)—a process that stretched into the nineteenth century (Plate 32). Socratic skepticism also sprouted. Tokugawa philosophers were inspired by a maxim of Zhu Xi, a Neo-Confucian from the Song dynasty: "Those with the major doubts make much progress."[92]

In 1720, the ban on the importation of Chinese books was relaxed after about ninety years. People now also pursued *Oranda gaku* ("Dutch learning"), or "*rangaku*" for short; until the nineteenth century, Japan's only window onto the wide world was Dutch books.[93] A pat example of the encounter between the two cultures is provided by Udagawa Shinsai's *Copperplate Illustrations of Internal Organs for the Compendium of Medicine*, which appeared in 1808 (Fig. 72, p. 843). The frontispiece features the Dutch anatomist Steven Blankaart, on whose *New Revised Anatomy* (published in Amsterdam in 1678) Shinsai had relied.

Dutch ships brought European astronomy, botany, chemistry, mathematics, and anatomy—plus, in 1783, the pump so useful to mining. Only after the shock of the First Opium War did the Japanese discover that Dutch was not the European lingua franca. So they began learning English, French, and German.

Japan took its own path, one that could not lead to a Scientific Revolution of the Western variety or to mathematical physics. For it had a totally different understanding of nature, indeed of reality. According to this conception—

shared by Japan and other East Asian cultures—all things were created by a spontaneous, omnipresent force.[94] We cannot explore this idea further here; in the broadest sense, it is a concept of being that was undermined in Europe by the systematic experiments of Francesco Redi and Antoni van Leeuwenhoek (pp. 822f.).

The power of tradition seemed invincible. Even when Shibukawa Kagesuke (1787–1856) taught his country about the heliocentric system, he still relied on what Chinese Jesuits had told him about it.[95] And although globes and world maps had long been known in Japan, most people continued to adhere to Confucian cosmology based on the principles of yin and yang. The heavens remained round, and they revolved around a motionless, cube-shaped Earth. The writings of Shizuki Tadao (1760–1806), including translations of introductions to Newton's theories, were not printed, and so the circle of those who could discuss them remained small.[96] It is conspicuous, though, that the same social world that embraced a more modern natural science and replicated muskets in the Tokugawa period became receptive early on to the Western perspective. With its cultural clubs and circles open to various social classes, it somewhat resembled the European society of humanism and the Enlightenment.[97]

The certainty that the Tokugawa regime would last for ten thousand generations turned out to be misplaced. The gunboats of the American Commodore Matthew Perry forced the country to end its isolation in 1853. Contemporaries compared the ensuing Meiji Revolution with the Italian Renaissance.[98] It put Japan on a path to Western-style modernity earlier than other Asian states. This process was facilitated by the country's high level of education, a side effect of its favorable economic development.[99] Schools and universities were founded, railroads built, telegraphs installed, scientific texts translated. The end of the shogunate meant the abolition of its caste system, thus enabling social mobility and unleashing creativity. A half-century after the revolution, Japan was on par with the European powers. The other side of its hectic modernization was the conviction of its own superiority—a mentality that would quickly drive the Land of the Rising Sun into the deadly adventure of imperialism.

The illusion of being the center of the universe also still held sway in the south, in China. The path to modernity was much more fraught there than in dynamic Japan.

47

Why Not China?

Dreams of Tranquility, Bustling Trade

In Beijing, the defeat of the oceanic faction was total after Yongle's sea expedition returned. Just building larger ships became a punishable offense. Foreign trade, if engaged in at all, was to be controlled by the government. With the exception of brief periods of relaxation, this policy remained in force down to the second half of the sixteenth century, although it did more to encourage smuggling and piracy than thwart merchant activity. We can only speculate as to the reasons. The central motive may have come from the constant Mongol threat on the northern border—China's biggest nightmare after famine. It seemed more prudent to invest available resources not in a costly fleet but rather in defensive measures.[1] Around 1470, construction began on the famous wall; it was completed at the turn of the seventeenth century. The largest manmade construction on the globe, a symbol of China's isolation from the outside world, is a monument to fear—not to mention militarily useless, a mammoth white elephant. Never sufficiently manned, enemies went around it or broke through. Not until powerful offensives were launched by the Qing dynasty would the danger from the steppe be banished for good.[2]

The emperors who succeeded the Renaissance man Yongle included skilled calligraphers and painters but no Machiavellians. They handed over the job of governing to eunuchs and officials, sank into the arms of courtesans, or drowned their boredom in alcohol. Horizontal power had no chance, even though Confucianism and Taoism theoretically justified resistance to tyrannical rule and limited power via tradition, ritual, and other means.[3] Slowly, local officials managed "from the bottom up" to transform a confused conglomeration of payments in kind into a well-ordered tax system based on monetary payments.[4] Otherwise, the Ming state was hardly capable of reform. No technological breakthroughs were made.[5] Great scientists like Li Shizhen (1518–1593), the "prince of the pharmacists,"[6] and open, critical minds like Xie Zhaozhe (1567–1624), who questioned ancient knowledge and customs like the binding of women's feet, were exceptions.[7] The taxes sucked out of the people went to nourishing an army of corrupt officials, ten thousand greedy eunuchs, and courtly luxury. The Ming military, now a gigantic force of four million, was poorly trained and technologically behind the times.

The global crisis aggravated the situation.[8] Cold and rainy weather blighted agriculture; famine and heavy taxation provoked revolts. Commerce slackened, and there was not enough capital to finance the importation of silver. The army, embroiled alongside Japan in a war for Korea in the late sixteenth century, could no longer be properly paid. Thus, a lack of money also drained Ming power. The end came in the form of Manchu attacks and a rebellion of hundreds of thousands of starving subjects. The rebels laid waste to the north, ultimately capturing Beijing. The last Ming emperor hanged himself in 1644. Desperate, one of his generals called in a Manchu army to put down the revolt. Yet the victorious force itself now seized power. After decades of extremely brutal war, the resistance of Ming stalwarts was ultimately extinguished. The rule of the Manchus—who called their dynasty "Qing"—entailed increased isolation from foreign influence, including Christian missionaries.[9]

Let us return to Needham's big question: why did China, once such a dynamic land friendly to innovation, not take a path that led to Western-style modernity? Why were there no further scientific breakthroughs? Why no Industrial Revolution? Some scholars have found an answer in China's spirituality. Did Buddha and Confucius erect hurdles to development while Europe's Protestants, heeding their work ethic and driven by the yearning to find signs of their elect status on Earth, chased after money and success? There seem to be arguments in support of this thesis. Competition, industriousness, and greed are anathema to Buddhism and Confucianism. A virtuous man speaks about moral principles, whereas only people of lower rank talk about profit—thus Sima Guang, citing Confucius, argued during the debate over Wang Anshi's reform proposals (p. 140).[10] Trade and financial transactions raised the specter of greed and usury; only agriculture was considered necessary by Confucian scholars.[11] The poet Lu You (1125–1210) captured this spirit in an idyllic scene:

> It's late; the children come home from school;
> braids unplaited, they ramble the fields;
> . . .
> Father sternly calls them to lessons;
> grandfather indulgently feeds them candy.
> We don't ask you to become rich and famous
> but when the time comes, work hard in the fields![12]

Nevertheless, this picture does not account for the fact that China never appeared as a mere population of frugal farmers. Metropolises like Beijing, Hangzhou, and Suzhou never appeared as quiet abodes of introspective self-discovery. One Korean who visited Hangzhou in the late fifteenth century reported that gold and silver were piled high in the marketplaces and that people accumulated beautiful clothing and embellishments. Ships from foreign lands were anchored in a tight row like the teeth of a comb, and the streets featured variety theaters next to wine shops.[13] China's economy experienced periods of dynamic development. Craftsmen shaped and painted porcelain that was exported as far as Dresden, where it was sent as a gift by Grand Duke Ferdinando de' Medici (Fig. 79, p. 886). They built wooden furniture shimmering with lacquer; tea and silk made it to Japan or, via Manila, into Spanish hands. They even engaged in product differentiation: Muslims drank their Chinese tea from porcelain cups without human portraits; Japanese taste was also catered to, as was that of European customers. Upon request, the latter received goods adorned with their family crests and Christian motifs. Admittedly, scholars disagree as to the dimensions reached by China's foreign trade.[14] They agree, however, that the Chinese were great, ambitious traders active all over Southeast Asia. The dreams of tranquility fed by Buddhism, Confucianism, and Taoism clearly had no retarding effect on their industriousness. When the head of a family clan of the middle Ming dynasty lamented how city life corrupted traditional values,[15] it reflected the same melancholy that gripped Ibn Khaldun in the Maghreb and Sannazaro in Naples.

One explanation for these contradictions might be that only the elite had the opportunity to live out tranquil Confucian values. The lower classes, whom Sima Guang looked down upon, needed to make their tiny profit if they were to survive—in China as everywhere else in the world. Comprising the vast majority of Chinese society, *they* were the source of increasing economic prosperity—not the officials engrossed in painting calligraphy nor the gentry busy with collecting antiquities. The Ming minister Zhang Han (1511–1593) put it in a nutshell: it was human nature for people to strive after what made them profit. Never satisfied with what they had, they plunged after it like a waterfall into a valley; coming and going without letup, restless day and night, never reaching the point at which the raging torrents inside of them could find peace.[16] Zhang Han knew what he was talking about, seeing that he came from a rich family of textile traders from exuberant Hangzhou.

Religious norms and real life always differ. The traditional distaste of India's Brahmins for merchants dampened the latter's industriousness as little as Confucian spirituality lessened commercial activity in Ming China. The Bible itself is anything but a manifesto for capitalism. It teaches that it is easier for a camel to pass through the eye of a needle than for a rich man to get into Heaven. It depicts Jesus driving merchants and money changers out of the temple and traces human misery back to the tasting of the fruit of the Tree of Knowledge. Nevertheless, it was capitalists and scholars who constructed European modernity, with all its highs and lows. In fact, religions tend to *respond* to the confusion of the world more than they are ever able to contain it. They provide support in uncertain times and enclaves of tranquility amidst the clamor of everyday life. If the case were different, the European Middle Ages would have produced only societies of peace-loving, pious, and humble people—not capitalists. We would thus do well not to overemphasize the significance of religious doctrines for the everyday lives of working people.

China's trade boomed in the seventeenth and eighteenth centuries. In early modern times, the Yangtze Delta enjoyed higher agricultural productivity than anywhere else. In the north, Jingdezhen shone as the world center of porcelain manufacture. But the economy was largely driven by small household production and state revenues. The Chinese Leviathan lived on taxes, monopolies, and customs duties. Its need for credit was nothing like the European monarchs' hunger for gold.[17] Unlike in Europe—one thinks of the difficult marriage between the Fuggers and the Habsburgs—the imperial court never entered into a liaison with capitalism. In addition, the land that invented paper money and elaborated the first theory of monetary value did not create a banking system.

Of course, none of this had to hinder scientific progress or the development of new technology. Several prerequisites for industrialization were present: hardworking people, manufactories, coal, and let us not forget a state that safeguarded order and peace. Capital also could have been mobilized in spite of the underdeveloped credit system.[18] What was lacking were technical innovations. At most, agricultural methods were improved, and old inventions were tinkered with. China's economy continued to work on the same power that had driven it for millennia: the muscles of millions. Prometheus remained chained to his rock in the Caucasus. He did not make it to the Yangtze.

An Arrogant Giant

The fate of printing illustrates China's technological stagnation. It was not peculiar to the Middle Kingdom. Korea and Japan—the countries that had first grasped the principle underlying all printing—did not progress beyond a medieval technical state. Here and there, experiments were made with movable type, both in China and in Korea, where metal types appeared by the thirteenth century.[19] However, since no one had the idea of using a press to print texts, each sheet of paper still had to be applied to the dyed woodblock and rubbed from the back side. Staying with wood accorded with the Chinese delight in calligraphy, as the soft material allowed for a more flexible design.[20] Gradually, people started using types made of bronze, but still no presses. It must be said, however, that printing with movable type does not offer nearly as many advantages for fonts based on word or syllable characters rather than letters.

China's "great inertia"[21] was not hidden from contemporary visitors. The Jesuit father Diego Pantoja, who went to the country in 1602, wrote, "There are to be found many good things, but not put into practice."[22] Why was that the case? Let us first consider political and social conditions. In the late Ming dynasty, the system of civil service exams remained the filter for achieving higher positions, which naturally were open only to a tiny minority. The European system was doubtless less rational than that of China, Vietnam, or Korea.[23] But it was more open. Humanist careers like that of Bartolomeo Platina (1421–1481)—who became prefect of the Vatican Library after a youthful stint as a mercenary—or Leonardo Bruni would have been impossible in the Middle Kingdom. Bruni supposedly got his position as papal secretary by writing a dictated letter more beautifully than a competitor.[24] If Bruni had succeeded neither in Rome nor in Florence, a hundred other options would have presented themselves to a man of his qualities. In China, such talents found no multitude of competing courts and cities that might provide a livelihood, nor was there the wide variety of universities, academies, monasteries, museums, alchemical laboratories, intellectual circles, and libraries that, reflecting Latin Europe's political map, gave long stability to research and debate.[25]

The lack of patronage opportunities was doubtless one of the most important reasons that no great breakthroughs were made in China anymore. Since there was no hereditary landed aristocracy, the large estates that in Europe provided a great deal of money for science, scholarship, and the arts barely existed in China (as in the Ottoman Empire).[26] The success or failure of all costly research ultimately depended on a word from the imperial court. Emblematic of its weight, even in debates over philosophical questions, is the fate of the teachings of Zhu Xi, the encyclopedically learned "Chinese Aristotle" and a preeminent Confucian. Within the space of a mere fifty years, they were first declared heretical and then enshrined as official state doctrine, with their author given a memorial tablet in the Confucian Temple.[27] His *Great Learning*, which he combined with the *Analects of Confucius*, the *Doctrine of the Mean*, and the *Mencius* to form the Four Books, continued to be examination material for civil servants down to the twentieth century.

Another impediment to the development of innovations was the kingdom's rigid social structure. Artisanal techniques were usually passed down from father to son, from master to student. It was an enormous hindrance to innovation, as the system was opposed to establishing new trades for new specialized sectors, as happened in Europe, such as those devoted to making precision instruments or even just threads and screws. Whereas two-thirds of the population of late medieval England worked as free wage laborers, it was at most five percent in Qing China.[28] Many skills were taught only locally. At least handbooks circulated in the countryside to spread knowledge of agricultural techniques and propagate the planting of melons, sugar cane, cotton, and other fruits. Book production only increased in the late Ming dynasty.[29] However, fewer than fifty titles per year were produced, lagging far behind European output. Hardly any of the books were the work of scholars. A 1637 technical encyclopedia was intended for dilettantes or to entertain courtiers, not to disseminate its contents among the masses. In sum, despite everything China did not have, it did have a functioning medium of communication and widespread literacy.[30] Lacking, however, were the *messages* that in Europe led to radical upheavals. Only a few of the large libraries in the country were open to a broad spectrum of readers. The first public library was established in 1905.

Small renaissances of ancient knowledge were usually driven by initiatives from Beijing. Astronomy and history were centered in their own offices at the court and in a few academies. One searches in vain for a critical historiography that accounted for complexity and change in past developments. Like in the citadels of Islam (and unlike in Europe), the number of those involved in scientific or scholarly discourse was vanishingly small—and not only compared to the size of the country. Academies, initially places where literati and civil servants gathered for discussion and to pursue learning for learning's sake, ended up largely under state supervision until the end of the eighteenth century. They functioned chiefly as training centers for passing the sterile civil service exams.[31]

The hierarchical order of society was set in stone.[32] When learned Ming officials of the sixteenth century argued that the emperor had to respect rituals dictated by the natural order, it was but a tiny step toward a constitutional monarchy. Communal autonomy developed solely in rudimentary form. Only village communities gained a certain degree of autonomy under the "ritual umbrella" of the state.[33] As in other non-European cultures, the iron ties of lineage were also inimical to social mobility. Only during the late Ming dynasty could greater elasticity be observed. Nevertheless, as in other countries outside Europe, no civil society took shape there.[34] If it is true that advanced machine technology was necessary for the outbreak of the Industrial Revolution, it was still as fully beyond the realm of possibility in eighteenth-century China as in Southeast Asia, Japan, Russia, and Africa. Only espionage (or, to put it more gently, learning from Europeans) would have enabled a "great leap forward." Yet the Chinese did not attempt it.

China's increasing isolation from foreign influence and thus also from the now abundantly available "wonders of the West" stemmed in part from an attitude that was also present in Japan: the *arrogance of the center*, and attending it the conviction that one did not need others, seeing as how they were as inferior to oneself as the Moon to the Sun. What is more, China, like other Asian states, had always lacked pathfinders. Apart from wood, furs, and slaves, Europe had little to offer East Asian traders until the time of the silver boom. Yet who but merchants could have blazed the trail to cultural exchange?

The number of those who visited the West was accordingly small. The tour of a group of young Japanese travelers who visited Portugal, Spain, and Italy between 1584 and 1586 had been arranged by Jesuits. A little later, in 1599, a Persian embassy set off for southern Europe.[35] The report that one member composed for Shah Abbas I provides one of the few glimpses of Europe as seen through Eastern eyes. It describes Florence, Madrid, and the gardens of Aranjuez, which it acclaimed as the "ninth wonder of the world." In contrast to this Persian account and a few others, Latin Europe possessed whole libraries of travel literature. Furthermore, Europe's geographers had long since gained a clear understanding of the Earth's surface as a whole. With the method developed by Gerhard Mercator (1512–1594), the globe could be projected onto a cylinder.[36] The number of globes and maps produced in Europe between 1472 and 1500 alone is estimated at fifty-six thousand; in the sixteenth century, the number shot into the millions.

In comparison, China, once so curious, had strange notions of the world beyond its intellectual walls, especially concerning the "far west," *yuan xi* or *tau xi*. Chinese scholars knew of Africa's triangular shape and labeled a Ming dynasty map "A-lu-man-ni-a" for Germany. Yet they thought the Earth was flat and rectangular, and China's greatest explorer, Xu Hongzu (1586–1641), crisscrossed the country but never left its borders.[37] Even in the nineteenth century, some Chinese people harbored the curious notion that all knowledge, even that of Europe, came from China.[38] The first authentic report of a Chinese person who saw the "West" with his own eyes was probably that of the translator Lin Qian, who traveled from Xiamen to New York in 1847, spent one and a half years in the United States, and then returned to his homeland. His enthusiasm for Western technology reached hymnic heights.

> Letters are cast in iron, contending heaven in speed and skill. For their bookprinting with movable type as well as in ships, wagons, flails, looms, and for hammering and casting they use steam-wheels and a machinery to transport movement, which is miraculously fast and effortless.[39]

And he observed in amazement,

> Following one's own mind and trusting one's hand, a person who invents a technique can make a name for himself. They do not honor empty literacy; instead, anybody who creates a new art that profits the world is richly rewarded.

Stoic, Not Dramatic

The desire for gain or simply the wish to survive and feed one's family may have trumped Confucian ideals in the quotidian world of work in China. Things were different in the realm of science, however. Ideological commitments were strong there, often overwhelming. The vast majority of China's scientists and technicians had passed a civil service examination. They knew their Confucius inside and out, and so they had internalized the principles underlying his natural philosophy. Their view of nature and the cosmos was fundamentally different from that of Europeans and their agonistic intellectual systems. One essential difference from the Western concept was that no almighty God seemed to be the lord of natural laws. As Needham notes,

> Universal harmony comes about not by the celestial fiat of some King of Kings, but by the spontaneous cooperation of all beings in the universe brought about by their following the internal necessities of their own natures.[40]

In his view, Chinese thought did not have

> confidence that the code of Nature's laws could be unveiled and read, because there was no assurance that a divine being, ever more rational than ourselves, had ever formulated a code capable of being read.[41]

Ideas such as that human beings are "the goal of nature" (Nicholas of Cusa) or that God wants us to know *everything* (Paracelsus) were as foreign to Chinese thinkers as the notion that man was the center of being.[42] Chinese natural philosophers saw themselves as part of the cosmos, connected with the heavens and the Earth, and subsumed in the highest end, the unity of yin and yang, the antagonistic forces responsible for all change. Chinese science thought holistically or, as Needham would say, in an "organicismic" way.[43] Paramount were not the analysis and dissection of nature, nor the mastery of it, but rather harmony with it. The point was to stand the test of a continuous cycle of birth and rebirth lasting eons.[44] The physics of ancient China was based on mutual influences, not causal laws. The "Mohist" school founded by Mozi (ca. 479–381 BC), which dealt inter alia with logic, geometric optics, economics, and mechanics, faded into obscurity—to the detriment of science.[45]

Rational research and economic activity were foreign to the spirit of Taoism, too. Its esoteric teachings quieted yearnings that Buddha's wisdom could not fulfill. It knew miracle-working practices, supplied its adherents with gods and a path to immortality, and enjoined them to seek harmony with the all-encompassing, ineffable "Tao," the "way."[46] Not logic and dialectic but rather rituals, meditation, and physical practices had been the methods to reach insight for many Far Eastern religions from time immemorial. Confucianism looked to family, social order, and the upbringing and education of the individual as the foundation of a well-ordered state. It barely touched on technology and natural science. Only a few isolated cracks appeared in the edifice.[47] Yet, like Buddhism, it did not erect insurmountable hurdles to the sciences. Admittedly, its dictum, "True preservers of the old must renew themselves daily,"[48] was seldom taken to heart. What is more, Chinese natural science was aimed at practical use. The construction of theoretical systems was foreign to it.

One undeniable difference from the intellectual history of Europe was that China was long ignorant of the Greek tradition and its critical method. Chinese thinkers engaged in intellectual practices that were very similar to those of European thinkers, such as weighing advantages and disadvantages, adducing analogies, and citing predecessors. However, concepts of proof and argumentation were unfamiliar, as was the dialectical game of refutation and rebuttal.[49] Even the dialogues by the critical Neo-Confucian Wang Yangming (1472–1529), which pit the inborn "good knowledge" of the heart against book learning, are built around a student asking reverent questions of a wise teacher—not discussion. An intense debate between two intellectuals, like the one engaged in by Li Zhi (1527–1602) and Geng Dingxiang (1524–1594), was very rare. Li Zhi defended intellectual autonomy against the authority of the ancients and the power of Confucius. Ultimately, his unconventional views landed him in trouble, and he committed suicide.[50]

The ideal Confucian scholar clearly differed from his European counterparts. He resembled a friendly Benedictine monk to whom nothing is more foreign than a loud dispute. He lived surrounded by students in a hut in the countryside, subsisting by the sweat of his brow. Only a few needs burdened him. After his morning ancestor worship rituals, Zhu Xi spent time in nature with his students and organized picnics that included the moderate enjoyment of wine. He recited texts by classical historians and philosophers. Benevolent and respectful even of the people, he dressed neatly. He scrupulously insisted on adhering to rituals.[51] He recommended committing a few canonical works to memory and meditating upon them. Questioning their message was not part of the exercise.

Confucian ideals were not the only reason for the lack of fruitful debate and thus the slackening of the desire for novelty in China. Confucianism was rooted in a strongly patrilineal society on which it had its own stabilizing influence in return. The clearest expression of this was the ancestor cult, which was thousands of years old and could take on bizarre forms. For example, medieval China knew the custom of bringing one's own flesh as a sacrifice to one's parents.[52] When one's father died, a three-year period of mourning was to be observed. During the Ming dynasty, one had to put one's career on hold.[53] Confucianism exalted honoring one's ancestors as highly as Buddhism and Hinduism did; it prescribed detailed guidelines for rituals. Since one's ancestors could only be properly worshipped in their place of origin, where their graves and cult sites were located, it was difficult to move to a new place. The development of novelties was hindered not only by excessive respect for one's forefathers but also by the steely strength of vertical power and the Confucian yearning for harmony. China never witnessed controversies even remotely comparable to European debates about forms of government, cosmological models, or religion. Imperial censorship had its eye on everything.

In the thirteenth century, Chinese science had clearly reached limits that it could scarcely have transcended even if there had been no invasions or political upheavals. A minimum of physics was kept in check by a maximum of metaphysics.[54] Chinese philosophy never expanded its reach like Renaissance European philosophy did. As has been amply demonstrated, the latter's intellectual horizon spanned from materialism to the metaphysics of light to self-renouncing mysticism, from deep skepticism to faith in reason—a rich conceptual pageant unknown anywhere else in the world.

In China, the pace of intellectual change was slow. New thoughts always had to be justified by way of ancient models whose authority could scarcely be questioned.[55] Chinese scholars calculated solar eclipses, worked out precise star charts, and supplied the emperor with astrological prognoses; it did not occur to them to question the cosmology handed down to them from ancient times.[56] They observed rock formations, animals, and plants and even developed taxonomies. Yet they were far from taking the step that had been decisive for the West, namely developing a physics based on mathematics, systematic observation, and experimentation.

Another example is provided by Chinese medicine. During the Ming dynasty, it was based on the same spiritual practices, breathing exercises, and acupuncture as fifteen hundred years earlier. Would not the study of the meridians—the channels through which, according to traditional teachings, life energy flows—have suggested anatomical investigation? By no means. Traditional China never pursued the medicine of dissection as pioneered by Vesalius's anatomy.[57] China's art of healing was gentle; it took individual physical constitution and social circumstances into consideration. Its adepts were interested in cosmic cycles lasting eons, which they hoped to illustrate in alchemical experiments. What they sought was connected to their deepest spiritual values. Understanding the enduring patterns, unity, and harmony of the cosmos behind the chaos of events required abandoning petty earthly finitude and the limited realm of things it sought to know. Greco-Western natural science was dramatic; the Chinese variety was stoic.[58] Perhaps the transition from progressive science to the restoration of the ancient, as the Chinese described their project, only began after Wang Yangming, but that is unclear.

When the Hellenic spirit finally arrived in China—first in the form of Euclid's geometry—it initially found lukewarm reception. The supernova of 1572, which moved Tycho Brahe to such deep insights, was also observed by the Chinese. They registered the event without comment. A bit more of Euclid and some Ptolemaic theories finally found their way to China in 1607, when Matteo Ricci (1552–1610) encouraged a Chinese translation of the *Almagest*. Since it was Christian monks who taught the Chinese about European astronomy, it was a long time before they became acquainted with the Copernican system.[59] In competition with official Ming astronomers, who were often Muslims, the Chinese adopted the cosmology of Tycho ("Ti-ku") and not that of "Ko-po-ni," Copernicus. They agreed with Ptolemy—"To-lu-mou"—in leaving Earth in the center of the universe. Brahe was, for them, merely the one who swept away a model recognized as false. In addition, they perceived the contradictions between Western theories as they became more aware of them. For a long time, they attempted to save their own "phenomena." As one saying had it, "Eastern sea, western sea: mind is the same, truth is the same."[60] After one Jesuit explained the Copernican system, the Qianlong Emperor (r. 1735–1796) replied serenely, "In Europe you have your way of explaining the celestial phenomena. As for us, we have ours too, without making the Earth rotate."[61]

Only after another century did Western concepts slowly gain ground. Until then, China stuck to its own harmonious cosmology, uninfluenced by the debates burning in Europe about the ancient world system. In Needham's summary,

> The Europeans suffered from a schizophrenia of the soul, oscillating forever unhappily between the heavenly host on one side and the "atoms and the void" on the other; while the Chinese, wise before their time, worked out an organic theory of the universe which included nature and man, church and state and all things past, present and to come.[62]

That may have made them happier. The distinctly European "restlessness of the mind," the *inquietudo* that Marsilio Ficino once saw as proof of the divinity of the human soul,[63] remained foreign to them.

In sum, the causes for the chasm that opened up between China and the West, beginning slowly in the thirteenth century and then widening ever faster during the Industrial Revolution, were rooted deep in China's society, in its spirituality, and in its system of rule. It does not suffice to look simply at the economy or to analyze conditions in Europe immediately before the Industrial Age.

In the early twentieth century, the Chinese legal system was still based in large part on laws that came from the Tang Code and were thus over a thousand years old. China remained the home of gunpowder without muskets, of printing without the printing press, of large boats without adjustable sails.[64] The telescope made its way to the imperial court a short decade after its European premiere, but it was treated as top secret. As in India and Turkey, it underwent no significant technical improvements. Finally, we must not overlook the fact that the fruitful collaboration between craftsmanship and learning that was key to Europe's Scientific Revolution never developed in China. One reason was that the number of craftsmen had declined dramatically since the Song dynasty.[65] The Kangxi Emperor's attempt to import the art of clockmaking to his court failed, in part because of a lack of technical know-how.[66] In the late seventeenth century, spectacles still had to be imported from Europe. Glass was not available locally; thus, the techniques for producing and working with glass were not developed. The poet Kong Shangren wrote at the time,

Clear glass from across the Western Seas
Is imported through Macao.
Fashioned into lenses big as coins,
They encompass one's vision in a double frame.
I put them on—things suddenly become clear.
I can see the very tips of things!
And read fine print by the dim-lit window
Just like in my youth.[67]

The Chinese paid a high price for their idyll. Occasionally, the fertile soil had to be exploited to the maximum to feed the booming population. In years with poor harvests, it was difficult to provide for the masses. Poor farmers sought to reduce the number of their children by killing "excess" offspring—by no means a practice peculiar to the Middle Kingdom.[68] The problem of overly high birth rates, which had been discussed in China as far back as the third century BC, remained on the agenda. The Malthusian crisis was unrelenting. "The land of the empire is the chief source of provision for the empire's people," noted the philosopher, poet, and civil servant Hong Liangji in 1793.

> If there are more people, there will be more producers. A large population is the basis of wealth. How could it on the contrary cause poverty? There is not much unused land in the empire, but *productivity* does not conform to any such restraints.[69]

In 1796, a rebellion broke out that required more than a decade to suppress. Famine, high taxes, and poverty soon bred turmoil in other regions as well. The multi-ethnic state seemed on the verge of breaking apart. Revolts became more and more common after 1850. Opium, imported by the ton from India to China by the English once silver became scarce, had its poisonous effect. When the Chinese government instituted drastic measures to stop the opium trade, the British feared for their lucrative business. An English army landed with steam-powered gunboats in 1840; they had an easy job of it. The Opium Wars—1840–1842 and 1856–1858—compelled China to sign treaties that safeguarded free trade with the narcotic and foresaw the opening of ports and the cession of the island of Hong Kong. Other European countries and America likewise extorted prodigiously favorable trade conditions. The phantasm of the ancient Chinese cosmic order faded away—forever. The gloomy setting for the endgame was the Taiping Rebellion, a religiously inspired uprising that rocked the country from 1850 to 1864. It resulted in the death of twenty to thirty million people.

The Chinese deemed it absolutely necessary to open up to Western knowledge. They visited countries beyond the seas, learning new things and becoming acquainted with the miracle of democracy. Books and periodicals transported the culture, technology, and science that had been amassed in the West since the Renaissance to an empire that now, like other East Asian states, lost its own version of modernity.[70] It was Europeans who, like colonial powers, laid railroads across China and, in concert with Japan, exploited the country. When the last emperor abdicated in 1912 and the republic was founded, the oldest kingdom in world history vanished from the stage.

48

Deep History

SOUNDINGS

The Benefits of Religious Conflict

Let us return to the ruins of Canossa, the symbolic location of a world-historical conflict that was played out in many arenas. It stands not only for the struggle between the emperor and the pope but also for the eternal antagonism between purity and pollution, religion and the secular world. As earth-shattering as this event may have seemed to some contemporaries, it was only one moment during the long process of the separation of church and state, religion and science. "Canossa" symbolizes the consolidation and rise of the papal church, as well as the clergy's exaggerated claims to worldly power. The castle in the Apennines was the starting point for paths leading to Avignon, Wittenberg, and Geneva, not to mention Gaeta, the exile of Pius IX—the especially fallible pope who proclaimed the doctrine of papal infallibility. Indeed, the Reformation and the wars of religion were sparked by the *institution* of the Church—an organization inextricably entangled with the world, one that pursued political goals, satisfied financial appetites, and possessed defects that stood in stark contrast with its towering moral pretensions. The "rise of the West" was ultimately owed in part to the fact that it had to suffer through the fire of religious conflict. From its ashes rose the beguilingly beautiful yet dire and deadly phoenix of "modernity."

The difference is clear not only with regard to Byzantium, Islamic societies, and—likely—indigenous New World societies but also those that followed Buddha, the Tao, or Hindu gods. Aggressive Crusader piety was foreign to them. One king of Siam announced in the mid-sixteenth century that he was a lord of bodies, not of souls, and thus that he did not engage in proselytizing.[1] The decentralized organization of Asia's major faith communities almost always gave greater power to the sword of temporal authority. Religiously motivated military violence was rare and, as in Japan during the Warring States period, remained a regional phenomenon. Priests in Asia never convulsed the governmental systems of entire empires. Similar to the Greek Orthodox Church and even more so to Russian Orthodoxy, Far Eastern religions and their functionaries were the wards of state power. They only had authority when they were allied with it.[2] Thus Brahmins—priests, scholars, and custodians of ancient Vedic texts—served as political teachers and trusted advisors. More like notables than priests, they were tasked with managing the affairs of the provinces.[3] When Buddhists were persecuted and monasteries destroyed (as in the European Reformation), monks were helpless victims and not, as during the Investiture Controversy, a powerful opponent of temporal authorities.[4]

Religious and secular power also seemed inextricably linked in the lands of the third major monotheistic religion, Islam. The caliphs were considered patrons of the faith, protectors of pilgrimage routes to Mecca, and guardians of the law. As successors to the Prophet, they combined the offices of emperor and pope in themselves—a role also claimed by lesser potentates over time.[5] As a result, there could be no war between religion and the world. "Happy Asia, happy rulers in the East, who need not fear the weapons of their subjects nor worry about the intrigues of their bishops!"—thus groaned a man who had been forced to experience what priestly power meant: Emperor Frederick II.[6]

Islam waged no wars to convert unbelievers. It also lagged far behind Christianity in the zealous persecution of heretics. A few exceptions confirm the rule.[7] Muslim conquerors' restraint rested from the outset on reason of state. Unless the "pagan" religions of the subjugated were tolerated, conquered territory could not be ruled. Whether or not followers of other religions were treated with clemency in Muslim states depended on whether power was in the hands of moderates or monsters. "People of the Book" like Jews and Christians, but also Zoroastrians, Hindus, and Buddhists, could receive the status of "protected persons," which guaranteed the integrity of their life and property.[8] These *dhimmis* had to pay a special tax, a powerful incentive to conversion to Islam—which could lead to its being forbidden in the interest of the fisc.[9] Admittedly, limits were placed on how non-Muslims practiced their faith. Their clothing often marked them as outsiders. All in all, however, they were treated better than religious minorities in Christian Europe and "pagans" in Africa and the Americas. Indeed, one contemporary observer, Alberico Gentili, regarded the Ottoman Empire as a model of religious tolerance, which he recognized as serving political interests.[10]

India went down both paths of dealing with religious plurality: integration via tolerance and hardline Islamization. Under the Mughal emperors, a distinct variant of Islam developed there that incorporated Hindu traditions.[11] Akbar dispensed with the usual tax on "infidels." The solution he arrived at for his reign was called *Sulh-i kul*, or universal peace.[12] His successor Jahangir (r. 1605–1627), although a devout Muslim, continued the policy. In the late period of the dynasty, Aurangzeb, an Indian Philip II, took the path of a rigid religious policy. For example, he had Hindu temples destroyed. His hardline stance may have contributed to his failure to integrate subject territories into his realm. The Mughal state began to decline even before his death.

One reason that the world outside Latin European Christendom seldom experienced religious wars or conflict between religious and secular power was that the rest of the world knew no comparable universal religious institution with the same claim to political sovereignty as the papacy. Caliphs and sultans united secular rule with priestly functions in themselves, as had the *basileus* before them. And the tsars of Moscow certainly never allowed themselves to be badgered by their patriarchs.

Of course, the emperors and kings of Latin Europe were not entirely of this world either.[13] The anointing some of them received set them apart from mere mortals; the kings of France and England were in the habit of healing the scrofulous by laying on their hands. Yet this hint of priestliness was hardly comparable with the grand shamanic roles played by Far Eastern rulers. Some, like Roman emperors, traced their ancestry back to gods. The emperor of Japan, for example, claimed to be descended from the sun god Amaterasu.[14] His chief duty was to honor the gods and, by observing traditional ceremonies, calibrate the relationship between them and the earthly world. He was aided by an office for divine affairs and the state cult.

The power of China's Sons of Heaven was likewise based on their mastery over ritual.[15] The Mongol emperors and even the Qing were somewhat similar to Christ. They claimed to be bodhisattvas: merciful beings who strove for Buddhahood and thus enlightenment, but who put off entering Nirvana to save others while walking the Earth.[16] The most important ruler of the Javanese Majapahit Empire, Hayam Wuruk (r. 1350–1389), was considered an incarnation of both Shiva and Buddha at the same time, a master of the masters of the world.[17]

The deities under Asia's skies—the Hindus alone worshipped 330 million of them—usually coexisted with one another as peacefully as rulers did with priests. The Jin dynasty in China did not merely patronize the worship of Buddha. It also tolerated popular Taoism and even Judaism. The ancient Jewish community in Kaifeng still exists today.[18] A Taoist could simultaneously follow Buddha and Shiva and, in everyday life, imitate Confucius. Monks belonging to different Buddhist sects sometimes even lived together in the same monastery.[19] The group dynamic of deities in Asia thus resembled the friendly relationship that the ancient gods of Europe enjoyed before monotheism infected the continent with intolerance.[20] Christian missionaries seeking to make their god the sole ruler in Asia were the first who had to pay the price for it. Violent conflicts did break out between Hindus and Muslims in India, and iconoclasm was not unknown, but such episodes were rare.

Like in Rome and Greece, Asia's gods underwent mild metamorphoses over space and time. For example, a Hindu mother deity could become Tara, the beautiful embodiment of selfless compassion. At her core was the merciful bodhisattva Avalokiteśvara.[21] She appeared as the androgynous goddess Guanshiyin in China, as Kannon in Japan, and in various other guises in other countries. Occasionally, attempts were made to unify the grand systems.[22] For a long time, the Middle Kingdom looked with unconcern upon Islam, the "little faith"[23] that Chinese merchants first encountered in the oasis towns of Central Asia. In 1307, the Great Khan even approved the creation of an archbishopric. And when Ibn Battuta visited Guangzhou a few decades later, he noted that Jews, Christians, and Zoroastrians could be found there. In Japan, Buddhists took comfort in their old Shinto deities, celebrating festivals with them, while Indian Hindus were inspired by mystical Islam.[24] One Indonesian mystic of the fourteenth century reduced the logic of Asian religious peace to a formula that recalls Lessing's ring parable: "The truth of Jina (Buddha) and the truth of Shiva is one; they are indeed different, but they remain one, as there is no duality in truth."[25]

For contemporaries, Asia's general state of religious peace was naturally a boon for business. Asia experienced no wars between church and state and hardly any battles among the religions themselves. That meant, however, that it produced no Reformation—much less an Enlightenment, whose victory in Europe was motivated primarily by opposition to the chaos of the confessional age and the omnipresence of religion. In the "West," a life lived in peace was cleaved from a life lived in truth.[26] That was one of the preconditions for the development of civil society in Europe and the freedom required by scientific rationality.

Demographic Regimes: Life, Survival, Death

When considering the reasons for the "great divergence," one need not fall into the trap of biological determinism to assign a possibly even more important role to a massive, tenacious force: demography. Its statistics tell the story of entire societies. They speak of epidemics and famine, economic growth and decline, fertility and birth control. They also give insight into mentalities, into sets of beliefs and disbeliefs.

Compared to East Asia, Europe always had much lower population numbers. We are, however, dependent on rough estimates. For India, more precise data only becomes available in the late nineteenth century.[27] Absolute numbers—perhaps twelve to fourteen million people in the Central Provinces, perhaps 400,000 in Istanbul, up to eighteen million in Japan around 1600—tell us little, as we do not know much about the size of families. Families in China seem to have been larger on average than those in Europe. Whereas the early modern European household seldom averaged more than three to five people, in Jin China, the number was between 6.33 and 6.71; a census dating to 1380 suggests about 7.5 people.[28] This evidence supports John Hajnal's oft-cited thesis (pp. 153f.).

The apparently high population in Asia may very well be a constant going back to ancient history. References to armies of millions, megacities, and monumental buildings indicate that Asia had a massive number of inhabitants. Compared to the sumptuous architectural complex of Samarra or the palaces of Chinese emperors, Charlemagne's palace chapel in Aachen, constructed around the same time, seems like a broom closet. And what were the few thousand cavalrymen mustered by the medieval German emperors for their marches to Rome compared with Mahmud of Ghazni's 100,000-man army, or with the 135,000 warriors that Harun al-Rashid was able to mobilize just for his campaign against Byzantium?[29] No modern European force could compare to the army of the Song, which for a while numbered over one million troops, to say nothing of the four million soldiers commanded by the Ming.

In Southeast Asia, 15 or more cities in the seventeenth century had populations between 50,000 and 100,000, including Pegu (modern Bago), Ayutthaya, Phnom Penh, and Thăng Long (modern Hanoi).[30] Gyeongju, capital of the Silla Kingdom (in the area that would later become Korea), had 178,396 tile-roofed buildings and numerous magnificent mansions, according to a precise contemporary report.[31] No European commune of the Middle Ages came anywhere close to the dimensions of Chinese cities at the time. Chang'an numbered over one million inhabitants during the Tang dynasty, as did Nanjing later, while the Song capital of Kaifeng reached 400,000.[32] At the end of the eleventh century, China is thought to have contained 95 million souls. By 1600 it was perhaps 150 million.[33] By 1800 the number was 313 million, compared to 200 million in all of Europe. The fact that China waged far fewer wars than European states only could have encouraged further population growth.[34]

It was only possible to feed the megacities thanks to far-reaching trade networks, canals dug by millions of forced laborers, and, above all, the rice economy.[35] Rice produces higher yields per seed than grain. A rice kernel has four times more calories than wheat. What is more, rice is less perishable and therefore easier to transport over long distances. It was the food of millions, and its availability was one of the reasons for East Asia's high population statistics. By opening up more land for crops, using fertilizers, and planting hitherto unknown New World fruits, it became more or less possible to feed an exponentially growing population in China, India, and Japan.[36] Yet foodstuffs only barely met demand, as frequent famines attest.

What role did demographic differences play in the "great divergence?" According to a hotly debated thesis, the mass availability of cheap muscle power meant that China was not forced to search for alternative production methods, such as by developing machines or harnessing steam power. As a result, the Chinese economy of industriousness did not transform into a capital-intensive economy. There was simply no need for industrialization. This theory likely accounts in part for China's "inertia"—and the fact that there was no Industrial Revolution in other Asian states.

According to another theory, this one uncontroversial, the necessity of feeding millions and millions of people may have strengthened vertical power—seeing that authoritarian regimes are better than others at managing complex organizational tasks such as irrigating fields and building canals.[37] In addition, famine can be highly explosive, as is well known—and not only in the case of China. If the masses cannot be fed, soldiers and weapons must be used to shoot them down if necessary. Indeed, the gargantuan armies of the Chinese emperors were more often involved in imposing deathly silence at home than fighting off savage invaders from abroad. Furthermore, authoritarian states are as inhospitable in the long run to science and research as those that collapse in revolt and revolution. Strict vertical power generally allows and promotes only what is useful to its own ends. Private property is at the mercy of state expropriation; industriousness—and thus also ingenuity—is less worthwhile than in more open societies where law checks authority.

The fact that the opposite case, "underpopulation," could have an impact is shown dramatically by the case of Africa. Other examples can be cited around the globe, from precolonial North America to Russian Central Asia.[38] Like "overpopulation," the term "underpopulation" must always be understood relatively. Here it is connected to the possibility of urbanization and thus to one of the conditions for the creation of sophisticated political organization, without which scientific discourse and significant technological progress are inconceivable. In prehistoric times, farms and pastures may have produced essential innovations. But Ibn Khaldun already recognized that "the sciences are numerous only where civilization is large and sedentary culture highly developed."[39]

Middle Class Power

Without cities, there would be no states of the kind known in Europe. And a specific social formation would also be lacking, one that had an indispensable share in the construction of "Western modernity": the middle class. The middle classes initially developed in cities, as can be seen in the etymology of words like "citizen" as well as "burgher," "burgess," and "bourgeoisie" (related to *Burg* and "borough"). Aristotle had praised the "middling element" as the guarantor of a moderate constitution. It was composed of free citizens who were neither poor nor rich.[40] In his view, the larger the middle class was with respect to the extremes, the better the community. The most salient characteristic of the middle class was—and is—its openness to movement up and down. Upward mobility occurred most easily through economic success. Wealth made one noble: a title could be bought, an aristocratic lifestyle adopted, even blue blood married into. That is what made such a deep impression on Lin Qian during his visit to New York; that is what marked the starkest contrast to conditions in his homeland. On the other hand, there was the danger of sinking into poverty. Ambition and fear could be spurs to work and industriousness. It is no coincidence that the European Middle Ages produced a work ethic that anticipated the Protestant one in certain respects.[41] There is a remarkable number of texts giving pride of place to nobility of the spirit, attained through achievement or "virtue," over nobility of blood.[42]

Europe's middle class cultivated literacy and arithmetic rationality. It supplied courts and churches with taxes, providing them with clever minds to boot. Thanks to its merchants, nearly all of whom were of middle-class origin, Europe's economy became a global economy, its culture a global culture—sometimes for the good of other countries, more often to their disadvantage. The "middling element" was possessed of inexhaustible creativity. Thucydides and Plato had already praised it for this quality.[43] Burghers had broken the educational monopoly of the Church, and they had filled the ranks of the humanists who carried the knowledge of the ancients and the Arabs forward into modernity.[44] In places lacking an urban middle class, the prospect was bleak for the economy, technology, and science.[45]

Most of the poets, artists, scholars, and inventors discussed in this book came from cities or at least received their training in an urban context. More than any social class outside of Latin Europe, the ambitious middle class inside Europe was wont to invest in the education of the next generation.[46] At any rate, the availability of highly skilled workers seems to have been greater than anywhere else. For example, the "qualification bonus"—the term economists use to distinguish between wages for skilled versus unskilled labor—was much lower in England than in most other countries around the world. Of course, this is no call to sing a paean to Europe's urban middle classes. They also included slave traders and murderous anti-Semites, reckless soldiers and martinets, zealots, skinflints, speculators, and freeloaders—the usual human bestiary in which good and evil know no class boundaries.

Cities with wide-ranging freedoms and a socially mobile middle class—ambitious to rise and anxious about falling—only could have emerged in the politically porous context of Latin Europe. A loosely comparable social class developed in India in the late nineteenth century, but it achieved almost no political power.[47]

Max Weber long ago recognized the "occidental city" and its "rational," prosperous,[48] educationally eager, and creative middle class as a singular phenomenon in world history.[49] Where it came from is unclear. Might the causes for the emergence of this peculiarity lie in Latin Europeans' distinctive marriage patterns, which we have so often had occasion to highlight? They tended to result in nuclear families (p. 153), whereas elsewhere we often find closely knit tribal lineages. As the social historian Michael Mitterauer has argued, social mobility was complicated in the latter world.[50] According to this view, endogamy—marriage within one's kinship network, excluding only a small circle of the closest relatives—entrenched these structures, thereby codifying connections for generations. In contrast, the world of nuclear families was more amenable to upward social mobility, for instance by means of shrewd marriage alliances.

Yet another sign of rifts that opened up long before the "great divergence" is that people outside Europe engaged much more seldom in cooperative decision-making along functional lines.[51] Nowhere else was there even close to the same number of corporations and communes, universities, academies, and parliaments, guilds, merchant associations, chivalric orders, sodalities, confraternities, and similar organizations; this was already the case in the Middle Ages.[52] The historian Otto Gerhard Oexle has even gone so far as to speak of "corporate" or "group societies." At any rate, this idiosyncrasy, albeit seemingly unimportant at first glance, is a further indication of the strength of horizontal power and of a substantial degree of freedom.

Corporate associations had been a thorn in the side of the ancient Roman emperors.[53] Did such circles perhaps hatch conspiracies, spawn rebellions, and organize strikes? The oldest law regarding corporate groups—the cultic communities and confraternities that structured everyday life in Rome—was focused on controlling them. The *lex Julia de collegiis*, drafted in the time of Augustus, distinguished between authorized and illicit groups.

Medieval rulers were also suspicious of the horizontal power then spreading its wings. Bishop Otto of Freising was disconcerted by the Lombard communes. In his view, they imitated ancient Roman practice and loved freedom so much that they preferred to be ruled by consuls elected annually by all strata of society rather than by a monarch.[54] What is more, they had no problem allowing young people of low birth and even those who practiced contemptible, even mechanical, trades to rise to military service or positions of dignity. And yet, somewhat to his chagrin, the snooty aristocrat recognized this as the very source of their power: "That is the reason they are superior in wealth and power to all other cities on the globe." In the eyes of a French author, Guibert of Nogent, "'commune' was a new name, and the worst possible one, for what it was."[55] Similar tones were sounded when the English king John Lackland made concessions to London's citizens in return for the city's support. As one chronicler commented, communes were "a cancer on the people, a terror of the realm, and an illness for the clergy."[56] Yet they were as hard to abolish or even to subdue as corporations and other associations. The thirteenth century gave them this juridical name using the Roman law construct of the *persona ficta*, a legal entity composed of several individuals.

Of course, horizontal power was not entirely absent outside Europe. Monasteries, where decisions were certainly reached by majority vote, were found all over the world. Communalism in Europe, the self-organization of rural communities, had equivalents in the assemblies of dignitaries in rural India and in fifteenth-century Dai Viet.[57] Merchant associations of guild-like organizations existed in East Asia, in the Byzantine Empire and under the Ottomans, as well as (albeit late) in China.[58] Yet they were not given legal recognition, nor did they exercise political influence.

The might of the middle class was confined to Latin Europe. Representatives of urban associations may have participated in choosing the *tlatoani*, the Aztec ruler, but this was an exception that proved the rule. So was the rise of the "people's parliaments" we just encountered in Japan's Warring States period. No Chinese emperor, no sultan, and certainly no Muscovite tsar had to deal with entities like the estates of the realm. Unlike Charles V or the Venetian doge, they did not have to sign a document limiting their authority when they assumed power.[59] Was there space outside of Europe for observations like that of Joannes Bassianus, a twelfth-century Bolognese jurist who claimed that the will of the people *alone* determined the power of law and custom? Could teachings be found similar to that of George Buchanan (1506–1582), who saw the king as subject to the law that was created by the people?[60]

Of course, there is no way to precisely measure the impact of corporate entities and the political influence of parliaments and other representative assemblies on the growth and innovative potential of European societies. Yet it is remarkable that horizontal power was especially strong in two incredibly successful early modern nations: the Netherlands and England.

In general, horizontal power injects a certain amount of rationalism into politics. Guilds, merchant associations, and other corporate bodies were able to represent political demands and economic interests more forcefully than individuals. The more clearly horizontal power made itself felt, the less likely it was for monarchs to plunder their own people or wage senseless wars. Guilds tended to oppose innovation, be closed to outsiders, and thus stymie up-and-coming talents, but they did guarantee artisanal excellence.[61] Their training systems had a significant share in helping European craftsmanship achieve its phenomenal level of quality. They prepared millions of potential aides to the Scientific and Industrial Revolutions. Neither Gutenberg's press nor the telescope nor the steam engine could have been built without "invisible technicians."[62]

Of great importance for the distant future, corporations of all kinds allowed people to gain experience of democracy before the age of democracy. They were a training ground for making speeches for and against propositions, reaching decisions by majority vote, and forging compromises. As far back as around 1222, one manual on government argued that "truth is better discovered from many because there is safety where council is broad [*multa consilia*]."[63] Whereas the drinking of coffee was banned in Istanbul because the government feared the uncontrolled fellowship it entailed,[64] information networks only expanded and solidified further westward. New manifestations of the public sphere took shape. Clubs and reading groups sprang up like mushrooms. To adapt an idea from the economic historian Joel Mokyr, the Renaissance and the Enlightenment created economic growth.[65] Thanks to this transformation, these first two intellectual movements in human history became irreversible.

The Long Grasp of History

What we would now call "culturally specific behavior"[66] was conceived in the sixteenth century as an astrologically influenced national character. Later it was dubbed a "national spirit" and then a "national psychology." Its tenacious power is one of the reasons why a society is or is not economically strong, technologically advanced, or amenable to innovation.[67] Those who want to survive in a corrupt, violent context must themselves be corrupt and willing to engage in violence; when security and order reign, those who threaten them will quickly pay the price. Finally, the might of mentality is related to whether people are highly egocentric and dominated by self-interest, whether achievement and originality are rewarded, or whether, not having many children, people invest in education.[68] Political and economic behavior can abide for centuries and survive profound upheavals, albeit sometimes only as a shadow.

Time and again, we recognize ourselves as the concrete heirs of the bygone times described in this book. For example, the imprint of the post-Tridentine confessional map can still be seen today. In Italy, Spain, and Bavaria, there are more Catholics than in Sweden or England. Economically strong, urbanized zones—like the one between northern Italy and southern England, which economic geographers call the "Blue Banana"—were already prosperous back in the Middle Ages.[69] The "conservatism" of the African economy clearly has a very long prehistory.[70] And the Russia of Ivan IV can be described in terms that recall contemporary characteristics of the country. Ivan's empire was an authoritarian state with close ties to the Orthodox Church and an economy lukewarm on innovation. It exported raw materials and imported more complex technology. Despite being massive, it was constantly hungry for more land to the west.

Especially striking is the *longevity* of the West's success (and here "success" is meant only in terms of economic data, innovative technological power, and scientific progress). The successor states to the Renaissance Europe of yesteryear, including its offshoots in the United States, Canada, and Australia, currently comprise a little more than 12 percent of the world population, but they account for more than half of gross world product and, by the turn of the third millennium, had secured by far the greatest number of patents. These trends seem only recently to have started to shift. Down to our own day, the greatest success has accrued to democratic, more-or-less ideologically neutral states.

Nevertheless, Europe itself did not present a monolithic picture. In the seventeenth century, cracks started forming within Europe itself: a "small divergence."[71] The north—and especially England—increasingly became the home of prospering economies and innovative societies, whereas the south fell behind. Reasons for this may be found in the declining importance of the Mediterranean region in the wake of the Cape Route's discovery. Another possible cause adduced by historians is that the European marriage model was less established in the south, and thus there was less social mobility.[72] Corruption and mismanagement are more widespread in the south, and so economic strength and innovation are accordingly weak.[73] When modern maps use different colors to designate such differences, how much of the deep past shimmers on the surface? Even today, the south bears the marks of its earlier repression and exploitation at the hands of foreign masters in its higher levels of corruption and poverty. In early modern Italy, illiteracy was already much more widespread in the south than in the north. In contrast, the north appears as prosperous, indeed rich, and as less corrupt. Can we espy there the distant reflection of the medieval tradition of independent communes, which lasted down to the fifteenth century? Brunetto Latini already speculated that corruption was less prevalent in cities with elected councils than in monarchies.[74] Even in modern Italy, the patrimony of the old city-republics registers a comparatively higher degree of civic participation.[75] Northern Italy also kept pace with Europe's grand developments. It was the home of significant participants in the Scientific Revolution. In Bologna, the physician Luigi Galvani (1737–1798) experimented with electricity, as did Giambattista Beccaria (1716–1781) in Turin. The latter's experiments were continued by Alessandro Volta (1745–1827) of Como. He built the first working battery and laid the foundations for telegraphy. Lombardy and the Veneto—forming the southern tip of the Blue Banana—continue to be among the economically strongest regions in the world.

The stagnation of Spain, the other leading country in southern Europe and the mother of the languishing Mezzogiorno, continued down to the eighteenth century. The double-edged sword of silver and gold from the New World long made it possible to import what was necessary. At the same time, it diminished the ambition to produce it at home. In the words of one contemporary, the country was poor because it was rich.[76] In addition, a fragmented legal system, regional and local customs duties, and taxes hampered domestic trade and market integration.[77] The dynamics that gave rise to the Scientific Revolution in the north were utterly absent on the Iberian Peninsula. The physician and scholar Juan de Cabriada (1665–1714) complained "how sad and shameful" it was "that, like savages, we have to be the last to receive the innovations and knowledge that the rest of Europe already has."[78] Enlightenment reforms were meant to promote economic growth and cement the absolute power of the crown. The people did not get any wiser. According to one (admittedly very rough) estimate, more than six times more books per capita were produced in eighteenth-century England than in Spain. In the Netherlands it was seven times more.[79]

In the Napoleonic Age, only the merest shadow of Spain's former glory on the world stage was visible. After its defeat in the Battle of Trafalgar in 1805, its days as a sea power were over for good. The viceroyalties in Latin America were perturbed by independence movements. By 1824, Madrid had lost nearly all its mainland possessions. In the Caribbean, only Puerto Rico and Cuba were retained until the end of the century. At that point, it was anyone's guess whether Spain's future would belong to monarchy, democracy, or the military.

In the rest of Latin Europe, global crises and religious wars had facilitated the creation of strong monarchies. In the process, horizontal power died many deaths. And yet, perhaps as a result of the continent's political fragmentation, it was also granted nine lives.[80] Horizontal regimes prevailed in the Netherlands, in England, and in the Swiss Confederacy, whose *libera libertà* ("broad freedom") had already been admired by Machiavelli.[81] In many German territories, princes succeeded in wresting power from the estates—but not in all of them. The Peace of Westphalia had confirmed the right of imperial cities to participate and vote in Imperial Diets, in line with longstanding practice. In the Scandinavian kingdoms, the gravitational center of power had long rested with the crowns. Yet their kings could not rule in the manner of Russian tsars. Thus, Sweden's chancellor Axel Oxenstierna (1583–1654) once recalled that his king could neither make a law nor alter one nor impose a tax without the consent of the assembly, consisting of representatives from the clergy, the towns, the farmers, and the nobility.[82] In France, the monarchy was victorious for the moment. As we know, however, it was an utterly Pyrrhic victory. At any rate, like most states north of the Alps, France possessed a strong, creative "third estate" whose existence was as favorable to prosperity and innovation as any de jure horizontal regime.

49

Epilogue

On the Shoulders of Giants

Europe's path traversed temperate zones, stayed close to the sea, and was often framed by pastures, woods, and fields. It led from *mythos* to *logos*, from forests to cities and across the oceans. Ultimately, it emerged from a closed world into an infinite universe. Labored breath metamorphosed into the world-conquering power of steam. The grand dialogue, which paved the way for the "West" and proved its constant companion, was favored not only by nature and geography. Thinkers of the twelfth century already recognized that they were, in the winged words of Bernard of Chartres, dwarves on the shoulders of giants.[1] Newton used the same metaphor. He had managed to see further than Descartes, as he wrote to Hook in 1676, "by standing on ye shoulders of giants."[2] And he honored them, both the moderns—Copernicus, Brahe, Kepler, Galileo—and men who belonged not to his own century nor the previous one

but rather who had lived over two thousand years earlier: Pythagoras, Philolaus, Plato and Aristotle, Euclid and Archimedes, Ptolemy and Pappus of
Alexandria.

It had taken millennia to assemble the ingredients of Europe's information
society: writing, the alphabet, Latin, Indo-Arabic numerals, paper, printing—
and let us not forget eyeglasses or the art of painting from nature! The ubiquitous computer of today had its first predecessors in the abacus and the
"bones" invented by John Napier (1550–1617). There were countless other
forerunners, including the architect Wilhelm Schickhard's (1592–1635)
Rechenuhr, or "calculating clock," and a calculating machine designed by
Blaise Pascal. Some devices were genuine European developments, such as
the mechanical clock with escapement. And they, in turn, were around for
centuries before the principles according to which they functioned were applied to totally different contexts, e.g., in steam engines.

It should be clear by now that Europe's place in the world cannot be explained solely with a view to developments since the seventeenth century or
on the basis of purely economic data.[3] Cultural, political, and social conditions
were of decisive importance for technological innovations. The communica-
tive élan of humanism and the Enlightenment, their zeal for scholarship, efficiency, and education fostered the systematization of research strategies and
the exponential increase of useful knowledge that turned the Industrial Revolution into a world-changing force. In contrast to what is often claimed,[4]
Europe's expansion was not the reason for its rise. The creative explosion that
buoyed the Scientific Revolution and sparked and attended the Industrial
Revolution was informed by the same dynamic of competition that centuries
earlier had sent Europe's ships to every corner of the globe. Without technical
know-how, social mobility, ambition, and greed for gain, early modern
Europe's venture to what it thought of as a "New World" would surely have
failed. Ultimately, both expansion and scientific and technological innovation
stood in a dynamic relationship with the process of industrialization. Newly
invented machines attended the birth of factories and accelerated their spread;
all this mobilized capital, further innovation, and even more capital.

All technological and scientific revolutions have relied on access to the intellectual legacies of the recent and more distant past. When forced to make
it on their own, societies are only innovative for short periods of time; this has
been called "Cardwell's Law," after the historian of technology Donald
Cardwell.[5] The European realm of possibility was home to several giants onto
whose shoulders the Europeans—long since taller than dwarves—could

climb. First was the Greek giant, who preserved the rich traditions of the East and bequeathed to Europe a *way of thinking* that would be indispensable for its modern science. He was followed by the Roman giant, who brought his law, his masterful engineering, his rational approach to the world, and his statesmanship. Then came the Byzantine giant, with his theology, his icons, and his shelves full of ancient manuscripts. Finally, there was the Arab giant, with his philosophy, his titanic translation efforts, and his medical, mathematical, and astronomical knowledge. They were even joined by the Indian giant, who contributed numerals, and the Chinese giant, who shared the seminal invention of paper. And let us not forget the great masters of the Middle Ages, with their translations, their razor-sharp logic, their first steps toward a new natural science, and their bold invention of a mechanized world.

Nowhere outside of Europe were there similarly "enlightened" cultures amenable to science in which such a large number of scholars, technicians, and tinkerers participated. Beginning in the Middle Ages, no other region of the globe was covered by a similarly dense communication network that facilitated the spread of useful knowledge.[6] Thanks to Gutenberg, the quantity of available knowledge mushroomed beyond measure. What others had to think up and develop for themselves, perhaps even rediscover since it had been lost, was ready to hand for Europeans—in black and white. They were able to develop ideas further, transcending what had come before.

Naturally, we cannot say for certain what significance each individual stream and factor had in cementing Latin Europe's special status. Even less can we distinguish between "contingency" and "path dependence." Theoretical curiosity clearly drove the scientific upheavals that started in the Renaissance, but its importance for the introduction of new techniques is disputed. Theory and practice often went their own separate ways. For example, it was not until the Napoleonic Age that artillerymen applied Galileo's insight that objects shot in the air follow the path of a parabola.[7] "Mere" craftsmen like Zacharias Janssen and Hans Lipperhey were just as much founders of telescopic astronomy as scholars like Giacomo Della Porta and Galileo. Henry Beighton designed an ingenious valve and also wrote treatises for the Royal Society. The instrument maker James Watt was highly educated, whereas Newcomen was a blacksmith—but also a lay preacher and anything but unlettered. And could clockmakers or even humble armorers, who laboriously made screws to hold their suits together, be erased from the prehistory of the machine age?

To formulate it a bit more complexly: we have observed chains of causality that took shape independently but then became increasingly intertwined, as well as ideas and achievements of individuals whose appearance at a specific point in time was *emergent*. A Copernicus, a Kepler, a Galileo, or a Newton is not born every day, nor even a Tycho Brahe. A broad realm of possibility was required just to produce these five individuals. It reached from Toruń in Poland to Weil der Stadt in southern Germany, from Pisa to Woolsthorpe-by-Colsterworth in Lincolnshire to Knutstorp Castle in the Swedish province of Scania. When and where these innovators were born was an accident. But it was no accident that they were *all* born in Latin Europe.

An overview of the opportunities that the region afforded does not explain how Kepler managed to calculate the orbit of Mars. But it does provide an explanation for why there was not only the possibility of a Kepler but also the potential for other greats, for hundreds of auxiliary minds, assistants, and creative thinkers. Contrary to the view of Achille Mbembe, the true "baptismal fonts of modernity" were not (or at least not primarily) in the region of the Atlantic slave trade.[8] They encompassed nearly all of Latin Europe, and its water, to stick with the metaphor, smacked of the salty Aegean Sea and carried the knowledge of Asia and Africa. This is not to say that the slave trade and colonialism were immaterial to Europe's economic superiority—rather that it is too shortsighted to view these factors as the most important or as the only true preconditions for the spectacular successes of Latin Europe's economy and technology. Their foundations lay much deeper.

Investigating such far-distant causes of the "great divergence" does not mean absolving the "West" of responsibility or justifying imperialism, colonialism, racism, and all their consequences. By the same token, ignoring the "home-made" problems of other cultures would remove guilt from the shoulders of corrupt elites, bloody dictators, and narrow-minded religious authorities. It would conceal the iron matrix of geography, the dark force of demography, the power of social structures, the tenaciousness of mentalities, and the fundamental importance of cultural transfer. Asking which of the factors that favored Europe's development did not exist elsewhere by no means entails engaging in *Defizitgeschichte*, i.e., enumerating the perceived deficits of the past of a group or region.[9] This would be a justifiable criticism if the procedure were used to substantiate civilizational or racial superiority—notions, incidentally, that seem close to the position of one author who argues that Europe's progress has its deepest roots in the "aristocratic warlike culture" of fierce "Indo-European speakers."[10]

I hope I have made it abundantly clear that I do not see the Western model as the sole path to salvation, nor do I consider it above reproach. It is obvious that unbound curiosity, once it abandons the realm of theory for real-world application, can be as good and useful as it can be dangerous, indeed murderous. It is equally obvious that Europe's creativity was not simply "good." As is well known, it produced not only medicines and democracy but also the *Hammer of Witches* and Zyklon B. Francis Bacon knew all too well: "instruments of lust and instruments of death" spring from the same source.[11] The following summary should be read with these caveats in mind.

The start was made by geography, followed by the state and its specialized, learned bureaucracy, its institutions, and its comparatively impartial legal system. We have described the outlines of its origins in the distant past and traced how it grew in the modern era into a mortal god, developing into an abstract entity detached from the person of its ruler. Its existence was one of the preconditions for the specifically "Western" form of modernity. By providing a minimum of security and freedom and by protecting property (including intellectual property) more effectively than other kinds of political entities, it unquestionably made a major contribution to Europe's creativity.

The existence of competitive societies, powerful middle classes led by educated laymen, and structures of horizontal power also helped Latin Europe achieve its place in the vanguard. It is particularly difficult to imagine England's "industrial enlightenment" without such elements. Indirect evidence of their importance is provided by Song China, which was also friendly to innovation. Its society seems to have been more open than that of the Yuan dynasty or the Ming dynasty. During the latter period, the principles behind the design of a water-powered multi-spindle spinning wheel (which had been known during the Yuan dynasty) were forgotten.[12] In 1065, the Song historian Sima Guang took the view that the emperor had to heed the majority, as communicated via meetings of high court officials, since it expressed the will of heaven.[13] An educational system independent of the court also took shape. But such developments remained rudimentary. No urban middle class emerged in China either. No other region of the world produced a similarly high number of functionally dynamic societies as Europe.[14]

As Needham noted, another key cause of Europe's rise was its political fragmentation, which, however, did not go so far that its states lost their ability to govern for extended periods of time.[15] This atomization contributed to the creation of a diverse market economy.[16] Without the money it generated, science and culture would have dried up. On the other hand, it has been objected that Asia was also divided into numerous states that often waged war against each other.[17] That is true. Yet the huge zone between the Mediterranean and the Pacific was dominated by massive kingdoms and short-lived steppe empires. In Renaissance Italy and the Holy Roman Empire alone—which around 1648 was not even half the size of Kazakhstan—several hundred more-or-less independent states were tucked away. They used money, arms, and diplomacy to constantly negotiate and impose new balances of power, mustering culture and science for the fray and financing scholars and inventors.

The rise of rhetoric to a kind of universal discipline is indicative of the climate of intellectual competition that ruled in Renaissance Europe from the time of Petrarca onward. No other classical text survives in more manuscripts— over one thousand—than the *Rhetorica ad Herennium*.[18] As we have seen, rhetoric assumed exceptional importance even in the realm of natural science. Outside of Europe, no society elaborated a theory of rhetoric with comparable enthusiasm. In China, rhetoric played a much smaller role than in Europe. It had almost no place in the public sphere.[19] The same can be said for Muslim societies. Rhetoric—Ibn Sina devoted a commentary to Aristotle's treatise on the topic—did not primarily provide a guide there to discussing or arguing about scientific discoveries or political issues. The ruler in al-Farabi's ideal state is a prophet, philosopher, and imam all in one; he is a paragon of virtue. He should be a master of rhetoric above all because it is his duty to impart his wisdom to the common people.[20] In contrast, Poliziano emphasized rhetoric's utility in the political realm: "There is nothing more fertile and useful than to persuade one's fellow citizens by means of words, so that they perform actions advantageous to the state and refrain from those that are damaging."[21]

Latin Europe's divided political landscape meant that there were always opportunities for patronage somewhere. In addition, those who wanted to publish questionable material had options. If an individual was not tolerated in a particular principality or city, the next court or church steeple was often hardly a day's journey away. Even Giordano Bruno ultimately met misfortune only because he arrived in otherwise liberal Venice at the wrong time and attached himself to the wrong patron. Galileo was free to pursue his research in Arcetri unmolested and to publish his *Discourses* in Leiden, the refuge of many unconventional thinkers. It seems that political fragmentation (and thus pluralism) is as closely connected to creativity as creativity, the middle classes, and strong horizontal power are to one another.

After the decline of the Western Roman Empire, Latin Europe never again experienced the collapse of whole states or societies. The money economy and the protection of private property subdued its wars. Unlike Africa, the Americas, and many states in Asia, Latin Europe was spared invasions after the tenth century. At most, the European system was reconfigured internally, such as when some states grew larger at the expense of others.[22] Permanent competition compelled the maintenance of complex structures at all costs—expensive institutions, bureaucracy, and even more expensive armies—even when their marginal usefulness diminished. Europeans had something that is indispensable for truly significant innovations: time—*a great deal of time*. That is what was required for research and tinkering to lead to paradigm shifts. Multifarious Latin Europe was always creative somewhere. It amassed knowledge and passed it down from generation to generation.

Although politically fragmented and religiously divided, Europe had become one large forum for dialogue thanks to the superlanguage of Latin and the supermedium of printing. Technical knowledge had roamed freely around Europe before Gutenberg—for example, Bohemia had learned from Venice how to make top-quality glass[23]—but such transfers had never occurred at the breathless pace that now set in, proceeding ever more swiftly. The innovation boom that led to the Industrial Revolution—to reiterate Eisenstein's powerful thesis—would have been unthinkable without printing.[24] Furthermore, in the early seventeenth century, newspapers began enlarging the scope of the public sphere: first in Strasbourg, then (starting in 1631) in Paris in the form of the *Gazette*; by the following century, newspapers were everywhere.[25] Books and periodicals provided the superstructure for a continental culture of knowledge without which there would have been neither a Scientific nor an Industrial Revolution. For example, Georg Agricola's 1556 treatise on mining had already spread the knowledge of how to build a piston pump from Saxony and Bohemia to the rest of Europe. The *Grubenhunt* (literally "tunnel dog") described in that book and other earlier writings—a car used to transport waste and ore out of mineshafts—belongs to the long prehistory of the railroad (Fig. 82, p. 921). For it familiarized people with the principle of conducting a vehicle over rails.[26] Agricola's book was only translated into German and Italian, as the difficulty of rendering its countless technical terms in the vernacular was almost unmanageable. Yet its woodblock illustrations were largely self-explanatory. The mere presence of dense communication networks can explain the accelerating pace at which Europe increased its stores of knowledge beginning in the fifteenth century, with innovation following upon innovation. A regularly issued court gazette first appeared in China in 1730. It had little in common with European periodicals.

No long list of major innovators readily comes to mind from post-medieval cultures in either East Asia or the Ottoman Empire, especially in the key disci-

plines of medicine, astronomy, and physics.[27] In contrast, when it comes to
Latin Europe from the thirteenth to the twentieth century, we can speak of a
vast mass of inventions and discoveries, including those that led to true paradigm shifts. In the form of letters, books, and oral discussions, thousands upon
thousands of individuals participated in a process of intellectual exchange that
crossed national and temporal boundaries. Centuries before the "great divergence," no other culture in the world possessed even close to the same number
of intellectuals and scholars, highly specialized craftsmen, and inventors from
all social classes—above all from the "third estate," the great source of Europe's
ideas. The richness and diversity of this group can be seen in the origin of a few
trailblazers who took decisive steps toward the mechanization of weaving and
mining. They include the gentleman amateur Somerset, the city councilman
Guericke, and Huygens, son of a diplomat and poet. We have encountered the
weavers Hargreaves and Kay, the clergyman Cartwright, and the smith Newcomen. James Watt was the son of a Scottish merchant, and Richard Trevithick,
who built the first functioning locomotive, the issue of an engineer. Expressions
of the burgeoning spirit of innovation can be found in fights over patents and
in an increase in disputes over who deserved credit for new ideas.

The notion that competition is good for creativity, as Vasari emphasized with
regard to Florentine art, was already familiar to antiquity. Velleius Paterculus

cited competition (*aemulatio*), jealousy, and admiration to explain the fact that certain ages abound with first-rate scholars and artists.[28] Periods of cultural flourishing in classical Greece, in the Spain of the *reyes de taifas*, and in fifteenth-century Indo-Islamic culture attest to this connection just as forcefully as do the multi-state Europe of the Renaissance and—rising to a unique level of world-historical significance—England during the Industrial Revolution.

A further factor of central importance was the *containment of religion*. As we have seen time and again, however, religion did not always have a stunting effect in the European realm of possibility. Kepler and Galileo both pursued science as a path to God. Ecclesiastics had always performed scientific research, and ecclesiastical princes had always provided patronage. Nor did Protestantism maintain the distance from science that Luther had initially adopted, as the case of England powerfully shows. The sociologist Robert K. Merton even argued that Puritan utilitarianism in the service of the honor of God was the true motor of the Scientific Revolution. In his view, it encouraged the pursuit of profit and active engagement with the world, as well as ennobling methodical scientific work.[29] This argument may hold for individual cases. But the European realm of possibility was much too complex for any such explanation to suffice for understanding the processes that led to European modernity. It is no secret that the history of Renaissance science includes countless Catholics eager for knowledge—from Jesuits like Clavius and Kircher to laymen like Galileo, Descartes, Torricelli, Volta, and Ampère. Catholic France produced more journals devoted to technical topics than even England.[30] In Protestant lands, fixated as they were on the reading of the Bible, widespread literacy enlarged the circle of potential innovators. As a general rule, however, none of the heroes of the Scientific Revolution, whether Catholic or Protestant, were religious fanatics. It is not even entirely clear that perhaps the greatest of them all, Isaac Newton, was a devout Christian.

If Europe's development ever became "path dependent"—and, if so, starting when—is difficult to say. The road toward a critical public sphere in which laymen participated and ultimately dominated was taken in the twelfth century. Dramatic technological advances cropped up in the fourteenth century,[31] becoming unmistakable with the invention of printing. The point after which the path was "locked in," achieving clear and stable contours, was probably reached at the latest with Gutenberg's invention. This view is not universal, however.

No one knows if and when there may have been opportunities to leave the path. One thinks of the butterfly effect—or the bullet that wounded William of Orange on the shoulder in the 1690 Battle of the Boyne. If it had struck the British king a few centimeters lower, he could have died. Whether in that case, as Jack Goldstone has argued,[32] England would have remained Catholic, France would have become the hegemonic power in Europe, and the Industrial Revolution would never have happened, we will never know.

The Uniqueness of the European Renaissance

In Arnold Toynbee's universal history, the term "renaissance" does not denote an epoch but rather a frequently recurring phenomenon in history: a cultural necromancer raises ancient things from the dead to achieve a specific, deliberate goal.[33] Renaissances appeared again and again in government, philosophical systems, law, language, and the arts, in all ages and all places. A similar argument was made half a century later by the anthropologist Jack Goody.[34] In his view, renaissances occurred in all literate cultures, as such revisions were inherent in the nature of written texts. However, his concept is focused essentially on looking backward, on attempts to translate ancient texts and use them in the present as tools for reform. In this very restricted sense, all kinds of "renaissances" can indeed be found: a Hindu renaissance in Gupta India, as well as Abbasid, Fatimid, and Buyid renaissances; in the late nineteenth century a "rebirth," *al-Nahda*, in Egypt and various Arab-speaking regions of the Ottoman Empire; a "Maori renaissance"; and, between 1920 and 1950, a *renacimiento colonial* in Latin America.[35]

The scholar Hu Shih (1891–1962) called the cultural revolution he and other young intellectuals initiated in 1917 the first phase of a "Chinese renaissance," one that, in the language of Nietzsche, would lead to a revaluation of all values. He did recognize, though, that the "true" Chinese renaissance occurred during the burst of innovation in the Song dynasty.[36] Meanwhile, knowledge of the European Renaissance spread in China thanks to translations and scholarly overviews. Finally, in the second decade of the twenty-first century, the Chinese Communist Party claimed that it was leading the country toward a "rebirth." The word for it, *fuxing*, was adopted by the Party as a slogan for its policy.[37] In 2009, China's most prominent blogger Han Han was forbidden from using it as the title for a magazine he was planning. Applied in this way to the current age of mass globalization, the twenty-first century, the term "renaissance" loses all connection to its historical foundation.[38]

Although it is remarkable how similar the conditions are that have led to true renaissances, "reactions against a new age,"[39] the European variant was nevertheless of an entirely different dimension. It lasted a long time. The first attempts to conjure the ancients, to stick with Toynbee's metaphor, were made under the Carolingians, followed by tentative efforts under the Ottonians and more vigorous ones under the Hohenstaufen. By the twelfth century at the latest, the ancient ghost was as good as omnipresent in Europe and about to grow to gigantic proportions. Yet the necromancers knew how to keep it within the chalk boundary of their control. They unleashed its thousand-year-old knowledge and began to play with it. And in contrast to their Muslim counterparts, they proceeded to clip the mighty wings of religion.[40]

The most important characteristic of the European Renaissance, the core of its identity, was the gargantuan range of its thought. Nowhere else in the world were there educational and research institutions that accommodated a similarly large number of disciplines, all the while training hundreds of thousands of students. Neither the universities of India nor the houses of wisdom and madrasas were anything like them. In Europe's universities, a host of now largely forgotten professors, *doctores*, and *magistri* amassed knowledge that ultimately provided an impetus to dialogue. The Middle Ages of Ockham and even of the Aristotelians—here we depart from the views of older generations of scholars—adopted and refined the critical, skeptical approaches of antiquity and passed them down to modern times. Just about all the greats of the Scientific Revolution had completed a university degree. Seen from this point of view, Eric Jones's "European miracle" was no miracle at all. Ultimately, the great breakthroughs were the *result of the large number* of attempts made to solve problems. It was a question of statistics that here and there—at first spread over centuries, then in ever quicker succession—some shots hit the mark. Even in Song China, in contrast, learned "gentlemen," the class of the *shi*, did not make up 5 percent of the population.[41]

Not just copying antiquity but rather developing its legacy further—this intention marked the cultural production of the European Renaissance from the very beginning. "It is senseless to put all one's faith in an old bag of bones," wrote Petrarca. "For those who invented these things were themselves only human beings. There is nothing so polished, nothing so perfect, that nothing can be added to it."[42] Bruni called for antiquity to be appropriated so that it could be assimilated to the needs of the present,[43] and Angelo Poliziano scoffed, "In my view, anyone who composes by imitation alone is like a parrot or a magpie, seeming to voice what he does not understand."[44] Indeed, Latin Europe's Renaissance was not simply a reincarnation. That was the essence of its world-historical importance. That is why we insist on the term, despite all polemics against it and the attempts at overly crisp periodization it has inspired.[45] Unlike fellow inheritors of the tradition in the Muslim and Byzantine intellectual worlds, Latin Europe exploited the rational and aesthetic potential of ancient thought and art to the utmost, creating something entirely new out of it. Lands beyond the borders of Latin Europe may have acquired this or that tool from the West; improving such imports was seldom attempted. Ideas may have cropped up here and there, but they did not lead to long-term research. And while Arabic letters were cast in sixteenth-century Italy,[46] the homelands of the Arabic language remained in the age of the manuscript.

The social dynamics of European societies were conspicuously reflected in rapidly shifting clothing styles. As Fernand Braudel pointed out, Europe was the continent of fashion crazes. "Almost every year we invent a new manner of dressing," observed Luís Fróis of Portugal in the sixteenth century. "In Japan the form is always the same and never varies."[47] The sparkling diversity of art in the late Renaissance had no counterpart outside of Europe, nor did the celebration of imagination, fêted in a flurry of ever-changing varieties. Imagination was what Renaissance artists and scholars had in common. It was the foundation of all creativity, whether manifested in *A Midsummer Night's Dream*, a portrait of Emperor Rudolph II composed of artfully arranged fruit, or the insight that Mars followed an elliptical orbit. All that and more was within reach in the European realm of possibility. It gave Arcimboldo, Shakespeare, Kepler, a few other great minds, and countless lesser lights the chance to make something out of their ideas. Sometimes, as with Alberti and Leonardo, a scientific mind and artistic talent were united in the same person.

We have approached the Renaissance, to adopt the words of the Japanese poet, as a "floating world" with blurry boundaries. Its beginnings became perceptible in the High Middle Ages with the massive change in speaking and writing, the "discursive revolution." What Burckhardt dubbed the "birth of the individual" was actually a discussion about earthly subjectivity. It emerged as early as the twelfth century, when secular topics started being discussed with greater frequency. It became one of the signatures of the West, in contrast to other major civilizations.[48] Developing organically with it was the formation of a lay culture. First, jurists and then other occupations and social classes took up the word. Thus, the first precursors of the group emerged that would go on to play such a phenomenal role in the history of the Renaissance and the prehistory of the Industrial Revolution: an educated, economically strong middle class that demanded a say in government and sometimes even achieved it.

The catalyzing function of ancient thought—we must not think of its reception simply as a "cause"—cannot be overestimated when it comes to Latin Europe's intellectual development. The technique of the critical dialogue passed down from the Greeks stimulated the constant questioning and challenging that characterized the learned culture of the Renaissance. Decisive for the major breakthroughs, however, was Latin Europe's insistence on conquering the ancient giants. It was not only errors and contradictions in the intellectual edifices of Aristotle and others that encouraged the project of demolition. It was also driven by other "streams": the concrete experience of sea captains, observations and systematic experiments, a mathematics that went beyond what was to be learned from Alexandria, and, last but not least, the patriotism produced in many places by the spirit of competition. The latter also fed the determination to show that Athens and Rome could be outdone.

The elements of political and social horizontal power that spread more forcefully across Europe than anywhere else—their most impressive manifestation was the English Parliament—facilitated experimentation, discussion, and printing; they expanded the opportunities to think "impure" thoughts. The broad diversity of the "Western" mind, which exploited the ancient tradition for all it was worth, was put in a nutshell by the French philosopher Omer Talon (ca. 1510–1562):

> When something in the speeches and writings of Plato is suitable and useful, I adopt it. When there is something good in the Garden of Epicurus, I do not scorn it. When Aristotle has something better for sale, I take it. When Zeno's wares are more attractive than Aristotle's, I abandon the latter and head to the former's shop. When everything I find in the stores of the philosophers is empty and useless, I do not buy anything at all.[49]

The significance of each individual factor leading to the Scientific and Industrial Revolutions may not be entirely clear. What is certain, though, is that Europe's realm of possibility transformed during the Renaissance into a realm of probability that provided a wealth of opportunities for innovation. Even democratic ideas emerged. The polis and the Roman Republic supplied practical models, whereas the writings of Plato, Aristotle, Thucydides, and Cicero provided theoretical foundations. The significance one ascribes to philosophical discourse for the genesis of Western democracies depends on the value one is willing to assign generally to ideas in historical processes. Max Weber noted that interests, not ideas, are the primary determiners of human action, but then he added: "Worldviews shaped by ideas have very often acted as switchmen to determine the tracks along which the dynamics of interest drive action."[50] Let us recall that Alexander Hamilton, James Madison, and John Jay, the authors of the *Federalist Papers*—those fascinating testimonials to political wisdom that helped to pave the way for the American Constitution and, thus, modern representative democracy—were written under the pseudonym "Publius." The reference was to Publius Valerius Publicola, who, according to Livy, was one of the first consuls of the Roman Republic and was therefore counted as one of its founders.

In this way, the legacy of humanism bore fruit for the future of Europe and the world. It prized the active over the contemplative life, the good over the true, the exceptional over the common. It retrained the focus from the hereafter to the here and now, and it made philosophy the master of the art of living a good life.[51] By the end of the Middle Ages, the model of popular government was also once again firmly in the world and no longer to be wished out of it. It was no coincidence that the same intellectual space that spawned civil society had earlier been the birthplace of the theory of democracy: Europe, along with its American colonies. For quite some time, both civil society and democracy only existed there. It is, therefore, not entirely incorrect to place the thought of Machiavelli and earlier writers (like Bruni and Salutati) in a tradition that produced the intellectual world of the English and American revolutions, and thus of the modern, Western style nation-state, as well. Machiavelli's republican project remained a design on paper. If it had been built—thus it has been observed—it would have been the "greatest of Renaissance creations."[52]

Twilight of a Faun

Dividing history into distinct periods means playing fast and loose with what Ernst Bloch called the *Gleichzeitigkeit des Ungleichzeitigen*, the "simultaneity of the non-simultaneous." It means simplifying the variety of millions upon millions of lives, ignoring the specific meaning that individuals and groups assigned to their everyday affairs. The age that we have traced was also bafflingly diverse.[53] It played with pagan gods. It made rationality and empiricism touchstones of a new science, while wizards and "wise women" helped when knowledge and faith faltered. The frescoes in Renaissance churches exulted in mathematically correct linear perspective; not far off, groups of clothed, life-sized votive figures made of wax hung from the ceiling, fetishes of those who commissioned them.[54] The period was as familiar with mysticism and the mathematical mindset as it was with a fanaticism that sought to purify with fire. It celebrated ostentatious triumphs in the ancient manner. It smiled with Erasmus and laughed raucously with Rabelais. It fostered fervent piety and cultivated the saturnine illness of melancholy. Its scholars and technicians completed projects that had been initiated in Athens and Alexandria. Its rugged physiognomy was shaped by people as various as Gutenberg, Ficino, Fugger, Botticelli, Bosch, Luther, Michelangelo, and Shakespeare. The characters who embodied its spirit included Prometheus, Odysseus, and Doctor Faustus, as well as Don Quixote and all the fools that Sebastian Brant placed on his ship. Incidentally, Nietzsche's Renaissance man was not among them. Only a few (in the jargon of the age) "illustrious" individuals like Alberti or Leonardo roamed through the epoch as its pale shadow. The philosopher of the hammer was also the stoutest purveyor of the legend of a thoroughly pagan Renaissance.[55] Yet the accusation of godlessness generally only helped to disqualify opponents in religious conflict. It would be difficult to find the "atheist monsters" demonized by the millenarian Reformer Pierre Viret. And when a zealot lamented that all Christian states were infected with "execrable atheism," it was simply a shorthand explanation for the ills of the age.[56] The few intellectuals who might be guilty of the charge of atheism include Leonardo and Machiavelli.

The swiftly increasing accumulation of ancient texts in the twelfth century provides the strongest argument for having the prehistory of the Renaissance start then at the latest. The massive impact that the "revived" classical tradition had on the sciences, technology, and cultural production in the broadest sense justifies using the much-debated term not only to refer to an artistic style but also to name a period of history. Only starting in fifteenth-century Italy, however, did architecture and painting display the enduring, widespread influence of classical forms. Just how problematic broad-brush periodization is can be seen in the fact that Renaissance style does not appear in some northern regions until Italy was already flirting with the High Baroque.

When should we say the Renaissance ended? The metamorphoses of the satyr provide clues.[57] From a fallen angel, the seventeenth century transformed it into a faun who was at times indifferent, at times friendly to humans. Bruno took this ugly creature with a beautiful soul as a simile for Socrates, and natural historians thought it was a monster begotten from the union of a human and an animal. The Age of Enlightenment considered it a primitive form of the human race and, finally, taking up older approaches, an ape. Likewise, the dragon shrunk to a lizard, the seductive mermaid became a sea ape, and the monsters of the East disappeared from world maps.[58] In a similar par-

allel, rhetoric, long so dominant, lost its place in the canon of the philosophical disciplines. Formal logic ascended in the wake of Cartesianism.[59]

In this way, the cultural foothills on the other side of the saddle age flattened out during the seventeenth century. Nevertheless, Giambattista Vico (1668–1744) of Naples, the last representative of a rhetorical humanism and an exponent of an Aristotelian concept of historical truth, can still rightly be considered a Renaissance thinker. Even "medieval" things survived. For example, Vincent of Beauvais's *Speculum maius* was reprinted in the Catholic stronghold of Douai in 1627—not as a curious historical source but as a schoolbook. Supporters of Tycho Brahe's model could still be found in eighteenth-century Portugal and France,[60] to say nothing of "popular" conceptions of the universe. Galen and Hippocrates continued to heal. But experiments and the anatomist's knife slowly led their concepts to be revised. Ancient spirits wafted away from bodies, which became mechanically functioning apparatuses. Chemistry, only destined to become a full-fledged university discipline in the nineteenth century, began to dissociate itself from alchemy, shedding its magical and astrological facets as well.[61]

Savonarola's pious putsch and Luther's Reformation did not initiate new periods in history, although some contemporaries thought they did.[62] The Council of Trent seemed to Eugenio Battisti to be the sign of an "anti-Renaissance," and Hiram Haydn placed the climax of his "counter-Renaissance" in the seventeenth century.[63] The thundering rumble of the religious wars may, for a while, have drowned out the grand dialogue, Herder's "breath of our mouth." But it did not silence it. The continuities endured from the scientific fervor, the passion for antiquity, and the secularism of the twelfth century down to the enlightened, classicizing eighteenth century, when the Renaissance concept of civic freedom buried by Hobbes in 1651 (pp. 807f.) celebrated its resurrection. The pedagogical eros of humanism survived. Indeed, it grew more forceful than ever in the nineteenth century. In contrast, confessional controversies became less important. In England, even Protestant dissenters were tolerated after 1688. Spaces for the profane expanded. For example, the number of religious images in the inventories of private residences in Calvinist Dordrecht dropped by three-quarters between 1620 and 1680.[64] From the perspective of the history of science, the birth and death dates of Kepler and Galileo mark a watershed. Ultimately, the high point of a long development toward the triumph of observation and experience as the sources of all knowledge was reached with Newton's *Principia* of 1687 and Locke's *Essay concerning Human Understanding* of 1690.[65]

The last great witchcraft panic haunted Europe around 1660. Frances Yates placed the end of the Renaissance in 1614, the year in which the Genevan philologist Isaac Casaubon debunked the *Corpus hermeticum*, proving that it was a more recent work than previously believed.[66] Newton still engaged with Hermes, however. He took him as evidence for the fact that the will of God was at work in gravitation. This notion is strangely close to the view of an al-Ghazali.

The Mediterranean world experienced a profound transformation. Its economy was on the decline. After more than twenty years of war, Venice lost Crete, its last bastion in the Aegean. The sea of the future was the Atlantic, the power of the future England. The fact that new dynasties took over in Russia (the Romanovs) and China (the Qing) was in part related to the global climate crisis. It contributed to the widespread breakdown of order not only in Europe but also in Southeast Asia.[67] There are therefore good reasons for seeing *it*— and thus the seventeenth century—as the periodization boundary stone.

Perhaps the owl of Minerva had taken flight again, unnoticed. The world-historical era that began with the Renaissance may have reached its end while a new one was dawning in the eastern half of the globe. At any rate, in the "floating world" of history, the light of the next morning always shimmers the night before. Whether Altdorfer's *Battle of Alexander at Issus* intended the Greek victory to signify the dawn of the West or the dusk of the East is unclear, nor does it matter (Fig. 81, p. 914). Describing the end or the beginning of an epoch always means keeping one's eye on both the Sun's afterglow and the first rays of daybreak. Giordano Bruno was already uncertain if he was witnessing the morning of a new day or the evening of an old one.[68] Perhaps the Renaissance and the "great divergence" were nothing more than a precondition for the current "great convergence"—and thus a mere phase in one long process: global modernization.[69]

The World a Dream

Starting with Petrarca, the Renaissance occasionally even considered itself to be "modern." Just as imagination and originality were prized in the arts, progress and *novelty*, often discredited in the Middle Ages, became increasingly attractive. Striking a keynote, some humanists were convinced they had inaugurated a new age of the arts and sciences. "The die is cast. I have ventured it!" proclaimed Ulrich von Hutten's motto.[70] In 1499, Polydore Vergil produced the first history of technology in the form of his *On Discovery*, an account of all inventions and discoveries from antiquity on.[71] It was no longer about going "back," as "*re*-formations" seek to do. Scholars in the generation of Galileo—such as Telesio and Campanella—were already being praised or chided as *novatores*, innovators. Patrizi promised a "new philosophy," John Dee a "new discipline," and Fernel a "new medicine." Bacon held out the prospect of a "great instauration" of the sciences. Copernicus and Kepler wanted a "new astronomy."[72] Finally, Descartes claimed modernity for his century and for his own mathematical method, which aimed at gaining absolute truth. In his view, his times were entirely different from the previous age, which had produced nothing more than opinion;[73] its *historia*, furthermore, had discovered only what was already known and preserved in books.

In Descartes's day, antiquity continued to be an admired source of inspiration, a supplier of topics and characters for art, literature, and the sciences. But its "re*birth*" was now finished; the "Renaissance," understood literally, was over. Jacopo Nardi's 1568 translation of Livy, the fifth to date, was to be the last until the nineteenth century. A similar fate was shared by other classics. Grand monuments of antiquity like the Laocoon group could become objects of mockery. Aristotle, Ptolemy, and other thinkers could be mummified as objects of philological or historical research.

Science still pursues Bacon's project unperturbed. Without Vesalius and Harvey there would be no medicine of the kind we know, and without mechanical clocks and steam engines there would be no automobiles. Without Kepler's astronomy, without Galileo's and Newton's physics, space travel would only be science fiction. The Renaissance even took up the Greek project of studying magnetism and electricity. The latter was dubbed *vis electrica* by William Gilbert in the sixteenth century. And yet Prometheus was still chained to a rock, bound to pay the price of knowledge with his own flesh. That is how the Aristotle translator Louis Le Roy (1510–1577) saw it.[74] Did nature not show how progress and decline were entangled with one another? The air pummeled the Earth with storms and gales; fire ravaged it; water ate away at its land, carving out bays and ripping open gorges and lake basins; mountains eroded. Like Montaigne, Le Roy knew the ambivalent nature of the innovations that would drag Europe into its modernity. He saw printing as a gift of divine inspiration, artillery as the work of the devil.

The foundation of existence teetered, no matter how much certainty reason and mathematics promised. Pascal noted that he huddled between the two abysses of the infinite and nothingness.[75] Skeptical philosophy and Cartesian doubt turned human beings into demiurges of their world in an entirely different sense than would have occurred to the Renaissance—indeed, even to Descartes himself. An unbridgeable gap opened up between the nature of things and what was perceptible to the senses and reason. With the divine guarantor of truth taken out of the game, the human perspective on nature and the universe was now the only one possible.[76] The suspicion crept in that human beings could not help but project their own concepts and claims onto the world. It is thus formed out of their images, and in that sense it is entirely their creation. As a result, "reality" would be nothing but a figment of the imagination, a dream.

The oft-quoted words spoken by Prospero to the son of the King of Naples in *The Tempest* sound like the swan song of the epoch that we call the Renaissance.

> You do look, my son, in a moved sort,
> As if you were dismay'd: be cheerful, sir.
> Our revels now are ended. These our actors,
> As I foretold you, were all spirits and
> Are melted into air, into thin air:
> And, like the baseless fabric of this vision,
> The cloud-capp'd towers, the gorgeous palaces,
> The solemn temples, the great globe itself,

Ye all which it inherit, shall dissolve
And, like this insubstantial pageant faded,
Leave not a rack behind. We are such stuff
As dreams are made on, and our little life
Is rounded with a sleep.[77]

Boastful certainty sounds different. Indeed, the epoch did not have much in common with the drama shaped by the nineteenth-century cult of the Renaissance, in which daggers flashed in the night, poison dripped into crystal goblets, and titian-red sunsets romanticized delight and death. The ice-cold seekers of power and their "tremendous dream" imagined by the "hysterical Renaissance," a literary trend around 1900, were nothing but ghosts born of dissatisfaction with modernity.[78] The Renaissance was not, as Nietzsche thought, large, hard, and clear.[79] Rather, like all history, it was contradictory and complicated.

It has bequeathed to us a few simple teachings. Religion should have its place in the heart and not in politics. Apostles of purity are a deathly danger. No culture buds and blossoms without cross-pollination. There is no alternative to tolerance, which is born from staring into the "abyss of doubts"[80] revealed by Skeptics like Montaigne and Bayle. Tolerance provides strategic advantages and is thus politically and economically useful. Moreover, it is in line with the ethics of the Sermon on the Mount. Societies that encourage competition and enable upward mobility regardless of origin, religion, and sex are good for scientific and technological progress. So is good governance. Institutions can be bastions of freedom. Without the useful knowledge accumulated over long periods of time, the Western version of modernity would not have been possible (whether it was *desirable* or not is an entirely different question). Capital matters a lot, but minds matter most. In general, innovation promotes growth more than growth pushes innovation. Breakthroughs require freedom, peace and quiet, and communication. As Samuel Johnson knew, "The seeds of knowledge may be planted in solitude, but must be cultivated in public."[81]

The nature of freedom and human dignity was discussed in greater depth in the Renaissance than in any previous age. The poet John Donne recalled in 1624—the Thirty Years' War had only recently begun—that each and every individual is part of a larger whole.

No man is an island,
Entire of itself,

Every man is a piece of the continent,
A part of the main.
If a clod be washed away by the sea,
Europe is the less.
[...]
Any man's death diminishes me,
Because I am involved in mankind,
And therefore never send to know for whom the bell tolls;
It tolls for thee.[82]

Some of the most important thinkers of the Renaissance paved the way for a grand idea: that human rights are neither Christian nor Muslim, neither European nor Asian, but rather apply to everyone. The prehistory of this idea includes the sixteenth-century debates over freedom of conscience, tolerance, and the treatment of the indigenous peoples of the Americas and Africa. The Enlightenment philosopher Denis Diderot observed in amazement that the most arrogant of all civilizations was also the most radical in its self-criticism.[83] Even today, that may be the greatest strength of the West.

POSTSCRIPT TO THE FIRST
GERMAN EDITION

ZURICH. JULY 22, 2017. So, that's it. The last corrections have been made. A few final mistakes were caught in the net; more than a few—thus one must fear—slipped through. Now it is time to bid farewell to a capricious and captivating comrade, a companion on distant travels through space and time. It departed this morning without ceremony in the direction of Munich, to the publisher, to start a brand-new life. What for many years was a mental game of thoughts and phrases will soon coalesce as paper and ink. My intimate, mercurial friend will become something neutral, an object: a book. It will now travel its own paths.

The long road to this short farewell began over a decade ago, when the publisher C. H. Beck engaged me to write a history of the seventeenth century. Other endeavors—including a book about a painting by Piero della Francesca, the *Flagellation of Christ*—got in the way. Then my research interests shifted, and it made sense to refocus the topic. We decided to undertake a cultural history of the Renaissance. The project was shepherded along by Detlef Felken. With a delicate mixture of friendliness and tenacity, as well as oblique appeals to the author's conscience, he made sure that mind ultimately became matter. Wolfgang Beck supervised the initial stages of the work, as he had numerous earlier joint book projects, with critical interest and benevolence. So did his successor, Jonathan Beck. The text was edited by Stefanie Hölscher, whose keen sense of style, supreme command of grammar, and general expertise improved the manuscript in so many ways. Beate Sander and Christa Schauer created a physical book whose beauty reflected their passion and aesthetic sense. Alexander Goller compiled the index. I warmly thank them all. I am also grateful to the Gerda Henkel Foundation for accepting the book into its renowned "Historische Bibliothek."

While developing the concept for this book, it became clear that yet another survey in the venerable tradition of Jacob Burckhardt, Peter Burke, and

John Hale was unlikely to yield truly new insights. I therefore decided to place Latin Europe's Renaissance in a comparative perspective, as a means of highlighting its significance in world history. Whether I have succeeded in the difficult tasks of combining narrative and analysis, engaging with various theoretical approaches, and still writing something halfway entertaining is for the reader to decide. Whenever possible, I have provided new translations of primary sources. As a result, there are occasional discrepancies with the form in which they appear in the secondary literature cited.

Working on a project that investigates numerous major world cultures is like walking a tightrope. You have to make sure there is a reliable net below you, namely by securing the advice and assistance of all manner of experts. My efforts proved highly successful. Many colleagues came to my aid, critically assessing chapters or sections of the book: Rainer Babel (Paris), Andreas Beyer (Basel), Floris Cohen (Amsterdam), Alexander Demandt (Berlin), Martin Dusinberre (Zurich), Ulrike Freitag (Berlin), Henner Fürtig (Hamburg), Carsten Goehrke (Zurich), Adam Jones (Leipzig), Robert Jütte (Stuttgart), Anne Kolb (Zurich), Gesine Krüger (Zurich), Thomas Leinkauf (Münster), Christian Marek (Zurich), Gert Melville (Dresden), Sergiusz Michalski (Tübingen), Maurus Reinkowski (Basel), Dietmar Rothermund (Heidelberg), Helwig Schmidt-Glintzer (Wolfenbüttel), Ludwig Schmugge (Rome), Sebastian Scholz (Zurich), Peter Schreiner (Cologne), Peter Schulthess (Zurich), Raji Steineck (Zurich), Simon Teuscher (Zurich), Sven Trakulhun (Constance), and Peer Vries (Amsterdam). Engaging with their multifaceted critical comments on the manuscript was one of the most positive aspects of the entire project. Thanking these colleagues and friends, however, in no way means that I claim their authority for my view of things. Furthermore, all the errors that remain are mine and mine alone. If Chinese, Arabic, Persian, or Slavic names and terms are written correctly, it is because Sabine Höllmann (Munich), Petra Rehder (Munich), and Renate Stephan (Rott am Inn) checked them for me.

I would like to thank not only these individuals but also others who improved the book with all manner of suggestions and practical assistance: David Abulafia (Cambridge), Pablo Blitstein (Heidelberg), Peter Burke (Cambridge), Paolo Castelo (Cusco), Cesare de Seta (Naples), Johannes Fried (Frankfurt am Main), Toby Huff (Cambridge, MA), Nicolas Jaspert (Heidelberg), Klaus Jonas (Zurich), Yasuo Kamata (Tokyo), Christiane Liermann (Loveno/Turin), Robert Muchembled (New York), Gherardo Ortalli (Venice), John Pearson (Zurich), George Saliba (New York), Manfred G. Schmidt

(Heidelberg), Martina Stercken (Zurich), and Joseph Tainter (Salt Lake City). Countless discussions with Andreas Tönnesmann (1953–2014) and Eberhard Weis (1925–2013) have also left their mark on this book.

It was helpful to present and discuss various considerations on the history and reception of Renaissance culture at guest lectures. My heartfelt thanks to those who presented me with these opportunities (I have listed the institutions where the lectures were held): Wolfgang Behringer (Universität des Saarlandes, Saarbrücken), Joseph Connors (Villa I Tatti, The Harvard University Center for Italian Renaissance Studies, Florence), Uwe Fleckner (Warburg-Haus, Hamburg), Andreas Gestrich (German Historical Institute, London), Jongsook Lee (Center for Medieval and Renaissance Studies, Seoul National University, Seoul), Heinrich Meier (Carl Friedrich von Siemens Foundation, Munich), Martin Mulsow (Forschungszentrum Gotha/Universität Erfurt), Hans Ottomeyer (Deutsches Historisches Museum, Berlin), Jae Woo Park (Hankuk University, Seoul), Heinz Schilling (Humboldt-Universität zu Berlin), Sebastian Schütze (Queen's University, Kingston, Canada), Gerd Schwerhoff (Technische Universität, Dresden), Shai Shu Tzeng (National Taiwan University, Taipei), Aldo Venturelli (Italienisches Kulturinstitut, Berlin), Martin Warnke (Warburg-Haus, Hamburg), Shengmin Yang (Minzu University of China, Beijing), Hofang Yu (Nan Hua University, Taipei).

Martin Baumeister not only invited me to give a guest lecture on the topic of "Renaissances" at the Deutsches Historisches Institut in Rome, but he also allowed me, along with Alexander Koller, to organize a conference on the topic of "Global Renaissances? The European Renaissance in Transcultural Comparison" (October 13–14, 2016). I would like to thank him and Alexander for their excellent collaboration. Looking back further into the past, there were two projects that especially sensitized me to the transdisciplinary view: the Bonn *Graduiertenkolleg* "Die Renaissance in Italien und ihre europäische Rezeption" (1996–2002), and the European Science Foundation program "Cultural Exchange in Europe, c. 1400–c. 1600" (1999–2003). I had the special privilege of coming into very close contact with several magical masterpieces of the Renaissance as co-curator of two large exhibitions: "Florenz!" (Bundeskunsthalle, Bonn, with Katharina Chrubasik, Annamaria Giusti, and Gerhard Wolf, 2013) and "Europa in der Renaissance. Metamorphosen, 1400–1600" (Schweizerisches Nationalmuseum, Zurich, with Denise Tonella, 2016).

I would like to thank my assistants in Zurich, Noemi Bearth, Rosemary Bor, Jose Caceres, Janina Gruhner, Samuel Haffner, Thomas Manetsch, and Stephan Sander-Faes, for providing me with Pantagruelian piles of books and for helping to correct the proofs. Jose saved me from various errors in judgment about the history of his South American homeland. With kindness, firmness, and efficiency, Rosemary and Janina made sure that the present was not neglected while still not letting it intrude too insolently into the author's study.

My greatest debt is to the woman I married just about thirty years ago, who has gracefully put up with my longstanding liaison with the Renaissance. This book is dedicated to her and to our children Tassilo, Martin, and Priscilla. The precise words with which I would like to thank Gabi for her love and indulgence are for her ears alone.

POSTSCRIPT TO THE NEW GERMAN EDITION

DER MORGEN der Welt has been received very positively. Accordingly, it has been reprinted three times so far. Translations, including into Chinese, are in progress. The occasional complaint that the book's perspective is Eurocentric requires no rebuttal. A thorough, unbiased reading should suffice to dismiss it. Apart from some stylistic polishing and the correction of a few errors, the text in this new edition therefore appears unchanged.

I would like to thank Klaus F. Steinsiepe (Bern) for checking the footnotes and for his numerous suggestions for improvement.

Zurich, May 2019

NOTES

Preface to the English Edition

1. McNeill; Jones 2003; Goody 2010b.
2. Hong Kong: Wen Hui Publishing Co., 2022.
3. Mittler.
4. Elvin 2005, 300. The reference to Sivin is drawn from Mittler 312.
5. Mann 2023, 197.
6. Lepore 17.
7. Collet; Ó Gráda/Paping/Vanhaute.
8. Göle 114; Eisenstadt 11, 25.
9. Douthat 205–232. Douthat speaks *inter alia* of a renaissance of religion or faith and of technological innovations.
10. Roeck 2024b.
11. Roeck 2022; Roeck 2024a.

1. Europe's Grand Dialogue

1. Galilei 1967, 105; Moss 215–256.
2. Swinford 153.
3. For Cicero's significance in the Italian Renaissance, see Baker 133–183.
4. Roeck 2009, 451–455.
5. As quoted in Heidegger 136.
6. Burke 1993, 98–108; Cox 1992; Roeck 2022.
7. Jones 2003; Goody 2010b; Pomeranz; Vries 2013, 15–17; on the "West": Osterhammel 87.
8. Blaut; Symes; Lepore 17.
9. Frank.
10. For a different view: Chakrabarty 63f.
11. Keating/Markey; Wiele; Roeck 2001; Roeck 2004, 19–25; Gordon Campbell in Campbell 2019, 1–3; Roeck 2024b.
12. Trakulhun/Weber xvi; against such a teleological view: Hobson 295; Blaut 1.
13. Clark 2007, 13f.
14. Clark 2007, 13f.
15. Kingdon 86–89.
16. Greve/Schnabel 9f.; Cardwell 490f.; Landes 1994, 644f.
17. E.g., Amin 13–23.
18. Ferguson 2011, 12.
19. Acemoglu/Robinson 2012, 75–84.
20. Lewis 1982, 68.

21. Analogous to the *Sattelzeit* ("saddle age") between 1750 and 1850 posited by Reinhart Koselleck in Brunner et al. I: xv.

22. Ferguson 1948, 90, 71, 96f.; Otto 16f.

23. Reid 2011, 135–155.

24. Shryock/Smail.

25. Foucault 2002, 138–140.

26. Stark 2005.

27. Greenblatt.

28. Dirlik 143–177.

29. Gombrich 1997, 151.

2. The Luck of Geography

1. Buck 1969, 1f.

2. Taagepera 124; Jones 2003, 57.

3. Diamond 1997, 176–191; Bellwood; for the Fertile Crescent: Bellwood 44–66; for Greece: Wesson 21–32.

4. Fortson 47f.; April McMahon et al. in Shryock/Smail 114; Bellwood 201–207.

5. Marek 2010, 83f.; on Uruk: Modelski 177f.

6. Service 280–282.

7. Diamond 1997, 134–136; Morris 2010, 85–134, on proto-scripts: 101, 123; Horden/Purcell 51–172.

8. Edzard 77–83.

9. Larsen.

10. Morris 2010, 233.

11. Haarmann 2007, 76–94; Marek 1993.

12. Demandt 2011, 54.

13. Horden/Purcell 172.

14. Jaspers 1–21, 51–60; Hodgson 1974, I: 111f.

15. Cohen 2010, xxii.

16. Troeltsch 1035: "nicht auf Rezeption und nicht auf Loslösung von der Antike, sondern auf einer durchgängigen und bewußten Verwachsung mit ihr."

17. Leppin 2010, 25–40; Kolb 59, 66; but cf. Stephen Bowd in Lee et al. 2010, 5f.; Szlezák.

3. Greek Thought

1. Abulafia 2011, 83 f., 101–105; Braudel et al. 2000; Catlos/Kinoshita.

2. Braudel et al. 2000, 8 f.; Horden/Purcell 257–263.

3. Timothy Earle et al. in Shryock/Smail 214–216.

4. Plato, *Phaedrus* 109b.

5. Abulafia 2011, 89.

6. Meier 2004, 7: "Nadelöhr der Weltgeschichte"; for a different view: Demandt 2011, 83–88; for Mardonius: Herodotus 6.43.

7. Flaig 455–471; for what follows: Klaus Rosen in Fenske et al. 55f.

8. Leppin 2010, 17–19, 74–81; Ostwald 35–63.

9. Burkert 2003, 20f., 55–78, 80.

10. Bernal.

11. Wesson 43f.

12. Plato, *Theaetetus* 155d; Hölscher.

13. Lach I: 5–12.

14. Heinen 2013, 41.

15. Szlezák.

16. Kirk/Raven 90–92, for the sundial: 99n96; Hölscher 38–40.

17. Kirk/Raven 104–110, 142.

18. Riedweg 2002, on the Pythagoreans as a sect: 129–135.

19. The relevant texts are in Bieri 39f.; Flashar 1998–2007, II.1: 201, 293f.

20. Kirk/Raven 132.

21. Hölscher 135f.; Kirk/Raven 184, 192.

22. Theophrastus, *Opinions of the Natural Philosophers* fr. 6a; Diels 482; Diogones Laertius 9.3.21; Fehling 195–231, 203f.

23. Assmann 12.

24. Kirk/Raven 287.

25. Kirk/Raven 168–170.

26. Osborne 62.

27. Diels 1934, 80 B4; Flashar 1998–2007, II.1: 38, for Prodicus 60; for Euhemerus: Kohl 169.

28. Waterfield 211; Rapp 102f.; Diogones Laertius 9.51; Plato, *Theaetetus* 152a–e.

29. Blumenberg 1987, 485.

30. Näf 46f., 181; Rowe 1965, 2.

31. Thucydides (tr. Warner) 48 (1.22.2).

32. Thucydides 5.85-111.

33. Böckenförde 2006, 35, 57–59, 138–140.

34. Flashar 1998–2007, II.1: 44f.

35. Wilfried Nippel in Lieber 21; in general Szlezák 153–172.

36. Hösle 81f.

37. Forke 39f., 92f.

38. Malinar 257, 263.

39. Berlin 20–48, 54.

40. Capelle 135.

41. Erasmus 1965, 68.

42. Hösle 84.

43. Plato, *Philebus* 16; for what follows: Kranz 1971, 135.

44. Hösle 101f.

45. Klaus Döring in Flashar 1998, II.1: 161–164.

46. Ricken 12 (also for what follows).

47. Horn/Rapp 124f.

48. Diogenes Laertius 8.36; Xenophanes B 7.

49. Hösle 187f.

50. Klaus Döring in Flashar 1998, II.1: 285.

51. Flashar 2013, 18–24.

52. Plato, *Republic* 527b.

53. Sturlese 180.

54. Plato, *Timaeus* 40b.

55. Müller 2009.

56. John Marenbon in Brower/Guilfoy 35–38.

57. Taylor 1989, 115–126.

58. Erler 528–540; Horn et al. 2009; for Plotinus: Theiler 124–139; John Marenbon in Pasnau 2014, 37.

59. Fürst 88–97; Riedweg 2002, 165f.

60. Flashar 2013.

61. Mote 2003, 338f.

62. Flashar 2013, 41f.
63. Grieb 27–36.
64. Irwin.
65. Brennan.
66. Cleanthes.
67. Brennan 235–237.
68. Cicero, *Familiar Letters* 15.19.2.
69. Marcus Aurelius, *Meditations*, 3.8; 12.36.
70. Horn/Rapp 350f.
71. Kranz 216.
72. Herodotus 2.73.1-3.
73. Cicero, *De finibus* 5.3.7.
74. Cohen 2010, 24f.
75. Galen, *On Hippocrates' Epidemics* 3.2.4; Kühn vol. 17a, 606.
76. Julia Becker et al., "Pergament" in Meier 2015, 337.
77. Krafft.
78. Eisenstein I: 193f.
79. Trzaskoma et al. 434.
80. Heinen 96.
81. Demandt 2011, 65.
82. George Ovitt in Lindberg/Shank 632.
83. Deming 124.
84. Noll 10.

4. Rome

1. Seeley 8.
2. Tacitus, *Annals* 11.24 (English translation J. Jackson).
3. Chua XXI.
4. Virgil, *Aeneid* 6.851–853.
5. Kolb 143; Alföldy 104.
6. Horace, *Epistles* 2.1.156 (trans. Alcock 1); for what follows: Vogt-Spira/Rommel.
7. Abulafia 2011, 98.
8. Kolb 148.
9. Jehne.
10. Zimmermann.
11. Lucian, *How To Write History* 42.
12. Whitmarsh 58; Reardon 40f.
13. Näf 80.
14. Tacitus, *Histories* 1.1.4.
15. Ptak 90; Frankopan.
16. Tainter 188.
17. Polybius 4.38.2.
18. Mommsen 1992, 517: "im Witwenstand, schmollend, grollend, kritisierend."
19. Matthew 16:18f.
20. Acts 24:5.
21. Horn/Rapp 431–433, 440–442; Colish 18f.
22. Clauss 16.
23. Mitterauer 157.
24. Edwards 2012 (also for what follows).
25. Kohl 2020, 31.

26. Romans 13:1–7.
27. Schimmelpfennig 34f.; Herbers 30–32; for an overview: Hamilton.
28. Fowden 75.
29. Hanns Christof Brennecke in Berndt/Steinacher 1–19 (with bibliography).
30. Lattimore.
31. Heather 209f.
32. Frankopan 103–105.
33. Socrates of Constantinople, *Historia ecclesiastica* 7.15.
34. McLynn 166f.; Gemeinhardt 152–160; Cameron 1984, 48–52; Symmachus quotation in Barrow 41.
35. Buzás 2.
36. Stemberger 32–35.
37. Ward-Perkins 2005; Börm; Sarris 33–83.
38. Alföldy 217; Salvian 190.
39. Doyle 98–103.
40. Wolters 2011, 96.
41. Williams/Friell 170f.
42. Ammianus 31.13.19.

5. The Roman Legacy

1. Pliny, *Natural History* 3.5.39 (English translation John Bostock and H. T. Riley).
2. Lach 562, n. 347.
3. Lactantius, *Divine Institutes* 7.25; Bede the Venerable PL XCIV: 543.
4. Daniel 7:23–27; Schmidt-Biggemann 620–645.
5. Dandelet 3.
6. Polybius 6.11; Bringmann 12; Wilfried Nippel in Lieber 39–41.
7. Wickham 2009.
8. Wolters 2011, 93f.
9. Kolb 169f. (also for what follows).
10. Kolb 193, Trajan quote: 178; Buzás 1f.
11. Kolb 176.
12. Horn 1995, 28; Augustine, *City of God* 8.9.
13. Augustine, *City of God* 9.1, 9.13, 9.19; Psalms 96:5; Götz; Moos 249.
14. Augustine, *City of God* 5.21.
15. Horn 1995, 36f.
16. Näf 161f.; Demandt 2011, 64f., 69.
17. Lal 91–94.

6. New Powers, Scribal Monks

1. Anderson 1991, 6; Geary 16–19, 186; Watson Andaya/Andaya 46.
2. Geary 155–157.
3. Lane 3.
4. Service 14f.; Tilly 14f., 66–95; North et al. 2009, 19–23; Sahlins 28–47.
5. Scholz 11–17.
6. Sarris 170f.
7. Cassius Dio 56.18.3.
8. Fowden 152.
9. Scholz 32–34.
10. Liebs 157–163, 166–176.

11. Flasch 2011, 55–85; Jan A. Aertsen in Pasnau 77f.

12. Boethius, *Consolation of Philosophy* 3.m9.

13. Gibbon ch. 39, p. 33.

14. Näf 2010, 85.

15. Andrew Louth in Shepard 115f.; Haldon; Michael Kaplan in Haldon 143–167; Schreiner 2011, 78–80; Cameron 1993, 26f.; Lilie 170f.

16. Wesel 50–58.

17. Ware 315.

18. Tertullian, *The Prescription against the Heretics* 7.9f. (trans. Holmes).

19. Fried 2004, 345–349.

20. Buzás 36, for what follows: 104.

21. Horn 1995, 154–160, 112; Lindberg 2013, 28.

22. Lindberg in Lindberg/Shank 2013, 28.

23. Flasch 1994; Horn 1995, 58–61; Curtius 83f., 212.

24. Galileo, *Opere* V, 340; Drake 207f.

25. Grant 2004, 93f.

26. Ovid, *Metamorphoses* 12.210–535.

27. Flasch 2008, 162f.

28. Scholz 28f., 117–119.

29. Cassiodorus 12f., 21.

30. North 2005, 147–153.

31. Van Zanden 2009, 44.

32. Thompson 1965, 589; seven pages: Ganz 22.

33. Avrin 224.

34. Legner 188f.: "Pessime mus, saepius me provocas ad iram. Ut te deus perdat."

35. Strabo 2.5.8.

36. Scholz 199–204.

37. Otto Gerhard Oexle in Meinhardt et al. 171f.

38. Stephen C. McCluskey in Lindberg/Shank 291.

39. Thompson 1965, 109; James 2001, 180–184.

40. Dohrn-van Rossum 46f.

41. Thompson 1965, 313.

42. Greenblatt 30f; Buzás 33.

43. Lilie 54.

44. For what follows: Robinson 2010; Donner xiii–xxxi, esp. xxvii; Berkey 2003; Krämer 17–35; Lapidus 1998, 194f., 218; Egger; Halm 2001.

45. Khalidi 2001.

46. Surah 2:190–191.

47. Timothy Earle et al. in Shryock/Smail 231f.; Hartmann 70–72.

48. For what follows: Berkey 2003, 74f., 93, 160f., 167–169; Crone 2005, 358–392.

49. Rohe 9.

50. Madelung; Krämer 38–41; Albrecht Noth in Halm 2001, 75, 99f.; Crone 2004, 128f.

51. Schadeina.

52. Schimmel 2014.

53. Werner 369.

54. Blankinship; Paul M. Cobb in Robinson 2010, 261–268.

55. Djebbar 32; Foltz 14.

56. Kennedy 2004b, 11f.

57. Freely 255.

58. Kraemer 4f., 57–60.

59. Ben-Shammai 20.

60. Lückerath.

61. Pirenne 234.

62. Schimmelpfennig 59–76, 95; Michael McCormick in Shepard 409–414.

63. Belting 1993, 41–45.

64. Costambeys et al. 51–65; Busch; Fried 2016; for what follows: Herbers 2012, 70f.

65. Fried 2007; Valla 2007, 181.

66. Curta 213–217.

7. First Rebirths and the Striving for a New Order

1. Herbers 75–78; Hartmann 1995, 53–58; English translation of the Royal Frankish Annals (*Annales regni Francorum*): King 1987, 93.

2. Williams/Friell 65; McLynn 298–330.

3. Einhard 30f.

4. Witt 2012, 18f.

5. Scholz 196; for what follows: Fried 2016, 268–278; Costambeys et al. 144–153.

6. Bullough 1993, 124 (modified).

7. Steckel 171.

8. Veyard-Cosme 107–129.

9. Thompson 1965, 56f.

10. Buzás 39.

11. Patzold 39.

12. Fried 2016, 349, 351–354.

13. Bullough 1991; Dodds/Shaffer.

14. Veyard-Cosme 126; Godman 192–193 (translation modified).

15. Bolgar 117–129.

16. MGH Poetae latini aevi Carolini 2:335–350.

17. Stephen C. McCluskey in Lindberg/Shank 297; Bruce S. Eastwood in Lindberg/Shank 315f.

18. Forschner 32f.

19. Kreuzer.

20. Steckel 632–636.

21. Steckel 441–454; for York: Buzás 15f.

22. MGH Capitularia 2, Nr. 254, 253–255.

23. Althoff 2004.

24. Stein 1980, 264–266; Kulke/Rothermund 2010, 134f.; but also: Beaujard II: 197f.

25. Doyle; Menzel 43f.

26. Trompf 225, n. 214.

27. For what follows: Krautheimer 1980, 161–163.

28. Pauler.

29. Althoff 114–125; Krautheimer 1980, 163–166.

30. Kortüm.

31. McCormick 569.

32. Curta 59–61.

33. Abulafia 2011, 122; Lübke 93, 96; Costambeys et al. 338–347.

34. Jordanes 6.

35. Duczko 253f.; Hildermeier 39–47.

36. Duczko 217–238, 68.

37. Obolensky.

38. Padokh; Zeuske 221.

39. Goehrke 2010, 185.

40. Lübke 104; for Africa: Dierk Lange in Fried/Hehl 2010, 114f.; Fynn-Paul.

41. Fine 113–126; Clewing/Schmitt 43–52, 70f.; Alexander 19–30.

42. Nordeide 307–318, 322f.

43. Sawyer/Sawyer 196f.

44. Sawyer/Sawyer 60, 101.

45. Flaig 98–100; Sawyer/Sawyer 103f.

46. Gudmundsson 11; Claude H. Christensen in Thompson 1965, 508.

47. Richards 2005, 115.

48. April McMahon et al. in Shryock/Smail 103–127.

49. James 253f.; Bullough 1991, 299.

50. Lübke 97; Levtzion/Hopkins 32; Cadamosto 109.

51. Schreiner 2011, 92f.

52. Nebrija 97: "siempre la lengua fue compañera del imperio: y de tal manera lo siguió: que junta mente començaron. crecieron. y florecieron. y después junta fue la caída de entrambos."

53. Splett 2.

54. Witt 2012, 30f.

55. Sturlese 37–41, 44–50.

56. Witt 2012, 81f.

57. Colish 99; Zwierlein; Classen 1982, 400.

58. Bellwood 185–189.

8. Arab Spring, Byzantine Autumn

1. Ashtor 71.

2. Watson.

3. Lübke 97.

4. Frankopan 57.

5. Lombard 147f.

6. Hendrich 68f.

7. Chaudhuri 1985, 167–169, 107, 190, 58, 60; Beaujard II: 113–126, for Aden: 218f.

8. Beaujard II: 269; Abu-Lughod 212–241; Modelski 169f., 219.

9. Pedersen 1984, 123f.

10. Starr 332–380.

11. Robinson 2003, 39.

12. Chaudhuri 1985, 48; Tilman Nagel in Haarmann 1987, 137–139.

13. Lübke 108; for what follows: Krämer 2005, 76; Fowden 150.

14. Chaudhuri 1985, 47; Murray 1985, 40.

15. Freely 255; for Baghdad's population: Modelski 184.

16. Fehérvari; Kraemer 84–86; Kennedy 2004a, 256f.

17. Rosenfeld/Ihsanoŝlou 56; Sabra 2018c, 125.

18. F. Jamil Ragep in Lindberg/Shank 34; Hoodbhoy; for what follows: Gutas.

19. Cassiodorus 24–26.

20. Shahbazi.

21. Gutas 56–60; Sabra 2018a, 105.

22. Kennedy 2004a, 255.

23. Horden/Purcell 289.

24. Hill 1998, art. II, 233 and art. III; Ahmad Dallal in Esposito 194.

25. Robinson 2003, 44, 87f., 143–148.

26. Monschi 443.

27. Saliba 2002, 360–367.

28. S. K. Padover in Thompson 1965, 341f.; Goldstein in Iqbal IV.

29. Bacon 1905, 275

30. For the use of the term: Adamson/Taylor 3.

31. Gutas; F. Jamil Rageb in Lindberg/Shank 27–61; Khalidi 2005, I.

32. Mahdi.

33. Richter-Bernburg; Ahmad Dallal in Esposito 201–203; Rudolph 2004, 23–26.

34. Khalidi 2005, 11, 167; Stroumsa 103f.

35. Niewöhner.

36. Sabra 2018c, 125.

37. David C. Lindberg/Katherine H. Tachau in Lindberg/Shank 492–496; Summers 53–55.

38. Robert Wisnovsky in Adamson/Taylor 92–136; Emilie Savage-Smith in Lindberg/Shank 139–167.

39. Kraemer 1986, 10f.

40. Ess 2017, 295–352; Stroumsa; Lindstedt.

41. Sabra 2018a, 106; Crone 2004, ch. 6.

42. Gutas 83–95, 165.

43. Ibn Sina 33.

44. Thompson 1965, 353.

45. Pedersen 1984, 118f.; for what follows: Michael Brett in Robinson 2010, 575f. (with bibliography).

46. Robinson 2003, 7; McDermott 49–53.

47. Makdisi 70.

48. Kunitzsch 3–21; for al-Khwarizmi: J. L. Berggren in Lindberg/Shank 64f., 71f., 77f.

49. Bhattacharyya 185–192.

50. Thompson 1965, 190–213; Witt 2012, 94f.

51. Haefele 194f.

52. Hartmann 164–177; Ciggaar 60.

53. Sturlese 42f.

54. For what follows: Murray 1985, 162–165; Darlington; LaGrandeur 84f.; Truitt.

55. Richer of Saint-Remi 196 (3.50).

56. Freely 107; Pedersen 1984, 120

57. Kunitzsch 11.

58. Juan Vernet/Julio Samsó in Rashed 1996, 254; for Gerbert's letter to Lupitus: Gerbert of Aurillac 46f.

59. Cardwell 56.

60. Bergmann.

61. Touwaide; Schantz 122f.; Rosenthal 6f.; Juan Vernet/Julio Samsó in Rashed 1996, 30f.; Ventura.

62. Hoffmann 2012, 590f.

63. Schauer 102f.

64. Ciggaar 63; Schultberger/Neumann 137.

65. Ciggaar 55.

66. Ostrogorsky 193–197.

67. Colish 125.

68. Michael Angold in Shepard 605; Barber/Jenkins; Kaldellis 191–224.

69. Magdalino 46–48.

70. Baldwin 71f., 74f.; Kaldellis 281–283.

71. Treadgold 1984a, 94; Schreiner 2011, 389f.

72. Williamson 76–83.

9. The Centers of the World

1. Kulke/Rothermund 2006, 208f.

2. For what follows see Chaudhuri 1985, 34–62; Rothermund/Weigelin-Schwiedrik; Findlay/O'Rourke 67–71; Gunn; Beaujard.

3. Abu-Lughod 8, 12.

4. Campbell 1995.

5. Lieberman 2003, I: 23–25.

6. Chaudhuri 54; Riello 17–27.

7. Malinar 172f.

8. Grousset 165f.

9. Stein 2010, 121f., 166, 282; Kulke/Rothermund 2010, 90f.

10. Chaudhuri 1985, 37.

11. Pearson 62–112.

12. What follows is based on Maria Verna Blümmel and Detlev Taranczewski in Kreiner 52–148.

13. Hurst 31.

14. Ganz 14.

15. Detlev Taranczewski in Kreiner 120f.

16. Modelski 155.

17. Stanley-Baker 63.

18. Winchester.

19. Needham 1969, 148.

20. Elvin 1973; Gernet; Mote 2003; Kuhn 2009; Vogelsang 2013.

21. Obata 101.

22. Mote 2003, 31–71.

23. Charles Hartman in Chaffee/Twitchett 53; for Wang Anshi see Paul Jakov Smith in Twitchett/Smith 347–483.

24. Mote 2003, 131–135, 342f.; Roman senators: Wickham 2009, 28f.

25. McMullen 11.

26. Mallory; Kuhn 2009, 17.

27. McDermott/Shiba Yoshinobu 355–367.

28. Elvin 1973, 127; Findlay/O'Rourke 62; Bray 1994, 203.

29. Kuhn 2009, 246–249.

30. Findlay/O'Rourke 61f.

31. Chaudhuri 1985, 102; Lach 513f.

32. Villiers 79.

33. Deng 122.

34. For what follows: Mote 2003, 393, 365, 155.

35. Charles Harman in Chaffee/Twitchett 22f.; for what follows: Kuhn 2009, 202.

36. For what follows: Vogelsang 313–332; Elvin 1973, 179–199; McDermott 13f.; Kuhn 2009, 183–186; Beaujard II: 161–191.

37. Robert Hymes in Chaffee/Twitchett 542–568.

38. Vogelsang 300–302.

39. For Kuo: Sivin 1995b; Sivin 1995e, 47.

40. Kuhn 2009, 182f., 127.

41. Elvin 1973, 149, 160f.; Kuhn 2009, 234–241.

42. Gernet, Part V.

43. Barnhart et al. 110.

44. Kuhn 2009, 260; for soap: 257f.

45. Yoshinobu 205.

46. Goody 2010a, 226; Mote 2003, 325–346; Barnhart 100; Brinker 72; Kuhn 2009, 129; Robert Hymes in Chaffee/Twitchett 621.

47. Kuhn 2009, 10.

48. Mote 2003, 580, 637.

49. Ronan 67, 211f.

50. Kuhn 2009, 3; Bodde.

51. John W. Chaffee in Chaffee/Twitchett 309–313; Peter K. Bol in Chaffee/Twitchett 710.

52. Vogelsang 284–286; Lewis 2012, 237; Mote 2003, 139–144.

53. Bol 1992, 148; Peter K. Bol in Chaffee/Twitchett 672f., 682–689 for Wang Anshi.

54. Kuhn 2009, 143f.

55. Brinker 72.

56. Völkel 167.

57. Robert Hymes in Chaffee/Twitchett 662f.

58. Elvin 1973, 84.

59. Kuhn 2009, 207.

60. Bol 1992, 148.

61. Kuhn 2009, 78f.

10. Takeoff under the Sun

1. Duby 1981, 5; Van Zanden 2009, ch. II; Mauelshagen 62f.

2. Jones 1997, 92–103; Sawyer/Sawyer 42f.

3. Lübke 276–289.

4. George Ovitt in Lindberg/Shank 636–639.

5. Theophilus/Ilg 5.

6. Adas 27f.

7. Wickham 2009, 369; Murray 1985, 43–45; Kluge.

8. Jacob 2010, 31.

9. Marks 80.

10. Violante 123–137.

11. D. E. Luscome/G. R. Evans in Burns 2010, 307.

12. White 1961, 97–111; Vernet/Samsó 29.

13. For what follows: Peter Blickle, "Grundherrschaft," in *EdN* IV: 1159–1160; Kuchenbuch.

14. Mitterauer 56f.

15. Werner Troßbach, "Dorfgemeinde" in *EdN* II: 1095–1097 (with bibliography).

16. Hajnal; for what follows: Mitterauer 59–65; Van Zanden 2009, ch. 4; Cerman.

17. Laslett in Laslett/Wall 23.

18. Mitterauer 72–75, 107; Ubl 242f.

19. Glaber 114–117 (3.4.13); Fried 1989, 448.

20. LeGoff 1965, 22f.

21. Jacob (1927) 2010, 12f.; Lübke 366.

22. Jones 1997, 96.

23. Feldbauer 1995, 102f.; for Amalfi: Tangheroni 96–98; G. A. Loud in Shepard 577f.

24. Marks 79.

25. Olgiati.

26. Jones 2003, 95.

27. Fried 2015, 119f.; Wollasch 105.

28. Ennen 1987, 124f.

29. Isenmann 192–195.

30. Schimmelpfennig 74f.; Chaucer, *The Miller's Tale*, 3480; Fenn 127.

31. Curtius 122.

11. Latin Europe Falls Apart

1. Malinar/Vöhler; Bley et al.; Angenendt 2011.

2. Rev. 21:8.

3. Moore.

4. Ezra 9–10.

5. Otloh/Gäbe 243–369.

6. Heesterman 26.

7. Dundas 179–181; Franke/Twitchett 317f.; Borst 213.

8. Malinar 184–201; Harald Fischer-Tiné, "Kaste" in *EdN* VI: 423–429.

9. Fenn 127–140; Cohn 1970.

10. Jantzen 7–20.

11. For what follows: Panofsky 1948; Flasch 2011, 85–92; Angenendt 2000, 150.

12. Fried 2015, 118.

13. Melville 89–124.

14. Melville 209.

15. Wollasch 144–147, 168, 240.

16. Parker 2013, 179.

17. Curtius 52.

18. Herbers 117f.

19. Hartmann 1995, 146.

20. MGH Poetae Latini medii aevi 5,1.2: 480.12: "sub caesaris potentia purgat papa secula."

21. For what follows: Weinfurter 2006a; Schieffer 2012; Laudage; Zey.

22. Herbers 128–130.

23. Zey 16.

24. Wilfried Hartmann in Gabriel et al. 101–133.

25. Schieffer 2013, 227; on Latin: Herbert Bloch in Benson and Constable 621.

26. Wong 96.

27. Weinfurter 2006a, 169.

28. Guillaume de Pouille 138f.

29. Paul Magdalino in Shepard 647.

30. Barton 147.

31. For what follows: Jaspert; Zouache (with bibliography); wicked race: Munro 1895, 7.

32. Riley-Smith/Riley-Smith 76–77 (translation adapted).

33. McGinn 1994, 12.

34. Abulafia 1995b, 1–20; Tangheroni 162–164.

35. Ibn Jubayr 301; Tolan 101–112.

36. Borgolte 265f.

37. Iogna-Prat 337–339, 442n8: "maximus precursor Antichristi et electus diaboli Muhamet"; Tolan 46–63.

38. Boshof 102.

39. Boshof 79.

40. Heather 610–614.

41. As quoted by Lübke 248 (Lübke translates the term as *das jüngere Europa*; the original Polish is *młodsza Europa*, which may also be rendered as "younger Europe").

42. Borgolte 143 (citing Bernard F. Reilly); on what follows: Dinzelbacher 2006, 701–706.

43. Horden/Purcell 457f.

44. Wickham 2009, 159; Engel 15–18; Gudmundsson 282–284.
45. Kolga et al. 359.
46. Nabokov 76; Zernack 90f.
47. Schieffer 2013, 251–253.
48. Fried 2008, 239.
49. Grundmann 1973, 14.
50. For a different view see Teschke 35–62.
51. Morgan 74.
52. Duby 1990, 136.
53. Holt; Vincent, 80, 89, 96.
54. Laudage 66.
55. LeGoff 2014, 704.

12. Vertical Power, Horizontal Power

1. For a different view: Hui.
2. Patzold 120f.; Spieß; Reynolds 1994.
3. Kin'ichi Tomobe in Bernholz/Vaubel 114f.; Brochlos 171–173; Adolphson et al. 3.
4. Hurst 33, 40f.; Hall 1966, 138–141.
5. Paul 134.
6. Ennen 1987, 123.
7. Hartmann 404–409.
8. Moor.
9. Jones 1997, 333: "civitas dicitur civium libertas, habitantium immunitas."
10. Scott 20–22; Borgolte 68, 109.
11. Jones 1997, 407.
12. Jones 1997, 403.
13. Najemy 2006, 69; for Rome: Goez 192.
14. Wim Blockmans in Allmand 41f.
15. Selzer; Dollinger.
16. Scott 130.
17. Skinner 1978, II: 130f.
18. Knackstedt 157f., 121, 128f.
19. Granberg 224; Goehrke 2010, 191f.
20. Günther 2011, 58f., 107.
21. Sigrist.
22. Wickham 2009, 100f.
23. Georg Schmidt in *EdN* III: 1149.
24. Scott 48f.
25. Wim Blockmans in Allmand 29.
26. Van Zanden et al. 838.
27. Kamen 2014a, 13.
28. North/Thomas 100f.
29. Sawyer/Sawyer 96.
30. Sabean et al. 4f.
31. North et al.
32. Rüegg; Michael H. Shank in Lindberg/Shank 214–236; Witt 2012.
33. Curtius 97.
34. Horace, Epistle 1.1.54; Seneca, Letter 119.7.9.
35. Kamp 94, 98; Murray 1985, 73–76; Wolverton 178.

36. Bumke I: 97.
37. Witt 2012, 59f., and n. 170; Bretone 255f.
38. David E. Luscombe/Gillian R. Evans in Burns 2010, 314.
39. Stelzer 121, 145.
40. LeGoff 1993.
41. Schrage 59.
42. Lange 1997, 345.
43. Boshof 267.
44. Claude H. Christensen in Thompson 1965, 478f.; for the "nations": Hirschi 125f.
45. Rainer Christoph Schwinges in Rüegg 210.
46. Rader 149–151.
47. Gorochov 131f.
48. Shank 226f.
49. Fleck 39.
50. Adcock 47.
51. Koch 147f., 152, 168f.; Weinfurter 2006b, 46.
52. Miethke 32, 36, 40.
53. Pinker xxiv, 79–81, 235.
54. Repgen 27–50.
55. Kantorowicz 240.
56. Armitage 2000, 37f., 45; Hirschi 65.
57. Dinzelbacher 2008, 604–615.
58. Signori 104.
59. Hechberger 2004, 27–34; Goetz 2008, 45.
60. Bates; Patzold 86f.
61. Acemoglu/Robinson 2012; Vries 2013, 120–139, 318–323; for a definition: Greif 30.
62. Cicero, *Republic* 1.34.
63. For institutions as a concept: Acemoglu/Robinson 2012, 104–115.
64. Kölmel 36.
65. Voltaire 410.
66. Reynolds 65f.
67. Vincent 35.

13. Origins of the "Great Divergence"

1. For what follows: Mote 2003, 410–412; Krämer 171–184; Lübke 325–332, 354f.; Vogelsang 348–351.
2. Jackson 2005, 139–168.
3. Morgan 76.
4. Pipes 55.
5. Morgan 90–94.
6. Service 321.
7. Franke/Twitchett 457f., 460, 468.
8. Allsen 83–102, 179.
9. Franke 19f.
10. Wong 102, 106.
11. Franke/Twitchett 627–640.
12. Chia 129.
13. Brinker 79, 81; McCausland 110f., 333f.
14. Zheng 47; Mote 2003, 483.

15. Wong 54; Qian.

16. Robert G. Morrison in Lindberg/Shank 129–135; Burnett in Lindberg/Shank 364.

17. Vogelsang 362; for what follows: 236f.

18. Morgan 194f.; Allsen 174.

19. Franke/Twitchett 300.

20. Hendrich 87–107; Josef Puig Montada in Adamson/Taylor 155–179; Vernet/Samsó; Colish 151f.; Langerman.

21. Thérèse-Anne Druart in McGrade 108; Puig Montada in Adamson/Taylor, 175.

22. Hendrich 78–86; Michael E. Marmura in Adamson/Taylor 137–154; Baharuddin; Grunebaum 116–118.

23. Wohlmann 36.

24. Bosworth.

25. Gimaret 788; Sardar 107.

26. Wohlmann; John Haldane in Pasnau 2014, 295f.

27. Machiavelli, *Discourses* 1.11.12.

28. Khoury 7.

29. Schreiner 2011, 73, 80, 88.

30. Marie-France Auzépy in Shepard 283; Anne Tihon in Lindberg/Shank 190–206; Borgolte 53.

31. Fodor; Ševčenko; Katerina Ierodiakanou in Pasnau 2014, 39–49.

32. Angeliki E. Laiou in Shepard 824–827.

33. Ciggaar 13f.

34. Michael Agnold in Shepard 614f.

35. Grant 1996, 186–191.

36. Bolgar 88f.; for what follows: Schreiner 2011, 114f.

14. First "Renaissances"

1. Thompson 1965, 368.

2. Flasch 2015, 58.

3. Dronke.

4. Nykrog 599.

5. Boshof 174–180.

6. Chrétien de Troyes 2; Ciggaar 94, 185.

7. Witt 2012, 222–225.

8. Krohn 205.

9. Bell 93 (*Der arme Heinrich*, vv. 1–3).

10. Ciggaar 345f.

11. Gottfried von Strassburg, *Tristan*, vv. 4736f. (trans. Lee Stavenhagen).

12. Jezler et al.

13. Goetz 268–272; Jones 1997, 90f., 127f.

14. Glauser 11f., 40–50.

15. Trompf 226–229; Goetz 188–193, 205f.

16. Boshof 187; for Cosmas of Prague: Goetz 386.

17. Müller 2002a, 94–100; Zernack 43–46; Cross/Sherbowitz-Wetzor 51.

18. Witt 2000, 47–50; Praloran/Morato.

19. Mark 16:1; Zielske, esp. 418, 422, 438.

20. Adcock.

21. Chaucer, *The Nun's Priest's Tale*.

22. Autrand (with bibliography).

23. Weigand 292: "auf einem grünen Wiesenrain . . . der stand voll heller Blüte."

24. Krohn 210, 220.

25. *CB* 3.

26. *CB* 222.

27. Kasper.

28. *CB* 191.

29. Vollmann 4f.; Dinzelbacher 2006, 87f.

30. Neidhart von Reuental/Beyschlag, Poem L 84, 462–467, VI.1.

31. Schaller et al.

32. Charles Burnett in Lindberg/Shank 372.

33. Borgolte 125.

34. Moos 4, 246, 251.

35. Haskins; Goetz 57–61; Krautheimer 181–225; Charles Burnett in Lindberg/Shank 365–384; translation of Hildebert: William of Malmesbury 613–615; Gregorius Magister/Huygens 20.

36. Bloch in Benson/Constable 631–633.

37. Hugh of St. Victor 61–62 (*Didascalicon* 2.1).

38. Hagedorn 35.

39. Nigellus/Mozley/Raymo.

40. Matthew 122.

41. Sunesen/Ebbesen/Mortensen 76f.; Glauser 20.

42. Goetz 56.

43. Bumke I: 154, 156.

44. Schnell; Rader 266–268; Watson Andaya/Andaya 50f.

45. Montgomery 141; Classen 1981, 25f.

46. Southern I: 30f.

47. Chenu.

48. Steckel 903–907; Brian Leftow in Pasnau 735–738.

49. Anselm of Canterbury 53 (*Proslogion*, ch. 1).

50. Steckel 1184f.

51. Ratkowitsch.

52. Blumenberg 1985, 43.

53. Brower/Guilfoy.

54. Brian Patrick McGuire in Sergent 27; E. Rozanne Elder in Sergent 111 (adapted); Steckel 1179.

55. Putallaz.

56. Nadja Germann in Pasnau 225–229.

57. Kouamé; for what follows: Boshof 160.

58. Angenendt 2000, 50 and 764n168 (quotation of Gottfried of Clairvaux, *Vita Bernardi*, 3.5 and 3.13, *PL* CLXXXV); Sturlese 179 (with quotation of Otto of Freising, *Gesta Friderici regis* 1.49: "qui humanis rationibus saeculari sapientia confisi nimium inherebant abhorreret"); for his agitation for Crusade: Mayer 124–126; English translation of "What did the apostles teach": Fichtenau 203; for "God's watchdog" (*catulus qui domus dei custos*): *PL* CLXXXV: 651.17.

59. Chenu 11.

60. M.A.F. Sabot in Anderson 1995, 64f.

61. Steckel 827; Sturlese 66–77.

62. Sanford 42.

63. Boshof 205–207.

64. Thorndike 1972, 23; for Gregory IX: Imbach 1989, 27; Levi 2002, 226.

65. Nadja Germann in Pasnau 222–225; Bergmann 217.

66. Ciggaar 89.

67. For what follows: Charles Burnett in Lindberg/Shank 343–345; Montgomery 141–179; Glick 257; Speer/Wegener.

68. Keil.

69. Panofsky 1974.

70. Melville 136f., 141–145.

71. Melville 103–107.

72. Oudart 246, 419f.

73. Fine 171–179.

74. Borst 2012, 109, 196–205.

75. Andrews 1999.

76. Goez 176.

77. Vicaire; Feld 2007.

78. Grundmann 1995, 45.

79. Melville 239f., 245–247.

80. David Luscombe in Pasnau 72–75.

81. Bonaventure 1978, 206.

82. Ertl 89–100, 105; for poverty: Michael F. Cusato in Pasnau 589–591.

83. Ertl 50.

84. Christel Gärtner in Gabriel et al. 9.

85. Schimmelpfennig 230f.

86. *Inferno* 27.70: "gran prete."

87. Bleienstein 227.

88. Ciggarr 294.

89. Charles Burnett in Lindberg/Shank 342.

90. Matthew 118f.; Ciggaar 286–292.

91. Khair 85–101.

92. Rader 219f., for the Constitutions: 152–161.

93. Rader 16–22.

94. Rader 276–285.

95. Park 2011, 15–44, 17f.; Imbach 1989, 95.

96. Elliott 2006, 107; Valdeón Baruqe 159–166, 172–177; John North in Lindberg/Shank 468f.

97. Bolgar 226.

98. McEvoy 9.

99. Moseley 50.

100. Montgomery 145f.; Borgolte 283.

101. Thompson 1965, 367.

102. McEvoy 84f.

103. Keen 4f.; Couliano 29–31.

104. Steven Baldner in Resnick 205f.; Edward Grant in Lindberg/Shank 439f.

105. Albertus Magnus/Simon 1978, 504; English translation: Maurer 154.

106. Forschner 2006.

107. Linsenmann 59–72 (on Augustine) and passim.

108. Signori 134.

109. David C. Lindberg in Lindberg/Shank 277f.; William R. Newman in Lindberg/Shank 392–394; Hackett.

110. Allsen 175.

111. Grant 2004, 181–184; for "manifest and detestable errors" (*manifestos et exsecrabiles errores*): Thijssen.

112. Grant 1994, 155–168.

113. Duhem 412; Blumenberg 1987, 164; Grant 1988, 537–539; Wei.

114. Pasnau/Toivanen.

115. Tolan 125–129; Enders; Imbach 1989, 102–130; Schmidt-Biggemann 129–148.

15. New Horizons, New Things

1. Burckhardt 93; for criticism of this passage: Martin 2004.

2. For what follows: Cary J. Nederman in Pasnau 552–557; Ertl 255–270; Rosenwein 31–52.

3. Wimthrop Wetherbee in Brower/Guilfoy 47–51; Sturlese 201f.; Morris 1972, 66.

4. H. Darrel Rutkin in Resnick 494.

5. Bacon/Steele II: 94f.

6. Cross.

7. Flasch 2011, 454f.

8. John of Salisbury/Nederman, 160 (7.8), 176 (7.25).

9. Miethke 295: "dignitati enim humani generis derogaret si omnes essent servi imperatoris"; Bonnie Kent in McGrade 239–241; Imbach 1989, 30.

10. Cary J. Nederman in Pasnau 556; Southern I: 45–48.

11. Benton 282f.; Johnston 12.

12. Legner 117f.

13. Finlay et al. 76–84.

14. Disney 141.

15. Zeuske 176.

16. *Inferno* 21.7-21.

17. Seibt 75; also Cochrane 75.

18. Jones 1997, 645.

19. Najemy 13–17.

20. *Purgatorio* 6.149–151.

21. Krieger.

22. Isenmann 289–291.

23. Lübke 338–340.

24. Favier 31–37.

25. Borgolte 115.

26. Maddicott 204, 208f.; Krüger 1877, 489 (5.59.5.2).

27. Commynes 2007, II: 244f. (4.1)

28. Sawyer/Sawyer.

29. Tuchtenhagen 2008, 37.

30. Pipes 56; Goehrke 2010, 72.

31. Polo 33; for what follows: Münkler 1998.

32. Polo 40–41.

33. Khair et al.

34. Ibn Jubayr /Broadhurst 348–351.

35. Zheng 209; for Bar Sauma: Lach 39.

36. Sawyer/Sawyer 154.

37. Gunn 2–4, 17–20.

38. Wilhelmus Rubruquensis/Van den Wyngaert 187; Lach 31–34.

39. Wilke; Edson.

40. Rachewiltz 191–201; Brincken.

41. Volker Schmidtchen in Ludwig/Schmidtchen 550; Biondo Flavio 348–349.

42. Jones 1997, 183.

43. Taylor 2011, 39–63.

44. Egel 153: "Didicimus miracula semper fugere."

45. Papal bull *Antiquorum habet*, 22 February 1300 in Denzinger/Hünermann 384, nr. 868: "in huiusmodi praesenti et quolibet centesimo secuturo annis."

46. Krautheimer 180.

47. *Paradiso* 12.140; Schmidt-Biggemann 1998, 602–620.

48. Jones 1997, 208; Greif 23f.

49. Witt 2012, 452, n. 32, for trade: 451, n. 25.

50. Pierre de Jean Olivi 68f.

51. Charles Burnett in Lindberg/Shank 344.

52. Burns 2001; Leu 2016b, 43f.

53. Landes 1998, 46f.

54. Willach 37.

55. David C. Lindberg/Katherine H. Tachau in Lindberg/Shank 505–507; Flasch 2007; Topdemir.

56. Kischlat 205; for Salimbene: Cochrane 95; for reactions to this view: Black 2010, 30–32.

57. North 2005, 159; for Amalfi: Biondo Flavio 348–349.

58. White 1978, 221, n. 16 (adapted).

59. Paula Clark in Dale et al. 131 (*Nuova cronica* 9.36).

16. Italian Overture

1. Huizinga 1991, 17.

2. Witt 2000, 162; Buck 1969, 4.

3. Witt 2012, 69, 71f., for what follows: 360, 469; Jones 1997, 157.

4. Isenmann 420.

5. Ibn Sina/Gohlman 27.

6. Rucellai/Battista 223: "Scripta leggibile di buono inchiostro."

7. Grendler 114; Bolgar 197.

8. Najemy 47f.

9. Witt 2012, 384, 438–455, for Latini: 455–457.

10. Skinner 1978, 41f.

11. Witt 2000, 53, 93f.; Witt 2012, 458, 462f.; for Antenor: Billanovich 94–98.

12. Werner 38f.; Cochrane 84f., 245f.

13. Pirożyński 313.

14. Beschorner.

15. Witt 2012, 466; Witt 2000, 99, for the following poem: 98, n. 46.

16. Billanovich; Witt 2000, 118–173.

17. Jäger 1764, col. 1203: "der die schönen Wissenschaften treibet"; Leinkauf 2017, 113–128; Rabil.

18. Witt 2000, 112.

19. Nauert 29; Hankins 1994, I: 31, for Rinuccini: 33.

20. Barbaro/Branca I: 96: "duos agnosco dominos, Christum et litteras"; Levi 2002, 167; for Salutati: Trompf 220f.

21. Joachimsen 419.

22. Makdisi 354.

23. Viti 1993; Sabbadini I: 140–142.

24. E.g., Lorenzo Valla: Nauta.

25. Witt 2000, 118.

26. Witt 2000, 115.

27. Most recently Stierle 2014.

28. *Inferno* 4.144.

29. *Inferno* 32.124–139; 33.1–90.

30. *Paradiso* 33.55f., 142–145; Lang/McDannell 94–107.

31. Buck 1969, 4f.: "per istum enim poetam resuscitata est mortua poesis . . . ipse vero poeti-cam scientiam suscitavit et antiquos poetas in mentibus nostris reminiscere fecit."

32. *Inferno* 15.97.

33. *Convivio* 1.3, 4.

34. Witt 2000, 214.

35. See Dante's letter to Cangrande della Scala, in Alighieri 1965, 863: "in qua et muliercule comunicant."

36. *Inferno* 20.61; *Purgatorio* 6.76f.

37. *Paradiso* 30.133–138.

38. Billanovich 83f.

39. Miethke 156–160.

40. Favier 328–333, for what follows: 335–357; English translation of *Unam Sanctam*: Ogg 388.

41. *Inferno* 19.52–123.

42. Fried 2015, 390; text of the letter: Gieseler 244n20: "Sciat maxima tua fatuitas in tempo-ralibus nos alicui non subesse . . . secus autem credentes fatuos et dementes reputamus."

43. Patrick N. R. Zutschi in Jones 2000, 653–673, 669; for the Chinese embassy: Hennig 239f.

44. Manfredi 271.

45. Fried 2015, 400; Feld 2007, 496–501.

46. Miethke 204–247.

47. Menzel 40–42: "hegemoniales Königtum."

48. Goez 197–201.

49. Green.

50. Machiavelli 1988, 89.

51. Goldthwaite 2009, 48–57.

52. Villani/Porta 12.94; Doren I: 405; Goldthwaite 2009, 265–340; John H. Munro in *RIE* IV: 115–125.

53. Barrie Dobson in Allmand 139.

54. Tripodi.

55. Pegolotti/Evans.

56. Hunt 121.

57. Ennen 1987, 165f.

58. Villani/Porta III: 331–342 (13.17).

59. Villani/Porta, III: 424–426 (13.55); Hunt 268–271; Goldthwaite 2009, 242.

60. Goldthwaite 2009, 147; Witt 1983, 274.

61. Edson 133; for what follows: Cochrane 10–13.

62. Hughes.

63. Gleeson-White 19; Morelli/Tangheroni; Murray 1985, 162–187; English translation: Leonardo Fibonacci 17.

64. Villani/Porta III: 197–202 (12.94); Najemy 100–109.

65. Murray 1985, 162; Rose; Robert Black in *RIE* II: 297f.

66. Baxandall 1972.

67. Guasti 11, document 15: "ad reverentiam et decus omnipotentis Dei et beate Virginis Marie matris eius et beate Reparate virginis, et ad honorem et decorem Fiorentine civitatis."

68. Vasari I: 370–372; Legner 194–196; Boccaccio 488–489 (*Decameron* 6.5).

69. *Purgatorio* 11.94–96.

70. Belting 1993, 153f.; Nagel/Wood.

71. Lowden 164.

72. For an in-depth discussion: Didi-Huberman 24–26.

73. Bacon/Bridges 210 (4.1).

74. Belting 1993; Alexander Perrig in Toman 40–45; Sauerländer.

75. Krüger 2001, 35–44; Didi-Hubermann 33f.

76. Dunlop.

77. Wirth 2015.

78. Sauerländer 705f.

79. Panofsky 1960, 59.

80. Aceto.

81. Stierle 2003, 115–118, 292–317; English translation: Petrarca 2017, I: 44–61, at 53; for Augustine: Petrarca 2017, I: 57 (*Confessions* 10.8.15).

82. Colish 81f.; Morris 1972, 114f.

83. Cicero, *Pro Archia* 16 (trans. Yonge and London); Looney 136f.

84. *Canzoniere* (Sonnet 126).

85. Catullus 1861, 17.

86. Stierle 2003, 390: "Il buon re cicilian che n'alto intese / e lunge vide."

87. For what follows: Looney.

88. Stierle 2003, 432–438.

89. Petrarca, *Familiares* 23.19.8 (Petrarca 1859–1863, III: 238): "quasi ad aliud quam ad legendum sit inventa."

90. Bishop 318–319.

91. Gruzinski 2012, 82–84.

92. Erler 535.

93. Stierle 2003, 669.

94. Eisner.

95. Trompf 243; Mommsen 1942, 232.

96. Mommsen 1942, 240; Stierle 2003, 13.

97. *Canzoniere* (Sonnet 272).

17. A World(view) Falls Apart

1. Grimm/Hartwig 91f.

2. Mauelshagen 63, 87.

3. Burkert 2003, 40–42; Voigtländer/Voth 169–171; for criticism of this view: Vries 2013, 66–79 (with bibliog.).

4. Le Roy Ladurie.

5. Petrarca 1807, 123 (*Triumphus mortis* 1.73–81).

6. Benedictow.

7. *Ephemerides Urbevetanae*..., in *RIS* XV: col. 639–654, 653: "Et era sì grande la mortalità, e lo sbigottimento delle genti, che morivano di subito; e la mattina erano sani, e l'altra mattina morti."

8. *Cortusii Patavini duo, sive Guglielmi et Albrigeti Cortusiorum Historia*..., in *RIS* XII: col. 926: "Uxor fugiebat amplexum cari viri, pater filii, frater fratris."

9. Rodolico, 231: "poi la terra addosso à sulo, e suolo, con poca terra, come si minestrasse lasagne a fornire di formaggio."

10. Haeser 161: "ubi est caput mundi et terre principium."

11. Schilling 1999, 256.

12. *RIS* XIV: col. 15: "usavano dissolutamente il peccato della gola, I conviti, le taverne, e delitie, con le dilicate vivande, I guochi, scorrendo senza freno alla lussuria."

13. Voigtländer/Voth 168; for what follows: Epstein.

14. Cohn 2007.

15. Bosl/Weis 143–146.

16. Perrig in Toman, 78.

17. Bergdolt 1994, 208f.

18. Johannes von Saaz, 1.

19. Ormrod 2011, 212; Harriss.

20. Curry 31.

21. Stierle 2003, 272: "non disuptantium, ubi nunc auditur sed bellantium fragor, non librorum sed armorum cumuli cernentur, non syllogismi, non sermones, sed excubiae atque arietes muris impacti resonant."

22. Froissart.

23. Seibt 209, 217; Esch 2016, 18–20.

24. Gabrielli 45: "Spiritus Sancti miles (Nicolaus) severus et clemens, liberator Urbis, zelator Italie, amator orbis et tribunus augustus."

25. *RIS* XV.6: 652; Cohn 2006, 76105.

26. Seibt 95.

27. Isenmann 261; Ertl 213.

28. Voigtländer/Voth 176–178.

29. Caferro 75.

30. Eiden 149.

31. Dunn 59f.

32. *Henry VI, Part 2*, 4.2; Cohn 2013, 125.

33. Levy 2006, 316, 318.

34. Saul 74.

35. Cohn 2006, 242.

36. *Childe Harold's Pilgrimage* 114.

37. Kamen 2014a, 21f.

38. Kafka/Brod 14: "Mütterchen mit Krallen"; for Charles IV: Fried 2015, 407–427; Paravicini 304–311.

39. *Vita Caroli quarti*, ch. 3.

40. Benešovská 289–310, esp. 291.

41. Miethke 191 (with bibliography).

42. Stierle 2003, 462f.

43. Goez 229–231.

44. Trapp 17.

45. Moeglin/Müller 272: "als ein swin in sime stalle."

46. Caferro 2.

47. Najemy 151–176; for the Ciompi: Cohn 2006, 58–62.

48. Witt 1976, 50–52.

49. Caterina di Siena /Misciatelli et al. 573, 603f., 637, 686, 723, 731.

50. Pastor 1938, 137.

51. Schmitt 2009a.

52. Marion Turner in Saunders 2006, 16f.

53. Burckhardt 10; Limongelli 332f., 417f.; Cochrane 225.

54. Gamberini.

55. McKee 133–167.

56. Saul.

57. Saul 334, 358f.

58. Redondo 65.

59. Mühle 99–104, quote at 99: "magnum chaos errorum et licium"; Lübke 419–423; Davies 286–291.

60. Haumann 18f.

61. Mühle 106: "unus princeps, unus ius, una moneta in toto regno."

62. Etting.

63. Martin 2007, 220–260; Goehrke 2010, 79.

64. Lübke 403f. (also for the following quotation); Galeotti, 8.

65. Lübke 404; Sturm 170.

66. Matuz 29–32; Lapidus 1988, 306–309; Barkey.

67. Lowry 95; Findley 109.

68. Ćirković 82–85.

69. Jackson 1986, 55; Jackson 2005, 235–255; Clavijo/Lindgren 83.

18. Before the Great Renaissance

1. Buck 1969, 4f.; Boccaccio 488 (*Decameron* 6.5).

2. Schiltberger/Neumann 88f., 111: "groß wie Esel"; "den namen das rot mer, es ist aber nit rot."

3. Clavijo/Lindgren 145.

4. Boccaccio 5 (*Decameron* 1. Introduction).

5. Thompson 1965, 185f.

6. Branca; Kapp 77–81 (with bibliography).

7. Sacchetti/Faccioli 192.

8. Saunders 2.

9. Chaucer, *Parliament of Fowls* 24f.; Ingham 151.

10. Caferro 134; "wise poete": The Wife of Bath's Tale 1125.

11. Mirbt/Aland 475f.

12. William R. Newman in Lindberg/Shank 399f.

13. Witt 2000, 294.

14. Haas; Mojsisch/Summerell.

15. Ruh III: 507–510.

16. Honnefelder 140–142, 27–47, 113–117; Vos 2006, 397–430; Perler 98–109.

17. Levy 2015, 73.

18. Rossi 1998, 322: "entia non sunt multiplicanda praeter necessitatem."

19. Edith Dudley Sylla in McGrade; Crosby 1997; for Bradwardine: Kobusch 444–448.

20. Thijssen.

21. Imbach 2004, 93.

22. Edith Dudley Sylla in McGrade 183.

23. Grant in Lindberg/Numbers 58; Walter Roy Laird in Lindberg/Shank 411–415, 423–426.

24. Edward Grant in Lindberg/Shank 437.

25. F. Jamil Ragep in Lindberg/Shank 59; Dijksterhuis 181–185.

26. Edward Grant in Lindberg/Shank 450.

27. Grant 1994, 648, 65f.; Bieri 2007, 50–56, 432f.

28. Babbitt; Imbach 1989, 90–92.

29. Lindberg/Shank 10f.; Duhem vf; Butterfield 15f.

30. Gilson 86f.

31. Perler 15–18.

32. Chaucer, The Cook's Tale 4404; The Canon's Yeoman's Tale 762; Stromer.

33. Eisenstein I; 14; Grimm/Hartwig 87.

34. Bury 53.

35. Cursi.

36. Hoenen 137; Smith 2012; Kapp 46–49.

37. Partington 42–63.

38. Kirk 2005, 50f.

39. Hill, art. IV, 36–38.

40. Hill, art. I, 21; North 2005, 175–185.

41. Mayr 5; Landes 1983, 6–11; Dohrn-van Rossum 52–55, 102f.

42. Dohrn-van Rossum 106f.; North 2005, 193.

43. North 2005.

44. Shank 2007, 3–27, 19–22; North 2005, 179.

45. *Purgatory* 6.149–151; *Paradise* 15.96–99; Dohrn-van Rossum 266–289.

46. Popplow 65–67.

47. Stierle 2014, 36f., 41–47; Dante, *Inferno*, 26.94–99; Petrarca, *Canzoniere*, sonnet 189 (trans. A. S. Kline).

48. Stierle 2003, 43: "laboriosa virtus."

49. Saitta II: 148; Findlen 1994, 304–308.

50. Fernández-Armesto 101f.

51. Findlen 1994, 304.

52. Bornstein 43f., 55.

53. Rex 2002, xv.

54. Trevelyan 188.

55. Edwards 1999, 48–50.

56. Schürer.

57. Flasch 2011, 569–572; Leinkauf 2017, 1494–1497, 1544–1564, 19.

58. Huizinga 1996, 164; for what follows: Bergdolt 1994, 216f.

59. Mack; Campbell/Milner.

60. Behringer 2003, 52–60.

61. Hedeman.

62. Darwin 4–6.

63. Barfield.

64. Conermann 394.

65. Goetz 2008, 43 (with bibliography).

66. Moran 1991.

67. Gaukroger 197.

68. Angenendt 2000, 552: "im Höchsten der Seele."

69. Dante, *Convivio* 4.14,15.

70. Fried 2015, 363; Schröder 1998, 57–60.

71. Fairbank/Goldman 18f., 173–176.

72. Ennen 1991, 150f.

73. Origo 57; for Thomas: Bumke II: 456.

74. Autrand 76, for what follows: 154–163; Sabbadini II: 64–74.

75. Gudmundsson 79.

19. The Sun Sets in the East

1. Peter C. Perdue in Reinhard 2015, 154f.; Taranczewski 2006, 31–64, 46f.; Taranczewski in Kreiner 146–148.

2. Brook 2010, 14–23, for what follows: 86–91; Vogelsang 372–377.

3. Mote 2003, 603.

4. Beaujard II: 394–406 (with bibliog.).

5. Vogelsang 237, 378f.; Sprenkel.

6. Zheng 54.

7. Goldziher 205f.; for another viewpoint: Gutas 1998, 166f.

8. Szlezák 52f.

9. Rudolph 91f.; Sabra 2018b, 363–371; for a critique of this view: Thérèse-Anne Druart in McGrade 99f.

10. Sajjad H. Rizvi in Adamson/Taylor 240.

11. Roshdi Rashed in Iqbal I: 37–44; Vernet/Samsó 1996, 269–273; Brentjes; Issawi 85; Lal 55 (with bibliography); Timur Kuran in Bernholz/Vaubel; Van Zanden 2009, 62f.

12. Watson 32f.

13. Ibn Jubayr/Broadhurst 226.

14. Ziai in Adamson/Taylor 420.

15. Surah 33:40.

16. Modjtahedi.

17. Ze'evi 39f.; North et al. 2009, 241; for astronomy: Egger 39; King 1212; al-Jabri; for Ibn Khaldûn: Ibn Khaldûn/Rosenthal II: 431–434; in general: Juan Vernet and Julio Samsó in Rashed 1996, 244.

18. Wiedemann 18f

19. Saliba 2007, 186.

20. Bakar 239, in general: 229–262.

21. Ragep 2007, 73, 75.

22. Sabra 1998, 322.

23. Mottahedeh 91; Krämer 2005, 162–164; Huff 2011, 153–158; Livingstone.

24. Rizvi 24.

25. Makdisi 89.

26. Bhatt 29–36.

27. Vernet/Samsó 1996, 263.

28. Rizvi 31–36.

29. Brömer.

30. Whitfield 14–16.

31. Kellermann/Treue 155.

32. Machiavelli/Marchand 289.

20. Florence at First Light

1. Molà 549f., 554.

2. Alexander Perrig in Toman 80–84.

3. Ghiberti/Bartoli 92f., 97, quotation at 93: "pruova e conbattimento"; Rauterberg.

4. Villani, *Nuova Cronaca* 1.42.

5. Günther 2009, 44.

6. Ridde 945.

7. Alberti 1988 (*De re aedificatoria* 7.10).

8. Warren.

9. Sorci 612–615.

10. Tartuferi.

11. Vasari II: 217: "Oh che dolce cosa è questa prospettiva!"; Summers 16–42.

12. Belting 2011.

13. Cennini 15 (ch. 28).

14. Biggi 166f.

15. Vasari I: 247, II: 287.

16. For what follows: Bianca 2010, ix–xxiii, for "greenhorn": ix; Witt 1983; Witt 2000, 292–337; Brucker 1987; Cotroneo 29–38.

17. Salutati/Novati 145: "nichil novum fingimus, sed quasi sarcinatores de ditissime vetustatis fragmentis vestes, quas ut novas edimus, resarcimus."

18. Witt 2000, 308; Witt 1983, 212–220; Fubini 2003, 132.

19. Witt 1983, 301; for what follows: Cotroneo 30, 35.

20. Cotroneo 225; Hankins 1994, I: 37; Leinkauf 2017, 443–453, 479–487.

21. Witt 2000, 445f.

22. Prezziner 75–79.

23. Floerke xivf.

24. Vespasiano da Bisticci II: 232f.: "aveva in casa sua infinite medaglie di bronzo, d'ariento et d'oro, et molte figure antiche d'ottone"; 240: "chi gli volava gratificare gli mandava o statue di marmo, o vasi fatti dagli antichi o piture o iscolture di marmo, d'epitafi di marmo, di picture di mano di singulari maestri, di molte cose di musaico"; Martines 112–116; Manfredi 278–282.

25. Hankins 1994, I: 32.

26. Grafton 2000, 63.

27. Connors/Dressen 200f.

28. De la Mare.

29. Sacchetti 169.

30. Ghiberti 108f.; Schlosser.

31. Krautheimer/Krautheimer-Hess I: 167.

32. Schlosser 143.

33. Klöckner 29–31.

34. Kroeber.

35. Roeck 2013, 81.

36. Hartt.

37. Ianziti 2012; Pocock 86–91.

38. Bruni/Viti 703–749; Fubini 2003, 173f.

39. Witt 2000, 493.

40. Najemy 214.

41. Bruni/Viti 703–749.

42. Cochrane 3f., 18f.; Ianziti 2012, 119; Fubini 2003, 93–164.

43. Roover; Kent 1978; Kent 2000; Field 1988, 10–16.

44. Pius II 2004, 318f.

45. Schmidt 1998, quotation at 1.

21. From Constance to Constantinople

1. Esch 1969; Esch 2016, 50–55, 58f.

2. Schimmelpfennig 232.

3. Facetiae, nr. 35.

4. Ansgar Frenknen in Braun et al. 47–51 (with bibliography).

5. Helmrath 2014; Braun et al.; Buck 2010.

6. Dieter Mertens in Braun et al. 33–38.

7. Greenblatt 48–50; Vespasiano da Bisticci I: 542.

8. Hoensch 491.

9. Studt.

10. Vespasiano da Bisticci I: 470.

11. Šmahel II: 869f.

12. Moeglin/Müller 308: "wie die Hund."
13. Grant 2014, 23f.; Šmahel II: 392–428, 641.
14. Ceccopieri Baruti.
15. Angenendt 2000, 75–79.
16. Mormando.
17. Melville 297, 306–312.
18. Müller 2011.
19. Helmrath 2014, 35: "sicut quinta rota in curru."
20. Connors/Dressen 216.
21. Grimm/Hartwig 2014, 85; for Christine de Pizan: Leinkauf 2017, 842–846.
22. Starkey 148.
23. Tuetey 3: "on pouroit gueres veoir sans savoir pourquoy"; 6: "comme ce tout Paris fust plain de Sarazins, et si ne savoit nul pourquoy ils s'esmouvoient."
24. Adams 149–165.
25. Krynen 279–312; Barbey.
26. Weber 1977, 321.
27. Schilling 1999, 225–227.
28. Van Loo 340–427.
29. Geneva Drinkwater in Thompson 1965, 431f.
30. Roupnel 29.
31. Fallows 1.
32. Kantorowicz.
33. Villiers 197.
34. Huizinga 1996, 94.
35. Gombrich 1978, 176.
36. Harbison.
37. Roeck 2013, 60.
38. Warnke 1993, 37f., 131f., 204.
39. Hirschfeld 103–113; Gelfand.
40. Hirschfeld 103.
41. Vos 1999, 60f.
42. Baxandall 1964, 90–107; for what follows: Vos 1999, 67f.
43. Nuttall.
44. Vespasiano da Bisticci I: 24: "si tenevano le pecore e le vache in sino dove oggi e' banchi de mercatanti."
45. Kälin 170f.
46. Schmitt 2001, 295.
47. Ryder 316–357.
48. Lane 227; for what follows: Michael Mallet in Allmand 553.
49. Scott 2012, 81–87.
50. Soldi Rondinini.
51. Ianziti 1992, 503–505; Blastenbrei.
52. Cappelli.

22. Children of the Discursive Revolution

1. Black in *RIE* II: 292 f., 298f.
2. Vergerio's treatise in Kallendorf 1–91, quotations at 54–55.
3. Marullus/Schönberger 10.
4. Müller 1984a.

5. Brian P. Copenhaver in Schmitt 1988, 107.

6. Witt 2000, 466; Huizinga 1996, 387; Leinkauf 2017, 321; Baker, ch. 1 ("The Renaissance of Eloquence").

7. Keßler 2008, 25.

8. Vasoli 50f.; Hobbins 113–116.

9. Golinski 367–396, 372f.

10. Bruni/Viti 84; English translation: Cox 2017, 301.

11. Etting 178.

12. Trinkaus 103–170; Vasoli 67–121; Ryder 321–325; Leinkauf 2017, 173f., 185, 352f., 357f.

13. Mode.

14. Nauta 7, 45–47.

15. Skinner 1978, 106f.

16. Angenendt 2000, 15.

17. Fubini 2003, 262–286.

18. Figliuolo 82.

19. Westermann 40f.

20. *Paradiso* 4.49.

21. Borgolte 2002, 291.

22. Geneva Drinkwater in Thompson 1965, 422: "graecum est; non legitur."

23. Paul Oskar Kristeller in Schmitt 1988, 130.

24. Bolgar 276, also Appendix I.

25. Egel 132; Edson 114–140.

26. Stinger.

27. Viti 1997; Bianca 1999.

28. Hankins 1994, I: 165f.

29. Robin 22.

30. Schreiner 1994, 625.

31. Vespasiano da Bisticci 19: "Era una sedia al dirimpeto a quella del papa da l'altro lato, ornato di drappo di seta, et lo 'mperadore cor una veste alla greca di brocato domaschino molto rica cor uno capeletto alla greca, che v'era in su la punta una bellissima gioia."

32. Wind 282, n. 18.

33. Tambrun 60.

34. Otto 261.

35. Fürst 84–86.

36. Riedweg 1993, 44.

37. Demandt 2011, 111f.; Riedweg 2002, 165, for what follows:163.

38. Lewy 473–479; Erler 531–533.

39. Burns 2006, 165; Tambrun 94–104.

40. Walker.

41. Hankins 1994, I: 193–217.

42. Hankins 1994, I: 217–263.

43. For Cusanus, see most recently: Leinkauf 2017, 1061–1164; Leinkauf 2014.

44. Ebeling 84–86, for what follows: 69, 91; Keßler 2008, 103f.; Copenhaver 2015, 84–101.

45. Flasch 1998, 53.

46. Dieter Mertens in Fenske et al. 196; Flasch 1998, 79, 82–86; Leinkauf 2017, 1142.

47. Anthony Black in Burns 2010, 584.

48. Leinkauf 2017, 1110; Flasch 1998, 385f., 416, 455; for what follows: Schmidt-Biggemann 79, 88; Otto 39.

49. Leinkauf 2017, 1066f.

50. Schmidt-Biggemann 64: "gläubige menschliche Mutmaßung von den Zeichen Gottes."

51. Leinkauf 2017, 1068f.

52. Nicholas of Cusa, 88f.; Leinkauf 2017, 220, 661; Flasch 1998, 148f., 155, 255.

53. Flasch 1998, 318–324, 431.

54. Flasch 1998, 160.

55. Flasch 1998, 99f.

56. Blumenberg 1976, 34–36, 56f., 101–103.

57. Leinkauf 2017, 1017, 1097f., 1179.

58. Innocent III 78.

59. Trinkaus 247f.

60. Floerke; Fubini 2003, 114–126.

61. Greenblatt.

62. Lucretius 1.1–10, for Epicurus and religion: 1.79.

63. Hossenfelder 79–81.

64. Lucretius 1.932; 1.149; for what follows: Greenblatt 185–202.

65. Lucretius 6.389–421.

66. Greenblatt 197; Lucretius 4.1076–1081.

67. Blumenberg 1996, 25–28.; Lucretius 2.1–13, quotation at 2.7–8.

68. Leinkauf 2017, 706–724; Nauta 185–190; Keßler 2008, 80–82.

69. Valla 1970, 21: "laeta in animo commotia, suava jucunditas in corpore"; Leinkauf 2017, 711.

70. *Inferno* 10.13–15.

71. Prosperi; Drücke 121–138.

72. Virgil, *Georgics* 2.490–492 (trans. J. B. Greenough).

73. Esch 2016, 192–194; Fubini 2003, 53–89.

74. Esch 2008, 84–96.

75. Esch 2008, 97.

76. Justin Stagl in *EdN* I: 489–491.

77. Celenza 1999, 156; on Alberti see: Grafton 2000; Tavernor; Roeck 2006, 98.

78. Alberti/Tauber.

79. Alberti/Tauber 48f.: "scrutator fuit assiduus"; 66f.

80. Landino 120.

81. Hartung 100–102.

82. Grafton 2000, 221–224.

83. Alberti/Knight/Brown.

84. Marsh 55–58; Alberti 2003, 355–441; English translation: Alberti 1987, II: 189–279.

85. Skinner 1978, I: 98.

86. Alberti 1972, 55.

87. Didi-Huberman 43.

88. Baxandall 1971, 132f.

89. Alberti 2002, 102f.

90. Alberti 1988, 303 (9.5); Kruft 1994, 41–50; Wittkower 1998.

91. Alberti 1988, 156 (6.2); Aristotle, *Nicomachean Ethics* 1106b, 10–12; Roeck 2013, 76; Krüger 2001, 29–34.

92. Schoot 79–95.

93. Guidi Bruscoli 554–556.

94. Müller/Springeth; Schwob et al. For Wolkenstein's works in English, see Classen 2008, which has been consulted but not followed for the translations here.

95. Klein 18: "fiedeln, trommeln, pauken, pfeifen."

96. Klein 70: "Her wiert, uns dürstet . . . , pring her wein! pring her wein! pring her wein!"

97. Klein 33, 58, 61: "zwai hendlin smal"; 79: "die weissen hende mir geben hohen müt."

98. Klein 33: "Ihr Mund all Stund weckt mir die Gail / mit sehniglicher Klage"; "damit das Bettlin krache."

99. Klein 53: "Mund Mündlein gekusst / Zunge an Zünglin, Brüstlin an Brust."

100. Klein 84.

101. Klein 98, 123: "da ich gedacht an Bodensee / zur Stund tat mir der Beutel weh."

102. Klein 25: "Turniere und auch Stechen, / das war mir nie bekannt. / Ich habe einen vollen Beutel, / darin stoß' ich mein Hand, / Gold, Silber, Edelgesteine / zieh' ich daraus genug."

103. Klein 32.

104. Klein 18: "Ich habe gelebt wohl vierzig Jahr wohl minder zwei / mit toben, wüten, dichten, singen mancherlei."

105. Dopsch 2011, 13.

106. Klein 9.

107. Gerrit Walter in *EdN* V: 665–691, 684–686; Helmrath et al.

108. Gorochov; Müller 2002a.

109. Smoller.

110. Pascoe 11–51; Smoller 102–111.

111. Hobbins 1, 11.

112. Richards 2000.

113. Hobbins 70; Imbach 1989, 41f.

114. Ornato.

115. Stechow 139f.

116. Müller 2002a, 375.

117. Müller 2002a, 334.

118. Delogu et al.; for Seneca: Jean-Claude Mühlethaler in Delogu et al. 163.

119. Torres-Alcalá 49.

120. Ryder 317f.

121. Saygin 241–252.

122. Müller 2002a, 352–361.

123. Thompson 1965, 391–393; Saygin; Starkey 149.

124. Paasch; Sabbadini II: 10–16.

125. Baron 51–62.

126. Helmrath 2002, 99–141, 133f., 127f.; for Virgilius: Baron 68.

127. Baron 151.

128. Kidwell 1991, 55–59.

129. Hankins 1994, I: 81, 131f.; Findlen 1993, 83–86.

130. Rinaldi 342; Saitta I: 656–670.

131. Pontano, *Eridanus* (1.15), tr. Roman, 195–197; for Pontano: Cotroneo 86–120.

132. Dicke; Bernstein 62–90.

133. Bernstein 43–62.

134. Buzás 127: "doch mer die alten puecher, der neuen acht ich nit zu keiner Stund" (emphasis added).

135. Reichel.

136. Stark 2005, 187f.; Keßler 2008, 35f.

137. E.g. *Grand Testament* 12, 40, 139, 145; *Petit Testament* 37; Pinkernell 2002; Grimm/ Hartwig 108–110; Villon.

138. Villon 209, 47–49 (*Ballade des dames du temps jadis*), 64 (*Ballade de la belle Heaulmiere aux filles de joie*).

23. *Le tens revient*

1. Schmitt 2009b, 13–16.

2. Philippides/Hanak.

3. Riggs 76f. (Kritovoulos §256); Philippides/Hanak 585f.

4. Beaujard II: 387.

5. Faroqhi 2009, 67; Beaujard II: 441 (with bibliography).

6. Mansel.

7. Olivier de la Marche II: 340–380; Huizinga 1996, 305.

8. Bertrand Schnerb in Allmand 448.

9. Geertz.

10. Olivier de la Marche 381.

11. Flasch 1998, 341.

12. Soykut 25; Bisaha 2.

13. Pius II 2019, 129.

14. Lewis 2003, 29.

15. Goez 254–257; Suraiya Faroqhi in Reinhard 2015, 306–328.

16. Argenti I: 106–146.

17. Rösch 92f.

18. Esch 2016, 173–175.

19. Esch 2016, 243–263; Pellegrini.

20. *Aeneid* 1.378.

21. Coquelines III,3 101b. D: "Aeneam reiicite, Pium suscipite."

22. Tönnesmann 2013.

23. Fortini Brown 310f.

24. Hankins 1994, I: 118.

25. Najemy 341–474.

26. Buck 1969, 1f.

27. Machiavelli 1988, 283 (*Florentine Histories* 7.6); Brown 1992, 54f.

28. Brown 1992, 177.

29. Burckhardt 27.

30. Daniels 360: "nulla vis saevum potuit extinguere Xystum / audito nomine pacis obit."

31. Housley 56–58.

32. Koller.

33. Pangerl.

34. Wiesflecker I: 69.

35. Walsh 2005, 129–136.

36. *Richard III* 1.1.

37. Schilling 1999, 120–124; Alexander 67–71; Mączak 185–190.

38. Wiesflecker I: 281.

39. Sahlins 1968, 88–90.

40. *RIS* XXIV: 7 66; Frigo.

41. Settis/Cupperi.

42. Rucellai 551, 139.

43. Vespasiano da Bisticci II: 175.

44. Vespasiano da Bisticci II: 183: "tolsi in poco tempo quarantacinque iscrittori, et finii volumi dugento in mesi ventidua."

45. Smith/O'Connor 474.

46. Roeck 2006; Roeck/Tönnesmann (also for what follows).

47. Starr 484.

48. Connors/Dressen 208–211; Roeck/Tönnesmann 152–156.

49. Eiche 131f.: ". . . mostrarli lui proprio cum diligentia a le persone de auctorità e de doctrina cum farli cum bel modo intendere la prestantia belleza e gintileza d'essi e de caracteri e de miniature, e de vedere . . . che non se pighe alchuna charta . . . e quando se mustrano a

persona ignorante che per curiosità li volesse vedere, se non è de troppo auctorità basta una ochiata."

50. Vespasiano da Bisticci I: 387: "E che lettere! E che libri! E come degni!"

51. Kidwell 1991, 270f.

52. Strong.

53. Dorothy Robathan in Thompson 1965, 550f.

54. Saygin 219–232; Hankins 1994, I: 117–154.

55. Viti 1997.

56. White 1973, 247.

57. Burckhardt 387.

58. Hankins 1994, I: 15, 131.

59. Hankins 1994, I: 267–359, 277; Kristeller 1964; Field 1988, 177–201; Leinkauf 2017, 1165–1246.

60. Joost-Gaugier 83f.

61. Tambrun 241.

62. Assmann 76–78; Schmidt-Biggemann 68f., 91–93; for what follows: Ebeling 91–94.

63. Flasch 1998, 375f.

64. Ficino 1576/1959–1960, 1836; English translation: Campanelli 57.

65. Joost-Gaugier 27f.; Kristeller 1964, 74–91.

66. Allen/Hankins I: 14–17; for what follows: Keßler 2008, 107–110; Otto 270f.; Schmidt-Biggemann 414–416.

67. Kristeller 1964, 191; Vickers 1984a, 120; for what follows: Leinkauf 2017, 1256–1262, 1306–1327.

68. Ficino 1985, 130.

69. Grafton 1997, 116.

70. Most recently Dougherty.

71. Kamen 2014b, 6.

72. Pico della Mirandola 2018, 83: "secundum propriam opinionem."

73. Pico della Mirandola 1965; Keßler 1971, 122.

74. Zanato 421.

75. Pico della Mirandola/Caplan, ch. 7.

76. Zanato 391; English translation: Lucchi 103.

77. Mann 1936, 271–272.

78. Machiavelli 1988, 344 (*Florentine Histories* 8.22).

79. Brown 2011, 11.

80. Machiavelli 1988 (*Florentine Histories* 8.36); for Riniccuini: Garin I: 342–345; Jones 1997, 333.

81. Abulafia 1995a, 1–25.

82. Rabin 172f.

24 Media Revolution

1. For what follows: Matheus 2005b, 12; Leu 2016b.

2. Rothmann.

3. Leu 2016b, 43.

4. Allsen 180–185.

5. Mendoza 88r (3.14).

6. Wolff; Schnack.

7. Childress 62.

8. Franck; Mahal 15f.

9. Wirtz 159–161.
10. Alberti 1890, 310.
11. Máthé.
12. Füssel 46f.; Rothmann 47–49.
13. Panagiotakes 5; for Makarije: Ivana Nikolić in Biggins/Crane 85f.
14. Leu 2016b, 48f.
15. Eisenstein I: 46; Rothmann 48; Van Zanden 2009, 75–77; Marks 83.
16. Bezold 140; Celtis 1502, 49v (*Amores* 3.9): "Omnia pressor habet nil nunc absconditum in orbe est . . . Scimus enim coelo faciat quid Iuppiter alto / et quid sub terries Pluto sepultus agat."
17. Hirsch 78–81, 83.
18. Hobbins 19f.
19. R. F. Yeager in Saunders 52.
20. Touwaide.
21. Rothmann 58; Eisenstein I: 347.
22. Gilmore 186; Eisenstein.
23. Füssel 73; Vespasiano da Bisticci I: 398: "i libri tutti sono belli in superlative grado, tutti iscritti a penna, e non v'è ignuno a stampa, chè se ne sarebe vergognato"; Rothmann 41; for the contemporary discussion about printing in Venice, see Baker 229–231.

25. New Worlds

1. Church.
2. Ma Huan/Sheng-lan 9f., for the ship names: 18, for Mecca: 173–178.
3. Pearson 90.
4. Whitmore 103–107; Hall 2011, 246f.
5. Russell.
6. Levathes 180.
7. Pagden 2004, 194; Richardson 1993, 67–98; Lach 20–48.
8. Lach 27.
9. Moseley; Michelet.
10. Fernández-Armesto 105–107.
11. Rosen 1967, 11.
12. Edson 79, 96; for the Canary Islands: Abulafia 2008, 49–64.
13. Oliveira Marques 142–151, 217–238; Reinhard 2016, 77–96.
14. Witte 425.
15. Edson 141–164; Egel 171–174.
16. Edson 52 (for quotation), 151–155 ("Sources of the map").
17. Cadamosto, for "another world": 105r.
18. Black 2015, 28f.
19. Falola/Roberts x–xi; Mbembe 13–15; for fashion: Thornton 2012, Part 4; Bailey et al.
20. Angus MacKay in Allmand 606; Martín 2003, 9.
21. Edwards 2000; Kamen 2014a, 1–5.
22. Elliott 2006, 121 (with bibliography).
23. For what follows: Kamen 2014b; Kamen 2014a, 57; Edwards 2005; Edwards 2000, 68–100.
24. Kamen 2014b, 265–270.
25. Edwards 2000, 99.
26. Edwards 2005, 29–31.
27. Hering Torres 64; Kamen 2014b, 42, 303–327.

28. Harvey 81–97.
29. Harvey 109f., 115f.
30. Kamen 2014b, 2, 5–8.
31. Harvey 59f.
32. Harvey 222.
33. Feldbauer/Liedl 60–65; for what follows: Harvey 308–321; O'Callaghan 122–196.
34. Harvey 219.
35. For what follows: Thomas.
36. Grant 1994, 626, 41f.; Wey Gómez 64–66, 145.
37. Strabo 1, 1.1.3, 1.1.20, 1.3.3.
38. Strabo 2.1.30, 1.1.8.
39. Strabo 1.4.6; Colón 65.
40. Strabo 2.3.6.
41. Wey Gómez 88f., 369.
42. Thomas 83f.
43. Hamdani.
44. Lactantius, *Divine Institutes* 3.24; Blumenberg 1987, 29; Grant 1994, 628f.
45. Schedel/Füssel xii.
46. Pliny, *Natural History* 9.41; Marees/van Dantzig/Jones 3f.
47. Columbus/Markham 31–35; for what follows: Abulafia 2008, 162–174; Bitterli 57–67.
48. Columbus/Markham 38.
49. Columbus 54.
50. Columbus 84; Egel 242–267; Magasich-Airola/de Beer 25–30.
51. Columbus 90–91.
52. Brendecke 2016, 93–102; Thomas 329; Barrera-Osorio 28 and ch. 2.
53. Elliott 2006, 51.
54. Jurt 46; for sirens: Todorov 15f.
55. Todorov 5.
56. For what follows: Kamen 2014b, 25–35.
57. Findley 99.
58. Kamen 2014b, 61f., 65, 68.
59. Pérez 2014; Edwards 2005, 86f.
60. Kamen 2014b, 159; Coleman 6, 43.
61. Harvey 253.

26. Witches, High Finance, and the Authority of the State

1. Belting 2016.
2. Genesis 6:1–2.
3. Gombrich 1978, 276.
4. Leu 2016b, 46.
5. Barnes 142; Brendecke 1999, 71–73.
6. Savonarola/Besold II, Conclusio 7, 64f.: "tota ergo vita Christiana ad hoc tendit, ut purificetur ab omni infectione terrena."
7. Werner 420–423.
8. Celenza 2001, 41.
9. Hatfield 1995, 89–114, esp. 98–100.
10. Kamen 2014b, 53.
11. For an overview, see Levack.
12. Behringer 2004, 68.

13. Mackay I: 7f.

14. Mackay I: 8 ("Apologia auctoris").

15. Edwards 1999, 88f.

16. Bumke II: 456f.

17. Mackay I: 86

18. Girard; Bezold 148.

19. Celenza 2001, 42f.

20. Dinzelbacher 2008, 697; for dragons: Zedler VII: 1374.

21. Johnston 21, 53, 63: "Anderswelt."

22. Christopher Dyer in Allmand 106–120.

23. Walsh 1920, 84.

24. More 1995, 62; for Spain: Pérez 1989, 187f.

25. Ulrich Pfisterer in *EdN* I: 136–140; Cerman.

26. Bosl/Weis 14.

27. Tinagli 51; Van Zanden 2009, 25–28, 233–266, 271f.

28. Isenmann 999.

29. Goez 276.

30. Schilling 2017, 100 (quoting Lothar Suhling): "bedeutendste und folgenreichste montanwirtschaftliche Neuerung."

31. Kühlmann 1997, 78, l.35: "Sed volitant caeco tenebrosa ibi sydera mundo."

32. Ekkehard Westermann in *EdN* VIII: 740–743.

33. Reinhold Reith in *EdN* VIII: 416f.

34. Bibliography in Christoph Bartels in *EdN* VIII: 734–736; for what follows: Christoph Bartels in *EdN* VIII: 746–764.

35. Wiesflecker V: 482; Metzig 2, 5.

36. Wiesflecker I: 66f.

37. Jörg Rogge in Meinhardt et al., 116–120 (with bibliography); Moraw.

38. Zedler I: 522f.

39. Moeglin/Müller 418–426.

40. Svalduz 137f. (with bibliography).

41. Wiesflecker IV: 151.

42. Häberlein 2006, 56f.

43. Mandrou 1997.

44. The annual wage of a trained miner was 30 guilders in the late fifteenth century: Schilling 2012, 69.

45. Ehrenberg 111: "Es ist bekannt und liegt am Tage, dass Eure Kaiserliche Majestät die Römische Krone ohne meine Mithilfe nicht hätten erlangen können."

46. Pölnitz; Tracy 100f.

47. Häberlein 2006, 78f.

48. For this and what follows: Reinhard 2001, 84–86. Reinhard 2001.

27. *Raison d'État* Is Born

1. *RIS* XXXII: 3, 303.

2. Condivi 20r: "ch'io per me non so lettere."

3. Pastor 1908, 42.

4. Commynes 1912, 170, 169 (7.18).

5. Buck 1985, 29 (citing Jean-Jacques Marchand).

6. *Prince* 111.

7. Pocock 156–191, "drastic experiment": 190; Brown 2010, 168.

8. *Prince* 99, 101 (ch. 25).

9. *Prince* 69 (ch. 18).

10. *Prince* 67 (ch. 17).

11. *Discourses* 37 (1.12), 34–36 (1.11).

12. *Discourses* 38 (1.12).

13. *Prince* 66 (ch. 17).

14. Schmitt 2005, 5.

15. *Prince* 57 (ch. 13).

16. *Prince* 48f. (ch. 12)

17. *Prince* 105 (ch. 26).

18. Hoeges 114.

19. Machiavelli 1988, 122f. (3.13); Skinner 1978, I: 45–48, 180–186; for the old Florentine discourse: Keßler 1971, 35f., 41, 47.

20. Buck 1985, 143f.; Irwin 726f.

21. *Discourses* 115–119 (1.58), "brute animal": 44 (1.16).

22. Fubini 2003, 195–207.

23. *Prince* 108–110.

24. Petrarca 2017, Letter VIII.7 (*Familiar Letters* 24.8).

28. Travels to Utopia, Art Worlds

1. Pieper.

2. Kruft 1989, 20–33 (Pienza), 34–51 (Sabbioneta).

3. Tigler 52f.

4. Wendell; Roeck 2013, 83f.

5. Witt 2012, 42, 219; Curtius 157.

6. *Inferno* 23.95.

7. Tavernor 28f.; Colonna 1499.

8. Kruft 1994, 60.

9. Kretzulesco-Quaranta 46.

10. Colonna 1499, Fiiiv.

11. Frank-Rutger Hausmann in Kapp 105–107.

12. Sannazaro 152, 153 ("pilgrim of love").

13. Esch 2008, 18, for what follows: 26, 68.

14. Günther 2009, 168–178.

15. *VLH* I: 247–283, esp. 252–255 (Joachim Knape).

16. More 1995, 218.

17. Nipperdey 113–146.

18. McRae; Inagaki/Stewart; al-Azmeh 127, 172; Crone 2004, 318.

19. Lenin 471f., 478, 483.

20. Castiglione 40.

21. Castiglione 35f.

22. Castiglione 41.

23. Lowe 27.

24. Burke 1993; Burke 1995.

25. Dedekind: "Lies' wohl dies Büchlein oft und viel / und tu allzeit das Widerspiel."

26. Elias.

27. Kapp 142.

28. Thomasin von Zerklaere.

29. Thomasin von Zerklaere, 168: "vrume ritter, guote vrouwen, wise phaffen" (v. 14695f.).

30. Nichols 267f.

31. Castiglione 223.

32. Bonoldi/Centanni.

33. Settis 1990, 128.

34. For what follows: Burke 1972, 85–98; Warnke 1993; Baxandall 1972; Najemy 315–340 (with bibliography).

35. Kubersky-Piredda; Glasser.

36. Hirschfeld 136.

37. Welch; Fantoni et al.; Goldthwaite 1993.

38. Guerzoni 81 (with bibliography).

39. *Europe in the Renaissance* 278f.

40. Dürer 1956, I: 59; English translation: Dürer 2016, 159.

41. For the current state of research on Leonardo: Bambach; Renn.

42. Rosheim.

43. Capra 182.

44. Kemp; Keele.

45. Clayton/Philo; Keele 253–d54.

46. Ost, 29.

47. Villata 292, no. 337.

48. Leonardo da Vinci 1995, I: 32: "lettori di varie e belle opere."

49. *R* I: 116, no. 10; Leonardo da Vinci 1975–1980, I: 119*v*.

50. Leonardo da Vinci 1995.

51. *R* II: 324, no. 1339.

52. *R* II: 252–253, no. 1213.

53. *R* II: 245, no. 1178f.

54. Leonardo da Vinci 1995, I: 8; 78; for Dante: *Inferno* 11.102–105.

55. *R* II: 369, no. 1473; Leonardo da Vinci 1975–1980, III: 1067*r*: "Anassagora. Ogni cosa viene da ogni cosa e d'ogni cosa si fa ogni cosa e ogni cosa torna in ogni cosa."

56. Leonardo da Vinci 1986–1990, F 82, fol. 49*v*: "Guarda la luce e ammira la sua bellezza. Chiudi gli occhi e osserva: quello che hai visto non c'è più, quello che vedrai non c'è ancora. Chi è quel che lo rifà, se 'l fattore al continuo muore?"

57. Beck 123–133.

58. For what follows: Wallace 2011; Pfisterer (with bibliography).

59. Settis 2006, 118: "nec docta vetustas / nobilius spectabat opus, nunc celsa revisit / exemptum tenebris redviivae moenia Romae."

60. Hatfield 2003, 195–201.

61. Di Teodoro, 44: "di questa anticha madre de la gloria e grandezza italiana."

62. Kohl 2020, 190–192; Esch 2016, 34f.

63. Vasari IV: 383; for what follows: Beck.

64. Buonarroti 118.

65. Hall 2020, 48.

66. Buonarroti 302.

67. Leinkauf 2017, 1261.

68. Keßler 1971, 52f.

69. *Orlando Furioso* 33.2.4: "Michel, più che mortale, angel divino"; Emison 134f.

70. Ciriacono.

71. Wittkower 1998; Bertling Biaggini.

72. Lockwood 227.

73. Welch 245–273.

74. Kapp 125–130.

75. Kidwell 2004, 99–112; Leinkauf 2017, 1365–1371; for Bembo: Tavoni (with bibliography).
76. Bullegas.
77. Schmitt 1984c, esp. 299f.; Fusaro.
78. Collard 378–380; for a different view (for England): Saygin 266.

29. South Wind

1. Prietzel 402–404, 421.
2. Pagliaroli.
3. Märtl, for his library: 285–292; Manfredi 283.
4. Donald R. Kelley in Porter/Teich 130; Nauert 121f.; Leinkauf 2017, 128.
5. Cotroneo 348–352, 381f.; La Garanderie.
6. Lemaire; Grimm/Hartwig 131.
7. Stephenson 2004.
8. Marguerite de Navarre.
9. Müller 2002a, 361; Walsh 2005, 381; Huizinga 1996, 386f.
10. For the problem of time in Renaissance art: Nagel/Wood.
11. Howard in *RIE* VI: 332f.
12. Biersack (with bibliography).
13. Pérez 1989, 325–342; Edwards 2000, 261–281; Praloran/Morato 498.
14. Allés Torrent.
15. Rowe 1965, 13; for Pietro Martire: Biersack 568–576.
16. Bresc-Bautier 288, 292–297.
17. Marías 298–321.
18. Harasimowicz 415f., 420; Connors/Dressen 211–213.
19. Miggiano.
20. Hajnóczi.
21. Tibor Klaniczay in Porter/Teich 165.
22. Havas/Kiss 283.
23. Pipes 89.
24. Mączak 181; Füssel/Pirożyński; Harasimowicz 418f., 421–425.
25. Biggi 171.
26. Burke 2016, 62f.
27. Josef Macek in Porter/Teich 198f.; for the theater: Biggi 171.
28. Martínek.
29. Macek in Porter/Teich, 201–203, 208 (also for what follows).
30. Macek in Porter/Teich, 206, 211.
31. Nauert 122–124.
32. Donald Kelley in Porter/Teich 124–126; for Gaguin: Müller 2002a, 369f.
33. Kühlmann et al., 68–71; for what follows: *VLH* I: 375–427 (Jörg Robert).
34. Celtis/Schäfer 358.
35. Ott 92–95, 100–112; *VLH* III: 1–35 (Franz Josef Worstbrock).
36. Gerrit Walther in *EdN* I: 574–581, esp. 575 (with bibliography); *VLH* II: 819–840 (Franz Josef Worstbrock/Béatrice Hernad); Stauber.
37. Roeck 2013, 117–119.
38. Baxandall 1980.
39. *VLH* I: 1211 (Herbert Jaumann): "O saeculum! O litterae! Iuvat vivere!"
40. Blusch 357; Vasoli 225–273.
41. Johannes Helmrath in *EdN* XII: 144–147: "humanistische Horizontale."
42. Bezold 98; *E* II: 124–127.

43. Mundt 38f.; *VLH* II: 697–703 (Ulrich Muhlack); for Wimpfeling: *VLH* II: 1289–1375 (Dieter Mertens).
44. Szlezák 13f.
45. Sachs/Goetze II: 80; Holzberg.
46. Jardine 1995; for Erasmus: *VLH* I: 658–803 (Franz Josef Worstbrock); Rummel.
47. Elsa Strietman in Porter/Teich 78.
48. *E* VI: 78f.
49. *E* VII: 357–633, 372–375, 412f., 458f.; *VLH* I: 703–708 (Manfred Eikelmann).
50. *E* II: 146–157; *VLH* I: 719–723 (Franz Josef Worstbrock).
51. *E* I: 28f.
52. *E* VI: 94–97.
53. *E* I: 252f.
54. Kühlmann 2004, 286.
55. August Buck in Hammerstein 51.
56. Mout 23.
57. *E* II: 48–51, 101–110, 122f.
58. *E* II: 20–23, 57–59, 45–47.
59. *E* II: 208–211.
60. *E* II: 134f.
61. Soykut 39f.
62. Forst 108; *E* III: 252f.
63. *E* V: 362f.; *VLH* I: 770–773 (Franz Josef Worstbrock).
64. *E* V: 404f.; English translation: Erasmus 1917, 33.
65. *E* V: 412f.
66. *E* V: 448f.
67. *E* V: 430f.; English translation: Erasmus 1917, 60.

30. Empires and Emperors

1. Soykut 3–14; Bisaha.
2. Cochrane 326.
3. Kreutel 190.
4. Busbeq/Forster 112.
5. Khair 127–130.
6. Krämer 205–218; Faroqhi 2009; Inalcik.
7. Busbecq/Forster 60.
8. Lapidus 1988, 33; Kappeler 2013, 17f., 23; Mann 2005, I: 296.
9. Lowry 128–130.
10. Crane/Akin 124.
11. Faroqhi 2009, 44–55.
12. Haarmann 1987, 335.
13. Hildermeier 124, for what follows: 144–152; Crummey.
14. Goehrke 2010, 81f.
15. Granberg 193–198.
16. Onasch M 33f.
17. Crummey 127.
18. Onasch M 32.
19. Peter C. Perdue in Reinhard 2015, 114f.
20. Goehrke 2010, 72, 186.
21. Kappeler in Feldbauer et al., 200f.

22. Herberstein 84; Fletcher 13r; for Russian travelers: Szech 77.

23. Onasch M 67; Goehrke 2010, 193.

24. Heller 106–109.

25. Herberstein 113f.; Schilling 2017, 70–83.

26. Szech.

27. Vogel 384–392; Edson 220–226.

28. Israel 2016, 196 (with bibliography).

29. Grant 1994, 633; *VLH* II: 548–566 (Christoph Fassbender/Franz Josef Worstbrock); Hall 1954, 11: "hic non terra sed mare est in quo mire magnitudinis insulae sed Ptolomeo fuerunt incognite." The relevant sections of the map are found in: Reisch (VD 16 R 1033), Munich, Bayerische Staatsbibliothek, 4°PH Un 114, at VII, 1. I am grateful to Patrick Baker for his help in decoding a Latin abbreviation.

30. Vespucci/Northup, Translation 17f.; Ringmann: *VLH* II: 726–739 (Franz Josef Worstbrock/Beate Hintzen).

31. Abulafia 2008, 241–273.

32. Reinhard 2016, 311.

33. Schmitt 1984d, 323.

34. Barrera-Osorio 13–28.

35. Freedman 76–103.

36. Jones/Ruddock.

37. Reinhard 2016, 296.

38. Schmitt 1984d, 378f.; Thomas 375–377.

39. Magasich-Airola/Beer 49–51.

40. Todorov 55–57; Roys 111; Hassig 105.

41. Todorov 70–75; Reinhard 2016, 298.

42. Adorno 214f.

43. Lupher 39; Adorno 141.

44. Israel 2016, 188.

45. Sewell 90f.

46. Lach 61, 157, 527.

47. Edson 134.

48. Pires/Cortesão II: 287.

49. Pires/Cortesão I: 43, II: 269.

50. Lewis 2003, 13.

51. Abu-Lughod; Reid 2015, 72; De Vries 2003.

52. Pigafetta 18.

53. Pigafetta 16, 22; Magasich-Airola/Beer 175–184.

54. Chaplin.

55. As described in Bitterli 138.

56. Pigafetta 24.

57. For Charles V, see Parker 2019 and Kohler.

58. Parker 2019, 68f.

59. Kohler 195.

60. Kohler 73.

61. Brandi 106.

62. Brandi 185f.

63. Kohler 170, 196.

64. Lupher; Dandelet 138–198; Pagden 1995, 40–62; MacCormack 19.

65. Strong 140.

66. Kamen 2014a, 70–76; Pérez 2006.

67. Adorno 55.

68. Parker 2019, 391; O'Malley 1964, 193f.

69. Luther/Jacobs 9.

31. Religious Revolution

1. *WA* VI: 182f.

2. *WA*, Tischreden II: 669: "in termino civilitatis."

3. Kaufmann 2014, 201: "Rundumversorgung für die Lebenden und Toten"; Schilling 2017, 273; Angenendt 2000, 191, 655f.

4. Leppin 2010, 32, 83–86.

5. Leppin 2016, 93.

6. Kohl 2020, 49.

7. Benz 51f.

8. Kaufmann 2014, for "See of Avarice": 172 (Luther/Jacobs 33), for "pride": 244f. (Luther/Jacobs 53), for saints: 371 (Luther/Jacobs 77).

9. *WA* VI: 484–573; Schilling 2013, 191–201 (for what follows).

10. Schilling 2013, 192.

11. *WA* VII: 12–73; "most blessed father": Luther/Jacobs 266; "lamb": Luther/Jacobs 269.

12. Köpf 174–183; Leppin 2010, 177.

13. *WA*, Briefe II: 397: "Meinen Deutschen bin ich geboren, und ihnen diene ich."

14. Kalkoff 43: "al presente . . . tutta la Germania è involta"; Schilling 2012, 233; for Luther as a new saint: Warnke 1984, 32f.

15. MacCulloch 58–115.

16. Kaufmann 2016, 15.

17. Moeglin/Müller 403–414.

18. Moeglin/Müller 410f.: "Das geistliche Recht ist krank; das Kaisertum und alles, was zu ihm gehört, steht im Unrecht. Man muß es mit Kraft durchbrechen, und das muß sein. Wenn die Großen schlafen, so müssen die Kleinen wachen"; 406: "Der Schaden liegt an der Priesterschaft"; 411: "Es soll sich klar und überall scheiden das geistliche und das weltliche Leben, so klar, als es von Anfang an war und von unseren Altvordern gefordert war, und wie die Rechte es weisen heutzutage."

19. Hollegger 259f.

20. Bezold 139.

21. Celenza 1999, for references: 110, 116, 146, 180, 188.

22. Bellitto 33–37.

23. Pius II 1960, 500 (VII.9).

24. Miethke 134, for John XXII as a heretical pope: 271.

25. Takahashi Shogimen in Levy 2006, 217; Ian Christopher Levy in Levy 2006, 353f.

26. *WA*, Briefe II: 115.

27. Kamen 2014b, 87, for what follows: 94.

28. Price 3, 176f.; *VLH* II: 579–633 (Gerald Dörner).

29. Reuchlin III: xliiif.

30. *VLH* I: 646–658 (Gerlinde Huber-Rebenich).

31. Burkhardt 28f.

32. Murner/Neukirchen 174: Wenn der Ochs verwirft das Joch / Und das Roß sein Kummet noch / Und der Bauer läuft vom Pflug / So geschieht dem Ackern nicht genug."

33. Michalski.

34. Goertz 1987, 184f., for the Zwickau Prophets: 98.

35. Goertz 1987, 98; Schilling 2013, 290f.

36. Zwingli 250.

37. Kaufmann 2014, 336–339.

38. Ertl 201–209; also Jones 1997, 298.

39. Leppin 2010, 224.

40. Barnes 51; Cunningham/Grell 19–31; Cohn 1970.

41. Kaufmann 2014, 248–250, 224f.; Luther/Jacobs 45, 48.

42. Goertz 1989, 186–195. English translations of Müntzer's most important writings: Baylor.

43. Müntzer, *Sermon to the Princes (or An Exposition of the Second Chapter of Daniel)* in Baylor 98–114.

44. Müntzer 329: "Dr. Lügner"; "das sanftlebende Fleisch zu Wittenberg"; "Grundsuppe des Wuchers, der Räuberei und Dieberei"; "die Fisch im Wasser, die Vögel in der Luft, das Gewächs auf Erden."

45. Blickle 1981; Schilling 2017, 45–55.

46. Talkenberger 344f.

47. Köpf 254–260.

48. Müntzer 414: "Dran, dran, dieweil das Feuer heiß ist . . . dran, dran, weil ihr Tag habt! Gott gehet euch vor, folget, folget!"

49. Goertz 1989, 171: "omnia sunt communia."

50. Goertz 1989, 22: "mit dem gemeinen Mann hielt und nicht mit den großen Hansen."

51. Schilling 2012, 308f.: "lügenhaften Teufel"; "Weltfresser"; "räuberischen und mörderischen Rotten der Bauern."

52. Bücking.

53. Werner Troßbach in *EdN* II: 1048–1061, 1056f. (bibliography).

54. Richardson 2013, 2, 23f.

55. Jouanna 179–188.

56. On Philip, see most recently Parker 2014.

57. Esch 2014, 422: "lutherisches Gewitter."

58. Mörke 95f.

59. Dickens 182; Moeller 1972; Mörke 93–100.

60. Tuchtenhagen 2009, 62f.

61. Hamm 192–199.

62. Roth, chapters 7–8 (158–224).

63. Leppin 2016, 171.

64. MacCulloch 160f., 187–189.

65. Randolph Head in Kreis 220f.

66. Haug-Moritz.

67. E.g., *WA* LIII: 169.

68. Deppermann 338: "Träumer des Absoluten."

69. Dülmen.

70. Duchardt 63.

71. Bibliography in Berg 2016; Berg 2013.

72. Elton 1991, 167–169; qualifications in Coby; for what follows, see most recently Berg 2013, 144–148.

73. Cohn 2013, Part 3.

74. Dembek 10–12.

75. Act for the Advancement of True Religion (The UK Statute Law Database, 34/35, Henry VIII, c. 1).

76. Elton 1982, 353.

77. Kennedy 1987, 60.

78. Burke 1972, 152, 279; for the development of the nude as an artistic motif in the Renaissance, see Kren/Burke/Campbell.

79. Lastraioli.

80. O'Malley 2013, 64–67.

81. Nicholas Davidson in Porter/Teich 46.

82. Pastor 1905, 108: "e mi doglio in fine a le viscere de la poca religione de noi altri italiani."

83. Rozzo.

84. Overell 175f.

85. Rotondò.

86. Hernán 106–112; for Ochino see Overell 41–60.

87. Marx 1999, 35–49, 253–256.

88. Biersack 586f.

89. Teresa of Ávila 226 (29.17).

90. Hernán; Feld 2006, 142.

91. Sebastian Neumeister in Neuschäfer 89.

92. Cabanel 46.

93. Strohm; Opitz; Selderhuis; McKim.

94. Naphy 1994; Cabanel 173–189.

95. Feld 2006, 202f.

96. Strohm 116.

97. Stevenson 181–186.

98. Selderhuis 41: "Hirtenhund Gottes."

99. Naphy in McKim, 31f.

100. Weber 2002; Holder 260–262.

101. Jouanna 273: "lieu total."

102. Burke 1982, 34.

103. Hamm 174f.

104. Kohler 2013, 362.

105. Benzoni.

106. Brandi 427: "Alle Welt weiß, daß nur der Papst Euch in alle früheren und gegenwärtigen Schwierigkeiten gebracht hat. Welcher Fürst hat Euch mehr geschadet als er? Die Blinden vermögen zu sehen, daß auf ihn alles zurückgeht, was der Franzose Euch angetan hat."

107. O'Malley 2013, 87.

108. Kohler 311: "Dieses ist die Elbe, so oft von den Römern genannt, und so selten gesehen!"

109. Moeller 1999, 156.

110. Jedin II: 376.

111. Mehlhausen 134–136, 70–72.

112. Isenmann 244f., 267f.; Parker 2019, 335f.

113. Kohler 334.

114. Druffel III: 340–348, 340f., 346: "geliebten Vaterlands deutscher Nation"; "viehisch."

115. Parker 2019, 328.

116. Schilling 2012, 313f., 550–570; Kaufmann 2011.

117. WA LIII: 417–552, at 522 ("scharfe Barmherzigkeit"), 523f., 538.

118. Price 134f.

119. Schumann 66–71.

120. Leppin 2010, 109.

121. Kaufmann 2014, 411, 414.

122. Leinkauf 2017, 105: "non in Platonis academia, sed in ecclesia dei!"

123. Malinar 97f.; Schimmel 2014.

124. For Franck and what follows see Forst 124; Ebeling 116f.; for Schwenckfeld see Thomas Konrad Kuhn in NDB 24 (2010), 63f.

125. Leinkauf 2017, 1236.

126. Forst 125 (translation modified).
127. Bonaventure des Périers.
128. Noth 1993, 24; Khadduri 56.
129. Brecht II: 210–234; Leppin 2010, 246–257; Levi 2002, 299–302.
130. *E* IV: 190f.
131. *E* IV: 156f.
132. *E* IV: 162f.
133. *E* IV: 178f.
134. Luther 1989, 174; *WA* XVIII: 164: "die vernunfft des teuffels hure ist."
135. Jüngel 73f.
136. *E* IV: 182f.; for the reference to Valla: 178f.
137. Levi 2002, 3, 8f.
138. Leppin 2016, 19–21.
139. Joost-Gaugier 41.
140. Dürer/Rupprich II: 104: "Die Kunst ist groß, schwer und gut, und wir mögen sie mit großen Ehren in das Lob Gottes wenden."
141. Dürer/Rupprich II: 104: "Schönste aller Welt."
142. Legner 519.
143. *VLH* I: 700–703 (Judith Rice Henderson).
144. *WA* Tischreden I: 490, no. 968.
145. Kaufmann 2014, 428; Flashar 2013, 300; Leppin 2010, 93f., 105f.
146. *WA* VI: 508.
147. Maron.
148. Schilling 2012, 588: "Du versuche nicht, diese götliche Äneis zu erforschen, sondern beuge Dich nieder und bete ihre Spuren an."

32. Revolution of the Heavenly Spheres

1. Hegel 412.
2. Grimm/Hartwig 126f.
3. Schilling 2012, 633; Irwin 762–767.
4. Leinkauf 2017, 669–687, 1323.
5. Leonardo da Vinci 1975–80, 949v, 1743; Kirk/Raven 276.
6. Pico della Mirandola 2012, 116f.
7. Pico della Mirandola 2012, 142f.
8. Pico della Mirandola 2012, 168f.
9. Couliano 89.
10. Sutton 30–33; Keßler 1971, 171–183; Leinkauf 2017, 1601–1621.
11. Pine 116, 272.
12. Pine 342f.
13. *De fato* III: 7, 262; as quoted in Pine 343, n. 104.
14. Leinkauf 2017, 1: "oportet enim in philosophia haereticum esse, qui veritatem invenire cupit."
15. Pine 51.
16. Zimmern/Barack III: 530, 577; Arnold 185; Céard 120; Mahal 63f.; *VLH* II: 1089–1122 (Klaus Arnold).
17. *VLH* I: 23–35 (Wolf-Dieter Müller-Jahnke).
18. Schmidt-Biggemann 503–507; LaGrandeur 55–59; Ruderman 1995, 138–140.
19. Steiner 157–161.
20. Zanato 494: "dal saper troppo nasce inquietudine."

21. "Besser ist ruhe, dann vnrhue, Aber nützer vnrhue, dann rhue." See Bergdolt 2008, 190.

22. Kuhn 1962; Cohen 1994, 122–135, 148f.; Schurz/Weingartner 2–8.

23. Mittelstrass 1.

24. Vespucci/Northup, Translation 3.

25. Shapin 1992, 333–369.

26. Suter 6.

27. Copernicus/Rossmann 1966.

28. Pedersen 2011, 15.

29. Thorndike 1949, 1.

30. Grant 1994, 308–323; Kepler/Caspar 1982, 315.

31. *De anima* 2.1 (412a).

32. Goldstein 1973, 205; for what follows: Grant 1994; Edward Grant in Lindberg/Shank 436–455, 191, 210f., 422–428, 454–459, 224f., 630; Flashar 2013, 266–276.

33. Karfík 108f.; Sturlese 351–362.

34. Forke 113.

35. Grant 1994, 332–334.

36. Randles 7–31.

37. For Seuse: Angenendt 2000, 749f.; for Calvin: Selderhuis 309; Lang/McDannell 146–156; Randles 37f., 38f. (for Luther).

38. For what follows: Westman 2011; Grant 1994, 271–323; Henry 2001; Cohen 2010.

39. Carmody 571f.; Grant 1994, 302f.; Saliba 2007, 150f., also 119–123, 162, 193.

40. Boas Hall 76.

41. Barker 353f.

42. Robert G. Morrison in Lindberg/Shank 128f.

43. Huff 2011, 262 (with bibliography).

44. Wiedemann 22; Huff 2011, 60.

45. Zinner 92, 107.

46. Zinner 175–185; Lowood/Rider 4–8; John North in Rüegg 319.

47. Ragep 2007; Hugonnard-Roche; Saliba 2007, 124, 131f., 185, 193–232.

48. Burmeister I: 101.

49. Kühne/Kirchner 22: "gigantei cujusdam laboris instar."

50. Knoll.

51. Findlen 1994, 101f.

52. Copernicus/Zeller/Zeller 3–7, quotations at 4; Copernicus/Duncan 23–27, quotations at 25, 26; Westman in Lindberg/Westman 1990.

53. Moss vii.

54. Grant 1994, 312.

55. Joost-Gaugier 134.

56. Koyré 1973, 58f.; for what follows: Lakatos/Zahar 373.

57. Shea 24f., 115; Grant 1994, 514f.

58. Copernicus/Duncan 50.

59. *Summa contra gentiles* 4.11; Otto 2000, 220.

60. Camerota 96f.; Kuhn 1957, 189f.; Koyré 1973, 57.

61. Helden 1985, 27; Carrier 104.

62. Copernicus/Duncan 41f.

63. Burmeister III: 174, 178; Cunningham 30; Westman 1975, 4.

64. Bezold 120.

65. *De caelo* 271a33; Forrester 35.

66. Westman 2011, 128–130; Copernicus/Duncan 26–27.

67. Gingerich 2004, 128f.

68. Feingold 1984, 103; Kaufmann 1993a, 142.

69. *WA*, Tischreden IV: 412f. (no. 4638): "ego credo sacrae scripturae, nam Iosua iussit solem stare, non terram."

70. Joshua 10:12–13; Melanchthon IV: 679: "Sarmatischen Sternforscher"; Zinner 272, 246.

71. Hooykas 1974, 146f.; for the source: Bieri 496f.; Gingerich 2004, 80f.

72. Curtius 1948, 323: "Omnis mundi creatura / Quasi liber et pictura / Nobis est et speculum."

73. Cusa/Hopkins 88f.; Blumenberg 2022, 46–53, esp. 47; for Augustine: 40f.; Donald Kelley in Schmitt 1988, 751; for Islam: Ismail.

74. Grant 1994, 103f.

75. Elvin 2004, 62.

76. Clarke; Céard 251; for an example: Westman 2011, 241.

77. Barnes 91.

78. Robinson 2003, 129f., 149–155; Watson Andaya/Andaya 248f.

79. *Troilus and Cressida* 1.3; Grant 1996, 601; also Blair 116–152.

80. Jordan 190–192.

81. Barnes 92f.

82. Kermode.

33. The Great Chain of Being

1. Reiter 16, 66; Granet 274; Grözinger.

2. Schmidt-Biggemann, ch. 4; Granet 274–292; Leinkauf 2017, 129, 1149; Yoshida 71–73.

3. Foucault 1970, 17.

4. Ashworth 306; Charles H. Lohr in Schmitt 1988, 572f.

5. Ficino 1994, 244f.: "ars enim . . . per vapores, numeros, figuras, qualitates"; Copenhaver 2015, 55–126; Perrone Compagni; for India: Bhattacharya 3.

6. Vickers 1984a, 95f.

7. Pico/Borghesi et al., 244f.

8. Zika.

9. Roeck 1989, 96f.

10. Keßler 1971, 113.

11. Müller 1984b, 54.

12. Eamon 1994, 71f.

13. Ebeling 74.

14. Ebeling 77f. (English translation of quotations follows Ebeling's German).

15. Bianchi 19.

16. Copenhaver 1992.

17. Eamon 1994, 165.

18. Ebeling 77 (English translation of quotations follow's Ebeling's German).

19. Angenendt 2000, 150.

20. Schmidt-Biggemann 464–467; Leinkauf 2017, 1698–1702.

21. Grant 1994, 575; Danielle Jacquart in Lindberg/Shank 603.

22. Yates 1975, 17.

23. William Newman in Lindberg/Shank 389.

24. Westman 2011.

25. Rutkin.

26. North 1987, 6; Sachs 1568/2005, 13: "ob künftig komm' ein fruchtbar Jahr / Oder Teuerung und Kriegsgefahr / Und sonst mancherlei Krankheit."

27. Gascoigne 271, 274; Schmidt-Biggemann 478–485.

28. Westman 2011, 62–75.

29. Fabian; Caroti 77.

30. Ernst 259; Smoller 32–36.

31. *Canterbury Tales*, Franklin's Tale, 1131–1134.

32. Rosen 1984, 257; Angenendt 2000, 109.

33. Ebeling 45.

34. Rutkin 52.

35. Zinner 146; Field 1987, 144.

36. Pompeo Faracovi 60f.

37. Westman 1980, 116–121.

38. Westman 1980, 109, 161.

39. Jablonski/Schwabe I: 54; Moran 2005, 149f.

40. Boas Hall 174; for the prohibition of alchemy: William Newman in Lindberg/Shank 399.

41. Moran 2005, 5f.; Couliano.

42. Sherman; Clucas.

34. The Dissection of Man

1. For what follows: Dioscorides, preface; Gerabek 311–315.

2. Wear 22, 31f.; Ogilvie 219; Jütte 2013.

3. French 1994, 44.

4. Moran 2005, 96f.

5. Wittkower 1963.

6. Grafton 2000, 58.

7. Bergdolt 2008, 125.

8. Nicoud; for Elyot: Bergdolt 2008, 187.

9. Mikkeli 189; French 2003, 101.

10. Forrester/Henry 3–65.

11. Aristotle, *Generation of Animals* 2.3; Mulsow 207–209.

12. Siraisi 2.

13. Pagel; Dopsch et al.

14. Peuckert 426f.; French 2003, 148.

15. Paracelsus, "Vorrede," A[i]v: "wir sind des Gestirns Schüler, und das Gestirn ist unser Lehrmeister."

16. French 2003, 99; Ebeling 102f.

17. Jacobi 109; for *archeus*: Hall 1975, I: 184; Pagel 75; for his concept of man as a microcosm: Vickers 1984a, 126f.; for nature: Eamon 1994, 161.

18. Henry 1991, 191–221, 212f.; Hall 1975, I: 181.

19. Pagel 28; Pennuto 314f.

20. Peuckert 323: "Sind vier Paar Hosen eines Tuchs."

21. LaGrandeur 56, 59.

22. Pagel 1f.

23. Pagel 10f.

24. Leinkauf 2017, 1417, n. 52.

25. Robert Jütte in *NDB* 26 (2016), 773f. (bibl.).

26. French 1994, 19.

27. French 1999, 11f.; Cunningham 42–54; O'Malley 1964.

28. French 1994, 40f.

29. Bhattacharya 3f.
30. Vesalius 538f. (5.15).
31. Vesalius, Preface 3*v*.
32. Fracastoro/Wöhrle 34f.
33. Catani/Sandrone 154–157.
34. Cunningham 132f.; Gascoigne 238.
35. Burckhardt 130.

35. European Tableau I

1. Parker 2013; Mauelshagen; Reid 2015, 150f.
2. Westman 2011, 44.
3. Schilling 1999, 292.
4. Camporesi 26–28.
5. Saalfeld; Schilling 1999, 271f.
6. Schilling 1999, 303.
7. Parker 2013.
8. Münch 359f.
9. McCloskey; Münch 359: "Verfleißungskampagne."
10. Münch 135f.
11. Münch 106–113; Behringer 2004.
12. Chaudhuri 1990, 274; Brook 2010, 73–76; for scapegoats: Girard.
13. Behringer 2004; for India: Kapur.
14. Behringer 2004, 85f.
15. Ernst 1991, 260–262.
16. Mauer 327; for werewolves: Nordian Nifli Hein in *EdN* XIV: 999–1003.
17. Heesterman 26, 33f.; Burkert 1987, 19f.; Girard.
18. Roger Mols in Cipolla 68f.
19. Forst 130.
20. Pettegree 222.
21. Greef 52.
22. Köpf 477f.; Gotthard 2004.
23. O'Malley 2013, 159–161; for Paul V: Feld 2006, 183–187.
24. Kohler 348.
25. Haan.
26. Durot 125; Carroll.
27. O'Malley 2013, 227; Concilium Tridentinum, Canones et decreta, 98.
28. Göttler; Tönnesmann 2002, 133–136.
29. Gilbert 1980, xix; Roeck 2013, 130 (bibliography).
30. Caliari 103: "Nui pittori ci pigliamo la licenza che si pigliano i poeti e i matti."
31. For what follows: Rolf Decot in *EdN* VI: 8–12 (bibliography).
32. Ignatius of Loyola 1987, 49–51.
33. Köpf 467–470; Ignatius of Loyola 1959, 344.
34. Bolgar 329–369; Feld 2006, 223–236.
35. Melanie Wald in *EdN* VI: 12–15.
36. Feld 2006, 187–192.
37. Schmitt 1984c, 314.
38. François; Châtelier; Jütte 2008, 186–199.
39. Cook 261; for what follows: Cabanel 204–304.
40. Opitz 139f.; Greef 49.

41. Crouzet 17; Horace, *Odes* 3.3 (translation A. S. Kline): "Si fractus illabatur orbis / impavidum ferient ruinae."
42. For what follows: Israel 1995, 155–178.
43. Kamen 2014a, 128f.
44. Cabanel 263–278.
45. Forst 164.
46. *Mt* 796 (3.12).
47. Cabanel 307–391.
48. Neumahr (bibliography).
49. Neumahr 255f.
50. Neuschäfer 147 (bibliography).
51. Tracy 307.
52. Kamen 2014b, 164.
53. Stirling 7; Parker 2019, 465.
54. Kamen 2010.
55. Kamen 2014a, 137–139.
56. Parker 1972, 6; Kennedy 1987, 45–47.
57. Elton 1991, 198.
58. Kennedy 1987, 48.
59. Malettke 43.
60. Kennedy 1987, 52f.
61. Todorov 68f.
62. Häberlein 2006, 105.
63. Kamen 2014b, 108f.; Opitz 105–108.
64. Kamen 2014a, 104.
65. Kamen 2014a, 56.
66. Edwards 2000, 274.
67. Kamen 2014b, 151, for what follows: 123–159.
68. Manfred Tietz in Neuschäfer 167.
69. Kamen 2014a, 179; Bleichmar et al.
70. Pfandl 533–545.
71. Reinhard 1999, 317.
72. Pfandl 515.
73. Israel 1997.
74. Scott 2012, 131–136, 212; Koenigsberger 2001, 22, 66–72.
75. Israel 1995, 211.
76. Adams 1994, 41.
77. Parker 1999, 20–23.
78. Schilling 1999, 188f.
79. Israel 1995, 570.
80. Israel 1995, 328f.
81. De Vries/van der Woude 371.
82. Reinhard 2016, 180–182.
83. Israel 1995, 575; for the salaries of humanists: Grafton/Jardine 97f.
84. For bibliography: Berg 2016, 236.
85. Clegg 222f.
86. Johnston 70–72.
87. Elton 1991, 268.
88. Elizabeth I 97.
89. Loades; Hammer.

90. Mauer 258f.

91. Loades 224.

92. Kelsey 218f.

93. Martin/Parker 17f.; for what follows: 139–181; for numbers: 22–26; Parker 1999, 92–96.

94. Smith/Alston 48; Maddicott 228f.

95. Loughlin et al. 403.

36. European Tableau II

1. Schama 59, 103; Assmann 2010, 17f.; Zernack 74f.; for England: Berg 2013, 210.

2. Greenfeld 29–58.

3. Hans Peter Herrmann in *EdN* IX: 932–937, 933; Schmidt 2007, 423.

4. "Il ne faut plus faire de distinction de catholique et de huguenot. Il faut que tous soient bons Français."

5. Hale 1993, 60–63; for "German pigs": Dedekind, "Vorrede."

6. Starkey 1992, 156, 158f.

7. Hedinger 19; for van Mander: Roeck 2013, 170–173.

8. Tuchtenhagen 2008, 50–70.

9. Åkerman 34f., 53, 56; Glauser 51f.; Sawyer/Sawyer 232f.

10. For what follows: Alexander 82f., 107–122; Davies.

11. Davies 296.

12. Brüning 111–141.

13. Davies 301.

14. Harasimowicz 435.

15. Schmidt 2009, 136–141.

16. Hildermeier 253.

17. Goehrke 2010, 85.

18. Khodarkovsky 94.

19. Schmidt 2009, 12; for what follows: Hildermeier 279–282.

20. Schmidt 2009, 141–145.

21. Pipes 83.

22. Augustynowicz 47–68.

23. Manfred Rudersdorf in Schindling/Ziegler 79–97.

24. Roeck 1996, 63: "Rachen und Hände"; for Schwendi: Schmidt 2007, 226–240.

25. Edith Koller in *EdN* VI: 286–290.

26. Marshall; Evans.

27. Ruderman 77–82; for the Golem: Grün 33–35.

28. Priuli I: 153: "a Coluchut e a Adem in la India, citade principale, heranno capitate tre caravelle del re di Portogalo, el quali li haveanno mandate ad inquerir dele ixolle di speesse et che di quelle hera patron il Colombo . . . Questa nova et effecto mi par grandinisimo, se L'he vero"; Israel 2016, 185; Findlay/O'Rourke 204; for what follows: Feldbauer 2003, 163.

29. Scruzzi 78–80.

30. Findlay/O'Rourke 209.

31. Rösch 161.

32. Matthew 16:18f.; Angenendt 2000, 647; for Suárez: Quentin Skinner in Schmitt 1988, 406.

33. Lill 18–24.

34. Goldthwaite 2009, 607.

35. Sources in Cochrane 194.

36. Finlay et al. 132.

37. Levi 1947, 141.

37. Beyond the Pillars of Hercules

1. Or "semiperiphery" on a global scale: Wallerstein II: 236; in general: Thomas A. Kirk in *RIE* IV: 49–70.

2. Lamana.

3. Sebastian Neumeister in Neuschäfer 109.

4. Alemán 43: "que es la mar que todo lo sorbe y adonde todo va a parar"; Thomas 583–604.

5. Elliott 1970, 76; Lockhart.

6. Pérez 1989, 208.

7. Reinhard 2016, 310.

8. Oltmer 39.

9. Toribio de Ortiguera in Aguirre/Mampel González/Neuss-Escandell 109; letter to Philip: Aguirre 1961.

10. Ercilla y Zúñiga/Lerner 79: "Chile fertil Prouincia e señalada / En la region Antartica famosa"; MacCormack 214–218.

11. Magasich-Airola/Beer 69–74.

12. Waszkis.

13. Cabanel 301f.; Bitterli 118f.

14. Elliott 2006, 62f.

15. Brendecke 2016, 3, 137, 181; for what follows: Ingrid Kummels in *EdN* V: 814–825, 819.

16. Reinhard 2016, 384f.

17. Reinhard 2016, 378.

18. Durán 1971, 410f.; Gruzinski 1988, 231.

19. Durán /Heyden 1994, 98f.

20. Clendinnen 89–91, 206–208, for what follows: 63–79, for Toral: 106f.

21. Gruzinski 1988, 32 (quotation translated from Gruzinski's French).

22. Todorov 151.

23. Vries 2013, 37–39.

24. Crosby 1972, 40f.; Crosby 2004, 196–216.

25. Oltmer 56; Iliffe 135–140; Zeuske 207.

26. Wallerstein I: 336.

27. Schoenbaum 129; Hentzner 48f.

28. Mbembe 15.

29. Gunn 81, for what follows: 71, 69.

30. Crosby 1972, 77–85; Crosby 2004, 173–193.

31. Rowe 1965; Adorno 94.

32. *Timaeus* 24a; *Critias* 113–116; for the tribe of Israel: Durán/Heyden 1994, 3–11; for llamas: Cieza de León 378; Schmitt 1984d, 433; for Ophir: MacCormack 263–266; for mosques: Lisa Voigt in Bailey et al. 41; for the tapir of Castile: Clendinnen 137.

33. MacCormack 25, 121, 133; Elliott 2006, 41 (bibliography).

34. Bibliography: Carla Rahn Philipps in Bailey et al. 39.

35. MacCormack 74.

36. Magasich-Airola/Beer; for islands: Edson 162.

37. Burke 2016, 65–69.

38. Gruzinski 2012, 95; Gareis.

39. Gruzinski 2012, 84–86, 167–169 (also for what follows); for Perseus: Ovid, *Metamorphoses* 4.604–739; for the *tlacuilos*: Gruzinski 1988, 25f. and passim.

40. Gruzinski 1988, 85–88, 97.

41. Duffy/Metcalf; Staden's title: *Warhaftige Historia und beschreibung eyner Landtschafft der Wilden Nacketen, Grimmigen Menschfresser-Leuthen in der Newenwelt America gelegen.*

42. Groese.

43. Mancall 33.

44. Adorno 114f., 122; Mignolo 429, 431.

45. Reinhard 2016, 314: "Esta voz os dice que todos estáis en pecado mortal y en él vivís y morís por la crueldad y tiranía que usáis con estas inocentes gentes . . . los matáis por sacar y adquirir oro cada día!"; for Vitoria: 317f.

46. Adorno 88–95, 120–124; Lupher 103–150.

47. Todorov 219–241; Mignolo 186–202; Adorno 61–98, 205–212.

48. Sahagún, 49; Todorov 239.

49. Icazbalceta I: 274; Gareis 264f.

50. Münkler 2006, 109.

51. Abulafia 2008, 307; for what follows: Merediz.

52. MacCormack 48f.

53. Roys 31, 34, 76; Clendinnen 134–139, 151, 161–169.

54. Castillo/Léon-Portilla I: 328, 332–334; for the "land of the turkey and the deer": Clendinnen xv.

55. Durán/Heyden 1994, 99; for Dürer: Kruft 1994, 111.

56. MacCormack 62f., 227–236; for Noah: Poma de Ayala 25, 64, 80f. et al., for the fifth age of the world: 31, for Aristotle: 72, for Bartholomew: 91–94, for Potosí: 1057; see also Gruzinski 1988, 39.

57. Gebhard Poppenberg in Neuschäfer 87f.; Lupher 293f.; MacCormack 58f.

58. Fernández 59–94.

59. Kamen 2014a, 91.

60. For what follows: Reinhard 2016, 143–149.

61. Gruzinski 2014, 223f.

62. Lach I: 753; for what follows: Mendoza 91r–93v (3.18).

63. Watson Andaya/Andaya 167.

64. Vries 2009, 66–68; Findlay/O'Rourke 212–226; Liu 68–76; for India: Kulke/Rothermund 2010, 170–176.

65. Elton 1991, 339–348; Andrews 1991, 106f.

66. Andrews 1991, 76–86; Crummey 19f.

67. Grewe 155; Elizabeth Mancke in Armitage/Braddick 199.

68. Williams.

69. Hiatt 232f.

70. Veer.

71. Hayes, for Gilbert's demise: 295f.

72. Andrews 1991, 200–222.

73. Borge.

74. Herendeen 50, 180–242.

75. Pagden 2004, 198f.

76. Barnes 1988, 105f.

77. Völkel 222–226; Donald Kelley in Schmitt 1988, 151.

78. Bouwsma 1968, 568–623; for Baronius: Cochrane 458–463, for Sarpi: 472–478.

79. Pocock 219–271.

80. Crosby 1997, 90–92.

81. Cochrane 433; Fubini 2012.

82. Bouwsma 1968, 271f., 286f.; Cochrane 234–236.

83. E.g., Fubini 2012, 72–74.

84. Cochrane 366–375; for Vittoria Colonna: Giovio/Gouwens 510f.

85. Bouwsma 2000, 58.

86. Grafton et al. 1992, 126.

87. Donald Kelley in Schmitt 1988, 750.

88. *De oratore* 2.36; for the reception of this notion: e.g. MacCormack 247.

89. Leinkauf 2017, 459: "divinus furor . . . pedestre magis ac . . . servile officium"; for Robortello: Keßler 1971, 8.

90. Cotroneo; Donald Kelley in Schmitt 1988, 746–761; for Bodin: Leinkauf 2017, 1047–1060; for Patrizi: Leinkauf 2017, 961f., 1033–1047; Leinkauf 1998, 79–94.

91. Otto 203, 205–207, for Patrizi: Cotroneo 205–267, esp. 264f.

92. Patrizi 56v: "L'historia, ella non è gia opra di Dio? Nò. Ne della natura? Ne di lei. Ma si dell'huomo. Si di lui, rispose egli."

38. Autumn of the Renaissance

1. Bredekamp.

2. Bredekamp 90; originally "Lasciate ogni pensiero voi che entrate" ("Abandon all thought, ye who enter here"). Translations of other partial inscriptions follow Bredekamp's German.

3. Bredekamp 31–41.

4. Dall'Asta 64f.

5. Pulci 1000 (25.117); for Thélème: Jouanna 260f.

6. Stapleton 267.

7. Delumeau 217, 225: "Il m'est advis de ce monde que je voye un viell edifice ruineux duquel l'arène [le sable], le mortier et les pierres et toujours quelque petit quartier de muraille tombe petit à petit. Que pouvons-nous plus attendre d'un tel édifice qu'une ruine soudaine, voire à l'heure qu'on y pernera le moins?"

8. Loughlin et al. 199.

9. Bright 1.

10. Lund.

11. Kapp 150 162–165.

12. Tasso 71 (Act 1, Scene 2): "S'ei piace, ei lice."

13. *Mt* 363 (2.12: "Apology for Raymond Sebond").

14. Montaigne 1962, 1190.

15. *Mt* 629 (3.3).

16. Grimm/Hartwig 147f.; Popkin 44–63; Starobinski.

17. Maclean 1996, 105.

18. Maclean 1996, 10–13.

19. *Mt* 611 (3.2); Montaigne 1998, 399; Auerbach 285–311.

20. *Mt* 611 (3.2).

21. Bouwsma 2000, 64.

22. Montaigne 1962, 1204.

23. *Mt* 456 (2.12: "Apology for Raymond Sebond"), quoting Lucetius 5.830f.; Maclean 1996, 65.

24. Ricken 9f.

25. Burke 1982, 36; *Mt* 178 (1.39).

26. *Mt* 766 (3.9).

27. *Mt* 798 (3.12).

28. *Mt* 152 (1.31).

29. *Mt* 397 (2.12: "Apology for Raymond Sebond"); for Copernicus: Guthke 52f.

30. *Mt* 704 (3.8); for what follows: Compagnon 123–125.

31. Legros 425–429: "Homo sum humani a me nihil alienum puto"; "Οὐδὲν ὁρίζω" ("I determine nothing"); "Οὐ καταλαμβάνω"("I understand nothing"); "Επέχω" ("I withhold [judgment]"); "Σκέπτομαι"("I deliberate"); "Ἀκαταληπτῶ" ("I grasp nothing").

32. Terence, *Heauton Timorumenos* 1.1

33. Maclean 1996, 15.

34. Hall 2014, 75–101; Beyer.

35. Cole.

36. Vasari IV: 484: "Fu costui di bello ingegno, capriccioso, e molto destro in ogni cosa."

37. Rossi 1980.

38. Leinkauf 2017, 973; Bouwsma 2000, 28–34.

39. Barasch 295–301.

40. Haydn; for *Gargantua*: 395.

41. Rabelais/Raffel.

42. For "ass-wiping": Rabelais 1.13; for Pantagruel's tongue: 2.32; for Alexander: 2.18; for the dogs: 2.22; for Florence: 4.11, quotation on p. 414 of Rabelais/Raffel.

43. Caro 28: "Et non sarebbe gran fatto . . . che gli Apelli lo dipingessero: che I Policleti lo'ntagliassero: che Michelangelo ne l'un modo, et ne l'altro l'immortalasse . . . Naso perfetto. Naso principale. Naso divino. Naso, che benedetto sia fra tutti I nasi: et benedetta sia quella mamma, che vi fece cosi nasuto: et benedette tutte quelle cose che voi annasate."

44. For what follows: Roeck 2013, 43, 145–155, 215f.

45. Hills 1989.

46. Dürer/Rupprich I: 49f., n. 12; Pon.

47. Burns in *RIE* VI: 524–533.

48. Wittkower 1963, 102–114.

49. Biggi 167.

50. Mayer Brown 429f.

51. Dürer/Rupprich III: 292: "Traumwerck."

52. Isenmann 123.

53. Roeck 2015.

54. Frangenberg 90: "S'io havessi cotesta bella figura in casa . . . io la estimerei molto, e ne terrei gran conto per una delle piu dilicate, e morbide figure, che veder si possano."

55. Fortini Brown 325f.: "impudiche statue e immagini, che offendono gli occhi casti."

56. Rabelais 158 (2.8).

57. Findlen 1994, 324; for Cardano: Grafton 2001.

58. Ogilvie 83.

59. Gaukroger 2008, 147.

60. Findlen 1994, 65f.

61. Daston/Park 68–88; Kaufmann 1993b; Pomian; Barrera-Osorio 120–127.

62. Cochrane 426, 441.

63. Turner 220.

64. Schreurs 21.

65. Mokyr 2002, 5; Kelley 1997.

66. Hirsch 5f.; Eisenstein I: 100; Chartier 76; Blair 1997, 46–48.

67. Eisenstein I: 97; Leu 2016a.

68. Berns/Neuber; Couliano 97–122.

69. Otto 385–436; Leinkauf 2017, 193–198, 1452–1467.

70. Leinkauf 2017, 391–405; Vasoli 2007, Part V; Skalnik; Ogilvie 226f.

71. Elkana 37; Feingold 16, 19f.

72. Gascoigne 208.

73. Pyenson/Sheets-Pyenson 77–88.

74. Rinaldi 338: "La scienza sederà in mezzo d'un cortile ombroso, overo luogo boscareccio di villa con platani intorno . . . a discorrere de studi dilettevoli."

75. Eamon 1994, 149–151; Eamon/Paheau.

76. Baur 41f.; for voodoo: Eamon 1994, 232.

77. Balbiani; Boas Hall 187–189.

78. Blair 1997, 27.

79. Ashworth 1996, 20f.; Leu 2016a.

80. Boas Hall 186; Heilbron 160; Céard 240–243; Maclean 1984, 242f., 251n88; for the mosquito: Oettermann 60.

81. Findlen 1994, 21–31; Roling 614–620.

82. Vittori.

83. Zedler 29, 1609–1614.

84. Popkin 2003, 130.

85. Flashar 2013, 74f.

86. Cohen 1994, 160f.

87. Ogilvie 129, 131.

88. Cunningham 154.

89. Schmitt 1984b, 60; Schmitt 1984c, 302, 317f.

90. Lach I: 193.

91. Oliveira Marques 203f.

92. Acosta/Franch 141: "Aquí yo confieso que me reí e hice donaire de los meteoros de Aristóteles y de su filosofía, viendo que en el lugar y en el tiempo que, conforme a sus reglas, había de arder todo y ser un fuego, yo y todos mis compañeros teníamos frío"; Vogel 39, 47; Canizares-Esguerra 96–98; Barrera-Osorio 117f.

93. Blair 116f.

94. Ducheyne.

95. Richard H. Popkin in Schmitt 1988, 682.

96. For Telesio: Mulsow; for mathematics: Otto 226.

97. Cardano.

98. Lattis 87, 94, 96, 116; for 77 spheres: Gaukroger 99.

99. Lattis 103; Grant 1994, 306f.

100. Copernicus 1976, 44; Westman 1980, 111.

101. Johnson 164–166.

102. Gaukroger 98; Leinkauf 2017, 1642–1653.

103. Firpo 1993.

104. Firpo 1993, 348: "Finalmente stette senpre nella sua maledetta ostinazione."

105. For what follows: Spampanato 2000.

106. Bruno 1588, p. D: "ad vos pro laribus vestris perlustrandis pervenissem, natione exterus, exul, transfuga, ludicrum fortunae, corpore pusillus, rerum possessione tenuis, favore destitutus, multitudinis odio pressus, & ideo stultis & ignobilissimis contemptibilis."

107. Firpo 1993, 348: "mille errori e vanità."

108. *BW* VI: 89.

109. *BW* II: 38: "fatte svanir le fantastiche muraglia de le prime, ottave, none, decime, et altre, che vi s'avesser potute aggiongere, sfere per relazione de vani matematici e cieco veder di filosofi volgari."

110. Rowland 151–159; Pirillo.

111. *BW* II: 72: "O varie dialettiche, o nodosi dubii, o importuni sofismi, o cavillose capzioni, o scuri enigmi, o intricati laberinti, o indiavolate sfinge, risolvetevi, o fatevi risolvere."

112. *BW* IV: 197–199; Grant 1994, 449, 390–421.

113. Funkenstein 194; Guthke 36f., 64f.; Leinkauf 2017, 1716–1734.

114. *BW* IV: 73, 329; Schmidt-Biggemann 1998, 513f.

115. *BW* IV: 38f.; English translation: Waley Singer 246.

116. Bruno/Kuhlenbeck VI: 138.

117. *BW* IV: 176–178; English translation: Waley Singer 313f.

118. *BW* IV: 92f.

119. *BW* IV: 122–125.

120. Spampanato 664: "Salomon et Pythagoras. Quid est quod est? Ipsum quod fuit. Quid est quod fuit? Ipsum quod est. Nihil sub sole novum"; Ecclesiastes 1:9.

121. *BW* II: 154f.: "sette tanto differenti e contrarie, che ne parturiscono alter innumerabili contrariisime (*sic*) e differentissime."

122. Pirillo 30f.: "et altri heretici oltramontani . . . i quali non meritano nome di teologi ma di pedanti"; Firpo 1993, 28, 177f.

123. *BW* VI: 16–21.

124. *BW* V: 40, 370f.; English translation: Bruno/Imerti 86, 255.

125. *BW* V: 370, 374f., 507n327.

126. *BW* V: 168–171; English translation: Bruno/Imerti 150.

127. Firpo 1993, 351: "sacras litteras esse somnium."

128. Firpo 1993, 351: "Maiore forsan cum timore sentantiam in me fertis quam ego accipiam."

129. Spampanato 786.

130. *BW* IV: 248; English translation: Waley Singer 348.

131. Yates 1964, 244; Zinner 1968, 334.

132. Pumfrey 1989, 45–53.

133. Leinkauf 2017, 1220.

134. *BW* IV: 310f.; English translation: Waley Singer 378.

135. The following is based on Schoenbaum 118–142; Mancall 9–14, 73–76; Porter 1994, 34–65; Modelski 197.

136. Clegg 23.

137. Holderness; Ingeborg Boltz in Schabert 134–169; Honan.

138. Schoenbaum 70.

139. Schoenbaum 134f.

140. Suerbaum 33–36; in general: Bernhard Klein in Schabert 43–47.

141. Hans Walter Gabler in Schabert 301, 315.

142. Chambers I: 28.

143. Suerbaum 243–245.

144. Holderness 22.

145. *As You Like It* 2.7.165–166.

146. Sonnet 129.

147. Perry et al. 22–24.

148. *Richard II*, 2.1.40, 57f.

149. *Henry IV, Part 1*, 3.2.4–11; Bevington 125–157.

150. *Hamlet* 2.297f.; Tillyard; Suerbaum 83–109; *Merchant of Venice* 5.1.54–65.

151. *King Lear* 4.1.41f.

152. Antonio Poppi in Schmitt 1988, 660; Haydn 107f.

153. *King Lear* 4.2.48–51.

154. *A Winter's Tale* 3.3.

155. Bachmann.

39. Observation, Experimentation, Calculation

1. Amabile; Firpo 1998; Headley 1997.

2. Amabile III: 480–482, 496f.; Campanella/Ernst 244.

3. Amabile I: 1, 216, 219, 320, 363f.

4. Campanella/Ditadi 82.

5. Firpo 1998, 235–239: "hoimè che moro, à traditori figlioli di cornuti, bagasce . . . scenditimi che vi dico ogni cosa che volete . . . hoime che moro! hoime li coglioni, hoime che mi havete ammazzato . . . io piscio, frate . . . mi caco nelle calze . . . Lasciatemi cacare . . . non posso più . . . et bisogna che venga il Papa, se il papa non viene che rimedia ad ogni cosa, le cose non vanno bene."

6. Amabile II: 2: 289: "che in atra tomba i miei dolori / sol pianto rimbombando il ferro e il sasso."

7. Foucault 1972, 534; for Campanella's City of the Sun: Campanella 1981.

8. Campanella/Roush, 66f.

9. Amabile III: 550 (no. 439): "Sciolto e legato, accompagnato e solo, / gridando, cheto, il fiero stuol confondo: / folle all'occhio mortal del basso mondo, / saggio al Senno divin dall'altro polo."

10. Grant 1994, 81.

11. Barnes 152f., 206f.; Delumeau 228–231; Pirillo 41–75.

12. Trüper et al.; Subrahmanyam 746f., 756.

13. Campanella/Ditadi 106.

14. Butler 3–13.

15. Balbiani.

16. Behringer 2004, 204.

17. For Zabarella: Mikkeli; Wallace 1992, 186–188; Leinkauf 2017, 198–211; Schmitt 1969.

18. Daston 83–87.

19. Henry 2001.

20. Gilbert 75–77.

21. Gaukroger 164f.

22. Grafton 1992, 201f.

23. Feingold 9.

24. Bacon 1854, III: 345 (aphorism 3).

25. Brian P. Copenhaver in Schmitt 1988 296f.

26. Boas Hall 252.

27. Blair 227–231.

28. Hall 1975, I: 240.

29. Hooykas 1972, 65 (also 68); Bacon 1628.

30. Bacon/Spedding et al. XIV: 95, 79.

31. Bacon/Spedding et al. IV: 20; Eamon 1994, 320; Jacob 1997, 31.

32. Pollock 98f., 128f., 102, 111.

33. Hoorn 108f.

34. Cunningham 158; French 1999, 195f., 206–209.

35. Wear 371.

36. Pagel 15.

37. Porter 1997, 215f.

38. French 1994, 4.

39. French 1994, 2.

40. The Sun Rises in the West

1. Gaukroger 172.

2. Thoren 1, 186; Westman 1980, 122–126; Cohen 2010, 89f.

3. Thoren 1, 339.

4. Thoren 254–262; Westman 2011, 230–235.

5. Maeyama 1974.

6. Bucciantini 61.

7. Van Helden 49.

8. Westman 2011, 288–290; Grant 1994, 261, 327; Gaukroger 99.

9. Thoren 410–415.

10. Thoren 432–439; for what follows: Gaukroger 172–187; Martens; Bialas.

11. Caspar 97.

12. Butterfield 63.

13. Bialas 33; Kepler/Riekher; Field 1997, 183–186.

14. Kepler/Caspar et al. III: 178: "Dei beneficium."

15. Mittelstrass 216, 219.

16. Cohen 1994, 313; Hooykas 1972, 36; Martens 78f.

17. Csikzentmihalyi.

18. Kepler/Caspar et al. III: 7; English translation: Kepler/Donahue, 30.

19. Stephenson 1994a, 87–130.

20. Stephenson 1994a, 2f., 204f.

21. Pumfrey 1989, 48f.

22. Grant 1994, 544f.

23. Kepler/Caspar et al. I: 115f., 26*; Rosen 1984; Field 1984.

24. Cassirer 349.

25. Martens 81, 102.

26. Hadden; Henry 2008, 50; Westman 1980, 127.

27. Grant 1994, 216–218; Field 1997, 1; Henry 2008, 18f.

28. *Timaeus* 53b; Kepler/Aiton et al. 146f., 303f.; Keßler 1971, 132f.

29. Kepler/Aiton et al. 391; *Phaedrus* 243e–245a, 249d–250c, 265b; Hatfield in Lindberg/Westman 108–110; Field/Frank James 8.

30. Wisdom 11:20; Westman 2011, 328–332.

31. Field in Curry 167.

32. Westman 2011, 356–362; Gaukroger 176–181; Martens 39–65; Stephenson 1994b.

33. Westfall in Lindbergh/Numbers, 221; see also Saitta II: 172, 176.

34. Kepler/Aiton et al. 74.

35. De Pace; Hatfield in Lindberg/Westman 94; for Einstein: Born 91.

36. Grant 1994, 443; Helden 35–38.

37. Randles 106–108.

38. Swinford.

39. Rosen 1967, 22.

40. Camerota 160; English translation of the *Starry Messenger*: Drake 21–58, quotations at 27f.; Galilei 2009.

41. Thorndike 1949, 197, 245.

42. Campanella/Ditadi 226: "Tu purgasti oculos hominum, et novum ostendis caelum et novam terram!"

43. Swerdlow.

44. Willach 116.

45. Reeves 5.

46. Drake 137–141; for Galileo's life: Camerota.

47. Blumenberg 1987, 652.

48. Dupré.

49. Galilei/Favaro XI: 296: "il funerale o più tosto l'estremo et ultimo giuditio della pseudofilosofia."

50. Kepler/Caspar et al. IV: 344, 472: "O multiscium, et quovis sceptro pretiosius perspicillum: an, qui te dextra tenet, ille non Rex, non dominus constituatur operum Dei?"

51. Drake 108.

52. Lattis xv, 133; Grant 1994, 215f.

53. Corwin 2, 66–68.

54. Lowood/Rider 15.

55. Galilei, *Considerazioni al Tasso*, in Galilei/Favaro IX: 59–148, 69: "qualche ometto curioso."

56. Clavelin.

57. Rossi 2000, 83–85.

58. Galilei/Favaro VI: 197–372, quotation at 232: "Egli è scritto in lingua matematica, e i caratteri son triangoli, cerchi ed altre figure geometriche, senza i quali mezzi è impossibile a intenderne umanamente parola; senza questi è un aggirarsi vanamente per un oscuro labirinto"; Moss 243f.

59. Cohen 2010, 201f.

60. Galileo/Favaro VII: 355: "non posso trovar termine all' ammiration mia, come abbia possuto in Aristarco e nel Copernico far la ragion tanta violenza al senso, che contro a questo ella si sia fatta padrona della loro credulità"; Blumenberg 1987, 127.

61. Pitt 97; Cohen 1994, 86, 510.

62. Clavelin 184223.

63. Drake 274, 277.

64. Koyré 1957, 95f.; Grant 1994, 324–370.

65. Galilei/Favaro V: 187; English translation: Drake 123f.

66. Shea 1972, 166.

67. Galilei/Favaro VI: 350; English translation: Drake 277f.; Rossi 2000, 84.

68. Galilei/Favaro VI: 489: "atomi realmente indivisibili" (emphasis added).

69. Mauthner II: 219f.

70. Galileo/Favaro V: 319: "l'intenzione dello Spirito Santo essere insegnarci come si vadia al cielo, e non come vadia il cielo".

71. Carrier 169.

72. Fantoli 143, 193; Camerota 285–292, 310–325; Henry 2008, 85f.; Westman 2011, 217–219; Feldhay; Santillana.

73. Redondi 234–237, 272–280.

74. Redondi 260; Galilei/Favaro XIX: 405.

75. Zahlten 733f.

76. Galilei/Favaro XIX: 406f.

77. Galilei/Favaro VII: 540; English translation: Boas Hall 331.

78. Biagioli 339, 332.

79. Camerota 541: "publicas seu secretas conversationes."

80. Galilei/Favaro VII: 470, 486.

81. Gingerich 1973, 307.

82. Koyré 1948.

83. Shapin 1996, 32.

84. Cohen 2010, 118; for what follows: 112–117.

85. Feldhay 143f.

86. More in Bleichmar et al.

87. Cohen 2010, 126; Gaukroger 169; Westman 2011, 496.

88. Willach 108.

89. Eamon 1994, 97.

90. Pavey 161f.

91. Kruft 1989, 68–81.

92. Maclean 1996, 122.

93. Descartes/Adam/Tannery IX: 2, 18; for what follows: VI: 31–40.

94. Markie.

95. Rossi 2000, 99–107.

96. Koyré 1957, 100f.

97. Garber 1995, 321.

98. Roger Ariew in Pasnau 120f.

99. Ertz.

41. In the Age of Leviathan

1. Nahrstedt.

2. Schiebinger 22f.

3. Kelly; Nauert 54–59.

4. Saul 356.

5. Kaufmann 2014, 30.

6. Marchi/Van Miegroet 89n61; Israel 1995, 555.

7. Wolfgang Reinhard in Fenske et al. 251; Bodin.

8. Skinner 1978, I: 248–254; Gerrit Walther in *EdN* XIII: 209-212; MacCormack 86.

9. Lipsius 392f. (4.3): "Clementiae non hic locus. Ure, seca, ut membrorum potius aliquod, quam totum corpus intereat" ("This is not the place for clemency. Burn and cut so that a part of the body may be lost but the rest saved").

10. Toulmin 107.

11. Forst 168, 172f.

12. Hobbes/Gaskin 254.

13. "Non est potestas super terram quae comparetur ei." Hobbes's frontispiece gives the Bible verse as Job 41:24, in line with its numbering in the Vulgate.

14. Hobbes/Malcolm II: 520.

15. Hobbes/Malcolm III: 678f.

16. Hobbes/Malcolm I: 133; Quentin Skinner in Schmitt 1988, 452 (also for what follows).

17. Reinhard 1999, 175.

18. Popper 148.

19. Voigtländer/Voth 172.

20. Procacci 153.

21. Parker 2013, 290.

22. Loades 8.

23. Mancall 80–82, 94f., 139-151; Armitage 2000, 74f.; for Raleigh: Raleigh 199.

24. Parker 1999, 132; Reinhard 2016, 223.

25. Darwin 113f.; Hammer.

26. Marks 100.

27. De Vries/Van der Woude 382–396; for what follows: Ormrod 2003; Israel 2002.

28. Grotius/Hakluyt 10.

29. Reid 2015, 136.

30. Reinhard 2016, 414f., 199.

31. Armitage/Braddick.

32. Parker 1999, 133.

33. Reinhard 2016, 216.

34. Armin Reese in *EdN* VI: 936-942; Findlay/O'Rourke 248f.

35. Oltmer 34–39; Alison Games in Armitage/Braddick 43.

36. Perdue 2005, 1677; Crosby 2004, 37.

37. Kwan.

38. Armitage 2000, 119.

39. Conermann 498f.

40. Josef Kreiner in Kreiner 194–197; Tsutsui 86f.; Bayly 81; Findlay/O'Rourke 197.

41. Pomeranz 190.

42. Wiesner-Hanks 147.

43. *Richard II*, 2.1.40–50.

44. Mielants 70–83.

45. Elliott 2006, 37; Osterhammel 330f., 347.

46. Acemoglu/Robinson 2008.

47. Jensen 186.

48. Reinhard 2016, 509: "einer der folgenreichsten Schritte der nordamerikanischen Geschichte."

49. Brooks.

50. Reinhard 2016, 522–526.

51. Behringer 2004, 145f. (with bibliography).

52. Forst 182–186.

53. MacFarlane.

54. Fortescue.

55. Macpherson, ch. 3.

56. Jacob 1997, 81–85, 60f.

57. Israel 2001, 265f.

58. Smith 1906, 39; Bernhard Klein in Schabert 38.

59. Nate 299f.; Jardine 2000.

60. Pepys VIII: 243f.; for what follows: 105–115, 14; Mokyr 2002 58f.

61. Hooykas 1972, 88–92.

62. Van Zanden 2009, 258, 262f.

42. The Mechanical Universe

1. Cohen 2010, 219f.

2. Gribbin 31.

3. Jardine 2000, 42–50.

4. Wilson 1995, 201; for Leeuwenhoek: 134–137.

5. Findlen 2004; Asmussen.

6. Kepler/Caspar et al. I: 253: "quae sola cogitatio, nescio quid horroris occulti prae se fert; dum errare sese quis deprehendit in hoc immenso; cujus termini,cujus medium, ideoque et certa loca, negantur."

7. Grierson I: 237; Toulmin 64f.

8. *All's Well That Ends Well* 2.3.1–6.

9. *King Lear* 1.2.121–136; Bevington 10f.

10. Bevington 129.

11. Popkin 2003, 219–238.

12. Leinkauf 2017, 1427f. (citing Luigi Firpo).

13. Monod 172f.

14. Headley 1997, 346.

15. Lovejoy 187; Bouwsma 2000, 81.

16. Bergerac (ch. 3); Guthke 190.

17. Rossi 2000, 117f.

18. For Pascal's wager, see Jordan.

19. Israel 2001, 230f., 268.

20. Israel 2001, 159–174.
21. Wilson 1995, 190.
22. Scheuchzer.
23. Gaukroger 263; Westman 2011, 496.
24. Busche 57f., 525–528.
25. Toulmin 100–103.
26. Leduc et al.
27. Kahn 336–338.
28. McClellan/Dorn 501 (with bibl.).
29. Rossi 2000, 228.
30. Kepler/Aiton et al., 391.
31. Cohen 2010, 237.
32. Cohen 2010, 238–245.
33. Westfall 1973, ix.
34. Newton 1729, 388.
35. Rossi 2000, 218; Westman 2011, 513.
36. Manuel 103.

43. The Archaeology of Modernity

1. Clark 1–3, 19–39; Acemoglu/Robinson 2012, 72–75; Van Zanden 2009, 298; Pomeranz 16; Goldstone 2009, 80f.; Wong ; Bray 2000a; Landes 1998; Parthasarathi; Malanima 286f.; Bayly; for a more nuanced approach: Vries 2013, 11–33.
2. Lee 1999, 6, 13f.; Wong 30f.; Voth; Vries 2013, 23f.; Pratt 90f.
3. E.g., Gupta/Ma 268.
4. Maddison.
5. Vries 2013, 40f., 428; Van Zanden 2009, 276–279; Clark 69f.
6. Overton 82.
7. Ulrich Pfisterer in *EdN* X: 505–514; Epstein 10f., 27–44; Osterhammel 645f.
8. Landes 2003; for an overview of theories of industrialization: Osterhammel 640–642.
9. For a different view: Schmidtke.
10. Vries 2013, 419f.; for a different view: e.g., Goldstone 2009, 67f.; Pomeranz 264.
11. Marks 104–120.
12. Trakulhun/Weber; Given 256; Marcon 23f.
13. Hollister-Short 141.
14. Grant 1981, 260–264; Flashar 2013, 253f.; Dolza.
15. Torricelli xviii: "viviamo immersi nel fondo di un oceano d'aria."
16. Marr 151–153, 157–160.
17. Phin 53f.; for Verbiest: Carolyn Dougherty in *EdN* VII: 1007.
18. Cohen 2010, 199–202; Shapin/Schaffer.
19. Beckert 67–77; Riello.
20. Hills 1989, 117; for what follows: 13 and Goldstone 2009, 126f.
21. Huff 1993; Huff 2014; Pomeranz 169; for India: Chaudhuri 1985, 210–214, 228; for the Ottoman Empire: Inalcik/Quataert 51; for China: Wong 133.
22. North in Davis 1995; in general North/Thomas 2f.
23. Dent; Acemoglu/Robinson 2012, 235–237.
24. Radkau 102f.
25. Sieferle 168. For the significance of coal: Pomeranz 2001, 65f.; Allen 2009.
26. Parthasarathi 22–46, esp. 26.
27. Riello 211–237.

28. Cohen 2010, 185f., 248f.; Mokyr 2002, 36.

29. Seherr-Thoss 1–3.

30. Ulrich Troitzsch in *EdN* XI: 853–856; Kellermann/Treue 134–157, 191–194; for Leupold: Müller-Sievers 205n9: "eine der allernützlichsten [Erfindungen] in der Welt."

31. Parker 1999, 128.

32. Mokyr 2003b; Jardine 2000.

33. Marx 1908, 534.

34. For what follows: Huff 2011; Morris 2010; Murray 2003, 245–258, 301–303, 296f.; Henry 2008, 107–109.

35. Schiller.

36. Weber 1988, 266–290; Lorenz, Appendix I, 179–182.

37. Mokyr 2002, 19.

38. Landes 1994, 653.

39. Halsberghe 163–193.

44. Vertical Power, Sky High

1. Pipes 77; for Ivan: Goehrke 2010, 266–268 (with bibliography).

2. Martin 2007, 321–327.

3. Fletcher 22*v* (ch. 8).

4. Goehrke 2003, 233.

5. Onasch 58; Funke 181f., 184, 252f.

6. Martin 2007, 379.

7. Herberstein 49; for the council: Crummey 150.

8. Marker 17.

9. Heller 73.

10. Pipes 12; for what follows: Goehrke 2010, 111 114, 122f.

11. For what follows: Inalcik/Quataert; Matuz; Faroqhi 2009.

12. Findlay/O'Rourke 224.

13. Van Zanden 2009, 272.

14. Inalcik/Quataert 218–255; for what follows: Timur Kuran in Bernholz/Vaubel 161–169, 174–177; Kuran 2011, 147–150.

15. Huff 2014, 288; Kuran 2011, 97–116; for waqfs: 110–115.

16. Greif; Kuran 2012, 63–79, 126.

17. Timur Kuran in Bernholz/Vaubel 175; for what follows: Inalcik 1973, 186.

18. Lewis 2003, 11.

19. Matuz 134; for what follows: 146–159; for the opposite view: Darling.

20. Faroqhi 2009, 85f.

21. Timur Kuran in Bernholz/Vaubel 152–157.

22. Matuz 110f.

23. Lewis 2003, 40; but see also Huff 2011, 130, 206.

24. Yenen 157f.

25. Huff 2011, 128; Sayili 292.

26. Emilie Savage-Smith in Porter 2003, 660; Barkey 233.

27. Reichmuth.

28. Atiyeh 235.

29. Duchesne 179–181; Kornicki 1998, 114.

30. Faroqhi 2000, 94–96.

31. Lewis 2003, 141.

32. Gdoura 115.

33. King 2000; Starr 8; for Ibn Khaldun: Simon 2002, 16–21.

34. Edward S. Kennedy, as quoted in Sabra 2018a, 114; Elkana 55f. (for what follows).

45. Pastoral Power

1. Pagden 1995.

2. Gentile 2006.

3. Huntington 35; White 2011, 111f.

4. Foucault 1982, 782–784.

5. Mauro Zonta in Speer/Wegener 89–105.

6. Bendix 99, 223.

7. Ruderman 51.

8. Langermann.

9. Ruderman 58.

10. Ruderman 69–76.

11. Ibn Nahmias.

12. Neher; Ruderman 64f., n. 36.

13. Haberman.

14. Bonaventure 1891, 332 (1.17): "si vero declinamus ad notitiam rerum in experientia, investigantes amplius, quam nobis conceditur; cadimus a vera contemplatione et gustamus de ligno vitito scientiae boni et mali, sicut fecit lucifer."

15. Biersack 572.

16. Sardar 109.

17. Berkey 2003, 202; *Sunan an-Nasa'i* 1578 (19: The Book of the Prayer for the Two 'Eids, chap. 22).

18. Nasr 1990, 97f.

19. Kamali 83.

20. Starr 495; Gutas 159–164.

21. Morrison in Lindberg/Shank 137.

22. Bucaille.

23. Tameli Kukkonen in Pasnau 237–243.

24. Westfall 1973, 80–82; Ward 31; for what follows: Grant 1994, 240, 559–562.

25. *BW* II: 154: "Le quali tutte [Jews, Christians, Muslims, and sects] vi [in Holy Writ] san trovare quel proposito che gli piace e meglio li vien comodo: non solo il proposito diverso e differente, ma ancor tutto il contrario; facendo de un 'sì' un 'non' e di un 'non' un 'sì'"; Noth 1978, 190f.

26. Dimitri Gutas in Pasnau 804–814; for exceptions: Vernet/Samsò in Rashed 1996, 244–247; Seta; for skepticism: Kraemer 1986, 189f.; Ragep; Marwan Rashed in Adamson/Taylor 288–293.

27. Pulci 18.115.

28. Ahmed.

29. Crone 2004, 396, 398.

30. E.g., Hasan 72–76; Udovitch 261; Clark 2007, 216.

31. Huff 2014, 290, 295.

32. Crone 2004, 316–318.

33. Berkey 2003, 202, 252; Berkey 1995; Adang et al.

34. Lewis 2003, 105.

35. al-Jabri 40–73.

36. Lewis 2003, 47.

37. Abdus Salam in Hoodbhoy ix.

38. Kuran 2011, 14; Derviş 1.
39. Sardar 112.
40. Lapidus 1973, 47; Glick 155; Robinson 2003, 139; Schatkowski-Schilcher 219.
41. Wirth 2000, I: 328–336.
42. Wirth 2000, I: 442.
43. Jones 2003, 5.
44. Gruber et al. 2013.
45. Lapidus 1988, 332f.; Feldbauer 2002, 191f.
46. Marcus 332; for Tripoli et al.: Lafi.
47. al-Farabi/Walzer 257; Crone 2004, 280; Mahdi 145f.; for Averroes: Crone 2004, 190.
48. Ibn Khaldûn/Rosenthal; Simon 2002, 148–152; Robinson 2003, 102.
49. Ertl 211f.
50. Gutas 156f.
51. Franz 2005, 38–41.
52. Huff 2011, 183; Krämer 185; French 1999, 24–26; Gutas 118f.; for India: Scharfe 262.
53. Brömer 350f.
54. Freedberg; Assmann 2010, 67–75; Kohl 2020, 27–32.
55. Naef 12–26, 73, 37; Lapidus 1988, 83.
56. Belting 1993, 41–45.
57. Reiter 2000, 100f.
58. Belting 1993, 40f.
59. Kren/Burke/Campbell.
60. Geoffroy-Schneiter.
61. Wujastyk 202, 204 (with bibliography, also for Sangye Gyamtso).
62. Harbison.
63. Ferguson 1992, xi.
64. Bhattacharya; Wujastyk.

46. Lost Civilizations, Stubborn States

1. Jack Stoneman in Shirane 30; Maclean 1996, 102; H. Paul Varley in Hall 1990, 448.
2. Diamond 2005; Tainter 191, 196f.; Acemoglu/Robinson 2012, 185–193.
3. Lal 35.
4. Hall 1995; Dierk Lange in Fried/Hehl 103–116; Patricia Pearson in Falola/Roberts 10–16 (with bibliography).
5. Goody 1968; Diop 179–186.
6. Levtzion/Hopkins 79f.; for what follows: 497 and Cadamosto 110v.
7. Goody 1971; Jones 2016, 273–277; Acemoglu/Robinson 2012, 174–177.
8. Jeff Hoover in Shillington 859–863.
9. Abulafia 2008, 92; Jones 1990, 125–129.
10. Jones 2016, 390; Thornton 2012, 78f.
11. Rauchenberger 27f.; Jones 2016, 130, 145, 253; for what follows: 128f.
12. Levtzion/Hopkins 266, 290f.; Diop 77–86, 92.
13. Diop 54; Rauchenberger 276-279; Amadori 516.
14. Thornton 2012, 414; in general: 412-418 and Davidson 67f.; for slaves: Reinhard 2016, 412.
15. Heywood/Thornton.
16. Service 72–75, 94–97.
17. Rauchenberger 206–211.
18. Jones 2016, 219–226.
19. Zeuske 508, 454.
20. Jones 2016, 352.

21. Rauchenberger 220, 327; Amadori 528: "Terra Negresca" or "Le Terre de li Nigri."

22. Austen 23f. (commentary on the contribution by John Thornton in the same volume; see also Thornton 2012, 68f.); Adas 38.

23. Kohl 2020, 14f.

24. Lowe.

25. Abulafia 2008, 94; Cadamosto 113, 114r.

26. Amadori 174f., Rauchenberger 370f.: "vivono come le Bè[stie] . . . Excepto alcunj chè habitano in lè ciptadj grandj chè ivj hanno un poco piu dè la rationalita & qualchè sentimento humano"; for Marees: Marees/Van Dantzig/Jones 31.

27. Fra-Molinero.

28. Connah 2001, 13.

29. Marees/Van Dantzig/Jones 77.

30. Freeman-Grenville 192.

31. Connah 2016, 260–298 (Great Zimbabwe); Iliffe 107f.; Marees/Van Dantzig/Jones 226f. (Benin).

32. Connah 2016, 156; Olupona 109.

33. Lange 1987; for the Kotoko city-states: Hansen.

34. Sahlins 1968, 12f.; Reinhard 2016, 906f.

35. Jones 2016, 381.

36. Findley 107.

37. Starr 111; for Nishapur: 196.

38. Morgan 2007, 73.

39. Starr 455; for what follows: 463–466, 472–474.

40. Findley 102.

41. Findley 104; Goehrke 2010, 44f.

42. Krämer 234f.

43. For what follows: Reid 2015; Watson Andaya/Andaya; Khair 112–118.

44. Chandler 76; Villiers 218, 231.

45. Lach I: 523.

46. Lieberman 2003; Findlay/O'Rourke 195–201; Wolters 1999, 27–40, 126–154; Watson Andaya/Andaya 46–49.

47. Watson Andaya/Andaya 123.

48. Watson Andaya/Andaya 220.

49. Lieberman 2014, 31; Watson Andaya/Andaya, 169.

50. Terwiel 22–29; Lieberman 2014; in general: Aung-Thwin.

51. Trakulhun 2006, 133.

52. Dahm 114; for Barros: Lach 529.

53. Pigafetta 71.

54. Topich/Leitich 31–36.

55. Parker 2013, 410–413; Watson Andaya/Andaya 210–233; Reid 2015, 143, 149–158, quotation at 156.

56. Kulke/Rothermund 2010, 83; Lieberman 2003, 3f.

57. Lieberman 2003, 261; Watson Andaya/Andaya 260f.

58. Reid 2015, 134–137, 84f., 139 (also for what follows); for Europe: Poulle.

59. Mukund.

60. Reid 2015, 94; Van Zanden 2009, 22f.; for what follows: Watson Andaya/Andaya 250f.

61. Yangwen.

62. Kulke/Rothermund 2010, 151–170.

63. Findley 129–132; Dale 23f.

64. Hasan 34–40, 60–65, 105f.; Weber 1978, 231f.

65. Blake 83–103.
66. Stein 1980, 419; Juneja 116; Mukund 36f.
67. André Wink in Mokyr 2003, 27; Leonard; Findlay/O'Rourke 270f.
68. Mukund; Vries 2013, 123–129; Scharfe 59.
69. Scharfe 316, 59.
70. Parthasarathi 191–198.
71. Watson Andaya/Andaya 270; for what follows, see Lal 28–35 and Deepak Lal in Bernholz/Vaubel 128–141.
72. Mallison 171–183, 172.
73. Dohrn-van Rossum 153f.
74. Starr 512f.; Scharfe 32; Allsen 185n45.
75. Gunn 94; Pearson 139.
76. Müller 1988, 103f.
77. Nagahara Keiji in Hall 1990, III: 330–341.
78. Tsang 191, 228f.
79. Ikegami 133, 188f.; for the term *ikki*, see White 1995, 125f., 139f.
80. McClain 9, 85–88; Pratt 87f.; Rüttermann 182, 183 (for *kaisho*); see also Tonomura.
81. Müller 1988, 201, 203; for what follows, see Lidin 28f.
82. Goodman 90; Gunn 281.
83. Summary in Toby xiii–xvi; Nosco 109–112.
84. Reid 2015, 158.
85. Toby 216–224; for the "land of the gods": 213–215.
86. Salter; Kornicki 1998, 493.
87. Günther Distelrath in Bernholz/Vaubel 106f.
88. Lawrence E. Marceau in Tsutsui 117–136.
89. Marks 92 (with bibliography).
90. Nosco 104–108, 111f.; for China, see Vogelsang 424.
91. Marcon 3–6, 9–12.
92. Tucker 9; for Zhu Xi, see Ess 2003, 74–84.
93. Nosco 108f.; for India: Parthasarathi 214f.
94. Marcon 20.
95. Nakayama 200–202; Goodman 98f., 8.
96. Goodman 104f.
97. Marcon 179–206.
98. Luo 68.
99. Hayami/Kitô 240–243.

47. Why Not China?

1. Zheng 50; Filipiak 117.
2. Perdue 2005, 256–299; Goldstone 2002.
3. Carreiro.
4. Peter C. Perdue in Reinhard 2015, 68f.
5. Mo 63–65.
6. Needham et al. VI.1: 308.
7. Rolf Trauzettel in Eggert et al. 270; Elvin 2004, 61–63; for Li Shizhen: Marcon 32–38.
8. Parker 2013, 111; Brook 2010; Vogelsang 402–409.
9. Mungello 31–39.
10. Ebrey 1993, 153.
11. Needham et al. VII.2: 53n24; Ebrey 1993, 60.

12. Mote 372f.

13. Brook 1998, 43.

14. Vries 2013, 401–408; De Vries 2015.

15. Brook 1998, 159.

16. Ebrey 1993, 216; Brook 1998, vii, 210–218; Yu-Lan 313–315; Chang 1962; Chang 1994; for India: Lal 35.

17. Kuhn 2009, 55f.; Mote 768.

18. Vries 2013, 352–354.

19. Park 2014; McDermott 13.

20. Chow 59.

21. Qian.

22. Lee 2012, 1.

23. Woodside.

24. Vespasiano da Bisticci I: 465; for Platina: Esch 2016, 196f.

25. Elvin 2004, 58.

26. Osterhammel 221.

27. Hoyt Cleveland Tillman in Chaffee/Twitchett, ch. 10; Vogelsang 347f.

28. Van Zanden 2009, 117, 145–176; for a more nuanced view: Vries 2013, 357f.; for what follows: Van Zanden 2009, ch. 5.

29. Chow 2004, 22; Van Zanden 2009, 188; Sivin 1995c, 168.

30. Brook 1998, 131; for libraries: 169f.; McDermott 126.

31. Grimm 478.

32. Vogelsang 372–377.

33. Faure 13.

34. Denis Twitchett in Twitchett 1979, 29–31; Kuhn 2009, 190.

35. Lach I: 688–706; Khair 173–183.

36. Uta Lindgren in *EdN* VI: 407–421; Pagden 2004, 193; Mignolo 219–221, 455; for the following numbers: David Woodward in Woodward 11.

37. Allsen 109f.; Brook 2010, 173–179; Adas 64.

38. Jenco 67–91.

39. Eggert 2006, 89.

40. Needham 1969, 121f.

41. Needham 1951, 41–42.

42. Flasch 1998, 80: "quasi finis naturae"; Copernicus/Zeller/Zeller 5; Blumenberg 1987, 206f; Leinkauf 2017, 134–139, also 217–219.

43. Needham 1928.

44. Malinar 2009, 243–245; Needham et al. II: 281; Hooykas 1972, 9–13.

45. Qian 50f., 58–60.

46. Ess 2011, 10–16.

47. Chang 1962; Vogelsang 388f.; Nosco 104.

48. Luo 77, but also 84.

49. Graham 62f.; Lloyd/Sivin.

50. Brook 2010, 179–182.

51. Kuhn 2009, 104; Thompson 2020.

52. Kuhn 2009, 114.

53. Chang 1962, 8f.; Ebrey 1991; Bray 2000a, 56–59; cf. Mitterauer 82–88; for Hinduism: Malinar 211–213.

54. Qian 68.

55. Mote 966; Elvin 1973, 95.

56. Maeyama 2003, 530.

57. Sivin 1995c, 188.
58. Elkana 68; for what follows: Luo 84.
59. Sivin 1995a.
60. Brook 2010, 183.
61. Sivin 1995a, 57.
62. Needham 1969, 121f.; Lal 42f.; Finlay 2000, 286.
63. Charles H. Lohr in Schmitt 1988, 574.
64. Goody 2010b, 126; Qian 1985.
65. Charles Hartman in Chaffee/Twitchett 23.
66. Landes 1983, 41f.
67. Morris 2010, 477; Zheng 135–168.
68. Mote 155; Wong 24; Zhao 12, 14–16; Pratt 94f.; for a different view: Lee/Feng 146.
69. Elvin 1973, 309; Zhao 22f.
70. Woodside; Vogelsang 462f.; Wong 21.

48. Deep History

1. Lach I: 534.
2. Hurst in Tsutsui 32.
3. Kulke/Rothermund 2010, 91, 99–101; Conermann 416f.
4. Buswell II: 640–646.
5. Berkey 2003, 264.
6. Huillard-Bréholles 686: "O felix Asia, o felices orientalium potestates que subditorum arma non metuunt et adinventiones pontificum non verentur!"; Fried 2015, 273f.
7. Embree/Wilhelm 189f.; for what follows: 195, 199.
8. Noth 1978, 190–204; Crone 2004, 370.
9. Bulliet 41f.
10. Pirillo 54f.
11. Conermann 2006, 20–28.
12. Rothermund 2016, 10.
13. Bertelli 2001.
14. Verena Maria Blümmel in Kreiner 62, 64f., 70–81.
15. Franke/Trauzettel 205; see also Twitchett/Mote 111.
16. Analayo.
17. Reid 2015, 44f.
18. Xin.
19. Ibn Battúta 293.
20. For exceptions: Twitchett/Loewe 813–820, 859, 861; Malinar 259f.
21. MacGregor 347f.; Kuhn 2009, 110.
22. Ebrey 1993, 146–150; Ebrahim.
23. Israeli 304n26; Chaudhuri 1985, 172.
24. Malinar 91–93.
25. Reid 2015, 45.
26. Böckenförde 2007, 47.
27. For India: Parthasarathi 172f.; for the Ottoman Empire: Suraiya Faroqhi in Reinhard 2015, 256–259; in general: Livi-Bacci 31
28. Franke/Twitchett 278f.; Heijdra; for Europe: Herlihy/Klapisch-Zuber 282–290; Roeck 1989, 303f.; for England: Laslett 66, 72.
29. Starr 333; Kennedy 2001, 99.
30. Reid 1988–1993, II: 69–72.

31. MacGregor 316.

32. For Chang'an: Modelski 150f., for Kaifeng: 44, for Nanjing: 66.

33. Brook 2010, 44f.; for Europe: Maddison 54; Malanima 9.

34. Voigtländer/Voth 178–181.

35. Bray 1994.

36. Wong 19f.; for what follows: 29f., 113f.; McDermott/Yoshinobu 342.

37. Wittfogel; Dorn; Lal 29; but see also Reid 2015, 41 (for Angkor); North in Davis 1995, 21f.

38. Findley 107.

39. Ibn Khaldûn/Rosenthal II: 431–434.

40. Aristotle, *Politics* 1295b.37f.; 1296b.38f.

41. Ertl 228; Jones 1997, 13.

42. *VLH* I: 1082f. (Gerlinde Huber-Rebenich/Sabine Lütkemeyer); Leinkauf 2017, 859–867; Quentin Skinner in Schmitt 1988, 447f.

43. Thucydides 1.41; Plato, *Republic* 463.

44. Martines 263.

45. Nasr 2009; Timur Kuran in Bernholz/Vaubel 152.

46. Lucas 159f.; Van Zanden 2009, 140; Grendler; Huppert 100.

47. Pernau 355–362; in general: Osterhammel 1087–1090.

48. Mann 2005, 412.

49. Weber 1986; for China: Michael Lessnoff in Mokyr 2003, 362.

50. Mitterauer 91–93; for China: Wong 100.

51. Glick 141f.; but see also Thornton 2012, 435–441.

52. Otto Gerhard Oexle in Meinhardt et al. 169–176: "Gruppengesellschaften"; Moor.

53. Groten 241f.

54. *MGH* Scriptores rerum Germanicarum 46, 116: "Ex quo factum est, ut caeteris orbis civitatibus divitiis et potentia (longe) premineant."

55. Guibert of Nogent, 127: "Communio autem novum ac pessimum nomen sic se habet."

56. Boshof 131f.; Borgolte 114: "communia est tumor plebis, timor regni, tepor sacerdotii."

57. Stein 1980; Watson Andaya/Andaya 124; for communalism: Blickle 1998.

58. For China: Vogelsang 229; Elvin 1973, 277, fig. 3; Peter J. Golas in Skinner 1977, 555–580; for Byzantium/Istanbul: Michel Kaplan in Haldon, 159f.; Schreiner 2011, 215, 83; for eastern Europe: Lübke 364, 366; for India: Embree/Wilhelm 158; Kulke/Rothermund 2010, 112, 88–90; Blake 112–114; Abu-Lughod 277f., 281; for Islam: Michael Bonner in Robinson 2010, 357; Paul 127f.; Inalcik/Quataert 545–636, 888-898; Blake 2002, 83–103.

59. Wong 83–87.

60. Mundy 127f.; Pirillo 128.

61. Stephan R. Epstein/Maarten Prak in Epstein/Prak 2008, 23.

62. Shapin 1989.

63. Mundy 130.

64. Faroqhi 2000, 217.

65. Mokyr 2005, 336.

66. Frey/Bierhoff 63–65; Simon 1990, 1665–1668; Cordes.

67. Cohen 2010, 276; Horden/Purcell 291–293.

68. Aronson et al. 405–407; Lucas 159f.; MacCormack 97f.

69. Schätzl 23.

70. Austen/Headrick.

71. Van Zanden 2009, 95–100, 117, 272, fig. 34; Van Zanden/Buringh/Bosker 843; Plejit/van Zanden; Mokyr 2005, 333, fig. 3; for a differentiated view: Kirk 2005, 67-69.

72. Van Zanden 2009, 104-120.

73. http://www.transparency.org/cpi2014/results; Van Zanden 2009, 200.

74. Mundy 128.

75. Putnam 150; Wickham 2015, 4.

76. Landes 1998, 171f.; Kamen 2014a, 237f.

77. Grafe.

78. Kamen 2014b, 153.

79. Buringh/Van Zanden; Plejit/Van Zanden 6; Van Zanden 2009, 193; Allen 2011, 25.

80. Tilly; Downing.

81. Ruggiero.

82. Koenigsberger in Davis 1995, 305; Wim Blockmans in Allmand, 46f.; Reinhard 1999, 75.

49. Epilogue

1. Goetz 59.

2. Newton/Turnbull et al. I: 416.

3. E.g., McCloskey.

4. See most recently Frankopan 258.

5. Mokyr 2002, 276.

6. Marks 77f.

7. Cohen 2010, 172.

8. Mbembe 13.

9. Osterhammel 639f.; cf. the debate between George Saliba and Toby Huff in *Bulletin of the Royal Institute for Inter-Faith Studies* 1:2 (1999), 139–152; 4:2 (2002), 115–141; for cultural transfer: Roeck 2007.

10. Duchesne 2011, x.

11. Studer 232.

12. Charles Hartman in Chaffee/Twitchett 37f.; for social mobility: Robert Hymes in Chaffee/Twitchett 650–655; for the educational system: Peter K. Bol in Chaffee/Twitchett 722; Hoyt Cleveland Tillman in Chaffee/Twitchett 727–790.

13. Riello 54f.

14. Mann 2005, 500; Qian 25f., 103f.; North in Davis 1995, 26f.; Borgolte 355f.

15. Baechler (and the comments by Michael Cook and Mark Elvin): 29–35.

16. Volckart.

17. Goldstone 2009, 97–102; Wong 74–79; Beaujard II: 542.

18. Brian Vickers in Schmitt 1988, 720.

19. Zhang 156.

20. Mahdi 135–137, 185f.; al-Farabi/Walzer 247, 437f.

21. Brian Vickers in Schmitt 1988, 730, 736.

22. Tainter 201f.

23. Epstein 19.

24. Marks; for a different view: Parthasarathi 214f. and Mokyr 2005, 298, 300.

25. Briggs/Burke 73–85; Marks 112f., 121f.

26. Cardwell 65; for the translations of Agricola: Agricola/Hoover/Hoover 21.

27. Cohen 1994, 441f.; Mokyr 2005, 285–351, 323f.; Vries 2013, 305–315.

28. Velleius Paterculus 1.6.6, 1.17; Demandt 2011, 83.

29. Merton ; Henry 2008, 100–102; Lal 99f.

30. Mokyr 2005, 331–333 (fig. 3); but see Marks 121f.

31. White 1978, 75–91, 80.

32. Goldstone 2006, 171; Landes 1994.

33. Toynbee IX: 120; Goody 2010b, 19.

34. Goody 2010b; Kraemer.

35. Schildgen/Zhou/Gilman; Bailey et al. 4.

36. Shih 272f.; see also Gamsa 641; Luo 95.

37. Gamsa 645.

38. Goldin/Kutarna.

39. Reardon 33.

40. Amin 67f.

41. Hymes in Chaffee/Twitchett 621, 625; Qian 119f.; Beaujard II: 171.

42. Stierle 283f.: "friuolum est soli senio fidere & qui haec inuenerunt homines erant . . . nil tam cultum nilque adeo cumulatum, cui non aliquid addi queat."

43. Otto 16.

44. Letter of Angelo Poliziano to Paolo Cortesi, in Dellaneva 3 (trans. Duvick).

45. Thus Rabb xxf.; for the debate: Gamsa 649f.

46. Pedersen 1984, 131–133.

47. Braudel 1967, 237; for Japan: Gunn 212.

48. Deepak Lal in Bernholz/Vaubel 139.

49. Talon 133: "si quid in Platonis sermonibus et scriptis commodum et utile est, accipio: si quid boni in hortis Epicuri prostat, non contemno: si quid melius Aristoteles vendit, quantum quomodo videtur, assumo: si magis sunt vendibiles Zenonis, quam Aristotelis merces, Aristotelem relinquo, ad Zenonis officinam diverto; si vana sunt et inutilia, que venduntur in tabernis philosophorum omnia, omnino nihil hinc emo"; see also Hooykas 1978, 15; Bouwsma 2000, 50.

50. Weber 1988, 252: "Die Weltbilder, welche durch Ideen geschaffen wurden, haben sehr oft als Weichensteller die Bahnen bestimmt, in denen die Dynamik der Interessen das Handeln fortbewegt."

51. Keßler 1971, 184.

52. Ardito 301; Skinner 1978, I; Armitage 2000, 125–145.

53. Lee et al.

54. Brückner 130.

55. Nietzsche 127; Roeck 2023; Schröder 1998, 60–63.

56. Blair 1997, 23.

57. Roling 288–293; for Socrates: Plato, *Symposium* 221e–222a.

58. Edson 202; Céard 300.

59. Toulmin 30f., 75f.

60. Gaukroger 189; Lattis 208f.

61. Moran 2005, 105.

62. Armitage 2000, 69.

63. Battisti; Haydn; Toulmin 45-87.

64. Loughman/Montias 48f.

65. Schmitt 1969, 80f.

66. Yates 1964, 398; for Newton: Moran 2005, 172.

67. Reid 2015, 143; Findlay/O'Rourke 277f.; Parker 2013.

68. Hans Blumenberg in Bruno/Fellmann 35; for attempts to define the boundaries of the early modern period: Osterhammel 55–58.

69. Grinin/Korotayev.

70. Schilling 2017, 170.

71. Ogilvie 3.

72. Rabb 148, 139; for Dee: Clucas 10; for *novatores*: Leinkauf 2017, 1630.

73. Otto 23f.

74. Céard 373–379, esp. 377f.; Toulmin.

75. Pascal, *Pensées* 72; Bouwsma 2000, 85; Wilson 1995, 190f.

76. Blumenberg 1987, 124-126.

77. *The Tempest* 4.1.147-158.
78. Mann 1987, 228: "ungeheurer Traum"; Rehm; O'Pecko.
79. Roeck 2023.
80. Popkin 2003, 125.
81. North 2005, 381.
82. Donne 108f.
83. Headley 2008, 4; Mignolo 440f.; Ibn Warraq.

ABBREVIATIONS

BW Bruno, Giordano. 2013–2018. *Werke.* Ed. Thomas Leinkauf. 7 vols. Hamburg:
Meiner (*BW II* = *La cena delle ceneri.* Ed. Angelika Bönker-Vallon; *BW IV* = *De
l'infinito, universo et mondi.* Ed. Angelika Bönker-Vallon; *BW V* = *Spaccio della
bestia trionfante.* Ed. Elisabeth Blum and Paul Richard Blum; *BW VI* = *Cabala del
cavallo pegaseo.* Ed. Sergius Kodera).

Canzoniere Petrarca, Francesco. 2001. *Canzoniere.* Trans. A. S. Kline. Poetry in Translation.
URL: www.poetryintranslation.com/klineascanzoniere.htm (accessed
January 18, 2021.

CB *Carmina Burana.* 2018. Ed. and trans. David A. Traill. 2 vols. Cambridge, MA:
Harvard University Press.

DBI *Dizionario Biografico degli Italiani.* 1960–2020. 100 vols. Rome: Istituto
dell'Enciclopedia Italiana.

Discourses Machiavelli, Niccolò. 1996. *Discourses on Livy.* Trans. Harvey C. Mansfield and
Nathan Tarcov. Chicago: University of Chicago Press.

E Erasmus of Rotterdam. 1968–1980. *Ausgewählte Schriften.* Ed. Werner Welzig.
8 vols., Darmstadt: WBG.

EdN Jaeger, Friedrich (ed.). 2005–2013. *Enzyklopädie der Neuzeit.* 15 vols. Stuttgart:
Metzler.

Inferno Alighieri 1995.

Mt Montaigne, Michel de. 1958. *The Complete Essays of Montaigne.* Trans. Donald M.
Frame. Stanford: Stanford University Press.

NDB *Neue Deutsche Biographie.* 1953–. 27 vols. to date. Berlin: Duncker & Humblot.

Purgatorio Alighieri 1995.

Paradiso Alighieri 1995.

PL *Patrologiae cursus completus . . . series latina.* 1844–1890. Ed. J.-P. Migne. 221 vols.
Paris: J.-P. Migne/Garnier Fratres.

Prince Machiavelli, Niccolò. 1998. *The Prince.* Trans. Harvey C. Mansfield. 2nd ed.
Chicago: University of Chicago Press.

R Richter, Jean Paul. 1970. *The Literary Works of Leonardo da Vinci.* 3rd ed.
New York: Phaidon.

RIE Fontana, Giovanni Luigi, and Luca Molà (eds.). 2005–2010. *Il rinascimento
italiano e l'Europa.* 6 vols. Treviso: Angelo Colla Editore.

RIS Muratori, Ludovico Antonio (ed.). 1723–1751/1900–1975. *Rerum Italicarum
Scriptores.* 25 vols. Milan: Typographia Societatis Palatinae in Regia Curia,
1723–1751. Second Series: Ed. Giosué Carducci. 34 vols. Città di Castello: Lapi /
Bologna: Zanichelli, 1900–1975.

VLH Worstbrock, Franz Josef (ed.). 2008–2015. *Deutscher Humanismus 1480–1520.*
Verfasserlexikon. 3 vols. Berlin: De Gruyter,.

WA *D. Martin Luthers Werke. Kritische Gesamtausgabe.* 1883–2009. Weimar:
Hermann Böhlaus Nachfolger.

BIBLIOGRAPHY

Standard works such as the Greek and Latin classics, the Bible, and the Quran are not listed unless a specific edition is cited.

al- at the beginning of Arabic names is ignored for purposes of alphabetization.

Abulafia, David (ed.). 1995a. *The French Descent into Renaissance Italy, 1494–95: Antecedents and Effects.* Aldershot: Ashgate.
———. 1995b. "Trade and Crusade, 1050–1250." In Michael Goodich, Sophia Menache, and Sylvia Schein (eds.), *Cross Cultural Convergences in the Crusader Period: Essays Presented to Aryeh Grabois on his Sixty-Fifth Birthday.* Bern: Peter Lang, 1–20.
———. 2008. *The Discovery of Mankind: Encounters in the Age of Columbus.* New Haven: Yale University Press.
———. 2011. *The Great Sea: A Human History of the Mediterranean.* Oxford: Oxford University Press.
Abu-Lughod, Janet L. 1989. *Before European Hegemony: The World System A.D. 1250–1350.* Oxford: Oxford University Press.
Acemoglu, Daron, and James A. Robinson. 2008. "The Persistence and Change of Institutions in the Americas." *Southern Economic Journal* 75:2, 282–299.
———. 2012. *Why Nations Fail: The Origins of Power, Prosperity, and Poverty.* New York: Profile Books.
Aceto, Francesco. 2013. "Nicola Pisano." *DBI.* Vol. 78, 453–460.
Acosta, Jose de. 1987. *Historia natural y moral de las Indias.* Ed. José Alcina Franch. Madrid: Dastin Historia.
Adams, Ann Jensen. 1994. "Competing Communities in the 'Great Bog of Europe': Identity and Seventeenth-Century Dutch Landscape Painting." In William J. T. Mitchell (ed.). *Landscape and Power.* Chicago: University of Chicago Press, 35–76.
Adams, Tracy. 2010. *The Life and Afterlife of Isabeau of Bavaria.* Baltimore: Johns Hopkins University Press.
Adamson, Peter, and Richard C. Taylor (eds.). 2005. *The Cambridge Companion to Arabic Philosophy.* Cambridge: Cambridge University Press.
Adang, Camilla et al. (eds.). 2015. *Accusations of Unbelief in Islam: A Diachronic Perspective on Takfir.* Leiden: Brill.
Adas, Michael. 1989. *Machines as the Measure of Man: Science, Technologies, and Ideologies of Western Divergence.* Ithaca: Cornell University Press.
Adcock, Fleur (ed.). 1994. *Hugh Primas and the Archpoet.* Cambridge: Cambridge University Press.
Adolphson, Mikael, Edward Kamens, and Stacie Matsumoto (eds.). 2007. *Heian Japan: Centers and Peripheries.* Honolulu: University of Hawai'i Press.

Adorno, Rolena. 2007. *The Polemics of Possession in Spanish America Narrative.* New Haven: Yale University Press.

Agricola, Georgius. 1950. *De re metallica.* Trans. Herbert Clark Hoover and Lou Henry Hoover. New York: Dover Publications.

Aguirre, Lope de. 1981. *Crónicas 1559–1561.* Ed. Elena Mampel González and Tur Neuss-Escandell. Barcelona: Edicions de la Universitat de Barcelona.

——. 1961. Letter to King Philip II of Spain. Trans. Tom Holloway. In Fordham University, *Modern History Sourcebook.* Originally published in A. Arellano Moreno (org.), *Documentos para la Historia economic de Venezuela.* Caracas: Univ. Central, 1961. https://sourcebooks .fordham.edu/mod/1561aguirre.asp (accessed September 16, 2022).

Ahmed, Shahab. 2015. *What is Islam? The Importance of Being Islamic.* Princeton: Princeton University Press.

Åkerman, Susanna. 1998. *Rose Cross Over the Baltic.* Leiden: Brill.

Alberti, Leon Battista. 1890. *Opera inedita et pauca separatim impressa.* Ed. Girolamo Mancini. Florence: Sansoni.

——. 1972. *On Painting and On Sculpture: The Latin Texts of De Pictura and De Statua.* Ed. and trans. Cecil Grayson. London: Phaidon.

——. 1987. *Dinner Pieces: A Translation of the Intercenales.* Trans. David Marsh. Binghamton: Medieval & Renaissance Texts & Studies.

——. 1988. *On the Art of Building in Ten Books.* Trans. Joseph Rykwert, Neil Leach, and Robert Tavernor. Cambridge, MA: MIT Press.

——. 2002. *Della pittura / Über die Malkunst.* Ed. Oskar Bätschmann and Sandra Gianfreda. Darmstadt: BWG.

——. 2003. *Momus.* Ed. Sarah Knight and Virginia Brown. Cambridge, MA: Harvard University Press.

——. 2004. *Vita.* Ed. and trans. Christine Tauber and Robert Cramer. Frankfurt: Stroemfeld.

Albertus Magnus. 1978. *Sancti Doctoris Ecclesiae Alberti Magni . . . Opera Omnia.* Vol. XXXVII. Ed. Paul Simon. 2nd ed. Münster: Aschendorff.

Alcock, Susan. 1996. *Graecia Capta: The Landscapes of Roman Greece.* Cambridge: Cambridge University Press.

Alemán, Mateo. 2003. *Guzmán de Alfarache.* Retamar: Ediciones Perdidas.

Alexander, Manfred. 2008. *Kleine Geschichte der böhmischen Länder.* Stuttgart: Reclam.

Alföldy, Géza. 1985. *The Social History of Rome.* Trans. David Braund and Frank Pollock. Totowa: Barnes & Noble.

Alighieri, Dante. 1995. *Divine Comedy.* Trans. Allen Mandelbaum. New York: Knopf.

——. 1965. *Tutte le opere.* Ed. Fredi Chiappelli. Milan: Mursia.

Allen, Robert C. 2009. *The British Industrial Revolution in a Global Perspective.* Cambridge: Cambridge University Press.

——. 2011. *Global Economic History: A Very Short Introduction.* Oxford: Oxford University Press.

Allés Torrent, Susanna. 2012. "Alfonso de Palencia y el humanismo italiano." *Cuadernos de Filologia Italiana* 19, 107–130.

Allmand, Christopher (ed.). 1998. *The New Cambridge Medieval History.* Vol. VII. Cambridge: Cambridge University Press.

Allsen, Thomas T. 2004. *Culture and Conquest in Mongol Eurasia.* Cambridge: Cambridge University Press.

Althoff, Gerd. 1996. *Otto III.* Darmstadt: WBG.

——. 2004. *Die Ottonen. Königsherrschaft ohne Staat.* Stuttgart: W. Kohlhammer.

Amabile, Luigi. 1882/2010. *Fra Tommaso Campanella, la sua congiura, i suoi processi e la sua pazzia*. 3 vols. Naples: Cav. Antonio Morano, 1882. Facsimile reprint: Whitefish: Kessinger Publishing, 2010.

Amadori, Gabriele (ed.). 2014. *Giovanni Leone Africano. Cosmographia de l'Affrica (Ms. V.E. 953 Biblioteca Nazionale Centrale di Roma—1526)*. Rome: ARACNE Editrice.

Amin, Samir. 2010. *Eurocentrism: Modernity, Religion, and Democracy: A Critique of Eurocentrism and Culturalism*. 2nd ed. New York: Monthly Review Press.

Analayo, Bhikkhu. 2010. *The Genesis of the Bodhisattva Ideal*. Hamburg: Hamburg University Press.

Anderson, Benedict. 1991. *Imagined Communities: Reflections on the Origins and Spread of Nationalism*. London: Verso.

Anderson, William S. 1995. *Ovid: The Classical Heritage*. New York: Garland.

Andrews, Frances. 1999. *The Early Humiliati*. Cambridge: Cambridge University Press.

Andrews, Kenneth R. 1991. *Trade, Plunder and Settlement: Maritime Enterprise and the Genesis of the British Empire, 1480–1630*. Cambridge: Cambridge University Press.

Angenendt, Arnold. 2000. *Geschichte der Religiosität im Mittelalter*. 2nd ed. Darmstadt: WBG.

———. 2011. "Reinheit und Unreinheit. Anmerkungen zu 'Purity and Danger.'" In Peter Burschel and Christoph Marx (eds.), *Reinheit*. Vienna: Böhlau, 47–74.

Anselm of Canterbury. 1962. *Basic Writings*. Trans. Sidney N. Deane. Peru, IL: Open Court.

Ardito, Alissa M. 2015. *Machiavelli and the Modern State: The Prince, the Discourses on Livy and the Extended Territorial Republic*. Cambridge: Cambridge University Press.

Argenti, Philip. 1958. *The Occupation of Chios by the Genoese and their Administration of the Island*. 3 vols. Cambridge: Cambridge University Press.

Armitage, David. 2000. *The Ideological Origins of the British Empire*. Cambridge: Cambridge University Press.

Armitage, David, and Michael J. Braddick. 2009. *The British Atlantic World, 1590–1800*. 2nd ed. Red Globe Press: Basingstoke.

Arnold, Klaus. 1991. *Johannes Trithemius (1462–1516)*. 2nd ed. Würzburg: Schöningh.

Aronson, Elliot et al. 2014. *Sozialpsychologie*. 8th ed. Hallbergmoos: Pearson.

Ashtor, Eliahu. 1976. *A Social and Economic History of the Near East in the Middle Ages*. London: Collins.

Ashworth, William B., Jr. 1990. "Natural History and the Emblematic World View." In Lindberg/Westman 1990, 303–332.

———. 1996. "Emblematic Natural History of the Renaissance." In Nicholas Jardine et al. (eds.), *Cultures of Natural History*. Cambridge: Cambridge University Press, 17–37.

Asmussen, Tina et al. (eds.). 2013. *Theatrum Kircherianum. Wissenskulturen und Bücherwelten im 17. Jahrhundert*. Harrassowitz: Wiesbaden.

Assmann, Jan. 2009. *The Prize of Monotheism*. Trans. Robert Savage. Stanford: Stanford University Press.

Atiyeh, George N. 1995. "The Book in the Modern Arabic World: The Cases of Lebanon and Egypt." In George N. Atiyeh (ed.), *The Book in the Islamic World: The Written Word and Communication in the Middle East*. Albany: State University of New York Press, 233–253.

Auerbach, Erich. 2013. *Mimesis: The Representation of Reality in Western Literature*. Trans. Willard R. Task. Intr. Edward W. Said. Princeton: Princeton University Press.

Augustynowicz, Christoph. 2010. "Kaiser Maximilian II. als electus Rex Poloniae und der Regensburger Reichstag von 1576. Implikationen des Nationenbegriffs im 16. Jahrhundert." In Marija Wakounig et al. (eds.), *Nation, Nationalitäten und Nationalismus im östlichen Europa*. Vienna: Böhlau, 47–68.

Aung-Thwin, Michael. 2012. *A History of Myanmar Since Ancient Times: Traditions and Transformations.* London: Reaktion Books.

Austen, Ralph A., and Daniel Headrick. 1983. "The Role of Technologies in the African Past." *African Studies* 26, 163–184.

———. 1990–1991. "On Comparing Pre-Industrial African and European Economies." *African Economic History* 19, 21–24.

Autrand, Françoise. 2009. *Christine de Pizan.* Paris: Fayard.

Avrin, Leila. 2010. *Scribes, Script, and Books: The Book Arts from Antiquity to the Renaissance.* 2nd ed. Chicago: American Library Association—The British Library.

al-Azmeh, Aziz. 2007. *The Times of History: Universal Topics in Islamic Historiography.* Budapest: Central European University Press.

Babbitt, Susan M. 1985. "Oresme's *Livre de Politiques* and the France of Charles V." *Transactions of the American Philosophical Society* 75:1, 1–158.

Bachmann, Ingeborg. "Bohemia Lies by the Sea." https://www.scottishpoetrylibrary.org.uk /poem/bohemia-lies-sea/ (accessed January 6, 2023).

Bacon, Francis. 1628. *The New Atlantis.* London: William Lee.

———. 1854. *Novum Organum.* Ed. and trans. Basil Montague. In *The Works.* Vol. III. Philadelphia: Parry & MacMillan.

———. 1860–1964. "Meditationes Sacrae." In Francis Bacon, *The Works of Francis Bacon.* Ed. James Spedding et al. 15 vols. Boston: Brown and Taggart.

———. 1905. *The Philosophical Works of Francis Bacon.* Ed. John M. Robertson. London: George Routledge and Sons.

Bacon, Roger. 1900. *The Opus majus of Roger Bacon.* Ed. and intr. John Henry Bridges. London: Williams and Norgate.

———. 1909–1940. *Opera hactenus inedita.* Ed. Robert Steele. 16 vols. Oxford: Clarendon.

Baechler, Jean. 2004. "The Political Pattern of Historical Creativity: A Theoretical Case." In Bernholz/Vaubel 2004, 18–28.

Baharuddin, Azizan. 2018. "The Significance of Sufi-Empirical Principles in the Natural Theology and Discourse on Science in Islam." In Iqbal 2018, I, 223–242.

Bailey, Gauvin Alexander et al. 2009. "Spain and Spanish America in the Early Modern Atlantic World: Current Trends in Scholarship." *Renaissance Quarterly* 62:1, 1–60.

Bakar, Osman. 1998. *Classification of Knowledge in Islam: A Study in Islamic Philosophies of Science.* Cambridge: Islamic Texts Society.

Baker, Patrick. 2015. *Italian Renaissance Humanism in the Mirror.* Cambridge: Cambridge University Press.

Balbiani, Laura. 2001. *La Magia naturalis di Giovan Battista Della Porta. Lingua, cultura e scienza in Europa all'inizio dell'età moderna.* Bern: Peter Lang.

Baldwin, Barry (ed. and trans.). 1984. *Timarion.* Detroit: Wayne State University Press.

Bambach, Carmen C. 2019. *Leonardo Da Vinci Rediscovered.* New Haven: Yale University Press.

Barasch, Moshe. 1985. *Theories of Art 1: From Plato to Winckelmann.* New York: New York University Press.

Barbaro, Ermolao. 1943. *Epistolae, Orationes, Carmina.* Ed. Vittore Branca. Florence: Bibliopolis.

Barber, Charles, and David Jenkins (eds.). 2006. *Reading Michael Psellos.* Leiden: Brill.

Barbey, Jean. 1983. *La Fonction royale. Essence et légitimité d'après les Tractatus de Jean de Terrevermeille.* Paris: Nouvelles Editions Latines.

Barfield, Thomas J. 1991. "Tribe and State Relations: The Inner Asian Perspective." In Philip S. Khoury and Joseph Kostiner (eds.). *Tribes and State Formation in the Middle East.* London: I. B. Tauris, 153–182.

Barker, Peter. 1999. "Copernicus and the Critics of Ptolemy." *Journal for the History of Astronomy* 30, 343–358.

Barkey, Karen. 2008. *Empire of Difference: The Ottomans in Comparative Perspective*. Cambridge: Cambridge University Press.

Barnes, Robin B. 1988. *Prophecy and Gnosis: Apocalypticism in the Wake of the Lutheran Reformation*. Stanford: Stanford University Press.

Barnhart, Richard et al. (eds.). 1997. *Three Thousand Years of Chinese Painting*. New Haven and Beijing: Yale University Press and Foreign Languages Press.

Baron, Frank E. 1966. "The Beginnings of German Humanism: The Life and Work of the Wandering Humanist Peter Luder." PhD dissertation, University of California at Berkeley.

Barrera-Osorio, Antonio. 2006. *Experiencing Nature: The Spanish American Empire and the Early Scientific Revolution*. Austin: University of Texas Press.

Barrow, Reginald H. 1973. *Prefect and Emperor: The Relationes of Symmachus AD 384*. Oxford: Clarendon.

Barton, Simon. 1997. *The Aristocracy in Twelfth-Century León and Castile*. Cambridge: Cambridge University Press.

Bates, David. 2013. *The Normans and Empire*. Oxford: Oxford University Press.

Battisti, Eugenio. 1962. *L'antirinascimento, con una appendice di manoscritti inediti*. Milan: Feltrinelli.

Baur, Otto. 1974. *Bestiarium humanum. Mensch-Tier-Vergleich in Kunst und Karikatur*. Gräfelfing: Heinz Moos.

Baxandall, Michael. 1964. "Bartholomaeus Facius on Painting: A Fifteenth-Century Manuscript of De viris illustribus." *Journal of the Warburg & Courtauld Institutes* 27, 90–107.

———. 1971. *Giotto and the Orators: Humanist Observers of Painting in Italy and the Discovery of Pictorial Composition, 1350–1450*. Oxford: Clarendon Press.

———. 1972. *Painting and Experience in Fifteenth Century Italy: A Primer in the Social History of Pictorial Style*. Oxford: Oxford University Press.

———. 1980. *The Limewood Sculptors of Renaissance Germany*. New Haven: Yale University Press.

Baylor, Michael G. (ed.). 1993. *Revelation and Revolution: Basic Writings of Thomas Müntzer*. Bethlehem: Lehigh University Press.

Bayly, Christopher. 2004. *The Birth of the Modern World: Global Connections and Comparisons, 1780–1914*. Oxford: Oxford University Press.

Beaujard, Philippe. 2012. *Les mondes de l'océan Indien*. 2 vols. Paris: Armand Colin.

Beck, James H. 1999. *Three Worlds of Michelangelo*. New York: W. W. Norton.

Beckert, Sven. 2014. *King Cotton. Eine Globalgeschichte des Kapitalismus*. Munich: C. H. Beck.

Behringer, Wolfgang. 2003. *Im Zeichen des Merkur. Reichspost und Kommunikationsrevolution in der Frühen Neuzeit*. Göttingen: Vandenhoeck & Ruprecht.

———. 2004. *Witches and Witch-Hunts. A Global History*. Cambridge: Polity Press.

Bell, Clair Hayden (ed. and trans.). 1931. *Peasant Life in Old German Epics: Meier Helmbrecht and Der arme Heinrich*. New York: Columbia University Press.

Bellitto, Christopher. 2001. *Nicolas de Clamanges: Spirituality, Personal Reform, and Pastoral Renewal on the Eve of the Reformations*. Washington, DC: The Catholic University of America Press.

Bellwood, Peter. 2005. *First Farmers: The Origins of Agricultural Societies*. Malden: Blackwell.

Belting, Hans. 1993. *Likeness and Presence: A History of the Image before the Era of Art*. Trans. Edmund Jephcott. Chicago: University of Chicago Press.

———. 2011. *Florence and Baghdad: Renaissance Art and Arab Science*. Trans. Deborah Locas Schneider. Cambridge, MA: Belknap Press.

———. 2016. *Hieronymus Bosch, Garden of Earthly Delights*. Munich: Prestel.

Bendix, Reinhard. 1977. *Max Weber: An Intellectual Portrait*. Berkeley: University of California Press.

Benedictow, Ole J. 2004. *The Black Death 1346–1353: The Complete History*. Woodbridge: The Boydell Press.

Benešovská, Klára. 2010. "Forgotten Paths to 'Another Renaissance': Prague and Bohemia, c. 1400." In Lee/Péporté/Schnitker 2010, 289–310.

Ben-Shammai, Haggai. 1997. "Jewish Thought in Iraq in the Tenth Century." In Norman Golb (ed.), *Judaeo-Arabic Studies: Proceedings of the Founding Conference of the Society for Judaeo-Arabic Studies*. Amsterdam: Harwood Academic Publishers, 15–32.

Benson, Robert Louis, and Giles Constable. (eds.). 1982. *Renaissance and Renewal in the Twelfth Century*. Cambridge, MA: Harvard University Press.

Benton, John F. 1982. "Consciousness of the Self and Perceptions of Individuality." In Benson/Constable 1982, 263–295.

Benz, Wolfgang. 2007. *Die Protokolle der Weisen von Zion. Die Legende von der jüdischen Weltverschwörung*. Munich: C. H. Beck.

Benzoni, Gino. 2000. "Paolo III." In Bray 2000b, 91–111.

Berg, Dieter. 2013. *Heinrich VIII. von England. Leben—Herrschaft—Wirkung*. W. Kohlhammer: Stuttgart.

———. 2016. *Die Tudors. England und der Kontinent im 16. Jahrhundert*. Stuttgart: W. Kohlhammer.

Bergdolt, Klaus. 1994. *Der Schwarze Tod in Europa. Die Große Pest und das Ende des Mittelalters*. Munich: C. H. Beck.

———. 2008. *Wellbeing: A Cultural History of Healthy Living*. Cambridge: Polity.

Bergerac, Cyrano de. 1899. *A Voyage to the Moon*. Trans. Archibald Lovell. New York: Doubleday. https://www.gutenberg.org/files/46547/46547-h/46547-h.htm (accessed January 27, 2023).

Bergmann, Werner. 1985. *Innovationen im Quadrivium des 10. und 11. Jahrhunderts. Studien zur Einführung vom Astrolab und Abakus im lateinischen Mittelalter*. Stuttgart: Steiner.

Berkey, Jonathan P. 1995. "Tradition, Innovation, and the Social Construction of Knowledge in the Medieval Islamic Near East." *Past & Present* 146, 38–65.

———. 2003. *The Formation of Islam: Religion and Society in the Near East, 600–1800*. Cambridge: Cambridge University Press.

Berlin, Isaiah. 2013. *The Crooked Timber of Humanity: Chapters in the History of Ideas*. Ed. Henry Hardy. 2nd ed. Princeton: Princeton University Press.

Bernal, Martin. 1987. *Black Athena: The Afroasiatic Roots of Classical Civilization*. Vol. I. New Brunswick: Rutgers University Press.

Berndt, Guido M., and Roland Steinacher (eds.). 2014. *Arianism: Roman Heresy and Barbarian Creed*. London: Routledge.

Bernholz, Peter, and Roland Vaubel (eds.). 2004. *Political Competition, Innovation and Growth in the History of Asian Civilizations*. Cheltenham: Edward Elgar Publishing.

Berns, Jörg Jochen, and Wolfgang Neuber. 1993. *Ars memorativa. Zur kulturgeschichtlichen Bedeutung der Gedächtniskunst 1400–1700*. Tübingen: Niemeyer.

Bernstein, Eckhard. 1978. *Die Literatur des deutschen Frühhumanismus*. Stuttgart: Metzler.

Bertelli, Sergio. 2001. *The King's Body: Sacred Rituals of Power in Medieval and Early Modern Europe*. Trans. R. Burr Litchfield. University Park: Penn State University Press.

Bertling Biaggini, Claudia. 2011. *Giorgione pictor et musicus amatus—Vom Klang seiner Bilder. Eine musikalische Kompositionsästhetik in der Malerei gegen die Aporie der Norm um 1500*. Hildesheim: Olms.

Beschorner, Andreas. 1992. *Untersuchungen zu Dares Phrygius*. Tübingen: Gunter Narr.

Bevington, David. 2002. *Shakespeare*. Malden: Blackwell.

Beyer, Andreas. 2002. *Das Porträt in der Malerei*. Munich: Hirmer.

Bezold, Friedrich von. 2019. "Konrad Celtis, 'der deutsche Erzhumanist.'" In Friedrich von Bezold, *Aus Mittelalter und Renaissance. Kulturgeschichtliche Studien*. Berlin: De Gruyter, 82–152.

Bhatt, Rakesh Kumar. 1995. *History and Development of Libraries in India*. New Delhi: Mittal Publications.

Bhattacharya, Jayanta. 2009. "The Knowledge of Anatomy and Health in Āyurveda and Modern Medicine: Colonial Confontation and Its Outcome." *Eä-Revista de humanidades médicas & estudios de ciencia y la tecnologia* 1, 1–51.

Bhattacharyya, R. K. 2011. "Brahmagupta: The Ancient Indian Mathematician." In B. S. Yadav and Man Mohan, *Ancient Indian Leaps into Mathematics*. New York: Springer, 185–192.

Biagioli, Mario. 1993. *Galileo, Courtier: The Practice of Science in the Culture of Absolutism*. Chicago: University of Chicago Press.

Bialas, Volker. 2004. *Johannes Kepler*. Munich: C. H. Beck.

Bianca, Concetta. 1999. "Gaza, Teodoro." In *DBI* 52, 737–746.

——— (ed.). 2010. *Coluccio Salutati e l'invenzione dell'umanesimo*. Rome: Edizioni di Storia e Letteratura.

Bianchi, Massimo Luigi. 1994. "The Visible and the Invisible. From Alchemy to Paracelsus." In Piyo Rattansi and Antonio Clericuzio (eds.). *Alchemy and Chemistry in the 16th and 17th Centuries*. Dordrecht: Kulwer Academic Publishers, 17–50.

Bieri, Hans (in collaboration with Virgilio Masciadri). 2007. *Der Streit um das kopernikanische Weltsystem im 17. Jahrhundert*. Bern: Peter Lang.

Biersack, Manfred. 2013. "'. . . umso gefährlicher ist es, sie zu kennen': Die kontroverse Aufnahme des Florentiner Renaissanceplatonismus im spanischen Humanismus (1486–ca. 1530)." *Zeitschrift für Historische Forschung* 40, 558–592.

Biggi, Maria Ida. "Il teatro italiano e l'Europa." In *RIE* VI, 159–173.

Biggins, Michael, and Janet Crayne (eds.). 2000. *Publishing in Yugoslavia's Successor States*. New York: Haworth Information Press.

Billanovich, Guido. 1976. "Il preumanesimo padovano." In Gianfranco Folena (ed.), *Storia della cultura veneta. Il Trecento*. Vicenza: Neri Pozza, 19–110.

Biondo Flavio. 2016. *Italia Illustrata*. Vol. II. Ed. and trans. Jeffrey A. White. Cambridge, MA: Harvard University Press.

Bisaha, Nancy. 2004. *Creating East and West: Renaissance Humanists and the Ottoman Turks*. Philadelphia: University of Pennsylvania Press.

Bishop, Morris. 1964. *Petrarch and His World*. London: Chatto and Windus.

Bitterli, Urs. 1999. *Die Entdeckung Amerikas. Von Kolumbus bis Alexander von Humboldt*. Munich: C. H. Beck.

Black, Jeremy. 2015. *The Atlantic Slave Trade in World History*. London: Routledge.

Black, Robert. 2010. "The Renaissance and the Middle Ages: Chronologies, Ideologies, Geographies." In Lee/Péporté/Schnitker 2010, 27–44.

———. "Le scuole e la circolazione del sapere." In *RIE* II, 287–307.

Blair, Ann. 1997. *The Theater of Nature: Jean Bodin and Renaissance Science*. Princeton: Princeton University Press.

Blake, Stephen P. 2002. *Shahjahanabad: The Sovereign City in Mughal India, 1639–1739*. Cambridge: Cambridge University Press.

Blankinship, Khalid Yahya. 1994. *The End of the Jihād State: The Reign of Hishā, 'Abd Al-Malik and the Collapse of the Umayyads*. Albany: State University of New York Press.

Blastenbrei, Peter. 1992. *Die Sforza und ihr Heer. Studien zur Struktur-, Wirtschafts- und Sozialgeschichte des Söldnerwesens in der italienischen Frührenaissance*. Heidelberg: Carl Winter.

Blaut, James M. 1993. *The Colonizer's Model of the World: Geographic Diffusionism and Eurocentric History*. New York: The Guilford Press.

Bleichmar, Daniela et al. (eds.). 2009. *Science in the Spanish and Portuguese Empires, 1500–1800*. Stanford: Stanford University Press.

Bleienstein, Fritz. 1969. *Johannes Quidort von Paris. Über königliche und päpstliche Gewalt.* Stuttgart: Klett.

Bley, Matthias, Nikolas Jaspert, and Stefan Köck (eds.). 2015. *Discourses of Purity in Transcultural Perspective (300–1600).* Leiden: Brill.

Blickle, Peter. 1981. *The Revolution of 1525: The German Peasants' War from a New Perspective.* Trans. Thomas A. Brady and H. C. Erik Midelfort. Baltimore: Johns Hopkins University Press.

———. 1998. *From the Communal Reformation to the Revolution of the Common Man.* Leiden: Brill.

Bloch, Herbert. 1982. "The New Fascination with Ancient Rome." In Benson/Constable 1982, 615–636.

Blumenberg, Hans. 1976. *Aspekte der Epochenschwelle. Cusaner und Nolaner.* Frankfurt: Suhrkamp.

———. 1987. *The Genesis of the Copernican World.* Trans. Robert M. Wallace. Cambridge, MA: MIT Press.

———. 1996. *Shipwreck with Spectator: Paradigm of a Metaphor for Existence.* Trans. Steven Rendall. Cambridge, MA: MIT Press.

———. 2022. *The Readability of the World.* Trans. Robert Savage and David Roberts. Ithaca: Cornell University Press.

Blusch, Jürgen. 1994. "Rudolf Agricola als Pädagoge und seine Empfehlungen *De formando studio.*" In Wilhelm Kühlmann (ed), *Rudolf Agricola, 1444–1485. Protagonist des nordeuropäischen Humanismus zum 550. Geburtstag.* Bern: Peter Lang, 355–385.

Boas Hall, Marie. 1962. *The Scientific Renaissance.* London: Collins.

Boccaccio, Giovanni. 2013. *The Decameron.* Trans. Wayne A. Rebhorn. New York: Norton.

Böckenförde, Ernst Wolfgang. 2006. *Geschichte der Rechts- und Staatsphilosophie.* 2nd ed. Tübingen: Mohr Siebeck.

———. 2007. "Die Entstehung des Staates als Vorgang der Säkularisierung." In Ernst Wolfgang Böckenförde, *Der säkularisierte Staat. Sein Charakter, seine Rechtfertigung und seine Probleme im 21. Jahrhundert.* Munich: Carl Friedrich von Siemens Stiftung.

Bodde, Derk. 1991. *Chinese Thought, Society and Science: The Intellectual and Social Background of Science and Technology in Pre-Modern China.* Honolulu: University of Hawai'i Press.

Bodin, Jean. 1986. *Les six livres de la République.* Paris: Fayard.

Bol, Peter K. 1992. *'This Culture of Ours': Intellectual Transitions in T'ang and Sung China.* Stanford: Stanford University Press.

Bolgar, Robert R. 1954. *The Classical Heritage and Its Beneficiaries.* Cambridge: Cambridge University Press.

Bonaventure. 1891. "Collationes in Hexaëmeron." In *S. Bonaventurae opera omnia.* Vol. V: *Opuscula varia theologica.* Florence/Ad Claras Aquas (Quaracchi): Ex Typographia Collegii S. Bonaventurae, 329–449.

———. 1978. *The Soul's Journey into God, The Tree of Life, The Life of St. Francis.* Trans. and Intr. Ewert Cousins. New York: Paulist Press.

———. 2018. *Collations of the Hexaemeron: Conferences on Six Days of Creation: The Illuminations of the Church* (Works of St. Bonaventure, Vol. XVIII). Trans. Jay Hammond. St. Bonaventure, NY: Franciscan Institute Publications.

Bonaventure des Périers. 1999. *Cymbalum mundi.* Ed. Peter Hampshire Nurse. 4th ed. Geneva: Droz.

Bonoldi, Lorenzo, and Monica Centanni. 2015. "Catena d'onore, catena d'amore: Baldassarre Castiglione e il gioco della 's.'" *Engramma* 126, online review: ISSN 1826–901X (accessed May 18, 2015).

Borge, Francisco J. 2012. "'We (upon peril of my life) shall make the Spaniards ridiculous to all Europe': Richard Hakluyt's 'Discourse' of Spain." In Daniel Carey and Claire Jowitt (eds.), *Richard Hakluyt and Travel Writing in Early Modern Europe.* Farnham: Ashgate, 167–176.

Borgolte, Michael. 2002. *Europa entdeckt seine Vielfalt, 1050–1250.* Stuttgart: Ulmer UTB.

Börm, Henning. 2013. *Westrom. Von Honorius bis Justinian.* Stuttgart: W. Kohlhammer.

Born, Max (ed.). 1971. *The Born-Einstein Letters: Correspondence between Albert Einstein and Max and Hedwig Born from 1916 to 1955.* Trans. Irene Born. New York: Walker and Company.

Bornstein, Daniel E. 1993. *The Bianchi of 1399: Popular Devotion in Late Medieval Italy.* Ithaca: Cornell University Press.

Borst, Arno. 2012. *Die Katharer.* 2nd ed. Vienna: Karolinger Verlag.

Boshof, Egon. 2007. *Europa im 12. Jahrhundert. Auf dem Weg in die Moderne.* W. Kohlhammer: Stuttgart.

Bosl, Karl, and Eberhard Weis. 1976. *Die Gesellschaft in Deutschland.* Vol. I: *Von der fränkischen Zeit bis 1848.* Munich: Lurz, 143–146.

Bosworth, Clifford E. 1987. "Aš ʿarī, Abu'l-Ḥasan." In *Encyclopaedia Iranica.* Vol. II.7, 702–703.

Bouwsma, William J. 1968. *Venice and the Defense of Republican Liberty: Renaissance Values in the Age of Counterreformation.* Berkeley: University of California Press.

———. 2000. *The Waning of the Renaissance, 1550–1640.* New Haven: Yale University Press.

Branca, Vittore. 1990. *Boccaccio medievale e nuovi studi sul* Decameron. 7th ed. Florence: Sansoni.

Brandi, Karl. 1937. *Kaiser Karl V. Werden und Schicksal einer Persönlichkeit und eines Weltreichs.* Munich: Bruckmann.

Braudel, Fernand. 1967. *Civilisation matérielle et capitalisme (XVe-XVIIIe siècle).* Vol. I. Paris: A. Colin.

———. 1995. *The Mediterranean and the Mediterranean World in the Age of Philip II.* Trans. Siân Reynolds. Vol. I. Berkeley: University of California Press.

Braudel, Fernand, Georges Duby, and Maurice Aymard. 2000. *Die Welt des Mittelmeeres. Zur Geschichte und Geographie kultureller Lebensformen.* 5th ed. Frankfurt: Fischer.

Braun, Karl-Heinz et al. (eds.). 2013. *Das Konstanzer Konzil, 1414–1418. Weltereignis des Mittelalters.* Darmstadt: Theiss.

Bray, Francesca. 1994. *The Rice Economies: Technology and Development in Asian Societies.* Berkeley: University of California Press.

———. 2000a. *Technology and Society in Ming China (1368–1644).* Washington, D.C.: American Historical Association, 2000.

Bray, Massimo (ed.). 2000b. *Enciclopedia dei Papi.* Vol. III: *I papi da Pietro a Francesco.* Rome: Istituto della Enciclopedia Italiana.

Brecht, Martin. 1981–1987. *Martin Luther.* 3 vols. Stuttgart: Calwer Verlag.

Bredekamp, Horst. 1991. *Vicino Orsini und der heilige Wald von Bomarzo. Ein Fürst als Künstler und Anarchist.* 2nd ed. Worms: Werner.

Brendecke, Arndt. 1999. *Die Jahrhundertwenden. Eine Geschichte ihrer Wahrnehmung und Wirkung.* Frankfurt: Campus.

———. 2016. *The Empirical Empire: Spanish Colonial Rule and the Politics of Knowledge.* Munich: De Gruyter.

Brennan, Tad. 2005. *The Stoic Life.* Oxford: Oxford University Press.

Brentjes, Sonja. 2012. "The Prison of Categories—'Decline' and Its Company." In Felicitas Opwis and David Reisman (eds.), *Islamic Philosophy, Theology, and Science.* Leiden: Brill, 131–156.

Bresc-Bautier, Geneviève. "I marmi." In *RIE* IV, 283–308.

Bretone, Mario. 1987. *Storia del diritto romano.* Bari: Laterza.

Briggs, Asa, and Peter Burke. 2010. *A Social History of the Media: From Gutenberg to the Internet.* 4th ed. Cambridge: Polity.

Bright, Timothy. 1940. *A Treatise of Melancholie.* New York: Columbia University Press.

Brincken, Anna-Dorothee von den. 1967. "Die universalhistorischen Vorstellungen des Johann von Marignola OFM. Der einzige mittelalterliche Weltchronist mit Fernostkenntnis." *Archiv für Kulturgeschichte* 49, 297–339.

Bringmann, Klaus. 2008. *Römische Geschichte. Von den Anfängen bis zur Spätantike.* 10th ed. Munich: C. H. Beck.

Brinker, Helmut. 2009. *Die chinesische Kunst.* Munich: C. H. Beck.

Brochlos, Astrid. 2001. *Grundherrschaft in Japan. Entstehung und Struktur des Minase no shô.* Wiesbaden: Harrassowitz.

Brokaw, Cynthia, and Peter Kornicki (eds.). 2013. *The History of the Book in East Asia.* London: Routledge.

Brömer, Rainer. 2012. "The Nature of the Soul and the Passage of Blood through the Lungs: Galen, Ibn al-Nafîs, Servetus, İtaki, 'Aṭṭār." In Manfred Horstmannshoff, Helen King, and Claus Zittel (eds.), *Blood, Sweat and Tears: The Changing Concepts of Physiology from Antiquity into Early Modern Europe.* Leiden: Brill, 339–362.

Brook, Timothy. 1998. *The Confusions of Pleasure: Commerce and Culture in China.* Berkeley: University of California Press.

———. 2010. *The Troubled Empire: China in the Yuan and Ming Dynasties.* Cambridge, MA: Belknap Press.

Brooks, Philip. 2005. *The Mayflower Compact.* Minneapolis: Compass Point Books.

Brower, Jeffrey E., and Kevin Guilfoy (eds.). 2004. *The Cambridge Companion to Abelard.* Cambridge: Cambridge University Press.

Brown, Alison. 1992. *The Medici in Florence: The Exercise and Language of Power.* Florence: Olschki.

———. 2010. "Philosophy and Religion in Machiavelli." In John M. Najemy (ed.), *The Cambridge Companion to Machiavelli.* Cambridge: Cambridge University Press, 157–172.

———. 2011. *The Return of Lucretius to Renaissance Florence.* Cambridge, MA: Harvard University Press.

Brucker, Gene Adam. 1987. *The Civic World of Early Renaissance Florence.* Princeton: Princeton University Press.

Brückner, Wolfgang. 2013. *Bilddenken. Mensch und Magie oder Missverständnisse der Moderne.* Münster: Waxmann.

Bruni, Leonardo. 1996. *Opere letterarie e politiche.* Ed. Paolo Viti. Turin: UTET.

Brüning, Alfons. 2008. *Unio non est unitas. Polen-Litauens Weg im konfessionellen Zeitalter (1569–1648).* Wiesbaden: Harrassowitz.

Brunner, Otto et al. (eds.). 2004. *Geschichtliche Grundbegriffe.* 8 vols. Stuttgart: Klett-Cotta.

Bruno, Giordano. 1588. *Oratio valedictoria a Jordano Bruno Nolano D. habita (. . .).* Wittenberg: Zacharias Crato.

———. 1969. *Das Aschermittwochsmahl.* Trans. Ferdinand Fellmann. Introduction by Hans Blumenberg. Frankfurt: Insel.

———. 1992. *The Expulsion of the Triumphant Beast.* Ed. and trans. Arthur D. Imerti. Lincoln: University of Nebraska Press.

———. 2003. *The Cabala of Pegasus.* Trans. Sidney L. Sondergard and Madison U. Sowell. New Haven: Yale University Press.

Bucaille, Maurice. 1978. *The Bible, the Qu'ran and Science: The Holy Scriptures Examined in the Light of Modern Science.* Indianapolis: American Trust Publication.

Bucciantini, Massimo. 2003. *Galileo e Keplero. Filosofia, cosmologia e teologia nell'Età della controriforma.* Turin: Einaudi.

Bucciantini, Massimo, Michele Camerota, and Sophie Roux (eds.). 2007. *Mechanics and Cosmology in the Medieval and Early Modern Period.* Florence: Olschki.

Buck, August. 1969. "Einleitung." In Buck (ed.), *Zu Begriff und Problem der Renaissance.* Darmstadt: WBG, 1–36.

———. 1985. *Machiavelli.* Darmstadt: WBG.

Buck, Thomas Martin (ed.). 2010. *Chronik des Konstanzer Konzils 1414–1418 von Ulrich Richental.* Ostfildern: Thorbecke.

Bücking, Jürgen. 1978. *Michael Gaismair, Reformer, Sozialrebell, Revolutionär. Seine Rolle im Tiroler 'Bauernkrieg' (1525–32).* Stuttgart: Klett-Cotta.

Bullegas, Sergio. 1993. *Angelo Beolco. La lingua contestata, il teatro violato, la scena imitata.* Alessandria: Edizioni dell'Orso.

Bulliet, Richard W. 1979. *Conversion to Islam in the Medieval Period: An Essay in Quantitative History.* Cambridge, MA: Harvard University Press.

Bullough, Donald A. 1991. *Carolingian Renewal: Sources and Heritage.* Manchester: Manchester University Press.

———. 1993. "What Has Ingeld to Do with Lindisfarne?" *Anglo-Saxon England* 22, 93–125.

Bumke, Joachim. 1986. *Höfische Literatur und Gesellschaft im hohen Mittelalter.* 2 vols. 2nd ed. Munich: dtv.

Buonarroti, Michelangelo. 1991. *The Poetry of Michelangelo: An Annotated Translation.* Trans. James M. Saslow. New Haven: Yale University Press.

Burckhardt, Jacob. 2002. *The Civilization of the Renaissance in Italy.* Trans. S. G. C. Middlemore. New York: Modern Library.

Buringh, Eltjo, and Jan Luiten van Zanden. 2009. "Charting the 'Rise of the West': Manuscripts and Printed Books in Europe, a Long-Term Perspective from the Sixth through Eighteenth Centuries." *Journal of Economic History* 69, 409–445.

Burke, Peter. 1972. *Culture and Society in Renaissance Italy, 1420–1540.* London: Batsford.

———. 1982. *Montaigne.* New York: Hill and Wang.

———. 1993. *The Art of Conversation.* Ithaca: Cornell University Press.

———. 1995. *The Fortunes of the Courtier: The European Reception of Castiglione's* Cortegiano. Cambridge: Polity Press.

———. 2016. *Hybrid Renaissance: Culture, Language, Architecture.* Budapest: Central European University Press.

Burkert, Walter. 1987. *Anthropologie des religiösen Opfers.* Munich: Carl-Friedrich-von-Siemens-Stiftung.

———. 2003. *Die Griechen und der Orient. Von Homer bis zu den Magiern.* Munich: C. H. Beck.

Burkhardt, Johannes. 2002. *Das Reformationsjahrhundert. Deutsche Geschichte zwischen Medienrevolution und Institutionenbildung, 1517–1617.* Stuttgart: Kohlhammer.

Burmeister, Karl Heinz. 1967. *Georg Joachim Rhetikus, 1514–1574. Eine Bio-Bibliographie.* 3 vols. Wiesbaden: Guido Pressler.

Burns, Dylan. 2006. "The Chaldean Oracles of Zoroaster, Hekate's Couch and Platonic Orientalism in Psellos and Plethon." *Aries* 6:2, 158–179.

Burns, Howard. "Castelli travestiti? Ville e residenze di campagna nel Rinascimento italiano." In *RIE* VI, 465–545.

Burns, James H. 2010. *The Cambridge History of Medieval Political Thought, c. 350–c. 1450.* 7th ed. Cambridge: Cambridge University Press.

Burns, Robert I. 2001. "Paper Comes to the West, 800–1400." In Uta Lindgren (ed.), *Europäische Technik im Mittelalter. Tradition und Innovation. 800 bis 1400.* 4th ed. Berlin: Gebrüder Mann, 413–422.

Bury, Richard de. 2013. *Philobiblon: A Treatise on the Love of Books.* Cambridge: Cambridge University Press.

Busbecq, Ogier Ghislain de. 2005. *The Turkish letters of Ogier Ghislain de Busbecq, Imperial Ambassador at Constantinople 1554–1562.* Trans. Edward Seymour Forster. Baton Rouge: Louisiana State University Press.

Busch, Jörg W. 2011. *Die Herrschaften der Karolinger 714–911.* Munich: Oldenbourg.

Busche, Hubertus. 1997. *Leibniz' Weg ins perspektivische Universum. Eine Harmonie im Zeitalter der Berechnung.* Hamburg: Meiner.

Buswell, Robert W. (ed.). 2004. *Encyclopedia of Buddhism*. New York: Macmillan Library Reference.

Butler, Elizabeth M. 1998. *The Fortunes of Faust*. University Park: Penn State University Press.

Butterfield, Herbert. 1973. *The Origins of Modern Science, 1300–1800*. London: Bell.

Buzás, Ladislaus. 1975. *Deutsche Bibliotheksgeschichte des Mittelalters*. Wiesbaden: Reichert.

Cabanel, Patrick. 2012. *Une histoire des protestants en France (XVIe-XXIe siècle)*. Fayard: Paris.

Cadamosto, Alvise. 1550. "Navigationi." In Giovanni Battista Ramusio. *Primo volume delle navigationi et viaggi. . . .* Venice: Eredi di Lucantonio Giunti.

Caferro, William. 2006. *John Hawkwood: An English Mercenary in Fourteenth-Century Italy*. Baltimore: Johns Hopkins University Press.

Caliari, Pietro. 1888. *Paolo Veronese, sua vita e sue opere*. Rome: Forzani.

Cameron, Alan. 1984. "The Latin Revival of the Fourth Century." In Treadgold 1984b, 42–58.

Cameron, Averil. 1993. *The Mediterranean World in Late Antiquity AD 365–600*. London: Routledge.

Camerota, Michele. 2004. *Galileo Galilei e la cultura scientifica nell'età della controriforma*. Rome: Salerno Editrice.

Campanella, Tommaso. 1977. *Articuli prophetales*. Ed. Germana Ernst. Florence: La Nuova Italia.

———. 1981. *The City of the Sun*. Ed. and trans. Daniel J. Donno. Berkeley: University of California Press.

———. 1992. *Apologia di Galileo. Tutte le lettere a Galileo Galilei e altri documenti*. Ed. Gibo Ditadi. Trans. Adriana Lotto. Este-Padua: Isonomia.

———. 2011. *Selected Philosophical Poems of Tommaso Campanella: A Bilingual Edition*. Ed. and trans. Sherry Roush. Chicago: University of Chicago Press.

Campanelli, Maurizio. 2019. "Marsilio Ficino's Portrait of Hermes Trismegistus and Its Afterlife." *Intellectual History Review* 29:1, 53–71.

Campbell, Gordon (ed.). 2019. *The Oxford Illustrated History of the Renaissance*. Oxford: Oxford University Press.

Campbell, Ian C. 1995. "The Lateen Sail in World History." *Journal of World History* 6:1, 1–23.

Campbell, Stephen J., and Stephen J. Milner (eds.). 2004. *Artistic Exchange and Cultural Translation in the Italian Renaissance City*. Cambridge: Cambridge University Press.

Camporesi, Piero. 1989. *Bread of Dreams: Food and Fantasy in Early Modern Europe*. Trans. David Gentilcore. Oxford: Polity Press.

Canizares-Esguerra, Jorge. 2004. "Iberian Science in the Renaissance: Ignored How Much Longer?" *Perspectives in Science* 12, 86–124.

Capelle, Wilhelm (ed.). 1968. *Die Vorsokratiker*. Stuttgart: Kröner.

Cappelli, Guido. 2014. "Pandoni, Porcelio." In *DBI* 80, 736–240.

Capra, Fritjof. 2007. *The Science of Leonardo da Vinci*. New York: Anchor.

Cardano, Girolamo. 2013. *Il Libro della mia vita*. Ed. Serafino Balduzzi, Milan: Luni.

Cardwell, Donald L. S. 1994. *The Fontana History of Technology*. London: Fontana.

Carmody, Francis. 1952. "The Planetary Theory of Ibn Rushd." *Osiris* 10, 556–586.

Caro, Annibale. 1574. *De le lettere familiari*. Vol. I. Venice: Aldo Manuzio.

Caroti, Stefano. 1987. "Nicole Oresme's Polemic Against Astrology in his 'Quodlibetica.'" In Curry 1987, 75–93.

Carreiro, Daniel. 2013. "The Dao Against the Tyrant: The Limitation of Power in the Political Thought of Ancient China." *Libertarian Papers* 5:1, 111–152.

Carrier, Martin. 2001. *Nikolaus Kopernikus*. Munich: C. H. Beck.

Carroll, Stuart. 2009. *Martyrs and Murderers: The Guise Family and the Making of Europe*. Oxford: Oxford University Press.

Caspar, Max. 1959. *Kepler*. Ed. and trans. C. Doris Hellman. London: Abelard–Schuman.

Cassiodorus Senator. 2014. *Einführung in die geistlichen und weltlichen Wissenschaften (Institutiones divinarum et saecularium litterarium)*. Ed. Andreas Pronay. Hildesheim: Georg Olms.

Cassirer, Ernst. 1967. "Mathematical Mysticism and Mathematical Science." In Ernan McMullin (ed.). *Galileo: Man of Science*. New York and London: Basic Books, 338–351.

Castiglione, Baldesar. 1976. *The Courtier*. Trans. George Bull. London: Penguin.

Castillo, Bernal Díaz de. 1984. *Historia verdadera de la conquista de la nueva España*. Ed. Miguel Léon-Portilla. 2 vols. Madrid: historia 16.

Catani, Marco, and Stefano Sandrone. 2015. *Brain Renaissance: From Vesalius to Modern Neuroscience*. Oxford: Oxford University Press.

Caterina di Siena. 1939–40. *Le lettere*. Ed. Pietro Misciatelli. 6 vols. Florence: Marzocco.

Catlos, Brian A., and Sharon Kinoshita (eds.). 2017. *Can We Talk Mediterranean? Conversations on an Emerging Field in Medieval and Early Modern Studies*. Cham: Palgrave Macmillan.

Catullus. 1861. *The Poems of Catullus*. Trans. Theodore Martin. London: Parker Son and Bourn West Strand.

Céard, Jean. 1977. *La Nature et les prodiges: l'insolite au XVIe siècle, en France*. Geneva: Droz.

Ceccopieri Baruti, Maria Vittoria (ed.). 1993. *Braccio da Montone e i Fortebracci, le compagnie di ventura nell' Italia del XV secolo*. Narni: Centro studi storici di Narni.

Celenza, Christopher S. 1999. *Renaissance Humanism and the Papal Curia: Lapo da Castiglionchio the Younger's* De curiae commodis. Ann Arbor: University of Michigan Press.

———. 2001. *Piety and Pythagoras in Renaissance Florence: The Symbolum Nesianum*. Leiden: Brill.

Celtis, Conrad. 2012. *Oden / Epoden / Jahrhundertlied: Libri Odarum quattuor, cum epodo et saeculari carmine (1513)*. Ed. and trans. Eckart Schäfer. 2nd. ed. Tübingen: Narr.

———. 1502. *Quattuor libri amorum*. Nuremberg: Sodalitas Celtica. https://www.bavarikon.de /object/BSB-HSS-00000BSB00007499?lang=de# (accessed July 18, 2022).

Cennini, Cennino. 1960. *The Craftsman's Handbook: The Italian* Il libro dell'arte. Trans. Daniel V. Thompson. New York: Dover.

Cerman, Markus. 2012. *Villagers and Lords in Eastern Europe, 1300–1800*. Basingstoke: Palgrave Macmillan.

Chaffee, John W., and Denis Twitchett (eds.). 2015. *The Cambridge History of China*. Vol. II. Cambridge: Cambridge University Press.

Chakrabarty, Dipesh. 2000. *Provincializing Europe: Postcolonial Thought and Historical Difference*. Princeton: Princeton University Press.

Chambers, Edmund K. 1930. *William Shakespeare: A Study of Facts and Problems*. 2 vols. Oxford: Clarendon.

Chandler, David. 2000. *A History of Cambodia*. 3rd ed. Boulder: Westview Press.

Chang, Carsun. 1962. *Wang-Yang Ming: Idealist Philosopher of Sixteenth-Century China*. Jamaica, NY: St. John's University Press.

Chang, Pin-tsun. 1994. "Work Ethics without Capitalism: The Paradox of Chinese Merchant Behaviour, c. 1500–1800." In Karl Anton Sprengard and Roderich Ptak (eds.), *Maritime Asia: Profit Maximisation, Ethics and Trade Structure c. 1300–1800*. Wiesbaden: Harrassowitz, 61–73.

Chaplin, Joyce E. 2012. *Round about the Earth: From Magellan to Orbit*. New York: Simon & Schuster.

Chartier, Roger. 1992. *L'ordre des livres: Lecteurs, auteurs, bibliothèques en Europe entre XIVe et XVIIIe siècle*. Aix-en-Provence: Alinéa.

Châtelier, Louis. 1989. *The Europe of the Devout: The Catholic Reformation and the Formation of a New Society*. Cambridge: Cambridge University Press.

Chaudhuri Kirti, N. 1985. *Trade and Civilization in the Indian Ocean: An Economic History from the Rise of Islam to 1750*. Cambridge: Cambridge University Press.

———. 1990. *Asia Before Europe: Economy and Civilization of the Indian Ocean from the Rise of Islam to 1750*. Cambridge: Cambridge University Press.

Chenu, Marie-Dominique. 1997. "The Platonisms of the Twelfth Century." In Marie-Domique Chenu, *Nature, Man, and Society in the Twelfth Century: Essays on New Theological Perspectives in the Latin West*. Ed. and trans. Jerome Taylor and Lester K. Little. Toronto: University of Toronto Press, Medieval Academy of America, 49–98.

Chia, Lucille. 2013. "*Mashaben*: Commercial Publishing in Jianyang from the Song to the Ming." In Brokaw/Kornicki 2013, 117–173.

Childress, Diana. 2008. *Johannes Gutenberg and the Printing Press*. Minneapolis: Twenty-First Century Books.

Cieza de León, Pedro. 1984. *La crónica del Perú*. Ed. Manuel Ballesteros. Madrid: historia 16.

Cipolla, Carlo M. 1974. *The Fontana Economic History of Europe: The Sixteenth and Seventeenth Centuries*. Glasgow: Collins.

Ciriacono, Salvatore. "Trasmissione tecnologica e sistemi idraulici." In *RIE* III, 439–456.

Chow, Kai-Wing. 2004. *Publishing, Culture, and Power in Early Modern China*. Stanford: Stanford University Press.

Chrétien de Troyes. 1966. *Cligés: A Romance*. Trans. L. J. Gardiner. New York: Cooper Square Publishers.

Chua, Amy. 2007. *Day of Empire: How Hyperpowers Rise to Global Dominance—and Why They Fall*. New York: Doubleday.

Church, Sally K. 2005. "The Colossal Ships of Zheng He: Image or Reality?" In Claudine Salmon and Roderich Ptak (eds.), *Zheng He: Images & Perceptions, Bilder & Wahrnehmungen*. Wiesbaden: Harrassowitz, 155–176.

Ciggaar, Krijnie N. 1996. *Western Travellers to Constantinople. The West and Byzantium, 962–1204*. Leiden: Brill.

Ćirković, Sima. 2004. *The Serbs*. Malden: Blackwell.

Clark, Gregory. 2007. *A Farewell to Alms: A Brief Economic History of the World*. Princeton: Princeton University Press.

Clarke, Angus G. 1987. "Metoposcopy: An Art to Find the Mind's Construction in the Forehead." In Curry 1987, 171–195.

Classen, Albrecht (trans.). 2008. *The Poems of Oswald von Wolkenstein: An English Translation of the Complete Works (1376/77–1445)*. New York: Palgrave Macmillan.

Classen, Peter. 1981. "Die geistesgeschichtliche Lage. Anstöße und Möglichkeiten." In Peter Weimar, *Die Renaissance der Wissenschaften im 12. Jahrhundert*. Zurich: Artemis und Winkler, 11–32.

———. 1982. "Res Gestae, Universal History, Apocalypse. Visions of Past and Future." In Benson/Constable 1982, 387–417.

Clauss, Manfred. 2007. *Konstantin der Große und seine Zeit*. 3rd ed. Munich: C. H. Beck.

Clavelin, Maurice. 1974. *The Natural Philosophy of Galileo: Essay on the Origin and Formation of Classical Mechanics*. Trans. Arnold J. Pomerans. Cambridge, MA: MIT Press.

Clavijo, Ruy González. 1993. *Clavijos Reise nach Samarkand 1403–1406*. Trans. Uta Lindgren. Munich: Institut für Geschichte der Naturwissenschaften.

Clayton, Martin, and Ron Philo. 2012. *Leonardo da Vinci, Anatomist*. London: Royal Collection Trust.

Cleanthes. *Hymn to Zeus*. Trans. M. A. C. Ellery. https://web.archive.org/web/20071224143142 /http://www.utexas.edu/courses/citylife/readings/cleanthes_hymn.html (accessed June 12, 2020).

Clegg, Cyndia Susan. 1997. *Press Censorship in Elizabethan England*. Cambridge: Cambridge University Press.

Clendinnen, Inga. 2003. *Ambivalent Conquests: Maya and Spaniard in Yucatan, 1517–1570*. 2nd ed. Cambridge: Cambridge University Press.

Clewing, Konrad, and Oliver Jens Schmitt (eds.). 2011. *Geschichte Südosteuropas. Vom frühen Mittelalter bis zur Gegenwart*. Regensburg: Pustet.

Clucas, Stephen (ed.). 2006. *John Dee: Interdisciplinary Studies in English Renaissance Thought*. Dordrecht: Springer.

Coby, Patrick J. 2009. *Thomas Cromwell: Machiavellian Statecraft and the English Reformation*. Lanham: Lexington Books.

Cochrane, Eric. 1981. *Historians and Historiography in the Italian Renaissance*. Chicago: University of Chicago Press.

Cohen, Floris. 1994. *The Scientific Revolution: A Historiographical Inquiry*. Chicago: University of Chicago Press.

———. 2010. *How Modern Science Came into the World: Four Civilizations, One 17th-Century Breakthrough*. Amsterdam: Amsterdam University Press.

Cohn, Norman. 1970. *The Pursuit of the Millennium: Revolutionary Millenarians and Mystical Anarchists of the Middle Ages*. Oxford: Oxford University Press.

Cohn, Samuel K., Jr. 2006. *Lust for Liberty: The Politics of Social Revolt in Medieval Europe, 1200–1425*. Cambridge, MA: Harvard University Press.

———. 2007. "After the Black Death: Labour Legislation and Attitudes Towards Labour in Late Medieval Western Europe." *Economic History Review* 60, 457–485.

———. 2013. *Popular Protest in Late Medieval English Towns*. Cambridge: Cambridge University Press.

Cole, Michael W. 2002. *Cellini and the Principles of Sculpture*. Cambridge: Cambridge University Press.

Coleman, David. 2003. *Creating Christian Granada: Society and Religious Culture in an Old-World Frontier City, 1492–1600*. Ithaca: Cornell University Press.

Colish, Marcia L. 1997. *Medieval Foundations of the Western Intellectual Tradition, 400–1400*. New Haven: Yale University Press.

Collard, Franck. 2002. "Paulus Aemilius' *De rebus gestis Francorum*. Diffusion und Rezeption eines humanistischen Geschichtswerks in Frankreich." In Helmrath/Muhlack/Walther 2002, 378–380.

Collet, Dominik. 2014. "Hungern und Herrschen. Umweltgeschichtliche Verflechtungen der Ersten Teilung Polens und der europäischen Hungerkrise 1770–72." *Jahrbücher für Geschichte Osteuropas* 62:2, 237–254.

Colón, Hernando. 1984. *Historia del Almirante*. Ed. Luis Arranz Márquez. Madrid: historia 16.

Colonna, Francesco. 1499. *Hypnerotomachia Poliphili*. Venice: Aldus Manutius.

Columbus, Christopher. 1893. *The Journal of Christopher Columbus (during his First Voyage, 1492–1493) and Documents relating to the Voyages of John Cabot and Gaspar Corte Real*. Trans. Clements R. Markham, London: Hakluyt Society.

Commynes, Philippe de. 1912. *The Memoirs of Philip de Commines*. Ed. Andrew Scroble. Vol. II. London: G. Bell & Sons.

———. 2007. *Mémoires*. Ed. Joël Blanchard. 2 vols. Geneva: Droz.

Compagnon, Antoine. 2019. *A Summer with Montaigne: On the Art of Living Well*. Trans. Tina Kover. London: Europa Editions.

Condivi de la Ripa, Ascanio. 1553. *Vita di Michelagnolo Buonarroti raccolta per Ascanio Transone*. Ed. Charles Davis. Rome: Antonio Blado. http://archiv.ub.uni-heidelberg.de/artdok /volltexte/2009/714/ (accessed July 16, 2022).

Conermann, Stephan. 2006. *Das Mogulreich. Geschichte und Kultur des muslimischen Indien*. Munich: C. H. Beck.

Connah, Graham. 2001. *African Civilizations: An Archaeological Perspective*. 2nd ed. Cambridge: Cambridge University Press.

———. 2016. *African Civilizations: An Archaeological Perspective*. 3rd ed. Cambridge: Cambridge University Press.

Connors, Joseph, and Angela Dressen. "Biblioteche: l'architettura e l'ordinamento del sapere." In *RIE* VI, 199–228.

Cook, Theodore Andrea. 2001. *Old Provence*. New York: Interlink Books.

Copenhaver, Brian B. 1992. *The Greek Corpus Hermeticum and the Latin Asclepius*. Cambridge: Cambridge University Press.

———. 2015. *Magic in Western Culture: From Antiquity to the Enlightenment*. Cambridge: Cambridge University Press.

Copernicus, Nicolaus. 1949. *De revolutionibus orbium coelestium libri sex*. Ed. Franz Zeller and Karl Zeller. Munich: Oldenbourg.

———. 1966. *Erster Entwurf seines Weltsystems sowie eine Auseinandersetzung Johannes Keplers über die Bewegung der Erde*. Ed. Fritz Rossmann. Darmstadt: WBG.

———. 1976. *On the Revolutions of the Heavenly Spheres*. Ed. and trans. A. M. Duncan. Newton Abbot: David & Charles.

———. 1984. *De revolutionibus libri sex*. Ed Heribert Maria Nobis/Bernhard Sticker. Hildesheim: Gerstenberg.

Coquelines, Charles (ed.). 1733/1964. *Magnum Bullarium Romanum*. Rome, 1733. Facsimile reprint: Graz: Akademische Druck- u. Verlagsanstalt, 1964.

Cordes, Christian. 2011. "Emergente kulturelle Phänomene und ihre kognitiven Grundlagen." In Greve/Schnabel 2011, 346–371.

Corwin, Lucille. 2008. "*Le Istitutioni Harmoniche* of Gioseffo Zarlino, Part 1: A Translation with Introduction." PhD Dissertation: City University of New York.

Costambeys, Marios, Matthew Innes, and Simon MacLean. 2011. *The Carolingian World*. Cambridge: Cambridge University Press.

Cotroneo, Girolamo. 1971. *I trattatisti dell'ars historica*. Naples: Giannini.

Cottingham, John (ed.). 1995. *The Cambridge Companion to Descartes*. Cambridge: Cambridge University Press.

Cox, Virginia. 1992. *The Renaissance Dialogue: Literary Dialogue in its Social and Political Context, Castiglione to Galileo*. Cambridge: Cambridge University Press.

———. 2017. "Dialogue." In Victoria Moul (ed.), *A Guide to Neo-Latin Literature*. Cambridge: Cambridge University Press, 289–307.

Couliano, Ioan-Peter. 1987. *Eros and Magic in the Renaissance*. Trans. Margaret Cook. 2nd ed. Chicago: University of Chicago Press.

Crane, Howard and Esra Akin. 2006. *Sinan's Autobiographies: Five Sixteenth-Century Texts*. Leiden: Brill.

Crone, Patricia. 2004. *God's Rule: Government and Islam*. New York: Columbia University Press.

———. 2005. *Medieval Islamic Political Thought*. Rev. ed. Edinburgh: Edinburgh University Press.

Crosby, Alfred W. 1972. *The Columbian Exchange: Biological and Cultural Consequences of 1492*. Westport: Greenwood.

———. 1997. *The Measure of Reality: Quantification and Western Society, 1250–1600*. Cambridge: Cambridge University Press.

———. 2004. *Ecological Imperialism: The Biological Expansion of Europe*. 2nd ed. Cambridge: Cambridge University Press.

Cross, Richard. 2014. "Medieval Theories of Haecceity." In *Stanford Encyclopedia of Philosophy* (Summer 2014 Edition). http://plato.stanford.edu/archives/sum2014/entries/medieval-haecceity/ (accessed May 29, 2021).

Cross, Samuel Hazzard, and Olgerd P. Sherbowitz-Wetzor (eds. and trans.). 1953. *The Russian Primary Chronicle: Laurentian Text*. Cambridge, MA: Medieval Academy of America.

Crouzet, Denis. 1998. *La sagesse et le malheur. Michel de l'Hospital, chancellier de France*. Seyssel: Champ Vallon.

Crummey, Robert O. 1987. *The Formation of Muscovy, 1304–1613*. London: Longman.

Csikzentmihalyi, Mihály. 1996. *Creativity: Flow and the Psychology of Discovery and Invention*. New York: HarperCollins.

Cunningham, Andrew. 1997. *The Anatomical Renaissance: The Resurrection of the Anatomical Projects of the Ancients*. Aldershot: Scholar Press.

Cunningham, Andrew, and Ole Peter Grell (eds.). 2000. *The Four Horsemen of the Apocalypse: Religion, War, Famine, Death in Reformation Europe*. Cambridge: Cambridge University Press.

Curry, Patrick (ed.). 1987. *Astrology, Science and Society: Historical Essays*. Woodbridge: Boydell Press.

Cursi, Marco. 2007. *Il Decameron: scritture, scriventi, lettori. Storia di un testo*. Rome: Viella.

Curta, Florin. 2006. *Southeastern Europe in the Middle Ages, 500–1250*. Cambridge: Cambridge University Press.

Curtius, Ernst Robert. 2013. *European Literature and the Latin Middle Ages*. Trans. Willard R. Trask. Intr. Colin Burrow. Princeton: Princeton University Press.

Dahm, Bernhard. 2004. "Handel und Herrschaft im Grenzbereich des Indischen Ozeans." In Rothermund/Weigelin-Schwiedrzik 2004, 105–143.

Dale, Sharon, Alison Williams Lewin, and Duane J. Osheim (eds.). 2009. *Chronicling History: Chroniclers and Historians in Medieval and Renaissance Italy*. University Park: Penn State University Press.

Dale, Stephen Frederic. 2004. *The Garden of the Eight Paradises: Babur and the Culture of Empire in Central Asia, Afghanistan and India, 1438–1530*. Leiden: Brill.

Dall'Asta, Matthias. 2008. *Philosoph, Magier, Scharlatan und Antichrist. Zur Rezeption von Philostrats Vita Apollonii in der Renaissance*. Winter: Heidelberg.

Dandelet, Thomas James. 2014. *The Renaissance of Empire in Early Modern Europe*. Cambridge: Cambridge University Press.

Daniels, Tobias. 2014. "Die italienischen Mächte und der Basler Konzilsversuch des Andreas Jamometic." *Zeitschrift der Savigny-Stiftung für Rechtsgeschichte, Kan. Abt.* 131, 339–367.

Darling, Linda T. 1996. *Revenue-Raising and Legitimacy: Tax-Collection and Finance Administration in the Ottoman Empire 1560–1600*. Leiden: Brill.

Darlington, Oscar G. 1947. "Gerbert, the Teacher." *American Historical Review* 52:3, 456–476.

Darwin, John. 2007. *After Tamerlane: The Global History of Empires Since 1405*. London: Allen Lane.

Daston, Lorraine. 2011. "The Empire of Observation, 1600–1800." In Daston/Lunbeck 2011, 81–113.

Daston, Lorraine, and Elizabeth Lunbeck (eds.). 2011. *Histories of Scientific Observation*. Chicago: University of Chicago Press.

Daston, Lorraine, and Katherine Park. 2001. *Wonders and the Order of Nature, 1150–1750*. New York: Zone Books.

Davidson, Basil. 1964. *The African Past: Chronicles from Antiquity to Modern Times*. Boston: Little, Brown.

Davies, Norman. 1984. *Heart of Europe: A Short History of Poland*. Oxford: Clarendon Press.

Davis, Richard W. (ed). 1995. *The Origins of Modern Freedom in the West*. Stanford: Stanford University Press.

Dedekind, Friedrich. 1551. *Grobianus. Von groben sitten und unhöflichen geberden*. Trans. Caspar Scheidt. Frankfurt: Christian Egenolff.

De la Mare, A. C. 1977. "Humanistic Script: The First Ten Years." In Fritz Krafft and Dieter Wuttke (eds.), *Das Verhältnis der Humanisten zum Buch*. Boppard: Boldt, 89–110.

Dellaneva, Joann (ed.). 2007. *Ciceronian Controversies*. Trans. Brian Duvick. Cambridge, MA: Harvard University Press.

Delogu, Daisy, Emma Cayley, and Joan E. McRae. 2015. *A Companion to Alain Chartier (c. 1385–1430): Father of French Eloquence*. Leiden: Brill.

Delumeau, Jean. 1978. *La Peur en Occident (XIVe-XVIIIe siècles). Une cité assiégée*. Paris: Fayard.

Demandt, Alexander. 2011. *Philosophie der Geschichte. Von der Antike bis zur Gegenwart*. Cologne: Böhlau.

Dembek, Arne. 2010. *William Tyndale (1491–1536). Reformatorische Theologie als kontextuelle Schriftauslegung*. Tübingen: Mohr Siebeck.

Deming, David. 2016. *Science and Technology in World History*. Vol. IV. Jefferson: McFarland & Co.

Deng, Gang. 1999. *Maritime Sector, Institutions, and Sea Power of Premodern China*. Westport: Greenwood.

Dent, Chris. 2009. "'Generally Inconvenient': The 1624 Statute of Monopolies as Political Compromise." *Melbourne Law Review* 33:2, 415–453.

Denzinger, Heinrich and Peter Hünermann (eds.). 2009. *Kompendium der Glaubensbekenntnisse und kirchlichen Lehrentscheidungen*. 42nd ed. Freiburg: Herder.

De Pace, Anna. 1993. *Le matematiche e il mondo: Ricerche su un dibattito in Italia nella seconda metà del Cinquecento*. Milan: FrancoAngeli.

Deppermann, Klaus. 1979. *Melchior Hofmann. Soziale Unruhen und apokalyptische Visionen im Zeitalter der Reformation*. Göttingen: Vandenhoeck & Ruprecht.

Derviş, Kemal. 2006. "Foreword." In *Arab Human Development Report 2005*. New York: United Nations Publications.

Descartes, René. 1973. *Œuvres*. Ed. Charles Adam and Paul Tannery. 12 vols. Paris: Librairie Philosophique J. Vrin.

De Vries, Jan. 2003. "Connecting Europe and Asia: A Quantitative Analysis of the Cape Route Trade, 1497–1795." In Dennis O. Flynn, Arturo Giraldez, and Richard von Glahn (eds.), *Global Connections and Monetary History, 1470–1800*. Aldershot: Taylor & Francis, 35–106.

———. 2015. "Understanding Eurasian Trade in the Era of the Trading Companies." In Maxine Berg et al. (eds.), *Goods from the East: Trading Eurasia, 1600–1800*. Houndmills, Basingstoke: Palgrave Macmillan, 7–39.

De Vries, Jan, and Ad van der Woude. 1997. *The First Modern Economy: Success, Failure, and Perseverance of the Dutch Economy, 1500–1815*. Cambridge: Cambridge University Press.

Diamond, Jared. 1997. *Collapse: How Societies Choose to Fail or Succeed*. New York: Viking.

———. 2005. *Guns, Germs and Steel: The Fates of Human Societies*. New York: W.W. Norton.

Dicke, Gerd. 1994. *Heinrich Steinhöwels Esopus und seine Fortsetzer. Untersuchungen zu einem Bucherfolg der Frühdruckzeit*. Tübingen: Niemeyer.

Dickens, Arthur G. 1974. *The German Nation and Martin Luther*. London: Edward Arnold.

Didi-Huberman, Georges. 1995. *Fra Angelico: Dissemblance and Figuration*. Trans. Jane-Marie Todd. Chicago: University of Chicago Press.

Diels, Hermann. 1934–1935. *Die Fragmente der Vorsokratiker*. Ed. Walter Kranz. 3 vols. 5th ed. Berlin: Weidmann.

Dijksterhuis, Eduard Jan. 1961. *The Mechanization of the World Picture: Pythagoras to Newton*. Oxford: Oxford University Press.

Dinzelbacher, Peter. 2006. *Das fremde Mittelalter. Gottesurteil und Tierprozess*. Essen: Magnus.

———. 2008. *Europäische Mentalitätsgeschichte*. 2nd ed. Stuttgart: Kröner.

Dio Cassius. 1924. *Roman History*. Trans. Earnest Cary. Vol. VII. Cambridge, MA: Harvard University Press.

Diop, Cheikh Anta. 1987. *Precolonial Black Africa: A Comparative Study of the Political and Social Systems of Europe and Black Africa, from Antiquity to the Formation of Modern States*. Trans. Harold J. Salemson. Westport: Lawrence Hill Books.

Dioscorides. 1570. *Pedacio Dioscórides Anazarbeo, acerca de la materia medicinal y de los venenos mortíferos*. Salamanca: Mathías Gast.

Dirlik, Arif. 2015. "Revisioning Modernity: Modernity in Eurasian Perspectives." In Trakulhun/ Weber 2015, 143–177.

Disney, Anthony R. 2009. *A History of Portugal and the Portuguese Empire*. Vol. I. Cambridge: Cambridge University Press.

Di Teodoro, Francesco Paolo. 2020. *Lettera a Leone X di Raffaello e Baldassarre Castiglione*. Florence: Olschki.

Djebbar, Ahmed. 2005. *L'âge d'or des sciences arabes*. Paris: Le Pommier.

Dodds, Jerilynn, and Jenny H. Shaffer. 2001. "Die karolingische Renaissance." In Eduard Carbonell and Roberto Cassanelli (eds.), *Von Mohammed zu Karl dem Großen. Aufbruch ins Mittelalter*. Stuttgart: Theiss, 171–190.

Dohrn-van Rossum, Gerhard. 1992. *Die Geschichte der Stunde. Uhren und moderne Zeitordnungen*. Munich: Hanser.

Dollinger, Philippe. 1989. *Die Hanse*. 4th ed. Stuttgart: Kröner.

Dolza, Luisa. "*Utilitas et delectatio*: libri di tecniche e teatri di machine." In *RIE* III, 115–143.

Donne, John. 1959. *Devotions Upon Emergent Occasions*. Ann Arbor: University of Michigan Press.

Donner, Fred M. (ed.). 1981. *The Early Islamic Conquests*. Princeton: Princeton University Press.

Dopsch, Heinz. 2011. "Oswald von Wolkenstein und seine Zeit." In Müller/Springeth 2011, 1–13.

Dopsch, Heinz, Kurt Goldammer, and Peter F. Kramml (eds.). 1993. *Paracelsus: 1493–1541*. "*Keines andern Knecht. . . .*" Salzburg: Pustet.

Doren, Alfred. 1901–1908. *Studien aus der Florentiner Wirtschaftsgeschichte*. 2 vols. Stuttgart: J. G. Cotta'sche Buchhandlung Nachfolger.

Dorn, Harold. 1991. *The Geography of Science*. Baltimore: Johns Hopkins University Press.

Dougherty, M. V. (ed.). 2008. *Pico della Mirandola: New Essays*. Cambridge: Cambridge University Press.

Douthat, Ross. 2020. *The Decadent Society: How We Became the Victims of Our Own Success*. New York: Simon and Schuster.

Downing, Brian M. 1992. *The Military Revolution and Political Change: Origins of Democracy in Early Modern Europe*. Princeton: Princeton University Press.

Doyle, Michael W. 1984. *Empires*. Ithaca: Cornell University Press.

Drake, Stillman (trans.). 1957. *Discoveries and Opinions of Galileo*. Garden City: Doubleday & Company.

Dronke, Peter. 1982. "Profane Elements in Literature." In Benson/Constable 1982, 569–592.

Drücke, Simone. 2001. *Humanistische Laienbildung um 1500. Das Übersetzungswerk des rheinischen Humanisten Johann Gottfried*. Göttingen: Vandenhoeck & Ruprecht.

Druffel, August von et al. (ed.). 1873–1913. *Briefe und Akten zur Geschichte des sechzehnten Jahrhunderts. Mit besonderer Rücksicht auf Bayerns Fürstenhaus*. 6 vols. Munich: M. Rieger'sche Universitäts-Buchhandlung.

Du Bellay, Joachim. 1996. *Les Regrets précédé de Les Antiquités de Rome*. Paris: Gallimard.

Duby, Georges. 1981. *The Age of the Cathedrals: Art and Society, 980—1420*. Trans. Eleanor Levieux and Barbara Thompson. Chicago: University of Chicago Press.

———. 1990. *The Legend of Bouvines: War, Religion, and Culture in the Middle Ages*. Trans. Catherine Tihanyi. Berkeley: University of California Press.

Duchardt, Heinz. 1984. "Das Tunisunternehmen Karls V. 1535." *Mitteilungen des österreichischen Staatsarchivs* 37, 35–72.

Duchesne, Ricardo. 2011. *The Uniqueness of Western Civilization*. Leiden: Brill.

Ducheyne, Steffen. 2005. "Newton's Training in the Aristotelian Textbook Tradition: From Effects to Causes and Back." *History of Science* 43, 217–237.

Duczko, Wladyslaw. 2004. *Viking Rus: Studies on the Presence of Scandinavians in Eastern Europe.* Leiden: Brill.

Duffy, Eve M., and Alida Metcalf. 2012. *The Return of Hans Staden: A Go-Between in the Atlantic World.* Baltimore: Johns Hopkins University Press.

Duhem, Pierre. 1955. *Études sur Léonard de Vince: Ceux qu'il a lus et ceux qui l'ont vu. III. Les précurseurs parisiens de Galilée.* 2nd ed. Paris: A. Hermann et fils.

Dülmen, Richard van. 1974. *Das Täuferreich zu Münster 1534–1535.* Munich: dtv.

Dundas, Paul. 2002. *The Jains.* London: Routledge.

Dunlop, Anne. 2009. *Painted Palaces: The Rise of Secular Art in Early Renaissance Italy.* University Park: Penn State University Press.

Dunn, Alastair. 2002. *The Great Rising of 1381: The Peasants' Revolt and England's Failed Revolution.* Stroud: Tempus.

Dupré, Sven. 2003. "Galileo's Telescope." *Journal of the History of Astronomy* 34, 364–399.

Durán, Diego. 1971. *Book of the Gods and Rites and the Ancient Calendar.* Ed. and trans. Fernando Horcasitas and Doris Heyden. Norman: University of Oklahoma Press.

———. 1994. *The History of the Indies of New Spain.* Trans. Doris Heyden. Norman: University of Oklahoma Press.

Dürer, Albrecht. 1956–1969. *Schriftlicher Nachlaß.* Ed. Hans Rupprich. 3 vols. Berlin: Deutscher Verein für Kunstwissenschaft.

———. 2016. *Masters of Art—Albrecht Dürer.* Hastings, East Sussex: Delphi Classics.

Durot, Éric. 2012. *François de Lorraine, duc de Guise entre Dieu et le Roi.* Paris: Classiques Garnier.

Eamon, William. 1994. *Science and the Secrets of Nature: Books of Secrets in Medieval and Early Modern Culture.* Princeton: Princeton University Press.

Eamon, William, and Françoise Paheau. 1984. "The Accademia Segreta of Girolamo Ruscelli: A Sixteenth-Century Italian Scientific Society." *Isis* 75, 327–342.

Earle, Thomas F., and Kate Lowe. 2005. *Black Africans in Renaissance Europe.* Cambridge: Cambridge University Press.

Ebeling, Florian. 2009. *Das Geheimnis des Hermes Trismegistos. Geschichte des Hermetismus.* 2nd ed. Munich: C. H. Beck.

Ebrahim, Alireza. 2018/2021. "Dārā Shukūh." Trans. Shahram Khodaverdian et. al. In Wilferd Madelung and Farhad Daftary (eds.), *Encyclopaedia Islamica Online.* First online January 8, 2018; last update June 17, 2021. https://doi.org/10.1163/1875-9831_isla_COM_037182 (accessed November 10, 2024).

Ebrey, Patricia Buckley. 1991. *Confucianism and Family Rituals in Imperial China: A Social History of Writing about Rites.* Princeton: Princeton University Press.

——— (ed.). 1993. *Chinese Civilization: A Sourcebook.* 2nd ed. New York: The Free Press.

Edson, Evelyn. 2007. *The World Map, 1300–1492: The Persistence of Tradition and Transformation.* Baltimore: Johns Hopkins University Press.

Edwards, John. 1999. *The Spanish Inquisition.* Stroud: Tempus.

———. 2000. *The Spain of the Catholic Monarchs 1474–1520.* Oxford: Blackwell.

———. 2005. *Torquemada and the Inquisitors.* Stroud: Tempus.

Edwards, Mark. 2012. *Christians, Gnostics and Philosophers in Late Antiquity.* London: Routledge.

Edzard, Dietz-Otto. 2014. *Geschichte Mesopotamiens. Von den Sumerern bis zu Alexander dem Großen.* Munich: C. H. Beck.

Egel, Nikolaus Andreas. 2014. *Die Welt im Übergang. Der diskursive, subjektive und skeptische Charakter der Mappamondo des Fra Mauro.* Heidelberg: Winter.

Egger, Vernon O. 2004. *A History of the Muslim World to 1405: The Making of a Civilization.* Upper Saddle River: Pearson Prentice Hall.

Eggert, Marion. 2006. "Discovered Other, Recovered Self: Layers of Representation in an Early Travelogue on the West (*Xihai jiyou cao*, 1849)." In Joshua A. Fogel (ed.), *Traditions of East Asian Travel*. New York: Berghahn Books, 70–96.

Eggert, Marion et al. (eds.). 2004. Geschichte der chinesischen Literatur. Vol. IV. Munich: Saur.

Ehrenberg, Richard. 1922. *Das Zeitalter der Fugger. Geldkapital und Kreditverkehr im 16. Jahrhundert.* Jena: G. Fischer.

Eiche, Sabine (ed.). 1999. *Ordine et officij de casa de lo illustrissimo signor duca de Urbino*. Urbino: Accademia Raffaello.

Eiden, Herbert. 1995. '*In der Knechtschaft werdet ihr verharren. . . .' Ursachen und Verlauf des englischen Bauernaufstandes von 1381.* Trier: thf-Verlag.

Einhard. 1911. *Einhardi Vita Karoli Magni*. Post G. H. Perz recensuit G. Waitz. Curavit O. Holder-Egger. MGH SS rer. Germ. 25. 6th ed. Hanover/Leipzig: Hahn.

Eisenstadt, Shmuel N. 2000. "Multiple Modernities." *Daedalus* 129:1, 1–29.

Eisenstein, Elizabeth L. 1979. *The Printing Press as an Agent of Change: Communications and Cultural Transformations in Early Modern Europe*. 2 vols. Cambridge: Cambridge University Press.

Eisner, Martin. 2014. "In the Labyrinth of the Library: Petrarch's Cicero, Dante's Virgil, and the Historiography of the Renaissance." *Renaissance Quarterly* 67:3, 755–790.

Elias, Norbert. 2000. *The Civilizing Process: Sociogenetic and Psychogenetic Investigations*. Rev. ed. Oxford: Blackwell.

Elizabeth I. 2000. *Collected Works*. Ed. Leah S. Marcus et al. Chicago: University of Chicago Press.

Elkana, Yehuda. 1981. "A Programmatic Attempt at an Anthropology of Knowledge." In Everett Mendelsohn and Elkana Yehuda (eds.), *Sciences and Cultures: Anthropological and Historical Studies of the Sciences*. Dordrecht: Reidel, 1–76.

Elliott, John H. 1970. *The Old World and the New, 1492–1650*. Cambridge: Cambridge University Press.

———. 2006. *Empires of the Atlantic World: Britain and Spain in America, 1492–1830*. New Haven: Yale University Press.

Elton, Geoffrey. 1982. *The Tudor Constitution: Documents and Commentary*. 2nd ed. Cambridge: Cambridge University Press.

Elton, Geoffrey. 1991. *England Under the Tudors*. 3rd ed. London: Routledge.

Elvin, Mark. 1973. *The Pattern of the Chinese Past*. Stanford: Stanford University Press.

———. 2004. "Some Reflections on the 'Use of Styles of Scientific Thinking' to Disaggregate and Sharpen Comparisons between China and Europe." *History of Technology* 25, 53–103.

———. 2005. Review of Joseph Needham, *Science and Civilisation in China. Volume 7: The Social Background. Part 2, General Conclusions and Reflections*. In *China Review International* 12:2, 297–307.

Embree, Ainslie T., and Friedrich Wilhelm. 1967. *Indien. Geschichte des Subkontinents von der Induskultur bis zum Beginn der englischen Herrschaft*. Frankfurt: Fischer.

Emison, Patricia A. 2004. *Creating the 'Divine' Artist: From Dante to Michelangelo*. Leiden: Brill.

Enders, Markus. 2006. "Das Gespräch zwischen den Religionen bei Raimundus Lullus." In Speer/Wegener 2006, 194–214.

Engel, Pál. 2001. *The Realm of St. Stephen: A History of Medieval Hungary, 895–1526*. Trans. Tamás Pálosfalvi. London and New York: I. B. Tauris.

Ennen, Edith. 1987. *Die europäische Stadt des Mittelalters*. 4th ed. Göttingen: Vandenhoeck & Ruprecht.

Ennen, Edith. 1991. *Frauen im Mittelalter*. 4th ed. Munich: C. H. Beck.

Epstein, Stephan R. "L'economia italiana nel quadro europeo." In *RIE* IV, 3–47.

Epstein, Stephan R., and Maarten Prak. 2008. "Introduction." In Epstein and Prak, *Guilds, Innovation and the European Economy*. Cambridge: Cambridge University Press, 1–24.

Erasmus, Desiderius. 1917. *Complaint of Peace*. Chicago: Open Court.

———. 1965. *The Colloquies*. Trans. Craig R. Thompson. Chicago: University of Chicago Press.

Ercilla y Zúñiga, Alonso. 1993. *La Araucana*. Ed. Isaías Lerner. Madrid: Cátedra.

Erler, Michael. 2007. "Platon." In Flashar 1998–2007, Vol. II.2, 528–540.

Ernst, Germana. 1991. "Astrology, Religion and Politics in Counter-Reformation Rome." In Pumfrey/Rossi/Slawinski 1991, 249–273.

Ertl, Thomas. 2006. *Religion und Disziplin. Selbstdeutung und Weltordnung im frühen deutschen Franziskanertum*. Berlin: De Gruyter.

Esch, Arnold. 1969. *Bonifaz IX. und der Kirchenstaat*. Tübingen: Niemeyer.

———. 2008. *Landschaften der Frührenaissance. Auf Ausflug mit Pius II*. Munich: C. H. Beck.

———. 2014. *Die Lebenswelt des europäischen Spätmittelalters. Kleine Schicksale erzählt in Schreiben an den Papst*. Munich: C. H. Beck.

———. 2016. *Rom. Vom Mittelalter zur Renaissance*. Munich: C. H. Beck.

Esposito, John L. (ed.). 1999. *Oxford History of Islam*. Oxford: Oxford University Press.

Ess, Hans van. 2003. *Der Konfuzianismus*. Munich: C. H. Beck.

———. 2011. *Der Daoismus. Von Laozi bis heute*. Munich: C. H. Beck.

Ess, Josef van. 2017. *Theology and Society in the Second and Third Centuries of the Hijra: A History of Religious Thought in Early Islam*. Vol. V. Trans. John O'Kane and Gwendolin Goldbloom. Leiden: Brill.

Etting, Vivian. 2004. *Queen Margrethe I, 1353–1412, and the Founding of the Nordic Union*. Leiden: Brill.

Europe in the Renaissance: Metamorphoses, 1400–1600. 2016. Exhibition Catalogue. Berlin: Hatje Cantz.

Evans, Robert J. W. 1973. *Rudolf II and His World: A Study in Intellectual History, 1576–1612*. Oxford: Oxford University Press.

Fabian, Seth Boniface. 2014. "Cecco vs. Dante: Correcting the Comedy with Applied Astrology." PhD Dissertation, Columbia University.

Fairbank, John K., and Merle Goldman. 2005. *China: A New History*. 2nd ed. Cambridge, MA: Harvard University Press.

Fallows, David. 1987. *Dufay*. London: J. M. Dent & Sons, 1987.

Falola, Toyin and Kevin D. Roberts (eds.). 2008. *The Atlantic Worlds, 1450–2000*. Bloomington: Indiana University Press.

Fantoli, Annibale. 2003. *Galileo: For Copernicanism and for the Church*. 3rd ed. Vatican City: University of Notre Dame Press.

Fantoni, Marcello, Louisa C. Matthew, and Sara F. Matthews-Grieco (eds). 2003. *The Art Market in Italy, 15th–17th Centuries*. Modena: F. C. Panini.

al-Farabi, Abu Nasr. 1985. *Al-Farabi on the Perfect State: Abū Naṣr Al-Fārābī's Mabādi' Ārā Ahl al-Madīna al-Fāḍila*. Ed. Richard Walzer. Oxford: Clarendon Press.

Faroqhi, Suraiya. 2000. *Subjects of the Sultans: Culture and Daily Life in the Ottoman Empire*. Trans. Martin Bott. I. B. Tauris Publishers: London.

———. 2009. *The Ottoman Empire*. Trans. Shelley Frisch. Princeton: Markus Wiener.

Faure, David. 2007. *Emperor and Ancestor: State and Lineage in South China*. Stanford: Stanford University Press.

Favier, Jean. 2005. *Un roi de marbre. Philippe le Bel-Enguerrand de Marigny*. Paris: Fayard.

Fehérvari, Géza. 1971. "Harran." In Victor Louis Ménage (ed.), *Encyclopedia of Islam*. Vol. III. 2nd ed. Leiden: Brill, 227–230.

Fehling, Detlev. 1985. "Das Problem der Geschichte des griechischen Weltmodells vor Aristoteles." *Rheinisches Museum für Philologie* 128:3/4, 195–231.

Feingold, Mordechai. 1984. *The Mathematician's Apprenticeship: Science, University and Society in England, 1560–1640*. Cambridge: Cambridge University Press.

Feld, Helmut. 2006. *Ignatius von Loyola. Gründer des Jesuitenordens*. Böhlau: Weimar.

———. 2007. *Franziskus von Assisi und seine Bewegung*. 2nd ed. Darmstadt: WBG.

Feldbauer, Peter. 1995. *Die islamische Welt 600–1250. Ein Frühfall von Unterentwicklung?* Vienna: Promedia.

———. 2002. "Die islamische Stadt im 'Mittelalter.'" In Feldbauer/Mitterauer/Schwentker 2002, 79–106.

———. 2003. *Estado da India. Die Portugiesen in Asien, 1498–1620*. Vienna: Mandelbaum.

Feldbauer, Peter, and Gottfried Liedl. 2008. *Die islamische Welt 1000–1517. Wirtschaft. Gesellschaft. Staat*. Vienna: Mandelbaum.

Feldbauer, Peter, Michael Mitterauer, and Wolfgang Schwentker (eds.). 2002. *Die vormoderne Stadt. Asien und Europa im Vergleich*. Böhlau: Vienna.

Feldhay, Rivka. 1995. *Galileo and the Church: Political Inquisition or Critical Dialogue?* Cambridge: Cambridge University Press.

Fenn, Richard K. 1997. *The End of Time: Religion, Ritual and the Forging of the Soul*. Cleveland: Pilgrim.

Fenske, Hans et al. (eds.). 1981. *Geschichte der politischen Ideen. Von Homer bis zur Gegenwart*. Königstein: Athenäum.

Ferguson, Eugene S. 1992. *Engineering and the Mind's Eye*. Cambridge, MA: MIT Press.

Ferguson, Niall. 2011. *Civilization: The West and the Rest*. London: Allen Lane.

Ferguson, Wallace K. 1948. *The Renaissance in Historical Thought: Five Centuries of Interpretation*. Cambridge, MA: Riverside Press.

Fernández, Christian. 2004. *Inca Garcilaso: Imaginación, memoria, e identidad*. Lima: Fondo Editorial, Universidad Nacional Mayor de San Marcos.

Fernández-Armesto, Felipe. 2007. *Amerigo: The Man Who Gave His Name to America*. New York: Random House.

Fichtenau, Heinrich. 1998. *Heretics and Scholars in the High Middle Ages, 1000–1200*. Trans. Denise A. Kaiser. University Park: Pennsylvania State University Press.

Ficino, Marsilio. 1576/1959–1960. *Opera omnia*. 2 vols. Basel: Officina Henricpetrina, 1576. Facsimile reprint: Turin: Bottega d'Erasmo, 1559–1960.

———. 1985. *Commentary on Plato's Symposium on Love*. Ed. and trans. Sears Reynolds Jayne. Dallas: Spring Publications.

———. 1994. *Über die Liebe oer Platons Gastmahl*. Ed. Paul Richard Blum. Hamburg: Meiner.

Field, Arthur M. 1988. *The Origins of the Platonic Academy in Florence*. Princeton: Princeton University Press.

Field, Judith V. 1984. "Kepler's Rejection of Numerology." In Vickers 1984b, 284–290.

———. 1987. "Astrology in Kepler's Cosmology." In Curry 1987, 143–170.

———1997. *The Invention of Infinity: Mathematics and Art in the Renaissance*. Oxford: Oxford University Press.

Field, Judith V., and Frank A. J. L. James (eds.). 1993. *Renaissance and Revolution: Humanists, Scholars, Craftsmen and Natural Philosophers in Early Modern Europe*. Cambridge: Cambridge University Press.

Figliuolo, Bruno. 2002. "Die humanistische Historiographie in Neapel und ihr Einfluß auf Europa." In Helmrath/Muhlack/Walther 2002, 77–98.

Filipiak, Kai. 2008. *Krieg, Staat und Militär in der Ming-Zeit (1368–1644). Auswirkungen militärischer und bewaffneter Konflikte auf Machtpolitik und Herrschaftsapparat der Ming-Dynastie*. Wiesbaden: Harrassowitz.

Findlay, Ronald, and Kevin H. O'Rourke. 2007. *Power and Plenty: Trade, War, and the World Economy in the Second Millennium*. Princeton: Princeton University Press.

Findlen, Paula. 1993. "Humanism, Politics, and Pornography in Renaissance Italy." In Lynn Hunt (ed.), *The Invention of Pornography: Obscenity and the Origins of Modernity, 1500–1800*. New York: Zone Books, 49–108.

———. 1994. *Museums: Collecting, and Scientific Culture in Early Modern Italy*. Berkeley: University of California Press.

——— (ed.). 2004. *Athanasius Kircher: The Last Man Who Knew Everything*. London: Routledge.

Findley, Carter Vaughn. 2005. *The Turks in World History*. Oxford: Oxford University Press.

Fine, John V. A., Jr. 1983. *The Early Medieval Balkans: A Critical Survey from the Sixth to the Late Twelfth Century*. Ann Arbor: University of Michigan Press.

Finlay, Moses I., Denis Mack Smith, and Christopher Duggan. 1968. *A History of Sicily*. London: Chatto & Windus.

Finlay, Robert. 2000. "China, the West, and World History in Joseph Needham's *Science and Civilization in China*." *Journal of World History* 11, 265–304.

Firpo, Luigi. 1993. *Il processo di Giordano Bruno*. Rome: Salerno.

———. 1998. *I processi di Tommaso Campanella*. Rome: Salerno.

Flaig, Egon. 2013. *Die Mehrheitsentscheidung. Entstehung und kulturelle Dynamik*. Paderborn: Schöningh.

Flasch, Kurt. 1994. *Augustin. Einführung in sein Denken*. 2nd ed. Stuttgart: Reclam.

———. 1998. *Nikolaus von Kues. Geschichte einer Entwicklung. Vorlesungen zur Einführung in seine Philosophie*. Frankfurt: Klostermann.

———. 2007. *Dietrich von Freiberg. Philosophie, Theologie, Naturforschung um 1300*. Frankfurt: Klostermann.

———. 2011. *Das philosophische Denken im Mittelalter. Von Augustin zu Machiavelli*. Stuttgart: Reclam.

———. 2015. *Der Teufel und seine Engel. Die Neue Biographie*. Munich: C. H. Beck.

Flashar, Hellmut (ed.). 1998–2007. *Die Philosophie der Antike*. Vol. II in two parts. Basel: Schwabe.

———. 2013. *Aristoteles. Lehrer des Abendlandes*. Munich: C. H. Beck.

Fleck, Ludwik. 1979. *Genesis and Development of a Scientific Fact*. Trans. Frederick Bradley and Thaddeus J. Trenn. Chicago: University of Chicago Press.

Fletcher, Giles, the Elder. 1591/1996. *Of the Russe Common Wealth*. London: Thomas Charde, 1591. Facsimile reprint: Ed. Richard Pipes. Cambridge, MA: Harvard University Press, 1966.

Floerke, Hanns. 1906. *Die Fazetien des Poggio Fiorentino*. Munich: Georg Müller.

Fodor, Nóra. 2004. "Die Übersetzungen lateinischer Autoren durch M. Planudes." PhD Dissertation, University of Heidelberg.

Foltz, Richard. 1999. *Religions of the Silk Road: Overland Trade and Cultural Exchange from Antiquity to the Fifteenth century*. New York: St. Martin's Press.

Forke, Alfred. 1927. *Die Gedankenwelt des chinesischen Kulturkreises*. Munich: Oldenbourg.

Forrester, John M., and John Henry (eds.). 2005. *Jean Fernel's On the Hidden Causes of Things: Forms, Souls, and Occult Diseases in Renaissance Medicine*. Leiden: Brill.

Forschner, Maximilian. 2006. *Thomas von Aquin*. Munich: C. H. Beck.

Forst, Rainer. 2013. *Toleration in Conflict: Past and Present*. Cambridge: Cambridge University Press.

Fortescue, Sir John. 1997. *On the Laws and Governance of England*. Ed. Shelley Lockwood. Cambridge: Cambridge University Press.

Fortini Brown, Patricia. "Le antichità." In *RIE* IV, 309–337.

Fortson, Benjamin. 2010. *Indo-European Languages and Culture: An Introduction*. 2nd. ed. Chichester: Blackwell.

Foucault, Michel. 1970. *The Order of Things: An Archaeology of the Human Sciences*. New York: Pantheon.

———. 1972. *Folie et déraison. Histoire de la folie à l'âge classique.* Paris: Gallimard.

———. 1982 "The Subject and Power." In Hubert L. Dreyfus and Paul Rabinow, "Afterword." *Michel Foucault: Beyond Structuralism and Hermeneutics.* Chicago: University of Chicago Press.

———. 2002. *The Archaeology of Knowledge.* 2nd ed. London: Routledge.

Fowden, Garth. 1994. *Empire to Commonwealth: Consequences of Monotheism in Late Antiquity.* Princeton: Princeton University Press.

Fracastoro, Girolamo. 1911. *Hieronymus Fracastor's Syphilis, from the Original Latin.* Trans. Solomon Claiborne Martin. St. Louis: The Philmar Company.

Fra-Molinero, Baltasar. 2015. "Juan Latino and his Racial Difference." In Earle/Lowe 2015, 326–344.

Franck, Jakob. 1883. "Krantz, Martin." In *Allgemeine Deutsche Biographie*, Vol. XVII. Leipzig: Duncker und Humblot, 45–47.

François, Etienne. 1993. *Protestants et catholiques en Allemagne. Identités et pluralisme, Augsbourg 1648–1806.* Paris: Michel.

Frangenberg, Thomas. 1990. *Der Betrachter. Studien zur florentinischen Kunstliteratur des 16. Jahrhunderts.* Berlin: Gebr. Mann.

Frank, Andre Gunder. 1998. *ReOrient: Global Economy in the Asian Age.* 4th ed. Berkeley: University of California Press.

Franke, Herbert. 1987. *From Tribal Chieftain to Universal Emperor and God: The Legitimation of the Yuan Dynasty.* Munich: C. H. Beck.

Franke, Herbert, and Rolf Trauzettel. 1968. *Das Chinesische Kaiserreich.* Frankfurt: Fischer.

Franke, Herbert, and Denis Twitchett (eds.). 1994. *The Cambridge History of China.* Vol. VI: *Alien Regimes and Border States, 907–1368.* Cambridge: Cambridge University Press.

Frankopan, Peter. 2015. *The Silk Road: A New History of the World.* London: Bloomsbury.

Franz, Edgar. 2005. "Deutsche Mediziner in Japan—ein Beitrag zum Wissenstransfer in der Edo-Zeit." *Japanstudien* 17, 31–56.

Freedberg, David. 1989. *The Power of Images: Studies in the History and Theory of Response.* Chicago: University of Chicago Press.

Freedman, Paul. 2008. *Out of the East: Spices and the Medieval Imagination.* New Haven: Yale University Press.

Freely, John. 2009. *Aladdin's Lamp: How Greek Science Came to Europe through the Islamic World.* New York: Vintage.

Freeman-Grenville, G. S. P. 1962. *The Medieval History of the Coast of Tanganyika.* Berlin: Akademie Verlag.

French, Roger. 1994. *William Harvey's Natural Philosophy.* Cambridge: Cambridge University Press.

———. 1999. *Dissection and Vivisection in the European Renaissance.* Aldershot: Ashgate.

———. 2003. *Medicine before Science: The Business of Medicine from the Middle Ages to the Enlightenment.* Cambridge: Cambridge University Press.

Frey, Dieter, and Hans Werner Bierhoff. 2011. *Sozialpsychologie—Interaktion und Gruppe.* Göttingen: Hogrefe.

Fried, Johannes. 1989. "Endzeiterwartung um die Jahrtausendwende." *Deutsches Archiv für Erforschung des Mittelalters* 45, 381–473.

———. 2004. *Der Schleier der Erinnerung. Grundzüge einer historischen Memorik.* Munich: C. H. Beck.

———. 2007. *Donation of Constantine and Constitutum Constantini: The Misinterpretation of a Fiction and its Original Meaning.* Berlin: De Gruyter.

———. 2015. *The Middle Ages.* Trans. Peter Lewis. Cambridge, MA: Harvard University Press.

———. 2016. *Charlemagne.* Trans. Peter Lewis. Cambridge, MA: Harvard University Press.

Fried, Johannes, and Ernst-Dieter Hehl (eds). 2010. *Weltdeutungen und Weltreligionen: 600 bis 1500*. Darmstadt: WBG.

Frigo, Daniela. "Il Rinascimento e le corti: Ferrara e Mantova." In *RIE* I, 309–330.

Froissart, Jean. 1857. *Chronicles of England, France, Spain, and the Adjoining Countries by Sir John Froissart*. Trans. Thomas Johnes. 2 vols. London: Henry G. Bohn.

Fubini, Riccardo. 2003. *Humanism and Secularization: From Petrarch to Valla*. Durham: Duke University Press.

———. 2012. "Nanni, Giovanni." In *DBI* 72, 726–732.

Funke, Fritz. 1999. *Buchkunde: Ein Überblick über die Geschichte des Buches*. 6th ed. Munich: Saur.

Funkenstein, Amos. 1975. "The Dialectical Preparation for Scientific Revolutions: On the Role of Hypothetical Reasoning in the Emergence of Copernican Astronomy and Galilean Mechanics." In Westman 1975, 165–203.

Fürst, Alfons. 2010. "Monotheism Between Cult and Politics: The Themes of the Ancient Debate between Pagan and Christian Monotheism." In Stephen Mitchell and Peter van Nuffelen (eds.), *One God: Pagan Monotheism in the Roman Empire (1st–4th cent. A.D.)*. Cambridge: Cambridge University Press, 82–99.

Füssel, Stephan. 1999. *Gutenberg und seine Wirkung*. Frankfurt: Insel.

Füssel, Stephan, and Jan Pirożyński (eds.). 1997. *Der polnische Humanismus und die europäischen Sodalitäten*. Wiesbaden: Harrasowitz.

Fusaro, Maria. "Gli uomini stranieri d'affari in Italia." In *RIE* IV, 369–395.

Fynn-Paul, Jeffrey. 2009. "Empire, Monotheism and Slavery in the Greater Mediterranean Region from Antiquity to the Early Modern Era." *Past and Present* 205, 3–40.

Gabriel, Karl, Christel Gärtner, and Detlef Pollack (eds.). 2012. *Umstrittene Säkularisierung. Soziologische und historische Analysen zur Differenzierung von Religion und Politik*. Berlin: Berlin University Press.

Gabrielli, Annibale (ed.). 1890. *Epistolario di Cola di Rienzo*. Rome: Forzani.

Galeotti, Mark. 2019. *Kulikovo 1380: The Battle That Made Russia*. Oxford: Osprey.

Galilei, Galileo. 1890–1909. *Le opere di Galileo Galilei*. Ed. Antonio Favaro. 20 vols. Florence: Giunti Barbèra.

———. 1967. *Dialogue Concerning the Two Chief World Systems—Ptolemaic & Copernican*. Trans. Stillman Drake. 2nd ed. Berkeley: University of California Press.

———. 2009. *Sidereus Nuncius or Sidereal Message*. Ed. and trans. William R. Shea and Tiziana Bascelli. Sagamore Beach: Science History Publications.

Gamberini, Andrea. 2000. "Gian Galeazzo Visconti." In *DBI* 54, 383–391.

Gamsa, Mark. 2013. "Uses and Misuses of a Chinese Renaissance." *Modern Intellectual History* 10:3, 635–654.

Ganz, David. 1996. "*Temptabat et scribere*: Vom Schreiben in der Karolingerzeit." In Rudolf Schieffer (ed.), *Schriftkultur und Reichsverwaltung unter den Karolingern*. Wiesbaden: Springer, 13–33.

Garber, Daniel. 1995. "Descartes' Physics." In Cottingham 1995, 286–334.

Gareis, Iris. 1999. "Wie Engel und Teufel in die Neue Welt kamen. Imaginationen von Gut und Böse im kolonialen Amerika." *Paideuma* 45, 257–273.

Garin, Eugenio. 1978. *Storia della filosofia italiana*. 3 vols. Turin: Einaudi.

Gascoigne, John. 1990. "A Reappraisal of the Role of Universities in the Scientific Revolution." In Lindberg/Westman 1990, 207–260.

Gaukroger, Stephen. 2006. *The Emergence of Scientific Culture: Science and the Shaping of Modernity, 1210–1685*. Oxford: Clarendon.

Gdoura, Wahid. 1985. *Le Début de l'Imprimérie Arabe à Istanbul et en Syrie. Évolution de l'Environment Culturel (1706–1787)*. Tunis: Institut Supérieur de Documentation.

Geary, Patrick. J. 2003. *Myth of Nations: The Medieval Origins of Europe*. Princeton: Princeton University Press.

Geertz, Clifford. 1980. *Negara: The Theatre State in Nineteenth-Century Bali*. Princeton: Princeton University Press.

Gelfand, Laura. 2009. "Piety, Nobility and Posterity: Wealth and the Ruin of Nicolas Rolin's Reputation." *Journal of Historians of Netherlandish Art* 1:1, 1–26.

Gemeinhardt, Peter. 2007. *Das lateinische Christentum und die antike pagane Bildung*. Tübingen: Mohr Siebeck.

Gentile, Emilio. 2006. *Politics as Religion*. Princeton: Princeton University Press.

Geoffroy-Schneiter, Berenice. 2001. *Gandhara: The Memory of Afghanistan*. Paris: Assouline.

Gerabek, Werner E. et al. 2007. *Enzyklopädie Medizingeschichte*. Berlin: De Gruyter.

Gerbert of Aurillac. 1966. *Die Briefsammlung Gerberts von Reims*. Ed. Fritz Weigle. MGH, Die Brife der deutschen Kaiserzeit, 2. Weimar: Hermann Böhlaus Nachfolger.

Gernet, Jacques. 2002. *A History of Chinese Civilization*. 2nd ed. Cambridge: Cambridge University Press.

Ghiberti, Lorenzo. 1998. *I commentarii*. Ed. Lorenzo Bartoli. Florence: Giunti.

Gibbon, Edward. 1788. *The History of the Decline and Fall of the Roman Empire*. Vol. IV. London: Strahan & Cadell.

Gieseler, Johann Karl Ludwig. 1836. *Text-Book of Ecclesiastical History*. Vol. II. Philadelphia: Carey, Lea, and Blanchard.

Gilbert, Creighton E. 1980. *Italian Art, 1400–1500: Sources and Documents*. Englewood Cliffs: Prentice-Hall.

Gilbert of Colchester, William. 1893/2010. *On The Loadstone and Magnetic Bodies, and On The Great Magnet the Earth*. Trans. Paul Fleury Mottelay. New York: J. Wiley & Sons, 1893. Facsimile reprint: Whitefish: Kessinger Publishing, 2010.

Gilmore, Myron P. 1952. *The World of Humanism, 1453–1517*. New York: Harper & Brothers.

Gilson, Étienne. 1937. *The Unity of Philosophical Experience*. New York: Scribner's.

Gimaret, Daniel. 1993. "Muʾtazila." In Clifford E. Bosworth et al. (eds.), *Encyclopédie de l'Islam*. Vol. VII. 2nd ed. Leiden: Brill, 783–793.

Gingerich, Owen. 1973. "Johannes Kepler." In *Dictionary of Scientific Biography*. Vol. VII. New York: Charles Scribner, 289–312.

———. 2004. *The Book Nobody Read: Chasing the Revolutions of Nicolaus Copernicus*. New York: Walker.

Giovio, Paolo. 2013. *Notable Men and Women of Our Time*. Ed. and trans. Kenneth Gouwens. Cambridge: Harvard University Press.

Girard, René. 1986. *The Scapegoat*. Baltimore: Johns Hopkins University Press.

Given, James. 1990. *State and Society in Medieval Europe: Gwynedd and Languedoc under Outside Rule*. Ithaca: Cornell University Press.

Glaber, Rodulfus. 1990. *The Five Books of the Histories*. Ed. and trans. John France. *And The Life of St. William*. Ed. Neithard Bulst. Trans. John France and Paul Reynolds. Oxford: Clarendon.

Glasser, Hannelore. 1990. *Artists' Contracts of the Early Renaissance*. New York: Garland.

Glauser, Jürg (ed.). 2006. *Skandinavische Literaturgeschichte*. Stuttgart: Metzler.

Gleeson-White, Jane. 2011. *Double Entry: How the Merchants of Venice Created Modern Finance*. New York: W.W. Norton & Co.

Glick, Thomas F. 1979. *Islamic and Christian Spain in the Early Middle Ages*. Princeton: Princeton University Press.

Godman, Peter. 1985. *Poetry of the Carolingian Renaissance*. London: Duckworth.

Goehrke, Carsten. 2003. *Russischer Alltag. Eine Geschichte in neun Zeitbildern vom Frühmittelalter bis zur Gegenwart*. Vol. I. Zurich: Chronos.

——. 2010. *Rußland. Eine Strukturgeschichte*. Zurich: Chronos.

Goertz, Hans-Jürgen. 1987. *Pfaffenhaß und Groß Geschrei. Die reformatorischen Bewegungen in Deutschland 1517–1529*. Munich: C. H. Beck.

——. 1989. *Thomas Müntzer. Mystiker, Apokalyptiker, Revolutionär*. C. H. Beck.

Goetz, Hans-Werner. 2008. *Geschichtsschreibung und Geschichtsbewusstsein im hohen Mittelalter*. 2nd ed. Berlin: Akademie Verlag.

Goez, Werner. 1988. *Geschichte Italiens im Mittelalter und Renaissance*. Darmstadt: WBG.

Goldin, Ian, and Chris Kutarna. 2016. *Age of Discovery: Navigating the Risks and Rewards of Our New Renaissance*. New York: Vijay Govindarajan.

Goldstein, Bernard R. 2018. "The Heritage of Arabic Science in Hebrew." In Iqbal 2018, IV, 65–74.

Goldstein, Thomas. 1973. "The Influence of the Geographic Discoveries upon Copernicus." *Organon* 9, 199–215.

Goldstone, Jack A. 2002. "Efflorescences and Economic Growth in World History: Rethinking the Rise of the West and the Industrial Revolution." *Journal of World History* 13, 323–389.

——. 2006. "Europe's Peculiar Oath: Would the World be 'Modern' if William III's Invasion of England in 1688 Had Failed?" In Philip Tetlock, Richard Ned Lebow, and Noel Geoffrey Parker (eds.). *Unmaking the West: 'What if'-Scenarios That Rewrite World History*. Ann Arbor: University of Michigan Press, 168–196.

——. 2009. *Why Europe? The Rise of the West in World History, 1500–1850*. Boston: McGraw-Hill Higher Education.

Goldthwaite, Richard A. 1993. *Wealth and the Demand for Art in Italy, 1300–1600*. Baltimore: Johns Hopkins University Press.

——. 2009. *The Economy of Renaissance Florence*. Baltimore: Johns Hopkins University Press.

Goldziher, Ignaz. 1981. "The Attitude of Orthodox Islam Toward the 'Ancient Sciences.'" In Merlin Swartz (ed.). *Studies on Islam*. Oxford: Oxford University Press, 185–215.

Göle, Ninifer. 2000. "Snapshots of Islamic Modernities," *Daedalus*, 129:1, 91–117.

Golinski, Jan V. 1990. "Chemistry in the Scientific Revolution." In Lindberg/Westman 1990, 367–396.

Gombrich, Ernst H. 1978. *The Story of Art*. Oxford: Phaidon.

——. 1997. *Aby Warburg: An Intellectual Biography*. Oxford: Phaidon.

Goodman, Grant K. 1986. *Japan: The Dutch Experience*. London: Athlone Press.

Goody, Jack. 1968. "Restricted Literacy in Northern Ghana." In Jack Goody (ed.). *Literacy in Traditional Societies*. Cambridge: Cambridge University Press, 198–264.

——. 1971. *Technology, Tradition, and the State in Africa*. Oxford: Oxford University Press.

——. 2010a. *Renaissances: The One or the Many?* Cambridge: Cambridge University Press.

——. 2010b. *The Eurasian Miracle*. Cambridge, MA: Polity.

Gorochov, Nathalie. 1997. *Le collège de Navarre de sa fondation (1305) au début du XVe siècle (1418): histoire de l'institution, de sa vie intellectuelle et de son recrutement*. Paris: Honoré Champion.

Gottfried von Strassburg. *Tristan*. Trans. Lee Stavenhagen. http://stavenhagen.net/GvS /Reviews.html (accessed December 17, 2020).

Gotthard, Axel. 2004. *Der Augsburger Religionsfrieden*. Münster: Aschendorff.

Göttler, Christine. 1996. *Die Kunst des Fegefeuers nach der Reformation. Kirchliche Schenkungen, Ablaß und Almosen in Antwerpen und Bologna um 1600*. Mainz: Philipp von Zabern.

Götz, Roland. 1987. "Der Dämonenpakt bei Augustinus." In Georg Schwaiger (ed.), *Teufels-glaube und Hexenprozesse*. C. H. Beck, 57–84.

Grafe, Regina. 2012. *Distant Tyranny: Markets, Power, and Backwardness in Spain, 1650–1800*. Princeton: Princeton University Press.

Grafton, Anthony. 1997. *Commerce with the Classics: Ancient Books and Renaissance Readers*. Ann Arbor: University of Michigan Press.

———. 2000. *Leon Battista Alberti: Master Builder of the Renaissance*. New York: Hill and Wang.

———. 2001. *Cardano's Cosmos: The Worlds and Works of a Renaissance Astrologer*. Cambridge, MA: Harvard University Press.

Grafton, Anthony, and Lisa Jardine. 1986. *From Humanism to the Humanities: Education and the Liberal Arts in Fifteenth- and Sixteenth-Century Europe*. London: Duckworth.

Grafton, Anthony, April Shelford, and Nancy Siraisi. 1992. *New Worlds, Ancient Texts: The Power of Tradition and the Shock of Discovery*. Cambridge, MA: Harvard University Press.

Graham, Angus C. 1968. "China, Europe, and the Origin of Modern Science: Needham's *The Grand Titration*." In Nakayama/Sivin 1968, 45–69.

Granberg, Jonas. 2004. "Veche in the Chronicles of Medieval Rus: A Study of Functions and Terminology." PhD dissertation, Goteborg University.

Granet, Marcel. 1971. *Das chinesische Denken—Inhalt, Form, Charakter*. Munich: Piper.

Grant, Edward. 1981. *Much Ado about Nothing: Theories of Space and Vacuum from the Middle Ages to the Scientific Revolution*. Cambridge: Cambridge University Press.

———. 1988. "The Effects of the Condemnation of 1277." In Norman Kretzman et al. (eds.), *The Cambridge History of Later Medieval Philosophy*. Cambridge: Cambridge University Press, 537–539.

———. 1994. *Planets, Stars, and Orbs: The Medieval Cosmos, 1200–1687*. Cambridge: Cambridge University Press.

———. 1996. *The Foundations of Modern Science in the Middle Ages: Their Religious, Institutional and Intellectual Contexts*. Cambridge: Cambridge University Press.

———. 2004. *Science and Religion from Aristotle to Copernicus, 400 B.C. to A.D. 1550*. Westport: Greenwood Press.

Grant, Jeanne. 2014. *For the Common Good: The Bohemian Land Law and the Beginning of the Hussite Revolution*. Brill: Leiden.

Greef, Wulfert de. 2004. "Calvin's Writings." In McKim 2004, 41–47.

Green, Louis. 1986. *Castruccio Castracani: A Study of the Origins and Character of a Fourteenth-Century Italian Despotism*. Oxford: Oxford University Press.

Greenblatt, Stephen. 2011. *The Swerve: How the Renaissance Began*. London: Bodley Head.

Greenfeld, Liah. 2003. *The Spirit of Capitalism: Nationalism and Economic Growth*. Cambridge, MA: Harvard University Press.

Gregorius Magister. 1970. *Narracio de Mirabilibus urbis Romae*. Ed. Robert B. C. Huygens. Leiden: Brill.

Greif, Avner. 2010. *Institutions and the Path to Modern Economy: Lessons from Medieval Trade*. 8th ed. Cambridge: Cambridge University Press.

Grendler, Paul F. 1986. *Schooling in Renaissance Italy: Literacy and Learning, 1300–1600*. Baltimore: Johns Hopkins University Press.

Greve, Jens, and Annette Schnabel (eds.). 2011. *Emergenz. Zur Analyse und Erklärung komplexer Strukturen*. Berlin: Suhrkamp.

Grewe, Wilhelm G. 2000. *The Epochs of International Law*. Berlin: De Gruyter.

Gribbin, John. 2002. *Science: A History, 1543–2001*. London: Allen Lane.

Grieb, Volker. 2008. *Hellenistische Demokratie. Politische Organisation und Struktur in freien griechischen Poleis nach Alexander dem Großen*. Stuttgart: Franz Steiner.

Grierson, Herbert J. C. 1912. *The Poems of John Donne*. 2 vols. Oxford: Oxford University Press.

Grimm, Jürgen, and Susanne Hartwig (ed.). 2014. *Französische Literaturgeschichte*. 6th ed. Stuttgart: Metzler.

Grimm, Tilemann. 1977. "Academies and Urban Systems in Kwangtung." In Skinner 1977, 475–498.

Grinin, Leonid, and Andrey Korotayev. 2015. *Great Divergence and Great Convergence: A Global Perspective*. Cham: Springer International Publishing.

Groese, Michiel van. 2008. *The Representation of the Overseas World in the de Bry Collection of Voyages (1590–1634)*. Leiden: Brill.

Groten, Andreas. 2015. *Corpus und* universitas: *Römisches Körperschafts- und Gesellschaftsrecht: zwischen griechischer Philosophie und römischer Politik*. Tübingen: Mohr Siebeck.

Grotius, Hugo. 2004. *The Free Sea*. Trans. Richard Hakluyt. Ed. David Armitage. Indianapolis: Liberty Fund.

Grousset, René. 1971. *In the Footsteps of the Buddha*. New York: Orion Press and Grossman Publishers.

Grözinger, Karl E. 1991. "Jüdische Wundermänner in Deutschland." In Karl E. Grözinger, *Judentum im deutschen Sprachraum*. Frankfurt: Suhrkamp, 190–221.

Gruber, Elisabeth et al. (eds.). 2013. *Mittler zwischen Herrschaft und Gemeinde. Die Rolle von Funktions- und Führungsgruppen in der mittelalterlichen Urbanisierung Zentraleuropas*. Innsbruck: Studien Verlag.

Grün, Nathan. 1885. *Der hohe Rabbi Löw und sein Sagenkreis*. Prag: Brendeis.

Grundmann, Herbert. 1973. *Wahlkönigtum, Territorialpolitik und Ostbewegung im 13. und 14. Jahrhundert*. Munich: dtv.

———. 1995. *Religious Movements in the Middle Ages*. Trans. Steven Rowan. Intr. Robert E. Lerner. Notre Dame: University of Notre Dame Press.

Grunebaum, Gustav Edmund von. 1969. *Islam: Essays in the Nature and Growth of a Cultural Tradition*. London: Routledge & Kegan Paul.

Gruzinski, Serge. 1988. *La colonisation de l'imaginaire. Sociétés indigènes et occidentales dans le Mexique espagnol. XVIe-XVIIIe siècle*. Paris: Gallimard.

———. 2012. *The Mestizo Mind: The Intellectual Dynamics of Colonization and Globalization*. Trans. Dele Dusinberre. London: Routledge.

———. 2014. *The Eagle and the Dragon: Globalization and European Dreams of Conquest in China and America in the Sixteenth Century*. Trans. Jean Birrell. Cambridge: Polity Press.

Guasti, Cesare. 1887. *Santa Maria del Fiore: La costruzione della Chiesa e del Campanile secondo i documenti*. Florence: M. Ricci.

Gudmundsson, Óskar. 2011. *Snorri Sturluson: Homer des Nordens. Eine Biographie*. Cologne: Böhlau.

Guerzoni, Guido. "Novità, innovazione, imitazione: i sintomi della modernità." In *RIE* III, 59–87.

Guibert of Nogent. 2011. *Monodies and On the Relics of Saints: The Autobiography and a Manifesto of a French Monk from the Time of the Crusades*. Trans. Joseph McAlhany, Jay Rubenstein. New York: Penguin.

Guidi Bruscoli, Francesco. "Le tecniche bancarie." In *RIE* IV, 543–566.

Guillaume de Pouille. 1961. *La geste de Robert Guiscard*. Ed. Marguerite Mathieu. Palermo: Istituto siciliano di studi bizantini e neoellenici.

Günther, Hubertus. 2009. *Was ist Renaissance? Eine Charakteristik der Architektur zu Beginn der Neuzeit*. Darmstadt: WBG.

Günther, Linda-Marie. 2011. *Griechische Antike*. 2nd ed. Tübingen: Francke.

Gunn, Geoffrey C. 2003. *First Globalization: The Eurasian Exchange, 1500–1800*. Lanham: Rowman & Littlefield.

Gupta, Bishnupriya, and Debin Ma. 2010. "Europe in an Asian Mirror: The Great Divergence." In Stephen Broadberry and Kevin O'Rourke (eds.). *The Cambridge Economic History of Europe*. Vol I: 1700–1870. Cambridge: Cambridge University Press, 264–285.

Gutas, Dimitri. 1998. *Greek Thought, Arabic Culture: The Graeco-Arabic Translation Movement in Baghdad and Early Abbasid Society*. London: Routledge.

Guthke, Karl S. 1990. *The Last Frontier: Imagining Other Worlds from the Copernican Revolution to Modern Science Fiction*. Trans. Helen Atkin. Ithaca: Cornell University Press.

Haan, Bertrand. 2010. *Une paix pour l'éternité. La negociation du traité du Cateau-Cambrésis*. Geneva: Droz.

Haarmann, Harald. 2007. *Geschichte der Schrift. Von den Hieroglyphen bis heute*. 4th ed. Munich: C. H. Beck.

Haarmann, Ulrich (ed.). 1987. *Geschichte der arabischen Welt*. Munich: C. H. Beck.

Haas, Alois M. 1995. *Meister Eckhart als normative Gestalt geistlichen Lebens*. 2nd ed. Freiburg: Johannes-Verlag.

Häberlein, Mark. 2006. *Die Fugger: Geschichte einer Augsburger Familie (1367–1650)*. Stuttgart: W. Kohlhammer.

Haberman, Jacob. 2007. "Delmedigo, Joseph Solomon." In Fred Skolnik and Michael Berenbaum (eds.), *Encyclopaedia Judaica*. Vol. V. 2nd ed. Detroit: Macmillan Reference, 543–544.

Hackett, Jeremiah (ed.). 1997. *Roger Bacon and the Sciences: Commemorative Essays*. Leiden: Brill.

Hadden, Richard W. 1994. *On the Shoulders of Merchants: Exchange and the Mathematical Conception of Nature in Early Modern Europe*. Albany: State University of New York Press.

Haefele, Hans F. (ed.). 1980. *Ekkehardi IV. Casus Sancti Galli (St. Galler Klostergeschichten)*. Darmstadt: WBG.

Haeser, Heinrich. 1882. *Lehrbuch der Geschichte der Medicin und der epidemischen Kankheiten*. Vol. III. 3rd ed. Jena: Gustav Fischer.

Hagedorn, Suzanne C. 2004. *Abandoned Women: Rewriting the Classics in Dante, Boccaccio, & Chaucer*. Ann Arbor: University of Michigan Press.

Hajnal, John. 1965. "European Marriage Patterns in Perspective." In David Glass and David E. C. Eversley, *Population in History*. London: Edward Arnold, 101–143.

Hajnóczi, Gábor. 1999. "Un discepolo del Ficino a Buda. Francesco Bandini." *Verbum* 1:1, 13–20.

Haldon, John F. (ed.). 2009. *A Social History of Byzantium*. Malden: Blackwell.

Hale, John. 1993. *The Civilization of Europe in the Renaissance*. London: HarperCollins.

Hall, Arthur R. 1954. *The Scientific Revolution, 1500–1800: The Formation of the Modern Scientific Attitude*. London: Longmans.

Hall, James. 2014. *The Self-Portrait: A Cultural History*. London: Thames & Hudson.

———. 2020. "Under Siege: The Aesthetics and Politics of Michelangelo's Attack on Flemish Painting." *Simiolus* 42, 45–86.

Hall, John W. 1966. *Government and Local Power in Japan, 500–1700: A Study Based on Bizen Province*. Princeton: Princeton University Press.

——— (ed.). 1990. *The Cambridge History of Japan*. Vol. III. Cambridge: Cambridge University Press.

Hall, Kenneth R. 2011. *A History of Early Southeast Asia: Maritime Trade and Societal Development, 100–1500*. Lanham, MD: Rowman & Littlefield.

Hall, Kim F. 1995. *Things of Darkness: Economies of Race and Gender in Early Modern England*. Ithaca: Cornell University Press.

Hall, Thomas S. 1975. *History of General Physiology*. 2 vols. 2nd ed. Chicago: University of Chicago Press.

Halm, Heinz (ed.). 2001. *Geschichte der arabischen Welt*. 4th ed. Munich: C. H. Beck.

Halsberghe, Nicole. 2011. "Introduction and Development of the Screw in Seventeenth-Century China: Theoretical Explanations and Practical Applications by Ferdinand Verbiest." *East Asian Science, Technology, and Medicine* 34, 163–193.

Hamdani, Abbas. 1979. "Columbus and the Recovery of Jerusalem." *Journal of the American Oriental Society* 99:1, 39–48.

Hamilton, Bernard. 2003. *The Christian World of the Middle Ages*. Cheltenham: The History Press.

Hamm, Berndt. 1996. *Bürgertum und Glaube. Konturen der städtischen Reformation*. Göttingen: Vandenhoeck & Ruprecht.

Hammer, Paul E. J. 2003. *Elizabeth's Wars: War, Government and Society in Tudor England, 1544–1604*. Basingstoke: Palgrave Macmillan.

Hammerstein, Notker (ed.). 1996. *Handbuch der deutschen Bildungsgeschichte*. Vol. I. Munich: C. H. Beck.

Hankins, James. 1994. *Plato in the Italian Renaissance*. 2 vols. Leiden: Brill.

Hansen, Mogens Herman. 2000. "The Kotoko City-States." In Mogens Herman Hansen (ed.), *A Comparative Study of Thirty City-State Cultures: An Investigation Conducted by the Copenhagen Polis Centre*. Copenhagen: Kongelige Danske Videnskabernes Selskab, 531–546.

Harasimowicz, Jan. "Il Rinascimento fuori dal *limes romanus*." In *RIE* I, 415–438.

Harbison, Craig. 2012. *Jan van Eyck: The Play of Realism*. 2nd ed. London: Reaktion Books.

Harriss, Gerald. 2005. *Shaping the Nation: England 1360–1461*. Oxford: Oxford University Press.

Hartmann, Wilfried (ed.). 1995. *Frühes und hohes Mittelalter, 750–1250*. Stuttgart: Reclam.

Hartt, Frederick. 1964. "Art and Freedom in Quattrocento Florence." In Lucy F. Sandler (ed.), *Essays in Memory of Karl Lehmann*. Locust Valley: Institute of Fine Arts, New York University, 114–131.

Hartung, Stefan. 2003. "Rehierarchisierungen und Systemverschiebungen in der paradoxen Lob- und Tadelliteratur der Renaissance." In Mark Föcking and Bernhard Huss (ed.), *Varietas und Ordo. Zur Dialektik von Vielfalt und Einheit in Renaissance und Barock*. Stuttgart: Franz Steiner, 91–114.

Harvey, Leonard P. 1990. *Islamic Spain, 1250–1492*. Chicago: University of Chicago Press.

Hasan, Farhat. 2004. *Locality in Mughal India. Power Relations in Mughal India, c. 1572–1730*. Cambridge: Cambridge University Press.

Haskins, Charles H. 1927. *The Renaissance of the Twelfth Century*. Cambridge, MA: Harvard University Press.

Hassig, Ross. 2006. *Mexico and the Spanish Conquest*. 2nd ed. Norman: University of Oklahoma Press.

Hatfield, Gary. 1990. "Metaphysics and the New Science." In Lindberg/Westman 1990, 93–166.

Hatfield, Rab. 1995. "Botticelli's Mystic Nativity, Savonarola and the Millennium." *Journal of the Warburg and Courtauld Institutes* 58, 89–114.

———. 2003. "The High End: Michelangelo's Earnings." In Fantoni/Matthew/Matthews-Grieco 2003, 195–201.

Haug-Moritz, Gabriele. 2002. *Der Schmalkaldische Bund, 1530–1540/41*. Leinfeld-Echterdingen: DRW.

Haumann, Heiko. 1990. *Geschichte der Ostjuden*. Munich: dtv.

Havas, Lázló, and Sebestýen Kiss. 2002. "Die Geschichtskonzeption Antonio Bonfinis." In Helmrath/Muhlack/Walther 2002, 281–307.

Hayami, Akira, and Hiroshi Kitô. 2004. "Demography and Living Standards." In Akira Hayami et al. (eds.), *The Economic History of Japan, 1600–1900*. Vol. I. Oxford: Oxford University Press, 213–247.

Haydn, Hiram. 1950. *The Counter Renaissance*. New York: Charles Scribner's Sons.

Hayes, Edward. 1910. "Sir Humphrey Gilbert's Voyage to Newfoundland, 1583." In Charles W. Eliot (ed.), *Voyages and Travels: Ancient and Modern*. New York: P. F. Collier & Son, 263–298.

Headley, John M. 1997. *Tommaso Campanella and the Transformation of the World*. Princeton: Princeton University Press.

———. 2008. *The Europeanization of the World: On the Origins of Human Rights and Democracy*. Princeton: Princeton University Press.

Heather, Peter. 2009. *Empires and Barbarians*. Oxford: Oxford University Press.

Hechberger, Werner. 2004. *Adel, Ministerialität und Rittertum im Mittelalter*. Munich: Oldenbourg.

Hedeman, Anne D. 1991. *The Royal Image: Illustrations of the Grandes Chroniques de France, 1274–1422*. Berkeley: University of California Press.

Hedinger, Bärbel. 1986. *Karten in Bilder. Zur Ikonographie der Wandkarte in holländischen Interieurgemälden des 17. Jahrhunderts*. Hildesheim: Olms.

Heesterman, Jan C. 1985. *The Inner Conflict of Tradition: Essays in Indian Ritual, Kinship, and Society*. Chicago: University of Chicago Press.

Hegel, Georg Wilhelm Friedrich. 1899. *The Philosophy of History*. Trans. John Sibree. Rev. ed. New York: The Colonial Press.

Heidegger, Martin. 2001. *Poetry, Language, Thought*. Trans. Albert Hofstadter. New York: Harper & Row.

Heijdra, Martin. 2008. "The Socio-Economic Development of Rural China During the Ming." In Twitchett/Mote 2008, 437–439.

Heilbron, John L. 1982. *Elements of Early Modern Physics*. Berkeley: University of California Press.

Heinen, Heinz. 2013. *Geschichte des Hellenismus. Von Alexander bis Kleopatra*. Munich: C. H. Beck.

Helden, Albert van. 1986. *Measuring the Universe: Cosmic Dimensions from Aristarchus to Halley*. Chicago: University of Chicago Press.

Heller, Klaus. 1987. *Russische Wirtschafts- und Sozialgeschichte*. Vol. I. Darmstadt: WBG.

Helmrath, Johannes. 2002. "*Vestigia Aeneae imitari*: Enea Silvio Piccolomini als 'Apostel' des Humanismus. Formen und Wege seiner Diffusion." In Helmrath/Muhlack/Walther 2002, 99–141.

———. 2014. "Das Konzil von Konstanz und die Epoche der Konzilien (1409–1449): Konziliare Erinnerungsorte im Vergleich." In Gabriela Signori and Birgit Studt (eds.), *Das Konstanzer Konzil als europäisches Ereignis: Begegnungen, Medien und Rituale*. Ostfildern: Thorbecke, 19–56.

Helmrath Johannes, Ulrich Muhlack, and Gerrit Walther (eds.). 2002. *Diffusion des Humanismus: Studien zur nationalen Geschichtsschreibung europäischer Humanisten*. Göttingen: Wallstein.

Hendrich, Geert. 2011. *Arabisch-islamische Philosophie. Geschichte und Gegenwart*. 2nd ed. Frankfurt: Campus.

Hennig, Richard. 1953. *Terrae Incognitae. Eine Zusammenstellung und kritische Bewertung der wichtigsten vorcolumbischen Entdeckungsreisen an Hand der darüber vorliegenden Originalberichte*. 2nd ed. Leiden: Brill.

Henry, John. 1991. "Doctors and Healers: Popular Culture and the Medical Profession." In Pumfrey/Rossi/Slawinski 1991, 191–221.

———. 2001. "Animism and Empiricism: Copernican Physics and the Origins of William Gilbert's Experimental Method." *Journal of the History of Ideas* 62, 1–19.

———. 2008. *The Scientific Revolution and the Origins of Modern Science*. 3rd ed. Basingstoke: Palgrave Macmillan.

Hentzner, Paul. 1757. *A Journey into England in the Year MDXCVIII*. London: Strawberry-Hill. https://archive.org/details/journeyintoengla00hentrich/page/n3 (accessed October 31, 2024).

Herbers, Klaus. 2012. *Geschichte des Papsttums im Mittelalter*. Darmstadt: WBG.

Herberstein, Sigmund von. 1557. *Moscovia der Haupstat in Reissen (…) sambt des Moscoviter Gepiet und seiner Anrainer … Beschreibung*. Vienna: Michael Zimmermann.

Herendeen, Wyman H. 2007. *William Camden: A Life in Context*. Woodbridge: The Boydell Press.

Hering Torres, Max Sebastián. 2006. *Rassismus in der Vormoderne. Die 'Reinheit des Blutes' im Spanien der Frühen Neuzeit*. Frankfurt: Campus.

Herlihy, David, and Christiane Klapisch-Zuber. 1985. *Tuscans and their Families: A Study of the Florentine Catasto of 1427*. New Haven: Yale University Press.

Hernán, Enrique García. 2013. *Ignacio de Loyola*. Madrid: Tauris/Fundación Juan March.

Heywood, Linda, and John Thornton. 2007. *Central Africans, Atlantic Creoles, and the Foundation of the Americas, 1585–1660*. Cambridge: Cambridge University Press.

Hiatt, Alfred. 2008. *Terra Incognita: Mapping the Antipodes Before 1600*. Chicago: University of Chicago Press.

Hildermeier, Manfred. 2013. *Geschichte Russlands. Vom Mittelalter bis zur Oktoberrevolution*. Munich: C. H. Beck.

Hill, Donald R. 1998. *Studies in Medieval Islamic Technology: From Philo to al-Jazari—from Alexandria to Diyar Bakr*. Aldershot: Ashgate.

Hills, Richard L. 1989. *Power from Steam: A History of the Stationary Steam Engine*. Cambridge: Cambridge University Press.

Hinrichs, Ernst. 1994. "Heinrich IV." In Peter Claus Hartmann (ed.), *Französische Könige und Kaiser der Neuzeit. Von Ludwig XII. bis Napoleon III., 1498–1870*. Munich: C. H. Beck, 143–170.

Hirsch, Rudolf. 1974. *Printing, Selling and Reading, 1450–1550*. Wiesbaden: Harrassowitz.

Hirschfeld, Peter. 1968. *Mäzene. Die Rolle des Auftraggebers in der Kunst*. Munich: Deutscher Kunstverlag.

Hirschi, Caspar. 2012. *The Origins of Nationalism: An Alternative History from Ancient Rome to Early Modern Germany*. Cambridge: Cambridge University Press.

Hobbes, Thomas. 1994. "The Verse Life." In John C. A. Gaskin (ed.), *The Elements of Law, Natural and Politic*. Oxford: Oxford University Press, 254–264.

———. 2012. *Leviathan*. Ed. Noel Malcolm. 3 vols. Oxford: Oxford University Press.

Hobbins, Daniel. 2009. *Authorship and Publicity before Print: Jean Gerson and the Transformation of Late Medieval Learning*. Philadelphia: University of Pennsylvania Press.

Hobson, John M. 2004. *The Eastern Origins of Western Civilization*. Cambridge: Cambridge University Press.

Hodgson, Marshall G. S. 1974. *The Venture of Islam: Conscience and History in a World Civilization*. 3 vols. Chicago: University of Chicago Press.

Hoeges, Dirk. 2000. *Niccolò Machiavelli. Die Macht und der Schein*. Munich: C. H. Beck.

Hoenen, Maarten J. F. M. 1999. "At the Crossroads of Scholasticism and Northern Humanism." In Fokke Akkerman, Arie Vanderjagt, and Adrie Lann (eds.), *Northern Humanism in European Context, 1469–1629: From the 'Adwert Academy' to Ubbo Emmius*. Leiden: Brill, 131–148.

Hoensch, Jörg K. 1997. *Kaiser Sigismund. Herrscher an der Schwelle zur Neuzeit (1368–1437)*. 2nd ed. Munich: C. H. Beck.

Hoffmann, Eva R. 2012. "Translating Image and Text in the Medieval Mediterranean World between the Tenth and Thirteenth Centuries." In Heather E. Grossmann and Alicia Walker (eds.), *Mechanisms of Exchange: Transmission in Medieval Art and Architecture of the Mediterranean, ca. 1000–1500*. Leiden: Brill, 584–623.

Holder, R. Ward. 2004. "Calvin's Heritage." In McKim 2004, 245–273.

Holderness, Graham. 2011. *Nine Lives of William Shakespeare*. London: Continuum.

Hollegger, Manfred. 2005. *Maximilian I. (1459–151). Herrscher und Mensch einer Zeitenwende*. Stuttgart: W. Kohlhammer.

Hollister-Short, Graham. 2004. "The Formation of Knowledge Concerning Atmospheric Pressure and Steam Power in Europe from Aleotti (1589) to Papin (1690)." *History of Technology* 25, 137–150.

Hölscher, Uvo. 1968. *Anfängliches Fragen. Studien zur frühen griechischen Philosophie.* Göttingen: Vandenhoeck & Ruprecht.

Holt, James Clarke. 1992. *Magna Carta: The Charter and Its History.* 2nd ed. Cambridge: Cambridge University Press.

Holzberg, Niklas. 1995. "Möglichkeiten und Grenzen humanistischer Antikenrezeption. Willibald Pirckheimer und Hans Sachs als Vermittler klassischer Bildung." In Stephan Füssel (ed.), *Hans Sachs im Schnittpunkt von Antike und Neuzeit.* Nuremberg: Hans Carl, 9–29.

Honan, Park. 1998. *Shakespeare: A Life.* Oxford: Oxford University Press.

Honnefelder, Ludger. 2005. *Johannes Duns Scotus.* Munich: C. H. Beck.

Hoodbhoy, Perez. 1991. *Islam and Science: Religious Orthodoxy and the Battle for Rationality.* London: Zed Books.

Hoorn, Willem van. 2011. "Servetus and the Non-Discovery of Lesser Circulation." In Juan Naya and Marian Hillar (eds.), *Heartfelt: Proceedings of the International Servetus Congress, Barcelona, 20–21 October 2006.* Lanham: University Press of America, 105–143.

Hooykas, Reijer. 1972. *Religion and the Rise of Modern Science.* Edinburgh: Scottish Academic Press.

———. 1974. "Calvin and Kopernikus." *Organon* 10, 139–148.

———. 1978. *Humanisme, science et réforme. Pierre de la Ramée (1515–1573).* Leiden: Brill.

Horden, Peregrine, and Nicholas Purcell. 2000. *The Corrupting Sea: A Study of Mediterranean History.* Oxford: Blackwell.

Horn, Christoph. 1995. *Augustinus.* Munich: C. H. Beck.

Horn, Christoph, and Christof Rapp (eds.). 2008. *Wörterbuch der antiken Philosophie.* 2nd ed. C. H. Beck, Munich.

Horn, Christoph, Joachim Müller, and Jörn Söder (eds.). 2009. *Platon-Handbuch: Leben— Werk—Wirkung.* Stuttgart: J. B. Metzler.

Hösle, Vittorio. 2006. *Der philosophische Dialog. Eine Poetik und Hermeneutik.* Munich: C. H. Beck.

Hossenfelder, Malte. 2006. *Epikur.* Munich: C. H. Beck.

Housley, Norman. 2013. *Crusade and the Ottoman Threat: 1453–1505.* Oxford: Oxford University Press.

Howard, Deborah. "'Un compendio del mondo intero': l'architettura di corte nei paesi del Mare del Nord." In *RIE* VI, 323–344.

Huff, Toby E. 1993. *The Rise of Early Modern Science: Islam, China, and the West.* Cambridge: Cambridge University Press.

———. 2011. *Intellectual Curiosity and the Scientific Revolution: A Global Perspective.* Cambridge: Cambridge University Press.

———. 2014. "The 'Eastern' Origins of Western Civilization?" *Academic Questions* 27:3, 286–299.

———. 2016. "Europe, Renaissance and the Emergence of Modern Science." In *Europe in the Renaissance,* 61–69.

Hugh of St. Victor. 1961. *The Didascalicon of Hugh of Saint Victor: A Medieval Guide to the Arts.* Ed. and trans. Jerome Taylor. New York: Columbia University Press.

Hughes, Barnabas B. 1989. *Robert of Chester's Latin Translation of al-Kwārizmī's al-Jabr: A New Critical Edition.* Stuttgart: Franz Steiner.

Hugonnard-Roche, Henri. 2018. "The Influence of Arabic Astronomy in the Medieval West." In Iqbal 2018, IV, 489–512.

Hui, Victoria Tin-bor. 2005. *War and State Formation in Ancient China and Early Modern Europa.* Cambridge: Cambridge University Press.

Huillard-Bréholles, Jean-Louis-Alphonse (ed.). 1861. *Historia diplomatica (…) Friderici Secundi.* Vol. VI.2. Paris: Henri Plon.

Huizinga, Johan. 1991. *Das Problem der Renaissance. Renaissance und Realismus.* Berlin: Wagenbach.

———. 1996. *The Autumn of the Middle Ages.* Trans. Rodney J. Payton and Ulrich Mammitzsch. Chicago: University of Chicago Press.

Hunt, Edwin S. 1997. *The Medieval Super-Companies: A Study of the Peruzzi Company of Florence.* Cambridge: Cambridge University Press.

Huntington, Samuel P. 1993. "The Clash of Civilizations?" *Foreign Policy* 72, 22–49.

Huppert, George. 1999. *The Style of Paris: Renaissance Origins of the French Enlightenment.* Bloomington: Indiana University Press.

Hurst, G. Cameron, III. 2007. "The Heian Period." In Tsutsui 2007, 30–46.

Ianziti, Gary. 1992. "Sforza." In Volker Reinhardt (ed.), *Die großen Familien Italiens.* Stuttgart: Kröner, 501–515.

———. 2012. *Writing History in Renaissance Italy: Leonardo Bruni and the Uses of the Past.* Cambridge, MA: Harvard University Press.

Ibn Battúta. 1929. *Travels in Asia and Africa, 1325 to 1354: Explorations of the Middle East, Asia, Africa, China and India from 1325 to 1354.* Ed. and trans. Hamilton A. R. Gibb. London: Broadway House.

Ibn Jubayr. 2017. *Travels of Ibn Jubayr.* Trans. Roland J. C. Broadhurst. London: Goodword Books.

Ibn Khaldûn. 1958–1986. *The Muqaddimah: An Introduction to History.* Ed. Franz Rosenthal. 3 vols. New York: Pantheon Books.

Ibn Nahmias, Joseph. 2016. *The Light of the World: Astronomy in al-Andalus.* Ed. Robert G. Morrison. Berkeley: University of California Press.

Ibn Sina. 1974. *The Life of Ibn Sina.* Ed. and trans. William E. Gohlman. Albany: State University of New York Press.

Ibn Warraq. 2007. *Defending the West: A Critique of Edward Said's Orientalism.* Amherst, NY: Prometheus Books.

Icazbalceta, Joaquín García (ed.). 1858–1866. *Colección de documentos para la historia de México.* 2 Vols. México: Librería de J.M. Andrade.

Ignatius of Loyola. 1959. *Letters of St. Ignatius of Loyola.* Trans. William J. Young. Chicago: Loyola University Press. https://archive.org/stream/lettersofst.ignatiusofloyola/Letters%20 of%20St.%20Ignatius%20of%20Loyola_djvu.txt (accessed March 30, 2023).

———. 1987. *Spiritual Exercises of Ignatius Loyola.* Trans. Elisabeth Meier Tetlow. Lanham: University Press of America.

Ikegami, Eiko. 1995. *The Taming of the Samurai: Honorific Individualism and the Making of Modern Japan.* Cambridge, MA: Harvard University Press.

Iliffe, John. 2017. *Africans: The History of a Continent.* 3rd ed. Cambridge: Cambridge University Press.

Imbach, Ruedi. 1989. *Laien in der Philosophie des Mittelalters: Hinweise und Anregungen zu einem vernachlässigten Thema.* Amsterdam: Grüner.

———. 2004. "*Virtus illiterata*: Zur philosophischen Bedeutung der Scholastikkritik in Petrarcas Schrift *De suis et multorum ignorantia*." In Jan A. Aertsen and Martin Pickavé (ed.), *Herbst des Mittelalters? Fragen zur Bewertung des 14. und 15. Jahrhunderts.* Berlin: De Gruyter, 84–104.

Inagaki, Hisao, and Harold Stewart. 2003. *The Three Pure Land Sutras.* Berkeley: University of California Press.

Inalcik, Halil. 1973. *The Ottoman Empire: The Classical Age 1300–1600.* London: Weidenfeld and Nicolson.

Inalcik, Halil, and Donald Quataert (eds.). 1997. *An Economic and Social History of the Ottoman Empire, 1300–1914.* 2 vols. Cambridge: Cambridge University Press.

Ingham, Patricia Clare. 2015. *The Medieval New: Ambivalence in an Age of Innovation*. Philadelphia: University of Pennsylvania Press.

Innocent III. 2001. *On the Misery of the Human Condition*. Trans. Margaret Mary Dietz. In Amélie Oksenberg Rorty (ed.), *The Many Faces of Evil*. London: Routledge, 78–83.

Iogna-Prat, Dominique. 2004. *Ordonner et exclure. Cluny et la société chrétienne face à l'hérésie, au judaïsme et a l'islam, 1000–1200*. Paris: Aubier.

Iqbal, Muzaffar (ed.). 2018. *Islam and Science: Historic and Contemporary Perspectives*. 4 vols. London: Routledge.

Irwin, Terence. 2007. *The Development of Ethics: A Historical and Critical Study*. Vol. I. Oxford: Oxford University Press.

Isenmann, Eberhard. 2012. *Die deutsche Stadt im Spätmittelalter, 1150–1550*. 2nd ed. Vienna: Böhlau.

Ismail, Mohd Zaidi b. 2018. "The Cosmos as the Created Book and its Implications for the Orientation of Science." In Iqbal 2018, I, 269–291.

Israel, Jonathan I. 1995. *The Dutch Republic: Its Rise, Greatness, and Fall*. Oxford: Clarendon.

———. 1997. *Conflicts of Empires: Spain, the Low Countries and the Struggle for World Supremacy, 1585–1713*. London: Hambledon.

———. 2001. *Radical Enlightenment: Philosophy and the Making of Modernity, 1650–1750*. Oxford: Oxford University Press.

———. 2002. *Dutch Primacy in World Trade 1585–1740*. Oxford: Oxford University Press.

Israel, Uwe. 2016. "Venedigs Welt im Wandel um 1500." In Ingrid Baumgärtner and Piero Falchetta (eds.), *Venezia e la nuova oikoumene: Cartografia del Quattrocento*. Rome: Viella, 176–200.

Israeli, Raphael. 1977. "Muslims in China: The Incompatibility between Islam and the Chinese Order." *T'oung Pao* 2nd series, 63, no. 4-5, 296–323.

Issawi, Charles. 1981. *The Arab World's Legacy*. Princeton: Princeton University Press.

Jablonski, Johann Theodor, and Johann Joachim Schwabe. 1767. *Allgemeines Lexicon der Künste und Wissenschaften*. Leipzig: Thomas Fritschen.

al-Jabri, Mohammed Abed. 1995. *Introduction à la critique de la raison arabe*. Paris: Le Découverte.

Jackson, Peter. (ed.). 1986. *The Cambridge History of Iran*. Vol. VI. Cambridge: Cambridge University Press.

———. 2005. *The Mongols and the West, 1221–1410*. London: Methuen.

Jacob, Georg (ed. and trans.). 2010. *Arabische Berichte von Gesandten an germanischen Fürstenhöfen aus dem 9 und 10. Jahrhundert*. Berlin: De Gruyter, 2010.

Jacob, Margaret C. 1997. *Scientific Culture and the Making of the Industrial West*. Oxford: Oxford University Press.

Jacobi, Jolande. 1958. *Paracelsus, Selected Writings*. New York: Pantheon Books.

Jäger, Wolfgang. 1764. *Nuovo Dizzionario italiano-tedesco*. Nuremberg: Gabriel Nicolaus Raspe.

James, Edward. 2001. *Britain in the First Millennium*. London: Arnold.

Jantzen, Hans. 2000. *Über den gotischen Kirchenraum und andere Aufsätze*. Berlin: Gebr. Mann.

Jardine, Lisa. 1995. *Erasmus, Man of Letters: The Construction of Charisma by Print*. Princeton: Princeton University Press.

———. 2000. *Ingenious Pursuits: Building the Scientific Revolution*. London: Anchor.

Jaspers, Karl. 2021. *The Origin and Goal of History*. Trans. Michael Bullock. London: Routledge.

Jaspert, Nikolas. 2008. *Die Kreuzzüge*. 4th ed. Darmstadt: WBG.

Jedin, Hubert. 1949–1975. *Geschichte des Konzils von Trient*. 4 vols. Freiburg: Herder.

Jehne, Martin. 1999. "Cato und die Bewahrung der traditionellen *Res publica*. Zum Spannungsverhältnis zwischen *mos maiorum* und griechischer Kultur im zweiten Jahrhundert v. Chr." In Vogt-Spira/Rommel 1999, 115–134.

Jenco, Leigh. 2015. *Changing Referents: Learning Across Space and Time in China and the West*. Oxford: Oxford University Press.

Jensen, Merill (ed.). 1955. *English Historical Documents*. Vol. IX: *American Colonial Documents, to 1776*. London: Eyre & Spottiswoode.

Jezler, Peter et al. (eds.). 2014. *Ritterturnier. Geschichte einer Festkultur*. Lucerne: Quaternio.

Joachimsen, Paul. 1930. "Der Humanismus und die Entwicklung des deutschen Geistes," *Deutsche Vierteljahrsschrift für Literaturwissenschaft und Geistesgeschichte* 8, 419–480.

Johannes von Saaz. 1958. *Death and the Plowman or, The Bohemian Plowman: A Disputatious and Consolatory Dialogue about Death from the Year 1400*. Trans. Ernest N. Kirrmann. Chapel Hill: University of North Carolina Press. https://doi.org/10.5149/9781469657646_von-Saaz (accessed January 19, 2021).

John of Salisbury. 2012. *Policraticus*. Ed. Cary J. Nederman. Cambridge.

Johnson, Francis R. 1968. *Astronomical Thought in Renaissance England: A Study of English Scientific Writing from 1500 to 1645*. New York: Octagon Books.

Johnston, Andrew James. 2013. *Robin Hood. Geschichte einer Legende*. Munich: C. H. Beck.

Jones, Adam. 1990. *Zur Quellenproblematik der Geschichte Westafrikas, 1450–1900*. Stuttgart: Franz Steiner.

———. 2016. *Afrika bis 1850*. Frankfurt: Fischer.

Jones, Eric. 2003. *The European Miracle: Environments, Economics and Geopolitics in the History of Europe and Asia*. 3rd ed. Cambridge: Cambridge University Press.

Jones, Evan T., and Alwyn Ruddock. 2008. "John Cabot and the Discovery of America." *Historical Research* 81, 212, 224–254

Jones, Michael (ed.). 2000. *The New Cambridge Medieval History*. Vol. VI. Cambridge: Cambridge University Press.

Jones, Philip. 1997. *The Italian City-State: From Commune to Signoria*. Oxford: Oxford University Press.

Joost-Gaugier, Christiane L. 2009. *Finding Heaven: Pythagoras and Renaissance Europe*. Cambridge: Cambridge University Press.

Jordan, Jeff (ed.). 1994. *Gambling on God: Essays on Pascal's Wager*. Lanham: Rowan and Littlefield.

Jordanes. 1882. *De originibus actibusque Getarum*. Ed. Alfred Holder. Freiburg: J. C. B. Mohr.

Jouanna, Arlette. 1996. *La France du XVIe siècle, 1483–1598*. Paris: Presses universitaires de France.

Juneja, Monika. 2002. "Vorkoloniale Städte Nordindiens. Historische Entwicklung, Gesellschaft und Kultur, 10–18. Jahrhundert." In Feldbauer/Mitterauer/Schwentker 2002, 107–132.

Jüngel, Eberhard. 2003. " . . . *unum aliquid assecutus, omnia assecutus*. . . . Zum Verständnis des Verstehens—nach M. Luther, *De servo arbitrio* (*WA* 18, 605)." In Eberhard Jüngel, *Ganz werden*. Tübingen: Mohr Siebeck, 54–75.

Jurt, Joseph. 2002. "Die Kannibalen: Erste europäische Bilder der Indianer—von Kolumbus bis Montaigne." In Monika Fludernik (ed.), *Der Alteritätsdiskurs des Edlen Wilden*. Würzburg: Ergon, 45–63.

Jütte, Robert. 2008. *Contraception: A History*. Cambridge: Polity.

———. 2013. *Krankheit und Gesundheit in der Frühen Neuzeit*. Stuttgart: W. Kohlhammer.

Kafka, Franz. 1958. *Briefe 1902–1924*. Ed. Max Brod. Frankfurt: Fischer.

Kahn, Paul W. 2007. *Adam and Eve and the Problem of Evil*. Princeton: Princeton University Press.

Kälin, Hans. 1974. *Papier in Basel bis 1500*. Basel: self-published.

Kaldellis, Anthony. 2007. *Hellenism in Byzantium: The Transformations of Greek Identity and the Reception of the Classical Tradition*. Cambridge: Cambridge University Press.

Kalkoff, Paul (ed.). 1886. *Die Depeschen des Nuntius Aleander vom Wormser Reichstag 1521*. Halle: Verein für Reformationsgeschichte.

Kallendorf, Craig (ed. and trans.). 2002. *Humanist Educational Treatises*. Cambridge, MA: Harvard University Press.

Kamali, Mohammad Hashim. 2018. "Islam, Rationality and Science: A Brief Analysis." In Iqbal 2018, II, 75–93.

Kamen, Henry. 2010. *The Escorial: Art and Power in the Renaissance*. New Haven: Yale University Press.

———. 2014a. *Spain, 1496–1714: A Society of Conflict*. 4th ed. London: Routledge.

———. 2014b. *The Spanish Inquisition: A Historical Revision*. 4th ed. New Haven: Yale University Press.

Kamp, Hermann. 2005. "Gutes Geld und böses Geld: Die Anfänge der Geldwirtschaft und der Gabentausch im hohen Mittelalter." In Klaus Grubmüller and Markus Stock (eds.), *Geld im Mittelalter. Wahrnehmung—Bewertung—Symbolik*. Darmstadt: WBG, 91–112.

Kantorowicz, Ernst H. 2016. *The King's Two Bodies: A Study in Medieval Political Theology*. Princeton: Princeton University Press.

Kapp, Volker (ed.). 2007. *Italienische Literaturgeschichte*. 3rd ed. Stuttgart: Metzler.

Kappeler, Andreas. 2002. "Stadtluft macht nicht frei! Die russische Stadt in der Vormoderne." In Feldbauer/Mitterauer/Schwentker 2002, 194–212.

———. 2013. *The Russian Empire: A Multi-Ethnic History*. Trans. Alfred Clayton. Milton Park: Routledge.

Kapur, Soheila. 1983. *Witchcraft in Western India*. Hyderabad: Sangam Books.

Karfík, Filip. 2004. *Die Beseelung des Kosmos. Untersuchungen zur Kosmologie, Seelenlehre und Theologie in Platons Phaidon und Timaios*. Munich: Saur.

Kasper, Christine. 1992/93. "Das Schlaraffenland zieht in die Stadt. Vom Land des Überflusses zum Paradies für Sozialschmarotzer." *Jahrbuch der Oswald von Wolkenstein-Gesellschaft* 7, 255–291.

Kaufmann, Thomas. 2011. *Luthers "Judenschriften."* Tübingen: Mohr Siebeck.

———. 2014. *An den christlichen Adel deutscher Nation von des christlichen Standes Besserung*. Tübingen: Mohr Siebeck.

———. 2016. *Geschichte der Reformation in Deutschland*. Frankfurt: Verlag der Weltreligionen.

Kaufmann, Thomas DaCosta. 1993a. "Astronomy, Technology, Humanism, and Art at the Entry of Rudolf II into Vienna, 1577." In Kaufmann 1993c, 136–150.

———. 1993b. "From Mastery of the World to Mastery of Nature: The Kunstkammer, Politics and Science." In Kaufmann 1993c, 174–194.

——— (ed.). 1993c. *The Mastery of Nature: Aspects of Art, Science, and Humanism in the Renaissance*. Princeton: Princeton University Press.

Keating, Jessica, and Lia Markey. 2018. "The Medievalists and the Early Modernists: A World Divided?" In Christina Normore (ed.), *A World within Worlds? Reassessing the "Global Turn" in Medieval Art*. Special edition of *The Medieval Globe*. Amsterdam: Amsterdam University Press, 203–218.

Keele, Kenneth D. 2014. *Leonardo da Vinci's Elements of the Science of Man*. New York: Academic Press.

Keen, Elizabeth. 2007. *The Journey of a Book: Bartholomew the Englishman and the Properties of Things*. Canberra: Australian National University Press.

Keil, Gundolf. 2010. "Secretum Secretorum." In Kurt Ruh et al. (eds.), *Die deutsche Literatur des Mittelalters. Verfasserlexikon*. Vol. VIII. 2nd ed. Berlin: De Gruyter, 993–1013.

Kellermann, Rudolf, and Wilhelm Treue. 1962. *Kulturgeschichte der Schraube*. 2nd ed. Munich: F. Bruckmann.

Kelley, Donald R. (ed.). 1997. *History and the Disciplines: The Reclassification of Knowledge in Early Modern Europe*. Rochester, NY: University of Rochester Press.

Kelly, Joan. 1984. "Did Women Have a Renaissance?" In Joan Kelly, *Women, History and Theory: The Essays of Joan Kelly*. Chicago: University of Chicago Press, 19–50.

Kelsey, Harry. 1998. *Sir Francis Drake, the Queen's Pirate*. New Haven: Yale University Press.

Kemp, Martin. 2006. *Leonardo da Vinci: The Marvellous Works of Nature and Man.* Oxford: Oxford University Press.

Kennedy, Hugh. 2001. *The Armies of the Caliphs: Military and Society in the Early Islamic State.* London: Routledge.

———. 2004a. *The Court of the Caliphs: The Rise and Fall of Islam's Greatest Dynasty.* London: Weidenfeld & Nicolson.

———. 2004b. "The Decline and Fall of the First Muslim Empire." *Der Islam* 81, 3–30.

Kennedy, Paul. 1987. *The Rise and Fall of the Great Powers: Economic Change and Military Conflict from 1500 to 2000.* New York: Random House.

Kent, Dale. 1978. *The Rise of the Medici: Faction in Florence 1426–1434.* Oxford: Oxford University Press.

———. 2000. *The Patron's Œuvre: Cosimo de' Medici and the Florentine Renaissance.* New Haven: Yale University Press.

Kepler, Johannes. 1937–2002. *Gesammelte Werke.* Ed. Max Caspar et al. 22 vols. Munich: C. H. Beck.

———. 1939/1990. *Weltharmonik.* Trans. and Intro. Max Caspar. Fünfter, unveränderter reprografischer Nachdruck der Ausgabe von 1939. Munich: Oldenbourg, 1990.

———. 1992. *New Astronomy.* Trans. William H. Donahue. Cambridge: Cambridge University Press.

———. 1997. *The Harmony of the World.* Trans. Eric J. Aiton, Alistair M. Duncan, and Judith V. Field. Philadelphia: American Philosophical Society.

———. 2008. *Schriften zur Optik 1604–1611.* Ed. Rolf Riekher. Frankfurt: Harri Deutsch.

Kermode, Frank. 2000. *The Sense of an Ending: Studies in the Theory of Fiction.* 2nd ed. Oxford: Oxford University Press.

Keßler, Eckhard. 1971. *Theoretiker humanistischer Geschichtsschreibung.* Munich: Fink.

———. 2008. *Die Philosophie der Renaissance. Das 15. Jahrhundert.* Munich: C. H. Beck.

Khadduri, Majid. 1955. *War and Peace in the Law of Islam.* Baltimore: Johns Hopkins University Press.

Khair, Tabish, et al. (eds.). 2005. *Other Routes: 1500 Years of African and Asian Travel Writings.* Bloomington: Indiana University Press.

Khalidi, Muhammad Ali. 2005. *Medieval Islamic Philosophical Writings.* Cambridge: Cambridge University Press.

Khalidi, Tarif. 2001. *The Muslim Jesus: Sayings and Stories in Islamic Literature.* Cambridge, MA: Harvard University Press.

Khodarkovsky, Michail. 2002. *Russia's Steppe Frontier: The Making of a Colonial Empire.* Bloomington: Indiana University Press.

Khoury, Raif Georges (ed.). 2002. *Averroes (1126–1198) oder der Triumph des Rationalismus.* Heidelberg: Winter.

Kidwell, Carol. 1991. *Pontano: Poet and Prime Minister.* London: Duckworth.

———. 2004. *Pietro Bembo: Lover, Linguist, Cardinal.* Montreal: McGill-Queen's University Press.

King, David A. 2000. "Taki al-Din." In Peri J. Bearman et al. (eds.). *Encyclopedia of Islam.* Vol. X. 2nd ed. Leiden: Brill.

———. 2018. "The Astronomy of the Mamluks." In Iqbal 2018, III, 317–341.

King, P. D. 1987. *Charlemagne: Translated Sources.* Lambrigg, Kendal, Cumbria: P. D. King.

Kingdon, John W. 1995. *Agendas, Alternatives, and Public Policies.* 2nd ed. New York: Longman.

Kirk, Geoffrey S., and John E. Raven (eds.). 1971. *The Presocratic Philosophers: A Critical History with a Selection of Texts.* Cambridge: Cambridge University Press.

Kirk, Thomas A. 2005. *Genoa and the Sea: Policy and Power in an Early Modern Maritime Republic, 1559–1684.* Baltimore: Johns Hopkins University Press.

———. "Le risposte italiane ai cambiamenti economici," in *RIE* IV, 49–69.

Kischlat, Harald. 2000. *Studien zur Verbreitung arabischer philosophischer Werke. Das Zeugnis der Bibliotheken, 1150–1400.* Münster: Aschendorff.

Klein, Karl Kurt et al. (eds.). 1987. *Die Lieder Oswalds von Wolkenstein.* 3rd ed. Tübingen: Max Niemeyer.

Klöckner, Jutta. 2012. "Von der Anschauung zur Anbetung. Götterbilder im antiken Griechenland." *Gießener Universitätsblätter* 45, 29–41.

Kluge, Bernd. 1991. *Deutsche Münzgeschichte von der Späten Karolingerzeit bis zum Ende der Salier (ca. 900–1125).* Sigmaringen: Thorbecke.

Knackstedt, Wolfgang. 1975. *Moskau. Studien zur Geschichte einer mittelalterlichen Stadt.* Wiesbaden: Steiner.

Knoll, Paul W. 1975. "The Arts Faculty at the University of Cracow at the End of the Fifteenth Century." In Westman 1975, 137–156.

Kobusch, Theo. 2011. *Die Philosophie des Hoch- und Spätmittelalters.* Munich: C. H. Beck.

Koch, Carl. 1960. *Religio. Studien zu Kult und Glauben der Römer.* Nuremberg: Hans Carl.

Koenigsberger, Helmut G. 1995. "Parliaments in the Sixteenth Century and Beyond." In Davis 1995, 269–311.

———. 2001. *Monarchies, States Generals and Parliaments: The Netherlands in the Fifteenth and Sixteenth Centuries.* Cambridge: Cambridge University Press.

Kohl, Karl Heinz. 2020. *Powerful Things: The History and Theory of Sacred Objects.* Trans. Jeremy Gaines. Canon Pyon: Sean Kingston Publishing.

Kohler, Alfred. 2013. *Karl V. Eine Biographie.* 2nd ed. C. H. Beck: Munich.

Kolb, Frank. 2005. *Die Stadt im Altertum.* Düsseldorf: Albatros.

Kolga, Margus et al. (eds.). 2001. *The Red Book of the Peoples of the Russian Empire.* Tallinn: NGO Red Book.

Koller, Heinrich. 2005. *Kaiser Friedrich III.* Darmstadt: WBG.

Kölmel, Wilhelm. 1970. *Regimen christianum. Weg und Ergebnisse des Gewaltenverhältnisses und des Gewaltverständnisses (8. bis 14. Jahrhundert).* Berlin: De Gruyter.

Köpf, Ulrich. 2001. *Reformationszeit, 1495–1555.* Stuttgart: Reclam.

Kornicki, Peter. 1998. *The Book in Japan: A Cultural History from the Beginnings to the 19th Century.* Leiden: Brill.

———. 2013. "Manuscript, Not Print: Scribal Culture in the Edo Period." In Brokaw/Kornicki 2013, 406–467.

Kortüm, Hans Henning. 1999. "Gerbertus qui et Silvester. Papsttum um die Jahrtausendwende." *Deutsches Archiv für Erforschung des Mittelalters* 55, 29–62.

Kouamé, Thierry. 2009. "Monachus non doctoris, sed plangentis habet officium. L'autorité de Jérôme dans le débat sur l'enseignement des moines aux XIᵉ et XIIᵉ siècles." *Cahiers de Recherches Médiévales et Humanistes* 18, 9–38.

Koyré, Alexandre. 1948. "From an Approximate World to a Universe of Precision." *Critique* 28, 806–823.

———. 1957. *From the Closed World to the Infinite Universe.* Baltimore: Johns Hopkins Press.

———. 1973. *The Astronomical Revolution: Copernicus—Kepler—Borelli.* Trans. Robert E. W. Maddison. Ithaca: Cornell University Press.

Kraemer, Joel L. 1986. *Humanism in the Renaissance of Islam: The Cultural Revival During the Buyid Age.* Leiden: Brill.

Krämer, Gudrun. 2005. *Geschichte des Islam.* Munich: C. H. Beck.

Krafft, Fritz. 1999. "Ktesibios." In Hubert Cancik, Helmuth Schneider, and August Fr. Pauly (eds.). *Der Neue Pauly.* Vol. VI. Stuttgart: Metzler, cols. 876–878.

Mackay, Christopher S. (ed.). 2006. *Henricus Institoris, O. P. and Jacobus Sprenger, O. P. Malleus maleficarum.* 2 vols. Cambridge: Cambridge University Press.

Kranz, Walther. 2006. *Die griechische Philosophie*. Munich: dtv.

Krautheimer, Richard. 1980. *Rome: Profile of a City, 312–1308*. Princeton: Princeton University Press.

Krautheimer, Richard, and Trude Krautheimer-Hess. 1970. *Lorenzo Ghiberti*. 2 vols. Princeton: Princeton University Press.

Kreiner, Josef (ed.). 2010. *Kleine Geschichte Japans*. Stuttgart: Reclam.

Kreis, Georg (ed.). 2014. *Die Geschichte der Schweiz*. Basel: Schwabe.

Kren, Thomas, Jill Burke, and Stephen J. Campbell. 2018. *The Renaissance Nude*. Los Angeles: J. Paul Getty Museum.

Kretzulesco-Quaranta, Emmanuela. 1987. *Les Jardins du Songe*. 2nd ed. Rome: Editrice Magma.

Kreutel, Richard F. 1978. *Der fromme Sultan Bayezid: Die Geschichte seiner Herrschaft (1481–1512) nach den altosmanischen Chroniken des Oruç und des Anonymus Hanivaldanus*. Graz: Styria.

Kreuzer, Johann. 2005. "Von der Insel der Heiligen ins Zentrum der karolingischen Renaissance: Johannes Scotus Eriugena." In Markus Knapp and Theo Kobusch (eds.), *Querdenker. Visionäre und Außenseiter in Philosophie und Theologie*. Darmstadt: WBG, 84–94.

Krieger, Karl-Friedrich. 2003. *Rudolf von Habsburg*. Darmstadt: WBG.

Kristeller, Paul Oskar. 1964. *The Philosophy of Marsilio Ficino*. Trans. Virginia Conant. Gloucester, MA: Peter Smith.

Kroeber, Alfred L. 1957. *Style and Civilizations*. Ithaca: Cornell University Press.

Krohn, Rüdiger. 1982. "Literaturbetrieb im Mittelalter." In *Propyläen Geschichte der Literatur. Literatur und Gesellschaft der westlichen Welt*. Vol. II. Berlin: Propyläen, 199–220.

Krüger, Klaus. 2001. *Das Bild als Schleier des Unsichtbaren. Ästhetische Illusion in der Kunst der frühen Neuzeit in Italien*. Munich: Fink.

Krüger, Paul (ed.). 1877. *Codex Iustinianus*. Berlin: Weidmann.

Kruft, Hanno-Walter. 1989. *Städte in Utopia: Die Idealstadt vom 15. bis zum 18. Jahrhundert zwischen Staatsutopie und Wirklichkeit*. Munich: C. H. Beck.

———. 1994. *A History of Architectural Theory: From Vitruvius to the Present*. Trans. Ronald Taylor, Elsie Callander, and Antony Wood. London: Zwemmer.

Krynen, Jacques. 1981. *Idéal du prince et pouvoir royal en France à la fin du moyen âge (1380–1440). Étude de la littérature politique du temps*. Paris: A. et J. Picard.

Kubersky-Piredda, Susanne. 2005. *Kunstwerke-Kunstwerte. Die Florentiner Maler der Renaissance und der Kunstmarkt ihrer Zeit*. Norderstedt: Books on Demand.

Kuchenbuch, Ludolf. 2004. "Abschied von der 'Grundherrschaft.' Ein Prüfgang durch das ostfränkisch-deutsche Reich (950–1050)." *Zeitschrift für Rechtsgeschichte* 121, 1–99.

Kühlmann, Wilhelm. 2004. "Literarisierung und Zivilisierung. Anmerkungen zur Kulturanthropologie und zu *De cvilitate morum puerilium* (1530) des Erasmus von Rotterdam." In Rüdiger Schnell (ed.), *Zivilisationsprozesse. Zu Erziehungsschriften der Vormoderne*. Cologne: Böhlau, 277–294.

Kühlmann, Wilhelm et al. (eds.). 1997. *Humanistische Lyrik des 16. Jahrhunderts*. Frankfurt: Suhrkamp.

Kuhn, Dieter. 2009. *The Age of Confucian Rule: The Song Transformation of China*. Cambridge, MA: Harvard University Press.

Kühn, Karl Gottlob (ed.). 1821–1833. *Galeni opera omnia*. 22 vols. Leipzig: Karl Cnobloch.

Kuhn, Thomas S. 1957. *The Copernican Revolution: Planetary Astronomy in the Development of Western Thought*. Cambridge, MA: Harvard University Press.

———. 1962. *The Structure of Scientific Revolutions*. Chicago: University of Chicago Press.

Kühne, Andreas, and Stefan Kirschner. 2004. *Biographia Copernicana. Die Copernicus-Biographien des 16. bis 18. Jahrhunderts*. Berlin: Akademie Verlag.

Kulke, Hermann, and Dietmar Rothermund. 2006. *Geschichte Indiens. Vom Mittelalter bis zur Gegenwart*. 2nd ed. Munich: C. H. Beck.

———. 2010. *A History of India.* 5th ed. London: Routledge.

Kunitzsch, Paul. 2018. "The Transmission of Hindu-Arabic Numerals Reconsidered." In Iqbal 2018, IV, 3–21.

Kuran, Timur. 2004. "Islamic Statecraft and the Middle East's Delayed Modernization." In Bernholz/Vaubel 2004, 150–183.

———. 2011. *The Long Divergence: How Islamic Law Held Back the Middle East.* Princeton: Princeton University Press.

Kwan, Jamie. 2019. "'Un roi, une loi, une foi.' Henri IV and the Portrait of the King." Ph.D. Dissertation, Princeton University.

Lach, Donald F. 1965–1969. *Asia in the Making of Europe.* 2 vols. Chicago: University of Chicago Press.

Lafi, Nora. 2007. "The Ottoman Municipal Reforms between Old Regime and Modernity: Towards a New Interpretative Paradigm." In Eminönü Belediyesi (ed.), *First International Symposium on Eminönü.* Istanbul: Eminönü Belediyesi, 348–355

La Garanderie, Marie-Madeleine de. 2010. *Guillaume Budé, philosophe de la culture.* Paris: Garnier.

LaGrandeur, Kevin. 2013. *Androids and Intelligent Networks in Early Modern Literature and Culture: Artificial Slaves.* London: Routledge.

Lakatos, Imre, and Elie Zahar. 1975. "Why Did Copernicus' Research Program Supersede Ptolemy's?" In Westman 1975, 354–383.

Lal, Deepak. 1999. *Unintended Consequences: The Impact of Factor Endowments, Culture and Politics on Long Run Economic Performance.* 2nd ed. Cambridge, MA: Harvard University Press.

Lamana, Gonzalo. 2008. *Domination Without Dominance: Inca-Spanish Encounters in Early Colonial Peru.* Durham: Duke University Press.

Landes, David S. 1983. *Revolution in Time: Clocks and the Making of the Modern World.* Cambridge, MA: Harvard University Press.

———. 1994. "What Room for Accident in History? Explaining Big Changes by Small Events." *The Economic History Review* 47:4, 637–656.

———. 1998. *The Wealth and Poverty of Nations: Why Some Are So Rich and Some So Poor.* New York: W.W. Norton.

———. 2003. *The Unbound Prometheus: Technological Change and Industrial Development in Western Europe from 1750 to the Present.* 2nd ed. Cambridge: Cambridge University Press.

Landino, Cristoforo. 1974. "Proemio al Commento dantesco." In Roberto Cardini (ed.), *Scritti critici e teorici.* Vol. I. Rome: Bulzoni, 100–164.

Lane, Frederic C. 1973. *Venice: A Maritime Republic.* Baltimore: Johns Hopkins University Press.

Lang, Bernhard, and Colleen McDannell. 2001. *Heaven: A History.* 2nd ed. New Haven: Yale University Press.

Lange, Dierk. 1987. *A Sudanic Chronicle: The Bornu Expeditions of Idris Alauma (1564–1576).* Stuttgart: Steiner.

Lange, Hermann. 1997. *Römisches Recht im Mittelalter.* Vol. I: *Die Glossatoren.* Munich: C. H. Beck.

Langermann, Y. Tzvi. 2013. "Science in the Jewish Community." In Lindberg/Shank 2013, 168–189.

Lapidus, Ira M. 1988. *A History of Islamic Societies.* Cambridge: Cambridge University Press.

———. 1973. "The Evolution of Muslim Urban Society." *Comparative Studies in Sociology and History* 15, 21–50.

Larsen, Mogens Trolle. 2015. *Ancient Kanesh: A Merchant Colony in Bronze Age Anatolia.* Cambridge: Cambridge University Press.

Laslett, Peter. 1965. *The World We Have Lost.* London: Methuen.

Laslett, Peter, and Richard Wall (eds.). 1972. *Household and Family in Past Time.* Cambridge: Cambridge University Press.

Lastraioli, Chiara. 2011. "Une pape *'fatto per necessitade.'* L'image d'Adrien VI dans la propagande européenne du XVIe siècle," *Pape et papauté: respect et contestation d'une autorité bifrons.* Saint-Etienne, Dec. 2011. https://shs.hal.science/halshs-00840698 (accessed June 14, 2021).

Lattimore, Owen. 1940. *Inner Asian Frontiers of China.* New York: American Geographical Society.

Lattis, James M. 1995. *Between Copernicus and Galileo: Christoph Clavius and the Collapse of Ptolemaic Cosmology.* 2nd. ed. Chicago: University of Chicago Press.

Laudage, Johannes. 2012. "Die papstgeschichtliche Wende." In Weinfurter 2012, 51–68.

Leduc, Christian, Paul Rateau, and Jean-Luc Solere (eds.). 2015. *Leibniz et Bayle. Confrontation et dialogue.* Stuttgart: Franz Steiner.

Lee, Alexander, Pit Péporté, and Harry Schnitker (eds.). 2010. *Renaissance? Perceptions of Continuity and Discontinuity in Europe, c. 1300–c. 1550.* Leiden: Brill.

Lee, Christina H. (ed.). 2012. *Western Visions of the Far East in a Transpacific Age, 1522–1657.* London: Routledge.

Lee, James, and Wang Feng. 2001. *One Quarter of Humanity: Malthusian Mythology and Chinese Realities: 1700–2000.* Cambridge, MA: Harvard University Press.

Lee, John. 1999. "Trade and Economy in Preindustrial Asia, c. 1500–c.1800." *Journal of Asian Studies* 58, 2–26.

Legner, Anton. 2010. *Artifex. Künstler im Mittelalter und ihre Selbstdarstellung.* Cologne: Greven.

LeGoff, Jacques. 1965. *Das Hochmittelalter.* Frankfurt am Main: Fischer.

———. 1993. *Intellectuals in the Middle Ages.* Trans. Teresa Lavender Fagan. Cambridge, MA: Blackwell.

———. 2014. *Saint Louis.* Paris: Gallimard.

Legros, Alain. 2000. *Essais sur poutres. Peintures et inscriptions chez Montaigne.* Paris: Klincksieck.

Leinkauf, Thomas. 1998. "Freiheit und Geschichte. Francesco Patrizi und die Selbstverortung der menschlichen Freiheit in der Geschichte." In Enno Rudolph (ed.), *Die Renaissance als erste Aufklärung.* Vol. I. Tübingen: Mohr Siebeck, 79–94.

———. 2014. *Cusanus, Ficino, Patrizi. Formen platonischen Denkens in der Renaissance.* Berlin: trafo.

———. 2017. *Grundriss Philosophie des Humanismus und der Renaissance (1350–1600).* 2 vols. Hamburg: Felix Meiner.

Lemaire, Jean. 1948. *Épîtres de l'amant vert.* Ed. Jean Frappier. Lille: Giard.

Lenin, Vladimir. 1918. *The State and Revolution: The Marxist Theory of the State & the Tasks of the Proletariat in the Revolution.* Lenin Internet Archive. https://www.marxists.org/archive/lenin/works/1917/staterev/ (accessed August 23, 2023).

Leonard, Karen. 1979. "The 'Great Firm' Theory of the Decline of the Mughal Empire." *Comparative Studies in Society and History* 21, 151–167.

Leonardo da Vinci. 1986–1990. *I manoscritti dell'Institut de France.* Ed. Augusto Marinoni. 12 vols. (A-K). Florence.

———. 1975–80. *Il Codice Atlantico di Leonardo da Vinci nella Biblioteca Ambrosiana di Milano.* Ed. Augusto Marinoni. 3 vols. Florence.

———. 1995. *Libro di Pittura: Il Codice Urbinate lat. 1270 nella Biblioteca Apostolica Vaticana.* Ed. Carlo Pedretti and Carlo Vecce. 2 vols. Florence: Giunti.

Leonardo Fibonacci. 2002. *Fibonacci's Liber Abaci: A Translation into Modern English of Leonardo Pisano's Book of Calculation.* Trans. Laurence E. Sigler. New York: Springer.

Lepore, Jill. 2018. *These Truths: A History of the United States.* New York: W. W. Norton.

Leppin, Hartmut. 2010. *Das Erbe der Antike.* Munich: C. H. Beck.

Leppin, Volker. 2010. *Martin Luther.* 2nd ed. Darmstadt: WBG.

———. 2016. *Die fremde Reformation. Luthers mystische Wurzeln.* Munich: C. H. Beck.

Le Roy Ladurie, Emmanuel. 1973. "Un concept. L'unification microbienne du monde (XIVe–XVIIe siècles)." *Schweizerische Zeitschrift für Geschichte* 23, 627–696.

Leu, Urs B. 2016a. *Conrad Gessner (1516–1665). Universalgelehrter und Naturforscher der Renaissance*. Zurich: NZZ Libro.

———. 2016b. "Der Buchdruck in Europa." In *Europe in the Renaissance*, 43–51.

Levack, Brian P. (ed). 2013. *The Oxford Handbook of Witchcraft in Early Modern Europe and Colonial America*. Oxford: Oxford University Press.

Levi, Anthony. 2002. *Renaissance and Reformation: The Intellectual Genesis*. New Haven: Yale University Press.

Levi, Carlo. 1947. *Christ Stopped at Eboli: The Story of a Year*. Trans. Frances Frenaye. New York: Farrar, Straus and Company.

Levtzion, Nehemia, and John F. P. Hopkins (eds.). 2000. *Corpus of Early Arabic Sources for West African History*. 2nd ed. Princeton: Markus Wiener Publishers.

Levy, Ian Christopher (ed.). 2006. *A Companion to John Wyclif, Last Medieval Theologian*. Leiden: Brill.

———. 2015. "The Study of Theology in the Middle Ages." In Robert N. Swanson (ed.), *The Routledge History of Medieval Christianity: 1050–1500*. Oxon: Routledge, 63–76.

Lewis, Bernard. 1982. *The Muslim Discovery of Europe*. New York: W.W. Norton.

———. 2003. *What Went Wrong? The Clash between Islam and Modernity in the Middle East*. New York: Perennial.

Lewis, Mark Edward. 2012. *China's Cosmopolitan Empire: The Tang Dynasty*. Cambridge, MA: Harvard University Press.

Lewy, Hans. 2011. *Chaldaean Oracles and Theurgy: Mystic Magic and Platonism in the Later Roman Empire*. 3d ed. Paris: Institut des Études Augustiniennes.

Lidin, Olof G. 2002. *Tanegashima: The Arrival of Europe in Japan*. Copenhagen: Nordic Institute of Asian Studies.

Lieber, Hans-Joachim (ed.). 1991. *Politische Theorien von der Antike bis zur Gegenwart*. Munich: Olzog.

Lieberman, Victor. 2003–2009. *Strange Parallels: Southeast Asia in Global Context, ca. 800–1830*. 2 vols. Cambridge: Cambridge University Press.

———. 2014. *Burmese Administrative Cycles: Anarchy and Conquest, 1580–1760*. Princeton: Princeton University Press.

Liebs, Detlef. 2002. *Römische Jurisprudenz in Gallien (2. bis 8. Jahrhundert)*. Berlin: Duncker und Humblot.

Lilie, Ralph-Johannes. 2005. *Byzanz. Geschichte des oströmischen Reiches*. 4th ed. Munich: C. H. Beck.

Lill, Rudolf. 1980. *Geschichte Italiens vom 16. Jahrhundert bis zu den Anfängen des Faschismus*. Darmstadt: WBG.

Limongelli, Marco Daniele. 2010. "*Lamento* di Bernabò Visconti: Edizione critica e commento." PhD dissertation, Università degli Studi di Trento.

Lindberg, David C., and Ronald Numbers (eds.). 1986. *God and Nature: Historical Essays on the Encounter between Christianity and Science*. Berkeley: University of California Press.

Lindberg, David C., and Michael H. Shank (eds.). 2013. *The Cambridge History of Science*. Vol. II. Cambridge: Cambridge University Press.

Lindberg, David C., and Robert S. Westman (eds.). 1990. *Reappraisals of the Scientific Revolution*. Cambridge: Cambridge University Press.

Lindstedt, Ilkka. 2011. "Anti-Religious Views in the Works of Ibn al-Rawandi and Abu l-'Ala' al-Ma'arri." *Studia Orientalia* 111, 131–158.

Linsenmann, Thomas. 2011. *Die Magie bei Thomas von Aquin*. Berlin: Akademie Verlag.

Lipsius, Justus. 2004. *Politica: Six Books of Politics or Political Introduction*. Ed. Jan Waszink. Assen: Royal Van Gorcum.

Liu, William Guanglin. 2015. *The Chinese Market Economy 1000–1500*. Albany: State University of New York Press.

Livi-Bacci, Massimo. 2006. *A Concise History of World Population*. Malden: Blackwell.

Livingstone, John. 1995. "Muhammad 'Abduh on Science." *The Muslim World* 85, 215–234.

Lloyd, Geoffrey E. R., and Nathan Sivin. 2002. *The Way and the Word: Science and Medicine in Early China and Greece*. New Haven: Yale University Press.

Loades, David. 1992. *The Tudor Navy: An Administrative, Political and Military History*. Aldershot: Ashgate.

Lockhart, James. 1999. "Letters and People to Spain." In James Lockhart, *Of Things of the Indies: Essays Old and New in Early American Latin History*. Stanford: Stanford University Press, 81–97.

Lockwood, Lewis. 2009. *Music in Renaissance Ferrara 1400–1505: The Creation of a Musical Center in the Fifteenth Century*. Oxford: Oxford University Press.

Lombard, Maurice. 1975. *The Golden Age of Islam*. Translated by Joan Spencer. New York: American Elsevier.

Looney, Dennis. 2009. "The Beginnings of Humanistic Oratory: Petrarch's Coronation Oration (*Collatio laureationis*)." In Victoria Kirkham and Armando Maggi (eds.), *Petrarch: A Critical Guide to the Complete Works*. Chicago: University of Chicago Press, 131–140.

Lorenz, Edward N. 1993. *The Essence of Chaos*. Seattle: University of Washington Press.

Loughlin, Marie H., Sandra Bell, and Patricia Brace (eds.). 2012. *The Broadview Anthology of Sixteenth-Century Poetry and Prose*. Peterborough: Broadview.

Loughman, John, and John Michael Montias. 2000. *Public and Private Spaces: Works of Art in Seventeenth-Century Dutch Houses*. Zwolle: Waanders.

Lovejoy, Arthur O. 2001. *The Great Chain of Being: A Study of the History of an Idea*. 22nd ed. Cambridge, MA: Harvard University Press.

Lowden, John. 2004. "Manuscript Illumination in Byzantium, 1261–1557." In Helen C. Evans, *Byzantium: Faith and Power (1261–1557)*. New Haven: Yale University Press.

Lowe, Kate. 2015. "The Stereotyping of Black Africans in Renaissance Europe." In Earle/Lowe 2015, 17–47.

Lowood, Henry E., and Robin E. Rider. 1994. "Literary Technology and Typographic Culture: The Instrument of Print in Early Modern Science." *Perspectives on Science* 2:1, 1–37.

Lowry, Heath W. 2003. *The Nature of the Early Ottoman State*. Albany: State University of New York Press.

Lübke, Christian. 2004. *Das östliche Europa*. Munich: Siedler.

Lucas, Robert E., Jr. 2002. *Lectures on Economic Growth*. Cambridge, MA: Harvard University Press.

Lucchi, Lorna de'. 1922. *An Anthology of Italian Poems 13th–19th Century*. New York: Alfred A. Knopf. https://elfinspell.com/MediciPoem.html (accessed March 1, 2021).

Lucretius Carus, Titus. 2007. *The Nature of Things*. Trans. Alicia Elsbeth Stallings. London: Penguin.

Lückerath, Karl August. 2003. "Die Diskussion über die Pirenne-These." In Jürgen Elvert and Susanne Krauß (eds.), *Historische Debatten und Kontroversen im 19. und 20. Jahrhundert*. Stuttgart: Steiner, 55–69.

Ludwig, Karl-Heinz, and Volker Schmidtchen (eds.). 1992. *Metalle und Macht: 1000–1600*. Berlin: Propyläen Verlag.

Lund, Mary Ann. 2010. *Melancholy, Medicine and Religion in Early Modern England: Reading 'The Anatomy of Melancholy'*. Cambridge: Cambridge University Press.

Luo, Zhitian. 2015. *Inheritance within Rupture: Culture and Scholarship in Early-Twentieth-Century China*. Leiden: Brill.

Lupher, David A. 2003. *Romans in a New World: Classical Models in Sixteenth-Century Spanish America*. Ann Arbor: University of Michigan Press.

Luther, Martin. 1970. *Three Treatises*. Trans. Charles M. Jacobs et al. 2nd ed. Minneapolis: Fortress Press.

———. 1989. *Martin Luther's Basic Theological Writings*. Ed. Timothy F. Lull. Minneapolis: Fortress Press.

Ma Huan. 1970. *Ying-yai Sheng-lan: The Overall Survey of the Ocean's Shores 1433*. Ed. and trans. J. V. G. Mills. Cambridge: Cambridge University Press.

MacCormack, Sabine. 2007. *On the Wings of Time: Rome, the Incas, Spain and Peru*. Princeton: Princeton University Press.

MacCulloch, Diarmaid. 2013. *Reformation: Europe's House Divided, 1490–1700*. London: Folio Society.

MacFarlane, Alan. 1979. *The Origins of English Individualism: The Family Property and Social Transition*. London: Cambridge: Cambridge University Press.

MacGregor, Neil. 2010. *History of the World in 100 Objects*. New York: Penguin.

Machiavelli, Niccolò. 1988. *Florentine Histories*. Trans. Laura F. Banfield and Harvey C. Mansfield. Princeton: Princeton University Press.

———. 1998. *L'arte della Guerra: Scritti politici minori*. Ed. Jean-Jacques Marchand, Denis Fachard, and Giorgio Masi. Rome: Salerno.

Mack, Rosamond E. 2001. *Bazaar to Piazza: Islamic Trade and Italian Art, 1300–1600*. Berkeley: University of California Press.

Maclean, Ian. 1984. "The Interpretation of Natural Signs. Cardano's *De subtilitate* versus Scaliger's *Exercitationes*." In Vickers 1984b, 231–252.

———. 1996. *Montaigne philosophe*. Vendôme: Presses Universitaires de France.

Macpherson, Crawford B. 1962. *The Political Theory of Possessive Individualism: Hobbes to Locke*. Oxford: Clarendon.

Mączak, Antoni. 1992. "Poland." In Porter/Teich 1992, 180–196.

Maddicott, John Robert. 2010. *The Origins of the English Parliament, 924–1327*. Oxford: Oxford University Press.

Maddison, Angus. 2001. *The World Economy: A Millennial Perspective*. Paris: OECD Development Centre Studies.

Madelung, Wilferd. 1997. *The Succession to Muhammad: A Study of the Early Caliphate*. Cambridge: Cambridge University Press.

Maeyama, Yasukatso. 1974. "The Historical Development of Solar Theories in the Late Sixteenth and Seventeenth Centuries." In Arthur Beer (ed.), *Vistas in Astronomy*. London: Pergamon, 35–60.

———. 2003. "Das Paradoxe in der Astronomiegeschichte. Naturgesetzlichkeit, Geo-, und Egozentrizität." In Maeyama, *Astronomy in Orient and Occident: Selected Papers on its Cultural and Scientific History*. Hildesheim: Olms, 526–531.

Magasich-Airola, Jorge, and Jean-Marc de Beer. 2007. *America Magica: When Renaissance Europe Thought It Had Conquered Paradise*. Trans. Monica Sandor. 2nd ed. London: Anthem Press.

Magdalino, Paul. 2002. "The Byzantine Reception of Classical Astrology." In Catherine Holmes and Judith Waring (eds.), *Literacy, Education and Manuscript Transmission in Byzantium and Beyond*. Leiden: Brill, 33–58.

Mahal, Günther. 1980. *Faust. Die Spuren eines geheimnisvollen Lebens*. Bern: Scherz.

Mahdi, Muhsin S. 2001. *Alfarabi and the Foundation of Islamic Political Philosophy*. Chicago: University of Chicago Press.

Makdisi, George. 1990. *The Rise of Humanism in Classical Islam and the Christian West*. Edinburgh: Edinburgh University Press.

Malanima, Paolo. 2009. *Pre-Modern European Economy: One Thousand Years (10th–19th Centuries)*. Leiden: Brill.

Malettke, Klau. 2008. *Die Bourbonen*. Vol. I: *Von Heinrich IV. bis Ludwig XIV. (1589–1715)*. Stuttgart: Kohlhammer.

Malinar, Angelika. 2009. *Hinduismus*. Göttingen: Vandenhoeck & Ruprecht.

Malinar, Angelika and Martin Vöhler (eds.). 2009. *Un/Reinheit: Konzepte und Erfahrungsmodi im Kulturvergleich.* Munich: Fink.

Mallison, Françoise. 2011. "The Teaching of Braj, Gujarati, and Bardic Poetry at the Court of Kutch: The Bhuj Brajbhasa Pathśala (1749–1948)." In Sheldon Pollock (ed.), *Forms of Knowledge in Early Modern Asia: Explorations in the Intellectual History of India and Tibet, 1500–1800.* Durham: Duke University Press, 171–182.

Mallory, Walter H. 1926. *China: Land of Famine.* New York: American Geographical Society.

Mancall, Peter C. 2007. *Hakluyt's Promise: An Elizabethan's Obsession for an English America.* New Haven: Yale University Press.

Mandrou, Robert. 1997. *Die Fugger als Grundbesitzer in Schwaben, 1560–1618.* Göttingen: Vandenhoeck & Ruprecht.

Manfredi, Antonio. "Gli umanisti e le biblioteche tra l'Italia e l'Europa." In *RIE* II, 267–286.

Mann, Heinrich. 1987. *Die Göttinnen. Die drei Romane der Herzogin von Assy.* Vol. I: *Diana.* Frankfurt: Fischer.

Mann, Michael. 2005. *The Sources of Social Power.* Vol I. Cambridge: Cambridge University Press.

———. 2023. *On Wars.* New Haven: Yale University Press.

Mann, Thomas. 1936. *Stories of Three Decades.* Trans. Helen Tracy Lowe-Porter. New York: Knopf.

Mansel, Philip. 1995. *Constantinople: City of the World's Desire 1453–1924.* London: John Murray.

Manuel, Frank E. 1974. *The Religion of Isaac Newton.* Oxford: Oxford University Press.

Marchi, Neil de, and Hans J. van Miegroet. 2006. "The History of Art Markets." In Victor A. Ginsburgh and David Throsby (eds.), *Handbook of the Economics of Art and Culture.* Vol. I. Amsterdam: Elsevier, 69–122.

Marcon, Federico. 2015. *The Knowledge of Nature and the Nature of Knowledge in Early Modern Japan.* Chicago: University of Chicago Press.

Marcus, Abraham. 1989. *The Middle East on the Eve of Modernity: Aleppo in the Eighteenth Century.* New York: Columbia University Press.

Marees, Pieter de. 1987. *Description and Historical Account of the Gold Kingdom of Guinea.* Ed. Albert van Dantzig and Adam Jones. Oxford: Oxford University Press.

Marek, Christian. 1993. "Euboia und die Entstehung der Alphabetschrift bei den Griechen." *Klio* 75, 27–44.

———. 2010. *Geschichte Kleinasiens in der Antike.* Munich: C. H. Beck.

Marguerite de Navarre. 2013. *L'Heptaméron.* Ed. Nicole Cazauran and Sylvie Lefèvre. Paris: Champion.

Marías, Fernando. "Il palazzo di Carlo V a Granada e l'Escorial." In *RIE* VI, 293–321.

Marker, Gary. 1985. *Publishing, Printing, and the Origins of Intellectual Life in Russia, 1700–1800.* Princeton: Princeton University Press.

Markie, Peter. 1995. "The Cogito and Its Importance." In Cottingham 1995, 140–173.

Marks, Stephen G. 2016. *The Information Nexus: Global Capitalism from the Renaissance to the Present.* Cambridge: Cambridge University Press.

Maron, Gottfried. 1988. *Martin Luther und Epikur: Ein Beitrag zum Verständnis des alten Luther.* Göttingen: Vandenhoeck & Ruprecht.

Marr, Alexander. 2006. "*Gentille curiositée*: Wonder-Working and the Culture of Automata in the Late Renaissance." In Robert J. W. Evans and Alexander Marr (eds.). *Curiosity and Wonder from the Late Renaissance to the Enlightenment.* Aldershot: Ashgate, 149–170.

Marsh, David. 1998. *Lucian and the Latins: Humor and Humanism in the Early Renaissance.* Ann Arbor: University of Michigan Press.

Marshall, Peter H. 2007. *The Mercurial Emperor: The Magic Circle of Rudolf II in Renaissance Prague.* London: Random House.

Martens, Rhonda. 2000. *Kepler's Philosophy and the New Astronomy.* Princeton: Princeton University Press.

Martin, Colin, and Geoffrey Parker. 2002. *The Spanish Armada.* 2nd ed. Manchester: Manchester University Press.

Martin, Janet. 2007. *Medieval Russia, 980–1548.* 2nd ed. Cambridge: Cambridge University Press.

Martin, John Jeffries. 2004. *Myths of Renaissance Individualism.* Basingstoke and New York: Palgrave/St. Martin's Press.

Martín, José Luis. 2003. *Enrique IV de Castilla. Rey de Navarra, príncipe de Cataluña.* Hondarribia: Nerea.

Martínek, Jan. 1980. "Bohuslaw von Lobkowicz und die Antike." *Listy filologické* 103, 24–30.

Martines, Lauro. 1963. *The Social World of the Florentine Humanists, 1390–1460.* Princeton: Princeton University Press.

Märtl, Claudia. 1996. *Kardinal Jean Jouffroy († 1473). Leben und Werk.* Sigmaringen: Thorbecke.

Marullus, Michael. 1998. *Institutiones principales / Prinzenerziehung.* Ed. and trans. Otto Schönberger. Würzburg: Königshausen u. Neumann.

Marx, Barbara. 1999. "Vittoria Colonna (1492–1547)." In Irmgard Osols-Wehden (ed.), *Frauen der italienischen Renaissance. Dichterinnen, Malerinnen, Mäzeninnen.* Darmstadt: WBG, 35–49, 253–256.

Marx, Karl. 1908. *Capital: A Critique of Political Economy.* Vol. I. Trans. Samuel Moore and Edward Aveling. Chicago: Charles H. Kerr.

Máthé, Piroska. 1972. "Heynlin de Lapide, Johannes." In *NDB* 9, 98–100.

Matheus, Michael (ed.). 2005a. *Lebenswelten Johannes Gutenbergs.* Stuttgart: Franz Steiner.

———. 2005b. "Mainz zur Zeit Gutenbergs." In Matheus 2005a, 9–37.

Matthew, Donald, 1992. *The Norman Kingdom of Sicily.* Cambridge: Cambridge University Press.

Matuz, Josef. 2006. *Das Osmanische Reich: Grundlinien seiner Geschichte.* 4th ed. Darmstadt: WBG.

Mauelshagen, Franz. 2010. *Klimageschichte der Neuzeit, 1500–1900.* Darmstadt: WBG.

Mauer, Benedikt. 2001. *"Gemain Geschrey" und "teglich Reden." Georg Kölderer—ein Augsburger Chronist des konfessionellen Zeitalters.* Augsburg: Wissner.

Maurer, Armand Augustine. 1982. *Medieval Philosophy: An Introduction.* Toronto: Pontifical Institute of Medieval Studies.

Mauthner, Fritz. 1921. *Der Atheismus und seine Geschichte im Abendlande.* Stuttgart: DVA.

Mayer, Hans Eberhard. 1988. *The Crusades.* Trans. John Gillingham. Oxford: Oxford University Press.

Mayer Brown, Howard. 1970. "How Opera Began: An Introduction to Jacopo Peri's *Euridice* (1600)." In Eric Cochrane (ed.), *The Late Italian Renaissance, 1525–1630.* London: Macmillan, 401–443.

Mayr, Otto. 1986. *Authority, Liberty and Automatic Machinery in Early Modern Europe.* Baltimore: Johns Hopkins University Press.

Mbembe, Achille. 2017. *Critique of Black Reason.* Ed. and trans. Laurent Dubois. Durham: Duke University Press.

McCausland, Shane. 2011. *Zhao Mengfu: Calligraphy and Painting for Khubilai's China.* Aberdeen, Hong Kong: Hong Kong University Press.

McClain, James. 1982. *Kanazawa: A Seventeenth-Century Castle Town.* New Haven: Yale University Press.

McClellan, James E., III, and Harold Dorn. 2015. *Science and Technology in World History: An Introduction.* 3rd ed. Baltimore: Johns Hopkins University Press.

McCloskey, Deirdre. 2010. *Bourgeois Dignity: Why Economics Can't Explain the Modern World.* Chicago: University of Chicago Press.

McCormick, Michael. 2001. *Origins of the European Economy: Communications and Commerce AD 600–900*. Cambridge: Cambridge University Press.

McDermott, Joseph. 2006. *A Social History of the Chinese Book: Books and Literati Culture in Late Imperial China*. Aberdeen, Hong Kong: Hong Kong University Press.

McDermott, Joseph, and Shiba Yoshinobu. 2015. "Economic Change in China, 960–1279." In Chaffee/Twitchett 2015, 321–385.

McEvoy, James. 2000. *Robert Grosseteste*. Oxford: Oxford University Press.

McGinn, Bernard. 1994. *Die Mystik im Abendland*. Vol. I. Freiburg: Herder.

McGrade, Arthur S. 2003. *The Cambridge Companion to Medieval Philosophy*. Cambridge: Cambridge University Press.

McKee, Sally. 2000. *Uncommon Dominion: Venetian Crete and the Myth of Ethnic Purity*. Philadelphia: University of Pennsylvania Press.

McKim, Donald K. (ed.). 2004. *The Cambridge Companion to John Calvin*. Cambridge: Cambridge University Press.

McLynn, Neil B. 1994. *Ambrose of Milan: Church and Court in a Christian Capital*. Berkeley: University of California Press.

McMullen, David. 1988. *State and Scholars in T'ang China*. Cambridge: Cambridge University Press.

McNeill, William H. 1963. *The Rise of the West: A History of the Human Community*. Chicago: University of Chicago Press.

McRae, Michael. 2004. *In Search of Shangri-La: The Extraordinary True Story of the Quest for the Lost Horizon*. London: Penguin.

Mehlhausen, Joachim (ed.). 1996. *Das Augsburger Interim von 1548*. 2nd ed. Neukirchen-Vluyn: Neukirchener.

Meier, Thomas et al. (eds.). 2015. *Materiale Textkulturen. Konzepte—Materialien—Praktiken*. Berlin: De Gruyter.

Meinhardt, Matthias, Andreas Ranft, and Stephan Selzer (eds.). 2007. *Mittelalter*. Munich: Oldenbourg.

Melanchthon, Philipp. 1834–1860. *Opera quae supersunt omnia*. Corpus reformatorum I-XXVIII. Ed. Karl Gottlieb Bretschneider. Halle: Schwetschke.

Melville, Gert. 2016. *The World of Medieval Monasticism: Its History and Forms of Life*. Trans. James D. Mixson. Collegeville, MN: Liturgical Press.

Mendoza, Juan Gonzáles de. 1586. *Historia de las cosas mas notables, ritos y costumbres del gran Reyno dela China*. Madrid: Querino Gerardo Flamenco.

Menzel, Ulrich. 2015. *Die Ordnung der Welt: Imperium oder Hegemonie in der Hierarchie der Staatenwelt*. Berlin: Suhrkamp.

Merediz, Eyda M. 2004. *Refracted Images: The Canary Islands through a New World Lens: Transatlantic Readings*. Tempe: Arizona Center for Medieval and Renaissance Studies.

Merton, Robert K. 1970. *Science, Technology and Society in Seventeenth-Century England*. New York: Howard Fertig.

Metzig, Gregor M. 2016. *Kommunikation und Konfrontation. Diplomatie und Gesandtschaftswesen Kaiser Maximilians I: (1486–1519)*. Berlin: De Gruyter.

Michalski, Sergiusz. 1992. *The Reformation and the Visual Arts*. London: Routledge.

Michelet, Fabienne L. 2006. "Reading and Writing the East in *Mandeville's Travels*." In Speer/Wegener 2006, 282–302.

Mielants, Eric. 2007. *The Origins of Capitalism and the Rise of the West*. Philadelphia: Temple University Press.

Miethke, Jürgen. 2008. *Politiktheorie im Mittelalter. Von Thomas von Aquin bis Wilhelm von Ockham*. Tübingen: Mohr Siebeck.

Miggiano, Gabriella. 2008. "Marzio, Galeotto." In *DBI* 71, 478–484.

Mignolo, Walter D. 2011. *The Darker Side of Modernity: Global Futures, Decolonial Options.* Durham: Duke University Press.

Mikkeli, Heiki. 2010. "Jacopo Zabarella (1533–1589): The Structure and Method of Scientific Knowledge." In Paul Richard Blum (ed.), *Philosophers of the Renaissance.* Washington, D.C.: Catholic University of America Press, 181–191.

Mirbt, Carl, and Kurt Aland (eds.). 1967. *Quellen zur Geschichte des Papsttums und des Römischen Katholizismus.* Vol. I. 6th ed. Tübingen: Mohr Siebeck.

Mittelstrass, Jürgen. 1962. *Die Rettung der Phänomene. Ursprung und Geschichte eines antiken Forschungsprinzips.* Berlin: De Gruyter.

Mitterauer, Michael. 2010. *Why Europe? The Medieval Origins of Its Special Path.* Trans. Gerald Chapple. Chicago: University of Chicago Press.

Mittler, Barbara. 2019. Review of Bernd Roeck, *Der Morgen der Welt.* In *Historische Anthropologie* 27:2, 311–315. https://www.vr-elibrary.de/doi/epdf/10.7788/hian.2019.27.2.310 (accessed October 11, 2023).

Mo, Pak Hung. 2004. "Lessons from the History of Imperial China." In Bernholz/Vaubel 2004, 57–95.

Mode, Robert L. 1973. "The Orsini Sala Theatri at Monte Giordano in Rome." *Renaissance Quarterly* 26:2, 167–172.

Modelski, George. 2003. *World Cities: -3000 to 2000.* Washington, D.C.: Faros.

Modjtahedi, Karim. 2004. "Kant im Iran." *Spektrum Iran* 17:2, 13–18.

Moeglin, Jean-Pierre, and Rainer A. Müller (eds.). 2000. *Deutsche Geschichte in Quellen und Darstellung.* Vol. II: *Spätmittelalter 1250–1495.* Stuttgart: Reclam.

Moeller, Bernd. 1972. *Imperial Cities and the Reformation: Three Essays.* Ed. and trans. H. C. Erik Midelfort and Mark U. Edwards, Jr. Philadelphia: Fortress Press.

———. 1999. *Deutschland im Zeitalter der Reformation.* Göttingen: Vandenhoeck & Ruprecht.

Mojsisch, Burkhard, and Orrin F. Summerell. 2011. "Meister Eckhart." In *Stanford Encyclopedia of Philosophy* (Summer 2011 Edition). https://plato.stanford.edu/archives/sum2011/entries/meister-eckhart/ (accessed June 14, 2021).

Mokyr, Joel. 2002. *The Gifts of Athena: Historical Origins of the Knowledge Economy.* Princeton: Princeton University Press.

——— (ed.). 2003a. *The Oxford Encyclopedia of Economic History.* Oxford: Oxford University Press.

———. 2003b. "The Riddle of the 'Great Divergence': Intellectual and Economic Factors in the Growth of the West." *Historically Speaking* 5:1, 2–6.

———. 2005. "The Intellectual Origins of Modern Economic Growth." *The Journal of Economic History* 65:2, 285–351.

Molà, Luca. "Stato e impresa: privilegi per l'introduzione di nuove arti e brevetti." In *RIE* III, 533–572.

Mommsen, Theodor E. 1942. "Petrarch's Conception of the 'Dark Ages.'" *Speculum* 17:2, 226–242.

———. 1992. *Römische Kaisergeschichte.* Ed. Barbara Demandt and Alexander Demandt. Munich: C. H. Beck.

Monod, Jacques. 1971. *Chance and Necessity: An Essay on the Natural Philosophy of Modern Biology.* Trans. Austryn Wainhouse. New York: Alfred A. Knopf.

Monschi, Nasrollah. 1996. *Kalila und Dimna. Fabeln aus dem klassischen Persien.* Ed. Seyfeddin Najmabadi and Siegfried Weber. Munich: C. H. Beck.

Montaigne, Michel de. 1962. *Œuvres complètes.* Ed. Albert Thibaudet and Maurice Rat. Paris: Gallimard.

Montgomery, Scott L. 2000. *Science in Translation: Movements of Knowledge through Cultures and Time.* Chicago: University of Chicago Press.

Moor, Tine de. 2008. "The Silent Revolution: A New Perspective on the Emergence of Commons, Guilds, and Other Forms of Corporate Action in Western Europe." *International Review of Social History* 53, 179–212.

Moore, Robert I. 1987. *The Formation of a Persecuting Society: Power and Deviance in Western Europe, 950–1250.* Oxford: Blackwell.

Moos, Peter von. 1965. *Hildebert von Lavardin (1056–1133). Humanitas an der Schwelle des höfischen Zeitalters.* Stuttgart: Hiersemann.

Moran, Bruce T. 1991. *Patronage and Institutions: Science, Technology and Medicine at the European Court.* Rochester: Boydell.

———. 2005. *Distilling Knowledge: Alchemy, Chemistry, and the Scientific Revolution.* Cambridge, MA: Harvard University Press.

Moraw, Peter. 1985. *Von offener Verfassung zu gestalteter Verdichtung. Das Reich im späteren Mittelalter.* Berlin: Propyläen.

More, Anna. 2009. "Cosmopolitanism and Scientific Reason in New Spain: Carlos de Sigüenza y Góngora and the Dispute over the 1680 Comet." In Bleichmar et al. 2009, 115–131.

More, Thomas. 1995. *Utopia.* Ed. George M. Logan. Trans. Robert M. Adams. Cambridge: Cambridge University Press.

Morelli, Marcello, and Marco Tangheroni (eds.). 1994. *Leonardo Fibonacci: il tempo, le opere, l'eredita scientifica.* Pisa: Pacini.

Morgan, David. 2007. *The Mongols.* 2nd ed. Oxford: Blackwell.

Mörke, Olaf. 2005. *Die Reformation. Voraussetzungen und Durchsetzung.* Munich: Oldenbourg.

Mormando, Franco. 1999. *The Preacher's Demon: Bernardino of Siena and the Social Underworld of Early Renaissance Italy.* Chicago: University of Chicago Press.

Morris, Colin. 1972. *The Discovery of the Individual, 1050–1200.* New York: Harper and Row.

Morris, Ian. 2010. *Why the West Rules—For Now: The Patterns of History, and What They Reveal about the Future.* London: Profile Books.

Morrison, Robert G. 2013. "Islamic Astronomy." In Lindberg/Shank 2013, 109–138.

Moseley, Charles (ed.). 2005. *The Travels of Sir John Mandeville.* London: Penguin.

Moss, Jean Dietz. 1993. *Novelties in the Heavens: Rhetoric and Science in the Copernican Controversy.* Chicago: University of Chicago Press.

Mote, Frederick W. 2003. *Imperial China, 900–1800.* Cambridge, MA: Harvard University Press.

Mottahedeh, Roy. 1985. *The Mantle of the Prophet: Religion and Politics in Iran.* New York: Pantheon Books.

Mout, Nicolette (ed.). 1998. *Die Kultur des Humanismus. Reden, Briefe, Traktate, Gespräche von Petrarca bis Kepler.* Munich: C. H. Beck.

Mühle, Eduard. 2011. *Die Piasten. Polen im Mittelalter.* Munich C. H. Beck.

Mukund, Kanakalatha. 1999. *The Trading World of the Tamil Merchant: Evolution of Merchant Capitalism in the Coromandel.* Himayatnagar: Orient Longman.

Müller, Gregor. 1984a. *Mensch und Bildung im italienischen Renaissance-Humanismus: Vittorino da Feltre und die humanistischen Erziehungs-Denker.* Baden-Baden: Koerner.

Müller, Heribert. 2002a. "Der französische Frühhumanismus um 1400. Patriotismus, Propaganda und Historiographie." In Helmrath/Muhlack/Walther 2002, 319–376.

———. 2011. "Das Basler Konzil und die europäischen Mächte: Universaler Anspruch und nationale Wirklichkeiten." *Historische Zeitschrift* 293, 593–629.

Müller, Jörn. 2009. "*Psychologie.*" In Horn/Müller/Söder 2009, 142–154.

Müller, Klaus. 1988. *Wirtschafts- und Technikgeschichte Japans (Handbuch der Orientalistik V.3.3).* Leiden: Brill.

Müller, Ludolf. 2002b. "*Nestorchronik.*" In Rosemarie Müller (ed.), *Reallexikon der Germanischen Altertumskunde.* Vol. XXI. 2nd ed. Berlin: De Gruyter, 94–100.

Müller, Rainer A. 1984b. *Edelsteinmedizin im Mittelalter. Die Entwicklung der spätantiken und mittelalterlichen Lithotherapie unter besonderer Berücksichtigung des Konrad von Megenberg.* Munich: Demeter.

Müller, Ulrich, and Margarete Springeth (eds.). 2011. *Oswald von Wolkenstein: Leben—Werk—Rezeption.* Berlin: De Gruyter.

Müller-Sievers, Helmut. 2012. *The Cylinder: Kinematiks of the Nineteenth Century.* Berkeley: University of California Press.

Mulsow, Martin. 1998. *Frühneuzeitliche Selbsterhaltung. Telesio und die Naturphilosophie der Renaissance.* Tübingen: Max Niemeyer.

Münch, Paul. 1990. *Lebensformen in der frühen Neuzeit, 1500–1800.* Berlin: Propyläen.

Mundt, Felix. 2008. *Beatus Rhenanus, Rerum Germanicarum libri tres (1531). Ausgabe, Übersetzung, Studien.* Tübingen: Niemeyer.

Mundy, John Hine. 1995. "Medieval Urban Liberty." In Davis 1995, 101–134.

Mungello, David E. 2013. *The Great Encounter of China and the West, 1500–1800.* 4th ed. Lanham: Rowman & Littlefield.

Münkler, Herfried. 2007. *Empires: The Logic of World Domination from Ancient Rome to the United States.* Cambridge: Polity.

Münkler, Marina. 1998. *Marco Polo. Leben und Legende.* Munich: C. H. Beck.

Munro, Dana C. (ed.). 1895. *Urban and the Crusaders: Translations and Reprints from the Original Sources of European History.* Vol. I.2. Philadelphia: University of Pennsylvania Press.

Munro, John H. "I panni di lana." In *RIE* IV, 105–141.

Müntzer, Thomas. 2010. *Kritische Gesamtausgabe.* Ed. Helmar Junghans and Armin Kohnle. Vol. II. Leipzig: Evangelische Verlagsanstalt.

Murner, Thomas. 2014. *Von dem grossen lutherischen Narren (1522).* Ed. Thomas Neukirchen. Heidelberg: Winter.

Murray, Alexander. 1985. *Reason and Society in the Middle Ages.* Oxford: Oxford University Press.

Murray, Charles. 2003. *Human Accomplishment: The Pursuit of Excellence in Arts and Sciences, 800 BC to 1950.* New York: Harper Perennial.

Nabokov, Vladimir (trans.). 1960. *The Song of Igor's Campaign: An Epic of the Twelfth Century.* New York: Vintage Books.

Naef, Silvia. 2007. *Bilder und Bilderverbot im Islam. Vom Koran bis zum Karikaturenstreit.* Munich: C. H. Beck.

Näf, Beat. 2010. *Antike Geschichtsschreibung. Form—Leistung—Wirkung.* Stuttgart: Urban.

Nagel, Alexander, and Christopher S. Wood. 2010. *Anachronic Renaissance.* New York: Zone Books.

Nahrstedt, Wolfgang. 1972. *Die Entstehung der Freizeit.* Göttingen: Vandenhoeck & Ruprecht.

Najemy, John M. 2006. *A History of Florence 1200–1575.* Oxford: Blackwell.

Nakayama, Shigeru. 1969. *A History of Japanese Astronomy: Chinese Background and Western Impact.* Cambridge, MA: Harvard University Press.

Nakayama, Shigeru, and Nathan Sivin (eds.). 1968. *Chinese Science: Explorations of an Ancient Tradition.* Cambridge, MA: MIT Press

Naphy, William G. 1994. *Calvin and the Consolidation of the Genevan Reformation.* Manchester: Manchester University Press.

———. 2004. "Calvin's Geneva." In McKim 2004, 25–37.

Nasr, Seyyed Hossein. 1990. *Man and Nature: The Spiritual Crisis of Modern Man.* London: Unwin Hyman.

Nasr, Vali. 2009. *The Rise of Islamic Capitalism: Why the New Muslim Middle Class is the Key to Defeating Extremism.* New York: Free Press.

Nate, Richard. 2006. "'I thought it worth the trial': Wissenschaftliche und literarische Experimente der englischen Restaurationszeit." In Helmar Schramm, Ludger Schwarte, and

Jan Lazardzig (eds.), *Spektakuläre Experimente. Praktiken der Evidenzproduktion im 17. Jahrhundert*. Berlin: De Gruyter.

Nauert, Charles G., Jr. 2006. *Humanism and the Culture of Renaissance Europe*. 2nd ed. Cambridge: Cambridge University Press.

Nauta, Lodi. 2009. *In Defense of Common Sense: Lorenzo Valla's Humanist Critique of Scholastic Philosophy*. Cambridge, MA: Harvard University Press.

Nebrija, Antonio de. 1980. *Gramática de la lengua castellana*. Ed. Antonio Quilis. Madrid: Editorial Universitaria Ramón Areces.

Needham, Joseph. 1928. "Organicism in Biology." *Journal of Philosophical Studies* 3:9, 29–40.

———. 1951. *Human Law and the Laws of Nature in China and the West*. Cambridge: Cambridge University Press.

———. *The Grand Titration: Science and Technology in East and West*. London: Routledge, 1969.

Needham, Joseph et. al. (eds.). 1954–2004. *Science and Civilization in China*. 7 vols. in 27 parts. Cambridge: Cambridge University Press.

Neher, André. 1986. *Jewish Thought and the Scientific Revolution of the Sixteenth Century: David Gans (1541–1613) and His Times*. Oxford: Oxford University Press.

Neidhart von Reuental. 1975. *Die Lieder Neidharts*. Ed. Siegfried Beyschlag. Darmstadt: WBG.

Neumahr, Uwe. 2015. *Miguel de Cervantes. Ein wildes Leben*. Munich: C. H. Beck.

Neuschäfer, Hans-Jörg (ed.). 2011. *Spanische Literaturgeschichte*. 4th ed. Stuttgart: Metzler.

Newton, Isaac. 1729. "General Scholium from the Mathematical Principles of Natural Philosophy." In Newton, *The Mathematical Principles of Natural Philosophy*. Vol. II. London: Benjamin Motte, 387–393.

———. 1959–1978. *The Correspondence of Isaac Newton*. Eds. Herbert W. Turnbull et al. 7 vols. Cambridge: Cambridge University Press.

Nicholas of Cusa. 1996. *On Wisdom and Knowledge*. Trans. Jasper Hopkins. Minneapolis: The Arthur J. Banning Press.

Nichols, Madaline W. 1932. "Las Siete Partidas." *California Law Review* 20, 260–285.

Nicoud, Marylin. 2016. "Reguardati, Benedetto." In *DBI* 86, 758–761.

Nietzsche, Friedrich. 2016. *Die Geburt der Tragödie oder Griechentum und Pessimismus*. Berlin: Holzinger.

Niewöhner, Friedrich. 1988. *Veritas sive Varietas. Lessings Toleranzparabel und das Buch von den drei Betrügern*. Heidelberg: Schneider.

Nigellus de Longchamps. 1960. *Speculum stultorum*. Ed. John H. Mozley and Robert R. Raymo. Berkeley: University of California Press.

Nipperdey, Thomas. 1975. "Die Utopia des Thomas Morus und der Beginn der Neuzeit." In Thomas Nipperdey, *Reformation, Revolution, Utopie. Studien zum 16. Jahrhundert*. Göttingen: Vandenhoeck & Ruprecht, 113–146.

Noll, Thomas. 2005. *Alexander in der nachantiken bildenden Kunst*. Mainz: Philipp von Zabern.

Nordeide, Saebjørg W. 2011. *The Viking Age as a Period of Religious Transformation: The Christianization of Norway from AD 560 to 1150/1200*. Turnhout: Brepols.

North, Douglass C. 1995. "The Paradox of the West." In Davis 1995, 7–34.

North, Douglass C., and Robert Paul Thomas. 1973. *The Rise of the Western World: A New Economic History*. Cambridge: Cambridge University Press.

North, Douglass C., John Joseph Wallis, and Barry R. Weingast (eds.). 2009. *Violence and Social Orders: A Conceptual Framework for Interpreting Human History*. Cambridge: Cambridge University Press.

North, John D. 1987. "Medieval Concepts of Celestial Influence: A Survey." In Curry 1987, 5–18.

———. 2005. *God's Clockmaker: Richard of Wallingford and the Invention of Time*. London: Hambledon Continuum.

Nosco, Peter. 2007. "Intellectual Change in Tokugawa Japan." In Tsutsui 2007, 101–116.

Noth, Albrecht. 1978. "Möglichkeiten und Grenzen islamischer Toleranz." *Saeculum* 29, 190–204.

———. 1993. "Der Dschihad: sich mühen für Gott." In Gernot Rotter (ed.), *Die Welten des Islam. Neunundzwanzig Vorschläge, das Unvertraute zu verstehen.* Frankfurt: Fischer, 22–32.

Nuttall, Paula. 2004. *From Flanders to Florence: The Impact of Netherlandish Painting, 1400–1500.* New Haven: Yale University Press.

Nykrog, Per. 1982. "The Rise of Literary Fiction." In Benson/Constable 1982, 593–612.

Obata, Shigeyoshi (ed. and trans.). 1923. *The Works of Li-Po, the Chinese Poet.* London: Dent.

Obolensky, Dimitri. 1971. *The Byzantine Commonwealth: Eastern Europe 500–1543.* New York: Praeger.

O'Callaghan, Joseph F. 2014. *The Last Crusade in the West: Castile and the Conquest of Granada.* Philadelphia: University of Pennsylvania Press.

Oettermann, Stephan. 1982. *Die Schaulust am Elefanten. Eine Elephantographia curiosa.* Frankfurt: Syndikat.

Ogg, Frederic Austin (ed.). 1908. *A Source Book of Medieval History.* New York: American Book Company.

Ogilvie, Brian W. 2006. *The Science of Describing: Natural History in Renaissance Europa.* Chicago: University of Chicago Press.

Ó Gráda, Cormac, Richard Paping, and Eric Vanhaute (eds.). 2007. *When the Potato Failed: Causes and Effects of the "Last" European Subsistence Crisis, 1845–1850.* Turnhout: Brepols.

Olgiati, Giustina. 2011. *Genova, porta del mondo. La città medievale e i suoi habitatores.* Genova: Brigati.

Oliveira Marques, António Henrique de. 1977. *History of Portugal.* 2 vols. New York: Columbia University Press.

Olivier de la Marche. 1884. *Mémoires d'Olivier de La Marche Maître d'Hotel et Capitaine des gardes de Charles le Téméraire.* Ed. Henri Beaune and J. Arbaumont. 2 vols. Paris: Renouard.

Oltmer, Jochen. 2012. *Globale Migration. Geschichte und Gegenwart.* Munich: C. H. Beck.

Olupona, Jacob K. 2011. *City of 201 Gods: Ilé-Ifẹ in Time, Space and Imagination.* Berkeley: University of California Press.

O'Malley, Charles Donald. 1964. *Andreas Vesalius of Brussels 1514–1564.* Berkeley: University of California Press.

O'Malley, John W. 2013. *Trent: What Happened at the Council.* Cambridge, MA: Harvard University Press.

Onasch, Konrad. 1967. *Grundzüge der russischen Kirchengeschichte.* Göttingen: Vandenhoeck & Ruprecht.

O'Pecko, Michael T. 1976. "Renaissancism and the German Drama, 1890–1910." Ph.D. Dissertation, Johns Hopkins University.

Opitz, Peter. 2009. *Leben und Werk Johannes Calvins.* Göttingen: Vandenhoeck & Ruprecht.

Origo, Iris. 1962. *The World of San Bernardino.* New York: Harcourt, Brace & World.

Ormrod, David. 2003. *The Rise of Commercial Empires: England and the Netherlands in the Age of Mercantilism, 1650–1770.* Cambridge: Cambridge University Press.

Ormrod, W. Mark. 2011. *Edward III.* New Haven: Yale University Press.

Ornato, Ezio. 1969. *Jean Muret et ses amis Nicolas de Clamanges et Jean de Montreuil. Contribution à l'étude des rapports entre les humanistes de Paris et ceux d'Avignon (1394–1420).* Geneva: Droz.

Osborne, Catherine. 2004. *Presocratic Philosophy: A Very Short Introduction.* Oxford: Oxford University Press.

Ost, Hans. 1975. *Leonardo-Studien.* Berlin: De Gruyter.

Osterhammel, Jürgen. 2014. *The Transformation of the World: A Global History of the Nineteenth Century.* Trans. Patrick Camiller. Princeton: Princeton University Press.

Ostrogorsky, George. 1956. *History of the Byzantine State*. Trans. Joan Mervyn Hussey. Oxford: Basil Blackwell.

Ostwald, Martin. 1995. "Freedom and the Greeks." In Davis 1995, 35–63.

Otloh von St. Emmeram. 1999. *Liber de temptatione cuiusdam monachi*. Ed. Sabine Gäbe. Bern: Lang.

Ott, Martin. 2002. *Die Entdeckung des Altertums: Der Umgang mit der römischen Vergangenheit Süddeutschlands im 16. Jahrhundert*. Kallmünz: Michael Laßleben.

Otto, Stephan. 2000. *Renaissance und frühe Neuzeit*. Stuttgart: Reclam.

Oudart, Hervé. 2010. *Robert d'Arbrissel, eremit et prédicateur*. Spoleto: Fondazione Centro italiano di studi sull'Alto medioevo.

Overell, M. Anne. 2016. *Italian Reform and English Reformations, c. 1535–c. 1585*. London: Routledge.

Overton, Mark. 1996. *Agricultural Revolution in England: The Transformation of the Agrarian Economy, 1500–1800*. Cambridge: Cambridge University Press.

Paasch, Kathrin (ed.). 2001. *Der Schatz des Amplonius. Die große Bibliothek des Mittelalters in Erfurt*. Exhibition Catalogue. Erfurt: Stadt- und Regionalbibliothek.

Padokh, Yaroslav. 1993. "Ruskaia Pravda." In Danylo Husar Struk (ed.), *Encyclopedia of Ukraine*. Vol. IV. University of Toronto Press, 444–445.

Pagden, Anthony. 1995. *The Lords of All the World: Ideologies of Empire in Spain, Britain and France c. 500–c. 1800*. New Haven: Yale University Press.

———. 2004. "Politics, Possession and Projection: Changing European Visions of the World." In Michael Matthiesen and Martial Straub (eds.), *Gegenwarten der Renaissance*. Göttingen: Wallstein, 181–206.

Pagel, Walter. 1962. *Das medizinische Weltbild des Paracelsus. Seine Zusammenhänge mit Neuplatonismus und Gnosis*. Wiesbaden: Franz Steiner.

Pagliaroli, Stefano. 2002. "Tifernate, Gregorio." In *DBI* 59, 260–265.

Panagiotakes, Nikolaos M. 2009. *El Greco—The Cretan Years*. Trans. John C. Davis. London: Routledge.

Pangerl, Daniel Carlo. 2010. "Sterndeutung als naturwissenschaftliche Methode der Politikberatung. Astronomie und Astrologie am Hof Kaiser Friedrichs III. (1440–1493)." *Archiv für Kulturgeschichte* 92, 309–327.

Panofsky, Erwin. 1948. *Abbot Suger on the Abbey Church of St.-Denis and its Treasures*. 2nd ed. Princeton: Princeton University Press.

———. 1960. *Renaissance and Renascences in Western Art*. Stockholm: Alqvist & Wiksell.

———. 1974. *Gothic Architecture and Scholasticism: An Inquiry into the Analogy of the Arts, Philosophy, and Religion in the Middle Ages*. New York: Plume.

Paracelsus. 1571. *Astronomia magna*. Frankfurt: Feyerabend Lechler. https://www.digitale -sammlungen.de/de/details/bsb10196224 (accessed March 30, 2023).

Paravicini, Werner (ed.). 2003. *Höfe und Residenzen im spätmittelalterlichen Reich. Ein dynastisch-topographisches Handbuch*. Ostfildern: Thorbecke.

Park, Hye-Ok. 2014. "The history of Pre-Gutenberg Woodblock and Movable Type Printing in Korea." *International Journal of Humanities and Social Science* 4:9, 9–17.

Park, Katharine. 2011. "Observation in the Margins, 500–1500." In Daston/Lunbeck 2011, 15–44.

Parker, Geoffrey. 1972. *The Army of Flanders and the Spanish Road 1567–1659: The Logistics of Spanish Victory and Defeat in the Low Countries War*. Cambridge: Cambridge University Press.

———. 1999. *The Military Revolution: Military Innovation and the Rise of the West, 1500–1800*. 2nd ed. Cambridge: Cambridge University Press.

———. 2013. *Global Crisis: War, Climate Change and Catastrophe in the Seventeenth Century*. New Haven: Yale University Press.

———. 2014. *Imprudent King: A New Life of Philip II*. New Haven: Yale University Press.

————. 2019. *Emperor: A New Life of Charles V.* New Haven: Yale University Press.

Parthasarathi, Prasannan. 2011. *Why Europe Grew Rich and Asia Did Not: Global Economic Divergence, 1600–1850.* Cambridge: Cambridge University Press.

Partington, James Riddick. 1999. *A History of Greek Fire and Gunpowder.* 2nd ed. Baltimore: Johns Hopkins University Press.

Pascoe, Louis B. 2005. *Church and Reform: Bishops, Theologians, and Canon Lawyers in the Thought of Pierre d'Ailly (1351–1420).* Leiden: Brill.

Pasnau, Robert. 2014. *The Cambridge History of Medieval Philosophy.* Cambridge: Cambridge University Press.

Pasnau, Robert, and Juhana Toivanen. 2013. "Peter John Olivi." In *Stanford Encyclopedia of Philosophy* (Summer 2013 Edition). http://plato.stanford.edu/archives/sum2013/entries/olivi / (accessed June 14, 2021).

Pastor, Ludwig von (ed.). 1905. *Die Reise des Kardinals Luigi d'Aragona durch Deutschland, die Niederlande, Frankreich und Oberitalien, 1517–1518, beschrieben von Antonio de Beatis.* Freiburg: Herder.

————. 1908. *The History of the Popes from the Close of the Middle Ages: Drawn from the Secret Archives of the Vatican and Other Original Sources.* Vol. VII. Ed. Ralph Francis Kerr. St. Louis: B. Herder.

————. 1938. *The History of the Popes from the Close of the Middle Ages: Drawn from the Secret Archives of the Vatican and Other Original Sources.* Vol. I. Ed. Frederick Ignatius Antrobius. 6th ed. London: Kegan Paul, Trench, Trubner & Co.

Patrizi, Francesco. 1560/2008. *Della historia diece dialoghi.* Venice: Andrea Arrivabene, 1560. Facsimile reprint: Ed. Cesc Esteve. Madrid: Universidad Carlos III, 2008.

Patzold, Steffen. 2012. *Das Lehnswesen.* Munich: C. H. Beck.

Paul, Jürgen. 2003. "Max Weber und die 'Islamische Stadt.'" In Hartmut Lehmann and Jean Martin Ouédraogo (eds.), *Max Webers Religionssoziologie in interkultureller Perspektive.* Göttingen: Vandenhoeck & Ruprecht, 109–137.

Pauler, Roland. 2001. "Giovanni XII, Papa." In *DBI* 55, 573–577.

Pavey, Don. 2008. *Colours and Humanism.* Parkland: Universal Publishers.

Pearson, Michael. 2003. *The Indian Ocean.* London: Routledge.

Pedersen, Johannes. 1984. *The Arabic Book.* Princeton: Princeton University Press.

Pedersen, Olaf. 2011. *A Survey of the Almagest.* New York: Springer.

Pegolotti, Francesco Balducci. 1936. *La pratica delle mercatura.* Ed. Allan Evans. Cambridge, MA: The Medieval Academy of America.

Pellegrini, Marco. 2000. "Pio II." In Bray 2000b, 663–685.

Pennuto, Concetta. "Pestilenze, contagi, epidemie." In *RIE* V, 397–322.

Pepys, Samuel. 1995. *Pepys's Diary.* Vol. VIII. Ed. Robert Latham and William Matthews. Berkeley: HarperCollins.

Perdue, Peter C. 2005. *China Marches West: The Qing Conquest of Central Eurasia.* Cambridge, MA: Harvard University Press.

Pérez, Joseph. 1989. *Ferdinand und Isabella. Spanien zur Zeit der katholischen Könige.* Munich: Callwey.

————. 2006. *Los Comuneros.* Madrid: La Esfera de los Libros.

————. 2014. *Cisneros, el cardenal de España.* Barcelona: Taurus.

Perler, Dominik. 2006. *Zweifel und Gewissheit. Skeptische Debatten im Mittelalter.* Frankfurt: Klostermann.

Pernau, Margit. 2008. *Bürger mit Turban. Muslime im Delhi des 19. Jahrhunderts.* Göttingen: Vandenhoeck & Ruprecht.

Perrone Compagni, Vittoria. "Matizare il mondo. Magia naturale ed ermetismo." In *RIE* V, 95–110.

Perry, Marvin et al. (eds.). 1995. *Sources of the Western Tradition*. Vol. II: *From the Renaissance to the Present*. 3rd ed. Boston: Houghton Mifflin.

Petrarca, Francesco. 1807. *The Triumphs of Petrarch*. Trans. Henry Boyd. London: Longman, Hurst, Rees, and Orme.

———. 1859–1863. *Epistolae de rebus familiaribus et variae*. Ed. Giuseppe Fracassetti. 3 vols. Florence: Le Monnier.

———. 2017. *Selected Letters*. Trans. Elaine Fantham. 2 vols. Cambridge, MA: Harvard University Press.

Pettegree, Andrew. 2004. "The Spread of Calvin's Thought." In McKim 2004, 207–224.

Peuckert, Will Erich. 1991. *Theophrastus Paracelsus*. Hildesheim: Olms.

Pfandl, Ludwig. 1973. *Philipp II. Gemälde eines Lebens und einer Zeit*. 7th ed. Munich: Callwey.

Pfisterer, Ulrich. 2019. *Raffael. Glaube, Liebe, Ruhm*. Munich: C. H. Beck.

Philippides, Marios and Walter K. Hanak. 2011. *The Siege and Fall of Constantinople in 1453: Historiography, Topography and Military Studies*. Farnham: Ashgate.

Phin, John (ed.). 1887. *An Exact Reprint of the Famous Century of Inventions by the Marquis of Worcester*. New York: Industrial Publication Co.

Pico della Mirandola, Gianfrancesco. 1930. *On the Imagination: The Latin Text with an Introduction, an English Translation, and Notes*. Ed. and trans. Henry Caplan. New Haven: Yale University Press.

Pico della Mirandola, Giovanni. 1965. *On the Dignity of Man, On Being and One, and Heptaplus*. Trans. Charles Glenn Wallis, Douglas Carmichael. Intro. Paul J. W. Miller. Indianapolis: Hackett.

———. 2012. *Oration on the Dignity of Man*. Ed. Francesco Borghesi, Michael Papio, and Massimo Riva. Cambridge: Cambridge University Press.

———. 2018. *Neunhundert Thesen*. Ed. and trans. Nikolaus Egel. Hamburg: Meiner.

Pieper, Jan. 2005. "Beispiel Sabloneta quadrata. Die römischen Grundlagen des Stadtplans von Sabbioneta." *Bauwelt* 40/41, 33–45.

Pierre de Jean Olivi. 2012. *Traité des contrats*. Ed. Sylvain Piron. Paris: Les Belles Lettres.

Pigafetta, Antonio. 2007. *The First Voyage around the World 1519–1522: An Account of Magellan's Expedition*. Ed. Theodore J. Cachey, Jr. Toronto: University of Toronto Press.

Pine, Martin L. 1986. *Pietro Pomponazzi (1462–1525): Radical Philosopher of the Renaissance*. Padua: Antenore.

Pinker, Steven. 2011. *The Better Angels of Our Nature: Why Violence Has Declined*. New York: Penguin.

Pinkernell, Gert. 2002. *François Villon: biographie critique et autres études*. Heidelberg: Winter.

Pipes, Richard. 1974. *Russia under the Old Regime*. London: Weidenfeld & Nicolson.

Pirenne, Henri. 1939. *Mohammed and Charlemagne*. Trans. B. Miall. New York: W. W. Norton.

Pires, Tome. 2005. *The Suma Oriental of Tome Pires: An Account of the East, from the Red Sea to Japan, Written in Malacca and India in 1512–1515, and The Book of Francisco Rodrigues, Rutter of a Voyage in the Red Sea, Nautical Rules, Almanack and Maps, Written and Drawn in the East before 1515*. Ed. Armando Cortesão. 2 vols. London: Routledge.

Pirillo, Diego. 2010. *Filosofia ed eresia nell'Inghilterra del tardo cinquecento: Bruno, Sidney e i dissidenti religiosi italiani*. Rome: Edizioni di storia e letteratura.

Pirożyński, Jan. 2002. "Humanistische Geschichtsschreibung in Polen." In Helmrath/Muhlack/Walther 2002, 308–318.

Pitt, Joseph C. 1992. *Galileo, Human Knowledge and the Book of Nature: Method Replaces Metaphysics*. Dordrecht: Springer.

Pius II. 1960. *Memoirs of a Renaissance Pope: The Commentaries of Pius II*. Trans. Leona C. Gabel and Florence Alden Gragg. London: Allen & Unwin.

———. 2004. *Commentaries*. Vol. 1. Ed. Margaret Meserve and Marcello Simonetta. Cambridge, MA: Harvard University Press.

———. 2019. *Oration "Constantinopolitana clades" of Enea Silvio Piccolomini (15 October 1454, Frankfurt)*. Ed. and trans. Michael Cotta-Schønberg. https://hal.archives-ouvertes.fr/hal -01097147/document (accessed February 25, 2021).

Plejit, Alexandra de, and Jan Luiten van Zanden. 2013. "Accounting for the 'Little Divergence.' What Drove Economic Growth in Pre-Industrial Europe, 1300–1800?" Working Papers 0046, Utrecht University, Centre for Global Economic History. https://ideas.repec.org/p /ucg/wpaper/0046.html (accessed February 2, 2016).

Pliny. 1893. *Natural History*. Trans. John Bostock and Henry Thomas Riley. London: George Bell & Sons.

Pocock, John G. A. 1975. *The Machiavellian Moment: Political Thought and the Atlantic Republican Tradition*. Princeton: Princeton University Press.

Pollock, Linda. 1993. *With Faith and Physic: The Life of a Tudor Gentlewoman*. London: Collins & Brown.

Pölnitz, Götz von. 1958–1986. *Anton Fugger*. 3 vols. Tübingen: Mohr Siebeck.

Polo, Marco. 1958. *The Travels of Marco Polo*. Trans. Ronald Latham. Harmondsworth: Penguin.

Poma de Ayala, Guaman. *Nueva corónica y buen gobierno*. Kopenhagen, Det Kongelige Bibliotek, GKS 2232 4. http://www5.kb.dk/permalink/2006/poma/info/es/frontpage.htm (accessed June 30, 2021).

Pomeranz, Kenneth. 2001. *The Great Divergence: China, Europe and the Making of the Modern World Economy*. Princeton: Princeton University Press.

Pomian, Krzysztof. 1990. *Collectors and Curiosities: Paris and Venice, 1500–1800*. Trans. Elizabeth Wiles-Portier. Cambridge: Polity Press.

Pompeo Faracovi, Ornella. "La riforma dell'atrologia." In *RIE* V, 59–72.

Pon, Lisa. 2004. *Raphael, Dürer and Marcantonio Raimondi: Copying and the Italian Renaissance Print*. New Haven: Yale University Press.

Pontano, Giovanni. 2014. *On Married Love: Eridanus*. Trans. Luke Roman. Cambridge, MA: Harvard University Press.

Popkin, Richard H. 2003. *The History of Scepticism from Erasmus to Spinoza*. Oxford: Oxford University Press.

Popper, Karl. 1945. *The Open Society and Its Enemies*. Vol. I: *The Spell of Plato*. London: Routledge.

Popplow, Marcus. 2007. "Setting the World Machine in Motion: The Meaning of Machina Mundi in the Middle Ages and the Early Modern Period." In Bucciantini/Camerota/Roux 2007, 45–70.

Porter, Roy. 1994. *London: A Social History*. 4th. ed. Cambridge, MA: Harvard University Press.

———. 1997. *The Greatest Benefit to Mankind: A Medical History of Humanity from Antiquity to the Present*. London: HarperCollins.

———. (ed.). 2003. *The Cambridge History of Science*. Vol. IV: *Eighteenth-Century Science*. Cambridge: Cambridge University Press.

Porter, Roy, and Mikuláš Teich (eds.). 1992. *The Renaissance in National Context*. Cambridge: Cambridge University Press.

Poulle, Emmanuel. "La produzione di strumenti scientifici." In *RIE* III, 345–366.

Praloran, Marco, and Nicola Morato. "Nostalgia e fascinazione della letteratura cavalleresca." In *RIE* II, 487–512.

Pratt, Edward E. 2007. "Social and Economic Change in Tokugawa Japan." In Tsutsui 2007, 86–100.

Prezziner, Giovanni. 1810/1975. *Storia del pubblico studio e delle società scientifiche e letterarie di Firenze*. Florence: Carli in Borgo SS. Apostoli, 1810. Facsimile reprint: Bologna: Forni, 1975.

Price, David H. 2011. *Johannes Reuchlin and the Campaign to Destroy Jewish Books*. Oxford: Oxford University Press.

Prietzel, Malte. 2001. *Guillaume Fillastre der Jüngere (1400/07–1473): Kirchenfürst und herzoglich-burgundischer Rat*. Stuttgart: Thorbecke.

Priuli, Girolamo. 1921. *I diarii di Girolamo Priuli (ca. 1494–1512)*. Ed. Arturo Segre. Città di Castello: S. Lapi.

Procacci, Giuliano. 1970. *History of the Italian People*. London: Weidenfeld & Nicholson.

Prosperi, Valentina. 2007. "Lucretius in the Italian Renaissance." In Stuart Gillespie and Philip R. Hardie (eds.), *The Cambridge Companion to Lucretius*. Cambridge: Cambridge University Press, 214–226.

Ptak, Roderich. 2007. *Die maritime Seidenstraße. Küstenräume, Seefahrt und Handel in vorkolonialer Zeit*. Munich: C. H. Beck.

Pulci, Luigi. 1989. *Il Morgante*. Milan: Garzanti.

Pumfrey, Stephen. 1989. "Magnetical Philosophy and Astronomy, 1600–1650." In René Taton and Curtis Wilson (eds.), *Planetary Astronomy from the Renaissance to the Rise of Astrophysics. Part A: Tycho Brahe to Newton*. Cambridge: Cambridge University Press, 45–53.

Pumfrey, Stephen, Paolo L. Rossi, and Maurice Slawinski (eds.). 1991. *Science, Culture, and Popular Belief in Renaissance Europe*. Manchester: Manchester University Press.

Putallaz, François-Xavier. 1995. *Insolenta liberta. Controverses et condamnations au XIIIe siècle*. Paris: Cerf.

Putnam, Robert D. 1993. *Making Democracy Work: Civic Traditions in Modern Italy*. Princeton: Princeton University Press.

Pyenson, Lewis, and Susan Sheets-Pyenson. 1999. *Servants of Nature: A History of Scientific Institutions, Enterprises and Sensibilities*. London: HarperCollins.

Qian, Wen-yuan. 1985. *The Great Inertia: Scientific Stagnation in Traditional China*. London: Croom Helm.

Rabb, Theodore K. 2007. *The Last Days of the Renaissance and the March to Modernity*. New York: BasicBooks.

Rabelais, François. 1990. *Gargantua and Pantagruel*. Trans. Burton Raffel. New York: W. W. Norton & Company.

Rabil, Albert, Jr. (ed.). 1988. *Renaissance Humanism: Foundations, Forms, and Legacy*. 3 vols. Philadelphia: University of Pennsylvania Press.

Rabin, Sheila J. 2008. "Pico on Magic and Astrology." In Dougherty 2008, 152–178.

Rachewiltz, Igor de. 1971. *Papal Envoys to the Great Khans*. Stanford: Stanford University Press.

Rader, Olaf B. 2010. *Friedrich II. Ein Sizilianer auf dem Kaiserthron*. Munich: C. H. Beck.

Radkau, Joachim. 1999. "Das hölzerne Zeitalter." In Ulrich Troitzsch (ed.), *"Nützliche Künste." Kultur und Sozialgeschichte der Technik im 18. Jahrhundert*. Münster: Waxmann, 97–117.

Ragep, F. Jamil. 2007. "Copernicus and His Islamic Predecessors: Some Historical Remarks." *History of Science* 14, 65–81.

Raleigh, Walter. 1997. *The Discoverie of the Large, Rich, and Bewtiful Empyre of Guiana*. Ed. Neil L. Whitehead. Manchester: Manchester University Press.

Randles, William G. L. 1999. *The Unmaking of the Medieval Christian Cosmos, 1500–1760: From Solid Heavens to Boundless Æther*. Aldershot: Ashgate.

Rapp, Christof. 2007. *Vorsokratiker*. 2nd ed. Munich: C. H. Beck.

Rashed, Roshdi. (ed.). 1996. *Encyclopedia of the History of Arabic Science. Vol. I: Astronomy—Theoretical and Applied*. London: Routledge.

———. 2018. "The End Matters." In Iqbal 2018, I, 37–44.

Ratkowitsch, Christine. 1995. *Die Cosmographia des Bernardus Silvestris: Eine Theodizee.* Cologne: Böhlau.

Rauchenberger, Dietrich. 1999. *Johannes Leo der Afrikaner: Seine Beschreibung des Raumes zwischen Nil und Niger nach dem Urtext.* Wiesbaden: Harrassowitz.

Reardon, Bryan P. 1984. "The Second Sophistic." In Treadgold 1984b, 23–41.

Redondi, Pietro. 1987. *Galileo: Heretic.* Trans. Raymond Rosenthal. Princeton: Princeton University Press.

Redondo, Augustin. 2000. "Chronique d'un avènement annoncé (Fernão Lopes et le Maître d'Aviz)." In Augustin Redondo, *La prophétie comme arme de guerre des pouvoirs (XVe-XVIIe siècles).* Paris: Presses De La Sorbonne Nouvelle, 57–68.

Reeves, Eileen. 2008. *Galileo's Glassworks: The Telescope and the Mirror.* Cambridge, MA: Harvard University Press.

Rehm, Walter. 1969. "Der Renaissancekult um 1900 und seine Überwindung." In Walter Rehm, *Der Dichter und die neue Einsamkeit. Aufsätze zur Literatur um 1900.* Göttingen: Vandenhoeck & Ruprecht, 34–77.

Reichel, Jörn. 1985. *Der Spruchdichter Hans Rosenplüt.* Stuttgart: Franz Steiner.

Reichmuth, Stefan. 2004. "Bildungskanon und Bildungsreform aus der Sicht eines islamischen Gelehrten der anatolischen Provinz. Muhammad al-Sājaīqli (Saçaqlii-zâde, gest. um 1145/1733) und sein Tartib al-'ulūm." In Rüdiger Arnzen and Jörn Thielmann (eds.), *Words, Texts and Concepts Cruising the Mediterranean Sea: Studies on the Sources, Contents and Influences of Islamic Civilization and Arabic Philosophy and Science.* Leuven: Peeters, 491–518.

Reid, Anthony. 1988–1993. *Southeast Asia in an Age of Commerce.* 2 vols. New Haven: Yale University Press.

———. 2015. *A History of Southeast Asia: Critical Crossroads.* Malden: Blackwell.

Reid, Richard. 2011. "Past and Presentism: The 'Precolonial' and the Foreshortening of African History." *Journal of African History* 52, 135–155.

Reinhard, Wolfgang. 1999. *Geschichte der Staatsgewalt: Eine vergleichende Verfassungsgeschichte von den Anfängen bis zur Gegenwart.* Munich: C. H. Beck.

———. 2001. *Probleme deutscher Geschichte 1495–1806: Reichsreform und Reformation 1495–1555.* Stuttgart: Klett-Cotta.

——— (ed). 2015. *Empires and Encounters, 1350–1750.* Cambridge, MA: Harvard University Press.

———. 2016. *Die Unterwerfung der Welt. Globalgeschichte der europäischen Expansion 1415–2015.* Munich: C. H. Beck.

Reisch, Gregor. 1503. *Margarita philosophica.* Freiburg: Johann Schott (Munich, Bayerische Staatsbibliothek, 4°Ph Un 114).

Reiter, Florian C. 2000. *Taoismus zur Einführung.* Hamburg: Junius.

Renn, Jürgen, et al. 2021. *Leonardo's Intellectual Cosmos.* Florence: Giunti.

Repgen, Konrad. 1985. "Kriegslegitimationen in Alteuropa. Entwurf einer historischen Typologie." *Historische Zeitschrift* 241, 27–50.

Resnick, Irven M. 2013. *A Companion to Albert the Great: Theology, Philosophy, and the Sciences.* Leiden: Brill.

Reuchlin, Johannes. 1999–2013. *Briefwechsel.* Ed. Matthias Dall'Asta and Gerald Dörner. 4 vols. Stuttgart-Bad Cannstatt: Frommann-Holzboog.

Rex, Richard. 2002. *The Lollards.* New York: Palgrave.

Reynolds, Susan. 1994. *Fiefs and Vassals: The Medieval Evidence Reinterpreted.* Oxford: Oxford University Press.

Richards, Earl Jeffrey. 2000. "Christine de Pizan and Jean Gerson: An intellectual Friendship." In John Campbell and Nadia Margolis (eds.), *Christine de Pizan 2000: Studies on Christine de Pizan in Honour of Angus J. Kennedy.* Leiden: Brill, 197–208.

Richards, Julian D. 2005. *The Vikings: A Very Short Introduction*. Oxford: Oxford University Press.

Richardson, Glenn. 2013. *The Field of Cloth of Gold*. New Haven: Yale University Press.

Richardson, William A. R. 1993. "Mercator's South Continent: Its Origins, Influence, and Gradual Decline." *Terrae Incognitae* 25, 67–98.

Richer of Saint-Remi. 2000. *Historiae*. Ed. Hartmut Hoffmann. MGH Scriptores, 38. Hanover: Hahnsche Buchhandlung.

Richter-Bernburg, Lutz. 2004. "ḤĀWI, AL-." In *Encyclopedia Iranica*. Vol. XII.1. London: Encyclopædia Iranica Foundation, 64–67.

Ricken, Friedo. 1994. *Antike Skeptiker*. Munich: C. H. Beck.

Ridde, Valéry. 2009. "Policy Implementation in an African State: An Extension of Kingdon's Multiple Stream's Approach." *Public Administration* 87:4, 938–954.

Riedweg, Christoph. 1993. *Jüdisch-hellenistische Imitation eines orphischen Hieros Logos— Beobachtungen zu OF 245 und 247 (sog. Testament des Orpheus)*. Tübingen: G. Narr.

———. 2002. *Pythagoras. Leben—Lehre—Nachwirkung. Eine Einführung*. Munich: C. H. Beck.

Riello, Giorgio. 2013. *Cotton: The Fabric that Made the Modern World*. Cambridge: Cambridge University Press.

Riggs, Charles T. 1954. *History of Mehmed the Conqueror: Kritovoulos*. Princeton: Princeton University Press.

Riley-Smith, Jonathan, and Louise Riley-Smith. 1981. *The Crusades, Idea and Reality, 1095–1274*. London: Edward Arnold.

Rinaldi, Massimo. "Le accademie del Cinquecento." In *RIE* II, 337–359.

Rizvi, Sajjad. 2007. *Mulla Sadra Shirazi: His Life, Works and Sources for Safavid Philosophy*. Oxford: Oxford University Press.

Robin, Diana. 1991. *Filelfo in Milan: Writings 1451–1477*. Princeton: Princeton University Press.

Robinson, Charles F. 2003. *Islamic Historiography*. Cambridge: Cambridge University Press.

Robinson, Chase F. (ed.). 2010. *The Formation of the Islamic World: Sixth to Eleventh Centuries*. Cambridge: Cambridge University Press.

Rodolico, Niccolò. 1903. *Chronaca Fiorentina di Marchionne di Coppo Stefani*. Città di Castello: S. Lapi.

Roeck, Bernd. 1989. *Eine Stadt in Krieg und Frieden. Studien zur Geschichte der Reichsstadt Augsburg zwischen Kalenderstreit und Parität*. Göttingen: Vandenhoeck & Ruprecht.

———. 1996. *Gegenreformation und Dreißigjähriger Krieg, 1555–1648*. Stuttgart: Reclam.

———. 2001. "Renaissance." In Neil J. Smelser and Paul B. Baltes (eds.), *International Encyclopedia of the Social and Behavioral Sciences*. Vol. XIX. Amsterdam: Elsevier, 13155–13160.

———. 2004. *Das historische Auge: Kunstwerke als Zeugen ihrer Zeit. Von der Renaissance zur Revolution*. Göttingen: Vandenhoeck & Ruprecht.

———. 2006. *Mörder, Maler und Mäzene. Piero della Francescas 'Geißelung': Eine kunsthistorische Kriminalgeschichte*. Munich: C. H. Beck.

———. 2007. "Introduction." In Hermann Roodenburg (ed.), *Forging European Identities, 1400–1700*. Cambridge: Cambridge University Press, 1–29.

———. 2009. "Religious Crisis 1400–1700: Some Considerations." In Troels Dahlerup and Per Ingesman (eds.), *New Approaches to the History of Late Medieval and Early Modern Europe*. Copenhagen: Det Kongelige Danske Videnskabernes Selskab, 445–462.

———. 2013. *Gelehrte Künstler. Maler, Bildhauer und Architekten der Renaissance über Kunst*. Berlin: Wagenbach.

———. 2015. "'. . . die ersten Gemälde der Welt.' Über die Entzauberung des Raumes in der europäischen Renaissance." In Dirk Syndram, Yvonne Wirth, and Doreen Zerbe (eds.), *Luther und die Fürsten*. Dresden: Michael Sandstein, 47–64.

———. 2022. "Die Renaissance der Konversation. Eine kurze Geschichte des Gesprächs im Zeitalter der Diskursrevolution." In Christoph Strosetzki (ed.), *Der Wert der Konversation. Perspectiven von der Antike bis zur Moderne*. Berlin/Heidelberg: Metzler, 71–99.

———. 2024a. "El giro icónico. Antecedentes, estudios de casos y perspectivas." In Gustavo Leyva (ed)., *Las Ciencas Sociales revisitadas*. Mexico City: Editorial Gedisa Mexicana, 351–377.

———. 2024b. "Jacob Burckhardt and His Heirs: The Construction of the Renaissance in the German-Speaking World." In Véronique Ferrer and Jean-Louis Fournel (eds.), *Renaissances*. Vol. I: *Constructions, usages et migrations d'une catégorie historiographique (XIXe-XXIe siècle)*. Geneva: Droz, 289–310.

Roeck, Bernd, and Andreas Tönnesmann. 2011. *Die Nase Italiens. Federico da Montefeltro, Herzog von Urbino*. 3rd ed. Berlin: Wagenbach.

Rohe, Mathias. 2011. *Islamisches Recht. Geschichte und Gegenwart*. 3rd ed. Munich: C. H. Beck.

Roling, Bernd. 2010. *Drachen und Sirenen. Die Rationalisierung und Abwicklung der Mythologie an den europäischen Universitäten*. Leiden: Brill.

Ronan, Colin A. 1981. *The Shorter Science and Civilization in China: An Abridgement of Joseph Needham's Original Text*. Cambridge: Cambridge University Press.

Roover, Raymond de. 1963. *The Rise and Decline of the Medici Bank, 1397–1494*. Cambridge, MA: Harvard University Press.

Rösch, Gerhard. 2000. *Venedig. Geschichte einer Seerepublik*. Stuttgart: W. Kohlhammer.

Rose, Paul Lawrence. 1975. *The Italian Renaissance of Mathematics: Studies on Humanists and Mathematicians from Petrarch to Galileo*. Geneva: Droz.

Rosen, Edward. 1967. *Kepler's Somnium: The Dream, or Posthumous Work on Lunar Astronomy*. Madison: University of Wisconsin Press.

———. 1984. "Kepler's Attitude toward Astrology and Mysticism." In Vickers 1984b, 253–272.

Rosenfeld, Boris A., and Ekmeleddin İhsanoğlu (eds.). 2003. *Mathematicians, Astronomers and Other Scholars of Islamic Civilisations and Their Works*. Istanbul: IRCICA.

Rosenthal, Franz. 1994. *The Classical Heritage in Islam*. London: Routledge.

Rosenwein, Barbara H. 2005. "Y avait-il un 'moi' au haut moyen-âge?" *Revue Historique* 129, 31–52.

Rosheim, Mark E. 2006. *Leonardo's Lost Robots*. New York: Springer.

Rossi, Paolo. 1998. *La nascita della scienza moderna in Europa*. Rome/Bari: Laterza.

———. 2000. *The Birth of Modern Science*. Trans. Cynthia De Nardi Ipsen. Oxford: Blackwell.

Rossi, Sergio. 1980. *Dalle botteghe alle Accademie. Realtà sociale e teorie artistiche a Firenze dal XIV al XVI secolo*. Milan: Feltrinelli.

Roth, Cecil. 1925. *The Last Florentine Republic (1527–1530)*. London: Methuen.

Rothermund, Dietmar. 2016. "Akbar and Philipp II of Spain: Contrasting Strategies of Imperial Consolidation." In Dietmar Rothermund, *Aspects of Indian and Global History: A Collection of Essays*. Baden-Baden: Nomos, 9–26.

Rothermund, Dietmar, and Susanne Weigelin-Schwiedrzik (eds.). 2004. *Der Indische Ozean. Das afro-asiatische Mittelmeer als Kultur- und Wirtschaftsraum*. Vienna: Promedia.

Rothmann, Michael. 2005. "'Das trojanische Pferd der Deutschen' oder die Vervielfältigung des Wissens—Johannes Gutenberg, der Buchdruck und der Markt." In Matheus 2005a, 40–58.

Rotondò, Antonio. 1977. "Bizzarri, Pietro." In *DBI* 11, 466–476.

Roupnel, Gaston. 1936. *La Bourgogne. Types et coutumes*. Paris: Horizons de France.

Rowe, John H. 1965. "The Renaissance Foundations of Anthropology." *American Anthropologist* 67:1, 1–20.

Rowland, Ingrid D. 2008. *Giordano Bruno: Philosopher, Heretic*. Chicago: University of Chicago Press.

Roys, Ralph L. 1933. *The Book of Chilam Balam of Chumayel*. Washington, D.C.: Carnegie Institution.

Rozzo, Ugo. 2008. *La strage ignorata: I fogli volanti a stampa nell'Italia dei secoli XV e XVI*. Udine: Forum.

Rucellai, Giovanni di Pagolo. 2013. *Zibaldone*. Ed. Gabriella Battista. Florence: SISMEL.

Ruderman, David B. 1995. *Jewish Thought and Scientific Discovery in Early Modern Europe*. New Haven: Yale University Press.

Rudersdorf, Manfred. 1990. "Maximilian II." In Anton Schindling and Walter Ziegler (eds.), *Die Kaiser der Neuzeit, 1519–1918. Heiliges Römisches Reich, Österreich, Deutschland*. Munich: C. H. Beck, 79–97.

Rudolph, Ulrich. 2004. *Islamische Philosophie*. Munich: C. H. Beck.

Rüegg, Walter (ed.). 1993. *Geschichte der Universität in Europa*. Vol. I. Munich: C. H. Beck.

Ruggiero, Raffaele. 2014. "Ritratto delle cose della Magna e altri scritti sulla Germania." *Enciclopedia Machiavelliana*. https://www.treccani.it/enciclopedia/ritratto-delle-cose-della-magna -e-altri-scritti-sulla-germania_%28Enciclopedia-machiavelliana%29/ (accessed August 10, 2023).

Ruh, Kurt. 1990–1999. *Geschichte der abendländischen Mystik*. 4 vols. Munich: C. H. Beck.

Rummel, Erika. 2004. *Erasmus*. London: Continuum.

Russell, Peter. 2000. *Prince Henry 'the Navigator': A Life*. New Haven: Yale University Press.

Rüttermann, Markus. 2002. "Städte im vormodernen Japan." In Feldbauer/Mitterauer/Schwent-ker 2002, 153–193.

Rutkin, H. Darrel. "L'astrologia da Alberto Magno a Giovanni Pico della Mirandola." In *RIE* V, 47–58.

Ryder, Alan. 1990. *Alfonso the Magnanimous: King of Aragon, Naples and Sicily, 1396–1458*. Oxford: Clarendon.

Saalfeld, Dieter. 1971. "Die Wandlungen der Preis- und Lohnstruktur während des 16. Jahrhun-derts in Deutschland." *Schriften des Vereins für Socialpolitik*, New Series 63, 9–28.

Sabbadini, Remigio. 1996. *Le scoperte dei codici Latini e Greci ne' secoli XIV e XV (1905/14)*. 2 vols. Florence: Sansoni.

Sabean, David Warren, Simon Teuscher, and Jon Mathieu (eds.). 2007. *Kinship in Europe: Ap-proaches to Long-Term Development (1300–1900)*. New York: Berghahn Books.

Sabra, Abdelhamid I. 1998. "Configuring the Universe: Aporetic, Problem Solving, and Kine-matic Modeling as Themes of Arabic Astronomy." *Perspectives on Science* 6, 288–330.

———. 2018a. "The Appropriation and Subsequent Naturalization of Greek Science in Medi-eval Islam." In Iqbal 2018, IV, 107–118.

———. 2018b. "Science and Philosophy in Medieval Islamic Theology." In Iqbal 2018, IV, 350–390.

———. 2018c. "Situating Arabic Science: Locality versus Essence." In Iqbal 2018, IV, 119–135.

Sacchetti, Franco. 1970. *Trecento Novelle*. Ed. Emilio Faccioli. Turin: Einaudi.

Sachs, Hans. 1568/2005. *Eygentliche Beschreibung Aller Stände auff Erden*. Frankfurt: Sigmund Feyerabend, 1568. Reprint: Leipzig: Seeman, 2005.

———. 1894. *Sämtliche Fabeln und Schwänke*. Ed. Edmund Goetze. Vol. II. Halle: Max Niemeyer.

Sahagún, Bernardino de. 1982. *General History of the Things of New Spain*. Vol. I. Santa Fe: School of American Research and the University of Utah.

Sahlins, Marshall 1968. *Tribesmen*. Englewood Cliffs: Prentice Hall.

Saitta, Giuseppe. 1949–1951. *Il pensiero italiano nell' Umanesimo e nel Rinascimento*. 3 vols. Bolo-gna: C. Zuffi.

Saliba, George. 2002. "Greek Astronomy and the Medieval Arab Tradition." *American Scientist* 90, 360–367.

———. 2007. *Islamic Science and the Making of the European Renaissance.* Cambridge, MA: MIT Press.

Salter, Rebecca. 2006. *Japanese Popular Prints from Votive Slips to Playing Cards.* Honolulu: University of Hawai'i Press.

Salutati, Coluccio. 1891–1905. *Epistolario.* Ed. Francesco Novati. 4 vols. Rome: Tipografia Forzani.

Salvian. 1930. *On the Government of God.* Trans. Eva M. Sanford. New York: Columbia Univ. Press.

Sanford, Eva Matthews. 1944. "The Study of Ancient History in the Middle Ages." *Journal of the History of Ideas* 5:1, 21–43.

Sannazaro, Jacopo. 1966. *Arcadia & Piscatorial Eclogues.* Trans. Ralph Nash. Detroit: Wayne State University Press.

Santillana, Giorgio de. 1967. *The Crime of Galileo.* 8th ed. Chicago: University of Chicago Press.

Sardar, Ziauaddin. 2018. "Islam and Science: Beyond the Troubled Relationship." In Iqbal 2018, I, 97–115.

Sarris, Peter. 2011. *Empires of Faith: The Fall of Rome to the Rise of Islam, 500–700.* Oxford: Oxford University Press.

Sauerländer, Willibald. 1982. "Architecture and the Figurative Arts: The North." In Benson/Constable 1982, 671–710.

Saul, Nigel. 1997. *Richard II.* New Haven: Yale University Press.

Saunders, Corinne. (ed.). 2006. *A Concise Companion to Chaucer.* Oxford: Blackwell.

Savonarola, Girolamo. 1615. *De simplicitate christianae vitae.* Ed. Christoph Besold. Strasbourg: Lazarus Zetzner.

Sawyer, Birgit, and Peter Sawyer. 1993. *Medieval Scandinavia: From Conversion to Reformation, circa 800–1500.* Minneapolis: University of Minnesota Press.

Saygin, Susanne. 2001. *Humphrey, Duke of Gloucester (1390–1447) and the Italian Humanists.* Leiden: Brill.

Sayili, Aydin. 1988. *The Observatory in Islam and Its Place in the General History of the Observatory.* Ankara: Türk Tarih Kurumu.

Schabert, Ina (ed.). 2000. *Shakespeare-Handbuch: Die Zeit—Der Mensch—Das Werk—Die Nachwelt.* 4th ed. Stuttgart: Kröner.

Schadeina, Abdulaziz. 1981. *Islamic Messianism: The Idea of the Mahdi in Twelver Shi'ism.* Albany: State University of New York Press.

Schaller, Dieter et al. 1983. "Carmina Burana." In *Lexikon des Mittelalters.* Vol. II. Munich: Artemis, coll. 1513–1517.

Schama, Simon. 1987. *The Embarrassment of Riches: An Interpretation of Dutch Culture in the Golden Age.* New York: Alfred A. Knopf.

Schantz, Peter. 2009. *Weißdorn und Herzgespann: Medizinhistorische Untersuchungen zur europäischen Tradition dieser Heilpflanzen vom Mittelalter bis zur Gegenwart.* Kassel: Kassel University Press.

Scharfe, Hartmut. 2002. *Education in Ancient India.* Leiden: Brill.

Schatkowski-Schilcher, Linda. 1985. *Families in Politics: Damascene Factions and Estates of the 18th and 19th Centuries.* Stuttgart: Franz Steiner.

Schätzl, Ludwig. 1991. *Wirtschaftsgeographie der Europäischen Gemeinschaft.* Paderborn: Schöningh.

Schauer, Alexander. 2000. *Muslime und Franken. Ethnische, soziale und religiöse Gruppen im Kitab al-I'tibar des Usama ibn Munqid.* Berlin: Klaus Schwarz.

Schedel, Hartmann. 2004. *Weltchronik.* Ed. Stephan Füssel. Augsburg: Weltbild.

Scheuchzer, Johann Jacob. 1726. *Homo diluvii testis et theoskopos.* Zurich: Johann Heinrich Bürklin.

Schiebinger, Londa. 1995. *Nature's Body: Gender in the Making of Modern Science*. Boston: Beacon Press.

Schieffer, Rudolf. 2012. "Papsttum und Königreiche im 11./12. Jahrhundert." In Weinfurter 2012, 69–80.

———. 2013. *Christianisierung und Reichsbildungen. Europa 700–1200*. Munich: C. H. Beck.

Schildgen, Brenda Deen, Gang Zhou, and Sander L. Gilman (eds.). 2006. *Other Renaissances: A New Approach to World Literature*. New York: Palgrave MacMillan.

Schiller, Friedrich. 1988. *What Is, and to What End Do We Study, Universal History*. Trans. Caroline Stephan and Robert Trout. Published by the Schiller Institute. https://archive.schillerinstitute.com/transl/Schiller_essays/universal_history.html (accessed January 30, 2023).

Schilling, Heinz. 1999. *Die Neue Zeit. Vom Christenheitseuropa zum Europa der Staaten, 1250 bis 1750*. Berlin: Siedler.

———. 2013. *Martin Luther. Rebell in einer Zeit des Umbruchs*. 2nd ed. Munich: C. H. Beck.

———. 2017. *1517. Weltgeschichte eines Jahres*. Munich: C. H. Beck.

Schiltberger, Johannes. 1859. *Reisen des Johannes Schiltberger aus München in Europa, Asien und Afrika: Von 1394 bis 1427*. Ed. Karl Friedrich Neumann. Munich: Karl Friedrich Neumann.

Schimmel, Annemarie. 2014. *Sufismus*. 5th ed. Munich: C. H. Beck.

Schimmelpfennig, Bernhard. 2009. *Das Papsttum: Von der Antike bis zur Renaissance*. 6th ed. Darmstadt: WBG.

Schindling, Anton, and Walter Ziegler (eds.). 1990. *Die Kaiser der Neuzeit, 1519–1918. Heiliges Römisches Reich, Österreich, Deutschland*. Munich: C. H. Beck.

Schlosser, Julius von. 1904. "Über einige Antiken Ghibertis." *Jahrbuch der kunsthistorischen Sammlungen des allerhöchsten Kaiserhauses* 24:4, 141–150.

Schmidt, Alexander. 2007. *Vaterlandsliebe und Religionskonflikt. Politische Diskurse im Alten Reich (1555–1648)*. Leiden: Brill.

Schmidt, Christoph. 2009. *Russische Geschichte 1547–1914*. Munich: Oldenbourg.

Schmidt, Victor. 1998. "A Humanist's Life Summarized: Leonardo Bruni's Epitaph." *Humanistica Lovaniensia* 47, 1–14.

Schmidt-Biggemann, Wilhelm. 1998. *Philosophia perennis. Historische Umrisse abendländischer Spiritualität in Antike, Mittelalter und Früher Neuzeit*. Frankfurt: Suhrkamp.

Schmidtke, Susann. 1997. "Das Entkommen aus der Bevölkerungsfalle durch kontinuierliche Wirtschaftsprozesse: Sensitivität des Komlos-Artzrouni-Modells." *Historical Social Research* 22:2, 162–194.

Schmitt, Carl. 2005. *Political Theology: Four Chapters on the Concept of Sovereignty*. Ed. and trans. George Schwab. Chicago: University of Chicago Press.

Schmitt, Charles B. 1969. "Experience and Experiment: A Comparison of Zabarella's View with Galileo's *De Motu*." *Studies in the Renaissance* 16, 80–138.

———. 1984a. *Aristotelian Tradition and Renaissance Universities*. London: Variorum Reprints.

———. 1984b. "Aristotle as a Cuttlefish: The Origin and Development of a Renaissance Image." In Schmitt 1984a, art. IV.

———. 1984c. "Philosophy and Science in Sixteenth-Century Italian Universities." In Schmitt 1984a, art. XV.

——— (ed). 1988. *The Cambridge History of Renaissance Philosophy*. Cambridge: Cambridge University Press.

Schmitt, Eberhard. (ed.). 1984d. *Dokumente zur Geschichte der europäischen Expansion*. Vol II. Munich: C. H. Beck.

Schmitt, Jean-Claude. 2009a. "Individuation et saisie du monde." In Patrick Boucheron (ed.), *Histoire du monde au XVe siècle*. Paris: Fayard, 769–790.

Schmitt, Oliver Jens. 2001. *Das venezianische Albanien (1392–1479)*. Munich: Oldenbourg.

———. 2009b. *Skanderbeg: Der neue Alexander auf dem Balkan*. Regensburg: Pustet.

Schnack, Jutta. 1990. "Meckenem, Israel van." In *NDB* 16, 587–88.

Schnell, Rüdiger. 1989. "Der 'Heide' Alexander im christlichen Mittelalter." In Willi Erzgräber (ed.), *Kontinuität und Transformation der Antike im Mittelalter*. Sigmaringen: Thorbecke, 45–64.

Schoenbaum, Samuel. 1987. *William Shakespeare: A Compact Documentary Life*. Oxford: Oxford University Press.

Scholz, Sebastian. 2015. *Die Merowinger*. Stuttgart: W. Kohlhammer.

Schoot, Albert van der. 2005. *Die Geschichte des goldenen Schnitts. Aufstieg und Fall der göttlichen Proportion*. Stuttgart: Frommann-Holzboog.

Schrage, Eltjo J. H. 1992. *Utrumque Ius. Eine Einführung in das Studium der Quellen des mittelalterlichen gelehrten Rechts*. Berlin: Duncker und Humblot.

Schreiner, Peter. 1994. "Giovanni Aurispa in Konstantinopel. Schicksale griechischer Handschriften im 15. Jahrhundert." In Johannes Helmrath, Heribert Müller, and Helmut Wolff (eds.), *Studien zum 15. Jahrhundert*. 2 vols. Munich: Oldenbourg, 623–633.

———. 2011. *Byzanz 545–1453*. 4th ed. Munich: Oldenbourg.

Schreurs, Anna. 2000. *Antikenbild und Kunstanschauungen des Pirro Ligorio*. Cologne: Walther König.

Schröder, Winfried. 1998. *Ursprünge des Atheismus. Untersuchungen zur Metaphysik- und Religionskritik des 17. und 18. Jahrhunderts*. Stuttgart: Frommann-Holzboog.

Schumann, Hans Wolfgang. 2004. *Der historische Buddha. Leben und Lehren des Gotama*. Munich: Diederichs.

Schürer, Markus. 2010. "Enzyklopädik als Naturkunde und Kunde vom Menschen. Einige Thesen zum *Fons memorabilium universi* des Domenico Bandini." *Mittellateinisches Jahrbuch* 45, 116–131.

Schurz, Gerhard, and Paul Weingartner (eds.). 1998. *Koexistenz rivalisierender Paradigmen. Eine post-kuhnsche Bestandsaufnahme zur Struktur gegenwärtiger Wissenschaft*. Opladen: Westdeutscher Verlag.

Schwob, Anton et al. 1999–2004. *Die Lebenszeugnisse Oswalds von Wolkenstein. Edition und Kommentar*. 3 vols. Vienna: Böhlau.

Scott, Tom. 2012. *The City-State in Europe, 1000–1600: Hinterland, Territory, Region*. Oxford: Oxford University Press.

Scruzzi, Davide. 2010. *Eine Stadt denkt sich die Welt. Wahrnehmung geographischer Räume und Globalisierung in Venedig von 1490 bis um 1600*. Berlin: Akademie Verlag.

Seeley, John Robert. 2005. *The Expansion of England: Two Courses of Lectures*. New York: Cosimo Classics.

Seherr-Thoss, Hans Christoph Graf von. 1965. *Die Entwicklung der Zahnradtechnik. Zahnformen und Trägheitsberechnung*. Berlin: Springer.

Seibt, Gustav. 1992. *Anonimo romano. Geschichtsschreibung in Rom an der Schwelle zur Renaissance*. Stuttgart: Klett-Cotta.

Selderhuis, Herman J. 2009. *Johannes Calvin, Mensch zwischen Zuversicht und Zweifel. Eine Biographie*. Gütersloh: Gütersloher Verlagshaus.

Selzer, Stephan. 2010. *Die Hanse*. Darmstadt: WBG.

Sergent, F. Tyler (ed.). 2019. *A Companion to William of Saint-Thierry*. Leiden: Brill.

Service, Elman R. 1975. *Origins of the State and Innovation: The Process of Cultural Evolution*. New York: W. W. Norton.

Seta, Adi. 2018. "Time, Motion, Distance, and Change in the Kalam of Fakhir al-Din-al-Razi: A Preliminary Survey with Special Reference to the Matalib Aliyah." In Iqbal 2018, III, 393–408.

Settis, Salvatore. 1990. *Giorgione's Tempest*. Chicago: University of Chicago Press.

———. 2006. *Laocoonte: Fama e stile*. Rome: Donzelli.

Settis, Salvatore, and Walter Cupperi (eds.). 2007. *Il Palazzo Schifanoia a Ferrara / The Palazzo Schifanoia in Ferrara*. Modena: Cosimo Panini.

Ševčenko, Ihor. 1984. "The Palaeologan Renaissance." In Treadgold 1984b, 144–171.

Sewell, Robert. 1900. *A Forgotten Empire (Vijayanagar): A Contribution to the History of India*. London: Swan Sonnenschein.

Shahbazi, A. Shapur. 2005. "Sasanian Dynasty." In *Encyclopædia Iranica*. Online edition, 2005. http://www.iranicaonline.org/articles/sasanian-dynasty (accessed June 21, 2016).

Shank, Michael H. 2007. "Mechanical Thinking in European Astronomy (13th–15th Centuries)." In Bucciantini/Camerota/Roux 2007, 3–27.

Shapin, Steven. 1989. "The Invisible Technician." *American Scientist* 77:6, 554–563.

———. 1992. "Discipline and Bounding: The History and Sociology of Science as Seen through the Externalism-Internalism Debate." *History of Science* 30, 333–369.

———. 1996. *The Scientific Revolution*. Chicago: University of Chicago Press.

Shapin, Steven and Simon Schaffer. 1985. *Leviathan and the Air Pump: Hobbes, Boyle, and Experimental Life*. Princeton: Princeton University Press.

Shea, William R. 1972. *Galileo's Intellectual Revolution*. London: Macmillan.

Shepard, Jonathan (ed.). 2008. *The Cambridge History of the Byzantine Empire, c. 500–1492*. Cambridge: Cambridge University Press.

Sherman, William H. 1995. *John Dee: The Politics of Reading and Writing in the English Renaissance*. Amherst: University of Massachusetts Press.

Shih, Hu. 1960. "The Renaissance in China." *Journal of the Royal Institute of International Affairs* 5:1, 265–283.

Shillington, Kevin (ed.). 2005. *Encyclopedia of African History*. 3 vols. London: Routledge.

Shirane, Haruo (ed.). 2002. *Early Modern Japanese Literature: An Anthology*. New York: Columbia University Press.

Shryock, Andrew, and Daniel Lord Smail (eds.). 2011. *Deep History and the Architecture of Past and Present*. Berkeley: University of California Press.

Sieferle, Rolf Peter. 2001. *The Subterranean Forest: Energy Systems and the Industrial Revolution*. Trans. Michael T. Osman. Cambridge: The White Horse Press.

Signori, Gabriela. 2007. *Das 13. Jahrhundert. Einführung in die Geschichte des spätmittelalterlichen Europa*. Stuttgart: W. Kohlhammer.

Sigrist, Christian. 1978. "Gesellschaften ohne Staat und die Entdeckung der 'social anthropology.'" In Ferdinand Kramer and Christian Sigrist (eds.), *Gesellschaften ohne Staat. Gleichheit und Gegenseitigkeit*. Frankfurt: Syndikat, 28–46.

Simon, Herbert A. 1990. "A Mechanism for Social Selection and Successful Altruism." *Science* 21, 1665–1668.

Simon, Róbert. 2002. *Ibn Khaldūn: History as Science and the Patrimonial Empire*. Budapest: Akadémiai Kiadó.

Siraisi, Nancy G. 1990. *Medieval and Early Renaissance Medicine: An Introduction to Knowledge and Practice*. Chicago: University of Chicago Press.

Sivin, Nathan. 1995a. "Copernicus in China or, Good Intentions Gone Astray." In Sivin 1995d, art. IV.

———. 1995b. "Shen Kua." In Sivin 1995d, art. III.

———. 1995c. "Science and Medicine in Chinese History." In Sivin 1995d, art. VI.

———. 1995d. *Science in Ancient China: Researches and Reflections*. Aldershot: Variorum.

———. 1995e. "Why the Scientific Revolution Did Not Take Place in China—or Didn't It?" In Sivin 1995d, art. VII.

Skalnik, James. 2002. *Ramus and Reform: University and Church at the End of the Renaissance*. Kirksville: Truman State University Press.

Skinner, G. William (ed.). 1977. *The City in Late Imperial China*. Stanford: Stanford University Press.

Skinner, Quentin. 1978. *The Foundations of Modern Political Thought*. 2 vols. Cambridge: Cambridge University Press.

Šmahel, František. 2002. *Die Hussitische Revolution*. Trans. Thomas Krzenck. 3 vols. Hanover: Hahnsche Buchhandlung.

Smith, Christine and Joseph O'Connor. 2006. *Building the Kingdom: Giannozzo Manetti on the Material and Spiritual Edifice*. Turnhout: Brepols.

Smith, Jennifer Anh-Thu Tran. 2012. "Reginald Pecock and Vernacular Theology in Pre-Reformation England." PhD dissertation, University of California, Los Angeles.

Smith, Sir Thomas. 1906. *De Republica Anglorum*. Ed. Leonard Alston. Cambridge: Cambridge University Press.

Smoller, Laura A. 1994. *History, Prophecy, and the Stars: The Christian Astrology of Pierre D'Ailly, 1350–1420*. Princeton: Princeton University Press.

Soldi Rondinini, Gigliola. 1997. "Filippo Maria Visconti." In *DBI* 43, 772–782.

Sorci, Alessandra. "L' 'invention del secul nostro nova': la prospettiva rinascimentale." In *RIE* V, 607–625.

Southern, Richard W. 1995–1997. *Scholastic Humanism and the Unification of Europe*. 2 vols. Oxford: Blackwell.

Soykut, Mustafa. 2010. *Image of the 'Turk' in Italy: A History of the "Other" in Early Modern Europe*. 2nd ed. Berlin: Klaus Schwarz.

Spampanato, Vincenzo. 1921. *Vita di Giordano Bruno con documenti editi ed inediti*. Messina: Casa editrice Giuseppe Principato.

Speer, Andreas, and Lydia Wegener (eds.). 2006. *Wissen über Grenzen. Arabisches Wissen und lateinisches Mittelalter*. Berlin: De Gruyter.

Spieß, Karl-Heinz (ed.). 2013. *Ausbildung und Verbreitung des Lehnwesens im Reich und in Italien im 12. und 13. Jahrhundert*. Stuttgart: Ostfildern.

Splett, Jochen. 1976. *Abrogans-Studien. Kommentar zum ältesten deutschen Wörterbuch*. Wiesbaden: Steiner.

Sprenkel, Sybille van der. 1977. "Urban Social Control." In Skinner 1977, 609–632.

Stanley-Baker, Joan. 1994. *Japanese Art*. London: Thames & Hudson.

Stapleton, Michael L. 1990. "Spenser, the 'Antiquitez de Rome,' and the Development of the English Sonnet Form." *Comparative Literature Studies* 27:4, 259–274.

Stark, Rodney. 2005. *The Victory of Reason: How Christianity Led to Freedom, Capitalism, and Western Success*. London: Random House.

Starkey, David. 1992. "England." In Porter/Teich 1992, 146–163.

Starobinski, Jean. 1982. *Montaigne en mouvement*. Paris: Gallimard.

Starr, S. Frederick. 2013. *Lost Enlightenment: Central Asia's Golden Age from the Arab Conquest to Tamerlane*. Princeton: Princeton University Press.

Stauber, Reinhard. 2002. "Hartmann Schedel, der Nürnberger Humanistenkreis und die 'Erweiterung der deutschen Nation.'" In Helmrath/Muhlack/Walther 2002, 159–185.

Stechow, Wolfgang. 1966. *Northern Renaissance Art, 1400–1600: Sources and Documents*. Englewood Cliffs: Prentice-Hall.

Steckel, Sita. 2011. *Kulturen des Lehrens im Früh- und Hochmittelalter. Autorität, Wissenskonzepte und Netzwerke von Gelehrten*. Cologne: Böhlau.

Stein, Burton. 1980. *Peasant State and Society in Medieval India*. Oxford: Oxford University Press.

———. 2010. *A History of India*. Ed. David Arnold. 2nd ed. London: Wiley-Blackwell.

Steiner, Reinhard. 1991. *Prometheus. Ikonologische und anthropologische Aspekte der bildenden Kunst vom 14. bis zum 17. Jahrhundert*. Grafrath: Boer.

Stelzer, Winfried. 1978. "Zum Scholarenprivileg Friedrich Barbarossas (*Authentica habita*)." *Deutsches Archiv zur Erforschung des Mittelalters* 34, 121–165.

Stephenson, Barbara. 2004. *The Power and Patronage of Marguerite de Navarre*. Aldershot: Ashgate.

Stephenson, Bruce. 1994a. *Kepler's Physical Astronomy*. Princeton: Princeton University Press.

———. 1994b. *The Music of the Heavens: Kepler's Harmonic Astronomy*. Princeton: Princeton University Press.

Stemberger, Günter. 1979. *Das klassische Judentum. Kultur und Geschichte der rabbinischen Zeit*. Munich: C. H. Beck.

Stevenson, William R., Jr. 2004. "Calvin and Political Issues." In McKim 2004, 173–182.

Stierle, Karlheinz. 2003. *Francesco Petrarca. Ein Intellektueller im Europa des 14. Jahrhunderts*. Munich: Hanser.

———. 2014. *Dante Alighieri. Dichter im Exil, Dichter der Welt*. Munich: C. H. Beck.

Stinger, Charles L. 1977. *Humanism and the Church Fathers: Ambrogio Traversari (1386–1439) and the Revival of Patristic Theology in the Early Italian Renaissance*. Albany: State University of New York Press.

Stirling, William. 1853. *The Cloister Life of the Emperor Charles the Fifth*. 3rd ed. London: John W. Parker and Son.

Strabo. 1917–1933. *The Geography*. Trans. Horace Leonard Jones. 8 vols. London: Heinemann.

Strohm, Christoph. 2009. *Johannes Calvin. Leben und Werk des Reformators*. Munich: C. H. Beck.

Stromer, Wolfgang von. 1960. "Das Handelshaus der Stromer von Nürnberg und die Geschichte der ersten deutschen Papiermühle." *Vierteljahresschrift für Sozial- und Wirtschaftsgeschichte* 47, 81–104.

Strong, Roy. 1973. *Art and Power: Renaissance Festivals, 1450–1650*. Woodbridge: Boydell Press.

Stroumsa, Sarah. 1999. *Freethinkers of Medieval Islam: Ibn al-Rawandi, Abu Bakr al-Razi, and Their Impact on Islamic Thought*. Leiden: Brill.

Studer, Heidi G. 1998. "Francis Bacon on the Political Dangers of Scientific Progress." *Canadian Journal of Political Science* 31, 219–234.

Studt, Birgit. 2013. "Martin V. Überwindung des Schismas und Kirchenreform." In Braun et al. 2013, 126–131.

Sturlese, Loris. 1993. *Die deutsche Philosophie im Mittelalter*. Munich: C. H. Beck.

Subrahmanyam, Sanjay. 1997. "Connected Histories: Notes towards a Reconfiguration of Early Modern Eurasia." *Modern Asian Studies* 31:3, 735–762.

Sturm, Gottfried. (trans.). 1982. "Sadonstschina. Die Lobpreisung des Fürsten Dimitri Iwanowitsch und seines Vetters, des Fürsten Wladimir Andrejewitsch, wie sie ihren Feind, den Khan Mamai, besiegten." In Graßhoff et. al. (eds.), *O Bojan, du Nachtigall der alten Zeit. Sieben Jahrhunderte altrussischer Literatur*. Berlin: Rütten & Loening, 159–170.

Suerbaum, Ulrich. 2001. *Shakespeares Dramen*. 2nd ed. Tübingen: Francke.

Summers, David. 2007. *Vision, Reflection, and Desire in Western Painting*. Chapel Hill: University of North Carolina Press.

Sunan an-Nasa'i. https://sunnah.com/nasai (accessed July 22, 2023).

Sunesen, Anders. 1985–1988. *Andreae Sunonis filii Hexaemeron post M. Cl. Gertz*. Ed. Sten Ebbesen and Boethius Laurentius Mortensen. 2 vols. Copenhagen: Reitzel.

Suter, Heinrich. 1900. *Die Mathematiker und Astronomen der Araber und ihre Werke*. Leipzig: Teubner.

Sutton, John. 1991. "Religion and the Failure of Determinism." In Stephen Gaukroger (ed.). *The Uses of Antiquity*. Dordrecht: Kluwer, 25–51.

Svalduz, Elena. "Palazzi pubblici: I luoghi di governo e le sedi dell'amministrazione cittadina." In *RIE* VI, 125–158.

Swerdlow, Noel. 1998. "Galileo's Discoveries with the Telescope and Their Evidence for the Copernican Theory." In Peter Machamer (ed.), *The Cambridge Companion to Galileo*. Cambridge: Cambridge University Press, 244–270.

Swinford, Dean. 2006. *Through the Daemon's Gate: Kepler's Somnium, Medieval Dream Narratives, and the Polysemy of Allegorical Motifs*. London: Routledge.

Symes, Carol. 2011. "When We Talk about Modernity." *The American Historical Review* 116:3, 715–726.

Szech, Anna. 2016. *Moskau—das dritte Rom? Einflüsse der italienischen Renaissance auf die russische Kunst der Frühen Neuzeit. Reiseberichte als eine Quellengattung der Kunstgeschichte*. Bern: Peter Lang.

Szlezák, Thomas A. 2010. *Was Europa den Griechen verdankt. Von den Grundlagen unserer Kultur in der griechischen Antike*. Tübingen: Mohr Siebeck.

Taagepera, Rein. 1978. "Size and Duration of Empires: Systematics of Size." *Social Science Research* 7, 108–127.

Tacitus. 1937. *Annals*. Books 4–6, 11–12. Trans. John Jackson. Cambridge, MA: Harvard University Press.

Tainter, Joseph A. 1988. *The Collapse of Complex Societies*. Cambridge: Cambridge University Press.

Talkenberger, Heike. 1990. *Sintflut*. Tübingen: Niemeyer.

Talon, Omer. 1577. *Petri Rami . . . Praefationes, Epistolae, Orationes*. Paris: Dionysius Valens.

Tambrun, Brigitte. 2006. *Pléthon. Le retour de Platon*. Paris: Vrin.

Tangheroni, Marco. 1996. *Commercio e navigazione nel Medioevo*. Bari: Laterza.

Taranczewski, Detlev. 2006. "Japan, der Feudalismus, Westeuropa, Ostasien." In Hans Martin Krämer, Tino Schölz, and Sebastian Conrad (eds.), *Geschichtswissenschaft in Japan. Themen, Ansätze und Theorien*. Göttingen: Vandenhoeck & Ruprecht, 31–64.

Tartuferi, Angelo. 2008. "Masaccio." In *DBI* 71, 496–509.

Tasso, Torquato. 2021. *Aminta*. Ed. Davide Colussi and Paolo Trovato. Turin: Einaudi.

Tavernor, Robert. 1998. *On Alberti and the Art of Building*. New Haven: Yale University Press.

Tavoni, Mirko. 2011. "Bembo, Pietro." In Raffaele Simone, Gaetano Berruto, and Paolo D'Achille, eds. *Enciclopedia dell'Italiano*. Vol. I. Rome: Istituto della Enciclopedia Italiana Treccani, 1526–1529.

Taylor, Charles. 1989. *Sources of the Self: The Making of Modern Identity*. Cambridge, MA: Harvard University Press.

Taylor, Christopher. 2011. "Prester John, Christian Enclosure, and the Spatial Transmission of Islamic Alterity in the Twelfth-Century West." In Jerold C. Frakes (ed.), *Contextualizing the Muslim Other in Christian Medieval Discourse*. New York: Palgrave Macmillan, 39–63.

Teresa of Ávila. 2011. *The Life of St. Teresa of Jesus*. Trans. David Lewis. New York: Cosimo Classics.

Tertullian. 2018. *The Prescription Against Heretics*. Trans. Peter Holmes. Fairfield: Lighthouse Publishing.

Terwiel, Barend J. 2011. *Thailand's Political History: From the 13th Century to Recent Times*. Bangkok: River Books.

Teschke, Benno. 2010. "Revisiting the 'War-Makes-States' Thesis: War, Taxation and Social Property Relations in Early Modern Europe." In Olaf Asbach and Peter Schröder (eds.). *War, the State and International Law in Seventeenth-Century-Europe*. Burlington: Ashgate, 35–62.

Theiler, Willy. 1966. "Plotin zwischen Platon und Stoa." In Theiler, *Forschungen zum Neuplatonismus*. Berlin: De Gruyter, 124–139.

Theophilus Presbyter. 1874. *Schedula diversarum artium*. Ed. Albert Ilg. Vienna: Wilhelm Braumüller.

Thijssen, Hans. 2018. "Condemnation of 1277." *The Stanford Encyclopedia of Philosophy* (Winter 2018 Edition). Ed. Edward N. Zalta. https://plato.stanford.edu/archives/win2018/entries/condemnation/ (accessed 24 May 2022).

Thomas, Hugh. 2003. *Rivers of Gold: The Rise of the Spanish Empire, from Columbus to Magellan.* New York: Random House.

Thomasin von Zerklaere. 2004. *Der welsche Gast: Text (Auswahl), Übersetzung, Stellenkommentar.* Ed. Eva Willms. Berlin: De Gruyter.

Thompson, James W. 1965. *The Medieval Library.* New York: Hafner.

Thompson, Kirill. 2020. "Zhu Xi." *The Stanford Encyclopedia of Philosophy* (Fall 2020 Edition). https://plato.stanford.edu/archives/sum2021/entries/zhu-xi/ (accessed August 3, 2023).

Thoren, Victor E. 1990. *The Lord of Uraniborg: A Biography of Tycho Brahe.* Cambridge: Cambridge University Press.

Thorndike, Lynn. 1949. *The Sphere of Sacrobosco and Its Commentators.* Chicago: University of Chicago Press.

———. 1972. *University Records and Life in the Middle Ages.* New York: Columbia University Press.

Thornton, John. 2012. *A Cultural History of the Atlantic World, 1250–1820.* Cambridge: Cambridge University Press.

Thucydides. 1985. *History of the Peloponnesian War.* Trans. Rex Warner. London: Penguin.

Tigler, Peter. 1963. *Die Architekturtheorie des Filarete.* Berlin: De Gruyter.

Tilly, Charles. 1990. *Coercion, Capital, and European States, AD 990–1990.* Cambridge: Blackwell.

Tillyard, Eustache M. W. 1998. *The Elizabethan World Picture: A Study of the Idea of Order in the Age of Shakespeare, Donne and Milton.* London: Pimlico Books.

Tinagli, Paola. 1997. *Women in Italian Renaissance Art: Gender, Representation and Identity.* Manchester: Manchester University Press.

Toby, Ronald. 1984. *State and Diplomacy in Early Modern Japan: Asia in the Development of the Tokugawa Bakufu.* Princeton: Princeton University Press.

Todorov, Tzvetan. 1987. *The Conquest of America: The Question of the Other.* New York: Harper & Row.

Tolan, John. 2008. *Sons of Ishmael: Muslims through European Eyes in the Middle Ages.* Gainesville: University Press of Florida.

Toman, Rolf (ed.). 2007. *Die Kunst der italienischen Renaissance. Architektur, Skulptur, Malerei, Zeichnung.* Potsdam: Ullmann.

Tönnesmann, Andreas. 2013. *Pienza. Städtebau und Humanismus.* Berlin: Wagenbach.

Tonomura, Hitomi. 1992. *Community and Commerce in Late Medieval Japan: The Corporate Villages of Tokuchin-ho.* Stanford: Stanford University Press.

Topdemir, Hüseyin Gazi. 2007. "Kamal Al-Din Al-Farisi's Explanation of the Rainbow." *Humanity & Social Sciences Journal* 2:1, 75–85.

Topich, William J., and Keith A. Leitich. 2013. *The History of Myanmar.* Santa Barbara: Greenwood.

Torres-Alcalá, Antonio. 1983. *Don Enrique de Villena: un mago al dintel del Renacimiento.* Madrid: Ediciones J. Porrúa Turanzas.

Torricelli, Evangelista. 1715. *Lezioni accademiche.* Florence: Jacopo Guiducci.

Toulmin, Stephen. 1990. *Cosmopolis: The Hidden Agenda of Modernity.* Chicago: University of Chicago Press.

Touwaide, Alain. 2005. "Dioscorides." In Thomas F. Glick, Steven Livesey, and Faith Wallis (eds.). *Medieval Science, Technology and Medicine: An Encyclopedia.* New York: Routledge, 152–154.

Toynbee, Arnold J. 1934–1954. *A Study of History.* 10 vols. Oxford: Oxford University Press.

Tracy, James D. 2002. *Emperor Charles V, Impresario of War: Campaign Strategy, International Finance, and Domestic Politics.* Cambridge: Cambridge University Press.

Trakulhun, Sven. 2006. *Siam und Europa. Das Königreich Ayutthaya in westlichen Berichten 1500–1670.* Laatzen: Wehrhahn.

Trakulhun, Sven, and Ralph Weber (eds.). 2015. *Delimiting Modernities: Conceptual Challenges and Regional Responses*. Lanham: Lexington Books.

Trapp, J. B. 2006. "Petrarchan Places: An Essay in the Iconography of Commemoration." *Journal of the Warburg and Courtauld Institutes* 69, 1–50.

Treadgold, Warren. 1984a. "The Macedonian Renaissance." In Treadgold 1984b, 75–98.

——— (ed.). 1984b. *Renaissances before the Renaissance: Cultural Revivals of Late Antiquity and the Middle Ages*. Stanford: Stanford University Press.

Trevelyan, George Macaulay. 1937. *History of England*. 2nd ed. London: Longmans, Green.

Trinkaus, Charles. 1995. *In Our Image and Likeness: Humanity and Divinity in Italian Humanist Thought*. South Bend: University of Notre Dame Press.

Tripodi, Claudia. 2010. "I fiorentini quinto elemento dell'universo. L'utilizzazione encomiastica di una tradizione/invenzione." *Archivio storico italiano* 625, 491–515.

Troeltsch, Ernst. 2008. *Der Historismus und seine Probleme*. Ed. Friedrich Wilhelm Graf. Berlin: De Gruyter.

Trompf, Garry W. 1979. *The Idea of Historical Recurrence in Western Thought: From Antiquity to the Reformation*. Berkeley: University of California Press.

Truitt, Elly R. 2012. "Celestial Divination and Arabic Science in Twelfth-Century England: The History of Gerbert of Aurillac's Talking Head." *Journal of the History of Ideas* 73:2, 201–222.

Trüper, Henning, Dipesh Chakrabarty, and Sanjay Subrahmanyam (eds.). 2015. *Historical Teleologies in the Modern World*. London: Bloomsbury.

Trzaskoma, Stephen M., R. Scott Smith, and Stephen Brunet (ed. and trans.). 2004. *Anthology of Classical Myth: Primary Sources in Translation*. Indianapolis: Hackett.

Tsang, Carol Richmond. 2007. *War and Faith: Ikko Ikki in Late Muromachi Japan*. Cambridge, MA: Harvard University Press.

Tsutsui, William M. (ed.). 2007. *A Companion to Japanese History*. Malden: Blackwell.

Tuchtenhagen, Ralph. 2008. *Kleine Geschichte Schwedens*. Munich: C. H. Beck.

———. 2009. *Kleine Geschichte Norwegens*. Munich: C. H. Beck.

Tucker, John A. (ed.). 2006. *Ogyū Sorai's Philosophical Masterworks: The Bendō and Benmei*. Honolulu: University of Hawai'i Press.

Tuetey, Alexandre (ed.). 1881. *Journal d'un bourgeois de Paris, 1405–1449*. Paris: Champion.

Turner, Gerard l'Estrange. 1985. "The Cabinet of Experimental Philosophy." In Oliver Impey and Arthur MacGregor (eds.), *The Origins of Museums: The Cabinet of Curiosities in Sixteenth- and Seventeenth-Century Europe*. Oxford: Ashmolean Museum, 214–222.

Twitchett, Denis C. (ed.). 1979. *Cambridge History of China*. Vol III. Cambridge: Cambridge University Press.

Twitchett, Denis C., and Michael Loewe (eds.). 1986. *The Cambridge History of China*. Vol. I: *The Ch'in and Han Empires, 221 B.C.–A.D. 220*. Cambridge: Cambridge University Press.

Twitchett, Denis C., and Frederick W. Mote (eds.). 2008. *The Cambridge History of China*. Vol. VIII.2: *The Ming Dynasty, 1368–1644*. Cambridge: Cambridge University Press.

Twitchett, Denis C., and Paul Jakov Smith (eds.). 2009. *The Cambridge History of China*. Vol. V. Cambridge: Cambridge University Press.

Ubl, Karl. 2008. *Inzestverbot und Gesetzgebung. Die Konstruktion eines Verbrechens (300–1100)*. Berlin: De Gruyter.

Udovitch, Abraham L. 1970. *Partnership and Profit in Medieval Islam*. Princeton: Princeton University Press.

Valdeón Baruqe, Julio. 2003. *Alfonso X el Sabio. La forja de la España moderna*. Madrid: Temas de Hoy.

Valla, Lorenzo. 1970. *De vero falsoque bono*. Ed. Maristella de Panizza Lorch. Bari: Adriatica.

———. 2007. *On the Donation of Constantine*. Trans. Glen W. Bowersock. Cambridge, MA: Harvard University Press.

Van Loo, Bart. 2020. *Burgund: Das verschwundene Reich. Eine Geschichte von 1111 Jahren und einem Tag*. 4th ed. Munich: C. H. Beck.

Van Zanden, Jan Luiten. 2009. *The Long Road to the Industrial Revolution: The European Economy in a Global Perspective, 1000–1800*. Leiden: Brill.

Van Zanden, Jan Luiten, Eltjo Buringh, and Erik Maarten Bosker. 2012. "The Rise and Decline of European Parliaments, 1188–1789." *The Economic History Review* 65:3, 635–861.

Vasari, Giorgio. 1966–1987. *Le vite de' più eccellenti pittori scultori e architettori: nelle redazioni del 1550 e 1568*. Ed. Rosanna Bettarini and Paola Barocchi. 6 vols. Florence: Sansoni.

Vasoli, Cesare. 2007. *La retorica e l'umanesimo. "Invenzione" e "metodo" nella cultura del XV e XVI secolo*. Milano: Feltrinelli.

Veer, Gerrit de. 1598/2010. *Die Reisen des Willem Barents über das Nordmeer in den Jahren 1594, 1595 und 1596*. Nuremberg: Levinus Hulsius, 1598. Facsimile reprint: Bremerhaven: Deutsches Schiffahrtsmuseum and Edition Stiedenrod, 2010.

Ventura, Iolanda. 2006. "Il *De materia medica* di Dioscoride nel Medievo: mediazione araba e ricezione occidentale." In Speer/Wegener 2006, 317–339.

Vernet, Juan, and Julio Samsó. 1996. "The Development of Arabic Science in Andalusia." In Rashed, Roshdi (ed.). *Encyclopedia of the History of Arabic Science*. Vol. I: *Astronomy—Theoretical and Applied*. London: Routledge, 243–275.

Vesalius, Andreas. 1543. *De humani corporis fabrica*. Basel: Johannes Oporinus.

Vespasiano da Bisticci. 1970–1976. *Le Vite*. Ed. and trans. Aulo Greco. 2 vols. Florence: INSR.

Vespucci, Amerigo. 1916. *Letter to Piero Soderini, Gonfaloniere. The Year 1504*. Trans. George Tyler Northup. Princeton: Princeton University Press.

Veyard-Cosme, Christiane. 2010. "La Renaissance carolingienne au miroir des contemporains." In Marie-Sophie Masse (ed.), *La Renaissance? Des Renaissances?* Paris: Éditions Klincksieck, 107–128.

Vicaire, Marie-Humbert. 1982. *Histoire de Saint Dominique*. 2 vols. 2nd ed. Paris: CERF.

Vickers, Brian. 1984a. "Analogy Versus Identity: The Rejection of Occult Symbolism, 1580–1680." In Vickers 1984b, 95–163.

———. (ed.). 1984b. *Occult and Scientific Mentalities in the Renaissance*. Cambridge: Cambridge University Press.

Villani, Giovanni. 1991. *Nuova Cronica*. Ed. Giuseppe Porta. 3 vols. Parma: Guanda.

Villata, Edoardo. 1999. *Leonardo da Vinci. I documenti e le testimonianze contemporanee*. Milan: Ente Raccolta Vinciana.

Villiers, John. 2001. *Südostasien vor der Kolonialzeit*. 7th ed. Frankfurt: Fischer.

Villon, François. 2013. *The Testament and Other Poems*. Trans. Anthony Mortimer. Richmond, Surrey: Alma Classics.

Vincent, Nicholas. 2012. *Magna Carta: A Very Short Introduction*. Oxford: Oxford University Press.

Violante, Cinzio. 1974. *La società milanese nell'età precomunale*. Bari: Laterza.

Virgil. 1900. *Bucolics, Aeneid, and Georgics*. Trans. James Bradstreet Greenough. Boston: Ginn.

Viti, Paolo. 1993. "Enoch d'Ascoli." In *DBI* 42, 695–699.

———. 1997. "Francesco Filelfo." In *DBI* 47, 613–626.

Vittori, Angelo. 1613. *Disputatio de palpitatione cordis (…) Beati Filippi Neri*. Rome: Typographia Camera Apostolica.

Vogel, Klaus Anselm. 1995. "Sphaera terrae—das mittelalterliche Bild der Erde und die kosmographische Revolution." PhD dissertation, Georg-August-Universität Göttingen.

Vogelsang, Kai. 2013. *Geschichte Chinas*. 3rd ed. Stuttgart: Reclam.

Vogt-Spira, Gregor, and Bettina Rommel (eds.). 1999. *Die kulturelle Auseinandersetzung Roms mit Griechenland als europäisches Paradigma*. Stuttgart: Franz Steiner.

Voigtländer, Nico, and Hans Joachim Voth. 2013. "Gifts of Mars: Warfare and Europe's Early Rise to Riches." *Journal of Economic Perspectives* 27:4, 165–186.

Volckart, Oliver. 1999. *Political Fragmentation and the Emergence of Market Economies: The Case of Germany, c. 1000–1800 A.D.* Jena: Max-Planck-Institute zur Erforschung von Wirtschaftssystemen.

Völkel, Markus. 2006. *Geschichtsschreibung. Eine Einführung in globaler Perspektive.* Cologne: Böhlau.

Vollmann, Benedikt Konrad. 2004. "Lateinisches Schauspiel des Spätmittelalters." In Hans-Joachim Ziegeler (ed.), *Ritual und Inszenierung. Geistliches und weltliches Drama des Mittelalters und der Frühen Neuzeit.* Tübingen: Niemeyer, 1–8.

Voltaire. 1817. *Oeuvres complètes. Histoire générale.* Vol. VII. Paris: Th. Desoer.

Vos, Antonie. 2006. *The Philosophy of John Duns Scotus.* Edinburgh: Edinburgh University Press.

Vos, Dirk de. 1999. *Rogier van der Weyden. Das Gesamtwerk.* Munich: Hirmer.

Voth, Hans-Joachim. 2001. *Time and Work in England 1750–1830.* Oxford: Clarendon.

Vries, Peer. 2009. *Zur politischen Ökonomie des Tees. Was uns Tee über die englische und chinesische Wirtschaft der frühen Neuzeit sagen kann.* Vienna: Böhlau.

———. 2013. *Escaping Poverty: The Origins of Modern Economic Growth.* Vienna: V & R Unipress.

Waley Singer, Dorothea. 1950. *Giordano Bruno: His Life and Thought, with Annotated Translation of His Work* On the Infinite Universe and Worlds. New York: Schuman.

Walker, Daniel P. 1958. *Spiritual and Demonic Magic from Ficino to Campanella.* London: Warburg Institute.

Wallace, William A. 1992. *Galileo's Logic of Discovery and Proof.* Dordrecht: Kluwer.

Wallace, William E. 2011. *Michelangelo: The Artist, the Man and His Times.* Cambridge: Cambridge University Press.

Wallerstein, Immanuel. 1974–1980. *The Modern World System.* 2 vols. New York: Academic Press.

Walsh, Richard J. 2005. *Charles the Bold and Italy (1467–1477): Politics and Personnel.* Liverpool: Liverpool University Press.

Walsh, Thomas (trans.). 1920. *Hispanic Anthology: Poems Translated from the Spanish and North American Poets.* New York: G. P. Putnam's Sons.

Walter, Gerrit. "Humanismus." In *EdN* V, 665–691.

Ward, Benedicta. 1987. *Miracles and the Medieval Mind: Theory, Record and Event, 1000–1215.* Philadelphia: University of Pennsylvania Press.

Ward-Perkins, Bryan. 2005. *The Fall of Rome and the End of Civilization.* Oxford: Oxford University Press.

Ware, Kallistos. 1993. "Eastern Christendom." In John McManners (ed.). *The Oxford Illustrated History of Christianity.* Oxford: Oxford University Press, 131–166.

Warnke, Martin. 1984. *Cranachs Luther. Entwürfe für ein Image.* Frankfurt: Fischer.

———. 1993. *The Court Artist: On the Ancestry of the Modern Artist.* Trans. David McLintock. Cambridge: Cambridge University Press.

Warren, Charles. 1973. "Brunelleschi's Dome and Dufay's Motet." *Musical Quarterly* 59, 92–105.

Waszkis, Helmut. 1993. *Mining in the Americas: Stories and History.* Cambridge: Woodhead.

Waterfield, Robin (ed. and trans.). 2000. *The First Philosophers: The Presocratics and Sophists.* Oxford: Oxford University Press.

Watson Andaya, Barbara, and Leonard Y. Andaya. 2015. *A History of Early Modern Southeast Asia, 1400–1830.* Cambridge: Cambridge University Press.

Watson, Andrew M. 1974. "The Arab Agricultural Revolution and Its Diffusion." *The Journal of Economic History* 34:1, 8–35.

Wear, Andrew. 2000. *Knowledge and Practice in English Medicine, 1550–1680.* Cambridge: Cambridge University Press.

Weber, Hermann. 1977. "Richelieu und das Reich." In Hans Ulrich Rudolf (ed.). *Der Dreißigjährige Krieg. Perspektiven und Strukturen.* Darmstadt: WBG, 304–321.

Weber, Max. 1978. *Economy and Society: An Outline of Interpretive Sociology*. Ed. Günther Roth and Claus Wittich. Trans. Ephraim Fischoff et al. Berkeley: University of California Press.

———. 1986. *The City*. Ed. Don Martindale and Gertrud Neuwirth. 2nd ed. Glencoe: Free Press.

———. 1988. "Objektive Möglichkeit und adäquate Verursachung in der historischen Kausalbetrachtung." In Max Weber, *Gesammelte Aufsätze zur Wissenschaftslehre*. Ed. Johannes Winckelmann. 7th ed. Tübingen: Mohr Siebeck, 266–290.

———. 2002. *The Protestant Ethic and the Spirit of Capitalism*. Ed. Peter Baehr and Gordon C. Wells. New York: Penguin.

Wei, Ian P. 2012. *Intellectual Culture in Medieval Paris: Theologians and the University, c. 1100–1300*. Cambridge: Cambridge University Press.

Weigand, Rudolf Kilian. 2000. *Der "Renner" des Hugo von Trimberg. Überlieferung, Quellenabhängigkeit und Struktur einer spätmittelalterlichen Lehrdichtung*. Wiesbaden: Reichert.

Weinfurter, Stefan. 2006a. *Canossa. Die Entzauberung der Welt*. 2nd ed. Munich: C. H. Beck.

———. 2006b. *Das Jahrhundert der Salier (1024–1125)*. Ostfildern: Thorbecke.

———. 2012. *Päpstliche Herrschaft im Mittelalter. Funktionsweise—Strategien—Darstellungsformen*. Ostfildern: Thorbecke, 69–80.

Welch, Evelyn. 2009. *Shopping in the Renaissance: Consumer Cultures in Italy, 1400–1600*. New Haven: Yale University Press.

Wendell, Charles. 1971. "Baghdad: *Imago Mundi*, and Other Foundation-Lore." *International Journal of Middle East Studies* 2:2, 99–128.

Werner, Thomas. 2007. *Den Irrtum liquidieren. Bücherverbrennungen im Mittelalter*. Göttingen: Vandenhoeck & Ruprecht.

Wesel, Uwe. 2000. *Juristische Weltkunde. Eine Einführung in das Recht*. 8th ed. Frankfurt: Suhrkamp.

Wesson, Robert G. 1978. *State Systems: International Pluralism, Politics, and Culture*. New York: The Free Press.

Westermann, Hartmut. 2006. "Wie disputiert man über das Gute? Lorenzo Vallas *De vero bono* als Debatte über die richtige Debatte." *Jahrbuch Rhetorik* 25, 30–54.

Westfall, Richard S. 1973. *Science and Religion in Seventeenth-Century England*. Ann Arbor: University of Michigan Press.

———. 1986. "Rise of Science and the Decline of Orthodox Christianity: A Study of Kepler, Descartes, and Newton." In Lindberg/Numbers 1986, 218–237.

Westman, Robert S. 1975. *The Copernican Achievement*. Berkeley: University of California Press.

———. 1980. "The Astronomer's Role in the Sixteenth Century: A Preliminary Study." *History of Science* 18, 105–147.

———. 1990. "Proof, Poetics, and Patronage: Copernicus's Preface to *De revolutionibus*." In Lindberg/Westman 1990, 167–205.

———. 2011. *The Copernican Question: Prognostication, Skepticism, and Celestial Order*. Berkeley: University of California Press.

Wey Gómez, Nicolás. 2008. *The Tropics of Empire: Why Columbus Sailed South to the Indies*. Cambridge, MA: MIT Press.

White, Hayden. 1973. *Metahistory: The Historical Imagination in Nineteenth-Century Europe*. Baltimore: Johns Hopkins University Press.

White, James W. 1995. *Ikki: Social Conflict and Political Protest in Early Modern Japan*. Ithaca: Cornell University Press.

White, Lynn. 1961. "Eilmer of Malmesbury, an Eleventh Century Aviator: A Case Study of Technological Innovation, Its Context and Tradition." *Technology and Culture* 2:2, 97–111.

———. 1978. *Medieval Religion and Technology*. Berkeley: University of California Press.

White, Matthew. 2011. *Atrocitology: Humanity's 100 Deadliest Achievements.* Edinburgh: Canongate.

Whitfield, Peter. 1998. *New Found Lands: Maps in the History of Exploration.* London: Routledge.

Whitmarsh, Tim. 2005. *The Second Sophistic.* Oxford: Oxford University Press.

Whitmore, John K. 2006. "The Rise of the Coast: Trade, State, and Culture in Early Dai Viet." *Journal of Southeast Asian Studies* 37:1, 103–122.

Wickham, Chris. 2009. *The Inheritance of Rome: A History of Europe from 400 to 1000.* London: Allen Lane.

———. 2015. *Sleepwalking into a New World: The Emergence of Italian City Communes in the Twelfth Century.* Princeton: Princeton University Press.

Wiedemann, Eilhard. 1976. "Ibn al-Shātir, ein arabischer Astronom aus dem 14. Jahrhundert." In Edward S. Kennedy and Imad Ghanem (eds.), *The Life and Work of Ibn al-Shatir: An Arab Astronomer of the Fourteenth Century.* Aleppo: Institute for the History of Arabic Science, 17–26.

Wiele, Mignon. 2003. *Die Erfindung einer Epoche. Zur Darstellung der italienischen Renaissance in der Literatur der französischen Romantik.* Tübingen: Gunter Narr Verlag.

Wiesflecker, Hermann. 1971–1986. *Kaiser Maximilian I.* 5 vols. Munich: Oldenbourg.

Wiesner-Hanks, Merry E. 2013. *Early Modern Europe 1450–1789.* 2nd ed. Cambridge: Cambridge University Press.

William of Ockham. 1967. *Opera theologica.* Ed. Gedeon Gál. New York: Franciscan Institute.

———. 2001. *Texte zu Theorie der Erkenntnis und der Wissenschaft.* Ed. Ruedi Imbach. Stuttgart: Reclam.

Wilhelmus Rubruquensis. 1929. "Itinerarium ad partes orientales." In Anastasius van den Wyngaert (ed.), *Sinica Franciscana.* Vol. I. Florence/Ad Claras Aquas (Quaracchi): apud Collegium s. Bonaventurae, 164–332.

Wilke, Jürgen. 2001. *Die Ebstorfer Weltkarte.* Bielefeld: Verlag für Regionalgeschichte.

Willach, Rolf. 2007. "Der lange Weg zur Erfindung des Fernrohres." In Jürgen Hamel and Inge Keil (eds.), *Der Meister und die Fernrohre. Das Wechselspiel zwischen Astronomie und Optik in der Geschichte.* Frankfurt: Harri Deutsch, 34–126.

William of Malmesbury. 1988. *Gesta regum anglorum: The History of the English Kings.* Ed. and trans. Roger A. B. Mynors with Rodney M. Thompson and Michael Winterbottom. Oxford: Oxford University Press.

Williams, Glyn. 2002. *Voyages of Delusion: The Quest for the Northwest Passage.* New Haven: Yale University Press.

Williams, Stephen, and Gerard Friell. 1994. *Theodosius: The Empire at Bay.* New Haven/London: Yale University Press.

Williamson, Paul. 2010. *Medieval Ivory Carvings: Early Christian to Romanesque.* London: V & A Publishing.

Wilson, Catherine. 1995. *The Invisible World: Early Modern Philosophy and the Invention of the Microscope.* Princeton: Princeton University Press.

Winchester, Simon. 2008. *Bomb, Book and Compass: Joseph Needham and the Great Secrets of China.* London: Viking.

Wind, Edgar. 1981. *Heidnische Mysterien der Renaissance.* Frankfurt: Suhrkamp.

Wirth, Eugen. 2000. *Die orientalische Stadt im islamischen Vorderasien und Nordafrika. Städtische Bausubstanz und räumliche Ordnung, Wirtschaftsleben und soziale Organisation.* 2 vols. Mainz: Philipp von Zabern.

Wirth, Jean. 2015. *Villard de Honnecourt, architecte du XIIIe siècle.* Geneva: Droz.

Wirtz, Carolin. 2006. *Köln und Venedig. Wirtschaftliche und kulturelle Beziehungen im 15. und 16. Jahrhundert.* Cologne: Böhlau.

Witt, Ronald G. 1976. *Coluccio Salutati and His Public Letters*. Geneva: Droz.

———. 1983. *Hercules at the Crossroads: The Life, Work, and Thought of Coluccio Salutati*. Durham: Duke University Press.

———. 2000. *"In the Footsteps of the Ancients": The Origins of Humanism from Lovato to Bruni*. Leiden: Brill.

———. 2012. *The Two Latin Cultures and the Foundation of Renaissance Humanism in Medieval Italy*. Cambridge: Cambridge University Press.

Witte, Charles Martial de. 1956. "Les bulles pontificales et l'expansion portugaise au XVe siècle." *Revue d'histoire ecclesiastique* 51, 413–453.

Wittfogel, Karl August. 1967. *Oriental Despotism: A Comparative Study of Total Power*. 6th ed. New Haven: Yale University Press.

Wittkower, Rudolf. 1963. *Born under Saturn: The Character and Conduction of Artists*. New York: Random House.

———. 1998. *Architectural Principles in the Age of Humanism*. 2nd ed. Hoboken: John Wiley & Sons.

Wohlmann, Avital. 2010. *Al-Ghazali, Averroës and the Interpretation of the Qu'ran: Common Sense and Philosophy in Islam*. Trans. David Burrell. Milton Park: Routledge.

Wolverton, Lisa. 2015. *Cosmas of Prague: Narrative, Classicism, Politics*. Washington, D.C.: Catholic University of America Press.

Woodside, Alexander. 2006. *Lost Modernities: China, Vietnam, Korea, and the Hazards of World History*. Cambridge, MA: Harvard University Press.

Wolff, Martha. 1990. "Meister der Spielkarten." In *NDB* 16, 720.

Wollasch, Joachim. 1996. *Cluny: Licht der Welt. Aufstieg und Niedergang der klösterlichen Gemeinschaft*. Zurich: Artemis und Winkler.

Wolters, Oliver W. 1999. *History, Culture and Region in Southeast Asian Perspectives*. Ithaca: Cornell University Press.

Wolters, Reinhard. 2011. *Die Römer in Germanien*. 6th ed. Munich: C. H. Beck.

Wong, Roy Bin. 1997. *China Transformed: Historical Change and the Limits of the European Experience*. Ithaca: Cornell University Press.

Woodward, David (ed.). 2007. *The History of Cartography*. Vol. III. Chicago: University of Chicago Press.

Wujastyk, Dominik. 2008. "A Body of Knowledge: The Wellcome Ayurvedic Man and His Sanskrit Context." *Asian Medicine: Tradition and Modernity* 4, 201–248.

Xin, Xu. 2003. *The Jews of Kaifeng, China*. Jersey City: KTAV Publishing House.

Yates, Frances A. 1964. *Giordano Bruno and the Hermetic Tradition*. Chicago: University of Chicago Press.

———. 1975. *The Rosicrucian Enlightenment*. London: Routledge & Kegan Paul.

Yenen, Osman Şadi. 2014. "History and Eradication of Smallpox in Turkey." *Microbiology Australia* 35:3, 156–164.

Yoshida, Mitukumi. 1968. "The Chinese Concept of Nature." In Nakayama/Sivin 1968, 71–89.

Yoshinobu, Shiba. 1970. *Commerce and Society in Sung China*. Ann Arbor: University of Michigan Press.

Yu-Lan, Fung. 1966. *A Short History of Chinese Philosophy*. Ed. Derk Budde. New York: Free Press.

Zahlten, Johannes. 2006. "Disputation mit Averroes oder Unterwerfung des 'Kommentators.' Zu seinem Bild in der Malerei des Mittelalters und der Renaissance." In Speer/Wegener 2006, 717–744.

Zanato, Tiziano (ed.). 1992. *Lorenzo de' Medici, Opere*. Turin: Einaudi.

Zaret, David. 2000. *Origins of Democratic Culture: Printing, Petitions and the Public Sphere in Early-Modern England*. Princeton: Princeton University Press.

Zedler, Johann Heinrich (ed.). 1731–1754. *Grosses vollständiges Universal-Lexicon aller Wissenschaften und Künste*. 68 vols. Leipzig: Zedler.

Ze'evi, Dror. 2006. *Producing Desire: Changing Sexual Discourse in the Ottoman Middle East, 1500–1900*. Berkeley: University of California Press.

Zernack, Klaus. 1994. *Polen und Rußland. Zwei Wege in der europäischen Geschichte*. Berlin: Propyläen.

Zeuske, Michael. 2013. *Handbuch Geschichte der Sklaverei. Eine Globalgeschichte von den Anfängen bis zur Gegenwart*. Berlin: De Gruyter.

Zey, Claudia. 2017. *Der Investiturstreit*. Munich: C. H. Beck.

Zhang, Zhenhua. 1991. *Chinesische und europäische Rhetorik. Ein Vergleich in Grundzügen*. Frankfurt: Peter Lang.

Zhao, Zhongwei. 2006. "Towards a Better Understanding of Past Fertility Regimes: The Ideas and Practice of Controlling Family Size in Chinese History." *Continuity and Change* 21:1, 9–35.

Zheng, Yangwen. 2011. *China on the Sea: How the Maritime World Shaped Modern China*. Leiden: Brill.

Zielske, Harald. 1982. "Die Entwicklung des geistlichen und weltlichen Dramas und Theaters im Mittelalter." In *Propyläen Geschichte der Literatur*. Vol. II. Berlin: Propyläen, 414–445.

Zika, Charles. 1998. *Reuchlin und die okkulte Tradition der Renaissance*. Sigmaringen: Thorbecke.

Zimmermann, Bernhard. 1999. "Cicero und die Griechen." In Vogt-Spira/Rommel 1999, 240–248.

Zimmern, Froben Christoph von. 1881–1882. *Die zimmerische Chronik*. Ed. Karl August Barack. 2nd ed. Tübingen: Mohr Siebeck.

Zinner, Ernst. 1968. *Leben und Wirken des Joh. Müller von Königsberg genannt Regiomontanus*. Ed. Otto Zeller, 2nd ed. Osnabrück: Zeller.

Zouache, Abbès. 2015. "Les croisades en Orient. Histoire, mémoire." In *Tabularia. Mémoires normandes d'Italie et d'Orient* (November 17, 2015). http://journals.openedition.org /tabularia/2187 (accessed October 3, 2024).

Zwierlein, Otto. 1970. "Das Waltharius-Epos und seine lateinischen Vorbilder." *Antike und Abendland* 16, 153–184.

Zwingli, Ulrich. 1911. *Huldreich Zwinglis Sämtliche Werke*. Vol. VII: *Zwinglis Briefwechsel*, Vol. I: *Die Briefe von 1510–1522*. Ed. Emil Egli, Georg Finsler et al. Corpus Reformatorum 94. Leipzig: Heinsius.

LIST OF IMAGES

p. 1   FIGURE 1. Aristotle, Ptolemy, and Coperni-
cus. Etching (23 × 16.5 cm) by Stefano della Bella.
Frontispiece in Galileo Galilei, *Dialogo sopra i due
massimi sistemi del mondo* (Florence, 1632). Florence,
Biblioteca Nazionale. © akg-images / Rabatti &
Domingie.

p. 13   FIGURE 2. Titian, *The Rape of Europa*
(ca. 1560/2). Oil on canvas, 178 × 205 cm. Boston,
Isabella Stewart Gardner Museum. © Photo Fine
Art Images / Heritage Images / Scala Archives.

p. 21   FIGURE 3. Raphael, *The School of Athens*
(1510/11). Fresco, ca. 500 × 770 cm. Vatican City,
Vatican Palace, Stanza della Segnatura. © Scala
Archives.

p. 44   FIGURE 4. Michelangelo, *Risen Christ*
(1521). Marble, 205 cm (height). Rome, Santa Maria
sopra Minerva. © Scala Archives / Fondo Edifici di
Culto / Min. dell'Interno.

p. 62 FIGURE 5. Boethius in prison and the allegory of Philosophy. From Petrus Comestor, *Sermons et al.* (early 13th century). Ink on parchment. ©Bayerische Staatsbibliothek, Munich, Clm 2559, fol. 106v; Aldersbacher Sammelhandschrift.

p. 70 FIGURE 6. Hildebert chasing a mouse from his table, with Everwinus in the foreground. Manuscript illumination (ca. 1140). Brown and red ink on parchment, 25.2 × 33.5 cm. From an excerpt of Augustine, *De civitate Dei*. Prague, Metropolitan Library, cod. A 21/1, fol. 153r. Source: Anton Legner, *Der Artifex. Künstler im Mittelalter und ihre Selbst-darstellung. Eine illustrierte Anthologie* (Cologne: Greven, 2009).

p. 93 FIGURE 7. Portrait (*imago clipeata*) of Terence. Paint on parchment. From Terence, *Comedies* (copied in Corvey [?], ca. 825). © 2017 Biblioteca Apostolica Vaticana, Vatican City, Vat. Lat. 3868, fol. 2r.

p. 111 FIGURE 8. Yahya al-Wasiti, "Al-Harith meets Abu Zayd in the library of Basra." Paint and gold on paper, 37 × 28 cm. In Al-Hariri, *Maqamat* (Baghdad, 1237). © BNF, Paris, MS Ar 5847, fol. 5v /Archives Charmet / Bridgeman Images.

p. 133 FIGURE 9. *Diamond Sutra*, frontispiece and text. Block print, ink on paper, 27.6 × 499.5 cm (total size). Printed scroll (868 AD). © The British Library Board, London, Or. 8210/P.2 / Scala Archives.

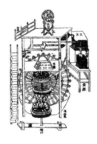

p. 143   FIGURE 10. Clock tower. In Su Song, *Xinyi Xiangfayao* (1092/94). Source: Needham et al. IV.2: 451, Figure 651.

p. 148   FIGURE 11. Novgorod, Cathedral of St. Sophia. Bronze, 360 × 240 cm. Right-side gate at the west entrance (1152/54), detail. © akg-images.

p. 159   FIGURE 12. Matilda of Tuscany and Hugh of Cluny intercede for Henry IV. Pen and ink on parchment. In Donizo of Canossa, *Vita Mathildis* (ca. 1115). © 2017, Biblioteca Apostolica Vaticana, Vatican City, Vat. Lat. 4922, fol. 49v.

p. 182   FIGURE 13. Edward I of England pays homage to Philip the Fair. Ink and gold on parchment, 46 × 35 cm. Manuscript illumination by Jean Fouquet (1455/60) from the *Grandes Chroniques de France*. Paris, Bibliothèque nationale de France, Français 6465, fol. 301v. © ullstein bild / Photo 12.

p. 202   FIGURE 14. Zhao Mengfu (1254–1322), "Horse and groom in the wind." Ink on paper, 22.7 × 49 cm. Album leaf. © National Palace Museum, Taipei / Bridgeman Images.

p. 214   FIGURE 15. Villard de Honnecourt, Standing and sitting nudes / Leaf faces (ca. 1220/30). Ink on parchment, 24.3 × 15.4 cm. . © Bibliothèque nationale de France, Paris; Français 19093, fol. 22r.

p. 225   FIGURE 16. Pythagoras. Limestone. Chartres Cathedral, royal portal (ca. 1150). © Chartres Cathedral, France / Bridgeman Images.

p. 247   FIGURE 17. Papermakers at work. Rough-grained paper, 65 × 54 cm. Votive image of the papermakers' guild of Fabriano (1559), detail. © Pia Università dei Cartai, Fabriano.

p. 266   FIGURE 18. Tommaso da Modena, portrait of Cardinal Hugh of St. Cher (1352). Fresco. Treviso, Chapter House of the former Monastery of San Niccolò. © Scala Archives.

p. 269   FIGURE 19. Giorgio Vasari, *Six Tuscan Poets* (ca. 1544). Dante surrounded by Petrarch, Boccaccio, Guido Cavalcanti, Marsilio Ficino, and Cristoforo Landino. Oil on wood, 132.1 × 131.1 cm. © Minneapolis Institute of Arts, Minneapolis, G 341 / The William Hood Dunwoody Fund / Bridgeman Images.

p. 344   FIGURE 25. Tang Yin, *The Thatched Hut of Dreaming of an Immortal* (16th century), detail. Scroll, ink and paint on paper, 29.6 × 682.1 cm. © Freer Gallery of Art, Smithsonian Institution, Washington, DC, F1939.60 / Bridgeman Images.

p. 355   FIGURE 26. Lucantonio degli Uberti (?), woodcut after Francesco Rosselli (?), *Florence* (*View with the Chain*), detail (ca. 1500). Paper, 57.8 × 131.6 cm. Berlin, Kupferstichkabinett, inv. no. 899-100. © bpk / Jörg P. Anders.

p. 365   FIGURE 27. Poggio Bracciolini, *Invectives against Lorenzo Valla* (ca. 1485). © University of Chicago Library, Chicago, MS 35, *Opuscula varia*, fol. 1r.

p. 372   FIGURE 28. Pisanello (attributed), portrait of Emperor Sigismund (1432/33). Tempera on parchment, mounted on wood, 58.6 × 42 cm. Vienna, Kunsthistorisches Museum, 2630. © Austrian Archives / Scala Archives.

p. 394   FIGURE 29. Giorgione, *The Three Philosophers* (1508/09). Oil on canvas, 124.5 × 126.5 cm. Vienna, Kunsthistorisches Museum, Gemäldegalerie 111. © DeAgostini Picture Library / Scala Archives.

p. 417   FIGURE 30. Santa Maria Novella, Florence. Facade by Leon Battista Alberti (1456–1470). © akg-images / Rabatti & Domingie.

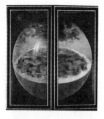

p. 486 FIGURE 36. Hieronymus Bosch, *The Garden of Earthly Delights* (ca. 1500), outer panels. Oil on oak wood, 220 × 193 cm. Madrid, Prado Museum, inv. no. P02823. © bpk /Alinari Archives / Raffaello Bencini.

p. 506 FIGURE 37. Michelangelo, *Moses* (1513–1516). Marble. Rome, San Pietro in Vincoli. © Scala Archives / Courtesy of the Ministero Beni e Attività Culturali e del Turismo.

p. 516 FIGURE 38. Unknown artist, *Ideal City* (ca. 1480). Tempera on wood, 67.5 × 239.5 cm. Urbino, Palazzo Ducale, Galleria Nazionale delle Marche , inv. no. 1990 D37. © bpk / Scala Archives.

p. 520 FIGURE 39. Poliphilo enters a pathless forest. Woodcut, 14 × 11.5 cm. In Francesco Colonna (?), *Hypnerotomachia Polifili* (Venice, 1499). © Art Media / Heritage Images / Scala Archives.

p. 536 FIGURE 40. Leonardo da Vinci, sketch of Michelangelo's *David* (1504/05). Ink, black chalk. Windsor Castle, Royal Collection Trust, RCIN 912591 / © His Majesty King Charles III 2022.

p. 544 FIGURE 41. Ludger tom Ring, portrait of Virgil (ca. 1558). Oil on oak wood, 44 × 31 cm. Westphalian State Museum of Art and Cultural History. © LWL-Museum für Kunst und Kultur (Westfälisches Landesmuseum), Münster, inv. no 1173 FG / Permanent loan from the Gesellschaft zur Förderung der westfälischen Kulturarbeit e. V. / Sabine Ahlbtrand-Donseif.

p. 547 FIGURE 42. Tapestry depicting Hector, Achilles, Agamemnon, and Menelaus (Tournai, ca. 1475/90). Wool and silk. Zamora, Cathedral Museum. © ullstein bild / Iberfoto / Fundación Carlos de Amberes / Iberfoto.

p. 550 FIGURE 43. Francesco Fiorentino and Bartolomeo Berrecci, courtyard of Wawel Castle, Cracow (1519–1536). © ullstein bild / Hein.

p. 555 FIGURE 44. Homer breathes inspiration into Virgil, Ovid, and Horace. Woodcut frontispiece in Simon Schaidenreisser, *Odyssea* (Augsburg, 1537). © Staats- und Stadtbibliothek Augsburg, 2 Math 99, title page of the supplementary volume.

p. 560 FIGURE 45. Martin Behaim, Georg Glockendon, et al., Behaim Globe (ca. 1491–1494). Various composite materials, paint, brass (horizontal ring), wrought iron (frame), 133 cm (height). © Nuremberg, Germanisches Nationalmuseum, WI 1826.

p. 569   FIGURE 46. Pier Antonio Solari, Palace of the Facets (1487–1491). Moscow, Kremlin. © akg-images / Elizaveta Becker.

p. 583   FIGURE 47. Hans Baldung Grien, *Martin Luther as an Augustinian Friar* (ca. 1520). Woodcut, 15.4 × 11.5 cm. Frontispiece in *Acta et res gestae D. Martini Lutheri*. Berlin, Staatliche Museen zu Berlin, 893–2. © akg-images.

p. 606   FIGURE 48. Memorial relief sculpture of an abbess (ca. 15th century) in the ambulatory of St. Paul's Cathedral in Münster. Sandstone. Damaged in 1534/35 during the rule of the Anabaptists. © Domverwaltung Münster / Dr. Michael Reuter.

p. 631   FIGURE 49. Piero di Cosimo, *Prometheus* (1510/20). Oil on poplar wood, 66 × 118.7 cm. Munich, Alte Pinakothek, inv. no. 8973. © bpk / Bayerische Staatsgemäldesammlungen.

p. 649   FIGURE 50. Johann Theodor de Bry, *The Microcosm (Man) and the Macrocosm (the World)*. Title page engraving in Robert Fludd, *Utriusque cosmi historia* (Oppenheim, 1617). © Bibliothèque de la Faculté de Médecine, Paris /Archives Charmet / Bridgeman Images.

p. 656   FIGURE 51. Jan van Calcar, engraving showing Vesalius dissecting a female body. 35.7 × 25.5 cm. Title page in Andreas Vesalius, *De humani corporis fabrica libri septem* (Basel, 1543).

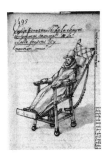

p. 725   FIGURE 57. Felipe Guaman Poma de Ayala, "The Rich Imperial Town of Potosí." Pen drawing, black ink, 14.5 × 20.5 cm. From *The First New Chronicle and Good Government* (1600–1615). Copenhagen, Royal Library, GKS 2232 4. Source: Carlos Gonzáles, Hugo Rosati, and Francisco Sánchez, *Guaman Poma: Testigo del mundo andino* (Santiago: LOM Ediciones, 2002).

p. 735   FIGURE 58. John White, "The Flyer" (1585–1593). Drawing of a Secotan Indian. Watercolor, black pencil, 24.6 × 15.1 cm. London, British Museum, inv. no. 1906,0509.1.16. © The Trustees of the British Museum.

p. 735   FIGURE 59. Giambologna, *Mercury* (1580). Bronze, 187 cm (height). Florence, Museo Nazionale del Bargello. © akg-images / Erich Lessing.

p. 737   FIGURE 60. "Mouth of Hell" (1564–1580). Bomarzo. © akg-images / Bildarchiv Monheim.

p. 747   FIGURE 61. Niccolò Boldrini, caricature of the Laocoon sculptural group (Venice, ca. 1540–1545). Woodcut, 27 × 40.6 cm. ETH Zurich, Graphics Collection, D 33. © akg-images.

p. 754 FIGURE 62. Book wheel. In Agostino Ramelli, *Le diverse et artificiose machine del capitano Agostino Ramelli* (Paris, 1588), fol. (656), 317r. Engraving, 35 × 23 cm. © Smithsonian Libraries, Washington, DC/ Bridgeman Images.

p. 758 FIGURE 63. The dragon of Bologna. In Ulisse Aldrovandi, *Serpentum, et draconum historiae libri duo* (Bologna, 1640), p. 404. Woodcut. © Alma Mater Studiorum Università di Bologna / Biblioteca Universitaria di Bologna, A.IV.H.III.11/8

p. 773 FIGURE 64. Simon de Passe, frontispiece in Francis Bacon, *Instauratio magna* (London, 1620). Engraving and etching, 23.8 × 15.4 cm. London, British Museum. © akg-images.

p. 783 FIGURE 65. Justus Sustermans, portrait of Galileo Galilei (1636). Oil on canvas, 66 × 56 m. Florence, Gallerie degli Uffizi. © Scala Archives / Courtesy of the Ministero Beni e Attività Culturali.

p. 803 FIGURE 66. Abraham Bosse, frontispiece in Thomas Hobbes, *Leviathan* (London, 1651). Engraving, 24.1 × 15.5 cm. London, British Museum. © Granger / Bridgeman Images.

p. 815   FIGURE 67. Pierre Lombart, *Britannia's Victory over Neptune* (based on an original by Francis Cleyn). Frontispiece in John Selden, *Of the Dominion, or, Ownership of the Sea* (London, 1652). Engraving, 23.1 × 16.5 cm. © The Bodleian Libraries, University of Oxford, Vet. A3 d.163.

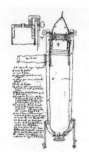

p. 821   FIGURE 68. Christiaan Huygens, design of a gunpowder engine (1637). Pen drawing. Leiden University Library, MS HUG 36 I, fol. 242v. © Deutsches Museum, Munich, Archiv, BN02713.

p. 823   FIGURE 69. Drawing of a flea, after an original by Christopher Wren (?). In Robert Hooke, *Micrographia* (London, 1665), schem. XXXIV, after p. 210. © Private Collection / Bridgeman Images.

p. 830   FIGURE 70. Francesco di Giorgio Martini, drawing of machinery for raising columns into position. In *Opusculum de architectura* (ca. 1480). London, British Museum, MS. Lat. 197 b. 21, fol. 27r. © The Trustees of the British Museum.

p. 837   FIGURE 71. Martin Löffelholz, drawing of a workbench with wing screws. In the Codex Löffelholz (Nuremberg, 1505). Cracow, Biblioteka Jagiellónska, MS Berol. Germ. Qu. 132'. © Uniwersytet Jagiellónski, Cracow.

p. 843   FIGURE 72. Udagawa Genshin (Shinsai), *Atlas of Medical Engravings of the Internal Organs* (1808). Frontispiece by Aodo Denzen, after an original in Steven Blankaart et al., *De nieuw hervormde anatomie* (Amsterdam, 1678). http://dl.ndl.go.jp/info:ndljp/pid/2532460.

p. 880 FIGURE 78. Aurangzeb reading the Quran, with his son Kam Bakhsh in the foreground (early 18th century). Paint on paper. Berlin, Museum fur Islamische Kunst, SMB, inv. no. I. 4593 fol. 45. © bpk.

p. 886 FIGURE 79. Bowl from Jingdezhen (Ming dynasty, 1540–1560). Porcelain, 10.5 cm (height). Staatliche Kunstsammlungen Dresden, PO 3226 / Jurgen Karpinski. © bpk.

p. 900 FIGURE 80. Hans Ulrich Franck, *The Armored Rider* (1643). Etching, 10.7 × 13.5 cm. Berlin, Museum of Prints and Drawings, G 5128. © bpk.

p. 914 FIGURE 81. Albrecht Altdorfer, *The Battle of Alexander at Issus* (1529). Tempera on limewood, 158.4 × 120.3 cm. Munich, Alte Pinakothek. Bayerische Staatsgemaldesammlungen, inv. no. 688. © bpk.

p. 921 FIGURE 82. Image of a *Grubenhunt* in Georg Agricola, *De re metallica* (Basel, 1556), bk. 6, fol. 113. Woodcut. © Royal Academy of Arts, London.

p. 929 FIGURE 83. *Homo sylvestris*, in Conrad Gessner, *Historia animalium* (Zurich, 1551; this image from a later German edition: *Allgemeines Thier-Buch*, Frankfurt am Main, 1669). © Ann Ronan / Heritage Images / Scala Archives.

COLOR PLATE CREDITS

Plate 1: Bequest of Cora Timken Burnett, 1956.

Plate 2: © bpk / Lutz Braun.

Plate 3: © Beijing, Palace Museum / Liu Zhigang.

Plate 4: © Werner Forman Archive / Scala Archives.

Plate 5: © Scala Archives.

Plate 6: © The National Gallery, London / Scala Archives.

Plate 7: © British Library Board. All Rights Reserved / Bridgeman Images.

Plate 8: © bpk / The Metropolitan Museum of Art, New York.

Plate 9: © The National Gallery, London / Scala Archives.

Plate 10: © De Agostini Picture Library /A. De Gregorio / Bridgeman Images.

Plate 11: © Scala Archives / Courtesy of the Ministero Beni e Att. Culturali.

Plate 12: © 2017 Biblioteca Apostolica Vaticana.

Plate 13: © Scala Archives / Courtesy of the Ministero Beni e Att. Culturali.

Plate 14: © bpk / BNF, Dist. RMN-GP.

Plate 15: © ullstein bild / IBERFOTO.

Plate 16: © bpk / Joseph Martin.

Plate 17: © The National Gallery, London / Scala Archives.

Plate 18: © Scala Archives / Courtesy of the Ministero Beni e Att. Culturali.

Plate 19: © Cracow, Franciscan Archives (OFMConv).

Plate 20: ullstein bild / United Archives / World History Archive.

Plate 21: © Walker Art Gallery, National Museums Liverpool / Bridgeman Images.

Plate 22: © Iowa State University Library, Special Collections and University Archives.

Plate 23: © ullstein bild / Heritage Images / Fine Art Images.

Plate 24: © Pinacoteca Ambrosiana, Milan / De Agostini Picture Library / Bridgeman Images.

Plate 25: © bpk /Alinari Archives / Serge Domingie.

Plate 26: © Woburn Abbey, Bedfordshire, UK / Bridgeman Images.

Plate 27: © DEA / ARCHIVIO J. LANGE / Kontributor.

INDEX OF NAMES

Note that *al-* at the beginning of Arabic names is ignored for purposes of alphabetization.